Schroeder's Collectible
TOYS
Antique to Modern
Price Guide

Fifth Edition

Edited by Sharon and Bob Huxford

COLLECTOR BOOKS
A Division of Schroeder Publishing Co., Inc.

Searching For A Publisher?

We are always looking for knowledgeable people considered to be experts within their fields. If you feel that there is a real need for a book on your collectible subject and have a large comprehensive collection, contact Collector Books.

On The Cover:

Liddle Diddle by Mattel, $75.00 (photo courtesy Cindy Sabulis); Marx Pluto windup, EX, $225.00; Star Wars figure, Luke Skywalker, Kenner, 12", NM, $200.00; Hopalong Cassidy game, 1950, complete, M in VG box, $150.00; Ohio Art pail and shovel, $25.00 – 50.00; Stump Speaker cast iron mechanical bank, Shepard Hardware, pat. 1886, $2,750.00; Sonny & Cher figures, Mego, 1975, 12", $25.00 – 35.00 each (photo courtesy Cindy Sabulis); Weird-Ohs Freddy Flameout model, complete, MIB, $60.00; Miss America clockwork speedboat, ca. 1920s, 15", $725.00; Barnacle Bill tin windup walker, Chein, 6½", ca. 1930s, EX, $450.00; Dollhouse, litho on fiberboard six-room bungalow, 1930s, VG, $200.00.

Editorial Staff:

Editors: Sharon and Bob Huxford

Research and Editorial Assistants: Michael Drollinger, Nancy Drollinger, Linda Holycross, Donna Newnum, Loretta Woodrow

Cover Design: Beth Summers

Layout: Terri Stalions and Beth Ray

COLLECTOR BOOKS
P.O. Box 3009
Paducah, Kentucky 42002-3009

Introduction

It seems that every decade will have an area of concentrated excitement when it comes to the antiques and collectibles market place. What Depression glass was to the late sixties, Fiesta to the seventies, and cookie jars were to the eighties, toys are to the nineties. No one even vaguely involved in the field can have missed all the excitement toys have stirred up among many, many collectors. There are huge toy shows nationwide; scores of newsletters, magazines, and trade papers that deal exclusively with toys; cataloged toy auctions with wonderful color photographs and several hundred lots each; and more and more toy collector's guides are appearing in the book stores each week.

If you've been using *Schroeder's Antiques Price Guide*, you know that we try very hard not to omit categories where we find even a minor amount of market activity — being collectors ourselves, we know how frustrating it can be when you are unable to find any information on an item in question. But that book is limited to a specific number of pages, and as we watched the toy market explosion taking place, we realized that if we were to do it justice, we would have to publish a companion guide devoted entirely to toys. And following the same convictions, we decided that rather than to try to zero in on only the larger, more active fields, we'd try to represent toys of all kinds, from the 19th century up to today. This is the format we chose to pursue.

Our concept is unique in the collectibles field. Though we designed the book first and foremost to be a price guide, we wanted to make it a buying/selling guide as well. So we took many of our descriptions and values from the 'toys for sale' lists of dealers and collectors around the country. In each of those listings we included a dealer's code, so that if you were looking for the particular model kit (or whatever) that (S5) had to offer, you'd be able to match his code with his name and address in the 'Dealer's Codes' section and simply drop him a line or call him to see if it were still available. Our experiment has been very successful. Feedback indicates that many of our sellers do very well, making productive contacts with collectors who not only purchase items from them on their initial call but leave requests for other merchandise they are looking for as well.

Each edition contains about 24,000 listings, but even at that we realize that when it comes to the toy market, that only began to scratch the surface. Our intent is to provide our readers with fresh information, issue after issue. The few categories that are repeated in their entirety in succeeding editions generally are those that were already complete or as nearly complete as we or our advisors could make them. But even those are checked to make sure that values are still current and our information up to date.

When we initially began to plan our layout, we soon discovered that organizing toys is mind-boggling. Collectors were quick to tell us that toys generally can't be sorted by manufacturer, as we were accustomed to doing in our other price guides. So we had to devise a sort that would not only be easy to use but one that our staff could work with. With this in mind, we kept our categories very broad and general. On the whole this worked very well, but we found that the character section was so large (4,000 lines) it was overwhelming to our advisors. So even though our original approach was probably the most user-friendly, we have broken the character collectibles down into several groups of collectibles and genres and created specific categories for them. But you'll find 'See Alsos' in bold, cross-references within the description lines, and a detailed index to help you locate the items you're looking for with ease.

What we want to stress is that our values are not meant to set prices. Some of them are prices realized at auction; you'll be able to recognize these by the 'A' at the end of the description line. The listings that have neither the 'A' code or the dealer code mentioned above were either sent to us for publication by very knowledgeable collectors who specialize in those specific types of toys or were originally dealer coded but altered at the suggestion of an advisor who felt that the stated price might be far enough outside the average market price range to be misleading (in which case, the dealer's code was removed). There are so many factors that bear on the market that for us to attempt to set prices is not only presumptuous, it's ludicrous. The foremost of these factors is the attitude of the individual collector — his personal view of the hobby. We've interviewed several by telephone; everyone has his own opinion. While some view auction prices as useless, others regard them as actual selling prices and prefer them to asking prices. And the dealer who needs to keep turning his merchandise over to be able to replenish and freshen his stock, will of necessity, sell at lower prices than a collector who will buy an item and wait for the most opportune time to turn it over for maximum profit. Where you buy affects prices as well. One of our advisors used this simple analogy: while a soda might cost you $2.50 at the ball park, you can buy the same thing for 39¢ at the corner 7-11. So all we (or anyone) can offer is whatever facts and information we can compile, and ask simply that you arrive at your own evaluations based on the data we've provided, adapted to your personal buying/selling arena, desire to own, and need to sell.

We hope you enjoy our book and that you'll be able to learn by using it. We don't presume to present it as the last word on toys or their values — there are many specialized books by authors who are able to devote an entire publication to one subject, covering it from 'A' to 'Z,' and when we're aware that such a text book exists, we'll recommend it in our narratives. If you have suggestions that you think will improve our format, let us hear from you — we value your input. Until next time — happy hunting! May you find that mint-in-the-box #1 Barbie or if you prefer that rare mechanical bank that has managed to so far elude you. But even if you never do, we hope that you'll find a generous measure of happiness and success, a treasure now and then, and new friends along the way.

— The Editors

Advisory Board

The editors and staff take this opportunity to express our sincere gratitude and appreciation to each person who has contributed their time and knowledge to help us. We've found toys to be *by far* the largest, most involved field of collecting we've ever tried to analyze, but we will have to admit, it's great fun! We've been editing general price guides for fifteen years now, and before ever attempting the first one, we realized there was only one way we would presume to publish such a guide — and that would be to first enlist the help of knowledgeable collectors around the country who specialized in specific areas. We now have more than 120, and we're still looking for help in several areas. Generally, the advisors are listed following each category's narrative, so if we have mentioned no one and you feel that you are qualified to advise us, have the time, and would be willing to help us out with that subject, please contact us. We'd love to have you on our advisory board. (We want to stress that even if an advisor is credited in a category narrative, that person is in no way responsible for errors. Errors are our responsibility.) Even if we currently list an advisor for your subject, contact us so that we'll have your name on file should that person need to be replaced. This of course happens from time to time due to changing interests or because they find they no longer have the time.

While some advisors sent us listings and prices, others provided background information and photographs, checked printouts, or simply answered our questions. All are listed below. Most are followed by a code; see the section called *Dealer Codes* for an explanation of how these are used in the listings.

Matt and Lisa Adams (A7)
Geneva Addy (A5)
Diane Albert (T6)
Sally and Stan Alekna (A1)
Jane Anderson (A2)
Pamela E. Apkarian-Russell (H9)
Bob Armstrong (A4)
Richard Belyski (B1)
Bill and Jeanne Bertoia
Larry Blodget (B2)
Bojo (B3)
Scott Bruce (B14)
Dick Borgerding (B4)
Sue and Marty Bunis (B11)
Bromer Booksellers, Inc. (B12)
Bill Campbell (C10)
Ken Clee (C3)
Candelaine (Candace Gunther) (G16)
Casey's Collectible Corner (C1)
Brad Cassity (C13)
Mark Chase and Michael Kelly (C2)
Arlan Coffman (C4)
Joel Cohen (C12)
Cotswold Collectibles (C6)
Marilyn Cooper (C9)
Cynthia's Country Store (C14)
Rosalind Cranor (C15)
Marl Davidson (D2)

Larry DeAngelo (D3)
Doug Dezso (D6)
Donna and Ron Donnelly (D7)
George Downes (D8)
Larry Doucet (D11)
Allan Edwards (E3)
Marcia Fanta (M15)
Paul Fink (F3)
Steve Fisch (F7)
Mike and Kurt Fredericks (F4)
Fun House Toy Co. (F5)
Lee Garmon
Carol Karbowiak Gilbert (G6)
Mark Giles (G2)
Joan Stryker Grumbaugh (G8)
Bill Hamburg (H1)
Don Hamm (H10)
George Hardy (H3)
Ellen and Jerry Harnish (H4)
Tim Hunter (H13)
Dan Iannotti (I3)
Roger Inouye (I1)
Kerry and Judy Irwin (K5)
Terri Ivers (I2)
Keith and Donna Kaonis (K6)
Ilene Kayne (K3)
David Kolodny-Nagy (K2)
Trina and Randy Kubeck (K1)
Tom Lastrapes (L4)
Kathy and Don Lewis (L6)
Val and Mark Macaluso (M1)
Helen L. McCale (M13)
John McKenna (M2)
Nancy McMichael (M18)
Michael and Polly McQuillen (M11)
Lucky Meisenheimer (M3)
Bill Mekalian (M4)
Steven Meltzer (M9)
Bruce Middleton (M20)
Ken Mitchell (M14)
Gary Mosholder (G1)
Judith Mosholder (M7)
Peter Muldavin (M21)
Natural Way (N1)
Roger Nazeley (N4)
Dawn Parrish (P2)
Diane Patalano (P8)
Sheri and John Pavone (P3)
The Phoenix Toy Soldier Co. (P11)
Pat and Bill Poe (P10)
Gary Pollastro (P5)
Judy Posner (P6)
Michael Paquin (P12)
Lorraine Punchard (P13)
John Rammacher (S5)
Jim Rash (R3)
Robert Reeves (R4)
Charlie Reynolds (R5)
David E. Richter (R1)
David Riddle (R6)
Cindy Sabulis (S14)
Scott Smiles (S10)
Carole and Richard Smythe (S22)
Steve Stephenson (S25)
Bill Stillman (S6)
Nate Stoller (S7)
Mark and Lynda Suozzi (S24)
Toy Scouts, Inc. (Bill Bruegman) (T2)
Richard Trautwein (T3)
Marcie and Bob Tubbs (T5)
Judy and Art Turner (H8)
Marci Van Ausdall (V2)
Norm Vigue (V1)
Randy Welch (W4)
Dan Wells (W1)
Larry and Mary White (W7)
Mary Young (Y2)
Henri Yunes (Y1)

How to Use This Book

Concept. Our design for this book is two-fold. Primarily it is a market report compiled from many sources, meant to be studied and digested by our readers, who can then better arrive at their own conclusion regarding prices. Were you to ask ten active toy dealers for their opinion as to the value of a specific toy, you would no doubt get ten different answers, and who's to say which is correct? Quite simply, there are too many variables to consider. Where you buy is critical. Condition is certainly subjective, prices vary from one area of the country to another, and probably the most important factor is how badly you want to add the item in question to your collection or at what price you're willing to sell. So use this as a guide along with your observations at toy shows, flea markets, toy auctions, and elsewhere to arrive at an evaluation that satisfies you personally.

The second function of this book is to put buyers in touch with sellers who deal in the type of toys they want to purchase. We contact dealers all over the country, asking them to send us their 'for sale' lists and permission to use them as sources for some of our listings, which we code so as to identify the dealer from whose inventory list the price and description are taken. Even though by publication much of their merchandise will have been sold since we entered our data early last spring, many of them tell us that they often get similar or even the same items in over and over, so if you see something listed you're interested in buying, don't hesitate to call any of them. Remember, though, they're not tied down to the price quoted in the book, since their asking price is many times influenced by what they've had to pay to restock their shelves. Let us know how well this concept works out for you.

Toys are listed by name. Every effort has been made to list a toy by the name as it appears on the original box. There have been very few exceptions made, and then only if the collector-given name is more recognizable. For instance, if we listed 'To-Night Amos 'n' Andy in Person' (as the name appears on the box lid), very few would recognize the toy as the Amos 'n' Andy Walkers. But these exceptions are few.

Descriptions and sizes may vary. When we were entering data, we often found the same toy had sold through more than one auction gallery or was listed in several dealer lists. So the same toy will often be described in various ways, but we left descriptions just as we found them, since there is usually something to be gleaned from each variation. We chose to leave duplicate lines in when various conditions were represented so that you could better understand the impact of condition on value. Depending on the source and who was doing the measuring, we found that the size of a given toy might vary by an inch or more. Not having the toy to measure ourselves, we had to leave dimensions just as they were given in auction catalogs or dealer lists.

Lines are coded as to source. Each line that represents an auction-realized price will be coded 'A' at the end, just before the price. Other letter/number codes identify the dealer who sent us that information. These codes are explained later on. Additional sources of like merchandise will be noted under the narratives. These are dealers whose lists arrived at our office too late to be included in the lines themselves.

As we said before, collectors have various viewpoints regarding auction results. You will have to decide for yourself. Some feel they're too high to be used to establish prices while others prefer them to 'asking' prices that can sometimes be speculative. We must have entered about 8,000 auction values, and here is what we found to be true: the really volatile area is in the realm of character collectibles from the '40s, '50s, and '60s — exactly where there is most interest, most collector activity, and hot competition when the bidding starts. But for the most part, auction prices were not far out of line with accepted values. Many times, compared to the general market place, toys in less-than-excellent condition actually sold under 'book.' Because the average auction-consigned toy is in especially good condition and many times even retains its original box, it will naturally bring higher prices than the norm. And auctions often offer the harder-to-find, more unusual items. Unless you take these factors into consideration, prices may seem high, when in reality, they may not be at all. Prices may be driven up by high reserves, but not all galleries have reserves. Whatever your view, you'll be able to recognize and consider the source of the values we quote and factor that into your personal evaluation.

Categories that have priority. Obviously there are thousands of toys that would work as well in one category as they would in another, depending on the preference of the collector. For instance, a Mary Poppins game would appeal to a games collector just as readily as it would to someone who bought character-related toys of all kinds. The same would be true of many other types of toys. We tried to make our decisions sensibly and keep our sorts simple. But to avoid sending our character advisors such huge printouts, we felt that it would be best to pull out specific items and genres to create specific categories, thereby reducing the size of the character category itself. We'll guide you to those specialized categories with cross-references and 'See Alsos.' If all else fails, refer to the index. It's as detailed as we know how to make it.

These categories have precedence over Character:

- Action Figures
- Battery-Operated Toys (also specific manufacturers)
- Books
- Bubble Bath Containers
- Celebrity Dolls (see Dolls)
- Character and Promotional Drinking Glasses
- Character Clocks and Watches
- Character Bobbin' Heads
- Chein
- Coloring, Activity, and Paint Books
- Corgi
- Dakins
- Disney
- Fisher-Price
- Games
- Guns
- Halloween Costumes
- Lunch Boxes
- Marx
- Model Kits
- Nodders
- Paper Dolls
- Pez Dispensers
- Pin-Back Buttons
- Plastic Figures
- Playsets
- Puppets
- Puzzles
- Radios
- Records
- Rock 'N Roll
- Snow Domes
- Sports Collectibles
- Telephones
- Trading Cards
- Toothbrush Holders
- View-Master
- Western
- Windups, Friction, and Other Mechanicals

Price Ranges. Once in awhile, you'll find a listing that gives a price range. These result from our having found varying prices for the same item. We've taken a mid-range — less than the highest, a little over the lowest — if the original range was too wide to really be helpful. If the range is still coded 'A' for auction, all that were averaged were auction-realized prices.

Condition, how it affects value, how to judge it. The importance of condition can't be stressed enough. Unless a toy is exceptionally rare, it must be very good or better to really have much collector value. But here's where the problem comes in: though each step downward on the grading scale drastically decreases a toy's value, as the old saying goes, 'beauty is in the eye of the beholder.' What is acceptable wear and damage to one individual may be regarded by another as entirely too degrading. Criteria used to judge condition even varies from one auction company to the next, so we had to attempt to sort them all out and arrive at some sort of standardization. Please be sure to read and comprehend what the description is telling you about condition; otherwise you can easily be mislead. Auction galleries often describe missing parts, repairs, and paint touch-ups, summing up overall appearance in the condition code. When losses and repairs were noted in the catalog, we noted them as well. Remember that a toy even in mint restored condition is never worth as much as one in mint original condition. And even though a toy may be rated otherwise 'EX' after losses and repairs are noted, it won't be worth as much as one with original paint and parts in excellent condition. Keep this in mind when you use our listings to evaluate your holdings.

These are the conditions codes we have used throughout the book and their definitions as we have applied them:

M — mint. Unplayed with, brand new, flawless.
NM — near mint. Appears brand new except on very close inspection.
EX — excellent. Has minimal wear, very minor chips and rubs, a few light scratches.
VG — very good. Played with, loss of gloss, noticeable problems, several scratches.
G — good. Some rust, considerable wear and paint loss, well used.
P — poor. Generally unacceptable except for a filler.

Because we do not use a three-level pricing structure as many of you are used to and may prefer, we offer this table to help you arrive at values for toys in conditions other than those that we give you. If you know the value of a toy in excellent condition and would like to find an approximate value for it in near mint condition, for instance, just run your finger down the column under 'EX' until you find the approximate price we've listed (or one that easily factors into it), then over to the column headed 'NM.' We'll just go to $100.00, but other values will be easy to figure by addition or multiplication. Even though at auction a toy in very good to excellent condition sometimes brings only half as much as a mint condition toy, the collectors we interviewed told us that this was not true of the general market place. Our percentages are simply an average based on their suggestions.

G	VG	EX	NM	M
40/50%	55/65%	70/80%	85/90%	100%
5.00	6.00	7.50	9.00	10.00
7.50	9.00	11.00	12.50	15.00
10.00	12.00	15.00	18.00	20.00
12.00	15.00	18.00	22.00	25.00
14.00	18.00	22.50	26.00	30.00
18.00	25.00	30.00	35.00	40.00
22.50	30.00	37.50	45.00	50.00
27.00	35.00	45.00	52.00	60.00
32.00	42.00	52.00	62.00	70.00
34.00	45.00	55.00	65.00	75.00
35.00	48.00	60.00	70.00	80.00
40.00	55.00	68.00	80.00	90.00
45.00	60.00	75.00	90.00	100.00

Condition and value of original boxes and packaging. When no box or packaging is referred to in the line or in the narrative, assume that the quoted price is for the toy only. Please read the narratives! In some categories (Corgi, for instance), all values are given for items mint and in original boxes. Conditions for boxes (etc.) are in parenthesis immediately following the condition code for the toy itself. In fact, any information within parenthesis at that point in the line will refer to packaging. Collector interest in boxes began several years ago, and today many people will pay very high prices for them, depending on scarcity, desirability, and condition. The more colorful, graphically pleasing boxes are favored, and those with images of well-known characters are especially sought-after. Just how valuable is a box? Again, this is very subjective to the individual. We asked this question to several top collectors around the country, and the answers they gave us ranged from 20% to 100% above mint-no-box prices.

Advertising. You'll notice display ads throughout the book. We hope you will contact these advertisers if they deal in the type of merchandise you're looking for. If you'd like your ad to appear in our next edition, please refer to the advertising rate chart in the back of the book for information.

Listing of Standard Abbreviations

These abbreviations have been used throughout this book in order to provide you with the most detailed descriptions possible in the limited space available. No periods are used after initials or abbreviations. When two dimensions are given, height is noted first. When only one measurement is given, it will be the greater — height if the toy is vertical, length if it is horizontal. (Remember that in the case of duplicate listings representing various conditions, we found that sizes often varied as much as an inch or more.)

Am — American
att — attributed to
bl — blue
blk — black
brn — brown
bsk — bisque
c — copyright
ca — circa
cb — cardboard
CI — cast iron
compo — composition
dbl — double
dia — diameter
dk — dark
dtd — dated
ea — each
emb — embossed
EX — excellent
F — fine
fr — frame, framed
ft, ftd — feet, foot, footed
G — good
gr — green
hdl — handle, handled
hdw — hardware
illus — illustrated, illustration
inscr — inscribed
jtd — jointed
L — long, length
litho — lithographed
lt — light, lightly
M — mint
MBP — mint in bubble pack
mc — multicolored
MIB — mint in box
MIP — mint in package
mk — marked
MOC — mint on card
MOT — mint on tree
NM — near mint
NP — nickel plated
NRFB — never removed from box
NRFP — never removed from package
orig — original
o/w — otherwise
P — poor
Pat — patented
pc — piece
pg, pgs — page, pages
pk — pink
pkg — package
pnt — paint, painted
pr — pair
prof — professional
rfn — refinished
rnd — round
rpl — replaced
rpr — repaired
rpt — repainted
rstr — restored
sq — square
sz — size
turq — turquoise
unmk — unmarked
VG — very good
W — width, wingspan
wht — white
w/ — with
w/up — windup
yel — yellow

Action Figures

Back in 1964, Barbie dolls had taken the feminine side of the toy market by storm. Hasbro took a risky step in an attempt to target the male side. Their answer to the Barbie craze was GI Joe. Since no self-respecting boy would admit to playing with dolls, Hasbro called their boy dolls 'action figures,' and to the surprise of many, they were phenomenally successful. Both Barbie and GI Joe were realistically modeled (at least GI Joe was) and posable 12" vinyl dolls that their makers clothed and accessorized to the hilt. Their unprecedented successes spawned a giant industry with scores of manufacturers issuing one 'action figure' after another, many in series. Other sizes were eventually made in addition to the 12" dolls. Some are 8" to 9", others 6", and many are the 3¾" figures that have been favored in recent years.

This is one of the fastest-growing areas of toy collecting today. Manufacturers of action figures are now targeting the collector market as well as the kids themselves, simply because the adult market is so active. You will find a wide range of asking prices from dealer to dealer; most of our listings are coded and represent only a sampling. Naturally, *where* you buy will also affect values. Be critical of condition! Original packaging is extremely important. In fact, when it comes to the recent issues, loose, played-with examples are seldom worth more than a few dollars. Remember, if no box is mentioned, values are for loose (unpackaged) dolls. When no size is given, assume figures are 3¾" or standard size for the line in question.

For more information we recommend *Collectible Action Figures* by Paris and Susan Manos, *Collector's Guide to Dolls in Uniform* by Joseph Bourgeois, and *Mego Toys* by Wallace M. Crouch (all published by Collector Books).

Advisors: George Downs (D8); Robert Reeves (R4), Best of the West.

Other Sources: B3, H12, I2, J2, J5, J7, M15, M17, O1, P3, S17, T1

See also Barbie Dolls; Character Collectibles; Dolls, Celebrity; GI Joe; Star Trek; Star Wars.

Action Jackson, accessory, Fire Rescue Pack, Mego, MIB, F1 .... **$15.00**
Action Jackson, accessory, Rescue Squad outfit, Mego, MIB, H4 .... **$10.00**
Action Jackson, accessory, Surf & Scuba outfit, Mego, MIB, H4 .... **$12.00**
Action Jackson, figure, Action Jackson, Mego, Army fatigues, red hair, 8", EX, H4 .... **$20.00**
Action Jackson, figure, Action Jackson, Mego, lt bl coveralls & wht boots, blk hair, 8", EX, H4 .... **$20.00**
Adventures of Indiana Jones, accessory, Map Room, MIB, B5 .... **$70.00**
Adventures of Indiana Jones, accessory, Wells of the Soul playset, Kenner, MIB **$100.00**
Adventures of Indiana Jones, figure, Cairo Swordsman, Toht or German Mechanic, Kenner, ea, from $25 to **$35.00**
Adventures of Indiana Jones, figure, Indiana Jones, Kenner, MOC **$125.00**
Adventures of Indiana Jones, figure, Indiana Jones, Raiders of the Lost Ark, Kenner, 12", MIB **$350.00**

Adventures of Indiana Jones, figure, Marion Ravenwood, Raiders of the Lost Ark, Kenner, 3¾", MOC, $200.00.

Aliens, accessory, Evac Fighter, Kenner, MIB, F1 .... **$30.00**
Aliens, accessory, Power Loader, Kenner, MIB, F1 .... **$20.00**
Aliens, accessory, Queen Hive playset, Kenner, MIB **$50.00**
Aliens, figure, Bishop, Gorilla, Killer Crab, Mantis, Night Cougar, Panther, Ripley or Wild Boar, Kenner, MOC, ea **$10.00**
Aliens, figure, King, Queen, Swarm or Arachnid, Kenner, MOC, F1, ea **$25.00**
Aliens, figure, Queen, Flying Queen or Atax, Kenner, w/trading cards, M (European cards), F1, ea **$25.00**
American West, figure, Cochise or Wild Bill Hickok, Mego, 8", M (NM box), B3, ea **$55.00**
Apollo 13, figure, Astronaut, Hasbro, 12", EX, F1 .... **$40.00**
Batman, accessory, Batmobile, Ertl, 1989, 1st series, MOC, H4 .... **$8.00**
Batman, accessory, Batmobile, Toy Biz, 1989, 2nd series, NRFB, H4 .... **$45.00**
Batman, see also Dark Knight, DC Comics Super Heroes, Legends of Batman, Marvel Super Heroes, Official World's Greatest Super Heroes and Super Powers
Batman (Animated Series), accessory, Batmobile, Kenner, MOC, F1 .... **$40.00**
Batman (Animated Series), accessory, Joker Mobile, Kenner, MOC, F1 .... **$30.00**
Batman (Animated Series), accessory, Nightsphere w/gr Batman figure, Kenner, MOC, F1 .... **$40.00**
Batman (Animated Series), accessory, Triple Attack Jet, Kenner, MOC, F1 .... **$20.00**
Batman (Animated Series), figure, Bane, Ras A Gual or Bruce Wayne, Kenner, MOC, F1, ea **$20.00**
Batman (Animated Series), figure, Manbat, Kenner, MOC, F1 .... **$25.00**
Batman (Animated Series), figure, Poison Ivy, Killer Kroc or Clayface, Kenner, MOC, F1, ea **$30.00**
Batman (Animated Series), figure, Scarecrow, Kenner, MOC, F1 .... **$30.00**
Batman Returns, accessory, Bruce Wayne's Custom Coupe, w/figure, Kenner, MIB, F1 .... **$40.00**

Batman Returns, accessory, Laser Blade Cycle, Kenner, MIB, F1 ....$15.00
Batman Returns, accessory, Robin Jet Foil Cycle, Kenner, MIB, F1 ....$30.00
Batman Returns, figure, Penguin, Applause, 10", EX, F1 .$12.00
Battlestar Galactica, accessory, Colonial Scarab, Mattel, M (NM Canadian box) $60.00
Battlestar Galactica, accessory, Colonial Viper, Mattel, M (NM Canadian box) $60.00
Battlestar Galactica, accessory, Cylon Raider, Mattel, M (NM Canadian box) $60.00
Battlestar Galactica, figure, Colonial Warrior, Mattel, 12", VG, H4 ....$30.00
Battlestar Galactica, figure, Commander Adama, Mattel, 3¾", VG, H4 ....$10.00
Battlestar Galactica, figure, Imperious Leader, Mattel, 3¾", MOC, H4 ....$20.00
Battlestar Galactica, figure, Lieutenant Starbuck, Mattel, 3¾", MOC (unpunched), H4 ....$30.00
Beetlejuice, accessory, Gross Out Meter, Kenner, 1990, MIB, P3 ....$15.00
Beetlejuice, accessory, Vanishing Vault, Kenner, 1990, MIB, D8/P3 ....$15.00
Beetlejuice, figure, Beetlejuice, talker, Kenner, 12", NRFB, H4 ....$150.00
Beetlejuice, figure, Showtime Beetlejuice or Shipwreck Beetlejuice, Kenner, 3¾", MOC, ea, from $10 to $14.00
Best of the West, accessory, Circle X Ranch, Marx, MIB $175.00
Best of the West, accessory, Jeep & Horse Trailer, Marx, MIB $150.00
Best of the West, accessory, Johnny West Adventure Jeep, Marx, VG, H4 ....$40.00
Best of the West, buffalo, Marx, NM, F5 ....$100.00
Best of the West, figure, Bill Buck, Marx, complete, M (EX box), H4, from $500 to $650.00
Best of the West, figure, Captain Maddox, Marx, complete, M (VG Fort Apache Fighters box), H4 ....$95.00
Best of the West, figure, Captain Maddox, Marx, missing few accessories, VG, H4 ....$50.00
Best of the West, figure, Chief Cherokee, Marx, complete, NM (NM box), F5 ....$160.00
Best of the West, figure, Chief Cherokee, Marx, missing few accessories, EX (EX box), H4 ....$80.00
Best of the West, figure, Fighting Eagle, Marx, complete, EX+, F5 ....$160.00
Best of the West, figure, Fighting Eagle, Marx, complete, NM (NM box), F5 ....$275.00
Best of the West, figure, General Custer, Marx, complete, M (VG Fort Apache Fighters box), H4 ....$70.00
Best of the West, figure, General Custer, Marx, missing few accessories, VG+, H4 ....$45.00
Best of the West, figure, Geronimo, Marx, complete, NM (EX box), F5 ....$140.00
Best of the West, figure, Geronimo, Marx, missing few accessories, EX (VG box), H4 ....$75.00
Best of the West, figure, Geronimo, Marx, missing few accessories, VG+, H4 ....$35.00
Best of the West, figure, Jaimie West, Marx, complete, M (NM box) $85.00
Best of the West, figure, Jaimie West, Marx, missing few accessories, EX, H4 ....$30.00
Best of the West, figure, Jane West, Marx, missing few accessories, EX, H4 ....$30.00
Best of the West, figure, Jane West, Marx, missing few accessories, NM (NM box), F5 ....$90.00
Best of the West, figure, Jay West, Marx, complete, M (NM box) $75.00
Best of the West, figure, Jay West, Marx, complete, NM, F5 ....$55.00
Best of the West, figure, Jed Gibson, Marx, complete, NM (EX box) $350.00
Best of the West, figure, Johnny West, Marx, complete, VG+, H4 ....$40.00
Best of the West, figure, Johnny West, Marx, missing paperwork, NM (EX 1st issue box), H4 ....$75.00
Best of the West, figure, Josie West, Marx, complete, MIB..$75.00
Best of the West, figure, Josie West, Marx, missing few accessories, EX (VG box), H4 ....$50.00
Best of the West, figure, Josie West, Marx, missing few accessories, VG, H4 ....$25.00
Best of the West, figure, Princess Wildflower, Marx, missing few accessories, NM, F5 ....$90.00
Best of the West, figure, Sam Cobra, Marx, missing few accessories, NM, F5 ....$110.00
Best of the West, figure, Sam Cobra, Marx, no accessories, VG, H4 ....$30.00
Best of the West, figure, Sheriff Garrett, Marx, missing few accessories, EX (G photo box), H4 ....$175.00
Best of the West, figure, Sheriff Garrett, Marx, missing most accessories, NM, F5 ....$55.00
Best of the West, figure, Zeb Zachary, Marx, complete, EX (EX box), minimum value $150.00

Best of the West, figure set, Geronimo and horse, EX, from $45.00 to $65.00.

Best of the West, figure set, Jane West & Flame, Marx, missing few accessories, EX (EX box), H4 ....$175.00

Best of the West, figure set, Johnny West & Thunderbolt, Marx, missing few accessories, VG (VG box), H4 ....$100.00
Best of the West, figure set, Sheriff Garret & Thunderbolt, Marx, complete, rare, NMIB, H4 ....$485.00
Best of the West, horse, Buckskin, Marx, dk brn, no accessories, NM, F5 ....$50.00
Best of the West, horse, Comanche, Marx, complete, EX (EX Fort Apache Fighters box), H4 ....$125.00
Best of the West, horse, Comanche, Marx, cream colored, complete, EX, H4 ....$55.00
Best of the West, horse, Flame, Marx, palomino, complete, MIB, H4 ....$125.00
Best of the West, horse, Pancho, Marx, cream colored, complete, VG, H4 ....$30.00
Best of the West, horse, Pancho, Marx, palomino, no accessories, EX, F5 ....$20.00
Best of the West, horse, Thunderbolt, Marx, blk, complete, VG, H4 ....$50.00
Best of the West, horse, Thunderbolt, Marx, blk w/blk tack, complete, NM from $50 to $70.00
Best of the West, horse, Thunderbolt, Marx, cream colored, complete, EX (VG box), H4 ....$80.00
Best of the West, horse, Thunderbolt, Marx, dk brn, complete, MIB, H4 ....$100.00
Best of the West, horse, Thunderbolt, Marx, dk brn, complete, EX, H4 ....$50.00
Big Jim, accessory, Kung Fu Studio, complete, MIB, H4 ..$85.00
Big Jim, accessory, Sky Commander Jet, MIB $50.00
Big Jim, figure, Big Jack, complete, MIB, H4 ....$40.00
Big Jim, figure, Captain Flint, complete, MIB, H4 ....$40.00
Big Jim, figure, Dr Steel, missing few accessories, VG, H4 ....$25.00
Big Jim, figure, Torpedo Fist, complete, VG, H4 ....$30.00
Big Jim, figure, Warpath, missing few accessories, VG, H4 ...$25.00

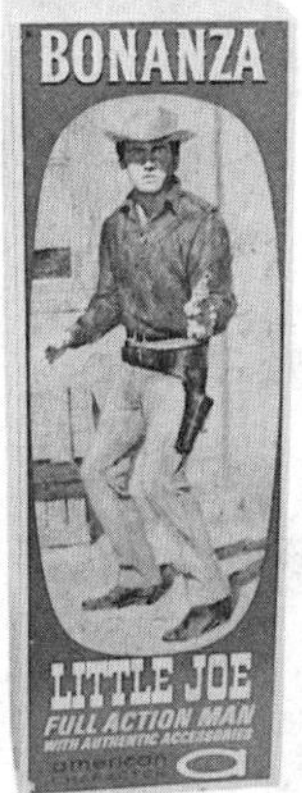

Photo courtesy June Moon

Bonanza, figures, Ben, Little Joe, Hoss, and Outlaw, J6, MIB, from $200.00 to $250.00 each.

Bonanza, figure set, Hoss w/Horse, Am Character, rare, 8", MIB, H4 ....$200.00
Bonanza, horse, Am Character, complete, EX, H4 ....$30.00
Buck Rogers in the 25th Century, accessory, Command Center, Mego, 1979, MIB, C1 ....$110.00
Buck Rogers in the 25th Century, figure, Buck, Dr Huer, Draco, Killer Kane or Walking Twiki, Mego, 12", NRFB, H4, ea $75.00
Buck Rogers in the 25th Century, figure, Walking Twiki, Draco or Killer Kane, Mego, 3¾", M, F1, ea $25.00
Captain Action, accessory, Parachute Pack, Ideal, complete, EX, H4 ....$70.00
Captain Action, accessory, Silver Streak Amphibian Car, Ideal, NM (EX box) $950.00
Captain Action, figure, Action Boy, Ideal, 12", complete, EX $400.00
Captain Action, figure, Aqualad, Ideal, 12", complete, EX, H4 ....$265.00
Captain Action, figure, Batman, Ideal, 12", complete, EX, H4 ....$200.00
Captain Action, figure, Captain Action, Ideal, 12", complete, EX, H4 ....$225.00
Captain Action, figure, Captain America, Ideal, 12", complete, VG, H4 ....$225.00
Captain Action, figure, Dr Evil, Ideal, 12", complete, NM (VG box) $450.00
Captain Action, figure, Robin, Ideal, 12", missing few accessories, EX, H4 ....$200.00
Captain Action, figure, Superman, Ideal, 12", MIB $950.00
Captain Action, outfit, Aquaman, Ideal, complete, NMIB .$400.00
Captain Action, outfit, Captain America, Ideal, complete, NMIB $700.00
Captain Action, outfit, Green Hornet, Ideal, complete, M (EX box) $3,000.00
Captain Peg-Leg, figure, Matchbox, 8", MIB, M17 ....$70.00
Captain Planet & the Planeteers, accessory, Eco Sub, Tiger/Kenner, MIB, F1 ....$30.00
Captain Planet & the Planeteers, accessory, Geo Cruiser, Tiger/Kenner, MIB, F1 ....$25.00
Captain Planet & the Planeteers, accessory, Skumm Copter, Tiger/Kenner, MIB, F1 ....$25.00
Captain Planet & the Planeteers, accessory, Toxic Cannon, Tiger/Kenner, MIB, F1 ....$15.00
Captain Planet & the Planeteers, figure, any character, Tiger/Kenner, 3¾", MOC, F1, ea $15.00
Captain Power, figure, Captain Power or Corp Pilot Chase, Mattel, MOC, F1, ea $15.00
Captain Power, figure, Tritor, Stingray Johnson or Scout Baker, Mattel, MOC, F1, ea $20.00
CHiPs, accessory, Highway Patrol Van, Empire Toys, rare, VG, H4 ....$45.00
CHiPs, accessory, Rescue Bronco, Fleetwood, MOC, J5 ..$25.00
CHiPs, figure, Jon, Mego, 8", MOC $35.00
CHiPs, figure, Ponch, Mego, 3¾", MOC, F1 ....$15.00
CHiPs, figure, Ponch, Mego, 8", MOC $25.00
CHiPs, figure, Sarge, Mego, 8", MOC $40.00
CHiPs, figure, Whilly Wheels, Mego, 3¾", MOC, F1 ......$20.00
Chuck Norris, figure, Chuck Norris, Ninja Warrior, Kimo or Super Ninja, Kenner, MOC, F1, ea $15.00
Clash of the Titans, figure, Kraken Sea Monster, MIB, H4 ...$190.00
Dark Knight, figure, Tec-Shield Batman, Shadow-Wing Batman, Iron Winch Batman or Bruce Wayne, Kenner, MOC, F1, ea $20.00

DC Comics Super Heroes, figure, Aquaman, Green Lantern, Hawkman or Two-Face, Toy Biz, 3¾", MOC, F1, ea ...$25.00
DC Comics Super Heroes, figure, Batman, Robin, Penquin, Joker, Riddler or Flash, Toy Biz, 3¾", MOC, F1, ea ..$20.00
Dr Evil, figure, Ideal, 1967, 12", NM (VG box), A $450.00
Dr Who, figure, Ace, Ice Warrior or Cyberman, Dapol, 4", MOC, H4, ea ...$30.00
Dukes of Hazzard, accessory, Hazzard County Sheriff's Car, Mego, rare, NM, H4 ...$100.00
Dukes of Hazzard, accessory, Two-Speed Stuntbusters, Knickerbocker, MIB (sealed), H4 ...$80.00
Dukes of Hazzard, figure, Bo, Luke, Daisy or Boss Hogg, Mego, 8", MOC, ea ...$35.00
Dukes of Hazzard, figure, Coy, Mego, 8", MOC, F1 ....$40.00
Dukes of Hazzard, figure, Daisy or Luke, Mego, 3¾", MOC, ea, from $20 to...$25.00

Dukes of Hazzard, figure, Uncle Jesse, MOC, $35.00.

Emergency, accessory, fold-out playset, vinyl, VG, H4.....$45.00
Emergency, figure, John or Roy, 8", EX, H4, ea $35.00
Emergency, figure, John or Roy, 8", MOC, H4, ea $70.00
ET, accessory, Stunt Spaceship, LJN, MOC, H4 ....$10.00
ET, figure, w/pop-up head, LJN, 4", MOC, H4 ....$20.00

Fighting Furies, figure, Hooded Falcon Adventure, MIB, $95.00.

Flash Gordon, figure, Flash Gordon, Mattel, MOC, H4...$25.00
Flash Gordon, figure set, Flash, Dr Zarkov & Thun, Mattel, MIB, H4 ...$40.00
Flash Gordon, figure set, Ming, Lizard Woman & Beastman, Mattel, MIB, H4 ...$40.00
Generation X, figure, any except Marrow or White Queen, Toy Biz, MOC, F1, ea ...$15.00
Generation X, figure, Marrow or White Queen, Toy Biz, MOC, F1, ea...$20.00
Ghost Rider, figure, any character, Toy Biz, MOC, F1, ea.$15.00
Girl From UNCLE, figure, April Dancer, complete, NM (EX box), F5...$400.00
Happy Days, accessory, Fonzie Garage, Mego, MIB..........$75.00
Happy Days, figure, any character, Mego, 8", MOC, ea, from $50 to...$60.00
He-Man, accessory, Monstroid, Mattel, MIB, H4.............$40.00
He-Man, accessory, Point Droid & Talon Fighter, Mattel, MIB, H4 ...$45.00
He-Man, figure, any character, Mattel, MOC, F1, ea.......$15.00
Honey West, figure, Honey West, Gilbert, 12", complete, NMIB...$250.00
How the West Was Won, figure, Zeb Macahan or Lone Wolf, Mattel, 9", MIB, H4, ea ...$45.00
Indiana Jones, see Adventures of Indiana Jones
James Bond, accessory, Dr No's Dragon Tank & Largos Hydrofoil Yacht, Gilbert, 1965, MOC, H4 ...$40.00
James Bond, accessory, Spin Top Pool Table & Deadly Laser Ray, Gilbert, 1965, MOC, H4...$40.00
James Bond, figure, Drax or Holly, Moonraker, Mego, 12", NMIB, ea ...$135.00
James Bond, figure, James Bond, Gilbert, w/scuba gear, 12", NM (NM box), A ...$800.00
James Bond, figure, Moonraker, Mego, 12", M (NM box), B3 ...$95.00
James Bond, figure, Oddjob, Gilbert, 12", M (EX box) ..$385.00
James Bond, figure, Thunderball, Gilbert, 12", M (NM box).$235.00
Justice League of America, figure, Aquaman, Robin or Wonder Woman, Ideal, 3", EX, H4, ea ...$65.00
Justice League of America, figure, Flash, Ideal, rare, 3", EX, H4 ...$75.00

Knight Rider, car and figure, EX, $40.00.

Knight Rider, figure, Michael Knight, Kenner, 6", MOC, H4 ...$30.00
Kojak, accessory, Police Emergency Access Set, Excel Toys, MOC, H4...$30.00
Land of the Lost, accessory, Land Master Jeep, MIB, F1...$20.00

Land of the Lost, figure, Talking Stink, Talking Annie or Talking Kevin, MOC, F1, ea $15.00
Land of the Lost, figure, Tom Porter, Annie Porter, Shung, Tasha or Kevin Porter, MOC, F1, ea $10.00
Last Action Hero, figure, any character except Evil Eye Bandit, Mattel, 1st or 2nd series, MOC, ea $5.00
Last Action Hero, figure, Evil Eye Bandit, Mattel, MOC.$10.00
Legends of Batman, figure, Crusader, Riddler, Firstmate, Laughing Man, Gladiator or Buccaneer, Kenner, MOC, F1, ea ..$10.00
Legends of Batman, figure, Flightpack, Silverknight, Catwoman or Joker, Kenner, MOC, F1, ea....$20.00
Legends of Batman, figure, Future, Cyborg, Nightwing, Knightquest, Viking, Knightsend or Samurai, Kenner, MOC, F1, ea $10.00
Legends of Batman, figure, Ultimate Batman, Kenner, 15", MIB, F1 ....$50.00
Legends of Batman, figure set, Egyptian Batman & Egyptian Catwoman, Kenner, MOC, F1 ....$25.00
Legends of Batman, figure set, Pirate Batman & Pirate Two-Face, Kenner, MOC, F1....$25.00
Legends of the Lone Ranger, figure, any character, Gabriel, 3¾", MOC, ea $20.00
Legends of the Wild West, figure, Wyatt Earp, Woolworth, 9", MIB, H4 ....$55.00
Lone Ranger Rides Again, accessory, Blizzard Adventure, Gabriel, NRFB (window cracked), H4....$35.00
Lone Ranger Rides Again, accessory, Hidden Silver Mine, Gabriel, NRFB, H4....$40.00
Lone Ranger Rides Again, accessory, Landslide Adventure, Gabriel, NRFB, H4....$40.00
Lone Ranger Rides Again, figure, Butch Cavendish or Little Bear, Gabriel, 9", NRFB, H4, ea....$50.00
Lone Ranger Rides Again, figure, Lone Ranger or Tonto, Gabriel, 9", EX, H4, ea $20.00
Love Boat, figure, any character, Mego, 3½", MOC, J5, ea .$25.00
M*A*S*H, figure, Klinger, Mego, 3¾", MOC, F1 ....$20.00
M*A*S*H, figure, Klinger in Drag outfit, Tri-Star, 3¾", MOC, H4 ....$40.00
Major Matt Mason, accessory, binoculars, Mattel, EX, H4.$8.00
Major Matt Mason, accessory, Cat Trak, Mattel, red or wht, EX, H4, ea....$10.00
Major Matt Mason, accessory, Gamma Ray Guard Pak, Mattel, MIB, D8 ....$95.00
Major Matt Mason, accessory, hammer, Mattel, EX, H4 ....$5.00
Major Matt Mason, accessory, Jet Pack, Mattel, complete, EX, H4 ....$15.00
Major Matt Mason, accessory, Rocket Launch Pack, Mattel, complete, EX, H4....$25.00
Major Matt Mason, accessory, Space Bubble, Mattel, complete, EX, H4 ....$35.00
Major Matt Mason, accessory, Space Shelter Pak, Mattel, MIB, D8....$95.00
Major Matt Mason, accessory, Space Sled, Mattel, complete, EX, H4 ....$15.00
Major Matt Mason, accessory, Space Travel Pak, Mattel, MIB, D8....$95.00
Major Matt Mason, accessory, Supernaut Power Limbs, Mattel, EX, H4 ....$25.00
Major Matt Mason, accessory, Supernaut Power Limbs, Mattel, MIB, D8 ....$95.00
Major Matt Mason, accessory, Talking Command Console, Mattel, non-working o/w EX, H4....$80.00
Major Matt Mason, accessory, Unitred & Space Bubble, Mattel, VG (G box), H4 ....$140.00
Major Matt Mason, accessory, Unitred Hauler, Mattel, EX (EX box), H4....$75.00
Major Matt Mason, accessory, walkie-talkie, Mattel, EX, H4...$10.00
Major Matt Mason, figure, Calisto, Mattel, M (M German card), A $400.00
Major Matt Mason, figure, Doug Davis, Mattel, w/helmet & visor, EX, H4....$80.00
Major Matt Mason, figure, Matt Mason, Mattel, w/helmet, EX, H4 ....$60.00
Major Matt Mason, figure, Sgt Storm, Mattel, fully jtd, 7", NM (NM box), A $665.00
Major Matt Mason, figure, Sgt Storm on Cat Trac, Mattel, 1967, fully jtd, 7", NM (NM card), A....$665.00
Man From UNCLE, accessory, Cap-Firing Tommy Gun, Gilbert, MIP $65.00
Man From UNCLE, accessory, Uncle Husky car, Gilbert, MOC, H4 ....$220.00
Man From UNCLE, figure, Illya Kuryakin, Gilbert, 12", VG (VG box), H4....$150.00
Marvel Super Heroes, accessory, Super Vator Playset, Mego, EX, H4 ....$50.00
Marvel Super Heroes, figure, Aqualad, Mego, complete, NM, H4....$120.00
Marvel Super Heroes, figure, Aquaman, Mego, complete, EX, H4 ....$42.00
Marvel Super Heroes, figure, Batman, Mego, complete, NM, H4....$75.00
Marvel Super Heroes, figure, Captain America, Mego, complete, NMIB, H4....$195.00
Marvel Super Heroes, figure, Catwoman, Mego, complete, EX, H4 ....$125.00
Marvel Super Heroes, figure, Conan, Mego, complete, NM (NM box), H4....$225.00
Marvel Super Heroes, figure, Daredevil, 1st issue, Toy Biz, MOC, F1 ....$40.00
Marvel Super Heroes, figure, Daredevil, 2nd issue, Toy Biz, MOC, F1 ....$15.00
Marvel Super Heroes, figure, Falcon, Mego, complete, NMIB, H4 ....$75.00
Marvel Super Heroes, figure, Green Arrow, Mego, complete, EX, H4 ....$95.00
Marvel Super Heroes, figure, Green Goblin, Mego, complete, NMIB, H4....$200.00
Marvel Super Heroes, figure, Human Torch, Mego, complete, NMIB, H4 ....$90.00
Marvel Super Heroes, figure, Invisible Woman, 2nd issue, Toy Biz, MOC, F1 ....$25.00
Marvel Super Heroes, figure, Iron Man, Mego, complete, NMIB, H4 ....$175.00
Marvel Super Heroes, figure, Joker, complete, VG, H4....$40.00
Marvel Super Heroes, figure, Joker, Mego, complete, NM (NM box), H4....$175.00

Marvel Super Heroes, figure, Lizard, Mego, wht jacket, complete, EX, H4 ....$95.00
Marvel Super Heroes, figure, Mr Fantastic, Mego, complete, NMIB, H4....$100.00
Marvel Super Heroes, figure, Mr Mxyzptlk, Mego, complete, NMIB, H4....$50.00
Marvel Super Heroes, figure, Penguin, Mego, complete, NM, H4 ....$40.00
Marvel Super Heroes, figure, Punisher, Annilus, Deathlok, Dr Doom, Dr Octopus or US Agent, Toy Biz, MOC, F1, ea $15.00
Marvel Super Heroes, figure, Riddler, Mego, complete, M (VG unpunched card), H4 ....$225.00
Marvel Super Heroes, figure, Robin, Mego, bendable, NM, H4....$25.00
Marvel Super Heroes, figure, Spider-Man, Mego, complete, NMIB, H4....$50.00
Marvel Super Heroes, figure, Thor, Green Goblin, Iron Man, Mr Fantastic or Human Torch, Toy Biz, MOC, F1, ea....$20.00
Marvel Super Heroes, figure, Thor, Mego, complete, NM, H4 ....$120.00
Marvel Super Heroes Secret Wars, figure, Constrictor, Mattel, 4", M (NM European card) $85.00

Marvel Super Heroes Secret Wars, figure, Daredevil and His Secret Shield, Mattel, 3¾", MOC, $40.00.

Marvel Super Heroes Secret Wars, figure, Hobglobin, 4", M (NM European card) $60.00
Marvel Super Heroes Secret Wars, figure, Iceman, 4", M (NM European card)....$85.00
Marvel Super Heroes Secret Wars, figure, Spider-Man or Wolverine, Mattel, 4", M (NM US card), J5, ea $35.00
Masters of the Universe, accessory, Blasterhawk, Mattel, MIB, F1 ....$40.00
Masters of the Universe, accessory, Dragon Walker, Mattel, MOC, F1....$20.00
Masters of the Universe, accessory, Fright Zone playset, Mattel, MIB $85.00
Masters of the Universe, accessory, Jet Sled, Mattel, MOC, F1 ....$20.00
Masters of the Universe, accessory, Land Shark, Mattel, MOC, F1 ....$20.00
Masters of the Universe, accessory, Masters Weapon Pak, Mattel, MOC, F1 ....$5.00
Masters of the Universe, accessory, Slit Stalker, Mattel, MOC, F1 ....$10.00
Masters of the Universe, accessory, Spydor, Mattel, MIB, F1....$40.00
Masters of the Universe, figure, Buzz-Off, Skeletor, Jitsu, Orko or Fisto, Mattel, MOC, H4, ea....$30.00
Masters of the Universe, figure, King Randor, Mattel, MOC, F1 ....$25.00
Masters of the Universe, figure, Moss Man, Two Bad, Roboto, Spikor or Sy-Klone, Mattel, MOC, H4, ea $20.00
Masters of the Universe, figure, Mousquitor, Dragstor, Clamp Champ, King Hiss, Rokkon or Rio Blast, Mattel, MOC, F1, ea....$15.00
Masters of the Universe, figure, Teela, Mattel, MOC, H4..$40.00
Masters of the Universe, figure, Thunder Punch He-Man, Dragon Blaster Skeletor or Buzz Saw Hordak, Mattel, MOC, F1, ea....$20.00
Masters of the Universe, figure, Zodiac, Tri-Clops, Ram Man or Mekaneck, Mattel, MOC, H4, ea $35.00
Micronauts, figure, Acroyear, Mego, 3¾", MOC, H4....$50.00
Micronauts, figure, Repto, Mego, 3¾", MOC, H4....$120.00
Mike Hazard, accessory, trench coat, Marx, NM, F5 ....$15.00
Mike Hazard, figure, Mike Hazard Double Agent, Marx, complete, NM (EX box), F5....$150.00
Muhammad Ali, figure, Mego, MOC (unpunched), H4...$160.00
Noble Knights, figure, Sir Gordon the Gold Knight, Marx, missing few accessories, NM, F5....$135.00
Noble Knights, figure, Sir Stuart the Silver Knight, Marx, missing few accessories, G, H4 ....$50.00
Official Scout High Adventure, accessory, Avalanche at Blizzard Ridge, Kenner, complete, EX, H4 ....$20.00
Official Scout High Adventure, accessory, Balloon Race to Devils Canyon, Kenner, MIB, H4....$25.00
Official Scout High Adventure, accessory, Pathfinder Jeep & Trailer, Kenner, EX (VG box), H4 ....$30.00
Official Scout High Adventure, Steve Scout or Craig Cub Scout, Kenner, NRFB, H4, ea $30.00

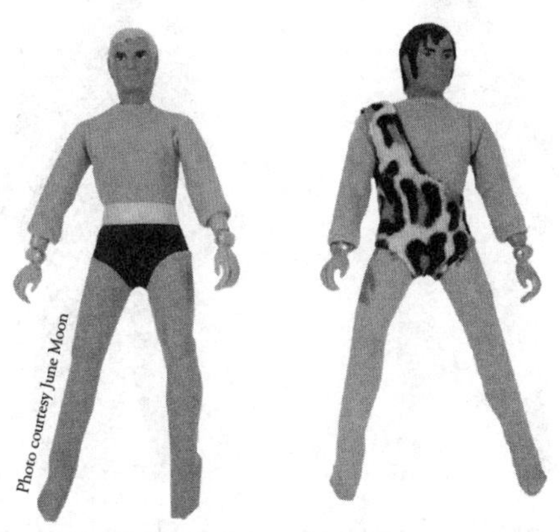

Official World's Greatest Super Heroes, figures, Aquaman and Tarzan, Mego, 8", EX, $45.00 each.

Official World's Greatest Super Heroes, figure, Batman, Bend'n Flex, Mego, 5", NMOC $50.00

Official World's Greatest Super Heroes, figure, Batman, Mego, 12", MIB...$75.00

Official World's Greatest Super Heroes, figure, Batman, Mego, 8", MIB $175.00

Official World's Greatest Super Heroes, figure, Captain America, Mego, 8", EX, $50.00.

Official World's Greatest Super Heroes, figure, Conan, Mego, 8", complete, M $160.00

Official World's Greatest Super Heroes, figure, Green Arrow, Mego, 8", no accessories, G $25.00

Official World's Greatest Super Heroes, figure, Human Torch, Mego, 8", complete, M, D8 ....$30.00

Official World's Greatest Super Heroes, figure, Human Torch, Mego, 8", MOC, D8 ....$50.00

Official World's Greatest Super Heroes, figure, Incredible Hulk, Mego, 8", MIB, T2..$100.00

Official World's Greatest Super Heroes, figure, Joker, Mego, 8", complete, M, D8 ....$55.00

Official World's Greatest Super Heroes, figure, Mr Mxyzptlk, Mego, 8", MOC (sealed), T2 ....$175.00

Official World's Greatest Super Heroes, figures, Mr. Mxyzptlk (smiling version), Mego, 8", EX, $45.00; Green Goblin, EX, $125.00.

Official World's Greatest Super Heroes, figure, Penguin, Mego, 8", MOC (sealed), T2..$125.00

Official World's Greatest Super Heroes, figure, Riddler, Fist Fighting, Mego, 8", M, D8.....................................$150.00

Official World's Greatest Super Heroes, figure, Riddler, Mego, 8", complete, NM, D8...$95.00

Official World's Greatest Super Heroes, figure, Robin, Fist Fighting, Mego, 8", M, D8.......................................$125.00

Official World's Greatest Super Heroes, figures, Spider-Man, Mego, 8", EX, $35.00; Shazam, EX, $50.00.

Official World's Greatest Super Heroes, figure, Spider-Man, Bend'n Flex, Mego, MOC, A $75.00

Official World's Greatest Super Heroes, figure, Spider-Man, Mego, 12", complete, M, D8.....................................$35.00

Official World's Greatest Super Heroes, figure, Spider-Man, Mego, 12", NRFB..$80.00

Official World's Greatest Super Heroes, figure, Supergirl, Bend 'n Flex, Mego, NMOC, A..$50.00

Official World's Greatest Super Heroes, figure, Superman, Bend 'n Flex, Mego, NMOC, A..$50.00

Official World's Greatest Super Heroes, figure, Superman, Bend'n Flex, Mego, MOC (sealed), T2....................$150.00

Official World's Greatest Super-Gals, figures, Invisible Girl, Mego, 8", EX, $35.00; Catwoman, EX, $95.00.

Official World's Greatest Super-Gals, figure, Supergirl, Mego, 8", MOC (sealed), T2 .... $200.00

Official World's Greatest Super-Gals, Wonder Woman, Mego, 8", MOC (sealed), T2 .... $200.00

Our Gang, figure, Alfalfa, Spanky, Mickey or Porkey, Mego, MOC (unpunched), H4, ea $40.00

Our Gang, figure, Buckwheat, Mego, MOC (unpunched), H4 .. $45.00

Our Gang, figure, Darla, Mego, MOC (unpunched), H4 . $55.00

Pee-Wee's Playhouse, figure, Miss Yvonne, Matchbox, 6", MOC, H4 .... $30.00

Pee-Wee's Playhouse, figure, Pee-Wee, Matchbox, 6", MOC, H4 .... $25.00

Pee-Wee's Playhouse, figure, Ricardo or Reba, Matchbox, 6", MOC, H4, ea $20.00

Planet of the Apes, accessory, Forbidden Zone Trap, Mego, MIB, H4 .... $350.00

Planet of the Apes, accessory, Throne, Mego, MIB, H4 ... $75.00

Planet of the Apes, accessory, Treehouse, Mego, MIB, H4 .. $225.00

Planet of the Apes, figure, Astronaut, Mego, 8", complete, VG $75.00

Planet of the Apes, figure, Cornelius, Mego, 8", complete, EX $65.00

Planet of the Apes, figure, General Ursus, Mego, 1967, bendable, 8", NM (NM card), A $200.00

Planet of the Apes, figure, General Ursus, Mego, 8", MOC. $155.00

Planet of the Apes, figure, Peter Burke, Mego, 8", complete, EX, H4 .... $75.00

Planet of the Apes, figure, Soldier Ape, Bend'n Flex, Mego, 5", MOC $65.00

Planet of the Apes, figure, Soldier Ape, Mego, 8", complete, EX, H4 .... $60.00

Planet of the Apes, figure, Soldier Ape, Mego, 8", rare brn outfit, EX, H4 .... $70.00

Planet of the Apes, horse, Stallion, Mego, MIB, H4 ...... $125.00

Power Rangers, figure, Billy (bl) or Zach (blk), Bandai, 1st issue, MIB, H4, ea $15.00

Power Rangers, figure, Jason (red), Bandai, 1st issue, MIB, H4 .... $15.00

Power Rangers, figure, Kimberly (pk) or Trina (yel), Bandai, 1st issue, MIB, H4, ea $20.00

Power Rangers, figure set, White Ranger & Tigerzord, Bandai, 1st issue set, MIB, H4 .... $50.00

Predator, figure, Lasershot, Lava, Nightstorm, Spiked Tail or Stalker, Kenner, MOC, F1, ea $20.00

Rambo, accessory, Savage Trike Cycle, Coleco, EX, F1 ... $15.00

Rambo, figure, Rambo, Coleco, 6", MOC, F1 .... $25.00

Rambo, figure, Sgt Havoc, Gripper or Turbo, Coleco, 6", MOC, F1, ea $20.00

Real Ghostbusters, figure, any character except Stay Puft Man or Slimer, Kenner, MOC, F1, ea $15.00

Real Ghostbusters, figure, Slimer, Kenner, MOC, F1 .... $25.00

Real Ghostbusters, figure, Stay Puft Man, Kenner, MOC, F1 ... $30.00

Robin Hood Prince of Thieves, accessory, Battle Wagon, Kenner, MIP $15.00

Robin Hood Prince of Thieves, figure, Azeem or Little John, Kenner, MOC, F1, ea $15.00

Robin Hood Prince of Thieves, figure, Dark Warrior or Will Scarlett, Kenner, MOC, F1, ea $25.00

Robin Hood Prince of Thieves, figure, Friar Tuck, Kenner, MOC, F1 .... $30.00

Robin Hood Prince of Thieves, figure, Robin Hood, Kenner, MOC $8.00

RoboCop, accessory, Skull Hog or Robocycle, Kenner, MOC, F1, ea $10.00

RoboCop, figure, any character except Gatlin Blast, Kenner, 3¾", MOC, F1, ea $15.00

RoboCop, figure, Gatlin Blast, Kenner, 3¾", rare, MOC, F1 . $25.00

Robotech, figure, Lynn Minmei, Dana Sterling or Lisa Hayes, Matchbox, 12", MIB, F1, ea $30.00

Robotech, figure, Max Sterling or Roy Fokker, Matchbox, MOC, ea $15.00

Robotech, figure, Rook Bartley, Matchbox, MOC, D8 .... $25.00

Rookies, figure, Mike or Willie, LJN, 8", MOC, H4, ea ... $70.00

Rookies, figure, Terry, LJN, 8", orig outfit, EX, H4 .... $35.00

Silverhawk, figure, Hardware, Steel Will, Moon Stryker, Windhammer or Condor, 2nd series, Kenner, MOC, F1, ea ... $15.00

Six Million Dollar Man, accessory, Bionic Mission Control Center, Kenner, missing few pcs, EX (VG box), H4 .... $60.00

Six Million Dollar Man, accessory, OSI Headquarters, Kenner, missing few pcs, NMIB, H4 .... $50.00

Six Million Dollar Man, figure, Bionic Bigfoot, Kenner, 12", complete, EX, H4 .... $70.00

Six Million Dollar Man, figure, Fembot, Kenner, 12", NRFB, H4 .... $125.00

Six Million Dollar Man, figure, Maskitron, Kenner, 12", NRFB, H4 .... $150.00

Six Million Dollar Man, figure, Oscar Goldman, Kenner, 12", NRFB, H4 .... $55.00

Six Million Dollar Man, figure, Steve, Kenner, New Bionic Arm, 12", rare, MIB, Y1 .... $75.00

Six Million Dollar Man, figure, Steve, Kenner, 2nd edition, New Bionic Grip, 12", MIB $50.00

Space: 1999, figure, Commander Koenig or Professor Bergman, Mattel, 9", MOC, ea $50.00

Spawn, accessory, Spawn Alley Playset, Todd Toys, MIB, F1 ... $40.00

Spawn, accessory, Spawnmobile, Todd Toys, MOC, F1 ... $30.00

Spawn, figure, any character from 1st or 2nd series, Todd Toys, MOC, F1, ea $30.00

Spawn, figure, any character from 3rd or 4th series, Todd Toys, MOC, F1, ea $15.00

Spider-Man, see Marvel Super Heroes and Official World's Greatest Super Heroes

Starsky & Hutch, figure, Chopper, Mego, 8", M (EX box), B3 .... $35.00

Starsky & Hutch, figure, Dobey, Mego, 8", MOC $50.00

Starsky & Hutch, figure, Starsky or Hutch, Mego, M (NM card), H4, ea $50.00

Steve Scout, see Official Scout High Adventure

Stony Smith, figure, Paratrooper, Marx, missing few accessories, NM (EX box), F5 .... $175.00

Super Mario Brothers, figure, any character, Ertl, 3¾", MOC, F1, ea $10.00

Super Powers, accessory, carrying case, Kenner, orig labels, EX, H4 .... $15.00

Super Powers, accessory, Darkseid Destroyer, Kenner, MIB, H4 .... $45.00

Super Powers, accessory, Kalibak Boulder Bomber, Kenner, EX (EX box), H4 ....$25.00
Super Powers, figure, Batman, Kenner, MOC (unpunched), H4 ....$55.00
Super Powers, figure, Brainiac, Kenner, complete w/ID card & comic book, NM, H4 ....$30.00
Super Powers, figure, Cyborg, Kenner, M (Mexico Super Amigos card), H4 ....$100.00
Super Powers, figure, Cyclotron, Kenner, MOC, H4 ....$50.00
Super Powers, figure, Cyclotron, Kenner, 3rd series, complete w/ID card, NM, H4 ....$40.00
Super Powers, figure, Darkseid, Kenner, complete w/ID card & comic book, NM, H4 ....$15.00
Super Powers, figure, DeSaad, Kenner, MOC, H4 ....$25.00
Super Powers, figure, Dr Fate, Kenner, complete, NM, H4 ....$25.00
Super Powers, figure, Firestorm, Kenner, complete w/ID card & comic book, NM, H4 ....$25.00
Super Powers, figure, Flash, Kenner, MOC, H4 ....$15.00
Super Powers, figure, Golden Pharaoh, Kenner, 3rd series, complete w/ID card, NM, H4 ....$60.00
Super Powers, figure, Hawkman, Kenner, complete w/ID card & comic book, NM, H4 ....$35.00
Super Powers, figure, Joker, Kenner, complete w/ID card & comic book, NM, H4 ....$35.00
Super Powers, figure, Kalibak, Kenner, MOC, H4 ....$15.00
Super Powers, figure, Lex Luther, Kenner, complete w/ID card & comic book, NM, H4 ....$15.00
Super Powers, figure, Mantis, Kenner, complete w/ID card & comic book, NM, H4 ....$25.00
Super Powers, figure, Mr Freeze, Kenner, 3rd series, complete w/ID card, NM, H4 ....$40.00
Super Powers, figure, Mr Miracle, Kenner, 3rd series, complete w/ID card & comic book, NM, H4 ....$90.00

Photo courtesy June Moon

Super Powers, figures, Orion, MOC, $55.00; Plastic Man, MOC, $125.00.

Super Powers, figure, Penguin, Kenner, complete w/ID card & comic book, NM $25.00
Super Powers, figure, Plastic Man, Kenner, complete, NM, H4 ....$70.00
Super Powers, figure, Red Tornado, Kenner, complete, NM, H4 ....$35.00
Super Powers, figure, Robin, Kenner, MOC (unpunched), H4 ....$55.00
Super Powers, figure, Samurai, Kenner, 3rd series, complete w/ID card & comic book, NM, H4 ....$60.00
Super Powers, figure, Shazam, Kenner, complete w/ID card & comic book, NM, H4 ....$50.00
Super Powers, figure, Steppenwolf, Kenner, complete w/ID card & comic book, NM, H4 ....$30.00
Super Powers, figure, Tyr, Kenner, MOC, H4 ....$60.00
Super Powers, figure, Tyr, Kenner, 3rd series, complete w/ID card & comic book, NM, H4 ....$40.00
Super Powers, figure, Wonder Woman, Kenner, M (NM card), H4 ....$30.00
Supergirl, figure, Ideal, 1967, 12", scarce, from $2,000 to $3,000.00
Swamp Thing, figure, Capture Swamp Thing or Climbing Swamp Thing, Kenner, 2nd series, MOC, F1, ea $10.00
SWAT, accessory, fold-out playset, vinyl, missing few pcs, VG, H4 ....$120.00
SWAT, figure, McCabe, 8", orig outfit, EX, H4 ....$35.00
SWAT, figure, Street, 8", orig outfit, EX, H4 ....$35.00
Tarzan, figure set, Young Tarzan & Kala, MOC $45.00
Teenage Mutant Ninja Turtles, figure, any character, Playmates, 3¾", MOC, F1, ea $20.00
Terminator 2, figure, Blaster T1000, Damage Repair, Power Arm, Secret Weapon or Techno Punch, Kenner, MOC, ea $20.00
Terminator 2, figure, John Conner, Kenner, MOC $25.00
Terminator 2, figure, Terminator, poseable, limited video offer w/release of 1st movie, 11", EX, H4 ....$20.00
Thundercats, accessory, Luna-Lasher, LJN, MIB $35.00
Thundercats, accessory, Mutant Skycutter, LJN, MIB $35.00
Thundercats, figure, any character, LJN, MOC, ea, from $35 to $45.00
Toxic Crusaders, figure, Toxic Crusader, Playmates, 5", MOC, F1 ....$15.00
Toy Story, figure, Kicking Woody, Quick Draw Woody or Karate Buzz Light-Year, Thinkway Toys, 6", MOC, ea $15.00
Universal Monsters, figure, Creature from the Black Lagoon, glow-in-the-dark, Remco, 3¾", MOC $45.00
Universal Monsters, figure, Dracula, glow-in-the-dark, Remco, 3¾", MOC $35.00
Universal Monsters, figure, Frankenstein, glow-in-the-dark, Remco, 3¾", MOC $35.00
Universal Monsters, figure, Mummy, glow-in-the-dark, Remco, 3¾", MOC $75.00
Universal Monsters, figure, Phantom, glow-in-the-dark, Remco, 3¾", MOC $35.00
Universal Monsters, figure, Wolfman or Mummy, Azrak, 8", EX, H4, ea $35.00
Viking Warrior, figure set, Erik the Viking & Horse, Marx, complete, NM (EX mailer), F5 ....$195.00
Viking Warriors, figure, Brave Erik, Marx, complete, NM (G box), F5 ....$165.00
Viking Warriors, figure, Erik the Viking, Marx, complete, EX, H4 ....$110.00
Viking Warriors, figure, Odin the Viking, Marx, missing few accessories, EX, H4 ....$160.00

Viking Warriors, horse, Marx, cream colored, complete, VG, H4 .... $45.00
Waltons, figure, any character, Mego, 8", complete, EX, H4, ea $20.00
Welcome Back Kotter, accessory, Grease Machine, AHI, MOC, H4 .... $70.00

Photo courtesy June Moon

Welcome Back Kotter, figure, Barbarino, Mattel, 9", MOC, $50.00.

Welcome Back Kotter, figure, Kotter, Epstein, Washington or Horshack, Mattel, 9", MOC, H4, ea $45.00
Willow, figure, any character except Ufgood, Tonka, 1988, MIP, F1, ea $5.00
Willow, figure, Kael w/Horse, Tonka, 1988, MIP, F1 .... $10.00
Willow, figure, Sorsha w/Horse, Tonka, 1988, MIP, F1 .... $10.00
Willow, figure, Ufgood w/Baby, Tonka, 1988, rare, MIP, F1 .... $10.00
Wizard of Oz, accessory, Munchkinland playset, Mego, complete, VG, H4 .... $150.00
Wizard of Oz, accessory, Wizard of Oz & His Emerald City, Mego, complete, MIB $300.00

Wizard of Oz, figures, Cowardly Lion and Glinda the Good Witch, Mego, 8", MIB, $45.00 each.

Wizard of Oz, figure, Cowardly Lion, Mego, 8", M, D8 .... $25.00
Wizard of Oz, figure, Scarecrow, Mego, 8", MIB, D8 .... $65.00
Wizard of Oz, figure, Scarecrow, Mego, 8", NM, D8 .... $25.00
Wizard of Oz, figure, Tin Woodsman, Mego, 8", MIB $35.00
Wizard of Oz, figure, Wicked Witch, Mego, 8", MIB, H4 .... $65.00
Wizard of Oz, figure, Wizard, Mego, 8", MIB, F1 .... $25.00

Photo courtesy June Moon

World Wrestling Federation, figure, Billy Jack Haynes, MOC, $85.00; Jesse Ventura, MOC, $45.00.

World Wrestling Federation, figure, Brutus Beefcake, Hasbro, MOC, F1 .... $30.00
World Wrestling Federation, figure, Bushwacker Butch, Hasbro, MOC, F1 .... $15.00
World Wrestling Federation, figure, Crush, Hasbro, MOC, F1 .... $25.00
World Wrestling Federation, figure, Earthquake, Hasbro, 4", MOC, F1 .... $30.00
World Wrestling Federation, figure, Headshrinker Fatu, Hasbro, MOC, F1 .... $15.00
World Wrestling Federation, figure, Honky Tonk Man, Hasbro, MOC, F1 .... $40.00
World Wrestling Federation, figure, Jake the Snake Roberts, Hasbro, MOC, F1 .... $20.00
World Wrestling Federation, figure, Jimmy Snuka, Hasbro, MOC, F1 .... $30.00
World Wrestling Federation, figure, Lex Luger, Hasbro, MOC, F1 .... $25.00
World Wrestling Federation, figure, Ludvig Borga, Hasbro, MOC, F1 .... $35.00
World Wrestling Federation, figure, Razor Ramon, Hasbro, MOC, F1 .... $25.00
World Wrestling Federation, figure, Roddy Piper, Hasbro, MOC, F1 .... $35.00
World Wrestling Federation, figure, Sgt Slaughter, Hasbro, MOC, F1 .... $30.00
World Wrestling Federation, figure, Ted Dibiase, gr outfit, Hasbro, MOC, F1 .... $20.00
World Wrestling Federation, figure, Texas Tornado, Hasbro, MOC, F1 .... $50.00
World Wrestling Federation, figure, Typhoon, Hasbro, 4", MOC, F1 .... $30.00

World Wrestling Federation, figure, Ultimate Warrior, gr trunks, Hasbro, MOC, F1 ....$35.00
World Wrestling Federation, figure, Ultimate Warrior, purple trunks, Hasbro, MOC, F1 ....$50.00
Wyatt Earp, figure, Wyatt Earp, Mego, Am West Series, 8", rare, M (EX Sears box), F1 ....$50.00
X-Force, figure, any except Deadpool, Domino or The Blob, MOC, F1, ea $15.00
X-Force, figure, Deadpool, Domino or The Blob, MOC, F1, ea...$20.00
X-Men Classics (Animated Series), figure, any character, Toy Biz, MOC, F1, ea $15.00
X-Men Robot Fighters, figure, Jubilee, Toy Biz, MOC, F1 .$20.00
X-Men Robot Fighters, figure, Storm, Wolverine, Gambit or Cyclops, Toy Biz, MOC, F1, ea $15.00
X-Men 2099, figure, any character, Toy Biz, MOC, F1, ea .$15.00
Zeroid, accessory, Robot Zogg Commander Set, Ideal, MIB, H4...$200.00
Zeroid, figure, Robot from Star Raiders, Ideal, EX, H4.....$45.00

Activity Sets

Activity sets that were once enjoyed by so many as children — the Silly Putty, the Creepy Crawlers, and those Mr. Potato Heads — are finding their way back to some of those same kids, now grown up, more or less, and especially the earlier editions are carrying pretty respectable price tags when they can be found complete or reasonably so. The first Thingmaker/Creepy Crawler (Mattel, 1964) in excellent but played-with condition will sell for about $65.00 to $75.00. For more information about Tinker Toys see *Collector's Guide to Tinker Toys* by Craig Strange (Collector Books).

Advisor: Bill Bruegman (T2).

See also Character, TV, and Movie Collectibles; Coloring, Activity, and Paint Books; Disney; Playsets; Western.

Adams' Hocus-Pocus Magic Set, SS Adams, 1962, complete & unused, NM (EX box) $85.00
Big Burger Grill, Kenner, 1967, complete, EX (EX box), F8 ..$30.00
Big Top Cotton Candy Machine, Hasbro, 1960s, unused, NMIB, J2...$125.00
Boy's World Thingmaker, Mattel, 1968, Deluxe edition, NMIB, from $200 to $250.00
Cartoon Charm Set, King Features Syndicate, complete w/48 plastic charms, chains & pins, NMIB, A $135.00
Charm Jewelry Kit, Ginny Gem, 1957, complete, MIB, F8 ..$35.00
Colorforms, 1950, 1st issue, complete w/100 geometric shapes, unused, rare, MIB, T2...$80.00
Cooky Cucumber w/Her Friend Mr Potato Head, Hasbro, 1966, complete, EX (VG box), M17/H4.............................$50.00
Creeple Peeple Thingmaker, Mattel, 1965, complete, MIB.$100.00
Creeple Peeple Thingmaker Pak, EX, T2..........................$50.00
Creepy Crawlers, Mattel, 1964, 1st issue, VG (VG box), from $65 to $75.00
Creepy Crawlers Collector's Case, Mattel, 1964, vinyl w/spider web design on front, NM, F8...................................$50.00
Creepy Crawlers II, Mattel, 1978, NMIB..........................$50.00
Crime Lab, Amsco, 1976, unused, MIB, from $25 to........$50.00

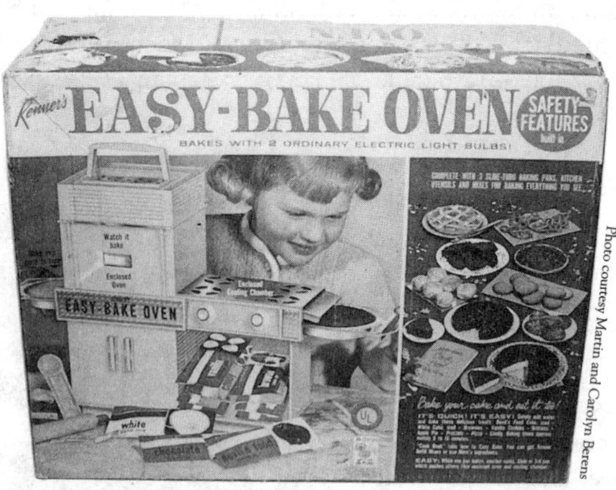

Photo courtesy Martin and Carolyn Berens

Easy-Bake Oven, Kenner, MIB, from $75.00 to $85.00.

Photo courtesy Martin and Carolyn Berens

Electric Mold Master, Kenner, MIB, $40.00.

Electrical Workshop, Remco, 1960s, unused, NMIB, J2...$100.00
Famous Comics Viewmaster & Films, Acme Plastics, 1947, complete, EX (VG box), A $125.00
Favorite Funnies Printing Set, Semco, 1930s, EX (EX box), J5...$85.00
Federal Agent Fingerprint Set, Transogram, 1938, MIB...$135.00
Girl's World Thingmaker, Mattel, 1968, complete, NMIB, F8 ....$50.00
Great Foodini Magic Set, Pressman, 1960, complete, rare, NMIB, F8...$150.00
Hanna-Barbera Stamp Set, Creative, 1974, complete, MIB (sealed), F8...$50.00
Harvey-Toon TV Flannel Funnies, Rand McNally, 1971, Colorforms-type playset featuring several characters, NMIB, F8 ....$30.00
Hingees, Reed & Assoc, 1944, features Popeye, Dick Tracy, Little Orphan Annie, etc, unused, NM (EX box), from $200 to...$300.00
Hocus Pocus Magic Set, 1976, complete, NMIB $50.00
Incredible Edibles Gobble-Degoop, Mattel, 1966, MOC, M17 ....$35.00

Incredible Edibles Kooky Kakes, Mattel, 1967, contents sealed, MIB, M17 ....$120.00
Jr Miss Costume Jewelry Set, 1940s, complete, EX (EX box) .$35.00
Jr Miss United Nations Jewelry Set, 1940s, complete, EX (EX box) $35.00
Krazy Ikes, Whitman, 1964, complete, EX (EX canister), T2..$25.00
Magic Kit of Tricks & Puzzles, Transogram, 1960s, complete, EX (EX box), M17 ....$55.00
Magnetic Comic Faces, Deluxe, 1950s, complete, EX (G box), F8 ....$15.00
Make Your Own Funnies, Jaymar, 1930s, complete w/10 jtd wood comic characters to assemble, NM (EX box), from $500 to $600.00
Martian Magic Tricks, Gilbert, 1963, complete, scarce, NMIB, from $250 to $300.00
Merry Milkman, Hasbro, 1955, complete, NMIB, F8.....$120.00
Microscope & Lab Set, Gilbert #13025, electric, MIB $40.00
Mister Funny Face, Peerless Playthings Inc, 1953, complete, NM (NM box), M17 ....$100.00

Monster Machine, Gabriel, MIB, $25.00.

Moon Rocks, Hasbro, 1970, 3-D, EX (EX box), J2 ....$35.00
Motorized Monster Maker, Topper, 1960s, few pcs missing, EX (EX box), F8 ....$75.00

Mr. and Mrs. Potato Head, Hasbro, MIB, $85.00.

Mr & Mrs Potato Head & Pets, Hasbro, complete, MIB, from $60 to $70.00
Mr Magic Set, Adams, 1960s, complete, NMIB, J2 ....$50.00
Mr Potato Head Frenchy Fry Set, Hasbro, complete, rare, EX (EX box) $85.00

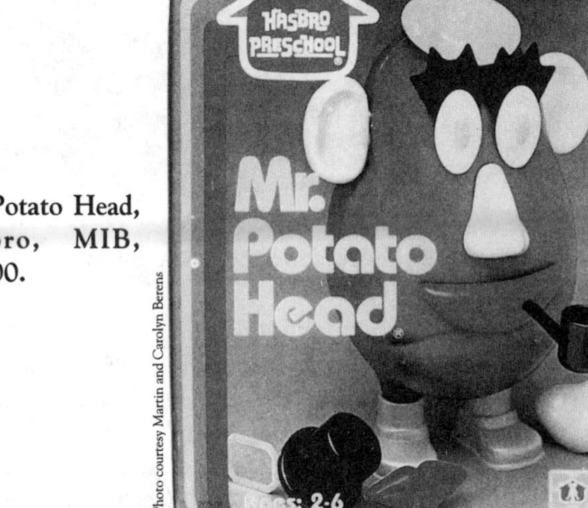

Mr. Potato Head, Hasbro, MIB, $25.00.

Mr Potato Head Funny Face Kit, Hasbro, 1950s, EX (EX box), J2 ....$50.00
My First Apron & Bead Set, 1940s, complete, EX (EX box)..$25.00
My House Printer Kit, Colorforms, 1962, complete, EX (EX box), F8 ....$25.00
Mysto Magic Exhibition Set, Gilbert, 1920s, NM (EX box) .$450.00
Play-Doh Wood-Doh Modeling Compound, Rainbow Crafts, 1959, complete, EX (EX canister) $35.00
Playstone Funnies Kasting Kit, Allied Mfg, 1936, features Little Orphan Annie, Sandy, Skeezix, etc, EX (VG box) .$150.00
Power Mite Workshop, Ideal, 1969, complete, EX (EX box)...$125.00
Pretzel Jetzel Factory, Transogram, 1965, complete, EX (G box), F8 ....$45.00
Science Magic, Remco, 1969, complete, NMIB, F8 ....$25.00
Scribblebug, Eberhard Faber, 1961, complete, NM (EX box), F8 ....$40.00
See 'N Say Talking Picture Puzzle, Mattel, 1968, complete w/plastic carrying case, NM (EX box), F8 ....$40.00
Shaker Maker Animals, Ideal, 1971, set #2, missing pnt o/w complete & unused, EX (EX box), F8 ....$30.00
Shaker Maker Bugglies Set, Ideal, 1972, MIB, F8 ....$30.00
Shrink Machine, Wham-O, 1968, complete, EX (EX box), F8 ....$70.00
Shrunken Head Apple Sculpture, Milton Bradley, 1975, complete, M (NM box), M17, from $45 to $65.00
Slinky Pop-Up, James Industries, 1950s, 5", MIB, M17....$40.00
Sneaky Pete's Magic Show, Remco, 1960s, complete, NMIB, F8 ....$150.00
Space Scientists Drafting Set, 1950s, EX (EX box), J2...$100.00
Spirofoil Set, Kenner, 1970, few pcs missing, EX (EX box), F8 ....$15.00
Strange Change Toy Featuring the Lost World, Mattel, 1967, complete, EX (EX box), F8 ....$80.00

Super Heroes Shaker Maker, Ideal, MIB (sealed), J5........**$45.00**
Suzy Homemaker Grill, Topper, MIB, C17......................**$65.00**

Photo courtesy Martin and Carolyn Berens

Suzy Homemaker Sweet Shoppe Soda Fountain, Topper, MIB, from $40.00 to $50.00.

Switch 'N Go Military Tank Set, Mattel, 1965, complete, EX (EX box), F8 ....**$45.00**
Talking Picture Puzzle w/Spellums, Mattel, 1968, NM (EX carrying case), F8 ....**$40.00**
Thingmaker Fright Factory, Mattel, MIB (sealed), J2 ....**$150.00**
Thingmaker Fun Flowers, Mattel, complete, EX, S15 ......**$35.00**
Thingmaker Mini Dragon Maker Pack, Mattel, 1967, MIB (sealed), J2 ....**$125.00**
Thingmaker Thingholder, Mattel, 1967, vinyl carrying case w/various images of Thingmaker sets on cover, EX, F8 ....**$40.00**
Trix Stix, Harry Dearly, 1952, complete, MIP, M17 ....**$50.00**
Vac-U-Form Casting Set, Mattel, 1960s, MIB, from $60 to...**$75.00**
Vac-U-Form Playset, Mattel, 1962, missing few minor pcs, EX (EX box), F8 ....**$80.00**

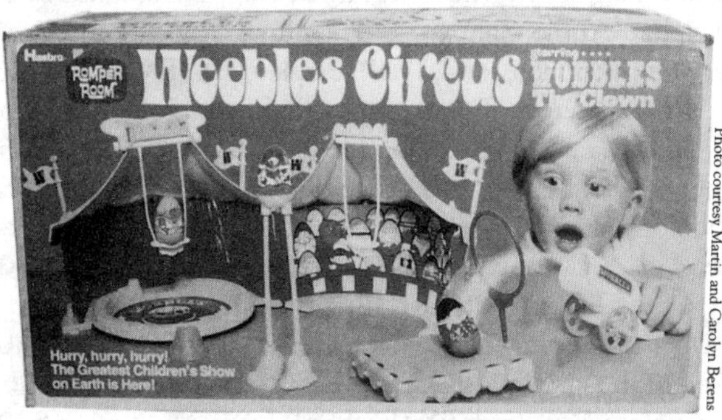

Photo courtesy Martin and Carolyn Berens

Weebles Circus, Romper Room, MIB, $25.00.

Winky Dink Paint Set, Pressman, 1950s, complete, EX...**$75.00**
Young Magician's Box of Tricks, Saalfield, 1958, complete, NM (VG box), F8 ....**$25.00**

Advertising

The assortment of advertising memorabilia geared toward children is vast — plush and cloth dolls, banks, games, puzzles, trucks, radios, watches, and much, much more. And considering the popularity of advertising memorabilia in general, when you add to it the crossover interest from the realm of toys, you have a real winning combination! Just remember to check for condition very carefully; signs of play wear are common. Think twice about investing much money in soiled items, especially cloth or plush dolls. (Stains are often impossible to remove.)

For more information we recommend *Zany Characters of the Ad World* by Mary Jane Lamphier; *Advertising Character Collectibles* by Warren Dotz; *Advertising Dolls Identification & Value Guide* by Joleen Ashman Robison and Kay Sellers; *Huxford's Collectible Advertising* by Sharon and Bob Huxford; *Cracker Jack Toys* by Larry White; *Pepsi-Cola Collectibles, Vols I, II, and III*, by Bill Vehling and Michael Hunt; and *Collectible Coca-Cola Toy Trucks* by Gael de Courtivron.

Advisors: Michael Paquin (P12), Jim Rash (R3), advertising dolls; Larry White (W7), Cracker Jack.

See also Bubble Bath Containers; Cereal Boxes and Premiums; Character, TV, and Movie Collectibles; Dakins; Disney; Fast-Food Collectibles; Halloween Costumes; Pin-Back Buttons; Premiums; Radios; Telephones; Western; and other specific categories.

A&P Super Market, horse & wagon, Marx, plastic, red & yel wagon w/yel spoke wheels, single brn horse, NM (NM box), A **$165.00**
A&W Root Beer, bear, 1975, plush, 13", EX, from $20 to..**$35.00**
Actigall, squeeze toy, Gall Bladder figure, Summit, 1989, vinyl, 4", M, J6 ....**$40.00**
Actigall, squeeze toy, Gall Bladder figure, Summit, 1989, vinyl, 8", M, from $40 to..**$65.00**

Admiral Appliances, figure, Admiral, vinyl, 7", M $15.00

Photo courtesy Dunbar Gallery

Aero Mayflower Transit Company, truck, Linemar, friction, MIB, D10, $350.00.

Allied Van Lines, doll, 1970s, stuffed cloth, 18", G, M15...$30.00
Bazooka, doll, Bazooka Joe, 1973, stuffed cloth, EX..........$20.00
Betty Crocker, doll, Kenner, 1974, stuffed cloth, 13", VG, M15 ....$20.00
Big Boy, bank, 1973, Big Boy figure, vinyl, 9", EX, F8......$20.00
Big Boy, doll, Big Boy, 1978, stuffed cloth w/Big Boy printed on chest, 14", MIP $30.00
Big Boy, doll, Dolly, 1978, stuffed cloth w/dotted dress, hands on hips, 14", MIP $30.00
Big Boy, kite, paper w/image of Big Boy, M, from $200 to ..$250.00
Borden, bag, 1980s, canvas, Cheese Is My Bag, EX, J5 .....$15.00
Borden, doll, Beauregard, 1950s, stuffed plush w/vinyl face & ears, 12", VG, M15 ....$55.00
Borden, doll, Elsie, 1973, stuffed cloth w/vinyl head & hooves, 13", VG, from $50 to $80.00
Borden, Elsie's Funbook Cut-Out Toys & Games, 1940s, EX, P6 ....$65.00

Photo courtesy Mary Jane Lamphier

Borden, figure, Elsie the Cow, 1993, PVC, 3½", M, from $10.00 to $20.00.

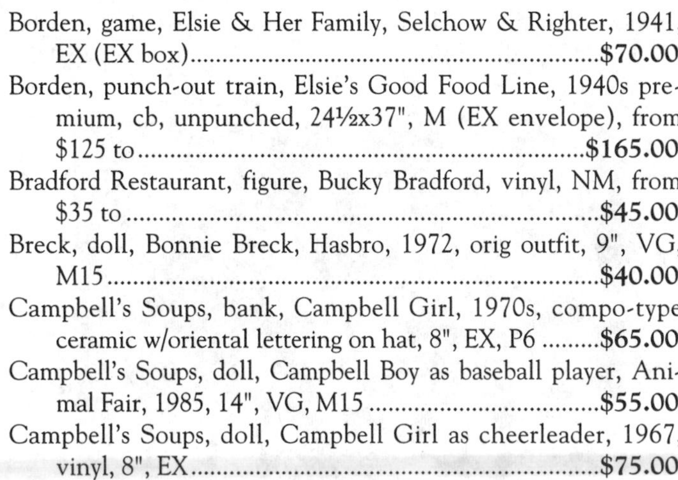

Borden, game, Elsie & Her Family, Selchow & Righter, 1941, EX (EX box)..$70.00
Borden, punch-out train, Elsie's Good Food Line, 1940s premium, cb, unpunched, 24½x37", M (EX envelope), from $125 to $165.00
Bradford Restaurant, figure, Bucky Bradford, vinyl, NM, from $35 to $45.00
Breck, doll, Bonnie Breck, Hasbro, 1972, orig outfit, 9", VG, M15 ....$40.00
Campbell's Soups, bank, Campbell Girl, 1970s, compo-type ceramic w/oriental lettering on hat, 8", EX, P6 ....$65.00
Campbell's Soups, doll, Campbell Boy as baseball player, Animal Fair, 1985, 14", VG, M15 ....$55.00
Campbell's Soups, doll, Campbell Girl as cheerleader, 1967, vinyl, 8", EX..$75.00

Photo courtesy June Moon

Campbell's Soups, doll, Campbell Girl in Scottish outfit, M, from $85.00 to $100.00.

Campbell's Soups, doll kit, 1989, MIP $35.00
Campbell's Soups, dolls, Campbell Kids, 1970s, rag-type, MIB, pr $125.00
Campbell's Soups, dolls, Campbell Kids, 1970s, vinyl, 9", MIB, pr $150.00
Campbell's Soups, game, Campbell Kids Shopping Game, Parker Bros, 1955, complete, scarce, EX (EX box)..............$300.00
Campbell's Soups, jigsaw puzzle, All Aboard, 1986, 28 pcs, VG $25.00
Campbell's Soups, tea set, 1982, plastic, Campbell Kids image, 4 cups, plates, tray, dish & utensils, MIB $50.00
Campbell's Soups, vacuum cleaner, Mirro/Pla-Vac, 1950s, aluminum, battery-op, MIB..$85.00
Cap'n Crunch, doll, Mighty Star, 1987, stuffed cloth, 18", EX $30.00
Cap'n Crunch, game, Island Adventure, Warren, 1987, NM (EX box), F8 ....$25.00
Caravelle Candy Bar, figure, Caravelle man on horse, bendable, rare, M, from $150 to...$200.00
Cheetos, doll, Cheetah, 1980s, stuffed plush, 18", EX, F8 ....$20.00

Chiffon Margarine, doll, Mother Nature, stuffed cloth w/yarn hair, 15", MIB, H4/M15 ....$30.00

Photo courtesy Mary Jane Lamphier

Chips Ahoy, figure, Nabisco, 1990s, 5", M, $20.00; Oreo Cookie, figure, Nabisco, 1990s, 4½", M, from $5.00 to $10.00.

Chiquita Bananas, football, 1970s, bright yel w/logo on front, 11", EX, J5 ....$25.00
Chiquita Bananas, walkie-talkies, M, B5/S15, from $65 to...$75.00
Chocks Vitamins, doll, Charlie Chocks, 1960s, stuffed cloth, 18", EX, J5 ....$25.00
Chrysler, bank, Mr Fleet, 1970s, scarce, M, from $300 to..$350.00
Chucky Cheese Pizza, bank, Chucky Cheese figure, vinyl, 7", EX, H4 ....$10.00
Coca-Cola, airplane, 1973-74 Albatross, red & wht, EX..$100.00
Coca-Cola, bang gun, Santa in sleigh, 1970s, paper, unused, M, A $10.00
Coca-Cola, bus, Ashi Toys, litho tin w/plastic windows, friction, 14", NM....................$1,300.00
Coca-Cola, car, Isetta, Bandai, 1950s, red & wht w/chrome detail & lithoed interior, 6½", NM $175.00
Coca-Cola, change purse, red leather w/Drink Coca-Cola in gold, triangular, NM....................$475.00
Coca-Cola, dispenser, Linemar, 1950s, insert coin & Coke dispenses into cup, tin, battery-op, 9½", NM (EX box), A...........$950.00
Coca-Cola, dispenser, 1970s, plastic, EX, N2 ....$25.00
Coca-Cola, doll, Buddy Lee, 1950s, composition, EX $875.00
Coca-Cola, doll, Frozen Coca-Cola mascot, 1960s, stuffed cloth, 1960s, NM $150.00
Coca-Cola, game, Safety & Danger, 1938, cb, complete, EX...$100.00
Coca-Cola, game, Santa Ring Toss, 1980s, 10", VG $10.00
Coca-Cola, game, Tic-Tac-Toe, EX (EX box)................$165.00
Coca-Cola, game set, complete w/target, table tennis, bingo & checkers, 1939, VG (EX box) $425.00
Coca-Cola, game set, complete w/2 decks of cards, cribbage board, checkers & dominos, Milton Bradley, 1943, NMIB $450.00
Coca-Cola, jigsaw puzzle, Crossing the Equator, EX (EX box)....................$150.00
Coca-Cola, jigsaw puzzle, Hawaiian Beach, rare, NMIB...$185.00
Coca-Cola, jigsaw puzzle, Teenage Party, NMIB............$100.00
Coca-Cola, key chain, 1950s, bottle shape, gold-tone metal, 1½", MIP, M15 ....$5.00

Coca-Cola, music box, 1950s, shaped like a cooler w/doll on revolving disk, red, EX $2,700.00

Photo courtesy Dunbar Gallery

Coca-Cola, truck, Buddy L, 1950s, pressed steel, 12", M, D10, $450.00.

Coca-Cola, truck, Buddy L #5117, 1970s, pressed steel w/contour logo, 9", EX....................$50.00
Coca-Cola, truck, Buddy L #5270J, 1980s, pressed steel w/clear plastic cab top, 14", NM $25.00
Coca-Cola, truck, Buddy L #5426, 1962-64, pressed steel w/2-tiered divided bay, 15", EX $155.00
Coca-Cola, truck, Budgie, 1950s, diecast, orange w/divided open bay, 5", EX $125.00
Coca-Cola, truck, Budgie, 1980s, diecast, red w/wht bed cover, NMIB $75.00
Coca-Cola, truck, Dinky #402, 1965-69, diecast, 4½", MIB .$425.00
Coca-Cola, truck, Goso/Germany, 1957, tin, red & yel w/2-tiered open bay, w/12 plastic cases, 13", NM, from $1,500 to $1,600.00
Coca-Cola, truck, Hartoy Inc, lights up & plays Coca-Cola song, diecast, 1/64th scale, MOC, M15 ....$20.00
Coca-Cola, truck, Japan, 1950, gr w/lithoed cases, friction, 9", rare, EX, A....................$1,100.00
Coca-Cola, truck, Japan, 1970s, tin & plastic, yel w/image of 2 bottles & red disk logo, friction, 4", NM....................$40.00
Coca-Cola, truck, Lincoln Toys/Canada, early 1950s, pressed steel, red, w/12 wooden blocks in back, 16", EX......$850.00
Coca-Cola, truck, Marusan, 1956-57, tin, yel & bl w/red detail, friction, w/2 removable bottle racks, 8", NMIB.......$850.00

Photo courtesy John Turney

Coca-Cola, truck, Marx, lithographed tin, 11", MIB, $450.00.

Coca-Cola, truck, Marx, metal, yel w/red detail, mk Delicious & Refreshing, case of Coke in back, 12", EX, A **$200.00**
Coca-Cola, truck, Marx, 1950-54, plastic, red & yel Chevy w/enclosed bed, top ad panel, 11", EX **$800.00**
Coca-Cola, truck, Marx, 1954-56, tin, yel w/red wheel covers, 12", NM (EX box) **$650.00**
Coca-Cola, truck, Marx, 1956-57, tin, open bay w/center ad panel, 7 cases of Coke, 17", EX **$500.00**
Coca-Cola, truck, Marx/Canada, 1949-52, pressed steel, red w/stake bed, wht logo, 20", EX, from $1,200 to....**$1,300.00**
Coca-Cola, truck, Matchbox #37A, 1950s-60s, diecast, yel w/red trim, 2", M (G box) **$85.00**
Coca-Cola, truck, Metalcraft, 1932, pressed steel, red & yel, complete w/10 bottles, 11", EX, from $600 to **$800.00**
Coca-Cola, truck, Mighty Midget #49, Benbros, 1950s, diecast, 2", MIB **$250.00**
Coca-Cola, truck, Sanyo, 1960s, tin, yel & wht w/red detail & logo, battery-op, 12", NMIB....................................**$275.00**
Coca-Cola, truck, Smith-Miller, pressed steel, yel w/4 cases, blk rubber tires, 13", NM (NM box), A **$2,200.00**
Coca-Cola, truck, Spain, red & yel plastic, mk Beba Coca-Cola in bed & on rear, w/6 cases, 8", scarce, EX, A **$235.00**
Coca-Cola, truck set, Buddy L #4969E, 1980s, 6 pcs, MIB.**$75.00**
Coca-Cola, truck set, Buddy L #4973, 1970s, 7 pcs, MIB, J6..**$85.00**

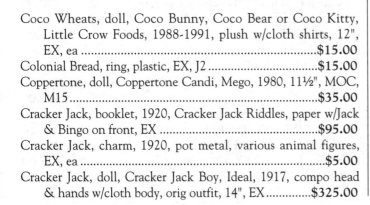

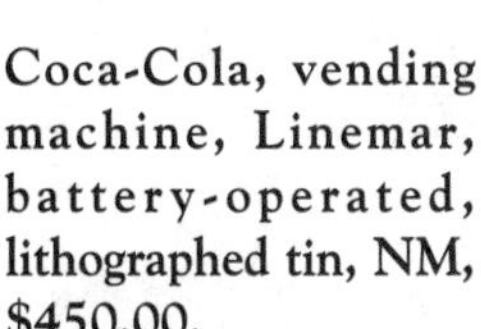
Coca-Cola, vending machine, Linemar, battery-operated, lithographed tin, NM, $450.00.

Coco Wheats, doll, Coco Bunny, Coco Bear or Coco Kitty, Little Crow Foods, 1988-1991, plush w/cloth shirts, 12", EX, ea **$15.00**
Colonial Bread, ring, plastic, EX, J2 ....**$15.00**
Coppertone, doll, Coppertone Candi, Mego, 1980, 11½", MOC, M15 ....**$35.00**
Cracker Jack, booklet, 1920, Cracker Jack Riddles, paper w/Jack & Bingo on front, EX **$95.00**
Cracker Jack, charm, 1920, pot metal, various animal figures, EX, ea **$5.00**
Cracker Jack, doll, Cracker Jack Boy, Ideal, 1917, compo head & hands w/cloth body, orig outfit, 14", EX.............**$325.00**
Cracker Jack, figure, astronaut, plastic, EX **$10.00**
Cracker Jack, Goofy Zoo Wheel Game, 1940, red, brn & gr paper, EX...**$40.00**

Cracker Jack, horse and wagon, 1910, lithographed metal, EX, $200.00.

Cracker Jack, magic picture, plastic w/image of man holding hoop, Who's Jumping Thru!..., EX............................**$10.00**
Cracker Jack, magic slate, 1980, paper & plastic, EX..........**$8.00**
Cracker Jack, magnifier, 1960, plastic, various shapes & colors, EX, ea, from $1 to **$5.00**
Cracker Jack, maze puzzle, 1970, paper & plastic, EX **$6.00**
Cracker Jack, mirror, 1900s, celluloid & glass, Eat Cracker Jack & Be Happy, EX **$85.00**
Cracker Jack, Mysticolor Paint Set, 1970, paper, EX **$8.00**
Cracker Jack, paint book, 1920, Cracker Jack Painting Book, EX **$80.00**
Cracker Jack, palm puzzle, plastic & paper w/Gee Cracker Jack Is Good, EX **$75.00**
Cracker Jack, palm puzzle, plastic & paper w/rising moon image, EX...**$85.00**
Cracker Jack, pocket clip, 1980, plastic, various animal figures, EX, ea **$4.00**
Cracker Jack, puzzle, 1940, Last Round-Up, red & gr paper, EX **$30.00**
Cracker Jack, squeaker, 1910, paper bellows, Me For Cracker Jack w/several different designs, EX, ea **$60.00**
Cracker Jack, sticker, 1970, glow-in-the-dark, blk on yel, EX **$4.00**
Cracker Jack, tilt card, 1950, magician, elephant, pirate, etc, plastic & paper, EX, ea..**$8.00**
Cracker Jack, top, 1900s, japanned metal, A-B-C around periphery, EX...**$50.00**
Cracker Jack, top, 1910, metal & wood, Always on Top, EX **$75.00**
Cracker Jack, trick mustache, 1940, paper, red or blk, ea .**$20.00**
Cracker Jack, whistle, metal, airplane w/patriotic images, EX...**$85.00**
Cracker Jack, whistle, 1930, metal w/playing card face, EX..**$60.00**
Curad, bank, Taped Crusader, vinyl, NM, P12 ....**$75.00**
Curtiss Candy, truck, Marx, red plastic w/5 rolls of candy in truck bed, 9", NM (NM box), A **$175.00**
Datsun-Nissan, dog, orig overalls & hat, 13", VG, M15...**$30.00**
Del Monte, doll, Yumkin Brawny Bear, 1985, plush w/cloth overalls, 12", EX...**$20.00**

Diaparene, figure, Diaparene Baby, 1980s, vinyl, w/orig diaper, M $50.00
Dole Pineapple, clock, rnd, EX, B5 .... $30.00
Dole Pineapple, doll, Bananimal Banabear, Trudy Toys, 1989, plush, w/orig tag, 10", M $15.00
Domino's Pizza, figure, Donny Domino, PVC, M $15.00
Dr Pepper, dart game, 1943, EX $300.00
Dr Pepper, paddle ball, Free!...w/Each Carton of Dr Pepper, EX $35.00
Emerson TV, bank, 1950s, Ultrawave TV w/clown on screen, wht plastic, 2½x4", EX, P4 .... $35.00
Eskimo Pie, doll, Eskimo Pie Boy, Chase Bag Co, 1975, stuffed cloth, 15", NM $20.00
Eveready Batteries, bank, blk cat, plastic, Save w/the Cat, MIB, J6 .... $35.00
Fanny Farmer Candies, truck, Marx, 1950s, plastic, wht w/brn lettering, 10", M (EX box), A $175.00
Frito Lay, eraser, Frito Bandito figure, 1960s, various colors, 1½", NM, ea, from $20 to $40.00
Frostie Root Beer, doll, 1972, stuffed cloth, 16", EX $25.00
Fruit Stripe Gum, figure, Yipe Zebra, bendable, scarce, EX, from $20 to $35.00
Gerber, bank, 1980, tin can-shape w/Gerber Orange Juice paper label, EX, G8 .... $15.00
Gerber, baseball cap, 1980s, blk & wht w/Gerber Baby image in center, EX, G8 .... $8.00
Gerber, boxcar, Bachmann, 1978, bl, HO scale, 5¾", MIB, G8 .... $95.00
Gerber, frisbee, 1980s, lettering surrounds image, Safety Comes in Cans..., bl on wht, EX, G8 .... $8.00
Gerber, Jingle Blox, 1950s, complete w/5 stacking blocks, EX (EX box), G8 .... $45.00
Gerber, patch, 1978, Fifty Years of Caring 1928-78 & image of Gerber Baby, bl & wht cloth, EX, G8 .... $6.00
Gerber, playing cards, 1955, features Sun Rubber Gerber doll, complete, NMIB, G8 .... $45.00
Gerber, record, What Is a Baby?, 1958, narrated by Rosemary Clooney, 33⅓ rpm, EX (EX sleeve), G8 .... $30.00
Gerber, reefer car, Lionel #6-9877, 1979, bl w/Gerber Baby image, O gauge, 11½", MIB, G8 .... $95.00
Gerber, squeak toy (may be a prototype), shaped like jar of baby food, 4", EX, G8 .... $250.00
Gerber, squeaker doll, Atlanta Novelty, 1985, vinyl, girl or boy, 8", EX, G8, ea $20.00

Photo courtesy Joan Stryker Grubaugh

Gerber, truck, Nylint, 1978, GMC 18-wheeler, pressed steel, 21½", M, G8, $85.00.

Gerber, teddy bear, Tender Loving Care Bear, Atlanta Novelty, 1978, plush w/red bow tie, 20", EX, G8 .... $25.00
Gerber, tote bag, 1990s, bl nylon, 11x14", EX, G8 .... $15.00
Goodyear Tire & Rubber Co, blimp, inflatable rubber, 32", MIP, M15 .... $15.00
Gordon's Farm Products, truck, Japan, w/driver, litho tin, opening rear doors & side door, friction, 7", EX, A $250.00
Grandma's Cookies, bank, Grandma figure, 1970, plastic, 7½", NM $30.00
Green Giant, doll, Jolly Green Giant, 1960s, stuffed cloth, 16", EX, from $20 to $40.00
Green Giant, doll, Little Sprout, 1974, stuffed cloth, 12", EX $20.00
Green Giant, figure, Little Sprout, 1970s, inflatable vinyl, 24", MIP $65.00

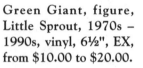

Green Giant, figure, Little Sprout, 1970s – 1990s, vinyl, 6½", EX, from $10.00 to $20.00.

Green Giant, flashlight, Little Sprout figure, MIB, P12 ... $45.00
Green Giant, jump rope, Little Sprout hdls, EX $15.00
Green Giant, kite, Jolly Green Giant, 1960s, thin plastic, 42x48", unused, M, from $20 to $30.00
Green Giant, pencil sharpener, Little Sprout, MIB $100.00
Green Giant, puppet, Little Sprout, EX $15.00
Harley-Davidson, doll, Harley Hog, logo on front & back of leather jacket, 9", M $20.00
Hawaiian Punch, doll, Punchy, stuffed cloth, 20", EX $50.00
Hawaiian Punch, game, Mattel, 1978, EX (EX box), H4 . $30.00
Hershey Kiss, bank, shaped like candy, M, B5 .... $10.00
Hershey's Chocolate, bear, Ideal, 1982, stuffed cloth w/vinyl face, 12", VG, M15 .... $30.00
Hood's Sarsaparilla, jigsaw puzzle, 1880s, EX (worn box), D10, from $300 to $400.00
Hostess, transfers, 1981, set of 6, M, B5 .... $30.00
Howard Johnson's, truck, Marx, 1950s, plastic, 11", scarce, NMIB, D10, from $300 to $400.00
Icee, ring, Icee bear, EX, J2 .... $15.00
Jack Frost Sugar, doll, Jack Frost, stuffed cloth, 17", EX ... $25.00
Jell-O, kite, 1950s, yel paper w/bold red lettering, M, J5 .. $25.00

Jif Peanut Butter, periscope, 1950s, features Jifaroo the kangaroo, yel cb, unused, 20", EX, from $15 to $25.00

Jordache Jeans, doll, cheerleader, Mego, 1981, 12", NRFB, H4/M15..........................$30.00

Jordache Jeans, doll, man or lady, Mego, 1981, 12", MIB, M15, ea..........................$25.00

Jordache Jeans, outfits, Mego, 1981, 8 different, NRFB, M15, ea from $8 to..........................$12.00

Keebler, doll, Keebler Elf, 1981, stuffed plush, 24", VG, from $25 to..........................$35.00

Kellogg's, doll cutouts, Dandy the Duck or Dinky the Dog, 1935, cloth, uncut, 17x13", M, P6, ea..........................$75.00

Kellogg's Frosted Flakes, tote bag, 1969, canvas, image of Tony licking his lips, 8", EX, F8..........................$50.00

Kellogg's Pop Tarts, bank, Milton the Toaster, 1970s, vinyl, rare, MIB, minimum value..........................$100.00

Ken-L Ration Sausages, wristwatch, Quartz premium, 1990s, blk plastic case & band, MIB, P4..........................$30.00

Kentucky Fried Chicken, bank, Colonel Sanders w/bucket of chicken, plastic, 10", EX, P6..........................$50.00

Kleenex, figures, Kleenex bears, mail-in premium, set of 3, NM, B5..........................$50.00

Kool-Aid, doll, Kool-Aid Kid, 1989, w/pigtails & freckles, 14", VG, from $15 to..........................$25.00

Kool-Aid, doll, Kool-Aid Kid, 1989, w/pigtails & freckles, 9", MIB, from $25 to..........................$35.00

Kool-Aid, doll, Mr Kool-Aid Awesome Dude, stuffed cloth, w/sunglasses & surfing shorts, MIP, M15..........................$15.00

Lee Jeans, teddy bear, 1988, wearing official Lee jeans, stuffed cloth, 15", VG, M15..........................$15.00

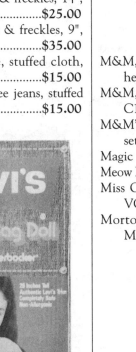

Levi's, rag doll, Knickerbocker, MIB, from $50.00 to $75.00.

Photo courtesy Martin and Carolyn Berens

Libby's, doll, Mattel, 1974, pull-string talker (not working), stuffed cloth w/yarn hair, 15", EX, J6..........................$40.00

Little Debbie, doll, 1984, vinyl with cloth outfit, 11", M, J6, $85.00.

Photo courtesy June Moon

M&M, dispenser, plain or peanut M&M in various colors, handheld, M, C11, ea from $3 to..........................$5.00

M&M, topper, plain or peanut M&M in several variations, M, C11, ea from $3 to..........................$5.00

M&M's, light set, 2" M&M's w/hands & feet in various colors, set of 20, NRFB, from $15 to..........................$20.00

Magic Chef, figure, vinyl, 7½", NM, from $10 to..........................$20.00

Meow Mix, figure, cat, 1970s, vinyl, NM, P12, from $38 to ..$45.00

Miss Clairol, doll, Glamour Misty, Ideal, 1965, 12", rpl robe, VG, M15..........................$35.00

Morton Salt, doll, Morton Girl, Mattel, 1974, 10", MIB, M15..........................$40.00

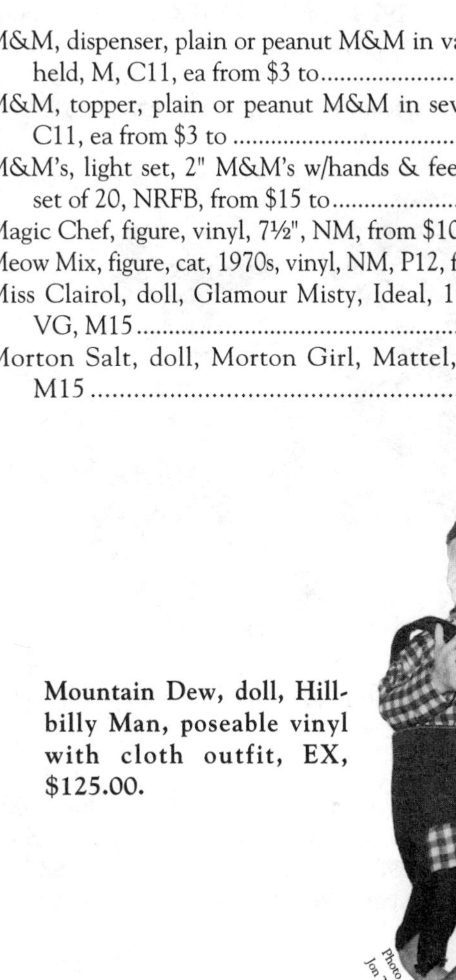

Mountain Dew, doll, Hillbilly Man, poseable vinyl with cloth outfit, EX, $125.00.

Photo courtesy Jon Thurmond

Moxie, kite, 1930s, Moxie Flyer, image of Moxie man, EX..**$150.00**
Moxie, Moxie-Mobile, 1917, horse & jockey in car, flat tin, 8", VG, A....**$1,200.00**
Mr Bubble, figure, Mr Bubble, vinyl, M....**$45.00**
Mr Clean, figure, vinyl, M, from $120 to....**$150.00**
Nabisco/National Biscuit Co, riding toy, yel van w/red stripe & logo, steering wheel on top, 22", VG, A....**$100.00**
National Biscuit Co, truck, Gibbs, pressed steel, 13", EX, D10....**$1,325.00**
Nestle, doll, Nestle Chocolate Man, Chase Bag Co, 1970, stuffed cloth, 15", NM....**$20.00**
Nestle, doll, Quik Bunny, stuffed plush, 14", M, P12....**$30.00**
Newberry's, truck, Marx, 1950s, bl & silver litho tin, You Always Find More..., 12", NM (NM box), A....**$300.00**
North American Van Lines, doll, Mary Ann, MIB, J2....**$70.00**
Northern Tissue, doll, 1986 or 1988, 16", VG, M15, ea...**$25.00**
Oscar Mayer, ring, Oscar Mayer kids, NM, J2....**$15.00**
Oscar Mayer, Weinermobile, pedal car, 1994-95, 2 different, P12, from $250 to....**$350.00**
Oscar Mayer, Weinermobile, remote control, MIB, P12..**$75.00**
Pappy Parker's Fried Chicken, figure, hillbilly, 1970s, vinyl, bl or brn outfit, NM, P12, ea....**$45.00**
Pepsi-Cola, dart board, 1950s, mk Pepsi-Cola Hits the Spot, 18", EX....**$125.00**
Pepsi-Cola, dispenser, 1970s, plastic, VG, N2....**$25.00**
Pepsi-Cola, jigsaw puzzle, 1970s, complete, EX (EX canister)....**$25.00**
Pepsi-Cola, kaleidoscope, 1981, can shape w/Catch the Pepsi Spirit, cb, VG, J5....**$15.00**
Pepsi-Cola, kite, 1960s, features Mary Poppins, EX....**$125.00**

Pepsi-Cola, pull toy, 1945, puppy with hot dog wagon, wood, 10", EX, $250.00.

Pepsi-Cola, Santa doll, Animal Fair Inc, stuffed plush w/fur beard, logo on belt buckle, 20", NM....**$55.00**
Pepsi-Cola, squirt gun, 1989, can shape, MOC....**$25.00**
Pepsi-Cola, transformer, Mattel, 1989, Pepsi can, VG, M15...**$15.00**
Pepsi-Cola, truck, Buddy L, wood & masonite, gr, 16", w/pressed steel hand cart, EX....**$800.00**
Pepsi-Cola, truck, Buddy L, 1943, van-type, Buy...Sparkling Satisfying on decal, mk Railway Express, 16", EX....**$500.00**

Photo courtesy Gary Metz

Pepsi-Cola, truck, Canadian, lithographed metal, NM, $500.00.

Pepsi-Cola, truck, Linemar, 1951, litho tin, 4", EX....**$175.00**
Pepsi-Cola, truck, Marx, 1940s, plastic, NMIB....**$450.00**
Pepsi-Cola, truck, 1956, litho tin w/plastic cab cover, 9", NM....**$175.00**
Pepsi-Cola, van, 1950s, litho tin, 11", EX....**$125.00**
Pepsi-Cola, van, 1970s, plastic, EX....**$40.00**
Pillsbury, book bag, Poppin' Fresh/Goofy Grape, 1969, rare, EX....**$85.00**
Pillsbury, decals, Poppin' Fresh, set of 18, MIP, P12....**$10.00**
Pillsbury, doll, Poppin' Fresh, 1972, stuffed cloth, 11", EX, I2 .**$20.00**
Pillsbury, doll, Poppin' Fresh, 1982, stuffed plush, scarce, M, from $30 to....**$45.00**
Pillsbury, figures, Grandmommer & Grandpopper, NM, pr....**$150.00**
Pillsbury, finger puppets, Poppin' Fresh & Pals, set of 3, rare, MIB, P12....**$235.00**
Pillsbury, gumball machine, Poppin' Fresh, MIB, P12....**$350.00**
Pillsbury, mug, Poppin' Fresh, 1979, plastic, EX, from $9 to .**$12.00**

Photo courtesy June Moon

Planters, vendor's costume, life-size, EX, from $800.00 to $900.00.

Pillsbury, playhouse, Poppin' Fresh, vinyl, w/4 finger puppets, NM, from $250 to..$300.00
Pillsbury, pop-up can, Poppin' Fresh, bl version, M, P12..$300.00
Pillsbury, pop-up can, Poppin' Fresh, orange version, M, P12 ....$200.00
Pillsbury, school box, Poppin' Fresh, w/pencils, erasers, etc, EX $100.00
Pizza Hut, bank, Pizza Hut Pete, 1969, plastic, NM, P12..$55.00
Planters, charm bracelet, 1941, 6 plastic charms on brass-colored chain, VG, P4 ....$50.00
Planters, doll, Mr Peanut, Chase Bag Co, 1967, stuffed cloth, 21", EX...$30.00
Planters, doll, Mr Peanut, Chase Bag Co, 1970, stuffed cloth, 18", NM $25.00
Planters, doll, Mr Peanut, stuffed plush, salesman's sample, 26", MIP, H4 ....$25.00
Planters, figure, Mr Peanut, bl hat version, jtd wood, 9", EX, A $200.00
Planters, pin, Mr Peanut figure, 1930s, diecut wood w/Mr Peanut lettered on hat, 2", EX, J5..$35.00
Planters, pop gun, 1930s-40s, paper w/image & Bang! for Planters Peanuts, 9", rare, VG................................$200.00
Poll Parrot Shoes, figure, bsk, Poll Parrot Shoes incised on back, 3½", VG, M15 ....$55.00
Poll Parrot Shoes, figures, Bride & Groom, Sonsco/Japan, celluloid, 4", EX, M15, pr $65.00
Poll Parrot Shoes, ring, 1950s, brass w/emb parrot, EX, J5..$65.00
Popsicle, figure, Popsicle Kids, Matchbox, 1988, 6 different, 6", NRFB, M15, ea $15.00
Quaker Oats, tic-tac-toe puzzle ring, EX, J2......................$55.00
Raid, Raid Bug, remote control, 14", M, from $300 to...$350.00

Photo courtesy John Turney

RCA Television Service Truck, Marx, plastic, MIB, $300.00.

Red Barn Restaurant, doll, Hamburger Hungry, 1970, plush & felt, EX $30.00
Red Barn Restaurant, trick-or-treat bag, 1964, orange w/image of witch & Red Barn logo, 13x13", EX, T2...................$20.00
Reddy Kilowatt, figure, 1960s, glow-in-the-dark, lg head version, rare, MOC (orig mail-order box), H4 ....$200.00

Revlon, doll, Little Miss Revlon, Ideal, 1958, orig red & wht striped dress w/red sunglasses & shoes, 10½", MIB....$75.00
Ritalin, figure, Ritalin Man, plastic, NM, P12................$125.00
Royal Gelatin, bank, King Royal, 1970s, vinyl, scarce, NM, P12..$225.00
Salamander Shoes, figures, vinyl, set of 6, sm, M, P12 ...$125.00
Salerno Bakery, truck, Marx, 1950s, tin, bl & wht w/red lettering, 11", NMIB, A $425.00
Seven-Up, doll, Fresh-Up Freddie, Canadian, stuffed cloth w/rubber head, 15", EX $75.00
Seven-Up, figure, Spot, Commonwealth Toy & Novelty, 1988, plush & felt w/suction cups on hands, 6", MIB..........$10.00
Seven-Up, figure, Spot, 1988, bendable, 5", M, from $10 to ..$20.00
Seven-Up, music box, can shape, plays Love Story, NM, J2 ..$50.00
Shakey's Pizza, doll, Shakey Chef, stuffed cloth, 18", EX .$25.00
Shoney's, bank, Shoney's bear, vinyl, M, P12...................$20.00

Photo courtesy Shirley Bertrand

Smokey the Bear, doll, Ideal, MIB, $250.00.

Spam, bank, litho tin, mail-in premium, M, P4 ....$10.00
Star-Kist, bank, Charlie Tuna, 1988, ceramic, 10", M, P12, from $45 to $65.00
Star-Kist, figure, Charlie Tuna, 1970s, vinyl, rare, EX, from $40 to $50.00
Star-Kist, figure, Charlie Tuna, 1970s, vinyl, rare, MIB, P12, from $125 to $150.00

Sun-Maid Raisins, van, gas-powered, early style with brass grille and headlights, 72", M, A, $700.00.

Sunbeam Bread, doll, Little Miss Sunbeam, stuffed cloth, 17", EX....$30.00
Swiss Miss, doll, Swiss Miss, 1978, stuffed cloth w/cloth dress, yarn hair, 17", EX....$20.00
Tagamet, figure, pk stomach shape, bendable, M, 6", H4.$22.00
Tango Orange Drink, figure, Tango Voodoo, British premium, vinyl, MIB, P12....$45.00
Tastee Freeze, doll, Miss Tastee Freeze, 1950s, hard plastic, 7", NM, H4/J5....$20.00
Tastee Freeze, puppet, Little T, 1960s-70s, plush & felt, M.$15.00
Texaco, doll, Texaco Cheerleader, 1973, 11", NRFB, M15, from $55 to....$60.00
Texaco, fire chief hat, Brown & Bigelow, 1950s, hard plastic, battery-op microphone & amplifier, MIB, D10, from $200 to....$300.00

Photo courtesy Bill Bruegman

Texaco, toy tanker, battery-operated, MIB, T2, from $150.00 to $200.00.

Texaco, truck, pressed steel, red & wht, 24", NMIB....$275.00
Tyson Chicken, doll, Chicken Quick, stuffed cloth, 13", VG, M15....$15.00
Vlasic Pickles, doll, Stork, Trudy Toys, 1989, fluffy wht fur w/glasses & bow tie, 22", NM, F8....$40.00

Photo courtesy June Moon

Wrangler, doll, Cody, Ertl, 1982, 11½", MIB, $55.00.

Wrangler, doll, Missy, Ertl, 1982, 11½", MIB, M15....$55.00
Wrangler, figure, Missy or Cody, Ertl, 1982, 4", MOC, M15, ea....$6.00

Advertising Signs, Ads, and Displays

A common advertising ploy used as far back as the late 1900s and still effective today is to catch the eye of the potential consumer with illustrations of well-known celebrities or popular fictional characters. Nowadays, with the intense passion character-collectibles buffs pour into their hobby, searching for these advertising items is a natural extension of their enthusiasm, adding even more diversity to an already multifaceted collecting field.

American Skyline Construction Set, display, cb, 24" L, EX, J2....$80.00
Batman, display, cb stand-up from 1st movie, 60", EX, H4..$40.00
Batman, display, Ideal, 1966, Batman figure, cb easel-back, 6-ft, scarce, NM, A....$550.00
Batman Batmobile, display, image of Batman & Robin running toward Batmobile, 3-D plastic diecut, 48x34", rare, EX, A....$1,100.00
Batman Records Are Here!, banner, 1966, blk lettering on fluorescent orange background, cb, 23", scarce, NM, A..$700.00
Buck Rogers Space Ranger Kit, ad, EX, J2....$20.00
Donald Duck Bread, sign, image of dwarf from Snow White holding loaf of bread, diecut cb, 11x8", NM, A....$100.00
Green Hornet Bike Badge, display, Burry's, 1966, 3-D Vacuform plastic, 30x45", EX, from $3,000 to....$4,000.00
Howdy Doody for Halo Shampoo, sign, 1950s, full-figure behind sign, Halo Everybody!..., diecut cb, 24", EX, A....$125.00
Howdy Doody for Royal Gelatins & Puddings, sign, Howdy holding glass w/product name, diecut cb, 30x40", VG, A....$450.00
Joker, display, cb stand-up from 1st movie, 60", EX, H4...$40.00
Lone Ranger & Lassie at Madison Square Garden Rodeo, 4-pg fold-out poster, 1950s, 8x14", EX, J5....$100.00
Lone Ranger Signal Siren Flashlight, display, Usalite/TLR Inc, litho cb, complete w/flashlight, 9", NM, A....$450.00
Mickey Mouse Flashlight, display, image of Mickey in clubhouse, diecut cb, 17", EX....$650.00
Mr Potato Head, poster, 1960s, Take Me Home... flanks image of Mr Potato Head, paper, 13x11", EX, from $200 to....$300.00
Popeye, display, 1929, full-figure of Popeye w/sign, I Sez Wheatena Makes Muskle..., cb easle-back, 9", EX, A....$855.00
Popeye, Olive Oyl & Wimpy for Westinghouse Mazda Lamps, display, 1934, diecut cb, 31x19", EX, A....$325.00
Popeye Bifbat, 1929, Free...From Octagon Products, diecut cb stand-up, 29x15", EX, A....$600.00
Popeye Creamsicle & Popsicle, display, 1938, image of Popeye & list of premiums, cb, 12", EX, A....$225.00
Popeye Popsicle, Fudgicle & Creamsicle, sign, 1939, Save Bags for Gifts, diecut cb, 17x13", EX, A....$350.00
Popeye the Sailor Man, sign, advertises 50¢ book, diecut cb stand-up, 14x9", EX, A....$225.00

Post Sugar Crisp, sign, 1950s, image of Sugar Bear eating cereal, Appetites Do Handsprings!, cb, 21x11", EX, J5.........**$65.00**

Ripley's Believe It or Not Hobby Kits, sign, Multiple, 1966, image & Ouch!...Are Great!, cb, rare, 12x17", EX, A **$200.00**

Roy Rogers Cookies, electric sign, diecut image of Roy w/lasso, 24x12", VG, A **$1,000.00**

Roy Rogers Trick Lasso, electric sign, diecut image of Roy w/lasso, 24x12", EX, A **$1,450.00**

Silly Putty, poster, 1960s, image of girl & boy playing w/Silly Putty & You See It on Television..., 18x11", EX, A..**$100.00**

Slinky, display, 1956, cardboard mechanical, 17", EX, A, $750.00.

Straight Arrow for Nabisco Shredded Wheat, sign, 1949, Straight Arrow holding box of cereal, diecut cb, 10", EX, A **$275.00**

Now You Can Give the "Little Feller" What His Heart Desires!
A Great Opportunity to Save On
Famous "STURDITOY" Trucks
RIGHT AT THE FACTORY!

How to reach our plant

Mail and Phone Orders Filled

PRESSED METAL CO.
Campbell Street and York Avenue

Sturditoy, newspaper ad, Evening Bulletin, December 14, 1928, framed, 27x19", EX, A, $450.00.

Tarzan Masks, poster, Northern Paper Mills, 1933, free masks w/purchase of Northern Tissue or Gauze, 26x19", EX, A **$600.00**

Tinker Toy, display, 1940, rotating Tinker Toy paddle wheel model on board, 19x19", EX...................................**$450.00**

Aeronautical

Toy manufacturers seemed to take the cautious approach toward testing the waters with aeronautical toys, and it was well into the second decade of the 20th century before some of the European toy makers took the initiative. The earlier models were bulky and basically inert, but by the '50s, Japanese manufacturers were turning out battery-operated replicas with wonderful details that advanced with whirling motors and flashing lights.

See also Battery Operated; Cast Iron, Airplanes; Model Kits; Windups, Friction, and Other Mechanicals.

Aero-Car XY 302, MSK/ST, 1950s, friction, litho tin, 11½" WS, rare, prop missing o/w EX, P4..........................**$450.00**

Air France, Arnold, cream, blue, and gray, 19½" wingspan, EX, A, $600.00; Air France, France, friction, two-tone blue, 20" wingspan, EX, A, $1,000.00.

American Airlines DC-7, Linemar, battery-op, 4-prop, silver w/red & bl detail, 19" W, EX (EX box), A **$400.00**

American Airlines Electra II, TN, friction, tin & plastic, 15" L, EX, J2 ....**$100.00**

American Airlines N-5024, Japan, battery-op, 4-prop, litho tin, 17" W, EX, A..**$155.00**

American Airlines NC-2100, Marx, 1940s, 4-prop, metal, 27" W, EX, A **$300.00**

Army Scout Plane, Steelcraft, single-prop, pressed steel, 22" W, rstr, A...**$250.00**

Photo courtesy Dunbar Gallery

BAC (Vickers) VC-10, marked BOAC, Japan, 1950s, friction, lithographed tin, 16" wingspan, NMIB, D10, $300.00.

Beechcraft Stagger, stick & tissue construction w/rubber band power, 27" W, EX, A $350.00

Biplane, German, clockwork mechanism, hand-pnt tin fuselage w/pilot, canvas cover over wings & tail fin, 7" W, NM, A $2,900.00

Black Knight BK-02, friction, litho tin, 13" L, NMIB, A .. $225.00

Blackhawk Monocoupe, stick & tissue model w/rubber wheels, 70" W, EX, A $50.00

Left: BOAC Radiant 5600, Schuco, battery-operated, lithographed tin and plastic, 19" wingspan, EX, A, $350.00; Back: Boeing Stratocruiser, Japan, friction, lithographed tin, 20" wingspan, EX, A, $350.00; Front: KLM Flying Dutchman Constellation, Germany, friction, lithographed tin, 20" wingspan, EX, A, $500.00.

Boeing 727, TT, friction, litho tin, 10" L, EX (EX box), A .. $125.00

Bristol Bulldog NF-125, Straco, battery-op, single-prop, bl w/red & yel detail, 14" W, NMIB, A $275.00

Comet DH 109, MT, friction, litho tin w/red plastic window inserts for sparking action, 7" W, EX (VG box), A . $200.00

Comet Jetliner, Japan, friction, 4-prop, litho tin, 19" W, EX, A $225.00

Curtiss Jenny Trainer, S&E, friction, single-prop, red-pnt tin, 14" W, MIB, A $300.00

Douglas Sky Rocket, friction, litho tin, 11" L, EX (worn box), A $85.00

Elektro Radiant 5600, Schuco, marked Clipper Nurnberg, battery-operated, lithographed tin with plastic props and dome, 19" wingspan, NM (NM box), A, $750.00.

Eastern Airlines Passenger Jet, Cragstan, 4-prop, battery-op, litho tin, 23" W, EX, A $250.00

Flying Tiger Line Cargo Plane, battery-op, 4-prop, 14" W, EX (EX box), A $185.00

Photo courtesy Dunbar Gallery

Flying Wonder, Arnold, lithographed tin, 10" wingspan, M (worn box), $175.00.

Four Motor Airplane, Linemar, friction, mk KLM & FH DSL on wings, litho tin w/plastic props, 16" W, NM (EX box), A . $250.00

Graf Zeppelin, clockwork, cream-pnt tin w/red lettering, celluloid prop, stylized molded gondola, 10", EX, A $650.00

Graf Zeppelin, Steelcraft, pressed steel, 30", rstr, A $225.00

Graf Zeppelin DLZ 127, mk Made in Germany, clockwork w/battery-op light, litho tin, Nazi flag on rear fins, 11", VG, A $385.00

Gyro Copter, 1930s, silver-pnt tin, 4½" L, scarce, EX $200.00

Hiller Ram Jet Helicopter, Japan, friction, litho tin, 10" L, NM (worn box), A $100.00

Hopewell Flyer Hanging Zeppelin, clockwork, litho tin, 9", EX, A $465.00

Japan Airlines DC-8, friction, 4-prop, litho tin & plastic, 23" W, VG, A $135.00

Japanese Bomber, clockwork, 4-prop, gr-pnt tin, 17" W, VG, A $100.00

Los Angeles Dirigible, Steelcraft, cream-pnt pressed steel, rubber rear wheels w/caster-style front wheel, 25", EX, A .. $500.00

Macon Airship, Japan, clockwork, litho tin, 7", no props o/w EX, A $250.00

Military Aeroplane, Marx, 1930s, w/up, 2-prop, rare silver & bl version, NM (NM box), A $775.00

Military Jet Plane, Marx, battery-op, 4-prop, tin & plastic, advances w/lights & sound, 15" W, NM (EX box), A $300.00

Northwest Airlines, friction, 4-prop, litho tin, 19" W, NM (worn box), A $350.00

PAA China Clipper, Chein, clockwork, litho tin, EX, A . $450.00

Pan American Airlines Strato Clipper, Acorn, friction, 4-prop, litho tin, 11" W, NM (EX box), A $250.00

Pan American Boeing Jet Clipper America, Marx, battery-op, 4-prop, litho tin, 18" W, EX, A $165.00

Pan American Clipper, Y, 1950s, friction, 4-prop, litho tin, 23" W, rare, EX, A $650.00

Pan American DC-8, battery-op, 4-prop, red, wht & bl litho tin, stop-&-go action, 13" W, NMIB, A $165.00

Pan American Passenger Plane, 4-prop, pressed steel, 27" W, EX, A $225.00

Pan American Super-7 Clipper, Chalmer, 4-prop, pressed steel w/blk rubber tires, 17½" W, NM (worn box), A $200.00

Pan American World Airways, Y, friction, 4-prop, silver w/red detail, 11" W, EX, A....................$145.00

Pan American 707 Jet, battery-op, litho tin, VG (worn box), A....................$165.00

Patrol Plane A-1026-S, Japan, friction, single-prop, litho tin, 13" W, NM (EX box), A $125.00

Republique Airship, clockwork, pnt & stained tin w/paper props, cast lead figure w/spyglass in gondola, 12", VG, A....................$1,600.00

Sabena Helicopter, Arnold, crank action, litho tin, 9", EX (worn box), A....................$125.00

Sky Taxi Cessna, TT, friction, single-prop, litho tin, 10" W, NM (EX box), A $125.00

Speedplane, bl-& red-pnt balsa wood w/Bantam ignition engine, teardrop wheel pods, 18" W, EX, A $250.00

Speedplane, 1946, red-pnt balsa wood w/Bantam ignition engine, 17" W, EX, A....................$200.00

Spirit of St Louis, United Electrical Mfg, 2 tin airplanes on rod connected to litho tin lighthouse, 19", NM, A $3,200.00

Stratoliner 700 Sky Cruiser, Marx, friction, 2-prop, litho tin, 18" W, NM (EX box), A $300.00

Stratoliner 700 Sky Cruiser, Marx, friction, 4-prop, litho tin, 18" W, NM (EX box), A $375.00

Trans-Atlantic Zeppelin, Marx, clockwork mechanism, silver-pnt tin, 9½", MIB, A....................$550.00

TWA DC-7C Airliner, Yonezawa, 1950s, battery-op, 4-prop, litho tin, several actions, 23½" W, NM (NM box), P4.......$750.00

TWA Passenger Plane, Marx, w/up, 4-prop, blk & gold tin w/celluloid props, lithoed captain & co-pilot, 18" W, EX, A $385.00

UN Rescue Plane, Japan, friction, silver-tone w/cross insignias, 9" W, VG (VG box), A....................$150.00

United Airlines DC-7, Japan, friction, 4-prop, litho tin, 23" W, VG, A $125.00

US Army Bomber, Marx, w/up, 2-prop, litho tin, 18" W, NM, A $225.00

USAF B-36 Convair, Japan, friction, litho tin, 26" W, EX, A....................$465.00

USAF B-45 Tornado Bomber, Bandai, friction, litho tin, 16" WS, VG, A....................$275.00

USAF BK-02VF Fighter Plane, Japan, friction, litho tin, 23" L, EX, A $185.00

USAF C-120 Pack Plane, Japan, friction, litho tin, 16" W, EX, A $185.00

USAF Rescue Battalion Helicopter, Marx, battery-op, litho tin, 17", EX, A....................$100.00

USS Macon Airship, no mechanism, pnt tin, 2 gondolas & 4 outboard motors, 15", EX, A $700.00

Vertol New York Airways Helicopter, Japan, battery-op, litho tin, 14", EX, A $100.00

Westland G-AMHK Helicopter, Alps, battery-op, litho tin, w/pilot, 14", EX, A $100.00

Zeppelin, American, clockwork, silver-pnt tin, 2 outboard motors, 9", EX, A....................$225.00

Zeppelin, clockwork mechanism, yel-pnt tin w/paper props, 2 gondolas, 16", EX, A $1,000.00

Zeppelin, Orobr, clockwork, tan-& red-litho tin w/celluloid props, 10", VG, A....................$750.00

Zeppelin R-101, mk Made in Germany, clockwork w/battery-op light, emb tin, 15", G, A $250.00

Zeppelin R-120, mk Made in Germany, clockwork, emb tin w/4 outboard motors, 17", EX (G box), A....................$1,750.00

Automobiles and Other Vehicle Replicas

Listed here are the model vehicles (most of which were made in Japan during the 1950s and '60s) that were designed to realistically represent the muscle cars, station wagons, convertibles, budget models, and luxury cars that were actually being shown concurrently on showroom floors and dealers' lots all over the country. Most were made of tin, many were friction powered, some were battery operated. In our descriptions, all are tin unless noted otherwise.

When at all possible, we've listed the toys by the names assigned to them by the manufacturer, just as they appear on the original boxes. Because of this, you'll find some of the same models listed by slightly different names. All vehicles are painted or painted and lithographed tin unless noted.

For more information we recommend *The Golden Age of Automotive Toys, 1925 – 1941*, by Ken Hutchison and Greg Johnson (Collector Books).

See also Promotional Cars; specific manufacturers.

Bonneville Salt-Flats Special #12, Mattel, friction, gold w/Mobilgas decals, NM (NM box), A $400.00

Buick, KO, friction, bl w/chrome detail, 10½", EX (EX box mk New Buick)....................$250.00

Buick, 1961, Ichiko, friction, red & wht, 18", NMIB, from $850 to....................$950.00

Buick Riviera Giant Door-Matic Car, Japan, friction, bl w/chrome detail, detachable roof, 11", EX (EX box), A $450.00

Buick Sedan, 1959, Yonezawa, friction, tan over brn w/chrome detail, 8", EX (EX box)....................$275.00

Cadillac, 1952, Alps, friction, blk 2-door w/chrome detail, red interior, 11", NMIB....................$900.00

Cadillac, 1954, Alps, friction, dk gr w/chrome detail, red interior, 11½", scarce, NM....................$1,400.00

Cadillac, 1954, Kiaeusa/Japan, bl-gray w/NP detail, 12½", M (worn box)....................$1,200.00

Cadillac, 1961, Yonezawa, friction, lt bl w/gr & wht interior, 14", rare color, NM (EX box)....................$600.00

Cadillac Convertible, 1954, Alps, friction, red w/chrome detail, 11", MIB, A....................$4,900.00

Cadillac Convertible, 1959, Bandai, friction, red w/chrome detail, 11", NM (VG box)....................$475.00

Cadillac Convertible, 1961, Bandai, battery-op, gold w/red interior, 17", EX (worn box)....................$550.00

Cadillac Police Car, Ichiko, friction, roof light swivels, 6", NM (EX box mk Polizei)....................$50.00

Cadillac Sedan, 1950, Marusan, battery-op, cream w/dk gr top & chrome detail, 11", MIB..$2,500.00
Cadillac Sedan, 1950, TN, battery-op, brn w/chrome detail & hood ornament, 8", NM..$165.00
Cadillac Sedan, 1959, Bandai, friction, blk w/chrome detail, plastic taillights, 11", EX..$300.00

Cadillac, 1959, Bandai, gold with chrome detail, MIB, $350.00.

Cadillac Sedan, 1963, Bandai, friction, red w/chrome detail, 8", NM (EX box)..$350.00
Chevrolet, 1954, Marusan, battery-op, red w/yel top, chrome detail, 11", MIB..$2,000.00
Chevrolet, 1954, Marusan, friction, beige w/blk roof, striped interior, 11", EX...$800.00
Chevrolet, 1955, Marusan, battery-op, 2-tone gr, celluloid head turns when door is opened, 10½", rare, NM........$2,800.00
Chevrolet Bel Air Station Wagon, 1961, friction, gr & wht w/plastic windshield & windows, 10", EX (EX box).$500.00
Chevrolet Convertible w/U-Haul Trailer, Japan, friction, bl car & red trailer, EX (NM box)....................................$200.00
Chevrolet Corvette Stingray, 1964, Bandai, friction, bl w/chrome detail, fancy hubs, 8", EX.......................$150.00
Chrysler, 1957, Japan, battery-op, wht & red w/chrome detail, 9½", EX...$275.00
Chrysler Imperial, 1961, Bandai, friction, red w/blk top, chrome detail, plastic taillights, 8", NM (NM box)............$275.00
Datsun Fair Lady Z, Ichiko, friction, bright yel w/chrome trim, 18", NM (EX box)...$250.00
Dodge Sedan, 1959, TN, friction, red w/wht top, chrome detail, fancy hubs, 9", EX...$325.00
Edsel Station Wagon, TN, friction, blk & red w/wht trim, opening rear gate, 10½", NM...$500.00
Fiat Convertible, Usagai, friction, lt metallic bl w/chrome detail, 6", NM (EX box), A..$175.00
Fiat Sedan, Usagai, friction, lt metallic bl w/chrome detail, 6", NM (EX box), A..$175.00
Ford Convertible, 1956, Irco, yel & red w/chrome detail, 7", VG...$275.00
Ford Convertible, 1958, Kosuge, battery-op, retractable roof, bl w/chrome detail, 9", VG, A...................................$225.00
Ford Crown Victoria, 1956, Yonezawa, friction, wht over red w/bl roof, chrome detail, 12", MIB......................$1,500.00
Ford Custom Ranch Wagon, 1955, Bandai, friction, red w/blk top, chrome detail, 11½", MIB...............................$375.00

Ford-Fairlane 500 Skyliner, Cragstan, remote control, blue and white with chrome detail, 11", VG (VG box), A, $350.00.

Ford Fairlane, 1956, SAN, friction, scarce chrome version, 13", EX (G box)..$750.00
Ford Mustang Coupe, 1965, Bandai, friction, metallic bl w/blk top, chrome detail, 8", NM.....................................$200.00
Ford Mustang 2+2, 1960s, friction, bl, 14", MIB............$150.00
Ford Red Cross Ambulance, 1956, Bandai, friction, wht w/red cross on roof, 12", EX (EX box)..............................$350.00

Ford Skyliner, 1958, TN, battery operated, red with chrome detail, detractable roof, NMIB, A, $300.00.

Ford Station Wagon, Japan, friction, red w/dk bl top, chrome detail, Ford hubs, 7", EX, A.....................................$135.00
Ford Station Wagon, 1960, Japan, friction, yel over blk w/Standard Fresh Coffee advertising, 11½", MIB............$2,400.00

House Trailer and Station Wagon, SSS Toys, friction, red car, white house trailer with red detail, MIB, $225.00.

Ford Sunliner, 1962, Y, red w/chrome detail, 10", EX (EX box) $350.00

Ford 2-Door Hardtop, 1957, Ichiko, friction, bl & wht w/chrome detail, 9½", VG+ $300.00

Graham Paige No 3, CK, w/up, red w/orange trim, chrome detail, mounted rear spare, 6", EX (EX box), A.......$350.00

Isetta 700, Bandai, friction, red & wht, jutting headlights, 6", EX, A $235.00

Jaguar Coupe, Bandai, friction, red with chrome detail, black top, 9", NM (EX box), A, $675.00.

Jaguar E-Type, TT, friction, red with chrome detail, 11", NM (NM box), A, $475.00.

Jaguar E-Type Convertible, Europe, friction, blk w/chrome detail, Cordatic tires, 10", EX (EX box), A................$65.00

Lincoln Futura, Alps, friction, red 2-door w/clear bubble roof, chrome detail, 11", MIB....................$4,200.00

Lincoln Mark III w/Shasta Trailer, 1958, Bandai, friction, gr & wht, 22", M $650.00

Mercedes Sedan 219, Bandai, friction, bl w/chrome detail, 8", MIB, A....................$250.00

Mercedes 190 SL, Schuco, w/up, red w/chrome detail, plastic interior, 8", NM (NM box), A $465.00

Mercedes 300 SL Convertible, SSS, friction, red w/chrome detail, blk rubber tires, 9", NM (NM box), A..........$250.00

Mercedes 300 SL Gullwing Coupe, 1955, Marklin, w/up, chrome, steerable front end, 13", MIB....................$325.00

MG II Convertible, Japan, friction, yel w/chrome detail, mounted rear spare, 8", EX (worn box), A $250.00

MG Magnetta Mark III Convertible, Japan, friction, 8", EX (EX box)....................$325.00

New Cunningham C-6R, Irco, friction, bl & wht convertible w/chrome detail, 8", NM (EX box), A....................$450.00

Oldsmobile Convertible, 1952, Y, friction, red w/chrome detail, 10", EX (EX box) $500.00

Oldsmobile Toronado, 1966, Bandai, battery-op, red w/blk tires, 11", NM $200.00

Packard Hawk Convertible, 1957, Schuco, battery-op, 10½", EX (VG box) $900.00

Packard Sedan, Alps, friction, red w/chrome detail, 16½", EX, A $3,000.00

Packard 52, Japan, friction, red w/chrome detail, bl tin tires, 7", EX (EX box), A $175.00

Plymouth Convertible, 1959, friction, red w/wht tail fins, chrome detail, 11", EX....................$600.00

Pontiac Deluxe Sedan, Asahitoy, friction, red & wht w/chrome detail, family lithoed in windows, 10", rare, NMIB, A..$700.00

Porsche, Bandai, battery operated, cream with chrome detail, features opening doors, with driver, 10", NM (EX box), A, $200.00.

Porsche Sedan, Joustra, friction, red w/passengers lithoed in windows, blk rubber tires, 8", EX (EX box), A $135.00

Porsche Sportomatic Coupe, TT, battery-op, red & bl, 11", EX (EX box) $185.00

Renault, Rossignol, w/up, red, bl & cream w/tin balloon tires, 8½", VG, A $250.00

Renault Floride, Ichiko, friction, red with black top, chrome detail, 8", EX (EX box), A, $150.00.

Renault Floride, Ichiko, friction, red w/blk top, chrome detail, 8", EX (EX box), A $150.00

Rolls Royce Silver Cloud, Bandai, friction, bl w/wht top, chrome detail, 12", scarce, NM (EX box) $350.00

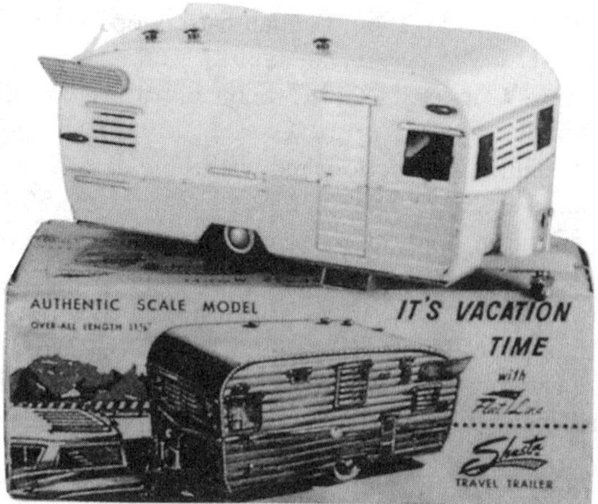

Shasta Travel Trailer, Fleet Line, 1950s, white and yellow with plastic windows, 11½", scarce, NM (EX box), A, $400.00.

Volkswagen Bug, 1963, Bandai, friction, bl w/chrome detail, 8", NM (EX box) $150.00

Volkswagen Convertible, Japan, friction, bl w/cream top, red plastic seats, lighted piston action, 9½", EX (EX box)......$125.00

Volkswagen Sedan, Bandai, battery-op, red w/chrome detail, vinyl driver, 10", EX (EX box), A $250.00

Banks

The impact of condition on the value of a bank cannot be overrated. Cast iron banks in near-mint condition with very little paint wear and all original parts are seldom found and might bring twice as much (if the bank is especially rare, up to five times as much) as one in average, very-good original condition with no restoration and no repairs. Overpainting and replacement parts (even screws) have a very negative effect on value. Mechanicals dominate the market, and some of the hard-to-find banks in outstanding, near-mint condition may exceed $20,000.00! (Here's a few examples: Girl Skipping Rope, Calamity, and Mikado.) Modern mechanical banks are also emerging on the collectibles market, including Book of Knowledge and James D. Capron, which are reproductions with full inscriptions stating that the piece is a replica of the original. Still banks are widely collected as well, with more than 3,000 varieties having been documented. Beware of unmarked modern reproductions.

For more information we recommend *The Dictionary of Still Banks* by Long and Pitman; *The Penny Bank Book* by Moore; *The Bank Book* by Norman; and *Penny Lane* by Davidson.

Advisors: Bill Bertoia, mechanicals; Dan Iannotti (I3), modern mechanicals; and Diane Patalano (P8).

See also Advertising; Battery-Operated; Character, TV, and Movie Collectibles; Disney; Diecast Collector Banks; Reynolds Toys; Rock 'n Roll; Santa; Western.

Mechanical Banks

Afghanistan Bank, Mechanical Novelty Works, pnt CI, G+ $1,500.00

Always Did 'Spise a Mule (Bench), J&E Stevens, pnt CI, EX $950.00

Always Did 'Spise a Mule (Bench), J&E Stevens, pnt CI, G, A..$650.00

Always Did 'Spise a Mule (Jockey), Book of Knowledge, NM, I3 ....$285.00

Always Did 'Spise a Mule (Jockey), J&E Stevens, painted cast iron, EX, $725.00.

Artillery Bank, Book of Knowledge, NM, I3 ....$345.00

Artillery Bank, J&E Stevens, bronze-pnt CI, VG, A......$600.00

Artillery Bank, J&E Stevens, pnt CI, VG, A..................$600.00

Auto Bank, John Wright, limited edition of 250, NM, I3 .$675.00

Bad Accident, J&E Stevens, pnt CI, upside-down letters, VG, A...$1,100.00

Bad Accident, James Capron, M, I3 ....$1,250.00

Bank of Education & Economy, Proctor-Raymond, NP CI, VG, A $400.00

Betsy Ross, Davidson/Imswiller, limited edition of 300, bl or yel dress, M, I3, ea $975.00

Bill E Grin, J&E Stevens, pnt CI, G, A $600.00

Billy Goat, J&E Stevens, pnt CI, NM, A $2,850.00

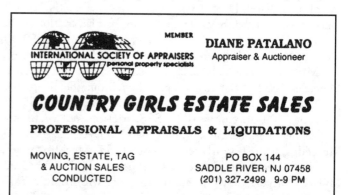

Bird on Roof, J&E Stevens, CI, EX, A $2,300.00
Bobby Riggs & Billie Jean King, John Wright, limited edition of 250, scarce, NM, I3 ....$1,275.00
Bowler's Strike, Richards/Utexiqual, scarce, NM, I3......$725.00
Boy on Trapeze, Barton & Smith, pnt CI, bl pants, VG, A..$1,550.00
Boy on Trapeze, Barton & Smith, pnt CI, gray pants, VG, A...$2,600.00
Boy on Trapeze, Book of Knowledge, NM, I3.................$675.00
Boy Robbing Bird's Nest, J&E Stevens, pnt CI, rpt $1,800.00
Boy Scout Bank, J&E Stevens, pnt CI, EX..................$6,700.00
Boy Stealing Watermelon, Kyser & Rex, pnt CI, VG.$3,600.00
Bulldog Bank, J&E Stevens, pnt CI, EX, A $1,300.00
Cabin Bank, Book of Knowledge, NM, I3 ....$285.00

Cat and Mouse, Book of Knowledge, M, I3, $425.00.

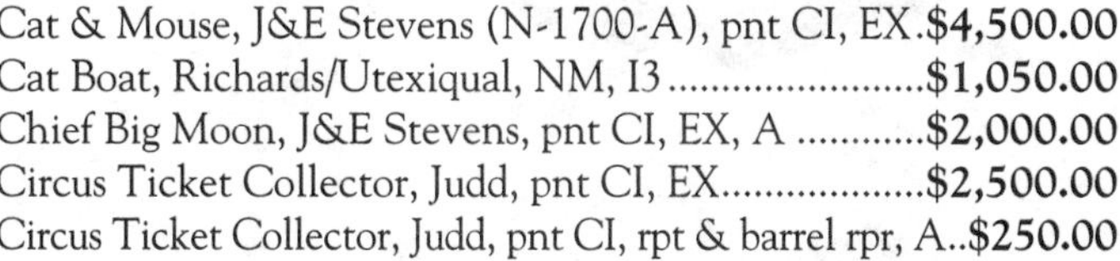
Cat & Mouse, J&E Stevens (N-1700-A), pnt CI, EX.$4,500.00
Cat Boat, Richards/Utexiqual, NM, I3 ....$1,050.00
Chief Big Moon, J&E Stevens, pnt CI, EX, A $2,000.00
Circus Ticket Collector, Judd, pnt CI, EX...................$2,500.00
Circus Ticket Collector, Judd, pnt CI, rpt & barrel rpr, A..$250.00

Dinah, John Harper, painted cast iron, NM, D10, $1,250.00.

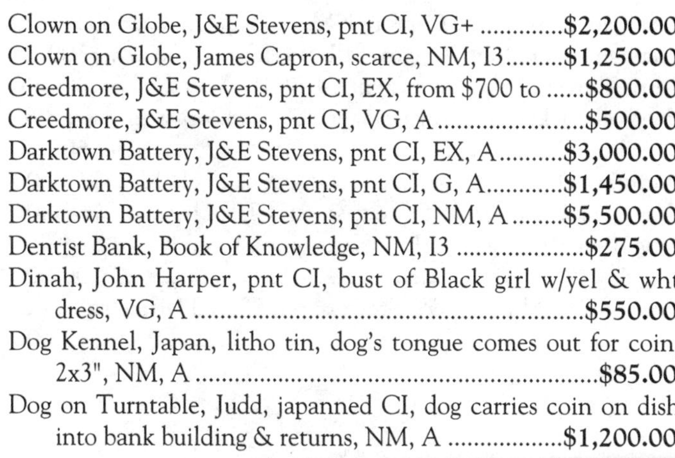
Clown on Globe, J&E Stevens, pnt CI, VG+ $2,200.00
Clown on Globe, James Capron, scarce, NM, I3.........$1,250.00
Creedmore, J&E Stevens, pnt CI, EX, from $700 to $800.00
Creedmore, J&E Stevens, pnt CI, VG, A $500.00
Darktown Battery, J&E Stevens, pnt CI, EX, A..........$3,000.00
Darktown Battery, J&E Stevens, pnt CI, G, A............$1,450.00
Darktown Battery, J&E Stevens, pnt CI, NM, A........$5,500.00
Dentist Bank, Book of Knowledge, NM, I3 ....$275.00
Dinah, John Harper, pnt CI, bust of Black girl w/yel & wht dress, VG, A $550.00
Dog Kennel, Japan, litho tin, dog's tongue comes out for coin, 2x3", NM, A $85.00
Dog on Turntable, Judd, japanned CI, dog carries coin on dish into bank building & returns, NM, A $1,200.00

Dog on Turntable, Judd, painted cast iron, NM, $1,450.00.

Eagle & Eaglets, Book of Knowledge, M, I3....................$425.00

Eagle and Eaglets, J&E Stevens, painted cast iron, EX, from $1,500.00 to $1,800.00.

Elephant Bank, James Capron, NM, I3 ....$275.00
Elephant Bank, John Wright, MIB, I3 ....$300.00
Ferris Wheel Bank, Hubley, pnt CI, VG+, A $5,000.00
Football Kicker, unknown maker, CI figure on steel base, 8½", EX, H7 ....$1,600.00
Fortune Telling Savings Bank, CI, G, A $150.00
Frog Bank (2 Frogs), J&E Stevens, pnt CI, rpl leg, A $660.00
Frog on Round Base, J&E Stevens, pnt CI, red lattice base, EX, A $1,000.00
Frog on Round Base, J&E Stevens, pnt CI, red lattice base, VG, A $525.00

Photo courtesy Dunbar Gallery

Frog on Stump, J&E Stevens, painted cast iron, VG, D10, $750.00.

Girl in Victorian Chair, WS Reed, pnt CI, EX, A, from $9,000 to $12,000.00
Girl Skipping Rope (Blue Dress), J&E Stevens, pnt CI, VG, A $18,700.00
Hall's Excelsior, J&E Stevens, pnt CI, EX+, A $1,200.00
Hall's Excelsior, J&E Stevens, pnt CI, rpt figure, VG, A ..$275.00
Hall's Liliput, J&E Stevens, gray- & bl-pnt CI, EX, A ...$770.00
Hen & Chick, J&E Stevens, pnt CI, VG, A $2,200.00
Home Bank, J&E Stevens, pnt CI, VG-, A $1,700.00
Hoopla Bank, John Harper, pnt CI, VG, A $1,200.00
Horse Race Bank, J&E Stevens, pnt CI, flanged base, EX, A $10,450.00
Humpty Dumpty, Book of Knowledge, MIB, I3 ....$400.00
Humpty Dumpty, Shepard Hardware, pnt CI, EX, from $2,750 to $3,000.00
Indian & Bear, Book of Knowledge, M, I3 ....$475.00
Joe Socko, Straits Corp, litho tin, NM $850.00
Jolly 'N' Bank, John Harper, pnt CI, red jacket w/butterfly tie, G+ $200.00
Jolly 'N' Bank, John Harper, pnt CI, red jacket w/wht collar, some overpnt $125.00
Jolly 'N' Bank, Starkies, pnt CI, bust of Black man in wht top hat, red lips, red shirt, 8", VG, A $350.00
Jolly Joe Clown, Saalheimer & Strauss, litho tin, VG, A ...$900.00
Jonah & the Whale, Shepard Hardware, pnt CI, VG+, A..$3,850.00
Leap Frog, Book of Knowledge, MIB, I3 ....$395.00
Leap Frog, Shepard Hardware, pnt CI, VG, A $2,500.00
Lion & Monkeys, James Capron, scarce, NM, I3 ....$1,250.00

Photo courtesy Dan Iannotti

John Deere Anvil Bank, painted diecast, MIB, I3, $150.00.

Lighthouse, unknown manufacturer, painted cast iron, NM, D10, $5,000.00.

Lion Hunter, J&E Stevens, painted cast iron, VG, $3,500.00.

Lion & Monkeys, Kyser & Rex, pnt CI, VG, A $1,100.00
Little Joe, att John Harper, pnt CI bust of Black man, EX, A $400.00

Magic Bank, J&E Stevens, pnt CI, EX $2,500.00
Magician Bank, Book of Knowledge, NM, I3 ....$425.00
Magician Bank, J&E Stevens, pnt CI, VG $2,800.00
Mason Bank, Shepard Hardware, pnt CI, VG $3,500.00
Milking Cow, Book of Knowledge, NM, I3 ....$345.00
Milking Cow, J&E Stevens, pnt CI, rpl boy & fence, A..$2,750.00

Milking Cow, J&E Stevens, painted cast iron, rare, EX, D10, $11,000.00.

Minstrel, Saalheimer & Strauss, litho tin, G, A $525.00
Monkey & Coconut, J&E Stevens, pnt CI, VG-, A ...$2,300.00
Monkey Bank, Hubley, pnt CI, VG, A $700.00
Monkey Bank, James Capron, NM, I3 ....$300.00

Mule Entering Barn, J&E Stevens, painted cast iron, EX, D10, $1,850.00.

Mule Entering Barn, J&E Stevens, pnt CI, M, A........$2,850.00
Mule Entering Barn, James Capron, NM, I3...................$750.00
National Savings Bank, NP CI, NM+, A $3,500.00
New Bank, J&E Stevens, pnt CI, EX, A.......................$1,500.00
Novelty Bank, J&E Stevens, pnt CI, M, A..................$5,000.00
Novelty Bank, J&E Stevens, pnt CI, VG, A $600.00
Organ Bank (Boy & Girl), Kyser & Rex, pnt CI, NM, A ..$3,400.00
Organ Bank (Monkey), Kyser & Rex, pnt CI, EX, A..$1,300.00
Owl (Turns Head), Book of Knowledge, M, I3 ....$300.00
Owl (Turns Head), J&E Stevens, pnt CI w/glass eyes, EX, A $525.00
Paddy & the Pig, Book of Knowledge, M, I3 ....$385.00
Paddy & the Pig, J&E Stevens, pnt CI, VG, A $1,550.00

Paddy and the Pig, J&E Stevens, painted cast iron, NM, D10, $3,300.00.

Panorama Bank, J&E Stevens, pnt CI, NM, A $8,800.00
Pay Phone Bank, J&E Stevens, NP CI, G, A $700.00
Peg-Leg Begger, Judd, 2nd casting, pnt CI, EX, A $300.00
Penny Pineapple, Wilton, commemorates Hawaii 50th State, NM, I3 ....$545.00
Picture Gallery, Shepard Hardware, pnt CI, VG, A .$13,750.00
Pig in Highchair, J&E Stevens, gold-pnt CI, VG, A......$600.00
Popeye Knockout Bank, Straits, litho tin, diecut Popeye & opponent boxing on rectangular base, EX, A $750.00

Professor Pug Frog, James Capron, scarce, NM, I3, $1,300.00.

Punch & Judy, Book of Knowledge, M, I3 ....$375.00
Punch & Judy, Book of Knowledge, MIB, I3 ....$425.00
Punch & Judy, Shepard Hardware, pnt CI, EX $2,500.00
Rabbit in Cabbage, Kilgore, pnt CI, G-, A $275.00
Race Course Trotters, James Capron, very scarce, EX, I3 ....$595.00
Reclining Chinaman, J&E Stevens, pnt CI, EX..........$3,500.00
Rooster, Kyser & Rex, pnt CI, missing lever...................$350.00
Saluting Sailor, Germany, litho tin, VG, A $1,100.00
Santa Claus, Shepard Hardware, pnt CI, place coin in Santa's hand & he tosses it into chimney, overpnt, A.........$575.00

Speaking Dog, Shepard Hardware, pnt CI, maroon base, EX, A $2,500.00
Stump Speaker, Shepard Hardware, pnt CI, blk jacket, EX, A $3,300.00
Stump Speaker, Shepard Hardware, pnt CI, gr jacket, VG, A $2,300.00
Tammany Bank, Book of Knowledge, NMIB, I3 ....$400.00
Tammany Bank, J&E Stevens, pnt CI, M, A $2,100.00

Tammany Bank, J&E Stevens, painted cast iron, VG, $550.00.

Photo courtesy Dunbar Gallery

Teddy & the Bear, Book of Knowledge, NM, I3.............$335.00
Teddy & the Bear, J&E Stevens, pnt CI, EX...............$2,500.00
Teddy Box, Czechoslovakia, litho tin w/images of children, EX, A $300.00
Toad on Stump, J&E Stevens, pnt CI, NM.................$1,500.00
Trick Dog, Hubley, pnt CI, bl base, EX+, A...................$800.00
Trick Dog, Hubley, pnt CI, yel & brn base, EX..............$900.00
Trick Dog, James Capron, NM, I3 ....$550.00
Trick Dog, Shepard Hardware, pnt CI, red & gr base, NM..$3,200.00
Trick Pony, Book of Knowledge, NMIB, I3 ....$395.00

Uncle Sam, Book of Knowledge, M, I3, $375.00.

Photo courtesy Dan Iannotti

Two Frogs, James Capron, NM, I3 ....$550.00
Uncle Bugs, Warner Bros, MIB, I3...................................$215.00
Uncle Remus, Book of Knowledge, MIB, I3 ....$450.00
Uncle Remus, Kyser & Rex, pnt CI, EX, A.................$1,750.00
Uncle Sam, Book of Knowledge, MIB, I3 ....$450.00
Uncle Sam, Shepard Hardware, pnt CI, EX+, A.........$3,300.00
Uncle Sam, Shepard Hardware, pnt CI, partial rpt, A ..$1,400.00
Uncle Sam & Arab, John Wright, commemorates 1975 Arab Oil Embargo, limited edition of 250, NM, I3 ....$1,300.00
US & Spain, Book of Knowledge, orig cannon ball, M, I3...$335.00

Photo courtesy Dan Iannotti

Washington at Rappahannock, John Wright, 1977, NM, I3, $700.00.

William Tell, J&E Stevens, pnt CI, G, A $500.00
William Tell, J&E Stevens, pnt CI, NM, A $2,000.00
World's Fair, Book of Knowledge, scarce bronze version, NM, I3...$400.00
Zoo Bank, Kyser & Rex, 1894, pnt CI, VG, A $1,000.00

Registering Banks

Ben Franklin, Marx, tin, MIB, I3 ....$350.00
Little Orphan Annie Dime Bank, 1936, litho tin, 3" dia, EX, A $450.00
Popeye Daily Quarter Bank, 1950s, litho tin, 4", EX+, A ..$150.00
Snow White & the Seven Dwarfs Dime Bank, WDE, 1938, litho tin, 2½x2½", VG, A $125.00
Superman Dime Register, 1940s, litho tin, sq w/canted corners, rare, EX $250.00

Still Banks

$100,000 Money Bag, US, chrome-plated CI, 3⅝", EX, A.$300.00
Andy Gump, Arcade, pnt CI, 4⅜", VG..........................$600.00
Apple, Kyser & Rex, pnt CI, red w/gr leaves, 3", G, A...$650.00
Arabian Safe, Kyser & Rex, japanned CI, 4¼", NM......$400.00
Arabian Safe, Kyser & Rex, japanned CI, 4¼", VG, A..$100.00
Aunt Jemima, AC Williams, pnt CI, bl w/silver apron, red bandana, 5⅞", EX, A...$200.00
Bank of Commerce, Kenton, NP CI, 6¾", NM, A.........$550.00

Bank of Industry, Kenton, red-pnt CI w/NP door, 5", NM ..**$175.00**
Baseball Player, AC Williams, pnt CI, 5¾", EX+, A **$575.00**
Baseball Player, AC Williams, pnt CI, 5¾", G, A..........**$175.00**
Bear Stealing Pig, gold-pnt CI, 5½", G, A......................**$525.00**

Bear Stealing Pig, gold-painted cast iron, 5½", EX, D10, $750.00.

Photo courtesy Dunbar Gallery

Bear w/Honey Pot, Hubley, brn-pnt CI w/bl & yel pot, 6½", NM, A **$600.00**
Blackpool Tower, Chamberlain & Hill, japanned CI, 7⅜", NM, A **$325.00**
Boston Bull Terrier, Vindex, brn- & wht-pnt CI, 5¾", NM....**$450.00**

Photo courtesy Dunbar Gallery

Boxer Dog, gold-painted cast iron, 4", VG, D10, $125.00.

Boxer Head, Germany, pnt lead, 2⅝", dent in back of head o/w EX, A **$130.00**
Bungalow Bank (Cottage w/Porch), Grey Iron, pnt CI, 3¾", VG **$325.00**
Bureaux Caisse, brass, 8¼", EX **$850.00**
Buster Brown & Tige, AC Williams, gold-pnt CI w/red highlights, 5½", EX, A..**$230.00**
Camel Kneeling, Kyser & Rex, 1889, japanned CI, 2½", EX, A **$825.00**
Castle, Kyser & Rex, gr-pnt CI, 3", VG, A....................**$300.00**
Cat w/Toothache, Germany, pnt lead, 4", EX, A **$100.00**
Champion Heater, red- & bl-pnt CI w/NP combination lock, 4⅛", NM, A..**$385.00**
Charlie Chaplin, Geo Borgfeldt & Co, pnt glass figure standing next to barrel, 3¾", EX, A **$225.00**
Chicago & NY Bank, Kenton Hardware, CI vault w/2 combination locks, 6", EX, A **$385.00**
Circus Elephant, seated, Hubley, pnt CI, 3¾", NM, A ..**$350.00**
City Bank w/Teller, Judd, japanned CI, 5½", EX **$325.00**
Columbia Bank, Kenton, wht-pnt CI, 5¾", missing trap o/w EX, A **$500.00**
Coronation Bank, Sydenham & McOustra, CI w/emb bust in center, 6⅝", NM, A **$200.00**
Cruise Ship, silvered lead, mk Souvenir Chicago on side, 8", EX **$850.00**
Cupola Bank, J&E Stevens, pnt CI, 3¼", EX, A **$350.00**
Cupola Bank, J&E Stevens, pnt CI, 4⅛", VG **$225.00**
Cupola Bank, J&E Stevens, pnt CI, 5½", EX, A **$475.00**
Darkey Sharecropper, US, pnt CI, 5¼", NM, A.............**$300.00**
Dresser, brn-& blk-pnt CI, columned panel w/simulated wood carving, 6¾", rare, EX, A **$1,000.00**
Duck, outstretched wings, Hubley, pnt CI, 4¾", NM, A..**$165.00**
Duck on Tub, Hubley, pnt CI, red tub, 5⅜", NM, A **$330.00**
Dutch Boy on Barrel, Hubley, pnt CI, 5⅝", VG, A........**$125.00**
Dutch Girl, Grey Iron, gold-pnt CI, 6½", EX, A **$525.00**
Egyptian Tomb, gr-pnt CI w/hieroglyphics on front panel, 6¼", scarce, EX, A **$275.00**
Elephant, US, red-pnt CI, Art Deco style w/trunk raised high, 4⅜", NM, A...**$250.00**

Photo courtesy Dunbar Gallery

Elephant on Wheels, AC Williams, gold-painted cast iron with red detail, 4⅜", EX, D10, $375.00.

Ferdinand the Bull, Crown, blk-& wht-pnt compo, 5⅛", EX, A **$300.00**
Fidelity Safe, Kyser & Rex, japanned CI w/gold highlights, 3", NM, A **$175.00**
Floral Safe, Kyser & Rex, pnt CI, 4⅝", NM, A **$385.00**

Foxy Grandpa, Wing, pnt CI, 5½", VG, from $200 to........$300.00
Gem Stove, Abendroth Bros, bronze-pnt CI, Gem Heaters Save Money on back, 4¾", NM, A $275.00
General Pershing, Grey Iron, CI, 7¾", G, A $55.00
General Sheridan on Base, Arcade, gold-pnt CI, 6", part of tail missing o/w VG, A $335.00
George Washington (Hollow Base), US, pnt CI, 6¼", NM, A $55.00
Globe Safe, Kenton, sphere w/claw feet, NP combination lock on hinged front door, 5", EX, A $100.00
Globe Savings Fund Bank, Kyser & Rex, japanned CI, 7⅛", NM $3,600.00
Gold Dollar Eagle Clock, Arcade, gold-pnt CI, 3½", EX, A....$250.00
Good Luck Horseshoe (depicts Buster Brown & Tige), pnt CI, 4¼", VG $250.00
Graf Zeppelin, AC Williams, silver-pnt CI, 6⅝", VG, A..$125.00
Guardian Bank, Atholf Bergman, hand-pnt tin, 1 of 2 known, VG, A..$6,000.00
Home Bank, Judd, bronze-pnt CI, 4", EX, A $500.00
Home Savings Bank, J&E Stevens, yel- & beige-pnt CI, 5⅞", EX, A $525.00
Horn of Plenty Safe, EM Roche Novelty, NP CI w/brass combination lock, 4", EX, from $475 to $550.00
House w/Basement, Ohio Foundry, red- & blk-pnt CI, 4⅝", EX, A...$2,400.00
Independence Hall, gold-pnt CI, 11", peak of roof broken o/w VG, A $965.00

Indian with Tomahawk, Hubley, gold-painted cast iron with red detail, 6", EX, D10, $275.00; Pig, AC Williams, gold-painted cast iron, 3" long, EX, D10, $125.00.

Photo courtesy Dunbar Gallery

Indiana Silo, CI, 3½", rare, G, A................................$1,100.00
Iron Masters House, Kyser & Rex, brn-pnt CI w/red roof, 4½", scarce, NM, A $1,375.00
IXL Safe Bank, Kyser & Rex, gr-pnt CI w/gold highlights, 4", EX, A $150.00
John Brown's Fort, CI, 2⅛", EX, A............................$1,100.00
Kodak Bank, J&E Stevens, NP CI, 4¼", EX, A..............$225.00
Lady's Shoe w/Mouse, Germany, 1920s, silvered lead, 3¼", NM, A $225.00

Lifeboat, yel- & bl-pnt pressed steel, decal on side: Contributions for Royal National..., 14", overpnt, scarce, A .$365.00

Lion, Hubley, gold-painted cast iron with red detail, 5" long, VG, D10, $185.00.

Photo courtesy Dunbar Gallery

Log Cabin, US, CI, 2½", EX, A $275.00
Main Street Trolley (No People), AC Williams, gold-pnt CI, 6¾", EX-, A $385.00
Main Street Trolley (w/People), AC Williams, gold-pnt CI, 6¾", rpl wheels, EX, A $350.00
Main Street Trolley (w/People), AC Williams, gold-pnt CI, 6¾", VG, A $250.00
Maine Bank, Grey Iron, 1900, japanned CI w/gold highlights, 4⅝", NM...$750.00
Mammy, hands on hips, Hubley, pnt CI, 5¼", EX, A $300.00
Mary & Her Lamb, US, pnt CI, 4⅜", G- $250.00
Merry-Go-Round, Grey Iron, NP CI, 4⅝", rpl shaft, A .$100.00
Metropolitan Bank, J&E Stevens, CI, 5⅞", VG, A........$300.00

Monkeys, AC Williams, gold-painted cast iron, 3½", EX, D10, $375.00.

Photo courtesy Dunbar Gallery

Moon & Star Safe, blk-pnt CI w/gold highlights, 5⅛", EX, A $150.00

Mosque Bank, Grey Iron, gold-pnt CI, 4¼", EX, A........**$165.00**
Mosque Bank (Combination Door), Grey Iron, gold-pnt CI, 5⅛", NM..........**$600.00**
Mutt & Jeff, AC Williams, gold-pnt CI, 4¼", VG, A....**$155.00**
National Safe Deposit, CI w/gold highlights, 5¾", NM, A.**$185.00**
New England Church, wht-pnt CI w/gr roof & gold steeple, 7½", EX, A..........**$600.00**
New Heatrola Bank, Kenton, red-pnt CI w/gold highlights, metal sides, 4½", EX, A..........**$145.00**
North Pole, Grey Iron, NP CI, 4¼", VG, A..........**$400.00**
North Side Savings Bank, Kenton, NP CI, 3½", NM, A .**$825.00**
Old Homestead Bank, Kyser & Rex, japanned CI w/NP combination lock, 4⅛", NM, A..........**$475.00**
Old Volunteer Bank, pnt CI fire hydrant, rare, EX, A ..**$1,850.00**
Our Kitchener, England, japanned CI, 6", NM, A..........**$200.00**
Pagoda Bank, England, CI w/gold highlights, 5", G-, A.**$250.00**
Parlor Stove, CI w/NP center bands & finial, 6⅞", NM, A...**$350.00**
Peters Weatherbird, Arcade, pnt CI, 4¼", NM, A......**$1,000.00**
Piano Bank, pnt CI w/instrument design, 5¾", rpt, A....**$325.00**
Pingree Potato Bank, US, CI, 5¼", rare, VG, A..........**$825.00**
Porky Pig, Hubley, 1930, pnt CI, base lettered Porky, 5¾", M..........**$300.00**
Pug Dog, Germany, lead, Hershey Park stenciled on side, 2¾", M, A..........**$300.00**
Puppo Dog (No Pillow), Hubley, 2nd casting, pnt CI w/emb bee, 4⅞", EX..........**$150.00**
Puppo on Pillow, Hubley, pnt CI, 6", EX, A..........**$450.00**
Radio Bank (Combination Door), Kenton, gr-pnt CI w/NP front panel, metal sides, 4½", NM, A..........**$435.00**
Radio Bank (2 Dials), Kenton, CI w/metal sides & back, 3⅜", VG, A..........**$385.00**
Radio Bank (3 Dials), Kenton, red-pnt CI w/NP front panel, metal sides, 3½, NM, A..........**$275.00**
Recording Bank, NP CI, 6⅝", EX, A..........**$350.00**
Reindeer, AC Williams, gold-pnt CI, 9½" L, NM, A....**$100.00**
Riverside Bank, Am Badge, lead, 5⅜", EX, A..........**$300.00**
Rocking Chair, CJ Manning, gold-pnt CI, 6¾", rare, EX..**$2,900.00**
Roper Stove, Arcade, wht-pnt CI & sheet metal, 3¾", NM, A..........**$1,000.00**

Scottie Dog, Hubley, painted cast iron, 6" long, EX, D10, $200.00.

Royal Bank (George V), Chamberlain & Hill, japanned CI, 5¾", EX, A..........**$225.00**
Rumplestiltskin, pnt CI, base lettered Do You Know Me?, 6", VG..........**$250.00**
Safety Vault w/Grill, Kenton, NP CI, 7¼", NM, A..........**$200.00**
Sampson Safe, NP CI w/emb eagle & shield on top panel, 5¼", rare, NM..........**$600.00**
Santa Claus, Wing, pnt CI, 5⅞", EX, A..........**$475.00**
Seal on Rock, Arcade, blk-pnt CI, 3½", VG, A..........**$225.00**
Sharecropper, AC Williams, pnt CI, toes visible on 1 foot, 5½", NM, A..........**$275.00**
Shell Out, J&E Stevens, pnt CI conch shell, 4¾" L, G, A .**$385.00**
Ship, hand-pnt tin w/2 masts & stacks, mounted on base w/ball feet, 9¼", NM..........**$5,000.00**
Skyscraper, AC Williams, CI, 6 posts on roof, 6½", EX, A ...**$300.00**
Squirrel w/Nut, US, gold-pnt CI, 4⅛", scarce, VG, A ...**$525.00**
State Bank, Am, japanned CI w/gold trim, 4⅛", NM, A .**$225.00**
State Bank, Kenton, japanned CI w/gold & bronze highlights, 3¼", NM, A..........**$175.00**
State Bank, Kenton, japanned CI w/gold highlights, 8½", NM, A..........**$1,750.00**

Statue of Liberty, AC Williams, gold-painted cast iron, 6½", VG, D10, $225.00.

Steamboat, AC Williams, bl-pnt CI w/red stacks, 7⅝", NM, A..........**$500.00**
Steamboat, Arcade, gold-pnt CI, 7½", G, A..........**$200.00**
Street Clock, AC Williams, pnt CI, 6", VG..........**$650.00**
Submarine, hand-pnt lead, 5¼" L, EX, A..........**$350.00**
Tabernacle Savings Bank, Keyless Lock Co, CI w/copper finish, 2½", NM..........**$3,600.00**
Tank Savings Bank, Ferrosteel, CI, spoke wheels, 9½", G, A..........**$385.00**
Templetone Radio, Kenton, gr-pnt CI w/gold highlights, steel sides, 4", EX..........**$350.00**
Tower Bank, John Harper, japanned CI, 9¼", G, A......**$265.00**
Tower Bank, Kyser & Rex, japanned CI w/red & gold highlights, 6⅞", EX..........**$850.00**
Traders Bank, Canada, CI, 8½", G..........**$1,200.00**
Trolley Car, Kenton, silver-pnt CI, 5¼", scarce, G, A...**$275.00**

Two Kids, Harper, pnt CI, gr base, 4½", VG $750.00
Two-Faced Black Boy, AC Williams, blk-pnt CI w/gold hat, 3⅛", G, A $150.00
United Bank, AC Williams, gold-pnt CI, 2¾", EX, A...$550.00
US Mailbox, no eagle, Kenton, silver-pnt CI w/red lettering, 4¾", EX, A $200.00

US Mailbox, with eagle, Kenton, green-painted cast iron with gold detail, NM, D10, $165.00.

US Mailbox, w/eagle, Kenton, silver-pnt CI w/red lettering, 5⅛", EX, A $175.00
Villa, Kyser & Rex, blk-pnt CI w/gold window trim & red finial, 5", EX, A..................$500.00
Washington Monument, AC Williams, gold-pnt CI, 6⅛", VG, A $200.00
Westminster Abbey, England, japanned CI, 6⅜", NM, A..$350.00
Wise Pig, Hubley, wht-pnt CI w/pk facial highlights, 6⅝", EX, A $135.00
World Time Bank, Arcade, CI w/paper timetables, 4⅛", NM, A $300.00
Yellow Cab, Arcade, pnt CI, stenciled doors, 7¾", NM..$3,200.00
Young America Bank, Kyser & Rex, japanned CI, 4⅜", NM..$350.00

Barbie Doll and Friends

No one could argue the fact that vintage Barbies are holding their own as one of the hottest areas of toy collecting on today's market. Barbie was first introduced in 1959, and since then her face has changed three times. She's been blond and brunette; her hair has been restyled over and over, and it's varied in length from above her shoulders to the tips of her toes. She's worn high-fashion designer clothing and pedal pushers. She's been everything from an astronaut to a veterinarian, and no matter what her changing lifestyle required, Mattel (her 'maker') has provided it for her.

Though even Barbie items from recent years are bought and sold with fervor, those made before 1970 are the most sought after. You'll need to do a lot of studying and comparisons to learn to distinguish one Barbie from another, but it will pay off in terms of making wise investments. There are several books available; we recommend them all: *The Wonder of Barbie* and *The World of Barbie Dolls* by Paris and Susan Manos; *The Collector's Encyclopedia of Barbie Dolls and Collectibles* by Sibyl DeWein and Joan Ashabraner; *The Story of Barbie* by Kitturah B. Westenhouser; *Barbie Doll Fashion, Vol. 1, 1959 – 1967*, and *Barbie Doll Fashion, Vol. II, 1968 – 1974*, by Sara Sink Eames; *Barbie Exclusives, Books I and II*, by Margo Rana; *Barbie, The First 30 Years, 1959 Through 1989*, by Stefanie Deutsch; *A Decade of Barbie Dolls and Collectibles, 1981 – 1991*, by Beth Summers; *The Barbie Doll Boom, 1986 – 1995*, *Collector's Encyclopedia of Barbie Doll Exclusives and More*, and *Thirty Years of Mattel Fashion Dolls* all by by J. Michael Augustyniak; *The Barbie Years, 1959 to 1996, First and Second Editions*, by Patrick C. Olds; *Skipper, Barbie's Little Sister* by Scott Arend, Karla Holzerland, and Trina Kent; *Collector's Guide to 1990s Barbie Dolls* by Maria-Martinez-Esguerra; *Collector's Guide to Barbie Doll Vinyl Cases* by Connie Craig Kaplan; and *Collector's Guide to Barbie Doll Paper Dolls* by Lorraine Mieszala (all published by Collector Books).

Remember that unless the box is mentioned in the line (orig box, MIB, MIP, NRFB, etc), values are given for loose items. As a general rule, a mint-in-the box doll is worth twice as much (or there about) as one mint, no box. The same doll, played with and in only good condition, is worth half as much (or even less). Never-removed-from-box examples sell at a premium.

Advisor: Marl Davidson (D2).

Dolls

Allan, 1963, pnt red hair, straight legs, MIB, D2..................$125.00
Allan, 1963, pnt red hair, straight legs, nude, EX, D2 ......$45.00
Allan, 1963, pnt red hair, straight legs, orig swimsuit & sandals, VG, M15 ....$65.00
Allan, 1964, pnt red hair, bendable legs, orig outfit, VG, M15 ....$165.00

Barbie #1 in Gay Parisienne, 1959, MIB, $6,500.00.

Barbie, #1, 1958-59, blond hair, MIB, D2 ....**$9,950.00**
Barbie, #1, 1958-59, brunette hair, MIB, D2.............**$10,000.00**
Barbie, #2, 1959, blond hair, MIB, D2.........................**$9,000.00**
Barbie, #2, 1959, brunette hair, MIB, D2 ....**$8,500.00**
Barbie, #3, 1960, blond hair, MIB, D2.........................**$2,400.00**
Barbie, #3, 1960, blond hair, orig swimsuit, NM, D2 .....**$950.00**
Barbie, #3, 1960, brunette hair, MIB, D2 ....**$2,250.00**
Barbie, #3, 1960, brunette hair, orig swimsuit, EX, D2...**$900.00**
Barbie, #4, 1960, blond hair, MIB, D2.........................**$1,100.00**
Barbie, #4, 1960, brunette hair, MIB, D4 ....**$1,500.00**
Barbie, #5, 1961, blond hair, orig swimsuit, NM, D2 .....**$325.00**
Barbie, #5, 1961, brunette hair, orig swimsuit, NM, D2 .**$400.00**
Barbie, #5, 1961, red hair, MIB, D2 ....**$1,300.00**
Barbie, #6, blond hair, orig swimsuit, NM, D2 ....**$325.00**
Barbie, #6, brunette hair, orig swimsuit, NM, D2 ....**$350.00**
Barbie, #6, red hair, replica swimsuit, NM, D2 ....**$600.00**
Barbie, African, 1996, Dolls of the World, NRFB, D2 .....**$20.00**
Barbie, American Girl, 1964, blond hair, orig swimsuit, NM, D2 ....**$550.00**
Barbie, American Girl, 1964, red hair, replica swimsuit, NM, D2 ....**$600.00**
Barbie, Angel Face, 1992, NRFB, D2 ....**$45.00**
Barbie, Angel Lights, 1993, NRFB, D2 ....**$85.00**
Barbie, Antique Rose, FAO Schwarz, 1996, NRFB, D2 .**$295.00**
Barbie, Army, 1989, American Beauty Series, NRFB, M15..**$45.00**
Barbie, Astronaut, 1985, NRFB...**$75.00**
Barbie, Ballerina on Tour, 1976, MIB, M15 ....**$100.00**
Barbie, Benefit Ball, 1992, Classique Collection, NRFB, D2 ....**$150.00**
Barbie, Benefit Performance, porcelain, 1987, NRFB, D2 ..**$600.00**
Barbie, Birthday Surprise, 1991, NRFB, M15 ....**$35.00**
Barbie, Blossom Beautiful, Sears Exclusive, 1992, rare, MIB ..**$400.00**
Barbie, Blue Starlight, 1996, Sears Exclusive, NRFB, D2 .**$60.00**
Barbie, Bubble-Cut, 1961, blond or brunette hair, MIB, D2, ea **$500.00**
Barbie, Bubble-Cut, 1961, blond or brunette hair, nude, EX, D2, ea..**$125.00**
Barbie, Bubble-Cut, 1961, brunette hair, orig swimsuit, NM, D2 ....**$200.00**
Barbie, Bubble-Cut, 1961, jet blk hair, MIB, D2 ....**$650.00**
Barbie, Bubble-Cut, 1961, jet blk hair, orig swimsuit, NM, D2 ....**$200.00**
Barbie, Bubble-Cut, 1961, red hair, MIB, D2 ....**$600.00**
Barbie, Bubble-Cut, 1961, red hair, orig swimsuit, NM, D2 ..**$200.00**
Barbie, Bubble-Cut w/side part, 1962-64, blond hair, MIB, D2 ....**$2,000.00**
Barbie, Bubble-Cut w/side part, 1962-64, blond hair, orig swimsuit, VG, M15 ....**$165.00**
Barbie, Busy, 1971, NRFB, M15...**$225.00**
Barbie, Busy Gal, 1994, NRFB, D2....................................**$55.00**
Barbie, Canadian, 1987, Dolls of the World, NRFB, D2 ..**$75.00**
Barbie, Chinese, 1993, Dolls of the World, NRFB, D2 ....**$45.00**
Barbie, Circus Star, 1994, FAO Schwarz, NRFB, D2 ....**$95.00**
Barbie, Color Magic, 1966, blond hair, nude, EX, D2 ....**$300.00**
Barbie, Color Magic, 1966, blond hair, orig swimsuit & hair band, NM, D2...**$650.00**
Barbie, Dance Club, 1989, NRFB.......................................**$50.00**
Barbie, Denim 'n Lace, 1992, MIB **$35.00**

Barbie, Disney Fun, 1994, NRFB, D2................................**$65.00**
Barbie, Doctor, 1987, NRFB, M15 ....**$35.00**
Barbie, Dramatic New Living, 1970, blond or red hair, NRFB, D2, ea...**$350.00**
Barbie, Dream Date, 1982, NRFB, M15............................**$35.00**
Barbie, Dream Fantasy, 1990, Walmart limited edition, NRFB **$45.00**
Barbie, Dream Glow, 1986, orig outfit, VG, M15.............**$15.00**
Barbie, Egyptian Queen, 1993, Great Eras, NRFB, D2...**$175.00**
Barbie, Elizabethan, 1994, Great Eras, NRFB, D2 ....**$55.00**
Barbie, Empress Bride, 1992, Bob Mackie, MIB, D2.......**$950.00**
Barbie, English, 1991, Dolls of the World, NRFB, D2......**$75.00**
Barbie, Evening Enchantment, 1989, Sears Exclusive, NRFB, M15 ....**$55.00**
Barbie, Evening Extravaganza, 1993, Classique Collection, NRFB, D2 ....**$95.00**
Barbie, Evening Pearl, porcelain, 1995, Presidential Series, NRFB, D2 ....**$300.00**
Barbie, Evergreen Princess, 1994, red hair, FAO Schwarz, NRFB, D2 ....**$595.00**
Barbie, Fabulous Fur, 1983, NRFB **$50.00**
Barbie, Fashion Photo, 1977, MIB, M15............................**$85.00**
Barbie, Fashion Queen, 1963, nude, EX, D2.....................**$75.00**

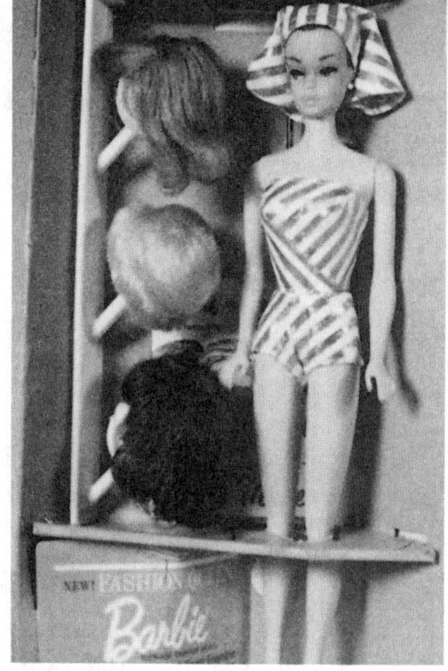

Barbie, Fashion Queen, 1963, original swimsuit and turban, complete with wigs and stand, NM, $275.00.

Barbie, Flapper Girl, 1993, Great Eras, NRFB, D2 ....**$275.00**
Barbie, Flight Time, 1989, NRFB, M15 ....**$40.00**
Barbie, Gibson Girl, 1993, Great Eras, NRFB, D2 ....**$165.00**
Barbie, Goddess of the Moon, 1996, Bob Mackie, NRFB, M15..**$175.00**
Barbie, Gold, 1990, Bob Mackie, NRFB, D2 ....**$650.00**
Barbie, Gold Jubilee, 1994, NRFB, D2.............................**$850.00**
Barbie, Gold Lace, 1989, Target, NRFB, M15 ....**$45.00**
Barbie, Gold Sensation, porcelain, 1993, MIB, D2 ....**$350.00**
Barbie, Golden Dream, 1980, NRFB, M15 ....**$45.00**
Barbie, Grecian Goddess, 1995, Great Eras, NRFB, D2 ...**$55.00**
Barbie, Greek, 1985, Dolls of the World, NRFB, D2........**$70.00**

Barbie, Growing Pretty Hair, 1971, 1st edition, orig outfit, complete w/wigs, NM, D2 ....$255.00
Barbie, Happy Birthday, 1990, NRFB $35.00
Barbie, Hawaiian, 1975, MIB, M15 ....$85.00
Barbie, Holiday, 1988, NRFB, D2...............................$1,000.00
Barbie, Holiday, 1989, NMIB, D2.................................$200.00
Barbie, Holiday, 1989, NRFB, D2 ....$250.00
Barbie, Holiday, 1990, NRFB, D2 ....$200.00

Photo courtesy Lee Garmon

Barbie, Holiday, 1991, NRFB, $195.00.

Barbie, Holiday, 1992, NRFB, D2 ....$150.00
Barbie, Holiday, 1993, NRFB, D2 ....$150.00
Barbie, Holiday, 1994, NRFB, D2 ....$175.00
Barbie, Holiday, 1995, NRFB, D2 ....$75.00
Barbie, Holiday, 1996, NRFB, D2 ....$50.00
Barbie, Holiday Dreams, 1994, NRFB, D2 ....$35.00
Barbie, Holiday Jewel, porcelain, 1995, NRFB, D2 ....$250.00
Barbie, India, 1981, Dolls of the World, NRFB, D2 ....$150.00
Barbie, International Holiday, 1994, NRFB, D2..............$95.00
Barbie, Japanese, 1984, Dolls of the World, NRFB, D2 .$150.00
Barbie, Jewel Jubilee, 1991, NRFB $85.00
Barbie, Jeweled Splendor, 1995, NRFB, D2....................$295.00
Barbie, Kenyan, 1993, Dolls of the World, NRFB, D2 .....$35.00
Barbie, Lilac & Lovely, 1987, Sears limited edition, NRFB..$55.00
Barbie, Live Action, 1971, orig outfit, NM, D2.............$150.00
Barbie, Magic Curl, 1981, NRFB.....................................$40.00
Barbie, Magic Moves (Black), 1985, NRFB, M15 ....$35.00
Barbie, Malaysian, 1990, Dolls of the World, NRFB, D2 .$60.00
Barbie, Malibu, 1971, orig swimsuit & towel, NM, D2.....$35.00
Barbie, Masquerade Ball, 1993, Bob Mackie, NRFB, D2..$450.00
Barbie, Mexican, 1988, Dolls of the World, NRFB, D2 ...$30.00
Barbie, Midnight Gala, 1994, Classique Collection, NRFB, D2 ....$95.00
Barbie, Midnight Waltz, 1996, Ballroom Beauties Series II, NRFB, D2 ....$60.00

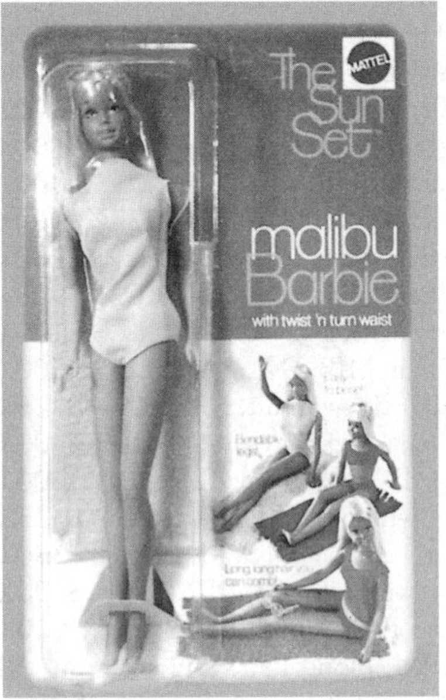

Barbie, Malibu, 1971, MIP, $85.00.

Barbie, Miss, 1964, pnt hair, NRFB, D2 ....$1,300.00
Barbie, Miss, 1964, pnt hair, orig swimsuit & hat, complete w/3 wigs & stand, NM, D2..$400.00
Barbie, Miss America, 1972, orig outfit, missing crown & roses, NM, D2..$75.00
Barbie, Moon Goddess, 1996, Bob Mackie, NRFB, D2 ..$160.00
Barbie, Moonlight Magic, 1993, NRFB, D2......................$90.00
Barbie, Native American, 1994, Dolls of the World, NRFB, D2 ....$55.00
Barbie, Newport, 1973, NRFB, M15 ....$175.00
Barbie, Nigerian, 1989, Dolls of the World, NRFB, D2....$65.00
Barbie, Norwegian, 1995, Dolls of the World, NRFB, D2 ..$25.00
Barbie, Olympic Gymnast, 1995, NRFB, D2 ....$75.00
Barbie, Oriental, 1980, Dolls of the World, NRFB, D2 ....$95.00

Barbie, Queen of Hearts, Bob Mackie, 1994, NRFB, $275.00.

Barbie, Parisienne, 1980, Dolls of the World, MIB, M15...**$200.00**
Barbie, Peach Pretty, 1989, NRFB **$45.00**
Barbie, Peruvian, 1985, Dolls of the World, NRFB, D2 ...**$75.00**
Barbie, Pink & Pretty, 1982, orig outfit, VG, M15...........**$15.00**
Barbie, Plantation Belle, porcelain, 1992, MIB, D2 ....**$150.00**
Barbie, Platinum, 1991, Bob Mackie, MIB, D2 ....**$600.00**
Barbie, Police, 1993, Toys 'R Us, NRFB, M15..................**$70.00**
Barbie, Ponytail, 1961, blond hair, orig red swimsuit, VG, M15 ....**$285.00**
Barbie, Quick Curl, 1972, NRFP, M15 ....**$165.00**

Barbie, Quick Curl Miss America, 1972, MIB, $125.00.

Barbie, Romantic Rose Bride, porcelain, 1995, NRFB, D2.**$300.00**
Barbie, Royal, 1979, Dolls of the World, NRFB, D2 ......**$195.00**
Barbie, Royal Splendor, porcelain, 1993, Presidential series, NRFB, D2 ....**$300.00**
Barbie, Russian, 1988, Dolls of the World, NRFB, D2/M15 .**$75.00**
Barbie, Russian, 1996, Dolls of the World, NRFB, D2 .....**$20.00**
Barbie, Sapphire Dream, 1995, NMIB, D2 ....**$75.00**
Barbie, Savvy Shopper, 1994, Bloomingdales, NMIB, D2..**$85.00**
Barbie, Silken Flame, porcelain, 1992, NRFB, D2 ....**$225.00**
Barbie, Silver Screen, 1993, FAO Schwarz, NRFB, D2..**$295.00**
Barbie, Silver Starlight, porcelain, 1993, NRFB, D2......**$500.00**
Barbie, Snow Princess, 1994, Seasons Series, NRFB, M15..**$135.00**
Barbie, Soda Fountain Sweetheart, 1996, Coca-Cola, NRFB, D2..**$195.00**
Barbie, Solo in the Spotlight, porcelain, 1989, NRFB, D2..**$200.00**
Barbie, Sophisticated Lady, porcelain, 1990, NRFB, M15 ..**$225.00**
Barbie, Spanish, 1991, Dolls of the World, NRFB, D2.....**$50.00**
Barbie, Spring Bouquet, 1994, Enchanted Seasons, NRFB, D2 ....**$150.00**
Barbie, Standard, 1970, blond hair, MIB, D2 ....**$700.00**
Barbie, Standard, 1970, red hair, orig swimsuit, NM, D2..**$1,000.00**
Barbie, Starlight Dance, 1996, Classique Collection, NRFB, D2 ....**$55.00**
Barbie, Starlight Waltz, 1995, Ballroom Beauty Series I, NRFB, D2 ....**$75.00**
Barbie, Starlily Bride, porcelain, 1994, NRFB, D2 ....**$325.00**
Barbie, Sterling Wishes, 1991, Spiegel, NRFB, D2 ....**$150.00**
Barbie, Swirl Ponytail, 1964, blond hair, MIB, D2......**$1,000.00**
Barbie, Swirl Ponytail, 1964, blond hair, orig swimsuit, NM, D2/M15...**$400.00**
Barbie, Swirl Ponytail, 1964, red hair, orig swimsuit, NM, D2 ....**$450.00**
Barbie, Swiss, 1983, Dolls of the World, NRFB, D2 ....**$50.00**
Barbie, Talking, 1968, blond or brunette hair, orig swimsuit, NM, D2, ea **$175.00**
Barbie, Truly Scrumptious, 1968, NRFB, D2..................**$500.00**
Barbie, Twirly Curls, 1982, NRFB...................................**$30.00**
Barbie, Twist 'N Turn, 1964, red hair, orig swimsuit & bow, EX, D2 ....**$350.00**
Barbie, Twist 'N Turn, 1966, blond hair, orig swimsuit & cover-up, NM, D2...**$250.00**
Barbie, Twist 'N Turn, 1967, blk hair, orig outfit & bow, NM, D2 ....**$325.00**
Barbie, Twist 'N Turn, 1967, blond hair, orig swimsuit & bow, NM, D2...**$265.00**
Barbie, Twist 'N Turn, 1968, brunette hair, NRFB, D2 .**$900.00**
Barbie, Twist 'N Turn, 1968, red hair, orig swimsuit, NM, D2 ....**$250.00**
Barbie, Twist 'N Turn, 1969, brunette hair, NRFB, D2 .**$900.00**
Barbie, Twist 'N Turn, 1969, brunette hair, orig swimsuit, NM, D2 ....**$275.00**
Barbie, Twist 'N Turn, 1970, brunette hair, orig swimsuit & bow, NM, D2 ....**$300.00**
Barbie, Vacation Sensation, 1986, NRFB **$55.00**
Barbie, Walk Lively, 1972, NRFB, D2 ....**$300.00**
Barbie, Walt Disney World 25th Anniversary, 1996, NRFB, D2 ....**$50.00**
Barbie, Wedding Day, porcelain, 1988, NRFB, D2 ....**$500.00**
Barbie, Winter Fantasy, 1990, FAO Schwarz, NRFB, D2..**$295.00**
Barbie, Winter Princess, 1993, NRFB, D2/M15 ....**$400.00**
Barbie, 35th Anniversary, 1993, brunette hair, NRFB, D2 ...**$50.00**
Barbie as Belle, 1996, NRFB, D2....................................**$100.00**

Photo courtesy J. Michael Augustyniak

Barbie as Dorothy, 1995, Hollywood Legends, NRFB, $85.00.

Barbie as Cinderella, 1996, Children's Collector Series, NRFB, D2 .... $35.00
Barbie as Glinda, 1995, Hollywood Legends, NRFB, D2 .. $85.00
Barbie as Little Bo Peep, 1995, Children's Classic Series, NRFB, D2 .... $125.00
Barbie as Maria (Sounds of Music), 1994, Hollywood Legends, NRFB, D2 .... $55.00
Barbie as My Fair Lady, Embassy Ball, 1995, Hollywood Legends, NRFB, D2 .... $90.00
Barbie as Scarlett, 1994, Hollywood Legends, gr & wht picnic dress, NRFB, D2 .... $55.00
Barbie as Scarlett, 1994, Hollywood Legends, gr velvet dress, NRFB, D2 .... $55.00
Barbie as Scarlett, 1994, Hollywood Legends, red dress, NRFB, D2 .... $75.00
Brad, Talking, 1971, M, D2 .... $125.00
Brad, 1969, bendable legs, NRFB, M15 .... $175.00

Cara, Deluxe Quick Curl, 1976, MIB, $65.00; PJ, Deluxe Quick Curl, 1976, MIB, $65.00.

Carla, 1976, NRFB, D2 .... $200.00
Chris, 1967, blond hair, orig outfit, NM, D2 .... $125.00
Christie, Kissing, 1979, NRFB, M15 .... $55.00
Christie, Sun Lovin', 1978, NRFB, M15 .... $65.00
Christie, Talking, 1968, orig swimsuit, EX, M15 .... $150.00
Christie, Twist 'N Turn, 1968, red hair, MIB, D2 .... $500.00
Curtis, Free Movin', 1975, MIB, M15 .... $115.00
Francie, Black, 1966, nude, M, D2 .... $800.00
Francie, Growin' Pretty Hair, 1970, MIB, D2 .... $200.00
Francie, Growin' Pretty Hair, 1970, orig outfit, EX, D2 . $125.00
Francie, Hair Happenin's, 1970, orig outfit, EX, D2 .... $150.00
Francie, Malibu, 1970, orig swimsuit, VG, M15 .... $55.00
Francie, Twist 'N Turn, 1966, blond hair, NRFB, D2 .... $800.00
Francie, Twist 'N Turn, 1967, blond hair, nude, EX, D2 .. $85.00
Francie, Twist 'N Turn, 1967, brunette hair, orig swimsuit, EX, D2 .... $155.00
Francie, 1966, blond hair, orig swimsuit, bendable legs, NM, D2 .... $200.00
Francie, 1967, brunette hair, bendable legs, nude, EX, D2 ... $125.00
Jamie, New & Wonderful Walking, orig outfit, NM, D2 . $300.00
Jamie, Walking, brunette hair, orig outfit, boots & hair band, NM, D2 .... $275.00
Jamie, Walking, red hair, dressed in Strolling in Style, M, D2 .... $350.00
Kelly, Quick Curl, 1972, orig outfit, NM, D2 .... $100.00
Kelly, Quick Curl, 1972, NRFB, M15 .... $175.00
Kelly, Yellowstone, 1973, NRFB, D2 .... $450.00
Ken, Busy Talking, 1972, orig outfit, VG, M15 .... $85.00
Ken, Doctor, 1987, NRFB, M15 .... $35.00
Ken, Earring Magic, 1992, NRFB, D2 .... $50.00
Ken, Free Movin', 1975, NRFB, M15 .... $100.00
Ken, Gold Metal Skier, 1975, NRFB, M15 .... $115.00
Ken, Mod Hair, 1972, NRFB, M15 .... $115.00
Ken, Roller Skating, 1980, NRFB $40.00
Ken, Sun Valley, 1973, NRFB, M15 .... $125.00
Ken, Superstar, 1976, orig outfit, VG, M15 .... $25.00

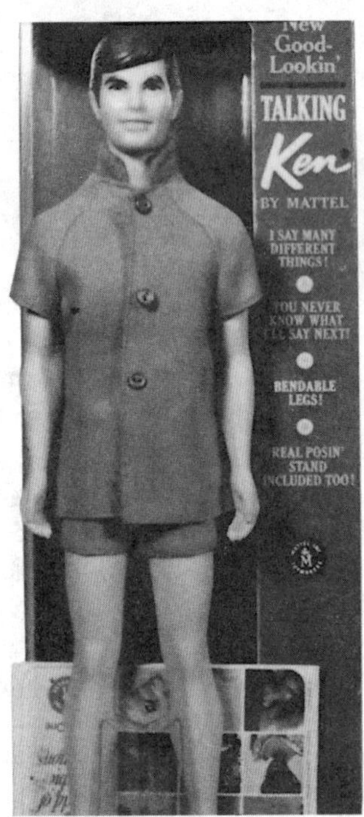

Ken, Talking, 1969, MIB, $275.00.

Ken, 1961, flocked blond or brunette hair, orig outfit, straight legs, VG (VG box), M15, ea $185.00
Ken, 1961, flocked blond or brunette hair, orig outfit, straight legs, NM, D2, ea $165.00
Ken, 1961, flocked brunette hair, straight legs, nude, EX, D2 ... $40.00
Ken, 1962, pnt brunette hair, straight legs, MIB, D2 ...... $225.00
Ken, 1965, pnt blond hair, bendable legs, nude, EX, D2 .. $125.00
Ken, 1965, pnt brunette hair, orig swimsuit, bendable legs, NM, D2 .... $225.00
Ken as Cowardly Lion, 1996, Hollywood Legends, NRFB, D2 .... $85.00
Ken as Rhett, 1994, Hollywood Legends, NRFB, D2 .... $65.00
Midge, 1963, blond hair, straight legs, MIB, D2 .... $150.00

Midge, 1963, blond hair, straight legs, nude, EX, D2........$75.00
Midge, 1963, brunette hair, orig swimsuit, VG, M15.....$100.00
Midge, 1963, red hair, orig swimsuit & ribbon, bendable legs, M, D2 ....$450.00
Midge, 30th Anniversary, porcelain, 1992, MIB, D2 .....$175.00

PJ, Free Moving, 1975, original swimsuit, NM, $85.00.

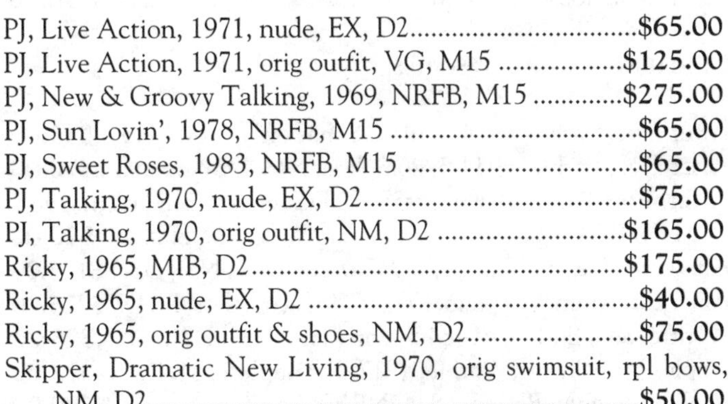

PJ, Live Action, 1971, nude, EX, D2...............................$65.00
PJ, Live Action, 1971, orig outfit, VG, M15 ....$125.00
PJ, New & Groovy Talking, 1969, NRFB, M15 ....$275.00
PJ, Sun Lovin', 1978, NRFB, M15 ....$65.00
PJ, Sweet Roses, 1983, NRFB, M15 ....$65.00
PJ, Talking, 1970, nude, EX, D2.......................................$75.00
PJ, Talking, 1970, orig outfit, NM, D2 ....$165.00
Ricky, 1965, MIB, D2...$175.00
Ricky, 1965, nude, EX, D2 ....$40.00
Ricky, 1965, orig outfit & shoes, NM, D2........................$75.00
Skipper, Dramatic New Living, 1970, orig swimsuit, rpl bows, NM, D2...$50.00

Skipper, Cool Tops, MIB, $35.00.

Skipper, Growing Up, 1974, NRFB, $125.00.

Skipper, Growing Up, 1974, orig outfit, EX, M15 ....$65.00
Skipper, Malibu, 1975, MIB, M15...................................$50.00
Skipper, Twist 'N Turn, 1969, blond hair, nude, EX, D2 .$45.00
Skipper, Twist 'N Turn, 1969, red hair, orig outfit & shoes, rpl headband, M, D2 ....$200.00
Skipper, 1964, red hair, orig swimsuit, rpl shoes, bendable legs, G, M15..$65.00
Skipper, 1965, red hair, orig swimsuit, bendable legs, NM, D2 ....$100.00
Skipper, 1970, brunette hair, straight legs, MIB, D2 ......$225.00
Skooter, 1963, blond hair, straight legs, nude, EX, D2 .....$50.00
Skooter, 1963, brunette hair, orig swimsuit & bows, MIB, D2 ....$175.00
Skooter, 1965, blond hair, bendable legs, MIB, D2 ....$225.00
Skooter, 1965, blond hair, re-dressed in Flower Girl outfit, bendable legs, VG, M15 ....$65.00
Stacey, Twist 'N Turn, 1968, blond hair, nude, EX, D2 ..$125.00
Stacey, Twist 'N Turn, 1968, blond hair, orig swimsuit, NM, D2 ....$300.00
Stacey, Twist 'N Turn, 1968, red hair, orig swimsuit, NM, D2 ....$300.00
Stacey, Twist 'N Turn, 1969, blond hair, orig swimsuit, VG, M15...$180.00
Steffie, Busy Talking, 1972, orig outfit, NM, M15 ....$275.00
Steffie, Walk Lively, 1968, nude, EX, D2.........................$95.00
Steffie, Walk Lively, 1968, orig outfit & scarf, NM, D2.$180.00
Steffie, Walk Lively, 1972, re-dressed, VG, M15.............$65.00
Todd, 1965, NRFB, D2...$225.00
Todd, 1966, orig outfit, NM, M15 ....$125.00
Tutti, 1966, brunette hair, dressed in Cookin' Goodies, EX, D2...$50.00
Tutti, 1966, brunette hair, orig outfit, NM, D2 ....$85.00
Tutti, 1966, red hair, nude, EX, D2 ....$50.00
Whitney, Jewel Secrets, 1986, NRFB, D2 ....$95.00
Whitney, Nurse, 1987, NRFB $80.00
Whitney, Perfume Pretty, 1987, NRFB, M15 ....$85.00

Whitney, Style Magic, 1988, NRFB, M15 .... **$65.00**

CASES

Barbie, Midge, Ken & Allan, 1963, red, NM, D2 .... **$45.00**

Barbie, 1963, black background, EX, $25.00.

Barbie, 1967, lavender w/wht cover, G, M15 .... **$15.00**
Barbie & Francie, 1965, G, M15 .... **$25.00**
Barbie & Ken, 1963, bl, rectangular, orig hangers & drawers, VG, M15 .... **$40.00**
Barbie & Midge, 1964, wearing Stormy Weather & Sorority Meeting, red, EX, D2 .... **$30.00**
Barbie & Midge Travel Pals, 1963, blk, rnd, NM, D2 .... **$150.00**
Barbie & the Rockers, 1985, dbl opening, VG, M15 .... **$35.00**

Photo courtesy Paris and Susan Manos

Barbie Goes Travelin', 1965, EX, $195.00.

Barbie in Pink & Pretty, 1982, M.................................... **$10.00**
Barbie in Red Flare, 1963, wht, G, D2 .... **$15.00**
Barbie's Playhouse Pavillion, Europe, 1978, plastic 2-room carrying case, NRFB, D2... **$65.00**
Francie, 1965, pk & wht, hexagon, NM, D2 .... **$35.00**
Ken, 1961, lavender, EX, D2 .... **$20.00**
Ken in Rally Days, 1962, teal, EX, D2/M15 .... **$20.00**
Madison Avenue, FAO Schwarz, 1991, EX, D2 .... **$75.00**
Miss Barbie, 1963, blk patent leather w/zipper closure, EX, D2 .... **$100.00**
Silver Screen Barbie, FAO Schwarz, 1994, M, D2........... **$55.00**
Skipper, 1964, beige, dbl opening, EX, D2 .... **$15.00**

Photo courtesy Mike's General Store

Skipper, 1964, blue background, rare, NM, $150.00.

Solo in the Spotlight, 1962, blk, G, D2 .... **$20.00**
Tutti, 1965, bl, VG, D2 .... **$25.00**
Tutti's Playhouse, 1965, M, D2 .... **$150.00**

CLOTHING AND ACCESSORIES

After Five, Barbie, #934-3, dress & hat only, VG, M15 ... **$35.00**
After Five, Barbie, #934-3, complete, NM, D2 .... **$70.00**
Afternoon Party, Barbie, #5835, Designer Collection, 1982, NRFP **$20.00**
Altogether Elegant, Francie, #1242-0, complete, NM, D2 .... **$125.00**
American Airlines Captain, Ken, #779-1, complete, M, D2 .**$225.00**
Antifreezers, Barbie, #1464-3, complete, NM, D2 .... **$75.00**
Apple Print Sheath, Barbie, #917-2, complete, M, D2 ..... **$75.00**
Arabian Nights, Barbie, #874, NRFB, D2...................... **$500.00**
Arabian Nights, Ken, #774-0, complete, NM, D2 .... **$165.00**
Army & Airforce, Ken, #797, NRFB, D2 .... **$150.00**
Astro Fashions, Barbie, #2738, 1985, NRFP **$30.00**
Baby Doll Pinks, Barbie, #3403-1, complete, M, D2......... **$45.00**
Ballerina, Barbie, #989-3, complete, NM, D2 .... **$45.00**
Ballet Lessons, Skipper, #1905-1, complete, M, D2 .... **$60.00**
Barbie Babysits, #953-0, complete, NM, D2 .... **$95.00**
Barbie in Hawaii, #1605-0, missing anklet & booklet, EX, D2 .... **$60.00**
Barbie in Holland, #823-2, complete, NM, D2............... **$125.00**
Barbie in Mexico, #820-1, replica booklet, NM, D2......... **$95.00**
Barbie Q, #962-0, complete, NM, D2 .... **$60.00**
Barbie's Boudoir Fashion Pak, #1834, MOC, D2............ **$165.00**
Beauty Bath Fashion Pak, #130, complete, NM, D2......... **$50.00**
Bermuda Holiday, Barbie, #1810-0, complete, NM, D2 .**$195.00**
Best Bow Fashion Pak, #118, complete, EX, D2 .... **$175.00**
Bold Gold, Ken, #1436-1, complete, M, D2....................... **$35.00**
Borderline, Francie, #1287-0, complete, M, D2.............. **$175.00**
Bride's Dream, Barbie, #947-2, complete, EX, D2 .... **$85.00**

Bubbles 'N Boots, Barbie, #3421, MOC, D2 ....$85.00
Busy Gal, Barbie, #981-3, replica sketches, EX, D2 ....$150.00
Busy Morning, Barbie, #956-1, complete, NM, D2 ....$150.00
Campus Hero, Ken, #770, complete, VG, M15 ....$35.00
Campus Sweetheart, Barbie, #1616-0, complete, M, D2 ..$595.00
Career Girl, Barbie, #954, jacket only, G, M15 ....$8.00
Career Girl, Barbie, #954-1, complete, NM, D2.............$130.00
Cheerleader, Barbie, #876-1, complete, EX, D2 ....$75.00
Cinderella, Barbie, #872-1, replica booklet, NM, D2.....$150.00
Clam Diggers, Francie, #1258-0, missing glasses, NM, D2..$75.00
College Student, Ken, #1416-1, jacket only, NM, D2......$50.00
Commuter Set, Barbie, #916-0, complete, NM, D2 ....$595.00
Confetti Cutie, Skipper, #1700-0, Sears Exclusive, complete, NM, D2...$250.00
Cool It Fashion Pak, #F4, complete, G, D2 ....$15.00

Photo courtesy June Moon

Country Clubbin', Ken, #1400, NRFB, $175.00.

Country Fair, Barbie, #1603-1, complete, NM, D2...........$45.00
Country Music, Barbie, #1055, NRFB, D2 ....$195.00
Cruise Stripes, Barbie, #918-1, complete, EX, D2............$35.00
Dancing Doll, Barbie, #1626-1, complete, NM, D2 ....$295.00
Dandy Lines, Ken, #3797, Designer Originals, 1981, NRFP ..$20.00
Day at the Fair, Skipper, #1911-0, complete, M, D2 ......$110.00
Dinner at Eight, Barbie, #946-0, complete, NM, D2 ....$75.00
Dr Ken, #793, complete, VG, M15 ....$45.00
Dream Boat, Ken, #785-0, complete, NM, D2..................$55.00
Dream Land, Barbie, #1669-0, gown only, M, D2 ....$45.00
Dreamtime, Skipper, #1901-1, replica phone book, NM, D2.....$40.00
Dreamy Blues, Barbie, #1456-0, complete, M, D2 ....$65.00
Dreamy Pink, Barbie, #1857-0, complete, NM, D2 ....$45.00
Dress Coat, Skipper, #1906-2, complete, EX, D2 ....$45.00
Drizzle Sizzle, Skipper, #1961, complete, VG, M15..........$65.00
Drum Major, Ken, #775-3, missing baton, NM, D2..........$50.00
Drum Majorette, Barbie, #875, complete, VG, M15 ....$50.00
Drum Majorette, Barbie, #875-3, complete, NM, D2 ....$85.00
Enchanted Evening, Barbie, #983-9, gown only, EX, D2 .$35.00
Entertainer, Francie, #1763-0, complete, M, D2..............$60.00

Fashion Accents Fashion Pak, #1830, MOC, D2 ....$250.00
Fashion Shiner, Barbie, #1691-3, coat only, NM, D2.......$25.00
Firelights, Barbie, #1481-0, complete, NM, D2 ....$75.00
First Things First, Francie, #1252-1, complete, NM, D2 ..$55.00
Flats 'N Heels Fashion Pak, #1837, MOC, D2................$150.00
Flower Girl, Skipper, #1904, NRFB, D2 ....$150.00
Flower Girl, Tutti, #3615, complete, NM, M15 ....$125.00
Flower Shower, Barbie, Classique Collection, #10150, 1993, NRFB, D2 ....$35.00
Fraternity Dance, Barbie, #1638-0, replica necklace, EX, D2 ....$225.00
Fraternity Meeting, Ken, #1408-0, complete, NM, D2.....$40.00
Fresh As a Daisy, Francie, #1254-1, complete, NM, D2 ...$75.00
Friday Night Date, Barbie, #979-2, complete, EX, D2 ......$95.00
Fun at the Fair, Barbie, #1624-2, missing cotton candy, NM, D2 ....$75.00
Gad Abouts, Francie, #1250-0, complete, NM, D2 ....$150.00
Garden Party, Barbie, #931-1, complete, EX, D2..............$45.00
Garden Wedding, Barbie, #1658-1, complete, NM, D2 .$195.00
Gay Parisienne, Barbie, #964-0, complete, M, D2 ......$1,395.00
Glimmer Glamour, Barbie, #1547-0, replica hose, VG, D2...$395.00
Glowin' Out, Barbie, #3404-2, complete, EX, D2 ....$55.00
Go Granny Go, Francie, #1267-0, missing album cover, NM, D2 ....$85.00
Going Bowling, Ken, #1403-0, complete, NM, D2............$25.00
Going Hunting, Ken, #1409-0, complete, NM, D2 ....$45.00
Gold 'N Glamour, Barbie, #1647-1, complete, NM, D2.$795.00
Gold Rush, Francie, #1222-0, complete, NM, D2 ....$85.00
Golden Elegance, Barbie, #992-3, complete, NM, D2....$195.00
Golden Girl, Barbie, #911-1, complete, NM, D2..............$70.00
Golfing Greats, Barbie, #3413-0, complete, NM, D2 .....$165.00
Graduation, Ken, #795, NRFB, D2 ....$75.00
Guinevere, Barbie, #873-4, complete, EX, D2 ....$150.00
Gypsy Spirit, Barbie, #1458-3, complete, NM, D2 ....$55.00

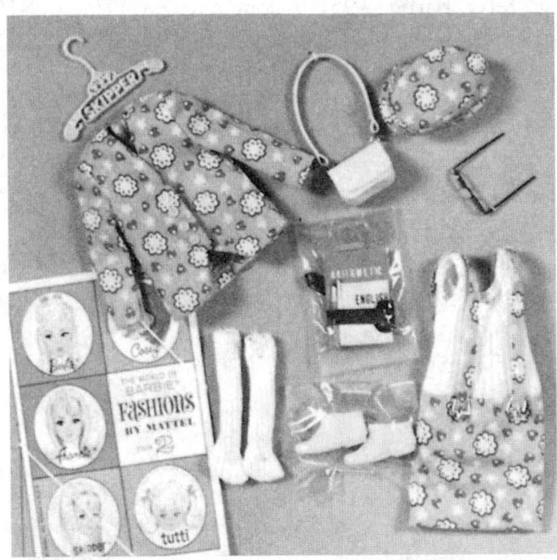

Hearts 'N Flowers, Skipper, #1945, complete, NM, $165.00.

Heavenly Holidays, Barbie, #4277, 1982, NRFP $55.00
Here Comes the Bride, Barbie, #1665-2, gown only, EX, D2....$25.00

Here Comes the Groom, Ken, #1426-0, missing vest, hat & gloves, NM, D2 .... $495.00
Hiking Holiday, Ken, #1412-3, complete, NM, D2 .... $85.00
Holiday Dance, Barbie, #1639-1, complete, EX, D2 .... $295.00
Hollywood Premiere, Barbie, Classique Collection, #01618, 1992, NRFB, D2 .... $50.00
Ice Breaker, Barbie, #942-1, complete, EX, D2 .... $40.00
In Training, Ken, #780-0, complete, NM, D2 .... $20.00
It's Cold Outside, Barbie, #819-1, complete, NM, D2 .... $45.00
Jump Into Lace, Barbie, #1823-0, complete, M, D2 .... $65.00
Junior Prom, Barbie, #1614-2, replica necklace, NM, D2 .. $250.00
Just for Fun Fashion Pak, #136, skates only, EX, D2 .... $5.00

Photo courtesy June Moon

King Arthur, Ken, #773, NRFB, $325.00.

Knit Hit, Barbie, #1804-0, complete, M, D2 .... $55.00
Knitting Pretty, Barbie, #957-5, complete, EX, D2 .... $195.00
Land & Sea, Skipper, #1917, jacket only, VG, M15 .... $10.00

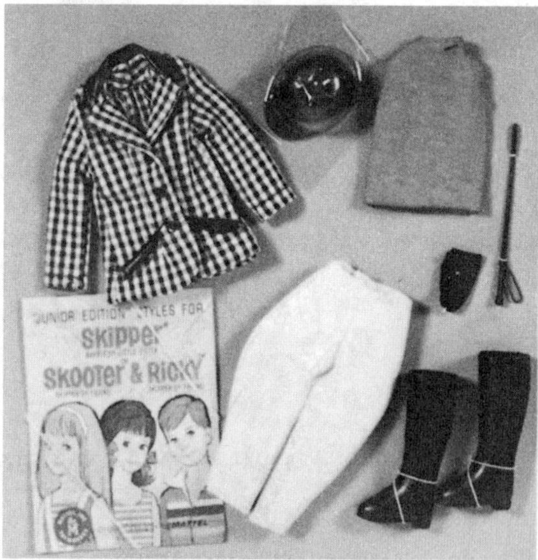

Learning to Ride, Skipper, #1935, complete, NM, $175.00.

Leather Weather, Barbie, #1751-1, complete, M, D2 .... $95.00
Let's Dance, Barbie, #978-1, complete, NM, D2 .... $55.00
Let's Have a Ball, Barbie, #1879-2, missing flower, VG, D2 ... $75.00
Lights Out, Ricky, #1501, NRFB, D2 .... $75.00
Lingerie Fashion Pak, #93A, blk, complete, EX, D2 .... $55.00
Lingerie Fashion Pak, #96A, pk, complete, EX, D2 .... $25.00
Little Red Riding Hood, Barbie, #880, NRFB, D2 .... $600.00
Lollapaloozas, Skipper, #1947-0, complete, M, D2 .... $75.00
Long 'N Fringy, Barbie, #3341-1, complete, NM, D2 .... $50.00
Loungin' Lovelies, Skipper, #1930-3, complete, NM, D2 . $50.00
Lunch Date, Barbie, #1600-0, complete, NM, D2 .... $55.00
Lunch on the Terrace, Barbie, #1649-1, complete, M, D2 .. $195.00
Masquerade, Ken, #794-0, complete, M, D2 .... $65.00
Me & My Dog, Tutti, #3554-0, coat only, EX, D2 .... $12.00
Me 'N My Doll, Skipper, #1913-0, complete, M, D2 .... $150.00
Midi Bouquet, Francie, #3446-0, dress only, NM, D2 .... $18.00
Midi Magic, Barbie, #1869-1, rpl hose, EX, D2 .... $45.00
Mini Chex, Francie, #1209-0, complete, NM, D2 .... $75.00
Miss Astronaut, Barbie, #1641, suit only, VG, M15 .... $55.00
Mood for Music, Barbie, #940-0, replica necklace, NM, D2 .... $110.00
Night Blooms, Francie, #1212-1, nightie only, EX, D2 .... $6.00
Night Scene, Ken, #1496-1, jacket & pants only, EX, D2 . $20.00
Nightly Negligee, Barbie, #965-6, complete, NM, D2 .... $45.00
Open Road, Barbie, #985-1, complete, NM, D2 .... $210.00
Orange Blossom, Barbie, #987-0, complete, NM, D2 .... $50.00
Oscar de la Renta, Series IV, Barbie, #9258, 1984, NRFB, D2 .... $40.00
Oscar de la Renta, Series VII, Barbie, #9261, 1984, NRFB, D2 .... $45.00
Outdoor Casuals, Skipper, #1915-3, complete, NM, D2 .. $45.00
Pants 'N Pinafore, Skipper, #1971-0, complete, NM, D2 . $55.00
Party Date, Barbie, #958-2, complete, NM, D2 .... $150.00
Party Pink Fashion Pak, #S2, complete, EX, D2 .... $10.00
Peachy Fleecy, Barbie, #915-1, complete, NM, D2 .... $95.00
Perfect Beginnings Fashion Pak, #250, pk slip only, EX, D2 .. $10.00
Picnic Set, Barbie, #967-6, replica fishing pole & fish, NM, D2 .... $135.00
Pink Fantasy, Barbie, #1754-2, complete, VG, D2 .... $45.00
Pink Moonbeams, Barbie, #1694-1, complete, NM, D2 . $125.00
Pink Sparkle Satin Fashion Pak, #106, coat only, NM, D2 .. $35.00
Plantation Belle, Barbie, #966-0, replica necklace, NM, D2 . $225.00
Platter Party, Skipper, #1914-0, complete, M, D2 .... $55.00
Play Ball, Ken, #792-4, complete, VG, D2 .... $35.00
Polka Dots & Rainbows, Francie, #1255-1, complete, NM, D2 .... $35.00
Pony Coat, Francie, #1240-1, complete, NM, D2 .... $25.00
Poodle Parade, Barbie, #1643-3, complete, M, D2 .... $550.00
Prince, Ken, #772-2, complete, NM, D2 .... $325.00
Prom Pinks, Francie, #1295-1, missing headband, EX, D2. $150.00
Rainy Day Checkers, Skipper, #1928-0, missing checkers, NM, D2 .... $95.00
Red Flare, Barbie, #939-2, complete, NM, D2 .... $55.00
Red Sensation, Skipper, #1901-0, complete, M, D2 .... $60.00
Registered Nurse, Barbie, #991-0, complete, NM, D2 .... $90.00
Resort Set, Barbie, #963-4, missing bracelet, NM, D2 .... $50.00
Riding in the Park, Barbie, #1668-0, complete, M, D2 .. $350.00
Roller Skate Date, Ken, #1405-1, complete, NM, D2 .... $55.00

Roman Holiday, Barbie, #968-3, replica necklace, NM, D2 ....$695.00
Romantic Ruffles, Barbie, #1871-1, missing earrings, NM, D2 ....$65.00
Sailor, Ken, #796, NRFB, D2 ....$125.00
Sand Castles, Tutti, #3603-0, missing socks, EX, D2 ....$50.00
Satin 'N Rose, Barbie, #1611-1, complete, NM, D2 ....$195.00
Satin Dreams, Barbie, Classic Collection, #10151, 1993, NRFB, D2 ....$25.00
Saturday Night Date, Ken, #786-0, complete, NM, D2 ....$45.00
School Days, Skipper, #1907-0, complete, M, D2 ....$55.00
Seein' the Sights, Ken, #1421-0, complete, NM, D2 ....$250.00
Senior Prom, Barbie, #951-2, complete, EX, D2 ....$70.00
Shape Ups, Barbie, #1782-1, complete, M, D2 ....$65.00
Sheath Sensation, Barbie, #986-3, complete, NM, D2 ....$60.00
Ship Ahoy, Skipper, #1918-2, complete, M, D2 ....$125.00
Ship Shape, Tutti, #3602-0, complete, NM, D2 ....$55.00
Silk 'N Fancy, Skipper, #1902-4, complete, M, D2 ....$55.00
Silken Flame, Barbie, #977-0, complete, NM, D2 ....$75.00
Silver Polish, Barbie, #1492-1, complete, M, D2 ....$135.00
Silver Sensation, Barbie, Collector Series III, #7438, 1983, NRFB, D2 ....$45.00
Singing in the Shower, Barbie, #988-0, complete, NM, D2 ..$30.00
Skater's Waltz, Barbie, #1629-0, complete, NM, D2 ....$175.00
Skating Fun, Skipper, #1908-0, complete, NM, D2 ....$45.00
Ski Queen, Barbie, #948-1, complete, EX, D2 ....$65.00
Sledding Fun, Skipper, #1936-0, complete, NM, D2 ....$175.00
Sleepy Time Gal, Barbie, #1674-1, robe only, NM, D2 ....$25.00
Snap Dash, Barbie, #1824-0, complete, M, D2 ....$95.00
Solo in the Spotlight, Barbie, #982-0, complete, NM, D2 .$165.00
Sorority Meeting, Barbie, #937-2, dress only, NM, D2 ....$25.00
Sport Shorts, Ken, #783, NRFB, D2 ....$50.00
Springtime Magic, Barbie, Collector Series II, #7092, 1983, NRFB, D2 ....$65.00
Stormy Weather, Barbie, #949-5, complete, NM, D2 ....$35.00
Stripes Are Happening, Barbie, #1545-1, top & skirt only, NM, D2 ....$50.00

Stripes Away, Barbie and Francie, #1775, MIB, $250.00.

Style Setters, Francie, #1268-3, missing hose, NM, D2 ....$95.00
Suburban Shopper, Barbie, #969, NRFB, D2 ....$350.00
Suede Scene, Ken, #26, complete, VG, M15 ....$15.00
Sunny Pastels, Skipper, #1910-1, complete, M, D2 ....$50.00
Sunshiners Fashion Pak, #76, complete, EX, D2 ....$25.00
Sweater Girl, Barbie, #976-2, complete, EX, D2 ....$55.00
Sweet Dreams, Barbie, #973-0, complete, NM, D2 ....$40.00
Swingin' Separates, Francie, #1042-0, complete, EX, D2 .$195.00
Swinging Easy, Barbie, #955-1, dress only, EX, D2 ....$25.00
Swirly Cue, Barbie, #1822-2, missing earrings, NM, D2 ...$50.00
Tennis Anyone, Barbie, #941-0, complete, NM, D2 ....$45.00
Tennis Time, Skipper, #3466-0, complete, NM, D2 ....$25.00
Tennis Tunic, Francie, #1221-0, complete, M, D2 ....$45.00
Terry Togs, Ken, #784-1, complete, NM, D2 ....$35.00
Time for Tennis, Ken, #790, NRFB, D2 ....$120.00
Top It Off Fashion Pak, #1800, MOC, D2 ....$75.00
Touchdown, Ken, #799-0, complete, NM, D2 ....$45.00

Photo courtesy June Moon

Touchdown, Ken, #779, MIB, $75.00.

Tuckered Out, Francie, #1253-2, complete, NM, D2 ....$45.00
Two for the Ball, Francie, #1232, complete, VG, M15 ..$125.00
Under Pretties, Skipper, #1900-0, complete, NM, D2 ....$25.00
Underliners, Barbie, #1821-2, complete, NM, D2 ....$65.00
Victory Dance, Ken, #1411-3, complete, NM, D2 ....$55.00
Way Out West, Ken, #1720, NRFB, D2 ....$75.00
What's New at the Zoo, Skipper, #1925-1, complete, EX, D2 ....$55.00
White Delight, Barbie, #3799, Designer Originals, 1981, NRFP $20.00
Wild 'N Wonderful, Barbie, #1856-1, blouse & skirt only, NM, D2 ....$50.00
Winter Holiday, Barbie, #975-2, complete, EX, D2 ....$65.00
Yachtsman, Ken, #789-1, missing hat, NM, D2 ....$30.00
5th Avenue Fashion, Barbie, Classique Collection, #01646, 1992, NRFB, D2 ....$65.00

Furniture, Rooms, and Houses

Barbie & Ken Little Theater, 1964, complete, NMIB, D2.$600.00
Barbie Deluxe Family House, 1966, complete, VG, D2..$135.00

Barbie Dream House, 1961, 1st edition, complete, NM, D2 .... $150.00
Barbie Fashion Plaza, 1975, NMIB, M15 .... $100.00
Barbie Fashion Shop, 1962, complete, EX, D2 .... $300.00
Barbie Housemate, 1966, complete, EX, D2 .... $150.00
Barbie's Cookin' Fun Kitchen, 1971, MIB $100.00
Barbie's Room-Fulls Country Kitchen, 1974, NRFB, D2 .$50.00
Barbie's Room-Fulls Firelight Living Room, 1974, NRFB, D2 .... $125.00
Barbie's Room-Fulls Studio Bedroom, #7405, 1974, NRFB, M15 .... $50.00
Francie & Casey Housemates, 1966, complete, NM, D2.$200.00
Francie's Mod A Go Go Bedroom, 1966, complete, EX, D2 .... $150.00

Go-Together Chair, Ottoman, and End Table, 1964, complete, MIB, $150.00.

Go-Together Lawn Swing & Planter, 1964, complete, MIB, D2 .... $150.00
Go-Together Lounge Chair, 1964, missing pillows, NM, D2 .... $65.00
Go-Together Swing, 1964, complete, M, D2 .... $100.00
Jamie's Studio Apartment, 1970, complete, EX, D2 .... $200.00
Lively Livin' House, 1970, EX (worn box), D2 .... $250.00
Magical Mansion, 1990, NRFB, D2 .... $1,000.00
Skipper's Dream Room, 1964, complete, M, D2 .... $500.00
Suzy Goose, Barbie or Midge Chifferobe, complete, VG, D2 ...$50.00
Suzy Goose, Skipper's Jeweled Bed, 1965, MIB, D2 .... $150.00
Suzy Goose Hope Chest, 1961, EX, D2 .... $5.00
Suzy Goose Vanity, 1963, complete, EX, D2 .... $35.00
Suzy Goose Wardrobe, 1962, complete, EX, D2 .... $50.00
Tutti & Chris House, 1967, complete, NM, D2 .... $125.00
Tutti's Ice Cream Stand, 1965, rare, NM, D2 .... $295.00
World of Barbie House, 1966, complete, EX, D2 .... $150.00

Gift Sets

Barbie, Ken & Midge Pep Rally, 1964, NRFB, from $1000 to $1,300.00
Barbie & Kelly Gardening Fun, 1996, NRFB, D2 .... $45.00
Barbie & Ken Campin' Out, 1983, NRFB $100.00
Barbie for President, Toys 'R Us, 1991, NRFB $75.00
Barbie Golden Groove, Sears, 1969, MIB $1,000.00
Barbie Loves Elvis, 1996, NRFB, D2 .... $75.00
Barbie Mix 'N Match Set, 1963, NRFB, from $2,000 to..$3,000.00

Barbie's 'Round the Clock Gift Set, 1963, NRFB, $5,500.00.

Birthday Fun at McDonald's, 1993, NRFB, D2 .... $50.00
Cinderella Gift Pack, Disney Classics, 1992, NRFB $125.00
Color Magic Set, 1965, rare, MIB, D2 .... $4,000.00
Dance Magic Barbie & Ken, 1990, NRFB $50.00
Disney Barbie & Friends, Toys 'R Us, 1991, NRFB $70.00
Dolls of the World, 1995, NRFB, D2 .... $60.00
Dressing Fun Barbie, 1993, MIB $20.00

Francie and Her Swingin' Separates, 1966, Sears, MIB, $1,000.00.

Francie Rise & Shine, 1971, NRFB $1,000.00
Happy Birthday Barbie, 1984, NRFB $75.00
Happy Halloween Barbie & Kelly, Target, 1996, NRFB, D2...$70.00
Island Fun Barbie & Ken, 1993, MIB $25.00
Jamie Strollin' in Style, Sears, 1972, MIB $425.00
Midge's Ensemble, 1964, NRFB, D2 .... $3,200.00

PJ Swingin' in Silver, Sears, 1970, MIB....$800.00
Rollerblade Snack & Surf Set, 1992, MIB....$25.00
Sharin' Sisters, 1992, NRFB, D2....$25.00
Skipper Bright & Breezy, 1969, MIB....$725.00
Skipper on Wheels, 1965, MIB, D2....$600.00
Skipper Party Time, 1964, MIB....$400.00
Tennis Stars Barbie & Ken, 1986, NRFB....$55.00
Travelin' Sisters, JC Penney Exclusive, 1995, MIB....$50.00
Wedding Party Midge, 1990, NRFB, D2....$150.00
Western Stampin' Barbie, 1993, MIB....$50.00

Vehicles

Austin Healy, Irwin, 1962, red & wht, very rare, NRFB, D2....$3,500.00
Barbie & Ken Dune Buggy, Irwin, 1970, pk, NRFB....$300.00
Barbie Dream Vette, 1982, pk, NRFB....$50.00
Barbie Goin' Boating, Sears Exclusive, 1973, NM, D2....$50.00
Barbie Silver 'Vette, 1984, silver, NRFB....$40.00
Classy Corvette, 1976, NRFB, D2....$35.00
Country Camper, 1971, MIB....$35.00
Ferrari, 1987, red, MIB, D2....$50.00
Ferrari, 1988, wht, MIB, D2....$50.00
Ken's Hot Rod, Irwin, 1961, NM, D2....$165.00
Mercedes, 1963, dk gr, VG, M15....$125.00

Photo courtesy Beth Summers

Porsche, 1991, pink, working headlights, NRFB, $50.00.

Star Traveler Motorhome, 1980, MIB....$75.00
Ten Speeder, 1973, MIB, D2....$25.00
Volkswagen Cabriolet, #3804, 1988, MIB....$35.00
1957 Belair Chevy, 1989, 1st edition, aqua, MIB....$150.00
1957 Belair Chevy, 1990, 2nd edition, pk, MIB....$125.00

Miscellaneous

Beauty Bath, Barbie, 1975, MIB, M15....$45.00
Book, Barbie & Ken, Random House, 1962, EX, D2....$25.00
Book, Barbie's New York Summer, Random House, 1962, EX, D2....$25.00
Book, Here's Barbie, Random House, 1962, G, D2....$15.00
Box, Allan, 1963, G, D2....$25.00
Box, Ken, 1961, EX, D2....$50.00
Box, Midge, 1962, G, D2....$50.00
Box, Ponytail Barbie, 1962, G, D2....$65.00

Photo courtesy Paris and Susan Manos

Barbie and Francie Color Magic Fashion Designer Set, 1966 – 67, MIB, $450.00.

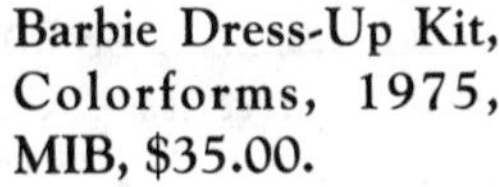

Barbie Dress-Up Kit, Colorforms, 1975, MIB, $35.00.

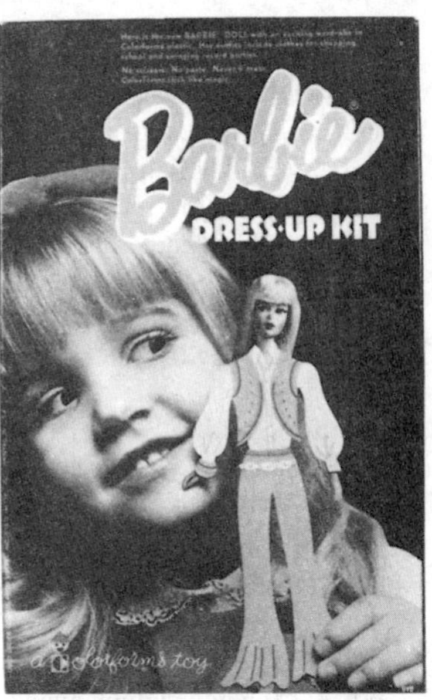

Box, Skipper, 1963, EX+, D2....$75.00
Box, Todd, 1965, EX, D2....$40.00
Catalog, Mattel, 1969, features Living Barbie on cover, 28 pgs, NM, F8....$15.00
Charm, 1995, sterling silver & 10k gold head figure of Ponytail Barbie, M, D2....$250.00
Charm Bracelet, Peter Brams Designs, 1989 Nostalgic Barbie, sterling silver, NRFB....$150.00
Color & Wipe-Off Board, Barbie, Western Publishing, 1985, NRFP....$10.00
Dictionary, Webster, 1963, red vinyl cover w/image of blond Bubble-Cut Barbie, EX, A....$50.00
Dictionary, 1963-65, Barbie's name & mc flowers, EX, D2....$110.00
Embroidery Set, Barbie, Ken & Midge, 1963, complete, MIB, from $200 to....$250.00
Hi-Fashion Grooming Set, Barbie, 1965, complete, MIB, D2....$375.00
Magazine, Barbie Bazaar, December, 1988, EX, D2....$75.00
Magazine, Barbie Bazaar, January/February, 1990, EX, D2..$30.00
Magazine, Barbie Bazaar, March/April, 1993, EX, D2....$25.00

Magazine, *Barbie Bazaar,* May/June, 1989, EX, $35.00.

Photo courtesy Beth Summers

Magazine, Barbie Bazaar, November/December, 1995, EX, D2 ....$10.00
Magazine, World of Barbie, 1964, NM, D2 ....$65.00
Mattel-O-Phone, Mattel, 1965, complete w/Barbie & Friends disk & Liddle Kiddles disk, NMIB, F8 ....$50.00
Night Light, Enesco, 1994, features Enchanted Evening Barbie, M, D2 ....$65.00
Ornament, Holiday Barbie, Hallmark, 1993, 1st in series, NRFB, from $100 to $125.00
Ornament, Holiday Barbie, Hallmark, 1994, 2nd in series, NRFB $50.00
Ornament, Holiday Barbie, Hallmark, 1995, 3rd in series, NRFB $35.00
Paper Dolls, Barbie, Christie & Stacey, Whitman #1978, 1968, uncut, M $80.00
Paper Dolls, Barbie, Ken & Midge, Whitman #1976, 1963, uncut, M $80.00
Paper Dolls, Barbie & Ken, Whitman #1976, 1970, uncut, M $45.00
Paper Dolls, Great Shape Barbie, Golden #1522, 1985, uncut, M $15.00
Paper Dolls, Meet Francie, Whitman #1980, 1966, uncut, M $85.00
Paper Dolls, New 'N Groovy PJ, Whitman #1981, 1970, uncut, M $50.00
Paper Dolls, Pretty Changes Barbie, Whitman #1982-42, 1981, uncut, M $20.00
Paper Dolls, Yellowstone Kelley, Whitman #1956, 1975, uncut, M $35.00
Pattern, Ken, Advanced Sew-Free, 1962, MIP, D2 ....$20.00
Pencil Case, 1961, blk vinyl w/Ponytail Barbie in profile, NM, D2 ....$95.00
Pencil Case, 1965, blk vinyl w/Swirl Ponytail Barbie, Ken & Midge on front, zipper closure, NM, D2 ....$150.00
Picture Maker, Barbie, Mattel, 1969, NMIB, F8 ....$45.00
Polly Pocket, Barbie, 1994, D2 ....$12.00
Polly Pocket, Stacey or Whitney, 1994, D2, ea $8.00
Puzzle, Skipper in School Days, 1965, complete, EX, D2 .$15.00
Quick Curl Boutique, Barbie, 1974, VG, M15 ....$45.00
Record, Barbie Sings, 1961, 3-record set, MIP, D2 ....$65.00
Scrapbook, 1964, features Swirl Ponytail Barbie, NM, D2 .$65.00

Tea Set, 25th Anniversary, NM, $125.00.

Video, Barbie & the Rockers Out of This World, Hi-Tops Video, 1987, NRFP $15.00
Wallet, Bubble-Cut Barbie wearing Enchanted Evening, 1962, bl vinyl, EX, D2 ....$50.00
Wristwatch, Ponytail Barbie, 1963, bl band, NM, D2 ....$150.00

Battery-Operated Toys

From the standpoint of being visually entertaining, nothing can compare with the battery-operated toy. Most (probably as much as 95%) were made in Japan from the '40s through the '60s, though some were distributed by American companies — Marx, Ideal, and Daisy, for instance — who often sold them under their own names. So even if they're marked, sometimes it's just about impossible to identify the actual manufacturer. Though batteries had been used to power trains and provide simple illumination in earlier toys, the Japanese toys could smoke, walk, talk, drink, play instruments, blow soap bubbles, and do just about anything else humanly possible to dream up and engineer. Generally, the more antics the toy performs, the more collectible it is. Rarity is important as well, but first and foremost to consider is condition. Because of their complex mechanisms, many will no longer work. Children often stopped them in midcycle, rubber hoses and bellows aged and cracked, and leaking batteries caused them to corrode, so very few have survived to the present intact and in good enough condition to interest a collector. Though it's sometimes possible to have them repaired, unless you can buy them cheap enough to allow for the extra expense involved, it is probably better to wait on a better example. Original boxes are a definite plus in assessing the value of a battery-op and can be counted on to add from 30% to 50% (and up), depending on the box's condition, of course, as well as the toy's age and rarity.

We have made every attempt to list these toys by the name as it appears on the original box. Some will sound very similar. Many toys were reissued with only minor changes and subsequently renamed. For more information we recommend *Collecting Toys* by Richard O'Brien (Books Americana) and *Collecting Battery Toys* by Don Hultzman (Collector Books).

Advisor: Tom Lastrapes (L4).

See also Aeronautical; Automobiles and Other Vehicle Replicas; Boats; Marx; Robots and Space Toys.

ABC Fairy Train, MT, children shake as train advances w/lights & sound, litho tin, 14", EX (EX box), A **$175.00**

ABC Toyland Express, MT, 1950s, several actions, litho tin, 14½", EX..**$160.00**

Accordion Player Hobo w/Monkey, Alps, seated hobo plays accordion while monkey plays cymbals, MIB, L4....**$575.00**

Accordion Playing Bunny w/Baby Bunny Playing Cymbals, Alps, 1950s, several actions, 12", EX **$400.00**

Acrobat Cycle, Aoshin, 1970s, advances & performs wheelie, plastic, 9", NM (EX box), A...................................**$150.00**

Acrobat Police Car, TPS, advances w/flashing light, tin, 10", EX..**$55.00**

Aerial Ropeway, TN, 1950s, EX (EX box), L4 ....**$175.00**

Air Control Tower, Bandai, 1960s, plane & helicopter circle tower, 11", EX...**$400.00**

Airmail Helicopter, KO, advances w/flashing lights & spinning props, mostly tin, 10", EX (EX box), A..................**$225.00**

Albino Gorilla, TN, MIB, L4 ....**$525.00**

Alitalia Jeep, Ichiko, advances w/flashing rear light as airplane appears on rear screen, litho tin, 7", EX (EX box), A .**$200.00**

All Stars Mr Baseball, K, baseball player swings at balls from batting machine, litho tin, 8", NM (NM box), A **$750.00**

Photo courtesy Martin and Carolyn Berens

Amazing Spider-Man Diesel Train, NMIB, $65.00.

American Circus Television Truck, Exelo, 1950s, several actions, litho tin w/full-figure clown driver, 9", rare, EX **$1,200.00**

Animal Helicopter, MT, rare, MIB, L4..........................**$575.00**

Animal Train, MT, MIB, L4 ....**$575.00**

Animated Squirrel, S&E, 1950s, several actions, 8½", EX..**$200.00**

Annie Tugboat, Y, 1950s, mystery action w/lights & sound, 12½", EX...**$175.00**

Antique Gooney Car, Alps, 1960s, wht open touring car w/animated driver, 4 actions, 9", MIB **$350.00**

Arctic Explorer Sled, Sears Exclusive, advances w/flashing lights & revolving propellers, tin & plastic, 16", NMIB, A.**$850.00**

Army Radio Jeep, Linemar, 1950s, several actions, remote control, 7", EX **$200.00**

Army Train Set, Haji, 1950s, w/6 sections of track, 15½", EX **$200.00**

Arthur-A-Go-Go Drummer, Alps, 1960s, several actions, 10", MIB, L4...**$750.00**

Artic Snowmobile, MT, MIB, L4..................................**$475.00**

Astro Dog (Snoopy look-alike), Y, 1960s, several actions, 11", EX **$200.00**

Atomic Fire Car, TN, 1950s, several actions, 9½", EX ..**$225.00**

Atomic Generator, Linemar, NMIB, L4 ....**$575.00**

Auto Scooter, France, carnival ride w/3 bumper cars, litho tin, 9x14", EX (EX box), A **$1,450.00**

B-Z Porter, MT, 1950s, figure on platform truck w/3 pcs of luggage, 7", MIB, L4 ....**$375.00**

B-Z Rabbit, MT, 1950s, several actions, litho tin, 7", EX.**$125.00**

Baby Bertha the Watering Elephant, Mego, 1960s, 3 actions, 10", rare, MIB, L4..**$1,250.00**

Baby Carriage, TN, 10", NMIB, L4...............................**$175.00**

Ball Playing Dog, Linemar, 1950s, 3 actions, tin & plush, 9", M, L4 ....**$175.00**

Balloon Blowing Monkey, Alps, 1950s, several actions, 11", MIB, L4...**$225.00**

Balloon Bunny, Y, remote control, rare, MIB, L4...........**$375.00**

Balloon Poodle, Y, 1960s, several actions, 11", EX.........**$125.00**

Batman and Robin Batcycle, Hong Kong, plastic, 7", NM (NM box), A, $465.00.

Bambi, see Walking Bambi
Barber Bear, TN, 1950s, barber clips & combs child's hair w/several other actions, tin & plush, 10", EX (EX box), L4........**$600.00**
Barney Bear the Drummer Boy, Alps/Cragstan, 1950s, plush & tin w/cloth clothes, remote control, 11", M, L4......**$250.00**
Bartender, Rosko, several actions, litho tin & vinyl w/cloth clothes, 11½", MIB, L4...**$85.00**
Batman & Robin Motorcycle w/Sidecar, Tam Toys, advances w/flashing lights, plastic, 10", NM (EX box), A......**$185.00**
Batmobile, AHI, 1977, forward & reverse action, plastic, radio control, 8", NM (NM box)......................................**$275.00**
Bear Target Game, MT, 1950s, several actions, litho tin, 9", EX...**$400.00**
Bear the Cashier, Modern Toys, 1950s, several actions, 7½", MIB...**$425.00**
Bear the Shoemaker, TN, 1950s, hammers shoe & smokes pipe, litho tin & plush, 9", NM (NM box), A..................**$300.00**
Bear Typist, TN, 1950s, several actions, litho tin & plush, 7½", rare, EX..**$800.00**
Beatles Car, Rico, 1964, bump-&-go action, litho tin Ford w/vinyl figures, musical, 19", scarce, NM (NM box), A **$4,000.00**
Beauty Parlor Bear w/Lighted Dryer Stand, S&E, 1950s, several actions, litho tin & plush, 9½", rare, EX.............**$1,000.00**
Big Dipper, Technofix, 1960s, 3 cars navigate track, litho tin, 21", EX...**$200.00**
Big John, Alps, 1960s, 3 actions, 12", EX........................**$125.00**
Big Machine Race Car, Taiyo, NMIB, L4.......................**$175.00**
Big Shot Cadillac, TN, advances as dog in back seat smokes pipe, tin w/rubber-headed figures, 10", NMIB, A....**$400.00**
Big Top Champ Circus Clown, Alps, 1960s, 3 actions, 14", EX...**$165.00**
Big Wheel Family Camper, Taiyo, 1970s, 3 actions, 10", EX...**$125.00**
Billy the Kid Sheriff, Y, 1950s, several actions, 10½", EX..**$350.00**
Bimbo the Drumming Clown, Cragstan, 1950s, MIB, L4.**$675.00**
Bingo the Clown, TN, 1950s, 13", rare, NM, L4............**$375.00**
Black Knight Batmobile (unauthorized), Alps, 1960s, several actions, 11½", EX..**$500.00**
Black Smithy Bear, TN, 1950s, litho tin & plush, 9", EX, L4..**$375.00**
Blacksmith Bear, A1, 1950s, several action, tin & plush w/cloth clothes, 10", NMIB..**$375.00**
Blinky the Clown, Amico, 1950s, advances & plays xylophone, light-up eyes, remote control, 10", EX, L4...............**$475.00**
Blushing Frankenstein, TN, sways, growls & loses his pants, tin, cloth & vinyl, 12", MIB, L4 ....**$325.00**
Blushing Gunfighter, Y, 1960s, several actions, 11", EX..**$225.00**
Blushing Willie, Y, 1960s, pours drink into glass w/several actions, tin w/cloth clothes, vinyl face, 10", NMIB, A **$150.00**
Bob Hope Golfer, 1984, radio control, MIB, B5.............**$125.00**
Bobby the Drinking Bear, Y, 1950s, several actions, 10", MIB, L4...**$675.00**
Bongo the Monkey, Alps, 1960s, 3 actions, MIB, L4 .....**$250.00**
Breakfast Chef, K, 1960s, 8", EX **$125.00**
Bruno Accordion Bear, Y, 1950s, slides side to side while playing, tin & plush, remote control, 10", EX, L4..........**$250.00**
Bubble Blowing Boy, Y, 1950s, litho tin, 7½", MIB, L4.**$375.00**
Bubble Blowing Dog, Y, 1950s, litho tin, 8", M, L4........**$275.00**
Bubble Blowing Lion, MT, 1950s, litho tin, 7½", M, L4..**$200.00**
Bubble Blowing Monkey, Alps, 1959, dips wand in solution & blows bubbles, 10", NM...**$200.00**
Bubble Blowing Musician, Y, 1950s, man blows bubbles w/trumpet behind podium, 11", EX, L4 ....**$225.00**
Bubble Blowing Popeye, Linemar, lifts light-up pipe to mouth & blows bubbles, litho tin, 12", NM (NM box), A ..**$2,600.00**
Bubble Kangaroo, MT, 1950s, litho tin, 9", rare, EX......**$400.00**
Bubble Locomotive, TN, 1950s, 3 actions, 9½", EX **$100.00**
Bubbling Bull, Linemar, 1950s, bull w/rider dips face in bubble solution, base mk Wild West Rodeo, 7", NM (EX box)..**$325.00**
Bubbling Pup, Linemar, 1950s, several actions, 7½", EX..**$150.00**
Bulldozer, TN, 1950s, bump-&-go action, litho tin, EX, J6..**$120.00**
Bunny the Magician, Alps, 1950s, several actions, plush & tin w/cloth clothes, 14½", EX......................................**$500.00**
Burger Chef, Y, 1950s, dog shakes pan & flips burger over barbeque pit w/several other actions, tin & plush, 10", MIB........**$275.00**
Busy Housekeeper Bear, Alps, 1950s, advances w/vacuum, tin & plush w/cloth clothes, 8", NM (NM box), A...........**$350.00**
Busy Secretary, Linemar, 1950s, several actions, 7½", EX ..**$300.00**
Calypso Joe, Linemar, Black man advances & plays drum, tin w/cloth clothes, remote control, 10", EX **$600.00**
Cappy the Happy Baggage Porter Dog, Alps, 1960s, 4 actions, 12", NM, L4 ....**$200.00**
Captain Blushwell, Y, 1960s, several actions, tin & vinyl w/cloth clothes, 11", MIB, L4...**$175.00**
Captain Kidd Pirate Ship, Yonezawa, 1960s, bump-&-go w/smoking action, litho tin, 13", rare, EX (EX box)..**$475.00**
Casino King Slot Machine, Waco, EX, L4......................**$100.00**
Central Choo Choo, MT, 1960s, 3 actions, 15", EX.........**$85.00**
Champion Weight Lifter, YM, 1960s, monkey lifts barbells & face turns red, 10", EX **$125.00**
Chap the Obedient Dog, Rosko, 1960s, 3 actions, MIB, L4 ....**$275.00**
Charley Weaver Bartender, TN, 1962, makes drinks w/several actions, 12", MIB, L4..**$135.00**
Charlie the Drumming Clown, Alps, 1960s, several actions, 9½", MIB, L4...**$325.00**
Charm the Cobra, Alps, 1960s, 3 actions, mostly plastic, w/whistle (flute), rare, 6", EX **$575.00**
Cheerful Dachshund, Y, 1960s, several actions, 8½", EX.**$85.00**
Chiefy the Fire Dog, Alps, 1969, 3 actions, 9", EX.........**$100.00**
Chimp & Pup Rail Car, Cragstan, 1950s, chimp & pup work handlebar, litho tin, 9", MIB, L4............................**$375.00**
Chippy the Chipmunk, Alps, 1950s, 4 actions, 12", MIB, L4..**$225.00**
Chirping Grasshopper, MT, 1950s, 3 actions, 8½", EX..**$175.00**
Chuckling Charlie the Hysterical Laughing Clown, SH, 1960s, several actions, EX..**$300.00**
Circus Fire Engine, MT, 1960s, 4 actions, 10", EX, L4...**$250.00**
Circus Jet, TN, 1960s, circles & fires machine gun, M, L4.**$175.00**
Circus Lion, Rock Valley Toy Co, 1950s, hit mat w/wand for several actions, tin & plush, 10", MIB, L4..............**$700.00**
Clancy the Great, Ideal, 1960s, 3 actions, MIB, L4........**$375.00**
Climbing Donald Duck on His Friction Fire Engine, Linemar, Pluto driving, 18", EX (EX box) **$1,500.00**

Clown Circus Car, MT, 1960s, several actions, 8½", EX..**$275.00**
Clown Magician, Alps, tips hat & flips stack of cards, tin, cloth & vinyl, 12", MIB, L4 ....**$450.00**
Clown's Popcorn Truck, TPS, 1960s, several actions, mostly plastic, 6", EX **$275.00**
Clucking Clara, CK, MIB, L4 ....**$225.00**
Cock-A-Doodle-Doo Rooster, Mikuni, 1950s, several actions, litho tin, 8", EX **$165.00**
Coffeetime Bear, TN, pours & drinks cup of coffee, plush & tin, not working o/w EX **$200.00**
Cola Drinking Bear, Alps, 1950s, rare yel version, 3 actions, NMIB **$185.00**
College Jalopy, Linemar, advances w/lights & sound, litho tin w/4 figures, remote control, 9½", EX (VG box) **$450.00**
Comic Tank, Tomy, mystery action, rare, MIB, L4 ....**$350.00**
Communication Truck, MT, 1950s, remote control panel & sends morse code signals, tin, 12", NM (NM box) ..**$300.00**
Coney Island Penny Machine, Remco, 1950s, w/plastic prizes, 13", EX **$225.00**
Coney Island Rocket Ride, Alps, 1950s, spins w/ringing bell & flashing lights, litho tin, 14", rare, M **$800.00**
Cragstan Beep Beep Greyhound Bus, 1950s, 3 actions, 20", EX **$225.00**
Cragstan Crapshooter, Y, 1950s, 4 actions, 9", MIB, L4.**$175.00**
Cragstan Dilly Dalmatian, MIB, L4 ....**$250.00**
Cragstan Jumping Princess Poodle, 1950s, several actions, 8", EX **$85.00**
Cragstan One-Arm Bandit, Y, 1960s, 3 actions, 6", MIB, L4 ....**$250.00**
Cragstan Rolling Honey Bear, Y, 1950s, 7½", EX **$85.00**
Cragstan Skin Diver, rare, EX (EX box), L4 ....**$475.00**

Photo courtesy Don Hultzman

Cragstan Telly Bear, S&E, 1950s, six actions, 9", MIB, $500.00.

Cragstan Tootin'-Chuggin' Locomotive, 1950s, 3 actions, 24", EX **$145.00**
Cragstan Tugboat, SAN, 1950s, 3 actions, 13", M, L4...**$275.00**
Cragstan Yo-Yo Clown, 1960s, 3 actions, 9", NM, L4....**$375.00**
Crazy Car, Marusan, 1950s, several actions, litho tin w/full-figure driver, 9", EX **$125.00**
Cuty Cook (Hippo Chef), Y, 1960s, 5 actions, 10", M, L4...**$650.00**
Cycling Daddy, Bandai, 1960s, several actions, tin & plastic w/cloth clothes, 10", VG, A **$100.00**
Cycling Daddy, Bandai, 1960s, several actions, tin & plastic w/cloth clothes, 10", MIB, L4 ....**$225.00**
Cyclist Clown, K, advances w/flashing light, tin w/cloth clothes, remote control, 7", EX (EX box), L4 ....**$675.00**
Daisy the Jolly Drumming Duck, Alps, 1950s, several actions, 9", MIB, L4 ....**$375.00**
Dalmatian One-Man Band, Alps, 1950s, plays drums & cymbals, 9", EX **$250.00**
Dancing Santa Lantern, Marko, 1950s, celluloid & plastic, 6", NMIB, A **$75.00**
Dandy the Happy Drumming Pup, Cragstan/Alps, 1950s, litho tin & plush, EX, L4 ....**$200.00**
Dashee the Derby Hat Dachshund, Mego, 1971, several actions, remote control, 8", EX **$85.00**
Dennis the Menace Xylophone Player, Rosko, 1950s, plays London Bridge, litho tin, MIB **$350.00**
Dentist Bear, S&E, 1950s, several actions, 9½", EX....**$400.00**

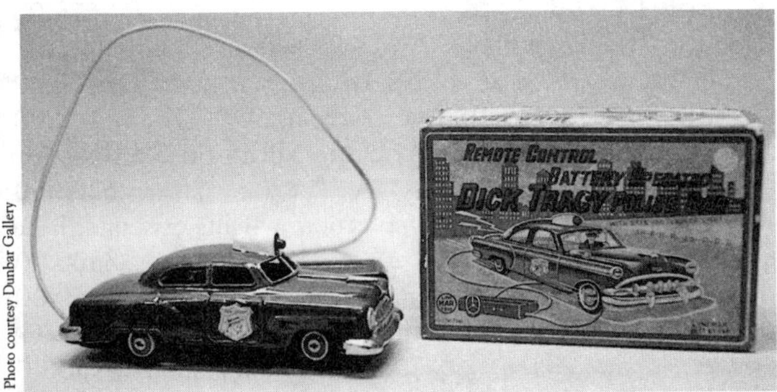

Photo courtesy Dunbar Gallery

Dick Tracy Police Car, Linemar, 1949, lithographed tin, remote control, 8", EX (VG box), $475.00.

Disneyland Fire Engine, Linemar, 1950s, several actions, 18", rare, EX **$700.00**
Dog Shuttling Train Set, Y, 1950s, several actions, 38" extended, EX **$400.00**
Dolly Seamstress, TN, 1950s, little girl at sewing machine, several actions, litho tin, 7", M (NM box), P4 ....**$385.00**
Donald Duck Locomotive, MT, 1970s, several actions, M, L4 ....**$475.00**
Donald Duck Piston Race Car, MT, advances w/lights, sound & several other actions, litho tin & plastic, 9", NMIB, A **$165.00**
Donald Duck Trolley, MT, 1960s, 3 actions, 11", EX.....**$325.00**
Donny the Smiling Bulldog, Tomiyama, 1961, 3 actions, 8½", EX **$150.00**
Dozo the Steaming Clown, Rosko, 1960s, litho tin w/cloth clothes, 10", MIB, L4 ....**$575.00**
Drinking Captain, S&E, 1960s, several actions, MIB, L4..**$200.00**
Drinking Dog, Y, pours milk into cup & drinks, light-up eyes, tin & plush, 9", scarce, NM (EX box), A **$225.00**
Drinking Licking Cat, TN, 1950s, pours & drinks from cup, plastic, plush & litho tin, 10", MIB, L4 ....**$325.00**
Drumming Bear, Alps, 1950s, Y, plays drum & eyes light, 12½", rare, NMIB, L4 ....**$1,600.00**

Drumming Mickey Mouse, Linemar, 1950s, plays drum & eyes light, plastic w/cloth clothes, remote control, 11", NMIB, A $1,900.00
Drumming Polar Bear, Alps, 1960s, 3 actions, w/3 tin fish, 12", EX $200.00
Drumming Target Bear, MT, EX, L4....$275.00
El Toro the Fighting Snorting Bull, TN, 1950s, w/detachable matador, litho tin & plush, 9½", EX....$250.00
Electric Cable Car, MIB, L4....$125.00
Electric Lucky Car, MT, 1950s, 3 actions, 7", EX....$400.00
Electric Vibraphone, TN, 1950s, litho tin, 3 actions, NMIB, A....$150.00
Electro Fire Engine, Linemar, MIB, L4 ....$175.00
Electro Sand Loader w/Conveyor, Linemar, MIB, L4....$225.00
Expert Motorcyclist, Modern Toys, 1950s, rider mounts & dismounts, litho tin, 11½", NM, L4....$1,000.00
Fantasy Land Ride, rare, EX, L4 ....$475.00
Father Bear, MT, 1950s, 4 actions, rare, MIB, L4....$500.00
Feeding Baby Bear, Y, EX, L4....$175.00
Feeding Bird Watcher, Linemar, 1950s, several actions, 10", MIB, L4....$675.00
Fido the Xylophone Player, Alps, 1950s, litho tin & plush, several actions, 9", scarce, MIB, L4 ....$475.00
Fighting Bull, Alps, 1960s, several actions, 9½", EX $140.00
Filling Station w/Studebaker, Distler, litho tin Shell station w/plastic car, NM (EX box), A $200.00
Fire Chief Car, TN, bump-&-go action w/lights & sound, litho tin, 10", NM (EX box), A $300.00
Fire Tricycle, TN, 1950s, several actions, 9½", EX $450.00
Firefly Bug, TN, 1950s, 3 actions, litho tin & plastic, 9", VG, A....$150.00
Firefly Racer #1, Mormac, 1950s, 10", EX....$400.00
Fishing Panda Bear, Alps, 1950s, several actions, litho tin & plush, 10", EX $300.00
Fishing Polar Bear, Alps, bear pulls fish out of pond, throws it in basket & squeals, plush & tin, 10", MIB, L4....$325.00
Flexie Pocket Monkey, Alps, 1960s, 3 actions, M, L4 ....$150.00
Flintstone Yacht, Remco, 1961, mostly plastic, 17", EX.$200.00
Flintstones Paddy Wagon, Remco, 1961, 18", NM (EX box), A $475.00
Flipper the Spouting Dolphin, Bandai, MIB, L4....$125.00

Photo courtesy Dunbar Gallery

Ford Mustang Stunt Car, Japan, 1969, NMIB, $175.00.

Flippy the Only Roller Skating Monkey That Skis, Alps, 1950s, 3 actions, 12", rare, EX $275.00
Flutterbirds, Alps, 2 birds fly above birdhouse as 1 chirps in door, litho tin & plush, 27", rare, EX (EX box), A $600.00
Flying Circus, Tomiyama, 1960s, 3 actions, MIB, L4..$1,200.00
Frankie the Roller Skating Monkey, Alps, 1950s, 3 actions, remote control, 12", MIB, L4 ....$250.00
Fred Flintstone's Bedrock Band, Alps, 1962, 8", EX, L4.$600.00
Friendly Jocko, Alps, 1950s, several actions, w/detachable cymbals, 8", rare, EX $300.00
Frontier Whistling Locomotive, MT, 1960s, 3 actions, 10", EX....$85.00
Funland Cup Ride, Sonsco, 1960s, kids spin around in cups, MIB $375.00
Funland Locomotive, Daiya, 1950s, 4 actions, 9", EX $100.00
General Patton Tank M-107, Daiya, forward & reverse w/several actions, remote control, litho tin, 8", NM (NM box), A....$200.00
Godzilla, Bullmark, advances as mouth lights up & emits smoke, litho tin & plastic, remote control, 10", NM (EX box), A $855.00
Godzilla, Mattel, 1977, advances on wheels w/flames & several other actions, plastic, 19", NM (NM box), A....$255.00
Gorilla, MT, shoot gorilla in chest & he roars and raises his arms, litho tin, complete w/gun, 10", NM (EX box) $375.00
Grand-Pa Panda, MT, sits in rocking chair & eats popcorn, eyes light, 9", MIB....$450.00
Green Hornet Secret Service Car (unauthorized), ASC, bump-&-go action w/lights & sound, litho tin, 11", EX, A $600.00
Greyhound Bus, Linemar, litho tin, remote control, 10", NMIB, A $200.00
Hamburger Chef, K, 1960s, 3 actions, litho tin, 9", EX..$225.00
Handy Hank Mystery Tractor, TN, 1950s, several actions, 10½", EX $200.00
Happy 'N Sad Magic Face Clown, Y, moves side to side & plays cymbals as facial expressions change, 10", MIB, L4.$475.00
Happy Band Trio, MT, 1970s, dog, rabbit & bear play instruments on litho tin stage, 11", MIB, L4....$675.00
Happy Clown Car, Y, 1960s, 3 actions, 6½", EX....$200.00
Happy Clown Theatre, Y, 1950s, w/puppet, 3 actions, 10", MIB, L4....$575.00
Happy Drive Car, Japan, little boy steers car, litho tin w/plastic figure, NMIB, A....$150.00
Happy Fiddler Clown, Alps, 1950s, litho tin w/cloth clothes, 10", NM, L4....$375.00
Happy Miner, Bandai, 1960s, 3 actions, 11", MIB, L4 .$1,100.00
Happy Naughty Chimp, Daishin, 1960s, several actions, 9½", EX $100.00
Happy Santa One-Man Band, Alps, 9", MIB, L4 ....$300.00
Happy the Clown Puppet Show, Y, 1960s, w/Pinocchio-type puppet, 3 actions, 10", EX $375.00
Hasty Chimp, Y, 1960s, 4 actions, 9", MIB, L4 ....$125.00
High Jinks at the Circus, Alps, clown w/performing monkey, several actions, MIB, L4....$375.00
Highway Patrol Helicopter, MT, 1960s, several actions, NMIB, L4....$200.00
Highway Patrol Police Special, Y, 1960s, several actions, full-figure driver, 11½", EX....$200.00

Hiller Hornet Helicopter, Alps, 1950s, several actions, 12", EX $225.00

Hoop Zing Girl, Linemar, 1950s, wiggles w/hula hoop, celluloid figure on tin base, 12", scarce, MIB, L4....................$575.00

Hoopy the Fishing Duck, Alps, 1950s, several actions, 10", MIB, L4 ....$575.00

Hooty the Happy Owl, Alps, 1960s, several actions, 9", MIB, L4 ....$185.00

Hopping Pup w/Cart, Alps, 1950s, 3 actions, 9", EX $85.00

Photo courtesy John Turney

Hot Rod 15B, TN, lithographed tin, with driver, MIB, $350.00.

Hot Rod Custom T Ford, Alps, 1960s, 4 actions, 10½", MIB, L4....................$300.00

Hot Rod Dream Boat, TN, 1950s, advances as driver's head spins, litho tin, 7", NM....................$325.00

Hot Rod Racer #7, Cragstan, 1950s, several actions, litho tin, 8", MIB, D10....................$325.00

Huey Helicopter, MIB, L4....................$100.00

Hungry Baby Bear, Y, 1950s, mama bear feeds baby bear w/several other actions, 10", MIB, L4....................$350.00

Indian Joe, Alps, 1960s, mixed materials, 11", EX (EX box), A, $165.00.

Hungry Cat, Linemar, 1960s, 7 actions, w/tray & fish, 9", MIB, L4....................$700.00

Hungry Hound Dog, Y, 1950s, MIB, L4....................$700.00

Hungry Sheep, MT, 1950s, 3 actions, 9", EX....................$200.00

Hy-Que Monkey, TN, 1960s, several actions, MIB, L4..$500.00

Ice Cream Vendor, TN, 1950s, advances w/ringing bell & lights, litho tin, 10", rare, EX (EX box)....................$1,400.00

Jaguar Stunt Car #15, MT, advances, rolls sideways & rights itself, litho tin, 9½", scarce, NMIB, A....................$125.00

James Bond's Aston Martin, Gilbert, 1966, several actions, tin, 11", NM (EX box)....................$4,750.00

Japanese Bullet Train, MT, litho tin train w/plastic track, MIB, L4....................$175.00

Jeepster, Daiya, 1960s, 10", EX....................$125.00

Jocko the Drinking Monkey, Linemar, 1950s, pours drink & lifts to mouth, light-up eyes, litho tin, 11", EX (EX box) .$225.00

John's Farm Truck, TN, 1950s, several actions, 9", MIB, L4.$325.00

Jolly Bambino the Eating Monkey, Alps, 1950s, eats candy w/several actions, tin & plush, 10", MIB, L4...........$700.00

Jolly Bear the Drummer Boy, K, 1950s, several actions, NM, L4....................$275.00

Jolly Bear w/Robin, MT, 1950s, 3 actions, 10", rare, MIB..$975.00

Jolly Daddy Smoking Elephant, Marusan, 1950s, several actions, EX, L4....................$225.00

Jolly Peanut Vendor, TN, NMIB, L4....................$525.00

Jolly Penguin, TN, 1950s, several actions, plush over tin, remote control, 7", EX....................$200.00

Jolly Popcorn Vendor, TN, bear pushes cart w/several actions, litho tin & plastic, 9", VG (VG box), A $325.00

Jolly Santa on Snow, Alps, 1950, several actions, MIB, L4....................$400.00

Josie the Walking Cow, Daiya, 1950s, several actions, EX, $200.00.

Josie the Walking Cow, Daiya, 1950s, several actions, MIB, L4....................$275.00

Jumbo the Bubble Blowing Elephant, Yonezawa, 1950, plush & litho tin, 7", MIB....................$185.00

Jumbo the Roaring Elephant, Alps, MIB, L4....................$200.00

Jungle Jumbo, BC, 1950s, 6 actions, 10", MIB, L4..........$800.00

Jungle Trio, Linemar, 1950s, monkeys & elephant play instruments on platform, NM, L4....................$750.00

Kiddie Trolley, MT, 1960s, several actions, 8", EX $100.00

Kissing Couple, Ichida, 1950s, bump-&-go car rolls as bird spins & chirps on hood, 10½", NMIB, L4 ....**$300.00**
Knitting Grandma, TN, 1950s, 3 actions, 8½", M, L4 ...**$275.00**
Lady Pup Tending Her Garden, Cragstan, 1950s, several actions, litho tin w/cloth clothes, 8", MIB, L4 ....**$500.00**
Laffin Head Indian Squaw, MIB, L4 ....**$150.00**
Lambo Elephant, Alps, 1950s, picks up logs, remote control, MIB, L4 ....**$675.00**
Laughing Clown, SH, 1960s, several actions, litho tin, 15", EX **$400.00**
Laurel & Hardy Old Timer Car (Yesin Tembleteo), Larry Harmon/Spain, mystery action, plastic, 11", NRFB, A..**$300.00**
Leo the Growling Pet Lion w/Magic-Face Change, Tomiyama, 1970s, plush over tin, remote control, 9", EX..........**$200.00**
Lite-O-Wheel Go Kart, Rosko, 1950s, 3 actions, MIB, L4 .**$185.00**
Loop the Loop Clown, TN, 1960s, performs on bar, 10", EX .**$125.00**
Los Walky Son, MIB, L4 ....**$350.00**
Lucky Car, Marusan, rare, VG, L4 ....**$250.00**
Lucky Crane, MT, 1950s, several actions, w/tin prizes, 8½", rare, EX **$1,000.00**
Lucky Seven Dice Throwing Monkey, Alps, shakes cup, throws dice & chatters, plush, tin & plastic, 12", MIB **$185.00**
Mac the Turtle, Y, 1960s, rolls over barrel w/several actions, NMIB, L4...**$250.00**
Magic Action Bulldozer, TN, 1950s, 3 actions, 9½", EX..**$200.00**
Magic Man Clown, Marusan, advances, tips hat & blows smoke from light-up pipe, tin w/cloth clothes, 11", NMIB.**$475.00**
Magic Snowman, MT, 1950s, several actions, 11", EX...**$300.00**
Major Tooty, Alps, 1960s, drum major plays drum, 14", MIB, L4 ....**$275.00**
Make-Up Bear, MT, 1960s, 9", MIB, L4 ....**$950.00**
Mambo the Jolly Drumming Elephant, Alps, 1950s, plays drum & cymbals, tin & plush, 9½", MIB, L4 ....**$375.00**
Marshal Wild Bill, Y, 1950s, several actions, litho tin w/cloth clothes, 10½", EX **$350.00**
Maxwell Coffee-Loving Bear, TN, 1960s, several actions, 10", NMIB, L4...**$250.00**

Merry-Go-Round Truck, TN, 1957, lithographed tin, remote control, 8", MIB, A, $725.00.

McGregor, TN, Scotsman sits up w/cane & smokes cigar, eyes roll, litho tin w/cloth clothes, 11½", EX (EX box), A.........**$200.00**
Melody Camping Car, Y, 1970s, 3 actions, 10", EX........**$125.00**
Mew-Mew Walking Cat, MT, 1950s, several actions, plush over tin, remote control, 7", EX **$125.00**
Mexicalli Pete, Alps, 1960s, 3 actions, MIB, L4 ....**$325.00**
Mickey Mouse Flying Saucer, MT, MIB, L4 ....**$275.00**

Photo courtesy Dunbar Gallery

Mickey Mouse Loop the Loop, Illco, MIB, $175.00.

Mickey Mouse Melody Railroad, Frankonia/WDP, 1967, rare, MIB, L4 ....**$1,600.00**
Mickey the Magician, Linemar, 1960s, 4 actions, litho tin, 10", rare, NMIB, L4 ....**$2,500.00**
Mickey Mouse, see also Drumming Mickey Mouse
Mighty Mike the Barbell Lifter Bear, K, 1950s, 4 actions, litho tin & plush, 12", M, L4 ....**$300.00**
Military Police Car, Linemar, advances as men fire machine gun in back seat, tin, remote control, 8½", NMIB, A **$225.00**
Mischievous Monkey, MT, monkey scoots up & down tree in front of doghouse, litho tin, EX (EX box)................**$375.00**
Miss Friday the Typist, TN, 1950s, girl types & bell rings, tin & vinyl, 7", NMIB, M5...**$350.00**
Moby Dick Whaling Boat, Linemar, 1950s, 3 actions, remote control, NM...**$200.00**
Monkee Mobile, Aoshin, 1967, w/4 figures, 12", EX **$600.00**
Monkey Handcar, TN, 1950s, 3 actions, NM, L4...........**$500.00**
Monkey the Shoe Maker, TN, 1950s, seated monkey smokes pipe & hammers shoe, rare, MIB, L4 ....**$875.00**
Mother Bear, MT, sits in rocking chair & knits, head nods & eyes light, tin & plush, 10", M, L4 ....**$300.00**
Mother Goose, Yonezawa, MIB, L4 ....**$250.00**
Mountain Cable Car, Cragstan, 1950s, litho tin, 9", EX ..**$125.00**
Mr Fox the Magician, Cragstan, fox lifts hat to reveal rabbit, litho tin, 9", MIB, L4...**$700.00**
Mr Fox the Magician Blowing Magical Bubbles, Y, 1960s, several actions, tin & plush w/cloth clothes, 9", EX.....**$400.00**
Mr MacPooch, SAN, 1950s, dog advances & lifts light-up & smoking pipe to mouth, remote control, 8", MIB, L4 .**$350.00**
Mr Magoo Car, Hubley, 1961, Mr Magoo steers as car rocks & rattles, tin w/cloth top, 9", M **$300.00**
Mr Traffic Policeman, A1, policeman blows whistle & turns as light changes, 13", MIB, L4...................................**$575.00**

Mumbo Jumbo the Hawaiian Drummer, Alps, 1960s, 3 actions, 10", MIB, L4 ....$400.00
Music Hall, Linemar, dogs plays piano, litho tin & plush, NMIB, A $250.00
Musical Bulldog, Marusan, 1950s, litho tin w/cloth clothes, EX, L4 ....$1,000.00
Musical Cadillac, Irco, 1950s, advances & plays music, tin, 9", VG (VG box), A $350.00
Musical Ice Cream Truck, Bandai, 1960s, bump-&-go action w/sound, tin & plastic, 10", VG (VG box), A $300.00
Musical Jackal, Linemar, 1950s, several actions, 10", rare, MIB, L4 ....$1,100.00
Musical Jolly Chimp, Lewis Galoob, 1960s, plays cymbals, shows teeth & chatters, plush & tin, MIB, J6 ....$125.00
Musical Marching Bear, Alps, 1950s, beats drum & blows horn, plush & tin w/cloth clothes, MIB, L4 ....$700.00
Musical Melody Mixer, Taiyo, 1970s, several actions, mostly plastic, 10½", EX $85.00

Musical Train, Japan, plastic, MIB, J6, $50.00.

Musical Vegetable Truck, Bandai, 1960s, several actions, MIB, L4 ....$275.00
Mystery Mike the Minstrel Man, Bell Products, 1960s, 14", EX $140.00
Nautilus Periscope, Cragstan, MIB, L4 ....$225.00
New Flip-Flap Flyer, Taiwan, 1960s, mostly plastic, 14", EX $100.00
Nutty Mads Car, Linemar, 1960s, 3 actions, MIB, L4 ....$275.00
Nutty Nibs, Linemar, 1950s, several actions, pnt tin w/red, wht & blk paper skirt, 12", VG, L4 ....$875.00
Ol' Sleepy Head Rip, Y, 1950s, bird wakes up man & he sits up, stretches & yawns, tin, cloth & vinyl, 9", NMIB, A .$300.00
Old Fashioned Fire Engine, MT, 1950s, several actions, MIB, L4 ....$300.00
Old Timer Car, Cragstan, 1950s, 3 actions, litho tin, 9", EX $175.00
Open Sleigh, MT, 1950s, bump-&-go action w/light-up lantern, litho tin & vinyl, 15", EX (EX box) $650.00

Pat O'Neill the Fun Loving Irishman, TN, several actions, 11", NM (NM box), A, $325.00.

Pat the Dog, Alps, 1950s, several actions, MIB, L4 ....$175.00
Patrol Auto-Cycle, TN, 1960s, driver works clutch, steers & blows whistle, litho tin, 10", scarce, NMIB, A $400.00
Pee Pee Puppy, TN, 1960s, several actions, plush over tin, 9", NM $150.00
Pepi the Tumbling Monkey, Yanoman, 1960s, MIB, L4 ..$100.00
Peppy Puppy w/Bone, Y, 1950s, several actions, 6½", EX.$100.00
Performing Circus Lion, VIA, MIB, L4 ....$500.00
Pete the Indian, Bandai, MIB, L4 ....$175.00
Pete the Pirate, Bandai, MIB, L4 ....$150.00
Pete the Policeman, Bandai, M, L4 ....$125.00
Pete the Talking Parrot, TN, 1950s, several actions, litho tin & plush, 18", EX $400.00
Peter the Drumming Rabbit, Alps, 1950s, several actions, MIB, L4 ....$250.00
Picnic Bear, Alps, 1950s, pours & drinks w/realistic motion, litho tin & plush, 10", EX (EX box), A $200.00
Picnic Bunny, Alps, 1950s, several actions, plush & tin, 10", MIB, L4 ....$200.00
Pierrot-Monkey Cycle, MT, 1950s, clown & monkey perform on cycle, 8", rare, EX $400.00
Piggy Cook, Yonezawa, 1950s, pig flips egg in pan & shakes pepper shaker, litho tin & vinyl, 11", MIB, L4 ....$300.00
Pink Panther One Man Band, Illco, 1970s, plays drums & cymbals, 11", EX $125.00
Pinkee the Farmer, TN, 1950s, several actions, 9½", EX..$225.00
Pinocchio Xylophone Player, TN, 1962, plays 'London Bridge,' tin w/rubber head, 9", MIB, L4 ....$350.00
Pioneer Covered Wagon, Ichida, 1960s, w/driver & horse, litho tin w/vinyl cover, NM $275.00
Playful Puppy, MT, 1950s, 4 actions, 5", M, L4 ....$200.00
Playland Octopus, Alps, 1950s, several actions, litho tin, 20", rare, EX $800.00
Pluto, Linemar, 1960s, several actions, litho tin, 10", rare, EX $400.00
Police Auto Cycle, Bandai, 1960s, several actions, VG, L4 ....$150.00

Police Jeep, TN, 1950s, several actions, 13", MIB, L4....$500.00
Polizei Volkswagen Bus, MT, litho tin, remote control, 5", NM (NM box), A....$85.00
Popcorn Eating Panda, MT, NM, L4....$175.00
Popcorn Vendor, S&E/Cragstan, bear pedals cart while umbrella spins & popcorn pops, litho tin & plush, 8", MIB, L4.$575.00
Popcorn Vendor, TN, duck pushes wagon w/bump-&-go action as popcorn pops, 8", MIB, L4....$600.00
Popcorn Vendor Truck, TN, 1960s, 3 actions, litho tin, 9", EX....$300.00
Popeye, see Bubble Blowing Popeye or Smoking Popeye
Portable Mixmaster, Daiya, MIB, L4....$65.00
Poverty Pup Bank, Poynter/Alabe, 1966, plastic doghouse w/puppy, several actions, 6", M, P4....$95.00
Pretty Peggy Parrot, Rosko, several actions, litho tin & plush, 10", EX (EX box), L4....$425.00
Professor Owl, Y, 1950s, several actions, litho tin, w/2 disks, 8", EX....$400.00
Puffy Morris, Y, 1960s, smokes real cigarette, 10", MIB, L4....$375.00
Puzzled Puppy, MT, 1950s, several actions, 7½", EX....$200.00
Rabbits & the Carriage, S&E, 1950s, mama pushes baby in carriage, MIB, L4....$425.00
Radicon Boat, MT, 1950s, 3 actions, remote control, 14", rare, MIB....$675.00
Rajah Rey the Indian Prince, TN, 1960s, several actions, 12", rare, EX....$675.00
Rambling Ladybug, MT, 1960s, litho tin, 8", EX....$125.00
Randy the Walking Monkey, A1, NMIB, L4....$175.00
RCA-NBC Mobile Color TV Truck, Cragstan, 1950s, forward & reverse action w/circus scene on lighted screen, 9", NMIB, A....$600.00
Reading Bear, Alps, 1950s, 5 actions, 9", M, L4....$525.00
Rembrandt the Monkey Artist, Alps, 1950s, several actions, litho tin & plush w/cloth clothes, 8", rare, EX....$400.00

Photo courtesy Don Hultzman

Roaring Lion, Rosko, 1950s, several actions, 11", NMIB, $200.00.

Rock 'N Roll Monkey, Rosko, 1950s, monkey plays guitar & sways, 13", MIB, L4....$350.00
Root Beer Counter, K, 1960s, 3 actions, litho tin & plastic, 8", EX....$200.00
Royal Cub, S&E, 1950s, mama bear pushes baby in carriage, litho tin & plush, 8", EX (EX box), A....$300.00
Sam the Shaving Man, Plaything Toy, 1960s, several actions, 11½", EX....$300.00
Santa Bank, Trim-A-Tree/HTC, 1960, several actions, litho tin w/cloth clothes, 11", EX....$300.00
Santa Copter, MT, 1950s, 3 actions, 8½", EX....$225.00

Photo courtesy Jeff Bub

Santa on Rotating Globe, HTC, 1950s, tin and cloth, 14", EX (EX box), $700.00.

Santa Sled, TN, 1950s, 4 actions, 14", M, L4....$350.00
Shaggy the Friendly Pup, Alps, 1960s, 3 actions, 8", EX..$85.00
Shoe Shine Bear, TN, 1950s, several actions, 9", EX....$250.00
Shoe Shine Joe w/Lighted Pipe, TN, 1950s, monkey buffs shoe, 11", MIB, L4....$300.00
Shooting Cowboys in Barrel, EX, L4....$575.00
Shooting Gallery Gorilla, MT, 1950s, shoot gorilla for action, litho tin, 10", rare, MIB, L4....$350.00
Singing Bird in Cage, TN, 1950s, several actions, litho tin, 9", EX....$200.00
Skating Circus Clown, TPS, 1950s, litho tin, 6", scarce, NM....$650.00
Sleeping Baby Bear, Linemar, 1950s, bear sits up in bed, yawns & squeals, tin & plush, 10", EX (EX box), A....$500.00
Slurpy Pup, TN, 1960s, several actions, 6½", MIB, L4...$125.00
Smarty Bird, Ideal, 1964, several actions, 16", EX....$125.00
Smokey Bear Jeep, MT, 1950s, advances w/lights & sound, litho tin, 10", rare, EX, L4....$675.00
Smokey Bear Jeep, MT, 1950s, advances w/lights & sound, litho tin, 10", rare, MIB, L4....$1,250.00
Smokey Bill, TN, 1960s, several actions, 9", MIB, L4....$250.00
Smoking Grandpa, SAN, 1950s, eyes closed, 9", rare, MIB, L4....$475.00
Smoking Grandpa, SAN, 1950s, eyes open, 9", MIB, L4..$300.00
Smoking Pa Pa Bear, SAN, 8", NM, L4....$100.00
Smoking Popeye, Linemar, 1950s, several actions, litho tin, 9", rare, EX, minimum value....$1,600.00

Smoking Volkswagen, Aoshin, 1960s, NM, $175.00.

Smoking Volkswagen, Aoshin, 1960s, 4 actions, MIB, L4..$275.00
Smoky (sic) Bear, SAN, 1950s, several actions, litho tin & plush, 9", NM $450.00
Snake Charmer, Linemar, plays flute as snake emerges from basket, litho tin & plastic, 8", EX, A $375.00
Snappy the Happy Bubble Blowing Dragon, TN, 1960s, several actions, litho tin, 30", scarce, NM $4,000.00
Sneezing Bear, Linemar, 1950s, raises tissue & sneezes, light-up eyes, litho tin, 9½", MIB, L4....................................$475.00
Snowman, Santa Creations, MIB, L4..............................$275.00
Spanking Bear, Linemar, 1950s, mama bear spanks baby w/several other actions, litho tin & plush, 9", EX, L4......$275.00
Sparky the Seal, MT, 1950s, 4 actions, plush over tin, 8", NM, L4...$150.00
Spin-A-Disk Monkey, Rosko, 1950s, several actions, 10", L4...$300.00
Strange Explorer, DSK, advances as gorilla tries to turn tank over, litho tin, 8", EX (G box), A $250.00
Strutting My Fair Dancer, Haji, 1950s, sailor girl dances atop base, litho tin, 12", EX..$200.00
Strutting Sam, Haji, 1950s, Black man dances atop platform, litho tin, 11", NMIB, A...$400.00
Stunt Plane, TPS, 1960s, 3 actions, MIB, L4..................$275.00
Sunbeam Motorcycle w/Sidecar, Marusan, 1950s, litho tin, w/rear spare, 9", EX (EX box), A $1,800.00
Super Susie, Linemar, 1950s, bear pushes groceries on conveyor belt w/several other actions, tin & plush, 8", EX.....$800.00
Superior Go-Kart, Japan, advances w/full-turning action & engine sound, litho tin w/plastic driver, 9", NM (EX box), A $125.00
Superman Tank, Linemar, 1959, Superman forces tank to turn over, litho tin, 11", not working o/w EX, A $1,450.00
Suzette the Eating Monkey, Linemar, 1950s, several actions, litho tin, 9", rare, EX $600.00
Swan the Queen on the River, Meiho, 1960s, several actions, 8½", EX...$125.00
Swimming Fish, Bandai, rare, MIB, L4 ....$275.00
Switchboard Operator, Linemar, 1950s, 7½", MIB, L4 ..$900.00
Teddy Bear Swing, Yonezawa, performs flips on bar, litho tin & plush, 13", MIB, L4..$575.00
Teddy Go-Kart, Alps, 1960s, 4 actions, EX, L4 ....$250.00
Teddy the Artist, Yonezawa, 1950s, simulates drawing, complete w/9 templates, M, L4 ....$500.00
Teddy the Champ Boxer, Y, 1950s, several actions, 9", EX...$300.00
Telephone Bear, Linemar, 1950s, 7½", MIB, L4 ....$450.00
Terry the Wonder Dog w/Lighted Eyes, Linemar, 1960s, 3 actions, 9", EX...$85.00
Tinkling Trolley, MT, 1950s, 4 actions, 10½", M, L4....$200.00
Titan the Tumbler, Cragstan, MIB, L4 ....$475.00
Tom & Jerry Helicopter, MT, 1960s, 3 actions, litho tin & plastic, 9½", EX $225.00
Tom & Jerry Jumping Jeep, MT, 1960s, 3 actions, 9", NM..$250.00
Tom & Jerry Locomotive, MT, bump-&-go action, litho tin & plastic, 9", NM (NM box), A.................................$165.00
Tom Tom Indian, Y, 1960s, several actions, litho tin w/cloth clothes, 10½", EX $165.00
Topo Gigio Xylophone Player, TN, 1960s, 3 actions, MIB, L4...$1,450.00
Traveler Bear, K, 1950s, 3 actions, 8", NM, L4 ....$375.00
Tric-Cycling Clown, MT, 1960s, several actions, litho tin & plastic, 12", rare, VG, A $450.00
Tricky Doghouse, Y, 1960s, several actions, litho tin, 7", EX $125.00
Trumpet Playing Monkey, Alps, 1950s, 9", MIB, L4......$350.00
Turn-O-Matic Gun Jeep, TN, 1960s, 10", NMIB, L4 ....$200.00
Twin Racing Cars, Alps, 1950s, 3 actions, MIB, L4.......$675.00

U-Control Racer #4, Cragstan, MIB, $550.00.

VIP Busy Boss Bear, S&E, 1950s, several actions, 8", EX, L4 ....$350.00
Waddles Family Car, Y, 1960s, MIB, L4 ....$175.00
Walking Bambi, Linemar, 1950s, several actions, MIB, L4.$675.00
Walking Dog, Linemar, 1950s, 6", EX...............................$125.00
Walking Donkey, Linemar, 1950s, 9", EX........................$175.00
Walking Knight in Armour, MT, 1950s, several actions, rare, NMIB, L4 ....$3,000.00
Walt Disney Airliner w/Cartoon Story Box, Reel/Italy/WDP, 1970s, advances w/blinking lights, plastic, 15", NMIB, A $100.00
Walt Disney Helicopter w/Cartoon Story Box, Reel/Italy/WDP, 1970s, plastic, 14", EX (EX box), A $100.00

Waltzing Matilda, TN, rare, MIB, L4 .... $900.00
Wee Little Baby Bear, see Reading Bear
Whirlybird Helicopter, Remco, 1960s, 3 actions, NMIB, L4 . $250.00
Willie the Walking Car, Y, 1960s, several actions, 8½", EX .. $225.00
Windy the Juggling Elephant, TN, 1950s, 10½", MIB, L4 .. $325.00
Worried Mother Duck & Baby, TN, 1950s, 3 actions, 11", MIB, L4 .... $225.00
Xylophone Bear, Linemar, non-walking version, rare, NM, L4 .... $675.00
Xylophone Bear, Linemar, walking version, rare, MIB, L4 . $575.00
Yo-Yo Monkey, Alps, 1960s, 9", MIB, L4 .... $300.00
Zoom Boat F-570, K, 1950s, forward & reverse action, litho tin, remote control, 10 ", EX (EX box), A $225.00

Beanie Babies

Who can account for this latest flash in collecting that some liken to the rush for Cabbage Patch dolls we saw many years ago! The appeal of these stuffed creatures is disarming to both children and adults, and excited collectors are eager to scoop up each new-found treasure. There is much to be learned about Beanie Babies. For instance, there are different tag styles and these indicate date of issue:

#1 Swing tag

#2 Swing tag

#3 Swing tag

#4 Swing tag

#1, Swing tag: single heart-shaped tag

#2, Swing tag: heart-shaped; folded, with information inside; narrow letters

#3, Swing tag: heart-shaped; folded, with information inside; wider lettering

#4, Swing tag: heart-shaped; folded, with information inside; wider lettering with no gold outline around the 'ty'; yellow star on front; first tag to include a poem and birthdate

(Note: for current Beanies with a #2 or #3 tag, add $30.00 to $40.00 to the prices suggested below.)

Unless information is given to the contrary, the following listings are for current issues in mint condition; discontinued (retired) items will be noted.

Advisors: Ellen and Jerry Harnish (H4).

See also Fast Food Collectibles.

Ally the Alligator, #4032, retired $65.00
Baldy the Eagle, #4074, retired $25.00
Bernie the St Bernard, #4109, from $8 to $10.00
Bessie the Cow, brn, #4009, retired $70.00
Blackie the Bear, #4011, from $8 to $10.00
Blizzard the Tiger, wht, #4163, retired $25.00
Bones the Dog, brn, #4001, retired $25.00
Bongo the Monkey, brn, #4067, retired, from $65 to $80.00
Bronty the Brontosaurus, bl, #4085, retired $900.00
Brownie the Bear, #4010, retired, minimum value $3,000.00
Bubbles the Fish, yel & blk, #4078, retired $185.00
Bucky the Beaver, #4016, retired $40.00
Caw the Crow, #4071, retired, minimum value $400.00
Chilly the Polar Bear, #4012, retired, minimum value . $1,600.00
Chip the Cat, calico, #4121, from $8 to $10.00
Chocolate the Moose, #4015, from $10 to $15.00
Chops the Lamb, wht w/blk face, retired $200.00
Claude the Crab, tie-dyed, #4083, from $8 to $10.00
Congo the Gorilla, #4160, from $8 to $10.00
Coral the Fish, tie-dyed, #4079, retired $125.00
Crunch the Shark, #4130, from $8 to $10.00
Cubbie the Bear, brn, #4010, retired $35.00
Curly the Bear, brn, #4052 .... $15.00
Daisy the Cow, blk & wht, #4006, from $8 to $10.00
Derby the Horse, brn, 2nd issue, #4008, from $20 to $25.00
Derby the Horse, brn w/yarn mane & tail, 1st issue, #4008 .. $500.00
Digger the Crab, orange, #4027, retired, minimum value . $700.00
Doby the Doberman, #4100, from $8 to $10.00
Doodles the Rooster, tie-dyed, #4171, retired $60.00
Dotty the Dalmatian, #4100, from $8 to $10.00
Ears the Rabbit, brn, #4018, retired $25.00
Echo the Dolphin, #4180, retired $25.00
Flash the Dolphin, #4021, retired $100.00
Fleece the Lamb, #4125, from $8 to $10.00
Flip the Cat, wht, #4012, retired $35.00
Floppity the Bunny, lilac, #4118, retired $25.00
Flutter the Butterfly, tie-dyed, #4043, retired, minimum value $850.00
Freckles the Leopard, #4066, from $8 to $10.00
Garcia the Teddy Bear, tie-dyed, #4051, retired, from $100 to $200.00
Gobbles the Turkey, from $8 to $10.00
Goldie the Goldfish, #4023, retired $35.00
Gracie the Swan, #4126, retired, from $15 to $25.00
Grunt the Razorback Pig, #4092, retired $175.00
Happy the Hippopotamus, lavender, 2nd issue, #4061, retired $25.00
Happy the Hippopotamus, gray, 1st issue, #4061, retired, minimum value $400.00
Hippity the Rabbit, lt gr, #4119, retired $25.00
Hoot the Owl, #4073, retired $40.00
Hoppity the Rabbit, pk, #4117, retired $25.00
Humphrey the Camel, #4060, retired, minimum value .. $850.00
Inch the Worm, mc, #4044, retired $25.00
Inky the Octopus, tan, 1st issue, #4028, retired, minimum value $400.00
Inky the Octopus, pk, 2nd issue, #4028, retired, from $15 to . $25.00
Jolly the Walrus, #4082, retired $25.00

Kiwi the Toucan, #4070, retired, minimum value..........$125.00
Lefty the Donkey, w/American flag, #4057, retired, minimum value..........$200.00
Legs the Frog, #4020, retired..........$35.00
Libearty the Bear, w/American flag, #4057, retired, minimum value..........$200.00
Lizzy the Lizard, #4033, retired, minimum value..........$425.00
Lucky the Ladybug, glued-on felt spots, #4040, retired...$500.00
Lucky the Ladybug, w/11 spots, #4040, retired, from $15 to .$25.00
Lucky the Ladybug, w/21 spots, #4040, retired..........$400.00
Magic the Dragon, #4088, retired, from $30 to..........$40.00
Manny the Manatee, #4081, retired..........$125.00
Maple the Bear, w/Canadian flag, Canadian Exclusive ..$175.00
Mel the Koala Bear, #4162, from $8 to..........$10.00
Mystic the Unicorn, 1st issue, #4007, retired..........$500.00
Nanook the Husky Dog, #4104, from $8 to..........$10.00
Nip the Cat, gold, 1st or 2nd issue, #4003, retired, minimum value..........$700.00
Nip the Cat, gold w/wht paws, 3rd issue, #4003, retired, from $25 to..........$30.00
Nuts the Squirrel, #4114, from $8 to..........$10.00
Patti the Platypus, hot pk & purple, #4025, from $20 to ..$25.00
Patti the Platypus, maroon, #4025, retired, minimum.$1,000.00
Peace the Bear, tie-dyed w/embroidered Peace sign, #4053 .$30.00
Peanut the Elephant, lt bl, #4062..........$25.00
Peanut the Elephant, royal bl, #4062, retired, minimum value..........$3,000.00
Peking the Panda Bear, #4013, retired, minimum value.$1,500.00
Pinchers the Lobster, #4026, retired, from $15 to..........$25.00
Pinky the Flamingo, #4072, from $8 to..........$10.00
Pouch the Kangaroo, #4161, from $8 to..........$10.00
Pugsly the Dog, #4105, from $8 to..........$10.00
Quackers the Duck, no wings, #4024, retired, minimum value..........$1,000.00
Quackers the Duck, w/wings, #4024, retired, from $15 to .$25.00
Radar the Bat, #4091, retired, minimum value..........$100.00
Rex the Tyrannosaurus, #4086, retired, minimum value ..$600.00
Righty the Elephant, w/American flag, #4086, retired, minimum value..........$200.00
Ringo the Raccoon, #4014, from $8 to..........$10.00
Roary the Lion, #4069, from $8 to..........$10.00
Rover the Dog, red, #4101, retired..........$25.00
Scoop the Pelican, #4107, from $8 to..........$10.00
Scottie the Terrier, #4102, retired, from $15 to..........$25.00
Seamore the Seal, wht, #4029, retired..........$125.00
Seaweed the Otter, #4080, from $8 to..........$10.00
Slither the Snake, #4031, retired, minimum value..........$750.00
Sly the Fox, all brn, 1st issue, #4115, retired..........$165.00
Sly the Fox, brn w/wht belly, 2nd issue, #4115, from $8 to ..$10.00
Snip the Siamese Cat, #4120, from $8 to..........$10.00
Snort the Bull, red w/beige ft, #4002, from $8 to..........$10.00
Sparky the Dalmatian, #4100, retired..........$85.00
Speedy the Turtle, #4030, retired, from $25 to..........$30.00
Spike the Rhinoceros, #4060, from $8 to..........$10.00
Splash the Whale, #4022, retired..........$100.00
Spooky the Ghost, #4090, retired, minimum value..........$40.00
Spot the Dog, blk spot on back, 2nd issue, #4000, retired..........$50.00
Spot the Dog, no spot on back, 1st issue, #4000, retired ..$1,600.00
Squealer the Pig, #4005, retired..........$30.00
Steg the Stegosaurus, tie-dyed, #4087, retired, minimum value..........$600.00
Sting the Stingray, tie-dyed, #4077, retired, minimum value..........$140.00
Stinky the Skunk, #4017, from $8 to..........$10.00
Stripes the Tiger, #4065, retired..........$450.00
Stripes the Tiger, #4065, 2nd issue, retired, from $15 to ..$25.00
Strut the Rooster, from $8 to..........$10.00
Tabasco the Bull, red, #4002, retired, minimum value...$225.00
Tank the Armadillo, #4031, retired, minimum value.....$150.00
Teddy Bear, brn, #4050, new face, retired, from $65 to....$70.00
Teddy Bear, brn, #4050, old face, retired..........$2,300.00
Teddy Bear, cranberry, #4052, new face, retired..........$2,000.00
Teddy Bear, cranberry, #4052, old face, retired..........$1,800.00
Teddy Bear, jade, #4057, new face, retired..........$2,000.00
Teddy Bear, jade, #4057, old face, retired..........$1,800.00
Teddy Bear, magenta, #4056, new face, retired..........$2,000.00
Teddy Bear, magenta, #4056, old face, retired..........$1,800.00
Teddy Bear, teal, #4051, new face, retired..........$2,000.00
Teddy Bear, teal, #4051, old face, retired..........$1,800.00
Teddy Bear, violet, #4055, new face, retired..........$2,000.00
Teddy Bear, violet, #4055, old face, retired..........$1,800.00
Trap the Mouse, #4042, retired, minimum value..........$1,000.00
Tuffy the Terrier, #4108, from $8 to..........$10.00
Tusk the Walrus, #4076, retired, minimum value..........$125.00
Twigs the Giraffe, #4068, retired..........$25.00
Valentino the Bear, wht w/red heart, #4058..........$15.00
Velvet the Panther, #4064, retired..........$35.00
Waddle the Penguin, #4075, retired..........$25.00
Waves the Whale, #4084, retired, from $10 to..........$25.00
Web the Spider, #4041, retired, minimum value..........$1,000.00
Weenie the Dachsund, #4013, retired..........$30.00
Wrinkles the Bulldog, #4103, from $8 to..........$10.00
Ziggy the Zebra, #4063, retired..........$25.00
Zip the Cat, all blk, #4004, retired, minimum value ...$1,500.00
Zip the Cat, blk w/wht paws, #4004, retired..........$35.00
Zip the Cat, blk w/wht tummy, #4004, retired, minimum value..........$450.00

Bicycles, Motorbikes, and Tricycles

The most interesting of the vintage bicycles are those made from the 1920s into the '60s, though a few even later models are collectible as well. Some from the '50s were very futuristic and styled with sweeping Art Deco lines; others had wonderful features such as built-in radios and brake lights, and some were decked out with saddlebags and holsters to appeal to fans of Hoppy, Gene, and many other western heroes. Watch for reproductions.

Condition is everything when evaluating bicycles, and one worth $2,500.00 in excellent or better condition might be worth as little as $50.00 in unrestored, poor condition. But here are a few values to suggest a range.

Advisor: Richard Trautwein (T3).

Bicycles

American Flyer Junior Roadmaster Spider-Man Bike, 1978, red w/spider web design on yel seat, 42", EX, J5 ....**$250.00**
Bowden, boy's, red futuristic design w/chrome trim, thin wht-wall tires, rear chrome carrier, wht grips, all orig, M, A **$3,850.00**

Bowden Space Lander, limited reissue of the 1950 issue, EX, $800.00.

BSA Paratrooper, Pat #543076, 1940, boy's, rstr, A **$475.00**
Colson Firestone Super Cruiser, 1950, girl's, EX, A **$325.00**
Columbia Deluxe, 1949, boy's, orig, 24", EX, A **$250.00**
Columbia Expert Ordinary, 1886, 52", EX, A **$1,600.00**
Columbia Ordinary, 1890, 58", VG, A **$1,200.00**
Columbia Roadster Ordinary, 1886, 57", EX, A.........**$3,200.00**
Eagle, boy's, pneumatic tires, no fenders, EX, A **$475.00**
Elgin Blackhawk, 1934, boy's, rstr, A **$2,000.00**
Gene Autry, girl's, brn & cream, w/horse head, gun & holster, 24", G, A **$800.00**
JC Higgins, 1951, boy's, jeweled tank, batwing headlight, EX, A **$800.00**
JC Higgins, 1951, girl's, full-skirted springer, wht-walls, rstr, A **$425.00**
JC Higgins Deluxe, 1947, girl's, NM, A **$450.00**
Monarch (Westfield), girl's, orig, EX, A **$350.00**
Monark Hex Custom Boardwalk Cruiser, 1947, boy's, G, A ..**$650.00**
Pacemaker Hard Tire Safety, Pat 1893, boy's, EX, A ..**$1,450.00**
Pennant Model 10, boy's, pneumatic tires, 1898, no seat, A **$450.00**
Pierce Arrow Pneumatic Safety, boy's, spring fork & cushion fr, 1900, EX, A **$950.00**
Roadmaster Luxury Liner, girl's, metallic gr w/chrome fenders, 26", EX, A **$500.00**
Schwinn B-6, 1946, boy's, rstr, A **$750.00**
Schwinn B-6, 1948, boy's, EX, A **$550.00**
Schwinn Black Phantom, boy's, 26", rstr, A **$850.00**
Schwinn Black Phantom, girl's, 26", rstr, A............**$400.00**
Schwinn Green Phantom, 1951, boy's, 26", EX, A **$700.00**
Schwinn Hornet, boy's, wht-walls, EX, A............**$200.00**
Schwinn Panther, 1952, boy's, EX, A **$650.00**
Schwinn Starlet, 1955, girl's, gr & cream, VG, A **$175.00**

Schwinn Autocycle, tan and cream with luggage rack, restored, A, $1,000.00.

Schwinn Black Phantom, complete with accessories, EX, A, $1,650.00.

Sears Spaceliner, girl's, bl-gr w/chrome fenders, electric light & horn, 67", EX, A **$200.00**
Shelby Donald Duck, 1949, girl's, 24", EX, A **$1,600.00**
Shelby Western Flyer Speedline Airflow, 1937, boy's, rstr, A **$3,800.00**
Silver King, 1834, girl's, light on front fender, EX, A.....**$350.00**
Western Strato Flyer, headlight in tank, chrome fenders w/front & rear carriers, wht-walls, G+, A **$85.00**
Wolf American, 1898, girl's, EX, A **$450.00**

Motor Vehicles

Elgin Motorbike/Bicycle, rear-wheel kickstand, rpl tires, G-, A .**$800.00**
Indian Motorcycle, Citan, 1940s-50s, blk & cream w/Indian Motorcycle logo, rstr, A **$4,200.00**
Monarch Super-Twin, ca 1949, blk w/red-orange trim, chrome fender headlight, rear-wheel kickstand, EX+, A ..**$3,200.00**
Spaceliner, Sears, girl's, bl-gr w/chrome fenders, wht seat & grips, electric light & horn, wht-walls, 67", EX, A ..**$200.00**
Speed Bike, Metal Specialties, ca 1930, red, rear-wheeled kickstand, 12" pneumatic tires w/red spokes, G, A.........**$850.00**

Whizzer Sportsman, w/windshield & spring seat, rear carrier, wht-walls, 20", rstr, A **$5,000.00**

Tricycles

Canterpony Riding Horse, Deeks Engineering Corp, 1930, pnt wood & aluminum w/glass eyes, 40", VG, A **$400.00**

Colson adult tricycle, 1900, 2-wheel drive w/rear differential, EX, A **$525.00**

Dandy Dan Horse-Drawn Sulky, Dan Patch Co, late 1800s-early 1900s, pnt iron & wood, 44", VG, A **$635.00**

Donaldson Jockey Cycle, scooter-type handlebars, rubber tires, 24½x37", old rpt, A **$8,500.00**

Ferbo, blk body w/bicycle chain, no fenders, 12", wide-spoked front wheels, G, A **$225.00**

Gendron Pioneer, red, no fenders, 19½", wide-spoked front wheel, G, A **$375.00**

Good Humor Trike, ca 1955, chain drive, opening door in rear compartment, 36", EX, A.................................. **$1,050.00**

Horse, articulated wooden horse w/stuffed saddle on CI fr, 2 spoked wheels, front pedals, 36", VG+, A **$850.00**

Iron Horse, 1940, child's, blk cast aluminum horse w/curved handlebars, red saddle & grips, EX, A..................... **$400.00**

Murray Airflow Jr, pnt pressed steel w/steel seat, 17½", G, A **$200.00**

Streamline Style, from Art Deco period, bl & cream, rstr, A **$715.00**

Velocipede, 1870, green, 16", rstr, A **$600.00**

Black Americana

Black subjects were commonly depicted in children's toys as long ago as the late 1870s. Among the most widely collected today are the fine windup toys made both here and in Germany. Early cloth and later composition and vinyl dolls are favorites of many; others enjoy ceramic figurines. Many factors enter into evaluating Black Americana, especially in regard to the handmade dolls and toys, since quality is subjective to individual standards. Because of this you may find wide ranges in dealers' asking prices. In order to better understand this field of collecting, we recommend *Black Collectibles Sold in America* by P.J. Gibbs; and *Black Dolls: 1820 – 1991* and *Black Dolls, Book II*, both by Myla Perkins.

Advisor: Judy Posner (P6).

See also Banks; Battery-Operated Toys; Schoenhut; Windups, Friction, and Other Mechanicals.

Acrobat Toy, articulated pnt wood native on wood fr, hand-operated, 8", VG **$75.00**

Book, All About Little Black Sambo, Cupples & Leon, 1917, John Gruelle illus (creator of Raggedy Ann), 48 pgs, EX, P6 .... **$200.00**

Book, Children's Stories That Never Grow Old, Reilly & Briton, 1908, 312 pgs, EX, P6..................................... **$95.00**

Book, Jasper & the Watermelons, by George Pal, 1945, 1st edition, hardcover, 32 pgs, w/dust jacket, EX, P6......... **$125.00**

Book, Kentucky Twins, Raphael Tuck, 1910, M Taylor illus, cb cover, EX, P6 .... **$300.00**

Book, Little Black Sambo, by Helen Bannerman, 1943, 1st animated edition, hardcover, rare, M, P6 .... **$235.00**

Book, Little Black Sambo, Whitman Top Top Tales, 1961, hardcover, 28 pgs, EX, P6 .... **$70.00**

Book, Little Brown Koko, 1940, 1st edition, hardcover, 96 pgs, EX, P6 .... **$95.00**

Book, Little Brown Koko's Pets & Playmates, by Blanche Seal Hunt, 1st edition, 1959, EX...................................... **$95.00**

Book, Meg & Moe, Lothrop, Lee & Shepard, 1938, hardcover, w/dust jacket, EX, P6.. **$125.00**

Book, Pickaninnies Little Redskins, 1800s, 15 pgs, rare, intact but brittle, P6... **$250.00**

Book, Pickaninny Twins, by Lucy Fitch Perkins, 1931, illus by author, 149 pgs, EX, P6 .... **$165.00**

Book, Pop-Up Little Black Sambo, 1934, EX **$265.00**

Book, Rufty Tufty Flies High, Heinemann Publishing, 1959, Ruth Ainsworth illus, EX, P6 .... **$70.00**

Book, Samantha Among the Colored Folks, Kemble, 1894, hardcover, EX **$125.00**

Book, Uncle Tom's Cabin, by Harriet Beecher Stowe, 1897, illus, hardcover, 542 pgs, EX, P6 .... **$95.00**

Book, Watermelon Pete (w/6 other stories), Elizabeth Gordon/Rand McNally, 1937, Clara Powers illus, EX, P6 .... **$95.00**

Book Set w/Doll, All About Little Black Sambo/Mother Goose/Little Red Riding Hood, Cupples & Leon, 1906, EX (EX box) **$950.00**

Card Game, Game of Dixieland, Fireside Game Co, 1897, EX (worn box), P6.. **$255.00**

Cinelin Theatre, Spain, 1920s, graphic stories w/performers on turning roller, mc cb stage, 8x7½", EX **$155.00**

Clicker, Minstrel Sam, 1920s, litho tin, 1¾", EX, P6....... **$95.00**

Coloring Book, Little Brown Koko, 1941, illus by Dorothy Wadstaff, 22 pgs, unused, EX, P6 .... **$125.00**

Crank Toy, Happy Jack Jigger, mk B&U/Germany, articulated litho tin figure dances when crank is turned, 7", EX..**$500.00**

Dancing Sambo Magic Trick, 1940s, jtd cb figure, M (NM envelope) **$95.00**

Dice Toy, Alco/Britain, activate plunger to spin laughing head & dice, 2" dia, NM **$120.00**

Doll, golliwog, hand-knit yarn, embroidered side-glance eyes, gr turtleneck & tweed pants, 17", EX, P6...................... **$95.00**

Doll, golliwog, stuffed cloth w/orange shirt & red pants, plush hair, 12", EX, P6 .... **$65.00**

Doll, golliwog, 1930s, hand-knit yarn w/felt features, red & wht striped jeans & bl jacket, 17", EX, P6 .... **$150.00**

Doll, golliwog, 1930s, hand-knitted wool w/felt features, bl dbl-breasted jacket w/red & wht striped pants, 17", EX, P6..**$100.00**

Doll, pickaninny, 1950s, inflatable plastic w/flasher eyes, yel skirt & hair bow, 10", EX, P6 .... **$50.00**

Doll, Raggedy Ann's Mammy friend (Belindy-type), 1950s, stocking-knit head & torso, cotton arms & legs, 14", EX, P6... **$75.00**

Doll, topsy-turvy, 1930s, changes to wht girl, stuffed cotton w/yarn hair, 14", EX, P6.. **$95.00**

Doll, 1900-30s, blk-pnt bsk body w/jtd arms & legs, molded & pnt features, 3 tufts of hair form pigtails, 6", G........ **$100.00**

Doll, 1930s, blk felt w/felt features & yarn hair, red organdy dress, wht hat & red ribbon, 8", EX, P6 ....**$55.00**

Doll Family, father, mother & boy golliwogs, stuffed cloth w/cloth clothes, yarn hair, button eyes, 18" & 22", EX **$100.00**

Doll Kit, Sambo, Bucilla Needlework, 1950s, complete, P6 ....**$95.00**

Dolls, unmarked, 1935 – 45, stuffed cloth with yarn hair, male: 17½", female: 19", EX, $175.00 for the pair.

Figure, Black man in tuxedo holding bouquet of roses, Japan, prewar, celluloid, 6½", NM, A....................**$110.00**

Figure, Dancing Dan, Bell Products, plastic figure on base moves to sound activation through microphone, NMIB....**$225.00**

Game of Little Black Sambo, Saalfield, 1923, missing spinner, EX (VG box), A, $125.00.

Game, Amos 'N Andy Card Party, AM Davis, 1930, complete, NM (NM box)....................**$165.00**

Game, Black Man Bagatelle or Black Woman Bagatelle, German, 1880s, put balls in mouth for teeth, 2½" dia, NM, ea **$100.00**

Game, Game of Dixieland, Fireside Game Co, 1897, complete, EX (worn box), P6....................**$265.00**

Game, Golli-Pop Target, Chad Valley, heavy cb w/paper litho figure, complete, EX (EX box) **$550.00**

Game, Jolly Darkie Target, Milton Bradley, NM............**$175.00**

Game, Skillets & Cakes, Milton Bradley, 1946, complete, EX (EX box), from $150 to **$200.00**

Game, The Game of Sambo, Parker Bros, 1915, rare, NMIB....................**$400.00**

Game, Zoo Hoo, Lubbers & Bell, 1924, complete, NM (EX box) **$165.00**

Noisemaker, 1930s, wood paddle w/2 balls attached to wires, imprinted w/2 humorous figures, 8¾", EX, P6 ....**$65.00**

Noisemaker, 1940s, man in hand-clapping & dancing pose, litho tin, EX, P6....................**$45.00**

Paper Dolls, Betty & Billy, Whitman, 1955, uncut, NM, P6 ....**$125.00**

Phonograph Jigger, Dancing Dandy, wood, EX, D10.......**$225.00**

Playette Moving Theatre, litho paper, theatre unit w/Little Black Sambo book & assorted cutouts, EX (EX box) **$225.00**

Pull Toy, Little Jasper, Wood Commodities, 1944, 10", NM (EX box), A, $300.00.

Pull Toy, Snowflake & Swipes, Nifty, 1920s, 8", EX, D10 .**$1,850.00**

Puppet, Jambo the Jiver Marionette, Talent Products, 1948, jtd wood w/cloth clothes, fiber hair, 14", VG................**$225.00**

Puppet, Tonga from the Congo Marionette, Talent Products, 1948, pnt wood & plastic, string skirt, 14", VG........**$225.00**

Puppet Theater, Little Black Sambo Playette, 1942, heavy cb, MIB, P6....................**$225.00**

Puzzle, fr-tray; Sifo, 1966, Little Black Sambo & Tiger in jungle w/Sambo under umbrella, 10x8", EX, P6 ....**$95.00**

Puzzle, Rastus, 1920s, celluloid, 4x3", EX (EX card), P6...**$165.00**

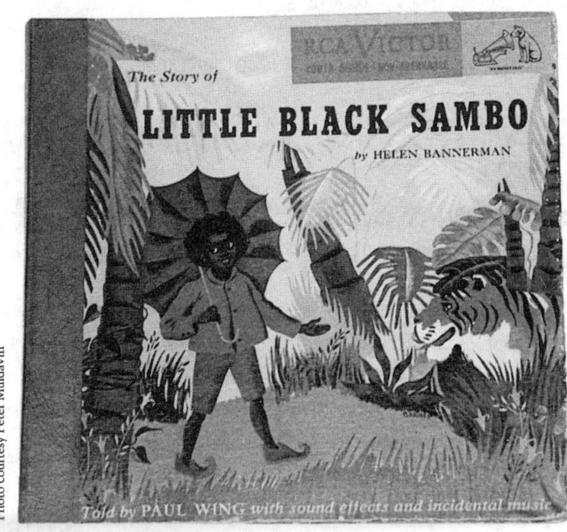

Record, Little Black Sambo, RCA Victor Y333, 1947, 78 rpm, two in album, EX, from $50.00 to $125.00.

Record & Book Set, Little Black Sambo, Music You Enjoy Inc, 1941, EX, P6 .... **$125.00**

Record & Book Set, Little Black Sambo's Jungle Band, written & narrated by Paul Wing, EX, P6 .... **$110.00**

Stacking Blocks, 1940s, set of 5 storybook blocks featuring Sambo & Tiger, EX, P6 .... **$125.00**

Storyland Box, Little Black Sambo, for cloth-type books, EX . **$75.00**

Tambourine, Amo's Singing Minstrells, unmarked, 1910 – 1920, tin, 6" dia, EX, $900.00.

Tea Set, ca 1904, matt porcelain w/golliwog graphics by Florence Upton, teapot, creamer & sugar, cup & saucer, M **$250.00**

Boats

Though some commercially made boats date as far back as the late 1800s, they were produced on a much larger scale during WWI and the decade that followed and again during the years that spanned WWII. Some were scaled-down models of battleships measuring nearly three feet in length. While a few were actually seaworthy, many were designed with small wheels to be pulled along the carpet or out of doors on dry land. Others were motor-driven windups, and later a few were even battery operated. Some of the larger manufacturers were Bing (Germany), Dent (Pennsylvania), Orkin Craft (California), Liberty Playthings (New York), and Arnold (West Germany).

Advisors: Richard Trautwein (T3); Dick Borgerding (B4).

See also Cast Iron, Boats; Battery-Operated Toys; Steam Powered; Tootsietoys; Windups, Friction, and Other Mechanicals; and other specific manufacturers.

Aeroboat, Bowman/England, wood hull w/tin bow, internal gears & orig rubber band intact, EX (EX wooden box) .. **$1,400.00**

Aircraft Carrier, Japan, friction, litho tin, w/Navy helicopter & 2 jets on deck, 9½", NM (EX box), A **$200.00**

Aircraft Carrier, Tudor-Rose, 1950s, gray plastic w/staight-deck carrier & red & yel snap-on accessories, 15", EX, P4 .. **$75.00**

Armada, Hess, clockwork, litho tin, complete w/5 cruisers & lg battleship, EX, A **$950.00**

Battleship, Bing, 1915, w/up, gray- & bl-pnt tin w/red trim, 3 observation towers, 2 British flags, 19", rstr, from $600 to **$900.00**

Battleship, Bliss, paper on wood, 16 wooden guns on upper deck, 2 masts w/gun towers, 36", EX **$4,000.00**

Battleship, Orobr, clockwork, litho tin w/paper flag, 2 stacks & lifeboats, pilot house on top deck, 11", EX, A **$700.00**

Battleship, Wolverine, w/up, litho tin, guns spark & props turn, 14½", rare, EX (worn box) **$200.00**

Battleship Dreadnaught, Marklin, 1st series, clockwork, pnt tin, 13 brass cannons, w/4 lifeboats, 42", prof rstr **$21,000.00**

Battleship HMS Albion, Marklin, 1902 – 1904, wheeled carriage, 22", EX, A, $13,700.00.

Battleship Indiana, litho tin hull w/wooden deck, crew station & pilot house, 2 smoke stacks, 31", EX, from $1,300 to **$1,500.00**

Battleship Philadelphia, Reed, 1877, paper on wood, 30", from $1,000 to **$1,500.00**

Cabin Cruiser, Orkin/Calwis Industries Ltd CA, 1930, steel hull & cabin, wooden deck, w/Am flag, 32", VG **$1,200.00**

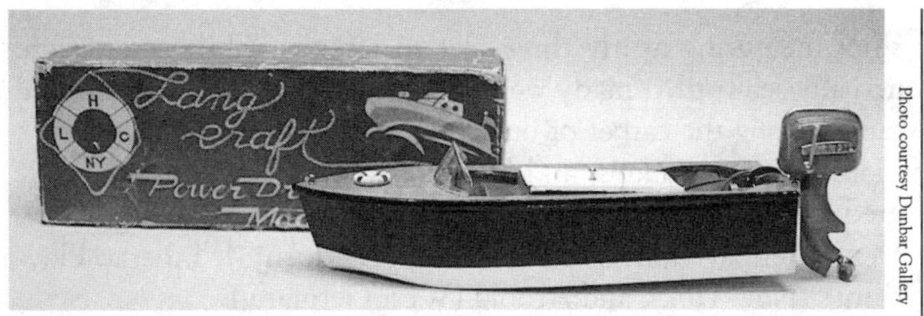

Boat and Motor, Langcraft, 1950s, EX (EX box), D10, $150.00.

Clipper Ship, Reed, 1877, paper on wood, 3 paper sails, 2 sailors & cargo on deck, 36", EX, from $1,100 to............**$1,600.00**

Cruiser, Bing, clockwork, wht- & bl-pnt tin w/yel stripe, brn deck, litho tin driver, 21", EX, A..........................**$1,200.00**

Endeavor III Yacht, wood w/2 cloth sails, 16", NMIB, A .**$300.00**

Ferryboat Union, Bing, clockwork, red- & bl-pnt tin w/yel detail, 2 paddle wheels & ventilators, 16", VG, A ..**$700.00**

Gunboat, Bliss, litho paper on wood, w/4 flags & mounted guns, 4 wooden wheels, 25½", G **$1,400.00**

Gunboat, Carette, w/up, red- & wht-pnt tin, 11", EX (EX box) **$650.00**

Gunboat, Ernst Plank, gray-pnt tin w/blk stripe on hull, gun, stack & funnel on deck, tin German flag, 11", VG, A **$475.00**

Gunboat, Germany, flywheel mechanism, litho tin w/center stack & railed sides, 9", EX, A **$150.00**

Gunboat Massena, Bing, w/up, bl- & gray-pnt tin w/red trim, 24", NM **$10,400.00**

Luxury Liner, Wolverine, w/up, red w/lithoed swimming pool, lifeboats & shuffleboard, 14½", NM (NM box), A .**$250.00**

Mighty Aircraft Carrier, Japan, friction, w/helicopter & 3 Navy planes, litho tin, 9", NM (NM box), A **$200.00**

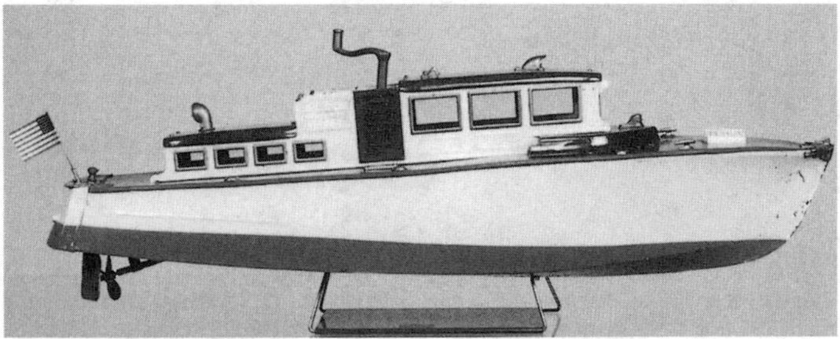

Motorboat, Orkin, clockwork mechanism, maroon and white with red hull, 30", EX, A, $3,500.00.

Nautilus Submarine SSN-58, SAN, crank-powered, bl-pnt tin, 13", NM (G box), A...**$285.00**

Northern Star Yacht, pnt wood w/3 cloth sails, 18", NMIB, from $300 to..**$375.00**

Ocean Liner, Arnold, w/up, red- & bl-pnt tin w/wht upper deck, 2 masts & stacks, 2 tiers of lifeboats, 13½", EX....**$1,000.00**

Ocean Liner, Arnold, w/up, wht-pnt tin w/red stripe, complete w/3 flags, 13", EX (EX box), from $450 to **$600.00**

Ocean Liner, Arnold, 1930s, flywheel mechanism, red- & bl-pnt tin w/red striping, 4 stacks, railed deck, 12½", EX...**$700.00**

Ocean Liner, Carette, 1905, clockwork, pnt tin, 16½", masts & lifeboat missing, G..**$1,000.00**

Ocean Liner, Bing, clockwork mechanism, red, white, and blue, three stacks and two masts, railed pilot house, 12", EX, from $700.00 to $850.00; Ocean Liner, Bing, clockwork mechanism, red, white, and blue, three stacks and two masts, two railed passenger decks, 16", EX, A, $1,900.00.

Ocean Liner, Falk, 1905, pnt tin, 4 stacks, railed deck, w/extra hull, 17", G...**$1,150.00**

Ocean Liner, Fleischmann, pnt tin, 2 lifeboats, 2 masts & stacks, w/pilot house, 12½", NM....................................**$1,000.00**

Ocean Liner, Germany, steam-powered, pnt tin, 13", G, A.**$575.00**

Ocean Liner Columbus, Marklin, pnt tin, 2 stacks, cut-out portholes, 20 lifeboats, 38", prof rstr...........................**$8,200.00**

Ocean Liner Luzern, Marklin, 1925, clockwork, pnt tin, 11½", missing 1 of 3 stacks & masts, VG **$2,000.00**

Ocean Liner Mauretania, Fleischmann, clockwork, pnt tin, 2 stacks & 2 masts, w/pilot house, 12", VG **$400.00**

Ocean Star Yacht, pnt wood w/3 cloth sails, 24", NMIB, A **$185.00**

Pacific Star Yacht, pnt wood w/3 cloth sails, 21", NMIB, A **$200.00**

Pond Yacht, 1880s, plank on fr racing boat w/weighted metal keel, mahogany finish, cloth sails, 34", EX, from $1,000 to **$1,200.00**

Pond Yacht, 1890s, wood hull w/early sloop in natural varnish, leaded keel, cloth sails, 33", EX, from $1,000 to ..**$1,200.00**

Racing Boat Seahawk, Bowman, wood hull w/tin bow, steam-powered boiler, 27", rpt, EX (EX wooden box), minimum value **$1,000.00**

Racing Shell, w/up, pnt & litho tin, 8-man rowing team & helmsman, 27", NM..**$12,000.00**

Riverboat, Bing, clockwork, pnt tin, 3 masts, 20", VG, A **$3,600.00**

Riverboat, Carette, white with red striping and brown hull, brass boiler, railed sides, 18", repaint, A, $665.00.

Riverboat Queen Mary, Marusan, battery-op, litho tin, advances w/sound & smoke, 14", EX (EX box), A..................**$275.00**

Side-Wheeler, Geo Brown, pnt & stenciled tin, 7", G...**$850.00**

Side-Wheeler Atlantic, Althof Bergmann, pnt tin, NM, D10 ....**$4,500.00**

Side-Wheeler Columbia, Fallows, pnt & stenciled tin, IXL emb on base, 11", G $3,300.00
Side-Wheeler Pacific, Bergmann, pnt & stenciled tin w/cast components, on wheels, 14", G $3,800.00
Side-Wheeler Priscilla, paper on wood, cream w/gr & red highlights, 2 blk stacks, 37", G $2,900.00
Side-Wheeler Union, Bliss, paper on wood, 2 decks, 2 lg stacks, w/gear housing & pilot house, 23", EX, from $1,200 to $1,500.00
Southern Star Yacht, pnt wood w/3 cloth sails, 21", NMIB, A $150.00
Speedboat, ca 1920, steam-powered, gray-pnt pressed steel w/brn deck, 26", EX, from $1,000 to $1,400.00
Speedboat, Fleet Line the Marlin, 1950s, battery-op, plastic hull w/wooden deck, canvas cover, 16", NM, from $200 to...$300.00
Speedboat, GFN, clockwork, wht-pnt tin w/bl stripe, brn deck, litho tin driver, 12", EX, A.....................................$700.00
Speedboat, Japan, battery-op, hand-pnt wood w/metal fittings, 18", EX, A $400.00
Speedboat, Kellermann, clockwork, pnt & stained wood, driver w/bsk head, 24", EX, A..$1,200.00

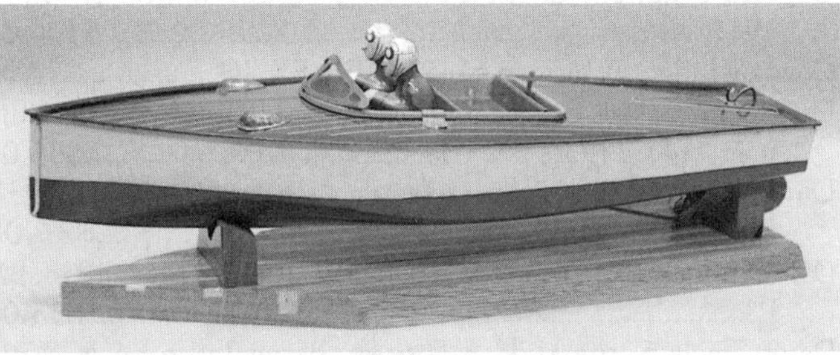

Speedboat, Lindstrom, with two figures, 18", NM, D10, $750.00.

Speedboat, Lionel, litho tin, orig stand, 18", VG $475.00
Speedboat, Metalcraft, battery-op, blk- & red-pnt metal, 24", G $150.00

Speedboat, Orkin, clockwork mechanism, black and red with simulated wood deck, with driver, 28", EX, A, $1,750.00.

Speedboat, w/Lindstrom outboard motor, litho tin & wood, 11", EX $450.00
Speedboat B-619, Bandai, crank-powered, litho tin, visible spinner in top, 12", EX, H7 ....$250.00
Speedboat Miss America, Mengel Playthings, clockwork, wood hull w/brass fittings, orig decals, 15", EX, from $450 to $550.00
Speedboat Sea-Fury, 1948, red & blk plastic w/metal motor, 16", EX, A $150.00
Steam Launch, Carette, cream-pnt tin w/red & blk trim, yel deck, 16", VG (worn box) $900.00
Steamboat, Bowman, gr- & brn-pnt tin w/exposed boiler & valves, rear seat on deck, 26", NM, A......................$475.00
Steamboat, Weeban, gray-pnt tin w/exposed brass boiler, 16", G, A $500.00
Submarine, Marklin, w/up, gr-pnt tin w/blk trim, deck railing, 16", EX..$1,100.00
Submarine, Marklin, w/up, gray-pnt tin w/blk stripe, lg side flippers, deck railing, 23", EX $3,000.00
Submarine Le Berrob, France, gray-pnt tin w/wht & red hatch, dives & rises when air is squeezed into tube, 9", NMIB $725.00
Torpedo Boat, Bing, w/up, gray- & blk-pnt tin, railed deck, red & yel flags, GBN emb on deck, 17", EX, from $1,200 to $1,400.00
Torpedo Boat, Bing, 2-tone gray-pnt tin w/blk trim, 2 torpedo chutes, guns & lifeboats, 16", VG $550.00
USS Farragut 072, Japan, battery-op, bl-pnt tin w/red detail, 15", NM, A $225.00

Books

Books have always captured and fired the imagination of children, and today books from every era are being collected. No longer is it just the beautifully illustrated Victorian examples or first editions of books written by well-known children's authors, but more modern books as well.

One of the first classics to achieve unprecedented success was *The Wizard of Oz* by author L. Frank Baum — such success, in fact, that far from his original intentions, it became a series. Even after Baum's death, other authors wrote Oz books until the decade of the 1960s, for a total of more than forty different titles. Other early authors were Beatrix Potter, Kate Greenaway, Palmer Cox (who invented the Brownies), and Johnny Gruelle (creator of Raggedy Ann and Andy). All were acomplished illustrators as well.

Everyone remembers a special series of books they grew up with, the Hardy Boys, Nancy Drew Mysteries, Tarzan — there were countless others. And though these are becoming very collectible today, there were many editions of each, and most are very easy to find. Generally the last few in any series will be the most difficult to locate, since fewer were printed than the earlier stories which were likely to have been reprinted many times. As is true of any type of book, first editions or the earliest printing will have more collector value. For more information on series books as well as others, we recommend *Collector's Guide to Children's Books, 1850 – 1950,* by Diane McClure Jones and Rosemary Jones (Collector Books).

Big Little Books came along in 1933 and until edged out by the comic-book format in the mid-1950s sold in huge volumes, first for a dime and never more than 20¢ a copy. They were printed by Whitman, Saalfield, Goldsmith, Van Wiseman, Lynn, and World Syndicate, and all stuck to Whitman's original layout — thick hand-sized sagas of adventure, the right-hand page with an exciting cartoon, well illustated and contrived so as to bring the text on the left alive. The first hero to be immortalized in this arena was Dick Tracy, but many more were to follow. Some of the more collectible today feature well-known characters like G-Men, Tarzan, Flash Gordon, Little Orphan Annie, Mickey Mouse, and Western heroes by the dozens. (Note: At the present time, the market for these books is fairly stable — values for common titles are actually dropping. Only the rare, character-related titles are increasing.) For more information we recommend *Big Little Books*, by Larry Jacobs (Collector Books).

Little Golden Books were first published in 1942 by Western Publishing Co. Inc. The earliest had spines of blue paper that were later replaced with gold foil. Until the 1970s the books were numbered from 1 to 600, while later books had no numerical order. The most valuable are those with dust jackets from the early '40s or books with paper dolls and activities. The three primary series of books are Regular (1-600), Disney (1-140), and Activity (1-52). Books with the blue or gold paper spine (not foil) often sell at $8.00 to $15.00. Dust jackets alone are worth $20.00 and up in good condition. Paper doll books are generally valued at about $30.00 to $35.00, and stories about TV Western heroes at $12.00 to $18.00. First editions of the 25¢ and 29¢ cover-price books can be identified by a code (either on the title page or the last page); '1/A' indicates a first edition while a number '/Z' will refer to the twenty-sixth printing. Condition is important but subjective to personal standards. For more information we recommend *Collecting Little Golden Books, Vols I and II*, by Steve Santi. The second edition also includes information on Wonder and Elf books.

For further study we also recommend *Whitman Juvenile Books* by David and Virginia Brown (Collector Books).

Advisors: Ron and Donna Donnelly (D7), Big Little Books; Joel Cohen (C12), Disney Pop-Up Books; Ilene Kayne (K3), Big Golden Books, Little Golden Books, Tell-a-Tale, and Wonder Books.

See also Black Americana; Coloring, Activity, and Paint Books; Rock 'n Roll.

Big Little Books

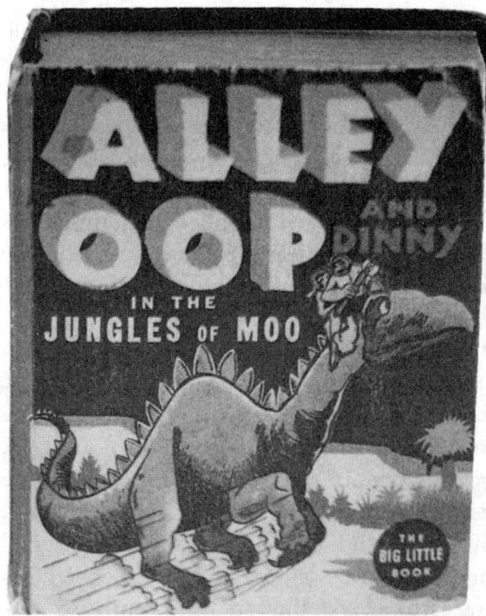

***Alley Oop in the Jungles of Moo*, Whitman #1473, 1938, M, $75.00.**

Andy Panda's Vacation, Better Little Book, Whitman #1485, 1946, EX, P3 ....**$35.00**
Bambi's Children, Whitman #1497, 1943, VG....................**$45.00**
Big Chief Wahoo & The Great Gusto, Better Little Book, Whitman #1443, 1938, EX, P3 ....**$35.00**
Billy the Kid, Whitman #773, 1935, EX, P3 ....**$35.00**
Blaze Brandon w/the Foreign Legion, Whitman #1447, 1938, EX, A **$25.00**
Blondie, Cookie & Daisy's Pups, Whitman #1491, 1943, EX..**$25.00**
Blondie & Baby Dumpling, Whitman #1415, 1937, NM .**$50.00**
Brenda Starr & the Masked Imposter, Whitman #1427, 1943, EX, F8....................**$30.00**
Buck Jones & the Two Gun Kid, Whitman #1404, 1937, EX, P3 ....**$35.00**
Buck Rogers & the Depth Men of Jupiter, Whitman #1169, 1935, EX....................**$60.00**
Buck Rogers & the Doom Comet, Whitman, 1935, VG+, J5....................**$45.00**
Bullet Benton, Saalfield #1169, 1937, EX, A....................**$25.00**
Captain Easy Behind Enemy Lines, Whitman #1474, 1943, VG+, F8....................**$18.00**
Captain Midnight & the Moon Woman, Better Little Book, Whitman #1452, 1943, EX, P3....................**$75.00**
Captain Midnight & the Secret Squadron, Whitman #1488, 1941, NM, A **$100.00**
Cowboy Lingo, Whitman #1457, 1938, EX, P3 ....**$30.00**
Dan Dunn & the Border Smugglers, Better Little Book, Whitman #1481, 1938, EX, P3 ....**$35.00**
Dan Dunn & the Crime Master, Whitman #1171, 1937, EX **$35.00**
Dan Dunn on the Trail of Wu Fang, Whitman #1454, 1938, EX, P3 ....**$35.00**
Desert Eagle & the Hidden Fortress, Better Little Book, Whitman, #1431, EX, P3 ....**$35.00**
Dick Tracy & the Boris Arson Gang, Whitman #1163, 1935, VG+, T2 ....**$35.00**
Dick Tracy & the Tiger Lily Gang, Whitman #1460, 1949, VG **$35.00**
Dick Tracy Solves the Penfield Mystery, Whitman #1137, VG **$55.00**
Donald Duck Off the Beam, Whitman #1438, 352 pgs, EX ...**$75.00**
Felix the Cat, Whitman #1129, 1936, 432 pgs, EX..........**$70.00**
Flash Gordon & the Monsters of Mongo, Whitman #1166, 1935, EX **$100.00**
Flash Gordon & the Red Sword Invaders, Whitman #1479, 1945, EX....................**$75.00**
Freckles & the Lost Diamond Mine, Whitman #1164, 1937, VG, T2....................**$25.00**
G-Man & the Radio Bank Robberies, Whitman #1434, 1937, EX....................**$40.00**
Gene Autry in Red Bandits Ghost, Better Little Book, Whitman #1461, 1949, EX, P3 ....**$35.00**
Gunsmoke, Whitman #1647, 1958, EX **$20.00**
Jack Armstrong & the Ivory Treasure, Whitman #1435, 1937, EX, F8....................**$40.00**
Jackie Cooper, The Story of; Whitman #714, 1933, VG..**$30.00**
Jimmy Allen in the Air Mail Robbery, Whitman #1143, 1936, EX, P3 ....**$35.00**

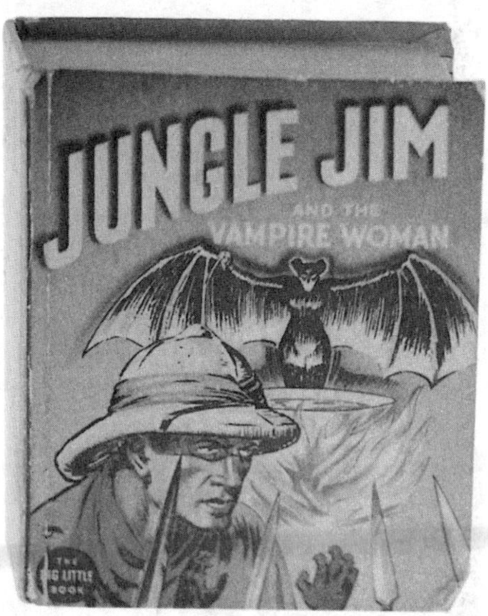

***Jungle Jim and the Vampire Woman*, Whitman #1139, 1937, NM, $90.00.**

Junior G-Men, Whitman #1442, 1937, EX, P3 ....**$40.00**
Lassie's Adventure in Alaska, Whitman #2004, 1967, EX, C1 ....**$15.00**
Li'l Abner in New York, Whitman #1198, 1936, EX........**$60.00**
Mandrake the Magician, Whitman #1167, 1935, VG, F8 ..**$30.00**
Maximo the Amazing Superman, Whitman #1436, 1941, EX, A...**$30.00**
Mickey Mouse & Pluto the Racer, Whitman #1128, 1936, EX...**$75.00**
Mickey Mouse & the Lazy Daisy Mystery, Whitman #1433, 1947, EX...**$65.00**
Mickey Mouse in the Race for Riches, Better Little Book, Whitman #1476, 1938, EX **$75.00**
Popeye & Queen Olive Oyl, Better Little Book, Whitman #1458, 1949, VG **$25.00**
Popeye Ghost Ship to Treasure Island, Whitman #2008, 1967, VG **$10.00**
Prairie Bill & the Covered Wagon, Whitman #758, 1934, VG, P3 ....**$30.00**

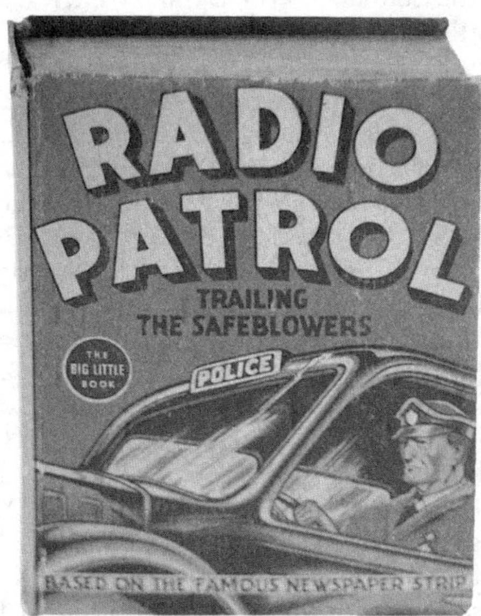

***Radio Patrol Trailing the Safeblowers*, Whitman #1173, 1937, EX, $35.00.**

Red Ryder in Circus Luck, Whitman #1466, 1947, EX **$35.00**

***Return of the Phantom*, Whitman #1489, 1942, VG, $40.00.**

Secret Agent K-7, Saalfield #1191, 1940, EX, P3 ....**$35.00**
Smitty & Herby Lost Among the Indians, Whitman #1404, 1941, EX...**$35.00**
Smokey Stover, Whitman #1413, 1942, EX **$35.00**
Speed Douglas & the Mole Gang, Whitman #1455, 1941, VG, P3 ....**$20.00**
Tarzan Twins, Whitman, 1934, 1st edition, rare, NM ...**$250.00**
Tim McCoy the Prescott Kid, Whitman #1152, 1935, VG, P3 ....**$40.00**
Tim Tyler's Luck, Adventure in the Ivory Patrol, Whitman #1140, 1937, VG, F8 ....**$40.00**
Tom Mix & His Circus on the Barbary Coast, Better Little Book Whitman #1482, 1940, EX.......................................**$45.00**
Zane Grey's King of the Royal Mounted Gets His Man, Whitman #1452, 1938, EX **$50.00**
Zane Grey's Tex Thorne Comes Out of the West, Whitman #1440, 1937, VG, P3 ....**$30.00**

Little Golden Books

A Day at the Beach, #110, A edition, EX, K3 ....**$25.00**
ABC Rhymes, #543, E edition, EX, K3 ....**$6.00**
Alvin's Daydreams, #107-73, A edition, EX, K3.................**$8.00**
Animal Counting Book, #584, A edition, EX, K3 ....**$10.00**
Baby's Day Out, #113-01, A edition, EX, K3 ....**$15.00**
Beauty & the Beast, #104-65, A edition, EX, K3 ....**$5.00**
Ben & Me, #D37, A edition, EX, K3 ....**$22.00**
Bible Stories of Boys & Girls, #174, A edition, EX, K3 ....**$10.00**
Big Bird's Day on the Farm, #200-50, C edition, EX, K3 ....**$2.00**
Big Brown Bear, #89, A edition, EX, K3 ....**$18.00**
Biskitts Double Trouble, #111-49, A edition, EX, K3.........**$8.00**
Bongo, #D9, F edition, EX, K3 ....**$10.00**
Bouncing Baby Bunny Finds His Friends, #129, A edition, EX, K3...**$10.00**
Bozo & the Hide 'N Seek Elephant, #598, D edition, EX, K3 ....**$6.00**

Bozo the Clown, #446, C edition, EX, K3 ....$8.00

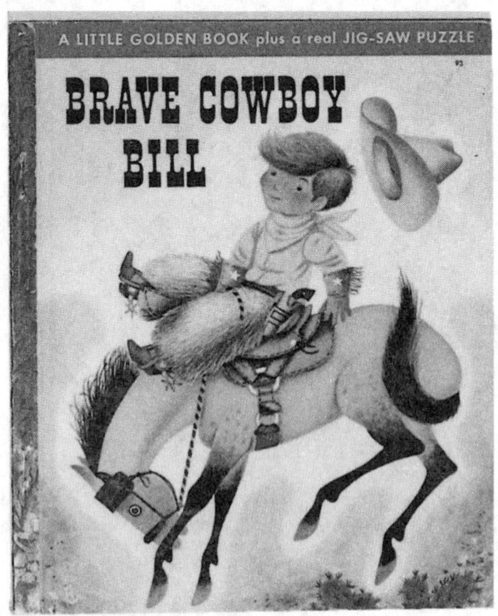

***Brave Cowboy Bill*, A edition, with puzzle: from $50.00 to $75.00; without puzzle: $18.00.**

Brave Eagle, #294, B edition, EX, K3 ....$8.00
Buffalo Bill Jr, #254, A edition, EX, K3 ....$15.00
Bugs Bunny & the Indians, #120, B edition, EX, K3 ....$12.00
Bugs Bunny at the Easter Party, #183, D edition, EX, K3 ....$10.00
Bugs Bunny Pioneer, #111-66, A edition, EX, K3 ....$6.00
Christmas Carols, #26, B edition, EX, K3 ....$12.00
Christmas Story, #158, E edition, EX, K3 ....$10.00
Corky, #486, A edition, EX, K3 ....$15.00
Dennis the Menace, #386, E edition, EX, K3 ....$8.00
Donald Duck Private Eye, #D94, A edition, VG, K3 ....$20.00
Dumbo, #D3, H edition, EX, K3 ....$15.00
Elves & the Shoemaker, #307-56, B edition, EX, K3 ....$2.00

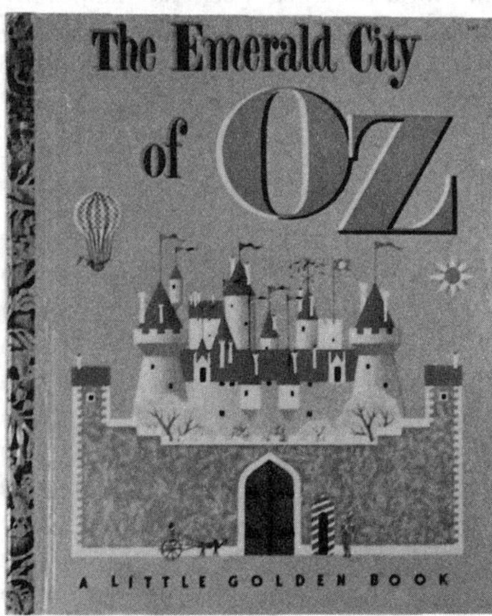

***Emerald City of Oz* #151, A edition, EX, $40.00.**

Farmyard Friends, #429, B edition, EX, K3 ....$10.00
Fly High, #599, A edition, EX, K3 ....$12.00
Fozzie's Funnies, #111-87, A edition, EX, K3 ....$5.00
Frosty the Snowman, #142, B edition, EX, K3 ....$6.00
Goof Troop, #107-87, A edition, EX, K3 ....$6.00
Grandpa Bunny, #D21, B edition, EX, K3 ....$22.00
Hansel & Gretel, #17, H edition, VG, K3 ....$10.00
Heidi, #258, C edition, EX, K3 ....$5.00
Hopalong Cassidy, #147, A edition, VG, K3 ....$15.00
Howdy Doody & Clarabell, #121, A edition, EX, K3 ....$20.00
Huckleberry Hound & the Christmas Sleigh, #403, D edition, K3 ....$10.00
Huckleberry Hound Builds a House, #376, B edition, EX, K3 ....$8.00

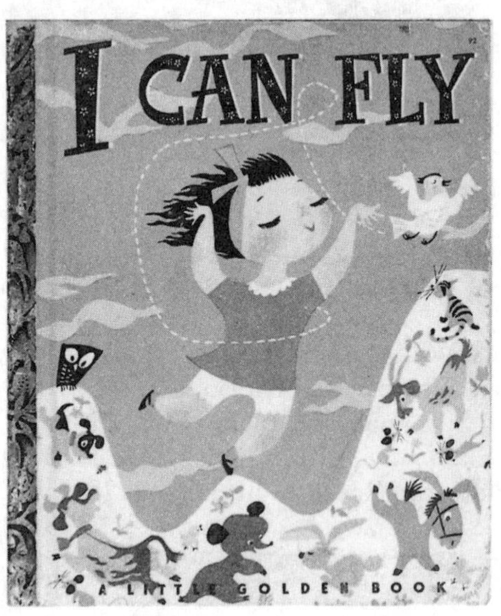

***I Can Fly*, A edition, EX, $15.00.**

Inspector Gadget in Africa, #107-49, A edition, EX, K3 ....$5.00
Jingle Bells, #553, 5th edition, EX, K3 ....$4.00
Jolly Barnyard, #200-44, A edition, EX, K3 ....$5.00
Katie the Kitten, #75, C edition, EX, K3 ....$16.00
Lassie & the Daring Rescue, #277, A edition, EX, K3 ....$12.00
Let's Fly a Kite Charlie Brown, #111-62, B edition, EX, K3 ....$6.00
Let's Go Shopping, #208-58, C edition, EX, K3 ....$3.00
Little Cottontail, #414, D edition, EX, K3 ....$5.00
Little Engine That Could, #548, I edition, EX, K3 ....$8.00
Little Lulu, #476, B edition, EX, K3 ....$16.00
Little Yip Yip & His Bark, #73, A edition, EX, K3 ....$20.00
Lively Little Rabbit, #15, E edition, EX, K3 ....$14.00
Magic Next Door, #106, D edition, EX, K3 ....$6.00
Mickey Mouse & His Spaceship, #D29, A edition, EX, K3 ....$20.00
Mickey Mouse Picnic, #D15, A edition, VG, K3 ....$25.00
Mickey's Christmas Carol, #459-42, A edition, EX, K3 ....$6.00
Mister Ed, #483, A edition, EX, K3 ....$18.00
More Mother Goose Rhymes, #317, A edition, EX, K3 ....$10.00
Mr Noah & His Family, #49, D edition, VG, K3 ....$12.00
My Kitten, #163, A edition, VG, K3 ....$28.00
My Little Dinosaur, #571, C edition, EX, K3 ....$5.00
My Own Grandpa, #208-56, A edition, EX, K3 ....$5.00
New House in the Forest, #24, C edition, EX, K3 ....$30.00
Nursery Songs, #348, D edition, EX, K3 ....$8.00
Old Mother Goose, #300-54, A edition, EX, K3 ....$6.00
Oscar's New Neighbor, #109-67, A edition, EX, K3 ....$5.00

Pete's Dragon, #D137, A edition, EX, K3 ....$10.00

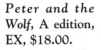

***Peter and the Wolf,* A edition, EX, $18.00.**

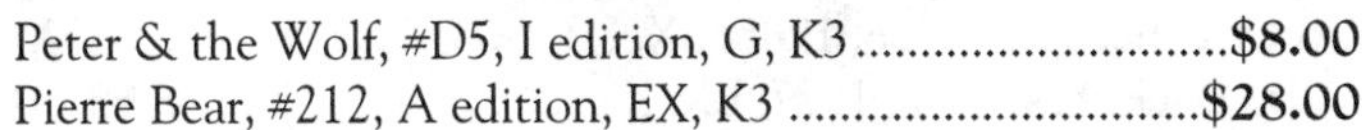

Peter & the Wolf, #D5, I edition, G, K3 ....$8.00
Pierre Bear, #212, A edition, EX, K3 ....$28.00

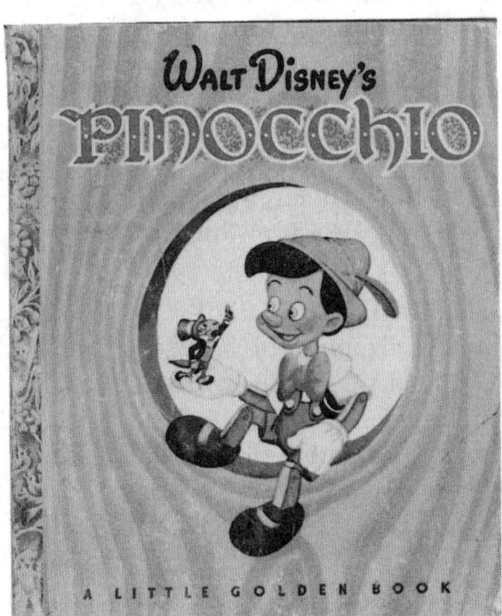

***Pinocchio,* A edition, EX, $8.00.**

Pinocchio, #D8, D edition, EX, K3 ....$18.00
Pinocchio & the Whale, #D101, A edition, VG, K3 ....$20.00
Poky Little Puppy, #506, C edition, EX, K3 ....$4.00
Poky Little Puppy's First Christmas, #461-01, A edition, EX, K3 ....$5.00
Prayers for Children, #5, J edition, EX, K3........................$12.00
Pussycat Tiger, #362, B edition, EX, K3 ....$16.00
Raggedy Ann & Andy & the Rainy Day Circus, #401, B edition, EX, K3 ....$5.00
Rainbow Brite, #107-48, A edition, EX, K3 ....$8.00
Robotman & Friends at School, #110-58, A edition, EX, K3 .$6.00
Rocky & His Friends, #408, A edition, EX, K3.................$22.00
Ronald McDonald & the Tale of the Talking Plant, #111-50, B edition, EX, K3 ....$10.00

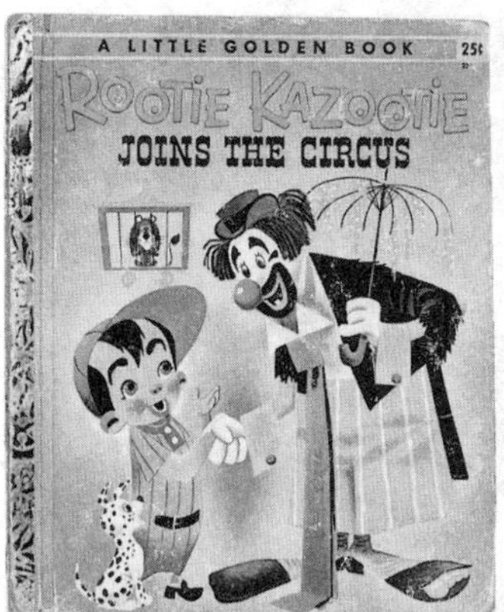

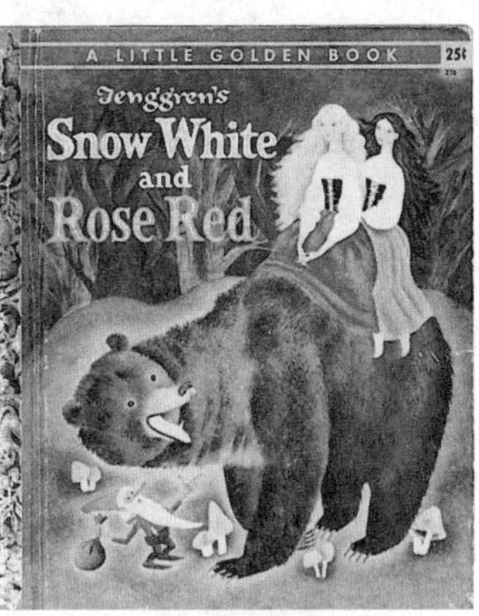

***Rootie Kazootie Joins the Circus,* A edition, EX, $20.00; *Tenggren's Snow White and Rose Red,* A edition, EX, $10.00.**

Rootie Kazootie the Detective, #150, A edition, EX, K3....$22.00
Ruff & Reddy, #378, A edition, EX, K3 ....$15.00
Rumpelstiltskin, #498, B edition, EX, K3 ....$8.00
Rupert the Rhinoceros, #201-57, E edition, EX, K3 ....$3.00
Santa's Toy Shop, #D16, A edition, EX, K3 ....$12.00
Seven Little Postmen, #504, G edition, EX, K3...............$10.00
Seven Sneezes, #51, B edition, VG, K3.........................$12.00
Shaggy Dog, #D82, B edition, EX, K3 ....$12.00
Sleepy Book, #46, D edition, EX, K3..............................$10.00
Snow White, #D4, C edition, VG, K3 ....$10.00
So Big, #574, E edition, EX, K3.......................................$12.00
Surprise for Sally, #84, A edition, VG, K3 ....$22.00
Tale of Peter Rabbit, #307-9, A edition, EX, K3................$5.00
Tawny Scrawny Lion, #138, K edition, EX, K3..................$5.00
Three Little Pigs, #D10, K edition, G, K3........................$10.00
Time for Bed, #301-55, B edition, EX, K3..........................$5.00
Tom & Jerry Christmas, #197, A edition, EX, K3 ....$12.00
Top Cat, #453, B edition, EX, K3 ....$18.00
Tweety & Sylvester in Birds of a Feather, #110-78, A edition, EX, K3 ....$5.00
Twelve Days of Christmas, #526, A edition, EX, K3 ....$12.00
Uncle Remus, #105-66, A edition, EX, K3 ....$12.00
Underdog & the Disappearing Ice Cream, #135, A edition, EX, K3..$15.00
We Like Kindergarten, #552, I edition, EX, K3 ....$4.00
When I Grow Up, #578, B edition, EX, K3........................$5.00
Wild Animal Babies, #309-58, A edition, EX, K3 ....$6.00
Willie Found a Wallet, #205-56, B edition, EX, K3............$4.00
Winnie the Pooh & the Honey Patch, #101-24, B edition, EX, K3 ....$4.00
Woody Woodpecker at the Circus, #149, B edition, EX, K3 ....$10.00
Zorro, #D68, B edition, EX, K3 ....$14.00

Pop-Up Books

Adventures in Oz, Derrydale, 1991, 1st edition, 3 pop-ups, 6 pgs, EX, K3 ....$10.00
Barbie Rockin' Rappin' Dancin' World Tour, Western Publishers, 1992, 1st edition, 5 pop-ups, EX, K3...................$20.00

***Buck Rogers Strange Adventures in the Spider-Ship,* Blue Ribbon, 1935, three pop-ups, M, $350.00.**

Child's Garden of Verses, Dutton, 1991, 1st edition, 5 pop-ups, 3 movable, 14 pgs, EX, K3 ....$15.00
Christmas Treasure Book, Simon & Schuster, 1950, 1 pop-up, EX, K3 ....$40.00
Disney's Aladdin, 1993, 1st edition, 4 pop-ups, 12 movable, M, K3 ....$12.00
Emerald City, Derrydale, 1991, 1st edition, 3 pop-ups, EX, K3 ....$10.00
First Christmas, Brown-Watson, 1988, 6 pop-ups, 6 movable, EX, K3 ....$15.00
Hopalong Cassidy & Lucky, EX, J2 ....$100.00
Huckleberry Hound & the Dog Cat, Modern, 1974, 4 pop-ups, EX, F8 ....$15.00
Jingle Bugs, Simon & Schuster, 1992, 1st edition, 1 pop-up, 13 movable, plays jingle bells, EX, K3 ....$20.00
Little Orphan Annie & Jumbo the Circus Elephant, Blue Ribbon, 3 pop-ups, M $250.00

***Mickey Mouse in King Arthur's Court,* M, C12, $1,500.00.**

Mickey Mouse Waddle Book, Blue Ribbon, 1934, M .$3,500.00
Minnie Mouse, WDE, 1930s, 3 pop-ups, M $400.00
Popeye w/the Hag of the Seven Seas, 1935, 3 pop-ups, EX, A $350.00
Rudolph the Red-Nosed Reindeer, by Robert L May, 1950, 5 pop-ups, NM, A $35.00
Terry & the Pirates, Blue Ribbon, 1935, 3 pop-ups, VG, J5 ..$125.00
Wings — A Pop-Up Book of Things That Fly, Random House, 1991, 1st edition, 6 pop-ups, 7 movable, EX, K3 ....$25.00

Tell-a-Tale by Whitman

Alonzo Purr the Seagoing Cat, #2406-3, 1974, EX, K3 ......$5.00
Bambi, #2548, 1972, EX, K3 ....$5.00
Benjamin Brownie & the Talking Doll, Top Top Tale #2499, 1962, EX, K3 ....$12.00
Billy Bunnyscoot the Lost Bunny, #888, 1948, VG, K3......$6.00
Bugs Bunny's Chimney Adventure, Top Top Tale #2464, 1963, EX, K3 ....$8.00
Bunny Button, #2526, 1953, EX, K3 ....$6.00
Christopher John's Fuzzy Blanket, #2672, 1959, VG, K3 .$15.00
Cinnamon Bear, #2674, 1961, fuzzy pgs, VG, K3 ....$15.00
Corky's Hiccups, #2428, 1968, EX, K3 ....$5.00
Daffy Duck, #2453-36, 1977, EX, K3 ....$5.00
Daniel's New Friend, #2560, 1968, EX, K3 ....$5.00
Donald Duck in Frontierland, #2445, 1957, VG, K3 ....$8.00
Dragon for Danny Dennis, Top Top Tale #2458, 1963, EX, K3 ....$15.00
Ernie the Cave King, #2604, 1975, EX, K3 ....$5.00
Fluffy & the Flyaway Fly, #2430, 1966, EX, K3 ....$6.00
Flying Sunbeam, #849, 1950, EX, K3 ....$10.00
Gingerbread Man, Top Top Tale #2472, 1960, EX, K3......$8.00
Grandpa's House, #2670, 1959, EX, K3 ....$12.00
Hildy's Hideaway, Top Top Tale #2473, 1961, EX, K3 ......$5.00
Ho-Hum, #2525, 1957, EX, K3 ....$5.00
Huffin Puff Express, #2415, 1974, EX, K3 ....$5.00
In, On, Under & Through, #2601, 1965, EX, K3 ....$6.00
Johnny Appleseed, #808, 1949, EX, K3 ....$20.00
Little Bitty Raindrop, #875, 1948, EX, K3 ....$9.00
Little Joe's Puppy, #2622, 1957, EX, K3 ....$6.00
Little Red Hen, #2431, 1953, EX, K3 ....$5.00
Ludwig Von Drake Dog Expert, Top Top Tale #2482, 1962, EX, K3 ....$15.00
Mary Poppins, #2606, 1964, EX, K3 ....$8.00
Mee-Yow, #2436, 1968, EX, K3 ....$8.00
Mickey Mouse & the Second Wish, #2454-31, 1973, EX, K3 ....$5.00
Mother Goose on the Farm, #2415-4, 1975, EX, K3 ....$5.00
My Little Book of Trains, #2421, Mattel giveaway, 1978, EX, K3 ....$10.00
Old Woman & Her Pig, #2610, 1964, EX, K3 ....$6.00
Paul Bunyan & the Babe Blue Ox, #2408, 1967, EX, K3....$8.00
Pink Panther Rides Again, #2403-1, 1976, EX, K3.............$6.00
Polka Dot Tots, #864, 1946, EX, K3 ....$10.00
Quick Draw McGraw, Badmen Beware, Top Top Tales, 1960, EX, T2 ....$20.00
Ricochet Rabbit's Showdown at Gopher Gulch Bakery, #2622, 1964, EX, K3 ....$10.00
Roy Rogers' Surprise for Donnie, #943, 1954, EX, K3 ......$20.00

Rudolph the Red-Nosed Reindeer, #2517-2, 1980, EX, K3 ..**$5.00**
Sleepy Puppy, #2400, 1961, EX, K3 ....**$5.00**
Snoozey, #2564, 1944, w/dust jacket, VG, K3 ....**$20.00**
Story of Christmas, #2446, 1965, EX, K3 ....**$5.00**
Sunny, Honey & Funny, #2640, 1951, EX, K3 ....**$12.00**
Three Bears, #2592, 1968, EX, K3 ....**$5.00**
Tom & Jerry & the Toy Circus, #2545, 1953, EX, K3 ......**$10.00**
Tommy Tractor, #381, 1947, EX, K3 ....**$8.00**
Tortoise & the Hare, Top Top Tale #2455, 1963, EX, K3..**$15.00**
Tweety & Sylvester at the Farm, #2642, 1978, EX, K3.......**$4.00**
Winnie the Pooh, #2526, 1974, EX, K3 ....**$4.00**
Wonderful Tony, #871, 1947, EX, K3 ....**$8.00**
Yogi Bear & the Cranky Magician, Top Top Tale #2494, 1963, EX, K3 ....**$10.00**
Yogi Bear Takes a Vacation, #2406, 1965, EX, K3 ....**$10.00**

Miscellaneous by Whitman

Andy Panda & His Friends, 1949, hardcover, 40 pgs, VG, T2....**$14.00**
Andy Panda's Rescue, 1969, softcover, NM, F8 ....**$8.00**
Beverly Hillbillies — Saga of Wildcreek, 1963, NM, P3 ..**$12.00**
Bozo the Clown King of the Ring, 1960, softcover, EX, F8...**$5.00**
Bugs Bunny's Adventures, Story Hour series, 1948, hardcover, 32 pgs, scarce, EX, T2 ....**$18.00**
Captain Midnight in Joyce of the Secret Squadron, 1942, hardcover, w/dust jacket, NM, F8 ....**$25.00**
Circus Boy Under the Big Top, 1957, NM, F8..........**$15.00**
Dick Tracy Meets the Night Crawler, 1945, hardcover, EX, D11 ....**$15.00**
Donald Duck, 1935, 1st edition, hardcover, G+, H7......**$300.00**
Donald Duck Has His Ups & Downs, 1937, 24 pgs, EX, A..........**$100.00**
Funny Company, Super Chief in the Big City, 1965, VG, F8 ....**$8.00**
Jetson's Birthday Surprise, 1963, NM, F8..........**$15.00**
Land of the Giants Flight of Fear, 1969, NM, F8..........**$15.00**
Little Orphan Annie & Her Dog Sandy, 1930s, softcover, VG, J5 ....**$15.00**
Mickey Mouse Has a Busy Day, 1937, 24 pgs, EX, A......**$120.00**
Mickey Mouse's Friends Wait for the County Fair, 1937, 24 pgs, EX, A **$120.00**
Mickey Mouse's Summer Vacation, 1949, softcover, NM, F8 ..**$18.00**
Mother Goose Rhymes, 1934, softcover, NM, T2 ....**$10.00**
Munsters Camera Caper, EX, P3 ....**$10.00**
Rebecca of Sunny Brook Farm, 1960, hardcover, EX, N2...**$15.00**
Rocky & Bullwinkle Go to Hollywood, 1961, softcover, EX, F8..........**$12.00**
Snow White & the Seven Dwarfs, 1938, softcover, 96 pgs, VG, J5 ....**$35.00**
Walt Disney's Famous Seven Dwarfs, hardcover, VG, M8 .**$45.00**
Woody Woodpecker's Peck of Trouble, 1951, VG, F8 ....**$4.00**

Wonder Books

A Horse for Johnny, #754, 1952, EX, K3 ....**$5.00**
A Surprise for Felix, 1959, 1st edition, NM, F8 ....**$12.00**
ABC & Counting Rhymes, #823, EX, K3 ....**$3.00**
Alice in Wonderland, #574, 1951, EX, K3..........**$8.00**
Baby Elephant, #541, 1950, EX, K3 ....**$10.00**
Bedtime Stories, #507, 1946, illus by Masha, EX, K3 ....**$15.00**
Brave Little Steam Shovel, #555, 1951, EX, K3..........**$5.00**
Buzzy the Funny Crow, 1963, EX, F8 ....**$15.00**
Casper & Wendy, #805, 1963, EX, K3 ....**$10.00**
Christmas in Song & Story, #586, 1953, illus by Catherine Scholz, EX, K3 ....**$6.00**
Copycat Colt, #545, 1951, illus by Charlotte Steiner, EX, K3 ....**$10.00**
Cozy Little Farm, #749, 1946, EX, K3 ....**$8.00**
Donkey Who Wanted To Be Wise, #771, 1961, EX, K3 ....**$4.00**
Famous Fairy Tales, #505, 1949, EX, K3 ....**$10.00**
Fred Flintstone the Fix-It Man, #917, 1976, EX, K3..........**$8.00**
Gandy Goose, #695, 1957, EX, K3 ....**$10.00**
Heckle & Jeckle Visit the Farm, 1958, EX, J5 ....**$25.00**
Hector Heathcote and the Knights, 1965, EX, F8 ....**$18.00**
Heidi, #532, 1950, EX, K3 ....**$5.00**
Hoppy the Curious Kangaroo, #579, 1952, EX, K3..........**$10.00**
How Peter Cottontail Got His Name, #668, 1957, by Thorton Burgess, EX, K3 ....**$8.00**
I Can Do Anything...Almost, #822, 1963, EX, K3 ....**$5.00**
Insects We Know, #747, 1960, EX, K3 ....**$5.00**
Kewtee Bear's Christmas, #867, 1956, EX, K3 ....**$8.00**
Let's Pretend, #680, 1959, EX, K3 ....**$4.00**
Little Car That Wanted a Garage, #573, 1952, EX, K3 ......**$8.00**
Little Duck Said Quack Quack Quack, #636, 1955, EX, K3 ...**$6.00**
Littlest Christmas Tree, #625, 1954, by Thorton Burgess, EX, K3 ....**$10.00**
Mary Alden's Cookbook for Children, #2518, 1955, softcover, EX, K3 ....**$25.00**
Minute-&-A-Half-Man, #758, 1960, EX, K3..........**$15.00**
Moppets Surprise Party, #794, 1955, Crosby Newell, EX, K3 ....**$12.00**
My ABC Book, #670, 1953, illus by Art Seiden, EX, K3....**$8.00**
Once There Was a House, #842, 1965, EX, K3..........**$8.00**
Peter Cottontail & Reddy Fox, #843, 1954, EX, K3 ....**$10.00**
Picture Story of Davy Crockett, #2525, 1955, EX, K3 ....**$5.00**
Pony Engine, #626, 1957, EX, K3 ....**$8.00**
Raggedy Ann & Marcella's First Day at School, #588, 1952, EX, K3 ....**$10.00**
Raggedy Ann's Merriest Christmas, 1952, EX, F8 ....**$12.00**
Romper Room Book of Happy Animals, #687R, 1957, EX, K3 ....**$8.00**
Sleepy Time for Everyone, #612, 1954, EX, K3 ....**$6.00**
Soupy Sales & the Talking Turtle, #960, 1965, EX, K3 ...**$10.00**
Surprise Doll, #519, 1949, EX, K3 ....**$30.00**
Tom Corbett's Trip to the Moon, #713, 1953, EX, K3 .....**$16.00**
Traveling Twins, #596, 1953, w/play money, EX, K3 ....**$22.00**
Tuggy the Tugboat, #696, 1958, EX, K3 ....**$8.00**
Visit to the Hospital, #690, EX, K3 ....**$5.00**
Water Water Everywhere, #607, 1953, EX, K3 ....**$8.00**
What Am I?, #832, illus by Dellwyn Cunningham, EX, K3 ..**$5.00**
Who Likes Dinner?, #598, 1953, EX, K3 ....**$8.00**
Why the Bear Has a Short Tail, #508, 1946, EX, K3........**$10.00**
Wonder Book of Christmas, #575, 1951, EX, K3 ....**$8.00**
Wonder Book of Firemen & Fire Engines, #637, 1956, EX, K3 ....**$8.00**
Yogi Bear Mosquito Flying Day, #924, 1976, EX, K3 ....**$5.00**
10 Rabbits, #601, EX, K3 ....**$5.00**

MISCELLANEOUS

ABC Nursery Rhymes, McLoughlin, ca 1900, EX, $225.00.

Photo courtesy Marvelous Books

Addams Family Monster Rally, Simon & Schuster, 1950, 1st edition, oversized softcover, EX+, F8 .... **$25.00**
Adventures of Mickey Mouse, McKay, 1st edition, gr version, hardcover, EX+, M8 .... **$165.00**
Adventures of Robin Hood & His Merry Men, Elf/Rand McNally, 1955, EX, K3.. **$10.00**
Adventures of Superman, by George Lowther, 1942, hardcover, w/dust jacket, scarce, EX, A **$200.00**
Aladdin & the Wonderful Lamp, McLoughlin Bros, 1940, EX, K3... **$20.00**
Alice in Wonderland, Random House, 1955, hardcover, EX, K3 .... **$60.00**
Batman & Robin From Alfred to Zowie, Golden Press, 1966, softcover, EX, A.. **$35.00**
Batman Vs the Joker, Signet, 1966, 1st edition, softcover, M, J5... **$25.00**

***Black Beauty,* by Anna Sewell, Winston publisher, 1927, cloth cover, EX, $60.00.**

Photo courtesy Marvelous Books

Berenstain's Baby Book, MacMillian, 1951, 1st edition, hardcover, EX, F8 .... **$15.00**
Bible Stories for Children, Samuel Lowe, 1945, hardcover, EX, K3 .... **$10.00**
Black Beauty, Lowe, 1959, softcover, EX, P3 .... **$5.00**
Blondie's Family, Treasure Book by Chic Young, 1954, EX, K3.. **$25.00**
Bobby Bear's Busy Day, Saalfield, 1952, hardcover, EX, K3 .**$15.00**
Brownie the Little Bear Who Likes People, McLoughlin Bros, 1939, EX, K3 .... **$20.00**
Buddy the Taxi, Elf/Rand McNally, 1958, EX, K3........... **$10.00**
Buffalo Bill, Tab Books, 1950, softcover, 275 pgs, EX, P3 ..**$6.00**
Captain January & Little Colonel, Random House, 1950s, hardcover, w/dust jacket, EX, A **$35.00**
Cold Blooded Penguin, Simon & Schuster, 1946, hardcover, w/dust jacket, NM, F8... **$25.00**
Contented Little Pussy Cat, by Frances Ruth Keller, 1949, hardcover, w/dust jacket, EX, G16 .... **$40.00**
David & Nancy's Train Ride, Jr Elf/Rand McNally, 1946, EX, K3.. **$15.00**
Dennis the Menace, Elf/Rand McNally, 1956, EX, K3..... **$12.00**
Dennis the Menace, Holt, 1953, hardcover, scarce, EX, T2 .**$30.00**
Dick Tracy & the Woo Sisters, Dell, 1947, softcover, NM, D11 .... **$75.00**
Dick Tracy Meets the Punks, Tempo, 1980, softcover, NM, D11 .... **$10.00**

***Donald Duck,* Whitman, 1st edition, EX, rare, $1,200.00.**

Photo courtesy Joel Cohen

Dr Seuss, How the Grinch Stole Christmas, late 1960s, hardcover, NM, F8 .... **$15.00**
Dr Seuss, Scrambled Eggs, Random House, 1953, hardcover, EX, F8... **$8.00**
Emmett Kelly in Willie the Clown, Elf/Rand McNally, 1957, EX, K3 .... **$15.00**
Felix the Cat, Treasure Books, 1953, EX, F8.................... **$15.00**
Five Busy Bears, Elf/Rand McNally, 1955, EX, K3............. **$8.00**
Flash Gordon in the Caverns of Mongo, Grosset & Dunlap, 1936, hardcover, 220 pgs, w/dust jacket, EX, A......... **$85.00**

Garfield on the Town, Ballantine, 1978, hardcover, NM, P3 ..$5.00
Gingerbread Man, McLoughlin Bros, 1939, EX, K3 ....$20.00
Ginny's First Secret, by Lee Kingman, 1958, hardcover, w/dust jacket, NM, G16 ....$125.00
Green Lantern & Green Arrow, Paperback Library, 1972, EX, A..$15.00
Hansel & Gretel, Samuel Lowe, 1944, softcover, EX, K3.$10.00

Honey Bear, **by Dixie Wilson, 1923, EX, $55.00.**

Hopalong Cassidy & the Bar 20 Cowboy, Golden, 1952, 1st edition, EX, F8..$20.00
House That Jack Built, Elf Jr/Rand McNally, 1942, EX, K3..$10.00
Humpty Dumpty, Jr Elf/Rand McNally, 1941, EX, K3 .....$20.00
It's a Great Pumpkin Charlie Brown, World Publishing, 1967, 1st edition, hardcover, EX, H11 ....$10.00
Jerry Lewis Book of Tricks & Magic, Random House, 1962, photo cover, worn spine o/w EX, F8.........................$20.00
King Kojo, by Ruth Plumly Thompson, 1938, hardcover, VG, A..$60.00
Land of Peek-A-Boo, Treasure Books, 1955, EX, K3 ....$20.00
Leave It to Beaver, Berkley, 1960, softcover, EX, F8 ....$15.00
Liddle Kiddles Shape Book, Golden/Mattel, 1968, diecut, softcover, EX, J5 ....$30.00
Little Bear's Ups & Downs, by Frances Margaret Fox, 1925, hardcover, EX, G16 ....$55.00
Little Lulu on Parade, David McKay, 1941, hardcover, w/dust jacket, EX, A...$80.00
Little Red Riding Hood, Jr Elf/Rand McNally, 1933, EX, K3..$20.00
Magic of Disneyland & Walt Disney World, Mayflower, 1979, hardcover, w/dust jacket, NM, F8 ....$30.00
Meet Dr Dolittle, Random House, 1967, hardcover, EX, F8.$15.00
Mickey Mouse & the Magic Carpet Book, Whitman/WDE, 1935, hardcover, 144 pgs, VG, A............................$110.00
Mickey Mouse Air Pilot, Walt Disney, 1937, hardcover, EX+, A $160.00
Mickey Mouse Circus, Birn Bros/England, 1930s, hardcover, NM, A $300.00
Mickey Mouse Sky High, England, hardcover, EX, A $175.00
Mickey Mouse Stories, David McKay/WD, 1934, hardcover, 62 pgs, EX, A $150.00
Mister Wizard's Junior Science Show, Elf/Rand McNally, 1957, EX, K3 ....$10.00
Mother Goose Favorites, Saalfield, 1904, linen cover, NM, G16..$45.00
Mr Snitzel's Cookies, Jr Elf/Rand McNally, 1950, EX, K3 .$10.00
Muggins' Becomes a Hero, Elf/Rand McNally, 1965, EX, K3 ....$12.00
Nanny & the Professor, Lancer, 1970, softcover, VG, F8...$8.00
Night Before Christmas, MA Donohue, 1920s, linen cover, VG+, P3 ....$35.00
One, Two, Cock-A-Doodle Doo, Jr Elf/Rand McNally, 1944, EX, K3 ....$10.00

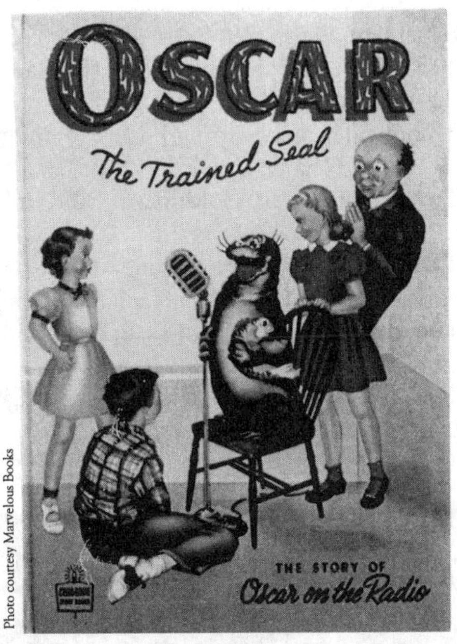

Oscar the Trained Seal, **by Mabel Neikirk, Whitman, 1948, EX, $35.00.**

Peppy the Lonely Little Puppy, Elf/Rand McNally, 1958, EX, K3 ....$15.00
Peter Pan, Grosset & Dunlap, 1942, hardcover, EX, T2...$15.00
Pinocchio, Jr Elf/Rand McNally, 1939, EX, K3................$15.00
Play It Again Charlie Brown, World Publishing, 1971, hardcover, EX, H11...$10.00
Popeye & the Pirates, 1945, spiral-bound hardcover, EX, A ..$35.00
Prince Valiant, Treasure Books, 1954, softcover, EX, F8..$12.00
Prince Valiant & the Golden Princess, by Hal Foster, Nostalgia, 1976, hardcover, w/dust jacket, NM, F8 ....$35.00
Prince Valiant in the Days of King Arthur, Treasure Books, 1950s, hardcover, EX, T2 ....$15.00
Puppy Dog Tales, Random House, 1964, EX, K3 ....$10.00
Puss in Boots, Samuel Lowe, 1944, softcover, EX, K3 ......$10.00
Raggedy Ann & Andy, Camel w/the Wrinkled Knees, Bobbs-Merrill, 1960, hardcover, VG, F8.............................$12.00
Raggedy Ann & the Golden Butterfly, by Johnny Gruelle, Bobbs-Merrill, 1961, hardcover, NM, F8 ....$35.00
Raggedy Ann & the Laughing Brook, Perks, 1946, softcover, EX, J5 ....$35.00
Raggedy Ann in Cookie Land, by Johnny Gruelle, Bobbs-Merrill, 1960, hardcover, NM, F8 ....$35.00

Raggedy Ann's Magical Wishes, Donohue publisher, 1928, hardcover, w/dust jacket, NM, G16..................................$95.00
Raggedy Ann's Mystery, by John Gruelle, Saalfield, 1962, softcover, EX, J5 ....$35.00
Rat Patrol in Desert Masquerade, Paperback Library #6, 1968, EX, F8..$15.00
Roy Rogers King of the Cowboys, by Frank Rasky, Messner, 1955, hardcover, EX, P4 ....$20.00
Rudolph the Red-Nosed Reindeer, by Robert L May, 1939, 1st printing, hardcover, 32 pgs, EX, D10 ....$50.00
Runaway Airplane, Jr Elf/Rand McNally, 1943, EX, K3...$15.00
Space Flight, Golden, 1959, NM, F8.................................$65.00
Superboy & the Legions of Super Heroes, Tempo Books, 1977, softcover, EX, A...$20.00
Superman, Lowther-Random House, 1942, hardcover, 215 pgs, EX, A $125.00
Superman, Signet, 1966, 1st edition, softcover, EX, F8....$12.00
Teddy Bear of Bumpkin Hollow, Elf/Rand McNally, 1956, VG, K3...$15.00
Thimble Theater Starring Popeye, Sonnet Publishing Co, 1931, series 1, hardcover, EX, A..$75.00
Three Bears Visit Goldilocks, Elf/Rand McNally, 1950, EX, K3...$15.00
Thumper, Grosset & Dunlap, 1942, hardcover, w/full-color wraparound, EX, J5 ....$25.00
Timothy the Little Brown Bear, Jr Elf/Rand McNally, 1949, EX, K3...$10.00
Traveling Bears' Birthday, by Seymour Eaton, 1921, hardcover, w/dust jacket, rare, NM, G16 ....$145.00

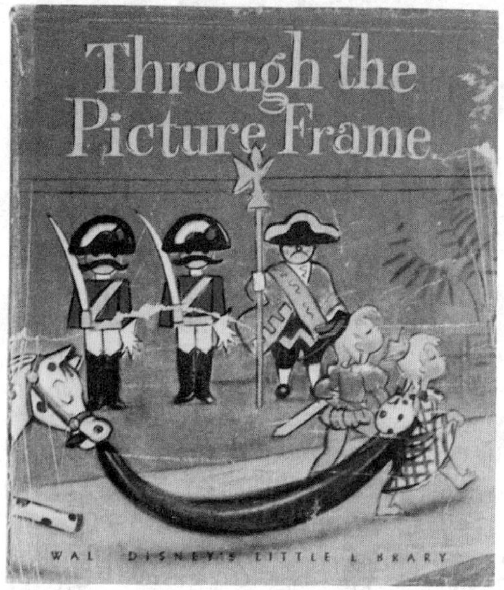

***Through the Picture Frame*, Hans Christian Andersen, 1944, 1st edition, VG, $45.00.**

'Twas the Night Before Christmas, McLoughlin Bros, 1910, hardcover, rare, NM, A $650.00
Uncle Remus, Golden, 1947, 1st edition, EX, F8 ....$16.00
Uncle Wiggily's Woodland Games, by Howard R Garis, 1931, hardcover, NM, G16 ....$45.00
Walt Disney Annual, Whitman, 1937, hardcover, 123 pgs, w/dust jacket, EX, A $140.00
Waltons Trouble on the Mountain, 1975, softcover, EX, F8 .$4.00
Wild Bill Hickok & Deputy Marshall Joey, Elf/Rand McNally, 1954, EX, K3 ....$12.00
Wizard of Oz, Grosset & Dunlap, Jr Library edition, illus by Evelyn Copelman, hardcover, EX (EX cb slip case), A ...$50.00
Wonderful Treasure Hunt, Treasure Books, 1952, EX, K3 .$8.00

Breyer

Breyer collecting seems to be growing in popularity, and though the horses dominate the market, the company also made dogs, cats, farm animals, wildlife figures, dolls, and tack and accessories such as barns for their models. They've been in continuous production since the '50s, all strikingly beautiful and lifelike in both modeling and color. Earlier models were glossy, but since 1968 a matt finish has been used, though glossy and semiglossy colors are now being re-introduced, especially in special runs. (A special run of Family Arabians was done in the glossy finish in 1988.)

One of the hardest things for any model collector is to determine the value of his or her collection. The values listed below are for models in excellent to near mint condition. This means no rubs, no scratches, no chipped paint, and no breaks — nothing that cannot be cleaned off with a rag and little effort. Any model which has been altered in any way, including having the paint touched up, is considered a customized model and has an altogether different set of values from an original finish model. The models listed herein have their original finishes, meaning they have not been altered or customized in any way. For more information, see *Breyer Animal Collector's Guide* by Felicia Browell (Collector Books).

Advisor: Carol Karbowiak Gilbert (G6).

Classic Scale Models

Andalusian Foal, dk chestnut, 1979-93, G6......................$15.00
Andalusian Mare, dapple gray, 1979-93, G6....................$15.00
Arabian Foal, alabaster, 1973-82, G6...............................$30.00
Arabian Foal, matt gray, 1973-82, G6..............................$25.00
Arabian Mare, matt chestnut, 1973-91, G6.....................$15.00
Arabian Stallion, matt sorrel, 1980-93, G6......................$15.00
Black Stallion (Black Stallion Returns Set), 1983-93, G6 .$15.00
Bucking Bronco, matt gray, 1961-67, G6.......................$150.00
Ginger (Black Beauty Family), matt chestnut, 1980-93, G6..$15.00
Jet Run (US Equestrian Gift Set), matt bay, 1980-93, G6..$15.00
Johar (Black Stallion Returns Set), matt alabaster, 1980-93, G6 ....$15.00
Kelso, matt dk bay, 1975-90, G6 ....$20.00
Lipizzan Stallion, matt alabaster, 1975-80, G6 ....$40.00
Man O'War, matt red chestnut, 1975-90, G6..................$25.00
Merrylegs (Pony for Keeps Set), matt alabaster, 1990-91, G6...$15.00
Mesteno the Messenger, 1992-1997, G6..........................$15.00
Might Tango (US Equestrian Team Gift Set), matt dapple gray, 1980-91, G6..$15.00
Mustang Foal, matt chestnut, 1976-90, G6......................$15.00
Mustang Mare, matt chestnut pinto, 1976-90, G6............$20.00

Mustang Stallion, matt chestnut, 1976-90, G6 .... **$15.00**
Polo Pony, matt bay, 1976-82, G6 .... **$60.00**
Quarter Horse Foal, matt red bay, 1975-82, G6 .... **$20.00**
Quarter Horse Mare, matt bay, 1974-93, G6 .... **$20.00**
Quarter Horse Stallion, matt palomino, 1974-93, G6 ...... **$15.00**
Rearing Stallion, matt bay, 1965-80, G6 .... **$30.00**
Ruffian, matt bay, 1977-90, G6 .... **$35.00**
Silky Sullivan, matt brn, 1975-90, G6 .... **$25.00**
Swaps, matt chestnut, 1975-90, G6 .... **$25.00**
Terrang, matt dk brn, 1975-90, G6 .... **$25.00**

Traditional Scale

Action Stock Horse Foal, matt bay pinto, 1984-86, G6 ... **$20.00**
Adios Famous Standardbred, 1969-80, G6 .... **$40.00**
Appaloosa Performance Horse, 1974-80, G6 .... **$40.00**
Appaloosa Performance Horse (Brenda Breyer Gift Set), chestnut blanket, 1980-85, w/doll & tack, G6 .... **$50.00**
Appaloosa Performance Horse (JC Penney), gray blanket, 1984, G6 .... **$95.00**
Appaloosa Stock Horse Foal, 1984-88, G6 .... **$20.00**

Bear Cub, brown-faced version, 1967 – 73, $25.00; Mother Bear, brown-faced version, 1967 – 73, $35.00.

Bison, $50.00.

Balking Mule, liver chestnut, 1968-71, G6 .... **$150.00**
Balking Mule, matt bay, 1968-73, G6 .... **$150.00**
Belgian, chestnut w/red & yel ribbon, 1965-80, G6 .... **$100.00**
Belgian, glossy dapple gray or blk, 1964-67, G6, ea **$650.00**
Belgian, woodgrain, 1964-65, G6 .... **$1,000.00**
Belgian (Disney World), semi-gloss blk w/wht & bl ribbon, 1984, G6 .... **$100.00**
Belgian Brabant, matt grulla, 1991-93, G6 .... **$40.00**
Black Beauty, 1979-88, G6 .... **$30.00**
Black Stallion, 1981-88, G6 .... **$30.00**
Buckshot Famous Spanish Barb, 1985-88, G6 .... **$40.00**

Boxer, 1954 – 73, $30.00.

Calf, $30.00; Cow, $35.00.

Calypso Quarter Horse, matt red dun, 1995-96, G6 .... **$20.00**
Cantering Welsh Pony, matt bay w/yel ribbons, 1971-73, G6 .... **$100.00**
Cantering Welsh Pony, matt chestnut w/red ribbons, 1971-76, G6 .... **$55.00**
Cantering Welsh Pony, seal brn w/bl ribbons, 1971-74, G6 .. **$125.00**
Cantering Welsh Pony (Small World), dapple gray w/gold ribbons, 1987, G6 .... **$150.00**
Cantering Welsh Pony (Small World), red roan w/yel ribbons, 1988, G6 .... **$100.00**
Clydesdale Foal (JC Penney Clydesdale Family Set), matt bay, 1982-84, G6 .... **$75.00**

Clydesdale Mare, matt lt bay, 1990-91, G6 .... $30.00
Clydesdale Stallion, glossy dapple gray w/gold bobs, 1961-65, G6 .... $150.00
Clydesdale Stallion, woodgrain, 1960-65, G6 .... $250.00
Cricket Quarter Horse Foal, 1995-present, G6 .... $15.00
Donkey, 1958-74, G6 .... $25.00
Dream Weaver, 1991 limited edition, G6 .... $40.00
El Pastor Paso Fino, 1974-81, G6 .... $50.00
Family Arabian Foal, glossy gray blanket appaloosa, 1963-67, G6 .... $20.00
Family Arabian Foal, glossy palomino, 1961-66, G6 .... $15.00
Family Arabian Foal, matt liver chestnut, 1988, G6 .... $25.00

Photo courtesy Carol Karbowiak Gilbert

Family Arabian Mare, 1967 – 87, $20.00; Rearing Stallion, 1965 – 76 and 1978 – 86, $25.00.

Family Arabian Mare, glossy alabaster, 1961-66, G6 .... $30.00
Family Arabian Mare, woodgrain, 1963-67, G6 .... $100.00
Family Arabian Stallion, glossy bay, 1959-66, G6 .... $35.00
Family Arabian Stallion, glossy gray blanket appaloosa, 1963-67, G6 .... $40.00
Fighting Stallion, glossy florentine, 1963-65, G6 .... $1,000.00
Five-Gaiter Commander, glossy palomino w/red & yel ribbons, 1962-71, G6 .... $125.00
Five-Gaiter Commander, Wedgewood w/blk & bl ribbons, 1964-65, G6 .... $1,500.00
Five-Gaiter Commander, woodgrain w/bl & wht ribbons, 1963-65, G6 .... $200.00
Foal (Frisky Foals Set), matt yel dun, 1992, G6 .... $20.00
Foal (Sears Collectible Stock Horse Family Set), matt buckskin, 1984, G6 .... $30.00
Foundation Stallion, matt blk, 1977-87, G6 .... $40.00
Fury Prancer, glossy dk plum, w/Davy Crockett rider, 1954-58, G6 .... $150.00
Fury Prancer Black Beauty, glossy, 1954-64, G6 .... $125.00
Galiceno, matt bay, 1978-82, G6 .... $50.00
Grayingham Lucky Lad (Breyerfest Dinner Model), 1993, G6 .... $125.00
Grazing Mare Buttons, matt bay, 1964-76 & 1978-82, G6, ea $50.00

Haflinger, matt sorrel, 1979-84, G16 .... $40.00
Hanoverian, matt bay, 1980-84, G6 .... $55.00
Indian Pony, matt alabaster, 1970-71, G6 .... $225.00
Indian Pony, matt brn pinto, 1970-76, G6 .... $75.00
John Henry, 1988-90, G6 .... $40.00
Jumping Horse, seal brn, Sears, 1982-83, G6 .... $100.00
Justin Morgan, matt dk bay, 1990-92, G6 .... $35.00
King the Fighting Stallion, glossy charcoal, 1961-71, G6 .... $150.00
King the Fighting Stallion, woodgrain, 1963-73, G6 .... $125.00
Kipper, 1986, G6 .... $80.00
Lady Phase (Sears Spirit of the West Gift Set), matt bay pinto, G6 .... $50.00
Lady Roxanna, 1986-88, G6 .... $40.00
Legionario Spanish Pride, matt bay, 1991-92, G6 .... $35.00
Lying Foal, matt red roan, 1969-73, G6 .... $75.00
Majestic Arabian Stallion, 1989-90, G6 .... $40.00
Man O'War, 1969-95, G6 .... $25.00
Man O'War (Sears Race Horse Set), glossy chestnut, 1990, G6 .... $40.00
Misty, flocked palomino pinto, Sears, 1984, G6 .... $70.00
Misty's Twilight, 1991-95, G6 .... $25.00
Morgan, matt lt bay, 1988-89, G6 .... $40.00
Morgan, woodgrain, 1963-85, G6 .... $750.00
Mustang, glossy alabaster, red eyes, semi-rearing, 1961-66, G6 .... $200.00
Mustang, glossy alabaster, red eyes, 1961-66, G6 .... $200.00
Mustang, glossy charcoal, semi-rearing, 1961-70, G6 .... $150.00
Mustang, glossy Copenhagen, semi-rearing, 1963-65, G6 .... $1,500.00
Old Timer, glossy dapple gray, 1966-87, G6 .... $80.00
Old Timer, matt bay, 1988-90, G6 .... $40.00
Pacer, matt dk bay, 1967-87, G6 .... $45.00
Palomino (Breyer Rider Gift Set), 1976, w/doll & tack (only 5 made), G6 .... $250.00
Pluto, lt dapple gray, Spiegel, 1993, G6 .... $90.00
Pony of the Americas, chestnut leopard appaloosa, 1976-80, G6 .... $50.00
Porcelain Icelandic Horse, 1992, G6 .... $250.00
Porcelain Premier Arabian Mare, 1995, G6 .... $225.00
Porcelain Saddlebred Parade Horse, 1996, G6 .... $225.00

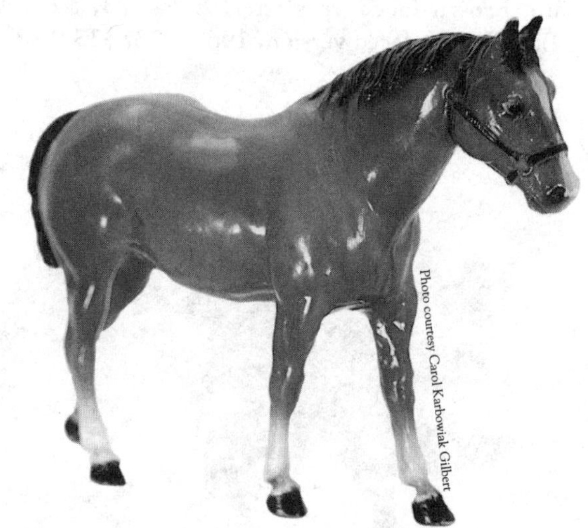

Photo courtesy Carol Karbowiak Gilbert

Quarter Horse Gelding, glossy bay, 1959 – 66, $150.00.

Porcelain Shire, 1993, G6 ....$250.00
Prancing Arabian Stallion, matt palomino, 1989-91, G6.$40.00
Proud Arabian Foal, glossy alabaster, 1956-60, G6 ....$40.00
Proud Arabian Foal, glossy gray blanket appaloosa, 1956-60, G6 ....$125.00
Proud Arabian Foal, woodgrain, 1956-60, G6 ....$1,250.00
Proud Arabian Stallion, dapple rose gray, 1991-94, G6....$40.00
Quarter Horse Gelding, buckskin, 1961-80, G6 ....$50.00
Quarter Horse Gelding, woodgrain, 1963-65, G6...........$225.00
Quarter Horse Stallion, matt blk roan, 1990, G6 ....$35.00
Quarter Horse Yearling, matt palomino, 1970-80, G6......$40.00
Racehorse, glossy chestnut, 1956-67, G6 ....$150.00
Racehorse, woodgrain, 1958-66, G6 ....$250.00
Reigseckers Palomino, red & yel ribbon, 1984, G6 ....$150.00
Running Foal, alabaster, 1963-71, G6.............................$45.00
Running Foal, glossy Florentine, 1963-65, G6...............$800.00
Running Foal, matt alabaster, 1963-71, G6 ....$45.00
Running Mare, glossy Copenhagen, 1963-64, G6.......$1,500.00
Running Mare (JC Penney Spirit of the West Set), soft gray, 1994, G6 ....$40.00
Running Stallion, blk blanket appaloosa, 1968-81, G6....$40.00
Running Stallion, matt alabaster, 1968-71, G6 ....$125.00
Saddlebred Weanling, matt chestnut, 1973-80, G6..........$50.00
San Domingo, blanket appaloosa, 1988-89, G6................$40.00
Scratching Foal, matt liver chestnut, 1970-71, G6.........$125.00
Secretariat, 1987-95, G6....................$25.00
Sherman Morgan, matt chestnut, 1987-90, G6 ....$50.00
Shetland Pony, glossy & matt alabaster, 1960-72, G6......$50.00
Shire, dapple gray, 1972-73 & 1975-76, G6, ea.............$100.00
Stallion (Princess of Arabia Set), lt dapple gray, 1995 limited edition, w/rider & tack, G6 ....$50.00
Stallion (Sears Running Horse Family), matt red bay, 1984, G6 ....$50.00
Stock Horse Foal, appaloosa, smooth coat, 1983-86, G6..$25.00
Stock Horse Mare, matt sorrel, 1983-86, G6 ....$35.00
Stock Horse Stallion, appaloosa, 1981-86, G6.................$40.00
Stud Spider, chestnut blanket appaloosa, 1990-91, G6 ....$35.00

Trakehner, semi-gloss and matt bay, 1979 – 84, $30.00.

Western Horse, glossy blk, 1959-62, G6 ....$150.00
Western Pony, glossy palomino, 1956-67, G6...................$40.00
Western Prancer, matt buckskin, 1961-73, G6 ....$60.00
Winchester (Breyerfast Raffle Model), 1994, G6 ....$1,700.00

Bubble Bath Containers

Since back in the 1960s when the Colgate-Palmolive Company produced the first Soaky, hundreds of different characters and variations have been marketed, bought on demand of the kids who saw these characters day to day on TV by parents willing to try anything that might make bathtime more appealing. Purex made their Bubble Club characters, and Avon and others followed suit. Most Soaky bottles came with detachable heads made of brittle plastic which cracked easily. Purex bottles were made of a softer plastic but tended to loose their paint.

Rising interest in US bubble bath containers has created a collector market for those made in foreign countries, i.e, UK, Canada, Italy, Germany, and Japan. Licensing in other countries creates completely different designs and many characters that are never issued here. Foreign containers are generally larger and are modeled in great detail, reminiscent of the bottles that were made in the US in the '60s. Prices may seem high, considering that some of these are of fairly recent manufacture, but this is due to their limited availablity and the costs associated with obtaining them in the United States. We believe these prices are realistic, though many have been reported much higher. Rule of thumb: pay what you feel comfortable with — after all, it's meant to be fun. And remember, value is affected to a great extent by condition. Unless noted otherwise, our values are for examples in near-mint condition. Bottles in very good condition are worth only about 60% to 65% of these prices. For slip-over styles, add 100% if the bottle is present. For more information we recommend *Collector's Guide to Bubble Bath Containers* by Greg Moore and Joe Pizzo (Collector Books).

Advisors: Matt and Lisa Adams (A7).

Alvin (Chipmunks), Soaky, red sweater w/wht A, w/contents, neck tag & puppet, M, A7....................$75.00
Alvin (Chipmunks), Soaky, wht sweater w/blk A, cap head, NM, A7....................$30.00
Atom Ant, Purex, orange body w/red accents, EX, A7.....$50.00
Augie Doggie, Purex, orange body w/gr shirt, orig tag & card, EX+, A7 ....$50.00
Baba Louie, Purex, brn w/bl scarf & gr hat, NM, A7........$35.00
Baby Bop, Kid Care, M, A7 ....$5.00
Baloo Bear, Colgate-Palmolive, 1960s, slipover only, NM, A7 ....$25.00
Bambi, Soaky, sitting & smiling, NM, A7 ....$25.00
Bamm-Bamm, Purex, gr suspenders w/wht & blk accents, NM, A7 ....$40.00
Barney, Kid Care, dressed as Santa, M, A7 ....$8.00
Barney Rubble, Milvern (Purex), bl outfit w/yel accents, NM, A7 ....$40.00
Barney Rubble, Purex, 1960s, brn & yel, NM, A7............$30.00
Batman, Avon, MIB $25.00

Beatles, Ringo Starr, Colgate-Palmolive, EX, from $100.00 to $125.00.

Beatles, Colgate-Palmolive, any member, EX, from $100 to .$125.00
Bert (Sesame Street), Minnetonka, holding boat, orig tag, NM, A7.....$8.00
Betty Bubbles, Lander, pk dress & red hair, EX, A7.........$20.00
Big Bad Wolf, Tubby Time, 1960s, gray & red w/cap head, NM, A7.....$40.00
Big Bird, Minnetonka, holding scrub brush & soap, w/tag, NM, A7.....$8.00
Bozo the Clown, Step Riley, cap head, EX, A7.........$30.00
Brontosaurus, Avon, 1970s, MIB, A7.........$15.00
Broom Hilda, VG.........$35.00
Brutus (Popeye), red shorts w/red & wht striped shirt, EX, A7.....$40.00
Bugs Bunny, Colgate-Palmolive, 1960s, gray, wht & orange, cap ears, NM, A7.....$30.00
Bullwinkle, Soaky, all brn, NM, A7.........$40.00
Bullwinkle, Soaky, striped shirt, NM.........$50.00

Cecil Sea Serpent, Purex, 1960s, MIB, A7, $75.00.

Cinderella, Soaky, 1960s, movable arms, NM, A7.........$35.00
Concertina, Avon, 1970, yel, MIB, A7.........$15.00
Cookie Monster, Minnetonka, holding sailboat, w/tag, NM, A7.....$8.00

Deputy Dawg, Colgate-Palmolive, 1960s, NM, $30.00; Dick Tracy, Soaky, EX, $45.00.

Donald Duck, Colgate-Palmolive, 1960s, wht & bl, NM, A7.....$30.00
Dopey, Colgate-Palmolive, 1960s, bank, purple & yel, NM, A7.....$30.00
Dragon Heart, Cosrich, dragon sitting on well, w/contents & orig tag, NM, A7.....$5.00
Droop-A-Long Coyote, Purex, pk w/bl & orange accents, gr hat, EX, A7.....$40.00
Dum Dum, Purex, 1966, scarce, NMIB.........$145.00
El Cabong, Knickerbocker, 1960s, blk, yel & wht, rare, NM, A7.....$75.00
Elmer Fudd, Soaky, in hunting outfit, NM, A7.........$30.00
ET, Avon, 1983, wearing bathrobe, NM, A7.........$15.00
Felix the Cat, Soaky, red body, EX+, A7.........$35.00
Fire Truck, Colgate-Palmolive, 1960s, red w/ladder & movable wheels, NM, A7.....$40.00
Flintstones Fun Bath, Roclar (Purex), 1970s, MIB (unopened), A7.....$75.00
Flipper, Kid Care, riding a wave, M, A7.........$8.00
Fozzie Bear, Calgon, Treasure Island outfit, M, A7.........$10.00
Fred Flintstone, Purex, 1960s, blk & red, NM, A7.........$30.00
Freddie the Frog, Avon, 1970, wht mug-shape w/image of frog, orange top, MIB, A7.....$15.00
Goofy, Colgate-Palmolive, 1960s, red, wht & blk w/cap head, NM, A7.....$25.00
Gravel Truck, Colgate Palmolive, 1960s, orange & gray w/movable wheels, NM, A7.....$40.00
Gumby & Pokey, M&L, shampoo & conditioner, orig shrink-wrap & stickers, M, A7.....$40.00

Huckleberry Hound, Knickerbocker, bank, red & blk, w/contents & orig neck card, M, A7 ....$65.00
Huckleberry Hound, Selcol, 1960s, bank, bl w/yel bow tie, rare, EX, A7 ....$125.00
Irwin Troll, Lander, 1970s, w/contents, M, A7....................$25.00
Jiminy Cricket, Colgate-Palmolive, 1960s, gr, blk & red, NM, A7 ....$30.00
King Louie, Colgate-Palmolive, 1960s, slipover only, NM, A7 ....$25.00
Lippy the Lion, Purex, purple vest, EX, A7....................$40.00
Lucy (Peanuts), Avon, 1970, red dress, MIB, A7 ....$25.00
Lunar Leader, Koscot, Martian-type alien waving US flag, NM, A $45.00
Magilla Gorilla, Purex, 1960s, movable or non-movable arms, NM, A7, ea $60.00
Mickey Mouse, Soaky, dressed as band leader, NM, A7...$30.00
Mighty Mouse, Lander, 1970s, VG, A7 ....$25.00

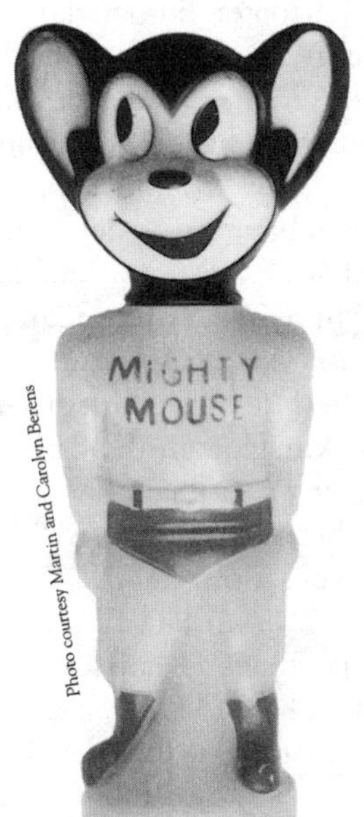

MIGHTY
MOUSE
Photo courtesy Martin and Carolyn Berens

Mighty Mouse, Soaky, NM, $25.00.

Miss Piggy, Calgon, Treasure Island outfit, M, A7 ....$10.00
Morocco Mole, Purex, rare, EX, A7 ....$100.00
Mousketeer Girl, Colgate-Palmolive, 1960s, red outfit w/orange or yel hair, NM, A7, ea....................$30.00
Mr Jinx w/Pixie & Dixie, Purex, 1960s, orange w/gray mice, NM, A7....................$30.00
Mr Magoo, Colgate-Palmolive, NM....................$50.00
Mush Mouse, Purex, purple vest, head & hat, EX, A7 .....$30.00
Muskie, Soaky, 1960s, NMIB, A7 ....$40.00
Oscar the Grouch, Minnetonka, holding trash can lid, M, A7 ....$10.00
Panda Bear, Tubby Time, 1960s, wht & blk w/cap head, NM, A7 ....$30.00
Pebbles Flintstone, Purex, 1960s, gr shirt w/yel shorts or purple shirt w/bl shorts, EX, A7, ea $40.00
Pluto, Colgate-Palmolive, 1960s, orange w/cap head, NM, A7 ....$25.00
Popeye, Soaky, 1960s, wht suit w/bl accents, MIB, A7.....$55.00

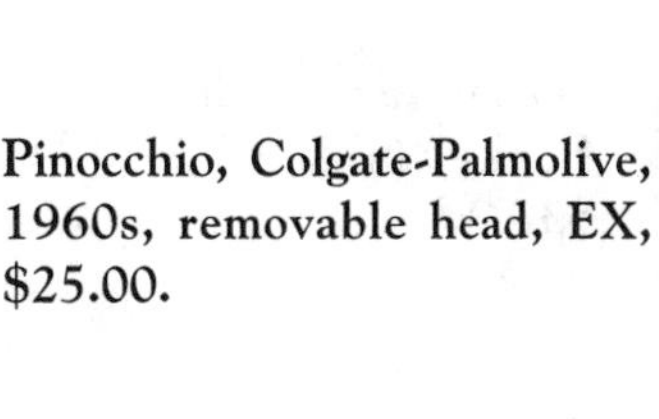

Pinocchio, Colgate-Palmolive, 1960s, removable head, EX, $25.00.

Porky Pig, Colgate-Palmolive, removable head, EX $25.00
Power Rangers, Kid Care, any character, M, A7, ea $8.00
Punkin' Puss, Purex, orange body w/bl clothing, VG, A7.$40.00
Ricochet Rabbit, Purex, 1960s, movable or non-movable arm, NM, A7, ea $50.00
Sailor, Avon, VG....................$12.00
Santa, Colgate-Palmolive, NMIB....................$30.00
Schroeder (Peanuts), Avon, 1970, MIB, A7....................$35.00
Secret Squirrel, Purex, yel w/purple hat, VG, A7 ....$50.00
Simon (Chipmunks), Soaky, gr sweater w/wht S, w/contents, tag & puppet, M, A7 ....$75.00
Skeletor (Masters of the Universe), Ducair Bio, NM, A7 .$20.00
Smokey Bear, Colgate-Palmolive, bl pants, yel cap hat, NM, A7 ....$30.00
Snaggle Puss, Purex, 1960s, pk w/gr hat, NM, A7 ....$65.00
Snoopy, Avon, 1969, Flying Ace outfit, MIB, A7 ....$30.00
Snow White, Colgate-Palmolive, 1960s, bank, bl & yel, NM, A7 ....$30.00
Snow White, Soaky, movable arms, NM, A7 ....$35.00
Spider-Man, Colgate-Palmolive, NMIB....................$55.00
Spouty Whale, Roclar, 1970s, orig label, M, J5....................$25.00
Squiddly Diddly, 1960s, purple & pk, NM, A7....................$75.00
Superman, Soaky, bl w/red outfit, EX, A7....................$50.00
Tasmanian Devil, Kid Care, standing in inner tube, EX, A7 ..$8.00
Teenage Mutant Ninja Turtles, Kid Care, pk shirt & swords, M, A7....................$8.00
Theodore (Chipmunks), Soaky, wht w/bl T, w/contents, neck tag & puppet, M, A7 ....$75.00
Tidy Toy Race Car, red or bl w/movable wheels, NM, A7, ea....................$50.00
Touche Turtle, Purex, 1960s, turq or red w/purple feathers, lying down, NM, A7, ea $50.00
Tweety Bird, Soaky, standing on cage, EX, A7 ....$30.00
Woodsy Owl, Lander, early 1970s, brn, gr & yel, NM, A7 .$45.00
Yakky Doodle Duck, Roclar (Purex), w/contents & neck card, M, A7....................$25.00
Yogi Bear, Purex, 1961, bank, NM $40.00

Wendy the Witch, Soaky, NM, A7, $30.00.

Photo courtesy Matt and Lisa Adams

Wolfman, Frankenstein, Creature From the Black Lagoon, Mummy, NM, $100.00 each.

FOREIGN

Action Man (Space Commando), Rosedew Ltd/UK, bl & gray uniform w/lg gun, M, A7 ....$10.00
Aladdin, Damascar/Italy, standing w/arms crossed, M, A7 ....$20.00
Aladdin, Grosvenor/UK, on flying carpet w/Jasmin & monkey, M, A7 ....$20.00
Algy Pug (Rupert), Euromark/UK, yel shirt & vest w/purple pants, red base, M, A7 ....$25.00
Alice in Wonderland, Aidee International Ltd/UK, 1993, standing in grass w/rabbit, NM, A7 ....$35.00
Angus the Panda (Creature Comforts), Rosedew Ltd/UK, blk & wht w/tan glasses, hand outstretched, M, A7 ....$20.00
Ariel (Little Mermaid), Damascar/Italy, 1995, sitting on purple rock, NM, A7 ....$25.00
Baloo (Jungle Book), Prelude/UK, dancing, M, A7 ....$20.00
Barbie, Grosvenor/UK, 1995, pk & wht wedding dress w/heart tag, NM, A7 ....$25.00
Barney Rubble, Damascar/Italy, 1995, wearing Water Buffalo hat w/bowling ball, M, A7 ....$50.00
Barney Rubble, Rosedew/UK, leaning on club, M, A7 ....$40.00
Barney Rubble, Rosedew/UK, standing at attention, M, A7 ..$40.00
Batman, Damascar/Italy, animated version, standing, M, A7 ..$20.00
Batman, Grosvenor/UK, 1992, c DC Comics, gray suit & blk cape, NM, A7 ....$30.00
Batmobile (Batman Forever), Prelude/UK, blk w/silver wheels, body lifts for bottle, M, A7 ....$20.00
Beast (Beauty & the Beast), Prelude/UK, 1994, movable arms, comes apart at waist, lg, NM, A7 ....$30.00
Belle (Beauty & the Beast), Centura/Canada, 1994, yel gown & gloves, NM, A7 ....$20.00
Boo Boo Bear, Damascar/Italy, sitting on 3 picnic baskets eating an apple, M, A7 ....$50.00
Bubba Saurus, Belvedere/Canada, bank, pk dinosaur, M, A7 ..$10.00
Budgie Helicopter, Euromark/UK, bl w/yel hat, M, A7 ....$20.00
Bugs Bunny, Centura/Canada, 1994, purple robe, holds carrot, NM, A7 ....$25.00
Bugs Bunny, Prelude/UK, gr trunks & red shoes, arms posed, M, A7 ....$20.00
Bump (Elephant), Rosedew/UK, bl w/yel overalls, bandaid on head, M, A7 ....$20.00
Buzz Lightyear, Centura/Canada, comes apart at waist, M, A7 ....$15.00
Casper the Friendly Ghost, Damascar/Italy, 1995, sitting on a pumpkin, glow-in-the-dark, NM, A7 ....$35.00
Cindy Bear (Yogi Bear), Damascar/Italy, sitting on purple rock, gray head & body, M, A7 ....$50.00
Daffy Duck, Prelude/UK, 1994, wearing shark suit, NM, A7 ....$30.00
Dino (Flintstones), Damascar/Italy, 1995, standing on food dish w/giant bone, M, A7 ....$50.00
Dino (Flintstones), Rosedew/UK, sitting up w/arms & legs at side, M, A7 ....$35.00
Dino Bubbles, Euromark/UK, gr or yel dinosaur, M, A7, ea..$15.00
Doc & Dopey, Grosvenor/UK, Fairytale Fragrance Foam Bath, M, A7 ....$10.00
Donald Duck, Grosvenor/UK, drying off back w/towel, M, A7 ....$20.00
Donald Duck, Mann & Schroder/German, 1970s, standing w/arms on hips, M, A7 ....$45.00
Donald Duck (Mickey & Pals), Centura/Canada, 1995, driving yel boat, NM, A7 ....$25.00
Dump Truck (Matchbox), Grosvenor/UK, yel, blk & red, cap on front, M, A7 ....$20.00
Fireman Sam, Woodand/UK, holding fire hose, M, A7....$20.00
Forever Friends, Grosvenor/UK, bear taking bath in wooden tub, M, A7 ....$15.00
Fred Flintstone, Damascar/Italy, 1994, standing w/golf club, M, A7 ....$50.00
Fred Flintstone, Rosedew/UK, standing at attention, M, A7...$40.00
Genie (Aladdin), Prelude/UK, sitting w/arms crossed, NM, A7 ....$25.00
Jafar (Aladdin), Grosvenor/UK, standing w/scepter & bird on shoulder, M, A7 ....$25.00

Jasmin (Aladdin), Prelude/UK, 1994, gr outfit, holds bird in hand, NM, A7 ....$25.00
Jemima Puddleduck (Beatrix Potter), Grosvenor/UK/Canada, bl bonnet, M, A7 ....$15.00
Little Mermaid, Grosvenor/UK, sitting in clam shell, M, A7....$25.00
Louie Duck, Rosedew/UK, gr outfit & hat, M, A7 ....$25.00
Mickey Mouse, Centura/Canada, red shirt w/bl pants & yel shoes, M, A7 ....$30.00
Mickey Mouse, Disney/Canada, 1994, blk tuxedo, red pants & yel tie, NM, A7....$30.00
Mickey Mouse (Fantasia), Centura/Canada, 1994, red robe, bl star & moon hat, NM, A7....$30.00
Minnie Mouse, Disney/Canada, 1994, pie-eyed, traditional 1930s outfit, NM, A7 ....$30.00
Mowgli & Kaa (Jungle Book), Prelude/UK, 1994, snake wrapped around boy, NM, A7....$30.00
Nala (Lion King), Centura/Canada, sitting on pk base, M, A7....$20.00
Noddy, Grosvenor/UK, red shirt & bl shorts, w/dog, M, A7 ....$25.00
Olive Oyl, Damascar/Italy, 1995, sitting w/hands clasped, M, A7....$50.00
Papa Smurf, IMPS Brussels/Germany, 1991, bl w/red pants & hat, wht beard, NM, A7 ....$30.00
Pebbles & Bamm-Bamm, Damascar/Italy, sitting on sabertooth tiger, M, A7 ....$50.00
Percy (Thomas the Tank), Grosvenor/UK, 1994, on blk tracks & gray bricks, NM, A7 ....$20.00
Pingu, Grosvenor/UK, penguin standing on igloo, M, A7.$20.00
Pink Panther, UK, 1972, standing at attention, M, A7....$75.00
Pocahontas, Centura/Canada, 1995, sitting on rock in grass, NM, A7....$25.00
Popeye, Damascar/Italy, standing on spinach crate, M, A7 .$50.00
Popeye, Rosedew Ltd/UK, 1987, holds spinach can, blk base, 10", NM, A7 ....$40.00
Power Rangers, Centura/Canada, any character, M, A7, ea .$20.00
Pumba & Timon (Lion King), Grosvenor/UK, Timon on Pumba's back, M, A7....$25.00
Race Car, Jackel/UK, orange & yel w/lg wheels, cap on back, M, A7 ....$20.00
RoboCop, Euromark/UK, 1995, movable, standing on gray bricks, NM, A7 ....$30.00
Rupert Bear, Euromark/UK, w/backpack, NMIB, A7 ....$30.00
Scooby Doo, Damascar/Italy, sitting, M, A7 ....$60.00
Scrappy Doo, Damascar/Italy, 1995, coming out of well w/water creature, NM, A7....$35.00
Sleeping Beauty, Damascar/Italy, 1994, standing w/rose, NM, A7 ....$30.00
Snow White, Grosvenor/UK, sitting on grass w/bunny & deer, M, A7....$30.00
Sonic Hedgehog, Matey/UK, 1990s, standing on red & bl game button, NM, A7....$30.00
Spider-Man, Euromark/UK, 1995, walking over trash can & tire, NM, A7....$30.00
SPV (Thunderbirds), Euromark/UK, 1993, gray, bl, wht & blk vehicle from cartoon, NM, A7....$35.00
Superman, Damascar Jr/Italy, flying pose, M, A7 ....$35.00
Sylvester & Tweety, Warner Bros/UK, Tweety sitting on Sylvester's head, M, A7 ....$25.00
Thomas the Tank, Bandai/Japan, 1991, red & bl, NM, A7 ..$25.00
Thunderbird, ITC Ent/UK, gr or yel, MIB, A7, ea $25.00
Tom (Tom & Jerry), Damascar/Italy, sitting in drum, M, A7....$35.00
Troll, German, bl, pk or yel hair, M, A7, ea $30.00
Ultimate Warrior, Grosvenor/UK, bath beads, M, A7 ....$25.00
Wile E Coyote, Prelude Ltd/UK, w/rocket backpack, M, A7 .$20.00
Wilma Flintstone, Damascar/Italy, 1995, washing clothes in pelican's bill, NM, A7 ....$35.00
Wilma Flintstone, Rosedew Ltd/UK, 1993, Topper, cartoon outfit, NM, A7 ....$20.00
Woodstock (Peanuts), unknown maker/UK, flying red plane, yel w/blk heart-shaped glasses, M, A7....$20.00
Yogi Bear, Damascar/Italy, standing on gr & purple grass, brn w/gr hat & tie, M, A7 ....$50.00
101 Dalmatians, Grosvenor/UK, pups on pillow w/red sunglasses, M, A7....$15.00

Buddy L

First produced in 1921, Buddy L toys have escalated in value over the past few years until now early models in good original condition (or restored, for that matter) often bring prices well into the four figures when they hit the auction block. The business was started by Fred Lundahl, founder of Moline Pressed Steel Co., who at first designed toys for his young son, Buddy. They were advertised as being 'Guaranteed Indestructible,' and indeed they were so sturdy and well built that they just about were. Until wartime caused a shortage, they were made of heavy-gauge pressed steel. Many were based on actual truck models; some were ride-ons, capable of supporting a grownup's weight. Fire trucks with hydraulically activated water towers and hoisting towers that actually worked kept little boys entertained for hours. After the war, the quality of Buddy Ls began to decline, and wood was used to some extent. Condition is everything. Remember that unless the work is done by a professional restorer, overpainting and amateur repairs do nothing to enhance the value of a toy in poor condition. Professional restorations may be expensive, but they may be viable alternatives when compared to the extremely high prices we're seeing today. In the listings that follow, toys are all pressed steel unless noted.

See also Advertising; Boats.

Cars and Busses

Country Squire Station Wagon, 1964, 15", EX $200.00
Dump Truck #634, 20½", EX....$200.00
Greyhound Bus, bl & wht w/blk rubber tires, clockwork mechanism, 16", EX, from $250 to $350.00
Greyhound Bus #755, MIB, from $550 to $600.00
Passenger Bus, ca 1929, 30", scarce, from $3,500 to $3,800.00
Scarab, red w/chrome detail, blk rubber tires, 10", VG, from $250 to $350.00

Photo courtesy Dunbar Gallery

Flivver Coupe, 1920s, black with red spoked wheels, 12", from $950.00 to $1,250.00.

Touring Car, blk w/aluminum wheels & red-pnt spokes, enclosed cab w/simulated soft top, 11", NM, A....**$1,900.00**
Transportation Bus, maroon w/blk & gold, 28", rstr, A.**$3,000.00**

Construction

Aerial Tramway #360, 1929-30, EX+ **$2,500.00**

Photo courtesy Dunbar Gallery

Concrete Mixer #280, 1926 – 30, 14x24", EX, D10, from $800.00 to $1,200.00.

Photo courtesy Dunbar Gallery

Sand Loader, 1933, 19½", EX, D10, from $500.00 to $700.00.

Derrick, blk base w/3 red braces joining a swinging boom rod, 21½", NM, from $350 to..**$450.00**
Mobile Power Digger, orange & yel w/red chassis, gr crane, 20", EX **$250.00**
Overhead Crane #250, 1924-27, NM, from $1,000 to .**$1,500.00**
Road Roller #290, 1930, 29", G, A **$2,400.00**

Photo courtesy Dunbar Gallery

Steam Shovel, 1930s, black with red detail, 24", EX, from $350.00 to $450.00.

Sand Loader, bl w/attached chained conveyors holding buckets, 18", NM, A..**$1,000.00**
Steam Shovel #220, 1921-31, NM, from $400 to...........**$500.00**
Trencher #400, 1928-31, NM, from $2,500 to **$3,000.00**

Firefighting

Photo courtesy Dunbar Gallery

Aerial Ladder Truck, 1926 – 30, 39", EX, D10, from $1,200.00 to $1,600.00.

Hook & Ladder Truck #205, 1924-31, EX, from $1,400 to **$1,500.00**
Hook & Ladder Truck #859, wood, 21½", EX................**$450.00**
Hydraulic Water Tower Truck #205D, 1930-31, red w/silver latticework tower, VG, A.......................................**$2,500.00**
Pumper Truck #205A, 1925-30, 23", EX, from $1,600 to **$1,800.00**
Pumper Truck #29, ride-on, 26", rstr **$1,200.00**

Outdoor Trains

Boxcar, red w/blk trucks, sliding center door, ladders on end, 22½", VG, from $350 to..**$450.00**
Caboose, 1921-31, red w/3017 decal, G......................**$1,500.00**

Caboose, red with black trucks, 20", overpaint, A, $350.00.

Coal Car (Gondola), blk w/red decals, retains orig Boston Dept Store tag, 21", EX, A $1,000.00
Coal Car (Gondola) #96834, blk w/ladders on 1 end, 22½", rare, EX, from $1,100 to $1,200.00
Freight Car, red, 21", EX, A $650.00
Hopper, 1928-31, blk, bottom dump, VG..................$2,500.00
Railway Steam Shovel, blk w/red corrugated roof, rotating cab on flat bed, 22½", EX, A $700.00
Stock Car #12457, red w/blk trucks, sliding center doors w/ladders on 1 end, 22½", EX......................................$1,100.00
Tank Car, yel w/blk fr & trucks, center ladder, 19½", missing couplers o/w VG, A...$1,000.00

TRUCKS AND VANS

Army Transport Truck, w/towed cannon, spoke wheels, 27", EX $275.00
Baggage Truck #203B, 1929-31, EX, from $2,000 to...$3,000.00
Big Show Circus Truck #484, 1947, wood, 25½", EX $900.00
City Dray Truck #439, 1934, gr & yel, 19", EX $500.00
Coal Truck #202, 1926-31, EX, from $3,000 to $4,000.00
Dump Truck #434, 1936, yel & red, electric headlights, 19½", G, A $300.00

Hydraulic Missile Launcher, MIB, $700.00.

Flivver Truck #210, 1925-30, blk w/aluminum wheels & red-pnt spokes, 12", NM, from $800 to $1,200.00
Ford Dump Truck #211A, 1926-30, blk w/open driver's seat, aluminum wheels w/red spokes, 11", NM, from $1,700 to..............$2,000.00
Ford 1-Ton Delivery Truck #212A, 1929-30, blk w/aluminum wheels & red-pnt spokes, 14", NM, from $3,000 to.$4,000.00
Huckster Truck, blk, 14", EX, A $4,000.00
Hydraulic Dump Truck #201A, 1926-31, 24½", G, A.$1,000.00
Ice Truck #207, 1926-31, EX, from $1,400 to $1,500.00
International Dump Truck, ride-on, 25", NM, from $550 to..$600.00
Merry-Go-Round Truck #5429, carousel w/horses in back, 12", NM..$250.00
Moving Van #204, 1920s, 25", G, A..............................$575.00
Parcel Delivery Truck, beige & brn, lg slant-back body w/rear doors, rubber tires, 24", G, A.................................$275.00

Railway Express Line Truck, red and green with simulated spoke wheels, 23½", EX, A, $700.00.

Robotoy Truck, red w/gr dump & blk chassis, moves forward & backward w/transformer, 21⅝", VG $1,000.00
Telephone Maintenance Repair Truck & Trailer #450, complete w/ladder & rope, 16", EX (VG box), A $450.00

Photo courtesy Dunbar Gallery

Texaco Tanker, 1950s, 25", NMIB, from $350.00 to $450.00.

US Mail Truck, #2592, khaki, w/decals, blk rubber tires, EX, A $350.00
Utility Delivery Truck #946, 1941-42, 25", EX $150.00
Wrecker #37, 1933, 24", NM, from $300 to $400.00
Zoo-A-Rama Truck & Cage, complete w/plastic monkeys & polar bears, 20", NMIB, A.......................................$250.00

Building Blocks and Construction Toys

Toy building sets were popular with children well before television worked its mesmerizing influence on young minds; in fact, some were made as early as the end of the eighteenth century. Important manufacturers include Milton Bradley, Joel Ellis, Charles M. Crandall, William S. Tower, W.S. Read, Ives Manufacturing Corporation, S.L. Hill, Frank Hornby (Meccano), A.C. Gilbert Brothers, The Toy Tinkers, Gebruder Bing, R. Bliss, S.F. Fischer, Carl Brandt Jr., and F. Ad. Richter (see Richter Anchor Stone Building Sets). Whether made of wood, paper, metal, glass, or 'stone,' these toys are highly prized today for their profusion of historical, educational, artistic, and creative features. For further information on Tinkertoys, read *Collector's Guide to Tinkertoys* by Craig Strange (Collector Books).

Richter's Anchor (Union) Stone Building Blocks were the most popular building toy at the beginning of the twentieth century. As early as 1880, they were patented in both Germany and the USA. Though the company produced more than six hundred different sets, only their New Series is commonly found today (these are listed below). Their blocks remained popular until WWI, and Anchor sets were one of the first toys to achieve international 'brand name' acceptance. They were produced both as basic sets and supplement sets (identified by letters A, B, C, or D) which increased a basic set to a higher level. There were dozens of stone block competitors, though none were very successful. During WWI the trade name Anchor was lost to A.C. Gilbert (Connecticut) who produced Anchor blocks for a short time. Richter responded by using the new trade name 'Union' or 'Stone Building Blocks,' sets considered today to be Anchor blocks despite the lack of the Richter's Anchor trademark. The A.C. Gilbert Company also produced the famous Erector sets which were made from about 1913 through the late 1950s.

Note: Values for Richter's blocks are for sets in very good condition; (+) at the end of the line indicates these sets are being reproduced today.

Advisors: Arlan Coffman (C4); George Hardy (H3), Richter's Building Blocks.

Aeroplane Builder, Schoenhut, assembles to 15" wingspan, missing few minor pcs, EX (VG box), A........................$650.00

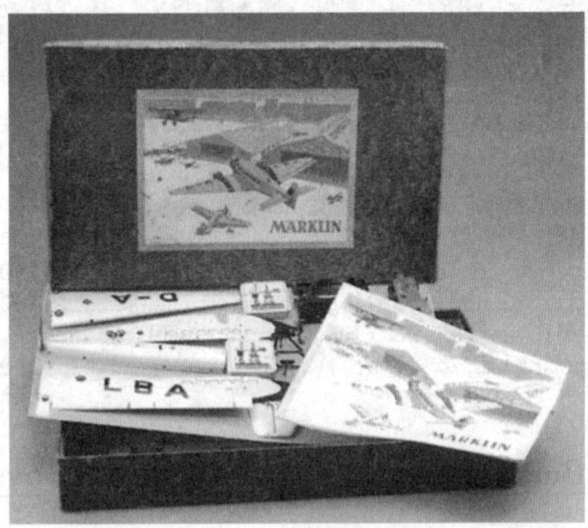

Aeroplane Construction Set, Marklin, complete, EX (EX box), A, $4,400.00.

American Model Builder, Mechanical Toy Co, VG (VG box), A $75.00

American Plastic Bricks, Halsam #705, complete, NM (EX canister), J6..$35.00

American Skyline, Elgo, 1950s, complete, NM (VG box), T2 ....$35.00

Arkitoy Construction Set, 1940s, complete, EX (EX box) .$75.00

Auto-Bouwdoos, Marklin, 2-door limousine, lt gr, assembled, w/up mechanism, 14½", M (EX box w/extra parts), A....$4,500.00

Bilt-E-Z Building, Scott, 1924, builds 3 tin buildings, complete w/instructions, EX (EX box), A $130.00

Build-A-Set, DA Pachter, 1943, complete, NM (VG box), S16 ....$50.00

Building Boats w/Blocks, Artwood #6050, complete, EX (EX box), P3..$25.00

Building Bricks, Auburn Rubber, 1950s, complete, EX (EX canister), T2 ....$40.00

D-A LBA Transport Plane Kit, Marklin #1151, complete, EX (EX box)..$2,000.00

Dirigible Builder, Schoenhut, assembles to 21", EX (VG box), A $1,250.00

Drawbridge Set, Renwal #155, complete, scarce, NM (EX box)..$250.00

Erector Set, Gilbert #3, MIB $175.00

Erector Set, Gilbert #5½, MIB, $175.00.

Erector Set, Gilbert #6½, MIB, $165.00.

Erector Set, Gilbert #7, EX (EX wooden box) $250.00

Erector Set, Gilbert #7½, complete w/catalog, EX (EX wooden box)..$350.00

Erector Set, Gilbert #8, EX (EX wooden box) $850.00
Giant Building Set, Ideal, 1960s, scaled to fit Motorific cars, complete, EX (EX box), J6 ....$150.00
Girder & Panel Bridge & Turnpike, Kenner, 1959, complete, NMIB $40.00
Girder & Panel Build-A-Home, Kenner, 1962, complete, EX (EX canister), T2 ....$35.00
Girder & Panel Monorail Skyway, Kenner, VG (VG box) $150.00
Lincoln Logs, paper label mk Original Lincoln Logs the All American Toy, complete, EX (G box), A..................$50.00
Lionel Construction Set, complete, MIB.........................$225.00
Mold Master Road Builder, Kenner, 1964, unused, NMIB, J2..$125.00
Mysto Erector Set, Mysto Mfg Co, complete, VG (VG box), A $125.00
Roger Robot Giant Playmate, Whitman, 1961, assembles to 4-ft, EX (EX box), M17..$250.00
Skyport Building Set, Ideal, 1968, complete, EX (EX box), F8 ....$85.00
Spirit of St Louis, Metalcraft #830, builds over 250 airplanes, EX (G box), A..$275.00
Super City Skyscraper Building Set, Ideal, 1960s, complete, EX (EX box) $135.00
Super City Town & Country, Ideal, complete, VG (VG box) $50.00
Tinker Zoo, Tinkertoy, 1961, complete, NM (NM canister), T2 ....$25.00
Tinkertoy Big Boy No 155, 1950s, complete, EX (EX canister), T2..$30.00
Tinkertoy Wonder Builder, complete, EX (EX canister), A..$50.00
Tru Model Erector Set, Gilbert #1, complete, EX (G box).$175.00
Tru Model New England Village, 1940s, complete, EX (EX box)..$75.00

Anchor Stone Building Sets by Richter

American House & Country House Set #206, VG, H3 .$600.00
American House & Country House Set #208, VG, H3 .$600.00
American House & Country House Set #210, VG, H3 .$700.00
DS Set #E3, w/metal parts & roof stones, VG, H3 ....$60.00
DS Set #03A, w/metal parts & roof stones, VG, H3.........$60.00
DS Set #05, w/metal parts & roof stones, VG, H3 ....$120.00
DS Set #05A, w/metal parts & roof stones, VG, H3 ......$150.00
DS Set #07, w/metal parts & roof stones, VG, H3 ....$270.00
DS Set #07A, w/metal parts & roofs, VG, H3 ....$200.00
DS Set #09A, w/metal parts & roof stones, VG, H3 ......$250.00
DS Set #11, w/metal parts & roof stones, VG, H3 ....$675.00
DS Set #11A, w/metal parts & roof stones, VG, H3 ......$300.00
DS Set #13A, w/metal parts & roof stones, VG, H3 ......$325.00
DS Set #15, w/metal parts & roof stones, VG, H3 ......$1,500.00
DS Set #15A, w/metal parts & roof stones, VG, H3 ......$475.00
DS Set #19A, w/metal parts & roof stones, VG, H3 ......$475.00
DS Set #21A, w/metal parts & roof stones, VG, H3 ......$975.00
DS Set #23A, w/metal parts & roof stones, VG, H3 ......$750.00
DS Set #25A, w/metal parts & roof stones, VG, H3 ...$1,500.00
DS Set #27, w/metal parts & roof stones, VG, H3 ......$6,000.00
Fortress Set #402, VG, H3..$100.00
Fortress Set #402A, VG, H3 ....$130.00
Fortress Set #404, VG, H3..$250.00
Fortress Set #404A, VG, H3 ....$275.00
Fortress Set #406, VG, H3..$500.00
Fortress Set #406A, VG, H3 ....$400.00
Fortress Set #408, VG, H3 ....$1,000.00
Fortress Set #408A, VG, H3 ....$800.00
Fortress Set #410, VG, H3 ....$1,800.00
Fortress Set #410A, VG, H3 ....$1,000.00
Fortress Set #412A, VG, H3 ....$1,500.00
Fortress Set #414, VG, H3 ....$5,000.00
German House & Country House Set #301, VG, H3 ....$500.00
German House & Country House Set #301A, VG, H3 .$500.00
German House & Country House Set #303, VG, H3 .$1,000.00
German House & Country House Set #303A, VG, H3 .$2,000.00
German House & Country House Set #305, VG, H3 .$3,000.00
GK-BK Great-Castle Set, VG, H3..............................$9,950.00
GK-NF Set #06, VG, H3 (+) $140.00
GK-NF Set #06A, VG, H3 (+) $160.00
GK-NF Set #08, VG, H3..$300.00
GK-NF Set #10, VG, H3..$480.00
GK-NF Set #10A, VG, H3 (+) $200.00
GK-NF Set #12, VG, H3..$680.00
GK-NF Set #12A, VG, H3 (+) $250.00
GK-NF Set #14A, VG, H3..$250.00
GK-NF Set #16, VG, H3 ....$1,180.00
GK-NF Set #16A, VG, H3..$300.00
GK-NF Set #18A, VG, H3..$400.00
GK-NF Set #20A, VG, H3..$500.00
GK-NF Set #22A, VG, H3..$500.00
GK-NF Set #24A, VG, H3..$600.00
GK-NF Set #28, VG, H3 ....$1,200.00
GK-NF Set #28A, VG, H3 ....$1,200.00
GK-NF Set #30A, VG, H3 ....$1,200.00
GK-NF Set #32B, VG, H3..$1,600.00
GK-NF Set #34, VG, H3 ....$7,000.00
GK-NF Set 08A, VG H3 (+) $120.00
KK-NF Set #05, VG, H3 ....$45.00
KK-NF Set #05A, VG, H3 ....$55.00
KK-NF Set #07, VG, H3 ....$100.00
KK-NF Set #07A, VG, H3 ....$90.00
KK-NF Set #09A, VG, H3 ....$100.00
KK-NF Set #11, VG, H3 ....$275.00
KK-NF Set #11A, VG, H3 ....$275.00
KK-NF Set #13A, VG, H3 ....$300.00
KK-NF Set #15A, VG, H3 ....$450.00
KK-NF Set #17A, VG, H3 ....$750.00
KK-NF Set #19A, VG, H3..$1,500.00
KK-NF Set #21, VG, H3..$3,500.00
Neue Reihe Set #102, VG, H3...$100.00
Neue Reihe Set #104, VG, H3...$150.00
Neue Reihe Set #106, VG, H3...$200.00
Neue Reihe Set #108, VG, H3...$300.00
Neue Reihe Set #110, VG, H3...$600.00
Neue Reihe Set #112, VG, H3 ....$1,000.00
Neue Reihe Set #114, VG, H3 ....$1,500.00
Neue Reihe Set #116, VG, H3 ....$2,000.00

California Raisins

The California Raisins made their first TV commercials in the fall of 1986. The first four PVC figures were introduced in 1987, the same year Hardee's issued similar but smaller figures, and three 5½" Bendees became available on the retail market. In 1988 twenty-one more Raisins were made for retail as well as promotional efforts in grocery stores. Four were graduates identical to the original four characters except standing on yellow pedestals and wearing blue graduation caps with yellow tassels. Hardee's increased their line by six.

In 1989 they starred in two movies: *Meet the Raisins* and *The California Raisins — Sold Out*, and eight additional characters were joined in figurine production by five of their fruit and vegetable friends from the movies. Hardee's latest release was in 1991, when they added still four more. All Raisins issued for retail sales and promotions in 1987 and 1988 (including Hardee's) are dated with the year of production (usually on the bottom of one foot). Of those released for retail sales in 1989, only the Beach Scene characters are dated, and these are actually dated 1988. Hardee's 1991 series are also undated.

Advisors: Ken Clee (C3) and Larry DeAngelo (D3).

Other Sources: W6

Applause, Captain Toonz, w/bl boom box, yel glasses & sneakers, Hardee's Second Promotion, 1988, sm, M.............**$3.00**

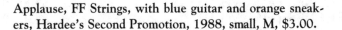

Applause, FF Strings, with blue guitar and orange sneakers, Hardee's Second Promotion, 1988, small, M, $3.00.

Applause, Michael Raisin, Special Edition, 1989, M........**$20.00**

Applause, Rollin' Rollo, w/roller skates, yel sneakers & hat mk H, Hardee's Second Promotion, 1988, sm, M..............**$3.00**

Applause, SB Stuntz, w/yel skateboard & bl sneakers, Hardee's Second Promotion, 1988, sm, M.................................**$3.00**

Applause, Trumpy Trunote, w/trumpet & bl sneakers, Hardee's Second Promotion, 1988, sm, M.................................**$3.00**

Applause, Waves Weaver I, w/yel surfboard connected to foot, Hardee's Second Promotion, 1988, sm, M...................**$4.00**

Applause, Waves Weaver II, w/yel surfboard not connected to foot, Hardee's Second Promotion, 1988, sm, M...........**$6.00**

Applause-Claymation, Banana White, yel dress, Meet the Raisins First Edition, 1989, M...................................**$20.00**

Applause-Claymation, Lick Broccoli, gr & blk w/red & orange guitar, Meet the Raisins First Edition, 1989, M.........**$20.00**

Applause-Claymation, Rudy Bagaman, w/cigar, purple shirt & flipflops, Meet the Raisins First Edition, 1989, M......**$20.00**

CALRAB, Blue Surfboard, board connected to foot, Unknown Promotion, 1988, M...**$35.00**

CALRAB, Blue Surfboard, board in right hand, not connected to foot, Unknown Promotion, 1987, M, $50.00.

CALRAB, Christmas Issue, with candy cane, 1988, M, $12.00.

CALRAB, Christmas Issue, 1988, w/red hat, M.................**$9.00**

CALRAB, Guitar, red guitar, First Commercial Issue, 1988, M...**$8.00**

CALRAB, Hands, left hand points up, right hand points down, Post Raisin Bran Issue, 1987, M **$4.00**

CALRAB, Hands, pointing up w/thumbs touching head, First Key Chains, 1987, M **$5.00**

CALRAB, Hands, pointing up w/thumbs touching head, Hardee's First Promotion, 1987, sm, M $3.00

CALRAB, Microphone, right hand in fist w/microphone in left, Post Raisin Bran Issue, 1987, M $6.00

Photo courtesy Larry DeAngelo

CALRAB, Microphone, right hand points up with microphone in left, Hardee's First Promotion, 1987, M, $3.00.

CALRAB, Microphone, right hand points up w/microphone in left, First Key Chains, 1987, M....................................$7.00

CALRAB, Saxophone, gold sax, no hat, First Key Chains, 1987, M..$5.00

CALRAB, Saxophone, gold sax, no hat, Hardee's First Promotion, 1987, sm, M..$3.00

CALRAB, Saxophone, inside of sax pnt red, Post Raisin Bran Issue, 1987, M $4.00

CALRAB, Singer, microphone in left hand not connected to face, First Commercial Issue, 1988, M..........................$6.00

CALRAB, Sunglasses, index finger touching face, First Key Chains, 1987, M $5.00

CALRAB, Sunglasses, index finger touching face, orange glasses, Hardee's First Promotion, 1987, M $3.00

CALRAB, Sunglasses, right hand points up, left hand points down, orange glasses, Post Raisin Bran Issue, 1987, M ..$4.00

CALRAB, Sunglasses II, eyes not visible, aqua glasses & sneakers, First Commercial Issue, 1988, M...........................$6.00

CALRAB, Sunglasses II, eyes visible, aqua glasses & sneakers, First Commercial Issue, 1988, M...............................$25.00

CALRAB, Winky, hitchhiking pose & winking, First Commercial Issue, 1988, M $6.00

CALRAB-Applause, AC, 'Gimme-5' pose, Meet the Raisins Second Edition, 1989, M..$150.00

CALRAB-Applause, Alotta Stile, w/purple boom box, pk boots, Hardee's Fourth Promotion, 1991, sm, MIP...............$12.00

CALRAB-Applause, Anita Break, shopping w/Hardee's bags, Hardee's Fourth Promotion, 1991, sm, MIP (w/collector's card) $12.00

CALRAB-Applause, Bass Player, w/gray slippers, Second Commercial Issue, 1988, M $8.00

CALRAB-Applause, Benny, w/bowling ball & bag, Hardee's Fourth Promotion, 1991, sm, MIP (w/collector's card)..$20.00

CALRAB-Applause, Boy in Beach Chair, orange glasses, brn base, Beach Theme Edition, 1988, M $15.00

CALRAB-Applause, Boy w/surfboard, purple board, brn base, Beach Theme Edition, 1988, M $15.00

CALRAB-Applause, Cecil Tyme (Carrot), Meet the Raisins Second Promotion, 1989, M $175.00

CALRAB-Applause, Drummer, Second Commercial Issue, 1988, M $8.00

Photo courtesy Larry DeAngelo

CALRAB-Applause, Girl with Boom Box, purple glasses, green shoes, brown base, Beach Theme Edition, 1988, M, $15.00.

CALRAB-Applause, Girl w/Tambourine, gr shoes & bracelet, Raisin Club Issue, 1988, M.......................................$12.00

Photo courtesy Larry DeAngelo

CALRAB-Applause, Girl with Tambourine (Ms Delicious), yellow shoes, Second Commercial Issue, 1988, M, $15.00.

CALRAB-Applause, Hands, Graduate w/both hands pointing up & thumbs touching head, Graduate Key Chains, 1988, M..$85.00

CALRAB-Applause, Hip Band Guitarist (Hendrix), w/headband & yel guitar, Third Commercial Issue, 1988, M..........$25.00

CALRAB-Applause, Hip Band Guitarist (Hendrix), w/headband & yel guitar, Second Key Chains, 1988, sm, M...$65.00

Photo courtesy Larry DeAngelo

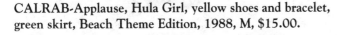

CALRAB-Applause, Hula Girl, yellow shoes and bracelet, green skirt, Beach Theme Edition, 1988, M, $15.00.

CALRAB-Applause, Lenny Lima Bean, purple suit, Meet the Raisins Second Promotion, 1989, M.......................$150.00

CALRAB-Applause, Microphone (female), yel shoes & bracelet, Third Commercial Issue, 1988, M................$9.00

CALRAB-Applause, Microphone (female), yel shoes & bracelet, Second Key Chains, 1988, sm, M...............$45.00

CALRAB-Applause, Microphone (male), left hand extended w/open palm, Second Key Chains, 1988, sm, M........$45.00

CALRAB-Applause, Mom, yel hair, pk apron, Meet the Raisins Second Promotion, 1989, M..................................$150.00

CALRAB-Applause, Piano, bl piano, red hair, gr sneakers, Meet the Raisins First Edition, 1989, M............................$35.00

CALRAB-Applause, Saxophone, blk beret, bl eyelids, Third Commercial Issue, 1988, M......................................$15.00

Photo courtesy Larry DeAngelo

CALRAB-Applause, Valentine, boy holding heart, Special Lover's Edition, 1988, M, $8.00.

CALRAB-Applause, Saxophone, Graduate w/gold sax, Graduate Key Chains, 1988, M $85.00

CALRAB-Applause, Singer (female), reddish purple shoes & bracelet, Second Commercial Issue, 1988, M $16.00

CALRAB-Applause, Sunglasses, Graduate w/index fingers touching face, orange glasses, Graduate Key Chains, 1988, M...$85.00

CALRAB-Applause, Valentine, girl holding heart, Special Lover's Edition, 1988, M...$8.00

CALRAB-Claymation, Sunglasses, Singer, Hands, Saxophone, Graduate on yel base, Post Raisin Bran, 1988, ea, from $50 to $65.00

Miscellaneous

Backpack, maroon & yel w/3 figures, 1987, EX, W6.........$35.00

Balloon, lead singer, CTI Industries, 1988, EX, W6 ....$8.00

Ballpoint Pen, set of 3 w/figures at top, M.........................$65.00

Bank, cereal box w/lid, plastic, EX, W6 ....$15.00

Baseball Cap, 1988, EX, W6..$5.00

Beach Towel, CALRAB, M $50.00

Belly Bag, bl or yel nylon fabric w/Conga Line, 1988, EX, W6, ea...$25.00

Belt, tan, 1988, M $30.00

Book, Birthday Boo Boo, 1988, EX, W6 ....$12.00

Book, Raisin the Roof, 1988, EX, W6 ....$12.00

Bulletin Board, Singer & Conga Line or Beach Scene, Rose Art, 1988, MIP, W6, ea...$35.00

Chalkboard, Singer & Conga Line, Rose Art, 1988, MIP, W6 ....$35.00

Clock, wall-type wristwatch, red or bl, 1987, EX, W6, ea..$85.00

Colorforms, MIB (sealed), P12 ....$35.00

Coloring Book, Sports Crazy, 1988, EX, W6.......................$5.00

Cross-Stitch Pattern, Leaflet #1, #3, #4 or #6, 1988, M, W6, ea $12.00

Doll, vinyl w/suction cups, 1987, lg version, EX, W6 ....$5.00

Doll, vinyl w/suction cups, 1987, sm version, EX, W6......$10.00

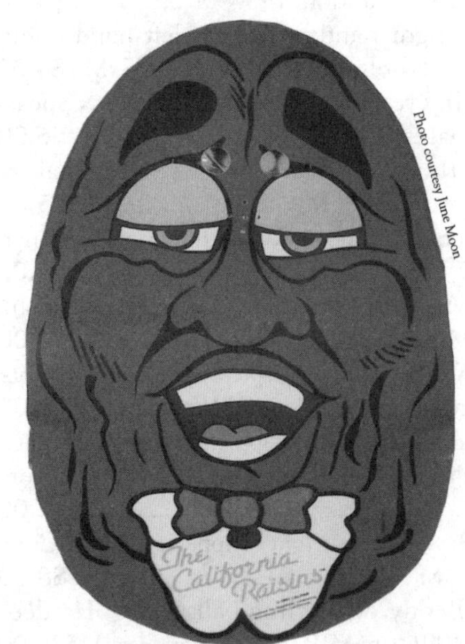

Photo courtesy June Moon

Halloween Costume, complete with gloves, M, $25.00 to $45.00.

Figure, bendable flat body, w/microphone, sunglasses or left hand pointing up, 1987, EX, W6, ea **$15.00**
Figure, Imperial Toy, 1987, inflatable vinyl, 42", MIB, W6 ..**$55.00**
Figure, w/bl tennis shoes, cloth, 1987, EX, W6 ....**$5.00**
Figure, w/microphone, sunglasses or yel high heels, cloth, 1988, EX, W6, ea **$4.00**
Figure, w/parasol & sunglasses, cloth, 1989, EX, W6 ....**$8.00**
Game, California Raisin board game, Decipher Inc, 1987, MIB, D3/W6 ....**$25.00**
Gloves, bl knit w/beige vinyl inserts, 1987, EX, W6.........**$35.00**

Key Chain, glasses and orange tennis shoes, 1988, MOC, J6, $12.00.

Photo courtesy June Moon

Punching Bag, Imperial Toys, 1987, inflatable, 36", MIB, $45.00 to $60.00.

Lapel Pin, girl, base player, or microphone, PVC, 1988, MOC, W6, ea **$15.00**
Mug, California Raisins marching, plastic, 1987, EX, W6 ..**$4.00**
Official Fan Club Watch Set, MIP, P12...........................**$50.00**
Patch, Ice Capades w/Raisin Singer, felt, 1988, EX, W6 ....**$8.00**
Picture Album, 1988, EX, W6...**$25.00**
Poster, Join the California Raisin Club, 1990, EX, W6 ....**$12.00**
Puffy Stick-On, 1987, EX, W6 ....**$10.00**
Puppet, female figure w/yel or gr shoes, Bendy/Sutton Happenings, 1988, MIB, W6, ea **$30.00**
Puppet, male w/yel shoes & glasses, Bendy/Sutton Happenings, 1988, MIB, W6 ....**$35.00**

Puzzle, American Publishing, 1988, 500 pcs, MIB, W6 ....**$20.00**
Puzzle, American Publishing, 1988, 75 pcs, MIB, W6 ......**$25.00**
Radio, AM/FM, figure w/posable arms & legs, 1988, MIB.**$75.00**
Record, California Raisins Sing the Hit Songs, 78 rpm, Priority Records, 1987, EX (EX sleeve), W6 ....**$20.00**
Record, I Heard It Through the Grapevine, 45 rpm, 1987, EX (EX sleeve)...**$20.00**
Record, Meet the Raisins, 33 1/3 rpm, EX (EX cover) **$20.00**
Record, Rudolph the Red-Nosed Reindeer, 45 rpm, 1988, EX (EX sleeve), W6..**$30.00**
Record, Signed, Sealed, Delivered I'm Yours, 45 rpm, 1988, EX (EX sleeve)...**$20.00**
Record, When a Man Loves a Woman, 45 rpm, 1987, EX (EX sleeve), W6 ....**$20.00**
Refrigerator Magnets, Hands, Orange Sunglasses, Microphone, Saxophone, 1988, ea...**$75.00**

Sandwich Stage, Del Monte Fruit Snacks, MIB, $75.00 to $100.00.

Photo courtesy Martin and Carolyn Berens

School Kit, w/promotion ideas, activities, recipes, etc, 1988, M, W6 ....**$30.00**
School Kit, w/ruler, pencil sharpener, eraser & pencil holder, 1988, MOC, W6...**$40.00**
Shoulder Bag, bl & orange w/dancing raisins, 1988, MOC, W6...**$25.00**
Sleeping Bag, purple, 1988, EX, W6................................**$40.00**
Slippers, fuzzy, children's, 1988, M................................**$55.00**
Sticker Album, w/slide-o-scope, Diamond Publishing, 1988, M, W6 ....**$15.00**
Sticker Book, unused, M, P12..**$25.00**
Suspenders, I Heard It Through the Grapevine, yel, 1987, EX, W6 ....**$35.00**
Tambourine, raisins on stage, 1987, EX, W6 ....**$15.00**
Tambourine & Kazoo, Imperial Toy Corporation, 1987, MOC, W6 ....**$35.00**
Tote Bag, aqua w/3 female singers, 1988, EX, W6 ....**$20.00**
Tote Bag, yel w/Conga Line, 1987, EX, W6.....................**$20.00**

Umbrella, lady raisins on the beach, 1988, EX, W6 ....$45.00
Video, Meet the Raisins, 1988, MIP, W6 ....$25.00
Video, Raisins Sold Out, 1990, MIP, W6 ....$25.00
Watercolor-By-Number Set, Rose Art, complete, 1988, EX, W6 ....$30.00
Wind-up Toy, figure w/hands up & gr bracelet, 1987, EX, W6 ....$12.00
Wind-up Toy, figure w/yel or gr shoes & bracelet, 1988, MOC, W6, ea $25.00
Wristwatch, lady w/yel tambourine, 1988, M, W6 ....$75.00

Candy Containers

As early as 1876, candy manufacturers used figural glass containers to package their candy. They found the idea so successful that they continued to use them until the 1960s. The major producers of these glass containers were Westmoreland, West Bros., Victory Glass, J.H. Millstein, J.C. Crosetti, L.E. Smith, and Jack and T.H. Stough. Some of the most collectible and sought after today are the character-related figurals such as Amos 'N Andy, Barney Google, Santa Claus, and Jackie Coogan, but there are other rare examples that have been known to command prices of $1,000.00 and more. Some of these are Black Cat for Luck, Black Cat Sitting, Quick Firer Cannon (with original carriage), and Mr. Rabbit with Hat (that books for $1,800.00, even in worn paint). There are many reproductions; know your dealer. For a listing of these reproductions, refer to *Schroeder's Antiques Price Guide.*

For more information we recommend *The Collector's Guide to Candy Containers*, written by Doug Dezso, our advisor for this category, and Leon and Rose Poirier (Collector Books). The plate numbers in the following listings refer to this book.

For other types of candy containers, see Halloween; Pez Dispensers; Santa Claus.

Baby Chick, plate #7, from $100.00 to 125.00.

Airplane (Boyd), plate #77, from $25 to $30.00
Airplane (Liberty Motor), plate #78, from $2,500 to ..$3,500.00
Barney Google on Pedestal, plate #189, from $250 to $350.00
Bear in Auto, plate #1, from $250 to $300.00
Black Cat Winking, plate #6, from $3,800 to..............$4,250.00
Blimp, plate #88, from $400 to......................................$500.00
Boat (Queen Mary), plate #103, from $350 to................$450.00

Cannon, plate #386, from $800.00 to $1,000.00.

Cannon on Truck, plate #382, from $2,200 to............$2,500.00
Car (Electric Runabout), plate #163, from $85 to $100.00
Car (Sedan), plate #177, from $100 to $125.00
Chick in Shell Auto w/Balloon Tires, plate #9, from $600 to..$725.00
Circus Dog w/Hat, plate #21, from $20 to........................$40.00
Circus Wagon, plate #527, from $325 to $425.00
Coal Car, plate #515, from $350 to...............................$400.00

Dog, paper and metal hat, plate #26, from $20.00 to $30.00.

Dog by Barrel, plate #19, from $225 to $250.00
Dolly's Milk Bottle, plate #109, from $50 to $75.00
Duck on Basket, plate #38, from $75 to $100.00
Dutch Windmill, plate #534, from $90 to.......................$100.00

Elephant (Genteel), plate #42, from $275 to..................**$350.00**

Felix by Barrel, plate #250, from $550.00 to $700.00.

Fire Engine (Three Dot USA), plate #260, from $100 to...**$125.00**
Fish, plate #44, from $200 to..**$250.00**
Goblin Face, plate #263, from $550 to............................**$650.00**
Greyhound Bus w/Luggage Rack, plate #151, from $275 to.....**$325.00**
Gun, beaded border grip, plate #390, from $18 to **$25.00**
Gun, grooved barrel, plate #392, from $25 to **$35.00**
Happifats on Drum, plate #199, from $250 to **$350.00**
Helicopter, plate #91, from $250 to **$300.00**

Rabbit on Dome, plate #65, from $450.00 to $525.00.

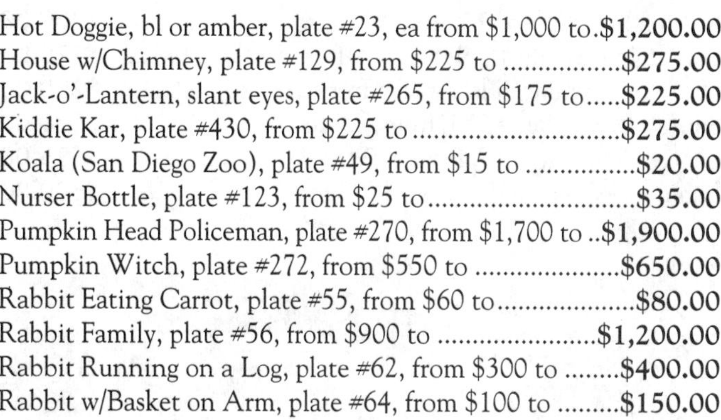

Hot Doggie, bl or amber, plate #23, ea from $1,000 to.**$1,200.00**
House w/Chimney, plate #129, from $225 to **$275.00**
Jack-o'-Lantern, slant eyes, plate #265, from $175 to.....**$225.00**
Kiddie Kar, plate #430, from $225 to **$275.00**
Koala (San Diego Zoo), plate #49, from $15 to **$20.00**
Nurser Bottle, plate #123, from $25 to..............................**$35.00**
Pumpkin Head Policeman, plate #270, from $1,700 to ..**$1,900.00**
Pumpkin Witch, plate #272, from $550 to **$650.00**
Rabbit Eating Carrot, plate #55, from $60 to....................**$80.00**
Rabbit Family, plate #56, from $900 to **$1,200.00**
Rabbit Running on a Log, plate #62, from $300 to **$400.00**
Rabbit w/Basket on Arm, plate #64, from $100 to **$150.00**

Rocking Horse with Rider, plate #47, from $175.00 to $225.00.

Skookum by Tree Stump Barrel, plate #207, from $550.00 to $650.00.

Rolling Pin, plate #310, from $250 to $300.00
Safe (Dime Savings), plate #312, from $90 to $120.00
Santa in Chimney, plate #281, from $125 to $200.00
Santa's Boot, plate #273, from $20 to $40.00
Scotty Dog, plate #35, from $20 to $35.00
Submarine, plate #104, from $500 to $600.00

Telephone, plate #222, from $1,000.00 to $1,250.00.

Telephone (Millstein Tot), plate #234, from $30 to $40.00
Turkey Gobbler, plate #75, from $175 to $225.00
Uncle Sam by Barrel, plate #215, from $750 to $900.00
Victory Lines Bus, plate #156, from $45 to $75.00
World Globe, plate #445, from $475 to $525.00
Yellow Taxi, plate #184, from $1,200 to $1,400.00

Cast Iron

Realistically modeled and carefully detailed cast-iron toys enjoyed their heyday from about the turn of the century (some companies began production a little earlier) until about the 1940s when they were gradually edged out by lighter-weight toys that were less costly to produce and to ship. (Some of the cast irons were more than 20" in length and very heavy.) Many were vehicles faithfully patterned after actual models seen on city streets at the time. Horse-drawn carriages were phased out when motorized vehicles came into use.

Some of the larger manufacturers were Arcade (Illinois), who by the 1920s was recognized as a leader in the industry; Dent (Pennsylvania); Hubley (Pennsylvania); and Kenton (Ohio). In the 1940s Kenton came out with a few horse-drawn toys which are collectible in their own right but naturally much less valuable than the older ones. In addition to those already noted, there were many minor makers; you will see them mentioned in the listings.

For more detailed information on these companies, we recommend *Collecting Toys* by Richard O'Brien (Books Americana).

Advisor: John McKenna (M2).

See also Banks; Pull and Push Toys.

Airplanes

Air France Fighter Plane, Arcade, bl w/yel pressed steel wings, NP propeller, 10" L, VG, A $250.00
America Airplane, Hubley, gray w/red lettering & stars on wings, 3 NP propellers, w/pilot & co-pilot, 17" wingspan, NM, A $5,000.00
Bremen Airplane, Kilgore, gr w/NP propeller & wheels, 7" L, rpt, A $325.00
Lindy Airplane, Hubley, bl w/emb lettering & stars on wings, NP single propeller, blk rubber tires, 3½" wingspan, M, A $750.00
Lindy Airplane, Hubley, gray w/red lettering, NP single propeller, 10" wingspan, NM, A $1,900.00

Photo courtesy Dunbar Gallery

Lindy Airplane, red with embossed lettering on wings, nickel-plated propeller, engine, and wheels, 4", EX, from $350.00 to $450.00.

Lindy Glider, Hubley, red w/yel wings, figure seated on front, 6½" L, VG, A $1,200.00
Lindy NR-211 Lockheed Sirius, red & blk w/NP propeller, rubber tires, w/pilot & co-pilot, rpt, EX, A $2,800.00
Seagull Airplane, Kilgore, red w/NP wing-mounted propeller & wheels, 7¾" L, VG, A $880.00
Travel Air Mystery Airplane, Kilgore, red w/NP propeller & wheels, 7" wingspan, M, A $1,100.00
UX-166 Airplane, AC Williams, red w/NP propeller, engine & wheels, 6½" L, EX, A $350.00
UX-166 Monoplane, AC Williams, silver w/NP propeller & motor, spoke wheels, 6" L, G, A $200.00

Boats

Battleship, Dent, wht & yel w/rpl bl mast, 2 battle stations, figure standing on pilot's deck, 19", G, A $2,500.00
City of New York Paddleboat, Wilkins, wht w/blk stacks & red trim, 15", G $1,000.00
Racing Scull, US Hardware, 4 oarsmen, 4 spoked wheels, G $850.00
Racing Scull, US Hardware, 8 oarsmen, yel & blk scull w/4 red spoked wheels, 14", rpt, EX $2,000.00
Speedboat, Hubley, mk Static, yel w/red detail, 3 rubber tires, driver w/hand on motor, 9½", EX, A $5,700.00

Speedboat, Hubley, 1930s, red w/2 NP wheels, integral driver, 5½", G, A $200.00

Static Boat, Hubley, red w/Static emb on both sides, driver w/hand on motor, 9½", EX, A $1,650.00

Steamboat, Wilkins, wht w/bl & red trim, 3 spoked wheels, 7½", G $150.00

Character

Andy Gump Car, Arcade, red w/NP grille & gr-pnt disk wheels, figure in gr suit, 7¼", EX, A $2,300.00

Andy Gump Car, Arcade, red w/NP grille & gr-pnt disk wheels, figure in blk suit, 7¼", VG, A $1,700.00

Chester Gump Cart, Arcade, figure in yel cart w/red spoke wheels, wht horse, 7½", rpt, A $200.00

Chester Gump Cart, Arcade, figure in yel cart w/red spoke wheels, 7½", EX, A $500.00

Foxy Grandpa Cart, Harris, figure standing in gr donkey-drawn cart, red spoke wheels, 7¼", EX, A $300.00

Popeye Spinach Wagon, Hubley, red w/blk rubber tires, mc figure, 6", EX, A $950.00

Circus Animals and Accessories

Overland Circus Band Wagon, Kenton, with six band members, driver, and two white horses with riders, spoke wheels, 15", EX, A, $800.00; Overland Circus Cage Wagon, Kenton, red with yellow spoke wheels, with bear, driver, and two white horses, 14", EX, A, $385.00.

Overland Circus Band Wagon, Kenton, w/6 band members, driver & 2 wht horses w/riders, spoke wheels, 15", MIB, A $1,000.00

Overland Circus Cage Wagon, Kenton, red w/yel spoke wheels, w/bear, driver & 2 wht horses, 14", MIB, A $700.00

Overland Circus Calliope Wagon, Kenton, red w/yel spoke wheels, w/2 wht horses & 4 figures, 14", EX, A....$1,650.00

Overland Circus Truck, Kenton, red w/gold trim & wht disk wheels, w/2 elephants & driver, 8", EX, A $1,300.00

Royal Circus Band Wagon, Hubley, red w/bl & gold spoke wheels, 4 gray horses & 6 musicians, EX $2,100.00

Royal Circus Cage Wagon, Hubley, bl w/gold trim, yel spoke wheels, w/lion, 2 gray horses & driver, 9½", VG.....$925.00

Construction

Buckeye Ditch Digger, Kenton, red & gr w/NP chain drive, digger & wheels, 12", G, A $475.00

Buckeye Ditch Digger, Kenton, red & gr w/NP digger, cast wheels w/chain treads, 9", EX, A $635.00

Caterpillar Tractor, Arcade, yel w/blk rubber treads, NP driver, 7¾", EX, A $700.00

Caterpillar Tractor, Arcade, 1929 model, gr w/red spoke wheels, orig chain tracks, NP driver, 5½", EX, A $1,750.00

Caterpillar Tractor, Arcade, 1936 model, yel w/silver engine, metal treads, NP driver, 7½", VG, A $900.00

Cement Mixer Truck, red & gr w/NP drum & side dump, wht rubber tires, w/driver, 8½", EX, A $1,200.00

Fairfield Ditch Digger, Kenton, 1930, red & gr w/wht rubber tires, 9½", EX, A $2,100.00

Galion Master Road Roller, Kenton, red w/wooden roller, NP spoke wheels, integral driver, 7½", EX, A $200.00

Huber Road Roller, Hubley, gr w/red spoke wheels, NP figure, 7½", NM, A $1,300.00

Jaeger Cement Mixer, Kenton, orange w/bl fr, aluminum drum & scoop, NP disk wheels, 9¼", VG, A $775.00

Jaeger Cement Mixer, Kenton, red & gr w/NP drum, scoop & disk wheels, 7", VG, A $385.00

Jaeger Cement Mixer, Kenton, red w/NP drum, rpl wht rubber tires, w/driver, 9", EX, A $800.00

Jaeger Cement Mixer, Kenton, silver with red and green drum support, nickel-plated drum, scoop, and levers, white rubber tires, 7", EX, A, $350.00; Jaeger Cement Mixer, Kenton, silver with red and green drum support, nickel-plated drum, scoop, and levers, white rubber tires, 9½", EX, A, $350.00.

Jaeger Cement Mixer, yel & bl w/silver drum, NP spoke wheels, 7", rpt, A $385.00

Jaeger Cement Mixer Truck, Kenton, red w/NP drum, wht rubber tires, 7½", EX, A $500.00

Photo courtesy Dunbar Gallery

Road Scraper, Dent, light blue with gold-painted spoke wheels, 5", EX, D10, $375.00.

Jaeger Cement Mixer Truck, Kenton, red w/NP drum, wht rubber tires, w/driver, 9", VG, A $1,450.00
Mack Cement Mixer Truck, Hubley, red & gr w/blk rubber tires, NP driver, 8", rstr, A $1,750.00
Panama Steam Shovel, Hubley, gr & red w/NP shovel, wht rubber tires, cast figures on trailer, 12", G, A $935.00
Steam Shovel Truck, Hubley, gr & red w/NP shovel, wht rubber tires, 4", VG, A $385.00
Steam Shovel Truck, Hubley, red & gr w/silver-pnt shovel, rpl wht rubber tires, 9¾", VG, A $350.00

Farm Toys

See also Horse-Drawn.

Allis Chalmers Tractor and Manure Spreader, Arcade, red and green with white rubber tires, 8", EX, D10, $350.00.

Case 3-Bottom Plow, Vindex, red w/gr spoke wheels, 10¼", EX+ $1,750.00
Ford Model N Tractor, Arcade, red w/gold highlights, blk rubber tires, w/driver, 6½", M, A $2,600.00
Fordson Tractor, Arcade, blk w/red spoke wheels, NP driver, 5½", EX, A $225.00
Fordson Tractor, Arcade, red w/gr spoke wheels, NP driver, 5½", NM, A $700.00
Fordson Tractor w/Land Scraper, Arcade, gray, Thorndike Co, Sioux City... stenciled on wheels, NP driver, 6", EX, A $525.00
Hay Wagon, Kyser & Rex, open seat wagon w/flared stake sides & spoke wheels pulled by steer, w/driver, 11½", EX, A $525.00
John Deere Harvester, Vindex, silver w/gr trim, complete w/combine attachment & figure, 13½", EX, A $7,100.00
John Deere Manure Spreader, Vindex, red w/gr shafts, yel spoke wheels, 9¼", very rare, M....................................$3,500.00
John Deere Thresher, Vindex, gray & gr w/yel spoke wheels, removable straw stacker & grain pipe, 7½", rare, EX+ $6,000.00
McCormick-Deering Thresher, Arcade, gr w/red highlights, wht spoke wheels, 12", M, A.................................$2,300.00
McCormick-Deering Thresher, Arcade, gray w/red striping, yel spoke wheels, 11", EX, A...$300.00
McCormick-Deering Thresher, Arcade, yel w/NP spoke wheels, 9½", rpl straw shoot, EX, A....................................$700.00
McCormick-Deering 10-20 Tractor, Arcade, gray w/red spoke wheels, NP driver, 7", EX $750.00
Oliver Row Crop Tractor, Arcade, 1939, gr w/red striping, blk rubber tires w/red hubs, NP driver, 7", MIB $2,500.00
Oliver Row Crop Tractor, Arcade, 1939, red, blk rubber tires w/yel hubs, NP driver, 7", EX $325.00
Oliver Superior Manure Spreader, Arcade, yel w/NP shafts & blk trim, 2 blk rubber tires, 9½", MIB $2,800.00
Plantation Cart, Kenton, horse-drawn cart w/driver, spoke wheels, 13", VG, A $550.00

Tractor, Hubley, green with spoke wheels, 4", EX, D10, $250.00.

Tractor Set, Arcade, 1930s, complete, NM, D10, $750.00.

Tractor, Skoglund & Olson, bl w/red spoke wheels, NP driver, scarce, EX, A $1,100.00
Tractor & Wagon, Arcade, red tractor w/gr open bed wagon, blk rubber tires, integral driver, 12", NM, A.................$400.00

Firefighting

Only motor vehicles are listed here; **see also Horse-Drawn.**

Fire Chief Car, Arcade, red w/NP bell on hood, wht rubber tires, 5", NM, A...$1,650.00
Fire Department Set, Hubley, w/fire chief car, hose reel truck, Harley Davidson motorcycle & accessories, MIB, A .$2,600.00
Fire Pumper, Kenton, red w/wht rubber tires, integral driver, 10", G+, A...$350.00
Ford Pumper Truck, Arcade, 1941 model, red w/blk rubber tires, 6 firemen, 13", VG, A $450.00
Ladder Truck, AC Williams, red w/NP grille, bell & running boards, 2 ladders, wht rubber tires, 7¼", EX, A....$1,300.00

Ladder Truck, Arcade, red w/NP grille, bumper & headlights, cast ladders & driver, wht rubber tires, 6¾", EX, A..$400.00
Ladder Truck, Arcade, red w/NP grille, 2 yel ladders, blk rubber tires, 2 firemen, 9¾", NM, A $1,300.00
Ladder Truck, Arcade, red w/yel ladders, blk rubber tires, 2 firemen, 15¾", missing hose reel, G, A........................$385.00
Ladder Truck, Hubley, red w/rpl NP ladders, wht rubber tires, integral driver, 12", EX, A.......................................$475.00

Photo courtesy Jacquie and Bob Henry

Ladder Truck, Hubley, red with replaced nickel-plated ladders, white rubber tires, two nickel-plated figures, 8½", EX, H7, $425.00.

Ladder Truck, Hubley, red w/silver highlights, chrome ladders, blk rubber tires w/spokes, NP driver, 13¼", EX, A..$650.00
Ladder Truck, Kenton, red w/NP extension ladder, disk wheels, w/driver, 9¼", VG, A...$950.00
Ladder Truck, Kenton, red w/4 yel ladders, spoke wheels, w/driver, 21", EX, A $975.00
Ladder Truck, red w/yel highlights, 2 wooden ladders, 2 firemen, 14", VG, A...$475.00
Ladder Truck, Skoglund & Olson, red w/NP supports, tin ladder, wht rubber tires, w/driver, 16", rpt, A $700.00
Mack Fire Truck, Arcade, red w/NP ladders & spoke wheels, integral driver, 9¾", G, A $950.00
Mack Ladder Truck, red w/yel ladders, NP spoke wheels & driver, 17¾", rpt, A $500.00
Pontiac Fire Truck, Arcade, red w/NP grille, wht rubber tires, integral firemen, 8⅝", missing 1 headlight, EX, A ..$250.00
Pumper Truck, AC Williams, red w/gold highlights, NP tires, integral driver, 10½", rpt, A...................................$350.00
Pumper Truck, AC Williams, red w/gold highlights, wht rubber tires, 3 firemen, 7½", EX, A $300.00
Pumper Truck, Hubley, red w/NP boiler, steam valves, cranks & firemen, blk rubber tires w/spokes, 13", EX, A $1,100.00
Pumper Truck, Hubley, red w/NP grille, wht rubber tires, NP firemen, 10", VG, A $525.00
Pumper Truck, Hubley, red w/NP grille & boiler, wht rubber tires, 2 firemen, 6½", EX, A $250.00
Pumper Truck, Hubley, red w/silver grille, running boards & boiler, wht rubber tires, 2 firemen, 8½", EX, A $450.00
Pumper Truck, Hubley, red w/silver highlights, blk rubber tires w/spokes, NP driver, 11", EX, A..............................$525.00
Pumper Truck, Kenton, red w/gold highlights, wht rubber tires, integral driver, 10½", EX, A $525.00
Water Tower Truck, Kenton, red w/bl extension crane, NP spoke wheels, integral driver, 16", rpt, A.............$1,450.00
Water Tower Truck, Kenton, red w/gr extension crane, NP disk wheels, 12", NM, A...$1,750.00

Horse-Drawn and Other Animals

Cement Mixer, Kenton, orange and green with nickel-plated drum and scoop, single black horse, with driver, 14", NM, A, $1,650.00; Contractor's Dump Wagon, Arcade, green with black rubber tires, one black and one white horse, with driver, 13", NM, A, $400.00.

Coal & Wood Wagon, Wilkins, gr w/yel spoke wheels, single blk horse, w/driver, 12", EX, A.....................................$775.00

Photo courtesy Dunbar Gallery

Farm Wagon, Arcade, 1940s, red with green detail, two dapple-gray horses, black rubber tires, 11", NM, D10, from $750.00 to $1,250.00.

Fire Hose-Reel Wagon, Ives, blk w/gold highlights, red spoke wheels, 2 blk horses, w/driver, 15", prof rstr, A........$500.00
Fire Ladder Wagon, Kenton, red w/2 yel ladders & spoke wheels, 2 blk & 1 wht horse on wheeled fr, w/driver, 16", NM, A $250.00
Fire Pumper, Carpenter, blk w/gold highlights, red spoke wheels, 1 blk & 1 wht horse, 18", VG, A $1,155.00
Fire Pumper, Kenton, red w/gold highlights, yel spoke wheels, 3 horses on wheeled fr, w/driver, 17", G, A $400.00
Hansom Cab, Kenton, bl w/yel spoke wheels, single wht horse, w/driver & lady passenger, 15¾", NM, A $385.00
Horse-Drawn Sleigh, Hubley, gr w/gold trim, single wht horse, lady driver in red, 15", EX, A $700.00
Ice Wagon, Hubley, red w/yel top, 4 yel spoke wheels, 2 blk horses, w/driver, 15½", VG, A $800.00
Log Cart, Kenton, red w/yel spoke wheels, single blk horse w/gold highlights, w/driver, 13", NM, A.................$650.00
Log Cart, Kenton, yel w/red spoke wheels, 2 blk oxen, driver atop tree trunk, 14", EX, A..$825.00

Milk Wagon, Kenton, wht w/red spoke wheels, single blk horse w/gold & silver highlights, w/driver, 12½", MIB, A..$500.00
Pony Cart, Dent, blk w/yel spoke wheels, lady driver, 9½", VG, A...$350.00
Sand & Gravel Wagon, Kenton, red w/gr spoke wheels, 1 blk & 1 wht horse, NP driver, 10", MIB, A...$200.00
Santa in Sleigh, Hubley, gr w/gold highlights, 2 brn reindeer on red spoke wheels, 17", EX, A...$1,100.00
Stake Wagon, Kenton, gr w/red spoke wheels, 1 blk & 1 wht horse, w/driver, 14", M, A...$300.00
Stake Wagon, Kenton, red w/gr spoke wheels, single blk horse w/silver & gold highlights, w/driver, 14", MIB, A...$300.00
Sulky, Kenton, yel w/NP spoke wheels, blk horse, w/driver, 7¼", MIB, A...$350.00
Surrey, Kenton, bl w/yel spoke wheels, cloth canopy, 2 wht horses, w/driver & lady passenger, 12½", MIB, A...$550.00
Surrey, Stanley, bl w/yel spoke wheels, cloth canopy, 2 blk horses & 2 female passengers, 11½", MIB, A...$155.00

Motor Vehicles

Note: Description lines for generic vehicles may simply begin with 'Bus,' 'Coupe,' or 'Motorcycle,' for example. But more busses will be listed as 'Coach Bus,' 'Coast-To-Coast,' 'Greyhound,' 'Interurban,' 'Mack,' or 'Public Service' (and there are other instances); coupes may be listed under 'Ford,' 'Packard,' or some other specific car company; and lines describing motorcycles might be also start 'Armored,' 'Excelsior-Henderson,' 'Delivery,' 'Policeman,' 'Harley-Davidson,' and so on. Look under 'Yellow Cab' or 'Checker Cab' and other cab companies for additional 'Taxi Cab' descriptions. We often gave any lettering or logo on the vehicle priority when we entered descriptions, so with this in mind, you should have a good idea where to look for your particular toy. Body styles (Double-Decker Bus, Cape-Top Roadster, etc) were also given priority.

Photo courtesy Dunbar Gallery

Ambulance, 1930s, integral medic on back, 4", EX, D10, from $200.00 to $300.00.

Ambulance, Arcade, bl w/wht rubber tires, 7⅝", G, A..$325.00
Ambulance, Arcade, wht w/red cross emb on sides, blk rubber tires, 5⅞", overpnt, A...$250.00
American Oil Co Truck, Dent, bl w/C-style cab, NP disk wheels, 10½", rpt, A...$350.00
Arctic Ice Cream Truck, Kilgore, bl & red w/NP disk wheels, 8", G, A...$400.00
Arctic Ice Cream Truck, Kilgore, bl & wht w/wht rubber tires, 6½", rpt, VG, A...$200.00
Auto Express Van, Hubley, orange w/blk roof, red spoke wheels, w/driver, 9½", EX, A...$1,265.00
Bell Telephone Truck, Hubley, bl w/wht rubber tires, integral driver, 9", EX, A...$200.00
Bell Telephone Truck, Hubley, brn w/NP winch, w/3 digging tools & trailer w/attached wood pole, 8", NM (G box), A...$350.00
Bell Telephone Truck, Hubley, gr w/gold highlights, wht rubber tires, w/driver, 5", EX, A...$400.00

Photo courtesy Dunbar Gallery

Bell Telephone Truck, Hubley, green with nickel-plated spoke wheels, 3¾", EX, D10, $300.00.

Bell Telephone Truck, Hubley, gr w/red detail, wht rubber tires, 9¼", EX, A...$650.00
Bell Telephone Truck, Hubley, gr w/silver sides, spoke wheels, 8¼", rpt, VG, A...$250.00
Bell Telephone Truck, Hubley, gr w/wht rubber tires, 4", NM, A...$225.00
Borden's Milk Truck, Arcade, gr milk bottle shape w/wht rubber tires, VG, A...$1,450.00
Borden's Milk Truck, Hubley, wht w/NP grille & spoke wheels, opening rear door, 7½", EX, A...$2,000.00

Photo courtesy Dunbar Gallery

Buick Sedan, Arcade, blue-green with black top, white rubber tires, nickel-plated driver, 8½", EX, $2,500.00.

Bus, AC Williams, take-apart model, orange & blk w/wht rubber tires, 4¾", NM, A..**$935.00**

Bus, Arcade, orange w/wht rubber tires & 2 mounted spares, 13¾", EX, A..**$2,200.00**

Bus, Arcade, 1920s, bl w/NP tires, 4½", G, A **$150.00**

Bus, Atlantic City NJ, Arcade, bl & wht w/wht rubber tires, 10", EX, A..**$300.00**

Bus, Atlantic City NJ, Arcade, bl & wht w/wht rubber tires, 7¼", NM, A..**$550.00**

Bus, Bowen Motor Coach 1936..., Arcade, silver & bl w/wht rubber tires, 10¾", NMIB, A **$4,400.00**

Bus, Dent, bl w/disk wheels, 8", G, A.............................**$450.00**

Bus, Dent, orange w/silver & yel disk wheels, 6¼", EX, A..**$475.00**

Bus, Hubley, orange streamlined style w/silver highlights, wht rubber tires, 8", EX, A **$200.00**

Bus, Kenton, orange w/blk roof, wht rubber tires, 9", rpt, A..**$135.00**

Bus, National Trailways System, Arcade, orange & beige w/wht rubber tires, 9", NM, A **$1,800.00**

Bus, Santa Fe Trails, Arcade, red & beige w/blk rubber tires, 9", NM, A **$2,500.00**

Car Carrier, AC Williams, green with three Austin sedans on slant-front trailer, nickel-plated tires, 12⅜", repaint, A, $475.00.

Car Carrier, AC Williams, red w/3 Austin sedans on gr slant-front trailer, NP tires, 12⅜", EX, A **$855.00**

Car Carrier, Arcade, gr w/3 Austin coupes on red flatbed trailer, wht rubber tires, 14", VG, A **$450.00**

Car Carrier, Arcade, gr w/3 Ford Model A cars on red flatbed trailer, spoke wheels, 20", VG, A **$1,300.00**

Car Carrier, Arcade, gr w/4 cars on red 2-tiered trailer, blk rubber tires, 15⅜", G, A **$450.00**

Car Carrier, Arcade, red w/3 cars on flatbed trailer, spoke wheels, 23½", EX, A..**$885.00**

Car Carrier, Hubley, red w/4 cars on 2-tiered trailer, wht rubber tires, 10¼", EX, A..**$365.00**

Car Carrier, Kenton, red w/4 vehicles on blk flatbed trailer, wht rubber tires, 18", VG, A.......................................**$1,550.00**

Chevrolet Coupe, Arcade, 1925 model, blk w/wht rubber tires & spoke wheels, NP driver, 7", NM, A **$825.00**

Chevrolet Coupe, Arcade 1928 model, blk & gray w/NP tires & mounted spare, 8¼", EX, A **$1,300.00**

Chrysler Airflow, AC Williams, orange w/NP grille & bumper, wht rubber tires, 4¾", EX, A..................................**$400.00**

Chrysler Airflow, AC Williams, red w/NP grille, bumper & chassis, wht rubber tires, 7", EX, A **$935.00**

Chrysler Airflow, Hubley, bl w/NP grille & bumper, mounted spare, wht rubber tires, 6¼", G-, A **$250.00**

Chrysler Airflow, Hubley, gr w/NP grille & bumper, mounted spare, wht rubber tires, 8", VG, A........................**$2,200.00**

Chrysler Airflow, Hubley, 1932 model, red w/NP grille & bumper, mounted spare, rpl wht rubber tires, 7⅞", VG, A..**$525.00**

Coal Truck, Hubley, yel & gr w/red spoke wheels, w/driver, 9½", M, A **$5,400.00**

Coal Truck, Kenton, red w/NP tires, 6½", VG, A..........**$450.00**

Coal Truck, Kenton, red w/wht rubber tires, 7¾", G, A .**$825.00**

Coast To Coast Truck, AC Williams, yel w/gr open stake trailer, NP spoke wheels, 10⅛", G, A **$275.00**

Contractor's Truck, Dent, red w/C-style cab, NP disk wheels, w/driver, 7½", EX, A...**$1,000.00**

Contractor's Truck, Kenton, red w/3 dump buckets in open bed, wht rubber tires, w/driver, 10", rpt, A **$450.00**

Contractor's Truck, Kenton, red w/3 dump buckets in open bed, yel spoke wheels, 8", rpt, EX, A **$300.00**

Coupe, AC Williams, take-apart model, maroon & brn w/NP grille & headlights, wht rubber tires, 6½", rpt, A....**$350.00**

Coupe, Kilgore, brn w/NP spoke wheels, 2 rpl passengers, 6¼", VG, A **$250.00**

Coupe, Skoglund & Olson, gray w/wht rubber tires & mounted spare, 8", rpt, A..**$550.00**

Photo courtesy Dunbar Gallery

Chevrolet Sedan, Arcade, green with nickel-plated tires, 8¼", EX, D10, $3,850.00.

Photo courtesy Dunbar Gallery

Delivery Cycle, marked Flowers, Hubley, blue-green with white rubber tires, integral driver, 3½", EX, D10, $1,350.00.

Delivery Truck, AC Williams, take-apart model, yel w/blk chassis, wht rubber tires, 7¼", EX, A $500.00
DeSoto Sedan, Arcade, gray w/NP grille & bumper, wht rubber tires, Sundial Shoes decal on trunk, 4", VG, A $125.00
DeSoto Sedan, Arcade, gray w/NP grille & bumper, wht rubber tires, 6⅛", G, A $155.00
Double-Decker Bus, AC Williams, red w/NP tires, 7¾", G-, A $175.00
Double-Decker Bus, Arcade, bl w/wht rubber tires, NP driver, 8", rpl rear steps, EX, A $385.00
Double-Decker Bus, Arcade, Chicago Motor Coach, red w/wht rubber tires, 8", EX, A $1,000.00
Double-Decker Bus, Arcade, gr w/blk rubber tires, 4 passengers on upper deck, 8", EX, A $350.00
Double-Decker Bus, Arcade, gr w/NP grille, orig decal on side, blk rubber tires, 8", NM, A $750.00
Double-Decker Bus, Arcade, Yellow Coach, bl w/gold highlights, wht rubber tires, 13⅜", VG, A $1,750.00
Double-Decker Bus, Freidag, gr w/orange stripe, disk wheels, passengers at windows, 9¼", G, A $600.00
Double-Decker Bus, Kenton, gr w/orange stripes, disk wheels, 6¼", missing rear steps o/w VG, A $350.00
Double-Decker Bus, Kenton, gr w/red stripe, wht rubber tires, 5 passengers on upper deck, 10", EX, A..................$1,100.00
Double-Decker Bus, Kenton, Pickwick Nite Coach, bl w/orange stripe, disk wheels & spare, 11", rpt, A................$1,000.00
Double-Decker Bus, Kenton, red w/gr stripe, wht rubber tires, 4 rpl NP passengers on upper deck, 6½", VG, A........$350.00

Photo courtesy Dunbar Gallery

Double-Decker Bus, Kenton, red with green stripe, white rubber tires, two original passengers on upper deck, 6½", NM, D10, $1,450.00.

Dump Truck, Arcade, gr w/red chassis, wht rubber tires, NP driver, 10½", rpt, A $450.00
Dump Truck, Hubley, gr & red w/C-style cab, wht rubber tires, NP driver, 10¾", EX, A..$900.00
Dump Truck, Hubley, red & silver w/extended roof guard, wht rubber tires, 7½", EX, A $350.00
Dump Truck, Kilgore, bl & red w/NP disk wheels, 8½", G, A $300.00
Express Stake Truck, Kilgore, take-apart model, bl & gr w/yel chassis, wht rubber tires, 5¾", M, A $1,100.00
Faegol Bus, Arcade, bl w/disk wheels, w/driver, 12", G, A.$300.00

Photo courtesy Dunbar Gallery

Faegol Bus, Arcade, 1930s, blue with nickel-plated disk wheels, 8", EX, D10, $750.00.

Faegol Bus, Arcade, mk Compliments of Faegol Companies, bl w/NP disk wheels, 8", EX, A $1,100.00
Faegol Bus, Arcade, mk Miss Lois, bl w/gold stripe, NP tires, 7¾", EX, A $500.00
Faegol Bus, Arcade, mk Reindeer Stages, bl w/NP disk wheels, 7¾", G-, A $135.00
Ford Coupe, Arcade, 1925 model, blk w/spoke wheels, NP driver, 6½", EX, A $350.00
Ford Coupe, Arcade, 1927 model, red w/gold stripe, NP spoke wheels & driver, 6¾", VG, A....................................$275.00
Ford Model A Coupe, Arcade, 1928 model, gr w/NP spoke wheels & driver, 6¾", NM, A $450.00
Ford Model T, Arcade, blk w/NP spoke wheels, 5", NM, A.$475.00
Ford Model T, Arcade, 1923 model, blk w/gold stripe, NP spoke wheels & driver, 6½", EX, A..................................$275.00
Ford Model T, Arcade, 1924 model, blk w/gold stripe, spoke wheels, 6½", EX, A..$300.00
Ford Touring Car, Arcade, blk w/spoke wheels, 6½", VG, A $325.00
Ford Tudor Sedan, Arcade, 1925 model, blk w/gold stripe, spoke wheels, w/driver, 6⅜", EX, A $350.00
Ford Wrecker, Arcade, red w/gr Weaver crane, NP crank & spoke wheels, 11", VG, A...$385.00
Ford Wrecker, Arcade, red w/gr Weaver crane, NP crank & spoke wheels, w/driver, 10", VG, A $425.00
Gasoline Truck, Champion, red w/C-style cab, wht rubber tires, 8", EX, A...$385.00
Gasoline Truck, Kenton, gr w/emb gold filler caps & cans on sides, disk wheels, w/driver, 8", rpt, A......................$350.00
Gasoline Truck, Skoglund & Olson, red w/2 fill caps, wht rubber tires w/bl hubs, 10", rpt, A......................................$600.00
Greyhound Bus, Arcade, Century of Progress, Chicago 1933, bl & wht w/wht rubber tires, 11½", EX, A..................$400.00
Greyhound Bus, Arcade, Century of Progress, Chicago 1934, bl & wht w/wht rubber tires, 5⅝", EX, A....................$475.00
Greyhound Bus, Arcade, City of Sacramento, bl & wht w/wht rubber tires, 9", NM, A...$950.00
Greyhound Bus, Arcade, Great Lakes 1936 Exposition, bl & wht w/wht rubber tires, 6¾", VG, A $350.00
Greyhound Bus, Arcade, Greyhound Lines, bl & wht w/wht rubber tires, 7½", NM, A...$550.00

Greyhound Bus, Arcade, Greyhound Lines GMC, bl & wht w/wht rubber tires, 5⅝", EX, A **$275.00**

Greyhound Bus, Arcade, Visit the World's Fair San Francisco, bl & wht w/blk rubber tires, 8¾", EX, A **$1,650.00**

Photo courtesy Dunbar Gallery

Greyhound New York World's Fair Motor Train, orange and blue with nickel-plated driver, EX, D10, $350.00.

Photo courtesy Dunbar Gallery

Harley-Davidson Motorcycle with Sidecar, Hubley, green with white rubber tires, 5", EX, D10, $750.00.

Photo courtesy Dunbar Gallery

Indian Motorcycle, Hubley, red with aluminum handlebars, black rubber tires with spoke wheels, policeman driver, 9¼", NM, $1,850.00.

Harley Davidson Motorcycle w/Sidecar, Hubley, olive gr, rubber tires w/spoke wheels, w/driver & passenger, 9", NM, A......**$3,400.00**

Hathaway's Bread Truck, Arcade, bl & wht w/lettering & children on side panels, rpl wht rubber tires, EX, A...**$1,650.00**

Hillclimber Motorcycle, Hubley, bl w/blk tank & motor, NP spoke wheels, w/driver, 6½", VG, A.....................**$1,200.00**

Ice Truck, Arcade, bl NP grille, wht rubber tires, 6¾", rpt, A **$200.00**

Indian Crash Car, Hubley, red w/blk rubber tires & spoke wheels, policeman driver, 6½", EX, A **$650.00**

International Dump Truck, Arcade, gr, red & yel w/blk rubber tires, 11¼", G, A **$275.00**

International Dump Truck, Arcade, red & gr w/NP grille, wht rubber tires, 9¼", VG, A **$450.00**

International Dump Truck, Arcade, red & gray w/rpl wht rubber tires, 11", VG, A...**$385.00**

International Pickup Truck, Arcade, yel w/blk rubber tires, 9¼", G, A **$350.00**

International Stake Truck, Arcade, gr w/NP grille & bumper, wht rubber tires, 11¾", G, A...............................**$500.00**

Lincoln Zephyr & Trailer, Hubley, gr w/NP grille & bumper, wht rubber tires, 13½", G, A..................................**$825.00**

Mack Dump Truck, Arcade, bl w/NP spoke wheels, 12", 2 rpl wheels, VG, A **$550.00**

Mack Dump Truck, Arcade, gr & red w/wht rubber tires, 11", VG, A **$275.00**

Mack Dump Truck, Arcade, gray w/wht spoke wheels, NP driver, 12", EX, A **$2,100.00**

Mack Dump Truck, Arcade, red w/cast chain drive, NP spoke wheels, w/driver, 8¼", VG, A **$385.00**

Mack Dump Truck, Arcade, red w/Coal stenciled on sides, blk rubber tires, 10", EX, A **$1,300.00**

Mack Dump Truck, Hubley, gr & red w/NP spoke wheels, 8¾", rstr, A **$635.00**

Mack Gasoline Truck, Arcade, yel w/3 fill caps, wht rubber tires, 13", rpt, A **$450.00**

Mack Ice Truck, Arcade, bl w/NP spoke wheels, w/driver, 8½", G-, A...**$275.00**

Mack Ice Truck, Arcade, bl w/wht rubber tires, 6⅞", VG, A **$275.00**

Mack Stake Truck, Arcade, gr w/NP spoke wheels, 8¾", rpt, A **$325.00**

Photo courtesy Dunbar Gallery

Mack Stake Truck, Hubley, orange with white rubber tires, 4½", EX, D10, $275.00.

Mack Stake Truck, Champion, bl w/C-style cab, NP spoke wheels, 6⅝", VG, A $385.00
Mack Wrecker, Arcade, red w/gr crane, Wrecker stenciled on sides, spoke wheels, no driver, 12½", G, A $600.00
Mack Wrecker, Arcade, red w/gr crane, Wrecker stenciled on sides, spoke wheels, NP driver, 12½", rare, G, A $775.00
Mack Wrecker, Arcade, red w/gr Weaver crane, NP crank & spoke wheels, w/driver, 8¼", EX, A $700.00
Motorcycle, Champion, bl w/NP tires, 5", EX, H7 .... $325.00
Motorcycle, Champion, gr w/wht rubber tires, integral driver, 5", EX, A $350.00
Panel Van, Champion, bl w/wht rubber tires, 7¾", VG, A $450.00
Pickup Truck, Skoglund & Olson, yel w/wht rubber tires & red hubs, 10¾", rpt, A $550.00
Police Motorcycle, Hubley, bl w/wht rubber tires & red-pnt hubs, 6¼", NM, A $825.00

Photo courtesy Dunbar Gallery

Police Patrol, Dent, red with spoke wheels, complete with four figures, 6½", MIB, D10, $1,850.00.

Pontiac Sedan, Arcade, red w/NP grille & bumper, rpl wht rubber tires, 6", rpt, A $125.00
Racer, AC Williams, early model, blk w/NP spoke wheels, integral driver, 7½", G, A $225.00
Racer, AC Williams, red w/cast cylinders on hood, wht rubber tires, NP driver, 8½", EX, A $575.00
Racer, Champion, red & gr w/rpl blk rubber tires, w/driver, 7¼", VG, A $525.00
Racer, Hubley, bl w/gold highlights, red pistons protruding from hood, blk rubber tires w/spokes, w/driver, 10", EX, A $2,300.00
Racer, Hubley, gr w/wht rubber tires, w/driver, 6½", EX, A $225.00
Racer, Hubley, silver & red w/opening hood doors, blk rubber tires w/NP spokes, w/driver, 8½", EX, A $2,100.00
Racer, Hubley, silver & red w/pistons protruding from hood, NP tires, w/driver, 8⅝", EX, A $1,000.00
Racer, Hubley, silver & red w/pistons protruding from hood, wht rubber tires, w/driver, 8½", EX, A $935.00
Racer, Kenton, bl w/red spoke wheels, w/driver, 7¼", rpt, A $185.00
Racer #1, Hubley, red w/wht rubber tires, integral driver, 7¾", VG, A $385.00
Racer #5, Hubley, gr w/NP tires & driver, hood opens, 9½", rpl hood doors, A $1,100.00
Racer #8, Hubley, red w/wht rubber tires, integral driver, 5½", VG, A $200.00

Photo courtesy Dunbar Gallery

Racer #8, Hubley, red with white rubber tires, integral driver, 5½", EX+, D10, $325.00.

Racer #9, Arcade, red w/NP side pipes, disk wheels & driver, 7¾", G, A $550.00
Racer #23, Freidag, gr w/NP disk wheels, NP driver, 4½", VG, A $225.00
Racer w/Headlight, Hubley, red w/wht rubber tires, w/driver, 6¼", EX, A $700.00
Roadster, Kilgore, 1928 model, bl open 2-seater w/NP spoke wheels, 6⅛", NM, A $825.00
Runabout, gr w/lt gr & gold highlights, NP spoke wheels, driver in open bench seat, 6", EX, A $525.00
School Bus, Dent, orange w/blk trim, disk wheels, 8½", rpt, A $325.00
Sedan, AC Williams, gr streamliner w/wht rubber tires, 8½", G-, A $250.00
Sedan, AC Williams, maroon streamliner w/wht rubber tires, 8½", rpt, A $200.00
Sedan, AC Williams, take-apart model, red w/bl chassis, wht rubber tires, 7¼", red rpt, A $250.00
Sedan, Arcade, red w/NP spoke wheels, orig decal on side, 5", VG, A $350.00
Sedan, Dent, bl w/NP tires & mounted spare, 7½", rpt, A $350.00
Sedan & Ramp, Skoglund & Olson, gray touring car w/wht rubber tires & gray hubs, mounted spare, 14" ramp, 8" car, EX, A $1,850.00
Sedan & Trailer, Arcade, red sedan & Mullens Red Cap trailer w/lift-up hood, wht rubber tires, 8¾", VG, A $450.00
Sedan & Trailer, Hubley, red sedan w/silver & red trailer, wht rubber tires, 9½", NM, A $700.00
Stake Truck, AC Williams, take-apart model, yel w/blk chassis, wht rubber tires, 7¼", VG, A $900.00
Stake Truck, Arcade, bl w/NP spoke wheels, 6⅞", VG, A . $225.00
Stake Truck, Arcade, gr w/NP spoke wheels, 7⅜", VG, A . $300.00
Stake Truck, Champion, red w/C-style cab, NP spoke wheels, 7", NM, A $650.00

Stake Truck, Freidag, gray & blk w/open-door cab, spoke wheels, 7½", rpt, A $350.00

Stake Truck, Hubley, red & bl w/wht rubber tires, 6½", EX, A $375.00

Photo courtesy Dunbar Gallery

Stake Truck, Kenton, 1930s, red with white rubber tires, 7", EX, D10, $350.00.

Standard Oil Co Truck, Arcade, gr w/red chassis, wht rubber tires, 12¾", overpnt, A $1,300.00

State Highway Truck, Kenton, red w/NP bumper & disk wheels, 10¼", rare, rpt, A $2,800.00

Studebaker Ice Truck, Arcade, bl w/NP grille & bumper, wht rubber tires, complete w/tongs & ice cubes, 6¾", EX, A $500.00

Photo courtesy Dunbar Gallery

Studebaker Roadster, Hubley, red with nickel-plated grille, bumper, and running boards, white rubber tires and mounted spare, 6¾", EX, $700.00.

Studebaker Sedan, Hubley, red w/NP grille, bumper & running boards, wht rubber tires & mounted spare, 6⅝", EX, A $475.00

Tanker Truck, Kenton, orange w/wht rubber tires, 8¼", VG, A $385.00

Taxi Cab, Arcade, bl w/blk trim, emb luggage rack, blk rubber tires, w/driver, 8¼", G, A $650.00

Taxi Cab, Arcade, orange & blk w/NP tires & spare, 5⅛", EX, A $600.00

Taxi Cab, Dent, orange & blk w/disk wheels & spare, w/driver, 7½", rpt wheels, VG, A $385.00

Taxi Cab Set, Kiddie Toys by Hubley, complete w/3 cars & street signs, MIB, A $950.00

Toy Town Bus, Kilgore, orange w/NP disk wheels, 7¾", scarce, rpt, A $165.00

Toytown Delivery Truck, Kilgore, red w/gold highlights, gold disk wheels, 6⅛", rpt, A $350.00

Wrecker, Arcade, red & gr w/NP spoke wheels & driver, VG, A $650.00

Photo courtesy Dunbar Gallery

Wrecker, Arcade, red with nickel-plated spoke wheels, 5½", EX, D10, $550.00.

Wrecker, Champion, red w/C-style cab, NP crank & barrel, wht rubber tires, 8¼", VG, A $350.00

Wrecker, Hubley, red w/NP grille & boom, wht rubber tires, 7½", EX, A $250.00

Wrecker, Hubley, take-apart model, red & yel w/wht rubber tires, 6¼", G, A $225.00

Wrecker, Skoglund & Olson, wht w/red winch & crane, wht rubber tires, Central Garage emb on sides, 12", EX, A $1,500.00

Yellow Cab, Arcade, bl & orange w/disk wheels, Compliments Little Club New Orleans on roof, 5", EX, A.........$1,100.00

Yellow Cab, Arcade, yel & blk w/wht rubber tires, w/driver, 7¾", EX, A $650.00

Yellow Cab, Hubley, orange Lincoln Zephyr w/blk trim, wht rubber tires, w/driver, 8", VG, A $400.00

Yellow Cab, Kenton, orange & blk w/disk wheels, 6½", G, A $500.00

10-Ton Stake Truck, Hubley, orange w/NP grille & stake sides, rpl wht rubber tires, 8½", VG, A $350.00

5-Ton Stake Truck, Hubley, yel w/red detail, spoke wheels, w/driver, 16½", EX, A $1,000.00

Trains

Freight Car No 4, Wilkins, orange w/gold stenciling, conductor mounted on top, NM, A $900.00

Locomotive & Tender, Hubley, blk w/red spoke wheels, locomotive mk 600, tender mk PRR Co, 16½", EX, A $450.00

Locomotive & Tender, Kenton, blk w/red detail, locomotive mk 999, tender mk NYCRR, 18", 2 wheels missing o/w EX, A $1,000.00

Pullman Railplane, Arcade, red w/wht lettering, 8½", VG, A $150.00

Train Set, Harris, NY Central & Hudson River Railroad baggage car w/locomotive & tender, red & blk, 18", NM, A.$550.00

Train Set, Wilkins, blk locomotive & tender w/red spoke wheels, red boxcar & caboose, 41", EX, A............**$1,100.00**

Miscellaneous

Arcadia Airport, Arcade, pnt & stenciled wood w/2 airplanes, missing canopy, EX, A...**$650.00**

Aviation Gas Trailer, Kilgore, traces of orig bl pnt, 7½", rare, VG, A...**$1,000.00**

Congo Fire Bug, sets off caps when stepped on, complete w/caps & instructions, 3", NMIB, A...................................**$400.00**

Photo courtesy Phil Helley

Road Construction Set, Arcade, complete, NMIB, H6, $600.00.

Road Construction Set, Arcade, missing few signs, EX (worn box), A, $525.00.

Engine Co No 99, Arcade, 1941, pnt & stenciled wood fire house w/pumper truck & ladder truck, NM, A.....**$1,375.00**

Gas Pump, Arcade, bl w/gold base, emb GAS, gallon dial revolves when crank is turned, rope hose, 6", EX.**$1,150.00**

Gas Pump, Arcade, gr w/gold base, emb GAS, gallon dial revolves when crank is turned, rope hose, 6", NM................**$2,600.00**

Grasshopper, Hubley, gr w/NP arms & wheels, 4½", EX, A..**$250.00**

Road Construction Set, Arcade, w/dump truck, tools, road signs, wheelbarrow, etc, missing few signs, EX, A **$525.00**

Sign, National Highway 41 To CPC, No Detours, Arcade, wht & yel w/blk trim, red base, 5¼", EX, A...................**$950.00**

Sign, US 30, Arcade, wht, 4¼", VG..............................**$200.00**

Catalogs

In any area of collecting, old catalogs are a wonderful source for information. Toy collectors value buyers' catalogs, those from toy fairs, and Christmas 'wish books.' Montgomery Ward issued their first Christmas catalog in 1932, and Sears followed a year later. When they can be found, these 'first editions' in excellent condition are valued at a minimum of $200.00 each. Even later issues may sell for upwards of $75.00, since it's those from the '50s and '60s that contain the toys that are now so collectible.

Advisor: Bill Mekalian (M4).

American Flyer, 1949, G, G1 ....**$25.00**

American Toy & Furniture Co, 1976, EX, M4 ....**$10.00**

Aurora Games, 1972, EX **$20.00**

Aurora Hobby Kits, 1973, EX..**$20.00**

Avalon Crafts & Activities, 1971, EX, M4.......................**$10.00**

Bachmann Trains, 1975, EX, M4 ....**$25.00**

Breyer Animal Creations, 1976, EX, M4..........................**$20.00**

Buddy L, 1965, pocket-sz, EX, M4...................................**$75.00**

Buddy L Train Sets, 1976, EX, M4..................................**$50.00**

Buddy L Wish Book, 1975, pocket-sz, EX, M4..................**$25.00**

Cadaco Games, 1976, EX **$10.00**

Gilbert Toys/American Flyer Trains, 1950, full color, 56 pages, EX, A, $50.00.

Chilton Toys, 1975, EX, M4 .... $15.00
Coleco Toys, 1972, EX, M4 .... $20.00
Colorforms, 1973, EX, M4 .... $10.00
Commonwealth Toy & Novelty, 1975, EX, M4 .... $20.00
Creative Playthings, 1970, EX, M4 .... $20.00
Creative Playthings, 1971, EX, M4 .... $10.00
Effanbee Dolls That Touch Your Heart, 1972, EX, M4 .... $20.00
Ertl Model Kits, 1973, EX, M4 .... $20.00
Fisher-Price, 1961, pocket-sz, EX $25.00
Fisher-Price Big Splash on a Rainy Day, 1976, EX $30.00
Fisher-Price Toys Make Learning Fun, 1968, EX $100.00
Furga Dolls, 1970, EX, M4 .... $50.00
Gabriel Learning Toys & Games, 1976, EX, M4 .... $20.00
Galoob, 1973, EX, M4 .... $30.00
Hall's Lifetime Toys, 1971, EX, M4 .... $10.00
Hasbro Dolls, 1972, EX, M4 .... $50.00
Hasbro Romper Room, 1972, EX, M4 .... $50.00
Hot Wheels, 1971, EX $25.00
Hubley, 1970, EX $25.00
Ideal, 1972, EX, M4 .... $75.00
Janex Toy Corp, 1973, EX, M4 .... $10.00
Knickerbocker, features Raggedy Ann & Andy, 1972, EX, M4 .... $65.00
Kusan Toys, 1968, EX $25.00
Lionel Trains, 1968, EX, M4 .... $20.00
Madame Alexander Dolls, 1968, EX, M4 .... $80.00
Marx Toys, 1972, EX, M4 .... $100.00
Matchbox, 1-75, 1976, EX, M4 .... $75.00
Matchbox, 1971, EX, M4 .... $175.00
Mattel Toys, 1968, EX $150.00
McKesson's Gift Book, 1955-56, EX, I2 .... $85.00
Mego Superstars, 1974, EX $250.00
Milton Bradley Games & Puzzles, 1970, EX, M4 .... $50.00
Movin' w/Mattel, 1976, EX, M4 .... $100.00
Nylint, 1967, EX $35.00

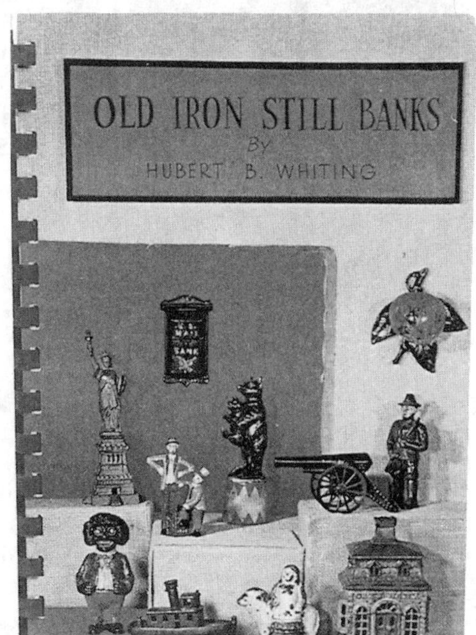

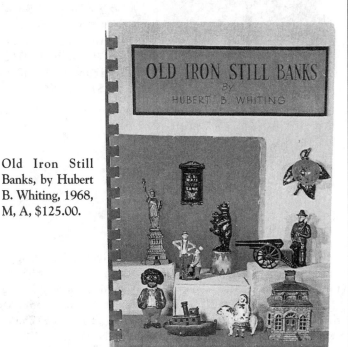

Old Iron Still Banks, by Hubert B. Whiting, 1968, M, A, $125.00.

Ohio Art World of Toys, 1970, EX $25.00
Parker Brothers Games & Toys, 1976, EX, M4 .... $80.00
Parker Games, 1968, EX, M4 .... $150.00
Playskool, 1968, w/Lincoln Log insert, EX $100.00
Playskool, 1975, EX $70.00
Remco Toys, 1957, rare, EX $50.00
Revell Model Kits, 1975, EX $75.00
Sears, 1967 Christmas, NM $100.00
Selchow & Righter Games, 1976, EX, M4 .... $10.00
Steiff, 1957, features 1950s animals, 15 pgs, M, G16 .... $35.00
Strombecker Tootsietoy, 100th Anniversary, 1976, EX, M4 .... $100.00
Strombecker Tootsietoy, 1972, EX, M4 .... $50.00
Superhero Catalog of Games, Books, Toys & Puzzles, 1977, EX $45.00
Thingmaker, Mattel, 1967, EX, F8 .... $15.00
Timeless Creations, 1991, EX, D2 .... $10.00
Tonka Toys, 1960, EX, M4 .... $35.00
Tonka 25th Anniversary, 1972, EX $150.00
Topper Toys, 1971, EX $35.00
Transogram, 1969, EX $75.00
Tyco, 1975, EX, M4 .... $25.00
View-Master Pictorial Products, 1976, EX, M4 .... $40.00
Vogue Dolls, 1974, EX, M4 .... $25.00
Wolverine Toys, 1973, EX $20.00

Cereal Boxes and Premiums

This is an area of collecting that attracts crossover interest from fans of advertising as well as character-related toys. What makes a cereal box interesting? Look for Batman, Huckleberry Hound, or a well-known sports figure like Larry Bird or Roger Maris on the front or back. Boxes don't have to be old to be collectible, but the basic law of supply and demand dictates that the older ones are going to be expensive! After all, who saved cereal boxes from 1910? By chance if Grandma did, the 1910 Corn Flakes box with a printed-on baseball game could get her $750.00. Unless you're not concerned with bugs, it will probably be best to empty the box and very carefully pull apart the glued flaps. Then you can store it flat. Be sure to save any prize that might have been packed inside. For more information we recommend *Cereal Box Bonanza, The 1950s, ID and Values* (Collector Books), and *Sixties Cereal Boxes and Premiums* by Scott Bruce.

Advisor: Scott Bruce (B14); Larry Blodget (B2), Post Cereal cars.
Other Sources: T2

General Mills Cap 'n Crunch, 1973, bank offer, side panel cut o/w EX, B14 .... $175.00
General Mills Cheerios, 1940, Lone Ranger on front, Lone Ranger town cutouts on back, NM, A $250.00
General Mills Cheerios, 1950s, shows Lone Ranger Rapid-Fire Revolver, VG, A $175.00
General Mills Cheerios, 1964, w/wild animal trading card cutouts, EX, B14 .... $12.00
General Mills Sir Grapefellow, w/biplane glider offer, NM, from $125 to $200.00

General Mills Wheaties, 1940s, w/Paul Bunyan mask, EX, B14 ....$20.00
General Mills Wheaties, 1940s, w/Princess Goldenhair mask, flaps torn o/w EX, B14 ....$15.00
General Mills Wheaties, 1995, Larry Bird Commemorative, NM $15.00
Kellogg's Apple Jacks, 1971, w/glow-in-the-dark stickers, flat, NM, B14 ....$80.00
Kellogg's Cocoa Krispies, 1963, Snagglepuss, flat, NM, B14 .$350.00
Kellogg's Corn Flakes, Canadian, 1956, w/Totem mask, flat, NM, B14 ....$40.00

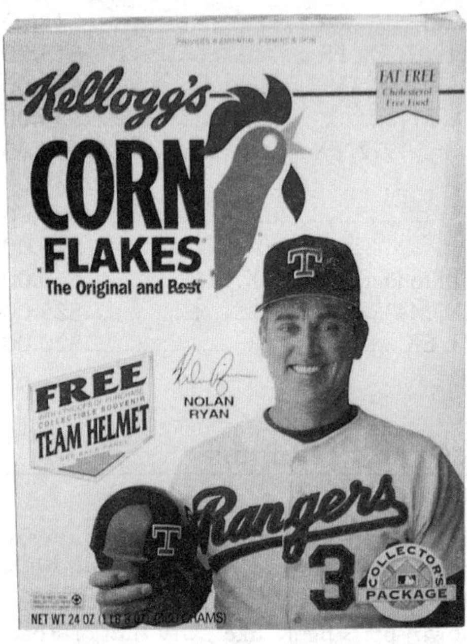

Kellogg's Corn Flakes, features Nolan Ryan, M (sealed), $25.00.

Kellogg's Corn Flakes, Max & Goofy, limited edition, NM $10.00
Kellogg's Corn Flakes, 1948, w/mask cutout, EX, B14......$30.00
Kellogg's Corn Flakes, 1960, Huckleberry Hound's Win a Pair of Fords contest, flat, NM, B14 ....$65.00
Kellogg's Corn Flakes, 1960s, back only, w/Huckleberry Hound mask, EX, A $15.00
Kellogg's Corn Flakes, 1960s, back only, w/Mr Jinx mask, EX, A....................$15.00
Kellogg's Corn Flakes, 1962, Yogi Bear Birthday Party, EX, B14....................$475.00
Kellogg's Frosted Flakes, Canadian, 1963, Yogi Bear's $5 a Week contest, EX, B14 ....$35.00
Kellogg's Frosted Flakes, 1966, Hokus-Pokus Fun #1, flat, NM, B14....................$75.00
Kellogg's Fruity Pebbles, 1972, Flintmobile, NM, B14 .....$95.00
Kellogg's OKs, 1963, features Yogi Bear, party mix recipe on back, flat, NM, B14 ....$325.00
Kellogg's Raisin Bran, 1950, Disney Joinies, EX, A........$150.00
Kellogg's Raisin Bran, 1992 Dream Team, NM $12.00
Kellogg's Rice Krispies, Howdy Doody & friends w/cut-out masks on back, NM, from $400....................$650.00
Kellogg's Rice Krispies, 1960, Woody Woodpecker bike contest, VG, B14....................$45.00
Kellogg's Rice Krispies, 1967, Woody Woodpecker swimmer toy, flat, NM, B14....................$125.00
Kellogg's Rice Krispies, 1973, Snap!, Crackle! & Pop! towel & washcloth offer, no flaps o/w VG, B14....................$25.00

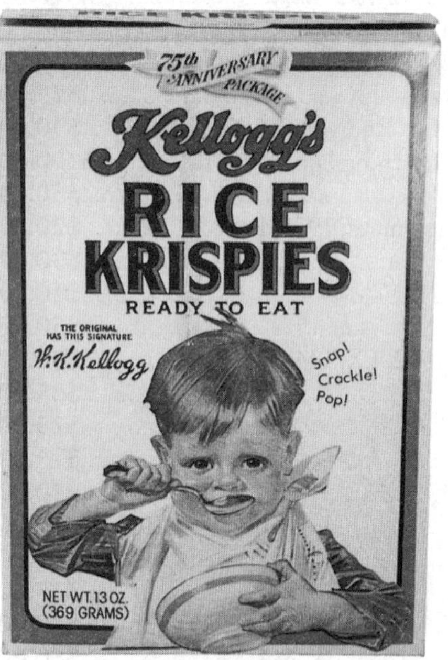

Kellogg's Rice Krispies, 75th Anniversary, 1982, EX, $15.00.

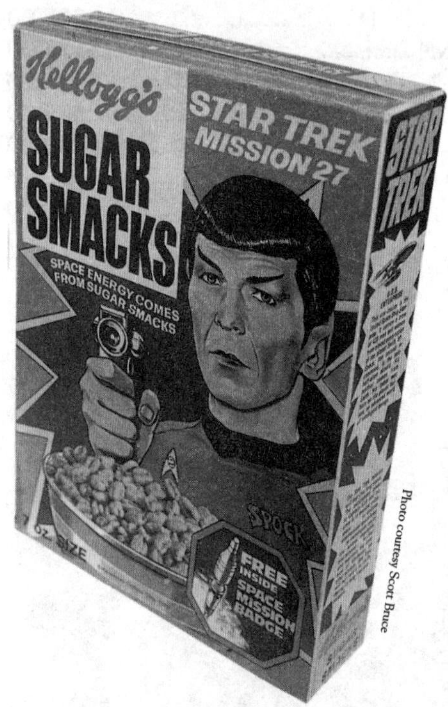

Photo courtesy Scott Bruce

Kellogg's Sugar Smacks, British, features Spock, 1969, NM, B10, from $750.00 to $1,000.00.

Kellogg's Sugar Smacks, Canadian, 1972, Tony the Tiger mug & bowl offer, flat, NM, B14....................$65.00
Kellogg's Sugar Smacks, 1964, Quick Draw McGraw w/road race game on back, flat, NM, B14....................$350.00
King Vitamin, 1972, Royal racing coach, NM, B14.......$125.00
Nabisco Great Honey Crunchers, Winnie the Pooh, NM, from $275 to....................$375.00

Nabisco Shredded Wheat, 1956, Rin Tin Tin insignia patch, NM, B14 ....**$95.00**
Nabisco Wheat Honeys, 1955, shows 12 Rin Tin Tin premium rings, EX, A **$80.00**
Post Alpha Bits, 1958, w/monkey & camel cutouts, VG, B14 ....**$30.00**
Post Grape-Nut Flakes, Hopalong Cassidy, NM, A **$700.00**
Post Grape-Nut Flakes, 1961, w/Bugs Bunny mask, flat, NM, B14 ....**$145.00**
Post Grape-Nuts, 1967, Dr Dolittle's carnival, flat, NM, B14 ....**$75.00**
Post Honeycombs, 1967, Dr Dolittle board games, NM, B14 ....**$125.00**
Post Raisin Bran, 1953, w/Roy Rogers pop-out card, M, B14 ....**$275.00**
Post Raisin Bran, 1966, Raisin Counter's Fun 'n Games series, flat, NM, B14 ....**$15.00**
Post Raisin Bran, 1988, California Raisins cassette offer, EX, W6 ....**$15.00**
Post Raisin Bran, 1988, California Raisins figure offer, EX, W6 ....**$15.00**
Post Rice Krinkles, 1954, w/Mighty Mouse blow pipe, NM, B14 ....**$75.00**
Post Sugar Crisp, Canadian, 1961, w/space launcher, NM, B14 ....**$55.00**
Post Sugar Crisp, 1957, back only, w/Yokel Duck mask, EX, J5 ....**$15.00**
Post Sugar Crisp, 1958, Mighty Mouse TV game, EX, B14.**$95.00**
Post Toasties, 1957, Mighty Mouse T-shirt, cape & playbook offer, NM, B14 ....**$175.00**
Post Toasties, 1958, w/Li'l Abner cutout, VG, B14 ....**$95.00**
Post Toasties, 1966, Billy Bird on back, flat, M, B14 ....**$50.00**
Post Toasties, 1966, Linus the Lion on back, flat, NM, B14 .**$65.00**
Post Toasties Corn Flakes, Roy Rogers advertising ranch set offer, EX, A **$295.00**

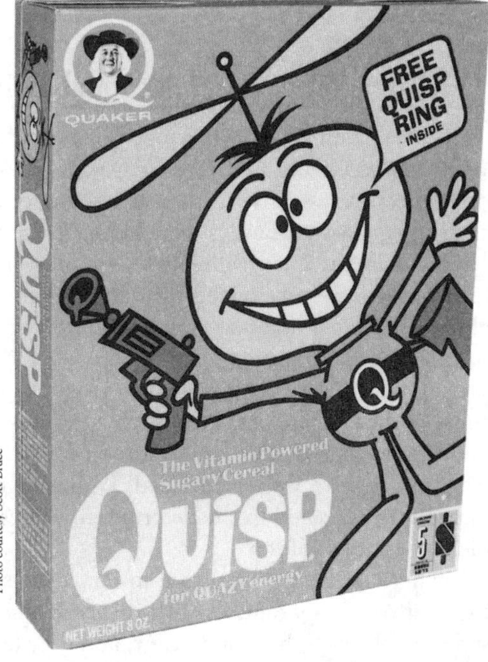

Photo courtesy Scott Bruce

Quaker Quisp, Quisp bank offer, M, from $600.00 to $750.00.

Post Toasties Corn Flakes, 1957, Mighty Mouse advertising t-shirt & cape offer, NM, A **$175.00**
Quaker Puffed Rice, 1950s, Sgt Preston's Yukon Trail, NM, A **$165.00**
Quaker Puffed Wheat Sparkies, Terry & the Pirates, NM, A **$95.00**
Ralston Wheat Chex, 1950, Cadet Happy advertising Space Patrol microscope kit, NM, A **$130.00**

Premiums

Sure, the kids liked the taste of the cereal too, but in families with more than one child there was more clammoring over the prize inside than there was over the last bowl! In addition to the 'freebies' included in the boxes, many other items were made available — rings, decoders, watches, games, books, etc. — often for just mailing in boxtops or coupons. If these premiums weren't free, their prices were minimal. Most of them were easily broken, and children had no qualms about throwing them away, so few survive to the present. Who would have ever thought those kids would be trying again in the '90s to get their hands on those very same prizes, and at considerable more trouble and expense. Note: Only premiums that specifically relate to cereal companies or their character logos are listed here. Other character-related premiums are listed in the Premiums category.

Alfie Dog, bike spoke reflector, 1980, bl plastic, EX, B14..**$10.00**
Apple Jack, mug & hat lid, 1967, plastic, VG, B14 ....**$50.00**
Apple Jack Kids, secret decoder, 1985, red plastic, M, B14..**$5.00**
Buffalo Bee, bowl rider, 1960s, plastic, NM, B14 ....**$10.00**
Bullwinkle & Cheerios Kid, plate, 1969, wht melmac, VG, B14 ....**$15.00**
Cap'n Crunch, Big Slick Gyro Car, 1972, blk plastic, MIP, B14 ....**$15.00**
Cap'n Crunch, binoculars, 1975, bl plastic, MIP, B14......**$15.00**
Cap'n Crunch, doll, plush, NM, P12 ....**$55.00**
Cap'n Crunch, imprint set, EX, J2 ....**$45.00**
Cap'n Crunch, Storyscope, 1972, plastic, MIP, B14.........**$15.00**
Cookie Crisp, Magic Club Magic Kit, MIB, P12 ....**$100.00**
Dig-'em, iron-on patch, 1974, glow-in-the-dark, MIP, B14.**$12.00**
Dig-'em, page marker/paper clip, 1979, gr plastic, NM, B14 ..**$5.00**

Photo courtesy June Moon

Fruit Brute, Frankenberry, Count Chocula, and Boo Berry, figures, vinyl, 8", EX, from $200.00 to $300.00 each.

Froot Loops, wallet, 1984, vinyl w/full-color image, EX ...$12.00
General Mills, pencil topper, 1973, skull & crossbones, rubber, MIP, B14 ...$10.00
Great Honey Crunchers, magnifying lens/blowpipe, moon-orbiter, 1972, bl plastic, MIP, B14 ...$35.00
Grins & Giggles, refrigerator magnet, 1976, MIP, B14, ea..$20.00

Photo courtesy Scott Bruce

Marky Maypo, bank, 1960s, EX, $100.00; Maypo Oat Cereal, box, 1956, EX, $250.00.

Ogg, sticker, 1973, Don't Litter...I Like a Clean Cave, paper, M, B14 ...$12.00
Pop!, canteen, 1973, yel, wht & red plastic, NM, B14 ...$20.00
Post Alpha Bits, bike streamers, 1970s, plastic, MIP, B14 ..$5.00
Post Alpha Bits, pocket printer, 1970s, plastic, MIP, B14 ..$5.00
Post Honeycomb, monster mitt, 1974, red w/eyeball, plastic, M, B14 ...$15.00
Post Honeycomb, yo-yo, 1970s, glow-in-the-dark, MIP, B14 ...$5.00
Post Raisin Bran, zig-zag ball, 1971, red plastic, MIP, B14...$5.00
Post Vehicle, F&F Mold, 1950 Ford, bl, no magnet, EX...$40.00
Post Vehicle, F&F Mold, 1950 Ford Custom Fordor, Magno-Power, red, M, orig mailer ...$50.00
Post Vehicle, F&F Mold, 1954 Club Coupe, Sierra Brown, M ...$30.00
Post Vehicle, F&F Mold, 1954 Mercury 4-door, yel, EX ..$20.00
Post Vehicle, F&F Mold, 1954 Ranch Wagon, Bloomfield, EX ...$30.00
Post Vehicle, F&F Mold, 1954 Sunliner, Torch Red, EX.$30.00
Post Vehicle, F&F Mold, 1955 Crown Victoria, Sea Sprite, EX ...$15.00
Post Vehicle, F&F Mold, 1955 Sunliner, Buckskin, EX......$5.00
Post Vehicle, F&F Mold, 1955 Thunderbird, red, EX $10.00
Post Vehicle, F&F Mold, 1956, Greyhound Super Sceni-cruiser, bl, rare, EX ...$35.00
Post Vehicle, F&F Mold, 1956 Ford/Fruehauf gasoline transport, aluminum, EX ...$20.00
Post Vehicle, F&F Mold, 1956 Greyhound Highway Traveler, bl, rare, EX ...$35.00
Post Vehicle, F&F Mold, 1957 Custom 4-door, Inca Gold, M ...$25.00

Photo courtesy Pat Webb

Post Vehicle, F&F Mold, 1957 Ford Fairlane 500 Town Victoria, Dresden Blue, NM, $45.00.

Post Vehicle, F&F Mold, 1960 Plymouth Hardtop, Twilight Blue, EX ...$15.00
Post Vehicle, F&F Mold, 1966 Mustang Convertible, Springtime Yellow, EX ...$10.00
Post Vehicle, F&F Mold, 1967 Couger, Fawn, lg early tires, EX ...$35.00
Quisp, Gyro Trail Blazer, 1960s, bl plastic, EX, B14 ...$25.00
Quisp, propellor beanie, 1966, M, B14, from $500 to.....$600.00
Snap! & Pop!, Magic Color Cards, 1933, EX, J2 ...$50.00
Sonny the Cuckoo Bird, card game, Sonny's Hearts, 1970s, MIP, B14 ...$15.00
Sugar Bear, padlock & key, 1970s, plastic, MIP, B14 ....$10.00
Sugar Bear, yo-yo, 1970s, 3-in-1, plastic, MIP, B14 ....$10.00
Tony the Tiger, iron-on patch, 1974, glow-in-the-dark, cloth, 2", MIP, B14 ...$12.00
Toucan Sam, bicycle license plate, 1973, bl plastic, 3x6", EX, B14 ...$10.00
Trix, whistle & magnifier, red, EX, J2 ...$15.00
Whippersnapper & Smacks, drawing template, 1970, gr plastic, 3x6", M, B14 ...$15.00

Character and Promotional Drinking Glasses

Once given away by fast-food chains and gas stations, a few years ago you could find these at garage sales everywhere for a dime or even less. Then, when it became obvious to collectors that these glass giveaways were being replaced by plastic, as is always the case when we realize no more (of anything) will be forthcoming, we all decided we wanted them. Since many were character-related and part of a series, we felt the need to begin to organize these garage-sale castaways, building sets and completing series. Out of the thousands available, the better ones are those with super heroes, sports stars, old movie stars, Star Trek, and Disney and Walter Lantz cartoon characters. Pass up those whose colors are worn and faded. Unless another condition or material is indicated in the description, values are for glass tumblers in mint condition.

There are some terms used in our listings that may be confusing if you're not familiar with this collecting field. 'Brockway' style tumblers are thick and heavy, and they taper at the bottom.

'Federal' is thinner, and top and diameters are equal. For more information we recommend *Collectible Drinking Glasses, Identification and Values* by Mark E. Chase and Michael J. Kelly (Collector Books) and *The Collector's Guide to Cartoon and Promotional Drinking Glasses* by John Hervey.

See also Clubs, Newsletters, and Other Publications.

Advisors: Mark E. Chase and Michael J. Kelly (C2).

Other Sources: B3, C1, C10, C11, D9, D11, F8, J2, H11, I2, J7, M8, M16, P3, P6, P10, R2, S20, T1, T2

Abbott & Costello, see Arby's Actor Series

Al Capp, Brockway, 1975, 16-oz, flat bottom, Joe Btsptflk, from $40 to **$60.00**

Al Capp, Brockway, 1975, 16-oz, flat bottom, Mammy, Pappy, Sadie, Lil' Abner, Daisy Mae, ea, from $30 to **$50.00**

Al Capp, Brockway, 1975, 16-oz, ftd, Mammy, Pappy, Sadie, Lil' Abner, Daisy Mae, ea, from $30 to....................**$50.00**

Animal Crackers, Chicago Tribune/NY News Syndicate, 1978, Louis, scarce, from $25 to **$50.00**

Animal Crackers, Chicago Tribune/NY News Syndicate, 1978, Lyle Dodo, Gnu, Lana, Eugene, ea, from $7 to **$10.00**

Annie Oakley, see Western Heroes

Apollo Series, Marathon Oil, Apollo 11, Apollo 12, Apollo 13, Apollo 14, ea, from $2 to **$4.00**

Apollo Series, Marathon Oil, carafe, from $6 to..............**$10.00**

Aquaman, see Super Heroes

Arby's, Actor Series, 1979, 6 different, smoke-colored glass w/blk & wht images, silver trim, numbered, ea, from $7 to **$10.00**

Arby's, Bicentennial Cartoon Character Series, 1976, 10 different, 5", ea, from $10 to **$18.00**

Arby's, Bicentennial Cartoon Character Series, 1976, 10 different, 6", ea, from, $15 to **$25.00**

Arby's, see also specific name or series

Archies, Welch's, 1971, 6 different w/many variations, ea ..**$3.00**

Archies, Welch's, 1973, 6 different w/many variations, ea ..**$3.00**

Avon, Christmas Issues, 1969-72, 4 different, ea, from $2 to **$5.00**

Baby Huey & Related Characters, see Harvey Cartoon Characters

Batman & Related Characters, see Super Heroes

Battlestar Galactica, Universal Studios, 1979, 4 different, ea, from $7 to....................**$10.00**

BC Ice Age, Arby's, 1981, 6 different, ea, from $3 to **$5.00**

Beatles, Dairy Queen, group photo & signatures in wht starburst, gold trim, Canadian, from $95 to....................**$125.00**

Buffalo Bill, see Western Heroes or Wild West Series

Bugs Bunny & Related Characters, see Warner Bros

Bullwinkle, Rocky & Related Characters, see Warner Bros or PAT Ward

Burger Chef, Burger Chef & Jeff, Now We're Glassified!, from $15 to **$25.00**

Burger Chef, Endangered Species Collector's Series, 1978, Tiger, Orang-Utan, Bald Eagle, ea, from $5 to **$7.00**

Burger Chef, Endangered Species Collector's Series, 1979, Giant Panda, from $7 to....................**$9.00**

Burger Chef, Friendly Monsters Series, 1977, 6 different, ea, from $20 to....................**$35.00**

Burger Chef, Presidents & Patriots, 1975, 6 different, ea, from $7 to **$10.00**

Burger King, Collector Series, 1979, 5 different Burger King characters featuring Burger Thing, etc, ea, from $4 to.**$6.00**

Burger King, Dallas Cowboys, Dr Pepper, 6 different, ea, from $7 to **$15.00**

Burger King, Have It Your Way 1776-1979 Series, 1976, 4 different, ea, from $4 to **$6.00**

Burger King, see also specific name or series

Calamity Jane, see Wild West Series

Captain America, see Super Heroes

Casper the Friendly Ghost & Related Charaters, see Arby's Bicentennial or Harvey Cartoon Characters

Chilly Willy, see Walter Lantz

Cinderella, Disney/Libby, 1950s-1960s, set of 8 ....**$120.00**

Cinderella, see also Disney Collector's Series or Disney Film Classics

Clarabell, see Howdy Doody

Currier & Ives, Arby's, 1975-76, 4 different, titled, ea, from $3 to **$5.00**

Currier & Ives, Arby's, 1978, 4 different, numbered, ea, from $3 to **$5.00**

Davy Crockett, from $12.00 to $15.00 each.

Daffy Duck, see Warner Bros
Daisy Mae, see Al Capp
Dick Tracy, 1940s, frosted, 8 different characters, 3" or 5", ea, from $50 to $75.00
Dilly Dally, see Howdy Doody
Disney Characters, 1936, Mickey, Minnie, Donald, Pluto, Clarabelle, Horace, F Bunny, 4¼" or 4¾", ea, from $40 to . $75.00
Disney Collector Series, Burger King, 1994, mc images on clear plastic, 8 different, MIB, ea $3.00
Disney Film Classics, McDonald's/Coca-Cola/Canada, Peter Pan, Cinderella, Fantasia or Snow White & the Seven Dwarfs, ea $15.00

Disney, First Dairy Series, 1930s, Mickey Mouse, from $40.00 to $60.00.

Disney's All-Star Parade, 1939, 10 different, ea, from $40 to $75.00
Disney, see also Wonderful World of Disney or specific character
Domino's Pizza, Avoid the Noid, 1988, 4 different, ea $7.00
Donald Duck, Donald Duck Cola, 1960s-70s, from $15 to . $20.00
Donald Duck or Daisy, see also Disney or Mickey Mouse (Happy Birthday)
Dudley Do-Right, see Arby's Bicentennial or PAT Ward
Dynomutt, see Hanna-Barbera
Elmer Fudd, see Warner Bros
Elsie the Cow, Borden, Elsie & Family in 1976 Bicentennial parade, red, wht & bl graphics, from $5 to $7.00
Elsie the Cow, Borden, 1950s, wht head image on waisted style, from $15 to $20.00
Elsie the Cow, Borden, 1960s, yel daisy image, from $10 to .. $12.00
Empire Strikes Back, see Star Wars Trilogy
ET, Army & Air Force Exchange Service, 1982, 4 different mc images, rnd bottom, ea, from $5 to $10.00
ET, Pepsi/MCA Home Video, 1988, 6 different, ea, from $15 to $25.00
ET, Pizza Hut, 1982, 4 different, ftd, from $2 to $4.00
Fantasia, see Disney Film Classics
Flintstone Kids, Pizza Hut, 1986, 4 different, ea, from $2 to... $4.00
Flintstones, Welch's, 1962 (6 different), 1963 (2 different), 1964 (6 different), ea, from $5 to $8.00
Flintstones, see also Hanna-Barbera
Foghorn Leghorn, see Warner Bros
Ghostbusters II, Sunoco/Canada, 1989, 6 different, ea, from $5 to $8.00
Goonies, Godfather's Pizza/Warner Bros, 1985, 4 different, ea, from $4 to $8.00
Great Muppet Caper, McDonald's, 1981, 4 different, 6", ea .. $2.00
Green Arrow, see Super Heroes
Green Lantern, see Super Heroes
Hanna-Barbera, Pepsi/Brockway, 1977, Yogi/Huck, Josie/Pussycats, Mumbly, Scooby, Flintstones, Dynomutt, ea, from $20 to $35.00
Hanna-Barbera, 1960s, jam glasses featuring Flintstones, Yogi Bear, Quick Draw, Cindy Bear, Huck, rare, ea from $75 to $110.00
Happy Days, Dr Pepper, 1977, Fonzie or Richie, ea, from $8 to $12.00
Happy Days, Dr Pepper, 1977, Ralph, Joanie, Potsie, ea, from $8 to $12.00
Happy Days, Dr Pepper/Pizza Hut, 1977, Fonzie or Richie, ea, from $10 to $15.00
Happy Days, Dr Pepper/Pizza Hut, 1977, Ralph, Joanie, Potsie, ea, from $8 to $12.00
Harvey Cartoon Characters, Pepsi, 1970s, action pose, Casper, Baby Huey, Wendy, Hot Stuff, ea, from $8 to $15.00
Harvey Cartoon Characters, Pepsi, 1970s, static pose, Casper, Baby Huey, Wendy, Hot Stuff, ea, from $12 to $20.00
Harvey Cartoon Characters, Pepsi, 1970s, static pose, Richie Rich, from $15 to $25.00
Harvey Cartoon Characters, Pepsi, 1970s, static pose, Sad Sack, scarce, from $25 to $35.00
Harvey Cartoon Characters, see also Arby's Bicentennial Series
He-Man & Related Characters, see Masters of the Universe
Hopalong Cassidy's Western Series, ea, from $25 to $30.00
Hot Dog Castle, Collector Series, 1977, Abilene Past, Abilene Present, Abilene Future, ea, from $6 to $8.00
Hot Stuff, see Arby's Bicentennial
Howard the Duck, see Super Heroes
Howdy Doody, Welch's/Kagran, 1950s, 6 different, emb bottom, ea, from $15 to $20.00
Huckleberry Hound, see Hanna-Barbera
Incredible Hulk, see Super Heroes
Indiana Jones & the Temple of Doom, 7-Up (w/4 different cosponsers), 1984, set of 4, ea, from $8 to $15.00
Indiana Jones: The Last Crusade, wht plastic, 4 different, ea, from $2 to $4.00
James Bond 007, 1985, 4 different, ea, from $10 to $15.00
Joe Btsptflk, see Al Capp
Joker, see Super Heroes
Josie & the Pussycats, see Hanna-Barbera
Jungle Book, Disney/Canada, 1966, 6 different, numbered, 4⅞", ea, from $40 to $75.00
Jungle Book, Disney/Canada, 1966, 6 different, numbered, 6½", ea, from $30 to $60.00
Jungle Book, Disney/Pepsi, 1970s, Bagheera or Shere Kahn, unmk, ea, from, $60 to $90.00

Jungle Book, Disney/Pepsi, 1970s, Mowgli, unmk, from $40 to **$50.00**

Jungle Book, Disney/Pepsi, 1970s, Rama, unmk, from $50 to **$60.00**

Keebler, Soft Batch Cookies, 1984, 4 different, ea, from, $7 to **$10.00**

Kellogg's, 1977, 6 different, ea, from $7 to **$10.00**

King Kong, Coca-Cola/Dino De Laurentis Corp, 1976, from $5 to **$8.00**

Laurel & Hardy, see Arby's Actor Series

Leonardo TTV Collector Series, Pepsi, Underdog, Go-Go Gophers, Sweet Polly, Simon Bar Sinister, 6", ea, from $15 to **$25.00**

Leonardo TTV Collector Series, Pepsi, Underdog, Sweet Polly, Simon Bar Sinister, 5", ea, from $8 to **$15.00**

Leonardo TTV, see also Arby's Bicentennial Series

Li'l Abner & Related Characters, see Al Capp

Little Rascals, see Arby's Actor Series

Lone Ranger, see Western Heroes

Mae West, see Arby's Actor Series

Mark Twain Country Series, Burger King, 1985, 4 different, ea, from $8 to **$10.00**

Masters of the Universe, Mattel, 1983, Teels, He-Man, Skeletor, Man-at-Arms, ea, from $5 to **$10.00**

Masters of the Universe, Mattel, 1986, Orko, He-Man/Battle Cat, Skeletor/Panthor, Man-at-Arms, ea, from $3 to ..**$5.00**

McDonald's, All-Time Greatest Steelers Team, 1982, 5 different, ea, from $5 to **$8.00**

McDonald's, McDonaldland Action Series, 1977, 6 different, ea **$5.00**

McDonald's, McDonaldland Collector Series, 1970s, 6 different, ea **$4.00**

McDonald's, McVote, 1986, 3 different, ea **$10.00**

McDonald's, Philadelphia Eagles, 1980, 5 different, ea, from $4 to **$6.00**

MGM Collector Series, Pepsi, 1975, Tom, Jerry, Tuffy, Barney, Droopy or Spike, ea, from $10 to **$15.00**

Mickey Mouse, Happy Birthday, Pepsi, 1978, Daisy & Donald, from $12 to **$15.00**

Mickey Mouse, Happy Birthday, Pepsi, 1978, Horace & Clarabelle, from $15 to **$20.00**

Mickey Mouse, Happy Birthday, Pepsi, 1978, Mickey, Minnie, Donald, Goofy, Pluto, Uncle Scrooge, ea, from $6 to **$10.00**

Mickey Mouse, Mickey's Christmas Carol, Coca-Cola, 1982, 3 different, ea **$10.00**

Mickey Mouse, Through the Years, Sunoco Canada, 1988, 6 different (1928, 1938, 1940, 1955, 1983 & 1988), ea from $6 to **$10.00**

Mickey Mouse, see also Disney Characters

Mister Magoo, Polomer Jelly, many different variations & styles, ea, from $25 to **$35.00**

NFL, Mobil Oil, helmets on colored bands, rocks, flat, Colts, Oilers, Steelers, Cowboys, ea, from $2 to **$4.00**

NFL, Mobil Oil, helmets on white bands, rocks, ftd, Redskins, Bills, Steelers, Eagles, Buccaneers, ea, from $3 to **$5.00**

Norman Rockwell, Saturday Evening Post Series, Arby's, early 1980s, 6 different, numbered, ea, from $2 to **$4.00**

Norman Rockwell, Saturday Evening Post Series, Country Time Lemonade, 4 different, w/authorized logo, ea, from $7 to **$10.00**

Norman Rockwell, Saturday Evening Post Series, Country Time Lemonade, 4 different, no logo, ea, from $5 to **$7.00**

Norman Rockwell, Summer Scenes, Arby's, 1987, 4 different, tall, ea, from $3 to **$5.00**

Norman Rockwell, Winter Scenes, Arby's/Pepsi, 1979, 4 different, short, ea, from $3 to **$5.00**

PAT Ward Collector Series, Holly Farms Restaurants, 1975, Bullwinkle, Rocky, Natasha, Boris, ea, from $50 to...**$75.00**

PAT Ward, Pepsi-Cola, Static Pose, Boris and Natasha, from $20.00 to $25.00; Snidely Whiplash, from $15.00 to $20.00.

PAT Ward, see also Arby's Bicentennial Series

Peanuts Characters, Camp Snoopy, McDonald's, 1983, wht plastic, Lucy or Snoopy, ea, from $5 to **$8.00**

Peanuts Characters, Snoopy for President, Dolly Madison Bakery, 4 different, ea, from $4 to **$6.00**

Peanuts Characters, Snoopy sitting on lemon or Snoopy sitting by lg red apple, pedestal bottom, ea, from $2 to **$3.00**

Peanuts Characters, Snoopy Sport Series, Dolly Madison Bakery, 4 different, ea, from $4 to **$6.00**

Peanuts Characters, I Have a Strange Team, Let's Break for Lunch!, I Got It! I Got It!, plastic, ea, from $5 to **$8.00**

Peanuts Characters, Kraft, 1988, Snoopy in pool, Lucy on swing, Snoopy on surfboard, Charlie Brown flying kite, ea..... **$2.00**

Penguin, see Super Heroes

Pepsi, Historical Advertising Posters, 1979, 4 different, blk & wht, ea, from $8 to **$10.00**

Pepsi, Night Before Christmas, 1982-83, 4 different, ea, from, $4 to **$6.00**

Pepsi, Twelve Days of Christmas, 1976, ea, from $1 to **$3.00**

Pepsi, see also specific names or series

Peter Pan, see Disney Film Classics

Pillsbury, Doughboy, 1991, mail-in premium, w/various musical instruments, from $6 to $12.00
Pinocchio, Dairy Promo/Libbey, 1938-40, 12 different, ea, from $15 to $25.00
Pinocchio, see also Disney Collector's Series or Wonderful World of Disney
Pluto, see Disney Characters
Pocahontas, Burger King, 1995, 4 different, MIB, ea $3.00
Popeye, Kollect-A-Set, Coca-Cola, 1975, Popeye $7.00
Popeye, Kollect-A-Set, Coca-Cola, 1975, 6 different, any except Popeye $5.00
Popeye, Pals, Popeyes Famous Fried Chicken, 1979, 4 different, ea, from $10 to $20.00
Popeye, 10th Anniversary Series, Popeye's Famous Fried Chicken/Pepsi, 1982, 4 different, ea, from $10 to......$15.00
Porky Pig, see Looney Tunes/Warner Bros
Quick Draw McGraw, see Hanna-Barbera

Rescuers, Pepsi/Brockway, 1977, from $8.00 to $15.00 each.

Return of the Jedi, see Star Wars Trilogy
Richie Rich, see Harvey Cartoon Characters
Riddler, see Super Heroes
Ringling Bros Circus Clowns Series, Pepsi/Federal, 1976, 8 different, ea $12.00
Ringling Bros Circus Poster Series, Pepsi/Federal, 1975, 6 different, ea....................$20.00
Road Runner & Related Characters, see Warner Bros
Robin, see Super Heroes
Rocky & Bullwinkle, see Arby's Bicentennial or PAT Ward
Roy Rogers Restaurant, 1883-1983 logo, from $8 to.........$12.00
Sad Sack, see Harvey Cartoon Characters
Sadie Hawkins, see Al Capp
Scooby Doo, see Hanna-Barbera
Sleeping Beauty, American, late 1950s, 6 different, ea, from $15 to $20.00
Sleeping Beauty, Canadian, late 1950s, 12 different, ea, from $20 to $20.00
Smurf's, Hardee's, 1982, 8 different, ea, from $1 to............$3.00
Smurf's, Hardee's, 1983, 6 different, ea, from $1 to............$3.00
Snidley Whiplash, see PAT Ward
Snoopy & Related Characters, see Peanuts Characters
Snow White & the Seven Dwarfs, Bosco, 1938, ea, from $25 to $45.00
Snow White & the Seven Dwarfs, Libbey, 1937-38, ea, from $15 to $24.00
Snow White & the Seven Dwarfs, Libbey, 1937-38, verses on back, various colors, 8 different, ea, from $60 to........$80.00
Snow White & the Seven Dwarfs, see also Disney Collector's Series or Disney Film Classics
Spider-Man or Spider-Woman, see Super Heroes
Star Trek, Dr Pepper, 1976, 4 different, ea, from $20 to...$25.00
Star Trek, Dr Pepper, 1978, 4 different, ea, from $30 to...$40.00
Star Trek II: The Search For Spock, Taco Bell, 1984, 4 different, ea, from $3 to $5.00
Star Trek: The Motion Picture, Coca-Cola, 1980, 3 different, ea, from $10 to....................$15.00
Star Wars Trilogy: Star Wars; Burger King/Coca-Cola, 1977, 4 different, ea, from $12 to $15.00

Star Wars Trilogy: Empire Strikes Back, Burger King/Coca-Cola, 1980, from $7.00 to $10.00.

Star Wars Trilogy: The Return of the Jedi; Burger King/Coca-Cola, 1983, 4 different, ea, from $4 to....................$6.00
Sunday Funnies, 1976, Broom Hilda, from $100 to........$150.00
Sunday Funnies, 1976, O Annie, Smilin' Jack, Moon Mullins, Gasoline Alley, Terry & Pirates, Brenda Starr, ea, from $8 to $15.00
Super Heroes, Marvel/Federal, 1978, Captain America, Hulk, Spider-Man, Thor, ea, $100 to....................$150.00
Super Heroes, Marvel/Federal, 1978, Spider-Woman, from $140 to $200.00

Super Heroes, Marvel/7-Eleven, 1977, Captain America, Fantasic Four, Howard the Duck, Thor, ea $20.00

Super Heroes, Marvel/7-Eleven, 1977, Incredible Hulk ...$25.00

Super Heroes, Marvel/7-Eleven, 1978, Amazing Spider-Man $30.00

Super Heroes (Moon) Series, Pepsi/DC Comics, 1976, Green Arrow, from $20 to $30.00

Super Heroes (Moon) Series, Pepsi/DC Comics, 1976, Riddler, Green Lantern, Joker, Penguin, ea, from $40 to $60.00

Super Heroes (Moon) Series, Pepsi/DC Comics or NPP, 1976, Batman, Batgirl, Robin or Shazam!, ea, from $10 to .$15.00

Super Heroes (Moon) Series, Pepsi/NPP, 1976, Green Arrow, ea from $10 to..$15.00

Super Heroes (Moon) Series, Pepsi/NPP, 1976, Riddler, Green Lantern, Joker or Penguin, ea, from $20 to $40.00

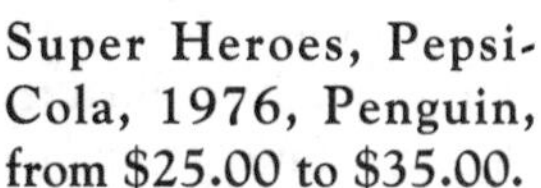

Super Heroes, Pepsi-Cola, 1976, Penguin, from $25.00 to $35.00.

Superman, National Periodical/M Polanar & Son, 1964, 6 different, various colors, 4¼" or 5¾", ea, from $20 to........$35.00

Superman, see also Super Heroes (Moon) Series

Sylvester the Cat, see Warner Bros

Tasmanian Devil, see Warner Bros

Tom & Jerry & Related Characters, see MGM Collector Series

Tweety Bird, see Looney Tunes or Warner Bros

Underdog & Related Characters, see Arby's Bicentennial or Leonardo TTV

Universal Monsters, Universal Studios, tapered, Frankenstein, Mummy, Wolfman, Creature from Black Lagoon, ea, from $35 to $50.00

Universal Monsters, Universal Studios, 1980, ftd, Frankenstein, Mummy, Mutant, Wolfman, Dracula, Creature, ea, from $75 to..$125.00

Urchins, Coca-Cola/American Greetings, 1976-78, swimming, baseball, skating, tennis, golf, bicycling, ea, from $3 to .$5.00

Walter Lantz, Pepsi, 1970, Cuddles, from $40 to $60.00

Walter Lantz, Pepsi, 1970s, Chilly Willy or Wally Walrus, ea, from $35 to...$55.00

Walter Lantz, Pepsi, 1970s, Space Mouse, from $150 to..$250.00

Walter Lantz, Pepsi, 1970s, Woody Woodpecker, from $10 to $20.00

Walter Lantz, Pepsi, 1970s-80s, Anty/Miranda, Chilly/Smedley, Wally/Homer, Cuddles/Oswald, ea, from $20 to........$30.00

Walter Lantz, Pepsi, 1970s-80s, Buzz Buzzard/Space Mouse, from $20 to $30.00

Walter Lantz, Pepsi, 1970s-80s, 2-sided, Woody Woodpecker/ Knothead & Splinter, ea, from $15 to.......................$20.00

Walter Lantz, see also Arby's Bicentennial Series

Warner Bros, Arby's, 1988, Adventures Series, ftd, 4 different, Bugs, Daffy, Porky, Sylvester & Tweety, ea, from $35 to $45.00

Warner Bros, Federal, 1973, Elmer Fudd, from $5.00 to $8.00.

Warner Bros, Federal, Tweety Bird, from $10.00 to $15.00.

Warner Bros, Marriott's Great America, 1975, 12-oz, 6 different, Bugs & related characters, ea, from $25 to................**$30.00**

Warner Bros, Marriott's Great America, 1989, 4 different, Porky, Bugs, Taz, Sylvester, ea, from $5 to................**$10.00**

Warner Bros, Pepsi, 1973, wht plastic, 6 different, Bugs, Daffy, Porky, Sylvester, Tweety, Road Runner, ea, from $3 to................**$5.00**

Warner Bros, Pepsi, 1973, 6 different, Bugs, Daffy, Porky, Sylvester, Tweety, Road Runner, 16-oz, each, from $5 to................**$12.00**

Warner Bros, Pepsi-Cola, Interaction series, 1976, Pepe LePew, from $5.00 to $7.00.

Warner Bros, Pepsi, 1979, Collector's Series, rnd bottom, Bugs, Daffy, Porky, Sylvester, Tweety, Road Runner, ea, $7 to .**$10.00**

Warner Bros, Welch's, 1974, action poses, 8 different, sayings around top, ea, from $2 to **$4.00**

Warner Bros, Welch's, 1976-77, 8 different, w/names around bottom, ea, from $5 to **$7.00**

WC Fields, see Arby's Actor Series

Welch's, Dinosaur Series, 1989, 4 different, ea................**$2.00**

Welch's, see also Archies, Howdy Doody or Warner Bros

Wendy's, Clara Pella (Where's the Beef?) or Clara Pella (no phrase), ea, from $4 to **$6.00**

Wendy's, Cleveland Browns, Dr Pepper, 1981, 4 different, ea, from $5 to................**$8.00**

Western Heroes, Annie Oakley, Buffalo Bill, Wild Bill Hickok, Wyatt Earp, ea, from $8 to **$12.00**

Western Heroes, Lone Ranger, from $10 to................**$15.00**

Wild Bill Hickok, see Western Heroes

Wild West Series, Coca-Cola, Buffalo Bill, Calamity Jane, ea, from $10 to **$15.00**

Wile E Coyote, see Warner Bros

Winnie the Pooh, Sears/WDP, 1970s, 4 different, ea, from $7 to **$10.00**

Wizard of Oz, Coca-Cola/Krystal, 1989, 50th Anniversary Series, 6 different, ea, from $10 to................**$15.00**

Wizard of Oz, Swift's, 1950s-60s, fluted bottom, Flying Monkeys or Emerald City, ea, from $15 to **$20.00**

Wizard of Oz, Swift's, 1950s-60s, fluted bottom, Glinda, from $15 to **$25.00**

Wizard of Oz, Swift's, 1950s-60s, fluted bottom, Wicked Witch, from $35 to................**$50.00**

Wonder Woman, see Super Heroes

Wonderful World of Disney, Pepsi, 1980s, Snow White, Pinocchio, Alice, Lady & the Tramp, Bambi, 101 Dalmatians, ea **$25.00**

Woody Woodpecker & Related Characters, see Arby's Bicentennial or Walter Lantz

Wyatt Earp, see Western Heroes

Yogi Bear, see Hanna-Barbera

Yosemite Sam, see Warner Bros

Ziggy, 7-Up Collector Series, 4 different, ea, from $4 to.....**$7.00**

Character Bobbin' Heads

Frequently referred to as nodders, these papier-mache dolls reflect accurate likenesses of the characters they portray and have become popular collectibles. Made in Japan throughout the 1960s, they were sold as souvenirs at Disney, Universal Studios, and Six Flags amusement parks, and they were often available at roadside concessions as well. Papier-mache was used until the

Andy and Barney, 1992, ceramic, 7", M, J6, $75.00 each.

mid-'70s when ceramic composition came into use. They were very susceptible to cracking and breaking, and it's difficult to find mint specimens — little wonder, since these nodders were commonly displayed on car dashboards!

Our values are for nodders in near-mint condition. To calculate values for examples in very good condition, reduce our prices by 25% to 40%.

Advisors: Matt and Lisa Adams (A7).

Beetle Bailey, NM, A7, from $100 to............................**$150.00**
Bugs Bunny, NM, A7, from $100 to..............................**$175.00**
Charlie Brown, Japan, ceramic w/gr baseball cap & mitt, NM, A7 ....**$60.00**
Charlie Brown, sq blk base, NM.......................................**$95.00**
Charlie Brown, 1970s, no base, sm, NM, A7 ....**$45.00**
Colonel Sanders, Kentucky Fried Chicken, 2 different styles, NM, A7, ea, from $100 to **$125.00**
Danny Kaye, kissing, NM, A7..**$100.00**
Danny Kaye & Girl, kissing, NM, A7, pr.......................**$150.00**
Dobie Gillis, NM, A7, from $250 to **$300.00**
Donald Duck, Walt Disney World, sq wht base, NM, A7 .**$75.00**
Donald Duck, 1970s, rnd gr base, NM, A7 ....**$75.00**
Donny Osmond, wht jumpsuit w/microphone, NM, A7, from $100 to..**$150.00**
Dr Ben Casey, NM, A7, from $100 to............................**$125.00**
Dr Kildare, NM, A7, from $100 to................................**$125.00**
Dumbo, rnd red base, NM, A7 ....**$100.00**
Eisenhower, bl coat, NM, A7, from $100 to **$125.00**
Elmer Fudd, NM, A7, from $100 to **$175.00**
Foghorn Leghorn, NM, A7, from $100 to.......................**$175.00**
Goofy, Disneyland, arms at side, sq wht base, NM, A7 ....**$75.00**
Goofy, Walt Disney World, arms folded, sq wht base, NM, A7 ....**$75.00**
Linus, Japan, ceramic, baseball catcher w/gr cap, NM, A7 .**$60.00**
Linus, Lego, sq blk base, NM, A7.....................................**$95.00**
Little Audrey, NM, A7, from $100 to............................**$150.00**
Lt Fuzz (Beetle Bailey), NM, A7, from $100 to **$150.00**
Lucy (Peanuts), Japan, ceramic, gr baseball cap & bat, NM, A7 ....**$60.00**
Lucy (Peanuts), Lego, sq blk base, NM, A7 ....**$95.00**
Lucy (Peanuts), 1970s, no base, sm, NM, A7 ....**$45.00**
Mammy (Dogpatch USA), NM, A7 ....**$75.00**
Mary Poppins, Disneyland, 1960s, wooden figure w/umbrella & satchel, 5¾", M, P6..**$95.00**
Maynard Krebs (Dobie Gillis), holds bongos, NM, A7, from $250 to..**$350.00**
Mickey Mouse, Disneyland, red, wht & bl outfit, sq wht base, NM, A7 ....**$100.00**
Mickey Mouse, Walt Disney World, bl shirt & red pants, NM, A7 ....**$75.00**
Mickey Mouse, yel shirt & red pants, rnd gr base, NM, A7 ...**$75.00**
Mr Peanut, moves at waist, w/cane, NM, A7, from $150 to **$200.00**
New York World's Fair Boy & Girl, in fair outfits, kissing, NM, A7 ....**$125.00**
Oodles the Duck (Bozo the Clown), NM, A7, from $150 to..**$200.00**
Pappy (Dogpatch USA), NM, A7...................................**$75.00**
Peppermint Patti, Japan, ceramic, gr baseball cap & bat, NM, A7 ....**$60.00**
Phantom of the Opera, sq base, rare, NM, A7...............**$500.00**
Phantom of the Opera, Universal Studios of California, gr face, NM, A7 ....**$150.00**

Photo courtesy June Moon

Pig Pen (Peanuts), Lego, NM, $95.00.

Schroeder (Peanuts), Lego, lg, NM, $95.00.

Pluto, 1970s, rnd gr base, NM, A7 ....$75.00
Porky Pig, NM, A7, from $100 to $175.00
Raggedy Andy, bank, mk A Penny Earned, NM, A7 ....$75.00
Raggedy Ann, bank, mk A Penny Saved, NM, A7....$75.00
Roy Rogers, Japan, 1962, compo, sq gr base, 6½", M, from $150 to....$200.00
Roy Rogers, NM, A7, from $150 to $200.00
Sgt Snorkel (Beetle Bailey), NM, A7, from $100 to $150.00
Smokey the Bear, holds shovel, rnd base, NM, A7, from $125 to....$200.00
Smokey the Bear, holds shovel, sq base, NM, A7, from $125 to....$200.00
Snoopy, as Flying Ace, 1970s, no base, NM, A7 ....$45.00
Snoopy, as Joe Cool, 1970s, no base, sm, NM, A7....$45.00
Snoopy, in Christmas outfit, 1970s, no base, sm, NM, A7 .$45.00
Snoopy, Japan, ceramic, gr baseball cap & mitt, NM, A7 ..$60.00
Snoopy, Lego, sq blk base, lg, NM, A7....$95.00
Space Boy, blk space suit & helmet, NM, A7....$75.00
Speedy Gonzales, NM, A7, from $100 to....$175.00
Three Little Pigs, bl overalls & yel cap, rnd red base, NM, A7, ea....$100.00
Topo Gigio, standing w/out fruit, standing w/apple, orange or pineapple, NM, A7, ea $75.00
Tweety, NM, A7, from $100 to....$175.00
Wile E Coyote, NM, A7, from $100 to....$175.00
Winnie the Pooh, 1970s, rnd gr base, NM, A7, from $100 to .$150.00
Wolfman, sq base, rare, NM, A7....$500.00
Woodstock, Japan, ceramic, w/bat, NM, A7....$60.00
Woodstock, 1970s, no base, sm, NM, A7....$45.00
Yosemite Sam, NM, A7, from $100 to....$175.00
Zero (Beetle Bailey), NM, A7, from $100 to $150.00

Character Clocks and Watches

Clocks and watches whose dials depict favorite sports and TV stars have been manufactured with the kids in mind since the 1930s, when Ingersoll made a clock, a wristwatch, and a pocket watch featuring Mickey Mouse. The #1 Mickey wristwatch came in the now-famous orange box commonly known as the 'critter box,' illustrated with a variety of Disney characters. There is also a blue display box from the same time period. The watch itself featured a second hand with three revolving Mickey figures. It was available with either a metal or leather band. Babe Ruth starred on an Exacta Time watch in 1949, and the original box contained not only the watch but a baseball with a facsimilie signature.

Collectors prize the boxes about as highly as they do the watches. Many were well illustrated and colorful, but most were promptly thrown away, so they're hard to find today. Be sure you buy only watches in very good condition. Rust, fading, scratches, or other signs of wear sharply devaluate a clock or a watch. Hundreds have been produced, and if you're going to collect them, you'll need to study *Comic Character Clocks and Watches* by Howard S. Brenner (Books Americana) for more information.

Note: Our values are typical of high retail. A watch in exceptional condition, especially an earlier model, may bring even more. Dealers (who will generally pay about half of book when they buy for resale) many times offer discounts on the more pricey items, and package deals involving more than one watch may sometimes be made for as much as a 15% discount.

Advisor: Bill Campbell (C10).

See also Advertising; California Raisins.

Clocks

Bambi Alarm Clock, Bayard, image of Bambi & Thumper looking at butterfly, rnd chrome case, bl base, 5", EX (EX box), from $175 to....$200.00
Bambi Wall Clock, 1970s, yel plastic w/image of Bambi & friends in forest, battery-op, 11x11", NM, J5 ....$65.00
Batman & Robin Talking Alarm Clock, Janex, 1974, 3-D image of Batman running behind car beside round clock, EX....$50.00

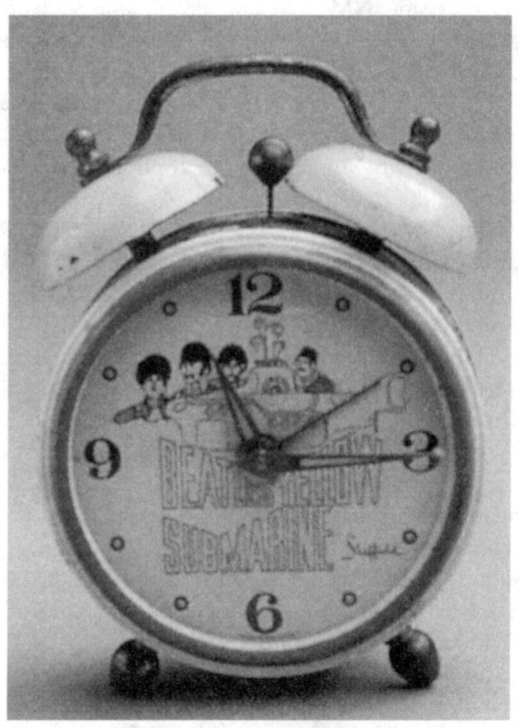

Beatles Yellow Submarine Alarm Clock, Sheffield, red and yellow, EX, A, $1,800.00.

Betty Boop Pendulum Clock, Poppo, pnt wood figure w/dial in middle, eyes move, 14½", EX **$500.00**

Big Bad Wolf Alarm Clock, Ingersoll, wolf w/nodding head surrounded by pigs, rnd red case, 4½", EX, A....... **$650.00**

Bozo Alarm Clock, Larry Harmon/French, 1960s, Bozo on face, rnd, rare, EX, A **$150.00**

Bugs Bunny Alarm Clock, Ingraham, Bugs laying down w/carrot in his mouth on face, rectangular case, 4", EX, A ... **$150.00**

Bugs Bunny Travel Alarm Clock, Seth Thomas, 1970, image of Bugs w/glow-in-the-dark hands, bl case, M, J5........... **$65.00**

Bugs Bunny Wall Clock, Seth Thomas, 1970, bl plastic case w/image of Bugs holding carrot, electric, 10" dia, NM, J5... **$85.00**

Cinderella Alarm Clock, Bradley/Japan, image of Cinderella leaving slipper on steps, 3" dia, scarce, MIB **$125.00**

Cinderella Wall Clock, Phinney Walker, 1970s, red metal w/image of Cinderella trying on slipper, 8" dia, NM, J5 .... **$65.00**

Davy Crockett Animated Clock, Haddon, 1950s, log cabin w/silkscreened image at right of clock face, 4x12", EX, A... **$425.00**

Disneyland Alarm Clock, Bradley, musical analog, image of Mickey as band leader w/parade of characters, EX, P6 .... **$125.00**

Donald Duck Alarm Clock, Bayard, 1930s, blue painted metal case and base, 5" dia, NM, A, $250.00.

Flintstones Alarm Clock, Sheffield, 1960s, ceramic figure of Fred w/dial in center, 8½", EX **$185.00**

Goofy Wall Clock, Welby by Elgin, 1970s, bl plastic w/full-color image of Goofy pointing time, 8" dia, NM, J5 .... **$65.00**

Howdy Doody Alarm Clock, Western Clock, 1954, mk Copyright 1954 Kagran Corp w/Howdy's image on face, metal case, 5", EX **$450.00**

Mickey Mouse Alarm Clock, Bayard, 1930s, Mickey in running pose on face, metal case, 4" dia, EX (EX box), A . **$1,800.00**

Mickey Mouse Alarm Clock, Ingersoll, 1930s, electric, lg rotating Mickey, gr gase, 4x4", NMIB **$2,200.00**

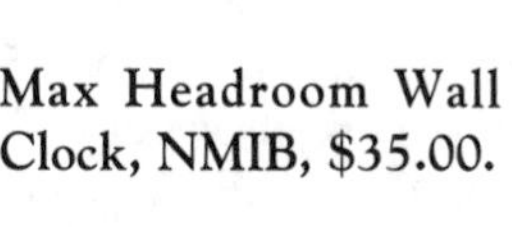

Max Headroom Wall Clock, NMIB, $35.00.

Photo courtesy Martin and Carolyn berens

Mickey Mouse Alarm Clock, Ingersoll, 1940s, Mickey's hands point time, tan case, 5" dia, VG (box mk Luminous Hands), A **$325.00**

Mickey Mouse Alarm Clock, Ingersoll, 1948, full-figure Mickey on face, wht plastic case, w/orig guarantee, MIB, A **$1,300.00**

Mickey Mouse Alarm Clock, Phinney-Walker, 1960s, analog movement, dbl bell, 4", EX, P6 .... **$75.00**

Mickey Mouse Wall Clock, Hamilton, 1970s, gr metal alarm clock shape w/Mickey's face, red hands, 10" dia, EX, J5 .... **$75.00**

Mighty Mouse Alarm Clock, 1960s, Mighty Mouse points time, orange case w/yel bells, NM, J5 .... **$85.00**

Minnie Mouse Alarm Clock, Bradley, 1976, Minnie in purple polka-dot dress, dbl bell, purple-pnt metal case, M, P4............ **$100.00**

Peanuts Alarm Clock, Janex, 1974, Charlie Brown & Snoopy sleeping next to round dial, EX, from $30 to **$45.00**

Pinocchio Alarm Clock, Bayard, 1939, Pinocchio w/animated Jiminy Cricket on his head, rnd, EX+, A................ **$250.00**

Planters, 1980, plaque style w/image of Mr Peanut & It's Always Time for Planters...1906, battery-op, 17x13", MIB, P4 . **$100.00**

Pluto Alarm Clock, Bayard, 1978, image of Pluto in front of doghouse on rnd dial, 5", MIB **$200.00**

Pluto Wall Clock, Allied, plastic figure w/clock attached to his chest, hands shaped as dog bones, 8", EX (EX box). **$450.00**

Popeye Alarm Clock, New Haven, litho tin w/colorful image on face, case & base, 4", EX, A **$850.00**

Popeye Alarm Clock, Smith Alarm/Great Britain, Popeye & Swee' Pea at play, rnd wht case, EX (EX box) **$385.00**

Raggedy Ann & Andy Talking Alarm Clock, Equity, rnd dial above raised image of Raggedy Ann & Andy, NM.... **$35.00**

Roy Rogers Alarm Clock, Ingraham, 1940, Roy on Trigger riding through canyon, sq gr case, 5", NM (VG box), A **$385.00**

Sesame Street Talking Alarm Clock, rnd dial in building w/Big Bird reading to Ernie & Oscar the Grouch, 11", EX..**$35.00**

Shmoo Pendulette Alarm Clock, Lux, 1950, figural w/dial in middle, 8", EX (EX box)........**$200.00**

Tweety Bird Talking Alarm Clock, Janex, 1978, battery-op, EX, J2........**$75.00**

Underdog Alarm Clock, Germany, 1970s, Underdog's hands keep time, yel plastic octagonal case, 3", NM, J5 ....**$195.00**

Winnie the Pooh Alarm Clock, Sunbeam, 1980s, MIB ...**$75.00**

Woody Woodpecker Alarm Clock, Columbia Time, image of Woody w/spatula in Woody's Cafe, rnd silver case, 4", EX, A........**$155.00**

Woody Woodpecker Alarm Clock, Westclox, image of nodding Woody w/spatula at Cafe tree, rnd wht case, 5½", EX, A..**$175.00**

Pocket Watches

Buck Rogers, colorful image of Buck & Wilma w/lightning bolt hands, 2" dia, EX, A........**$575.00**

Buck Rogers, Ingraham, 1935, NMIB, $650.00.

Mickey Mouse, Ingersoll, 1933, lithographed tin hands, NM, A, $1,500.00.

Dan Dare, Ingersoll/Great Britain, 1950s, space scene w/spaceship & gun ticking off seconds, MIB........**$800.00**

Hopalong Cassidy, unmk, 1950s, blk dial w/wht numbers surrounding bust-image of Hoppy, chrome case, 2" dia, EX........**$100.00**

James Bond 007 Spy Watch, Gilbert, w/secret lenses, EX (EX box)........**$300.00**

Mickey Mouse, Bradley, 1960s, full-figure Mickey on face, tin case, 2" dia, MIB, A........**$155.00**

Mighty Mouse, flexing his muscles, NP case, 1⅞" dia, EX........**$100.00**

Moon Mullins & Kayo, full-figure image in center, 2" dia, extremely rare, EX, A........**$350.00**

Popeye, Popeye in center w/various characters in between numbers, Popeye's arms keep time, 2" dia, EX, A **$650.00**

Three Stooges, mk FTTC, Moe pulling Curly's tooth out w/pliers, NP case, 2" dia, EX........**$100.00**

Three Little Pigs, Ingersoll, 1935, NMIB, $2,500.00.

Wristwatches

Alice in Wonderland, Ingersoll, image of Alice, pk fabric strap, EX (EX rnd pk box w/clear plastic teacup) **$250.00**

Archie, Rouan, 1960s, Archie's head revolves as it ticks, red band, NM, A........**$100.00**

Batman, Marcel, 1966, batwings keep time on rnd face encased in blk plastic wings, no band, EX, J5........**$200.00**

Batman Bat-Watch, NPPI, 1966, Batman on face, bat logo on band, MOC, A........**$750.00**

Big Jim, Bradley, 1973, figure in red shorts w/arms as hands, Big Jim in bl & red lettering, blk vinyl band, NM, J5........**$150.00**

Bozo the Clown, Bradley, 1960s, Bozo on face, rpl red band, EX, J5 ....$75.00
Buzz Lightyear, Fossil, 1996, limited edition of 7,500, complete w/certificate, plaque & rnd tin case, M, M8 ....$125.00
Captain Marvel, Fawcett, 1948, Captain Marvel holding airplane, rnd chrome case, vinyl strap, MIB, from $500 to $600.00
Casper the Ghost, Bradley, 1960s, Casper flies over mountains on bl dial, wht vinyl band, NM, J5 ....$150.00
Cinderella, Timex, 1958, Cinderella on face, pk band, complete w/plastic Cinderella figure, EX (EX box), A....$150.00
Cinderella, Timex/WDP, Cinderella's face covers dial, complete w/plastic slipper & storybook box, NMIB, A....$475.00
Cool Cat, Sheffield, 1960s, full-figure image, rpl band, VG, J5 ....$50.00
Dale Evans, Bradley, 1950s, rnd horseshoe image, rectangular gold-tone case, tan leather strap, EX (EX box)....$275.00
Davy Crockett, Disney version, 1950s, Davy holding rifle, gr plastic waterproof case, brn band, EX, A $75.00
Dennis the Menace, 1960s, bl-trimmed face w/image of Dennis & Ruff, rpl band, EX, J5 ....$75.00
Dick Tracy, New Haven/New Syndicate, 1948, Tracy pointing gun on face, orig beige band, EX (EX box), A....$300.00
Donald Duck, Bradley, 1985, 50th Anniversary Registered Edition, battery-op, complete w/paperwork, MIB, P6...$150.00
Donald Duck, Ingersoll/US Time, image of Donald w/lg dial arms, chrome case, bl strap, EX (EX box) $635.00

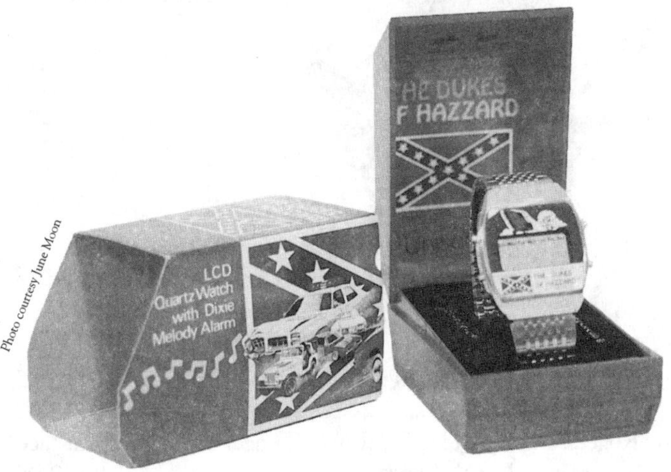

Dukes of Hazzard, LCD Quartz, Unisonic, 1981, stainless steel band, MIB, $35.00.

Dukes of Hazzard, LCD Quartz, Unisonic, 1981, stainless steel band, NRFB, H4 ....$40.00
Elmer Fudd, Sheffield, 1960s, Elmer in hunting outfit, wht vinyl band, NMIB, J5 ....$150.00
Evil Knievel, Bradley, 1976, Evil on motorcycle in stunt position, wht vinyl band, EX, A $125.00
Flintstones, Bradley, 1960s, close-up image of Fred & Pebbles, rpl red band, NM, J5 ....$65.00
Flipper, 1960s, gr image of Flipper jumping on blk face, rpl band, EX, J5 ....$65.00
Gerber Baby, 1970s, Gerber Baby's face covers face, brn vinyl band, EX $35.00
Goofy, Helbros, 1971, Goofy & numbers run backwards, rare, NM (NM plastic box) $1,000.00
Hazel, 1971, bust image, red band, NM, A $65.00
Hopalong Cassidy, US Time, 1950, bust-portrait on face, western motif on blk band, complete w/saddle display, MIB, A $625.00

Howdy Doody, Ideal Watch Co., MIB, $500.00.

Josie & the Pussycats, 1971, Josie playing guitar & music notes in pk & yel, rpl red vinyl band, EX, A $200.00
Lassie, 1960s, image of Lassie sitting, wht w/name in bl, NM $75.00

Lone Ranger, Everbrite/TLR, 1951, rare round version, complete with pop-up Lone Ranger figure, NMIB, A, $650.00.

Man From UNCLE, 1966, line drawing of Napolean talking on communicator, rpl band, EX.....$75.00

Mickey Mouse, Bradley, 50th Anniversary, image w/lg dial arms, rnd chrome base, blk lizard strap, NMIB.....$85.00

Mickey Mouse, Ingersoll, 1933, Mickey w/lg dial hands & seconds dial, rnd chrome case, chrome bracelet strap, EX.....$550.00

Mickey Mouse, Ingersoll/Mickey Mouse Electric, image w/lg dial arms, blk vinyl strap, NMIB.....$100.00

Mickey Mouse, Ingersoll/US Time, 1947, Mickey on rectangular face, red vinyl band, NM (EX box), A.....$350.00

Mickey Mouse, Timex, 1958, red band, complete with figure, NM; Minnie Mouse, Timex, 1958, yellow band, complete with figure, NM, $225.00 each.

Nightmare Before Christmas, Timex, digital, MIP, $45.00.

Photo courtesy Pamela Apkarian-Russel

Mickey Mouse, US Time, 1958, Mickey on face, red band, complete w/plastic Mickey figure, EX (EX box), A.....$200.00

Minnie Mouse, Bradley, 1970s, Minnie's hands point time, rpl band, EX, J5.....$35.00

Miss Piggy, Timex, 1982, image of Miss Piggy w/animated hearts, digital, MIB.....$65.00

Nightmare Before Christmas, Timex, features Lock, Shock & Barrel, MIB.....$175.00

Porky Pig, Sheffield, 1960s, Porky tipping his hat, bl band, NM (NM box), J5.....$150.00

Raggedy Ann, Bobbs-Merrill, 1971, image w/arms as hands, rpl band, EX.....$50.00

Ricochet Rabbit, 1960s, full-figure image & Ricochet Rabbit in blk & wht letters, wht band, NM, A.....$500.00

Rocketeer, Fossel, only 1,000 made, NM, $200.00.

Rocketeer, Hope, 1991, digital, metal w/plastic band, NMOC, M8.....$35.00

Roy Rogers, Ingraham, 1951, Roy & Trigger on rectangular face, brn strap, NM (NM box).....$400.00

Rudolph the Red-Nosed Reindeer, USA, rectangular chrome case, red vinyl strap, EX.....$75.00

Smokey Bear, Hamilton, 1960s, Smokey points time w/shovels, orig band, MIB, J5.....$150.00

Snow White, USA/WDP, image of Snow White, rnd plastic case, yel strap, complete w/wall hanging, EX (EX box).....$175.00

Space Mouse, Webster, 1960s, blk & wht image on face, red band, MIB, J5.....$65.00

Superman, Bradley, Superman image, rnd gold-tone case, gold-tone stretch band, EX (EX lt bl cylindrical box).....$175.00

Superman, colorful image of Superman, brn leather band, EX, A.....$85.00

Tom Corbett Space Cadet, Ingraham, 1951, image of Tom w/lightning bolt hands, chrome base, metal stretch band, NM, P4.....$165.00

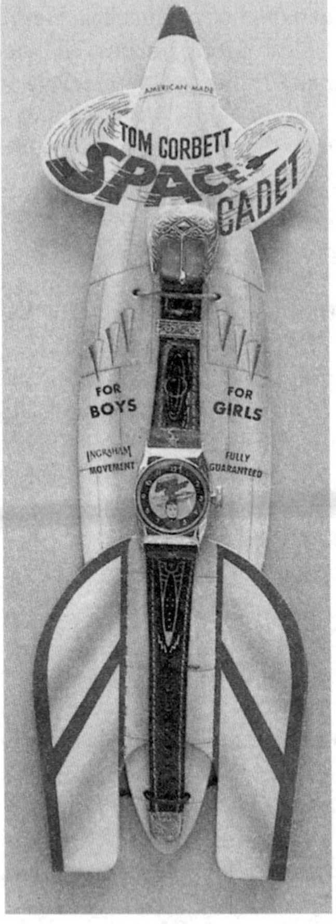

Tom Corbett Space Cadet, Ingraham, 1951, MOC, $1,200.00.

Tweety Bird, Topolino/Swiss, image w/lg dial arms, rnd chrome case, red leather strap, EX (EX box)..........................**$50.00**

Woody (Toy Story), Fossil, limited edition of 7,500, complete w/certificate, plaque & rnd tin case, M, M8...........**$125.00**

Woody Woodpecker, Ingraham, image of Woody, chrome case, red strap, NMIB...**$475.00**

Zorro, US Time, name in script, chrome case, blk leather strap w/silver-stamped designs, w/display hat, EX (EX box)..........**$400.00**

Character, TV, and Movie Collectibles

To the baby boomers who grew up glued to the TV set and addicted to Saturday matinees, the faces they saw on the screen were as familiar to them as family. Just about any character you could name has been promoted through retail merchandising to some extent; depending on the popularity they attain, exposure may continue for weeks, months, even years. It's no wonder, then, that the secondary market abounds with these items or that there is such wide-spread collector interest. For more information, we recommend *Collector's Guide to TV Memorabilia, 1960s & 1970s, 1st and 2nd edition* by Greg Davis and Bill Morgan; *Howdy Doody* by Jack Koch; *Character Toys and Collectibles, Vols I and II*, and *Cartoon Toys and Collectibles Identification and Value Guide* by David Longest; and *Cartoon Friends of the Baby Boom Era* by Bill Bruegman.

Note: Though most characters are listed by their own names, some will be found under the title of the group, movie, comic strip, or dominant character they're commonly identified with. The Joker, for instance, will be found in the Batman listings.

Advisors: Lisa Adams (A7), Dr. Dolittle; Jerry and Ellen Harnish (H4); Larry Doucet (D11), Dick Tracy; Trina and Randy Kubeck (K1), The Simpsons; Norm Vigue (V1); TV Collector (T6); Casey's Collectible Corner (C1); Bill Stillman (S6), Wizard of Oz.

See also Action Figures; Battery-Operated; Books; Chein; Character Clocks and Watches; Coloring, Activity, and Paint Books; Dakins; Disney; Dolls, Celebrity; Fisher-Price; Games; Guns; Halloween Costumes; Lunch Boxes; Marx; Model Kits; Paper Dolls; Pin-Back Buttons; Plastic Figures; Playsets; Puppets; Puzzles; Records; Toothbrush Holders; View-Master; Western; Windups, Friction, and Other Mechanicals.

A-Team, Colorforms Adventure Set, 1983, MIB (sealed), J2..**$25.00**

Addams Family, doll, Gomez, Ace, 1992, stuffed cloth, orig tag, NM, F8...**$15.00**

Addams Family, doll, Morticia, stuffed cloth, 27", NM, F8...**$50.00**

Addams Family, key chain, Thing, EX, F1.........................**$5.00**

Agent Zero, camera/pistol, Mattel, 1964, plastic, EX+, P3....**$45.00**

Alf, lap tray, 1987, Let's Do Lunch!, metal, EX, I2...........**$15.00**

Aliens, bop bag, Kid Dimension, 1993, inflatable plastic, 48", MIB, M17...**$45.00**

Photo courtesy Martin and Carolyn Berens

Alvin and the Chipmunks, doll, Alvin, Ideal, talker, plush with cloth clothes, 18", $55.00.

Alvin & the Chipmunks, music box doll, Alvin, Monarch, 1959, stuffed plush w/real harmonica, 10", not working, EX, F8..**$50.00**

Alvin & the Chipmunks, squeeze toy, Alvin, Holland, 1964, rubber, EX, C17 ....$60.00
Alvin & the Chipmunks, Treat Mobile, Ideal, 1984, MIB, H4....................$40.00
Amazing Chan Clan, handcuffs, Larami, 1972, MIP (sealed), F8 ....$15.00
Amos 'N Andy, figures, Japan, prewar, bsk, 8" & 7", EX, A ...$575.00
Amos 'N Andy, figures, Jaymar, 1930s, jtd wood, 6", NM, A.$300.00
Amos 'N Andy, figures, Pepsodent premium, 1931, litho cb, set of 6, complete w/punchout sheet, NM, A...............$500.00
Andy Brown, sparkler, Germany, 1930s, push lever & eyes spark, tin, 7", NM, A $725.00
Andy Gump, bank, litho tin, features Andy & Uncle Bim, 4", VG, A $165.00
Andy Gump, doll, Bucherer, jtd metal & compo w/cloth clothes, 8", rare, VG, A $400.00
Andy Gump, record & mask, Listerine premium, EX (EX card), A $100.00
Andy Panda, doll, stuffed cloth w/red felt overalls, retains orig tag, NM, T2, from $250 to $450.00
Annie, doll, Knickerbocker, 1982, 12", NRFB, M15........$25.00
Annie, doll, Knickerbocker, 1982, 7", NRFB, M15..........$12.00
Annie, puffy stickers, Gordy Int'l, 1981, MIP, M17 ....$10.00
Archie, sticker, Everything's Archie, 1968, 5" dia, EX (EX paper backing) $35.00
Archies, doll, Archie, 1960s, stuffed cloth, 18", complete w/comic book, MIP, J5 ....$75.00
Archies, Jughead Jr Shaving Kit, 1986, MOC, H4 ....$15.00
Archies, stencil set, 1983, MOC, H4 ....$15.00
Arnold Schwarznegger, Commando Vest, rare, MIB, P12.$100.00
Astro Boy, figure, Japan, 1960s, ceramic, 8", NM, F8.....$200.00
Astro Boy, music box, Japan, 1980s, ceramic, red w/blk specks & gold trim, plays theme song, NM, C1 ....$175.00
Baby Huey, figure, Alvimar, 1960s, inflatable vinyl w/bells inside, bl, wht & yel, 9", EX, J5 ....$25.00
Banana Splits, flute set, Larami, 1973, plastic, set of 3, MOC, C1 ....$55.00

Barney Google and Spark Plug, figures, Schoenhut, jointed wood with cloth clothes, MIB, A, $3,100.00.

Banana Splits, pajama bag, Fleegle, Animal Creations Ltd, 1970s, plush w/orig ribbons, 18" wide, rare, NM, A.............$600.00
Banana Splits, pillow, Fleegle or Snork, Kellogg's, 1960s, 10", minor fading o/w EX, J5, ea $50.00
Barney Google & Spark Plug, drum, KFS, 1929, litho tin, 10½" dia, VG, A $225.00
Barney Google & Spark Plug, figures, mk 1922-24 King Features..., DeBeck facsimile signature on base, bsk, 3", EX, A, pr $185.00
Barney Google & Spark Plug, pull toy, KFS, 1924, litho tin, 8", EX, A $850.00
Batman, bank, Transogram, 1966, standing pose, plastic, mk Owosso Federal Savings..., 19", EX, A $150.00
Batman, Bat Coders, Mego, 1976, plastic walkie-talkies w/alarm & danger signals, 14", NM (NM card), A $150.00
Batman, Batarang, Ideal, 1966, blk plastic, came w/utility belt, 8", NM, A $100.00
Batman, Batboat, Duncan, early 1970s, blk plastic w/molded Batman & Robin figures, decal on both sides, 8", VG, A $85.00
Batman, Batcuffs, Ideal, 1966, came w/utility belt, 4", NM, A $100.00
Batman, Batmobile, Polistil/Italy, diecast w/integral figures, 6", scarce, NM (EX box), A $1,300.00
Batman, Batmobile, Premier Products, plastic w/Batman & Robin figures, 8", NMIP, A $235.00
Batman, Batmobile pedal car, 1966, plastic, 34", EX, A $575.00

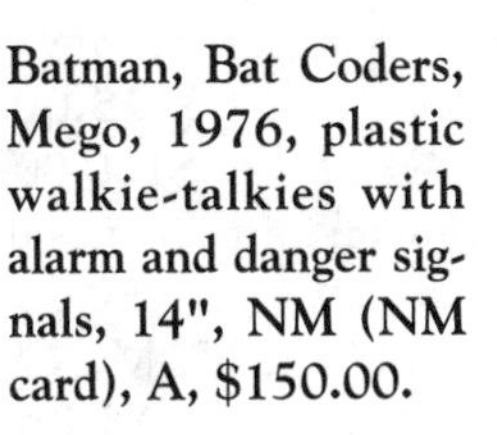

Batman, Bat Coders, Mego, 1976, plastic walkie-talkies with alarm and danger signals, 14", NM (NM card), A, $150.00.

Batman, bicycle license plate, 1966, emb metal, 2F3567 Batmobile, 4x7", NM, A **$50.00**
Batman, bike horn, Durham, 1960s, plastic Batman figure, battery-op, 6", EX (EX box), J5 ....**$85.00**
Batman, bubble bath (unauthorized), Beardmore, cb tube w/image & Fun in the Tub w/Bathman, w/contents, rare, NM, A **$165.00**
Batman, Cartoon-a-Rama Animation Art Set, 1977, MIB (sealed), F8..**$50.00**
Batman, charm bracelet, NPPI, 1966, gold-colored metal, 6 different figures, NMOC, A, from $100 to..................**$125.00**
Batman, clip-on tie, Omega, 1966, red w/Batman's face in center, Batman in yel letters, 11", NMIB, J5 ....**$100.00**
Batman, Colorforms, 1966, few pcs missing, NMIB, F8....**$40.00**
Batman, figure, Batman, Fun Things/NPPI, 1966, rubber w/elastic string, 5", NM (EX card), A...............................**$125.00**
Batman, figure, Robin, Chromoplasto/NPPI, 1960s, hard rubber, 5", VG, A..**$115.00**
Batman, figure, Robin, Fun Things/NPPI, 1966, rubber w/elastic string, 5", NM (EX card), A **$65.00**
Batman, figure set, Batman, Robin & Joker, Ideal, 1966, hard plastic, 3", NMIP, A **$125.00**
Batman, figure set, Batman & Robin, Italy, 1966, diecut vinyl w/foam layer to make them puffy, 3", NM, A **$35.00**
Batman, flicker ring, plastic, NM, J2 ....**$20.00**
Batman, Follow the Color Magic Rub-Off Set, Whitman, 1966, complete, EX (EX box), A **$100.00**
Batman, gloves, Wells Lamont Corp, 1966, simulated blk leather w/logo, 3 hooks on outside, MIP, A **$100.00**
Batman, hat, Joker, 1989, replica of hat worn in movie, EX, F1 ....**$15.00**
Batman, hat/mask, 1966, felt hat w/drop-down mask, Pow! patch on front, NM, F8...**$25.00**
Batman, helmet & cape, Ideal, 1966, plastic helmet w/vinyl cape, NM (EX box), A **$200.00**
Batman, license plate, 1966, diecut metal w/Batman lettered over image, 6x12", EX, A **$100.00**
Batman, magic slate, Golden, 1989, MIP (sealed), P3 ....**$5.00**
Batman, magic slate, Watkins-Strathmore, 1966, VG, A..**$50.00**
Batman, make-up kit, Joker, 1989, EX, F1 ....**$5.00**
Batman, music box, Catwoman, Price, 1978, ceramic figure on spinning base, 7", EX, F8 ....**$90.00**
Batman, night light, Snap-It, 1966, hard plastic head & Batwings, 2x3", NM, A...**$35.00**
Batman, Official Batman Chute, NPPI, 1966, MOC, D9.**$40.00**
Batman, paddle ball paddle, 1960s, wht plastic w/image of Batman on 1 side & Joker on the other, 10", EX, J5 .....**$125.00**
Batman, pillow, 1966, red fabric w/Batman & Robin logo above Gotham City, 14x21", rare, EX, A **$250.00**
Batman, pillow, 1966, wht felt w/image of colorful image of Batman & Robin running below logo, 11x12", M, from $75 to..**$100.00**
Batman, poncho & mask, 1976, MIP, V1 ....**$35.00**
Batman, Punch A-Loon, National Latex Products, 1966, red inflatable balloon w/rubber band, 16" dia, EX (EX card) **$65.00**
Batman, shopping bag, 1970s, wht vinyl w/full-color image of Batman & Robin on both sides, 15x18", EX, J5 ....**$15.00**
Batman, sleeping bag, 1975, various scenes w/Batman, Robin, Catwoman, etc, sm tears at bottom o/w EX, F8 ....**$30.00**
Batman, slippers, 1966, bl simulated leather boot-type w/colorful image, M, from $100 to **$150.00**
Batman, stamp set, Kellogg's premium, 1966, complete w/stamps & ink pad in blk plastic case, scarce, NM, A **$65.00**
Batman, String Art Kit, Smith, 1976, MIB (sealed), F8...**$45.00**
Batman, telephones, Remco, 1960s, red plastic w/cb Batman decals, battery-op, EX, A, pr **$185.00**
Batman, Thingmaker mold, Mattel, 1965, for rings or rubber stamps, EX, F8..**$35.00**

Beany and Cecil, doll, Cecil, Mattel, 1962, stuffed plush, VG, L6, $45.00.

Batman, Utility Belt, Ideal, 1966, soft yel plastic belt complete w/accessories, scarce, NMIB, A............................**$7,000.00**

Batman, wallet, Standard Plastic/Mattel, 1966, yel w/Batman swinging from rope on 1 side & Robin on the other, EX, A..**$25.00**

Batman, wastebasket, 1966, litho tin w/image of Batman & Robin in action pose, 10", VG, A.............................**$65.00**

Batman, wrist compass, 1966, compass inset in plastic logo, blk simulated leather band w/gold clasp, 7", NMOC, A..**$35.00**

Batman Returns, magic slate, Golden, 1992, MIP (sealed), P3..**$4.00**

Batman Returns, mask, Penguin, Morris, 1992, latex, EX, F1...**$50.00**

Battlestar Galactica, Colorforms Adventure Set, 1978, complete, NM (NM box), F8..**$25.00**

Battlestar Galactica, Poster Art Set, Craftmaster, 1978, complete, MIB, H4...**$30.00**

Beany & Cecil, Beany-Copter, Mattel, 1960s, MOC............**$140.00**

Beetle Bailey, doll, Presents, cloth w/vinyl head, orig tags, M .**$40.00**

Beetle Bailey, puffy stickers, Ja-Ru, 1983, MIP (sealed), C1 ....**$20.00**

Ben Casey, nurse kit, Transogram, 1962, complete, NM (EX box), F8..**$30.00**

Ben Casey, Paint-By-Number-Set, Transogram, 1960s, unused, EX, J5...**$15.00**

Betty Boop, display, cb stand-up, life-size, EX, F1.............**$30.00**

Betty Boop, doll, compo & wood, orig decal, 12", EX, A..**$685.00**

Betty Boop, doll, Play by Play Toys, 1992, stuffed cloth w/vinyl head, 14", EX, H4...**$15.00**

Betty Boop, doll, stuffed cloth w/mask face, redressed, EX, rare, A..**$100.00**

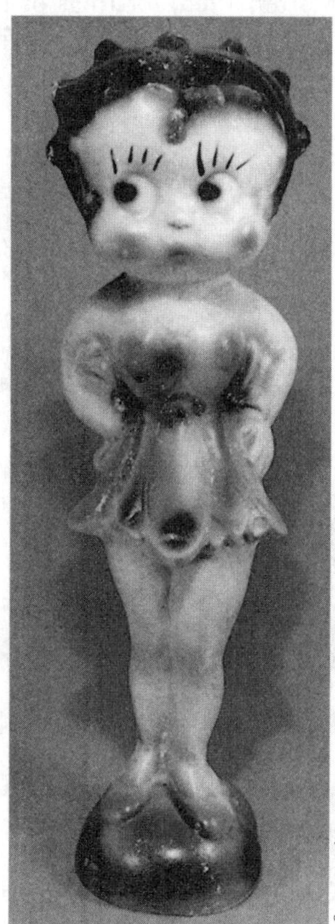

Photo courtesy David Longest

Betty Boop, figure, chalkware, classic pose, 14", NM, $275.00.

Betty Boop, fan, Japan, prewar, image of Betty w/movable eyes, 12", NM **$400.00**

Betty Boop, figure, Bimbo, Fleischer Studios, wood w/leatherette ears, 6", VG, A **$300.00**

Betty Boop, figure, celluloid figure on metal base, head nods back & forth w/rubber band action, 7", EX (worn box), A..**$1,000.00**

Betty Boop, figure, Japan, prewar, bsk, playing drum, 3½", EX, A **$125.00**

Betty Boop, figure, Jaymar, 1930s, jtd wood, 4¼", M, A..**$100.00**

Betty Boop, figure, mk Made in USA, cb w/metal joints on wood base, 9", EX, A..**$450.00**

Betty Boop, figure, NJ Croce, 1988, bendable, 8", MOC, H4...**$15.00**

Betty Boop, figure set, Bimbo Orchestra, Fleischer Studios/Japan, set of 3 in different poses, MIB.........**$500.00**

Betty Boop, figure set, Russia, 1980s, 5 hand-pnt wood figures that fit inside ea other, M, F8....................................**$75.00**

Betty Boop, mask, Bimbo, celluloid, 6x6", NM **$175.00**

Betty Boop, music box, Vandor, 1980s, ceramic, Betty seated at piano, plays I Want To Be Loved by You, MIB, F8 .**$100.00**

Betty Boop, transfers, Japan, 1935, set of 12, NMOC, A..**$25.00**

Betty Boop, ukelele, wood w/silkscreened image of Betty, Bimbo & Koko, 21", EX, A...**$230.00**

Beverly Hillbillies, car, Ideal, bl & red plastic w/seated figures, 23", EX (EX box) **$475.00**

Beverly Hillbillies, Colorforms, 1963, missing few pcs, EX (VG box), J5...**$25.00**

Big Bird, see Sesame Street

Bionic Woman, bank, Animals Plus, 1976, vinyl, 10", EX, M17...**$50.00**

Blippy, jack-in-the-box, Mattel, M, from $100 to **$150.00**

Blondie & Dagwood, Blondie Paints, 1946, watercolor pnts in litho tin box, EX, P6..**$40.00**

Blondie & Dagwood, kazoo, Dagwood, KFS, 1947, shaped like a sandwich, tin, 6", NM (G box), A **$150.00**

Bonanza, see Western category

Bonzo, pull toy, Chein, early mk, litho tin, 7", NM, A ..**$400.00**

Boo-Boo, see Huckleberry Hound

Bozo the Clown, Circus Train or Circus Wagon, Multiple Toys, 1970, MIB, ea...**$20.00**

Bozo the Clown, doll, Mattel, 1963, talker, 18", VG, M15 ....**$45.00**

Bozo the Clown, figure, Jesco, 1988, bendable, 6", MIP, M15 ....**$6.00**

Bozo the Clown, figure, Knickerbocker, 1960, bendable, 8", MIP (sealed), F8...**$25.00**

Bozo the Clown, Laurel & Hardy & Three Stooges, stamp set, Creative, 1974, complete, NMIB, F8 ....**$40.00**

Bozo the Clown, sticker, 1960s, from gumball machine, full-color diecut face, 3x4", NM, T2 ....**$8.00**

Bozo the Clown, sticker board, 1983, MIB........................**$15.00**

Bozo the Clown, Stitch-A-Story, Hasbro, 1967, MOC (sealed), J2 ....**$50.00**

Bozo the Clown, talking book, MIP (sealed), J2 ....**$55.00**

Breezy the Polar Bear, doll, Ideal, 1964, stuffed felt w/vinyl head, wire arms & legs, 8", M, T2...................................**$115.00**

Brenda Starr, Cub Reporter Camera, Seymour Prod, scarce, EX (EX box), A **$325.00**

Buck Rogers, Cosmic Conquests Printing Set, Stamperkraft/Dille, missing few stamps, VG (VG box), A $225.00

Buck Rogers, Electronic Communications Outfit, Remco/Dille, complete w/phones, decoder & electric wire, EX (VG box), A $100.00

Buck Rogers, Midget Caster Set, 1934, extremely rare, VG (VG box), J2 .... $750.00

Bugs Bunny, bag, Mighty Star, 1971, head figure of Bugs Bunny w/felt features, zipper closure in back, 17", NM, F8 ... $25.00

Bugs Bunny, bank, pnt metal, Bugs w/carrot leaning on tree trunk, 6", EX, A $135.00

Bugs Bunny, bank, Uncle Bugs, Great America, 1978, vinyl figure, EX $25.00

Bugs Bunny, bank, 1972, Bugs in bushel of carrots, plastic, 13", NM, F8 .... $25.00

Bugs Bunny, Chatterchum, Mattel, 1976, 7", VG, M15 ... $30.00

Bugs Bunny, doll, stuffed felt w/mask face, 24", EX, A ... $175.00

Bugs Bunny, doll, 1950s, dressed as Davy Crockett, EX . $325.00

Bugs Bunny, figure, 1988, bendable, 8", EX, N2 .... $20.00

Bugs Bunny, magic slate, Golden, 1987, MIP (sealed), P3 . $5.00

Bugs Bunny, pull toy, Bugs on tricycle, paper litho on wood w/bells on back wheels, NM $350.00

Bugs Bunny, purse, Mighty Star, 1971, cloth head figure of Bugs w/felt features, zipper closure, 17", NM, F8 .... $20.00

Bugs Bunny, ring toss, Larami, 1981, MOC, F1 .... $15.00

Bugs Bunny, Silly Putty, Ja-Ru, 1980, MOC, H4 .... $5.00

Bugs Bunny, Skediddler, Mattel, 1966, MIB $85.00

Bugs Bunny, sleeping bag, 1977, features Bugs, Porky Pig, Tweety Bird & several other characters, VG, F8 .... $15.00

Bullwinkle, see Rocky & Bullwinkle

Buttercup, doll, mk Geo MacManus-Made in Germany, jtd wood & compo w/cloth clothes, 10", EX, A $200.00

Captain America, bicycle license plate, Marx, 1967, pressed steel w/emb image & name on gr, 2x4", NM, F8 .... $40.00

Captain America, doll, Amsco, 1970s, Super Baby series, stuffed cloth w/vinyl head, 8", NM (VG box), J5 .... $45.00

Captain America, figure, Flying Captain America, Transogram/Marvel, 1966, Vacuform plastic, MOC (sealed), A $150.00

Captain America, pendant, Dell Plastics, 1966, yel vinyl w/paper insert picturing Captain America, 7", EX (EX pkg), J5 .. $65.00

Captain Kangaroo, Fun-Damental Activity Set, Lowe, 1977, NM (sealed), T2 .... $20.00

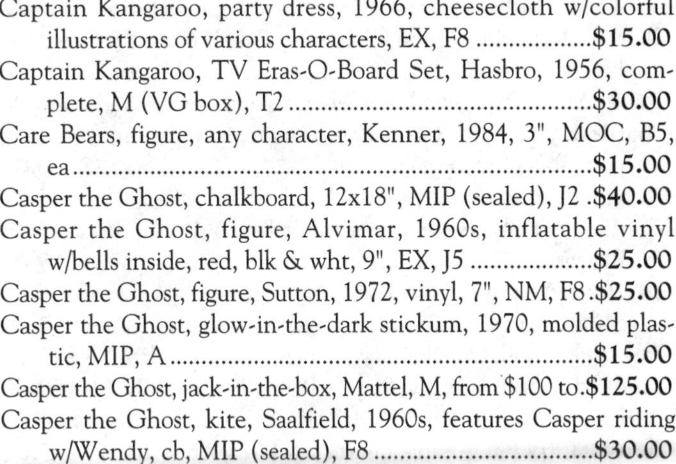

Captain Kangaroo, party dress, 1966, cheesecloth w/colorful illustrations of various characters, EX, F8 .... $15.00

Captain Kangaroo, TV Eras-O-Board Set, Hasbro, 1956, complete, M (VG box), T2 .... $30.00

Care Bears, figure, any character, Kenner, 1984, 3", MOC, B5, ea $15.00

Casper the Ghost, chalkboard, 12x18", MIP (sealed), J2 . $40.00

Casper the Ghost, figure, Alvimar, 1960s, inflatable vinyl w/bells inside, red, blk & wht, 9", EX, J5 .... $25.00

Casper the Ghost, figure, Sutton, 1972, vinyl, 7", NM, F8 . $25.00

Casper the Ghost, glow-in-the-dark stickum, 1970, molded plastic, MIP, A $15.00

Casper the Ghost, jack-in-the-box, Mattel, M, from $100 to . $125.00

Casper the Ghost, kite, Saalfield, 1960s, features Casper riding w/Wendy, cb, MIP (sealed), F8 .... $30.00

Casper the Ghost, pull toy, Casper plays xylophone, paper lithograph on wood, 10", rare, EX, A, $225.00.

Casper the Ghost, 3-D Cartoon Paint Set, Hasbro, 1971, MIB, F8 .... $40.00

Charlie Brown, see Peanuts

Charlie Chaplin, balancing toy, Am Flyer, 1925, travels on bicycle along string, 7", EX, A $250.00

Charlie Chaplin, doll, 1915, straw-stuffed cloth body w/compo head, blk molded hair, 16", rare, EX+, A $600.00

Charlie Chaplin, pin, mk Made in Japan, flat litho tin, pull string & he tips his hat, 4", EX, A $125.00

Charlie McCarthy, coloring set, Whitman, 1938, complete, NM (NM box), A $165.00

Charlie McCarthy, doll, 1930s, compo, moveable mouth, 13", EX, J2 .... $250.00

Charlie McCarthy, figure, 1930s, chalkware, wearing bl tux highlighted w/silver sparkles, red shoes, 16", EX, J5 .. $65.00

Charlie McCarthy, Flexy figure, pnt wood, 5", rare, EX, A.$350.00
Charlie McCarthy, pencil sharpener, Bakelite, bust figure, 1½", EX, A $65.00
Charlie McCarthy, pencil sharpener, Bakelite, rnd, EX, A..$50.00
Charlie McCarthy, Radio Party Game, radio premium, complete, NM (EX orig envelope)....................$100.00
Charlie's Angels, dresser set, Rack Toy, 1977, MOC, P12..$45.00
Charlie's Angels, poster, Sabrina or Kelly, 1970s, 36x24", EX, F1, ea....................$15.00
Charlie's Angels, Talk Time Telephone, Fleetwood, 1977, MOC, M15 ....$50.00
Child's Play, doll, Chucky, Play by Play, 1992, 15", EX, F1 .$25.00
Child's Play, doll, Chucky, Play by Play, 1992, 24", EX, F1 .$50.00
CHiPs, Colorforms, 1981, NMIB, J2 ....$30.00
Chitty-Chitty Bang-Bang, charm braclet, 1968, MIB.......$95.00
Cookie Monster, see Sesame Street
Creature From the Black Lagoon, figure, Remco, 4", NM, J2 ..$40.00
Curious George, magic slate, Fairchild, 1968, 12x9", M, T2....$10.00
Daffy Duck, bank, pnt metal, Daffy leaning on tree trunk, 6", EX, A $135.00
Daffy Duck, doll, Mighty Star, 1971, stuffed plush, 19", NM, F8 ....$25.00
Dagwood, see Blondie & Dagwood

Photo courtesy Cindy Sabulis

Dennis the Menace, night light, $30.00; record, 78 rpm, $10.00; Margret hand puppet, $25.00.

Dennis the Menace, Colorforms, 1961, complete, NMIB, F8 .$50.00
Dennis the Menace, Creepy Bugs, Larami, 1988, MOC, C1...$15.00
Dennis the Menace, doll, Joey, Presents, 1980s, cloth, EX......$25.00
Dennis the Menace, figure, 1960s, wood pull-string puppet, 6", G, F8 ....$20.00
Dennis the Menace, mug, 1962, red-pnt plastic, EX, B14 .$12.00
Dennis the Menace, Paint-by-Number Set, Determined, 1971, MIB (sealed), M17....................$40.00
Dennis the Menace & Ruff, ornament set, 1977, MIB, B5 ..$20.00
Deputy Dawg, doll, Ideal, 1960s, stuffed cloth w/vinyl head, minor fading o/w EX, H4....................$50.00
Deputy Dawg, pencil case, Hasbro, 1961, red cb w/school scene on lg decal, w/few accessories, 8x4", EX, T2 ....$25.00

Dick Tracy, belt buckle, 1960s, plastic image of Tracy in profile mounted on gold or silver buckle, EX, D11, ea..........$20.00
Dick Tracy, camera, Seymour, 1950s, 127mm, scarce, NMIB, D11 ....$100.00
Dick Tracy, Cartoon Kit, Colorforms, 1962, complete, EX (EX box), A....................$75.00
Dick Tracy, charm, any character, plastic head figures, from gumball machine, EX, D11, ea from $20 to $25.00
Dick Tracy, Crimestoppers Set, Larami, 1967, complete w/handcuffs, nightstick & badge, NMIP, D11 ....$40.00
Dick Tracy, Dick Tracy's Handcuffs for Junior, John Henry, 1940s, EX (yel 5x10" card or red 3x9" card), D11, ea ..$75.00
Dick Tracy, doll, Sparkle Plenty, Ideal, 1947-50, plastic head w/rubber body, yel yarn hair, 14", EX....................$175.00
Dick Tracy, figure, Bonnie Braids, Charmore, 1951, plastic, 1¼", NMOC, D11....................$50.00
Dick Tracy, figure, Dick Tracy, Rubb'r Niks, complete, NMOC, D11....................$45.00
Dick Tracy, figure, Dick Tracy, 1930s, pnt lead, EX, D11 .$30.00
Dick Tracy, film, Trick or Treat, 1960s, 8mm, EX (EX box), A $50.00
Dick Tracy, Fingerprint Lab, Parliament Toy, 1953, complete, EX (EX box) $135.00
Dick Tracy, flashlight, 1950s, bl & red w/etched image of Tracy on side, pocket sz, NMIB, D11 ....$75.00
Dick Tracy, greeting cards, Norcross, 1960s, several styles w/neon backgrounds, NM, D11, ea $20.00
Dick Tracy, ID Composit Kit, Playmates, 1990, MIB, P3.$15.00
Dick Tracy, magnifying glass, Larami, 1979, MOC, C1 ...$20.00
Dick Tracy, mask, Einson-Freeman, 1933, paper, rare, EX, D11....................$100.00
Dick Tracy, Mini Color Televiewer, Larami, 1972, NMIP, D11 ....$25.00
Dick Tracy, note pad, 1970s, cover shows profile of Dick Tracy & Rick Fletcher signature, 7x3½", M, D11 ....$15.00
Dick Tracy, Special Agent Set, Larami, 1972, complete w/dart gun, handcuffs & badge, EX, NMIP, D11 ....$40.00
Dick Tracy, Transistor Radio Receiver, American Doll & Toy, 1961, MIB, D11 ....$100.00
Dick Tracy, TV Watch, Ja-Ru, NMOC, D11 ....$20.00

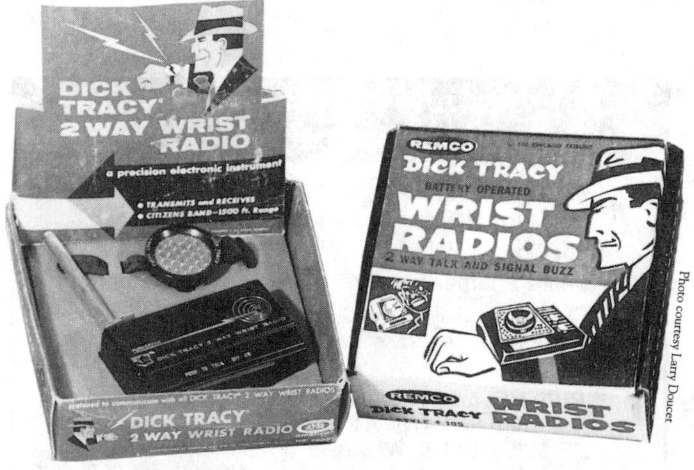

Photo courtesy Larry Doucet

Dick Tracy, Wrist Radios, Remco, MIB, $100.00.

Dick Tracy, valentine, 1940s, Say, Valentine, You May Detect It..., NM (orig envelope), D11 ....**$50.00**
Dick Tracy, wallet, 1973, blk vinyl, w/6 Crimestopper textbook cards, NM, D11...**$20.00**
Ding Dong School, Mr Bumps figure set, Barry Products, 1955, MIB, T2 ....**$60.00**
Ding Dong School, record player, Miss Frances on front, EX, T2..**$130.00**
Dondi, figure, 1960, vinyl w/moveable head, 12", NM, F8....**$70.00**
Dr Dolittle, bath toy, Fun Sponge, Amsco, NM, A7........**$30.00**
Dr Dolittle, Cartoon Kit, Colorforms, 1967, NMIB, from $25 to..**$35.00**
Dr Dolittle, doll, Mattel, 1969, talker, 24", NMIB, A7..**$150.00**
Dr Dolittle, jack-in-the-box, Giraffe, 1967, plays 'The Bear Went Over the Mountain,' NM.................................**$40.00**
Dr Dolittle, medical playset, Hasbro, NM, A7..................**$75.00**
Dr Dolittle, Mystery Chamber Magic Set, Remco, 1939, NMIB, A7 ....**$30.00**
Dr Dolittle, periscope, Bar-Zim, NMIP, A7......................**$30.00**
Dr Dolittle, playhouse, Mattel #5125, vinyl w/image of various characters, NM, A7 ....**$60.00**
Dr Dolittle, projector, Ugly Mugly, Remco, w/slides from movie, NMIB, A7...**$50.00**
Dr Dolittle, Ride-Em Rocker, Pushmi-Pullyu, AJ Renzi, 1974, NM, A7..**$50.00**
Dr Dolittle, Spelling & Counting Board, Bar-Zim, NMIP, A7 ....**$35.00**
Dr Dolittle, Stitch-a-Story, Hasbro, NMIP, A7................**$25.00**
Dr Dolittle, wrist flashlight, Bantamlite, NM, A7 ....**$30.00**
Dr Kildare, magic slate, Lowe, 1962, cb w/lift-up erasable film sheet, 12x8", unused, NM..**$50.00**
Dr Seuss, book bag, Cat in the Hat, 1970s, cloth w/image & I Like to Read, 12x9", EX, F8 ....**$15.00**

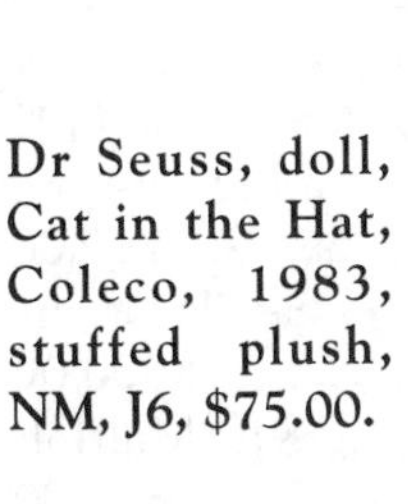

Dr Seuss, doll, Cat in the Hat, Coleco, 1983, stuffed plush, NM, J6, $75.00.

Dr Seuss, doll, Cat in the Hat, Mattel, 1970s, talker, NM.**$250.00**
Dr Seuss, doll, Cat in the Hat, stuffed cloth, 28", VG, J2.**$75.00**
Dr Seuss, doll, Cat in the Hat (unlicensed), Korea, 1980s, stuffed plush, 14", NM, F8..**$15.00**
Dr Seuss, doll, Horton the Elephant, Coleco, 1983, stuffed plush, EX..**$35.00**
Dr Seuss, doll, Thidwick the Big Hearted Moose, Coleco, 1983, plush, 16", NM, F8..**$90.00**
Dr Seuss, doll, Yertle the Turtle, Coleco, 1983, stuffed plush, EX...**$35.00**
Dr Who, doll, Harbert/BBC/Italian, 1979, vinyl, jtd, 9", NM (NM box), A **$200.00**
Dracula, doll, Hamilton Presents, 14", MIB, J2.................**$25.00**
Dracula, figure, Milton Bradley, 1974, foam rubber w/red felt cape, 11½", VG, H4 ....**$22.00**
Droopy Dog, squeeze toy, Alan Jay, 1960s, rubber, 4", EX, J5...**$35.00**
Dudley Do-Right, pen, 1970s, yel plastic w/silver Dudley figure on clip, NM, J5 ....**$25.00**
Dukes of Hazzard, Colorforms, 1981, NM (NM box), C1..**$30.00**
Dukes of Hazzard, Paint-By-Number Sun Catcher, NMOC, J2 ....**$25.00**
Dukes of Hazzard, Presto Magix Rub-Down Transfers, 1981, 5 variations, MIP, H4, ea...**$10.00**
Eloise, doll, cloth w/mask face, bl pleated skirt & wht blouse, 22", EX..**$175.00**
Elvira, makeup kit, MOC, from $15 to............................**$20.00**

Emergency, fire hats and oxygen mask, plastic, NM, J6, $55.00.

Emmett Kelly Circus, Colorforms, 1960, complete, NMIB, F8 ....**$40.00**
ET, doll, Showtime, 1982, plush, 8", NM, P3 ....**$6.00**

ET, night light, chest glows, MIB, B5 .....$35.00
ET, pillow, bl or purple, EX, B5, ea $20.00
ET, puffy stickers, Diamond Toymakers, 1982, MIP, D9 ....$3.00
ET, ring, head figure, MIP, B5 .....$20.00
ET, sponge ball, 1982, M, F1 .....$6.00

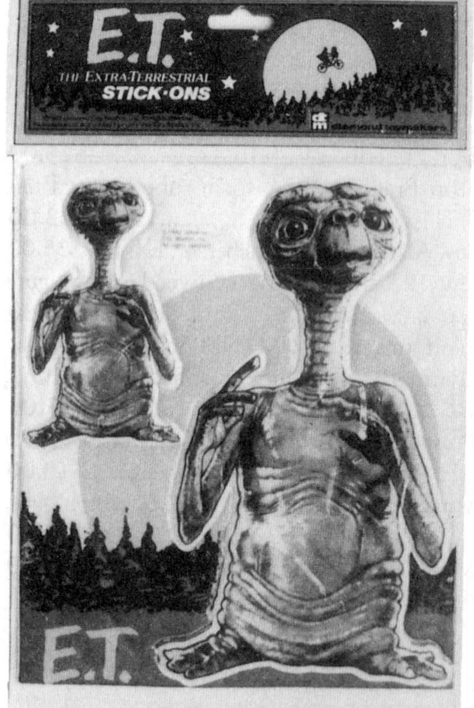

ET, Stick-Ons, MIP, B5, $5.00.

Photo courtesy Martin and Carolyn Berens

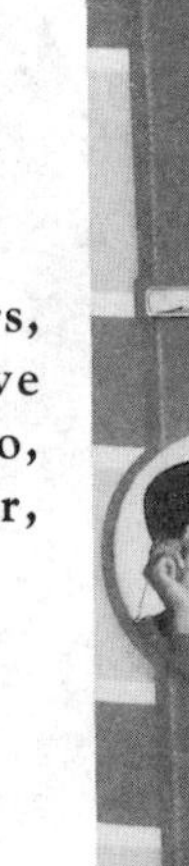
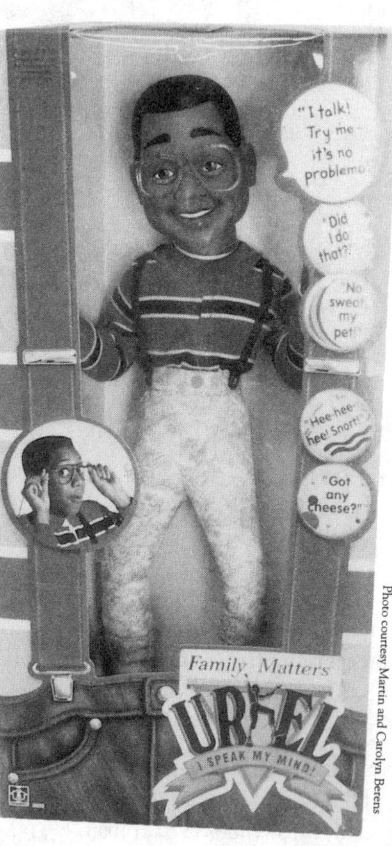

Family Matters, doll, Steve Urkel, Hasbro, 1991, talker, MIB, $40.00.

Photo courtesy Martin and Carolyn Berens

ET, windup walker, LJN, 1982, 3", MOC, C1.....$20.00
Family Affair, doll, Mrs Beasley, Mattel, talker, stuffed cloth w/vinyl head, 24", missing glasses o/w VG+, H4 .....$35.00
Family Affair, figure, Buffy & Mrs Beasley, 6", missing glasses o/w VG+, H4 .....$50.00
Family Affair, magic slate, features Buffy & Jody, 1970, EX, J2 .....$25.00
Fanny Price, doll, Ideal, compo & wood w/wire mesh arms & legs, orig outfit, 12", VG, A.....$75.00

Photo courtesy June Moon

Farrah Fawcett, Farrah's Glamour Center, Mego, NMIB, J6, $85.00.

Felix the Cat, doll, 1982, stuffed plush, 14", NM, F8.....$25.00
Felix the Cat, drum, 1930s, litho tin, scarce, EX $185.00
Felix the Cat, figure, compo w/cloth tail, jtd arms, 13", EX, A $350.00
Felix the Cat, figure, Fun-E-Flex, 1930s, Felix smoking pipe, wood, 3", rare, EX, A $335.00
Felix the Cat, figure, Germany, bsk, 1½", NM, V1 .....$350.00
Felix the Cat, figure, Japan, celluloid, Felix playing violin, 5", EX, A $110.00
Felix the Cat, figure, Pat Sullivan Copyr, 1924 on label under foot, jtd wood, 8", EX, A $375.00
Felix the Cat, figure, red-pnt wood w/cloth-covered wire arms, legs & tail, orig paper label on chest, 3", EX, A.....$350.00
Felix the Cat, figure, Schoenhut, jtd wood, orig decals on chest & foot, 5½", rare, EX, A $1,200.00
Felix the Cat, figure, Schoenhut, jtd wood w/leather ears, orig paper labels on chest & foot, 8", EX, A $750.00
Felix the Cat, hand toy, pnt wood, raise & lower handle for running action, 11", VG, A $300.00
Felix the Cat, Magna-Slide Cartoon Drawing Kit, Multiple Toys, 1960s, EX, F8 .....$75.00
Felix the Cat, pencil case, 1930s, fall scene w/scarecrow on front, winter scene w/snowman on back, EX, F8 .....$50.00
Felix the Cat, pull toy, 1936, Felix on delivery wagon, pnt wood, 10", rare, EX, A.....$275.00
Felix the Cat, sparkler, Nifty, litho tin, lever action, 5", NM (worn box), A $3,200.00
Felix the Cat, squeak toy, Germany, paper litho w/wood & paper squeaker, 6", EX, A.....$400.00

Felix the Cat, stencil set, Spears Bavaria by Pat Sullivan, incomplete, EX (EX box), A $150.00
Felix the Cat, tea set, Germany, 1920s, iridescent lusterware, service for 6, M, A $900.00
Felix the Cat, TV Color Set, Lido, 1950s, complete, NMIB, A $175.00
Flash Gordon, beanie w/fins & goggles, 1950s, NM, J2 ..$400.00
Flash Gordon, Colorforms, 1980, MIB, M17 ....$35.00
Flash Gordon, compass, 1950s, silver plastic w/yel wristband, MOC, P4....................$65.00
Flash Gordon, figure, chalkware, EX, C10 ....$500.00
Flash Gordon, outfit, Esquire Novelty, unused, MOC, J2 ..$200.00
Flintstone Kids, figure, any character, Coleco, MOC, H4, ea..$15.00

Photo courtesy Marcia Fanta

Flintstones, Baby Pebbles Cave House, Ideal, 1964, M, $175.00.

Flintstones, bank, Fred, 1977, Fred holding bowling ball, vinyl, 11", EX, J5....................$35.00
Flintstones, bubble pipe, Bamm-Bamm, 1960s, 8", EX, J2 .$20.00
Flintstones, Building Boulders, Kenner, MIB, T2, from $75 to $100.00
Flintstones, Cockamamies, 1961, complete, NMIB, J2 ....$30.00
Flintstones, coin purse, Barney, 1975, NM, J2 ....$25.00
Flintstones, doll, Barney, Knickerbocker, 1960s, plush & vinyl, 12", EX, C17 ....$75.00
Flintstones, doll, Fred, Knickerbocker, 1960s, plush & vinyl, 12", NM $85.00
Flintstones, doll, Pebbles, Mighty Star Ltd, 1982, cloth & vinyl, 12", MIB, H4 ....$60.00
Flintstones, dolls, Pebbles & Bamm-Bamm in cradle, Ideal, plastic, 14½" cradle, EX $125.00
Flintstones, figure, any character, Just Toys, bendable, MOC, J8, ea....................$10.00
Flintstones, figure set, Whitman, 1961, cb stand-up figures, Fred, Wilma, Barney & Betty, w/accessories, 18", EX, F8......$40.00
Flintstones, gumball machine, Fred, Hasbro, 1968, plastic head figure, 8", EX, F8 ....$50.00
Flintstones, Pencil-By-Number Coloring Set, Transogram, 1960s, complete, EX (EX box), A $130.00
Flintstones, Play Fun Set, Whitman, 1965, complete, EX (EX box), F8....................$65.00
Flintstones, puffy stickers (vending display), Hanna-Barbera, 1976, set of 8, M, M17....................$30.00
Flintstones, squeeze toy, any character, Lanco, 1960s, NMIP, ea $135.00
Flintstones, telephone, gr & red plastic w/cb dial, 6", VG, A....................$100.00
Flipper, doll, Knickerbocker, plush, NM, C17 ....$25.00
Flipper, jack-in-the-box, Mattel, M, from $100 to $125.00
Flipper, stick-ons, 1965, plastic, MIP (sealed), V1...........$50.00
Flub-A-Dub, see Howdy Doody
Foghorn Leghorn, flicker ring, EX, J2....................$40.00
Frankenstein, Show 'N Tell Record & Filmstrip, GE, 1965, complete, EX, F8....................$12.00
Freddy Krueger, see Nightmare on Elm Street
G-Man, pocket siren, Cortland, litho tin, crank action, 2x3", NMIP, A $150.00
G-Men, pencil box, 1930s, mk G-Men Clues, cb, 11x6", VG, J2 ....$100.00
Garfield, doll, Mattel, 1983, talker, 10", EX, M15 ....$60.00
Garfield, figure, Enesco, Garfield as referee, It's Official I Love You on base, 3", B5 ....$20.00
Garfield, figure, Enesco, Garfield as Uncle Sam, I Want You on base, 3", B5....................$20.00

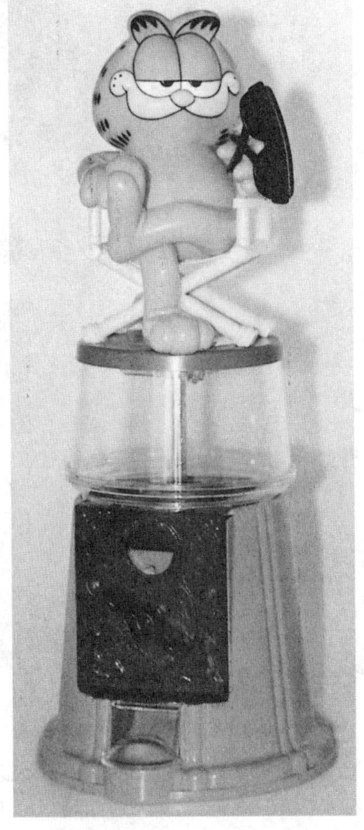

Garfield, gumball machine, Superior, 1988, EX, $20.00.

Garfield, figure, Garfield as Santa, vinyl, 6", B5 ....$25.00
Garfield, figure, Garfield as tennis player, ceramic, 4", B5.$20.00
Garfield, figure, Garfield as witch, vinyl, 6", B5...............$25.00
Garfield, figure, Garfield in workout suit, ceramic, 4½", B5 ..$20.00
Garfield, figure, Garfield on roller skates, ceramic, 2", EX, W2 ....$10.00
Garfield, figure, PVC w/suction cup, several variations, EX, W2, ea $5.00
Garfield, figure, To Dad From a Chip Off the Old Block, ceramic, EX, W2 ....$12.00
Garfield, jack-in-the-box, Pop Goes the Odie, MIB, W2.$30.00
Garfield, music box, Baby's First Christmas, train circles & plays 'Toyland,' M, W2...$25.00
Garfield, necklace, Avon, MIB, B5 ....$10.00
Garfield, night light, Garfield on cloud, MOC, B5...........$15.00
Garfield, night light, head figure, MOC, B5 ....$15.00
Garfield, play money, MIP, W2..$3.00
Garfield, slide-tile puzzle, MIP, W2...................................$5.00
Garrison's Gorillas, Garrison's Gorillas' Gear, Auburn Rubber/ABC, 1968, complete, EX (EX box), A $100.00
Gasoline Alley, doll, Rachel, screen-printed oilcloth, 17", NM, A $250.00
Gasoline Alley, dolls, Uncle Walt & Skeezix, screen-printed oilcloth, VG, A, pr $125.00
Get-Along Gang, figures, Am Greetings, ceramic on wood base, 7 different, B5, ea...$15.00
Goldilocks & the Three Bears, figure set, Japan, 1930s, bsk, complete w/Mama, Papa & Baby bear, rare, MIB, G16...$225.00

Photo courtesy Martin and Carolyn Berens

Goldilocks, Storybook Small-Talk Doll, Mattel, 1968, MIB, B5, $150.00.

Green Hornet, balloons w/strings, 20th Century Fox, 1960s, MOC, H12...$175.00
Green Hornet, Cartoon Kit, Colorforms, 1965, complete, NM (NM box) $100.00
Green Hornet, charm bracelet, w/5 charms, NMOC, B3 .$100.00
Green Hornet, flasher ring, Vari-Vue, 1960s, flashes from Green Hornet to Kato, NM, C1 ....$70.00
Green Hornet, Oil Painting by Numbers Set, Hasbro, MIB, T2, from $300 to $500.00
Green Hornet, rub-ons, Hasbro, rare, MIB $425.00
Green Hornet, wallet, Mattel, vinyl, M, P12.................$100.00
Gremlins, doll, Gizmo, Quiron, 1984, plush, 14", rare, MIB, D4/F1, from $150 to $200.00
Gremlins, doll, Gizmo, Quiron, 1984, plush, 9", M, D4/F1, from $75 to...$100.00
Gremlins, figure, Gizmo, LJN, 1984, bendable, MOC, H4 ..$35.00
Gremlins, Rub 'N Play Transfers, Colorforms, MIP, F1....$10.00
Gremlins II, magic slate, Golden, 1990, M, F1 ....$8.00
Grizzly Adams, doll, donkey, 1977, stuffed plush, 17", EX, N2 ....$40.00
Gulliver's Travels, boat, Rich Toys, wood w/cloth sails, 17", rare, EX, A $450.00
Gulliver's Travels, doll, King Little, Ideal, wood & compo, orig decal, 12", EX, A $575.00
Gulliver's Travels, doll, Prince David, Ideal, 1939, compo w/cloth cape & tights, 11", EX...............................$350.00
Gulliver's Travels, magic slate, Adventures of Gulliver, Watkins-Strathmore, 1969, unused, NM, F8............$35.00
Gumby & Pokey, Colorforms, 1988, MIB.......................$10.00
Gumby & Pokey, doll, Gumby, Applause, 1989, stuffed cloth, w/guitar & headband, 6", NM, J8.............................$10.00
Gumby & Pokey, figure, Pokey, Jesco, 1980s, bendable, 12", MOC, C11 ....$15.00
Gumby & Pokey, figure, Pokey, Lakeside, 1965, bendable, MOC, M17 ....$55.00
Gumby & Pokey, Lolly Pop-Up Puppet, 1967, unused, MIB, J2...$65.00
Gumby & Pokey, paint set, rare, NM, P12 ....$200.00
Gumby & Pokey, pencil top eraser, Pokey, 1967, 1", NM, T2 ....$15.00
Gunsmoke, see Western category
Happy Days, Colorforms, Fonzie, unused, EX (EX box), J2..$30.00
Happy Days, Fonz Viewer, Larami, 1981, 5", EX, F1 ....$15.00
Happy Days, guitar, Fonzie, 1976, MIB (sealed), J2..........$75.00
Happy Hooligan, figure, papier-mache w/movable arms & legs, 5", EX, A $85.00
Happy Hooligan, figure, Schoenhut, jtd wood w/cloth clothes, 9", VG, A $1,200.00
Hardcastle & McCormick, handcuffs, Ja-Ru, 1983, plastic, MOC, C1 ....$20.00
Harold Teen, ukelele, wood w/colorful decals, 21", EX, A..$65.00
Harry & the Hendersons, doll, Harry, Galoob, 1990, talker, 24", EX, N2 ....$30.00
Herman & Katnip, kite, Saalfield, 1960s, cb, MIP, F8 .....$25.00
Homey the Clown, see In Living Color
Howdy Doody, Bee-Nee Kit, 1950s, NMIB, J5 ....$65.00
Howdy Doody, booklet, Howdy Doody's Big Prize Doodle List, 1954-55, 4 pgs, EX, M17..$40.00

Howdy Doody, boxing gloves, Parvey, 1950s, tan w/blk image of Howdy, 6", NMIB, A $325.00
Howdy Doody, bubble pipes, Lido, complete w/2 plastic pipes, cup & bubbles, NM (NM box), A $175.00
Howdy Doody, catcher's mit, 1950s, brn vinyl w/silver image of Howdy, VG, A $100.00
Howdy Doody, Clock-A-Doodle, 1950s, litho tin w/up, NMIB $1,600.00
Howdy Doody, doctor kit, Ja-Ru, 1987, MOC, H4/J5 ....$15.00

Howdy Doody, doll, Princess, Beehler, plastic with cloth clothes, eyes open and close, 7", NM (EX box), A, $225.00; Howdy Doody, doll, Beehler, plastic with cloth clothes, jaws move, 7", NM (NM box), A, $255.00.

Howdy Doody, doll, Effanbee, 1947, compo & cloth, sleep eyes, orig outfit, 20", EX, minimum value $325.00
Howdy Doody, doll, Ideal, 1950s, talker, stuffed cloth w/plastic head, movable eyes & jaw, 19", complete, NMIB $1,800.00
Howdy Doody, doll, Noma Electrical/Cameo Product, jtd wood w/compo face, 13", scarce, NM (EX box), A $1,300.00
Howdy Doody, figure, Flub-A-Dub, Tee-Vee Toys/Kagran, plastic, push lever & his mouth moves, 3", NM (NM box), A $350.00
Howdy Doody, figure set, Tee-Vee Toys, 1950s, set of 5 different characters, EX, J5 ....$150.00
Howdy Doody, Flip-A-Ring, Flub-A-Dub, Flip-A-Ring Inc, 1950s, MIP, J5 ....$45.00
Howdy Doody, handkerchief, 1950s, colorful image of Howdy spinning lasso, 8x8", EX, J5 ....$25.00

Howdy Doody, Hoop Head, Patti-Plastics/Kagran, yel plastic hat w/attached hoop, 14", NM, A $75.00
Howdy Doody, Magic Piano, Kagran, yel w/colorful image of Howdy & friends, 15x10", EX (EX box), A $575.00
Howdy Doody, mitten kit, 1953, features Howdy Doody & Clarabelle, complete, NMIB, J5 ....$65.00
Howdy Doody, musical ball, 1950s, rolls in crazy pattern w/bell inside, plastic, 4" dia, EX, A $100.00
Howdy Doody, musical toy, Clarabell, 1950s, mk Howdy Doody's Clarabell, twist nose for action, diecut cb, 9x7", EX $1,900.00
Howdy Doody, paint set, Milton Bradley, complete, NM (NM box), A $200.00
Howdy Doody, pen, Leadworks, 1988, posable plastic figure, 6", M, P4 ....$5.00
Howdy Doody, pencil case, 1950s, red vinyl w/lg image of Howdy on front, 4x8", EX, J5 ....$65.00
Howdy Doody, pencil topper, Leadworks, 1988, vinyl, head figure, 1½", M, P4 ....$5.00
Howdy Doody, Phono Doodle, 1950s, sq record player w/colorful images, EX $250.00
Howdy Doody, Put on Your Own Puppet Show, Tee-Vee Toys/Kagran, plastic figures w/movable jaws, set of 5, NMOC, A $125.00
Howdy Doody, Put-in-Head Set, Tee-Vee Toys/Kagran, makes 100 different faces, complete, NM (EX box), A $225.00
Howdy Doody, raft, Ideal/Kagran, inflatable vinyl w/images of all characters, 9x9", NM, A $175.00
Howdy Doody, Ranch House Tool Box, Kagran, 1950s, metal, EX $200.00
Howdy Doody, sewing cards, Princess Summerfall-Winterspring, Milton Bradley, 1950s, EX (EX box), A $100.00
Howdy Doody, sparkler, Ja-Ru, 1987, MOC, H4 ....$10.00
Howdy Doody, squeak toy, 13", NM, J6 ....$85.00
Howdy Doody, stationery, Graphic Products, 1971, different character on each sheet, w/envelopes, MIB, J5 ....$25.00
Howdy Doody, suitcase, 1955, cb w/image of Howdy's face & Welcome to the 1955 Toy Fair, 10x14", VG, J5 ....$300.00
Howdy Doody, Uke, Emenee, plastic, 17", NM (EX box), A ..$165.00
Huckleberry Hound, bank, Knickerbocker, 1960, Huck in tuxedo & top hat, plastic, 10", EX, F8 ....$25.00
Huckleberry Hound, charm bracelet, 1959, gold-colored metal w/6 different characters, MOC, P4 ....$30.00
Huckleberry Hound, Colorforms, 1960, complete, NMIB, F8 ....$50.00
Huckleberry Hound, cuff links & tie clasp, 1959, gold-tone metal w/figure of Huck as ringmaster, MOC, P4 ....$20.00
Huckleberry Hound, doll, Boo-Boo, Knickerbocker, 1960s, gr cloth body w/pk bow tie, vinyl face, rare, EX $75.00
Huckleberry Hound, doll, Knickerbocker, red plush tuxedo body w/blk felt hat, rubber face, 18", NM, A $55.00
Huckleberry Hound, Flip Show, 1961, EX (EX box), J2 ...$40.00
Huckleberry Hound, Huck's Candy Factory, 1960, litho tin w/plastic dome, 11", G, F8 ....$40.00
Huckleberry Hound, speedboat, Regal Toy, 1960s, plastic, 17", NM, A $200.00
Huckleberry Hound, squeak toy, Dell, 1960, Huck holding top hat & cane, 6", NM, F8 ....$45.00

Hugga Bunch, tray, 1984, litho metal, VG, N2 ....$10.00
I Love Lucy, doll, Lucy, ca 1952, stuffed cloth w/pnt features, yarn hair, w/scarf, pants & apron, 26", rare, NRFB .$800.00
I Love Lucy, doll, Ricky Jr, Am Character, 1950s, vinyl w/bl overalls, wht shirt, blk tie & wht shoes, 20", EX (EX box) $500.00
In Living Color, doll, Homey the Clown, Acme, 1992, stuffed cloth, 24", MIB, H4/M15, from $25 to.......................$35.00
Incredible Hulk, bank, Renzi, 1979, gr plastic bust figure, 15", VG, T2, from $15 to..................$20.00
Incredible Hulk, candy bucket, Renzi, 1979, gr plastic head figure, 10", minor pnt flakes o/w VG, T2 ....$12.00
Incredible Hulk, switchplate, 1976, glow-in-the-dark, MIP (sealed), C1..................$25.00
Incredible Hulk, wallet, 1976, vinyl, unused, NM, C1 .....$20.00
Indiana Jones & the Temple of Doom, sleeping bag, 1984, various scenes from the movie, VG, F8 ....$30.00
Inspector Gadget, Detective Kit, Avalon, 1984, scarce, MIB, M17..................$55.00
Inspector Gadget, Shrinky Dinks, Colorforms, 1983, MIB, C1..................$30.00

Jack and Jill, Effanbee, NRFB, $150.00.

James Bond, pencil case, 1960s, blk vinyl w/target logo, zipper closure, 4x8", EX, J5 ....$125.00
James Bond, wallet, mk Glidrose Productions, 1966, vinyl, NM, H4..................$80.00
Jaws, figure, shark, 1975, plastic, 15", EX (EX box), N2...$25.00
Jerry Mahoney, bank, molded compo, 10", rare, EX, A $75.00
Jetsons, doll, Elroy, 1985, plush w/plastic hat, 14", NM, J8..$15.00
Jetsons, doll, George, Nanco, 1989, stuffed cloth, 13", EX, H4..................$10.00
Jetsons, figure, any character, Just Toys, bendable, MOC, J8, ea..................$10.00
Jetsons, film, 1960s, 8mm, NMIB, J5..................$15.00
Jetsons, Slate & Chalk Set, 1960s, unused, MIB $100.00
Jingle Dingle, Karbon Kopee Kit, KKK, 1954, complete, M (NM box), F8..................$40.00
Jingle Dingle, Ring-O-Bell Set, Gilmar, 1954, missing support bar o/w EX, F8..................$30.00
Josie & the Pussycats, pendant, 1970s, MOC, J5 ....$10.00
Kermit the Frog, see Muppets
King Kong, bank, plastic figure, 17", NM, J2 ....$35.00
King Kong, doll, 1970s, stuffed cloth, 20", VG, J2...........$40.00
King Kong, jewelry box, M, J2..................$30.00
Knight Rider, Colorforms Adventure Set, 1982, MIB, C1..$35.00
Krazy Kat, doll, Averill, stuffed felt w/applied face, orig orange neck ribbon, 18", VG, A $500.00
Krazy Kat, doll, stuffed velvet w/applied felt feet, orig red felt boots, 13", NM, A $1,000.00
Krazy Kat, figure, Chein, jtd wood w/stenciled face, orig decal & felt bow, 7", rare, EX, A..................$600.00
Krazy Kat, pull toy, Chein, litho tin w/wood & paper bellows, 7", EX, A $700.00
Land Before Time, doll, Little Foot, JC Penney Exclusive, stuffed cloth, EX, H4 ....$35.00

Photo courtesy June Moon

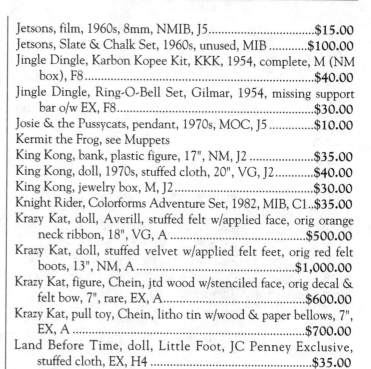

Land of the Lost, doll, Stink, Tiger, pull-string talker, MIB, J6, $85.00.

Lassie, doll, Knickerbocker, 1960s, plush w/vinyl face, glass eyes, 12", VG, T2 ....$15.00
Lassie, Trick Trainer, Mousely Inc, 1956, complete, scarce, NM (EX box) $275.00
Lassie, wallet, 1950s, brn vinyl w/full-color image of Lassie, EX, J5 ....$35.00
Laugh-In, Electric Drawing Set, 1969, EX (EX box), J2.$100.00
Laugh-In, flicker rings, set of 5, EX, H4 ....$20.00

Laurel and Hardy, figures, 1971, hand-painted plastic, 16", J6, $150.00 for the pair.

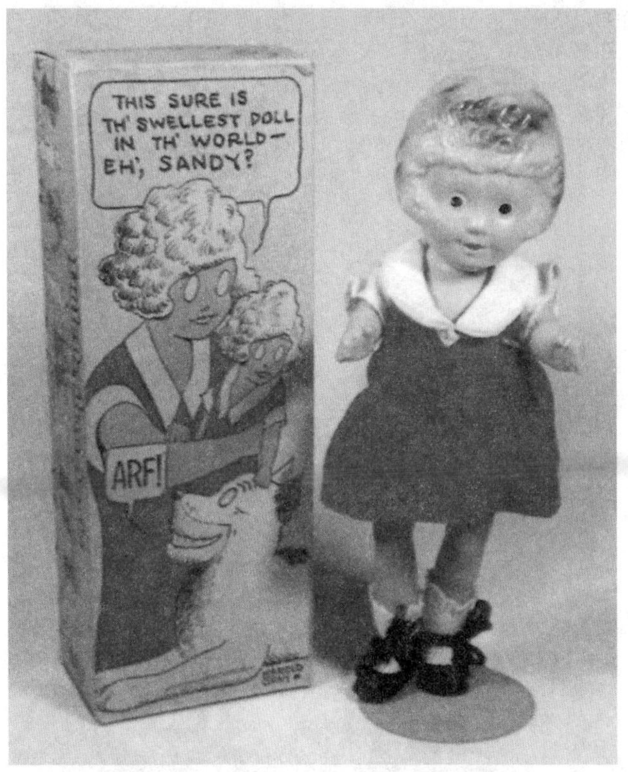

Little Orphan Annie, doll, Harold Gray copyright, 1930s, composition, original outfit, NMIB, $1,000.00.

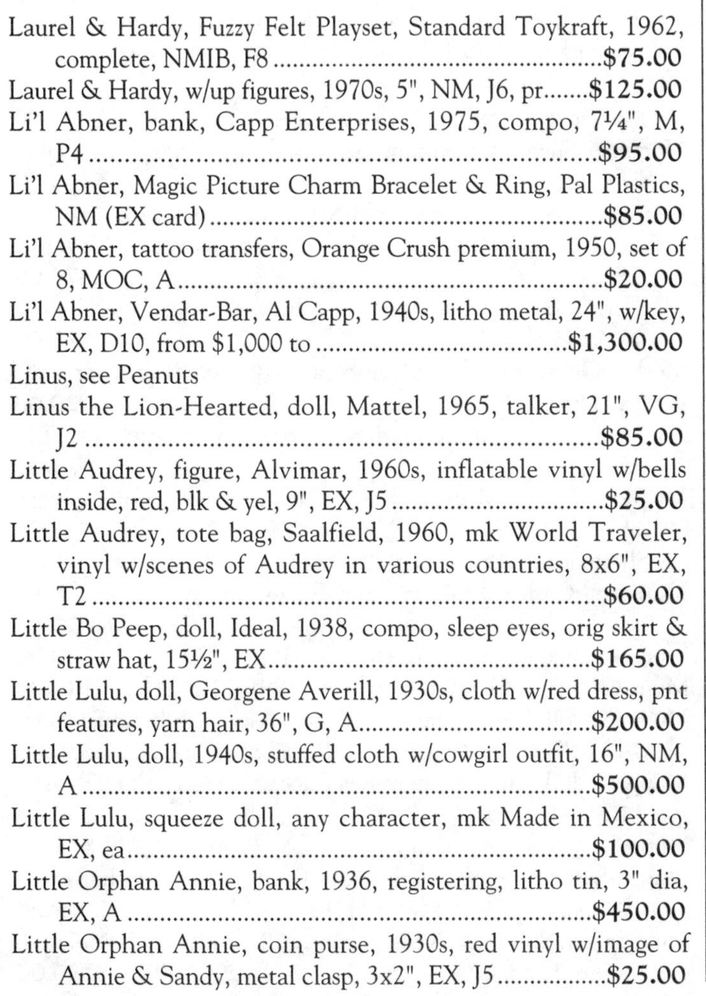

Laurel & Hardy, Fuzzy Felt Playset, Standard Toykraft, 1962, complete, NMIB, F8 ....**$75.00**

Laurel & Hardy, w/up figures, 1970s, 5", NM, J6, pr.......**$125.00**

Li'l Abner, bank, Capp Enterprises, 1975, compo, 7¼", M, P4 ....**$95.00**

Li'l Abner, Magic Picture Charm Bracelet & Ring, Pal Plastics, NM (EX card) **$85.00**

Li'l Abner, tattoo transfers, Orange Crush premium, 1950, set of 8, MOC, A **$20.00**

Li'l Abner, Vendar-Bar, Al Capp, 1940s, litho metal, 24", w/key, EX, D10, from $1,000 to **$1,300.00**

Linus, see Peanuts

Linus the Lion-Hearted, doll, Mattel, 1965, talker, 21", VG, J2 ....**$85.00**

Little Audrey, figure, Alvimar, 1960s, inflatable vinyl w/bells inside, red, blk & yel, 9", EX, J5 ....**$25.00**

Little Audrey, tote bag, Saalfield, 1960, mk World Traveler, vinyl w/scenes of Audrey in various countries, 8x6", EX, T2 ....**$60.00**

Little Bo Peep, doll, Ideal, 1938, compo, sleep eyes, orig skirt & straw hat, 15½", EX **$165.00**

Little Lulu, doll, Georgene Averill, 1930s, cloth w/red dress, pnt features, yarn hair, 36", G, A **$200.00**

Little Lulu, doll, 1940s, stuffed cloth w/cowgirl outfit, 16", NM, A **$500.00**

Little Lulu, squeeze doll, any character, mk Made in Mexico, EX, ea **$100.00**

Little Orphan Annie, bank, 1936, registering, litho tin, 3" dia, EX, A **$450.00**

Little Orphan Annie, coin purse, 1930s, red vinyl w/image of Annie & Sandy, metal clasp, 3x2", EX, J5 ....**$25.00**

Little Orphan Annie, figure, Sandy, Jaymar, 1930s, jtd wood, 4", M, A **$95.00**

Little Orphan Annie, paint box, Milton Bradley/FAS, image of Annie painting portrait of Sandy on lid, 10x16", EX, A .**$100.00**

Little Orphan Annie, teapot, 1930s, porcelain lusterware, sgn Licensed by Famous Artists Syndicate, 3", M, P6 ......**$70.00**

Little Orphan Annie, toy stove, 1930s, metal, w/upper deck baking oven & electric warmer, NM **$200.00**

Little Orphan Annie & Sandy, figure, copyright 1973, plaster, scarce, M, D10, from $300 to **$400.00**

Little Orphan Annie & Sandy, figures, Jaymar, jtd wood, 5", EX, I2, pr **$165.00**

Little Rascals, pencil sharpener, Spanky, 1930s, Bakelite, 1⅛", scarce, NM, A **$60.00**

Little Red Riding Hood, tea set, early 1900s, litho tin w/various scenes from the story, 8 pcs, EX **$375.00**

Little Red Riding Hood, tray, 1930s, litho tin, 6x9", minor scratches o/w VG, G16 ....**$65.00**

Lucy, see Peanuts

Ludwig Von Drake, doll, Gund, talker, rubber w/cloth clothes, complete w/RCA Victor tapes, 12½", NM (VG box), A **$200.00**

Maggie & Jiggs, figures, Schoenhut, jtd wood w/cloth clothes, complete w/rolling pin & pail, 8" & 6", EX, A, pr .**$1,200.00**

Magilla Gorilla, doll, Nanco, 1990, stuffed plush, 7", NM, F8 ....**$15.00**

Magilla Gorilla, squeeze toy, Screen Gems/Spain, 1967, vinyl w/hand-pnt features, 8", NM, A **$300.00**

Mama Katzenjammer, doll, Steiff, stuffed felt w/cloth apron, 16", EX, A **$350.00**

Maggie and Jiggs, dolls, Germany, papier mache with cloth clothes, wire arms and legs, 13", rare, NM, A, $650.00 for the pair.

Mork and Mindy, doll, Mork, Mattel, 1979, pull-string talker, stuffed cloth, 16", EX, J6, $35.00.

Mammy & Pappy Yokum, bank, Mammy, Al Capp, 1975, compo, 7", M, P6 ....$95.00
Man From Atlantis, Dip Dot Painting Kit, Kenner, 1977, NRFB, H4 ....$130.00
Man From UNCLE, Foto Fantastiks Coloring Set, Faber, 1965, MIB, P3 ....$165.00
Man From UNCLE, Invisible Writing Pen, Platignum House/MGM, 1965, NMOC, A $200.00
Man From UNCLE, Secret Print Putty, Colorforms, 1965, complete, NMOC, A $80.00
Marvel Super Heroes, bumper sticker, Marvel Comics, 1978, Warning: I Brake for Marvel Super Heroes, 4x14", M ..$15.00
Marvel Super Heroes, light-up drawing desk, Lakeside, 1976, plastic, EX (EX box), M17 ....$40.00
Marvel Super Heroes, Lite-Brite Picture Refill, Hasbro, 1980, MIP (sealed), F8 ....$15.00
Marvel Super Heroes, notebook, Mead, 1970s, unused, M, J2 ....$25.00
Matt Mason, Man in Space Talking Command Console, Mattel, EX, J6 ....$95.00
Mighty Mouse, boat, Ideal, 1950s, inflatable vinyl, red & yel w/Mighty Mouse image, 28x24", EX (VG box), A $80.00
Miss America, Colorforms, 1972, complete, MIB, J6 ....$35.00
Miss Piggy, see Muppets
Mork & Mindy, doll, Mork, Mattel, 1979, pull-string talker, stuffed cloth, 16", MIB $50.00
Mork & Mindy, Magic Show, Colorforms, MIB, V1 ....$30.00
Mork & Mindy, poster, Mork from Ork, 1970s, 36x24", EX, F1 .$15.00
Mortimer Snerd, doll, compo & wood w/wire arms & legs, cloth clothes, 12", EX, A $165.00
Mother Goose, dishes, Ideal, 1940s, plastic, 26 pcs, MIB .$150.00
Mother Goose, doll, 1985, plush, talks w/moving facial features, 18", VG, M15 ....$70.00
Mother Goose, jack-in-the-box, plays 'Mother Goose' song, NM $25.00
Mother Goose, magic slate set, Strathmore, 1945, complete, VG (VG box), F8 ....$20.00
Mr Magoo, doll, Ideal, 1961, stuffed cloth & vinyl, 16", EX, V1 ....$75.00
Mr Magoo, ring, Macman Ent, 1956, complete w/interchangeable head of Charlie & Waldo, NMOC, T2 ....$35.00
Mr Sherman, see Rocky & Bullwinkle
Munsters, Castex-5 Casting Set, Emenee, 1964, unused, MIB, J2 ....$1,000.00
Munsters, figure, Grandpa, Applause, 1991, MIP, H4 ....$40.00
Munsters, figure, Herman, Applause, 1991, MIP, H4 ....$40.00
Muppets, doll, Kermit the Frog, Fisher-Price, 1981, stuffed cloth, 14", MIB $30.00
Muppets, doll, Miss Piggy, Fisher-Price, 1981, stuffed cloth, 14", MIB, M15 ....$30.00
Muppets, Miss Piggy Latch Hook Kit, MIB (sealed), P12.$55.00
Muppets, stick puppet, Kermit the Frog or Rowlf, Fisher-Price, 1979, plastic, 3½", MOC, H4, ea $5.00
Mutt & Jeff, drum, Converse, litho tin, Bud Fisher facsimile signature, 12" dia, VG, A $250.00

Mutt & Jeff, figure, Mutt, Buco/Switzerland, compo w/cloth clothes, bendable, 7½", NM (EX box), A $200.00
Mutt & Jeff, figures, HC Fisher, celluloid, 4" & 5", VG, A, pr $100.00
Nancy & Sluggo, doll, Nancy, stuffed cloth w/mask face, cloth outfit, 13", EX, A $175.00
Nancy Drew, Mystery Pictures To Color, 1977, M $15.00
Nightmare on Elm Street, doll, Freddy Krueger, Matchbox, talker, 18", NRFB, H4 ....$50.00
Olive Oyl, see Popeye
Oswald Rabbit, figure, Irwin, prewar, jtd celluloid w/felt ears, 7", NM, A $675.00
Oswald Rabbit, magic slate, Saalfield, 1962, EX, F8 ....$20.00
Oswald Rabbit, stencil set, Universal Toy & Novelty, incomplete, VG, A $165.00
Our Gang, note pad, 1930s-40s, image above Members of Our Gang Appearing in MGM..., 5x9", EX, F8................$40.00
Peanuts, bank, Snoopy as tennis player, Hat Series, ceramic, 4", M, H11...$30.00
Peanuts, bank, Woodstock, ceramic, 6", M, H11..............$15.00
Peanuts, beach bag, Beagle Beach, Colgate premium, wht w/zipper closure, 9x8", M, H11...$20.00
Peanuts, bicycle license plate, Woodstock, Powered by Woodstock, red, MOC, H11 ....$10.00
Peanuts, bookmark, Snoopy, plastic w/image of Snoopy on doghouse, 4", M, H11 ....$8.00
Peanuts, Colorforms, How's the Weather Lucy, EX (EX box), H11 ....$30.00
Peanuts, Colorforms, Lucy's Winter Carnival, MIB, H11..$50.00
Peanuts, Colorforms, Peanuts Preschool, VG (VG box), H11 ....$25.00
Peanuts, Colorforms, Snoopy & Woodstock, EX (EX box), H11 ....$25.00
Peanuts, Colorforms, What's on Sale Snoopy, EX (EX box), H11 ....$25.00
Peanuts, doll, Bedtime Snoopy, Applause, plush, 11", MIB, H11 ....$15.00
Peanuts, doll, Charlie Brown, 1950s, vinyl, 9", VG, J2.....$75.00
Peanuts, doll, Linus, Hungerford, in red shirt w/hand out, 8", MIP, H11 ....$75.00
Peanuts, doll, Lucy, Hungerford, in yel dress & hat, 9", MIP, H11 ....$95.00
Peanuts, doll, Lucy, Ideal, rag-type, red dress, 14", VG, H11.$20.00
Peanuts, doll, Peppermint Pattie, Determined Toys, 1970s, rag-type, 14", MIB...$30.00
Peanuts, doll, Snoopy, World Wonder, 1986, talker, MIB, H11 ....$100.00
Peanuts, doll, Snoopy as chef, rag-type, 6", VG, H11.......$10.00
Peanuts, doll, Snoopy as Santa, Applause, 1992, plush, 15", MIP, H11 ....$35.00
Peanuts, doll, Snoopy w/rattle, plush, 9", MIP, H11.........$10.00
Peanuts, doll, Woodstock as Santa, Applause, plush, 9", MIP, H11 ....$20.00
Peanuts, figure, Linus w/blanket, 3", M, H11 ....$8.00
Peanuts, figure, Lucy in hula skirt, 1989, 3", M, H11..........$6.00
Peanuts, figure, Snoopy, Determined, plush clip-on, 3", MOC, H11...$5.00
Peanuts, figure, Snoopy as Joe Cool, 3", M, H11................$8.00
Peanuts, figure, Snoopy as mailman, 1970s, squeaker, EX, C17 ....$15.00
Peanuts, figure, Snoopy in rowboat, 4", M, H11 ....$10.00
Peanuts, fishing rod & reel, Snoopy, Zebco, orange plastic, VG, H11 ....$10.00
Peanuts, jack-in-the-box, Mattel, 1969, plays 'Where Did My Little Dog Go,' EX, H11 ....$50.00
Peanuts, jump rope, Snoopy, wht plastic, M $15.00
Peanuts, Mattel-O-Phone, 1969, MIB..............................$95.00
Peanuts, megaphone, Charlie Brown, Chein, 1970, rare, EX, H11 ....$25.00
Peanuts, pajama bag, Snoopy, Commonwealth, plush w/zipper closure, 18", M, H11 ....$15.00
Peanuts, pencil sharpener, Snoopy fire truck, KFS, 1958, NM $15.00
Peanuts, purse, Snoopy, canvas, image of Snoopy blowing bubbles, 9x8", M, H11 ....$10.00
Peanuts, ring, Snoopy, cloisionne, Snoopy lying on bed of hearts, M, H11 ....$5.00
Peanuts, See & Say, Snoopy Says, Mattel, VG, H11 ....$50.00
Peanuts, Sing-Along Radio, Snoopy, Determined, EX, H11 ...$80.00
Peanuts, sleeping bag, Snoopy, 1972, w/image & To Dance Is To Love & Snoopy Come Home, VG, F8 ....$20.00
Peanuts, Snoopy Sign-Mobile Coloring Set, Avalon, 1977, MIB, H11 ....$70.00
Peanuts, Snoopy Sno-Cone Machine, Hasbro, 1979, MIB, M15...$25.00
Peanuts, tea set, Snoopy, Chein, complete, MIB, H11 .....$50.00
Peanuts, telephone, Snoopy, Romper Room, 10", EX, J2 .$25.00
Peanuts, video tape, It's Christmas Time Again Charlie Brown, 1992, M, H11..$10.00
Peanuts, wallet, Snoopy & Woodstock, wht vinyl, NM ...$25.00

Photo courtesy Martin and Carolyn Berens

Peanuts, windup figures, MOC, B5, $10.00 each.

Pee Wee's Playhouse, Colorforms, 1988, MIB (sealed), D9 ..$20.00
Pee Wee's Playhouse, doll, Pee Wee Herman, Matchbox, 1987, talker, MIB, B5 ....$45.00
Peppermint Pattie, see Peanuts
Peter Potamus, doll, Ideal, 1964, stuffed cloth w/wire arms & legs, vinyl face, 8", M, A $125.00
Peter Rabbit, doll, Bucherer, jtd metal & compo w/cloth clothes, 8", VG, A...$650.00
Phantom of the Opera, figure, Hong Kong, 1950s, hard plastic w/vinyl head, 7", rare, NM, A $150.00
Phantom of the Opera, iron-on patch, 1965, classic pose w/logo below, 4x8", NM, T2, from $20 to $25.00
Pink Panther, doll, plush, 6", M, D4 ....$10.00

Pink Panther, figure set, Comic Spain, PVC, 4", set of 4, M, B5 ....$50.00
Pink Panther, Silly Putty, Ja-Ru, 1980, MOC, H4 ....$10.00
Pink Panther, slide-tile puzzle, Ja-Ru, 1981, MOC, M17 .$15.00
Pinky Lee, figure, rubber, squeeze body & head pops off, 9", NM, H4 ....$95.00
Pinky Lee, paint set, Gabriel, 1950s, complete, EX (EX box), J5 ....$75.00
Planet of the Apes, bank, General Ursus, Apac Prod, 1967, plastic, 18", NM, J6....................$30.00
Planet of the Apes, belt buckle, raised image, mk 20th Century...APJack 1967 from Lee Belt Buckle on bk, 2" dia, EX, A $150.00
Planet of the Apes, Colorforms Adventure Set, 1967, EX (EX box) $30.00
Planet of the Apes, Mix N' Mold Set, Burke, rare, MIB, P12....................$100.00

Photo courtesy Martin and Carolyn Berens

Planet of the Apes, Mix N' Mold Set, Dr. Zaius or Astronaut Virdon, rare, MIB, $100.00 each.

Planet of the Apes, squirt gun, Cornelius, AHI, 1970s, plastic, M, P12 ....$145.00
Planet of the Apes (Astro Apes), figure, Myra, Hong Kong, vinyl w/cloth outfit, fully jointed, 8", NMIP, A $165.00
Pokey, see Gumby & Pokey
Popeye, acrobat toy, Cooper/Shower Detroit, 1929, jtd cb figure on high bar, squeeze handle for action, 6", rare, EX, A $275.00
Popeye, bank, pnt ceramic, 7", EX, A $135.00
Popeye, boxing gloves, Everlast, 1950s, red, MIP, A $55.00
Popeye, Color & Re-Color Book, Jack Built, 1957, 16 cb pgs to color & wipe off, spiral-bound, VG, F8....................$25.00
Popeye, Daily Quarter Bank, 1950s, litho tin, 4", EX+, A.$150.00
Popeye, doll, Popeye, Cameo/KFS, 1960s, squeezeable vinyl w/jtd limbs, 14", NM (EX box), A $450.00
Popeye, doll, Popeye, felt w/oilcloth hat, 20", rare, EX, A.$385.00
Popeye, doll, Popeye, Lars/Italy, cloth-covered wire, 24", EX, A $155.00
Popeye, doll, Olive Oyl, Effanbee, stuffed cloth w/rubber head & compo feet, orig heart-shaped tag, 16", EX, A.........$330.00
Popeye, figure, Bluto, Italy/KFS, 1940s-50s, rubber w/hand-pnt details, 8", NM (EX pkg), A....................$125.00
Popeye, figure, Popeye, Chein, 1931, jtd wood & compo w/plastic hat brim, orig decal on foot, 8", EX, A $400.00
Popeye, figure, Popeye in boxing shorts & gloves, pnt wood cutout on rectangular base, 13", EX, A $250.00
Popeye, figure, Popeye, KFS, jtd wood, 6", EX+, H7 ......$125.00
Popeye, figure, Olive Oyl, mk Olive Oyl by KFS & Made in USA, jtd wood, 5", EX, A $85.00
Popeye, figure, Popeye, plaster, 7", EX, A $165.00
Popeye, figure, Popeye, 1930s, celluloid, 4", NM, D10...$275.00
Popeye, figure, Popeye, 1930s, chalkware, 12", EX, D10, from $400 to....................$500.00
Popeye, figure, Popeye, 1935, jtd wood, compo head, 13½", EX, A $350.00
Popeye, figure, Popeye, 1940s, celluloid, 5", EX, P6 ....$125.00
Popeye, figure set, pnt wood cutout figures w/balloons, set of 4, EX, A $150.00
Popeye, flicker ring, any character, NM, J2, ea from $20 to $25.00
Popeye, Flip-Show, 1961, EX (EX box), J2 ....$40.00
Popeye, Glow Putty, MOC, J2....................$25.00
Popeye, Great Big Popeye Paint & Crayon Book, McLoughlin Bros, 1935, NMIB, M17 ....$75.00
Popeye, harmonica, metal w/full-color decal, 4", EX (EX box), A....................$165.00
Popeye, hat & pipe, Empire, complete w/kazoo pipe & bl vinyl hat, NM (EX card), A $150.00
Popeye, ladder toy, wood, 2 Popeye figures flip down ladder, 18", VG, A $75.00
Popeye, lantern, pnt tin & glass figure, 11", EX.............$125.00
Popeye, Magic Play Around, Amsco, complete, NM (NM box), A $300.00

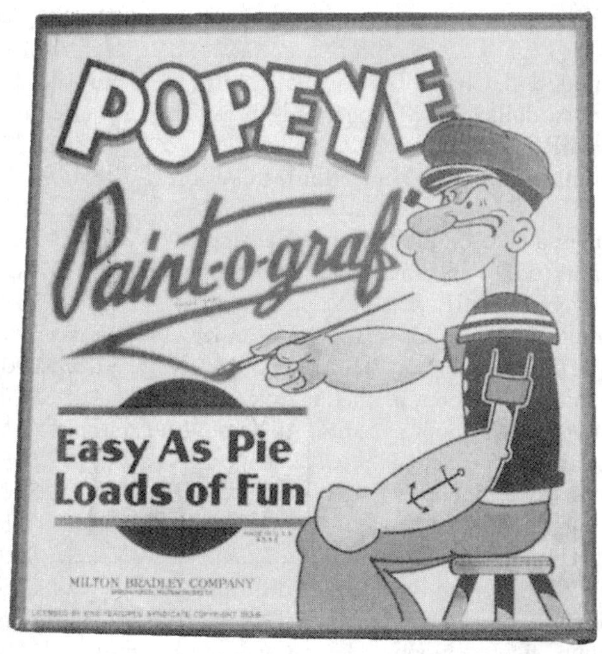

Popeye, Paint-o-graf, Milton Bradley, 1935, complete, EX (EX box), A, $350.00.

Popeye, Menu Bagatelle, Durable Toy & Novelty, 1935, litho tin, 23x14", EX, A $500.00
Popeye, night light, Aurolux, 1920s, pot metal ship w/glowing Popeye figure in bulb, 4", rare, EX, A $600.00
Popeye, Oil Painting by Numbers Set, Hasbro, 1950s, complete, NMIB, J5/T2, from $75 to $100.00
Popeye, Paint 'N Foil Kit, Crafco, 1978, MIP (sealed), M17..$25.00
Popeye, pencil sharpener, Bakelite, figural, 1½", EX, A...$85.00
Popeye, pencil sharpener, litho tin, 3", EX, A $325.00
Popeye, Pencil-by-Number Set, 1959, unused, MIB, V1 ..$35.00
Popeye, Popeye the Printer Stamp Set, Stamper Kraft, EX (EX box), A....................$175.00
Popeye, Popeye's Luck Jeep Spinner, litho cb figure & reversible disk on wood hdl, 7", EX (G box), A....................$400.00
Popeye, Presto-Paints, Kenner, 1961, complete & unused, NM (NM box), F8....................$50.00
Popeye, puffy magnet, EX, J2....................$15.00
Popeye, puzzle, Popeye the Juggler, Bar-Zim, 1929, tin & glass, 5x4", EX, A....................$125.00
Popeye, Red Cross booklet, Ahoy Sailor!, Sagendorf, 1940s, EX, J5....................$65.00
Popeye, Roly Poly Popeye Target, Knickerbocker, 1958, complete, NM (NM box), A....................$275.00
Popeye, squeak toy, Swee' Pea, 1930s, rubber, 6", VG, J2...$75.00
Popeye, Stardust Touch of Velvet Art, Hasbro, 1960s, complete, MIB, A....................$65.00
Popeye, Stitch-a-Story, Hasbro, 1967, MOC (sealed), F8/J2, from $40 to....................$50.00
Popeye, Stow-A-Way Slate, Lowe, 1957, 12x8", unused, NM, T2....................$30.00
Popeye, watering can, T Cohn, litho tin w/image of Popeye, Olive Oyl & Swee Pea in spinach patch, 7", EX, A ..$350.00
Porky Pig, bank, mk Japan, pnt bsk, bust figure, 5", EX, A...$50.00
Porky Pig, bubble gum machine, Banko Matic, 1970s, plastic figure, 9½", EXIB, J5....................$25.00
Porky Pig, figure, Sun Rubber, 1950s, 6", EX (EX box)..$100.00
Porky Pig, figure, 1930s, chalkware, 7", EX, H12..............$75.00
Porky Pig, jack-in-the-box, Mattel, M, from $100 to $150.00

Photo courtesy Martin and Carolyn Berens

Princess of Power, Butterflyer, Mattel, MIB, B5, $40.00.

Punch & Judy, theatre, England/Peter Pan Series, litho tin stage w/cb back, 7", EX (EX box), A....................$300.00
Punkin' Puss, doll, Ideal, 1960s, plush w/hard rubber face, felt clothes, 13", rare, EX, F8....................$175.00
Punky Brewster, doll, Galoob, 1984, 18", NRFB, M15.....$40.00
Quick Draw McGraw, bank, 1960, orange plastic, 9½", VG, N2....................$25.00
Quick Draw McGraw, doll, Nanco, 1989, plush w/felt hat, 12", NM, F8....................$15.00
Quick Draw McGraw, pencil sharpener, China, 1960s, ceramic figure, EX, F8....................$15.00
Raggedy Andy, doll, Playskool, 1987, 12", MIB, M15......$15.00
Raggedy Ann, bank, 11", VG, M15....................$10.00
Raggedy Ann, Colorforms Dress-Up Kit, 1967, M, V1.....$25.00
Raggedy Ann, doll, Hasbro, 1983, 17", MIB, M15 ....$25.00
Raggedy Ann, doll, Knickerbocker, 1983, 12", EX, M15..$20.00
Raggedy Ann, jewelry box, 1972, 9" L, VG, N2 ....$15.00
Raggedy Ann, TV chair, 1970s, inflatable, NMIB, J2 ......$35.00
Raggedy Ann & Andy, dolls, Knickerbocker, 1970s, beanbag style, 12", EX, ea....................$25.00
Raggedy Ann & Andy, manicure set, Larami, 1979, MOC (sealed), F8....................$10.00
Rainbow Brite, figures, PVC, set of 5, B5....................$25.00
Rambo, bank, vinyl, MIB, P12....................$45.00
Rambo, walkie-talkies, LarGo, 1985, complete w/headband, MOC, M17....................$30.00
Rambo, White Dragon Throw Knife, Largo, 1986, plastic knife & sheath from cartoon series, M, F1....................$15.00
Rat Fink, decal, 1990, NM....................$5.00
Rat Fink, key chain, figural, yel, EX, J2....................$25.00
Rat Fink, ring, Macman Ent, 1963, plastic w/detachable figure, MIP, T2....................$30.00
Real Ghostbusters, Glow-in-the-Dark Makeup Kit, Spearhead Industries, 1989, MOC, M17....................$25.00
Reg'lar Fellas, doll, Aggie, Bucherer, jtd metal & compo w/cloth clothes, 8", EX, A....................$450.00
Reg'lar Fellas, doll, Jimmy, Bucherer, jtd metal & compo w/cloth clothes, 8", EX, A....................$385.00
Reg'lar Fellas, doll, Puddin' Head, Bucherer, jtd metal & compo w/cloth clothes, 8", EX, A....................$385.00
Reg'lar Fellers, Microscope Set, complete, NMIB $275.00
Ringling Bros & Barnum & Bailey Circus, printing set, TST, 1940s-50s, complete, NMIB, F8....................$50.00
Ripley's Believe It or Not, kaleidoscope, 1950s, cb, EX (EX box), M17....................$60.00
Road Runner, doll, Mighty Star, 1971, stuffed plush w/wire frame, 17", EX, F8....................$35.00
Road Runner, Magic Cartoon Board, 1971, unused, M, P12..$25.00
Robin, see Batman
RoboCop, figure, RoboCop (unlicensed), made in Taiwan, talker, vinyl, 12", MIB, H4....................$100.00
RoboCop, pencil sharpener, MIP, J8....................$5.00
Rocky & Bullwinkle, bank, Mr Sherman, Pat Ward, 1960, glazed ceramic, 6", NM, A....................$550.00
Rocky & Bullwinkle, bank, Rocky, Play Pal, 1973, Rocky in front of tree, vinyl, 11", F8....................$70.00
Rocky & Bullwinkle, Bullwinkle Electric Quiz Game, 1971, MOC (sealed), J2....................$40.00
Rocky & Bullwinkle, Bullwinkle's Spelling & Counting Board, Larami, 1969, plastic, complete, 7" dia, MOC, P4.....$25.00

Rocky and Bullwinkle, doll, Bullwinkle, Mattel, 1971, talker, 11", EX, $125.00.

Rocky & Bullwinkle, figure, any character, Wham-O, MOC, ea....$25.00
Rocky & Bullwinkle, Make Your Badge Set, Larami, 1969, complete, MOC, P4....$25.00
Rocky & Bullwinkle, pen, 1970s, red plastic w/silver Bullwinkle figure on clip, NM, A....$25.00
Rocky & Bullwinkle, Rocky & His Friends Cartoon Kit, Colorforms, 1961, complete, NMIB....$100.00
Rocky & Bullwinkle, telescope, Larami, 1970s, MOC, H4 .$25.00
Romper Room, ring, 1960s premium, silver metal w/jack-in-the-box image, NM, A....$50.00
Romper Room, Stand-Up Rub-Ons, Hasbro, 1969, complete, NMIB, F8....$25.00

Scrappy, paint set, New Jersey Crayon Co., 1930s, complete, NM (EX box), A, $100.00.

Rookies, helmet, 1970s, plastic w/sticker on top, VG, J5 .$15.00
Rootie Kazootie, drum, 1950s, litho tin w/spring attachments, 8" dia, scarce, EX, A....$125.00
Rootie Kazootie, Fix-A-Rootie Tool Box, RK Inc, litho tin, 6x14", scarce, EX, A....$185.00
Rudolph the Red-Nosed Reindeer, magic slate, Lowe, 1946, 12x8", unused, M, T2....$35.00
Scooby Doo, doll, stuffed plush, 16", EX, C17....$40.00
Scrappy, bank, mk CPC, 1930s, material on metal w/emb image of Scrappy, 3", NM, A....$225.00
Sesame Street, doll, Big Bird, Ideal, talks w/tape player, 25", VG, M15....$55.00
Sesame Street, doll, Big Bird, Playskool, 1970s, pull-string talker, 22", VG, M15....$25.00
Sesame Street, doll, Cookie Monster, Hasbro, 1970s, stuffed plush w/ping-pong ball eyes, 12", VG, F8....$15.00
Sesame Street, doll, Ernie, stuffed cloth, 18", EX....$20.00
Sesame Street, figure, Kermit the Frog, Bend 'Ems, MOC, J8...$10.00
Sesame Street, figure set, Applause, 1993, PVC, set of 8, F1 ..$20.00
Shirley Temple, Bath Drum, Kerk Guild, originally held Castille soap, cb w/Shirley in drum major hat, 4" dia, EX, A .$75.00
Shirley Temple, figure, chalkware, 12½", EX....$275.00
Shirley Temple, figure, chalkware, 6", EX....$185.00
Shirley Temple, scrapbook, Saalfield, 1936, image of Shirley in bonnet, spiral-bound, EX....$50.00
Simpsons, bank, Bart, Street Kids, plastic, any color variation, MIB, K1, ea....$12.00
Simpsons, bulletin board, Roseart, 1990, cork w/full-color image, 16x20", EX, F1....$15.00
Simpsons, Crayon-By-Number, Rose Art, w/6 pictures & numbered crayons, MIB, K1....$6.00
Simpsons, doll, Bart, Dandee, rag-type w/suction cups on hands & feet, 8", MIB, K1....$10.00
Simpsons, doll, Bart, Dandee, soft vinyl, 10", MIB, K1 ....$10.00
Simpsons, doll, Bart, Dandee, stuffed cloth w/vinyl head, arms & legs, 16", MIB, K1....$15.00
Simpsons, doll, Bubble Blowin' Lisa, Mattel, blows bubbles w/saxaphone, 18", MIB, K1....$35.00
Simpsons, figure, Bart, PVC, various poses, MIP, ea....$4.00
Simpsons, figure, Lisa, Jesco, bendable, 3½", MOC, K1 .....$6.00
Simpsons, figure, Maggie, Jesco, bendable, 2", MOC, K1 ...$6.00
Simpsons, Fun Dough Model Maker, MIB, K1....$20.00
Simpsons, Homer Simpson Pop Gun Target Set, Ja-Ru, MOC, K1....$5.00
Simpsons, pogs, complete set of 50, M, F1....$15.00
Simpsons, Rad Rollers, Spectra Star, set of 6 marbles w/different characters magnified in center, MOC, K1....$8.00
Sinbad Jr, Magic Belt, Voplex, 1965, red plastic w/bl & wht plastic diamond-shaped buckle, battery-op, NM (NM box), T2....$160.00
Six Million Dollar Man, bank, Animals Plus, 1976, vinyl, 10", EX, M17....$50.00
Six Million Dollar Man, slide-tile puzzle, Am Publishing, 1977, MOC, M17....$30.00
Smokey the Bear, doll, Ideal, 1960s, 13", EX, J5....$20.00
Smokey the Bear, doll, 1967, 15", MIB, M15....$125.00
Smurfs, banner, Happy Smurfday, MIP, B5....$20.00
Smurfs, chalkboard, Smurfette, EX, B5....$25.00

Smurfs, coin purse, To Paint a Rainbow Life, cloth, EX, B5 .$10.00
Smurfs, Colorforms, complete, EX (EX box), B5 ....$35.00
Smurfs, figure, Papa Smurf, ceramic, VG, B5...................$30.00
Smurfs, figure, Smurf Village, ceramic, VG, B5 ....$30.00
Smurfs, Fun Club Packet, w/newsletters & stickers, EX, B5..$45.00
Smurfs, sand bucket & shovel, plastic, EX, B5.................$10.00
Smurfs, sewing cards, MIB (sealed), B5...........................$25.00
Smurfs, Smurf Amaze-ing Action Maze, EX, B5..............$20.00
Smurfs, Smurfettes Amaze-ing Action Maze, EX, B5 ....$20.00
Snoopy, see Peanuts
Soupy Sales, doll, Ideal, 1960s, stuffed cloth w/vinyl head & real hair, orig clothes, 24", EX, A.................................$275.00
Soupy Sales, doll, Sunshine Dolls, 1965, 6", MIB (sealed), J2..$235.00
Spark Plug, see Barney Google
Spider-Man, bank, Renzi, 1979, plastic bust figure, 15", EX, from $15 to $20.00
Spider-Man, bicycle, Am Flyer Jr Roadmaster, 1978, red & yel w/spider-web design on seat, 42", VG, J5................$165.00
Spider-Man, binder, Mead, 1970s, paper w/colorful image of several characters, NM, F8 ....$40.00
Spider-Man, Buddy L gift set, 1980s, w/figure & 4 vehicles, MIB..$55.00
Spider-Man, candy bucket, Renzi, 1979, red plastic head figure, 10", minor pnt flakes o/w VG, T2 ....$15.00
Spider-Man, Code Breaker, Gordy Int'l, 1980, plastic dial rotates to various letters, MOC, M17 ....$20.00

Photo courtesy Martin and Carolyn Berens

Spider-Man, siren, Empire, 1978, MIB, B5, $50.00.

Spider-Man, Colorforms Adventure Set, 1974, unused, MIB..$15.00
Spider-Man, Fly 'Em High Parachutist & Launcher, AHI, 1976, MOC, C1 ....$30.00
Spider-Man, roller skates, 1979, red, blk & bl plastic, EX, I2 .$15.00
Spider-Man, sunglasses, Nasta, 1986, MOC, M17............$10.00
Super Friends, Add-On-Bike Safety Flag, Robin, Cycle Safety Flag Co, 1954, MOC, D9 ....$20.00
Super Friends, Lite-Brite Picture Refill, Hasbro, 1980, MIP (sealed), F8..$20.00
Super Powers, book & cassette, Earth Core, 1985, M, N2 ..$12.00
Superman, bank, 1940s, dime register, litho tin, sq w/canted corners, rare, EX $250.00
Superman, belt buckle, Pioneer, 1940s, bronze w/emb image, rectangular, EX, A $450.00
Superman, Cartoonist Stamp Set, 1966, complete, MOC, A..$75.00
Superman, doll, Applause, 1988, 18", NM, B10 ....$25.00
Superman, figure, jtd wood & compo w/cloth cape, 13", rare, NM, A $1,500.00
Superman, Flip Flashlight, Bantamlite, 1966, bl plastic w/decal, complete w/key chain, MOC, A $150.00
Superman, floating ring, Ideal, 1967-72, inflatable plastic, 22" dia, MIP, from $20 to..$30.00
Superman, kite, Hi-Flier, 1984, MIP, M17 ....$30.00
Superman, magic slate, Whitman, 1965, diecut top w/Superman in action pose, EX..$45.00
Superman, Paint-by-Number Watercolor Set, Transogram, 1954, complete, unused, scarce, EX (EX box), A $200.00
Superman, playsuit, Funtime Playwear, 1954, complete w/Superman's Buddy comic book, rare, EX (EX box), from $400 to..$500.00
Superman, slide-tile puzzle, Tot Guidance, 1966, image of Superman flying over skyscrapers, plastic, 9x9", EX, A..........$50.00
Superman, smock, Miss Boutique, 1976, red vinyl w/full-color image of Superman, M, J5 ....$45.00
Superman, Sparkle Paints, 1966, w/5 pictures to pnt, NMIB....$65.00
Superman, Thingmaker Accessory Kit, Mattel, 1960s, complete, MOC, J5...$85.00
Superman, Wipe-Off Coloring Cloth, Howe, 1966, unused, MIP, from $50 to $60.00
Superman & Wonder Woman, Super-Sounds record player, Dee-Jay, 1970s, wht plastic, EX, M17 ....$75.00
Sword in the Stone, ring, 1970s cereal premium, bl or pk, EX, M8, ea $15.00
Sylvester the Cat, roly poly, EX, J2 ....$25.00
Tales From the Crypt, mask, Cryptkeeper, Ace Novelty, 1994, latex, EX, F1..$75.00
Tales of Wells Fargo, Paint-by-Number Set, Transogram, 1959, complete, NM (EX box), F8.....................................$70.00
Tarzan, Jungle Animals Set, Salco/Banner, 1966, complete, unused, NM (EX box), A $200.00
Tasmanian Devil, bank, Goad, 1990, ceramic, w/Looney Tunes tag, 5½", NM $45.00
Tasmanian Devil, doll, Mighty Star, 1970s, stuffed cloth, EX, C17..$40.00
Tasmanian Devil, doll, 1980, stuffed plush, 13", J7 ....$15.00
Tasmanian Devil, figure, vinyl, 6", NM $25.00
Tasmanian Devil, magic slate, Golden, 1992, M (sealed), P3 ..$5.00
Teddy Ruxpin, doll, Baby Teddy Ruxpin, 1986, VG, M15.$70.00

Teenage Mutant Ninja Turtles, cassette, Coming Out of Their Shells Tour, MCA, 1990 Pizza Hut premium, M, F1 ...$8.00

Terminator, doll, Classic Plastic, 1992, 11½", EX+, D9...$10.00

Terminator 2, figure, Terminator (unlicensed), made in China, vinyl, NRFB, H4 ...$50.00

Terrytoons, Monkey Stix, Ideal, 1960, M (NM sealed container), F8 ...$70.00

Thor, sew-on patch, 1970s, blk cloth w/mc image & yel stitched border, 3" dia, NM, T2...$6.00

Three Stooges, Colorforms, few pcs missing o/w MIB, H4..$40.00

Three Stooges, dolls, Exclusive Premiere/Target, 10", set of 3, NM, F1 ...$160.00

Three Stooges, dolls, Made in China, stuffed cloth w/vinyl heads, prison uniforms, set of 3, 13", EX, H4 ...$40.00

Three Stooges, figures, Applause, 1988, orig tags & stands, set of 3, 14", M, H4 ...$140.00

Three Stooges, flasher rings, Curly, Larry or Moe, EX, H4, ea.$20.00

Three Stooges, Photo Printing Set, Yankee/Maurer, complete, EX (VG box), from $500 to ...$600.00

Tom & Jerry, dolls, Georgene, 1949, stuffed cloth, 16" & 7", M, D10, pr, from $375 to ...$400.00

Tom & Jerry, figure, pnt plaster, 5", EX, A ...$85.00

Tom & Jerry, guitar, Mattel, 1965, musical w/up, EX, B10..$40.00

Tom & Jerry, jack-in-the-box, Mattel, M, from $75 to ..$100.00

Tom & Jerry, motorcycle w/sidecar, Bulgaria, Tom driving w/2 figures in sidecar, plastic, 13", scarce, NM, A...$200.00

Tom & Jerry, water pistols, Marx, 1960s, M, P12 ...$65.00

Uncle Wiggily, doll, Georgene, stuffed cloth, original clothes, retains original tag, 20", NM, A, $550.00.

Top Cat, figure, 1960s, vinyl, yel w/red jacket & hat, 8", VG, J5 ...$15.00

Top Cat, figure set, Top Cat, Benny the Ball & Spook, Knickerbocker, 1960s, vinyl, 8", VG+, F8 ...$95.00

Tweety Bird, doll, Chatter Chum, Mattel, 1976, MIB, P12.$45.00

Tweety Bird, doll, Chatter Chum, Mattel, 1976, NM, M15 ...$30.00

Universal Monsters, iron-on transfers, 1964, set of 6, MOC, H4 ...$200.00

Weird-Ohs, magic slate, Daddy the Way Out Suburbanite, 1963, cb w/lift-up erasable film sheet, 11x8", M (sealed), T2.$35.00

Weird-Ohs, magic slate, Davey the Way Out Cyclist, 1963, cb w/lift-up erasable film sheet, 11x8", M (sealed), T2 ..$50.00

Welcome Back Kotter, record player, 1976, EX, I2 ...$100.00

Welcome Back Kotter, wastebasket, metal, oval, VG+, H4.$40.00

Where's Waldo, doll, Waldo, Mattel, MIB, B5, $60.00.

Photo courtesy Martin and Carolyn Berens

Where's Waldo, doll, Woof, Mattel, 1990, stuffed plush w/sewn-on clothes, 9½", NM ...$30.00

Where's Waldo, figures, Waldo & Wenda, Mattel, 1990, cloth over wire bodies w/vinyl heads, 18", NM, pr...$65.00

Winky Dink, outfit, 1950s, yel, red & wht felt, scarce, EX, J5 ...$85.00

Winky Dink, Super Magic TV Kit, Winky Dink & You!, Standard Toycraft, 1968, EX (EX box), J5 ...$85.00

Wizard of Oz, bank, Dorothy, Arnart Imports, 1960s, hand-pnt, orig paper tag, 7", NMIB, S6 ...$825.00

Wizard of Oz, bank, Scarecrow, Arnart Imports, 1960s, hand-pnt, orig paper tag, 7", NMIB, S6...$100.00

Wizard of Oz, bank, Tin Woodsman, Arnart Imports, 1960s, hand-pnt, orig paper tag, 7", MIB, S6 ...$135.00

Wizard of Oz, bath beads, Ansehi, 1976, set of 12 in plastic tray, EX (EX box), S6 ....$75.00
Wizard of Oz, doll, Scarecrow, Ideal, 1939, cloth w/pnt mask face & yarn hair, 17", NM....................$800.00
Wizard of Oz, figure, Cowardly Lion, Multiple, 1960s, rubber, 6", EX, A $55.00
Wizard of Oz, figure, Tin Woodsman, Multiple, 1960s, rubber, 6", EX, A $55.00
Wizard of Oz, figurine, Dorothy, Avon, 1985, Images of Hollwood series, porcelain, 5½", NM, S6 ....$45.00
Wizard of Oz, flasher ring, Cowardly Lion or Tin Woodsman, M, C10, ea....................$100.00
Wizard of Oz, jack-in-the-box, Scarecrow, 1967, plays 'Hail Hail the Gang's All Here,' NM $50.00
Wizard of Oz, Magic Kit, Fun Inc, 1960s, complete w/10 tricks, NMIB, F8 ....$50.00
Wizard of Oz, sunglasses, Scarecrow, Multi-Kids/Lowes, 1989, yel plastic, MOC, M17 ....$20.00
Wizard of Oz, toy watch, Scarecrow & Tin Woodsman, Occupied Japan, 1940s, red fabric band, M, S6 ....$50.00
Wizard of Oz, trinket box, ruby slipper, Presents, 1989, MIB....$15.00
Wizard of Oz, valentine, Am Colortype, 1940-41, several variations, S6, ea from $100 to....................$125.00
Wolfman, doll, Hamilton Presents, 1992, vinyl w/cloth outfit, 14", EX, F1 ....$30.00
Wonder Woman, Colorforms Adventure Set, 1976, EX (EX box), J2....................$30.00
Wonder Woman, figure, Ideal, 1966, pnt plastic, 4", EX, J5 .$45.00
Wonder Woman, mirror, Avon, 1978, plastic figural hdl, NM (EX box) $20.00
Wonder Woman, slide-tile puzzle, 1978, EX, M17 ....$30.00
Wonder Woman, sunglasses, Nasta, 1988, MOC, M17....$20.00
Wonder Woman & Flash, figure set, Ideal, 1967, plastic, 3", scarce, NMOC, A $1,300.00
Woodstock, see Peanuts
Woody Woodpecker, film, 1960s, 8mm, NMIB, J5 ....$15.00
Woody Woodpecker, harmonica, early, plastic figure, 6", EX, J2....................$30.00
Woody Woodpecker, jack-in-the-box, Mattel, M, from $100 to $150.00
Woody Woodpecker, Juggle Puzzles, Gaston, 1950s, 6 different characters make over 40,000 combinations, NMIB, F8 .$30.00
Woody Woodpecker, kazoo, Linden, 1960s, red plastic figure, 7", EX, F8....................$25.00
Woody Woodpecker, mug, 1965-73, brn plastic w/pnt face, NM, B14 ....$15.00
Woody Woodpecker, Picture Dominoes, Saalfield, 1963, MIB (sealed), F8....................$45.00
Woody Woodpecker, ring, 1970s, cloisonne, M, J8..........$15.00
Woody Woodpecker, stamp ring, 1960s, wht w/image of Woody on top, yel plastic sides w/emb Woody Woodpecker Club, EX, A $150.00
Yogi Bear, bank, plastic, 14", EX, J2 ....$35.00
Yogi Bear, bank, plastic, 8", EX, P6 ....$35.00
Yogi Bear, doll, Applause, 1970s-80s, stuffed plush, 9", NM, F8....................$20.00
Yogi Bear, doll, Playtime, 1960s, plush w/felt hat, collar & tie, 17", EX, F8 ....$50.00
Yogi Bear, doll, 1977, pillow-type w/bells inside, 15", EX, J8 ....$20.00
Yogi Bear, figure, Japan, 1962, rubber w/movable head & arms, 6", NM, F8 ....$50.00
Yogi Bear, Lovable Smoking Traveler's Pet, plastic, MOC, P6 ....$20.00
Yogi Bear, mug, 1961, pnt plastic, NM, B14 ....$20.00
Yogi Bear, night light cover, 1960s, hollow figure w/hole at bottom, 7", EX, F8....................$20.00
Yogi Bear, Play Fun Set, Whitman, 1964, complete w/play mat of the park, NM (NM box), F8 ....$50.00
Yogi Bear, riding stick, AJ Renzi, 1961, wood w/plastic head figure of Yogi, 34", EX, F8....................$55.00

Chein

Though the company was founded shortly after the turn of the century, this New Jersey-based manufacturer is probably best known for the toys it made during the '30s and '40s. Wind-up merry-go-rounds and Ferris wheels as well as many other carnival-type rides were made of beautifully lithographed tin even into the '50s, some in several variations. The company also made banks, a few of which were mechanical and some that were character-related. Mechanical, sea-worthy cabin cruisers, space guns, sand toys, and some Disney toys as well were made by this giant company; they continued in production until 1979.

Advisor: Scott Smiles (S10).

See also Banks; Disney; Sand Toys.

Windups, Frictions, and Other Mechanicals

Photo courtesy Scott Smiles

Bear, 5", EX, $200.00.

Aquaplane, 1939, advances w/spinning prop, 8½", NM (EX box), A $500.00

Barnacle Bill Floor Puncher, 1930s, figure punches bag on rectangular base, litho tin & celluloid, 7", EX $700.00

Barnacle Bill in Barrel, 1930s, advances in waddling motion w/swaying head, 7", NM, A....................$350.00

Bass Drummer, 1930s, drum major advances & plays drum, 9", MIB, A....................$450.00

Big Top, 1961, tent spins & opens to reveal clown, tin w/plastic tent dome, lever action, 10", NM (EX box), A $200.00

Bonzo on Scooter, gray dog on gr & red scooter, 7", G ..$350.00

Broadway Trolley, early mk, 8", EX, A $200.00

Clown Barrel Walker, 1925, waddles around as head & barrel twist, 8", rare, NM (worn box), A....................$600.00

Clown Floor Puncher, clown hits punching bag, 8½", EX..$700.00

Disneyland Ferris Wheel, spins with bell sound, 17", M, A, $800.00.

Felix the Cat on Scooter, 7", EX, A....................$650.00

Happy Days Cash Register, press keys for actions, 4", EX ...$100.00

Happy Hooligan, 1932, advances in waddling motion, 6", NM, from $1,400 to....................$1,500.00

Hercules Ferris Wheel, spins w/ringing bell, 17", NM, A ..$385.00

Hercules Jazz Band, early, 13", rare, EX (G box) $850.00

Hopping Rabbit, early mk, pk & brn, 5", EX, A $150.00

Indian in Headdress, 1930s, EX, from $150 to................$175.00

Junior Truck, mk 220 on doors, gr & red w/yel tires, half-figure driver, 8", EX $400.00

Junior Truck, mk 420 on doors, gr w/red tires, half-figure driver, 8", EX....................$350.00

Monkey Bank, 1930s, tips hat when coin is dropped in slot, 5", EX $100.00

Musical Aero Swing, 4 gondolas spin & fly around center pole, 11", scarce, NMIB $1,000.00

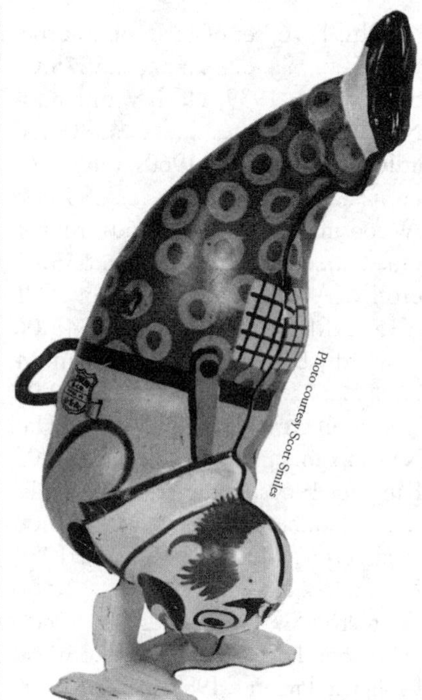

Hand-Standing Clown, balances on hands, 5", EX, from $125.00 to $150.00.

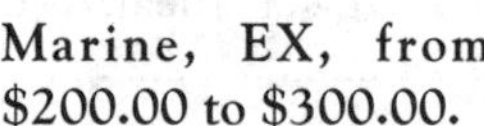

Marine, EX, from $200.00 to $300.00.

Native on Alligator, advances as mouth opens & closes, litho tin, 15", EX, A $250.00

Native on Turtle, 1930s, advances w/moving head, 8", NM (EX box), A....................$450.00

Navy Frog Man, litho tin w/plastic flippers, 12", NMOC, A..$125.00

Opera Sedan, gr & pinkish-lavender color w/balloon cord tires, 7", EX, A....................$200.00

Penguin, advances in waddling motion, 4", EX................$75.00

Pig, 1938, 5", EX, from $125 to $150.00

Playland Merry-Go-Round, 5 horses & 5 swans circle w/bell sound, 10", NM (EX box), A $650.00

Playland Whip, 4 kids in cars fly around base w/bobbing heads, 20" base, EX (EX box) $800.00
Popeye Floor Puncher, litho tin figure on platform hits celluloid bag, 7", EX, A $1,000.00
Popeye in Barrel, waddles back & forth in barrel, 7", EX..$675.00
Popeye Overhead Puncher, 1932, 9½", rare, NM $2,500.00
Popeye Shadow Boxer, advances in vibrating motion w/swinging arms, litho tin, 7", scarce, VG, A....................$1,700.00
Popeye Waddler, 1932, advances in waddling motion, 6½", NM, A....................$1,300.00
Rabbit w/Cart, rabbit pulls cart w/lithoed rabbits carrying a pumpkin & other animal scenes, 8", NM, from $125 to......$150.00

Photo courtesy John Turney

Racer #52, tin with wooden wheels, EX, $200.00.

Ride-A-Rocket Carousel, 4 rockets w/figures circle tower, litho tin w/celluloid props, 18", NM, A....................$900.00
Roller Coaster, 1930s, w/2 cars & bell, 19", NM (NM box) .$450.00

Photo courtesy Dunbar Gallery

Roller Coaster, 1950s, 19", EX, $300.00.

Santa Walker, advances in waddling motion w/gift in his hands, 6", EX, A....................$700.00
Santa's Gnome, early mk, advances in waddling motion, 6", EX+ $375.00
Ski Boy, advances on snow skis, 8", NM, A....................$250.00
Ski Ride, kids travel to top of ride, 19½", NM (EX box) .$1,100.00
Skin Diver, flippers move, 11½", NM (EX box), A........$200.00
Toyville Dump Truck, red, gr & yel, 9", NM, A............$350.00
US Army Soldier, 5", MOC, A $150.00
Yellow Taxi, early, mk Yellow Taxi Main 7570, 6", EX, A..$200.00

Miscellaneous

Photo courtesy Dunbar Gallery

Cathedral Organ, turn crank and music plays, lithographed tin, 9½", NMIB, from $175.00 to $225.00.

Drum, litho tin & paper w/image of children dressed as soldiers, orig drumsticks, 6¼" dia, NM, G16 ....$135.00
Easter Basket, 1950s, litho tin, 8", EX, N2 ....$50.00
Easter Egg, 1930s, take-apart w/lithoed scenes, 5", NM....$75.00
Hen on Egg, early mk, opens in center, litho tin, 5x5", NM, A....................$100.00
Hercules Motor Express Truck, blk C-style cab, blk chassis, yel stake bed w/name panel, wht wheels, red hubs, 22", EX $1,000.00
Krazy Kat Express Pull Toy, 1932, pnt wood w/litho tin lion on front, 12", scarce, EX, A....................$1,600.00
Popeye Sparkler, 1959, sparks fly behind clear red window inserts, plunger action, EX (EX box) $275.00
Rabbit Roly Poly, litho tin, 7", scarce, M, A....................$250.00
Top, 1930s, litho tin w/several images of children's toys, NM....................$100.00
Tray, 1984, teddy bear images, litho tin, 12x17", VG, N2.$25.00

Chinese Tin Toys

China has produced toys for export since the 1920s, but most of their tin toys were made from the 1970s to the present. Collectors are buying them with an eye to the future, since right now, at least, they are relatively inexpensive.

Government-operated factories are located in various parts of China. They use various numbering systems to identify types of toys, for instance, ME (metal-electric — battery operated), MS (metal-spring — windup), MF (metal friction), and others. Most toys and boxes are marked, but some aren't; and since many of the toys are reproductions of earlier Japanese models, it is often difficult to tell the difference if no numbers can be found.

Prices vary greatly depending on age, condition, availability, and dealer knowledge of origin. Toys currently in production may be discontinued at any time and may often be as hard to find as the earlier toys. Records are so scarce that it is difficult to pinpoint the start of production, but at least some manufacture began in the 1970s and '80s. If you have additional information (toy name and number; description as to size, color variations, actions, type, etc.; and current market), please contact our advisor. In the listings below, values are for new-in-the-box items.

Advisor: Steve Fisch (F7).

#ME021, police car, current, 16½x5x5", F7, from $55 to ..**$125.00**

#ME060, tank, remote control, 1970s, 7x4x4", F7, from $35 to **$75.00**

#ME084, jet plane, current, 12½x13x5", F7, from $35 to..**$75.00**

#ME086, Shanghai bus, F7, from $85 to **$150.00**

#ME087, jetliner, 1980s, 19x18x3", F7, from $55 to **$125.00**

#ME089, Universe car, 1970s, F7, from $85 to..............**$150.00**

#ME093, open-door trolley, discontinued, 10x5x4", F7, from $25 to **$35.00**

#ME095, fire chief car, current, 12½x5x5", F7, from $35 to .**$75.00**

#ME097, police car, 13x5x5", F7, from $35 to..................**$75.00**

#ME099, UFO spaceship, current, 8x8x5", F7, from $35 to..**$75.00**

#ME100, robot (resembles 1980s Star Strider robot), current, 12x4x6", F7, from $35 to..........**$125.00**

#ME102, spaceship, blows air, current, 13x5x4", F7, from $35 to **$75.00**

#ME104, locomotive, 15½x4x7", F7, from $35 to............**$75.00**

#ME105, locomotive, 9½x5½x5½", F7, from $35 to **$75.00**

#ME379, dump truck, discontinued, 13x4x3", F7, from $25.00 to $50.00.

#ME603, hens & chickens, F7, from $35 to **$50.00**

#ME610, hen laying eggs, current, 7x4x6", F7, from $25 to..**$50.00**

#ME611, News car or World Cap car, 5x16½x5", F7, ea, from $55 to **$125.00**

#ME614, automatic rifle, current, 23x2x8", F7, from $25 to ..**$65.00**

#ME630, Photo car, older version, 12½x5x5", from $35 to .**$125.00**

#ME677, Shanghai convertible, 1970s, 12x5x3", F7, from $35 to **$100.00**

#ME679, dump truck, discontinued, 13x4x3", F7, from $25 to **$50.00**

#ME699, fire chief car, current, 10x5x2", from $25 to......**$50.00**

#ME756, anti-aircraft armoured tank, F7, from $35 to **$75.00**

#ME767, Universe boat, current, 10x5x6", F7, from $35 to.**$75.00**

#ME767, Universe boat, 1970s, 10x5x6", F7, from $75 to.**$150.00**

#ME770, Mr Duck, current, 9x7x5", F7, from $25 to **$50.00**

#ME774, tank, remote control, 1970s, 9x4x3", F7, from $45 to **$75.00**

#ME777, Universe Televiboat, current, 15x4x7", F7, from $35 to **$75.00**

#ME777, Universe Televiboat, 1970s, 15x4x7", F7, from $75 to..........**$150.00**

#ME782, locomotive, 1970s-80s, battery-op, 10x4x7", from $35 to **$75.00**

#ME801, Lunar Explorer, 1970s, 12x6x4", F7, from $75 to..**$125.00**

#ME809, anti-aircraft armoured car, 1970s, 12x6x6", F7, from $75 to..........**$100.00**

#ME821, Cicada, 1970s, 10x4x4", F7, from $50.00 to $125.00.

#ME824, patrol car, 1970s, 11x4x3½", F7, from $35 to ...**$75.00**

#ME842, camel, discontinued, 10x4x7", F7, from $35 to .**$50.00**

#ME884, police car, VW bus style, current, 11½x5x5", F7, from $35 to **$75.00**

#ME895, fire engine, 1970x, 10x4x4", F7, from $50 to **$85.00**

#ME972, open-door police car, 9½x4x4", F7, from $35 to .**$100.00**

#ME984, jet plane, 13x14x4½", F7, from $35 to **$75.00**

#MF032, Eastwind Sedan, current, 6x2x2", F7, from $8 to..**$15.00**

#MF033, pickup truck, current, 6x2x2", F7, from $8 to....**$15.00**

#MF044, sedan, Nissan style, 9x3½x3", F7, from $10 to ..**$25.00**

#MF046, sparking carbine, 18x5x1", F7, from $20 to **$35.00**

#MF052, sedan, 8x3x2", F7, from $15 to..........**$25.00**

#MF083, sedan, current, 6x2x2", F7, from $8 to..............**$15.00**

#MF107, airplane, 6x6x2", F7, from $20 to..........**$35.00**

#MF111, ambulance, current, 8x3x3", F7, from $15 to **$20.00**
#MF127, Highway patrol car, 9½x4x3", F7, from $20 to..**$50.00**
#MF132, ambulance, 1980s, 10x4x4", F7, from $15 to.....**$35.00**
#MF134, tourist bus, current, 6x2x3", F7, from $15 to **$25.00**
#MF135, red flag convertible, current, F7, from $35 to **$75.00**
#MF136, double-decker train, current, 8x2x3", F7, from $15 to....................**$20.00**
#MF146, Volkswagen, 5x2x2", F7, from $10 to **$20.00**
#MF151, Shanghai pickup, 1970s, 12x4x4", F7, from $35 to .**$100.00**
#MF154, tractor, 1970s, 5x3x4", F7, from $25 to.............**$50.00**
#MF162, motorcycle, 6x2x4", F7, from $15 to.................**$35.00**
#MF163, fire truck, current, 6x2x3", F7, from $35 to **$75.00**
#MF164, construction truck, 1970s, 7x3x5", F7, from $35 to....................**$75.00**
#MF164, Volkswagen, current, 4x2x3", F7, from $10 to ..**$15.00**
#MF170, train, current, 10x2x4", F7, from $15 to **$25.00**
#MF171, convertible, current, 5x2x2", F7, from $8 to **$15.00**
#MF184, coach bus, 12½x4x4", F7, from $15 to **$30.00**

Photo courtesy Steve Fisch

#MF185, double-decker bus, current, 11x5x3", F7, from $15.00 to $25.00.

#MF193, soft-cover truck, 1970s, 11x3x4", F7, from $50 to..**$75.00**
#MF201, oil tanker, 1970s, 14x4x4", F7, from $15 to.......**$25.00**

Photo courtesy Steve Fisch

#MF249, flying boat, 1970s, 6x6x2", F7, from $35.00 to $75.00.

#MF203, sedan, 10½x4x2½", F7, from $25 to **$50.00**
#MF206, panda truck, current, 6x3x2", F7, from $10 to...**$20.00**
#MF216, airplane, discontinued, 9x9x3", F7, from $15 to .**$35.00**
#MF234, sedan, 6x2x2", F7, from $15 to..........................**$25.00**
#MF239, tiger truck, 10x3x4", F7, from $15 to **$30.00**
#MF240, passenger jet, 13x11x4", F7, from $30 to **$35.00**
#MF254, Mercedes Sedan, current, 8x4x3", F7, from $15 to ...**$25.00**
#MF274, tank, 1970s, 3x2x2", F7, from $8 to **$15.00**
#MF294, Mercedes Sedan, friction, 7x3x2", F7, from $12 to .**$20.00**
#MF298, traveling car, 8½x4x3½", F7, from $15 to.........**$25.00**

Photo courtesy Steve Fisch

#MF304, race car, discontinued, 10x4x3", F7, from $15.00 to $35.00.

#MF309, sedan, 9x2x3½", F7, from $20 to **$35.00**
#MF310, Corvette, 3x2x3", F7, from $10 to **$15.00**
#MF316, 1953 Corvette, current, F7, from $20 to **$50.00**
#MF317, Corvette convertible, current, 10x4x3", F7, from $20 to....................**$50.00**
#MF320, Mercedes sedan, current, 7x3x2", F7, from $10 to....................**$20.00**
#MF321, Buick convertible, current, 11x4x3", F7, from $20 to **$50.00**
#MF322, Buick sedan, current, 11x4x3", F7, from $20 to.**$50.00**
#MF326, Mercedes gull-wing sedan, current, 9x3x2", F7, from $15 to **$25.00**

Photo courtesy Steve Fisch

#MF714, fire chief car, current, 5x2x2", F7, from $8.00 to $15.00.

#MF329, 1956 Corvette convertible, current, 10x4x4", F7, from $20 to $50.00
#MF330, Cadillac Sedan, current, 11x4x3", F7, from $15 to .$35.00
#MF339, 1956 Corvette, current, 10x4x4", F7, from $20 to ..$50.00
#MF340, Cadillac convertible, current, 11x4x3", F7, from $20 to $50.00
#MF341, convertible, 12x4x3", F7, from $20 to $50.00
#MF342, sedan, 12x4x3", F7, from $20 to........................$50.00
#MF712, locomotive, current, 7x2x3", F7, from $10 to....$15.00
#MF713, taxi, current, 5x2x2", F7, from $8 to.................$15.00
#MF716, ambulance, 1970s, 8x3x3", F7, from $15 to.......$30.00
#MF717, dump truck, discontinued, 10x3x5", F7, from $15 to $35.00
#MF718, ladder truck, 10x3x4", F7, from $15 to $35.00
#MF721, light tank, current, 6x3x3", F7, from $15 to......$20.00
#MF722, jeep, current, 6x3x3", F7, from $15 to $20.00
#MF731, station wagon, current, 5x2x2", F7, from $8 to .$15.00
#MF735, rocket racer, current, 7x3x3", F7, from $15 to...$35.00
#MF742, flying boat, current, 13x4x4", F7, from $15 to...$35.00

#MF743, Karmann Ghia Sedan, current, 10x3x4", F7, from $15.00 to $45.00.

#MF753, sports car, current, 8x3x2", F7, from $15 to.......$25.00
#MF782, circus truck, current, 9x3x4", F7, from $15 to ...$25.00
#MF787, Lucky open car, current, 8x3x2", F7, from $15 to.$25.00
#MF798, patrol car, current, 8x3x3", F7, $15 to $25.00
#MF800, race car #5, current, 6x2x2", F7, from $10 to $20.00

#MF804, locomotive, current, 16x3x5", F7, from $15.00 to $25.00.

#MF832, ambulance, current, 5x2x2", F7, from $8 to $15.00
#MF844, double-decker bus, current, 8x4x3", F7, from $15 to $20.00
#MF861, space gun, 1970s, 10x2x6", F7, from $45 to.......$75.00
#MF893, animal van, current, 6x2x3", from $15 to..........$20.00

#MF900, police car, current, 6x3x2", F7, from $8.00 to $15.00.

#MF910, airport limo bus, current, 15x4x5", F7, from $20 to..$35.00
#MF923, torpedo boat, 8x3x3", F7, from $15 to $25.00
#MF951, fighter jet, 1970s, 5x4x2", F7, from $15 to.........$20.00
#MF956, sparking tank, current, 8x4x3", F7, from $15 to ..$20.00
#MF957, ambulance helicopter, 7½x2x4", F7, from $15 to ..$35.00
#MF958, poultry truck, current, F7, from $15 to $20.00
#MF959, jeep, discontinued, 9x4x4", F7, from #15 to $20.00
#MF974, circus truck, 6x2x4", F7, from $15 to $20.00
#MF985, fowl transporter, current, 12x3x4", F7, from $25 to $50.00
#MF989, noisy locomotive, 1970s, 12x3x4", F7, from $25 to $50.00
#MF993, mini car, current, 5x2x2", F7, from $8 to...........$15.00
#MF998, sedan, current, 5x2x2", F7, from $8 to...............$15.00
#MS002, jumping frog, current, 2x2x2", F7, from $8 to ...$15.00
#MS006, pecking chicken, 1970s, 2x1x1", F7, from $8 to.$15.00
#MS011, roll-over plane, current, 3x4x2", F7, from $10 to...$20.00
#MS014, single-bar exerciser, 1970s, 7x6x6", F7, from $25 to..$50.00
#MS057, horse & rider, 1970s, 6x2x5", F7, from $20 to...$35.00
#MS058, old-fashion car, current, 3x3x4", F7, from $15 to ..$20.00
#MS082, jumping frog, current, 2x2x2", F7, from $8 to ...$15.00
#MS083, jumping rabbit, current, 3x3x2", F7, from $8 to .$15.00
#MS085, xylophone girl, current, 7x3x9", F7, from $20 to..$35.00
#MS107, jumping Bambi, current, 5½x6", F7, from $15 to .$20.00
#MS134, sparking jet, current, F7, from $15 to $30.00
#MS166, crawling baby, vinyl head, current, 5x4x5", F7, from $15 to $20.00
#MS405, ice-cream vendor, current, F7, from $10 to $20.00
#MS405, jumping zebra, current, 5x2x4", F7, from $10 to..$20.00
#MS565, drumming panda/wheel, current, 5x3x5", F7, from $10 to $20.00
#MS568, sparrow, current, 5x2x2", F7, from $10 to $15.00
#MS569, oriole, current, 5x2x2", F7, from $10 to $15.00

#MS575, bear with flash camera, current, 6x3x4", F7, from $15.00 to $35.00.

#MS702, motorcycle, current, 7x4x5", F7, from $15 to....$35.00
#MS704, bird music cart, 1970s, 3x2x5", F7, from $15 to .$25.00

#MS709, motorcycle with sidecar, current, 7x4x5", F7, from $15.00 to $35.00.

#MS710, tricycle, current, 5x3x5", F7, from $15 to..........$20.00
#MS713, washing machine, 3x3x5", F7, from $15 to $20.00
#MS765, drummer, 5x3x6", F7, from $15 to....................$25.00
#MS827, sedan, steering, 1970s, 9x3x3", F7, from $50 to $75.00
#MS858, girl on goose, current, 5x3x3", F7, from $15 to .$25.00
#MS858, girl on goose, older style, 5x3x3", F7, from $25 to $50.00
#PMS102, rolling cart, current, 3x2x1", F7, from $15 to..$20.00
#PMS105, jumping dog, current, 3x2x6", F7, from $15 to.$25.00
#PMS106, jumping parrot, current, 3x2x6", F7, from $15 to $25.00
#PMS108, duck family, current, 10x2x3", F7, from $15 to ..$25.00
#PMS113, Fu dog, current, 4x2x3", F7, from $15 to.........$25.00
#PMS119, woodpecker, current, 3x2x6", F7, from $15 to .$25.00
#PMS210, clown riding bike, current, 4x2x5", F7, from $15 to..$25.00
#PMS212, elephant on bike, current, 6x3x8", F7, from $15 to..$35.00
#PMS213, duck on bike, current, 6x3x8", F7, from $15 to ..$35.00
#PMS214, lady bug family, current, 13x3x1", F7, from $15 to..$25.00
#PMS215, crocodile, current, 9x3x1", F7, from $15 to.....$20.00
#PMS217, jumping rabbit, current, 3x2x6", F7, from $15 to...$25.00
#PMS218, penguin, current, 3x2x6", F7, from $15 to $30.00

#PS013, boy on tricycle, current, 2x4x4", F7, from $12.00 to $25.00.

Circus Toys

If you ever had the opportunity to go to one of the giant circuses as a child, no doubt you still have very vivid recollections of the huge elephants, the daring trapeze artists, the clowns and their trick dogs, and the booming voice of the ringmaster, even if that experience was a half century ago. Most of our circus toys are listed in other categories.

See also Battery-Operated Toys; Cast Iron, Circus; Chein, Windups; Marx, Windups; Schoenhut; Windups, Friction, and Other Mechanicals.

Aero Circus, Newton, 1930s, MIB................................$475.00
Britains Mammoth Circus, complete, NM (EX box)......$800.00

Clever Clowns, Greycraft, Grey Iron Casting, 1930s, diecast figures, EX (EX box), D10 .... $750.00
Clicker, circus elephant, mk Made in Japan, litho tin elephant balances on log, 2½", NM $125.00
Clown Roly Poly, France, pnt compo, 8", VG $200.00
Crandall's Great Show the Acrobats, Pat 1867, wood blocks assemble to 10", EX (EX box), A $500.00
Jackie Acrobats, National Toy Mfg, 1920s, wood figures, VG (VG box), A $150.00

Kiddy Circus Pull Toy, UNK, wood, complete, NM, $275.00.

Mammoth Show Circus Wagon, Reed, 1890s, paper on wood, w/3 animals & 2 trainers, 14", VG, A $2,000.00
One-Ring Circus, probably Gibbs, 1920s, carved wood, 21 pcs, EX, D10, from $1,200 to $1,600.00
Ringling Bros Performing Animals on Circus Wagon, wooden clown & bear balance ball & spin on tin wheels, EX (VG box) $200.00
Ringling Bros Toy Circus, Mattel, MIB $85.00

Coloring, Activity, and Paint Books

Coloring and activity books from the early years of the twentieth century are scarce indeed and when found can be expensive if they are tied into another collectibles field such as Black Americana or advertising; but the ones most in demand are those that represent familiar movie and TV stars of the 1950s and '60s. Condition plays a very important part in assessing worth, and though hard to find, unused examples are the ones that bring top dollar — in fact, as much as 50% to 75% more than one even partially used.

Advisor: Diane Albert (T6).

See also Advertising.

Adventures of Electro-Man, coloring book, Lowe, 1967, few pgs colored, scarce, EX, from $40 to $50.00
Adventures of Rin-Tin-Tin, coloring book, Whitman, 1955, few pgs colored, VG+, T2 .... $12.00
Agent Zero, coloring book, Whitman, 1966, unused, NM, F8 .... $25.00
Aladdin & His Magic Lamp, coloring book, Saalfield, 1970, unused, EX, T2 .... $20.00
Ali Baba & the Forty Thieves, coloring book, Karas, 1962, unused, NM, J5 .... $15.00
Alice in Wonderland, punch-out book, Whitman/WDP, 1951, unused, EX, P6 .... $175.00
Alvin & the Chipmunks, sticker book, Whitman, 1966, stickers applied, VG, F8 .... $12.00
Andy Panda, coloring book, Whitman, 1944, few pgs colored, EX, F8 .... $25.00
Annette, coloring book, Whitman, 1961, unused, NM, F8 .. $25.00
Archies, coloring book, Whitman, 1970, few pgs colored, EX, F8 .... $16.00
Aristocats, sticker book, Whitman, 1970, 1 pg w/stickers applied, NM, F8 .... $25.00
Bambi, coloring book, Watkins-Strathmore, 1966, few pgs colored, EX, F8 .... $15.00
Bambi, paint book, Whitman, 1942, few pgs pnt, VG, M8 .. $35.00
Banana Splits, coloring book, Whitman, 1969, most pgs colored, EX, J5 .... $25.00
Barbie & Her Little Sister Skipper, coloring book, Whitman, 1965, few pgs colored, EX, F8 .... $20.00
Barney Google & Snuffy Smith, Lowe, 1963, few pgs colored, EX, T2 .... $20.00
Batman, coloring book, Holloway Candy premium, 1966, unused, NM, A $50.00
Batman, coloring book, Whitman, 1967, unused, NM, T2 .. $30.00
Batman, Robin & Penguin Giant Comics To Color, Whitman, 1976, unused, NM, A $15.00
Batman Meets Blockbuster, coloring book, Whitman, 1966, most pgs colored, EX, T2 .... $12.00
Batman Returns, coloring book, Golden, 1992, unused, NM, P3 .... $8.00
Batman Saves the Town, coloring book, Holloway Candy premium, 1966, scarce, unused, EX, A $125.00
Batman w/Robin the Boy Wonder, dot-to-dot book, Bertdan International, 1967, unused, M $50.00
Beany & Cecil, coloring book, Whitman, 1955, few pgs colored, EX, F8 .... $30.00
Beatles, coloring book, Saalfield, 1964, unused, EX, R2 ... $75.00
Bedknobs & Broomsticks, coloring book, Whitman, 1971, few pgs colored, EX, F8 .... $14.00
Beetle Bailey, coloring book, Lowe, 1961, unused, NM, T2 .... $25.00
Ben-Hur, coloring book, Lowe, 1959, few pgs colored, EX, T2 .... $15.00
Ben-Hur, punch-out book, Golden Press, 1959, unused, M, F8 .... $50.00
Benny the Beaver, Funny Animal Paint Book, Fawcett, 1945, unused, NM, F8 .... $16.00
Betsy McCall in Hawaii, coloring book, Whitman, unused, EX, V2 .... $25.00
Beverly Hillbillies, coloring book, Whitman, 1964, several pgs colored, EX, F8 .... $25.00

Beverly Hillbillies, punch-out book, Whitman, 1960s, unused, EX, J5 ....$85.00
Billy the Kid & Oscar, Funny Animal Paint Book, Fawcett, 1945, unused, NM, F8 ....$20.00
Blackbeard's Ghost, coloring book, Whitman, 1968, few pgs colored, EX, P3 ....$15.00

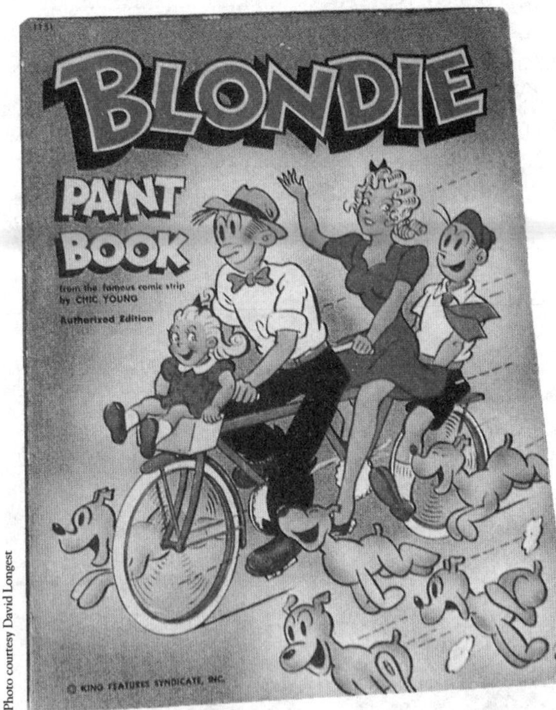

Photo courtesy David Longest

Blondie, paint book, Whitman, 1947, unused, EX, $35.00.

Bobby Benson's B-Bar-Riders, coloring book, Whitman, 1950, few pgs colored, EX, F8 ....$25.00
Bobby Sherman Paint & Color Album, Artcraft, 1971, few pgs colored, NM, F8 ....$30.00
Bon Voyage!, coloring book, Whitman, 1962, few pgs colored, NM, F8 ....$15.00
Bonanza, coloring book, Artcraft, 1960, unused, NM, F8..$25.00
Boots & Saddles, coloring book, 1958, unused, M, V1.....$35.00
Bozo the Clown, coloring book, Whitman, 1972, unused, EX, F8 ....$16.00
Buccaneer, coloring book, Saalfield, 1959, 1 pg colored, EX, T2 ....$15.00
Buffalo Bill & Calamity, coloring book, Whitman, 1957, several pgs colored, EX, F8 ....$25.00
Buffy & Jody, coloring book, Whitman, 1969, several pgs colored, VG+, F8 ....$14.00
Bugs Bunny, coloring book, Watkins-Strathmore, 1964, unused, NM, J5 ....$15.00
Bugs Bunny, coloring book, Whitman, 1956, few pgs colored, VG, F8 ....$15.00
Bugs Bunny & Porky Pig, paint book, Whitman, 1947, several pgs pnt, VG, F8 ....$18.00
Bugs Bunny Private Eye, coloring book, Whitman, 1957, unused, VG, T2 ....$15.00
Bullwinkle, coloring book, 1969, unused, M, V1 ....$25.00
Bullwinkle & Dudley Do-Right, coloring book, Saalfield, 1970, unused, EX, A $25.00
Captain & the Kids, coloring book, Abbott, 1950s, several pgs colored, EX, F8 ....$18.00
Captain America, coloring book, Whitman, 1966, few pgs colored, EX, T2 ....$25.00
Champ, coloring book, Merrill, 1935, few pgs colored, EX, F8 ....$15.00
Charlie Brown, coloring book, 1970, unused, M $15.00
Cheyenne, coloring book, Whitman, 1950s, several pgs colored, missing 1st pg o/w EX, F8 ....$25.00
Chitty-Chitty Bang-Bang, coloring book, Whitman, 1968, few pgs colored, EX+, F8 ....$15.00
Choo Choo Charlie, coloring book, Whitman, 1970, rare, few pgs colored, EX, F8 ....$50.00
Circus Boy, coloring book, Whitman, 1958, photo cover, several pgs colored, NM, F8 ....$40.00
Cisco Kid, coloring book, Saalfield, 1954, few pgs colored, VG, J5 ....$25.00
Davy Crockett, coloring book, Whitman, 1950s, few pgs colored, VG, J5 ....$25.00

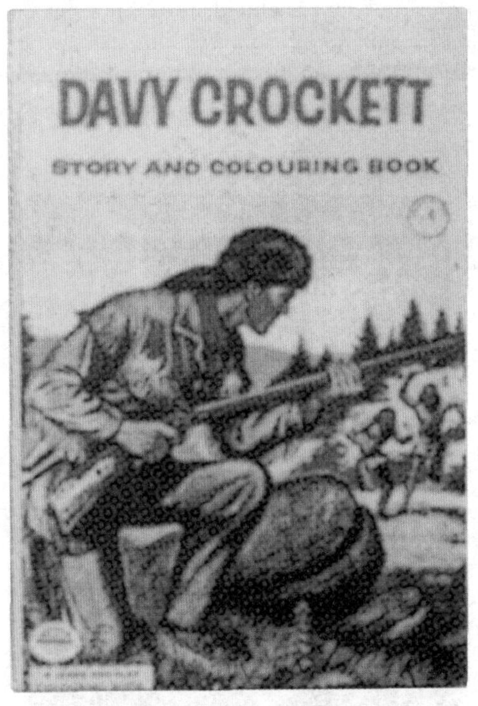

Davy Crockett, story and colouring book, Topline/ England, 1950s, unused, scarce, EX, A, $75.00.

Dear Santa, coloring book, Lowe, 1958, unused, NM, F8..$12.00
Devlin, coloring book, Saalfield, 1975, few pgs colored, EX, F8 ....$10.00
Dick Tracy, coloring book, Saalfield, 1946, unused, EX, D11 ....$45.00
Dick Tracy Junior Detective Kit, punch-out book, 1962, unused, M, D11 ....$25.00
Disneyland, coloring book, Whitman, 1968, few pgs colored, EX, F8 ....$15.00

Donald Duck, coloring book, Watkins-Strathmore, 1963, unused, EX, J5 ....$25.00
Donald Duck, coloring book, Whitman, 1960, several pgs colored, VG, F8 ....$15.00
Donald Duck Dots, dot-to-dot book, Whitman, 1954, unused, NM, F8....................$25.00
Dondi, coloring book, Saalfield, 1962, unused, NM, F8 ...$28.00
Donny Osmond, activity book, Artcraft, 1973, unused, NM, C1 ....$30.00
Doris Day, coloring book, Whitman, 1954, few pgs colored, NM, F8 ....$35.00
Dr Dolittle, coloring book, Watkins-Strathmore, 1962, several pgs colored, VG, F8 ....$12.00
Dune, activity book, Putnam, 1984, unused, NM, P3 ....$5.00
Elizabeth Taylor, coloring book, Whitman, 1952, few pgs colored, EX, J5 ....$35.00
Ellsworth Elephant, coloring book, Saalfield, 1962, most pgs colored, VG+, T2 ....$12.00
Emergency!, coloring book, Lowe, 1977, unused, NM, F8..$14.00
Etta Kett Color & Comics, Artcraft/Saalfield, 1960, unused, NM, J5 ....$15.00
Eve Arden, coloring book, Treasure Books, 1958, few pgs colored, EX, J5 ....$25.00
F-Troop, coloring book, Saalfield, 1960s, few pgs colored, EX, F8 ....$28.00
Family Affair, trace & color book, Whitman, 1969, few pgs colored, EX, F8 ....$16.00

Fantasia, paint book, Whitman, 1940, unused, rare, EX, A, $300.00.

Farm Animals, punch-out book, Lowe, 1961, unused, EX, T2 ....$12.00
Felix the Cat, coloring book, 1957, unused, M, V1 ....$50.00
Felix the Cat, sticker book, 1957, unused, M, V1 ....$60.00
Flintstones Meet the Gruesomes, Whitman, 1965, several pgs colored, rare, EX, F8 ....$55.00
Flipper, coloring book, Lowe, 1963, several pgs colored, VG, F8 ....$12.00
Frankenstein Jr, sticker book, Whitman, 1967, few stickers applied, NM, F8 ....$55.00
Freddie, coloring book, Playmore, 1978, few pgs colored, VG, F8 ....$8.00
Fun w/Elmer Fudd, coloring book, Watkins-Strathmore, 1963, few pgs colored, NM, F8 ....$30.00
Funday School, coloring book, Lowe, 1950s, unused, M, T2...$10.00
Funky Phantom, coloring book, Whitman, 1972, few pgs colored, VG, F8 ....$18.00
Fuzzy Bear, Funny Animal Paint Book, Fawcett, 1940s, unused, VG+ $15.00
Garrison's Gorillas, coloring book, Whitman, 1968, few pgs colored, EX, F8 ....$25.00

Gene Autry Cowboy Adventures, coloring book, Merrill, 1941, unused, EX, A, $85.00.

Gentle Ben, coloring book, Whitman, 1968, unused, EX, F8...$20.00
Get Smart, coloring book, Saalfield, 1965, 1 pg colored, VG+, T2 ....$20.00
Gilligan's Island, coloring book, Whitman, 1965, several pgs colored, NM, F8 ....$55.00
Goonies, coloring book, Simon & Schuster, 1985, unused, NM, P3 ....$5.00
Grace Kelly, coloring book, Whitman, 1956, few pgs colored, EX, J5 ....$45.00
Green Hornet, coloring book, Watkins-Strathmore, 1966, few pgs colored, EX, F8 ....$45.00
Gumby & Pokey, coloring book, Western Publishing, 1966, unused, NM, T2 ....$30.00
Hardy Boys, coloring book, 1957, unused, EX, V1 ....$12.00

Hayley Mills in Search of the Castaways, Whitman, 1962, unused, EX+, F8 ....$25.00

Heckle & Jeckle, coloring book, Treasure, 1957, few pgs colored, VG, F8 ....$16.00

Hee Haw, coloring book, Artcraft, 1963, unused, EX, J5 .$15.00

Hey There It's Yogi Bear, coloring book, Whitman, 1964, few pgs colored, EX, F8 ....$30.00

Hong Kong Phooey, coloring book, Saalfield, 1975, few pgs colored, VG, F8..........$6.00

Howdy Doody, coloring book, Whitman, 1951, few pgs colored, VG, F8 ....$20.00

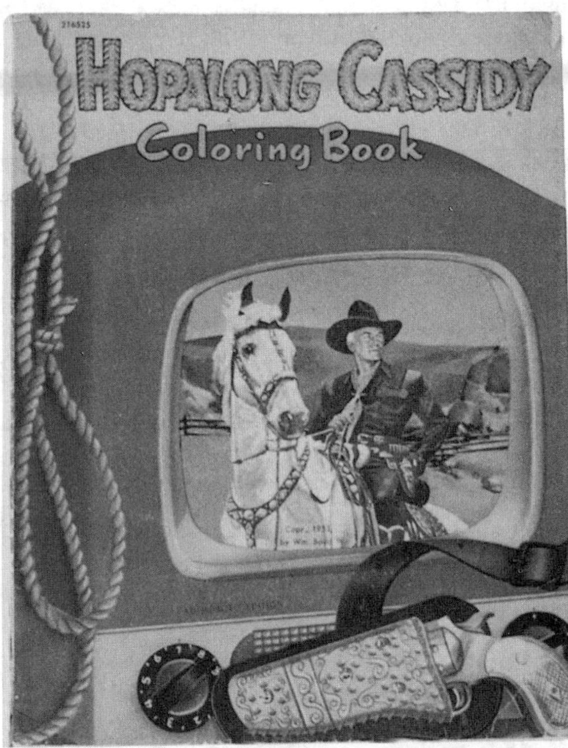

Hopalong Cassidy, coloring book, Lowe, 1950, unused, EX, from $55.00 to $75.00.

Howdy Doody, dot-to-dot book, Whitman, 1955, unused, EX, J5..........$40.00

Huck & Magilla Join the Circus, coloring book, Modern, 1977, unused, NM, F8 ....$25.00

Humpty Dumpty, coloring book, Lowe, 1950s, unused, NM, T2..........$10.00

Incredible Hulk, sticker book, Whitman, 1979, unused, NM, C1..........$18.00

Jetsons, color-by-number book, Whitman, 1963, few pgs colored, VG+, F8..........$25.00

Johnny Tremain, coloring book, Whitman, 1957, few pgs colored, EX, F8 ....$25.00

Kit Carson, coloring book, Lowe, 1957, several pgs colored, NM, F8 ....$25.00

Korg, coloring book, Artcraft, 1975, unused, EX, H4.......$15.00

Krazy Cat, coloring book, Lowe, 1963, unused, M, F8......$25.00

Land of the Giants, coloring book, Whitman, 1969, unused, NM, F8..........$45.00

Land of the Lost, coloring book, Whitman, 1975, several pgs colored, EX, F8..........$15.00

Lassie, coloring book, Whitman, 1961, several pgs colored, EX, F8 ....$18.00

Laugh-In, sticker book, 1968, unused, M, V1 ....$25.00

Laurel & Hardy, coloring book, Whitman, 1968, unused, NM, J5 ....$25.00

Little Lulu, coloring book, Whitman, 1944, several pgs colored, EX, F8..........$40.00

Little Lulu, paint book, Kleenex premium, 1951, unused, EX, A $50.00

Little Monsters, coloring book, Watkins-Strathmore, 1965, few pgs colored, EX, F8 ....$35.00

Little Orphan Annie, coloring book, Saalfield, 1930, all pgs colored, VG, F8 ....$35.00

Love Bug, coloring book, Hunts premium, 1969, several pgs colored, VG+, F8..........$15.00

Lucky Locket Kiddles, coloring book, Whitman, few pgs colored, EX, P2 ....$75.00

Magilla Gorilla, coloring book, Whitman, 1967, few pgs colored, VG, F8 ....$15.00

Magilla Gorilla Vs Yogi Bear for President, coloring book, Whitman, 1964, unused, EX, F8 ....$30.00

Major Matt Mason, punch-out book, Whitman, 1969, unpunched, NM, A $175.00

Mary Poppins, coloring book, Whitman, 1964, few pgs colored, EX, F8..........$25.00

Mary Poppins, dot-to-dot book, Whitman, 1973, few pgs colored, VG, F8 ....$15.00

Merrie Melodies, coloring book, Whitman, 1935, few pgs colored, EX, A $60.00

Mighty Mouse, activity book, Lowe, 1954, unused, NM, from $50 to $75.00

Millie the Lovable Monster, coloring book, Artcraft, 1963, several pgs colored, EX, F8 ....$18.00

Miracle of the White Stallions, Whitman, 1963, few pgs colored, EX+, F8..........$15.00

Mister Ed, coloring book, Whitman, 1963, few pgs colored, EX, F8 ....$25.00

Monroes, coloring book, Saalfield, 1966, unused, VG+, T2........$30.00

Photo courtesy David Longest

Mother Goose, paint book, Saalfield, 1908, unused, EX, $40.00.

Mr Magoo Trace & Color, Mayflower, 1980, unused, M, F8.......$20.00
Mr Peabody, coloring book, Whitman, 1977, unused, NM, J5....$15.00
My Favorite Martian, coloring book, Whitman, 1964, few pgs colored, EX, F8..$40.00
My Three Sons, coloring book, Whitman, 1967, unused, NM, C1...$45.00
National Velvet, coloring book, Whitman, 1961, several pgs colored, VG, F8 ....$15.00
Parade of Comics, sticker book, Saalfield, 1968, unused, NM, A..$35.00
Partridge Family, coloring book, Saalfield, 1970, several pgs colored, VG, F8 ....$25.00
Partridge Family, Pictorial Activity Album, Artcraft, 1973, unused, EX, F8 ....$30.00
Pat Brady, coloring book, Whitman, 1956, few pgs colored, EX, F8 ....$30.00
Pebbles & Bamm-Bamm, coloring book, Whitman, 1964, unused, NM, J2 ....$25.00
Pebbles & Bamm-Bamm, sticker book, Whitman, 1964, few stickers applied, EX, F8..$25.00
Pepper at School, sticker book, Whitman, 1966, unused, VG $20.00
PJ, coloring book, Whitman, 1971, few pgs colored, EX, F8 ....$15.00
Play Safe, coloring book, Lowe, 1968-72, unused, M, T2 ...$6.00

Popeye, A Great Big Punchout, Whitman, 1961, unused, NM, A, $125.00; Donald Duck and His Friends, A Great Big Punchout, Whitman, 1961, unused, NM, A, $100.00; Yogi Bear and His Friends, A Great Big Punchout, Whitman, 1961, unused, NM, A, $100.00.

Popeye, dot-to-dot book, Whitman, 1972, unused, NM, J5..$25.00
Porky Pig, coloring book, Saalfield, 1938, several pgs colored, NM, T2 ....$70.00
Raggedy Ann, coloring book, Whitman, 1968, few pgs colored, NM, F8..$30.00
Ramar of the Jungle, coloring book, Saalfield, 1956, several pgs colored, VG, F8 ....$25.00
Rango, coloring book, Saalfield, 1967, unused, NM, F8...$35.00
Reg'lar Fellers, paint book, Whitman, 1932, unused, EX, T2 ...$30.00
Reluctant Astronaut, coloring book, Artcraft, 1967, few pgs colored, EX, F8 ....$28.00
Ricochet Rabbit, coloring book, Whitman, 1964, few pgs colored, NM, F8...$35.00
Ripcord, coloring book, Saalfield, 1963, unused, NM, F8..$30.00
Robin Hood, coloring book, Saalfield, 1950s, unused, EX, T2 ....$12.00
Roger & Anita, coloring book, Watkins-Strathmore, 1961, few pgs colored, EX, F8 ....$25.00
Roy Rogers & Dale Evans, coloring book, Whitman, 1958, several pgs colored, VG, J5 ....$25.00
Rudolph the Red-Nosed Reindeer, coloring book, Lowe, 1963, unused, EX, T2..$15.00
Sabrina, coloring book, Whitman, 1971, few pgs colored, VG, T2...$20.00
School Days, coloring book, Lowe, 1965, unused, M, T2 .$10.00
Shari Lewis & Her Puppets, coloring book, Saalfield, 1958, few pgs colored, EX, F8 ....$28.00
Shazam! Double Trouble, Giant Comics To Color, Whitman, 1975, unused, NM, F8 ....$15.00
Shirley Temple, coloring book, Saalfield, 1935, all pgs colored, VG, F8 ....$25.00
Six Million Dollar Man, coloring book, Whitman, 1977, unused, EX, F8..$10.00
Sky Rocket, coloring book, Lowe, 1959, unused, NM, T2..$15.00
Smokey Bear, coloring book, Whitman, 1958, few pgs colored, EX, J5 ....$15.00
Snow White & the Seven Dwarfs, coloring book, Whitman, 1952, few pgs colored, NM, F8 ....$18.00

Snow White and the Seven Dwarfs, cutout book, Deans, 1939, unused, NM, A, $285.00.

Space Mouse, coloring book, Saalfield, 1966, unused, NM, F8 ....$30.00
Space: 1999, coloring book, Whitman, 1970s, unused, EX, F8 ....$10.00
Spin & Marty, coloring book, Whitman, 1956, several pgs colored, EX, F8 ....$25.00
Spooky, coloring book, Saalfield, 1969, several pgs colored, EX, F8 ....$20.00

Star Trek, coloring book, Saalfield, 1975, unused, NM, F8 .... **$25.00**
Steve Canyon, coloring book, Saalfield, 1952, few pgs colored, EX, T2 .... **$30.00**
Stingray, coloring book, Whitman, 1966, few pgs colored, EX, F8 .... **$30.00**
Stingray, sticker book, Whitman, 1966, all stickers applied, EX, F8 .... **$30.00**
Strange World of Mr Mom, coloring book, 1962, unused, M, V1 .... **$30.00**
Super Circus, coloring book, Whitman, 1953, unused, NM, F8 .... **$30.00**
Sword in the Stone, sticker book, Whitman, 1963, several stickers applied, VG, F8 .... **$15.00**
Tales of the Texas Rangers, coloring book, Saalfield, 1958, few pgs colored, NM, F8 .... **$30.00**
Tales of the Vikings, coloring book, Saalfield, 1960, few pgs colored, NM, F8 .... **$25.00**
Tammy's Vacation, coloring book, Watkins-Strathmore, 1960s, unused, M **$20.00**
Tarzan, coloring book, Whitman, 1966, 1 pg colored, EX, F8 .... **$15.00**
Tennessee Tuxedo, coloring book, Whitman, 1975, unused, NM, J5 .... **$25.00**
Terry & the Pirates, coloring book, Saalfield, 1946, few pgs colored, EX, T2 .... **$18.00**
Three Stooges, activity book, Playmore, 1983, few pgs colored, EX, H4 .... **$12.00**
Thunderbirds, coloring book, Whitman, 1968, few pgs colored, NM, F8 .... **$28.00**
Tom & Jerry, coloring book, Whitman, 1952, few pgs colored, EX, F8 .... **$20.00**
Tommy Tortoise, coloring book, Saalfield, 1966, few pgs colored, VG+, T2 .... **$12.00**
Top Cat, coloring book, Whitman, 1961, several pgs colored, EX, F8 .... **$35.00**
Treasure Island Adventure, coloring book, Lowe, 1950s, unused, NM, T2 .... **$10.00**
Tweety Bird, coloring book, Whitman, 1955, few pgs colored, EX, T2 .... **$20.00**
Underdog, dot-to-dot book, Whitman, 1980, few pgs colored, VG, F8 .... **$12.00**
Wacky Races, coloring book, Whitman, 1971, unused, NM, F8 .... **$35.00**
Wagon Train, coloring book, Whitman, 1959, several pgs colored, EX, F8 .... **$25.00**
Walt Disney Around the World, coloring book, Whitman, 1957, few pgs colored, VG, F8 .... **$10.00**
Walt Disney's Fairy Tales, coloring book, Whitman, 1960s, few pgs colored, EX, F8 .... **$35.00**
Walt Disney's Fun With a Camera, coloring book, Whitman, 1957, few pgs colored, EX, F8 .... **$12.00**
Walt Disney's Fun With Music, coloring book, Whitman, 1957, few pgs colored, EX, F8 .... **$12.00**
Walt Disney's Magic Forest, coloring book, Watkins-Strathmore, 1959, few pgs colored, EX, T2 .... **$15.00**
Walt Disney's Swim Fun, coloring book, Whitman, 1957, few pgs colored, VG, F8 .... **$10.00**
Walt Disney's True-Life Adventures, coloring book, Whitman, 1964, few pgs colored, EX, F8 .... **$10.00**
Waltons, coloring book, Whitman, 1975, unused, EX, F8 .. **$15.00**
Winnie the Pooh, sticker book, Whitman, 1965, few stickers applied, NM, F8 .... **$25.00**
Wonder Woman & the Menace of the Mole Men, Giant Comics to Color, Whitman, 1975, unused, NM, F8 .. **$25.00**
Wonders of the Animal Kingdom, sticker book, Golden Glow, 1959, few stickers applied, scarce, EX, T2 .... **$20.00**
Woody Woodpecker, Magic Paintless Paint Book, Whitman, 1959, several pgs pnt, VG, F8 .... **$15.00**
World's Fair, coloring book, Spertus, 1963, unused, M, F8 .. **$25.00**
Zorro, trace & color book, Whitman, 1958, few pgs colored, NM, C1 .... **$35.00**
101 Dalmatians, coloring book, Whitman, 1960, few pgs colored, VG+, F8 .... **$20.00**

Comic Books

For more than a half a century, kids of America raced to the bookstand as soon as the new comics came in for the month and for 10¢ an issue kept up on the adventures of their favorite super heroes, cowboys, space explorers, and cartoon characters. By far most were eventually discarded — after they were traded one friend to another, stacked on closet shelves, and finally confiscated by Mom. Discount the survivors that were torn or otherwise damaged over the years and those about the mundane, and of those remaining, some could be quite valuable. In fact, first

All-Flash Quarterly, DC Comics #1, NM, $1,500.00.

editions of high-grade comics books or those showcasing the first appearance of a major character often bring $500.00 and more. Rarity, age, and quality of the artwork are prime factors in determining value, and condition is critical. If you want to seriously collect comic books, you'll need to refer to a good comic book price guide such as Overstreet's.

Advisor: Ken Mitchell (M14).

Other Sources: A3, P3, K1 (for Simpson's Comics)

Adventures of Bob Hope, #30, VG, M14..........................$25.00
Al Capp's Wolf Gal, #2, 1952, VG+, M14 ....$55.00
Apache Trail, #3, 1958, NM, M14...................................$15.00
Avengers, Marvel Comics #1, 1963, VG $300.00
Bat Masterson, Dell Four-Color #1013, 1959, EX, F8.......$35.00

Photo courtesy Bill Bruegman

Batman, DC Comics #4, NM, $3,000.00.

Batman & Robin Battle Mutiny in the Big House, DC Comics #46, 1948, scarce, EX, A $145.00
Ben Casey, Dell #9, 1964, photo cover, NM, F8...............$15.00
Best of Donald Duck & Scrooge, #2, 1967, EX, M14 ....$40.00
Bonanza, #207, 1962, EX, M14 ....$60.00
Brave & the Bold Justice League of America, DC Comics #28, 1960, VG, A $250.00
Buck Jones, Dell Four-Color #652, 1955, EX+ $10.00
Bugs Bunny, Dell Four-Color #164, VG, M14..................$30.00
Bugs Bunny, Dell Four-Color #298, 1950, VG, F8 ....$15.00
Bugs Bunny Christmas Funnies, #7, EX, M14...................$45.00
Bullwinkle & Rocky, Gold Key #9, 1973, EX, F8 ....$12.00
Captain Midnight, #37, EX, M14......................................$85.00
Challengers of the Unknown, #28, EX, M14....................$40.00
Cheyenne, Dell #16, 1960, EX $15.00
Christmas & Archie, Archie Comics #1, 1974, EX..........$10.00
Christmas in Disneyland, #1, EX, M14 ....$90.00

Cisco Kid, Dell, 1952, NM, $15.00.

Conan the Barbarian, Marvel Treasury #4, 1975, oversized, NM, F8...$8.00

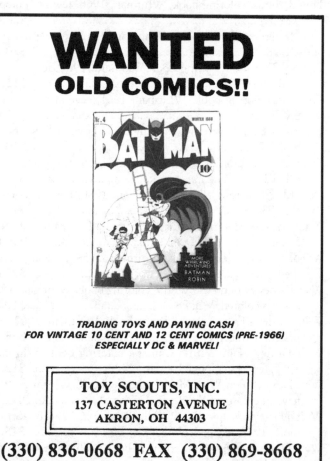

Daredevil, Marvel Comics #1, 1964, VG, A $165.00
Dark Shadows, Gold Key #5, 1970, NM, F8 ....$50.00
David & Goliath, Dell Four-Color #1205, 1961, VG, F8 .$20.00
Dennis the Menace, #9, G, M14 ....$10.00
Dick Tracy, Dell #4, NM, D11 ....$100.00
Dick Tracy, Harvey #58, VG $17.00
Donald Duck, Dell Four-Color #62, 1945, NM, M14 .$1,200.00
Donald Duck in Disneyland, #1, NM, M14 ....$125.00
Dr Who & the Daleks, Dell #1, 1966, VG, T2 ....$15.00

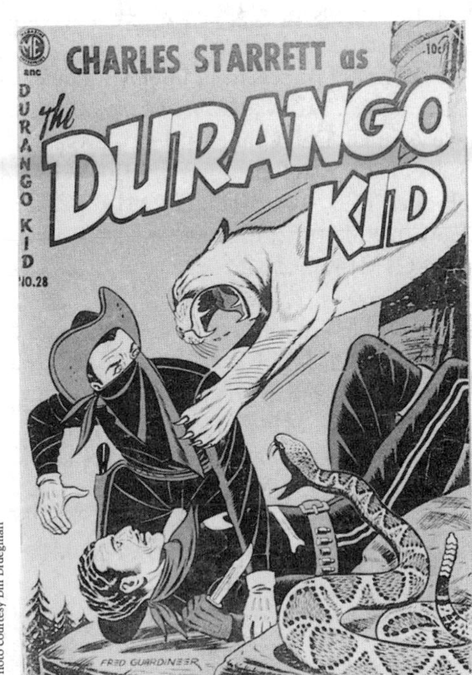

Photo courtesy Bill Bruegman

Durango Kid, #28, NM, $15.00.

Photo courtesy Bill Bruegman

Gene Autry Comics, Dell, EX, $10.00.

Felix the Cat, Dell #18, 1953, VG, F8 ....$10.00
Felix the Cat, Dell #2, 1948, VG, F8 ....$25.00
Felix the Cat, Dell Four-Color #162, 1947, EX................$40.00
Garrison's Gorillas, Dell #3, 1968, photo cover, EX, F8 ...$10.00
Gentle Ben, Dell #4, 1968, photo cover, VG, F8...............$6.00
George of the Jungle, Dell Giant #1, EX, M14 ....$40.00
Hand of Zorro, Dell Four-Color #574, 1954, EX..............$40.00
Hot Wheels, DC Comics #1, 1970, NM $30.00
Howdy Doody, Dell #15, 1952, EX....................................$25.00
Huey, Dewey & Louie Back to School, Dell Giant #22, NM, M14 ....$85.00
Human Torch Battling the Submariner, #8, NM, from $2,200 to $2,600.00

Incredible Hulk, Marvel Comics, 1962, EX, $1,000.00.

Incredible Hulk, Marvel Comics #6, 1963, EX, A $300.00
Josie & the Pussycats, Archie #18, 1966, EX $10.00
Josie & the Pussycats, Archie #6, 1964, EX $15.00
Lone Ranger, Dell #70, 1954, EX $20.00
Marge's Little Lulu, Dell #42, 1951, VG $20.00
Men Into Space, Dell Four-Color #1083, 1960, photo cover, NM, F8..$30.00
Mighty Crusaders, Archie #2, 1966, VG $5.00
Mod Squad, Dell #5, 1970, NM...$10.00
Mutt & Jeff, DC Comics #39, 1948, EX, F8 ....$12.00
No Time for Sergeants, Dell #2, 1965, EX, F8 ....$12.00
Oswald the Rabbit, Dell Four-Color #102, 1946, VG.......$25.00
Outer Limits, Dell #4, 1964, EX, F8 ....$15.00
Playful Little Audry, #1, EX, M14..................................$110.00
Popeye, Dell #48, 1959, EX, F8 ....$12.00
Raggedy Ann & Andy, Dell Giant #2, 1965, EX, M14 ......$8.00
Rawhide Kid, #5, VG, M14 ....$30.00
Red Ryder, Dell #69, 1949, EX..$20.00
Regards from Captain Wonder, Kid Komics #1, NM ..$2,000.00
Restless Gun, #1045, EX, M14 ....$55.00

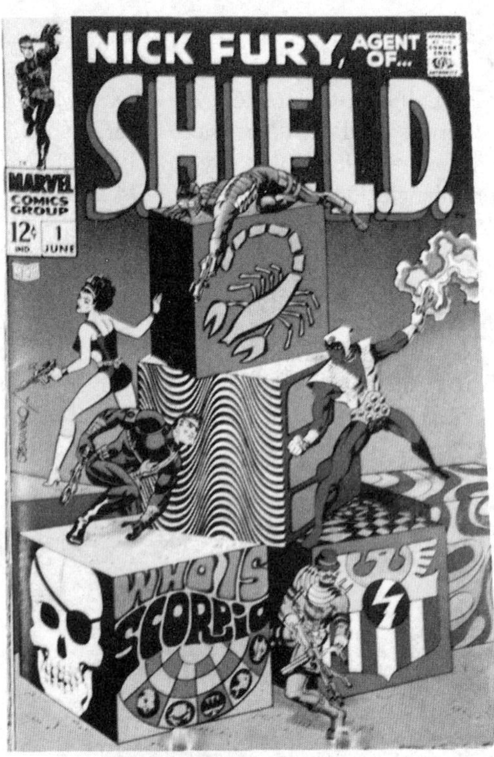

Nick Fury, Agent of Shield, Marvel Comics, EX, $15.00.

Richie Rich, #23, VG, M14...$15.00
Rifleman, Dell #5, 1960, photo cover, EX.........................$30.00
Rifleman, Gold Key #16, 1963, VG, F8 ....$15.00
Road Runner, Gold Key #39, 1973, NM $5.00
Rudolph the Red-Nosed Reindeer, DC Comics, 1952, EX ..$25.00

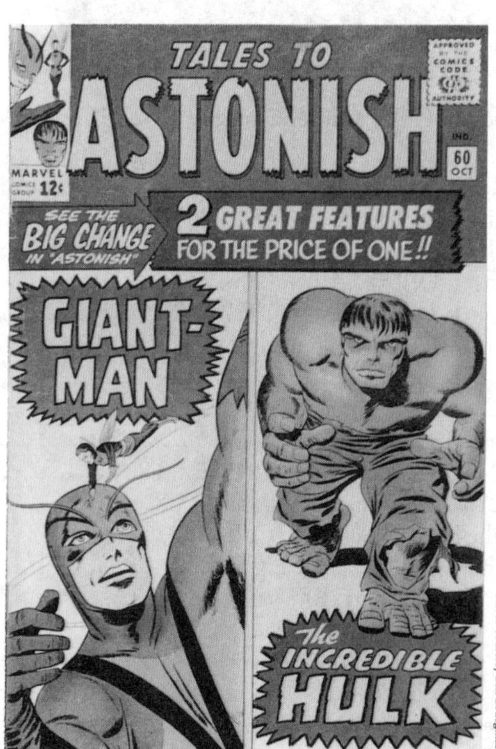

Photo courtesy Bill Bruegman

Tales to Astonish, Marvel Comics, NM, $50.00.

Ruff & Reddy, #7, EX, M14...$35.00
Savage Sword Conan, #3, NM, M14................................$15.00
Secret Agent, Gold Key #1, 1966, photo cover, EX $30.00
Sergeant Preston of the Yukon, #18, NM, M14................$35.00
Silly Symphonies, #7, NM, M14....................................$100.00
Sleeping Beauty, #984, 1959, NM, M14 ....$90.00
Space Busters, #2, 1952, EX, M14.................................$175.00
Space Mouse, Dell Four-Color #132, 1960, VG, F8..........$15.00
Steve Canyon, Dell Four-Color #641, 1955, NM $35.00
Superman, #8, 1941, EX, M14...$595.00
Superman's Pal Jimmy Olsen, #23, G+, M14....................$15.00
Tales of the Unexpected, #74, EX, M14 ....$25.00
Tarzan Saves the Proud Princess from Enemy Raiders, Dell #119, 1960, EX..$25.00
Tarzan's Jungle Annual, Dell Giant #4, 1955, EX $25.00
Teddy Roosevelt & His Rough Riders, Avon, 1950, VG, M14.$35.00
Terry & the Pirates, Dell #101, 1945, EX, M14...............$80.00
Tex Ritter, Fawcett #11, 1952, EX $20.00
Texas Kid, #9, VG, M14..$15.00
Thunder Agents, Tower #12, EX, M14 ....$10.00
Tillie the Toiler, Dell Four-Color #195, 1948, EX............$15.00
Tom Corbett Space Cadet, #9, EX, M14 ....$50.00
Tom Mix, Fawcett #10, 1948, VG....................................$40.00
Twilight Zone, #1288, EX, M14 ....$25.00
Uncle Scrooge Goes to Disneyland, #1, EX, M14 ....$235.00
Untouchables, Dell #207, EX, M14.................................$40.00
Voyage to the Bottom of the Sea, Gold Key #1, 1964, EX..$20.00
Walt Disney's Merry Christmas, Dell Giant #39, NM, M14....$190.00

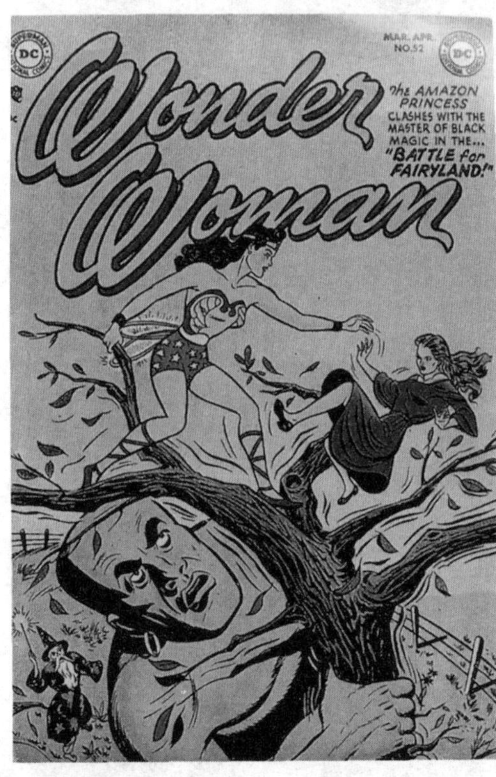

Wonder Woman, DC Comics #52, EX, $25.00.

Woody Woodpecker, #1, 1947, EX, M14..........................$90.00
Woody Woodpecker, Dell Four-Color #374, 1952, NM, F8 ..$25.00

World's Finest Comics, DC Comics #32, 1948, features Batman & Superman, EX....................$125.00
Zane Grey's Stories of the West, #270, VG, M14....................$15.00
Zorro, Dell #13, 1961, EX+....................$35.00
101 Dalmatians, Dell Four-Color #1183, 1961, EX, F8....................$25.00

Corgi

Corgi vehicles are among the favorites of the diecast collectors; they've been made in Great Britain since 1956, and they're still in production today. They were well detailed and ruggedly built to last. Some of the most expensive Corgi's on today's collector market are the character-related vehicles, for instance, James Bond (there are several variations), Batman, and Man From U.N.C.L.E.

Values are for mint-in-the-box or mint-in-package examples.

Other Sources: G2, L1, N3, W1

#050, Massey-Ferguson 50B Tractor....................$50.00
#050, Massey-Ferguson 65 Tractor....................$110.00
#051, Massey-Ferguson Tipper Trailer....................$25.00
#053, Massey-Ferguson Tractor Shovel....................$100.00
#054, Fordson Half-Track Tractor....................$160.00
#054, Massey-Ferguson Tractor Shovel....................$50.00
#055, David Brown Tractor....................$50.00
#055, Fordson Major Tractor....................$100.00
#056, Plough....................$25.00
#057, Massey-Ferguson Tractor & Fork....................$110.00
#058, Beast Carrier....................$40.00
#060, Fordson Power Major Tractor....................$100.00
#061, Four-Furrow Plough....................$20.00
#062, Ford Tipper Trailer....................$20.00
#064, Conveyor on Jeep....................$75.00
#066, Massey-Ferguson Tractor....................$85.00
#067, Ford Super Major Tractor....................$90.00
#069, Massey-Ferguson Tractor Shovel....................$100.00
#071, Fordson Disc Harrow....................$20.00
#072, Ford 5000 Tractor & Trencher....................$130.00
#073, Massey-Ferguson Tractor & Saw....................$125.00
#074, Ford 5000 Tractor & Scoop....................$100.00
#100, Dropside Trailer....................$20.00
#101, Platform Tractor....................$20.00
#102, Pony Trailer....................$25.00
#104, Dolphin Cabin Cruiser....................$30.00
#107, Batboat & Trailer....................$125.00
#109, Penny Burn Trailer....................$50.00
#112, Rice Horse Box....................$45.00
#150, Surtees TS9....................$40.00
#150, Vanwall, regular....................$70.00
#151, Lotus XI, regular....................$80.00
#151, McLaren Yardley M19A....................$30.00
#152, BRM Racer....................$80.00
#152, Ferrari 312 B2....................$35.00
#153, Bluebird Record Car....................$125.00
#153, Team Surtees....................$35.00
#154, Ferrari Formula I....................$50.00
#154, Lotus John Player....................$45.00
#154, Lotus Texaco Special....................$45.00
#155, Shadow F1 Racer....................$40.00
#156, Shadow F1, Graham Hill....................$40.00
#158, Lotus Climax....................$50.00
#158, Tyrrell-Ford Elf....................$40.00
#159, Cooper Maserati....................$50.00
#159, Indianapolis Racer....................$45.00
#160, Hesketh Racer....................$45.00
#161, Elf-Tyrrell Project 34....................$50.00
#161, Santa Pod Commuter....................$45.00
#162, Quartermaster Dragster....................$40.00
#162, Tyrell P34 Racer....................$40.00
#163, Santa Pod Dragster....................$50.00
#164, Wild Honey Dragster....................$50.00
#165, Adams Bros Dragster....................$40.00
#166, Ford Mustang....................$45.00
#167, USA Racing Buggy....................$35.00
#169, Starfighter Jet Dragster....................$40.00
#170, John Wolfe's Dragster....................$40.00
#190, Lotus John Player Special....................$60.00
#191, McLaren Texaco-Marlboro....................$65.00
#200, BMC Mini 1000....................$50.00
#200, Ford Consul, dual colors....................$200.00
#200, Ford Consul, solid colors....................$175.00
#200m, Ford Consul, w/motor....................$200.00
#201, Austin Cambridge....................$160.00
#201, Saint's Volvo....................$150.00
#201m, Austin Cambridge, w/motor....................$200.00
#202, Morris Cowley....................$150.00
#202, Renault R16....................$40.00
#202m, Morris Cowley, w/motor....................$175.00
#203, Detomaso Mangust....................$40.00
#203, Vauxhall Velox, dual colors....................$200.00
#203, Vauxhall Velox, solid colors....................$175.00
#203, Vauxhall Velox, w/motor, dual colors....................$300.00
#203, Vauxhall Velox, w/motor, red or yel....................$200.00
#204, Morris Mini-Minor, bl....................$200.00
#204, Rover 90, other colors....................$175.00
#204, Rover 90, wht & red....................$300.00
#204m, Rover 90, w/motor....................$200.00
#205, Riley Pathfinder, bl....................$175.00

#206, Hillman Husky, metallic blue and silver, $175.00.

#205, Riley Pathfinder, red.....$130.00
#205m, Riley Pathfinder, w/motor, bl.....$175.00
#205m, Riley Pathfinder, w/motor, red.....$225.00
#206, Hillman Husky Estate, solid colors.....$130.00
#206m, Hillman Husky Estate, w/motor.....$175.00
#207, Standard Vanguard.....$125.00
#207m, Standard Vanguard, w/motor.....$175.00
#208, Jaguar 2.4 Saloon.....$140.00
#208m, Jaguar 2.4 Saloon, w/motor.....$180.00
#208s, Jaguar 2.4 Saloon, w/suspension.....$135.00
#209, Riley Police Car.....$120.00
#210, Citroen DS19.....$90.00
#210s, Citroen DS19, w/suspension.....$100.00
#211, Studebaker Golden Hawk.....$125.00
#211m, Studebaker Golden Hawk, w/motor.....$175.00
#211s, Studebaker Golden Hawk, plated, w/suspension.$125.00
#213, Jaguar Fire Chief.....$150.00
#213s, Jaguar Fire Chief, w/suspension.....$200.00
#214, Ford Thunderbird.....$125.00
#214m, Ford Thunderbird, w/motor.....$300.00
#214s, Ford Thunderbird, w/suspension.....$100.00
#215, Ford Thunderbird Sport.....$125.00
#215s, Ford Thunderbird Sport, w/suspension.....$100.00
#216, Austin A-40, red & blk.....$175.00
#216, Austin A-40, 2-tone bl.....$100.00
#216m, Austin A-40, w/motor.....$300.00
#217, Fiat 1800.....$80.00
#218, Austin Martin DB4.....$110.00
#219, Plymouth Suburban.....$95.00
#220, Chevrolet Impala.....$80.00
#221, Chevrolet Impala Cab.....$110.00
#222, Renault Floride.....$90.00
#223, Chevrolet Police.....$110.00
#224, Bentley Continental.....$100.00
#225, Austin 7, red.....$100.00
#225, Austin 7, yel.....$300.00
#226, Morris Mini-Minor.....$100.00
#227, Mini-Cooper Rally.....$275.00
#228, Volvo P-1800.....$80.00
#229, Chevrolet Corvair.....$70.00
#230, Mercedes Benz 222, red.....$75.00
#231, Triumph Herald.....$100.00
#232, Fiat 2100.....$75.00

Photo courtesy of Al Rapp

#234, Ford Consul Classic, $85.00.

#233, Heinkel Trojan.....$90.00
#235, Oldsmobile Super 88.....$75.00
#236, Motor School, right-hand drive.....$90.00
#237, Oldsmobile Sheriff's Car.....$100.00
#238, Jaguar MK10, metallic gr or silver.....$190.00
#238, Jaguar MK10, metallic red or bl.....$125.00
#239, VW Karmann Ghia.....$90.00
#240, Fiat 500 Jolly.....$145.00
#241, Chrysler Ghia.....$80.00
#242, Fiat 600 Jolly.....$175.00
#245, Buick Riviera.....$95.00
#246, Chrysler Imperial, metallic turq.....$250.00
#246, Chrysler Imperial, red.....$110.00
#247, Mercedes Benz 600 Pullman.....$75.00
#248, Chevrolet Impala.....$80.00
#249, Morris Mini-Cooper, wicker.....$130.00
#251, Hillman Imp.....$100.00
#252, Rover 2000, metallic bl.....$80.00
#252, Rover 2000, metallic maroon.....$165.00
#253, Mercedes Benz 220SE.....$90.00
#255, Motor School, left-hand drive.....$225.00
#256, VW 1200 East Africa Safari.....$200.00
#258, Saint's Volvo P1800.....$165.00
#259, Citroen Le Dandy, bl.....$180.00
#259, Citroen Le Dandy, maroon.....$120.00
#259, Penguin Mobile.....$50.00
#260, Renault R16.....$45.00

Photo courtesy of Al Rapp

#261, James Bond's Aston Martin DB5, $235.00.

#261, Spiderbuggy.....$100.00
#262, Capt Marvel's Porsche.....$65.00
#262, Lincoln Continental Limo, bl.....$180.00
#262, Lincoln Continental Limo, gold.....$100.00
#263, Rambler Marlin.....$75.00
#264, Incredible Hulk.....$75.00
#264, Oldsmobile Toronado.....$85.00
#265, Supermobile.....$65.00
#266, Chitty-Chitty Bang-Bang, orig.....$350.00
#266, Chitty-Chitty Bang-Bang, replica.....$125.00
#266, Superbike.....$60.00
#267, Batmobile, red 'Bat'-hubs.....$400.00
#267, Batmobile, w/red whizzwheels.....$500.00
#267, Batmobile, w/whizzwheels.....$140.00
#268, Batman's Bat Bike.....$70.00

#269, James Bond's Lotus $100.00
#270, James Bond's Aston Martin, w/tire slashers, 1/43 scale $250.00
#270, James Bond's Aston Martin, w/whizzwheels, 1/43 scale $120.00
#271, Ghia Mangusta De Tomaso $65.00
#271, James Bond's Aston Martin $90.00
#272, James Bond's Citroen 2CV $60.00
#273, Honda Driving School $40.00
#273, Rolls Royce Silver Shadow $100.00
#274, Bentley Mulliner $80.00
#275, Mini Metro, colors other than gold $25.00
#275, Mini Metro, gold $75.00
#275, Rover 2000 TC, gr $75.00
#275, Rover 2000 TC, wht $160.00
#275, Royal Wedding Mini Metro $25.00
#276, Oldsmobile Toronado, metallic red $70.00
#276, Triumph Acclaim $20.00
#277, Monkeemobile $300.00
#277, Triumph Driving School $25.00
#279, Rolls Royce Corniche $30.00
#280, Rolls Royce Silver Shadow, other colors $50.00
#280, Rolls Royce Silver Shadow, silver $80.00
#281, Metro Datapost $20.00
#281, Rover 2000 TC $150.00
#282, Mini Cooper Rally Car $90.00
#283, DAF City Car $40.00
#284, Citroen SM $45.00
#285, Mercedes Benz 240D $25.00
#286, Jaguar XJ12C $45.00
#287, Citroen Dyane $25.00
#288, Minissima $20.00
#289, VW Polo $25.00
#290, Kojak's Buick, no hat $125.00

Photo courtesy of Al Rapp

#290, Kojak Buick, with hat, $75.00.

#291, AMC Pacer $20.00
#291, Mercedes Benz 240 Rally $35.00
#292, Starky & Hutch's Ford Torino $85.00
#293, Renault 5TS $20.00
#294, Renault Alpine $20.00
#298, Magnum PI's Ferrari $50.00
#299, Ford Sierra 2.3 Ghia $20.00
#300, Austin Healey, red or cream $150.00
#300, Austin Healey Sports Car, bl $300.00
#300, Chevrolet Corvette $100.00
#300, Ferrari Daytona $25.00
#301, Iso Grifo 7 Litre $60.00
#301, Lotus Elite $25.00
#301, Triumph TR2 Sports Car $150.00
#302, Hillman Hunter Rally, kangaroo $130.00
#302, MGA Sports Car $140.00
#302, VW Polo $20.00
#303, Mercedes Benz 300SL $100.00
#303, Porsche 924 ....$20.00
#303, Roger Clark's Ford Capri $75.00
#303s, Mercedes Benz 300SL, w/suspension $100.00
#304, Chevrolet SS350 Camaro $65.00
#304, Mercedes Benz 300SL, yel & red $100.00
#304s, Mercedes Benz 300SL, w/suspension $100.00
#305, Mini Marcos GT 850 ....$65.00
#305, Triumph TR3 ....$145.00
#306, Fiat X1/9 ....$30.00
#306, Morris Marina $65.00
#307, Jaguar E-Type $125.00
#307, Renault $20.00
#308, BMW M1 Racer, gold plated $110.00
#308, BMW M1 Racer, yel $25.00
#308, Monte Carlo Mini $100.00
#309, Aston Martin DB4 ....$125.00
#309, Aston Martin DB4, w/spoked hubs $175.00
#309, VW Turbo $20.00
#310, Chevrolet Corvette, bronze $165.00
#310, Chevrolet Corvette, red or silver $65.00
#310, Porsche 924 ....$20.00
#311, Ford Capri, orange $125.00
#311, Ford Capri, red $80.00
#311, Ford Capri, w/gold hubs $150.00
#312, Ford Capri S $35.00
#312, Jaguar E-Type $100.00
#312, Marcos Mantis $50.00
#313, Ford Cortina, bronze or bl $100.00
#313, Ford Cortina, yel $300.00
#314, Ferrari Berlinetta Le Mans $65.00
#314, Supercat Jaguar $30.00
#315, Lotus Elite $35.00
#315, Simca Sports Car, metallic bl $190.00
#315, Simca Sports Car, silver $65.00
#316, Ford GT 70 ....$50.00
#316, NSU Sports Prinz $90.00
#317, Mini Cooper Monte Carlo $200.00
#318, Jaguar XJS $25.00
#318, Lotus Elan, copper $300.00
#318, Lotus Elan, metallic bl $110.00
#318, Lotus Elan, wht $250.00
#319, Jaguar XJS $35.00

#319, Lamborghini P400 GT Miura $35.00
#319, Lotus Elan, gr or yel $140.00
#319, Lotus Elan, bl $100.00

Photo courtesy of Al Rapp

#319, Lotus Elan, red, $100.00.

#320, Saint's Jaguar XJS $85.00
#321, Monte Carlo Mini Cooper, 1965 .... $300.00
#321, Monte Carlo Mini Cooper, 1966, w/autographs ... $600.00
#321, Porsche 924, metallic gr $70.00
#321, Porsche 924, red $25.00
#322, Rover Monte Carlo $180.00
#323, Citroen DS19 Monte Carlo $180.00
#323, Ferrari Daytona 365 GTB4 .... $25.00
#324, Marcos Volvo 1800 GT $70.00
#325, Chevrolet Caprice $65.00
#325, Ford Mustang Competition $80.00
#326, Chevrolet Police Car $40.00
#327, Chevrolet Caprice Cab $40.00
#327, MGB GT $130.00
#328, Hillman Imp Monte Carlo $125.00
#329, Ford Mustang Rally $50.00
#329, Opel Senator, bl or bronze $40.00
#329, Opel Senator, silver $50.00
#330, Porsche Carrera 6, wht & bl $120.00
#330, Porsche Carrera 6, wht & red $60.00
#331, Ford Capri Rally $90.00

Photo courtesy of Al Rapp

#337, Chevrolet Stingray, $65.00.

#332, Lancia Fulvia Sport, red or bl $60.00
#332, Lancia Fulvia Sport, yel & blk $125.00
#332, Opel, Doctor's Car $50.00
#334, Ford Escort $20.00
#334, Mini Magnifique $90.00
#335, Jaguar 4.2 Litre E-Type $125.00
#336, James Bond's Toyota 2000GT $365.00
#338, Chevrolet SS350 Camaro $75.00
#338, Rover 3500 .... $30.00
#339, Rover 3500 Police Car $30.00
#339, 1967 Mini Cooper Monte Carlo, w/roof rack $300.00
#340, Rover Triplex $25.00
#340, 1967 Sunbeam IMP Monte Carlo $135.00
#341, Chevrolet Caprice Racer $25.00
#341, Mini Marcos GT850 .... $60.00
#342, Lamborghini P400 GT Miura $60.00
#342, Professionals Ford Capri $80.00
#342, Professionals Ford Capri, w/chrome bumpers $100.00
#343, Pontiac Firebird $55.00
#344, Ferrari 206 Dino Sport $70.00
#345, Honda Prelude $25.00
#345, MGC GT, orange $300.00
#345, MGC GT, yel $125.00
#346, Citroen 2 CV $20.00
#347, Chevrolet Astro 1 .... $50.00
#348, Pop Art Mustang Stock Car $140.00
#348, Vegas Ford Thunderbird $85.00
#349, Pop Art Morris Mini, minimum value $1,500.00
#350, Thunderbird Guided Missile $125.00
#351, RAF Land Rover $80.00

Photo courtesy of Al Rapp

#352, RAF Vanguard Staff Car, $100.00.

#353, Road Scanner $60.00
#354, Commer Military Ambulance $110.00
#355, Commer Military Police $135.00
#356, VW Personnel Carrier $135.00
#357, Land Rover Weapons Carrier $180.00
#358, Oldsmobile Staff Car $125.00
#359, Commer Army Field Kitchen $165.00
#370, Ford Cobra Mustang $25.00
#371, Porsche Carrera $40.00
#373, Peugeot 505 .... $25.00
#373, VW Police Car, Polizei $150.00
#374, Jaguar 4.2 Litre E-Type $90.00

#374, Jaguar 5.3 Litre $70.00
#375, Toyota 2000 GT $75.00
#376, Chevrolet Stingray Stock Car $50.00
#377, Marcos 3 Litre, wht & gray $100.00
#377, Marcos 3 Litre, yel or bl $60.00
#378, Ferrari 308 GT $25.00
#378, MGC GT $140.00
#380, Alfa Romeo P33 $45.00
#380, Beach Buggy $40.00
#381, Renault Turbo $20.00
#382, Lotus Elite $25.00
#382, Porsche Targa 911S $50.00
#383, VW 1200, red or orange $70.00
#383, VW 1200, Swiss PTT $130.00
#383, VW 1200, yel ADAC $200.00
#384, Adams Bros Probe 15 $50.00
#384, Renault 11 GTL, cream $20.00
#384, Renault 11 GTL, maroon $40.00
#384, VW 1200 Rally $70.00
#385, Porsche 917 $40.00
#386, Bertone Runabout $50.00
#387, Chevrolet Corvette Stingray $100.00
#388, Mercedes Benz C111 $40.00
#389, Reliant Bond Bug 700, gr $100.00
#389, Reliant Bond Bug 700 ES, orange $60.00

Photo courtesy of Al Rapp

#391, James Bond 007 Ford Mustang, $250.00.

#392, Bertone Shake Buggy $40.00
#393, Mercedes Benz 350 SL, metallic gr $100.00
#393, Mercedes Benz 350 SL, wht or bl $65.00
#394, Datsun 240Z, East African Safari $45.00
#396, Datsun 240Z, US Rally $45.00
#397, Can Am Porsche Audi $35.00
#400, VW Driving School, bl $65.00
#400, VW Driving School, red $140.00
#401, VW 1200 $60.00
#402, Ford Cortina GXL, wht w/red stripe $80.00
#402, Ford Cortina GXL Police, wht $50.00
#402, Ford Cortina GXL Polizei $150.00
#403, Bedford Daily Express $150.00
#403, Thwaites Dumper $45.00
#403m, Bedford KLG Plugs, w/motor $230.00
#404, Bedford Dormobile, cream, maroon & turq $110.00
#404, Bedford Dormobile, yel & 2-tone bl $200.00
#404, Bedford Dormobile, yel w/bl roof $125.00
#404m, Bedford Dormobile, w/motor $160.00
#405, Bedford Utilicon Fire Department, gr $160.00
#405, Bedford Utilicon Fire Department, red $200.00
#405, Chevrolet Superior Ambulance $40.00
#405, Ford Milk Float $25.00
#405m, Bedford Utilicon Fire Tender, w/motor $225.00
#406, Land Rover $80.00
#406, Mercedes Ambulance $35.00
#406, Mercedes Benz Unimog $50.00
#407, Karrier Mobile Grocers $150.00
#408, Bedford AA Road Service $150.00
#409, Allis Chalmers Fork Lift $30.00
#409, Forward Control Jeep $50.00
#409, Mercedes Dumper $50.00
#411, Karrier Lucozade Van $160.00
#411, Mercedes 240D, orange $80.00
#411, Mercedes 240D Taxi, cream or blk $65.00
#411, Mercedes 240D Taxi, orange w/blk roof $35.00
#412, Bedford Ambulance, split windscreen $130.00
#412, Bedford Ambulance, 1-pc windscreen $250.00
#412, Mercedes Police Car, Police $50.00
#412, Mercedes Police Car, Polizei $40.00
#413, Karrier Bantam Butcher Shop $150.00
#413, Mazda Maintenence Truck $50.00
#413s, Karrier Bantam Butcher Shop, w/suspension $200.00
#414, Bedford Military Ambulance $120.00
#414, Coastguard Jaguar $45.00
#415, Mazda Camper $50.00
#416, Buick Police Car $40.00
#416, Radio Rescue Rover, bl $125.00
#416, Radio Rescue Rover, yel $400.00
#416s, Radio Rescue Rover, w/suspension, bl $100.00
#416s, Radio Rescue Rover, w/suspension, yel $425.00
#417, Land Rover Breakdown $110.00
#417s, Land Rover Breakdown, w/suspension $85.00
#418, Austin Taxi, w/whizzwheels $50.00
#419, Ford Zephyr, Rijks Politie $350.00
#419, Ford Zephyr Politie $300.00
#419, Jeep $30.00
#420, Airbourne Caravan $100.00
#421, Bedford Evening Standard $200.00
#422, Bedford Van, Corgi Toys, bl w/yel roof $500.00
#422, Bedford Van, Corgi Toys, yel w/bl roof $200.00
#422, Riot Police Wagon $45.00
#423, Rough Rider Van $45.00
#424, Ford Zephyr Estate $85.00
#424, Security Van $30.00
#425, London Taxi $25.00
#426, Chipperfield's Circus Booking Office $300.00
#426, Pinder's Circus Booking Office $50.00
#428, Mister Softee's Ice Cream Van $200.00
#428, Renault Police Car $25.00
#429, Jaguar Police Car $40.00
#430, Bermuda Taxi, metallic bl & red $400.00
#430, Porsche 924 Polizei $30.00

Photo courtesy of Al Rapp

#430, Bermuda Taxi, white, $125.00.

#431, VW Pickup, metallic gold $300.00
#431, VW Pickup, yel....$100.00
#432, Vanatic Van....$30.00
#433, VW Delivery Van....$100.00
#434, Charlie's Angels Van....$50.00
#434, VW Kombi....$100.00
#435, Karrier Dairy Van....$125.00
#435, Superman Van....$50.00
#436, Citroen Safari....$100.00
#436, Spider Van....$50.00
#437, Cadillac Ambulance....$100.00
#437, Coca-Cola Van....$50.00
#438, Land Rover, gr....$60.00
#438, Land Rover, Lepra....$400.00
#439, Chevrolet Fire Chief....$100.00
#440, Ford Cortina Estate, w/golfer & caddy....$160.00
#440, Mazda Pickup....$30.00
#441, Jeep....$25.00
#441, VW Toblerone Van....$135.00
#443, Plymouth US Mail....$110.00
#445, Plymouth Suburban....$90.00
#447, Walls Ice Cream Van....$275.00
#448, Police Mini Van, w/dog & handler....$200.00
#448, Renegade Jeep....$20.00

Photo courtesy of Al Rapp

#450, Austin Mini Van, $100.00.

#450, Austin Mini Van, w/pnt grille....$160.00
#450, Peugeot Taxi....$25.00
#452, Commer Lorry....$130.00
#453, Commer Walls Van....$200.00
#454, Commer Platform Lorry....$130.00
#455, Karrier Bantam 2-Ton....$120.00
#456, ERF Dropside Lorry....$110.00
#457, ERF Platform Lorry....$100.00
#457, Talbot Matra Rancho, gr or red....$25.00
#457, Talbot Matra Rancho, wht or orange....$45.00
#458, ERF Tipper Dumper....$85.00
#459, ERF Moorhouse Van....$375.00
#459, Raygo Road Roller....$40.00
#460, ERF Cement Tipper....$90.00
#461, Police Vigilant Range Rover, Police....$35.00
#461, Police Vigilant Range Rover, Politie....$80.00
#462, Commer Van, Co-op....$125.00
#462, Commer Van, Hammonds....$170.00
#463, Commer Ambulance....$100.00
#464, Commer Police Van, City Police, minimum value ..$300.00
#464, Commer Police Van, County Police, bl....$110.00
#464, Commer Police Van, Police, bl....$100.00
#464, Commer Police Van, Police, gr....$750.00
#464, Commer Police Van, Rijks Politie, bl, minimum value...$300.00
#465, Commer Pickup Truck....$65.00
#466, Commer Milk Float, Co-op....$170.00
#466, Commer Milk Float, wht....$70.00
#467, London Routemaster Bus....$75.00
#468, London Transport Routemaster, Church's Shoes, red ..$200.00
#468, London Transport Routemaster, Design Centre, red...$250.00
#468, London Transport Routemaster, Gamages, red.....$200.00
#468, London Transport Routemaster Bus, Corgi Toys, brn, gr or cream....$1,000.00
#468, London Transport Routemaster Bus, Corgi Toys, red..$100.00
#468, London Transport Routemaster Bus, Madame Tussand's, red....$200.00
#468, London Transport Routemaster Bus, Outspan, red .$60.00
#470, Disneyland Bus....$40.00
#470, Forward Control Jeep....$60.00
#470, Greenline Bus....$20.00
#471, Karrier Snack Bar, Joe's Diner....$140.00
#471, Karrier Snack Bar, Potates Frites....$300.00
#471, Silver Jubilee Bus....$40.00
#471, Woolworth Silver Jubilee Bus....$40.00
#472, Public Address Land Rover....$150.00
#474, Ford Musical Walls Ice Cream Van....$250.00
#475, Citroen Ski Safari....$150.00
#477, Land Rover Breakdown, w/whizzwheels....$60.00
#478, Forward Control Jeep, Tower Wagon....$75.00

Photo courtesy of Al Rapp

#481, Chevrolet Police Patrol Car, $125.00.

#479, Mobile Camera Van $150.00
#480, Chevrolet Impala Cab $80.00
#480, Chevrolet Police Car $80.00
#482, Chevrolet Fire Chief Car....................$100.00
#482, Range Rover Ambulance....................$50.00
#483, Dodge Tipper $50.00
#483, Police Range Rover, Belgian $75.00
#484, AMC Pacer Rescue....................$30.00
#484, AMC Pacer Secours....................$50.00
#484, Livestock Transporter $60.00
#484, Mini Countryman Surfer, w/silver grille $175.00
#485, Mini Countrynman Surfer, w/unpnt grille....................$225.00
#486, Chevrolet Kennel Service $100.00
#487, Chipperfield's Circus Parade $200.00
#489, VW Police Car....................$30.00
#490, Touring Caravan....................$25.00
#490, VW Breakdown Truck....................$95.00
#491, Ford Escort Estate $100.00
#492, VW Police Car, Politie....................$275.00
#492, VW Police Car, Polizie $80.00
#492, VW Police Car, w/gr mudguards $300.00
#493, Mazda Pickup $35.00
#494, Bedford Tipper, red & silver....................$175.00

Photo courtesy of Al Rapp

#494, Bedford Tipper Truck, red and yellow, $80.00.

#495, Opel Open Truck....................$20.00
#497, Man From UNCLE, bl....................$250.00
#497, Man From UNCLE, wht, minimum value $600.00
#499, Citroen, 1968 Olympics $175.00
#500, US Army Rover....................$400.00
#503, Chipperfield's Circus Giraffe Transporter....................$125.00
#506, Sunbeam Imp Police....................$125.00
#508, Holiday Minibus $110.00
#509, Porsche Police Car, Polizie $80.00
#509, Porsche Police Car, Ritjks Politie $150.00
#510, Citroen Tour De France $125.00
#511, Chipperfield's Circus Poodle Pickup $600.00
#513, Alpine Rescue Car....................$350.00
#647, Buck Rogers' Starfighter $75.00
#648, Space Shuttle $50.00
#649, James Bond's Space Shuttle....................$80.00
#650, BOAC Concorde, all others (no gold logo on tail)...$30.00
#650, BOAC Concorde, gold logo on tail....................$100.00
#651, Air France Concorde, all others (no gold tail design) $50.00
#651, Air France Concorde, gold tail design....................$140.00
#651, Japan Air Line Concorde $400.00
#653, Air Canada Concorde $325.00
#681, Stunt Bike....................$250.00
#700, Motorway Ambulance $20.00
#701, Intercity Minibus $20.00
#703, Breakdown Truck....................$20.00
#703, Hi Speed Fire Engine $20.00
#801, Ford Thunderbird....................$25.00
#801, Noddy's Car $450.00
#801, Noddy's Car, w/Black-face golly....................$1,000.00
#802, Mercedes Benz 300 Sl $25.00
#802, Popeye's Paddle Wagon....................$550.00
#803, Beatle's Yellow Submarine $550.00
#803, Jaguar XK120 ....$20.00
#804, Jaguar XK120 Rally....................$20.00
#804, Jaguar XK120 Rally, w/spats $50.00
#804, Noddy's Car, Noddy only $275.00
#804, Noddy's Car, w/Mr Tubby $350.00
#805, Hardy Boy's Rolls Royce....................$300.00
#805, Mercedes Benz 300 SC $20.00
#806, Lunar Bug....................$150.00
#806, Mercedes Benz 300 SC $20.00
#807, Dougal's Car....................$300.00
#808, Basil Brush's Car $225.00
#809, Dick Dastardly's Racer....................$150.00
#810, Ford Thunderbird....................$25.00

Photo courtesy of Al Rapp

#811, James Bond's Moon Buggy, $500.00.

#831, Mercedes Benz 300 SL $25.00
#851, Magic Roundabout Train $350.00
#852, Magic Roundabout Carousel $800.00
#853, Magic Roundabout Playground....................$1,500.00
#859, Mr McHenry's Trike $250.00
#900, German Tank....................$50.00
#901, British Centurion....................$50.00
#902, American Tank....................$50.00
#903, British Chieftain Tank....................$50.00
#904, King Tiger Tank....................$50.00
#905, SU100 Tank Destroyer $50.00

#906, Saladin Armoured Car....$50.00
#907, German Rocket Launcher....$75.00
#908, French Recovery Tank....$75.00
#909, Quad Gun Tank, Trailer & Field Gun....$60.00
#920, Bell Helicopter....$30.00
#921, Hughes Helicopter....$30.00
#922, Sikorsky Helicopter....$30.00
#923, Sikorsky Helicopter Military....$30.00
#925, Batcopter....$75.00
#926, Stromberg Helicopter....$75.00
#927, Chopper Squad Helicopter....$60.00
#928, Spidercopter....$90.00
#929, Daily Planet Helicopter....$65.00
#930, DAAX Helicopter....$60.00
#931, Jet Police Helicopter....$50.00

Corgitronics

#1001, Corgitronics Firestreak....$80.00
#1002, Corgitronics Landtrain....$50.00
#1003, Ford Torino....$30.00
#1004, Corgitronics Beep Beep Bus....$40.00
#1005, Police Land Rover....$30.00
#1006, Roadshow, Radio....$50.00
#1007, Land Rover & Compressor....$50.00
#1008, Chevrolet Fire Chief....$40.00
#1009, Maestro MG1600....$50.00
#1011, Firestreak....$40.00

Exploration Models

#2022, Scanotron....$60.00
#2023, Rocketron....$60.00
#2024, Lasertron....$60.00
#2025, Magnetron....$60.00

Gift Sets

#1, Car Transporter Set....$850.00
#1, Ford Sierra & Caravan....$40.00
#1, Ford 500 Tractor & Beast Trailer....$160.00

Photo courtesy of Al Rapp

#2, Land Rover with Pony Trailer, $180.00.

#2, Unimog Dumper....$150.00
#3, Batmobile & Batboat, w/'Bat'-hubs....$400.00
#3, Batmobile & Batboat, w/whizzwheels....$210.00
#3, RAF Land Rover & Missile....$250.00
#4, Country Farm Set....$75.00
#4, RAF Land Rover & Missile....$500.00
#5, Agricultural Set....$300.00
#5, Country Farm Set, w/no hay....$90.00
#5, Racing Car Set....$300.00
#6, Rocket Age Set....$1,000.00
#6, VW Transporter & Cooper Maserati....$175.00
#7, Daktari Set....$150.00
#7, Tractor & Trailer Set....$130.00
#8, Combine Harvester Set....$400.00
#8, Lions of Longleat....$200.00
#9, Corporal Missile & Launcher....$600.00
#9, Tractor w/Shovel & Trailer....$200.00
#10, Centurion Tank & Transporter....$140.00
#10, Jeep & Motorcycle Trailer....$40.00
#10, Rambler Marlin, w/kayaks....$210.00
#11, ERF Truck & Trailer....$200.00
#11, London Set, no Policeman....$135.00
#11, London Set, w/Policeman....$600.00
#12, Chipperfield's Circus Crane Truck & Cage....$300.00
#12, Glider Set....$80.00
#12, Grand Prix Set....$450.00
#13, Fordson Tractor & Plough....$150.00
#13, Peugeot Tour De France....$90.00
#13, Renault Tour De France....$150.00
#14, Giant Daktari Set....$500.00
#14, Tower Wagon....$100.00
#15, Land Rover & Horsebox....$100.00
#15, Silvertone Set....$1,800.00
#16, Ecurie Ecosse Set....$500.00

Photo courtesy Al Rapp

#17, Land Rover and Ferrari, $200.00.

#17, Military Set....$85.00
#18, Emergency Set....$80.00
#18, Fordson Tractor & Plough....$125.00
#19, Chipperfield's Circus Rover & Elephant Trailer....$325.00
#19, Emergency Set....$80.00
#19, Flying Club Set....$85.00
#20, Car Transporter Set, minimum value....$900.00

#20, Emergency Set........$70.00
#20, Golden Guinea Set........$300.00
#21, Chipperfield's Circus Crane & Trailer, minimum value........$1,600.00
#21, ERF Milk Truck & Trailer........$350.00
#21, Superman Set........$250.00
#22, James Bond Set........$265.00
#23, Chipperfield's Circus Set, w/Booking Office........$1,000.00
#23, Spiderman Set........$200.00
#24, Construction Set........$150.00
#24, Mercedes & Caravan........$50.00
#25, Mantra Rancho & Trailer........$50.00
#25, Shell or BP Garage Set, minimum value........$1,600.00
#25, VW Transporter & Cooper Masarati........$160.00
#26, Beach Bug Set........$50.00
#26, Matra Rancho & Racer........$75.00
#27, Priestman Shovel Set........$195.00
#28, Mazda Pickup & Dinghy, w/trailer........$60.00
#28, Transporter Set........$800.00
#29, Ferrari Racing Set........$80.00
#29, Jeep & Horsebox........$40.00
#29, Tractor & Trailer........$140.00
#30, Grand Prix Set........$285.00
#30, Pinder's Circus Rover & Trailer........$135.00
#31, Buick Riviera & Boat........$225.00
#31, Safari Set........$100.00
#32, Lotus Racing Set........$110.00
#32, Tractor & Trailer........$170.00
#33, Fordson Tractor & Carrier........$150.00
#35, Chopper Squad........$60.00
#35, London Set........$175.00
#36, Tarzan Set........$250.00

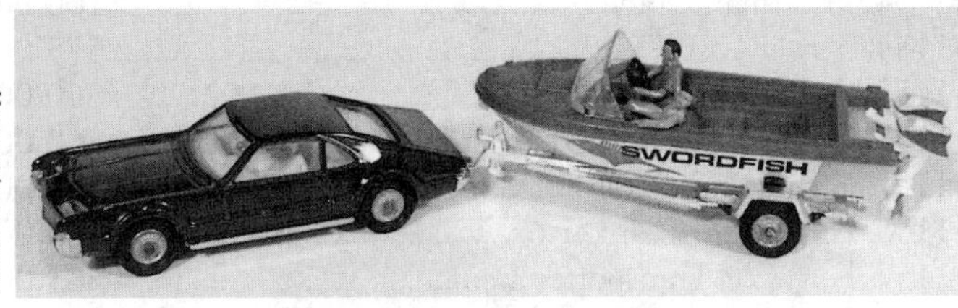

Photo courtesy of Al Rapp

#36, Tornado with Speedboat, $250.00.

#37, Fiat & Boat........$60.00
#37, Lotus Racing Team........$500.00
#38, Jaguar & Powerboat........$75.00
#38, Mini Camping Set........$100.00
#38, Monte Carlo Set........$600.00
#40, Avenger Set, w/Bentley, gr........$800.00
#40, Avenger Set, w/Bentley, red........$650.00
#40, Batman Set........$275.00
#41, Ford Transporter Set........$850.00
#41, Silver Jubilee State Landau........$40.00
#42, Agricultural Set........$80.00
#43, Silo & Conveyor........$65.00
#44, Police Rover Set........$65.00
#45, All Winners Set........$800.00
#45, Royal Canadian Mounted Police........$85.00
#46, All Winners Set........$600.00
#46, Super Karts........$30.00
#47, Ford Tractor & Conveyor........$195.00
#47, Pony Club Set........$50.00
#48, Ford Transporter Set........$600.00
#48, Jean Richards' Circus Set........$200.00
#48, Scammell Transport Set........$900.00
#49, Flying Club Set........$50.00

Huskies

Huskies were marketed exclusively through the Woolworth stores from 1965 to 1969. In 1970, Corgi Juniors were introduced. Both lines were sold in blister packs. Models produced up to 1975 (as dated on the package) are valued from $15.00 to $30.00 (MIP), except for the character-related examples listed below.

#1001A, James Bond's Aston Martin, Husky on base....$200.00
#1001B, James Bond Aston Martin, Junior on base........$175.00
#1002A, Batmobile, Husky on base........$200.00
#1003A, Bat Boat, Husky on base........$125.00
#1003B, Bat Boat, Junior on base........$85.00
#1004A, Monkeemobile, Husky on base........$200.00
#1004B, Monkeemobile, Junior on base........$175.00
#1005A, UNCLE Car, Husky on base........$175.00
#1005B, UNCLE Car, Junior on base........$1,500.00
#1006A, Chitty-Chitty Bang-Bang, Husky on base........$200.00
#1006B, Chitty-Chitty Bang-Bang, Junior on base........$175.00
#1007, Ironside Police Van........$140.00
#1008, Popeye Paddle Wagon........$200.00
#1011, James Bond Bobsleigh........$300.00
#1012, Spectre Bobsleigh........$300.00
#1013, Tom's Go-Kart........$75.00
#1014, Jerry's Banger........$75.00
#1017, Ford Holmes Wrecker........$175.00

Major Packs

#1100, Carrimore Low Loader, red cab........$140.00
#1100, Carrimore Low Loader, yel cab........$225.00
#1100, Mack Truck........$900.00
#1101, Carrimore Car Transporter, bl cab........$250.00
#1101, Carrimore Car Transporter, red cab........$135.00
#1101, Hydraulic Crane........$50.00
#1102, Crane Fruehauf Dumper........$65.00
#1102, Euclid Tractor, gr........$150.00
#1102, Euclid Tractor, yel........$200.00
#1103, Airport Crash Truck........$85.00
#1103, Euclid Crawler Tractor........$125.00
#1104, Machinery Carrier........$150.00
#1104, Racehorse Transporter........$125.00
#1105, Berliet Racehorse Transporter........$60.00
#1106, Decca Mobile Radar Van........$170.00
#1107, Berliet Container Truck........$60.00
#1107, Euclid Tractor & Dozer, red........$375.00
#1107, Euclid Tractor & Dozer, orange........$300.00
#1108, Bristol Bloodhound & Launching Ramp........$125.00
#1108, Michelin Container Truck........$50.00

#1109, Bristol Bloodhound & Loading Trolley...............$130.00
#1109, Michelin Truck...............$50.00
#1110, JCB Crawler Loader...............$60.00
#1110, Mobilgas Tanker...............$300.00
#1110, Shell Tanker...............$3,000.00
#1111, Massey-Ferguson Harvester...............$150.00
#1112, Corporal Missile on Launching Ramp...............$160.00
#1112, David Brown Combine...............$120.00
#1113, Corporal Erector & Missile...............$375.00
#1113, Hyster...............$50.00
#1113, Hyster Sealink...............$135.00
#1115, Bloodhound Missile...............$110.00
#1116, Bloodhound Missile Platform...............$100.00
#1116, Refuse Lorry...............$30.00
#1117, Bloodhound Missile Trolley...............$65.00
#1117, Faun Street Sweeper...............$30.00
#1118, Airport Emergency Tender...............$70.00
#1118, International Truck, Dutch Army...............$300.00
#1118, International Truck, gr...............$150.00
#1118, International Truck, US Army...............$275.00
#1119, HDL Hovercraft...............$100.00
#1120, Midland Coach...............$220.00
#1121, Chipperfield's Circus Crane...............$250.00
#1121, Corgimatic Ford Tipper...............$50.00
#1123, Chipperfield's Circus Animal Cage...............$140.00
#1124, Corporal Missile Launching Ramp...............$80.00
#1126, Ecurie Ecosse Transporter...............$200.00
#1126, Simon Snorkel Dennis Fire Engine...............$60.00
#1127, Simon Snorkel Bedford Fire Engine...............$110.00

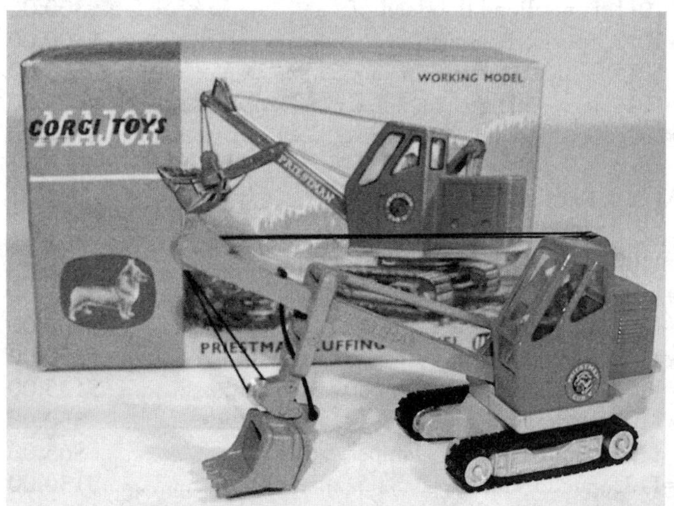

From the collection of Al Rapp

#1128, Priestman Cub Shovel, $75.00.

#1129, Mercedes Truck...............$25.00
#1129, Milk Tanker...............$275.00
#1130, Chipperfield's Circus Horse Transporter...............$275.00
#1130, Mercedes Tanker, Corgi...............$25.00
#1131, Carrimore Machinery Carrier...............$135.00
#1131, Mercedes Refrigerated Van...............$20.00
#1132, Carrimore Low Loader...............$250.00
#1132, Scania Truck...............$20.00
#1133, Troop Transporter...............$250.00
#1134, Army Fuel Tanker...............$400.00
#1135, Heavy Equipment Transporter...............$435.00
#1137, Ford Tilt Cab w/Trailer...............$125.00
#1138, Carrimore Car Transporter, Corgi...............$150.00
#1140, Bedford Mobilgas Tanker...............$300.00
#1140, Ford Transit Wrecker...............$25.00
#1141, Milk Tanker...............$300.00

From the collection of Al Rapp

#1142, Holmes Wrecker, $150.00.

#1143, American LaFrance Rescue Truck...............$125.00
#1144, Berliet Wrecker...............$80.00
#1144, Chipperfield's Circus Crane Truck...............$600.00
#1145, Mercedes Unimog Dumper...............$50.00
#1146, Tri-Deck Transporter...............$185.00
#1147, Ferrymaster Truck...............$130.00
#1148, Carrimore Car Transporter...............$160.00
#1150, Mercedes Unimog Snowplough...............$60.00
#1151, Scammell Co-op Set...............$350.00
#1151, Scammell Co-op Truck...............$250.00
#1152, Mack Truck, Esso Tanker...............$85.00
#1152, Mack Truck, Exxon Tanker...............$140.00
#1153, Priestman Boom Crane...............$80.00
#1154, Priestman Crane...............$100.00
#1154, Tower Crane...............$75.00
#1155, Skyscraper Tower Crane...............$60.00
#1156, Volvo Cement Mixer...............$60.00
#1157, Ford Esso Tanker...............$50.00
#1158, Ford Exxon Tanker...............$75.00
#1159, Ford Car Transporter...............$85.00
#1160, Ford Gulf Tanker...............$55.00
#1161, Ford Aral Tanker...............$85.00
#1163, Circus Cannon Truck...............$70.00
#1164, Dolphinarium...............$145.00
#1169, Ford Guiness Tanker...............$85.00
#1170, Ford Car Transporter...............$70.00

Dakins

Dakin has been an importer of stuffed toys as far back as 1955, but it wasn't until 1959 that the name of this San Francisco-based company actually appeared on the toy labels. They produced three distinct lines: Dream Pets (1960 – early 1970s), Dream Dolls (1965 – mid-1970s), and licensed characters and advertising figures, starting in 1968. Of them all, the latter series was the most popular and the one that holds most interest for collectors. Originally there were seven Warner Brothers characters. Each was made with a hard plastic body and a soft vinyl head, and all were under 10" tall. All in all, more than fifty cartoon characters were produced, some with several variations. Advertising figures were made as well. Some were extensions of the three already existing lines; others were completely original.

Goofy Grams was a series featuring many of their character figures mounted on a base lettered with a 'goofy' message. They also utilized some of their large stock characters as banks in a series called Cash Catchers. A second bank series consisted of Warner Brothers characters molded in a squatting position and therefore smaller. Other figures made by Dakin include squeeze toys, PVCs, and water squirters.

Advisor: Jim Rash (R3).

Alice in Wonderland, set of 3 w/Alice, Mad Hatter & White Rabbit, artist Faith Wick, 18", MIB **$300.00**
Baby Puss, Hanna-Barbera, 1971, EX+, R3....................**$100.00**
Bambi, Disney, 1960s, MIP, R3 ....**$35.00**
Bamm-Bamm, Hanna-Barbera, w/club, 1970, EX, R3 ......**$35.00**
Barney Rubble, Hanna-Barbera, 1970, EX, R3/B10..........**$40.00**
Benji, 1978, cloth, VG..**$30.00**
Bozo the Clown, Larry Hagman, 1974, EX, R3 ....**$35.00**
Bugs Bunny, Warner Bros, 1971, MIP, R3 ....**$30.00**
Bugs Bunny, Warner Bros, 1976, MIB (TV Cartoon Theater box) **$40.00**
Bugs Bunny, Warner Bros, 1978, MIP (Fun Farm bag).....**$20.00**
Bullwinkle, Jay Ward, 1976, MIB (TV Cartoon Theater box), R3 ....**$60.00**

Droopy dog, 1971, 8½", EX, J6, $25.00.

Cool Cat, Warner Bros, w/beret, 1970, EX+, R3 ....**$40.00**
Daffy Duck, Warner Bros, 1968, EX, R3 ....**$30.00**
Daffy Duck, Warner Bros, 1976, MIB (TV Cartoon Theater box), R3 ....**$40.00**
Deputy Dawg, Terrytoons, 1977, EX, R3 ....**$40.00**
Dewey Duck, Disney, straight or bent legs, EX, R3..........**$40.00**
Dino Dinosaur, Hanna-Barbera, 1970, EX, R3 ....**$40.00**
Donald Duck, Disney, 1960s, straight or bent legs, EX, R3...**$20.00**
Donald Duck, Disney, 1960s, straight or bent legs, NMIP..**$30.00**
Dream Pets, Bull Dog, cloth, EX **$15.00**
Dream Pets, Hawaiian Hound, cloth, w/surfboard & orig tag, EX **$15.00**
Dream Pets, Kangaroo, cloth, w/camera, wearing beret, EX..**$15.00**
Dream Pets, Midnight Mouse, cloth, w/orig tags, EX........**$15.00**
Dudley Do-Right, Jay Ward, 1976, MIB (TV Cartoon Theater box), R3 ....**$75.00**
Dumbo, Disney, 1960s, cloth collar, MIB, R3..................**$25.00**
Elmer Fudd, Warner Bros, 1968, hunting outfit w/rifle, EX, R3...**$125.00**
Elmer Fudd, Warner Bros, 1968, tuxedo, EX, R3 ....**$30.00**
Elmer Fudd, Warner Bros, 1978, MIP (Fun Farm bag), R3 ..**$35.00**
Foghorn Leghorn, Warner Bros, 1970, EX+, R3 ....**$75.00**
Fred Flintstone, Hanna-Barbera, 1970, EX, R3/B10, from $35 ....**$40.00**
Goofy, Disney, cloth cothes, EX...**$20.00**
Goofy Gram, Bull, I'm Mad About You, EX, R3..............**$25.00**
Goofy Gram, Dog, Congratulations Dumm-Dumm, EX, R3.**$25.00**
Goofy Gram, Frog, Happy Birthday, EX, R3 ....**$25.00**
Goofy Gram, Kangaroo, World's Greatest Mom!, EX, R3 ..**$25.00**
Goofy Gram, Pepe Le Peu, You're a Real Stinker, 1971, EX ..**$55.00**
Goofy Gram, Tiger, To A Great Guy, EX, R3 ....**$25.00**
Hokey Wolf, Hanna-Barbera, 1971, EX+, R3.................**$250.00**
Hoppy Hopperoo, Hanna-Barbera, 1971, EX+, R3 ....**$100.00**
Huckleberry Hound, Hanna-Barbera, 1970, EX+, R3 ......**$75.00**
Huey Duck, Disney, straight or bent legs, EX, R3 ....**$30.00**
Jack-in-the-Box, bank, 1971, EX, R3 ....**$25.00**
Lion in Cage, bank, 1971, EX, R3 ....**$25.00**
Louie Duck, Disney, straight or bent legs, EX, R3 ....**$30.00**
Merlin the Magic Mouse, Warner Bros, 1970, EX+..........**$25.00**
Mickey Mouse, Disney, 1960s, cloth clothes, EX, R3 ....**$20.00**
Mighty Mouse, Terrytoons, 1978, EX, R3......................**$100.00**
Minnie Mouse, Disney, 1960s, cloth clothes, EX, R3 ....**$20.00**
Monkey on a Barrel, bank, 1971, EX, R3 ....**$25.00**
Olive Oyl, King Features, 1974, cloth clothes, MIP, R3...**$50.00**
Olive Oyl, King Features, 1976, MIB (TV Cartoon Theater box), R3 ....**$40.00**
Oliver Hardy, Larry Harmon, 1974, EX+, R3 ....**$30.00**
Opus, 1982, cloth, w/tag, 12", EX, B10 ....**$15.00**
Pebbles Flintstone, Hanna-Barbera, 1970, EX, R3............**$35.00**
Pepe Le Peu, Warner Bros, 1971, EX **$55.00**
Pink Panther, Mirisch-Freleng, 1971, EX+, R3 ....**$50.00**
Pink Panther, Mirisch-Freleng, 1976, MIB (TV Cartoon Theater box), R3 ....**$50.00**
Pinocchio, Disney, 1960s, EX..**$20.00**
Popeye, King Features, 1974, cloth clothes, MIP, R3 ....**$50.00**
Popeye, King Features, 1976, MIB (TV Cartoon Theater box), R3...**$50.00**
Porky Pig, Warner Bros, 1968, EX, R3 ....**$30.00**

Porky Pig, Warner Bros, 1976, MIB (TV Cartoon Theater box), R3 ....$40.00

Practical Pig, EX, $45.00.

Ren & Stimpy, water squirters, Nickelodeon, 1993, EX, R3 ...$10.00
Road Runner, Warner Bros, 1968, EX, R3 ....$30.00
Road Runner, Warner Bros, 1976, MIB $45.00

Snagglepuss, 1971, EX, $100.00.

Rocky Squirrel, Jay Ward, 1976, MIB (TV Cartoon Theater box), R3 ....$60.00
Scooby Doo, Hanna-Barbera, 1980, EX, R3......................$75.00
Scrappy Doo, Hanna-Barbera, 1982, EX+, R3 ....$75.00
Seal on Box, bank, 1971, EX, R3......................................$25.00
Second Banana, Warner Bros, 1970, EX, R3 ....$35.00
Smokey Bear, 1976, MIB (TV Cartoon Theater box), R3..$30.00
Speedy Gonzalez, Warner Bros, MIB (TV Cartoon Theater box), R3 ....$50.00
Stan Laurel, Larry Harmon, 1974, EX+, R3 ....$30.00
Swee'Pea, beanbag doll, King Features, 1974, VG, R3 .....$20.00
Sylvester, Warner Bros, 1968, EX, R3 ....$20.00
Sylvester, Warner Bros, 1976, MIB (TV Cartoon Theater box), R3 ....$40.00
Sylvester, Warner Bros, 1978, MIP (Fun Farm bag), R3...$20.00
Tasmanian Devil, Warner Bros, 1978, rare, EX (Fun Farm bag) $400.00
Tiger in Cage, bank, 1971, EX, R3 ....$25.00
Top Banana, Warner Bros, NM, C17 ....$25.00

Tweety Bird, 1969, EX, $20.00.

Tweety Bird, Warner Bros, 1976, MIB (TV Cartoon Theater box), R3 ....$40.00
Underdog, Jay Ward, 1976, MIB (TV Cartoon Theater box), R3 ....$150.00
Wile E Coyote, bank, 1971, EX, C17............................$230.00
Wile E Coyote, Warner Bros, 1968, MIB, R3 ....$30.00
Wile E Coyote, Warner Bros, 1976, MIB (TV Cartoon Theater box), R3 ....$40.00
Woodsey Owl, 1974, missing clothes, EX $30.00

Yogi Bear, Hanna-Barbera, 1970, EX, R3 .... $60.00
Yosemite Sam, Warner Bros, 1968, MIB $40.00
Yosemite Sam, Warner Bros, 1976, MIP (Fun Farm bag), R3 ... $40.00

Advertising

Bay View, bank, 1976, EX+, R3 .... $30.00
Bob's Big Boy, missing hamburger o/w VG, H4 .... $80.00
Bob's Big Boy, 1974, w/hamburger, EX+, R3 .... $180.00
Budding Meats, Buddi Bull, 1970s, cloth, EX $30.00
Christian Bros Brandy, St Bernard, 1982, cloth, VG, M15 ... $30.00
Crocker National Bank, Cocker Spaniel, 1979, cloth, 12", VG, M15 .... $20.00
Diaperene Baby, Sterling Drug Co, 1980, EX, R3 .... $40.00
Freddie Fast, 1976, M, P12 .... $100.00
Glamour Kitty, 1977, EX, R3 .... $150.00
Kernal Renk, American Seeds, 1970, rare, EX+, R3 ...... $350.00
Li'l Miss Just Rite, 1965, EX+, R3 .... $75.00
Miss Liberty Bell, 1975, MIP, R3 .... $75.00
Quasar Robot, bank, 1975, NM, R3 .... $150.00
Sambo's Boy, 1974, EX+, R3 .... $75.00
Sambo's Tiger, 1974, EX+, R3 .... $125.00
Woodsy Owl, 1974, MIP, R3 .... $60.00

Diecast

Diecast replicas of cars, trucks, planes, trains, etc., represent a huge corner of today's collector market, and their manufacturers see to it that there is no shortage. Back in the 1920s, Tootsietoy had the market virtually by themselves, but one by one other companies had a go at it, some with more success than others. Among them were the American companies of Barclay, Hubley, and Manoil, all of whom are much better known for other types of toys. After the war, Metal Masters, Smith-Miller, and Doepke Ohlsson-Rice (among others) tried the market with varying degrees of success. Some companies were phased out over the years, while many more entered the market with fervor. Today it's those fondly remembered models from the '50s and '60s that many collectors yearn to own. Solido produced well-modeled, detailed little cars; some had dome lights that actually came on when the doors were opened. Politoy's were cleanly molded with good detailing and finishes. Mebetoys, an Italian company that has been bought out by Mattel, produced several; and some of the finest come from Brooklyn, whose Shelby (signed) GT-350H Mustang can easily cost you from $900.00 to $1,000.00 when you can find one.

In 1968 the Topper Toy Company introduced its line of low-friction, high-speed Johnny Lightning cars to be in direct competition with Mattel's Hot Wheels. To gain attention, Topper sponsored Al Unser's winning race car, the 'Johnny Lightning,' in the 1970 Indianapolis 500. Despite the popularity of their cars, the Topper Toy Company went out of business in 1971. Today the Johnny Lightnings are highly sought after and a new company, Playing Mantis, is reproducing many of the original designs as well as several models that never made it into regular production.

If you're interested in Majorette Toys, we recommend *Collecting Majorette Toys* by Dana Johnson; ordering information is given with Dana's listing under Diecast, in the section called Categories of Special Interest in the back of the book. Dana is also the author of *Collector's Guide to Diecast Toys & Scale Models*, published by Collector Books.

Advisor: Dan Wells (W1).

Other Sources: P3, N3, S5

See also Corgi; Dinky; Diecast Collector Banks; Farm Toys; Tootsietoys; Hot Wheels; Matchbox; Tekno.

Aurora Cigarbox, AC Cobra, metallic purple w/silver stripe, EX $20.00
Aurora Cigarbox, Camaro, yel w/tan interior, NM, W1 ... $50.00
Aurora Cigarbox, Cobra, lt bl w/2 thin blk stripes, M, W1 .. $25.00
Aurora Cigarbox, Dune Buggy, red w/blk interior, wht-w/red-striped top, M, W1 .... $24.00
Aurora Cigarbox, Ferrari Berlinetta, orange chrome w/silver stripe, tan interior, NM $12.00
Aurora Cigarbox, Firebird, orange chrome, tan interior, NM, W1 .... $32.00
Aurora Cigarbox, Ford GT, red w/thin wht stripe, tan interior, M, W1 .... $11.00
Aurora Cigarbox, Mako Shark, lt bl, tan interior, M, W1 .. $26.00
Aurora Cigarbox, Stingray, red, tan interior, NM, W1 .... $20.00
Aurora Cigarbox, Toronado, yel, tan interior, M, W1 ..... $23.00
Barlux, Brabham-Ford, #73008, 1:66, M $10.00
Barlux, Fiat Wrecker, #100, 1:24, M $30.00
Barlux, Fiat 697 Dump Truck & Loader, #762, 1:43, M ... $16.00
Bburago, Bugatti Atlantic, 1936, #503, VIP - 1:24, M $20.00
Bburago, Chevrolet Corvette, 1957, #3024, Diamonds - 1:18, M $30.00
Bburago, Ferrari GTO, #572, 1984, VIP - 1:24, M $20.00
Bburago, Porsche 911S, #102, Super - 1:24, M $20.00
Bburago, Porsche 959, #121, Super - 1:24, M $20.00
Best Toys of Kansas, Racer #76, 4¼" L, M $30.00
Best Toys of Kansas, Sedan #100, Pontiac, 4", M $30.00
Best Toys of Kansas, Sedan #90, 2-door airflow, hood reaches front bumper w/no grille, 3½", M $30.00
Budgie, Austin A95 Station Wagon, orange, metal wheels, 1950s, NM+, W1 .... $25.00
Budgie, Cattle Truck, cream & tan, plastic wheels, 1960s, NM, W1 .... $8.00
Budgie, Dump Truck, #18, 1:64, M $15.00
Budgie, Packard Convertible, tan, metal wheels, 1950s, complete, NM, W1 .... $40.00
Budgie, Routemaster Double-Decker Bus, #236, 4", M $16.00
Budgie, Salvage Crane, red & bl, England, 1959, no hook, VG+, W1 .... $25.00
Budgie, VW Microbus, lt bl, plastic wheels, 1950s, NM, W1 .. $40.00
Budgie, VW Pickup, 1960, Coca-Cola, 1:43, M $115.00
CD, Bugatti Sports Car, M $100.00
CD, Peugeot Sans Soupape, M $100.00
CD, Rosengart Super Traction Roadster, M $100.00
Danbury Mint, Buick Skylark Convertible, 1953, bl/bl-gray, 1:24, M $125.00
Danbury Mint, Chevrolet Bel Air Convertible, 1957, bl/lt & dk bl, M $125.00

Dugu, 1911 Fiat 4 Closed Tourer, 1962, M $50.00
Dugu, 1912 Itala 25/35HP Closed Tourer, 1965, M $50.00
Dugu, 1921 Duesenburg SJ, red, folded blk top, Italy, 1968, M (NM plastic display box) $80.00
Dugu, 1934 Rolls Royce Silver Ghost, top down, 1969, M .. $120.00
Dugu, 1936 Fiat 500A Topolino Coupe, dk red, 1966, M, W1 .... $30.00
Eligor, 1930 Talbot Pacific Limousine, red, 1970s, MIB, W1 .... $23.00
Eligor, 1934 Ford V8 Milk Truck, lt bl & wht, MIB, W1 . $23.00
Ertl, Bobby Allison, 1980 Gatorade Chevrolet, #88, wht, M (EX+ card), W1 .... $100.00
Ertl, Cale Yarborough, Valvoline Buick, wht, #27, M (NM card), W1 .... $55.00

Ertl, Campbell's produce truck, MIB, $30.00.

Photo courtesy Dana Johnson

Ertl, 1951 Chevrolet, green, M, $10.00.

Ertl, Weyerhaeuser log truck, MIB, $30.00.

Ertl, Darrel Waltrip, Mountain Dew Buick, wht, #11, M (NM card), W1 .... $70.00
Ertl, Richard Petty, STP Buick, red & bl, #43, M (NM card), W1 .... $80.00
Goodee, Land Speed Racer, 3", M $15.00
Goodee, Military Jeep, 6", M $25.00
Goodee, 1953 Ford Pickup Truck, 6", M $25.00
Goodee, 1953 Ford Police 2-Door Sedan, 3", M $28.00

Photo courtesy June Moon

Hubley, airplane, two-tone blue, NM, J6, $85.00.

Hubley, Car Carrier, red truck cab w/3 sedans on flatbed trailer, 12½", NMIB, A $650.00
Hubley, Fish Hatchery Truck, red w/plastic aquarium body, w/8 fish, 10", MIB, A $450.00
Hubley, Hook & Ladder Truck, red w/silver detail & ladders, 9¾", NMIB, A $125.00

Hubley, road grader, Mighty-Metal series, 13", MIB, A, $85.00; Hubley, dump truck, Mighty-Metal series, 12", MIB, A, $85.00.

Hubley, Log Truck, yel & wht w/blk rubber tires, complete w/logs & chain, NM (EX box), A **$165.00**

Hubley, Log Truck #1911, complete w/wooden logs, 8", NM (NM box), A..**$75.00**

Hubley, Lumber Truck, red & silver, complete w/chained logs, 12½", MIB, A **$300.00**

Hubley, Midget Racers #5, complete set of 3 w/NP drivers, MIB, A..**$1,000.00**

Hubley, Navy Fighter Bomber, Mighty-Metal series, 9", NM (EX box), A **$75.00**

Hubley, P-38 Fighter, Mighty-Metal series, silver w/red detail, 9", NM (EX box), A **$165.00**

Hubley, Pipe Truck, bl w/silver grille, blk rubber tires, complete w/wooden pipes, 10½", NMIB, A **$80.00**

Hubley, School Bus, 1969, yel, 9", NM (EX box), A........**$75.00**

Hubley, Taxi Cab Assortment, Kiddie Toys, complete, MIB, A, $935.00.

Hubley, Tow Truck, red w/NP winch, hook & crank, blk rubber tires, 1950s, 9½", NM (NM box), A.......................**$300.00**

Hubley, Tow Truck, red w/NP CI crane, searchlight & reel, 9½", MIB, A **$425.00**

Hubley, Tractor, Kiddie Toy series, red w/blk rubber tires, spring seat, 9", VG (G box), A **$100.00**

Imperial Toy, Boat Transporter Truck, orange, plastic wheels, 1976, MBP, W1 ....**$13.00**

Imperial Toy, Circus Truck, aqua, plastic wheels, 1976, M (NM+ card), W1 ....**$20.00**

Imperial Toy, Container Truck, orange, plastic wheels, 1976, M (NM+ card), W1 ....**$13.00**

Impy, Ford Corsair, purple w/wht interior, plastic wheels, 1970s, M, W1 ....**$20.00**

Johnny Lightning, AJ Foyt, metallic purple, complete, NM+, W1 ....**$60.00**

Johnny Lightning, Baja, metallic purple, NM+, W1 ....**$50.00**

Johnny Lightning, Custom '32 Ford, 1969, M **$30.00**

Johnny Lightning, Custom Dragster, 1969, M **$25.00**

Johnny Lightning, Custom El Camino, metallic orange, wht interior, doors open, scarce mirror finish, EX, W1 ..**$130.00**

Johnny Lightning, Custom Eldorado, metallic brn, wht interior, doors open, scarce color, NM, from $75 to **$85.00**

Johnny Lightning, Custom Ferrari, closed doors, 1969, M..**$30.00**

Johnny Lightning, Custom Ferrari, doors open, M **$110.00**

Johnny Lightning, Custom GTO, metallic red, wht interior, blk roof, doors open, VG, W1 ....**$80.00**

Johnny Lightning, Custom Mako Shark, doors open, M ..**$100.00**

Johnny Lightning, Custom Mako Shark, metallic lime, red interior, slight toning, NM, W1 ....**$40.00**

Johnny Lightning, Custom Spoiler, metallic purple, complete, NM+, W1 ....**$35.00**

Johnny Lightning, Custom Thunderbird, metallic lime, red interior, doors open, ½ blk roof, rare mirror finish, EX+, W1 ....**$150.00**

Johnny Lightning, Custom Toronado, 1969, M **$100.00**

Johnny Lightning, Custom Turbine, painted interior, 1969, M **$100.00**

Johnny Lightning, Custom Turbine, unpainted interior, 1969, M **$20.00**

Johnny Lightning, Custom XKE, doors open, M **$100.00**

Johnny Lightning, Custom XKE, metallic purple, wht interior, closed doors, NM+, W1...**$38.00**

Johnny Lightning, Double Trouble, metallic aqua, complete, M, W1 ....**$150.00**

Johnny Lightning, Flame Out, metallic orange, complete, NM, W1 ....**$40.00**

Johnny Lightning, Frantic Ferrari, metallic red, complete, NM+, W1 ....**$40.00**

Johnny Lightning, Frantic Ferrari, purple, 1969, MOC....**$65.00**

Johnny Lightning, Glasser, metallic lime, M (EX+ Power card), W1 ....**$110.00**

Johnny Lightning, Mad Maverick, 1970, M.....................**$30.00**

Johnny Lightning, Monster, jet powered, 1970, M **$20.00**

Johnny Lightning, Monster, metallic magenta, M (G Power card), W1 ....**$80.00**

Johnny Lightning, Parnelli Jones, metallic purple, complete, NM+, W1 ....**$60.00**

Johnny Lightning, Sand Stormer, metallic dk aqua, complete, M (NM card), W1 ....**$80.00**

Johnny Lightning, Sand Stormer, yel, 1969, MOC **$65.00**

Johnny Lightning, Screamer, metallic lime, M (VG+ Power card), W1 ....**$110.00**

Johnny Lightning, Smuggler, metallic bl, complete, NM+, W1 ....**$32.00**

Johnny Lightning, Spoiler, yel, 1969, MOC **$65.00**

Johnny Lightning, Stiletto, metallic yel, complete, NM, W1..**$32.00**

Johnny Lightning, TNT, 1970, M..................................**$30.00**

Johnny Lightning, Triple Threat, metallic purple, complete, NM+, W1 ....**$32.00**

Johnny Lightning, Twin Blaster, metallic purple, M (EX Customs card), W1 ....**$200.00**

Johnny Lightning, Vicious Vette, metallic lt purple, complete, EX+, W1 ....**$28.00**

Johnny Lightning, Vulture, metallic dk brn, orig engine/canopy, missing wing, dk reddish brn, NM, W1 .....$65.00
Johnny Lightning, Wasp, metallic red, complete, EX+, W1....$25.00
Johnny Lightning, Wedge, metallic purple, M (VG Jet Power card), W1 .....$110.00
Johnny Lightning, Whistler, metallic orange, complete, NM, W1 .....$40.00
Les Routiers, Mobile Crane, 1:90, M $50.00
Les Routiers, Panhard Tank Truck, 1:90, M $50.00
Linemar, Elegant Miniatures, set of 10 construction vehicles & trucks, NMIB, A $150.00

Photo courtesy Dana Johnson

Lledo, Greyhound Scenicruiser, EX, $20.00.

Lledo, Mack Breakdown Truck, M $10.00
Lledo, 1953 Pontiac Van, M $10.00
Londontoy, Beverage Truck, 4", M $25.00
Londontoy, Canadian Greyhound Bus, 6", M $40.00
Londontoy, Oil Tanker, 6", M $30.00
Majorette, Bank Security Armored Truck, M $2.00
Majorette, BMW 3.0 CSI, lime, plastic wheels, 1970s, M, W1 .....$13.00
Majorette, Chrysler 180, M $10.00
Majorette, Hotchkiss Jeep w/Cattle Trailer, M $16.00
Majorette, Mobile Hope Camper, hot pk w/beige camper, M ..$4.00
Majorette, Renault 5 LeCar, no rear view mirrors or antenna, 1:51, M $6.00
Majorette, Road Eaters Campbell's Teddy Bears, red, M ..$30.00
Majorette, Rock Motorcycle, M $15.00
Majorette, Ski-doo Snowmobile, yel, 1970s, EX+, W1 .....$4.00
Majorette, VW 1302 Beetle, closed trunk, lime gr, M $3.00
Marx, Jaguar XKE, red, litho tin interior, 1 orig label, no window version, 1970s, plastic wheels, MIP, W1, from $25 to $35.00
Mebetoys, Alfa Romeo Duetto Spyder, med gr, orig top, Italy, 1967, M, W1 .....$30.00
Mebetoys, Chaparral 2F, wht, Italy, 1968, M, W1 .....$30.00
Mebetoys, Corvette Rondine, med bl, Italy, 1968, M, W1 ..$40.00
Mebetoys, Innocenti Mini Minor, orange, Monte Carlo Rallye stickers, wht top, 1968, EX+, W1 .....$65.00
Mebetoys, Rolls Royce Silver Shadow, med gold, Italy, 1968, EX, W1 .....$30.00
Mercury, Alfa Romeo Giulietta Sprint, 1956, 1:48, M $45.00
Mercury, Areo, 1945, 1:40, M $100.00
Mercury, Bianchina Panoramica, 1962, 1:48, M $25.00
Mercury, Caravan Trailer, 1946, 1:40, M $50.00
Mercury, Chapparal 2F, 1968, 1:43, M $60.00
Mercury, Ferrari 250LM, 1951, 1:43, M $40.00
Mercury, Fiat Campagnola, 1975, 1:43, M $35.00
Mercury, Fiat 124, 1976, 1:43, M $35.00
Mercury, Fiat 697 Cement Mixer, 1977, 1:43, M $55.00
Mercury, Fiat 850 Bertone, 1965, 1:43, M $30.00
Mercury, Grand Prix Car: Jarama, 1:66, M $55.00
Mercury, Lanica Fulvia Rally, 1973, 1:43, M $25.00
Mercury, Little Toy, Michigan Scraper, yel, rubber wheels, 1960s, MBP, W1 .....$40.00
Mercury, Peugeot Convertible, lt bl, blk interior, plastic wheels, 1960s, M (EX+ card), W1 .....$30.00
Mercury, Warner & Swasey Gradall, 1961, M $50.00
Midgetoy, Army Troop Truck & Cannon Trailer, olive, US, 1950s, MIB, W1 .....$25.00
Midgetoy, Army Truck, ca 1950, 4½", M $14.00
Midgetoy, Corvette, gr, ca 1970s, 2", M $2.50
Midgetoy, El Camino, red, ca 1970s, 3", M $2.50
Polistil, Niki Lauda Ferrari #12, red w/blk tires, orig decals, EX, rare, A $100.00
Politoys, Drago Rear Engine Dragster, dk yel, Italy, complete, NM+, W1 .....$200.00
Politoys, Porsche 912, silver, blk interior, Italy, 1969, NM+, W1 .....$30.00
Road Champs, BJ & the Bear Truck, red, plastic wheels, 1981, M (EX+ card), W1 .....$20.00
Road Champs, Cadillac Eldorado, magenta, plastic tires, 1970s, M (NM card), W1 .....$20.00
Road Champs, Cadillac Fleetwood Brougham, magenta, plastic wheels, 1970s, M (EX+ card), W1 .....$15.00
Schuco, Audi 100-LS, 1971, 2¾", M $10.00
Schuco, BMW 630-CS, 1976, M $25.00
Schuco, Boeing 727, M $50.00
Schuco, Coles Hydraulic Crane, M $75.00
Schuco, Faun Street Sweeper, 1962, 2¼", M $60.00
Schuco, Junkers FD-13, M $40.00
Schuco, Mercedes Benz Low Loader, 1960, 4", M $60.00
Schuco, Mercedes Benz 200 Police Car, 1971, 2¼", M $10.00
Schuco, Mercedes Benz 350-DE, 1972, M $25.00
Schuco, Tipping Trailer, 1962, 3", M $60.00
Schuco, VW 1300, 1971, 2½" $10.00
Siku, Ford OSI 20M-TS, 1968-72, M $35.00
Siku, Lincoln Continental Mark III, 1969-72, M $30.00
Siku, Magirus Garbage Truck, 1967-74, M $50.00
Siku, Opel Caravan 1500, 1964-66, M $30.00
Siku, Pontiac Bonneville Convertible, 1966-71, M $70.00
Siku, Refuse Truck, 1992, M $5.00
Solido, Dodge WC 56 Hose & Ladder, 1995 variation, M .$20.00

Photo courtesy Dana Johnson

Solido, 1946 Chrysler Windsor Taxi, M, $20.00.

Solido, Ferrari 330 P3, red w/blk tires, opening engine compartment w/supports, 3¾", EX, A $25.00
Solido, Peugeot 604, 1:43, M.....$15.00
Solido, Saviem First Aid, M $20.00
Solido, 1968 Chevrolet Corvette, 1994, M.....$10.00
Solido, 1987 Bentley Continental, M $15.00
Solido, 1991 Citroen ZX Aura, M.....$15.00
Tomica, Bugatti Royale Coupe DeVille 1927, 186-F46, ca 1978, 1:80, M $6.00
Tomica, Ford Lotus Europa John Player Special, 161-F36/164-F25, M $6.00
Tomica, Hino Big Rig Semi, 89-24, M.....$10.00
Tomica Grehound Bus Americruiser, 222-F49, ca 1979, M.$25.00

Diecast Collector Banks

Thousands of banks have been produced since Ertl made its first model in 1981, the 1913 Model T Parcel Post Mail Service #9647. The Ertl company was founded by Fred Ertl, Sr., in Dubuque, Iowa, back in the mid-1940s. Until they made their first diecast banks, most of what they made were farm tractors. Today they specialize in vehicles made to specification and carrying logos of companies as large as Texaco and as small as your hometown bank. The size of each 'run' is dictated by the client and can vary from a few hundred up to several thousand. Some clients will later add a serial number to the vehicle; this is not done by Ertl. Other numbers that appear on the base of each bank are a 4-number dating code (the first three indicate the day of the year up to 365 and the fourth number is the last digit of the year, '5' for 1995, for instance). The stock number is shown only on the box, never on the bank, so it is extremely important that you keep them in their original boxes.

Other producers of these banks are Scale Models, incorporated in 1991, First Gear Inc., and Spec-Cast, whose founders at one time all worked for the Ertl company.

In the listings that follow, unless another condition is given, all values are for banks mint and in their original boxes. (#d) indicates a bank that was numbered by the client, not Ertl.

Advisors: Art and Judy Turner (H8), who provided us with all listings that do not include the codes of other dealers.

Other Sources: S5, T4

Key: JLE — Joseph L. Ertl

Ertl

A&W Rootbeer, 1932 Ford, #2190 .....$35.00
A-Treat Beverages, 1956 Ford Pickup, #F548.....$26.00
Aberfoyle Antique Market, 1938 Chevy, #4868.....$35.00
Ace Hardware, Stearman Plane, 1st edition, #F398 .....$85.00
Ace Hardware, 1925 Kenworth, #F397 .....$20.00
Adelt Mechanical, 1913 Ford, #9938.....$45.00
Agway, 1918 Ford, #9705 .....$25.00
Alka Seltzer, 1918 Ford, #9155 .....$95.00
Allen Organ Co, 1931 Hawkeye, #9892 .....$45.00
Allied Van Lines, 1950 Chevy Tractor Trailer, #1354.....$25.00
Alzheimer Association, 1913 Ford, #9680 .....$65.00
American Red Cross, 1926 Mack Truck, #7616 .....$40.00
Amoco, 1929 International Tanker, JLE, #4032.....$25.00
Amoco Stanolind Polarine, 1932 Ford, #7657.....$125.00
Amoco-Standard Oil Co, 1935 Mack Tanker, JLE, #3006 ...$20.00
Anheuser Busch, 1926 Mack & 1918 Ford Gift Set, #2124.$225.00
Anheuser Busch, 1931 Hawkeye, #7574 .....$35.00
Ar-Jay Sales, 1938 Chevy, #B072.....$20.00
Arm & Hammer, 1923 Chevy, #2096.....$75.00
Atlanta Falcons, 1913 Ford, #1248 .....$35.00
Atlas Van Lines, 1926 Mack Truck, #9514.....$40.00
Aunt Jemima Pancakes, 1923 Chevy, #2085 .....$95.00
Baltimore Gas & Electric, 1931 Hawkeye, #9848.....$45.00
Bank of the Eastern Shore, 1956 Ford Pickup, #F799.....$35.00
Barq's Rootbeer, 1932 Ford, #9072.....$45.00
Bell Telephone, 1932 Ford, #9803 .....$35.00
Ben Franklin, 1918 Ford, #1319 .....$35.00
Big A Auto Parts, 1926 Mack, #9094.....$45.00
Big Bear Family Center, 1938 Chevy, #3520 .....$25.00
Blue Ball National Bank, 1913 Ford, #9029.....$45.00
Boston Celtics, 1918 Ford, #B480 .....$22.00
Boston Red Sox, 1905 Ford, #B140.....$25.00
BP Gasoline, Stearman Plane, #F905 .....$55.00
Breyers Ice Cream, 1905 Ford, #9028.....$65.00
Buehlers Supermarket, 1955 Cameo Pickup, #F931 .....$26.00
Buffalo Bills, Stearman Plane, #F699 .....$30.00
Bumper To Bumper Auto Parts, 1923 Chevy, #2973.....$30.00
California Highway Patrol, Air Express Plane, #F502 .....$32.00
Cam-2 Motor Oil, 1931 International, JLE, #4103.....$32.00
Campbell's Soup, 1957 Chevy Stake Truck, #F603 .....$30.00
Campbell's Soup Seasons Greetings, 1931 Hawkeye, #B623...$25.00
Canada Dry, 1913 Ford, #2133.....$125.00
Carlisle Prod Spring Car Show, 1926 Mack Truck, #9340 .$25.00
Carnation, 1913 Ford, #9178.....$34.00
Caterpillar, 1931 Hawkeye, #2353 .....$25.00
Caterpillar, 1932 Ford, #2432.....$30.00
Central Tractor Farm & Family, 1951 Ford Pickup, #H278 ....$30.00
Charlotte Hornets, 1956 Ford Pickup, #B887 .....$20.00
Cherry Smash, 1905 Ford, #9252 .....$65.00
Cherry Smash, 1932 Ford, #B062 .....$50.00
Chevrolet, Vega Plane, #35011 .....$55.00
Chevrolet GM Parts, 1955 Cameo Pickup, #B071 .....$32.00
Chevrolet Motor Co, 1926 Fire Truck, gr, #9071 .....$25.00
Chicago Cubs, 1926 Mack Truck, #7545 .....$40.00
Chiquita Bananas, 1913 Ford, #9662 .....$65.00
Citgo, Vega Plane, #35012 .....$32.00
Citgo Lubricants, 1925 Kenworth, #3779 .....$45.00
Classic Motorbooks, 1950 Chevy, #7567 .....$45.00
Coast To Coast Hardware, 1932 Ford, #2932 .....$25.00
Coca-Cola, 1925 Kenworth, #B398 .....$25.00
Coca-Cola, 1929 International Tanker, JLE, #4075 .....$35.00
Coker Tire, 1931 Hawkeye, #F424 .....$30.00
Colorado Rockies, 1917 Ford, #B350 .....$35.00
Conoco Oil, 1926 Mack Truck, #9750 .....$225.00
Continental Insurance, 1932 Ford, #9665.....$30.00
Country Fresh, 1925 Kenworth, #B069.....$22.00
Crown Petroleum, 1931 Hawkeye Tanker, #9652 .....$30.00
Cushman Motor Scooter Club, 1938 Chevy, #3266.....$50.00

Custom Chrome, 1931 International, JLE, #5030 ....$95.00
Dairy Queen, 1918 Ford, #9033...$95.00
Dairy Queen, 1950 Chevy, #9178 ....$135.00
Dallas Cowboys, 1955 Cameo Pickup, #B327 ....$30.00
Daytona Bike Week, 1920 International, JLE, #3111.......$95.00
Diamond Rio, 1940 Ford, #67503 ....$24.00
Dobyns-Bennett High School, 1950 Chevy, #7516..........$95.00
Dr Pepper, 1923 Chevy, #3907...$35.00
Drake Hotel, 1913 Ford, #2113 ....$125.00
Dubuque Golf & Country Club, 1913 Ford, #9726 ....$75.00
Dupont, 1923 Chevy, #1353...$75.00
Dutch Girl Ice Cream, 1931 Hawkeye, #9049 ....$30.00
East Coast Nationals, 1932 Ford, #9470...........................$28.00
Eastview Pharmacy, 1913 Ford, #9896 ....$25.00
Eastwood Co, 1926 Fire Truck, #1666 ....$60.00
Eastwood Co II, 1939 Dodge Airflow, #B315 ....$34.00
Edelbrock, 1932 Ford, #9027 ....$325.00
Elmers Glue, 1918 Ford, #F608 ....$20.00
Ephrata Fair, 1950 Chevy, #7541 ....$40.00
Ertl Replica Club, 1931 Hawkeye, #2088.........................$25.00
Ertl 50th Anniversary, 1913 Ford, #B945 ....$35.00
Exxon, P51 Mustang Plane, #47004 ....$45.00
Farm Bureau Co-op, 1918 Ford, #9220.............................$25.00
Farmers Almanac, 1938 Chevy, #3595 ....$25.00
Federal Express, Step Van, #9334....................................$45.00
Field of Dreams, 1905 Ford, #7617 ....$40.00
Fina Oil, 1913 Ford, #9407 ....$65.00
Food City 500, 1923 Chevy, #B019 ....$40.00
Ford, 1905 Ford, #B245..$35.00
Ford Motor Co, 1912 Ford, #9348 ....$40.00
Ford Motorsports, Stearman Plane, #0500 ....$30.00
Gilmore Oil Co, 1931 International Tanker, JLE, #4010.$25.00
Global Van Lines, 1913 Ford, #1655................................$45.00
Golden State Pickup Parts, 1955 Cameo Pickup, #3286 ..$20.00
Goodyear, 1950 Chevy, #7538 ....$40.00
Goodyear Tire 25th Anniversary, 1931 Hawkeye, #4957.$28.00
Granny Goose Chips, 1913 Ford, #9979 ....$50.00
Grapette Soda, 1932 Ford, #9885 ....$65.00
Green Spot Beverage, 1931 International, JLE, #4107 .....$25.00
Gulf Oil, 1926 Mack Tanker, #7652 ....$45.00
Gulf Oil, 1956 Ford Pickup, #H017 ....$32.00
Gulf Oil (Station Issue), 1925 Kenworth Wrecker, #B107.$125.00
Hamm's Beer, 1913 Ford, #2145.......................................$75.00
Harbor Freight Tools, 1923 Chevy, #F040.......................$30.00
Harley Davidson of Baltimore, 1931 International, JLE, #5033 ....$95.00
Harvard Rescue Squad, 1951 GMC, #F314 ....$35.00
Heim Electric, 1932 Ford, #9616.....................................$295.00
Henny Penny, 1950 Chevy, #9692.....................................$35.00
Hershey Antique Auto Club, 1926 Fire Truck, #9779 .....$75.00
Hershey Chocolate Almonds, 1912 Ford, #1351 ....$24.00
Hershey Cocoa, 1905 Ford, #9665.....................................$55.00
Hershey Milk Chocolate, 1912 Ford, #1350 ....$30.00
Hills Bank & Trust, 1950 Chevy, #9109..........................$95.00
Hollycliff Farms, 1926 Mack Truck, #9972.......................$25.00
Home Hardware, 1931 Hawkeye, #9200 ....$25.00
Hostess Cupcakes, 1913 Ford, #9422................................$30.00
House of Books, 1913 Ford, #9256 ....$40.00
Houston Rockets, 1956 Ford Pickup, #B882.....................$20.00
Humble Oil Co, 1950 Chevy Pickup, #F855.....................$35.00
HWI Hardware, 1905 Ford, #9674 ....$25.00
IGA, 1917 Ford, #F951 ....$20.00
IGA 60th Anniversary, 1932 Ford, #9350 ....$45.00
Indian Motorcycle, 1920 International, #3069 ....$30.00
Indianapolis Colts, Stearman Plane, #F708 ....$24.00
International Harvester, 1959 Chevy El Camino, #4450 .$28.00
Iowa Hawkeyes, 1951 GMC, #B782.................................$25.00
Iowa State Cyclones, 1912 Ford, #B783...........................$30.00
Iowa 106th Fireman Association, 1913 Ford, #2137.........$85.00
Jasper Racing Engines, 1932 Ford, #3774..........................$65.00
JC Penney, 1918 Ford, #1328 ....$40.00
JC Whitney, 1923 Chevy, #9364 ....$38.00
JF Good Co, 1913 Ford, #9524 ....$40.00
JI Case, 1931 International, JLE, #0734............................$20.00
Jiffy Lube, 1955 Cameo Pickup, #B997 ....$25.00
Jim Beam Dist 1-1996, 1938 Chevy, #F324 ....$25.00
Jim Beam Dist 5-1993, Step Van, #3772...........................$40.00
John Deere, Vega Plane, #35024.......................................$55.00
John Deere, 1931 Hawkeye, #5687 ....$25.00
John Deere Servicegard, 1938 Chevy, #F072.....................$95.00
K-Mart, 1931 International, JLE, #5043 ....$32.00
Kansas City Chiefs, 1951 GMC, #B838.............................$20.00
Kauffmans Fruit Farm, 1931 Hawkeye, #9758..................$40.00
Kerr-McGee, 1913 Ford, #9130..$55.00
Key Aid Distributors, 1931 Hawkeye, #9648 ....$25.00
Kingsport Time News, 1923 Chevy, #B672 ....$35.00
Kodak, 1905 Ford, gold spokes, #9985 ....$225.00
Kodak, 1905 Ford, red wheels, #9985...............................$65.00
Kraft Foods, 1905 Ford, #B203 ....$45.00
Lake of the Ozarks, 1923 Chevy, #B380 ....$30.00
Lawson Products, 1931 Hawkeye, #9261...........................$35.00
Leinkenkugel Brewing Co, 1913 Ford, #F163 ....$38.00
Lennox, 1905 Ford, #9323 ....$35.00
Lincoln Fire Co, 192a6 Tire Truck, #1665 ....$35.00
Lion Oil Co, 1931 Hawkeye, #7617 ....$24.00
Lionel Trains, Stearman Plane, #37525 ....$55.00
Lipton Tea Co, 1932 Ford, #9087 ....$35.00
Lone Star Beer, 1926 Mack Truck, #9168.........................$55.00
Los Angeles Dodgers, 1938 Chevy, #F728 ....$20.00
Los Angeles Lakers, 1918 Ford, #B462.............................$22.00
Los Angeles Police Dept, 1912 Ford, #B992 ....$25.00
Ludens Candies, 1923 Chevy, #F105 ....$35.00
Lyken & Wisconsico Ambulance, 1918 Ford, #B695 ....$24.00
Maine Cycle, 1938 Chevy, #B041 ....$40.00
Manning Equipment 40th Anniversary, 1912 Ford, #F380..$30.00
Marathon Oil, 1929 International Tanker, JLE, #4044 ....$30.00
Marathon Oil, 1931 Hawkeye Tanker, #9361 ....$24.00
Marlin Plumbing & Heating, 1950 Chevy, #7678............$25.00
Marsh Supermarket, 1912 Ford, #B015 ....$25.00
Marsh Supermarket, 1931 Hawkeye Crates, #B761 ....$25.00
Martins Potato Chips, Step Van, #9856............................$40.00
Massey Ferguson, 1955 Cameo Pickup, #2305 ....$24.00
Massey Harris, 1913 Ford, #1092 ....$25.00
Maurice's, 1932 Ford, #9476...$34.00
McDonalds, Air Express Plane, #H302 ....$25.00
McDonalds Racing, Vega Plane, #00327 ....$40.00

Medicine Shoppe, 1913 Ford, #B701 ....$35.00
Meijer Foods, 1913 Ford, #9352 ....$20.00
Merit Oil Co, 1926 Mack Tanker, #9980 ....$75.00
Merita Bread, 1913 Ford, #9316 ....$22.00
Miami Dolphins, Stearman Plane, #F690 ....$24.00
Michelin Tires, 1931 International, JLE, #5046 ....$28.00
Mike Parsons Creative Services, 1938 Chevy, #H184 ....$24.00
Miller Beer, 1913 Ford, #9277 ....$45.00
Miller Beer, 1950 Chevy Tractor Trailer, #9270 ....$25.00
Miller High Life, 1950 Chevy, #9269 ....$30.00
Millers Paint & Wallpaper Store, 1917 Ford, #F044 ....$32.00
Mills Farm & Fleet, 1918 Ford, #H156 ....$22.00
Mills Ford Lincoln Mercury, 1913 Ford, #H157 ....$22.00
Minnesota Industrial Tools, Step Van, #9308 ....$25.00
Minnesota State Patrol, 1932 Ford, #4943 ....$50.00
Minnesota Vikings, 1955 Cameo Pickup, #B337 ....$30.00
Mobil Oil, 1918 Ford, #7519 ....$40.00
Mobil Oil, 1931 Hawkeye, #9742 ....$60.00
New York Farm Show, 1931 International, JLE, #5040 ....$35.00
New York Fire Department, Step Van, #H292 ....$35.00
Northwest Hardware Co, 1955 Cameo Pickup, #3859 ....$22.00
Oklahoma Oil Marketers, 1931 Hawkeye Tanker, #9592 ....$50.00
Old El Paso, 1905 Ford, #7636 ....$45.00
Old Milwaukee Beer, 1918 Ford, #9173 ....$35.00
Old Style Beer, Stearman Plane, #F579 ....$24.00
Olympia Beer, Vega Plane, #35022 ....$30.00
Orchard Supply, 1932 Ford, #B081 ....$40.00
Orlando Magic, 1918 Ford, #B484 ....$22.00
Otasco, 1926 Mack Truck, #2134 ....$55.00
Our Own Hardware, 1960 Ford Pickup, #F985 ....$24.00
Owatonna Tool Co, 1932 Ford, #B198 ....$75.00
Pabst Beer, 1938 Chevy, #F587 ....$20.00
Pennsylvania Power & Light, 1923 Chevy, #F020 ....$38.00
Pennzoil, 1918 Ford, #7676 ....$30.00
Pennzoil, 1931 Hawkeye Wrecker, #7528 ....$25.00
Peoples National Bank, 1913 Ford, #9877 ....$95.00
Pepsi-Cola, Stearman Plane, #37504 ....$80.00
Pepsi-Cola, 1905 Ford, #9736 ....$65.00
Pepsi-Cola, 1931 International, JLE, #5025 ....$75.00
Pepsi-Cola, 1950 Chevy, #9635 ....$45.00
Pepsi-Cola, 1955 Cameo Pickup, #7506 ....$50.00

Prairie Farms Milk, 1923 Chevy, #3958, $20.00.

Pepsi-Cola, 1957 Chevy Nomad, JLE, #2003 ....$65.00
Pepsi-Cola, 1959 Chevy El Camino, #F844 ....$34.00
Perkasie Lions Club, 1932 Ford, #2162 ....$32.00
Philadelphia Cream Cheese, 1913 Ford, #9835 ....$38.00
Philadelphia Eagles, Stearman Plane, #F713 ....$30.00
Philgas, 1938 Chevy, #B039 ....$125.00
Phillips 66, 1926 Mack Truck, #9231 ....$250.00
Phillips 66, 1940 Ford Pickup, #F440 ....$50.00
Phillips 66 75th Anniversary, 1929 International, JLE, #4030 ....$125.00
Phoenix Cardinals, 1931 Hawkeye, #B157 ....$30.00
Pittsburgh Steelers, 1957 Chevy, #F634 ....$24.00
Police Department, 1938 Chevy, #B686 ....$25.00
Pro Hardware, 1956 Ford Pickup, #B456 ....$28.00
PSI Energy, Bucket Truck, #3593 ....$32.00
Publix, 1913 Ford, #B498 ....$18.00
Publix, 1931 Hawkeye Box, #F991 ....$22.00
Publix (Dairi-Fresh), 1905 Ford, #9001 ....$25.00
Publix (Danish Bakery), 1913 Ford, #9249 ....$35.00
Publix (Deli), 1905 Ford, #7689 ....$25.00
Publix (Food & Pharmacy), 1950 Chevy, #9692 ....$35.00
Publix (Produce), 1917 Ford, #9148 ....$25.00
Publix (Shop/Pleasure), 1918 Ford, #9149 ....$35.00
Pumpkin World USA, 1950 Chevy, #1315 ....$25.00
Purina Mills Inc, 1913 Ford, #9103 ....$35.00
Quaker Oats, 1912 Ford, #F539 ....$40.00
Quaker Oats, 1925 Kenworth, #B268 ....$125.00
Quaker Oats, 1931 Hawkeye, #F569 ....$45.00
Quaker Oats, 1955 Cameo Pickup, #H359 ....$35.00
Quaker State Oil, 1913 Ford, #9195 ....$95.00
Quaker State Oil, 1926 Mack Truck, #9196 ....$32.00
Quakertown National Bank, 1905 Ford, #9979 ....$65.00
Quakertown National Bank, 1950 Chevy, #9972 ....$85.00
Quality Farm & Fleet, 1925 Kenworth, #B552 ....$20.00
Quality Farm & Fleet, 1932 Ford, #3951 ....$95.00
Radio Flyer, 1931 Hawkeye, #3549 ....$55.00
Radio Shack, 1931 Hawkeye, #9646 ....$38.00
Rajah Temple, 1925 Kenworth, #4895 ....$34.00
Randy Hundley Baseball Camps, 1931 Hawkeye, #3606 ....$34.00
RC Cola, 1917 Ford, #9827 ....$35.00
RCA, 1926 Mack Truck, #9275 ....$45.00
Red Crown Gasoline, P51 Mustang Plane, #47005 ....$25.00
Red Crown Gasoline, 1918 Ford, #1367 ....$24.00
Red Crown Gasoline, 1931 Hawkeye, 1st issue, #7654 ....$50.00
Red Rose Tea, 1913 Ford, #2130 ....$34.00
Reese's Peanut Butter Cups, 1923 Chevy, #9808 ....$28.00
Reese's Pieces, 1950 Chevy, #9809 ....$28.00
Relco Refrigeration, 1931 Hawkeye, #9130 ....$40.00
Remington Arms 175th Anniversary, 1931 Hawkeye, #7547 ....$65.00
Reminisce Magazine, 1918 Ford, #9628 ....$25.00
Respond First Aid, 1950 Chevy, #2793 ....$40.00
Richard Petty, 1913 Ford, #9573 ....$150.00
Richard Petty, 1931 International, JLE, #4101 ....$38.00
Richard Petty, 1950 Chevy, #2170 ....$85.00
Richlandtown Centennial, 1926 Mack Tanker, #9290 ....$35.00
Ringling Bros Circus, 1913 Ford, #9027 ....$145.00
Riverview Nursery, 1926 Mack Tanker, #9121 ....$35.00

Roanoke Life Saving & First Aid Crew, 1923 Chevy, #B736...$40.00
Roche Vitamins 25th Anniversary, 1917 Ford, #B540.....$45.00
Ronald McDonald House, 1920 International, JLE, #3083 .$22.00
Royalite Oil Co, 1931 Hawkeye, #9568..........................$30.00
Rumsey Electric, 1917 Ford, #F473..............................$40.00
Ryder Truck Rental, 1931 International, JLE, #5054.......$28.00
Safeguard Soap, 1950 Chevy, #7508...............................$35.00
Safety Kleen, Step Van, #9289......................................$45.00
Salem Rescue Squad, 1938 Chevy, #F510.......................$30.00
San Antonio Fire Department, 1926 Fire Truck, #2871...$75.00
San Francisco Police Department, 1932 Ford, #9039.......$85.00
San Francisco 49ers, Stearman Plane, #F692..................$30.00
San Francisco 49ers, 1913 Ford, #1297..........................$95.00
Sara Lee, 1950 Chevy, #9941...$65.00
Schneiders Meats, 1913 Ford, #1332..............................$35.00
Schneiders Meats, 1926 Mack Truck, #9228...................$95.00
Schwan's Ice Cream, 1950 Chevy, #9210........................$95.00
Scott Tissue, 1917 Ford, #9652......................................$30.00
Seagrams Ginger Ale, 1931 Hawkeye, #F964..................$45.00
Sealed Power/Speed-Pro, 1913 Ford, #2161....................$25.00
Sears, 1913 Ford, #2129...$45.00
Seattle Mariners, 1905 Ford, #B146................................$25.00
Seattle Supersonics, 1956 Ford Pickup, #B879...............$20.00
Seitz Meat Co, 1931 Hawkeye, #2787.............................$35.00
Sentry Hardware, Vega Plane, #35051............................$30.00
Service Team, 1955 Cameo Pickup, #9544......................$20.00
Servistar Hardware, 1932 Ford, #3843............................$25.00
Seven-Eleven, 1926 Mack Truck, #9155..........................$40.00
Seven-Up, 1913 Ford, #1662..$125.00
Seven-Up, 1955 Cameo Pickup, #F095...........................$20.00
Shaws Supermarket, 1938 Chevy, #H013........................$25.00
Shell Oil Co, P51 Plane, #47011.....................................$65.00
Shell Oil Co, 1935 Mack Truck, JLE, #3011...................$40.00
Shell Oil Co, 1938 Chevy, #3894...................................$28.00
Shell Oil Co, 1939 Dodge Airflow, #4866.......................$35.00
Shoprite, 1918 Ford, #9163..$30.00
Sidney Fire Department, 1913 Ford, #1335....................$28.00
Signal Motor Oil, 1931 Hawkeye, #2164.........................$26.00
Signal Oil Co, 1931 International, JLE, #4015................$30.00
Silver Springs Flea Market, 1918 Ford, #9619................$25.00
Sinclair, 1918 Ford, #9483...$40.00
Sinclair, 1926 Mack Truck, #2120..................................$65.00
Skelly Oil Co, 1931 International Tanker, JLE, #3035....$28.00
Slatington Lions Club, 1938 Chevy, #B716.....................$30.00
Smith Brothers Garage, 1931 Hawkeye Wrecker, #1659 .$30.00
Smithsonian Institution, 1912 Ford, #3616.....................$50.00
Smokecraft, 1918 Ford, #9493..$30.00
Smokey Bear, 1913 Ford, #9124.....................................$85.00
Smokey Bear, 1937 Ford Tractor Trailer, #2147..............$55.00
Snap On Tools, 1918 Ford, #B667...................................$40.00
Snyder Drugs, 1925 Kenworth, #F104.............................$30.00
Sohio, 1926 Mack Truck, #9269...................................$275.00
Sohio, 1938 Chevy, #3940..$50.00
Southern States Oil, 1918 Ford, #9322...........................$45.00
Southern States Oil, 1926 Mack Truck, #9199..............$195.00
Southwest Airlines, 1950 Chevy, #9976..........................$50.00
Sovereign Bank, 1932 Ford, #F488..................................$24.00
Sparklettes Water, 1926 Mack Truck, #9741...................$24.00
Spartan Food Stores, 1917 Ford, #9583............................$20.00
Spring Grove School, 1931 Hawkeye, #B299...................$34.00
Springettsburg Fire Co, 1926 Fire Truck, #1338..............$25.00
Spur Gasoline, 1937 Ford Tractor Trailer, #3901............$24.00
St Ignace Car Show, 1950 Chevy, #7629.........................$35.00
St Ignace Car Show, 1959 Chevy El Camino, #F369.......$25.00
State College Centennial, 1926 Fire Truck, #F885..........$38.00
State Line Auto Auction, 1932 Ford, #1655..................$175.00
Steamtown USA, 1926 Mack Truck, #9167......................$85.00
Steelcase, 1913 Ford, red w/gold trim, #1657..................$95.00
Steelcase, 1926 Mack Truck, Vintage series, #9041.........$38.00
Steve Thompson Trucking, 1937 Ford Tractor Trailer, #9613.....$28.00
Stewart & Stevenson Auto Accessories, 1917 Ford, #F051 ..$28.00
Storey Wrecker, 1931 Hawkeye Wrecker, #9006............$40.00
Street Cycles Harley Davidson, 1955 Cameo Pickup, #B174...$55.00
Strohs Beer, 1918 Ford, #7679...$45.00
Sturgis 53rd Annual Ralley, 1955 Cameo Pickup, #3612.$75.00
Sturgis 54th Annual Ralley, 1931 International, JLE, #5086.....$55.00
Sun Holiday Travel, 1918 Ford, #9618............................$24.00
Sunbeam Bread, 1932 Ford, #1330..................................$25.00
Sunbeam Bread, 1950 Chevy, #1329................................$45.00
Sunmaid Raisins, 1905 Ford, #9575................................$35.00
Sunoco, Vega Plane, #35004..$45.00
Sunoco, 1926 Mack Tanker, #9796..................................$50.00
Super Bowl XXVII, 1931 Hawkeye, #9346.......................$35.00
Super Valu, Air Express Plane, #B419.............................$30.00
Supertest Petroleum, 1938 Chevy, #9538........................$32.00
Sweet & Low, 1950 Chevy, #7631...................................$60.00
Swiss Farm Stores, 1931 Hawkeye, #B114.......................$28.00
Tabasco Sauce, 1925 Kenworth, #F504............................$30.00
Take Two Video, 1913 Ford, #2997.................................$25.00
Tampa Bay Buccaneers, 1951 GMC, #B829.....................$20.00
Tastykake, 1917 Ford, #F846...$35.00
Terminex Pest Control, 1932 Ford, #9346........................$30.00

Texaco Petroleum Products, Gasoline Truck, #9238, $600.00.

Texaco, Stearman Plane, #F121......................................$30.00
Texaco, 1905 Ford, #9321..$165.00
Texaco, 1925 Kenworth Stakebed Truck, #9385..............$35.00
Texaco, 1926 Mack Truck, #9040....................................$75.00
Texaco Lubricants, 1929 International, JLE, #4028.........$95.00
Texas A&M University, 1931 Hawkeye, #F437...............$30.00

Third Savings & Loan, 1923 Chevy, #B715 ....**$26.00**
Thomas English Muffins, 1932 Ford, #9128.....................**$50.00**
Thunderhills Golf Classic, 1905 Ford, #9433...................**$65.00**
Thunderhills Golf Classic, 1918 Ford, #7566 ....**$150.00**
Tide Laundry Detergent, 1913 Ford, #7509 ....**$45.00**
Tiny Lund Fish Camp, 1955 Cameo Pickup, #3264 ....**$65.00**
Tisco, 1917 Ford, #9983 ....**$18.00**
Titlist Golf Balls, 1913 Ford, #9489 ....**$55.00**
Tom's Snack Foods, Step Van, #1337 ....**$25.00**
Tonka, 1913 Ford, #9739...**$35.00**
Tower City Ambulance, 1917 Ford, #9142 ....**$25.00**
Toy Farmer Country Store, Trolley Car, #B814 ....**$30.00**
Toy Farmer Country Store, 1913 Ford, #1664 ....**$22.00**
Toy Shop, 1926 Mack Truck, #9442 ....**$22.00**
Toy Town Museum, 1931 Hawkeye, #F779 ....**$40.00**
Toys-R-Us, 1918 Ford, #4587 ....**$28.00**
Tractor Supply Co, 1913 Ford, #1349 ....**$35.00**
Tractor Supply Co, 1917 Ford, #9356 ....**$25.00**
Tractor Supply Co, 1926 Mack Truck, #9133.....................**$35.00**
Tractor Supply Co, 1950 Chevy, #9207 ....**$65.00**
Tremont Ambulance Association, 1932 Ford, #7665 ....**$40.00**
Tri-Cities Christian Schools, 1918 Ford, #B971 ....**$28.00**
Trico Industries, 1932 Ford, #9495 ....**$75.00**
Tropicana Orange Juice, 1932 Ford, #9798........................**$35.00**
Truckstops of America, 1932 Ford, #9687 ....**$35.00**
True Value Hardware, 1905 Ford, #9301 ....**$40.00**

True Value, 1926 Mack Bulldog, #9105, $32.00.

True Value Hardware, 1931 Hawkeye, #9501...................**$18.00**
True Value Hardware, 1951 GMC, #F266 ....**$25.00**
Trustworthy Hardware, 1905 Ford, #9395..........................**$95.00**
Trustworthy Hardware, 1918 Ford, #9744..........................**$50.00**
Tucson Miniature Auto Club, 1950 Chevy, #9222 ....**$40.00**
Tulsa Fire Department, 1926 Fire Truck, #9846 ....**$26.00**
Turkey Hill Markets, 1913 Ford, #9614 ....**$22.00**
Turner Hydraulics, 1931 Hawkeye, #2106 ....**$25.00**
Twentieth Street Bank, 1932 Ford, #2198 ....**$30.00**
Tydol Flying A, 1931 Hawkeye Tanker, #9123 ....**$30.00**
Ukrop's Market, 1932 Ford, #B487 ....**$44.00**
United Airlines, 1913 Ford, #9233 ....**$40.00**
United Airlines, 1926 Mack Truck, #9152 ....**$35.00**
United Parcel Service, 1912 Ford, #9704...........................**$35.00**
United Van Lines, 1917 Ford, #9715 ....**$26.00**
United Van Lines, 1925 Kenworth, #B725.........................**$36.00**
Universal Tire Co, 1955 Cameo Pickup, #3288 ....**$25.00**
University of Auburn Tigers, 1918 Ford, #F449 ....**$40.00**
University of Florida Gators, 1905 Ford, #9821...............**$75.00**
University of Kentucky Wildcats, 1918 Ford, #F920 ....**$50.00**
University of Notre Dame, 1938 Chevy, #B714 ....**$35.00**
University of Tennessee, 1913 Ford, #B520.......................**$95.00**
US Army Air Corps, Vega Plane, #12700...........................**$20.00**
US Mail, Stearman Plane, #37522 ....**$40.00**
US Mail, 1905 Ford, #7641 ....**$35.00**
US Mail, 1913 Ford, #9532 ....**$30.00**
US Mail, 1918 Ford, #9843 ....**$45.00**
US Mail, 1932 Ford, #9051 ....**$75.00**
US Mail, 1950 Chevy Tractor Trailer, #7640....................**$65.00**
US Navy, Air Express Plane, #F017 ....**$25.00**
USA Baseball, 1905 Ford, #9795.......................................**$35.00**
USAF Thunderbirds, F16 Plane, #46002 ....**$20.00**
V&S Variety Store, 1905 Ford, #9622 ....**$45.00**
V&S Variety Store, 1913 Ford, #9522 ....**$25.00**
Valley Forge, 1926 Mack Truck, #9616 ....**$95.00**
Valvoline, 1937 Ford Tractor Trailer, #9260 ....**$30.00**
Very Fine Juice, 1923 Chevy, #B109.................................**$25.00**
Vintage Chevrolet Club, 1938 Chevy, #B629 ....**$34.00**
Walgreen Drug Store, 1913 Ford, #9531...........................**$30.00**
Washington Apples, 1931 Hawkeye, #9559 ....**$38.00**
Washington Redskins, Stearman Plane, #F712.................**$30.00**
Washington State Apples, 1955 Cameo Pickup, #B378...**$40.00**
Watkins Inc, 1913 Ford, #F435 ....**$45.00**
Weaver's Meats 75th Anniversary, 1932 Ford, #F138 ......**$32.00**
Weil-McLain Boilers, 1905 Ford, #2122 ....**$30.00**
Weil-McLain Boilers, 1926 Mack Truck, #8580...............**$45.00**
West Bend, 1913 Ford, #9237 ....**$34.00**
West Friendship Fire Co, 1926 Fire Truck, #B763............**$28.00**
Westlake Hardware 90th Anniversary, 1912 Ford, #F567 ..**$30.00**
Wheelers, 1913 Ford, #1358..**$35.00**
White Castle, 1931 International, JLE, #5045.................**$30.00**
White Rose Gasoline, 1931 Hawkeye Tanker, #1657 ......**$30.00**
Wilwerts Harley Davidson, 1920 International, JLE, #3031 .**$350.00**
Wilwerts Harley Davidson, 1931 International, JLE, #5024....**$65.00**
Winchester, Stearman Plane, #3754 ....**$40.00**
Winn Dixie, 1918 Ford, #9116...**$25.00**
Winn Dixie, 1923 Chevy, #9144...**$20.00**
Winn Dixie, 1932 Ford, #9707 ....**$35.00**
Wireless, 1931 Hawkeye, #F080 ....**$35.00**
Wisconsin Farm Bureau, 1918 Ford, #B700 ....**$34.00**
Wix Filters, 1932 Ford, #9810 ....**$125.00**
Wix Filters, 1955 Cameo Pickup, #9756...........................**$65.00**
Wolfgang Candy, 1913 Ford, #9440..................................**$35.00**
Wonder Bread, 1913 Ford, #9161......................................**$48.00**

First Gear

All American Plaza, 1957 International Wrecker, #19-1467..**$40.00**
All States Transmissions, Mack B-61 Tractor Trailer, #19-1469 ....**$58.00**

Allegheny Coal Co, B-61 Mack Dump Truck, #19-1828 .$85.00
American Flyer, 1951 Ford Stake Truck, #19-0118..........$50.00
Anheuser Busch Eagle Snacks, 1951 Ford Van, #19-1121.$75.00
Anheuser Busch Eagle Snacks, 1952 GMC, #19-1407.....$32.00
Armstrong Tires, Mack B-61 Tractor Trailer, #19-1465 ..$74.00
BASF Corp, 1951 Ford Van, #29-1042...........................$95.00
Bechtel Construction, B-61 Mack Dump Truck, #19-2033 .$48.00
Blue Diamond Co, B-61 Mack Dump Truck, #19-1934 .$150.00
BP Gasoline, Mack B-61 Tractor Trailer, #19-2006.........$65.00
Budweiser, Mack B-61 Tractor Trailer, #19-1912.............$65.00
Burlington Truck Lines, 1956 White Tractor Trailer, #18-1545 ....$65.00
Busch Light Beer, 1952 GMC Van, #19-1622.................$38.00
Campbell's Soup, Mack B-61 Tractor Trailer, #19-1314..$65.00
Cape Cod Potato Chips, Mack B-61 Tractor Trailer, #19-1279..$58.00
Cape Cod Potato Chips, 1957 International Van, #19-1193..$32.00
Carlisle Collector Events, Mack B-61 Tractor Trailer, #19-1781 ....$49.00
Carlisle Collector Events, 1957 International Wrecker, #19-1732 ....$38.00
Chevrolet, 1949 Chevy Van, #19-1410...........................$30.00
Chevrolet - See the USA, 1949 Chevy Van, #19-1410 ...$30.00
Chevrolet Motor Co, 1949 Chevy, #10-1328..................$32.00
Chevrolet Rock Solid, 1949 Chevy, #10-1329................$30.00
Chevron Gasoline, 1951 Ford Tanker, #19-1021.............$40.00
Citgo, 1957 International Tanker, #29-1248...................$60.00
Civil Defense, 1949 Chevy, #19-1355.............................$30.00
Coker Tire, 1951 Ford Stake Truck, #19-1249................$45.00
Cole's Express, Mack B-61 Tractor Trailer, #19-1826......$85.00
Conrock Corporation, B-61 Mack Dump Truck, #19-1956 ...$50.00
CP Ward Construction, B-61 Mack Dump Truck, #19-1827..$75.00
Custom Chrome, 1951 Ford Stake Truck, #18-1161........$54.00

Ford, 1951 Ford F-6 Dry Goods Van, $30.00.

Custom Chrome 25th Anniversary, 1952 GMC Box, #18-1361 ....$95.00
Daisy Air Rifles, 1952 GMC Van, #10-0126....................$30.00
Daisy Red Ryder, 1957 International, #10-0125...............$30.00
Eastern Express, 1953 Ford Box, #19-1481.......................$32.00
Eastwood Co, 1952 GMC Wrecker, #19-0109.................$80.00
Eastwood Museum, 1951 Ford Van, #19-1010...............$115.00
Erector (AC Gilbert), 1957 International Van, #19-0111..$30.00
Esso, Mack B-61 Tractor Trailer, #19-1670......................$75.00
Esso, 1957 International Tanker, #19-1197......................$50.00
Exxon, Mack B-61 Tractor Trailer, #19-1708..................$45.00
Exxon Aviation, 1957 International Tanker, #19-1800...$35.00
First Gear Inc, 1951 Ford Stake Truck, #19-0120............$40.00
Ford Motorcraft, 1951 Ford Tanker, #20-1124................$25.00
Ford Quality Parts, 1951 Ford Box, #20-1123..................$25.00
Frank Dibella Moving, 1957 International Moving Van, #19-1450 ....$45.00
Global Van Lines, 1957 International Moving Van, #19-1801 ....$50.00
Graham Trucking Co, 1952 GMC Box, #19-1066...........$35.00
Grapette Soda, Mack B-61 Tractor Trailer, #19-1619......$75.00
Great Northern Railway, 1957 International Box, #19-1175..$32.00
Gulf Oil, 1957 International Wrecker, #19-1336.............$80.00
Hamm's Beer, 1953 Ford, #29-1480................................$35.00
Hershey Cocoa, 1952 GMC Sack, #19-1273....................$38.00
Hooker Headers, 1957 International Van, #10-1284........$40.00
Hostess Cupcakes, Mack B-61 Tractor Trailer, #19-1530...$58.00
Howard Johnsons, Mack B-61 Tractor Trailer, #18-1796.$65.00
Humble Oil Co, Mack B-61 Tractor Trailer, #19-1395..$175.00
Iowa Hawkeyes, 1952 GMC Van, #29-1268.....................$42.00
JC Whitney, 1957 International Wrecker, #10-1207.......$45.00
Lanser's Garage, 1952 GMC Wrecker, #19-1049.............$40.00
Lone Star Beer, 1952 GMC Van, #10-1258......................$32.00
Marathon Oil, 1953 Ford Tanker, #29-1588.....................$34.00
Marble King, 1957 International Flatbed, #19-1709........$52.00
Marx Toys, 1957 International F/T, #19-0113.................$48.00
Mayflower Transit Co, 1953 Kenworth Tractor Trailer, #19-1803 ....$80.00
McDonald's, 1957 International Box, #19-1797..............$40.00
McLean Trucking Co, 1956 White Tractor Trailer, #18-1845..$65.00
Mercury Marine, Mack B-61 Tractor Trailer, #19-1266...$75.00
Michelin Tires, Mack B-61 Tractor Trailer, #19-1502.....$65.00
Mobil Oil, Mack B-61 Tractor Trailer, #19-1556.............$65.00
Mobil Oil, 1952 GMC Tanker, #29-1231.........................$45.00
Mobilgas, 1957 International Wrecker, #18-1381............$95.00
Mobilgas Parkway, 1952 GMC Tanker, #29-1446..........$125.00
Moon Pie Chocolate, 1951 Ford Box, #19-1626...............$28.00
Motor City Ford, 1953 Ford Pickup, #307000...................$40.00
Mushroom Transportation, 1956 White Tractor Trailer, #19-1854 ....$60.00
National Motorcycle Museum, 1951 Ford Van, #29-1274.$48.00
New York Central System, 1953 Ford Box, #19-1436......$28.00
New York Fire Department, 1957 International Wrecker, #19-1401 ....$55.00
Northern Pacific Railroad, Mack B-61 Tractor Trailer, #19-1560..$58.00
Olympia Beer, 1952 GMC, #29-1482..............................$25.00

Paul Arpin Moving Co, 1957 International Moving Van, #19-1382 ....$45.00
Peach State Motorsports, 1949 Chevy, #19-1419 ....$35.00
Pennsylvania Railroad, Mack B-61 Tractor Trailer, #19-1435 ....$45.00
Pennzoil, 1952 GMC Wrecker, #19-1062 ....$50.00
Pepsi-Cola, Mack B-61 Tractor Trailer, #19-1357 ....$95.00
Pepsi-Cola, 1952 GMC Bottle, #10-1349 ....$30.00
Pepsi-Cola, 1953 Ford Pickup, #19-1582 ....$45.00
Pepsi-Cola, 1953 Ford Van, #10-1351 ....$30.00
Pez Candy, 1957 International Box, #29-1714 ....$50.00
Philadelphia Fire Department, 1953 Ford Pickup, #18-1585 ..$45.00
Philadelphia Wrecking, 1957 International Wrecker, #18-1347 ....$80.00
Phillips 66, 1957 International Fire Truck, #19-1337 ....$85.00
Phillips 66 Pipeline, 1949 Chevy Panel, #19-1831 ....$40.00
Phillips 66 Pipeline, 1951 Ford Flatbed, #19-1427 ....$50.00
Phillips 66 Trop-Artic Oil, Mack B-61 Tractor Trailer, #19-1722 ....$65.00
PIE Trucking, 1952 GMC Van, #10-1043 ....$50.00
Police Department, 1957 International Wrecker, #19-1264 .$35.00
Quaker Oats, Buckboard & Horses, #0004 ....$65.00
Railway Express, Mack B-61 Tractor Trailer, #19-1654 ...$65.00
RC Cola, 1951 Ford Bottle, #19-1131 ....$45.00
Reading Anthracite Co, Mack B-61 Dump Truck, #18-1872...$55.00
Remington, Mack B-61 Tractor Trailer, #10-1292 ....$75.00
Remington I-Goose, 1952 GMC Van, #10-1134 ....$35.00
Remington I-Turkey, 1951 Ford Van, #10-1133 ....$35.00
Remington II- Squirrel, 1953 Ford Van, #10-1571 ....$28.00
Remington II-Deer, 1953 Ford Van, #10-1485 ....$28.00
Roadrunner Express, 1951 Ford Van, #19-1108 ....$45.00
Roadway Express, 1953 Ford, #10-1379 ....$38.00
Santa Barbara Fire Department, 1957 International Fire Truck, #19-1408 ....$38.00
Santa Fe Trails Transportation, 1957 International Van, #10-1168 ....$85.00
Schultz Co Grand Pianos, 1957 International Box, #19-1332..$42.00
Seekonk Speedway, 1951 Ford w/Stock Car, #19-1516 ....$45.00
Shell Oil Co, Mack B-61 Tractor Trailer, #19-1392 ....$175.00
Shell Oil Co, 1952 GMC Tanker, #28-0105 ....$50.00
Shell Oil Co, 1953 Ford Pickup, #19-1554 ....$40.00
Shell Oil Co, 1957 International Tanker, #29-1270 ....$35.00
Skelly Oil Co, 1951 Ford Fire Truck, #19-1927 ....$38.00
Smith & Wesson, Mack B-61 Tractor Trailer, #18-1219 .$75.00
Smith & Wesson, 1952 GMC Stake Truck, #10-1326 ....$30.00
Special Export, 1951 Ford Stake Truck, #10-1259 ....$32.00
Spring Township, Mack B-61 Dump Truck, #19-2000 ....$52.00
State Highway Department, Mack B-61 Dump Truck, #19-1813 ....$75.00
Storey Wrecker, 1957 International Wrecker, #19-1665 .$38.00
Strohs Beer, 1952 GMC Van, #10-1353 ....$40.00
Sunshine Biscuits, Mack B-61 Tractor Trailer, #10-1472.$55.00
Sunshine Biscuits, 1957 International, #10-1473 ....$32.00
Texaco Pipeline, 1949 Chevy Panel, #19-1391 ....$175.00
Texaco Pipeline, 1953 Ford Pickup, #19-1688 ....$95.00
TNT Trucking, Mack B-61 Tractor Trailer, #10-1598 ....$50.00
Tollway & Tunnel, 1957 International Wrecker, #19-1439 ....$55.00
True Value Hardware, Mack B-61 Tractor Trailer, #10-1486 .$55.00
True Value Hardware, 1953 Ford Van, #19-1490 ....$34.00
Tydol Flying A, 1957 International Wrecker, #19-1707 ..$34.00
United Ice & Coal, Mack B-61 Dump Truck, #18-1850 ..$75.00
US Army Ambulance, 1949 Chevy, #19-1388 ....$25.00
US Army Fuel, 1957 International Tanker, #29-1380 ....$30.00
US Mail, Mack B-61 Tractor Trailer, #19-1302 ....$65.00
US Mail, 1953 Ford Van, #19-1441 ....$40.00
Utica Club Beer, Mack B-61 Tractor Trailer, #18-1697...$70.00
Valley Asphalt Co, Mack B-61 Dump Truck, #19-1958 ..$65.00
Von Der Ahe Moving, 1957 International Moving Van, #19-1448 ....$45.00
Winchester, Mack B-61 Tractor Trailer, #18-1320 ....$70.00
Wonder Bread, Mack B-61 Tractor Trailer, #19-1529 ....$58.00

Spec-Cast

Allied Van Lines, 1929 Ford, #2551 ....$20.00
Allis Chalmers, 1929 Ford Freight Truck, #2028 ....$25.00
American Airlines, 1929 Ford Fire Pumper, #02053 ....$22.00
Amoco, Vintage Plane, #0805 ....$75.00
Bell System, 1931 Ford, #1004 ....$24.00
Big A Auto Parts, 1929 Ford Wrecker, #1075 ....$20.00
Big A Auto Parts, 1936 Dodge Panel, #74028 ....$22.00
Big A Auto Parts, 1948 Ford Pickup, #68506 ....$28.00
Billy Ray Cyrus, 1929 Ford, #2588 ....$24.00
Brickyard 400, 1955 Chevy Convertible, #0459 ....$60.00
California Highway Patrol, 1937 Chevy, #15023 ....$24.00
Campbell's Soup, 1936 Dodge Convertible, #70002 ....$24.00
Campbell's Soup, 1955 Chevy, #50013 ....$28.00
Canada Tire, 1940 Ford Pickup, #3888 ....$28.00
Cheerios, 1942 Chevy Box, #75005 ....$28.00
Chevrolet Motor Co, 1937 Chevy Convertible, #0489 ....$22.00
Chevrolet Parts & Service, 1955 Chevy Sedan, #50020 ..$22.00
Chevrolet Racing, 1955 Chevy Convertible, #0490 ....$25.00
Chevron Employee Club of Houston, 1955 Chevy Convertible, #55015 ....$28.00
Chicago 10th Anniversary Bike Show, 1937 Chevy, #12504 ....$34.00
Chrome Specialties, 1955 Chevy, #50045 ....$45.00
Citgo, 1929 Ford, #2514 ....$30.00
Clark Oil & Refining, 1929 Ford Pickup, #1082 ....$24.00
Classic Auto Series, 1955 Chevy Convertible, #55002 ....$22.00
Classic Motorbooks, 1955 Chevy, #50032 ....$28.00
Classic Street Rods, 1929 Ford, #2578 ....$25.00
Coca-Cola, Kenworth Tractor Trailer, #30001 ....$48.00
Coca-Cola, 1929 Ford, #2711 ....$55.00
Conoco Oil, 1929 Ford, #2002 ....$30.00
Cooper Tire, 1914 Studebaker, #22508 ....$35.00
Cooper Tire, 1929 Ford, #1509 ....$55.00
Coors Field, 1942 Chevy Box, #75025 ....$38.00
Crown Petroleum, 1929 Ford Tanker, #2043 ....$30.00
Cycle Fabricators, 1955 Chevy, #50027 ....$40.00
Darlington 500, 1929 Ford, #2706 ....$65.00
Daytona Bike Week, 1929 Ford, #2589 ....$90.00
Diamond Rio, 1940 Ford, #67503 ....$24.00
Dick Spadaro Reproductions, 1948 Ford Panel, #327000.$38.00
Drag Specialties, 1931 Ford, #2524 ....$95.00
Dubuque Country Club, 1929 Ford, #1079 ....$20.00

Ducks Unlimited, 1937 Chevy, #15014 ....$45.00
Eastwood Club, 1929 Ford, #1735 ....$65.00
Eastwood Co, Vega Plane, #35000 ....$75.00
Eastwood Co II, 1936 Dodge Convertible, #264000 ....$65.00
Eatons of Canada, 1929 Ford, #0178 ....$28.00
Essolube Motor Oil, 1936 Dodge, #74003 ....$32.00
Fina Oil, 1929 Ford, #2004 ....$28.00
Ford, 1929 Ford Fire Truck, #2025 ....$20.00
Ford Sales & Service, 1940 Ford, #67502 ....$22.00
Frito-Lay, 1936 Dodge Pickup, #72041 ....$28.00
Gilmore Oil Co, 1940 Ford Tanker, #65504 ....$25.00
Gold Medal Flour, 1916 Studebaker, #25025 ....$22.00
Goodyear, 1937 Chevy, #15001 ....$20.00
Goodyear Tire Co, 1955 Chevy Convertible, #55006 ....$20.00
Gulf Oil, 1940 Ford Tanker, #65505 ....$25.00
Gumout Carburetor Cleaner, 1942 Chevy Box, #75002 ....$26.00
Hamm's Beer, 1929 Ford, #1014 ....$30.00
Harley Davidson, Kenworth Tractor Trailer, #99197 ....$75.00
Harley Davidson, 1929 Ford, #1516 ....$60.00
Harry Gant, 1929 Ford, #0228 ....$44.00
Heinz 57, 1916 Studebaker, #22502 ....$22.00
Hemmings Motor News, 1940 Ford Panel, #67506 ....$35.00
Hershey Chocolate Milk, 1916 Studebaker, #27503 ....$32.00
Hershey Milk Chocolate, 1936 Dodge, #74012 ....$24.00
HJ Heinz 57, 1929 Ford Pickup, #1027 ....$25.00
Hooters Atlanta 500, 1929 Ford, #2709 ....$75.00
Hot Wheels, 1929 Ford Panel, #316500 ....$50.00
Humble Oil Co, 1936 Dodge Tank, #72032 ....$28.00
Iola Old Car Show, 1940 Ford, #62504 ....$25.00
James Dean, 1955 Chevy, #50043 ....$24.00
JC Penney, 1940 Ford Pickup, #4737 ....$28.00
JC Whitney, 1916 Studebaker, #22520 ....$30.00
JC Whitney, 1936 Dodge Pickup, #72005 ....$35.00
Jewel Tea, 1931 Ford, #2584 ....$65.00
John Deere, 1936 Dodge Panel, #74042 ....$24.00
K&R Toy Show, Ballys 93, 1955 Chevy, #50028 ....$32.00
Kentucky Fried Chicken, 1940 Ford Panel, #67519 ....$22.00
Lennox 100th Anniversary, 1916 Studebaker, #22510 ....$95.00
Lennox 100th Anniversary, 1940 Ford, #62525 ....$55.00
Lionel Trains, 1955 Chevy, #303500 ....$32.00
Little Debbie Snacks, 1929 Ford, #2503 ....$28.00
Louisville Slugger, 1931 Ford, #1036 ....$25.00
Meisch Racing, 1929 Ford Convertible, #1535 ....$20.00
Mello Yello, 1929 Ford, #2710 ....$20.00
Miller Genuine Draft, 1929 Ford Chop Top, #1757 ....$30.00
Miller Lite Beer, 1929 Ford Tanker, #2044 ....$22.00
Mobil Oil, 1940 Ford Tanker, #65506 ....$35.00
Mobilgas, 1936 Dodge Tanker, #72007 ....$28.00
Model A Ford Club of America, 1929 Ford, #2542 ....$25.00
Moon Pie 75th Anniversary, 1957 Ford Sedan, #58009 ....$32.00
Mooseheart Farms, 1916 Studebaker, #22511 ....$25.00
Mopar, 1936 Dodge Panel, #321000 ....$34.00
Motorcraft #15 Racing, 1929 Ford, #0307 ....$20.00
Nabisco, 1929 Ford, #2508 ....$28.00
Olympia Beer, 1929 Ford, #2528 ....$15.00
Oreo Cookies, 1916 Studebaker, #25013 ....$22.00
Pabst Beer, 1929 Ford, #1512 ....$30.00
Penn State Nittany Lions, 1937 Chevy Convertible, #10044 .$25.00
Pennzoil, 1929 Ford, #1062 ....$28.00
Pennzoil, 1936 Dodge Tanker, #72010 ....$30.00
Pepsi-Cola, 1916 Studebaker, #22519 ....$30.00
Pepsi-Cola, 1936 Dodge Fire Truck, #72034 ....$34.00
Pepsi-Cola, 1936 Dodge Panel, #74013 ....$25.00
Pepsi-Cola, 1957 Ford Ranchero, #57006 ....$28.00
Planters Peanuts, 1957 Ford Sedan, #58008 ....$22.00
Police Department, 1937 Chevy Convertible, #10008 ....$24.00
Posies Racing, 1929 Ford, #1993 ....$34.00
Quaker State Racing, 1929 Ford, #0308 ....$22.00
Randy Travis, 1937 Chevy, #15019 ....$15.00
Red Crown Gasoline, 1940 Ford Tanker, #65502 ....$25.00
Richard Petty Hooters 500, Kenworth Tractor Trailer, #0316 ....$35.00
Richard Petty/Rick Wilson, 1937 Chevy, #0362 ....$40.00
Richmond Pontiac 400, 1929 Ford, #0212 ....$32.00
Rockingham Raceway, 1929 Ford, #0210 ....$65.00
Santa-Seasons Greetings, 1929 Ford, #1569 ....$20.00
Seacoast Harley Davidson, 1929 Ford Pickup, #1040 ....$295.00
Sentry Hardware, 1955 Chevy, #50030 ....$20.00
Sentry Hardware, 1957 Chevy Convertible, #55017 ....$28.00
Shell Oil Co, 1929 Ford, gold, #2007 ....$175.00
Shell Oil Co, 1936 Dodge Tanker, #72008 ....$32.00
Snap On Tools, 1929 Ford, #2598 ....$40.00
St Ignace Car Show, 1955 Chevy Sedan, #50041 ....$24.00
State Highway Patrol, 1940 Ford Convertible, #60004 ....$24.00
State Patrol, 1955 Chevy Panel, #50003 ....$20.00
Street Cycles Harley Davidson, 1929 Ford, #2563 ....$120.00
Sturgis 53rd Annual Ralley, 1937 Chevy, #15004 ....$125.00
Sunsweet, 1929 Ford, #1012 ....$35.00
Sunsweet, 1936 Dodge Panel, #74023 ....$20.00
Super Bell Axle Co, 1940 Ford, #326500 ....$35.00
Sweet & Low, 1929 Ford Roadster, #1554 ....$30.00
Talladega Speedway, 1929 Ford, #0235 ....$24.00
Tanya Tucker, 1937 Chevy Convertible, #10021 ....$24.00
Texaco, 1929 Ford, #2012 ....$40.00
Texaco Havoline, 1929 Ford, #2529 ....$45.00
Tootsie Roll, 1916 Studebaker, #22516 ....$45.00
Total Performance, 1931 Ford, #1169 ....$22.00
Toy Farmer Zeke, 1929 Ford, #1532 ....$25.00
Tractor Supply Co, 1916 Studebaker, #22537 ....$28.00
True Value Hardware-Conovor, 1948 Ford Pickup, #68503 ....$20.00
True Value Hardware-Green Thumb, 1955 Chevy Panel, #50049G $20.00
True Value Hardware-Tru-Test, 1937 Chevy, #15026T $18.00
Trustworthy Hardware, 1916 Studebaker, #22500 ....$18.00
Trustworthy Hardware, 1929 Ford, #1013 ....$25.00
Trustworthy Hardware 10th Anniversary, 1940 Ford, #62502 ....$45.00
US Army Ambulance, 1937 Chevy, #15018 ....$20.00
US Mail, 1916 Studebaker, #25019 ....$26.00
Wheaties, 1940 Ford, #67518 ....$24.00
Wheaties, 1955 Chevy, #50044 ....$20.00
Wheels of Time Car Show, 1936 Dodge Panel, #74049 ....$35.00
Winchester, Peterbilt Tractor Trailer, #32509 ....$32.00
Winchester, 1929 Ford, #02601 ....$30.00
Wire Works, 1957 Ford Ranchero, #324500 ....$32.00
Wolfs Head Motor Oil, 1942 Chevy Box, #75004 ....$25.00

Dinky

Dinky diecasts were made by Meccano (Britain) as early as 1933, but high on the list of many of today's collectors are those from the decades of the '50s and '60s. They made commercial vehicles, firefighting equipment, farm toys, and heavy equipment as well as classic cars that were the epitome of high style, such as the #157 Jaguar XK120, produced from the mid-'50s through the early '60s. Some Dinkys were made in France; since 1979 no toys have been produced in Great Britain. Values are for examples mint and in the original packaging unless noted otherwise.

See also Soldiers.

#100, Lady Penelope's Fab 1, luminous pk....................**$400.00**
#100, Lady Penelope's Fab 1, pk....................**$250.00**
#101, Sunbeam Alpine....................**$175.00**
#101, Thunderbird II & IV, gr....................**$300.00**
#101, Thunderbird II & IV, metallic gr....................**$400.00**
#102, Joe' Car....................**$135.00**
#102, MG Midget....................**$250.00**
#105, Triumph TR2....................**$200.00**
#106, Austin Atlantic, bl or blk....................**$150.00**
#106, Austin Atlantic, pk....................**$350.00**
#106, Prisoner Mini Moke....................**$260.00**
#106, Thunderbird II & IV....................**$120.00**
#107, Sunbeam Alpine....................**$150.00**
#108, MG Midget....................**$200.00**
#108, Sam's Car, gold, red or bl....................**$160.00**
#108, Sam's Car, silver....................**$120.00**
#109, Aston Healey 100....................**$160.00**
#109, Gabriel Model T Ford....................**$150.00**
#110, Austin Martin DB5....................**$110.00**
#111, Cinderella's Coach....................**$50.00**
#111, Triumph TR2....................**$160.00**
#112, Austin Healey Sprite....................**$125.00**
#112, Purdey's Triumph TR7....................**$75.00**
#113, MGB....................**$110.00**

#114, Triumph Spitfire, red, $125.00.

#114, Triumph Spitfire, gray or gold....................**$125.00**
#114, Triumph Spitfire, purple....................**$170.00**
#115, Plymouth Fury....................**$125.00**
#116, Volvo 1800S....................**$100.00**
#117, Four Berth Caravan....................**$60.00**
#120, Happy Cab....................**$60.00**
#120, Jaguar E-Type....................**$110.00**
#121, Goodwood Racing Gift Set....................**$2,000.00**
#122, Touring Gift Set....................**$2,000.00**
#122, Volvo 265 Estate Car....................**$50.00**
#123, Mayfair Gift Set....................**$3,000.00**
#123, Princess 2200 HL....................**$60.00**
#124, Rolls Royce Phantom V....................**$80.00**
#125, Fun A'Hoy Set....................**$250.00**
#128, Mercedes Benz 600....................**$80.00**
#129, MG Midget....................**$400.00**
#129, VW 1200 Sedan....................**$80.00**
#130, Ford Consul Corsair....................**$85.00**
#131, Cadillac El Dorado....................**$150.00**
#131, Jaguar E-Type, 2+2....................**$150.00**
#132, Ford 40-RV....................**$60.00**
#132, Packard Convertible....................**$165.00**
#133, Cunningham C-5R....................**$130.00**
#134, Triumph Vitesse....................**$100.00**
#135, Triumph 2000....................**$100.00**
#136, Vauxhall Viva....................**$80.00**
#137, Plymouth Fury....................**$130.00**
#138, Hillman Imp....................**$100.00**
#139, Ford Cortina....................**$115.00**
#139a, Hudson Commodore Sedan, dual colors....................**$350.00**
#139a, Hudson Commodore Sedan, solid colors....................**$225.00**
#139a, US Army Staff Car....................**$350.00**
#140, Morris 1100....................**$80.00**
#141, Vauxhall Victor....................**$80.00**
#142, Jaguar Mark 10....................**$100.00**
#143, Ford Capri....................**$100.00**
#144, VW 1500....................**$100.00**
#145, Singer Vogue....................**$100.00**
#146, Daimler V8....................**$100.00**
#147, Cadillac 62....................**$100.00**
#148, Ford Fairlane, gr....................**$125.00**
#148, Ford Fairlane, metallic gr....................**$225.00**
#149, Citroen Dyane....................**$50.00**
#149, Sports Car Gift Set....................**$1,800.00**
#150, Rolls Royce Silver Wraith....................**$100.00**
#151, Triumph 1800 Saloon....................**$150.00**
#151, Vauxhall Victor 101....................**$100.00**
#152, Rolls Royce Phantom V....................**$85.00**
#153, Aston Martin....................**$100.00**
#153, Standard Vanguard-Spats....................**$145.00**
#154, Ford Taunus 17M....................**$85.00**
#155, Ford Anglia....................**$120.00**
#156, Mechanized Army Set....................**$5,000.00**
#156, Rover 75, dual colors....................**$300.00**
#156, Rover 75, solid colors....................**$150.00**
#156, Saab 96....................**$100.00**
#157, BMW 2000 Tilux....................**$100.00**
#158, Riley....................**$140.00**

#158, Rolls Royce Silver Shadow....................................$100.00
#159, Ford Cortina MKII...$100.00
#159, Morris Oxford, dual colors...................................$300.00
#159, Morris Oxford, solid colors $140.00
#160, Austin A30 ....$125.00
#160, Mercedes Benz 250 SE $90.00
#161, Austin Somerset, dual colors $300.00
#161, Austin Somerset, solid colors $150.00
#161, Ford Mustang $100.00
#162, Ford Zephyr...$135.00
#162, Triumph 1300 ....$85.00
#163, Bristol 450 Coupe $100.00
#163, VW 1600 TL, metallic bl $150.00
#163, VW 1600 TL, red...$75.00
#164, Ford Zodiac MKIV, bronze $200.00
#164, Ford Zodiac MKIV, silver $100.00
#164, Vauxhall Cresta $125.00
#165, Ford Capri $90.00
#165, Humber Hawk..$150.00
#166, Renault R16 ....$60.00
#166, Sunbeam Rapier...$135.00
#167, AC Acceca, all cream...$300.00
#167, AC Acceca, dual colors $140.00
#168, Ford Escort $100.00
#168, Singer Gazelle $140.00
#169, Fire Corsair $100.00
#169, Studebaker Golden Hawk $160.00
#170, Ford Fordor, dual colors $300.00
#170, Ford Fordor, solid colors $125.00
#170, Lincoln Continental..$120.00
#170m, Ford Fordor US Army Staff Car $350.00
#171, Austin 1800 ....$100.00
#171, Hudson Commodore, dual colors $350.00
#172, Fiat 2300 Station Wagon...$75.00
#172, Studebaker Land Cruiser, dual colors....................$300.00
#172, Studebaker Land Cruiser, solid colors $165.00
#173, Nash Rambler $110.00
#173, Pontiac Parisienne $85.00
#174, Mercury Cougar $85.00
#175, Cadillac El Dorado...$100.00
#175, Hillman Minx $140.00
#176, Austin A105, gray $150.00
#176, Austin A105, cream $150.00
#176, Austin A105, cream w/bl roof, or gray w/red roof.$250.00
#176, NSU R80, metallic bl $180.00
#176, NSU R80, metallic red $80.00
#177, Opel Kapitan..$100.00
#178, Mini Clubman...$60.00
#178, Plymouth Plaza, bl w/wht roof $400.00
#178, Plymouth Plaza, pk, gr or 2-tone bl $150.00
#179, Opel Commodore $70.00
#179, Studebaker President $170.00
#180, Rover 3500 Sedan $40.00
#181, VW...$100.00
#182, Porsche 356A Coupe, cream, red or bl...................$130.00
#182, Porsche 356A Coupe, dual colors...........................$325.00
#183, Fiat 600 ....$100.00
#183, Morris Mini Minor...$100.00

#181, Volkswagen, $100.00.

#184, Volvo 122S, red $130.00
#184, Volvo 122S, wht $375.00
#185, Alpha Romeo 1900...$125.00
#186, Mercedes Benz 200 ....$100.00
#187, De Tomaso Mangusta 5000 ....$75.00
#187, Volkswagen Karmann-Ghia Coupe.........................$135.00
#188, Ford Berth Caravan $60.00
#188, Jensen FF $75.00
#189, Lamborghini Marzal...$65.00
#189, Triumph Herald..$120.00
#191, Dodge Royal Sedan, cream w/bl flash $300.00
#191, Dodge Royal Sedan, cream w/brn flash, or gr w/blk flash $170.00
#192, Desoto Fireflite $165.00
#192, Range Rover..$50.00
#193, Rambler Station Wagon $115.00

#194, Bentley S Coupe, $130.00.

#195, Range Rover Fire Chief $60.00
#196, Holden Special Sedan..$75.00
#197, Austin Countryman, orange $325.00
#197, Morris Mini Traveller, wht & brn $100.00
#197, Morris Mini Traveller, dk gr & brn $400.00

#197, Morris Mini Traveller, lime gr.....$300.00
#198, Rolls Royce Phantom V.....$115.00
#199, Austin Countryman, bl.....$115.00
#200, Matra 630.....$75.00
#201, Plymouth Stock Car.....$75.00
#201, Racing Car Set.....$750.00
#202, Customized Land Rover.....$50.00
#202, Fiat Abarth 2000.....$50.00
#203, Customized Range Rover.....$50.00
#204, Ferrari.....$55.00
#205, Talbot Labo, in bubble pkg.....$325.00
#206, Customized Corvette Stingray.....$70.00
#207, Triumph TR7.....$50.00
#208, VW Porsche 914.....$65.00
#210, Alfa Romeo 33.....$65.00
#210, Vanwall, in bubble pkg.....$200.00
#211, Triumph TR7.....$80.00
#213, Ford Capri.....$75.00
#214, Hillman Imp Rally.....$100.00
#215, Ford GT Racing Car.....$70.00
#216, Ferrari Dino.....$70.00
#217, Alfa Romeo Scarabo.....$50.00
#218, Lotus Europa.....$65.00
#219, Jaguar XJS Coupe.....$65.00
#220, Ferrari P5.....$55.00
#221, Corvette Stingray.....$60.00
#222, Hesketh Racing Car, dk bl.....$60.00
#222, Hesketh Racing Car, Olympus Camera.....$100.00
#223, McLaren M8A Can-Am.....$50.00
#224, Mercedes Benz C111.....$55.00
#225, Lotus Formula 1 Racer.....$55.00
#226, Ferrari 312/B2.....$50.00
#227, Beach Bunny.....$55.00
#228, Super Sprinter.....$60.00
#236, Connaught Racer.....$125.00
#237, Mercedes Benz Racer.....$125.00
#238, Jaguar Type-D Racer.....$140.00
#239, Vanwall Racer.....$125.00
#240, Cooper Racer.....$70.00
#240, Dinky Way Gift Set.....$130.00
#241, Lotus Racer.....$80.00
#241, Silver Jubilee Taxi.....$50.00
#242, Ferrari Racer.....$85.00
#243, BRM Racer.....$80.00
#243, Volvo Police Racer.....$50.00
#244, Plymouth Police Racer.....$50.00
#245, Superfast Gift Set.....$225.00
#246, International Car Gift Set.....$235.00
#249, Racing Car Gift Set, in bubble pkg.....$1,800.00
#250, Mini Cooper Police Car.....$75.00
#251, USA Police Car, Pontiac.....$80.00
#252, RCMP Car, Pontiac.....$100.00
#254, Austin Taxi, yel.....$120.00
#254, Police Range Rover.....$65.00
#255, Ford Zodiac Police Car.....$80.00
#255, Mersey Tunnel Police Van.....$100.00
#255, Police Mini Clubman.....$50.00
#256, Humber Hawk Police Car.....$140.00
#257, Nash Rambler Candian Fire Chief Car.....$100.00
#258, USA Police Car, Cadillac, Desoto, Dodge or Ford..$150.00
#259, Bedford Fire Engine.....$130.00
#260, Royal Mail Van.....$160.00
#260, VW Deutsch Bundepost.....$185.00
#261, Ford Taunus Polizei.....$275.00
#261, Telephone Service Van.....$150.00
#262, VW Swiss Post PTT Car, casting #129.....$250.00
#262, VW Swiss Post PTT Car, casting #181, minimum value.....$600.00
#263, Airport Fire Rescue Tender.....$70.00
#263, Superior Criterion Ambulance.....$115.00
#264, RCMP Patrol Car, Cadillac.....$175.00
#264, RCMP Patrol Car, Fairlane.....$135.00
#265, Plymouth Taxi.....$170.00
#266, ERF Fire Tender.....$75.00
#266, ERF Fire Tender, Falck.....$100.00
#266, Plymouth Taxi, Metro Cab.....$150.00
#267, Paramedic Truck.....$75.00
#267, Superior Cadillac Ambulance.....$100.00
#268, Range Rover Ambulance.....$60.00
#268, Renault Dauphine Mini Cab.....$135.00
#269, Ford Transit Police Accident Unit, Faulk Zonen...$60.00
#269, Jaguar Motorway Police Car.....$140.00
#270, AA Motorcycle Patrol.....$75.00
#270, Ford Panda Police Car.....$70.00
#271, Ford Transit Fire, Appliance.....$75.00
#271, Ford Transit Fire, Falck.....$150.00
#271, TS Motorcycle Patrol.....$265.00
#272, ANNB Motorcycle Patrol.....$300.00
#272, Police Accident Unit.....$60.00
#273, RAC Patrol Mini Van.....$165.00
#274, Ford Transit Ambulance.....$50.00
#275, Brink's Armoured Car, no bullion.....$75.00
#275, Brink's Armoured Car, w/gold bullion.....$200.00
#275, Brink's Armoured Car, w/Mexican bullion.....$1,000.00
#276, Airport Fire Tender.....$100.00
#276, Ford Transit Ambulance.....$60.00
#277, Police Range Rover.....$60.00
#277, Superior Criterion Ambulance.....$115.00
#278, Plymouth Yellow Cab.....$50.00
#278, Vauxhall Victor Ambulance.....$100.00
#279, Aveling Barford Diesel Roller.....$80.00
#280, Midland Mobile Bank.....$140.00
#281, Fiat 2300 Pathe News Camera Car.....$175.00
#281, Military Hovercraft.....$65.00
#282, Austin 1800 Taxi.....$85.00
#282, Land Rover Fire, Appliance.....$60.00
#282, Land Rover Fire, Falck.....$80.00
#283, BOAC Coach.....$130.00
#283, Single-Decker Bus.....$80.00
#284, London Austin Taxi.....$70.00
#285, Merryweather Fire Engine.....$80.00
#285, Merryweather Fire Engine, Falck.....$150.00
#286, Ford Transit Fire, Falck.....$160.00
#288, Superior Cadillac Ambulance.....$85.00
#288, Superior Cadillac Ambulance, Falck.....$150.00
#289, Routemaster Bus, Esso, purple.....$750.00

#289, Routemaster Bus, Esso, red $100.00
#289, Routemaster Bus, Festival of London Stores.........$200.00
#289, Routemaster Bus, Madame Tussaud's....................$150.00
#289, Routemaster Bus, Silver Jubilee..............................$40.00
#289, Routemaster Bus, Tern Shirts or Schwepps $150.00
#290, Double-Decker Bus $150.00
#290, SRN-6 Hovercraft...$60.00
#291, Atlantean City Bus $70.00
#292, Atlantean City Bus, Regent or Ribble $150.00
#293, Swiss Postal Bus $60.00
#295, Atlantean City Bus, Yellow Pages $70.00
#296, Duple Luxury Coach..$50.00
#296, Police Accident Unit...$100.00
#297, Silver Jubilee Bus, National or Woolworth.............$60.00
#298, Emergency Services Gift Set, minimum value...$8,000.00
#299, Crash Squad Gift Set $80.00
#299, Motorway Services Gift Set, minimum value $700.00
#299, Post Office Services Gift Set, minimum value......$650.00
#300, London Scene Gift Set $85.00
#302, Emergency Squad Gift Set....................................$100.00
#303, Commando Gift Set $120.00
#304, Fire Rescue Gift Set...$120.00
#305, David Brown Tractor $85.00
#308, Leyland 384 Tractor..$75.00
#309, Star Trek Gift Set $150.00
#319, Week's Tipping Farm Trailer...................................$40.00
#320, Halesowen Harvest Trailer $60.00
#321, Massey-Harris Manure Spreader.............................$60.00
#322, Disc Harrow $50.00
#323, Triple Gang Mower $50.00
#324, Hay Rake..$50.00
#325, David Brown Tractor & Harrow $135.00
#340, Land Rover...$85.00
#341, Land Rover Trailer...$40.00
#342, Austin Mini Moke $70.00
#342, Moto-Cart $75.00
#344, Estate Car...$95.00
#344, Land Rover Pickup...$50.00
#350, Tony's Mini Moke $150.00
#351, UFO Interceptor $80.00
#352, Ed Straker's Car, red $100.00
#352, Ed Straker's Car, yel or gold-plated......................$140.00
#353, Shado 2 Mobile..$85.00
#354, Pink Panther $60.00
#355, Lunar Roving Vehicle...$60.00
#357, Klingon Battle Cruiser $80.00
#358, USS Enterprise...$80.00
#359, Eagle Transporter..$75.00
#360, Eagle Freighter $75.00
#361, Galactic War Chariot $75.00
#362, Trident Star Fighter..$75.00
#363, Cosmic Zygon Patroller, for Marks & Spencer........$70.00
#364, NASA Space Shuttle, w/booster..........................$100.00
#366, NASA Space Shuttle, w/no booster.........................$60.00
#367, Space Battle Cruiser..$80.00
#368, Zygon Marauder $80.00
#370, Dragster Set..$70.00
#371, USS Enterprise, sm version $60.00
#372, Klingon Battle Cruiser, sm version.........................$60.00
#380, Convoy Skip Truck..$30.00
#381, Convoy Farm Truck...$30.00
#382, Wheelbarrow..$25.00
#382 Convoy Dumper...$30.00
#383, Convoy NCL Truck..$40.00
#384, Convoy Fire Rescue Truck $35.00
#384, Grass Cutter $25.00
#384, Sack Truck $25.00
#385, Convoy Royal Mail Truck $40.00
#386, Lawn Mower $100.00
#389, Med Artillery Tractor...$100.00
#390, Customized Transit Van $50.00
#398, Farm Equipment Gift Set $2,000.00
#399, Farm Tractor & Trailer Set $200.00
#400, BEV Electric Truck...$70.00
#401, Coventry-Climax Fork Lift, orange $70.00
#401, Coventry-Climax Fork Lift, red.............................$500.00
#402, Bedford Coca-Cola Truck $230.00
#404, Conveyancer Fork Lift $50.00
#405, Universal Jeep $50.00
#406, Commer Articulated Truck.......................................$165.00
#407, Ford Transit...$60.00
#408, Big Ben Lorry, bl & yel, or bl & orange $350.00
#408, Big Ben Lorry, maroon & fawn $200.00
#408, Big Ben Lorry, pk & cream...................................$2,000.00
#409, Bedford Articulated Lorry $175.00
#410, Bedford Van, Danish Post or Simpsons...............$125.00
#410, Bedford Van, MJ Hire, Marley or Collectors' Gazette .$60.00
#410, Bedford Van, Royal Mail $40.00
#411, Bedford Truck $140.00
#412, Bedford Van AA $60.00
#413, Austin Covered Wagon, lt & dk bl, or red & tan ..$650.00
#413, Austin Covered Wagon, maroon & cream, or med & lt bl $200.00
#413, Austin Covered Wagon, red & gray, or bl or cream.$450.00
#414, Dodge Tipper, all colors other than Royal bl........$100.00
#414, Dodge Tipper, Royal bl...$175.00
#416, Ford Transit Van...$50.00
#416, Ford Transit Van, 1,000,000 Transits $200.00
#417, Ford Transit Van...$50.00
#417, Leyland Comet Lorry...$175.00
#418, Leyland Comet Lorry...$175.00
#419, Leyland Comet Cement Lorry..................................$250.00
#420, Leyland Forward Control Lorry...............................$125.00
#421, Hindle-Smart Electric Lorry....................................$100.00
#422, Thames Flat Truck, bright gr...................................$200.00
#422, Thames Flat Truck, dk gr or red $100.00
#425, Bedford TK Coal Lorry $160.00
#428, Trailer, lg...$50.00
#429, Trailer...$45.00
#430, Commer Breakdown Lorry, all colors other than tan & gr..$1,000.00
#430, Commer Breakdown Lorry, tan & gr.....................$175.00
#430, Johnson Dumper $60.00
#432, Foden Tipper...$60.00
#432, Guy Warrior Flat Truck...$400.00
#433, Guy Flat Truck w/Tailboard $350.00

#434, Bedford Crash Truck $125.00
#435, Bedford TK Tipper, gray or yel cab $100.00
#435, Bedford TK Tipper, wht, silver & bl $250.00
#436, Atlas COPCO Compressor Lorry..........................$100.00
#437, Muir Hill Loader $50.00
#438, Ford D 800 Tipper, opening doors..........................$50.00
#439, Ford D 800 Snow Plough & Tipper........................$85.00
#440, Mobilgas Tanker $175.00
#441, Petrol Tanker, Castrol $175.00
#442, Land Rover Breakdown Crane $50.00
#442, Land Rover Breakdown Crane, Falck.....................$70.00
#442, Petrol Tanker, Esso $175.00
#443, Petrol Tanker, National Benzole...........................$175.00

#449, Chevrolet El Camino Pickup Truck, $120.00.

#449, Johnson Road Sweeper $70.00
#450, Bedford TK Box Van, Castrol $150.00
#451, Johnston Road Sweeper, opening doors $70.00
#451, Trojan Van, Dunlop $175.00
#452, Trojan Van, Chivers..$175.00
#454, Trojan Van Cydrax..$175.00
#455, Trojan Van, Brooke Bond Tea $175.00
#470, Austin Van, Shell-BP $175.00
#475, Ford Model T $100.00
#476, Morris Oxford $100.00
#477, Parsley's Car..$100.00
#480, Bedford Van, Kodak $160.00
#481, Bedford Van, Ovaltine $160.00
#482, Bedford Van, Dinky Toys $175.00
#485, Ford Model T w/Santa Claus...............................$150.00
#486, Morris Oxford, Dinky Beats.................................$150.00
#490, Electric Dairy Van, Express Dairy $100.00
#491, Electric Dairy Van, NCB or Job Dairies................$150.00
#492, Election Mini Van $350.00
#492, Loudspeaker Van $125.00
#500, Citroen 2-CV $65.00
#501, Citroen Police, DS-19 ....$100.00
#501, Foden Diesel 8-Wheel, 2nd cab $600.00
#502, Foden Flat Truck, 1st or 2nd cab $1,000.00
#503, Foden Flat Truck, 1st cab $1,200.00
#503, Foden Flat Truck, 2nd cab, bl & orange $400.00
#503, Foden Flat Truck, 2nd cab, bl & yel $1,200.00
#503, Foden Flat Truck, 2nd cab, 2-tone gr.................$3,000.00
#504, Foden Tanker, red...$800.00
#504, Foden Tanker, 2nd cab, red.................................$600.00

#504, Foden Tanker, two-tone blue, $500.00.

#505, Foden Flat Truck w/Chains, 1st cab..................$3,000.00
#505, Foden Flat Truck w/Chains, 2nd cab $450.00
#505, Maserati 2000 ....$135.00
#506, Aston Martin $125.00
#509, Fiat 850 ....$55.00
#510, Peugeot 204..$60.00
#511, Guy 4-Ton Lorry, red, gr or brn.........................$900.00
#511, Guy 4-Ton Lorry, 2-tone bl................................$350.00
#512, Guy Flat Truck, all colors other than bl or red $750.00
#512, Guy Flat Truck, bl or red $400.00
#512, Lesko Kart $125.00
#513, Guy Flat Truck w/Tailboard $400.00
#514, Alfa Romeo Giulia...$85.00
#514, Guy Van, Lyons...$2,000.00
#514, Guy Van, Slumberland..$600.00
#514, Guy Van, Spratt's $600.00
#514, Guy Van, Weetabix...$3,500.00
#515, Ferrari 250 GT $135.00
#517, Renault R8 ....$95.00
#518, Renault 4L..$50.00
#519, Simca 100...$50.00
#520, Chrysler New Yorker $225.00
#521, Bedford Articulated Lorry $175.00
#522, Big Bedford Lorry, bl & yel................................$350.00
#522, Big Bedford Lorry, maroon & fawn $200.00
#522, Citroen DS-19 ....$225.00
#523, Simca 1500..$60.00
#524, Panhard 24-CT $75.00
#524, Renault Dauphine...$145.00
#525, Peugeot 403-U $90.00
#526, Mercedes-Benz 190-SL $180.00
#527, Alfa Romeo 1900..$110.00
#529, Vespa 2-CV...$125.00
#530, Citroen DS-23...$60.00
#531, Leyland Comet Lorry, bl or brn..........................$500.00
#532, Bedford Comet Lorry w/Tailboard $250.00
#532, Lincoln Premiere $225.00

#531, Leyland Comet Lorry, orange and blue, $250.00.

#533, Leyland Cement Wagon.....$200.00
#533, Peugeot.....$100.00
#534, BMW 1500.....$90.00
#535, Citroen 2-CV.....$60.00
#538, Buick Roadmaster.....$300.00
#538, Renault 16-TX.....$45.00
#539, Citroen ID-19.....$11.00
#540, Opel Kadett.....$65.00
#541, Simca Versailles.....$130.00
#542, Simca Taxi.....$125.00
#543, Renault Floride.....$125.00
#545, De Soto Diplomat.....$150.00
#546, Austin-Healey.....$200.00
#548, Fiat 1800 Familiare.....$100.00
#550, Chrysler Saratoga.....$275.00
#551, Ford Taunus, Polizei.....$175.00
#551, Rolls Royce.....$285.00
#551, Trailer.....$60.00
#552, Chevrolet Corvair.....$120.00
#555, Fire Engine, w/extension ladder.....$135.00
#555, Ford Thunderbird.....$200.00
#556, Citroen Ambulance.....$150.00
#558, Citroen.....$95.00
#559, Ford Taunus.....$95.00
#561, Blaw-Knox Bulldozer.....$100.00
#561, Blaw-Knox Bulldozer, plastic.....$500.00
#561, Citroen Van, Gervais.....$225.00
#561, Renault Mail Car.....$65.00
#562, Muir-Hill Dumper.....$80.00
#563, Blaw-Knox Heavy Tractor.....$100.00
#563, Estafette Pickup.....$90.00
#564, Armagnac Caravan.....$70.00
#564, Elevator Loader.....$100.00
#566, Citroen Police Van.....$130.00
#568, Ladder Truck.....$150.00
#569, Dump Truck.....$165.00
#570, Peugeot Van.....$75.00
#571, Coles Mobile Crane.....$140.00
#572, Dump Truck, Berliet.....$140.00
#576, Panhard Tanker, Esso.....$350.00
#577, Simca Van, Bailly.....$200.00
#578, Simca Dump Truck.....$165.00
#580, Dump Truck.....$135.00
#581, Container Truck, Bailly.....$200.00
#581, Horse Box, British Railway.....$200.00
#581, Horse Box, Express Horse Van.....$800.00
#582, Pullman Car Transporter.....$160.00
#584, Covered Truck.....$135.00
#585, Dumper.....$135.00
#587, Citroen Van, Philips.....$110.00
#589, Berliet Wrecker.....$135.00
#590, City Road Signs Set.....$70.00
#591, AEC Tanker, Shell.....$225.00
#591, Country Road Signs Set.....$70.00
#592, Gas Pumps, Esso.....$80.00
#593, Road Signs Set.....$45.00
#595, Crane.....$265.00
#595, Traffic Signs Set.....$45.00
#597, Fork Lift.....$80.00
#601, Austin Para Moke.....$85.00
#602, Armoured Command Car.....$50.00
#603, Army Personnel, box of 12.....$125.00
#604, Land Rover Bomb Disposal Unit.....$70.00
#609, 105mm Howitzer & Gun Crew.....$50.00
#612, Commando Jeep.....$50.00
#615, US Jeep & 105mm Howitzer.....$60.00
#616, AEC Articulated Transporter & Tank.....$110.00
#617, VW KDF w/Antitank Gun.....$75.00
#618, AEC Articulated Transporter & Helicopter.....$100.00
#619, Bren Gun Carrier & Antitank Gun.....$65.00
#620, Berliet Missile Launcher.....$140.00
#621, 3-Ton Army Wagon.....$100.00
#622, Bren Gun Carrier.....$50.00
#622, 10-Ton Army Truck.....$140.00
#623, Army Covered Wagon.....$80.00
#625, 6-Pounder Antitank Gun.....$40.00
#626, Military Ambulance.....$100.00
#640, Bedford Military Truck.....$300.00
#641, Army 1-Ton Cargo Truck.....$75.00
#642, RAF Pressure Refueller.....$130.00
#643, Army Water Carrier.....$110.00
#650, Light Tank.....$160.00
#651, Centurion Tank.....$120.00
#654, Mobile Gun.....$50.00
#656, 88mm Gun.....$50.00
#660, Tank Transporter.....$130.00
#661, Recovery Tractor.....$150.00
#662, Static 88mm Gun & Crew.....$60.00
#665, Honest John Missile Erector.....$175.00
#666, Missile Erector Vehicle w/Corporal Missile & Launching Platform.....$350.00
#667, Armoured Patrol Car.....$50.00
#667, Missile Servicing Platform Vehicle.....$250.00
#668, Foden Army Truck.....$50.00
#670, Armoured Car.....$65.00
#671, MKI Corvette (boat).....$40.00
#671, Reconnaissance Car.....$165.00

#672, OSA Missile Boat $40.00
#673, Scout Car $50.00
#674, Austin Champ, olive drab $60.00
#674, Austin Champ, wht, UN version $500.00
#674, Coast Guard Missile Launch $45.00
#675, Motor Patrol Boat $45.00
#676, Armoured Personnel Carrier $80.00
#676, Daimler Armoured Car, w/speedwheels $60.00
#677, Armoured Command Vehicle $110.00
#677, Task Force Set $100.00
#678, Air Sea Rescue $60.00
#680, Ferret Armoured Car $60.00
#681, DUKW $60.00
#682, Stalwart Load Carrier $60.00
#683, Chieftain Tank $55.00
#686, 25-Pounder Field Gun $40.00
#687, Convoy Army Truck $25.00
#687, Trailer $35.00
#688, Field Artillery Tractor $60.00
#690, Mobile Antiaircraft Gun $100.00
#690, Scorpion Tank $50.00
#691, Striker Antitank Vehicle $60.00
#692, Leopard Tank $60.00
#692, 5.5 Med Gun $60.00
#693, 7.2 Howitzer $60.00
#694, Hanomag Tank Destroyer $60.00
#695, Howitzer & Tractor $250.00
#696, Leopard Antiaircraft Tank $60.00
#697, 25-Pounder Field Gun Set $150.00
#698, Tank Transporter & Tank $230.00
#699, Leopard Recovery Tank $70.00
#699, Military Gift Set $400.00
#700, Spitfire MKII RAF Jubilee $150.00
#701, Shetland Flying Boat $650.00
#702, DH Comet Jet Airliner $200.00
#704, Avro York Airliner $175.00
#705, Viking Airliner $100.00
#706, Vickers Viscount Airliner, Air France $150.00
#708, Vickers Viscount Airliner, BEA $150.00
#710, Beechcraft S35 Bonanza $85.00
#712, US Army T-42A $85.00
#715, Beechcraft C-55 Baron $60.00
#715, Bristol 173 Helicopter $85.00
#716, Westland Sikorsky Helicopter $90.00
#717, Boeing 737 .... $85.00
#718, Hawker Hurricane $85.00
#719, Spitfire MKII $85.00
#721, Junkers Stuka $80.00
#722, Hawker Harrier $80.00
#723, Hawker Executive Jet $60.00
#724, Sea King Helicopter $75.00
#725, Phantom II $100.00
#726, Messerschmitt, desert camouflage $100.00
#726, Messerschmitt, gray & gr $200.00
#727, US Air Force F-4 Phantom II $300.00
#728, RAF Dominie $80.00
#729, Multi-Role Combat Aircraft $75.00
#730, US Navy Phantom $100.00
#731, SEPECAT Jaguar $80.00
#731, Twin-Engine Fighter $60.00
#732, Bell Police Helicopter, M*A*S*H $100.00
#732, Bell Police Helicopter, wht & bl $60.00
#733, German Phantom II $200.00
#733, Lockhead Shooting Star Fighter $50.00
#734, Submarine Swift $60.00
#735, Glouster Javelin $60.00
#736, Bundesmarine Sea King $90.00
#736, Hawker Hunter $60.00
#737, P1B Lightning Fighter $90.00
#738, DH110 Sea Vixen Fighter $70.00
#739, Zero-Sen $100.00
#741, Spitfire MKII $100.00
#749, RAF Avro Vulcan Bomber $3,500.00
#750, Call Telephone Box $50.00
#751, Lawn Mower $100.00
#752, Goods Yard Crane $70.00
#752, Police Box $50.00
#755, Standard Lamp, single arm $30.00
#756, Standard Lamp, dbl arm $30.00
#760, Pillar Box $40.00
#766, British Road Signs, Country Set A $100.00
#767, British Road Signs, Country Set B $100.00
#768, British Road Signs, Town Set A $100.00
#769, British Road Signs, Town Set B $100.00
#770, Road Signs, set of 12 .... $150.00
#771, International Road Signs, set of 12 .... $160.00
#772, British Road Signs, set of 24 .... $200.00
#773, Traffic Signal $30.00
#777, Belisha Beacon $30.00
#781, Petrol Pumping Station, Esso $100.00
#782, Petrol Pumping Station, Shell $80.00
#784, Dinky Goods Train Set $80.00
#785, Service Station $200.00
#786, Tire Rack $50.00
#787, Lighting Kit $40.00
#796, Healy Sports Boat $65.00
#798, Express Passenger Train $170.00
#801, Mini USS Enterprise $60.00
#802, Mini Klingon Cruiser $60.00
#815, Panhard Armoured Tank $150.00
#817, AMX 13-Ton Tank $125.00
#822, M3 Half-Track $150.00
#893, UNIC Pipe-Line Transporter $275.00
#894, UNIC Boilot Car Transporter $275.00
#900, Building Site Gift Set $1,500.00
#901, Guy 4-Ton Lorry, see #501
#902, Foden Flat Truck, see #502
#903, Foden Flat Truck w/Tailboard, see #503
#905, Foden Flat Truck w/Chains $450.00
#911, Guy 4-Ton Lorry, see #511
#912, Guy Flat Truck, see #512
#913, Guy Flat Truck w/Tailboard, see #513
#914, AEC Articulated Lorry $150.00
#915, AEC Flat Trailer $100.00
#917, Guy Van, Spratts $350.00
#917, Mercedes Benz Truck & Trailer $120.00

#917, Mercedes Benz Truck & Trailer, Munsterland $300.00
#918, Guy Van, Ever Ready $500.00
#919, Guy Van, Golden Shred....................$1,000.00
#920, Guy Warrior Van, Heinz....................$3,000.00
#921, Bedford Articulated Lorry $175.00
#922, Big Bedford Lorry....................$175.00
#923, Big Bedford Van, Heinz Baked Beans can............$600.00
#923, Big Bedford Van, Heinz Ketchup bottle $2,000.00
#924, Aveling-Barford Dumper....................$110.00
#925, Leyland Dump Truck....................$235.00
#930, Bedford Pallet-Jekta Van, Dinky Toys $250.00
#931, Leyland Comet Lorry, all colors other than bl & brn $200.00
#931, Leyland Comet Lorry, bl & brn....................$500.00
#932, Leyland Comet Wagon w/Tailboard....................$200.00
#933, Leyland Comet Wagon....................$200.00
#934, Leyland Octopus Wagon, all colors other than bl & brn....................$300.00
#934, Leyland Octopus Wagon, bl & yel....................$2,000.00
#936, Leyland 8-Wheel Test Chassis $150.00
#940, Mercedes Benz Truck....................$85.00
#943, Leyland Octopus Tanker, Esso $300.00
#944, Shell-BP Fuel Tanker $300.00
#944, Shell-BP Fuel Tanker, red wheels $500.00
#945, AEC Fuel Tanker, Esso....................$150.00
#945, AEC Fuel Tanker, Lucas $150.00
#948, Tractor-Trailer, McLean $365.00
#949, Wayne School Bus....................$350.00
#950, Foden S20 Fuel Tanker, Burmah....................$100.00
#950, Foden S20 Fuel Tanker, Shell....................$100.00
#951, Trailer $50.00
#952, Vega Major Luxury Coach $140.00

#953, Continental Touring Coach, $400.00.

#954, Fire Station $300.00
#954, Vega Major Luxury Coach, no lights $130.00
#955, Fire Engine....................$140.00
#956, Turntable Fire Escape, Bedford $125.00
#956, Turntable Fire Escape, Berliet $225.00
#957, Fire Services Gift Set....................$600.00
#958, Snow Plough....................$260.00
#959, Foden Dump Truck....................$175.00
#960, Lorry-Mounted Concrete Mixer....................$125.00
#961, Blaw-Knox Bulldozer, see #561
#961, Vega Major Luxury Coach $250.00
#962, Muir-Hill Dumper....................$80.00
#963, Blaw-Knox Heavy Tractor....................$100.00
#963, Road Grader....................$75.00
#964, Elevator Loader....................$100.00
#965, Euclid Rear Dump Truck $80.00
#965, Terex Dump Truck $275.00
#966, Marrel Multi-Bucket Unit $130.00
#967, BBC TV Mobile Control Room....................$250.00
#967, Muir-Hill Loader & Trencher $80.00
#968, BBC TV Roving Eye Vehicle....................$260.00
#969, BBC TV Extending Mast Vehicle....................$275.00
#970, Jones Cantilever Crane $100.00
#971, Coles Mobile Crane....................$145.00
#972, Coles 20-Ton Lorry, mounted crane, yel & blk $200.00
#972, Coles 20-Ton Lorry, mounted crane, yel & orange..$130.00
#973, Eaton Yale Tractor Shovel $80.00
#973, Goods Yard Crane....................$90.00
#974, AEC Hoyner Transporter....................$110.00

#975, Ruston Bucyrus Excavator, $375.00.

#976, Michigan Tractor Dozer....................$75.00
#977, Commercial Servicing Platform Vehicle $250.00
#977, Shovel Dozer....................$75.00
#978, Refuse Wagon....................$100.00
#979, Racehorse Transporter....................$400.00
#980, Coles Hydra Truck....................$85.00
#980, Horse Box, British Railways $200.00
#980, Horse Box Express $800.00
#984, Atlas Digger $85.00
#984, Car Carrier....................$225.00
#985, Trailer for Car Carrier $125.00
#986, Mighty Antar Low Loader w/Propeller $400.00
#988, ABC TV Transmitter Van $375.00
#989, Car Carrier, Autotransporters....................$2,000.00
#990, Pullman Car Transporter w/4 Cars $2,500.00
#991, AEC Tanker, Shell Chemicals....................$225.00
#992, Avro Vulcan Delta Wing Bomber $3,000.00
#994, Loading Ramp for #992....................$30.00
#997, Caravelle, Air France $300.00
#998, Bristol Britannia Canadian Pacific....................$300.00
#999, DH Comet Jet....................$225.00

#987, ABC TV Mobile Control Room, $375.00.

Disney

Through the magic of the silver screen, Walt Disney's characters have come to life, and it is virtually impossible to imagine a child growing up without the influence of his genius. As each classic film was introduced, toy manufacturers scurried to fill department store shelves with the dolls, games, battery-ops, and windups that carried the likeness of every member of its cast. Though today it is the toys of the 1930s and '40s that are bringing exorbitant prices, later toys are certainly collectible as well, as you'll see in our listings. Even characters as recently introduced as Roger Rabbit already have their own cult following.

For more information we recommend *Character Toys and Collectibles, First and Second Series*, and *Antique & Collectible Toys, 1870 – 1950*, by David Longest; *Stern's Guide to Disney Collectibles* by Michael Stern (there are three in the series); *The Collector's Encyclopedia of Disneyana* by Michael Stern and David Longest; *Disneyana* by Cecil Munsey (Hawthorne Books, 1974); *Disneyana* by Robert Heide and John Gilman; *Walt Disney's Mickey Mouse Memorabilia* by Hillier and Shine (Abrams Inc., 1986); *Tomart's Disneyana Update Magazine*; and *Elmer's Price Guide to Toys* by Elmer Duellman (L-W Books).

Advisors: Joel J. Cohen (C12); Don Hamm (H10), Rocketeer.

See also Battery-Operated; Books; Bubble Bath Containers; Character and Promotional Drinking Glasses; Character Clocks and Watches; Chein; Coloring, Activity, and Paint Books; Dakins; Fisher-Price; Games; Lunch Boxes; Marx; Paper Dolls; Pez Dispensers; Pin-Back Buttons; Plastic Figures; Puppets; Puzzles; Ramp Walkers; Records; Sand Toy; Toothbrush Holders; View-Master; Western; Windups, Friction, and Other Mechanicals.

Aladdin, doll, Genie or Prince Ali, Applause, 10", M, F1, ea..$15.00
Aladdin, figure set, 1993, PVC, set of 4, M, F1................$15.00
Alice in Wonderland, doll set, cloth bodies w/posable heads, arms & legs, set of 8, 8½" to 10", EX, P6................$950.00
Alice in Wonderland, figure, March Hare, Marx, 1960s, plastic w/bendable arms & legs, cloth clothes, 6", scarce, EX, M8..$75.00
Alice in Wonderland, figure, Tweedle Dum, Shaw, 1940s, ceramic, EX, P6 ....$300.00
Alice in Wonderland, paint set, Hasbro, 1969, M (sealed), F8 ....$45.00
Alice in Wonderland, Stitch-A-Story, Hasbro, 1969, complete, NMIB, F8..$25.00
Alice in Wonderland, tea set, WDP, 1960s, china, various images, 11 pcs, MIB, P6.......................................$150.00
Aristocats, doll, Duchess, 1970, stuffed plush, 15", NM, F8..$50.00
Aristocats, doll, Marie the Cat, General Electric giveaway, plush, orig tag, NM..$15.00
Babes in Toyland, doll, Toyland Soldier, Gundikins, 1961, plush w/rubber head, 9½", scarce, EX, M8 ....$40.00
Babes in Toyland, Printer Set, Colorforms, 1961, complete, NM (EX box), F8 ....$25.00
Bambi, Colorforms, 1966, complete, NM (EX box), F8 ...$25.00
Bambi, doll, Bambi, Character Novelty/WDP, 1940s, plush velvet, 12½", EX, P6 ....$85.00

Bambi, dolls, Steiff, velvet with black glass eyes, M, 5½": $125.00; 9": $175.00.

Bambi, figure, Bambi, Japan, 1970s, ceramic, butterfly on tail, 5½", M, M8...$50.00
Bambi, figure, Bambi, Shaw Pottery, bl butterfly, 8", M.$175.00
Bambi, figure, Thumper, Am Pottery, 1930s, no label, 4", NM, M8 ....$75.00
Bambi, fork & spoon set, Walt Disney Stainless, 5", EX, P6, pr $50.00
Bambi, pencil sharpener, Plastic Novelties, Bakelite, 1¾", EX $65.00

Beauty & the Beast, doll, Beast or Lumiere, Applause, 12", M, F1, ea $15.00
Big Bad Wolf, see Three Little Pigs
Black Hole, Colorforms, 1970s, complete, NMIB, J5 ....$15.00
Casey Jr, pencil sharpener, Bakelite, figural, 1½", EX, from $50 to $70.00
Cinderella, apron, cloth w/colorful image, NM, J2 ....$25.00
Cinderella, doll, Cinderella, Ideal, 1938, compo w/real hair, orig gown, tiara & shoes, 13½", minimum value $275.00
Cinderella, dolls, Cinderella & Prince Charming, Effanbee, hard plastic, orig wrist tags, 14", EX, pr $450.00
Cinderella, handcar, Gus & Jaq, WD Mickey Mouse Ltd/England, tin w/compo figures, 8", NM, A $500.00
Cinderella, purse, 1970s, gr slipper w/zipper closure, 5", MIP, M17 ....$20.00
Disney, bank, Chein/WDP, slide open door & Donald's tongue slides out for coin, litho tin, 4x6", NM, A $300.00
Disney, Character Blox, New Enterprises, 1940s, 24 wooden blocks w/7 pgs of stickers, EX (EX box), M8 ....$75.00
Disney, embroidery set, features Snow White, Donald, Mickey, Ferdinand, etc, complete, EX (EX box), M8 ....$85.00
Disney, hat, WDE, paper, features several characters, scarce, EX, M8 ....$120.00
Disney, kaleidoscope, WDP, 1950s, litho cb, 9", EX, A $75.00
Disney, kaleidoscope, West Germany, 1970s-80s, litho cb, EX $35.00
Disney, Magic Erasable Pictures, Transogram, 1950s, unused, MIB, F8 ....$50.00
Disney, Scramble 4 Faces, Halsam Products, 1950s, MIP, J2 ..$50.00
Disney, Sketch-A-Graph Set, Ohio Art, 1955, complete, NM (EX box), F8 ....$55.00
Disney, tea set, Beswick of England, 1940s, features Pluto, Figaro, Bambi & Thumper, 4 pcs, M, M8 ....$155.00
Disney, top, WDP, 1973, various characters on bl & wht striped top w/red plunger, 6", NM $50.00
Disney, top, 1930s, litho tin, 9" dia, VG, J5 ....$65.00
Disney, toy wristwatch, Marx, 1971, shows Mickey, Donald, Goofy & Pluto, MOC, P6 ....$55.00
Disney, Walt Disney's Character Alphabet, WDP, diecut cb letters w/wood base for spelling words, NMIB, A $75.00
Disney, Walt Disney's Frontierland Logs, Halsam, 1955, complete w/instruction booklet, NM (EX box), A $75.00
Disneyland, Character Play World, fold-away, unused, MIB, J2 ....$125.00
Disneyland, charm bracelet, Little Miss Disneyland, 1950s, souvenir, MIB, P6 ....$35.00
Disneyland, map, Tom Sawyer Island, 1957, 1st version, EX, M8 ....$35.00
Disneyland, tea set, 1950s, features several characters, litho tin, 14 pcs, MIB, D10 ....$250.00
Disneyland, xylophone, Original Concert Grand, w/music stand, NMIB, P6 ....$135.00
Donald Duck, bank, Japan, Donald in tent, ceramic, 5", EX, from $25 to $35.00
Donald Duck, bank, Ucago, 1960s, 5", MIB, P6 ....$55.00
Donald Duck, camera, Herbert George/WDP, 3x5", MIB ..$75.00
Donald Duck, doll, Dancing Donald Duck, Romper Room, MIB, P12 ....$100.00
Donald Duck, doll, Italy, 1970s, stuffed felt, gr jacket & blk hat w/feather, NM $525.00

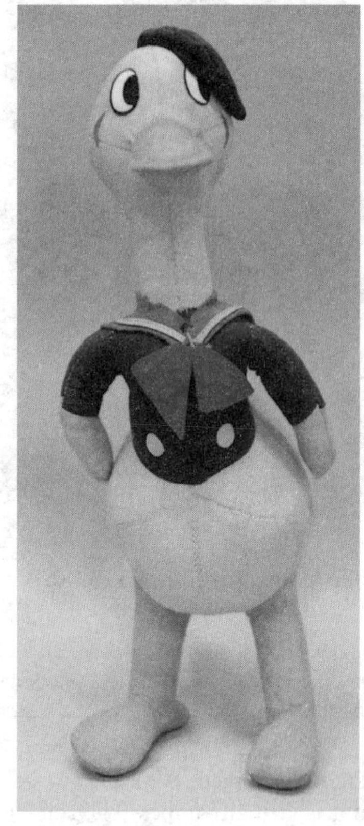

Photo courtesy Dunbar Gallery

Donald Duck, doll, Knickerbocker, 1936, 13", EX, D10, from $650.00 to $850.00.

Donald Duck, doll, Walking Donald Duck, Hasbro, 1960s, MIB $75.00
Donald Duck, figure, Enesco, 1970s, ceramic, 4", M, J5 ...$15.00
Donald Duck, figure, Italy, 1949, porcelain, in golfing pose, 8½", rare, NM, A $1,500.00
Donald Duck, figure, Lakeside, 1968, bendable, 7", EX (VG card), J5 ....$25.00
Donald Duck, figure, Seiberling, rubber, long-billed Donald, 6", VG $200.00
Donald Duck, figure, 1930s, bsk, long-billed Donald, 1¾", NM, M8 ....$75.00
Donald Duck, figure, 1930s, chalkware, EX $125.00
Donald Duck, Funnee Movee Viewer, Irwin, 1960s, w/4 films, EX, J5 ....$35.00
Donald Duck, jack-in-the-box, early, celluloid, EX+, A..$850.00
Donald Duck, jack-in-the-box, Spear, compo figure w/felt clothes, wood box, EX $300.00
Donald Duck, magic slate, Whitman, 1970s, NM, J6 ....$25.00
Donald Duck, paint box, Transogram, 1948, Donald painting on cover, litho tin, EX, M8 ....$50.00
Donald Duck, pop-apart figure, plastic, 9", MOC (sealed), J2 ....$45.00
Donald Duck, pull toy, Chad Valley, Donald in boat, wood, EX $425.00
Donald Duck, pull toy, Donald's Dairy, Salco/England, Donald in Pure Milk cart pulled by Pluto, pot metal, 4", EX $275.00
Donald Duck, roly poly, jtd celluloid figure sitting atop, 4", EX $325.00

Donald Duck, soap, Cussons, 1939, 5", M (M red lift-top box), P4 .... $150.00

Donald Duck, tea cup, Wadeheath of England, 1930s, features long-billed Donald in bl sailor suit, 2", M, M8 .... $100.00

Donald Duck, Tricky Toe, Gardner/WDP, complete & unused w/store display sign, NM (NM box), A $75.00

Donald Duck, watering can, Ohio Art, litho tin, EX $200.00

Donald Duck's Nephew, figure, Lars of Italy, 1940s, dressed as cowboy, felt w/plastic eyes & gun, 14", scarce, EX, P6 .... $225.00

Dumbo, balancing toy, Brazil, 1950s, balances on pole & rides back & forth on string, plastic & tin, 10", rare, NMIB, A $1,800.00

Dumbo, doll, compo w/felt ears & celluloid eyes, orig decal, 8", EX, A $275.00

Dumbo, figure, Am Pottery, 1940s, no label, 5", NM, M8 .... $100.00

Dumbo, figure, Shaw Pottery, wearing bonnet, 5", M, P6 .... $125.00

Fantasia, figure, centaurette, Vernon Kilns #17, 1940, reclining $635.00

Fantasia, figure, donkey unicorn, Vernon Kilns #116, 1940 .... $475.00

Fantasia, figure, elephant, Vernon Kilns, 1940s, standing $385.00

Fantasia, figure, satyr, Vernon Kilns, 1940, 4½", from $250 to $275.00

Fantasia, figure, unicorn, Vernon Kilns #14, 1940, setting $365.00

Ferdinand the Bull, bank, Crown Toy & Novelty, 1938, compo, EX $150.00

Ferdinand the Bull, doll, Knickerbocker, compo, 10", NM, A $575.00

Ferdinand the Bull, figure, Seiberling, rubber, 6", VG $75.00

Ferdinand the Bull, figure, 1930s, bsk, 3", EX, M8 .... $45.00

Ferdinand the Bull, pull toy, NN Hill Brass/WDE, 1938, Ferdinand on 4-wheeled platform, EX $300.00

Ferdinand the Bull, purse, WDE, 1938, EX, $125.00.

Goofy, doll, Merry Thoughts/England, stuffed cloth, 12", EX $75.00

Goofy, doll, 1980s, stuffed cloth, 15", NM, F8 .... $15.00

Horace Horsecollar, crib toy, compo w/wire arms & legs, EX $250.00

Horace Horsecollar, figure, Fun-E-Flex, wood w/rope tail, rare, EX $1,000.00

Jiminy Cricket, see Pinocchio

Jungle Book, doll set, Gund, 1966, stuffed velvet-type material, set of 7, 4" to 7", EX $350.00

Jungle Book, Ex-pan-dees Instant Sponge, James Industries, 1966, MIB, H4 .... $30.00

Jungle Book, figure, Baloo, Japan, 1966, velvet & felt, 6", NM, G16 .... $50.00

Jungle Book, figure, Kaa or Vulture, 1967, stuffed cloth, M, P6, ea $40.00

Lady & the Tramp, Colorforms Cartoon Kit, 1962, complete, NMIB, F8 .... $50.00

Lady & the Tramp, figure, Lady, Hagen-Renaker, 1950s, 1¼", NM $65.00

Lady & the Tramp, figure, Tramp, 1950s, ceramic, seated, 4½", EX $65.00

Lady & the Tramp, figures, Lady & Tramp, Schuco, Noah's Ark, 1950s, 2½" & 2¾", NMIB (separate boxes), G16 .... $450.00

Ludwig Von Drake, Erase-a-Board, 1960s, MIB (sealed), J2 .... $65.00

Ludwig Von Drake, figure, vinyl, squeaks, 9", NM, J2 .... $35.00

Ludwig Von Drake, Pencil- & Paint-by-Number Set, MIB (sealed), J2 .... $150.00

Mary Poppins, tea set, 1964, plastic, MIB, P6 .... $100.00

Mickey Mouse, ball, Eagle, 1950s, rubber, EX (EX box), J2 .... $45.00

Mickey Mouse, bank, Australia/WDP, 1950s, house mk State Savings of Victoria on roof, litho tin, 5", NM, A $250.00

Mickey Mouse, bank, Enesco, 1970s, ceramic, 4", NM, J5 .... $25.00

Mickey Mouse, bank, Ucago, 1960s, 5", MIB, P6 ....$55.00
Mickey Mouse, bank, Zell Products, 1934, leatherette book shape, 4x3", EX, M8 ....$175.00
Mickey Mouse, blocks, WDE, wood w/various images of Disney characters, set of 16, EX (VG box), A $200.00
Mickey Mouse, Bubble Buster, Kilgore, 1930s, 7", NM, D10 .$275.00
Mickey Mouse, camera, Mick-A-Matic, plastic head figure w/flash cube on top, MIB..$50.00
Mickey Mouse, Candy Factory, Remco, 1973, NMIB, F8..$75.00
Mickey Mouse, Christmas tree light set, Noma, complete, EX (EX box), A $200.00
Mickey Mouse, climbing toy, Dolly Toy, 1935, cb figure w/metal mechanism, NMIB, A $900.00
Mickey Mouse, Colorforms, 1970s, complete, EX (EX box), J5 ....$20.00
Mickey Mouse, doll, Borgfeldt, cloth & felt, 12", VG....$350.00
Mickey Mouse, doll, Charlotte Clark, 1930s, stuffed cloth, 19", NM $2,200.00
Mickey Mouse, doll, Chatterchum, Mattel, 1976, 7", VG, M15..$30.00
Mickey Mouse, doll, Dean's Rag Book Co, orig tag, 5", EX..$700.00
Mickey Mouse, doll, Hasbro, 1975, squeeze hands & he walks, 20", VG, M15 ....$25.00

Photo courtesy David Longest

Mickey Mouse, doll, Knickerbocker, 1930s, dressed as cowboy, EX, $2,000.00.

Mickey Mouse, doll, Knickerbocker, 1936, cloth & compo, 12", EX, D10, from $500 to..$700.00
Mickey Mouse, doll, Posie, Ideal, 1950s, EX (EX box), J2 ...$50.00
Mickey Mouse, doll, Steiff, orig button & tag, 10", EX, A.$750.00
Mickey Mouse, doll, Steiff, rare open mouth version, 7½", NM, D10, from $1,000 to $2,500.00
Mickey Mouse, doll, Steiff, velour, mk WD...George Borgfelt & Co, 7", EX, A...$1,375.00
Mickey Mouse, doll, Sun Rubber, 1950s, 10", VG, M15 ..$65.00

Photo courtesy Dunbar Gallery

Mickey Mouse, dominoes, Halsam, 1935, complete, EX, from $125.00 to $175.00.

Mickey Mouse, figure, American, 1931-32, jtd wood, 5", rare, D10 ....$750.00
Mickey Mouse, figure, Japan, celluloid w/spring arms & tail, 4", NM, A $485.00
Mickey Mouse, figure, Japan/WDE, compo w/spring arms & legs, hand-pnt details, 8", EX, A $600.00
Mickey Mouse, figure, 1960s, plastic, Mickey in yel space suit w/clear helmet, 4", NM, P4 ....$50.00
Mickey Mouse, figure, 1970s, bsk, Mickey on sled, 4", M, M8...$20.00
Mickey Mouse, figure, 1970s, bsk, Mickey w/kite, 4", M, M8...$20.00
Mickey Mouse, figure set, bsk, set of 4 w/Mickey holding various instruments, MIB, D10 ....$950.00
Mickey Mouse, gas mask, Happynak, 1936, series #50, extremely rare, VG (VG container) $3,000.00
Mickey Mouse, gumball machine, Hasbro, 1968, head form on red base, NM..$50.00
Mickey Mouse, Kodak Theatre, MIP, B5 ....$35.00
Mickey Mouse, lantern, WDP, 1977, figural, battery-op, MIB, P6 ....$100.00
Mickey Mouse, moccasins, box only, Athletic Shoe, 1930s, features Disney characters on all sides, 9x6", scarce, NM, A .$1,000.00
Mickey Mouse, music box, Schmid, Mickey as cowboy, 6", M, P6 ....$85.00
Mickey Mouse, music box, Schmidt, 50th Birthday, Mickey as Magician, plays It's a Small World, M, P6 ....$75.00
Mickey Mouse, paint set, Transogram, 1952, complete, EX (EX box), C1 ....$100.00
Mickey Mouse, pencil box, Dixon, figural, rare, G $400.00
Mickey Mouse, pencil box, Dixon, 1930s, cb w/image of Mickey on front, Donald & Pluto on back, 6x9", EX, T2 ......$80.00
Mickey Mouse, piano, Marks Bros, push keys & Mickey & Minnie figures dance, 10", rare, EX $2,400.00
Mickey Mouse, Picture Printing Set, Fulton/WDE, 1935, complete, EX (VG box), A $185.00
Mickey Mouse, Pin the Tail on Mickey Mouse, Hallmark/WDP, MIP $25.00
Mickey Mouse, projector, Johnson's/England, 1948, complete w/tin battery-op projector & 6 filmstrips, EX (G box), A $150.00
Mickey Mouse, pull toy, Toy Kraft/WDE, 1935, dog pulling sleigh-type wagon w/image of Mickey, 15", EX $250.00

Mickey Mouse, pull toy, WDE, 1935, Mickey between 2 wheels, wood & metal, 15", rare, EX, A $750.00

Mickey Mouse, purse, Am, 1930s, mesh w/chain hdl, NM, D10 ....$550.00

Mickey Mouse, rattle, celluloid w/rubber ring, image of Mickey tossing ball & baby Mickey in highchair, 7", NM, A .$150.00

Mickey Mouse, scarf, WDP, 1960s, red, wht & bl cotton w/allover print of pie-eyed Mickey, 31x15", MIB, P6..$30.00

Mickey Mouse, Shooting Gallery, Classic Toy, 1970s, MOC, J6 ....$55.00

Mickey Mouse, sled, Allen Co...Mickey Mouse Flexible Flyer stamped on bottom, 1930s, oak w/metal fr, 32", EX, A..$650.00

Mickey Mouse, Slugaroo, Gardner/WDP, complete & unused w/cb display sign, NM (NM box), A....................$75.00

Mickey Mouse, snow shovel, Ohio Art, mk WD, litho tin w/wood hdl, EX $250.00

Mickey Mouse, soap, Cussons, 1939, 4½", M (M red lift-top box), P4 ....$125.00

Mickey Mouse, Soldier Set, Marks Bros, 1930s, cb Mickey figures w/wooden holders, EX (EX box)....................$425.00

Mickey Mouse, squeeze toy, Germany, 1933, w/saxaphone & cymbals, flat tin, 6", NM, A....................$575.00

Mickey Mouse, stamp pad, WDE, 1930s, tin w/ink pad, 2x3", EX, A $50.00

Mickey Mouse, Talkie Jecktor, 1935, w/1 record & 6 paper litho films, EX, A $800.00

Mickey Mouse, Talking Telephone, Hasbro, 1964, battery-op, w/2 records, 12", EX $175.00

Mickey Mouse, Tinkersand Pictures, Toy Tinkers Inc, complete, EX (worn box)....................$125.00

Mickey Mouse, tool chest, 1930s, litho metal, EX..........$275.00

Mickey Mouse, top, WDE, 1935, litho tin w/image of various characters playing instruments, 9½" dia, VG, A.....$175.00

Mickey Mouse, toy chest, Odora, 1935, EX, D10, from $375.00 to $475.00.

Mickey Mouse, toy telephone, Hill Brass, cb Mickey figure pops up when receiver is picked up, EX $450.00

Mickey Mouse, tricycle, Triang, 1930s, gr- & red-pnt metal w/sq image of Mickey on seat, 18x7", EX, A....................$200.00

Mickey Mouse, uniform, Fisch & Co/Felt Ideas, red felt vest w/image of pie-eyed Mickey, w/hat & tassel, NM, A...$400.00

Mickey Mouse, washing machine, Ohio Art, litho tin, EX.$400.00

Mickey Mouse, wastebasket, Chein, 1974, litho tin, 13", EX, J2 ....$25.00

Mickey Mouse's Weebles Magic Kingdom, Romper Room, 1974, MIB, $125.00.

Mickey Mouse & Donald Duck, figure, Windsor/Canada, 1930s, bsk, Mickey & Donald in canoe, rare, EX, M8.....$1,350.00

Mickey Mouse & Donald Duck, fire truck, red rubber, 6½", EX, H7 ....$100.00

Mickey Mouse & Donald Duck, pull toy, Chad Valley, Donald & Mickey in boat, wood, EX....................$425.00

Mickey Mouse & Minnie, coin purse, Cohn & Rosenberger, 1934, hand-pnt enamel w/chain hdl, silk interior, 2", EX, A $600.00

Mickey Mouse & Minnie, masks, WDE, 1933, paper, 9", VG, A $75.00

Mickey Mouse & Minnie, party horn, Marks Bros, 1930s, litho cb w/wooden tip, EX....................$100.00

Mickey Mouse & Minnie, tambourine, Noble Cooley/WDE, EX $250.00

Mickey Mouse & Minnie, tea set, mk WD Japan, 1936, lustreware w/caramel trim, service for 6, EX+, A $335.00

Mickey Mouse & Minnie Mouse & Pluto, figure set, Borgfeldt, 1930s, bsk, NM (NM box mk The Three Pals), A..$900.00

Mickey Mouse & Pluto, figure, Japan, prewar, bsk, Mickey on Pluto, 3", NM, A $145.00

Mickey Mouse Club, bank, Mattel, 1957, tin & plastic clubhouse, EX, I2 ....$55.00
Mickey Mouse Club, Build-Up Blocks, Eldon, 1950s, M (NM box), C1 ....$45.00
Mickey Mouse Club, CB Radio, Durham Industries, 1977, MIB, J6 ....$25.00
Mickey Mouse Club, Dance-A-Tune, Jaymar, complete, MIB $125.00
Mickey Mouse Club, magazine, Vol 1, #4, NM, M8 ....$60.00

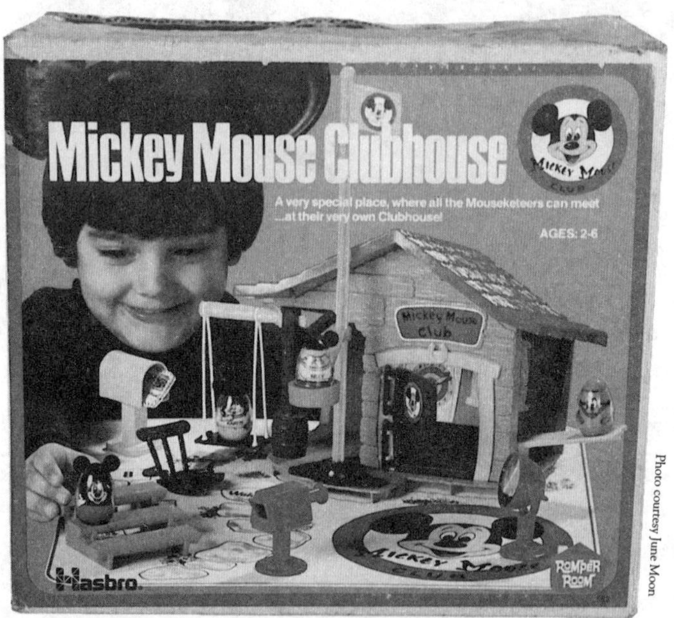

Mickey Mouse Club, Mickey Mouse Clubhouse, Hasbro/Romper Room, 1970s, MIB, $125.00.

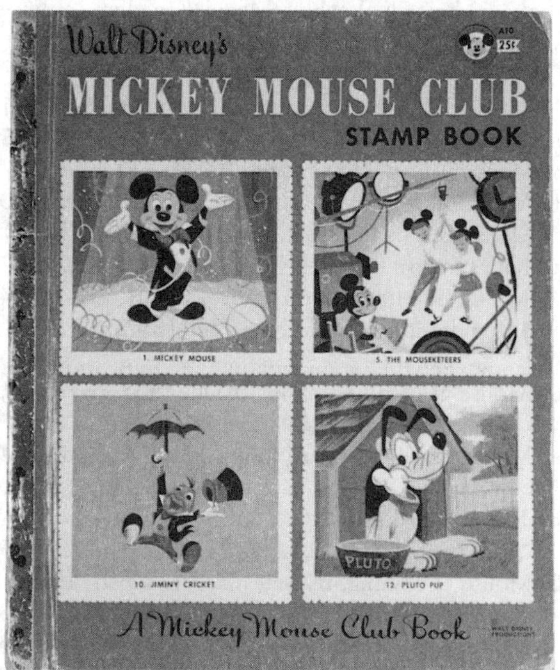

Mickey Mouse Club, stamp book, by Kathleen N. Daly, Golden Press, 1956, EX, $40.00.

Mickey Mouse Club, Mousegetar Jr, Mattel, 1950s, plastic 4-string w/crank, EX, M8 ....$200.00
Mickey Mouse Club, Mouseketeer Ears, Kohner, MIP $75.00
Mickey Mouse Club, Mousketeer Handbag Kit, Connecticut Leather/WDP, complete, EX (EX box) $50.00
Mickey Mouse Club, Professor Wonderful's Wonder Lab, Gilbert, 1964, complete, NMIB, F8 ....$45.00
Mickey Mouse Club, projector, Stephens, 1950s, plastic, complete w/4 films, MIB $125.00
Mickey Mouse Club, wallet, features Donald Duck, NMIB, D10 ....$75.00
Minnie Mouse, bank, Enesco, 1960s, sitting w/hands clasped in pk & wht dress, ceramic, 6", EX, M8 ....$35.00
Minnie Mouse, bank, Ucago, 1960s, 5", MIB, P6 ....$55.00
Minnie Mouse, doll, Applause, 1981, plush w/vinyl face & hands, 16", VG, M15 ....$15.00
Minnie Mouse, doll, Sun Rubber, 1950s, 10", VG, M15 ..$65.00
Minnie Mouse, figure, Am Pottery, 1940s, ceramic, w/broom in hand, 7", M, M8 ....$265.00
Minnie Mouse, figure, Japan, celluloid, pie-eyed Minnie w/yel flower on hat, 6", NM, A $625.00
Minnie Mouse, figure, Japan, prewar, bsk, long upturned nose, 2¾", EX, A $60.00
Minnie Mouse, figure, Japan, 1930s, bsk, hands on hips looking up, 3½", M $250.00
Minnie Mouse, figure, Japan, 1930s, bsk, in nightshirt, 4", EX $225.00
Minnie Mouse, figure, 1930s, bsk, w/umbrella & purse, 4", M, M8 ....$100.00
Minnie Mouse, figure, 1970s, bsk, w/golf clubs, 4", M, M8 ..$20.00
Mouseketeers, mug, Enesco, 1960s, emb image of Mickey's face, orig foil label, EX, P6 ....$50.00
Mouseketeers, TV Story Teller, T Cohn, 1956, phonograph combining pictures which move as records play, complete, NMIB $150.00
Nightmare Before Christmas, doll, Jack, Applause, MIB, J6 ....$225.00
Nightmare Before Christmas, doll, Sally, Applause, MIB, J6 ....$350.00
Nightmare Before Christmas, doll, Santa, Applause, 1994, stuffed cloth, orig tag, M, H4 ....$55.00
Nightmare Before Christmas, figure, Lock, Shock & Barrel in bathtub on wheels, Applause, PVC, M, H4 ....$10.00
Nightmare Before Christmas, figure, Sally, Hasbro, 1993, MOC, H4 ....$100.00
Nightmare Before Christmas, figure set, Lock, Shock & Barrel, Hasbro, 1993, w/3 masks, MIB, J6 ....$125.00

Nightmare Before Christmas, pins, MOC, from $25.00 to $35.00 each.

Nightmare Before Christmas, key chain, Applause, 1993, any character, M, F1, ea $5.00
Peter Pan, figure, Tinkerbell, 1980s, porcelain, w/gold string for hanging, 6", M, P6..$75.00
Peter Pan, hat, Weatherbird Shoes premium, 1950s, gr paper w/various characters around rim, EX, M8 ....$35.00
Peter Pan, place mat, Tinkerbell, 1960s, vinyl w/image of Tinkerbell & the magic castle, 12x18", EX, A $25.00
Peter Pan, Tinker Bells, Peter Puppet, move handle & Tinker Bell plays bells, tin & plastic, 16", rare, NMIB, A...$500.00
Piglet, see Winnie the Pooh
Pinocchio, clicker, Jiminy Cricket, yel plastic head figure, EX, M8..$20.00
Pinocchio, doll, Figaro, jtd compo, 7", EX, A................$465.00
Pinocchio, doll, Geppetto, Chad Valley, wood w/cloth clothes, orig tag, EX..$1,250.00
Pinocchio, doll, Jiminy Cricket, compo w/jtd arms, blk felt coat w/red piping & bl hat, 10", NM, A.........................$500.00
Pinocchio, doll, Jiminy Cricket, Ideal, jtd wood, orig felt hat brim & collar, 8½", EX, from $300 to.....................$500.00

Pinocchio, doll, Jiminy Cricket, Ideal, 1940, 8½", EX, from $300.00 to $500.00.

Pinocchio, doll, Pinocchio, Ideal, jtd wood & compo, orig collar & feathers, 7", EX, A..$100.00
Pinocchio, doll, Pinocchio, Ideal, jtd wood & compo, orig satin bow & decal, 20", EX, A $225.00
Pinocchio, doll, Pinocchio, Ideal, 1940s, jtd wood & compo, 11", NM (M rare box), A $550.00
Pinocchio, doll, Pinocchio, Ideal, 1940s, jtd wood & compo, orig hat & feather, 11", EX, A $250.00

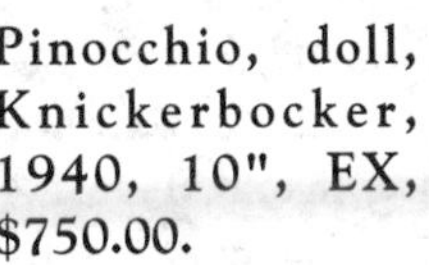

Pinocchio, doll, Knickerbocker, 1940, 10", EX, $750.00.

Pinocchio, doll, Pinocchio, Knickerbocker, 1963, stuffed cloth w/vinyl head, 13", NM, F8...$50.00
Pinocchio, figure, Geppetto, Multi-Products, 1940s, bsk, 2¼", EX, M8..$100.00

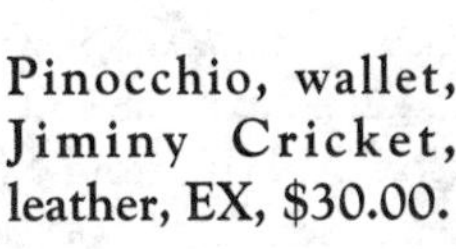

Pinocchio, wallet, Jiminy Cricket, leather, EX, $30.00.

Pinocchio, figure, Honest John, 1930s, bsk, 3", EX, M8...$40.00
Pinocchio, figure, Pinocchio, Bulgaria, Pinocchio on scooter, plastic, 12", EX, A ...$135.00
Pinocchio, figure, Pinocchio, Fun-E-Flex, wood, mk Pinocchio...Geo Borgfeldt Corp New York on foot, 5", EX ...$225.00
Pinocchio, figure, Pinocchio, Japan, prewar, hands in pockets, celluloid, 5½", NM, A...$100.00
Pinocchio, figure, Pinocchio, Multi-Products, 1940s, bsk, 2¼", EX, M8...$100.00
Pinocchio, figure, Pinocchio, Occupied Japan, ceramic, 5", NM, V1...$55.00
Pinocchio, jack-in-the-box, Marx, compo figure w/cloth clothes, paper litho box, 6x6", EX, A ...$250.00
Pinocchio, pencil sharpener, Figaro, Bakelite, figural, 1½", EX, A ...$50.00
Pinocchio, pencil sharpener, Jiminy Cricket, Plastic Novelties, Bakelite, 1¾", EX ...$65.00
Pinocchio, roly poly, celluloid, 5", EX, M5 ...$175.00
Pinocchio, stationery, Whitman, 1939, paper & envelopes in 3-way cb folder w/illus inside & out, EX, M8 ...$85.00
Pinocchio, tea set, ceramic trimmed in red, 8 pcs, EX....$250.00
Pluto, doll, WDP/Character Novelty, velour & felt w/oilcloth eyes, 12", EX, A ...$110.00
Pluto, figure, Come Alives, Kohner, plastic, turn knob & Pluto pets turtle sitting beside him, NM (EX box), A $250.00
Pluto, figure, Fun-E-Flex, wood w/felt ears & rope tail, EX ...$350.00
Pluto, figure, 1930s, bsk, Pluto sitting, 2½", EX, M8 ....$85.00
Pluto, pencil sharpener, Bakelite, 1½" dia, EX, M8..........$35.00
Pluto, pull toy, unmk, 1940s, litho wood w/fabric ears & rope tail, orig pull-string w/ball end, 12", NM, A...........$135.00
Pluto, rocking chair, 1950s, gray & red stuffed vinyl w/wood rockers, Pluto playing w/pups on back, 32", EX, J5..$200.00
Pluto the Pup, figure, Borgfeldt/WDE, jtd wood w/cloth ears, 6", NM (EX box mk Mickey Mouse's Dog), A.............$600.00
Pluto the Pup, figure & doghouse, Fun-E-Flex, wood w/felt ears, EX ...$400.00
Pocahontas, figure set, Applause, PVC, set of 7, 3", EX, F1 .$15.00
Rocketeer, backback, leather-like, promo for AMC Theatres, H10, from $75 to ...$125.00
Rocketeer, figure, Applause, vinyl, 9", EX, H10 ....$20.00
Rocketeer, Gee Bee plane, Spectra Star, MIB, H10 ....$45.00
Rocketeer, Poster Pen Set, Rose Art #1921, 1991, complete, MOC, from $20 to ...$30.00
Rocketeer, sleeping bag, H10 ...$45.00
Rocketeer, umbrella, Pyramid Handbag Co, EX, H10, from $75 to ...$100.00
Roger Rabbit, See Who Framed Roger Rabbit
Silly Symphony, Christmas tree light set, Noma, complete, rare, EX (EX box), A ...$250.00
Silly Symphony, fan, WDE, 1935, picnic scene w/various characters, litho paper w/wood hdl, 9", NM, A $135.00
Sleeping Beauty, booklet, Sleeping Beauty's Castle, 1957, EX, M8...$30.00
Sleeping Beauty, Dress Designer Kit, Colorforms, 1959, MIB, P6...$65.00
Sleeping Beauty, Magic Bubble Wand, 1950s, MIP..........$40.00

Sleeping Beauty, paint-by-number set, Transogram, 1959, complete, MIB, from $75.00 to $95.00.

Sleeping Beauty, sewing set, Transogram, 1959, unused, scarce, EX, M8 ...$65.00
Snow White & the Seven Dwarfs, bank, Dopey, Crown, compo, EX ...$200.00
Snow White & the Seven Dwarfs, bank, WDE, 1938, dime registering, litho tin, 2½x2½", VG, A...$125.00
Snow White & the Seven Dwarfs, charms, Japan, 1930s, hand-pnt celluloid, ea w/names on back, set of 8, NM, M8........$185.00
Snow White & the Seven Dwarfs, Cut-Out Book, Whitman, 1937, unused, EX, C12 ...$120.00
Snow White & the Seven Dwarfs, doll, Bashful, Ideal, stuffed cloth w/molded oilcloth face mask, 12", EX $225.00

Photo courtesy Dunbar Gallery

Snow White and the Seven Dwarfs, doll, Dopey, Ideal, 1937, stuffed cloth, 12", NM, from $250.00 to $450.00.

Snow White & the Seven Dwarfs, doll, Grumpy, Knickerbocker, 8", scarce, EX, M8..$250.00

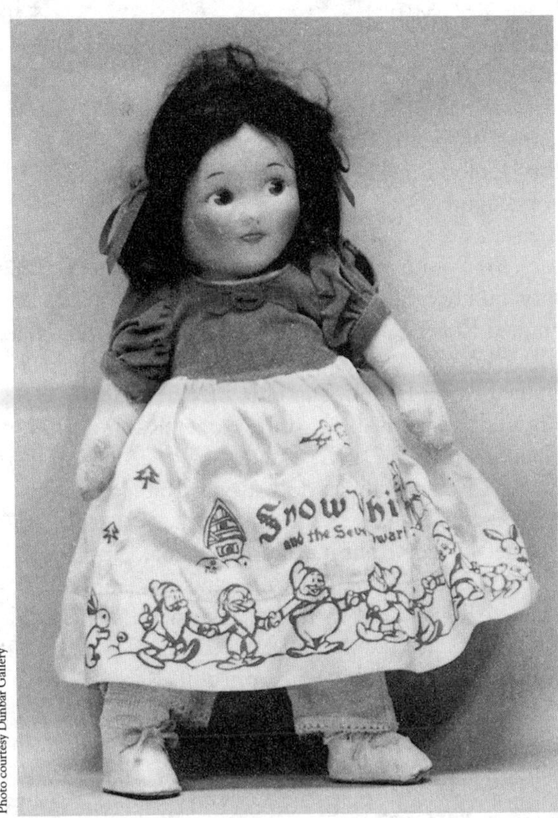

Photo courtesy Dunbar Gallery

Snow White and the Seven Dwarfs, doll, Ideal, 1937, 16", NM, from $350.00 to $450.00.

Snow White & the Seven Dwarfs, doll, Snow White, Reliable/WDE, compo w/mohair wig, pk & blk satin dress, 15", EX, A...$400.00

Snow White & the Seven Dwarfs, doll set, Knickerbocker, 1938, molded faces, orig velvet clothing, 11" to 16", VG, A..$1,000.00

Snow White & the Seven Dwarfs, figure, Dopey, 1930s, bsk, 3", EX, M8...$50.00

Snow White & the Seven Dwarfs, figure, Dopey, 1930s, bsk, 5", EX, M8...$75.00

Snow White & the Seven Dwarfs, figure, Dopey, 1930s, chalkware, 13", EX..$125.00

Snow White & the Seven Dwarfs, figure, Happy, Enesco, 1960s, ceramic, no label, 4½", NM, M8...............................$30.00

Snow White & the Seven Dwarfs, figure, Sleepy, Am Pottery, 5½", NM, M8..$275.00

Snow White & the Seven Dwarfs, figure, Sneezy, Am Pottery, 5½", NM, M8..$275.00

Snow White & the Seven Dwarfs, figure, Sneezy, Enesco, 1960s, no label, 4½", NM, M8..$30.00

Snow White & the Seven Dwarfs, figure, Snow White, Enesco, ceramic, 4½", NM, M8...$35.00

Snow White & the Seven Dwarfs, figure, Snow White, Seiberling Rubber, 1939, G..$900.00

Snow White & the Seven Dwarfs, figure, Snow White, 1930s, bsk, 5½", EX, M8..$75.00

Snow White & the Seven Dwarfs, figure set, dwarfs, Seiberling Rubber, 1939, VG, C12..$550.00

Snow White & the Seven Dwarfs, figure set, 1939, pnt bsk, MIB, C12...$1,200.00

Snow White & the Seven Dwarfs, house, Bully Co/West Germany, NM, B5...$125.00

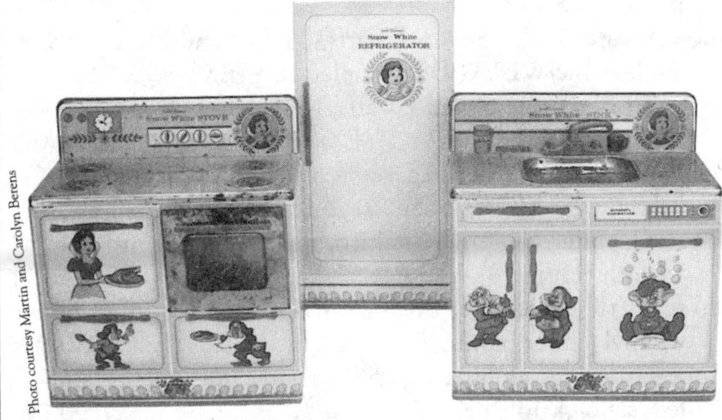

Photo courtesy Martin and Carolyn Berens

Snow White and the Seven Dwarfs, kitchen set, Wolverine, 1970s – 80s, lithographed tin, EX, $110.00.

Snow White & the Seven Dwarfs, musical sweeper, Dopey, Fisher-Price, plays Whistle While You Work, EX...$150.00

Snow White & the Seven Dwarfs, nightlight, Dopey, WDE, 1938, wood Dopey figure & tin battery case on rnd base, 3", EX, A...$165.00

Snow White & the Seven Dwarfs, pencil sharpener, Dopey, Bakelite, figural, 1½", rare, EX, A...........................$130.00

Snow White & the Seven Dwarfs, pencil sharpener, Snow White, Bakelite, figural, 1½", EX, A.......................$100.00

Photo courtesy Michael Stern

Snow White and the Seven Dwarfs, tea set, Aluminum Goods Mfg, 1937, 10 pieces, MIB, $300.00.

Snow White & the Seven Dwarfs, pull toy, Bashful, Sneezy & Doc, European, 1930s, EX $450.00
Snow White & the Seven Dwarfs, Stardust Touch of Velvet Art, Hasbro, 1960s, complete, MIB, A $65.00
Snow White & the Seven Dwarfs, Talking Telephone, Hasbro, 1967, complete w/8 records, MIB, J6 .... $225.00
Snow White & the Seven Dwarfs, tea set, Marx/WDP, china, 23 pcs, EX (EX box) $375.00
Snow White & the Seven Dwarfs, Tinkersand Pictures, Toy Tinkers Inc/WDE, 1937, complete, EX (EX box) ...$125.00
Snow White & the Seven Dwarfs, trinket box, Dopey, 1960s, ceramic w/gold trim, 2½x2", EX, P6 .... $60.00
Snow White & the Seven Dwarfs, xylophone, Larami, 1960s, litho tin, 9", MOC, J5 .... $35.00
Three Caballeros, doll, Panchito, made in Peru, jtd compo w/cloth clothes, 8", EX, A $275.00
Three Little Pigs, doll, Big Bad Wolf, Gund, stuffed plush w/vinyl face & hands, EX $50.00
Three Little Pigs, dolls, Lars/Italy, playing instruments, stuffed felt, set of 3, 13", EX $1,100.00
Three Little Pigs, drum, Ohio Art, litho tin w/image of Three Little Pigs playing instruments, 6½" dia, VG, A $150.00
Three Little Pigs, figure, Big Bad Wolf, Japan, 1930s, bsk, in overalls & top hat, 3½", EX $75.00

Three Little Pigs, figure set, Fun-E-Flex, wood, EX, A, $400.00.

Three Little Pigs, tea set, Ohio Art/WDE, 1935, green lithographed tin, complete, NM, $350.00.

Three Little Pigs, figures, Borgfeldt, bsk, playing instruments, 3", NM (EX box mk Who's Afraid of the Big Bad Wolf), A.......$600.00
Three Little Pigs, pull toy, 2 pigs in canoe, Wm Rogers, silver-plated, 8x5", MIB $400.00
Three Little Pigs, tea set, Ohio Art/WDE, 1935, gr litho tin, 8 pcs, NM, A $225.00
Thumper, see Bambi
Tigger, see Winnie the Pooh
Toy Story, Colorforms, 1993, MIB, M17 .... $15.00
Toy Story, figure, Woody or Buzz Light-Year, PVC, 3", MOC, F1, ea $6.00
Toy Story, Mr Potato Head, Hasbro, MIB, F1 .... $20.00
Toy Story, pull toy, Slinky Dog, MIB, F1 .... $20.00
Who Framed Roger Rabbit, bop bag, LJN, 1988, inflatable, 36", MIP, M17 .... $25.00
Who Framed Roger Rabbit, Dip Flip, LJN, 1987, MIB.....$25.00
Who Framed Roger Rabbit, doll, Roger Rabbit, LJN, 1987, inflatable vinyl, 36", EX, F1 .... $10.00
Who Framed Roger Rabbit, doll, Roger Rabbit, stuffed plush, 24", M $75.00
Who Framed Roger Rabbit, figure, Jessica, Applause, 1987, PVC, 3", EX, F1 .... $10.00
Who Framed Roger Rabbit, figure, Jessica, LJN, bendable, 6", MOC $30.00
Who Framed Roger Rabbit, stick-on doll, Roger Rabbit, LJN, 1987, 8", M, F1 .... $15.00
Winnie the Pooh, doll, Piglet, Gund, 1960s, stuffed cloth, 12", NM, F8 .... $50.00
Winnie the Pooh, doll, Piglet, Sears, 1964-68, stuffed cloth, 7", NM, F8 .... $100.00
Winnie the Pooh, doll, Pooh, Gund, 1960s, stuffed cloth w/name on sweater, 9", EX $225.00
Winnie the Pooh, doll, Pooh, Japan, stuffed velvet, Hand Made Novelty on paper label, 5", M, G16 .... $40.00
Winnie the Pooh, doll, Pooh, Knickerbocker, 1963, bl shirt, 13", EX, J2 .... $75.00
Winnie the Pooh, doll, Pooh, 1979, wearing red velvet shirt w/Disneyland Grad Night ribbon, 12", VG, M15 ......$55.00
Winnie the Pooh, figure, Pooh, Kanga, Piglet or Tigger, Beswick, ceramic, M, P6, ea $75.00
Winnie the Pooh, figure, Pooh, 1966, vinyl, sitting, 5½", EX, N2 .... $25.00
Winnie the Pooh, figure set, PVC, set of 6, NM, B5 ....$40.00
Winnie the Pooh, squeeze toy, Roo or Tigger, NM, ea.....$30.00
Winnie the Pooh, top, Ohio Art, 1960s, clear plastic cone-shaped dome w/wooden hdl & lithoed graphics, EX, P6 ....$75.00
101 Dalmatians, Colorforms, 1961, complete w/booklet, NM (EX box), F8 .... $40.00
101 Dalmatians, figure, Blot or Penny, Enesco, 1960s, ceramic, M, P6, ea $125.00
101 Dalmatians, squeeze toy, EX $30.00

Dollhouse Furniture

Back in the '40s and '50s, little girls often spent hour after hour with their dollhouses, keeping house for their imaginary families, cooking on tiny stoves (that sometimes came with scaled-to-fit pots and pans), serving meals in lovely dining rooms, making beds, and rearranging furniture, most of which was plastic, much of which was made by Renwal, Ideal, Marx, Irwin, and Plasco. Jaydon made plastic furniture as well but sadly never marked it. Tootsietoy produced metal items, many in boxed sets.

Of all of these manufacturers, Renwal and Ideal are considered the most collectible. Renwal's furniture was usually detailed; some pieces had moving parts. Many were made in more than one color, often brightened with decals. Besides the furniture, they made accessory items as well as 'dollhouse' dolls of the whole family. Ideal's Petite Princess line was packaged in sets with wonderful detail, accessorized down to the perfume bottles on the top of the vanity. Ideal furniture and parts are numbered, always with an 'I' prexif. Most Renwal pieces are also numbered.

Advisor: Judith Mosholder (M7).

Acme/Thomas, seesaw, red w/yel horse heads, M7 ....$10.00
Acme/Thomas, shoofly rocker, gr w/wht horse head, M7 .$10.00
Acme/Thomas, stroller, pk w/bl or wht wheels, M7, ea $6.00
Acme/Thomas, Tommy horse, red w/yel horse head & seat, M7 ....$18.00
Allied, chair, dining; red, M7 ....$2.00
Allied, hutch, red, M7 ....$4.00
Allied, stove, wht, M7 ....$4.00
Allied, vanity, pk, M7 ....$3.00
Ardee, lamp, floor; M7 ....$15.00
Best, bed, pk, M7 ....$5.00
Best, doll, baby; hard plastic, 3⅜", M7 ....$4.00
Best, rocking horse, pk, M7 ....$12.00

Bliss, paper lithograph on wood, eight pieces, EX, A, $775.00.

Block House Inc, table, coffee; Swedish blond maple, M7 .$18.00
Block House Inc, table, end; Swedish blond maple, 3-legged, M7 ....$20.00
Blue Box, chair, kitchen; avacado gr, M7 ....$2.00
Blue Box, sink, bathroom; w/shelf unit, M7 ....$4.00
Blue Box, table, dressing; wht w/pk, M7 ....$4.00
Blue Box, vanity, tan w/heart-shaped mirror, M7 ....$3.00
Donna Lee, chair, kitchen; wht, M7 ....$5.00
Donna Lee, sink, kitchen; wht, M7 ....$6.00
Donna Lee, stove, wht, M7 ....$6.00
Donna Lee, table, kitchen; wht, M7 ....$6.00
Endeavor, armoire, wht w/red, M7 ....$5.00
Endeavor, hutch, dining room; wht w/red, M7 ....$5.00
Endeavor, refrigerator, ivory, opening door, M7 ....$5.00
Endeavor, stove, ivory, M7 ....$5.00
Fisher-Price, shower, bright gr w/wht trim, M7 ....$12.00
Fisher-Price, toilet/vanity, bright gr w/wht trim, M7 ....$10.00
Grand Rapids, chest of drawers, wood w/stained finish, 1½" scale, M7 ....$20.00
Grand Rapids, dresser w/mirror, wood w/stained finish, 1½" scale, M7 ....$20.00
Grand Rapids, hutch, wood w/stained finish, 1½" scale, M7 ...$20.00
Grand Rapids, rocker, wood w/stained finish, 1½" scale, M7 ..$18.00
Ideal, buffet, dk brn or dk marbleized maroon, M7, ea $10.00
Ideal, chair, dining room; brn w/bl or yel seat, M7, ea $10.00
Ideal, chair, dining room; dk marbleized maroon w/bl, red or yel seat, M7, ea $10.00
Ideal, chair, sq back; yel, rose, gr or bl swirl w/brn base, M7, ea $15.00
Ideal, china closet, dk marbleized maroon or dk brn swirl, M7, ea $15.00
Ideal, cradle, bl, M7 ....$40.00
Ideal, doll, baby; w/diaper, M7 ....$10.00
Ideal, hamper, bl, M7 ....$6.00
Ideal, highboy, dk marbleized maroon, M7 ....$15.00
Ideal, highboy, ivory w/bl, M7 ....$18.00
Ideal, lamp, floor; dk brn w/wht shade, M7 ....$25.00
Ideal, lamp, table; dk brn w/rose swirl shade, M7 ....$20.00
Ideal, nightstand, brn, M7 ....$6.00
Ideal, nightstand, ivory w/bl, M7 ....$8.00
Ideal, picnic table, wht, M7 ....$20.00
Ideal, potty chair, bl, M7 ....$15.00
Ideal, radio, floor; brn or dk marbleized maroon, M7, ea ..$10.00

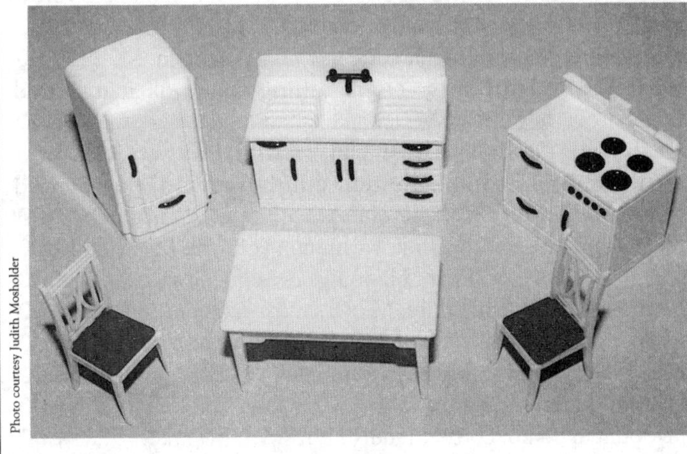

Ideal, refrigerator, $15.00; sink, $15.00; stove, $15.00; kitchen table, $6.00; kitchen chairs, $5.00 each.

Ideal, sewing machine, dk marbleized maroon or brn, M7, ea $20.00
Ideal, shopping cart, wht w/red basket, M7 ....$40.00
Ideal, sink, bathroom; bl w/yel, M7 ....$10.00
Ideal, sofa, bl or rose swirl w/brn base, M7, ea $20.00
Ideal, table, coffee; brn, M7 ....$10.00
Ideal, table, dining; dk marbleized maroon, M7 ....$20.00
Ideal, table, tilt-top; dk maroon swirl, M7 ....$25.00
Ideal, tub, corner; bl w/yel, M7 ....$18.00
Ideal, tub, ivory w/blk, M7 ....$10.00
Ideal, vanity, dk marbleized maroon, M7 ....$15.00
Ideal, vanity, ivory w/bl, M7 ....$18.00

Ideal, vanity bench, brn w/red seat or ivory w/bl seat, M7, ea $5.00
Ideal Petite Princess, boudoir chaise lounge, bl, M7 ....$25.00
Ideal Petite Princess, chair, dining; guest or host, M7, ea ...$8.00
Ideal Petite Princess, dressing table set, #4417-2, complete, M7 ....$28.00
Ideal Petite Princess, Fantasy family, #9710-5, M7 ....$75.00
Ideal Petite Princess, Fantasy telephone set, #4432-1, M7.$22.00
Ideal Petite Princess, Heirloom table set, #4428-9, M7 ....$27.00
Ideal Petite Princess, kitchen sink/dishwasher, #4508-8, M7 ....$100.00
Ideal Petite Princess, Little Princess bed, #4416-4, bl, M7.$40.00
Ideal Petite Princess, Lyre table set, #4426-3, complete, M7 ....$20.00
Ideal Petite Princess, Palace chest, #4420-6, w/picture, M7 ....$15.00
Ideal Petite Princess, refrigerator/freezer, #4505-4, complete, M7 ....$190.00
Ideal Petite Princess, Regency hearthplace, #4422-2, w/accessories, M7 ....$25.00
Ideal Petite Princess, rolling tea cart, #4424-8, complete, M7 ....$25.00
Ideal Petite Princess, Royal buffet, #4419-8, complete, M7 ..$25.00
Ideal Petite Princess, Royal candelabra, #4439-6, M7 ......$17.00
Ideal Petite Princess, Royal grand piano, #4425-5, complete, M7 ....$30.00
Ideal Petite Princess, sofa, #4407-3, brocade, M7 ....$25.00
Ideal Petite Princess, table, dining room; #4421-4, M7 ....$15.00
Ideal Petite Princess, Treasure Trove cabinet, #4418-0, M7...$12.00
Ideal Petite Princess, vanity, #4502-1, M7 ....$50.00
Ideal Young Decorator, bed, rose-colored spread, M7.......$35.00
Ideal Young Decorator, buffet, dk marbleized maroon, M7 ..$20.00
Ideal Young Decorator, chair, dining room; dk marbleized maroon w/yel seat, M7 ....$10.00
Ideal Young Decorator, diaper pail, yel w/bl, M7 ....$25.00
Ideal Young Decorator, hutch, dining room; dk marbleized maroon, M7 ....$25.00
Ideal Young Decorator, sink, bathroom; yel w/bl, M7 ......$40.00
Irwin, accessory, dust pan, bl, orange or yel, M7, ea............$4.00
Irwin, accessory, pail, dk bl, M7 ....$6.00
Irwin, accessory, tray, lt bl, M7 ....$3.00
Jaydon, bed, reddish brn swirl, w/spread, M7 ....$18.00
Jaydon, buffet, reddish brn, M7 ....$4.00
Jaydon, cupboard, corner; reddish brn swirl, M7 ....$4.00
Jaydon, piano w/bench, reddish brn swirl, M7 ....$12.00
Kilgore, baby buggy, bl-pnt CI, M7 ....$75.00
Kilgore, bed, gr-pnt CI, M7 ....$60.00
Kilgore, buffet, bl-pnt CI, M7 ....$50.00
Kilgore, chair, bedroom; gr-pnt CI, M7 ....$40.00
Kilgore, chair, dining; CI, no pnt, M7 ....$35.00
Kilgore, chair, living room; red-pnt CI, rpt, M7 ....$45.00
Kilgore, icebox, ivory-pnt CI, M7 ....$50.00
Kilgore, potty chair, bl-pnt CI, M7 ....$60.00
Kilgore, sink, bathroom; bl-pnt CI, M7 ....$50.00
Kilgore, sink, kitchen; tan-pnt CI, M7 ....$75.00
Kilgore, stove, bl-pnt CI, M7 ....$60.00
Kilgore, table, dressing; gr-pnt CI, M7 ....$60.00
Marx, accessory, frying pan, gray, M7 ....$4.00
Marx, accessory, pitcher, gray, M7 ....$4.00
Marx, Babyland Nursery Set, #3379, complete, unused, NMIB, A $465.00
Marx, bathroom set, dk ivory, hard plastic, ¾" scale, 4 pcs, M7 ....$20.00
Marx, bedroom set, dk ivory, hard plastic, ¾" scale, 8 pcs, M7 ....$40.00
Marx, buffet, maroon or brn swirl, hard plastic, ½" scale, M7, ea $3.00
Marx, buffet, maroon swirl, hard plastic, ¾" scale, M7 ....$5.00
Marx, buffet, tan w/molded fruit, hard plastic, ½" scale, M7..$3.00
Marx, chair, armless; bright yel, hard plastic, ½" scale, M7 .$3.00
Marx, chair, living room; red, hard plastic, ½" scale, M7 ...$3.00
Marx, chair, living room; yel or red, tufted, hard plastic, ¾" scale, M7, ea $5.00
Marx, chest of drawers, pk, hard plastic, ¾" scale, M7........$5.00
Marx, console TV, gr or yel, hard plastic, ½" scale, M7, ea .$3.00
Marx, crib, gr w/molded bottle & rattle, hard plastic, ½" scale, M7 ....$5.00
Marx, dining room set, brn, soft plastic, ¾" scale, 7 pcs, M7.$20.00
Marx, dining room set, brn swirl, hard plastic, ¾" scale, 7 pcs, M7 ....$30.00
Marx, doll, baby w/arms up, M7 ....$4.00
Marx, dresser, tan, w/mirror, hard plastic, ½" scale, M7 .....$3.00
Marx, hamper, ivory, hard plastic, ½" scale, M7 ....$3.00
Marx, hamper, pk, peach, bl or ivory, hard plastic, ¾" scale, M7, ea $5.00
Marx, highboy, yel, hard plastic, ½" scale, M7 ....$3.00
Marx, highboy, yel, hard plastic, ¾" scale, M7 ....$5.00
Marx, hutch, brn, soft plastic, ¾" scale, M7 ....$3.00
Marx, hutch, maroon swirl, hard plastic, ¾" scale, M7 ....$5.00
Marx, lamp, floor; yel w/red shade, hard plastic, ¾" scale, M7 ....$10.00
Marx, laundry basket, chartreuse, soft plastic, ¾" scale, M7 .$3.00
Marx, laundry basket, gr, hard plastic, ¾" scale, M7 ....$5.00
Marx, mangle, wht, hard plastic, ½" scale, M7 ....$4.00
Marx, nightstand, yel, hard plastic, ¾" scale, M7 ....$5.00
Marx, piano, red or yel, hard plastic, ½" scale, M7 ....$15.00
Marx, playpen, pk, soft plastic, ¾" scale, M7 ....$3.00
Marx, playpen, pk w/emb Donald Duck, hard plastic, ½" scale, M7 ....$8.00
Marx, refrigerator, wht, hard plastic, ½" scale, M7 ....$3.00
Marx, refrigerator, yel, soft plastic, ¾" scale, M7 ....$3.00
Marx, sink, kitchen; yel or ivory, soft plastic, ¾" scale, M7 .$3.00
Marx, sofa, lt gr or bright yel, hard plastic, ½" scale, M7, ea .$3.00
Marx, sofa, red or yel, soft plastic, ¾" scale, M7, ea $3.00
Marx, sofa, yel or red, hard plastic, ¾" scale, M7, ea $5.00
Marx, stool, peach or ivory, ftd, hard plastic, ¾", M7, ea ...$5.00
Marx, stove, ivory or wht, hard plastic, ¾" scale, M7, ea....$5.00
Marx, stove, yel or ivory, soft plastic, ¾" scale, M7, ea.......$3.00
Marx, table, coffee; lt gr, hard plastic, ½" scale, M7 ....$10.00
Marx, table, dining room; dk maroon swirl, hard plastic, ½" scale, M7 ....$3.00
Marx, toilet, ivory, hard plastic, ½" scale, M7 ....$3.00
Marx, toilet, pk, peach, bl or ivory, hard plastic, ¾" scale, M7, ea $5.00
Marx, tub, corner; peach, bl or ivory, hard plastic, ¾" scale, M7, ea $5.00
Marx, TV/phono, red, soft plastic, ¾" scale, M7 ....$3.00

Marx, vanity, yel, hard plastic, ¾" scale, M7 ....$5.00
Marx, vanity & bench, yel, soft plastic, ¾" scale, M7.........$5.00
Marx Little Hostess, chaise lounge, ivory w/pk, M7 ....$10.00
Marx Little Hostess, chest of drawers, rust, block front, M7..$10.00
Marx Little Hostess, lowboy, red, M7..............................$10.00
Marx Little Hostess, piano & bench, MIB, M7................$35.00
Marx Little Hostess, table, tilt-top; blk w/gold stenciling, M7 ....$10.00
Marx Little Hostess, vanity, ivory, M7 ....$10.00
Mattel Littles, armoire, M7 ....$8.00
Mattel Littles, bed, w/cover & pillow, MIB, M7 ....$15.00
Mattel Littles, chair, living room; M7 ....$4.00
Mattel Littles, doll, Belinda; w/chairs & pop-up room setting, MIB, M7...$25.00
Mattel Littles, doll, Hedy; w/sofa & pop-up room setting, MIB, M7 ....$22.00
Mattel Littles, dresser & lamp, MIB, M7 ....$12.00
Mattel Littles, sink/icebox, MIB, M7 ....$12.00
Mattel Littles, sofa, M7 ....$8.00
Mattel Littles, stove, w/kettle & coffeepot, MIB, M7.......$15.00
Mattel Littles, table, drop-leaf; w/plates & cups, MIB, M7 ..$15.00
Plasco, bathroom set, tub, toilet, vanity, bench & hamper, w/paper floor plan, MIB, M7 ....$65.00
Plasco, buffet, brn, tan or marbleized reddish brn, M7, ea ..$4.00
Plasco, chair, dining room; brn, M7 ....$3.00
Plasco, chair, dining room; brn w/striped paper seat cover, M7 ....$4.00
Plasco, dining room set, table, buffet, 4 chairs & 2 side tables, MIB, M7...$55.00
Plasco, doll, baby; pk, M7 ....$25.00
Plasco, dresser, tan w/yel detail, 3 drawers, M7 ....$15.00
Plasco, hamper, pk, w/opening lid, M7...............................$5.00
Plasco, highboy, brn, tan, maroon or brn swirl, M7, ea.......$8.00
Plasco, kitchen counter, pk, no-base style, M7 ....$3.00
Plasco, kitchen counter, wht w/bl base, M7 ....$6.00
Plasco, nightstand, brn, tan or mauve, M7, ea $3.00
Plasco, nightstand, ivory, stenciled, M7 ....$5.00
Plasco, refrigerator, pk or wht, no-base style, M7, ea $3.00
Plasco, refrigerator, wht w/bl base, M7 ....$5.00
Plasco, sink, bathroom; pk or turq, M7, ea $4.00
Plasco, sink, kitchen; pk or wht, no-base style, M7, ea $3.00
Plasco, sofa, lt bl w/brn base, M7 ....$8.00
Plasco, sofa, teal or turq, no-base style, M7, ea...................$3.00
Plasco, stove, pk, no-base style, M7 ....$3.00
Plasco, stove, wht w/bl base, M7...$5.00
Plasco, table, coffee; brn or marbleized brn, M7, ea $3.00
Plasco, table, dining; tan, M7 ....$8.00
Plasco, table, kitchen; lt bl, M7 ....$5.00
Plasco, table, patio; bl w/ivory legs, M7...............................$4.00
Plasco, toilet, turq w/wht seat, M7.......................................$8.00
Plasco, tub, pk, turq or rose, M7, ea......................................$4.00
Plasco, vanity, marbleized brn, no-mirror style, M7 ....$5.00
Plasco, vanity, pk, no-mirror style, w/bench, M7 ....$8.00
Plasco, vanity, pk, w/mirror, M7..$5.00
Pyro, cupboard, corner; lt gr, M7 ....$5.00
Renwal, baby bath, #122, bl, no decal, M7 ....$8.00
Renwal, baby bath, #122, pk w/duck or bunny decal, M7, ea $15.00
Renwal, bed, #81, brn w/ivory spread, M7...........................$8.00
Renwal, buffet, #D55, brn, opening drawer, M7 ....$8.00

Renwal, Busy Little Mother, MIB, $350.00.

Renwal, carpet sweeper, $85.00; mop, 45.00; vacuum cleaner, $25.00.

Renwal, carriage, #114, bl w/pk wheels, no insert, M7 .....$25.00
Renwal, carriage, #114, pk w/bl wheels, spread insert, M7 .$30.00
Renwal, chair, barrel; #77, bl w/brn base, stenciled, M7...$10.00
Renwal, chair, barrel; #77, dk red w/brn base, M7 ....$12.00
Renwal, chair, club; #76, bl w/brn base, M7........................$8.00
Renwal, chair, club; #76, ivory w/brn base, stenciled, M7...$10.00
Renwal, chair, rocking; #65, yel w/red, M7 ....$8.00
Renwal, chair, teacher's; #35, bl, M7 ....$18.00
Renwal, china closet, #K52, brn, stenciled, M7................$15.00
Renwal, china closet, #52, blk, stenciled, non-opening door, M7 ....$25.00
Renwal, clock, kitchen; #11, ivory or red, M7, ea.............$20.00
Renwal, clock, mantle; #14, ivory or red, M7, ea..............$10.00

Renwal, cradle, #119, pk, spread insert, M7 ....$30.00
Renwal, cradle, #120, pk or bl w/doll insert, M7, ea $30.00
Renwal, desk, student's; #33, red, brn or yel, M7, ea $12.00
Renwal, desk, teacher's; #34, bl, M7 ....$25.00
Renwal, doll, brother; #42, plastic rivets, M7 ....$25.00
Renwal, doll, brother; #42, tan or lt gr w/red tie, metal rivets, M7, ea $30.00
Renwal, doll, father; #44, bl suit, metal rivets, M7 ....$30.00

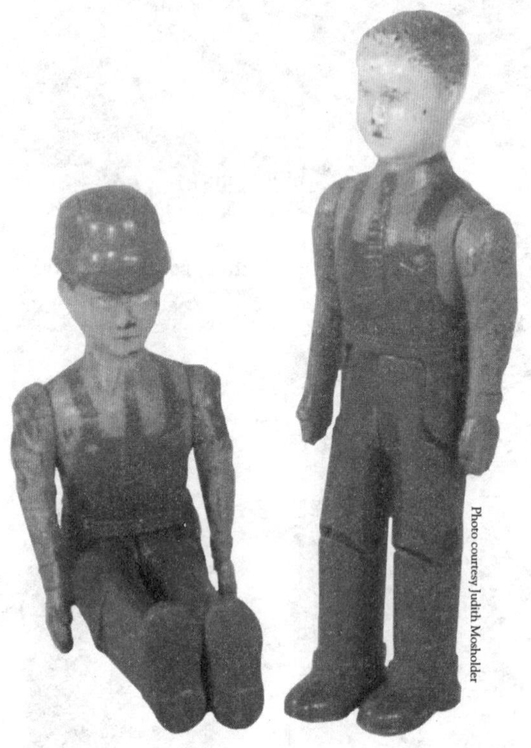

Photo courtesy Judith Mosholder

Renwal, doll, mechanic; with cap: $150.00; no cap: $100.00.

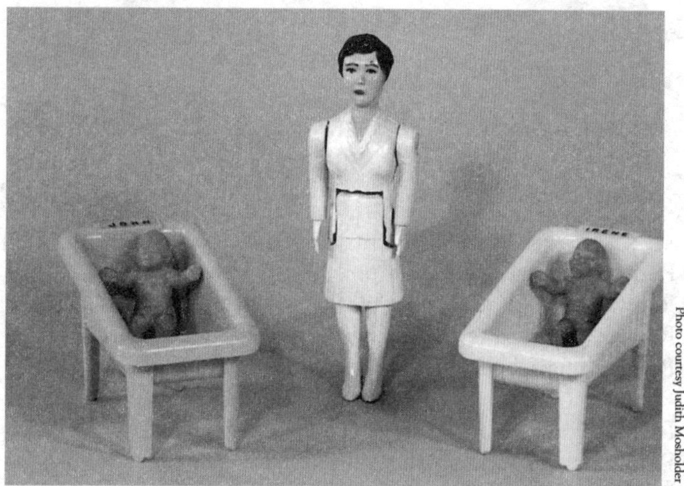

Photo courtesy Judith Mosholder

Renwal, doll, nurse, $40.00; baby, $12.00; nursery crib, $15.00.

Renwal, doll, mother; #43, pk, plastic rivets, M7 ....$25.00
Renwal, doll, sister; #41, yel dress, metal rivets, M7 ....$25.00
Renwal, fireplace, #80, brn or ivory w/ivory insert, brn logs & andirons, M7, ea $35.00
Renwal, hamper, #T98, ivory, M7 ....$2.00
Renwal, hamper, #T98, lime gr, opening lid & cb backing, M7 ....$10.00
Renwal, hamper, #T98, pk, opening lid, M7 ....$4.00
Renwal, highboy, #B85, brn, opening drawers, M7 ....$8.00
Renwal, highboy, #85, pk or bl, M7, ea $15.00
Renwal, ironing board, #32, pink or bl, w/iron, M7, ea $22.00
Renwal, lamp, floor; #70, red w/ivory shade, M7 ....$15.00
Renwal, lamp, floor; #70, yel w/ivory shade, M7...............$20.00
Renwal, lamp, table; #71, red, brn or marbleized brn w/ivory shade, M7, ea $10.00
Renwal, lamp, table; #71, yel w/ivory or wht shade, M7, ea..$10.00

Photo courtesy John Turney

Renwal, Little Red School House and Furniture, MIB, from $300.00 to $325.00.

Renwal, piano, #74, marbleized brn, M7 ....$30.00
Renwal, piano/vanity bench, #75, lt gr, M7 ....$4.00
Renwal, playground slide, #20, bl w/red, M7.....................$22.00
Renwal, playpen, #118, bl w/pk bottom or pk w/bl bottom, M7, ea $15.00
Renwal, refrigerator, #66, turq, w/opening door & 2 shelves, M7 ....$15.00
Renwal, scale, #10, red, M7 ....$10.00
Renwal, server, #D54, lt brn swirl, opening drawer, M7 .....$8.00
Renwal, server, #D54, reddish-brn, stenciled, opening drawer, M7 ....$12.00
Renwal, sink, #T96, pk w/lt bl, M7 ....$5.00
Renwal, sink, #T96, turq w/blk, M7 ....$8.00
Renwal, sink, #68, ivory w/blk, opening door, M7............$15.00
Renwal, smoking stand, #13, red w/ivory or ivory w/red, M7, ea $12.00
Renwal, sofa, #78, ivory w/brn base, M7 ....$18.00
Renwal, sofa, #78, pale pk w/brn base, M7........................$15.00
Renwal, sofa, #78, red w/brn base, M7 ....$15.00

Renwal, stool, #12, red w/ivory seat or ivory w/red seat, M7, ea..$10.00
Renwal, stove, #K69, ivory w/blk or red, opening door, M7, ea $15.00
Renwal, stove, #K69, lt turq, non-opening door, M7 ....$12.00
Renwal, table, #67, brn, yel or lt gr, M7, ea $8.00
Renwal, table, #67, ivory, M7 ....$5.00
Renwal, table, cocktail; #72, brn, M7 ....$10.00
Renwal, table, cocktail; #72, metallic red, M7 ....$15.00
Renwal, table, dining; #D51, brn, stenciled, M7................$20.00
Renwal, table, folding; #108, copper, M7........................$18.00
Renwal, table, folding; #108, gold, M7............................$15.00
Renwal, table, lamp; #73, brn, stenciled, M7 ....$10.00
Renwal, table, lamp; #73, metallic red, M7......................$10.00
Renwal, telephone, #28, yel w/red, M7 ....$22.00
Renwal, toilet, #T97, turq or ivory w/blk, M7, ea $9.00
Renwal, toydee, #36, bl or pk, M7, ea $6.00
Renwal, toydee, #36, bl w/Little Boy Blue decal, M7 ....$12.00
Renwal, tub, #T95, pk w/bl hdls, M7...................................$7.00
Renwal, vacuum cleaner, #37, red w/yel hdl, w/decal, M7.$25.00
Renwal, vanity, #82, brn, stenciled, simplified style, M7..$10.00
Renwal, washing machine, #31, bl or pk w/bear decal, M7, ea .$30.00
Sonia Messer, sofa, lt gr fabric, M7..................................$80.00
Sonia Messer, table, walnut stain w/lighter wood inlaid design, M7 ....$60.00
Strombecker, baby grand piano, walnut, ¾" scale, M7 .....$20.00
Strombecker, bathroom set, 1936, complete w/sandpaper & instructions, MIB, M7 ....$90.00
Strombecker, bedroom set, 1936, complete w/sandpaper & instructions, MIB, M7 ....$75.00
Strombecker, chair, living room; aqua, ¾" scale, M7 ....$10.00
Strombecker, lamp, table; aqua, gr or yel w/ivory shade, ¾" scale, M7, ea....$12.00
Strombecker, living room set, 1936, complete w/sandpaper & instructions, MIB, M7 ....$75.00
Strombecker, radio, floor; walnut w/etched detail, ¾" scale, M7....$12.00
Strombecker, sink, ivory or aqua, ¾" scale, M7, ea.............$8.00
Strombecker, sofa, red, ¾" scale, M7...............................$10.00
Strombecker, toilet, yel, ivory or aqua, ¾" scale, M7, ea..$10.00
Strombecker, tub, ivory or aqua, ¾" scale, M7, ea............$10.00

Superior, chair, $5.00; vanity with bench, yellow, $9.00; chest of drawers, $5.00; bed, $5.00.

Superior, bed, bright yel, ¾" scale, M7 ....$5.00
Superior, chair, dining room; yel, ¾" scale, M7 ....$3.00
Superior, chair, kitchen; olive gr, ¾" scale, M7 ....$3.00
Superior, chest of drawers, bl, gr, yel, turq or plum, ¾" scale, M7, ea $5.00
Superior, hutch, pk or red, ¾" scale, M7, ea $5.00
Superior, refrigerator, wht, ¾" scale, M7...........................$5.00
Superior, sofa, brn, ¾" scale, M7 ....$5.00
Superior, table, coffee; bright yel, ¾" scale, M7 ....$8.00
Superior, tub, yel or red, ¾" scale, M7, ea $5.00
Superior, vanity, bl, w/mirror, ¾" scale, M7........................$5.00
Superior, washing machine, wht, ¾" scale, M7...................$5.00
Tomy Smaller Homes, armoire, M7 ....$10.00
Tomy Smaller Homes, bar, kitchen; M7 ....$12.00
Tomy Smaller Homes, Bentwood rocker, M7 ....$8.00
Tomy Smaller Homes, lamp, table; M7............................$18.00
Tomy Smaller Homes, refrigerator, w/drawers, M7...........$12.00
Tomy Smaller Homes, sink w/dishwasher, 2 racks, M7 ....$12.00
Tomy Smaller Homes, sofa, 2-pc, M7 ....$12.00
Tomy Smaller Homes, sofa, 3-pc, M7 ....$15.00
Tomy Smaller Homes, table, coffee; M7 ....$10.00
Tomy Smaller Homes, table, end; M7...............................$8.00
Tootsietoy, bed, bl or pk w/slotted headboard & footboard, M7, ea $18.00
Tootsietoy, chair, dining room; brn or ivory, M7, ea $7.00
Tootsietoy, chair, living room; gold wicker-style w/cushion, M7 ....$18.00

Tootsietoy, dining room furniture set, diecast, complete, MIB, A, $225.00; Tootsietoy, girl's bedroom set, diecast, complete, MIB, A, $125.00; Tootsietoy, living room furniture set, diecast, complete, MIB, A, $225.00.

Tootsietoy, rocker, gold or ivory wicker-style w/cushion, M7, ea $22.00
Tootsietoy, sofa, gold or ivory wicker-style w/cushion, M7, ea$25.00
Tootsietoy, table, living room; gold, M7 ....$20.00
Tootsietoy, toilet, lavender w/flocked lid & wht seat, M7.$18.00
Tootsietoy, vanity bench, pk w/bl speckled seat, M7........$15.00
Wolverine, bed w/headboard, M7 ....$12.00
Wolverine, dresser w/mirror, M7....................................$10.00
Wolverine, playpen, M7 ....$8.00

Dollhouses

Dollhouses were first made commercially in America in the late 1700s. A century later, Bliss and Schoenhut were making wonderful dollhouses that even yet occasionally turn up on the market, and many were being imported from Germany. During the '40s and '50s, American toy makers made a variety of cottages; today they're all collectible.

Advisor: Bob and Marcie Tubbs (T5).

Other Sources: M15

Bliss, 2-story, paper litho on wood, wht w/brn roof, 4 bow windows w/curtains, sm porch w/2 columns, 13x9", EX, A $650.00

Photo courtesy David Longest

Bliss, two-story, paper lithograph on wood, early 1900s, EX, $1,500.00.

Bliss, 2-story Colonial mansion, paper litho on wood, hinged dbl front doors, 2 columns & 4 front steps, 18x16", G, A $300.00

Fisher-Price, #0250, 3-story w/5 rooms, spiral staircase, w/2 figures & instructions, 1978-79, M, C13........................$40.00

Fisher-Price, 3-story light-up w/5 rooms, spiral staircase, battery-op w/7 outlets, 1981, M, C13 ....$30.00

Jayline, 2-story w/5 rooms, litho tin, gr siding over wht w/red bricks, purple roof, 1949, 14½x18½", VG, T5 ....$50.00

Mansford, 2-story Victorian mansion w/belvedere, CI fence & lions, wood outhouse, late 1800s, 49" sq base, EX, A $2,800.00

Mansford, 3-story w/2 rooms on ea floor, front opening w/lift-off roof, orig wallpaper, late 1800s, 29x26", VG, A...$2,200.00

Marx, red siding, gray roof, patio above garage, VG, M7..$60.00

Marx, split-level, wht roof, gray siding & yel brick, w/fireplace, set of steps & breakfast bar, EX, M7..........................$80.00

German, two-story, hand painted and paper lithograph on wood, 1905, 25", EX, A, $1,650.00.

Hand-Made, two-story with opening front, green clapboard siding, simulated brick chimney, furnished, 22x19", EX, A, $355.00.

Marx, split-level, wht roof, gray siding & yel brick, w/pool, doorbell, light fixture & 60 pcs of furniture, EX, M7......**$125.00**
Marx, 2-story, litho tin, wht clapboard over mc stone, red roof, 14x38", VG, T5......**$100.00**
Marx, 2-story, red roof, patio above garage, ABC nursery, ½" scale, EX, M7......**$50.00**

Photo courtesy John and Sheri Pavone

Marx, two-story with attached garage, with 40 pieces of furniture, NM, $100.00.

McLoughlin Bros, Dolly's Play House, folding 2-room house, litho paper on board, late 1800s, 18½", EX (worn box), A......**$375.00**
Meritoy, Cape Cod, litho tin w/ivory clapboard over gray stone, red roof, plastic window inserts, 1949, 21x14", M...**$150.00**
Rich, bungalow, Arts & Crafts-style litho cb, wht w/red roof, 4 windows, 2 chimneys, 1930s, 32x21", VG, T5......**$200.00**
Rich, litho fiberboard w/red roof, bl shutters, 1940s, 16x24", VG, T5......**$135.00**
Schoenhut, 2-story colonial style w/4 rooms & attic, wood, 4 windows w/shutters, gr shingled roof, 1930, 17x17", VG...**$750.00**
T Cohn, litho tin w/bl shutters & red roof, 1951, furnished, 16x24", VG......**$200.00**
Tootsietoy, 2-story Victorian cottage w/3 rooms, pressed board, yel w/red trim, gr shingled roof, 1900s, 23", EX, A..**$475.00**
Unknown Maker, 2-story, Tudor-style, yel w/brn trim & maroon roof, furnished w/Tootsietoy furniture, 16x14", VG, A......**$500.00**
Unknown Maker, 2-story w/4 rooms & attic, pnt faux brick w/glass windows, lift-off roof, late 1800s, 38x26", VG, A......**$1,000.00**
Wolverine, Colonial Mansion, no garage, ½" scale, EX, M7..**$50.00**
Wolverine, Country Cottage #800, 1986, ½" scale, EX, M7.**$50.00**

Shops and Single Rooms

Drawing Room, Thorne, paneled walls, complete w/Chippendale couch, 3 chairs, dressing table, etc, 1940s, 15x28", EX, A......**$3,000.00**
Grocery Shop, wood w/wallpapered interior, molded metal labels, w/compo figure & tins, 10x19", VG, A **$475.00**
Kitchen, emb tin w/stove & several tin utensils, 10x19", EX, A......**$525.00**
Kitchen, Germany, wood w/center stove alcove, wallpapered, wood table, assorted tinware & accessories, 12x22", VG......**$700.00**

Modern Kitchen Set, Marx, lithographed tin, complete, NMIB, A, $250.00.

Newlyweds Bathroom, Marx #192, 3-sided litho tin room complete w/furniture, 1925, 3x5x3", MIB......**$400.00**
Newlyweds Dining Room, Marx #194, 3-sided litho tin room complete w/furniture, 1925, 3x5x3", MIB......**$300.00**
Newlyweds Kitchen, Marx #190, 3-sided litho tin room complete w/furniture, 1925, 3x5x3", MIB......**$400.00**
Newlyweds Parlor, Marx #193, 3-sided litho tin room complete w/furniture, 1925, 3x5x3", MIB......**$300.00**
Retail Shop, faux tortoise-shell columns & fitted shelves w/miscellaneous merchandise, 1800s, 15x21", VG......**$2,000.00**
Retail Shop, wood w/compo embellishments, wallpapered interior, molded metal labels, 10x18", VG, A......**$650.00**

Dolls and Accessories

Obviously the field of dolls cannot be covered in a price guide such as this, but we wanted to touch on some of the later plastic dolls from the '50s and '60s, since so much of the collector interest today is centered on those decades. For in-depth information on dolls of all types, we recommend the many lovely doll books written by authority Pat Smith; all are available from Collector Books. Other great publications by Collector Books are *Doll Values, Antique to Modern*, and *Modern Collectible Dolls* both by Patsy Moyer; *Madame Alexander Collector's Dolls Price Guide #22* by Linda Crowsey; *The World of Raggedy Ann Collectibles* by Kim Avery; and *Collector's Guide to Ideal Dolls* by Judith Izen.

See also Action Figures; Barbie and Friends; Character, TV, and Movie Collectibles; GI Joe; and other specific categories.

Baby Dolls

Remnants of baby dolls have been found in the artifacts of most primitive digs. Some are just sticks or stuffed leather or animal skins.

Baby dolls teach our young nurturing and caring. Mothering instincts stay with us and aren't we lucky as doll collectors that we can keep 'mothering' even after the young have 'flown the nest.'

Baby dolls come in all sizes and mediums: vinyl, plastic, rubber, porcelain, cloth, etc. Almost everyone remembers some baby doll they had as a child. The return to childhood is such a great trip. Keep looking and you will find yours.

Advisor: Marcia Fanta (M15).

Baby Brother Tender Love, Mattel, NFRB, B5, $75.00.

Photo courtesy Martin and Carolyn Berens

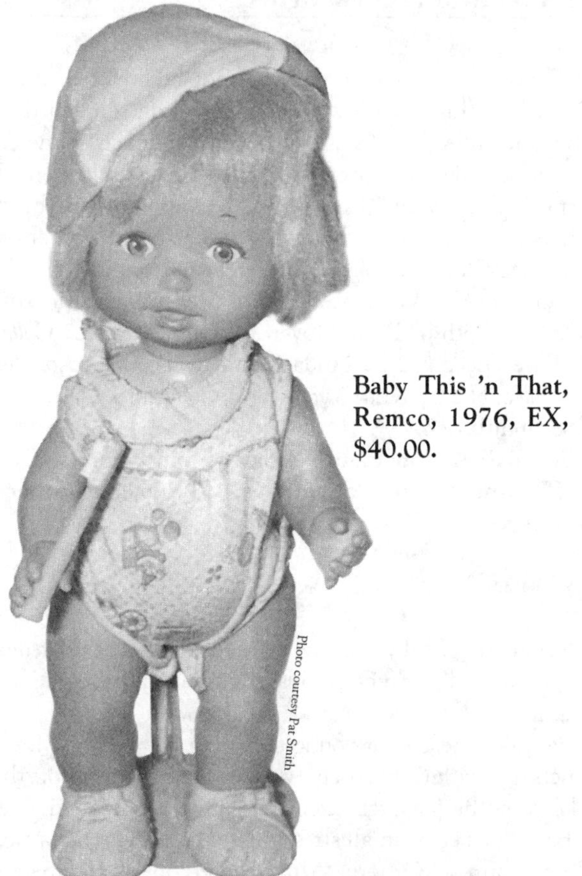

Baby This 'n That, Remco, 1976, EX, $40.00.

Photo courtesy Pat Smith

Baby First Step, Mattel, 1964, orig outfit, VG, M15.........**$45.00**
Baby Giggles, Ideal, 1967, re-dressed, 18", VG, M15........**$55.00**
Baby Go Bye-Bye & Her Bumpety Buggy, Mattel, VG (worn box), M15..........**$125.00**
Baby Heartbeat, Kenner, 1977, 13", MIB, M15...............**$35.00**
Baby Kissy, Ideal, 1962, 23", NRFB, M15.....................**$155.00**
Baby Pat-A-Burp, Mattel, 1963, orig outfit, 17", VG, M15 .**$70.00**
Baby Skates, Mattel, 1983, vinyl, orig outfit, 16", EX.......**$40.00**
Baby Small Walk, Mattel, 1967, orig outfit, 11", not working, MIB, M15..........**$15.00**
Baby Talk, Galoob, 1986, 18", MIB, M15.......................**$60.00**
Baby Talk, Hispanic, Galoob, 1986, 18", MIB, M15 ....**$90.00**
Baby Tenderlove, Mattel, 1971, orig outfit, 16", VG, M15 .**$25.00**
Baby That Away, Black, Mattel, 1974, orig outfit, 16", rare, VG, M15..........**$35.00**
Baby Tippee Toes, Mattel, 1967, all orig w/trike & horse, 16", VG, M15..........**$75.00**
Baby Walk & Play, Mattel, 1967, orig outfit, 11", VG, M15..**$30.00**
Baby Whoopsie, Ideal, 1978, 14", VG, M15 ....**$55.00**
Baby Won't Let Go, Kenner, 1977, 18", re-dressed, G, M15..**$20.00**
Baby Wrinkles, Coleco, 1984, 10", MIB, M15.................**$25.00**
Bathrobe Baby, Ideal, 1933, rubber & compo, orig outfit & diaper, 12", EX..........**$125.00**
Betsy Wetsy, Ideal, 1937-38, orig outfit, 15", EX (VG box) ...**$300.00**
Cabbage Patch Preemie, Coleco, w/pacifier & orig pk sleeper, VG, M15..........**$35.00**
Chew Suzy Chew, Black, Ideal, 1980, 15", NRFB, M15...**$30.00**
Dottie Dimples, Ideal, 1915, cloth & compo, orig outfit & bonnet, EX..........**$225.00**
Drinkie Walker, Horsman, 1988, plastic & vinyl, orig outfit, M..........**$25.00**
Gabbigale, Kenner, 1972, 19", MIB, M15........................**$65.00**
Ginny Toddles, Vogue, 1940s, compo, orig outfit, 7½", NM, G16..........**$325.00**
Heartbeat Baby, Effanbee, 1942, compo w/clockwork mechanism, orig outfit, 15", minimum value **$200.00**
Hush Lil' Baby, Mattel, 1975, 15", MIB, M15 ....**$25.00**
Hush-A-Bye Baby, Ideal, 1935, compo head & arms w/cloth body & legs, orig outfit, 14", EX..............................**$200.00**
I Love You Dolly, Uneeda, 1989, vinyl w/cloth body, orig outfit, 14", EX..........**$15.00**
Lil' Miss Fashion, Deluxe Reading, 1960, 20", MIB, M15 .**$125.00**
Little Baby Tenderlove, Mattel, 1976, 12", MIB, M15.....**$35.00**
Little Debbie Eve, Skippy Doll Corp, 1950s, orig outfit, 20", MIB, M17..........**$150.00**
Little Miss No Name, Hasbro, 1965, MIB, J2 ....**$325.00**
Living Baby Love 'N Touch, Black, Mattel, 1981, 14", NRFB, M15..........**$30.00**
Magic Baby Tenderlove, Mattel, 1978, 14", MIB, M15....**$30.00**
Newborn Thumbelina, Ideal, 1968-72, vinyl w/foam-stuffed body, 9", MIB..........**$85.00**
Patsy, Effanbee, 1927, compo, orig outfit, 14", minimum value..........**$400.00**
Patti Prays, Ideal, 1957, cloth & vinyl, orig outfit, 20", EX..........**$50.00**
Patty Playpal, Ideal, 1959, vinyl w/orange rooted saran hair, redressed, 35", EX, from $300 to **$350.00**
Patty Playpal, Ideal, 1980s, reissue, 36", MIB, M15........**$265.00**

Pigtail Sally, Ideal, 1941, compo, orig outfit, 18", EX.....$175.00

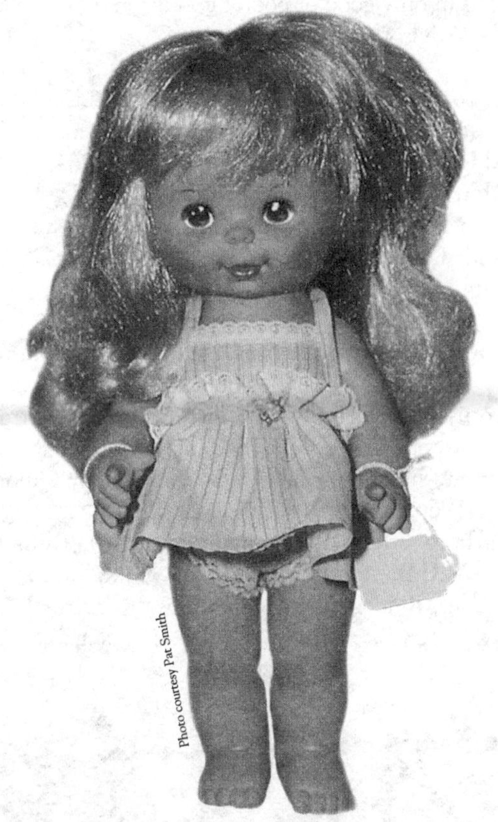

Pretty Curls, Ideal, EX, $40.00.

Rub-A-Dub Dolly, Black, Ideal, 1979-80, 16", NRFB, M15 .$50.00
Ruthie, Horsman, 1964, orig outfit, 16", VG, M15 ....$65.00
Sally Singer, Ideal, 1924, compo, orig outfit, 20", EX.....$200.00
Saucey Makes Faces, Mattel, 1973, 15", MIB, M15........$125.00
Saucy Walker, Ideal, 1951, hard plastic, orig outfit, 16", EX.$165.00
Snuggles & Her Rocking Horse, Ideal, 1979, cloth & vinyl, 12½", EX..$35.00
Special Blessings Christina, Kenner, 1987, 16", MIB, M15..$30.00
Talking Goody Two Shoes, Ideal, 1966, vinyl, orig outfit, 27", EX $125.00
Talking Patty Playpal, Ideal, 1986, 27", MIB, M15 ....$225.00
Talking Tot, Ideal, 1950, cloth & plastic, orig outfit, 22", EX $165.00
Tearful Tenderlove, Mattel, 1971, 16", VG, M15 ....$45.00
Tearie Dearie Twins, Ideal, 1963, vinyl, orig outfits, 9", EX...$65.00
Tender Love & Kisses, Mattel, 1976, 14", MIB, M15.......$25.00
Thumbelina, Ideal, 1961-62, cloth & vinyl, orig outfit, 20", EX $135.00
Tickletoes, Ideal, 1931-39, compo head w/rubber arms & legs, orig outfit, 24", EX..$175.00
Tiny Baby Tenderlove, Mattel, 1971, orig outfit, 11½", VG, M15 ....$35.00
Tiny Tears, American Character, 1950s, orig outfit, 12", VG, M15 ....$125.00
Toni, Ideal, 1949, hard plastic, brunette hair, orig outfit, 14", MIB $500.00
Winnie Walker, Madame Alexander, 1950, orig outfit, 23", VG+, M15 ....$375.00

Betsy McCall

The tiny 8" Betsy McCall doll was manufactured by the American Character Doll Co. from 1957 through 1963. She was made from high-quality hard plastic with a bisque-like finish and hand-painted features. Betsy came in four hair colors — tosca, red, blond, and brunette. She had blue sleep eyes, molded lashes, a winsome smile, and a fully jointed body with bendable knees. On her back there is an identification circle which reads McCall Corp. The basic doll wore a sheer chemise, white taffeta panties, nylon socks, and Maryjane-style shoes and could be purchased for $2.25.

There were two different materials used for tiny Betsy's hair. The first was a soft mohair sewn into fine mesh. Later the rubber scullcap was rooted with saran which was more suitable for washing and combing.

Betsy McCall had an extensive wardrobe with nearly one hundred outfits, each of which could be purchased separately. They were made from wonderful fabrics such as velvet, taffeta, felt, and even real mink. Each ensemble came with the appropriate footwear and was priced under $3.00. Since none of Betsy's clothing was tagged, it is often difficult to identify other than by its square snap closures (although these were used by other companies as well).

Betsy McCall is a highly collectible doll today but is still fairly easy to find at doll shows. Prices remain reasonable for this beautiful clothes horse and her many accessories. For further information we recommend *Betsy McCall, A Collector's Guide*, by Marci Van Ausdall.

Advisor: Marci Van Ausdall (V2).

See also Clubs, Newsletters, and Other Publications.

Doll, TV Time, #9153, all original, V2, $150.00.

Doll, American Character, in Playtime outfit, 14", EX, V2 .$250.00
Doll, American Character, in Town & Country outfit, 8", M $165.00
Doll, American Character, orig outfit, multi-jtd, 22", MIB, V2 ....$250.00
Doll, Ideal, all orig, 14", M, V2 ....$200.00
Doll, orig outfit w/pk tissue & booklet, 8", MIB, V2 ......$225.00
Doll, starter kit #9300, blond hair w/side part, complete, EX (worn card), minimum value....$175.00
Doll, Uneeda, all orig, 11½", EX, V2 ....$45.00
Doll, wearing pk Prom Time formal, 8", EX, V2....$135.00
Doll, wearing 1959 gr ballerina outfit & slippers, EX, V2 ..$150.00
Outfit, April Showers, complete, EX, V2....$35.00
Outfit, Bar-B-Que, MOC, V2....$75.00
Outfit, fur stole & muff, MIB, V2....$150.00
Outfit, Prom Time Formal, bl, EX, V2 ....$50.00
Outfit, Sunday Best, 1957, complete, EX, V2 ....$85.00
Outfit, Zoo Time, complete, VG, V2 ....$45.00
Pattern, McCall's #2247, uncut, V2 ....$25.00

Blythe by Kenner

Blythe by Kenner is an 11" doll with a slender body and an extra large head. You can change her eye color by pulling a string in the back of her head. She came with different hair colors and had fashions, cases, and wigs that could be purchased separately. She was produced in the early 1970s which accounts for her 'groovy' wardrobe.

Advisor: Dawn Parrish (P2).

Case, #33241, image of blond-haired doll wearing Pow-Wow Poncho on orange background, vinyl, EX, P2....$50.00
Doll, brunette, wearing Medieval Mood, EX, P2 ....$50.00
Doll, lt red hair, wearing Golden Goddess, EX, P2 ....$50.00
Doll, red hair, wearing Love 'N Lace, EX, P2....$50.00
Outfit, Aztec Arrival, complete, EX, P2....$50.00
Outfit, Golden Goddess, NRFB, P2 ....$75.00
Outfit, Kozy Kape, complete, EX, P2....$50.00
Outfit, Lounging Lovely, NRFB, P2 ....$75.00
Outfit, Love 'N Lace, NRFB, P2....$75.00
Outfit, Pleasant Peasant, missing shoes, EX, P2....$40.00
Outfit, Pow-Wow Poncho, complete, EX, P2 ....$50.00
Outfit, Priceless Parfait, missing 1 boot, EX, P2....$45.00
Wig, Lemon, complete w/instructions, M, P2 ....$75.00

Celebrity and Personality Dolls

Celebrity and character dolls have been widely collected for many years, but they've lately shown a significant increase in demand. Except for the rarer examples, most of these dolls are still fairly easy to find at doll shows, toy auctions, and flea markets, and the majority are priced under $100.00. These are the dolls that bring back memories of childhood TV shows, popular songs, favorite movies, and familiar characters. Mego, Mattel, Remco, and Hasbro are among the largest manufacturers.

Condition is a very important worth-assessing factor, and if the doll is still in the original box, so much the better! Should the box be unopened (NRFB), the value is further enhanced. Using mint as a standard, add 50% for the same doll mint in the box and 75% if it has never been taken out. On the other hand, dolls in only good or poorer condition drop at a rapid pace.

Advisor: Henri Yunes (Y1).

Abbott & Costello (Who's On First), Ideal, 1984, gift set, 12", MIB, Y1 ....$100.00
Al Lewis (Grandpa Munster), Remco, 1964, 6", MIB....$200.00
Alan Alda (Hawkeye from M*A*S*H), Woolworth, 1976, MOC, Y1 ....$30.00
Andy Gibb, Ideal, 1979, 7½", NRFB $50.00
Angie Dickinson (Police Woman), Horsman, 1976, 9", MIB $60.00
Annissa Jones (Buffy from Family Affair), Mattel, 1967, talker, 10" w/5" Mrs Beasley doll, MIB, Y1 ....$300.00
Annissa Jones (Buffy from Family Affair), Mattel, 1967, 6" w/3" Mrs Beasley doll, MIB $125.00
Barbara Eden (I Dream of Jeannie), Libby Majorette Doll Corp, 1966, 20", rare, NRFB $500.00
Barbara Eden (I Dream of Jeannie), Remco, 1972, 6½", NRFB....$100.00
Beatles, Remco, 1964, ea member w/instrument, MIB, ea from $150 to....$200.00

Photo courtesy June Moon

Beverly Hills 90210, Mattel, 1991, Dylan and Brandon, MIB, $65.00 each.

Beverly Hills 90210, Mattel, 1991, 5 different, 11½", MIB, ea....$65.00
Beverly Johnson, Real Models Collection, Matchbox, 1989, 11½", NRFB $40.00
Bobby Orr, Regal, 1975, 12", rare, MOC....$800.00
Boy George, LJN, 1984, 11½", scarce, MIB....$135.00
Brooke Shields, LJN, 1983, 2nd issue, in swimsuit w/suntan body, 11½", rare, NRFB $95.00
Brooke Shields, LJN, 1983, 3rd issue, Prom Party outfit, 11½", rare, NRFB....$200.00
Captain & Tenille, Mego, 1970s, 12", MIB, ea....$60.00

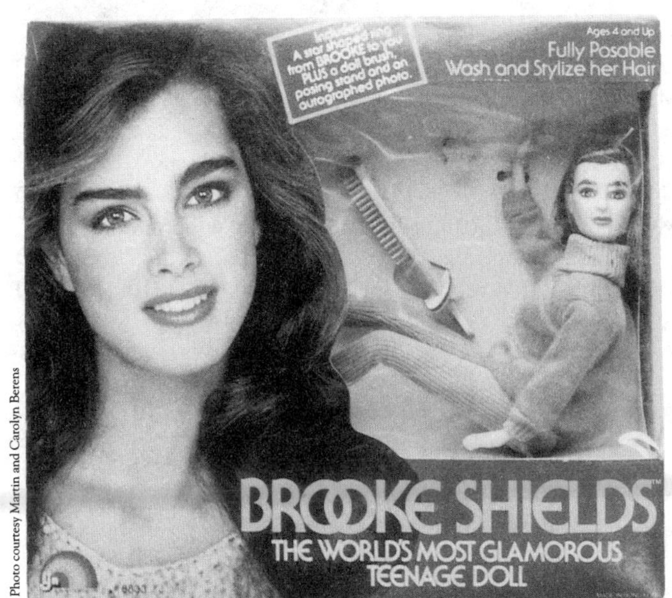

Photo courtesy Martin and Carolyn Berens

Brooke Shields, LJN, 1982, 1st issue, 11½", NRFB, $50.00.

Carol Channing (Hello Dolly), Nasco Dolls, 1962, rare, MIB **$250.00**

Charlie Chaplin, World Doll, 1989, 100th Anniversary, 11½", NRFB **$45.00**

Cher, Mego, 1976, 1st issue, pk dress, 12", NRFB (orange box) **$70.00**

Cher, Mego, 1977, 2nd issue, Growing Hair, 12", NRFB (photo on pk box) **$80.00**

Cher, Mego, 1981, 3rd issue, red swimsuit, 12", rare, NRFB (photo on box) **$95.00**

Cheryl Ladd (Kris from Charlie's Angels), Hasbro, 1977, jumpsuit & scarf, 8½", MOC **$40.00**

Cheryl Ladd (Kris from Charlie's Angels), Mattel, 1978, 12", NRFB **$80.00**

Cheryl Tiegs, Real Models Collection, Matchbox, 1989, 11½", NRFB **$40.00**

Christy Brinkley, Real Models Collection, Matchbox, 1989, 11½", NRFB **$40.00**

Clark Gable (Rhett Butler), World Dolls, 1980, 1st edition, 12", NRFB **$65.00**

Claudia Schiffer, Top Models Collection, Hasbro, 1995, 11½", rare, MIB **$100.00**

Debbie Boone, Mattel, 1978, 11", MIB, H4 ....**$50.00**

Dennis Rodman (Bad As I Wanna Be), Street Players, 1995, 11½", MIB, Y1 ....**$55.00**

Desi Arnez (Ricky Ricardo), Applause, 1988, 17", MIB...**$50.00**

Desi Arnez (Ricky Ricardo), Hamilton Presents, 1991, w/stand, 15½", MIB **$40.00**

Diahann Carroll (Julia), Mattel, 1969, 1st edition, gold & silver jumpsuit, straight hair, talker, 11½", NRFB **$200.00**

Diahann Carroll (Julia), Mattel, 1969, 1st edition, 2-pc nurse uniform, 11½", NRFB **$200.00**

Diahann Carroll (Julia), Mattel, 1970, 2nd edition, 1-pc nurse uniform, 11½", NRFB, Y1 ....**$200.00**

Diahann Carroll (Julia), Mattel, 1971, 2nd edition, gold & silver jumpsuit, Afro hair style, talker, 11½", NRFB....**$200.00**

Diana Ross, Mego, 1977, wht & silver dress, 12", NRFB.**$125.00**

Diana Ross (of the Supremes), Ideal, 1969, 19", NRFB..**$150.00**

Dolly Parton, Eegee, 1980, 1st edition, red jumpsuit, 12", NRFB **$65.00**

Dolly Parton, Eegee, 1987, 2nd edition, blk jumpsuit or cowgirl outfit, 11½", NRFB, ea **$50.00**

Dolly Parton, Goldberger, 1996, red checked dress or long blk dress, NRFB, ea **$30.00**

Dolly Parton, World Doll, 1987, red gown, 18", NRFB, M15 ....**$100.00**

Donna Douglas (Ellie Mae from Beverly Hillbillies), 1964, jeans w/rope belt or yellow dress, MIB, Y1 ....**$65.00**

Donny & Marie Osmond, Mattel, 1976, gift set, NRFB.**$100.00**

Dorothy Hamill, 1977, red olympic outfit w/medal, 11½", NRFB....**$75.00**

Dr J (Julias Erving), Shindana, 1977, w/basketball, 9½", MIB **$100.00**

Dr J (Julius Erving), Shindana, 1977, w/outfits, 9½", MIB **$400.00**

Elizabeth Montgomery (Samantha from Bewitched), Ideal, 1965, 12", rare, MIB **$350.00**

Elizabeth Taylor (Butterfield 8 or Cat on a Hot Tin Roof), Tristar, 1982, 11½", MIB, ea **$125.00**

Elizabeth Taylor (Father of the Bride, Butterfield 8 or Cat on Hot Tin Roof), World Doll, 1989, 11½", MIB, ea **$65.00**

Elizabeth Taylor (The Bluebird), Horsman, 1976, w/3 outfits, 12", NRFB....**$150.00**

Elvis Presley, Eugene, 1984, issued in 6 different outfits, 12", MIB, ea....**$65.00**

Elvis Presley (Aloha Hawaii), World Dolls, 1984, porcelain, wht jumpsuit, MIB **$200.00**

Elvis Presley (Burning Love), World Doll, 1984, 21", MIB..**$110.00**

Elvis Presley (Teen Idol, Jail House Rock or '68 Special), Hasbro, 1993, numbered edition, 12", MIB, ea **$40.00**

Farrah Fawcett (Jill from Charlie's Angels), Hasbro, 1977, jumpsuit & scarf, 8½", MOC....**$40.00**

Farrah Fawcett (Jill from Charlie's Angels), Mego, 1976, 1st edition, wht jumpsuit, 12", NRFB (photo on gr box).....**$60.00**

Farrah Fawcett (Jill from Charlie's Angels), Mego, 1981, lavender swimsuit, 12", rare, NRFB (photo on purple box) **$95.00**

Flip Wilson/Geraldine, Shindana, 1970, plush w/vinyl head, 2-sided, 16", MIB, M15 ....**$65.00**

Flo-Jo, LJN, 1989, pk & bl athletic outfit w/bag, 11½", MIB ..**$60.00**

Fran Dresher (Nanny), Street Players, 1995, 3 different outfits, talker, 11½", MIB **$55.00**

Fred Gwynne (Herman Munster), Presents, 1990, plush w/vinyl head, 12", MIB **$35.00**

Fred Gwynne (Herman Munster), Remco, 1964, MIB...**$150.00**

Grace Kelly (The Swan or Mogambo), Tri-Star, 1982, 11½", MIB, ea **$125.00**

Groucho Marx, Effanbee, 1983, 17", MIB, M15 ....**$90.00**

Jaclyn Smith (Kelly from Charlie's Angels), Hasbro, 1977, jumpsuit & scarf, 8½", MOC **$40.00**

Jaclyn Smith (Kelly from Charlie's Angels), Mego, 1978, bl dress, 12", rare, NRFB....**$125.00**

Jaleel White (Urkel), Hasbro, 1991, cloth & vinyl, 17", MIB....**$50.00**

James Dean, DSI, 1994, Rebel Rouser or City Streets outfit, 12", NRFB, M15, ea **$75.00**

Jimmy Osmond, Mattel, 1978, 9", MIB....**$65.00**

Jimmy Walker (JJ from Good Times), Shindana, 1975, cloth body w/vinyl head, 15", MIB, Y1 ....$50.00

Joe Namath, Mego, 1970, 11½", rare, MIB....$400.00

John Stamos (Jesse from Full House), Tiger, 1993, 11½", MIB, Y1 ....$40.00

John Travolta (On Stage...Superstar), Chemtoy, 1977, 12", NRFB, M15 ....$85.00

John Wayne, Effanbee, 1981, Great Legends series, Spirit of the West outfit, 17", MIB $125.00

John Wayne, Effanbee, 1982, Great Legends series, Guardian of the West outfit, 18", MIB....$125.00

Judy Garland (Wizard of Oz), Multitoys, 1984, 50th Anniversary, rare, MIB $100.00

Judy Garland (Wizard of Oz), Effanbee, 1984, Great Legends series, w/Toto & basket, 14½", MIB $100.00

Julie Andrews (Mary Poppins), Horsman, 1964, 1st edition, 12", MIB, Y1 ....$125.00

Julie Andrews (Mary Poppins), Horsman, 1964, 3-pc gift set, 11" w/5" Michael & Jan dolls, rare, NRFB....$250.00

Julie Andrews (Mary Poppins), Horsman, 1973, 2nd edition, 11", MIB, Y1 ....$75.00

Karen Mulder, Top Models Collection, Hasbro, 1995, 11½", rare, MIB....$100.00

Kate Jackson (Sabrina from Charlie's Angels), Hasbro, 1977, jumpsuit & scarf, 8½", MOC $40.00

Kate Jackson (Sabrina from Charlie's Angels), Mattel, 1978, red & wht dress, 11½", NRFB $60.00

KISS, Ace Frehley, Gene Simmons, Paul Stanley or Peter Criss, Mego, 1978, 12", NRFB, ea....$125.00

Kristy McNichol (Buddy from Family), Mattel, 1978, w/extra outfit, 9¼", MIB $45.00

Kristy McNichol (Buddy from Family), Mego, 9½", MIB, Y1....$40.00

Laurel & Hardy, Knickerbocker, 1960s, cloth bodies w/vinyl heads, 9½", MIB, ea....$65.00

Laurel & Hardy (Music Box), Peggy Nisbet Dolls, 1970s, MIB, ea....$50.00

Laverne & Shirley (Penny Marshall as Laverne & Cindy Williams as Shirley), Mego, 1977, 12", NRFB, pr ...$125.00

Lenny & Squiggy (Michael McKean as Lenny & David Lander as Squiggy), Mego, 1977, 12", NRFB, pr....$200.00

Linda Carter (Wonder Woman), Mego, 1976, 1st issue, w/military uniform, rare, 12", MIB (photo on box) $85.00

Lucille Ball (I Love Lucy), 1952, cloth, 26", rare, NRFB, Y1....$800.00

Macaully Caulkin (Kevin from Home Alone), THQ Inc, 1989, screams, MIB, Y1 ....$25.00

Madonna (Breathless Mahoney), Applause, 1990, blk evening gown w/gold trim & heels, 10", MIB....$40.00

Madonna (Breathless Mahoney), Playmates, 1990, plastic, bl dress, 19", NRFB....$60.00

Mae West, Effanbee, 1982, Great Legends series, 18", MIB.$120.00

Marie Osmond, Mattel, 1976, 11", MIB....$50.00

Marie Osmond, Mattel, 1976, 30", MIB $115.00

Marilyn Monroe, DSI, 1993, issued in 6 different outfits, 11½", NRFB, ea....$60.00

Marilyn Monroe, Tristar, 1982, issued in 4 different outfits, 16", NRFB, ea $110.00

Marilyn Monroe, Tristar, 1982, issued in 8 different outfits, 11½", NRFB, ea....$100.00

Marla Gibbs (Florence from The Jeffersons), 1978, 16", MIB, M15....$100.00

Mary Kate/Ashley Olsen (Michelle from Full House), cloth body w/vinyl head, talker, 15", MIB....$40.00

MC Hammer, Mattel, 1991, gold outfit w/boombox, 11½", MIB....$85.00

MC Hammer, Mattel, 1991, purple outfit, 11½", MIB.....$70.00

Michael Jackson, LJN, 1984, issued in four different outfits, 11½", NRFB, $70.00.

Mr T, Galoob, 1983, 1st edition, bib overalls, 12", MIB...$60.00

Mr T, Galoob, 1983, 2nd edition, talker, vest & jeans, 12", MIB....$75.00

Naomi Campbell, Top Models Collection, Hasbro, 1995, 11½", rare, MIB....$100.00

New Kids on the Block, 1990, 1st issue, Hangin' Loose, 5 different dolls, 12", MIB, ea $40.00

New Kids on the Block, 1990, 2nd issue, In Concert, 5 different dolls, 12", MIB, ea....$50.00

OJ Simpson, Shindana, Deluxe Set, 1975, w/several outfits & accessories, 9½", MIB....$250.00

OJ Simpson, Shindana, 1975, in football uniform, 9½", MIB....$125.00

Pam Dawber (Mork & Mindy), Mattel, 1979, 8½", MIB .$50.00

Parker Stevenson (Frank from Hardy Boys), Kenner, 1978, 12", NRFB, H4 .... **$50.00**
Patty Duke (Patty Duke Show), Horsman, 1967, 12½", rare, NRFB **$400.00**
Prince Charles, Goldberger, 1982, military wedding outfit, 12", NRFB **$250.00**
Prince Charles, Goldberger, 1982, Palace Guard outfit, 12", rare, NRFB **$350.00**
Prince Charles, Peggy Nesbit/England, 1984, wedding outfit, 8", MIB **$100.00**
Prince Charles & Princess Diana, Goldberger, 1982, wedding outfits, gift set, 12", very rare, NRFB **$600.00**
Princess Diana, Danbury Mint, 1985, pk dress, 15", MIB .**$110.00**
Princess Diana, Goldberger, 1982, silver dress, 11½", rare, NRFB **$350.00**
Princess Diana, Goldberger, 1982, wedding gown, 11½", NRFB **$250.00**
Princess Diana, Peggy Nisbet/England, 1984, wedding gown, 8", M **$100.00**
Redd Fox, Shindana, 1977, cloth, talker, MIB **$45.00**
Rex Harrison (Dr Dolittle), Mattel, 1969, cloth body w/vinyl head, talker, 24", MIB **$130.00**

Rex Harrison (Dr. Dolittle), Mattel, 1967, with Polynesia Parrot, 6", NRFB, $65.00.

Rex Harrison (Dr Dolittle), Mattel, 1967, w/Pushmi-Pullyu & Polynesia, 6", MIB **$90.00**
Richard Chamberlin (Dr Kildare), Bing Crosby Productions, 1962, rare, MIB **$350.00**
Robin Williams (Mork & Mindy), Mattel, 1979, w/space pak, 9", MIB **$45.00**
Roger Moore (James Bond in Moonraker), Mego, 1979, 12", MIB **$100.00**
Sally Ann Howes (Truly Scrumptious from Chitty-Chitty Bang-Bang), Mattel, 1969, wht dress, 11½", MIB **$400.00**
Sally Ann Howes (Truly Scrumptious from Chitty-Chitty Bang-Bang, Mattel, 1969, pk dress, talker, MIB, 11½" **$450.00**

Sally Field (Flying Nun), Hasbro, 1967, 12", MIB, $200.00.

Sally Field (Flying Nun), Hasbro, 1967, 5", MIB **$80.00**
Sarah Stimson (Little Miss Marker), Ideal, 1980, 12", MIB.**$40.00**
Selena, Arm Enterprises, 1996, 11½", MIB **$45.00**
Shaun Cassidy (Joe from The Hardy Boys), Kenner, 1978, 12", NRFB **$50.00**
Shirley Temple, Ideal, 1934, Stand Up & Cheer outfit, 15", EX **$700.00**
Shirley Temple, Ideal, 1957, orig bl & pk flocked dress, 12", VG, M15 .... **$150.00**
Shirley Temple, Ideal, 1972, Stand Up & Cheer outfit, 16", MIB, M15 .... **$160.00**
Shirley Temple, Ideal, 1982, issued in 6 different outfits, 8", MIB, M15, ea **$60.00**

Shirley Temple, Ideal, 1959, in Wee Willie Winkie outfit, 15", missing jacket and purse, $250.00.

Shirley Temple, Ideal, 1984, Glad Rags to Riches outfit, 16", rare, MIB, M15 .... **$125.00**
Sonny Bono, Mego, 1976, 12", NRFB (orange box) **$80.00**
Soupy Sales, Sunshine Dolls, 1965, 6", NRFB, J2 .... **$235.00**
Susan Dey (Laurie from Partridge Family), Remco, 1973, 16", rare, MIB **$250.00**
Suzanne Sommers (Chrissy from Three's Company), Mego, 1975, 12½", MIB **$85.00**
Sylvester Stallone (Over the Top), Lewco Toys, 1986, 20", NRFB **$35.00**
Sylvester Stallone (Rocky), Phoenix Toys, 1983, 8", MOC, H4 .... **$40.00**
Tatum O'Neal (International Velvet), Kenner, 1979, 11½", MIB **$85.00**
Three Stooges, Collins, 1982, set of 3, 13", MOC **$140.00**
Twiggy, Mattel, 1967, 11½", rare, MIB **$350.00**
Vanilla Ice, THQ, 1991, issued in 3 different outfits, 12", NRFB, ea **$45.00**
Vanna White, Pacific Media/Home Shopping Network, 1990, issued in 20 different outfits, 11½", NRFB, ea **$50.00**
Vanna White, Totsy Toys, 1990, limited edition, wedding dress, rare, MIB **$125.00**
Vince Edwards (Ben Casey), Bing Crosby Productions, 1962, 12", rare, MIB **$400.00**
Vivian Leigh (Scarlett), World Dolls, 1980, 1st issue, 12", NRFB **$65.00**
Wayne Gretsky, Mattel, 1982, The Great Gretsky/Le Magnifique, 11½", MIB **$150.00**
WC Fields, 1980, 16", M, J6 .... **$85.00**
Xuxa Brazilian Superstar, Roseart, 1993, available in 6 different outfits, 11½", MIB, ea **$65.00**
Yvonne De Carlo (Lily Munster), Remco, 1964, MIB ... **$150.00**

Chatty Cathy

In their book, *Chatty Cathy Dolls, An Identification & Value Guide*, authorities Kathy and Don Lewis (L6) tell us that Chatty Cathy (made by Mattel) has been the second most popular doll ever made. She was introduced in the 1960s and came as either a blond or a brunette. For five years, she sold very well. Much of her success can be attributed to the fact that Chatty Cathy talked. By pulling the string on her back, she could respond with eleven different phrases. During her five years of fame, Mattel added to the line with Chatty Baby, Tiny Chatty Baby and Tiny Chatty Brother (the twins), Charmin' Chatty, and finally Singing' Chatty. Charmin' Chatty had sixteen interchangeable records. Her voice box was activated in the same manner as the above-mentioned dolls, by means of a pull string located at the base of her neck. The line was brought back in 1969, smaller and with a restyled face, but it was not well received.

Advisor: Kathy and Don Lewis (L6).

See Also Coloring, Activity, and Paint Books; Paper Dolls; Puzzles.

Armoire, Chatty Cathy, L6 .... **$175.00**
Bedspread, Chatty Baby, twin-sz, L6 .... **$400.00**

Doll, Singin' Chatty, blond hair, M, L6, $250.00.

Carrying Case, Chatty Baby, pk or bl, L6 **$45.00**
Carrying Case, Tiny Chatty Baby, bl or pk, L6 **$35.00**
Case, Chatty Baby, 1962, vinyl w/5 images on lid, EX **$15.00**
Cover & Pillow Set, Tiny Chatty Cathy, L6 **$75.00**
Crib, Tiny Chatty Baby, MIB, L6 **$300.00**
Doll, Black Chatty Baby, M, L6 **$650.00**
Doll, Black Chatty Baby, w/pigtails, M, L6 **$1,500.00**
Doll, Black Chatty Cathy, 1962, pageboy-style hair, M, L6 **$1,200.00**
Doll, Black Tiny Chatty Baby, M, L6 **$650.00**
Doll, Charmin' Chatty, auburn or blond hair, bl eyes, 1 record, M, L6 **$250.00**
Doll, Chatty Baby, brunette hair, red pinafore over wht romper, orig tag, MIB, L6 **$250.00**
Doll, Chatty Baby, open speaker, blond hair, bl eyes, M, L6 **$250.00**
Doll, Chatty Baby, open speaker, brunette hair, bl eyes, M, L6 **$250.00**
Doll, Chatty Baby, open speaker, brunette hair, brn eyes, M, L6 **$375.00**
Doll, Chatty Cathy, brunette hair, brn eyes, M, L6 **$375.00**
Doll, Chatty Cathy, later issue, open speaker, blond hair, bl eyes, M, L6 **$750.00**
Doll, Chatty Cathy, later issue, open speaker, brunette hair, bl eyes, M, L6 **$750.00**
Doll, Chatty Cathy, later issue, open speaker, brunette hair, brn eyes, M, L6 **$850.00**
Doll, Chatty Cathy, mid-year or transitional, brunette hair, brn eyes, M, L6 **$650.00**

Photo courtesy Kathy Lewis

Dolls, Tiny Chatty Twins, M, L6, $250.00 each.

Doll, Chatty Cathy, mid-year or transitional, brunette hair, bl eyes, M, L6 **$650.00**
Doll, Chatty Cathy, mid-year or transitional, open speaker, blond hair, bl eyes, M, L6 **$600.00**
Doll, Chatty Cathy, patent pending, brunette hair, bl eyes, M, L6 **$750.00**
Doll, Chatty Cathy, patent pending, cloth over speaker or ring around speaker, blond hair, bl eyes, M, L6 **$750.00**
Doll, Chatty Cathy, porcelain, 1980, MIB, L6 **$750.00**
Doll, Chatty Cathy, reissue, blond hair, bl eyes, MIB, L6 **$80.00**
Doll, Chatty Cathy, soft face, w/pigtails, blond, brunette or auburn hair, M, L6 **$550.00**
Doll, Chatty Cathy, unmk prototype, brunette hair, bl eyes, M, L6 **$900.00**
Doll, Chatty Cathy, unmk prototype, brunette hair, brn eyes, M, L6 **$1,000.00**
Doll, Chatty Cathy, unmk prototype, cloth speaker, blond hair, M, L6 **$900.00**
Doll, early Chatty Baby, blond hair, bl eyes, ring around speaker, M, L6 **$250.00**
Doll, early Chatty Baby, brunette hair, brn eyes, M, L6 **$160.00**
Doll, early Chatty Cathy, brunette hair, bl eyes, M, L6 **$85.00**
Doll, Singin' Chatty, brunette hair, M, L6 **$275.00**
Doll, Tiny Chatty Baby, blond hair, bl eyes, M, L6 **$250.00**
Doll, Tiny Chatty Baby, brunette hair, bl eyes, M, L6 **$275.00**
Doll, Tiny Chatty Baby, brunette hair, brn eyes, M, L6 **$300.00**
Jewelry Set, Chatty Cathy, MIP, L6 **$150.00**
Nursery Set, Chatty Baby, NRFB, L6 **$200.00**
Outfit, Charmin' Chatty, Cinderella, MIP, L6 **$115.00**
Outfit, Charmin' Chatty, Let's Go Shopping, MIP, L6 **$85.00**
Outfit, Charmin' Chatty, Let's Play Birthday Party, MIP, L6 **$100.00**
Outfit, Charmin' Chatty, Let's Play Nurse, MIP, L6 **$90.00**
Outfit, Charmin' Chatty, Let's Play Pajama Party, MIP, L6 **$100.00**
Outfit, Charmin' Chatty, Let's Play Tea Party, MIP, L6 **$100.00**
Outfit, Charmin' Chatty, Let's Play Together, MIP, L6 **$75.00**
Outfit, Chatty Baby, Leotard set, MIP, L6 **$75.00**
Outfit, Chatty Baby, Outdoors, MIP, L6 **$75.00**
Outfit, Chatty Baby, Overall Set, pk or bl, MIP, L6 **$65.00**
Outfit, Chatty Baby, Party Pink, MIP, L6 **$100.00**
Outfit, Chatty Baby, Playsuit, MIP, L6 **$45.00**
Outfit, Chatty Baby, Sleeper Set, MIP, L6 **$55.00**
Outfit, Chatty Cathy, Nursery School, MIP, L6 **$145.00**
Outfit, Chatty Cathy, Party Coat, MIP, L6 **$150.00**
Outfit, Chatty Cathy, Party Dress, bl gingham, MIP, L6 **$250.00**
Outfit, Chatty Cathy, Pink Peppermint Stick, MIP, L6 **$150.00**
Outfit, Chatty Cathy, Playtime, MIP, L6 **$145.00**
Outfit, Chatty Cathy, Red Peppermint Stick (Candystripe), MIP, L6 **$400.00**
Outfit, Chatty Cathy, Sleepytime, MIP, L6 **$125.00**
Outfit, Chatty Cathy, Sunday Visit, MIP, L6 **$200.00**
Outfit, Chatty Cathy, Sunny Day, MIP, L6 **$200.00**
Outfit, Tiny Chatty Baby, Bye-Bye, MIP, L6 **$65.00**
Outfit, Tiny Chatty Baby, Dashin' Dots, MIP, L6 **$175.00**
Outfit, Tiny Chatty Baby, Fun Time, MIP, L6 **$140.00**
Outfit, Tiny Chatty Baby, Night-Night, MIP, L6 **$90.00**
Outfit, Tiny Chatty Baby, Pink Frill, MIP, L6 **$125.00**
Outfit, Tiny Chatty Baby, Playmate, bl gingham, MIP, L6 **$250.00**

Pattern, Chatty Baby, uncut, L6 ....$18.50
Pattern, Chatty Cathy, uncut, L6 ....$18.50
Pencil-Point Bed, Chatty Cathy, L6 ....$350.00
Play Hats, Charmin' Chatty, L6 ....$55.00
Play Table, Chatty Baby, L6..$175.00
Stroll-a-Buggy, Chatty Baby, 9-way, complete, L6 ....$300.00
Stroller, Chatty Baby, Walkin' Talk, L6 ....$500.00
Stroller, Chatty Cathy, 5-way, complete, L6 ....$225.00
Tea Cart, Chatty Cathy, w/2 trays, L6 ....$100.00
Teeter-Totter, Tiny Chatty Baby Twins, L6..................$500.00

Crissy and Her Family

Ideal's 18" Crissy doll with growing hair was very popular with little girls of the early 1970s. She was introduced in 1969 and continued to be sold throughout the 1970s, enjoying a relatively long market life for a doll. During the 1970s, many different versions of Crissy were made. Numerous friends followed her success, all with the growing hair feature like Crissy's. The other Ideal 'grow hair' dolls in the line included Velvet, Cinnamon, Tressy, Dina, Mia, Kerry, Brandy, and Cricket. Crissy is the easiest member in the line to find, followed by her cousin Velvet. The other members are not as common, but like Crissy and Velvet loose examples of these dolls frequently make their appearance at doll shows, flea markets, and even garage sales. Only those examples that are in excellent or better condition and wearing their original outfits and shoes should command book value. Values for the rare black versions of the dolls in the line are currently on the rise, as demand for them increases while the supply decreases.

Advisor: Cindy Sabulis (S14).

Photo courtesy Marcia Fanta

Crissy, Magic Hair; 1977, NRFB, $100.00.

Baby Crissy, 1973-76, pk dress, EX....................................$45.00
Baby Crissy, 1973-76, pk dress, MIB, M15.....................$125.00
Baby Crissy (Black); 1973-76, pk dress, EX.......................$80.00
Brandi, (Black); 1972-73, orange swimsuit, EX $75.00
Cinnamon, Curly Ribbons (Black); 1974, EX..................$70.00
Cinnamon, Curly Ribbons; 1974, EX...............................$45.00
Cinnamon, Hairdoodler (Black); 1973, EX $70.00
Cinnamon, Hairdoodler; 1973, EX...................................$40.00
Cinnamon, 1972-74, EX..$40.00
Crissy, Beautiful; 1969, orange lace dress, EX $40.00
Crissy, Country Fashion; 1982-83, EX $20.00
Crissy, Country Fashion; 1982-83, MIB, M15 ....$45.00
Crissy, Look Around; 1972, EX $40.00
Crissy, Magic Hair (Black); 1977, EX $75.00
Crissy, Magic Hair; 1977, EX..$30.00
Crissy, Movin' Groovin' (Black); 1971, EX $80.00
Crissy, Movin' Groovin'; 1971, EX..................................$35.00
Crissy, Swirla Curler (Black); 1973, EX $80.00
Crissy, Swirla Curler; 1973, EX $35.00
Crissy, Twirly Beads; 1974, MIB, M15 ....$65.00
Dina, 1972-73, purple playsuit, EX..................................$50.00
Kerry, 1971, gr romper, EX $55.00
Mia, 1971, turq romper, EX $50.00
Tara (Black); 1976, yel gingham outfit, EX $75.00
Velvet, Beauty Braider; 1973, EX $35.00
Velvet, Look Around (Black); 1972, EX..........................$75.00
Velvet, Look Around; 1972, EX $35.00
Velvet, Movin' Groovin'; 1971, EX $35.00
Velvet, Swirly Daisies (Black); 1974, EX $75.00
Velvet, Swirly Daisies; 1974, EX $35.00
Velvet, 1970, 1st issue, purple dress, EX..........................$55.00
Velvet, 1982 reissue, EX $30.00

Dawn

Dawn and her friends were made by Deluxe Topper, ca 1970s. They're becoming highly collectible, especially when mint in the box. Dawn was a 6" fashion doll, part of a series sold as the Dawn Model Agency. They were issued in boxes already dressed in clothes of the highest style, or you could buy additional outfits, many complete with matching shoes and accessories.

Advisor: Dawn Parrish (P2).

Dawn's Apartment, complete w/furniture, MIB................$50.00
Doll, Dancing Angie, NRFB...$30.00
Doll, Dancing Dale, NRFB $50.00
Doll, Dancing Dawn, NRFB $30.00
Doll, Dancing Gary, NRFB...$40.00
Doll, Dancing Glory, NRFB $30.00
Doll, Dancing Jessica, NRFB $30.00
Doll, Dancing Ron, NRFB..$40.00
Doll, Dancing Van, NRFB..$50.00
Doll, Dawn Head to Toe, pk & silver dress, NRFB...........$90.00
Doll, Dawn Majorette, NRFB...$75.00

Photo courtesy Pat Smith

Doll, Daphne, Dawn Model Agency, green and silver dress, NRFB, $75.00.

Doll, Denise, NRFB **$75.00**
Doll, Dinah, NRFB **$75.00**
Doll, Gary, NRFB **$30.00**
Doll, Jessica, NRFB **$30.00**
Doll, Kevin, NRFB **$30.00**
Doll, Kip Majorette, NRFB **$45.00**
Doll, Longlocks, NRFB **$30.00**
Doll, Maureen, Dawn Model Agency, red & gold dress, NRFB **$90.00**
Doll, Ron, NRFB **$30.00**
Outfit, Black Tie 'n Tux, #8393, NRFB, P2 .... **$65.00**
Outfit, Bluebelle, #0722, dress & shawl, NM, P2 .... **$10.00**
Outfit, Dinner Date, #0610, dress only, VG, P2 .... **$5.00**
Outfit, Down the Aisle, #0816, dress & veil, NM, P2 .... **$10.00**
Outfit, Fuchsia Flash, #0612, NRFB, P2 .... **$35.00**
Outfit, Furbulous Fake, #0821, hat & coat, NM, P2 .... **$8.00**
Outfit, Gold Glow Swirl, #0721, dress & shawl, NM, P2 . **$10.00**
Outfit, Green Fling, #8113, MIB **$25.00**
Outfit, Long 'N Leather, #8125, wht version, NRFB, P2.. **$40.00**
Outfit, Party Parfay, #0810, MIB **$25.00**
Outfit, Skinny Minny, #0611, NRFB, P2 .... **$30.00**
Outfit, Twinkle Twirl, #8114, dress only, M, P2 .... **$5.00**
Outfit, What a Racket, #8116, MIB **$25.00**

Dolly Darlings by Hasbro

Dolly Darlings by Hasbro are approximately 4" tall and have molded or rooted hair. The molded hair dolls were sold in themed hatboxes with small accessories to match their theme. The rooted hair dolls were sold separately and came with a small brush and comb. There were four plastic playrooms that featured the rooted hair dolls. Hasbro also produced the Flower Darling series which were 2" dolls in flower corsages. The Dolly Darlings and Flower Darlings were available in the mid to late 1960s.

Advisor: Dawn Parrish (P2).

Beth at the Supermarket, #8500, NRFB, P2 .... **$50.00**
Daisy Darling, #8572, complete, EX, P2 .... **$25.00**
Honey, #8533, NRFB, P2 .... **$50.00**
Rose Darling, #8575, NRFB, P2 .... **$40.00**
Shary Takes a Vacation, #8504, doll only, EX, P2 .... **$10.00**
Slick Set, #8541, doll only, EX, P2 .... **$25.00**
Slumber Party, #8512, doll only, EX, P2 .... **$25.00**
Tea Time, #8510, NRFB, P2 .... **$50.00**
Violet Darling, #8571, doll only, EX, P2 .... **$10.00**

Flatsys

Flatsy dolls were a product of the Ideal Novelty and Toy Company. They were produced from 1968 until 1970 in 2", 5", and 8" sizes. There was only one boy in the 5" line; all were dressed in '70s fashions, and not only clothing but accessory items such as bicycles were made as well.

In 1994 Justoys reissued Mini Flatsys. They were sold alone or with accessories such as bikes, rollerblades, and jet skis.

Advisor: Dawn Parrish (P2).

Photo courtesy Martin and Carolyn Berens

Flatsy's Townhouse, EX, complete, $100.00.

Baby Flatsy, EX, P2 ....$10.00
Bonnie Flatsy, sailing, NRFB, P2.....................................$55.00
Candy Mountain Flatsy, lavender ice-cream truck w/pk wheels, P2 ....$15.00
Cookie Flatsy, w/bl & red stove, EX, P2...........................$15.00
Cory Flatsy, print mini-dress, NRFB, P2 ....$60.00
Dale Fashion Flatsy, hot pk maxi, NRFB, P2 ....$60.00
Dale Fashion Flatsy, 2-pc wet-look outfit, NRFB, P2 ....$60.00
Dewie Flatsy, missing hat & umbrella, EX, P2 ....$15.00
Fall Mini Flatsy Collection, NRFB, P2.............................$65.00
Filly Flatsy, complete, EX, P2 ....$15.00
Flatsy Casey, NRFP...$65.00
Flatsy in Locket/Frame, MIP...$50.00
Flatsy Townhouse, house only, P2....................................$50.00
Flower Time Mini Flatsy, missing plastic fr, EX $25.00
Gwen Fashion Flatsy, gr hair, peach poncho & boots, NRFB, P2 ....$65.00
Munch-Time Flatsy, Lemonade boy or girl, EX, ea...........$15.00
Munch-Time Flatsy Clock, NRFB, P2 ....$75.00
Nancy Flatsy, nurse w/baby carriage, EX, P2....................$20.00
Play Time Flatsy, NRFB $75.00

Photo courtesy Martin and Carolyn Berens

Rally Flatsy, NM, $40.00.

Rally Flatsy, w/car in picture fr, VG, M15 ....$35.00
Sandy Flatsy, beach outfit, NRFB, P2 ....$50.00
Spinderella Flatsy, complete, M $50.00
Spinderella Flatsy, doll only, EX, P2 ....$20.00
Summer Mini Flatsy Collection, NRFB, P2.......................$65.00
Susie Flatsy, complete, EX, P2..$15.00

Galoob's Baby Face Dolls

Galoob's Baby Face dolls were first available on the toy market in 1991. By the end of 1992 the short-lived dolls were already being discounted by toy stores. Although they were targeted as play dolls for children, it didn't take long for these adorable dolls to find their way into adult collectors' hearts. The most endearing quality of Baby Face dolls are their expressive faces. Sporting big eyes with long soft eyelashes, cute pug noses, and mouths that are puckered, pouting, smiling, or laughing, these dolls are delightful and fun. The 13" heavy vinyl Baby Face dolls are jointed at the shoulders, elbows, knees, and hips. Their jointed limbs allow for posing them in more positions than the average doll and adds to the fun of displaying or playing with them. Old store stock of Baby Face dolls was plentiful for several years, and since these dolls are still relatively new as collectibles, it isn't difficult to find never-removed-from-box examples.

Advisor: Cindy Sabulis (S14).

Photo courtesy Cindy Sabulis

Left to right: So Innocent Cynthia, So Loving Laura, So Shy Sherri; Back row: So Sorry Sarah, So Sweet Sandi, from $40.00 to $50.00 each.

Activity Stroller, MIB, S14 ....$25.00
Asian Versions, NRFB, S14, from $65 to.........................$80.00
Asian Versions, re-dressed, S14, from $20 to...................$25.00
Bathtub Babies, NRFB, from $40 to $50.00
Bathtub Babies, re-dressed, S14, from $10 to...................$15.00
Black Versions, NRFB, S14, from $60 to $75.00
Black Versions, re-dressed, S14, from $20 to $25.00
Hispanic Versions, NRFB, S14, from $65 to....................$85.00
Hispanic Versions, re-dressed, S14, from $20 to $25.00
Outfits, NRFB, S14, from $20 to $25.00
White Version, So Silly Sally, NRFB, S16, minimum value....$200.00
White Versions, any other than So Silly Sally, NRFB, S16, from $40 to $50.00
White Versions, re-dressed, S14, from $10 to $15.00

Gerber Babies

The first Gerber Baby dolls were manufactured in 1936. These dolls were made of cloth and produced by an unknown manufacturer. Since that time, six different companies working with leading artists, craftsmen, and designers have attempted to capture the charm of the winsome baby in the charcoal drawing done by Dorothy Hope Smith of her friend's baby, Ann Turner (Cook). This drawing became known as the Gerber Baby and was adopted as the trademark of the Gerber Products Company, located in Fremont, Michigan. For further information see *Ger-*

ber Baby Dolls and Advertising Collectibles by Joan S. Grubaugh.
Advisor: Joan S. Grubaugh (G8).

Amsco, 1972-73, baby & feeding set, vinyl, complete, 14", NMIB, G8 .....$70.00
Amsco, 1972-73, pk & wht rosebud sleeper, vinyl, 10", NM, G8 .....$50.00
Amsco, 1972-73, re-dressed in red checked dress, vinyl, 14", M, G8 .....$40.00
Arrow Rubber & Plastic Corp, 1965-67, pk & wht bib & diaper, 14", MIB, G8 .....$100.00
Arrow Rubber & Plastic Corp, 1965-67, re-dressed in playsuit, 14", EX, G8 .....$45.00
Atlanta Novelty, 1979, snowsuit w/matching hood, 17", NRFB, G8 .....$95.00

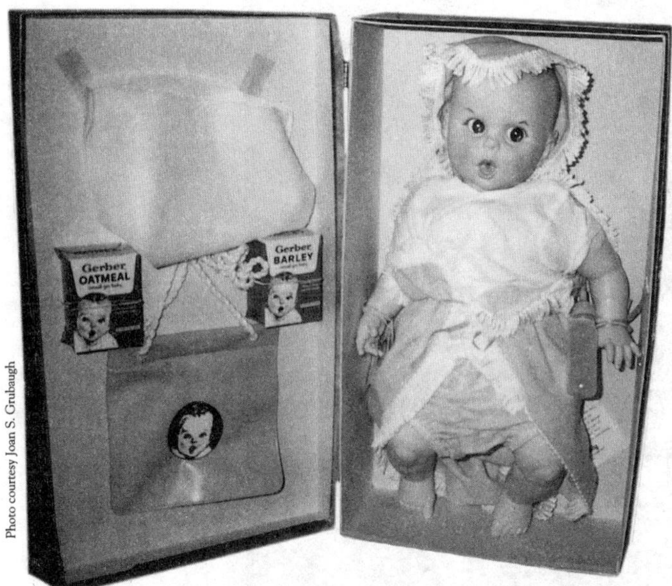

Photo courtesy Joan S. Grubaugh

Atlanta Novelty, Baby Drink and Wet, 1979 – 81, 17", complete in trunk, M, G8, $110.00.

Atlanta Novelty, 1979-81, w/'mama' voice, several different outfits, 17", NRFB, G8, ea $100.00
Atlanta Novelty, 1979-85, cloth body w/vinyl head, arms & legs, red checked bodysuit w/wht eyelet, 17", NRFB, G8 .....$90.00
Atlanta Novelty, 1981, collector's edition, vinyl w/eyelet lace christening dress in wicker basket, 12", NRFB, G8 .$100.00
Atlanta Novelty, 1981, porcelain w/soft body, wht eyelet christening gown, limited edition, 14", NRFB, G8 .....$350.00
Atlanta Novelty, 1984, rag doll, in pk or bl, 11½", EX, G8, ea $20.00
Lucky Ltd, 1989, Birthday Party Twins, 6", NRFB, G8 .....$40.00
Lucky Ltd, 1989-92, re-dressed in playsuit, 14", EX, G8...$25.00
Sun Rubber, 1955-58, red polka-dot dress, 12", VG, G8..$65.00
Sun Rubber, 1955-58, 2-pc pajamas, 12", VG, G8 .....$65.00
Toy Biz, 1994-95, Food & Playtime Baby, NRFB, G8 .....$25.00
Toy Biz, 1994-95, Potty Time Baby, vinyl, 15", NRFB, G8 .....$25.00

Holly Hobbie

Sometime around 1970 a young homemaker and mother, Holly Hobbie, approached the American Greeting Company with some charming country-styled drawings of children. Her concepts were well received by the company, and since that time over four hundred Holly Hobbie items have been produced, nearly all marked HH, H. Hobbie, or Holly Hobbie. See also Clubs, Newsletters, and Other Publications.

Advisor: Helen McCale (M13).

Doll, Country Fun Holly Hobbie, 1989, 16", NRFB $25.00
Doll, Grandma Holly, Knickerbocker, cloth, 14", MIB $20.00
Doll, Grandma Holly, Knickerbocker, cloth, 24", MIB $30.00
Doll, Holiday Holly Hobbie, 1988, scented, clear ornament around neck, 18", NRFB $40.00
Doll, Holly Hobbie, Heather, Amy or Carrie, Knickerbocker, cloth, 27", MIB, ea $35.00
Doll, Holly Hobbie, Heather, Amy or Carrie, Knickerbocker, cloth, 6", MIB, ea $10.00
Doll, Holly Hobbie, Heather, Amy or Carrie, Knickerbocker, cloth, 9", MIB, ea $15.00
Doll, Holly Hobbie, Heather, Amy or Carrie, Knickerbocker, cloth, 16", MIB, ea $25.00
Doll, Holly Hobbie, Heather, Amy or Carrie, Knickerbocker, cloth, 33", MIB, ea $45.00
Doll, Holly Hobbie Bicentennial, Knickerbocker, cloth, 12", MIB $30.00
Doll, Holly Hobbie Day 'N Night, Knickerbocker, cloth, 14", MIB $20.00
Doll, Holly Hobbie Dream Along, Holly, Carrie or Amy, Knickerbocker, cloth, 9", MIB, ea $15.00
Doll, Holly Hobbie Dream Along, Holly, Carrie or Amy, Knickerbocker, cloth, 12", MIB, ea $20.00

Photo courtesy Helen McCale

Dollhouse, M, $300.00.

Doll, Holly Hobbie Talker, Knickerbocker, cloth, 4 sayings, 16", MIB $30.00
Doll, Little Girl Holly, Knickerbocker, 1980, cloth, 15", MIB $30.00
Doll, Robby, Knickerbocker, cloth, 9", MIB $20.00
Doll, Robby, Knickerbocker, 1981, cloth, 16", MIB $30.00

Jem

The glamorous life of Jem mesmerized little girls who watched her Saturday morning cartoons, and she was a natural as a fashion doll. Hasbro saw the potential in 1985 when they introduced the Jem line of 12" dolls representing her, the rock stars from Jem's musical group, the Holograms, and other members of the cast, including the only boy, Rio, Jem's road manager and Jerrica's boyfriend. Each doll was posable, jointed at the waist, head, and wrists, so that they could be positioned at will with their musical instruments and other accessory items. Their clothing, their makeup, and their hairdos were wonderfully exotic, and their faces were beautifully modeled. The Jem line was discontinued in 1987 after being on the market for only two years. Our values are given for mint-in-box dolls. All loose dolls are valued at about $8.00 each.

Accessory, Jem Roadster, AM/FM radio in trunk, scarce, EX $150.00
Accessory, Jem Soundstage, Starlight House #17, from $40 to $50.00
Accessory, Jem Speaker & Dressing Room, 1986, complete, NM, J6 ....$100.00

Doll, Kimber, red hair, complete, MIB (not shown), $40.00.

Doll, Aja, complete, MIB $40.00
Doll, Ashley, curly blond hair, complete, MIB $25.00
Doll, Banee, waist-length straight blk hair, complete, MIB ..$25.00
Doll, Clash, straight purple hair, complete, MIB $40.00
Doll, Danse, pk & blond hair, complete, MIB $40.00
Doll, Jem/Jerrica, Glitter & Gold, complete, MIB $50.00
Doll, Jetta, blk hair w/silver streaks, complete, MIB $40.00
Doll, Krissie, dk skin w/brn curly hair, 11", complete, MIB .$25.00
Doll, Pizzaz (Misfits), chartreuse hair, complete, MIB $40.00
Doll, Raya, complete, MIB $40.00
Doll, Rio, Glitter & Gold, complete, MIB $50.00
Doll, Roxy, blond hair, complete, MIB $40.00
Doll, Shana (Holograms Band), purple hair, complete, MIB....$40.00

Doll, Stormer, blue hair, complete, MIB (not shown), $40.00.

Doll, Video, complete, MIB $40.00
Outfit, City Lights, MIP $15.00
Outfit, Fire & Ice, MIP $20.00
Outfit, Midnight Magic, MIP $20.00
Outfit, Music in the Air, MIP $15.00

Liddle Kiddles

From 1966 to 1971, Mattel produced Liddle Kiddle dolls and accessories, typical of the 'little kid next door.' They were made in sizes ranging from a tiny ¾" up to 4". They were all posable and had rooted hair that could be restyled. Eventually there were Animiddles and Zoolery Jewelry Kiddles, which were of course animals, and two other series that represented storybook and nursery rhyme characters. There was a set of extraterrestrials, and lastly in 1979, Sweet Treets dolls were added to the assortment.

In the mid-1970s Mattel reissued Lucky Locket Kiddles. The dolls had names identical to the earlier lockets but were not of the same high quality.

In 1994 – 95 Tyco reissued Liddle Kiddles in strap-on, clip-on, Lovely Locket, Pretty Perfume, and baby bottle collections.

Loose dolls, if complete and with all their original accessories, are worth about 50% less than the same mint in the box. Dressed, loose dolls with no accessories are worth 75% less. For more information, refer to *Little Kiddles, Identification and Value Guide*, by Paris Langford (Collector Books).

Advisor: Dawn Parrish (P2).

Other Sources: S14

Photo courtesy Cindy Sabulis

Alice in Wonderliddle, missing story book, M, $150.00.

Apple Blossom Kologne, #3707, MIP, P2 ....$60.00
Aqua Funny Bunny, #3532, MIP, P2 ....$100.00
Babe Biddle, #3502, missing windshield, NM, P2.............$50.00
Baby Din-Din, #3820, complete, M, P2 ....$75.00
Baby Rockaway, #3819, MIP, P2....................................$150.00
Beach Buggy, EX, P2...$55.00
Bluebell Kologne, #3709, complete, M, P2 ....$50.00
Bunson Burnie, #3501, complete, M, P2...........................$75.00
Bunson Burnie, #3501, NRFP, P2 ....$275.00
Calamity Jiddle, #3506, complete, M, P2.........................$75.00
Cinderiddles's Palace, #5068, plastic window version, M, P2..$85.00
Cookin' Kiddle, #3846, complete, M, P2 ....$125.00
Dainty Deer, #3637, complete, M, P2 ....$45.00
Flower Charm Bracelet, #3747, MIP, P2...........................$25.00
Flower Pin Kiddle, #3741, MIP, P2 ....$50.00
Flower Ring Kiddle, #3744, MIP, P2 ....$50.00
Freezy Sliddle, #3516, complete, M, P2...........................$65.00
Frosty Mint Kone, #3653, complete, M, P2 ....$75.00
Gardenia Kologne, #3710, MIP, P2..................................$75.00
Greta Grape, #3728, complete, M, P2..............................$50.00
Heart Charm Bracelet Kiddle, #3747, MIP, P2.................$25.00

Case, blue background, from $20.00 to $25.00.

Heart Pin Kiddle, #3741, MIP, P2......................................$50.00
Henrietta Horseless Carriage, #3641, complete, M, P2 ....$75.00
Honeysuckle Kologne, #3704, complete, M, P2...............$25.00
Honeysuckle Kologne, #3704, MIP, P2............................$60.00
Hot Dog Stand, EX, P2..$55.00
Howard Biff Boodle, #3502, complete, M, P2 ....$75.00
Howard Biff Boodle, #3502, NRFP, P2 ....$300.00
Kampy Kiddle, #3753, complete, M, P2.........................$150.00

Photo courtesy Martin and Carolyn Berens

Kiddle Komedy Theatre, missing boy, EX, $50.00.

King & Queen of Hearts, #3784, MIP, P2 ....$200.00
Lady Crimson, #A3840, NRFP, P2 ....$125.00
Lady Lace, #A3840, NRFP, P2..$125.00
Lady Lavendar, #A3840, NRFP, P2 ....$125.00
Laffy Lemon, #3732, complete, M, P2.............................$50.00
Larky Locket, #3539, complete, M, P2.............................$25.00
Laverne Locket, #3718, doll only, platinum hair, NM, P2..$25.00
Lenore Limousine, #3643, complete, M, P2......................$85.00
Liddle Biddle Peep, #3544, complete, M, P2 ....$125.00
Liddle Diddle, #3503, complete, M, P2 ....$75.00
Liddle Kiddles Kottage, EX, P2..$40.00
Liddle Lion Zoolery, #3661, complete, M, P2.................$200.00
Liddle Middle Muffet, #3545, complete, M, P2 ....$150.00

Photo courtesy Martin and Carolyn Berens

Liddle Kiddles Three-Story House, M, $75.00.

Liddle Red Riding Hiddle, #3546, complete, M, P2 ....$150.00
Lilac Locket, #3540, MIP, P2 ....$75.00
Lili of the Valley Kologne, MIP, P2 ....$60.00
Lois Locket, #3541, complete, M, P2 ....$85.00
Lola Locket, #3536, MIP, P2 ....$75.00
Lolli-Grape, #3656, complete, M, P2 ....$60.00
Lolli-Mint Kiddle, #3658, MIP, P2................................$75.00

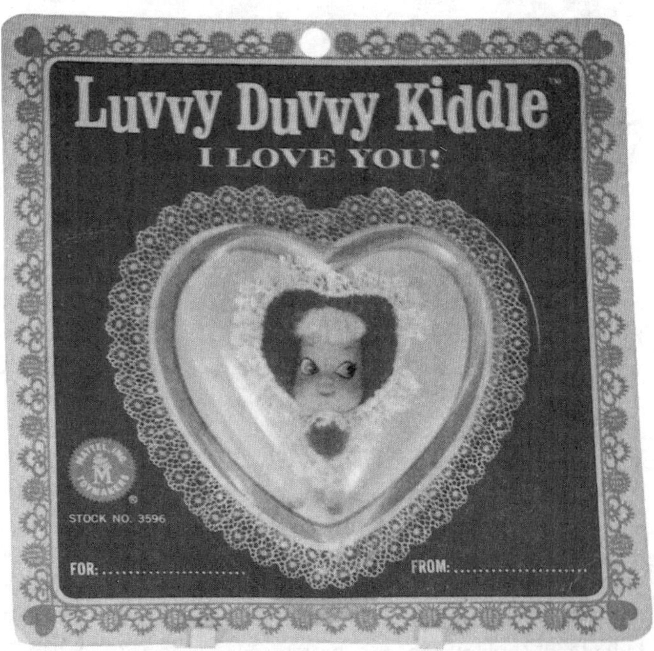

Luvvy Duvvy Kiddle, #3596, MIP, $100.00.

Lorelei Locket, #3717, 1976 version, MIP, P2 ....$25.00
Lottie Locket, #3679, complete, M, P2 ....$35.00
Lottie Locket, #3719, 1976 version, MIP, P2...................$25.00
Louise Locket, #3681, complete, M, P2 ....$30.00
Luana Locket, #3680, complete, M, P2...........................$35.00
Luana Locket, #3680, Gold Rush version, MIP, P2 ....$85.00
Lucky Lion, #3635, complete, M, P2..............................$45.00
Luscious Lime, #3733, complete, M, P2 ....$55.00
Luscious Lime, #3733, glitter variation, complete, M, P2 ....$75.00
Millie Middle, #3509, complete, M, P2 ....$125.00
Miss Mouse, #3638, complete, M, P2 ....$45.00
Nappytime Baby, #3818, complete, M, P2 ....$75.00
Nappytime Baby, #3818, doll only, M, P2........................$30.00
Nurse 'N Totsy Outfit, #LK7, no name sticker, MIP, P2 ..$25.00
Olivia Orange Kola Kiddle, #3730, MIP, P2 ....$80.00
Open-House, MIB..$75.00
Orange Meringue Skeididdler Outfit, #3585, MIP, P2 .....$25.00
Peter Paniddle, #3547, NRFP, P2..................................$400.00
Pink Funny Bunny, #3532, complete, M, P2.....................$25.00
Posies 'N Pink Skediddle Outfit, #3585, MIP, P2 ....$30.00
Pretty Priddle, #3549, complete, M, P2............................$75.00
Rah Rah Skediddle, #3788, complete, M, P2 ....$135.00
Rapunzel & the Prince, #3783, MIP, P2 ....$200.00
Robin Hood & Maid Marion, #3785, missing stands & necklace, M, P2..$70.00
Rolly Twiddle, #3519, missing shovel, NM, P2 ....$150.00
Romeo & Juliet, #3782, MIP, P2..................................$200.00
Rosebud Kologne, #3702, MIP, P2 ....$60.00

Photo courtesy Martin and Carolyn Berens

Snoopy Skediddler and His Sopwith Camel, M, $150.00.

Rosebud Kologne, #3702, silver glitter variation, complete, M, P2 ....$40.00
Rosemary Roadster, #3642, complete, M, P2 ....$75.00
Santa Kiddle, #3595, complete, M, P2 ....$25.00
Santa Kiddle, #3595, MIP, P2 ....$65.00
Shirley Skididdle, #3766, complete, M, P2 ....$25.00
Shirley Strawberry, #3727, complete, M, P2 ....$45.00
Sizzly Friddle, #3513, complete, M, P2 ....$75.00
Sleep 'N Totsy Outfit, #LK5, MIP, P2 ....$25.00
Sleeping Biddle, #3527, missing book & tiara, NM, P2....$75.00
Slipsy Sliddle, #3754, complete, M, P2 ....$125.00
Snap Happy Patio Furniture, #5171, MIP, P2 ....$30.00
Soapy Siddle, #3518, missing towel, NM, P2 ....$65.00
Suki Skediddle, #3767, complete, M, P2 ....$25.00

Suki'n Outfit, MIP, $25.00.

Surfy Skiddle, #3517, complete, M, P2 ....$75.00
Sweet Pea Kologne, #3705, MIP, P2 ....$60.00
Talking Townhouse, not working, NMIB, B5 ....$50.00
Teeter Time Baby, #3817, complete, M, P2 ....$75.00
Teresa Touring Car, #3644, complete, M, P2 ....$75.00
Tessie Tractor, #3671, missing 2 hair ribbons, M, P2 .....$150.00
Tiny Tiger, #3636, complete, M, P2 ....$45.00
Tracy Trikediddle, #3769, complete, M, P2 ....$65.00
Trikey Triddle, #3515, complete, M, P2 ....$75.00
Vanilly Lilly, #2819, MIP, P2 ....$25.00
Violet Kologne, #3703, complete, M, P2 ....$25.00
Violet Kologne, #3703, MIP, P2 ....$60.00
Windy Fliddle, #3514, complete, M, P2 ....$85.00

Littlechaps

In 1964 Remco Industries created a family of four fashion dolls that represented an upper-middle class American family. The Littlechaps family consisted of the father, Dr. John Littlechap, his wife, Lisa, and their two children, Judy and Libby. Their clothing and fashion accessories were made in Japan and are of the finest quality. Because these dolls are not as pretty as other fashion dolls of the era and their size and placement of arms and legs made them awkward to dress, children had little interest in them at the time. This lack of interest during the 1960s has created shortages of them for collectors of today. Mint and complete outfits or outfits never removed from box are especially desirable to Littlechap collectors. Values listed for loose clothing are for ensembles complete with all their small accessories. If only the main pieces of the outfit are available, then the value could go down significantly.

Advisor: Cindy Sabulis (S14).

Remco's Littlechap Family, Libby (front), Judy (left), John (back), and Lisa (right), EX, from $15.00 to $20.00 each.

Carrying Case, EX, S14 ....$25.00
Doll, Doctor John, MIB, S14 ....$60.00
Doll, Judy, MIB, S14 ....$65.00
Doll, Libby, MIB, S14 ....$45.00
Doll, Lisa, MIB, S14 ....$60.00
Family Room, Bedroom or Dr John's Office, EX, S14, ea .$125.00
Outfit, Doctor John, complete, EX, S14, from $15 to....$30.00
Outfit, Doctor John, NRFB, S14, from $30 to $50.00
Outfit, Judy, complete, EX, S14, from $25 to....$40.00
Outfit, Judy, NRFB, S14, from $35 to $75.00
Outfit, Libby, complete, EX, S14, from $20 to....$35.00

Outfit, Libby, NRFB, S14, from $35 to $50.00
Outfit, Lisa, complete, EX, S14, from $25 to $40.00
Outfit, Lisa, NRFB, S14, from $35 to $75.00

Mattel Talking Dolls

When a range is given, use the low side to evaluate dolls that have been played with and are nonworking. The high side reflects the value of a doll still mint and in the original box.

Advisor: Kathy Lewis (L6).

See also Disney; Character, TV, and Movie Memorabilia.

Baby Drowsey, Black, 1968, 15", MIB, M15 ....$125.00
Baby First Step, 1967, MIB, L6 ....$150.00
Baby Secret, 1966, red hair, 18", EX...............................$75.00
Baby See 'N Say, 1964, MIB, L6 ....$150.00
Baby Small Talk, 1968, MIB, L6 ....$75.00
Baby Teenietalk, 1966, orig dress, 17", VG, M15 ....$75.00

Photo courtesy Kathy Lewis

Matty the Talking Boy, 1961, MIB, $300.00.

Sister Belle, 1961, MIB, L6 ....$300.00
Sister Small Talk, 1968, plastic & vinyl, blond hair, EX..$55.00
Teachy Keen, 1966, MIB, L6 ....$125.00
Timey Tell, MIB, L6..$110.00

Rockflowers by Mattel

Rockflowers were introduced in the early 1970s as Mattel's answer to Topper's Dawn Dolls. Rockflowers are 6½" tall and have wire articulated bodies that came with mod sunglasses attached to their heads. There were four girls and one boy in the series with eighteen groovy outfits that could be purchased separately. Each doll came with their own 45 rpm record, and the clothing packages were also in the shape of a 45 rpm record.

Advisor: Dawn Parrish (P2).

Doll, Doug, #1177, NRFB, P2 ....$35.00
Doll, Heather, #1166, NRFB, P2......................................$35.00
Doll, Lilac, #1167, NRFB, P2 ....$35.00
Doll, Rosemary, #1168, NRFB, P2 ....$45.00
Outfit, Frontier Patchwork, #4068, NRFP, P2 ....$12.00
Outfit, Mini Lace, #4056, NRFP, P2...............................$12.00
Outfit, Overall Orange, #4065, NRFP, P2 ....$10.00
Outfit, Tie Dye Bells, #4054, NRFP, P2..........................$12.00
Outfit, Topped in Lace, #4058, NRFP, P2 ....$12.00

Strawberry Shortcake

It was around 1980 when Strawberry Shortcake came on the market with a bang. The line included everything to attract small girls — swimsuits, bed linens, blankets, anklets, underclothing, coats, shoes, sleeping bags, dolls and accessories, games, and many other delightful items. Strawberry Shortcake and her friends were short lived, lasting only until the middle of the decade.

Advisor: Geneva Addy (A5).

Atari Cartridge, Magical Matchups, VG, B5 ....$30.00
Book, Cooking Fun, EX, B5...$10.00
Candle, Apple Dumplin', MIP, B5 ....$20.00

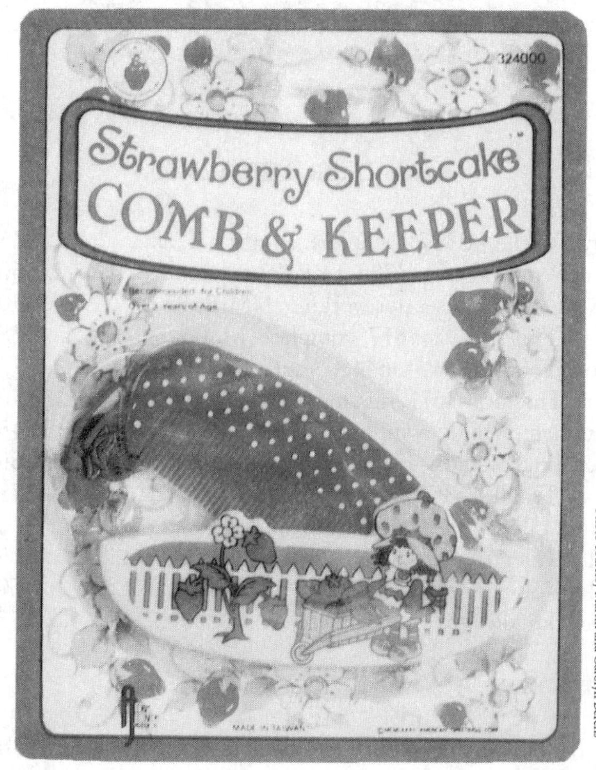

Photo courtesy Martin and Carolyn Berens

Comb and Keeper, MIP, from $15.00 to $20.00.

Charm, Strawberry Shortcake, NM, B5 ....$18.00
Clothes Rack, wood, MIB, B5 ....$75.00
Doll, Almond Tea, MIB $25.00
Doll, Angel Cake, 6", MIB $25.00
Doll, Apple Dumpling, MIB $25.00
Doll, Berry Baby Orange Blossom, 6", MIB....................$25.00
Doll, Butter Cookie, 6", MIB....................$25.00
Doll, Cafe Ole, MIB....................$25.00
Doll, Cherry Cuddler, 6", MIB $25.00
Doll, Lime Chiffon, 6", MIB....................$25.00
Doll, Mint Tulip, MIB $25.00
Doll, Orange Blossom, MIB, B5 ....$25.00
Doll, Raspberry Tart, MIB $25.00
Doll, Strawberry Shortcake, 12", NRFB....................$25.00
Doll, Strawberry Shortcake, 15", NM $35.00
Dollhouse $125.00
Dollhouse Furniture, attic, 6-pc, rare, M, A5....................$125.00
Dollhouse Furniture, bathroom, 5-pc basic, rare, M $65.00
Dollhouse Furniture, bedroom, 7-pc basic, rare, M $90.00
Dollhouse Furniture, kitchen, 11-pc basic, rare, M....................$100.00
Dollhouse Furniture, living room, 6-pc basic, rare, M $85.00
Figure, Almond Tea w/Marza Panda, PVC, 1", MOC, B5 .$10.00
Figure, Lemon Meringue w/Frappe, PVC, 1", MOC, B5...$10.00
Figure, Lime Chiffon w/balloons, PVC, MOC....................$10.00
Figure, Merry Berry Worm, MIB $20.00
Figure, Mint Tulip w/March Mallard, PVC, MOC, B5 ....$10.00
Figure, Purple Pieman w/Berry Bird, poseable, MIB..........$35.00

Figure, Sour Grapes with Dregs, Strawberryland Miniatures, MIP, from $15.00 to $20.00.

Figure, Raspberry Tart w/bowl of berries, MOC....................$10.00
Figure, Raspberry Tart w/Rhubarb, PVC, MOC, B5.........$10.00
Figure, Strawberry Shortcake on skateboard, PVC, MOC..$10.00
Lamp, ceramic, VG, B5 ....$50.00
Radio, transistor, M, A5 ....$35.00
Storybook Play Case, M, B5 ....$35.00
Stove, VG $30.00
Stroller, Coleco, 1981, M, J6....................$85.00
Suitcase, Strawberry Shortcake, cloth, VG, B5 ....$45.00
Tablecloth, rnd, EX, B5 ....$30.00
Telephone, Strawberry Shortcake figure, M, A5 ....$45.00
Toy Chest, M, A5 ....$40.00

Tammy

In 1962 the Ideal Novelty and Toy Company introduced their teenage Tammy doll. Slightly pudgy and not quite as sophisticated looking as some of the teen fashion dolls on the market at the time, Tammy's innocent charm captivated consumers. Her extensive wardrobe and numerous accessories added to her popularity with children. Tammy had a car, a house, and her own catamaran. In addition, a large number of companies obtained licenses to issue products using the 'Tammy' name. Everything from paper dolls to nurse's kits were made with Tammy's image on them. Her success was not confined to the United States; she was also successful in Canada and several other European countries.

Interest in Tammy has risen quite a bit in the past year according to Cindy Sabulis, co-author of *Tammy, the Ideal Teen* (Collector Books). Values have gone up and supply of quality mint-in-box items is going down. Loose, played-with dolls are still readily available and can be found for as low as $10.00 at doll shows. Values are given for mint-in-box dolls. Loose dolls are worth considerably less.

Advisor: Cindy Sabulis (S14).

Accessory Pak, #9181-80, w/curlers, brush, mirror & hairspray, NRFP, S14 ....$20.00
Accessory Pak, #9183-80, w/camera, luggage & airline ticket, NRFB, S14 ....$20.00
Accessory Pak, unknown #, w/frying pan & electric skillet, NRFP, S14, from $45 to $50.00
Accessory Pak, unknown #, w/snorkel, fins, watch & mask, NRFP, S14 ....$35.00
Doll, Bud, MIB, S14, minimum value....................$300.00
Doll, Dodi, MIB, S14 ....$75.00
Doll, Glamour Misty the Miss Clairol Doll, MIB, S14 ...$125.00
Doll, Grown Up Tammy, MIB, S14 ....$75.00
Doll, Grown Up Tammy (Black), MIB, S14, minimum value....................$250.00
Doll, Misty, MIB, S14....................$100.00
Doll, Misty (Black), MIB, S14, minimum value....................$300.00
Doll, Patti, MIB, S14....................$200.00
Doll, Pepper, MIB, S14....................$55.00
Doll, Pepper (Canadian version), MIB, S14 ....$65.00
Doll, Pepper (trimmer body & smaller face), MIB, S14....$75.00
Doll, Pepper w/'carrot'-colored hair, MIB, S14 ....$75.00
Doll, Pos'n Dodi, M (decorated box), S14 ....$150.00

Doll, Pos'n Dodi, M (plain box), S14..............................$75.00
Doll, Pos'n Misty & Her Telephone Booth, MIB, S14...$125.00
Doll, Pos'n Pepper, MIB, S14..$75.00
Doll, Pos'n Pete, MIB, S14...$125.00
Doll, Pos'n Salty, MIB, S14..$100.00
Doll, Pos'n Tammy, MIB, S14..$95.00
Doll, Pos'n Tammy & Her Telephone Booth, MIB, S14..$95.00
Doll, Pos'n Ted, MIB, S14...$100.00

Doll, Tammy, MIB, S14, $65.00.

Doll, Tammy's Dad, MIB, S14..$65.00
Doll, Tammy's Mom, MIB, S14...$65.00
Doll, Ted, MIB, S14 ....$65.00
Outfit, Dad & Ted, bathrobe & slippers, #9457-3, NRFP, S14...$20.00
Outfit, Dad & Ted, blazer & slacks, #9477-1, NRFP, S14..$20.00
Outfit, Dad & Ted, vest, tie & shoes, #9463-1, NRFP, S14..$20.00
Outfit, Pepper, Anchors Away, #9316-1, complete, M, S14.$30.00
Outfit, Pepper, Flower Girl, #9332-8, complete, M, S14..$45.00
Outfit, Pepper, Miss Gadabout, #9331-0, MIP, S14 ....$65.00
Outfit, Pepper, Sun 'n Surf, #9321-1, MIP, S14...............$65.00
Outfit, Pepper, Teacher's Pet, #9308-8, complete, M, S14..$40.00
Outfit, Tammy, Career Girl, #9945-7, complete, M, S14.$75.00
Outfit, Tammy, Cheerleader, #9131-4 or #9931-7, complete, M, S14, ea..$45.00
Outfit, Tammy, Fraternity Hop, #9137-1 or #9937-4, complete, M, S14, ea..$50.00
Outfit, Tammy, Jet Set, #9155-3 or #9943-2, complete, M, S14 ....$50.00
Outfit, Tammy, On the Avenue, #9944-0, complete, M, S14 ....$75.00
Outfit, Tammy, On the Town, #9168-6 or #9946-5, MIP, S14 ....$75.00
Outfit, Tammy, School Daze, #9133-0 or #9933-3, complete, M, S14, ea...$40.00
Outfit, Tammy's Mom, Evening in Paris, #9421-9, complete, M, S14 ....$35.00
Outfit, Tammy's Mom, Lounging Luxury, #9422-7, complete, M, S14 ....$35.00
Outfit, Tammy's Mom, Nighty Nite, #9415-1, MIP, S14 .$30.00
Pepper Case, hatbox style, S14..$40.00
Pepper Cases, any except hatbox style, S14, ea from $15 to $20.00
Pepper's Juke Box, M, S14..$50.00
Pepper's Treehouse, MIB, S14...$150.00
Tammy & Ted Catamaran, MIB, S14............................$200.00
Tammy Cases, S14, ea from $15 to $35.00
Tammy's Car, MIB, S14 ....$150.00
Tammy's Ideal House, M, S14, minimum value $100.00
Tammy's Juke Box, M, S14...$50.00
Tammy's Magic Mirror Fashion Show, NRFB, S14 ....$50.00

Tonka

The Aurora line of fashion dolls made by Tonka in 1987 is unique in that their Barbie-like bodies are metallic. There were

Crysta, MIB (not shown), $25.00.

four in the line, Aurora herself, Crysta, Lustra, and Mirra. Their costumes are futuristic, and their eyes are inset, faceted jewels. Their long tresses are shockingly bright — Aurora's is gold, Crysta's is pink, Mirra's blue, and Lustra's lavender. Mattel made a very similar line of dolls; the most notable difference is that they lacked the jewel eyes. Mattel's are dated 1975. Dolls from either series are valued at about $25.00 each, mint in box.

Tressy

American Character's Tressy doll was produced in this country from 1963 to 1967. The unique feature of this 11½" fashion doll was that her hair 'grew' by pushing a button on her stomach. Tressy also had a little (9") sister named Cricket. Numerous fashions and accessories were produced for these two dolls. Never-removed-from-box Tressy and Cricket items are rare, so unless indicated, values listed are for loose, mint items. A never-removed-from-box item's worth is at least double its loose value.

Advisor: Cindy Sabulis (S14).

Apartment, M, S14..........**$150.00**
Beauty Salon, M, S14..........**$125.00**
Case, Cricket, M, S14..........**$30.00**
Case, Tressy, M, S14..........**$25.00**
Doll, Pre-Teen Tressy, M, S14..........**$75.00**
Doll, Tressy, MIB..........**$90.00**

Doll, Tressy in Miss America Character outfit, NM, S14.**$65.00**
Doll, Tressy w/Magic Makeup Face, M, S14..........**$25.00**
Doll Clothes Pattern, M, S14..........**$10.00**
Gift Paks w/Doll & Clothing, NRFB, S14, minimum value ea..........**$100.00**
Hair Accessory Paks, NRFB, S14, ea..........**$20.00**
Hair Dryer, M, S14..........**$40.00**
Hair or Cosmetic Accessory Kits, M, S14, minimum value ea..........**$50.00**
Millinery, M, S14..........**$150.00**
Outfits, MOC, S14, ea..........**$25.00**
Outfits, NRFB, S14, minimum value ea..........**$40.00**

Upsy Downsys by Mattel

The Upsy Downsy dolls were made by Mattel during the late 1960s. They were small, 2½" to 3½", made of vinyl and plastic. Some of the group were 'Upsies' that walked on their feet, while others were 'Downsies' that walked or rode fantasy animals while upside-down.

Advisor: Dawn Parrish (P2).

Baby So-High, #3828, missing playland, P2..........**$50.00**
Downy Dilly, #3832, NRFB, P2..........**$150.00**
Downy Dilly & Foot Mobile, #3832, EX, P2..........**$35.00**
Flossy Glossy, #3827, doll & playland, EX, P2..........**$25.00**
Miss Information, #3831, doll only, EX, P2..........**$25.00**
Miss Information, #3831, NRFB, P2..........**$150.00**
Mother What Now, #3829, complete, EX, P2..........**$40.00**
Mother What Now, #3829, NRFB, P2..........**$150.00**
Pocus Hocus, #3820, missing playland, EX, P2..........**$50.00**
Pudgy Fudgy, #3826, NRFB, P2..........**$150.00**

Farm Toys

It's entirely probable that more toy tractors have been sold than real ones. They've been made to represent all makes and models, of plastic, cast iron, diecast metal, and even wood. They've been made in at least 1/16th, 1/32nd, 1/43rd, and 1/64th scale. If you buy a 1/16th-scale replica, that small piece of equipment would have to be sixteen times larger to equal the size of the real item. Limited editions (meaning that a specific number will be made and no more) and commemorative editions (made for special events) are usually very popular with collectors. Many models on the market today are being made by the Ertl company.

Advisor: John Rammacher (S5).

See also Cast Iron, Farm.

Agco Allis 6670 Row Crop, Ertl, 1/64th scale, #1214, MIB, S5 .**$4.00**
Agco Allis 6690 Tractor w/Duals, Ertl, 1/64th scale, #1286, MIB, S5..........**$4.00**
Agco Allis 6690 w/4 Post Rops, Ertl, 1/64th scale, #1239, MIB, S5..........**$4.00**
Agco 6680 w/Front Wheel Assist, Ertl, 1/64th scale, #1245, MIB, S5..........**$4.00**

Allis Chalmers D-19 Tractor, Ertl, 1/43rd scale, #2566, MIB, S5 ....$6.00

Allis Chalmers Tractor, Ertl, 1/16th scale, MIB, $30.00.

Brent Dual-Wheel Grain Cart, Ertl, 1996 Farm Show, red or gr, 1/64th scale, MIB, S5, ea $20.00
Case IH Forage Harvester, Ertl, 1/64th scale, #201, MIB, S5 ..$3.00
Case IH Hay Rake, Ertl, 1/64th scale, #210, MIB, S5 ....$3.00
Case IH Historical Set, Ertl, 1/64th scale, #238, 2 pcs, MIB, S5 ....$6.00
Case IH Milk Truck, Ertl, 1/64th scale, #648, MIB, S5 ....$6.00
Case IH Round Baler, Ertl, 1/64th scale, #274, MIB, S5 ....$4.00
Case IH Self-Prop Windrower, Ertl, 1/64th scale, #4405, MIB, S5 ....$8.00
Case IH Tractor w/End Loader, Ertl, 1/64th scale, #212, MIB, S5 ....$5.00
Case IH 12-Row Planter, Ertl, 900 series, 1/64th scale, #656, MIB, S5 ....$5.00
Case IH 1660 Combine, Ertl, 1/64th scale, #655, MIB, S5 ..$10.00
Case IH 2594 Tractor, Ertl, 1/64th scale, #227, MIB, S5 ...$3.00
Case IH 496 Wing Disk, Ertl, 1/64th scale, #694, MIB, S5 ..$5.00
Case IH 5130 Row Crop, Ertl, 1/64th scale, #229, MIB, S5 .$3.00
Case IH 5130 Row Crop, Ertl, 1991 Farm Show, 1/64th scale, #229, MIB, S5 ....$10.00
Case IH 7120 w/Duals, Ertl, 1/64th scale, #626, MIB, S5...$3.00
Case IH 7130 Magnum Tractor, Ertl, 1/64th scale, #458, MIB, S5 ....$3.00
Case IH 7220 w/Loader, Ertl, 1/64th scale, #460, MIB, S5.$5.00
Case IH 9260 4-Wheel Drive, Ertl, 1/64th scale, #231, MIB, S5 ....$5.00
Case IH 9260 4-Wheel Drive, Ertl, 1993 Farm Show, 1/64th scale, MIB, S5 ....$10.00
Case L Tractor, Ertl, 1/43rd scale, #2554, MIB, S5 ....$6.00
Case L Tractor, Ertl, 150 Year Collector's Edition, 1/16th scale, #252, MIB, S5 ....$35.00
Case Uniloader, Ertl, 1/64th scale, #455, MIB, S5 ....$5.00
CAT Flotation Liquid Fertilizer Spreader, Ertl, 1/64th scale, #2324, MIB, S5 ....$5.00
CAT Industrial Disc, Ertl, 1/64th scale, #2333, MIB, S5 ...$4.00
Caterpillar 2-Ton Tractor, Ertl, National Toy Show, 1/16th scale, #2438, MIB, S5 ....$65.00
Chevy Stake Truck, 1930, Ertl, 1/43rd scale, #2503, MIB, S5...$6.00
CIH Maxxum 5120 w/Duals, Ertl, 1/64th scale, #241, MIB, S5..$4.00
CIH 2188 Combine, Ertl, 1995 Farm Show, 1/64th scale, #4607, MIB, S5 ....$18.00
CIH 7150 Front Wheel Assist, Ertl, 1992 Farm Show, 1/64th scale, #285, MIB, S5 ....$10.00
Deluxe Farm Set, Slik Toy, complete w/tractor, harrow, raker & grader, NM (EX box), A $135.00
Deutz Allis Barge Wagon, Ertl, 1/64th scale, #2241, MIB, S5 ..$3.00
Deutz Allis Mixer Mill, Ertl, 1/64th scale, #2208, MIB, S5 .$3.00
Deutz Allis 6260 Tractor, Ertl, 1/64th scale, #1241, MIB, S5 .$3.00
Deutz Allis 7085 Tractor w/Loader, Ertl, 1/64th scale, #2233, MIB, S5 ....$4.00
Farmall Cub, 1956-58, Ertl, 1/16th scale, #235, MIB, S5 .$20.00
Farmall F-20, Ertl, 1/16th scale, #260, MIB, S5 ....$20.00
Farmall Super M-T-A Tractor, Ertl, 1/16th scale, #445, MIB, S5 ....$20.00
Farmall 140 Tractor, Ertl, 1995 Farm Show, 1/16th scale, MIB, S5 ....$35.00
Farmall 650 Tractor, Ertl, 1/16th scale, #246, MIB, S5 ....$22.00
Farmall 706 Diesel Tractor, Ertl, 1/16th scale, #2307, MIB, S5 ....$25.00
Ford F-250 Pickup w/Livestock Trailer, Ertl, 1/64th scale, #311, MIB, S5 ....$5.00
Ford New Holland Combine, Ertl, 1/64th scale, #815, MIB, S5 ....$10.00
Ford New Holland Hay Rake, Ertl, 1/64th scale, #369, MIB, S5 ....$3.00
Ford Pickup, 1940, Ertl, 50th Anniversary, 1/25th scale, MIB, S5 ....$22.00
Ford Powermaster Tractor, Hubley, #961, 11", NM (EX box), A $185.00
Ford Precision Classic 2N, Ertl, 1/16th scale, #354, MIB, S5 ..$95.00
Ford Precision Classic 8N, Ertl, 1/16th scale, #352, MIB, S5 ..$95.00
Ford Super Major 5000 Tractor, Ertl, 1/64th scale, #928, MIB, S5 ....$4.00
Ford Tractor, Aluminum Model Toys, silver & red plastic w/blk rubber tires, 9", NM (worn box), A $175.00
Ford 32 Roadster, Ertl, 1/43rd scale, #2501, MIB, S5 ....$6.00
Ford 5640 w/Loader, Ertl, 1/64th scale, #334, MIB, S5 ....$5.00

Fordson Super Major Tractor, Ertl, 1/16th scale, MIB, $30.00.

Ford 7740 w/Loader, Ertl, 1/64th scale, #387, MIB, S5.......**$5.00**
Ford 7740 w/4-Wheel Drive, Ertl, 1/64th scale, #333, MIB, S5..**$4.00**
Ford 7840 w/Duals, Ertl, 1/64th scale, #335, MIB, S5.........**$3.00**
Ford 8N Tractor, Ertl, 1/16th scale, #843, MIB, S5..........**$20.00**
Ford 8340 w/4-Wheel Drive, Ertl, 1/16th scale, #877, MIB, S5 ....**$50.00**
Ford 8730 Tractor, Ertl, 1/64th scale, #302, MIB, S5 ....**$3.00**
Ford 8730 w/Loader, Ertl, 1/64th scale, #303, MIB, S5.......**$5.00**
Ford 9N, Ertl, 1/64th scale, #926, MIB, S5 ....**$4.00**
Ford 901 Dealer Demo Tractor, Ertl, 1/16th scale, #363, MIB, S5 ....**$40.00**
Ford 901 Power Master Tractor, Ertl, 1/64th scale, #927, MIB, S5 ....**$4.00**
Fordson Model F Tractor, Ertl, 1/16th scale, #301, MIB, S5 ..**$18.00**
Fordson Tractor, Ertl, 1/43rd scale, #2526, MIB, S5 ....**$6.00**
Genesis 8770 Tractor, Ertl, 1/64th scale, #391, MIB, S5 ....**$4.00**
Genesis 8870 w/4-Wheel Drive, Ertl, 1/64th scale, #392, MIB, S5 ....**$4.00**
Hesston Forage Wagon, Ertl, 1/64th scale, #2266, MIB, S5..**$3.00**
Hesston SL-30 Skidsteer Loader, Ertl, 1/64th scale, #2267, MIB, S5 ....**$5.00**
Heston 8400 Self-Propelled Windrower, Ertl, 1/64th scale, #2261, MIB, S5 ....**$8.00**
IH Cub Tractor, 1976-79, Ertl, 1/16th scale, MIB, S5......**$18.00**
IH Farmall Cub, 1964-1976, Ertl, 1/16th scale, #653, MIB, S5........**$18.00**
IH I-D9 Tractor, Ertl, 1/16th scale, #4611, MIB, S5 ....**$35.00**
IH Wing Disk, Ertl, 1/64th scale, #1862, MIB, S5 ....**$3.00**
IH 1568 V-8 Tractor w/Duals, Ertl, Collector's Edition, 1/16th scale, #4603, MIB, S5 ....**$40.00**
IH 1586 Tractor, Ertl, 1/16th scale, #463, MIB, S5 ....**$18.00**
IH 1586 w/Loader, Ertl, 1/16th scale, #416, MIB, S5 ....**$25.00**
IHC Famous Engine, Ertl, 1/16th scale, #615, MIB, S5....**$20.00**
International 600 Diesel Tractor, Ertl, 1/16th scale, #282, MIB, S5 ....**$20.00**
John Deere Bale Processor, Ertl, 1/64th scale, #5568, MIB, S5 ....**$3.00**
John Deere Bale Throw Wagon, Ertl, 1/64th scale, #5755, MIB, S5 ....**$4.00**
John Deere Barge Wagon, Ertl, 1/64th scale, #5529, MIB, S5..**$3.00**
John Deere Combine, Ertl, 1/64th scale, #5604, MIB, S5...**$10.00**
John Deere Compact Utility Tractor, Ertl, 1/16th scale, MIB, S5........**$16.00**

John Deere Caterpillar, Ertl, MIB, $95.00.

John Deere Fertilizer Spreader, Ertl, 1/64th scale, #5558, MIB, S5 ....**$3.00**

John Deere Front-End Loader, 1/43rd scale, M, $8.00.

John Deere GP Standard, Ertl, Collector's Edition, 1/16th scale, #5767, MIB, S5 ....**$35.00**
John Deere GP Tractor, 1939, Ertl, 1/16th scale, #5801, MIB, S5........**$25.00**
John Deere Grain Cart, Ertl, 1/64th scale, #5565, MIB, S5 ..**$4.00**
John Deere Grain Drill, Ertl, 1/64th scale, #5528, MIB, S5..**$3.00**
John Deere Gravity Wagon, Ertl, 1/64th scale, #5552, MIB, S5........**$3.00**
John Deere Hay Rake, Ertl, 1/64th scale, #5751, MIB, S5..**$4.00**
John Deere Hydra-Push Spreader, Ertl, 1/64th scale, #574, MIB, S5 ....**$3.00**
John Deere MC Crawler, Ertl, 1/16th scale, #JDM-076, MIB, S5........**$45.00**
John Deere Mower Conditioner, Ertl, 1/64th scale, #5657, MIB, S5 ....**$3.00**
John Deere Mulch Tiller, Ertl, 1/64th scale, #578, MIB, S5 .....**$3.00**
John Deere Rotary Cutter, Ertl, 1/64th scale, #5600, MIB, S5........**$4.00**
John Deere Rotary Mower, Ertl, 1/16th scale, MIB, S5 ....**$22.00**
John Deere Row Crop, Ertl, 1/64th scale, #5571, MIB, S5 .**$3.00**
John Deere Skid Loader, Ertl, 1/64th scale, #5536, MIB, S5..**$5.00**
John Deere Skid Steer Loader, Ertl, 1/16th scale, #569, MIB, S5........**$18.00**
John Deere Skid Steer Loader, Ertl, 1/64th scale, #5622, MIB, S5 ....**$5.00**
John Deere Sprayer, Ertl, 1/64th scale, #5553, MIB, S5 .....**$3.00**
John Deere Tractor w/Front Wheel Drive, Ertl, 1/64th scale, #5612, MIB, S5 ....**$4.00**
John Deere Utility Tractor, Ertl, 1/16th scale, #516, MIB, S5.**$15.00**
John Deere Utility Tractor w/Loader, Ertl, 1/16th scale, #517, MIB, S5........**$20.00**
John Deere Waterloo Engine, Ertl, 1/16th scale, #5645, MIB, S5 ....**$20.00**

John Deere 12 A Combine, Ertl, 1/16th scale, #5601, MIB, S5 ....$45.00
John Deere 2510 Tractor, Ertl, 1/64th scale, #5756, MIB, S5 ..$4.00
John Deere 3010, Ertl, Collector's Edition, 1/16th scale, #5635, MIB, S5 ....$38.00
John Deere 4010 Diesel, Ertl, 1994 National Toy Show, 1/43rd scale, #5725, MIB, S5 ....$25.00
John Deere 5020 Tractor, Ertl, 1/64th scale, #5776, MIB, S5 ....$4.00
John Deere 535 Round Baler, Ertl, 1/64th scale, #577, MIB, S5 ....$3.00
John Deere 630 LP Tractor, Ertl, 1/43rd scale, #5599, MIB, S5 ....$5.00
John Deere 6400 Row Crop, Ertl, 1/16th scale, #5666, MIB, S5 ....$38.00
John Deere 6400 w/Duals, Ertl, 1/64th scale, #5734, MIB, S5..$4.00
John Deere 6400 w/Rops & Loader, Ertl, 1/64th scale, #5732, MIB, S5 ....$5.00
John Deere 6910 Self-Propelled Harvester, Ertl, 1/64th scale, #5658, MIB, S5 ....$10.00
John Deere 70 Tractor, Ertl, 1/16th scale, #5611, MIB, S5..$22.00
John Deere 7800 Row Crop, Ertl, 1/64th scale, #5538, MIB, S5 ....$4.00
John Deere 7800 w/Duals, Ertl, 1/64th scale, #5649, MIB, S5...$4.00
John Deere 7800 w/Loader, Ertl, 1/64th scale, #5652, MIB, S5.$5.00
John Deere 820 Diesel Tractor, Ertl, 1/16th scale, #5705, MIB, S5 ....$22.00
John Deere 8560 4-Wheel Drive, Ertl, 1/64th scale, #5603, MIB, S5 ....$5.00
John Deere 876 V-Tank Slurry Spreader, Ertl, 1/64th scale, #5928, MIB, S5 ....$5.00
John Deere 8870 4-Wheel Drive Tractor, Ertl, 1/64th scale, #5791, MIB, S5 ....$5.00
John Deere 95 Combine, Ertl, 1/64th scale, #5819, MIB, S5 .$10.00
Knudson 4400 4-Wheel Drive Tractor w/Duals, Ertl, 1/64th scale, #TF4400, MIB, S5 ....$20.00
Massey-Ferguson, Ertl, 1992 Farm Show, 1/43rd scale, #1131, MIB, S5 ....$25.00
Massey-Ferguson Challenger, Ertl, 1/16th scale, #1103, MIB, S5 ....$25.00
Massey-Ferguson 3070 Front-Wheel Drive, Ertl, 1/64th scale, #1107, MIB, S5 ....$4.00
Massey-Ferguson 3070 Tractor, Ertl, 1/64th scale, #1177, MIB, S5 ....$3.00
Massey-Ferguson 3070 w/Loader, Ertl, 1/64th scale, #1109, MIB, S5 ....$5.00
Massey-Ferguson 3140 w/Duals, Ertl, 1/64th scale, #1176, MIB, S5 ....$4.00
Massey-Ferguson 555 Tractor, Ertl, 1/16th scale, #1105, MIB, S5..$22.00
Massey-Ferguson 699 Tractor, Ertl, 1/64th scale, #1120, MIB, S5..$3.00
Massey-Harris Challenger Tractor, Ertl, 1/43rd scale, #2511, MIB, S5 ....$6.00
Massey-Harris 55 Wide-Front, Ertl, 1/16th scale, #1292, MIB, S5 ....$20.00
Minneapolis Moline G750, Ertl, 1994 National Tractor Show, 1/16th scale, #4375, MIB, S5 ....$80.00

McCormick-Deering Farmall, 1992 Lafayette Farm Toy Show Edition, MIB, $45.00.

New Holland Baler, Ertl, 1/64th scale, #337, MIB, S5........$3.00
New Holland Box Spreader, Ertl, 1/64th scale, #308, MIB, S5 ....$3.00
New Holland Mower Conditioner, Ertl, 1/64th scale, #322, MIB, S5 ....$4.00
New Holland Skid Loader, Ertl, 1/64th scale, #381, MIB, S5 ....$5.00
Oliver 1555 Diesel Tractor, Ertl, 1/16th scale, #2223, MIB, S5 ....$22.00
Oliver 1655 w/Wide Front, Ertl, 1/16th scale, #4472, MIB, S5 ....$20.00

Fast-Food Collectibles

Fast-food collectibles are attracting a lot of attention right now — the hobby is fun and inexpensive (so far), and the little toys, games, buttons, and dolls originally meant for the kids are now being snatched up by adults who are much more likely to appreciate them. They were first included in kiddie meals in the late 1970s. They're often issued in series of up to eight or ten characters; the ones you'll want to watch for are Disney characters, popular kids' icons like Barbie dolls, Cabbage Patch Kids, My Little Pony, Star Trek, etc. But it's not just the toys that are collectible. So are the boxes, store signs and displays, and promotional items (like the Christmas ornaments you can buy for 99¢). Supply dictates price. For instance, a test market box might be worth $20.00, a box from a regional promotion might be $10.00, while one from a national promotion could be virtually worthless.

Toys don't have to be old to be collectible, but if you can find them still in their original package, so much the better. Though there are exceptions, a loose toy is worth one half to two thirds the value of one mint in package. (The values given here are for MIP items unless noted otherwise.) For more information we recommend *McDonald's® Happy Meal® Toys — In the USA* and *McDonald's® Happy Meal® Toys — Around the World*, by Joyce and Terry Losonsky, and *Tomart's Price Guide to Kid's*

Meal Collectibles (Non-McDonald's) and *Kid's Meal Collectibles Update* '94 – '95 by Ken Clee. Both are listed under Fast-Food Collectibles in the Categories of Special Interest section of this book. We also recommend *McDonald's® Collectibles* by Gary Henriques and Audre Du Vall (Collector Books).

Advisors: Bill and Pat Poe (P10); Scott Smiles (S10), Foreign.

Other Sources: C3, C11, I2, K1 (Simpsons), M8, P3

Arby's

Babar's World Tour, finger puppets, 1990, ea....................$3.00
Babar's World Tour, pull-back racers, 1992, ea....................$3.00
Babar's World Tour, squirters, 1992, ea....................$2.00
Babar's World Tour, stampers, 1991, ea....................$3.00
Babar's World Tour, storybooks, 1991, ea....................$3.00
Babar's World Tour, vehicles, 1990, ea....................$3.00
Little Miss, 1981, ea....................$4.00
Looney Tunes Car Tunes, 1989, ea....................$3.00
Looney Tunes Characters, 1987, oval base, ea....................$5.00
Looney Tunes Characters, 1988, standing, ea....................$5.00
Looney Tunes Fun Fingers, 1989, ea....................$5.00

Photo courtesy Mary Jane Lamphier

Mr. Men, $5.00 each.

Snow Domes, 1995, Yogi or Snagglepuss, ea....................$5.00
Winter Wonderland Crazy Cruisers, 1995, ea....................$4.00
Yogi Bear Fun Squirters, 1994, ea....................$4.00

Burger King

Action Figures, 1991, ea....................$3.00
Aladdin, 1992, ea....................$3.00
Aladdin Hidden Treasures, 1994, ea....................$2.00

Archies, 1991, $4.00 each.

Beauty & the Beast, 1991, 4 different, ea....................$4.00
Beetlejuice, 1990, 6 different, ea....................$2.00
Bone Age, 1989, 4 different, ea....................$5.00
Bonkers, 1993, 6 different, ea....................$3.00
Capitol Critters, 1992, 4 different, ea....................$2.00
Captain Planet Flipover Star Cruisers, 1991, 4 different, ea....................$2.00
Cool Stuff, 1995, 5 different, ea....................$3.00
Crayola Christmas Bears, 1986, plush, 4 different colors, ea....................$5.00
Dino Crawlers, 1994, 5 different, ea....................$2.00
Gargoyles, 1995, 1st or 2nd set, ea....................$3.00
Glo Force, 1996, 5 different, ea....................$3.00
Glow-in-the-Dark Troll Patrol, 1993, 4 different, ea....................$2.00
Go-Go Gadget Gizmos, 1991, 4 different, ea....................$3.00
Good Goblin', 1989, 3 different, ea....................$3.00
Goof Troop Bowlers, 1992, 4 different, ea....................$3.00
Goofy & Max Adventures, 1995, any except yel runaway car, ea....................$3.00
Goofy & Max Adventures, 1995, yel runaway car....................$4.00
Hunchback of Notre Dame, 1995, hand puppets, 4 different, ea....................$10.00
Hunchback of Notre Dame, 1996, 8 different, ea....................$4.00
It's Magic, 1992, 4 different, ea....................$2.00
Kid Transporters, 1990, 6 different, ea....................$2.00
Life Savers Freaky Fellas, 1992, 4 different colors, ea....................$2.00
Lion King, 1994, 7 different, ea....................$3.00
Lion King, 1995, finger puppets, 6 different, ea....................$3.00
Little Mermaid, 1993, Urchin squirt gun, Flounder squirter or Sebastian w/up, ea....................$3.00
McGruff Cares for You, 1991, 4 different songbook & tapes sets, ea....................$6.00
Mini Record Breakers, 1989, 6 different, ea....................$2.00
Mini Sports Games, 1993, 4 different, ea....................$3.00
Minnie Mouse, 1992....................$6.00
Miss Daisy's Trolley w/Chip & Dale, 1993....................$6.00
Nerfuls, 1989, 3 different, ea....................$4.00
Oliver & Co, 1996, 5 different, ea....................$3.00
Pinocchio Summer Inflatables, 1992, 5 different, ea....................$4.00
Pocahontas, 1995, 8 different, ea....................$3.00
Pocahontas, 1996, finger puppets, 6 different, ea....................$3.00
Pranksters, 1994, 5 different, ea....................$3.00
Purrtenders, 1988, Free Wheeling Cheese Rider or Flip Top Car, ea....................$2.00
Purrtenders Sock-Ems, Christmas 1987, stuffed plush animals, 4 different, ea....................$5.00
Rodney Reindeer & Friends, 1986, 4 different, ea....................$5.00
Silverhawks, 1987, pencil topper....................$5.00

Photo courtesy Mary Jane Lamphier

Simpsons, 1990, $2.00 each.

Spacebase Racers, 1989, 4 different, ea....................$3.00
Sports All-Stars, 1994, 5 different, ea....................$4.00
Super Powers, door shield....................$8.00

Super Powers, 1987, Aquaman tub toy $6.00
Surprise Celebration Parade, 1992, 4 different, w/track, ea ... $6.00
Teenage Mutant Ninja Turtles Bike Gear, 1993, ea $3.00
Top Kids Wild Spinning Tops, 1994, 4 different, ea $2.00
Toy Story, 1995, Action Wing Buzz $6.00
Toy Story, 1995, Rex Dinosaur, RC Racer, Mr Potato Head or Army Recon Squadron, ea $3.00
Toy Story, 1995, Woody $8.00
Trak-Pak Golden Jr Classic Books, 1988, 4 different, ea $4.00
Water Mates, 1991, any except Snaps/rowboat w/pk shirt or Wheels/hovercraft w/bl control panel, ea $3.00
Water Mates, 1991, Sanps/rowboat w/pk shirt or Wheels/hovercraft w/bl control panel, ea $6.00
World Travel Adventure Kit, 1991, 4 different, ea $5.00
Z-Bots w/Pogs, 1994, 5 different, ea $2.00

Dairy Queen

Alvin & the Chipmunks Music Makers, 1994, 4 different, ea $5.00
Baby's Day Out Books, 1994, 4 different, ea $12.00
Bobby's World, 1994, 4 different, ea $5.00
Dennis the Menace, 1994, 4 different, ea $6.00
Radio Flyer, 1991, miniature wagon $5.00
Rock-A-Doodle, 1991, 6 different, ea $7.00
Space Shuttle, 6 different, ea $3.00
Tom & Jerry, 1993, 4 different, ea $6.00

Denny's

Adventure Seekers Activity Packet, 1993, ea $2.00
Dino-Makers, 5 different, ea $3.00
Flintstones, 1989, Fred & Wilma or Barney & Betty, plush, ea $8.00
Flintstones, 1989, Pebbles & Bamm-Bamm, plush, pr $12.00
Flintstones, 1990, vehicles, 3 different, ea $4.00
Flintstones Dino-Racers, 1991, 3 different, ea $4.00
Flintstones Fun Squirters, 1991, 5 different, ea $4.00
Flintstones Glacier Gliders, 1990, Barney playing hockey, Bamm-Bamm on sled or Dino, ea $3.00
Flintstones Rock 'N Rollers, 1991, Fred w/guitar or Barney w/saxaphone, ea $4.00
Jetson's Go Back to School, 1992, 4 different, ea $3.00
Jetson's Space Cards, 1992, 6 different, ea $4.00
Jetson's Space Travel Fun Books, 1992, 6 different, ea $3.00
Jetson's Space-Age Puzzle Ornaments, 1992, ea $3.00

Dominos Pizza

Avoid the Noid, 1988, 3 different, ea $5.00
Donnie Domino, 1989, 4" $6.00
Keep the Noid Out, 1987, 3 different, ea $5.00
Noid, 1989, bookmark $10.00

Hardee's

Apollo 13 Spaceship, 1995, 3-pc set $12.00
Balto, 1995, 6 different, ea $3.00
Beach Bunnies, 1989, 4 different, ea $2.00
Bobby's World (At the Circus), 1996, 5 different, ea $3.00
Breakman's World, 1995, 4 different, ea $3.00
Camp California, 1994, 4 different, ea $3.00
Dinobend Buddies, 1994, 4 different, ea $3.00
Dinosaur in My Pocket, 1993, 4 different, ea $3.00
Eek! The Cat, 1995, 6 different, ea $3.00
Eureka Castle Stampers, 1994, 4 different, ea $3.00
Fender-Bender 500 Racers, 1990, 5 different, ea $3.00
Flintstones First 30 Years, 4 different, ea $5.00
Gremlin Adventures Read Along Book & Record, 1984, 5 different, ea $6.00
Halloween Hideaway, 1989, 4 different, ea $2.00
Homeward Bound II, 1996, 5 different, ea $3.00
Kazoo Crew Sailors, 1991, 4 different, ea $3.00
Marvel Super Heroes in Vehicles, 1990, 4 different, ea $3.00
Mickey's Christmas Carol, 1984, plush figures, 4 different, ea $6.00
Micro Super Soakers, 1994, 4 different, ea $3.00
Mouth Figurines, 1989, 4 different, ea $3.00
Muppets Christmas Carol, 1993, finger puppets, 4 different, ea $4.00
Nickelodeon School Tools, 1995, 6 different, ea $3.00
Nicktoons Cruisers, 1994, 8 different, ea $3.00
Pound Puppies, 1986, plush, 4 different, ea $5.00
Pound Puppies & Pur-R-Ries, 1987, plush, 5 different, ea .. $5.00
Shirt Tales, 1990, plush figures, 5 different, ea $5.00
Smurfs Funmeal Pack, 1990, 6 different, ea $3.00
Speed Bunnies, 1994, 4 different, ea $3.00
Swan Princess, 1994, 5 different, ea $4.00
Tattoads, 1995, 4 different, ea $3.00
Tune-A-Fish, 1994, 4 different, ea $3.00
Waldo & Friends Holiday Ornaments, 1991, 3 different, ea ... $4.00
Waldo & Friends Straw Buddies, 1990, 4 different, ea $3.00
Walt Disney Animated Film Classic, 1985, plush, 5 different, ea $6.00
X-Men, 1995, 6 different, ea $3.00

Jack-in-the-Box

Bendable Buddies, 1975, 4 different, ea $10.00
Bendable Buddies, 1991, 5 different, ea $3.00
Finger Puppets, 1994, 5 different, ea $10.00
Garden Fun Seed Packages, 1994, 3 different, ea $5.00
Jack Pack Make-A-Scene, 1990, 3 different, ea $4.00
Star Trek Generations, 1994, 6 different, ea $5.00

Long John Silver's

Berenstain Bears Books, 1995, 4 different, ea $3.00
Fish Car, 1989, 3 different, ea $3.00
Free Willy II, 1995, 5 different, ea $4.00
I Love Dinosaurs, 1993, 4 different, ea $4.00
Map Activities, 1991, 3 different, ea $4.00
Once Upon a Forest, 1993, 2 different, ea $4.00
Sea Watchers, 1991, mini kaleidoscope, 3 different, ea $5.00
Treasure Trolls, 1992, pencil toppers, 4 different, ea $3.00
Water Blasters, 1990, 4 different, ea $4.00

McDonald's

Airport, 1986, Fry Guy Flyer, Grimace Ace or Birdie Bent Wing Blazer, ea **$4.00**
Airport, 1986, Ronald McDonald seaplane **$5.00**
Airport, 1986, under age 3, Fry Guy Flyer (floater) **$5.00**
Aladdin & the King of Thieves, 1996, any except under 3, ea **$3.00**
Aladdin & the King of Thieves, 1996, under age 3, Abu ... **$4.00**
Amazing Wildlife, 1995, ea **$2.00**
Animaniacs, 1995, any except under age 3, ea **$3.00**
Animaniacs, 1995, under age 3, ea **$5.00**
Babe, 1996, 7 different, ea **$3.00**
Bambi, 1988, 4 different, ea **$5.00**
Barbie/Hot Wheels, 1991, Barbie, any except under age 3, ea .. **$5.00**
Barbie/Hot Wheels, 1991, Barbie, under age 3, Costume Ball or Wedding Day Midge, ea **$8.00**
Barbie/Hot Wheels, 1991, Hot Wheels, ea **$4.00**
Barbie/Hot Wheels, 1993, Barbie, any except under age 3, ea. **$3.00**
Barbie/Hot Wheels, 1993, Barbie, under age 3, Rose Bride .. **$4.00**
Barbie/Hot Wheels, 1993, Hot Wheels, any except under age 3, ea **$3.00**
Barbie/Hot Wheels, 1993, Hot Wheels, under age 3, Hammer & Wrench, ea **$4.00**
Barbie/Hot Wheels, 1994, Barbie, any except Camp Teresa (variation) or under age 3, from $4 to **$5.00**
Barbie/Hot Wheels, 1994, Barbie, under age 3, Barbie Ball .. **$5.00**
Barbie/Hot Wheels, 1994, Camp Teresa (variation) **$8.00**
Barbie/Hot Wheels, 1995, Barbie, under age 3, Lil' Miss Candi Stripe **$4.00**
Barbie/Hot Wheels, 1995, Hot Wheels, any except under age 3, ea **$3.00**
Barbie/Hot Wheels, 1995, Hot Wheels, under age 3, Key Force truck **$4.00**
Barbie/Hot Wheels, 1996, Barbie, any except under age 3, ea ... **$3.00**
Barbie/Hot Wheels, 1996, Hot Wheels, under age 3, mini steering wheel **$4.00**
Barbie/HotWheels, 1995, Barbie, any except Afro-American Lifeguard Barbie & under age 3, ea **$3.00**
Barbie/Mini Streex, 1991, Barbie, any except under age 3, ea .. **$3.00**
Barbie/Mini Streex, 1992, Barbie, under age 3, Sparkle Eyes **$4.00**
Barbie/Mini Streex, 1992, Mini Streex, any except under age 3 .... **$2.00**
Barbie/Mini Streex, 1992, Mini Streex, under age 3, Orange Arrow **$4.00**
Barnyard (Old McDonald's Farm), 1986, 6 different, ea **$8.00**
Batman, 1992, 6 different, ea **$3.00**
Batman (Animated), 1993, any except under age 3, ea **$3.00**
Batman (Animated), 1993, under age 3, Batman **$4.00**
Beanie Babies, 1996, any except Pinky the Flamingo, from $8 to **$15.00**
Beanie Babies, 1996, Pinky the Flamingo, from $15 to **$25.00**
Bedtime, 1989, drinking cup, M **$3.00**
Bedtime, 1989, Ronald, set of 4, M, ea **$3.00**
Bedtime, 1989, wash mitt, bl foam **$5.00**
Berenstain Bears, 1987, any except under age 3, ea **$5.00**
Berenstain Bears, 1987, under age 3, Mama or Papa w/paper punchouts, ea **$8.00**
Boats & Floats, 1987, Fry Kids raft or McNuggets lifeboat, w/separate sticker sheet, ea, from $8 to **$10.00**
Cabbage Patch Kids/Tonka Trucks, 1992, Cabbage Patch Kids, any except under age 3, ea **$2.00**
Cabbage Patch Kids/Tonka Trucks, 1992, Tonka Trucks, under age 3, dump truck **$4.00**
Changeables, 1987, 6 different, ea **$5.00**
Chip 'N Dale Rescue Rangers, 1989, 4 different, ea **$4.00**
Circus Parade, 1991, ea **$5.00**
COSMc Crayola, 1988, under age 3, So Big, w/2 crayons & activity sheet **$5.00**
Crayola Stencils, 1987, any except under age 3, ea **$2.00**
Crayola Stencils, 1987, under age 3, Ronald **$6.00**
Crazy Creatures w/Popoids, 1985, 4 different, ea **$5.00**
Dink the Little Dinosaur, 1990, Regional, 6 different, M, ea .. **$5.00**
Dinosaur Days, 1981, 6 different, ea **$2.00**
Disney Favorites, 1987, activity book, Sword & the Stone ... **$5.00**
Disneyland — 40 Years of Adventures, 1995, ea **$3.00**
Ducktails, 1987, ea from $5 to **$6.00**
Ducktails II, 1988, launch pad in airport **$5.00**
Ducktails II, 1988, Scrooge McDuck in Car or Huey, Louie & Dewey on surf ski, ea **$7.00**
Ducktails II, 1988, Webby on tricycle **$8.00**
Fast Mac II, 1985, wht squad car, pk cruiser, red sports car or yel jeep, ea **$5.00**
Feeling Good, 1985, comb, Captain, red **$2.00**
Feeling Good, 1985, Fry Guy on duck **$4.00**
Feeling Good, 1985, mirror, Birdie **$3.00**
Feeling Good, 1985, soap dish, Grimace **$5.00**
Feeling Good, 1985, under age 3, Grimage in tub **$4.00**
Flintstone Kids, 1988, any except under age 3, ea **$8.00**
Flintstone Kids, 1988, under age 3, Dino **$12.00**
Friendly Skies, 1991, Ronald or Grimace, ea **$8.00**
Friendly Skies, 1994, United hangar w/Ronald in plane .. **$10.00**
Fun w/Food, 1989, ea **$10.00**
Funny Fry Friends, 1989, any except under age 3, ea **$2.00**
Funny Fry Friends, 1989, under age 3, Little Darling or Lil' Chief, ea **$6.00**
Ghostbusters, 1987, pencil case, Containment Chamber ... **$5.00**
Ghostbusters, 1987, pencil sharpener, ghost **$3.00**
Gravedale High, 1991, Regional, 5 different, ea **$5.00**
Halloween (What Am I Going To Be), 1995, any except under age 3, ea **$3.00**
Halloween (What Am I Going To Be), 1995, under age 3, Grimace in pumpkin **$4.00**
Halloween McNuggets, 1993, any except under age 3, ea .. **$3.00**
Halloween McNuggets, 1993, under age 3, McBoo McNugget **$4.00**
Happy Birthday 15 Years, 1994, any except Tonka or Muppet Babies, ea from $3 to **$5.00**
Happy Birthday 15 Years, 1994, Muppet Babies #11 train pc ... **$8.00**
Happy Birthday 15 Years, 1994, Tonka #7 train pc, from $10 to **$15.00**
Happy Pail, 1986, 5 different, M, ea **$5.00**
Hook, 1997, 4 different, ea **$3.00**
Jungle Book, 1989, set of 4, MIP **$15.00**
Jungle Book, 1990, under age 3, Junior or Mowgli, ea **$9.00**
Lego Building Set, 1986, helicopter or airplane, ea **$3.00**

Lego Building Set, 1986, race car or tanker boat, ea..........$6.00
Lego Motion, 1989, any except under age 3, ea................$5.00
Lego Motion, 1989, under age 3, Giddy Gator or Tuttle Turtle, ea..........$6.00
Little Gardener, 1989, Birdie shovel, Fry Kids planter, Grimace rake or Ronald water can, ea..........$2.00
Little Golden Book, 1982, 5 different, M, ea..........$3.00
Little Mermaid, 1989, 4 different, ea..........$5.00
Littlest Pet Shop/Transformers, 1996, any except under age 3, ea..........$3.00
Littlest Pet Shop/Transformers, 1996, under age 3, ea........$4.00
Looney Tunes Quack-Up Cars, 1993, 4 different, ea..........$2.00

Photo courtesy Mary Jane Lamphier

Mac Tonight, 1988, $6.00 each.

Mac Tonight, 1988, surf ski w/wheels..........$8.00
Mac Tonight, 1988, under age 3, skateboard..........$8.00
Marvel Super Heroes, 1996, any except under age 3, ea.....$3.00
Marvel Super Heroes, 1996, under age 3..........$4.00
McDino Changeables, 1991, any except under age 3, ea....$3.00
McDino Changeables, 1991, under age 3, Bronto Cheesburger or Small Fry Ceratops, ea..........$4.00
McDonaldland Band, 1986, Fry Kid Trumpet, Pan Pipes or Grimace Saxaphone, ea..........$3.00
McDonaldland Band, 1986, Hamburglar siren whistle, Ronald train whistle or Fry Guy boat whistle, M, ea..........$1.00
McDonaldland Band, 1986, Ronald harmonica..........$5.00
McDonaldland Dough, 1990, M, ea..........$5.00
McNugget Buddies, 1988, any except Corny w/red popcorn belt or Cowpoke w/scarf, ea..........$2.00
McNugget Buddies, 1988, Corny w/red popcorn belt or Cowpoke w/scarf, ea..........$4.00
Mickey's Birthdayland, 1988, any except under age 3, ea...$2.00
Mickey's Birthdayland, 1988, under age 3..........$6.00
Mix 'Em Up Monsters, 1989, Bibble, Corkle, Gropple or Thugger, ea..........$3.00
Moveables, 1988, any except Ronald, M, ea..........$8.00
Moveables, 1988, Ronald, M..........$9.00
Muppet Treasure Island, 1996, tub toys, any except under age 3, ea..........$3.00
Muppet Treasure Island, 1996, under age 3, book for bath.$4.00
Muppet Workshop, 1995, ea..........$2.00
Music — Mie, 1985, 4 different, M, ea..........$7.00
Mystery of the Lost Arches, 1992, Magic Lens Camera (recalled).$4.00
Mystery of the Lost Arches, 1992, micro-cassette/magnifyer, phone/periscope or flashlight/telescope, ea..........$3.00

Photo courtesy Martin and Carolyn Berens

New Archies, 1988, $6.00 each.

New Food Changeables, 1989, any except under age 3, ea.$2.00
New Food Changeables, 1989, under age 3, Pals Changeable Cube..........$4.00
Oliver & Co, 1988, 4 different, M, ea..........$2.00
Peanuts, 1990, any except under age 3, ea..........$3.00
Peanuts, 1990, under age 3, Charlie Brown egg basket or Snoopy's potato sack, ea..........$5.00
Piggsburg Piggs, 1991, Regional, 4 different, ea..........$5.00
Polly Pocket/Attack Pack, 1995, any except under age 3, ea..$2.00
Polly Pocket/Attack Pack, 1995, under age 3, ea..........$3.00
Potato Heads, 1992, 8 different, ea..........$4.00
Power Rangers, 1995, any except under age 3, ea..........$3.00
Power Rangers, 1995, under age 3..........$4.00
Rescuers Down Under, 1990, any except under age 3, ea...$1.00
Rescuers Down Under, 1990, under age 3, Bernard in cheese..$3.00
Runaway Robots, 1987, 6 different, M, ea..........$3.00
Safari Adventure, 1980, cookie molds, Ronald or Grimace, red or yel, M, ea..........$3.00
Safari Adventure, 1980, sponge, Ronald sitting cross-legged, M..........$5.00
School Days, 1984, eraser, Birdie or Grimace, M, ea..........$3.00
School Days, 1984, pencil, Grimace, Ronald or Hamburglar, M, ea..........$3.00
School Days, 1984, pencil sharpener, Grimace or Ronald, M, ea..........$3.00
School Days, 1984, ruler, M..........$4.00
School Days, 1985, pencil case, clear..........$6.00
Sea World of Texas, 1988, 4 different, M, ea..........$10.00
Snow White & the Seven Dwarfs, 1993, any except under age 3, ea..........$3.00
Snow White & the Seven Dwarfs, 1993, under age 3, Dopey or Sneezy, ea..........$4.00
Space Rescue, 1995, any except under age 3, ea..........$3.00
Space Rescue, 1995, under age 3, Astro Viewer..........$4.00
Spider-Man, 1995, any except under age 3, ea..........$3.00
Spider-Man, 1995, under age 3..........$4.00

Photo courtesy Mary Jane Lamphier

Sports Balls, 1990, $3.00 each.

Stomper Mini 4x4, 1986, 15 different, M, ea..........$8.00
Super Looney Tunes, 1991, any except under age 3, ea......$3.00

McDonald's, Star Trek, 1979, from $5.00 to $6.00 each.

Super Looney Tunes, 1991, under age 3, Daffy Duck as Bat Duck, ea $4.00
Super Mario Brothers, 1990, any except under age 3, ea $3.00
Super Mario Brothers, 1990, under age 3, Super Mario $4.00
Tale Spin, 1990, any except under age 3, ea $3.00
Tale Spin, 1990, under age 3, Baloo's Seaplane or Wildcat's Flying Machine, ea....................$4.00
Totally Toy Holiday, 1995, any except under age 3, ea from $3 to $4.00
Totally Toy Holiday, 1995, under age 3, ea from $4 to.......$5.00
Totally Toys, 1993, any except Magic Nursery (boy) or under age 3, ea....................$2.00
Totally Toys, 1993, under age 3, Key Force car..................$3.00
Totally Toys, 1993, under age 3, Magic Nursery (boy or girl), ea from $5 to....................$6.00
Turbo Macs, 1988, any except under age 3, M, ea $4.00
Turbo Macs, 1988, under age 3, Ronald in soft rubber car, M.....$6.00
VR Troopers, 1996, any except under age 3, ea $3.00
VR Troopers, 1996, under age 3 ....$4.00
Water Games, 1992, ea $4.00
Wild Friends, 1992, Regional, any except under age 3, ea..$4.00
Winter Worlds, 1983, ornament, Birdie or Mayor McCheese, M, ea $8.00
Winter Worlds, 1983, ornament, Grimace or Hamburglar, M, ea $6.00
Winter Worlds, 1983, ornament, Ronald McDonald, M....$3.00
Young Astronauts, 1992, any except under age 3, ea $2.00
Young Astronauts, 1992, under age 3, Ronald in lunar rover..$4.00
Zoo Face, 1988, 4 different, ea $4.00
101 Dalmatians, 1991, 4 different, ea $4.00

Pizza Hut

Air Garfield, kite, 1993 ....$6.00
Air Garfield, parachute, 1993 ....$8.00
Beauty & the Beast, 1992, hand puppets, 4 different, ea $4.00
Brain Thaws, 4 different, 1995, ea $4.00
Eureeka's Castle, 1990, hand puppets, 3 different, ea..........$5.00
Land Before Time, 1988, hand puppet, Cara, Littlefoot, Spike or Duckie, ea....................$5.00
Land Before Time, 1988, hand puppet, Sharptooth............$8.00
Marvel Comics, 4 different, 1994, ea $4.00
Mascot Misfits, 4 different, 1995, ea $4.00
Pagemaster, 4 different, 1994, ea $4.00
Squirt Toons, 5 different, 1995, ea $5.00
Universal Monsters, 1991, hologram cards, 3 different, ea .$5.00

Sonic

Airtoads, 6 different, ea....................$4.00
All-Star Mini-Baseballs, 1995, 5 different, ea $4.00
Animal Straws, 1995, 4 different, ea $3.00
Bone-A-Fide Friends, 1994, 4 different, ea....................$3.00
Brown Bag Bowlers, 1994, 4 different, ea $5.00
Brown Bag Buddies, 1993, 3 different, ea $4.00
Brown Bag Juniors, 1989, 4 different, ea....................$5.00
Creepy Strawlers, 1995, 4 different, ea $5.00
Flippin' Food, 1995, 3 different, ea $3.00
Food Train, 1995, set of 7 cars w/engine $22.00
Go Wild Balls, 1995, 4 different, ea $3.00
Holiday Kids, 1994, 4 different, ea....................$4.00
Monster Peepers, 1994, 4 different, ea....................$3.00
Shoe Biters, 1995, 4 different, ea $5.00
Squishers, 1995, 4 different, ea $5.00
Super Sonic Racers, 1995, 4 different, ea $3.00
Totem Pal Squirters, 1995, 4 different, ea $5.00
Very Fast Food, 1996, 4 different, ea $4.00
Wacky Sackers, 1994, set of 6....................$20.00

Subway

Battle Balls, 1995-96, 4 different, ea....................$3.00
Bobby's World, 1995, 4 different, ea....................$4.00
Bump in the Night, 1995, 4 different, ea....................$5.00
Cone Heads, 1993, 4 different, ea....................$4.00
Explore Space, 1994, 4 different, ea....................$4.00
Hackeysack Balls, 1991, 5 different, ea....................$4.00
Hurricanes, 1994, 4 different, ea....................$4.00
Inspector Gadget, 1994, 4 different, ea....................$4.00
Monkey Trouble, 1994, 5 different, ea $3.00
Santa Claus, 1994, any except under age 3, ea....................$4.00
Santa Claus, 1994, under age 3, Comet the Reindeer.........$5.00
Save the Wildlife, 1995, 4 different, ea $3.00
Tale Tale, 1995, any except under age 3, ea....................$4.00
Tale Tale, 1995, under age 3, Bunyon & Babe the Blue Ox .$5.00
Tom & Jerry, 1995, 4 different, ea....................$3.00

Taco Bell

Congo, 1995, watches, 3 different, ea....................$5.00
Happy Talk Sprites, Spark, Twinkle or Romeo, 1983, plush, ea $6.00
Hugga Bunch, Fluffer, Gigglet or Tuggins, 1984, plush, ea..$8.00
Mask, 1995, It's Party Time switchplate or Milo w/mask, ea..$4.00
Pebble & the Penguin, 1995, 3 different, ea....................$5.00

The Tick, 1995, finger puppet, Arthur Wall Climber or Thrakkorzog, ea....$4.00
The Tick, 1996, Arthur w/wings or Sewer Urchin, ea....$4.00

Target Markets

Adventure Team Window Walkers, 1994-95, 4 different, ea .$4.00
Muppet Twisters, 1994, 3 different, ea $4.00
Olympic Sports Weiner Pack, 1996, figures, 4 different, ea .$4.00
Roll-O-Fun Coloring Kit, 1995, 3 different, ea....$4.00
Targeteers, 1992, 5 different, ea....$5.00
Targeteers, 1994, 5 different, rooted hair, ea....$4.00

Wendy's

Alf Tales, 1990, 6 different, ea....$2.00
All Dogs Go To Heaven, 1989, 6 different, M, ea $2.00
Animalinks, 1995, 1995, 6 different, ea $2.00
Ballsasaurus, 1992, 4 different, ea $4.00
Cybercycles, 1994, 4 different, ea $3.00
Definitely Dinosaurs, 1988, 4 different, ea $4.00
Definitely Dinosaurs, 1989, 5 different, ea $4.00
Dino Games, 1993, 3 different, ea $3.00
Endangered Animal Games, 1993, any except under age 3, ea....$2.00
Endangered Animal Games, 1993, under age 3, elephant puzzle $3.00
Fast Food Racers, 1990, 6 different, ea $3.00
Felix the Cat, 1990, plush figure....$2.00
Felix the Cat, 1990, Story Board, Zeotrope, Milk Cap set or Ask Felix toy, ea....$3.00
Felix the Cat, 1990, under age 3, rub-on set....$4.00
Furskins Bears, 1986, 4 different, plush, M, ea $6.00
Gear Up, 1992, handlebar streamers or Back-Off license plate, ea....$2.00
Glo-Ahead, 1993, any except under age 3, ea....$2.00
Glo-Ahead, 1993, under age 3, finger puppet $3.00
Glofriends, 1989, 9 different, M, ea....$2.00
Gobots, 1986, Odd Ball/Monster, M $8.00
Jetsons Space Vehicles, 1989, 6 different, ea....$5.00
Jetsons: The Movie, 1990, 5 different, ea $3.00
Mega Wheels, any except under age 3, 1995, M, ea....$2.00
Mega Wheels, under age 3, circus wagon, 1995, M....$3.00
Mighty Mouse, 1989, 6 different, ea $4.00
Potato Head II, 1988, 5 different, M, ea $4.00
Rocket Writers, 1992, 4 different, ea....$2.00
Speed Bumpers, 1992, any except under age 3, ea $2.00
Speed Bumpers, 1992, under age 3, Truck Speed Roller....$3.00
Speed Writers, 1991, any except under age 3, ea $3.00
Speed Writers, 1991, under age 3, paint w/water book $4.00
Tecno Cows, 1995, any except under age 3, ea....$2.00
Tecno Cows, 1995, under age 3, Diamond tow truck $3.00
Too Cool! For School, 1992, pencil bat or gr pickle pen, ea ..$3.00
Wacky Windups, 1991, 5 different, ea....$4.00
Weird Writers, 1991, 3 different, M, ea....$2.00
World of Teddy Ruxpin, 1987, 5 different, ea from $3 to ...$4.00
World Wild Life, 1988, books, 4 different, ea $4.00
World Wild Life, 1988, plush figures, 4 different, ea....$5.00
Write & Sniff, 1994, any except under age 3, ea....$2.00
Write & Sniff, 1994, under age 3, stencil set $3.00
Yogi Bear & Friends, 1990, 6 different, ea....$3.00

White Castle

Bow Biters, 1989, Blue Meany....$5.00
Camp White Castle, 1990, fork & spoon, ea....$4.00
Castle Dude Squirters, 1994, 3 different, ea $3.00
Castle Meal Friends, 1991, Wendell, Princess or Woofles, ea ..$9.00
Castleburger Dudes, 1991, 4 different, ea $6.00
Castleburger Friends, 1989, 6 different, ea $5.00
Fat Albert & the Cosby Kids, 1990, 4 different, ea....$10.00
Glow-in-the-Dark Monsters, 1992, 3 different, ea $4.00
Holiday Huggables, 1990, 3 different, ea $6.00
Super Balls, 1994, 3 different, ea $5.00

Boxes and Bags

Burger King, Bone Age, Fairy Tales Cassettes or Tricy Treaters, 1989, ea from $6 to $7.00
Burger King, Critter Carton/Punch-Out Paper Masks, 1989, ea....$18.00
Burger King, Trak-Pak, 1988, ea....$8.00
Hardee's, Cruisin' Back to School or Muppet Christmas Carol, 1993, ea $2.00
Hardee's, Days of Thunder, Fender Bender 500 Racers, Marvel Super Heroes or Squirters, 1990, ea....$2.00
Hardee's, Eureka's Castle, Micro Soakers or Swan Princess, 1994, ea $1.00
Hardee's, Little Golden Books, 1987, ea $4.00
McDonald's, Amazing Wildlife, Barbie/Hot Wheels, Muppet Workshop, Power Rangers, Space Rescue or Toy Holiday, 1995, ea $1.00
McDonald's, Animaniacs, Bobby's World, Happy Birthday 15 Years, Making Movies or Mickey & Friends Epcot, 1994, ea $1.00
McDonald's, Back to the Future, Crayon Squeeze Bottle, Wild Friends or Yo-Yogi, 1992, ea from $2 to $3.00
McDonald's, Barbie/Hot Wheels, Gravedale High, Hook, Muppet Babies, Tiny Toons or 101 Dalmatians, 1991, ea from $2 to $3.00
McDonald's, Barbie/Mini Streex, Batman or Tiny Toon Adventures, 1992, ea from $1 to $2.00
McDonald's, Batman, Dino Dinosaurs, Field Trip, Halloween McNugget Buddies or Looney Tunes Quack-Up Cars, 1993, ea $1.00
McDonald's, Beach Toy, Jungle Book, Peanuts, Rescuers Down Under, Super Mario, Tale Spin or Valentine, 1990, ea from $2 to $3.00
McDonald's, Chip 'N' Dale Rescue Rangers, Garfield, Little Mermaid or Mickey's Birthdayland, 1989, ea from $3 to $4.00
McDonald's, Dink the Dinosaur, 1990....$10.00
McDonald's, Ducktails II, Fraggle Rock, Mac Tonight, McNugget Buddies, Oliver & Co or Zoo Face, 1988, ea from $4 to $5.00
McDonald's, Fry Benders or Sportsball, 1990, ea $5.00
McDonald's, Good Friends or Real Ghostbusters, 1987, ea ..$5.00

McDonald's, Happy Meal Workshop, Marvel, Masterpiece Home Video or Muppet Treasure Island, 1996, ea.......$1.00
McDonald's, Raggedy Ann Schoolhouse, 1989..................$5.00
McDonald's, Rain or Shine (no toys produced to match boxes), 1989, ea..$5.00
McDonald's, Snow White & the Seven Dwarfs, 1993........$3.00
Wendy's, Carmen Sandiego Code Cracker, 1994, ea..........$2.00
Wendy's, Fast Food Racers, Jetsons: The Movie, Micro Machines Super Sky Carrier or Yogi Bear, 1990, ea.....$4.00
Wendy's, Rhyme Time, Weather Watch or Wizard of Wonders, 1991, ea..$2.00
Wendy's, Wendy & the Good Stuff Gang, 1989, ea...........$3.00

Foreign

Burger King, Beauty & the Beast, 1992, set of 4, from $45 to..$55.00
Burger King, Cinderella, 1994, set of 3.............................$40.00
Burger King, Flintstones, 1994, set of 4............................$40.00
Burger King, Snow White, 1995, set of 4..........................$25.00
Burger King, X-Men, 1996, set of 4..................................$30.00
Burger King (England), Peter Pan, set of 5........................$35.00
Burger King (England), Robin Hood, 1993, set of 5.........$25.00
Burger King (England), Taz-Mania Crazies, 1994, set of 4.$20.00
Burger King (England), Tiny Toon Adventures, 1995, set of 4...$25.00
Burger King (England), Tom & Jerry, 1995, set of 4.........$25.00
McDonald's, Aristocrats, 1993, set of 4...........................$20.00
McDonald's, Dinosaurs, 1995, set of 4..............................$25.00
McDonald's, Hunchback of Notre Dame, 1994, set of 4 w/boxes..$35.00
McDonald's, Island Getaway, 1966, set of 4 w/boxes........$25.00
McDonald's, McFarm, 1995, set of 4 w/boxes..................$30.00
McDonald's, McRodeo, 1995, set of 4 w/boxes................$25.00
McDonald's, Pocahontas, 1996, set of 4 w/boxes.............$30.00
McDonald's, Toy Story, 1996, set of 4 w/boxes................$35.00
McDonald's, Winter Sports, 1995, set of 4.......................$25.00
McDonald's (Australia), Aladdin Straw Grippers, 1994, set of 4...$20.00
McDonald's (Australia), Batman Flicker Badges, 1995, set of 4...$15.00
McDonald's (Australia), Dark Wing Duck, 1994, set of 4.$20.00
McDonald's (Australia), Flintstone Stationary Series, 1994, set of 4...$20.00
McDonald's (Australia), Lion King stampers, 1995, set of 4....$15.00
McDonald's (Australia), McSports, 1995, set of 4...........$25.00
McDonald's (Australia), Pocahontas finger puppets, 1995, set of 4...$25.00
McDonald's (Australia), Summer Fun Toys, 1995, set of 4..$15.00
McDonald's (Australia), Winnie the Pooh cups, 1995, set of 4...$25.00
McDonald's (Australia), World Cup, 1994, set of 4.........$20.00
McDonald's (Australia), Zoomballs, 1995, set of 4...........$15.00
McDonald's (Australia), 101 Dalmatians, 1995, set of 4..$25.00
McDonald's (European), Airport, 1995, set of 4 w/boxes.$25.00
McDonald's (European), Aladdin, 1994, set of 4.............$25.00
McDonald's (European), Barbie, 1995, set of 4 w/boxes...$30.00
McDonald's (European), Connect-A-Car, 1991, set of 4.$20.00
McDonald's (European), Disneyland Paris, 1996, set of 4..$30.00
McDonald's (European), Euro Disney, 1992, set of 4.......$35.00
McDonald's (European), Flintstones, 1994, set of 4 w/boxes...$25.00
McDonald's (European), Fly & Drive, 1995, set of 4........$25.00
McDonald's (European), I Like Bikes, 1994, set of 4........$20.00
McDonald's (European), Kapt'n Baloo, 1993, set of 4......$20.00
McDonald's (European), Lion King, 1994, set of 4 puzzles...$25.00
McDonald's (European), McDonald's Band, 1993, set of 4 w/ups w/boxes..$25.00
McDonald's (Japan), Snoopy, 1996, set of 4....................$45.00
McDonald's (New Zealand), Batman Forever 3-D pop-up cards, 1995, set of 4..$20.00
McDonald's (New Zealand), Disney Fun Riders, 1994, set of 4...$25.00
McDonald's (New Zealand), Mystery Riders, 1993, set of 4..$20.00

Miscellaneous

This section lists items other than those that are free with kids' meals, for instance, store displays and memorabilia such as Christmas ornaments and plush dolls that can be purchased at the counter.

Burger King, doll, Magic King, Knickerbocker, 1980, complete w/magic scarf, 20", EX, F8..$35.00
Burger King, doll, Magic King, Knickerbocker, 1980, 20", MIB, M17..$65.00
Burger King, pencil pouch, ADI, 1982, w/ruler, eraser & sharpener, EX, D9..$12.00
Burger King, puppets, Toy Story, set of 4, MIP, J8...........$40.00
Chuck E Cheese, bank, 8", NM, B10.................................$6.00
Hardee's, backpack, orange, MIP.......................................$5.00
Hardee's, frisbee, yel letters on wht, 5", EX........................$5.00

Hardee's, Pound Puppy, MIB, $5.00.

Hardee's, rag doll, Gilbert Giddy Up, 15", EX, H4..........$15.00

Jack-in-the-Box, doll, Meatsa Meatsa Man, 1990, 5", EX...**$3.00**
Little Caesar's, doll, stuffed cloth, 6", H4........................**$15.00**
Long John Silver's, paint book, Adventure on Volcano Island, M...**$5.00**
McDonald's, Birthday Book, 1983, w/Ronald punch-out, M, C11...**$12.00**
McDonald's, birthday hat, 1978, w/Ronald, M, C11........**$12.00**
McDonald's, birthday hat, 1983, w/Ronald & Grimace, M, C11...**$8.00**
McDonald's, board game, Milton Bradley, 1975, VG (VG box), F8...**$25.00**
McDonald's, coloring board, Christmas, 1983, w/Ronald, Grimace & Hamburglar, M, C11.....................................**$8.00**
McDonald's, coloring board, 1981, w/Ronald, Grimace, Hamburglar & Birdie, M, C11...**$15.00**
McDonald's, coloring calendar, 1980, EX, from $8 to......**$12.00**

McDonald's, doll, Mayor, 1970s, stuffed cloth, 15", from $40.00 to $50.00.

McDonald's, display, Berenstain Bears, 1987, EX, from $65 to..**$85.00**
McDonald's, display, Halloween Nuggets, 1996, M, C11.**$25.00**
McDonald's, display, Jungle Book, w/plastic dome, M, C11 .**$85.00**
McDonald's, display, Mac Tonight, 1990, EX, from $75 to ..**$95.00**
McDonald's, display, New Food Changeables, 1989, EX, from $50 to...**$60.00**
McDonald's, display, Oliver & Co, 1988, EX, from $50 to..**$70.00**
McDonald's, display, Space Jam, M, C11.........................**$65.00**
McDonald's, display, Tiny Toons, 1991, EX, from $35 to ..**$50.00**
McDonald's, display, 101 Dalmatians, 1992, w/plastic dome, M, C11...**$100.00**

McDonald's, doll, Big Mac, early 1970s, stuffed cloth, 15", MIB...**$40.00**
McDonald's, doll, Big Mac, Remco, 1976, plastic w/cloth clothes, knob in back for head movement, EX, from $25 to...**$35.00**
McDonald's, doll, Fry Guy, 1987, stuffed cloth, 12", EX ..**$10.00**
McDonald's, doll, Grimace, Remco, 1976, plush fleece w/vinyl feet, knob in back for head movement, EX, from $25 to........**$35.00**
McDonald's, doll, Grimace, 1988, stuffed cloth, dressed as baseball player, 12", EX, from $5 to................................**$10.00**
McDonald's, doll, Hamburglar, 1970s, stuffed cloth, 1st version w/purple stripes, 15", MIB..**$40.00**
McDonald's, doll, Ronald McDonald, 1971, stuffed cloth, 17", EX...**$20.00**
McDonald's, doll, Ronald McDonald, 1978, inflatable, 37", EX...**$8.00**
McDonald's, growth chart, 1984, M, C11..........................**$8.00**
McDonald's, hand puppets, Grimace, Ronald or Hamburglar, cloth w/vinyl heads, MIB, ea.......................................**$15.00**
McDonald's, hat, cloth w/image of balloons & I Had My Party At McDonald's, EX...**$5.00**
McDonald's, kite, Movin' On-Movin' Up, M, C11 ....**$8.00**
McDonald's, mask, Ronald, paper punch-out, M.............**$75.00**
McDonald's, McDonaldland Picnic, 1981, only 500 produced, M, C11...**$100.00**
McDonald's, photo cube, 1981, w/Ronald, Grimace, Hamburglar & Birdie, M, C11...**$10.00**
McDonald's, place mats, 1970s, Remember Your Manners, 4 pcs, M, C11...**$20.00**
McDonald's, ring toss game, 1978, M, C11........................**$8.00**
McDonald's, sidewalk chalk in french fry box, M (sealed) .**$5.00**

McDonald's, stop watch, plastic, EX, $2.00.

McDonald's, suitcase, 1980, McKids, red w/image of Birdie & Hamburglar on bike, 10x15½", EX, from $20 to **$25.00**
McDonald's, sweater, 1976, embroidered image of Ronald McDonald, rare, NM, P12 ....**$125.00**
McDonald's, translite, Camp McDonaldland, 14x14", M, C11 ....**$10.00**
McDonald's, translite, Chip & Dale, 22x22", M, C11......**$15.00**
McDonald's, translite, Discover the Rain Forest, 22x22", M, C11 ....**$10.00**
McDonald's, translite, Muppet Workshop, 14x14", M, C11.**$8.00**
McDonald's, translite, Sleeping Beauty, 14x14, M, C11 ..**$12.00**
McDonald's, translite, 101 Dalmatians, 22x22", M, C11 .**$15.00**
McDonald's, yo-yo, bl or red w/logo, EX, ea from $4 to......**$7.00**
Pizza Hut, kite, Garfield, MIP, B5 ....**$15.00**

Fisher-Price

Fisher-Price toys are becoming one of the hottest new trends in the collector's market place today. In 1930 Herman Fisher, backed by Irving Price, Elbert Hubbard, and Helen Schelle, formed one of the most successful toy companies ever to exist. Located in East Aurora, New York, the company has seen many changes since then, the most notable being the changes in ownership. From 1930 to 1968, it was owned by the individuals mentioned previously and a few stockholders. In 1969 it became an aquisition of Quaker Oats, and in June of 1991 it became independently owned. In November of 1993, one of the biggest sell-outs in the toy industry took place: Fisher-Price became a division of Mattel.

There are a few things to keep in mind when collecting Fisher-Price toys. You should count on a little edge wear as well as some wear and fading to the paint. Unless noted otherwise, the prices in the listings are for toys in very good condition. Pull toys found in mint condition are truly rare and command a much higher value, especially if you find one with its original box. This also applies to playsets, but to command the higher prices, they must also be complete, with no chew/teeth marks or plastic fading, and with all pieces present. Another very important rule to remember is there are no standard colors for pieces that came with a playset. Fisher-Price often substituted a piece of a different color when they ran short. Please note that dates on the toys indicate their **copyright date and not the date they were manufactured.**

The company put much time and thought into designing their toys. They took care to operate by their five-point creed: to make toys with (1) intrinsic play value, (2) ingenuity, (3) strong construction, (4) good value for the money, and (5) action. Some of the most sought-after pull toys are those bearing the Walt Disney logo.

The ToyFest limited editions are a series of toys produced in conjunction with ToyFest, an annual weekend of festivities for young and old alike held in East Aurora, New York. It is sponsored by the Toy Town USA Museum and is held every year in August. Fisher-Price produces a limited-edition toy for this event; these are listed at the end of this category. (For more information on ToyFest and the museum, write to Toy Town Museum, P.O. Box 238, East Aurora, NY 14052; see display ad this section.) For more information on Fisher-Price toys we recommend *Fisher-Price, A Historical Rarity Value Guide*, by John J. Murray and Bruce R. Fox; and *A Pictorial Price Guide to the More Popular Fisher-Price Toys, 1931 – 1990*, by Brad Cassity and Gary Combs. (Available from the author; contact Mr. Cassity for ordering information.)

Additional information may be obtained through the Fisher-Price Collectors' Club who publish a quarterly newsletter; their address may be found in their display ad (this section) and in the Directory under Clubs, Newsletters, and Other Publications.

Advisor: Brad Cassity (C13). (Brad asks that he be allowed to thank his wife and three daughters, his brother Beau, Jeanne Kennedy, and Deanna Korth, all of whom he feels have been very instrumental in his life and hold a special place in his heart.)

Note: Collectors should be aware that since our last edition, values for Fisher-Price toys have decreased 15% on the overall average. Prices listed below are for examples that show only a little edge and paint wear and minimal fading (VG).

Other Sources: J2, J6, N2, O1, S20, T1

See also Dollhouse Furniture; Dollhouses.

#0005 Bunny Cart, 1948, C13 ....**$70.00**
#0006 Ducky Cart, 1948, C13 ....**$70.00**
#0007 Doggy Racer, 1942, C13 ....**$200.00**
#0007 Looky Fire Truck, 1950, C13.............................**$100.00**
#0008 Bouncy Racer, 1960, C13 ....**$40.00**
#0010 Bunny Cart, 1940, C13...**$75.00**
#0012 Bunny Truck, 1941, C13 ....**$75.00**
#0015 Bunny Cart, 1946, C13...**$70.00**
#0016 Ducky Cart, 1946, C13...**$70.00**
#0020 Animal Cutouts, 1942, duck, elephant, pony or Scotty dog, C13, ea **$50.00**
#0028 Bunny Egg Cart, 1950, C13 ....**$75.00**
#0050 Bunny Chick Tandem Cart, C13 ....**$100.00**
#0075 Baby Duck Tandem Cart, 1953, no number on toy, C13 ....**$100.00**
#0100 Dr Doodle, 1931, C13..**$800.00**
#0100 Dr Doodle, 1995, 1st Fisher-Price limited edition of 5,000, C13 ....**$125.00**
#0100 Musical Sweeper, 1950, plays Whistle While You Work, C13 ....**$175.00**
#0101 Granny Doodle, 1931, C13 ....**$800.00**
#0102 Drumming Bear, 1931, C13.................................**$700.00**
#0102 Drumming Bear, 1932, fatter & taller version, C13....**$700.00**
#0103 Barky Puppy, 1931, C13 ....**$700.00**
#0104 Looky Monk, 1931, C13..**$700.00**
#0105 Bunny Scout, 1931, C13..**$700.00**
#0107 Music Box Clock Radio, 1971, plays Hickory Dickory Dock **$5.00**
#0109 Lucky Monk, 1932, C13 ....**$700.00**
#0110 Chubby Chief, 1932, C13......................................**$700.00**
#0111 Play Family Merry-Go-Round, 1972-76, plays Skater's Waltz, w/4 figures, C13 ....**$40.00**
#0112 Picture Disk Camera, 1968-71, w/5 picture disks, C13...**$40.00**
#0114 Music Box TV, 1967, plays London Bridge & Row Row Row Your Boat as picture passes screen, C13............**$10.00**

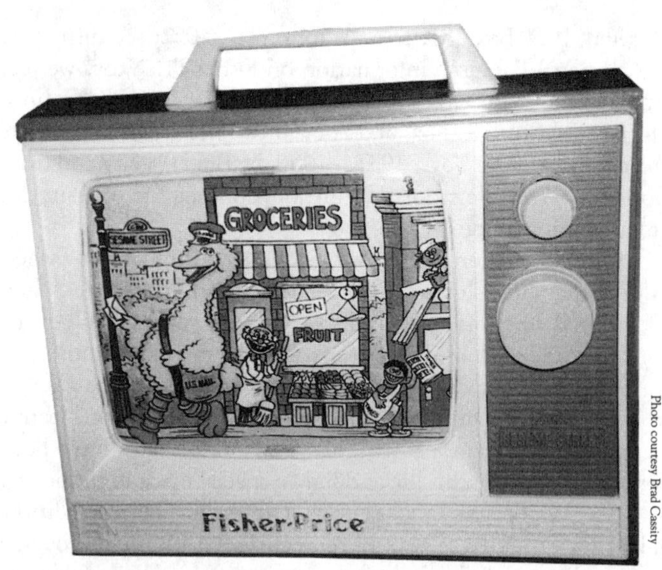

Photo courtesy Brad Cassity

#0114 Sesame Street Music Box TV, 1984 – 87, plays People in Your Neighborhood, C13, $10.00.

#0118 Tumble Tower Game, 1972-75, w/10 marbles, C13..$10.00
#0120 Cackling Hen, 1958, wht, C13..............................$40.00

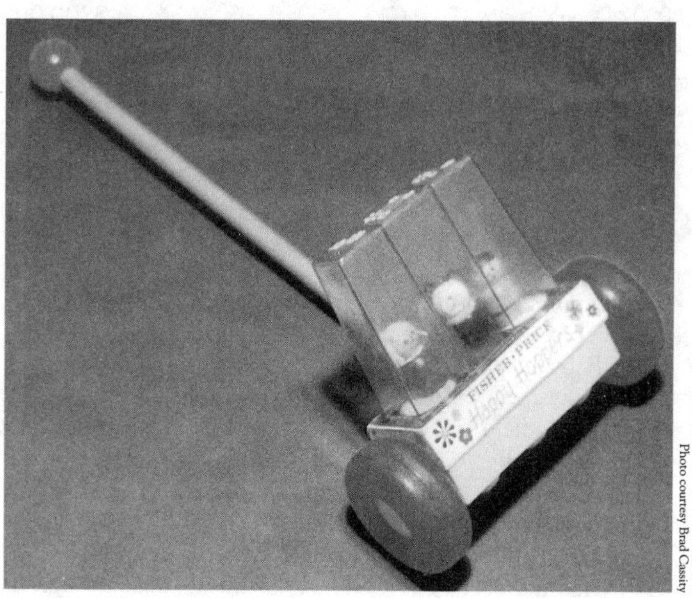

Photo courtesy Brad Cassity

#0121 Happy Hoppers, 1969 – 76, C13, $25.00.

#0122 Bouncing Buggy, 1974-79, 6 wheels, C13 ....$10.00
#0123 Cackling Hen, 1967, red litho, C13 ....$40.00
#0125 Uncle Tommy Turle, 1956, red shell, C13 ....$100.00
#0130 Wobbles, 1964-65, dog wobbles when pulled, C13..$50.00
#0131 Milk Wagon, 1964, truck w/bottle carrier, C13 .....$55.00
#0131 Toy Wagon, 1951, driver's head pops up & down when pulled by 2 musical horses, C13 ....$250.00
#0132 Dr Doodle, 1957, C13..$85.00
#0132 Molly Moo Cow, 1972-78, C13.............................$30.00
#0135 Play Animal Cicus, 1974-76, complete, C13 ....$55.00
#0136 Play Family Lacing Shoe, 1966-69, complete, C13..$50.00
#0137 Pony Chime, 1962, pk plastic wheel, C13 ....$40.00

#0138 Jack-in-the-Box Puppet, 1970-73, C13 ....$25.00
#0139 Tuggy Tooter, 1967-73 ....$30.00
#0139 Tuggy Turtle, 1959, C13 ....$100.00
#0140 Coaster Boy, 1941, C13..$700.00
#0140 Katy Kackler, 1954, C13...$70.00

Photo courtesy Brad Cassity

#0142 Three Men in a Tub, 1970 – 73, C13, $20.00.

#0145 Humpty Dumpty Truck, 1963, rnd heads w/wood nose, C13...$40.00
#0146 Play Pull-A-Long Lacing Shoe, 1970-75, w/6 figures, & 50" rnd lace, C13 ....$45.00
#0148 TV-Radio, 1959-67, Jack & Jill, wood & plastic, C13 ..$30.00
#0149 Dog Cart Donald, 1936, C13...............................$700.00
#0150 Barky Bubby, 1934, C31 ....$600.00
#0150 Pop-Up-Pal Chime Phone, 1968-78, C13.............$40.00
#0150 Teddy Turtle, 1940, C13 ....$400.00
#0150 Timmy Turtle, 1953, gr shell, C13 ....$100.00
#0152 Road Roller, 1934, C13 ....$700.00
#0154 Frisky Frog, 1971-83, squeeze plastic bulb & frog jumps, C13..$20.00
#0154 TV-Radio, 1964-67, Pop Goes the Weasel, wood & plastic, C13 ....$25.00
#0155 Skippy Sam, 1934, C13 ....$850.00
#0155 TV-Radio, 1968-70, Jack & Jill, wood & plastic w/see-through window on back, C13 ....$35.00
#0156 Circus Wagon, 1942, band leader in wagon, C13 .$400.00
#0156 Jiffy Dump Truck, 1971-73, squeeze bulb & dump moves, C13..$20.00
#0156 TV-Radio, 1966-67, Baa-Baa Black Sheep, wood & plastic, C13 ....$50.00
#0158 Katie Kangaroo, 1976-77, squeeze bulb & she hops, C13 ....$25.00
#0158 TV-Radio, 1967, Little Boy Blue, wood & plastic, C13..$50.00
#0159 TV-Radio, 1961-65 & Easter 1966, Ten Little Indians, wood & plastic, C13 ....$20.00
#0161 Creative Block Wagon, 1961-64, 18 building blocks & 6 wooden dowels fit into pull-along wagon, C13..........$75.00
#0161 Looky Chug-Chug, 1949, C13 ....$200.00
#0161 TV-Radio, 1968-70, Old Woman Who Lived in a Shoe, wood & plastic w/see-through window on back, C13 .$35.00
#0162 Roly Poly Sailboats, 1968-69, C13 ....$10.00

#0164 Chubby Cub, 1969-72, C13 .... $20.00
#0164 Mother Goose, 1964-66, C13 .... $40.00
#0166 Bucky Bullo, 1955, C13 .... $225.00
#0166 Piggy Bank, 1981-82, pk plastic, C13 .... $10.00
#0166 TV-Radio, 1963-66, Farmer in the Dell, C13 .... $25.00
#0168 Magnetic Chug-Chug, 1964-69, C13 .... $40.00
#0168 Snorky Fire Engine, 1960, gr litho, 4 wooden fireman & dog, C13 .... $150.00
#0169 Snorky Fire Engine, 1961, red litho, 4 wht wooden firemen, C13 .... $150.00
#0170 Change-A-Tune Carousel, 1981-83, music box w/crank hdl, 3 molded records & 3 child figures, C13 .... $35.00
#0171 Toy Wagon, 1942, ponies move up & down, bells rings, C13 .... $300.00
#0172 Roly Raccoon, 1980-82, waddles side to side, tail bobs & weaves, C13 .... $15.00
#0175 Gold Star Stagecoach, 1954, w/2 litho wood mail pouches, C13 .... $275.00
#0175 Kicking Donkey, 1937, C13 .... $450.00
#0175 TV-Radio, 1971-73, Winnie the Pooh, Sears distribution only, C13 .... $65.00
#0177 Donald Duck Xylophone, 1946, 2nd version w/'Donald Duck' on hat, C13 .... $300.00
#0177 Oscar the Grouch, 1977-84, C13 .... $30.00
#0178 What's in My Pocket, 1972-73, 10-pg cloth book w/8 pockets & 8 plastic replicas of boy's pocket items, C13 .... $20.00
#0183 Play Family Fun Jet, 1970-80, 1st version, red plastic wings w/bl engines, 4 wooden figures, no hole for gas, C13 .. $15.00
#0185 Donald Duck Xylophone, 1938, mk WDE, C13 .. $800.00
#0190 Gabby Duck, 1939, C13 .... $350.00
#0190 Molly Moo-Moo, 1956, C13 .... $225.00

#0190 Pull-A-Tune Pony Music Box, 1969 – 72, plays Shubert's Cradle Song, C13, $15.00; #0189 Pull-A-Tune Blue Bird Music Box, plays Children's Prayer, C13, $15.00.

#0191 Golden Gulch Express, 1961, C13 .... $100.00
#0192 Playland Express, 1962, C13 .... $100.00

#0194 Push Pullet, 1971-72, 16" push stick, C13..............$20.00
#0195 Double Screen TV Music Box, 1965-69, Mary Had a Little Lamb, wood & plastic, C13, from $20 to..............$30.00
#0195 Teddy Bear Parade, 1938, C13..............$600.00
#0196 Double Screen TV Music Box, 1964-69, Hey Diddle Diddle, wood & plastic, C13..............$30.00
#0200 Mary Doll, 1974-78, vinyl face & hands w/cloth body, removable apron & skirt, C13..............$20.00
#0200 Mary Doll, 1974-78, vinyl face & hands w/cloth body, removable apron & skirt, MIB, C13..............$50.00
#0200 Winky Blinky Fire Truck, 1954, C13..............$100.00
#0201 Jenny Doll, 1974-78, vinyl face & hands w/cloth body, removable skirt, C13..............$20.00
#0201 Jenny Doll, 1974-78, vinyl face & hands w/cloth body, removable skirt, MIB, C13..............$50.00
#0201 Woodsy-Wee Circus, 1931, complete, C13..............$700.00
#0202 Natalie Doll, 1974-78, vinyl face & hands w/cloth body, removable skirt & bonnet, C13..............$20.00
#0203 Audrey Doll, 1974-78, vinyl face & hands w/cloth body, removable jeans, C13..............$20.00
#0203 Audrey Doll, 1974-78, vinyl face & hands w/cloth body, removable jeans, MIB, C13..............$50.00
#0204 Baby Ann Doll, 1974-78, vinyl face & hands w/cloth body, removable nightgown & diaper, C13..............$20.00
#0204 Baby Ann Doll, 1974-78, vinyl face & hands w/cloth body, removable nightgown & diaper, MIB, C13......$50.00
#0205 Black Elizabeth Doll, 1974-78, vinyl face & hands w/cloth body, removable skirt, C13..............$20.00
#0205 Black Elizabeth Doll, 1974-78, vinyl face & hands w/cloth body, removable skirt, MIB, C13..............$50.00
#0205 Woodsy-Wee Zoo, 1931, complete w/camel, giraffe, lion, bear & elephant, C13..............$700.00
#0206 Joey Doll, 1975, vinyl face & hands w/cloth body, w/jacket, lace & tie sneakers, MIB, C13..............$50.00
#0206 Joey Doll, 1975, vinyl face & hands w/cloth body, w/jacket, lace & tie sneakers, C13..............$20.00
#0207 Woodsy-Wee Pets, 1931, complete w/goat, donkey, cow, pig & cart, C13..............$700.00
#0208 Honey Doll, 1978, yel & wht print, C13..............$20.00
#0208 Honey Doll, 1978, yel & wht print, MIB, C13......$45.00
#0209 Woodsy-Wee Dog Show, 1932, complete w/5 dogs, C13..............$700.00
#0215 Fisher-Price Choo-Choo, 1955, engine w/4 cars, C13..............$85.00
#0234 Nifty Station Wagon, 1960, removable roof, 4 wooden family figures & dog, C13..............$250.00
#0250 Big Performing Circus, 1932, complete w/figures, animals & accessories, C13..............$950.00
#0301 Bunny Basket Cart, 1957, C13..............$40.00
#0302 Chick Basket Cart, 1957, C13..............$40.00
#0303 Adventure People Emergency Rescue Truck, 1975-78, complete, C13..............$15.00
#0303 Bunny Push Cart, 1957, C13..............$75.00
#0304 Adventure People Safari Set, 1975-78, complete, C13..............$25.00
#0304 Running Bunny Cart, 1957, C13..............$75.00
#0306 Adventure People Short Plane, 1975-80, orange & wht plane w/gold pilot, C13..............$8.00
#0307 Adventure People & Their Wilderness Patrol, 1975-79, complete, C13..............$20.00
#0309 Adventure People & Their TV Action Team, 1977-78, complete, C13..............$25.00
#0310 Adventure People & Their Sea Explorer, 1975-80, complete, C13..............$15.00
#0310 Mickey Mouse Puddle Jumper, 1953, C13..............$140.00
#0312 Adventure People & Their North Woods Trailblazer, 1977-82, complete, C13..............$15.00
#0318 Adventure People Daredevil Sports Van, 1978-82, complete, C13..............$25.00
#0322 Adventure People Dune Buster, 1979-82, complete, C13..............$12.00
#0323 Aero-Marine Search Team, 1978-83, complete, C13...$20.00
#0325 Adventure People Alpha Probe, 1980-84, complete, C13..............$20.00
#0325 Buzzy Bee, 1950, 1st version, dk yel & blk litho, wooden wheels & antenna tips, C13..............$40.00
#0333 Butch the Pup, 1951, C13..............$75.00
#0334 Adventure People Sea Shark, 1981-84, complete, C13..............$20.00
#0344 Copter Rig, 1981-84, C13..............$15.00
#0345 Boat Rig, 1981-84, C13..............$15.00
#0345 Penelope the Performing Penguin, 1935, w/up, C13..$800.00
#0350 Adventure People Rescue Team, 1976-79, complete, C13..............$18.00
#0350 Go 'N Back Mule, 1931, w/up, C13..............$800.00
#0351 Adventure People Mountain Climbers, 1976-79, complete, C13..............$20.00
#0352 Adventure People Construction Workers, 1976-79, complete, C13..............$15.00
#0353 Adventure People Scuba Divers, 1976-81, complete, C13..............$12.00
#0354 Adventure People Daredevil Skydiver, 1977-81, complete, C13..............$12.00
#0355 Adventure People White Water Kayak, 1977-80, complete, C13..............$15.00
#0355 Go 'N Back Bruno, 1931, C13..............$800.00
#0356 Adventure People Cycle Racing Team, 1977-81, complete, C13..............$10.00
#0357 Adventure People Fire Star 1, blk & silver rocket sled, life-support cable & pilot figure, C13..............$15.00
#0358 Adventure People Deep Sea Diver, 1980-84, complete, C13..............$10.00
#0358 Donald Duck Back-Up, 1936, w/up, C13..............$800.00
#0360 Go 'N Back Jumbo, 1931, w/up, C13..............$800.00
#0365 Puppy Back-up, 1932, w/up, C13..............$800.00
#0367 Adventure People Turbo Hawk, 1982-83, complete, C13..............$15.00
#0368 Adventure People Alpha Interceptor, 1982-83, wht 2-stage space vehicle, astronaut & tether, C13..............$15.00
#0375 Bruno Back-Up, 1932, C13..............$800.00
#0377 Adventure People Astro Knight, 1979-80, foam plastic glider & figure, C13..............$15.00
#0400 Donald Duck Drum Major, 1946, C13..............$275.00
#0400 Donald Duck Drum Major Cart, 1946, C13..............$275.00
#0401 Stoopy Stork, 1931, Pop-Up Kritter, C13..............$200.00
#0404 Bunny Egg Cart, 1949, C13..............$80.00

#0405 Lofty Lizzy, 1931, Giraffe Pop-Up Kritter, C13 ...**$225.00**
#0407 Chick Cart, 1950, C13 ....**$50.00**
#0407 Dizzy Dino, 1931, Dinosaur Pop-Up Kritter, C13 ..**$225.00**
#0415 Lop-Ear Looie, 1934, Mouse Pop-Up Kritter, C13.**$225.00**
#0415 Super Jet, 1952, C13 ....**$225.00**
#0420 Sunny Fish, 1955, C13 ....**$200.00**
#0422 Jumbo Jitterbug, 1940, Elephant Pop-Up Kritter, C13 ...**$225.00**
#0425 Donald Duck Pop-Up, 1938, C13 ....**$400.00**
#0432 Mickey Mouse Choo-Choo, mk WDE, 1938, C13 .**$600.00**
#0432-532 Donald Duck Drum Major Cart, 1948, C13 .**$300.00**
#0433 Dizzy Donkey, 1939, Pop-Up Kritter, C13 ....**$125.00**
#0434 Ferdinand the Bull, 1939, C13 ....**$600.00**
#0435 Happy Apple, 1979, short stem, C13.......................**$3.00**
#0440 Goofy Gertie, 1935, Stork Pop-Up Kritter, C13 ..**$225.00**
#0440 Pluto Pop-Up, 1936, mk WDP, C13 ....**$100.00**
#0444 Queen Buzzy Bee, 1959, red litho, C13 ....**$40.00**
#0445 Hot Dog Wagon, 1940..**$225.00**
#0445 Nosey Pup, 1956, C13..**$75.00**
#0448 Mini Copter, 1971-83, bl litho, C3 ....**$20.00**
#0450 Donald Duck Choo-Choo, 1941, 8½", C13.........**$375.00**
#0450 Donald Duck Choo-Choo, 1942, bl hat, C13......**$200.00**
#0450 Music Box Bear, 1981-83, plays Schubert's Cradle Song, plastic, C13 ....**$15.00**
#0454 Donald Duck Drummer, 1949, C13 ....**$300.00**
#0460 Dapper Donald Duck, 1936, C13 ....**$600.00**
#0460 Movie Viewer, 1973-90, crank hdl, C13 ....**$5.00**
#0460-499 Movie Viewer Cartridge's, 1973-90, color, C13 ..**$6.00**
#0469 Donald's Cart, 1940, C13 ....**$400.00**
#0474 Bunny Racer, 1942, C13...**$225.00**
#0475 Walt Disney's Easter Parade, 1936, NM (EX box), A...**$1,600.00**
#0476 Cookie Pig, 1967, C13 ....**$50.00**
#0476 Mickey Mouse Drummer, 1941, C13 ....**$300.00**

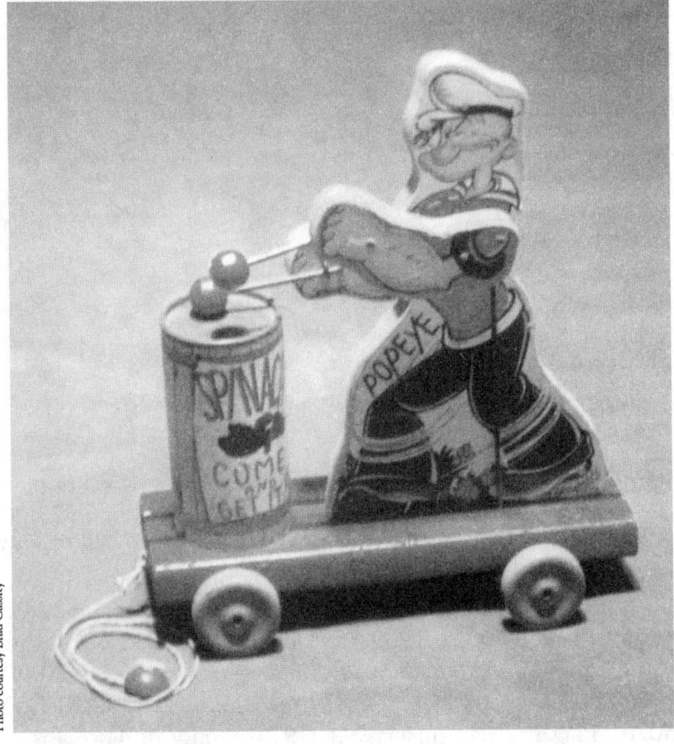

Photo courtesy Brad Cassity

#0488 Popeye Spinach Eater, 1939, C13, $600.00.

#0477 Dr Doodle, 1940, C13..**$225.00**
#0478 Pudgy Pig, 1962, C13..**$50.00**
#0480 Leo the Drummer, 1952, C13..............................**$225.00**
#0483 Disney Carnival, 1936-37, H7.............................**$750.00**
#0485 Mickey Mouse Choo-Choo, 1949, new litho version of #0432, C13 ....**$100.00**
#0494 Pinocchio, 1939, C13 ....**$600.00**
#0495 Sleepy Sue, 1962-Easter 1964, C13 ....**$55.00**
#0499 Kitty Bell, 1950, C13..**$125.00**
#0500 Donald Duck Cart, 1937, no number on toy, 3 colors, C13 ....**$700.00**
#0500 Donald Duck Cart, 1951, no baton, gr litho background, C13 ....**$350.00**
#0500 Donald Duck Cart, 1953, w/baton, new litho w/yel background, C13 ....**$350.00**
#0500 Pick-Up & Peek Puzzles, 1972-86, C13.................**$10.00**
#0510 Strutter Donald Duck, 1941, C13 ....**$300.00**
#0530 Mickey Mouse Band, 1935, C13 ....**$900.00**
#0533 Thumper Bunny, 1942, C13...............................**$500.00**
#0544 Donald Duck Cart, 1942, C13.............................**$300.00**
#0549 Toy Lunch Kit, 1962-79, red w/barn litho, w/thermos, C13..**$20.00**
#0550 Toy Lunch Kit, 1957, red, wht & gr plastic barn shape, no litho, C13..**$40.00**
#0600 Tailspin Tabby Pop-Up, 1947, 5", NM, A **$235.00**
#0604 Bunny Bell Cart, 1954, C13 ....**$100.00**
#0605 Donald Duck Cart, 1954, C13.............................**$300.00**
#0605 Woodsey Major Goodgrub Mole & Book, 1981, 32 pgs, C13..**$20.00**
#0606 Woodsey Bramble Beaver & Book, 1981, 32 pgs, C13 .**$20.00**
#0607 Woodsey Very Blue Bird & Book, 1981, 32 pgs, C13 ...**$20.00**
#0615 Tow Truck, 1960, C13..**$75.00**
#0616 Chuggy Pop-Up, 1955, C13 ....**$100.00**
#0616 Patch Pony, 1963, C13 ....**$50.00**
#0617 Prancing Pony, 1965-70, C13...............................**$40.00**
#0625 Playful Puppy, 1961, w/shoe, C13..........................**$50.00**
#0626 Playful Puppy, 1963, w/shoe, C13..........................**$50.00**
#0628 Tug-A-Bug, 1975-77, C13 ....**$15.00**
#0629 Fisher-Price Tractor, 1962, C13 ....**$40.00**
#0630 Fire Truck, 1959, C13..**$50.00**
#0634 Drummer Boy, 1967-69, drummer beats hollow drum w/spring-mounted mallets, plastic base, C13 ....**$50.00**
#0641 Toot-Toot Engine, 1962, bl litho, C13 ....**$65.00**
#0642 Dinky Engine, 1959, blk litho, C13.......................**$65.00**
#0642 Smokie Engine, 1960, blk litho, C13 ....**$65.00**
#0643 Toot-Toot Engine, 1964, plastic wheels, C13 ....**$5.00**
#0649 State Truck, 1960, C13..**$50.00**
#0653 Allie Gator, 1960, C13 ....**$85.00**
#0654 Tawny Tiger, 1962, C13..**$125.00**
#0656 Bossy Bell, 1960, w/bonnet, C13 ....**$50.00**
#0656 Bossy Bell, 1961, no bonnet, new litho design, C13..**$50.00**
#0658 Lady Bug, 1961-62, C13 ....**$55.00**
#0659 Puzzle Puppy, 1976, 8-pc take-apart & put-together dog, C13..**$15.00**
#0662 Merry Mousewife, 1962, C13...............................**$50.00**
#0677 Picnic Basket, 1975-79, plastic w/accessories & cotton tablecloth, C13 ....**$30.00**
#0678 Kriss Krickey, 1955, C13 ....**$100.00**

#0684 Little Lamb, 1964-65, C13 ....$50.00
#0685 Car & Boat, 1968-69, wood & plastic, 5 pcs, C13 .$40.00
#0686 Car & Camper, 1968-70, wood & plastic, 5 pcs, C13 ...$50.00
#0686 Perky Pot, 1958, C13 ....$75.00

#0693 Little Snoopy, 1964 – 87, C13, $3.00.

#0695 Pinky Pig, 1956, wooden eyes, C13......................$100.00
#0695 Pinky Pig, 1958, litho eyes, C13...........................$100.00
#0698 Talky Parrot, 1963, C13 ....$100.00
#0700 Cowboy Chime, 1951, C13 ....$250.00
#0700 Popeye, 1935, hitting bell, C13 ....$700.00
#0700 Woofy Wowser, 1940, C13 ....$400.00
#0703 Bunny Engine, 1954, C13 ....$100.00
#0703 Popeye the Sailor, 1936, C13 ....$700.00
#0705 Mini Snowmobile, 1971-73, w/sled, 2 figures & dog, C13 ....$50.00
#0705 Popeye Cowboy, 1937, on horse, C13.................$700.00
#0711 Cry Baby Bear, 1967-69, C13 ....$35.00
#0711 Huckleberry Hound, 1961, Sears only, C13.........$300.00
#0711 Raggedy Ann & Andy, 1941, C13 ....$850.00
#0712 Fred Flintstone Xylophone, 1962, Sears only, C13 ....$250.00
#0712 Teddy Tooter, 1957, C13 ....$250.00
#0714 Mickey Mouse Xylophone, 1963, Sears only, C13.$275.00
#0715 Ducky Flip Flap, 1964-65, 21" push stick, C13 ......$50.00
#0717 Ducky Flip Flop, 1937-40, Easter only, C13 ....$400.00
#0718 Tow Truck & Car, 1969-70, wood & plastic, C13 $30.00
#0719 Cuddly Cub, 1973-77, head turns & chimes when rocked, C13 ....$15.00
#0719 Fisher-Price Choo-Choo, 1963, engine, 3 cars, 3 figures & a dog, C13 ....$40.00
#0720 Fisher-Price Fire Engine, 1969, w/wood driver & 2 firemen, C13 ....$10.00
#0720 Pinnochio, 1939, C13..$500.00
#0721 Peter Bunny Engine, 1949, C13 ....$200.00
#0724 Jolly Jalopy, 1965-78, circus clown's roadster, C13 ..$10.00
#0725 Play Family Bath/Utility Room Set, 1972, 4 wooden figures & accessories, C13...$20.00
#0726 Play Family Patio Set, 1970, 3 figures w/dog & accessories, C13 ....$20.00
#0728 Buddy Bullfrog, 1959, yel body w/red litho coat, C13...$75.00
#0728 Buddy Bullfrog, 1961, gr coat w/red & wht pants, C13.$75.00
#0728 Play Family House Decorating Set, 1970, 4 figures w/accessories, C13 ....$20.00
#0729 Play Family Kitchen Set, 1970, 4 figures w/accessories, C13..$20.00
#0730 Racing Rowboat, 1952, C13 ....$300.00
#0732 Happy Hauler, 1968-70, wooden garden tractor w/plastic cart, C13 ....$35.00
#0733 Mickey Mouse Safety Patrol, 1956, C13 ....$250.00
#0734 Teddy Zilo, 1964-66, C13...$45.00
#0735 Juggling Jumbo, 1958, C13 ....$250.00
#0736 Humpty Dumpty, 1972-79, plastic, C13 ....$5.00
#0737 Galloping Horse & Wagon, 1948, C13................$250.00
#0738 Dumbo Circus Racer, 1941, rubber arms, C13.....$700.00
#0738 Shaggy Zilo, 1960, C13..$75.00
#0739 Poodle Zilo, 1962, C13 ....$75.00
#0741 Teddy Zilo, 1967, C13 ....$40.00
#0741 Trotting Donald Duck, 1937, C13 ....$800.00
#0742 Jingle Giraffe, 1958, C13 ....$225.00
#0745 Elsie's Dairy Truck, 1948, w/2 bottles, C13 ....$700.00
#0746 Pocket Radio, 1977-78, It's a Small World, wood & plastic, C13 ....$20.00
#0750 Hot Dog Wagon, 1938, C13.................................$400.00
#0750 Space Blazer, 1953, C13 ....$400.00
#0752 Teddy Zilo, 1948, 1st version, clown outfit w/red cheeks, C13 ....$350.00

#0752 Teddy Xylophone, 2nd version, C13, $325.00.

#0756 Pocket Radio, 1973, 12 Days of Christmas, wood & plastic, C13 ....$25.00
#0757 Humpty Dumpty, 1957, C13 ....$250.00
#0758 Pocket Radio, 1970-72, Mulberry Bush, wood & plastic, C13..$20.00
#0759 Pocket Radio, 1969-73, Do-Re-Me, wood & plastic, C13 ....$20.00
#0760 Peek-A-Boo Block, 1970-79, C13 ....$15.00
#0761 Play Family Nursery Set, 1973, family of 4 w/baby & accessories, C13 ....$20.00

#0762 Pocket Radio, 1972-77, Raindrops, wood & plastic, C13 ....$15.00
#0763 Music Box, 1962, Farmer in the Dell, yel litho, C13..$50.00
#0763 Pocket Radio, 1978, Whistle a Happy Tune, wood & plastic, C13 ....$20.00
#0764 Music Box, 1960-61 & Easter 1962, Farmer in the Dell, red litho, C13....................$50.00
#0764 Pocket Radio, 1975-76, My Name Is Michael, C13 ..$15.00
#0765 Pocket Radio, 1976, Humpty Dumpty, wood & plastic, C13 ....$25.00
#0765 Talking Donald Duck, 1955, C13 ....$125.00
#0766 Pocket Radio, 1968-70, Where Has My Little Dog Gone?, wood & plastic, C13....................$20.00
#0766 Pocket Radio, 1977-78, I'd Like To Teach the World To Sing, C13....................$20.00
#0767 Pocket Radio, 1977, Twinkle Twinkle Little Star, C13 ....$20.00
#0767 Tiny Ding-Dong, 1940, C13 ....$400.00
#0768 Pocket Radio, 1971-76, Happy Birthday, wood & plastic, C13 ....$15.00
#0770 Doc & Dopey Dwarfs, 1938, C13....................$1,000.00
#0772 Pocket Radio, 1974-76, Jack & Jill, C13....................$15.00
#0773 Tip-Toe Turtle, 1962, vinyl tail $15.00
#0774 Pocket Radio, 1967-71, Twinkle Twinkle Little Star, wood & plastic, C13....................$20.00
#0775 Pocket Radio, 1967-68, Sing a Song of Six Pence, C13 ....$25.00

#0785 Corn Popper, 1957, C13, $75.00.

#0775 Pocket Radio, 1973-75, Pop Goes the Weasel, wood & plastic, C13 ....$15.00
#0775 Teddy Drummer, 1936, C13 ....$675.00
#0777 Pushy Bruno, 1934, C13 ....$725.00
#0777 Squeaky the Clown, 1958, C13 ....$250.00
#0778 Ice Cream Wagon, 1940, C13 ....$350.00
#0778 Pocket Radio, 1967-68, Frere Jacques, wood & plastic, C13 ....$20.00
#0779 Pocket Radio, 1976, Yankee Doodle, wood & plastic, C13 ....$20.00
#0780 Jumbo Xylophone, 1937, C13 ....$275.00
#0784 Mother Goose Music Chart, 1955, C13 ....$100.00
#0785 Blackie Drummer, 1939, C13 ....$625.00
#0786 Perky Penguin, 1973-75, C13 ....$25.00
#0788 Rock-A-Bye Bunny Cart, 1940, C13 ....$300.00
#0791 Candy Man Tote-A-Tune Radio, 1979, Let's Go Fly a Kite, plastic, C13 ....$10.00
#0792 Music Box, 1980-81, Teddy Bear's Picnic, plastic, C13...$10.00
#0793 Jolly Jumper, 1963, C13 ....$50.00
#0793 Tote-A-Tune Radio, 1981, When You Wish Upon a Star, plastic, C13 ....$10.00
#0794 Big Bill Pelican, 1961, w/cb fish, C13 ....$85.00
#0794 Tote-A-Tune Radio, 1982-91, Over the Rainbow, plastic, C13 ....$5.00
#0795 Mickey Mouse Drummer, 1937, pie-eyed, C13....$700.00
#0795 Musical Duck, 1952, C13 ....$100.00
#0795 Tote-A-Tune Radio, 1984-91, Toyland, C13 ....$10.00
#0798 Chatter Monk, 1957, C13 ....$100.00
#0798 Mickey Mouse Xylophone, 1939, 1st version, w/hat, C13 ....$450.00
#0798 Mickey Mouse Xylophone, 1942, 2nd version, no hat, C13 ....$450.00
#0800 Hot Diggety, 1934, w/up, C13 ....$800.00
#0808 Pop'N Rig, 1956, C13 ....$85.00
#0810 Hot Mammy, 1934, w/up, C13 ....$800.00
#0870 Pull-A-Tune Xylophone, C13 ....$5.00
#0909 Play Family Rooms, 1972, Sears only, 4 figures w/dog & accessories, C13, from $150 to $200.00
#0910 Change-A-Tune Piano, 1969-72, Pop Goes the Weasel, This Old Man & The Muffin Man, C13 ....$40.00
#0910 This Little Pig, 1963, C13 ....$40.00
#0915 Play Family Farm, 1968-91, 1st version, complete, C13 ....$30.00
#0916 Fisher-Price Zoo, 1984-87, 6 figures w/accessories, C13 ....$20.00
#0919 Music Box Movie Camera, 1968-70, plays This Old Man, w/5 picture disks, C13 ....$40.00
#0923 Play Family School, 1971-78, 1st version, roof & side hinge open, 5 figures & accessories, C13 ....$20.00
#0926 Concrete Mixer, 1959, C13 ....$275.00
#0928 Play Family Fire Station, 1980-82, w/3 figures, dog & accessories, C13 ....$75.00
#0929 Play Family Nursery School, 1978-79, 6 figures & accessories, removable roof, 13¾x10x5½", C13 ....$70.00
#0930 Play Family Action Garage, 1970-85, 1st version, w/elevator ramp, 4 cars & 4 figures, masonite & plastic, C13 .$20.00
#0931 Play Family Hospital, 1976-78, w/figures & accessories, C13 ....$125.00
#0932 Amusement Park, 1963, park map, 5 wooden figures, musical merry-go-round & accessories, C13 ....$325.00
#0932 Ferry Boat, 1979-80, 3 figures, 2 cars & 2 life preservers, C13 ....$25.00
#0934 Play Family Western Town, 1982-84, 4 figures & accessories, C13 ....$75.00
#0937 Play Family Sesame Street Clubhouse, 1977-79, w/4 Sesame Street characters & accessories, C13 ....$70.00

Photo courtesy Brad Cassity

#0938 Play Family Sesame Street, 1975 – 78, C13, $70.00.

#0940 Sesame Street Characters, 1977, C13, ea $3.00
#0942 Play Family Lift & Load Depot, 1977-79, w/3 figures & accessories, C13 ....$50.00
#0945 Offshore Cargo Base, 1979-80, 3 platforms, 4 figures & accessories, C13 ....$55.00
#0952 Play Family House, 1969-79, 1st version, 2-story w/yel roof, figures & accessories (no cb delivery truck), C13 ....$30.00
#0952 Play Family House, 1980-87, 2nd version, new-style litho & brn roof, no staircase, C13 ....$20.00
#0952 Play Family House, 1987-88, 2-story w/brn roof, gr plastic base, complete, C13 ....$20.00
#0960 Woodsey's Log House, 1979, w/figures, accessories & 32-pg book, C13 ....$40.00
#0961 Woodsey's Store, 1980, hollow tree w/figures, accessories & 32-pg book, C13 ....$45.00
#0962 Woodsey's Airport, 1980, airplane, hangar, 1 figure & 32-pg book, C13 ....$30.00
#0969 Musical Ferris Wheel, 1966-72, 1st version w/4 wooden straight-body figures, rods in case, C13 ....$45.00
#0979 Dump Trucker Playset, 1965-70, w/3 figures & accessories, C13 ....$80.00
#0982 Hot Rod Roadster, 1983-84, riding toy w/4-pc take-apart engine, C13 ....$65.00
#0983 Safety School Bus, 1959, w/6 figures, Fisher-Price Club logo, C13 ....$250.00
#0985 Play Family Houseboat, 1972-76, w/2 deck lounges, figures & accessories, C13 ....$40.00
#0987 Creative Coaster, 1964-81 ....$75.00

#0990 Play Family A-Frame, 1974-76, w/4 figures, dog & accessories, C13 .... $65.00

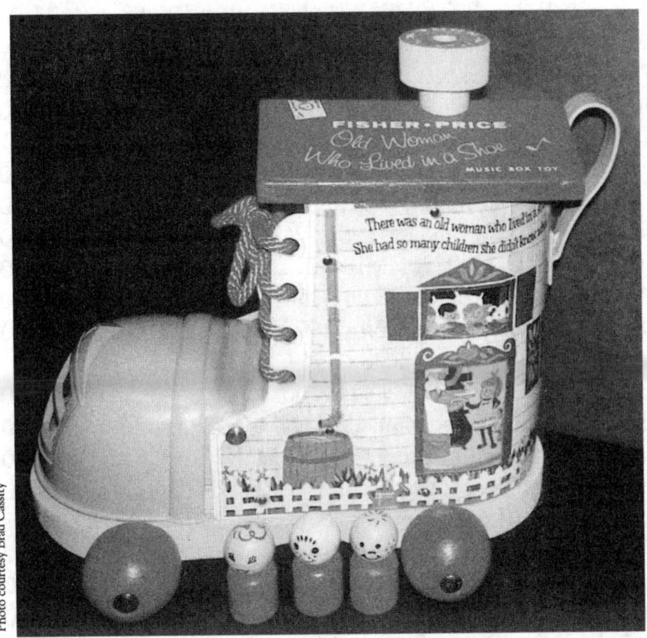

Photo courtesy Brad Cassity

#0991 Music Box Lacing Shoe, 1964 – 67, C13, $50.00.

#0991 Play Family Circus Train, 1973-78, 1st version, w/figures, animals & gondola car, C13 .... $25.00
#0991 Play Family Circus Train, 1979-86, 2nd version, w/figures & animals, no gondola car, C13 .... $15.00
#0992 Play Family Car & Camper, 1980-84, camper unfolds into tent, 4 figures & accessories, C13 .... $35.00
#0993 Play Family Castle, 1974-77, 1st version, w/6 figures & accessories, C13 .... $100.00
#0994 Play Family Camper, 1973-76, w/4 figures & accessories, C13 .... $70.00
#0996 Play Family Airport, 1972-76, 1st version, bl airport w/clear look-out tower, 6 figures & accessories, C13 . $70.00
#0997 Play Family Village, 1973-77, 2-pc village w/bridge, 8 figures, dog & accessories, C13 .... $70.00
#2500 Little People Main Street, 1986-90, 8 figures & accessories, C13 .... $45.00
#2525 Little People Playground, 1986-90, w/2 figures & accessories, C13 .... $15.00
#2526 Little People Pool, 1986-88, w/2 figures & accessories, C13 .... $15.00
#2551 Little People Neighborhood, 1988-90, 2-pc playset connects w/treehouse, 4 figures & accessories, C13 .... $55.00
#2552 McDonald's Restaurant, 1990, 1st version, bl car trash can, fry coaster, arches & figures, C13, from $75 to .. $80.00
#2552 McDonald's Restaurant, 1991-92, 2nd version, same pcs as 1st version but lg-sz figures, C13 .... $50.00
#6145 Jingle Elephant, 1993, ToyFest limited edition of 5,000, C13 .... $100.00
#6464 Grana'Pa Frog, 1994, ToyFest limited edition of 5,000, C13 .... $60.00
#6550 Buzzy Bee, 1987, ToyFest limited edition of 5,000, C13 .... $120.00
#6558 Snoopy Sniffer, 1988, ToyFest limited edition of 3,000, C13 .... $600.00
#6575 Toot-Toot, 1989, ToyFest limited edition of 5,000, C13 .... $100.00
#6588 Snoopy Sniffer, 1990, Fisher-Price Commemorative limited edition of 3,500, Ponderosa pine, C13 .... $150.00
#6590 Prancing Horses, 1990, ToyFest limited edition of 5,000, C13 .... $100.00
#6592 Teddy Bear Parade, 1991, ToyFest limited edition of 5,000, C13 .... $70.00
#6593 Squeaky the Clown, 1995, ToyFest limited edition of 5,000, C13 .... $150.00
#6599 Molly Bell Cow, 1992, ToyFest limited edition of 5,000, C13 .... $175.00
#8121 My Friend Karen Doll, 1990, only 200 made, C13 .. $125.00

Games

Early games (those from 1850 to 1910) are very often appreciated more for their wonderful lithographed boxes than their 'playability,' and you'll find collectors displaying them as they would any fine artwork. Many boxes and boards were designed by commercial artists of the day.

Though they were in a decline a few years ago, baby-boomer game prices have leveled off. Some science fiction and rare TV games are still in high demand. Games produced in the Art Deco era between the World Wars have gained in popularity — especially those with great design. Victorian games have become harder to find; their prices have also grown steadily. Condition and rarity are the factors that most influence game prices.

When you buy a game, check to see that all pieces are there. The games listed below are complete unless noted otherwise. For further information we recommend *Baby Boomer Games* by Rick Polizzi (Collector Books) and *Board Games of the '50s, '60s and '70s* (L-W Book Sales). Note: In the listings that follow, assume that all are board games (unless specifically indicated card game, target game, bagatelle, etc.), and that each is complete as issued, unless missing components are mentioned.

Advisor: Paul Fink (F3).

See also Advertising; Black Americana; specific categories.

$64,000 Question, Lowell, 1955, EX (EX box), F8 .... $50.00
ABC Education, card game, Ed-U, 1959, EX+ (EX+ box), P3 .... $10.00
Across the Continent, Parker Bros, 1952, NM (EX box), F8 .... $50.00
Addams Family, card game, Milton Bradley, 1965, NM (EX box), F8 .... $30.00
Adventures of Robin Hood, Betty-B, 1956, NM (EX box) .. $85.00
Adventures of Sir Lancelot, Lisbeth Whiting, 1957, VG (VG box), S16 .... $140.00
Alien, Kenner, 1979, missing 1 pawn, NM (EX box), F8 . $45.00
All in the Family, Milton Bradley, 1972, EX (EX box), F3 .. $15.00
All Star Baseball, Cadaco, 1969, VG (VG box), S16 ...... $40.00
Alvin & the Chipmunks Acorn Hunt, Hasbro, 1960, EX (EX box), F8 .... $55.00

Amazing Spider-Man, Milton Bradley, 1967, EX (EX box) .$125.00
America's Yacht Race, McLoughlin Bros, early 1900s, few pcs missing, VG (VG box), A $635.00
American Boys, McLoughlin Bros, early 1900s, EX (EX box), F3..$200.00
Amos 'N Andy Card Party, A Davis, 1930, unused, MIB, A...$200.00
Andy Gump in the White House, Sphinx, rare, EX (EX box), A $265.00
Animals, Birds & Fish, card game, Ed-U, 1959, NM (EX box), P3 ....$10.00
Annette's Secret Passage Game, Parker Bros, 1958, few pcs missing, rare, EX (EX box) $60.00
Annie Oakley, Milton Bradley, 1950s, VG (VG box)......$45.00
Apples Way, Milton Bradley, 1974, VG (VG box), S16..$20.00
Archie, Whitman, 1969, NM (EX box), F8.....................$50.00
Arnold Palmer's Inside Golf, David Bremson, 1961, VG (VG box)..$100.00
Around the World in 80 Days, Transogram, 1957, NM (EX box), F8...$40.00
Arrest & Trial, Transogram, 1963, NMIB $100.00
Art Linkletter's Game of People Are Funny, Whitman, 1954, NM (NM box), F8 ....$40.00
Art Linkletter's House Party, Whitman, 1968, NM (NM box), P3 ....$50.00
Ask Me Another, Marx, 1928, EX (EX box), A............$350.00
Assembly Line, Selchow & Righter, 1953, EX (EX box), F3...$60.00
Astro Launch, Ohio Art, 1960s, EX (EX box), F8...........$35.00
Axis & Allies, Milton Bradley, 1984, VG (VG box), F3..$20.00
Babes in Toyland, Parker Bros, 1961, EX (EX box), F8....$50.00
Bandersnatch, Mattel, 1969, NM (EX box), F8...............$75.00
Bang Box, Ideal, 1969, NMIB, F8.......................................$25.00
Barbie's Keys to Fame, Mattel, 1963, missing 1 card & key, EX (EX box), F8 ....$25.00
Barnabas Collins Dark Shadows, Milton Bradley, 1969, missing bonus fangs, EX (VG box), F8.................................$35.00
Barney Google & Spark Plug, Milton Bradley, 1923, EX (EX box), A..$100.00
Barney Miller, Parker Bros, 1977, VG (VG box), S16 .....$20.00
Bat Masterson, Lowell, 1958, VG (VG box) $60.00
Batman, card game, Ideal, 1966, NM (NM box), A.........$55.00
Batman, card game, Whitman, 1966, NM (NM box), A .$50.00

Batman and Robin, Hasbro, NMIB, $60.00.

Batman & Batgirl, Spanish Triang, 1966, EX (EX box), A $200.00
Batman & Robin, Hassenfeld, 1965, VG (VG box), S16.$75.00
Batman & Robin Pinball Game, Marx, 1966, EX, F8.....$175.00
Batman Jigsaw Puzzle Game, Milton Bradley, 1966, NM (NM box), C1 ....$100.00
Battle Line, Ideal, 1964, NM (NM box), F8 ....$90.00
Battle of the Planets, Milton Bradley, 1979, VG (VG box), S16 ....$50.00
Battle Stations, Burleson, 1952, NM (EX box), T2 ....$50.00
Battle-Cry, Milton Bradley, 1961, VG (VG box), S16.....$30.00
Battleboard, Ideal, 1972, NMIB, J2 ....$30.00
Battleship, Milton Bradley, 1965, NM, T2 ....$30.00
Battlestar Galactica, Parker Bros, 1978, NM (EX box), F8 ..$20.00
Beat the Clock, Milton Bradley, 1969, NM (EX box), F8 ..$40.00
Beatlemania Trivia, 1984, EX (EX box), N2 ....$20.00
Ben Casey MD, Transogram, 1961, NM (EX box), F8 .....$30.00
Ben-Hur, McLoughlin Bros, 1899, VG (VG box), F3.$1,800.00
Bermuda Triangle, Milton Bradley, 1976, NMIB, J2 ....$35.00
Beverly Hillbillies, Standard Toykraft, 1963, EX (EX box), S16...$80.00
Beverly Hillbillies Set-Back, card game, 1963, NMIB, J2.$25.00
Bewitched, Game Gems, 1965, EX (EX box) $125.00
Bewitched, Stymie card game, Milton Bradley, 1964, EX (VG box), F8 ....$45.00
Beyond the Stars, House of Ideas, 1964, NMIB, F8 ....$35.00
Bible Boys, card game, Zondervan, 1930s-40s, NM (EX box), F8 ....$15.00
Bicycle Race, McLoughlin Bros, 1890, EXIB, F5............$925.00
Big Board, Dadem Inc, 1960, VG (VG box)......................$50.00
Big Sneeze, Ideal, 1968, NM (NM box), F8.......................$30.00
Billionaire, Parker Bros, 1973, VG (VG box), S16...........$35.00
Bing Crosby's Game Call Me Lucky, Parker Bros, 1954, NM (EX box) $65.00
Bionic Woman, Parker Bros, 1976, VG (VG box), S16...$30.00
Black Beauty, Transogram, 1958, NM (EX box), F8 ....$25.00
Black Cat, Parker Bros, 1950s, EX (EX box), F3...............$55.00
Black Hole Space Alert, Whitman, 1979, MIB, F8/J2......$35.00
Blockade, Corey Games, 1941, VG (VG box), S16..........$85.00

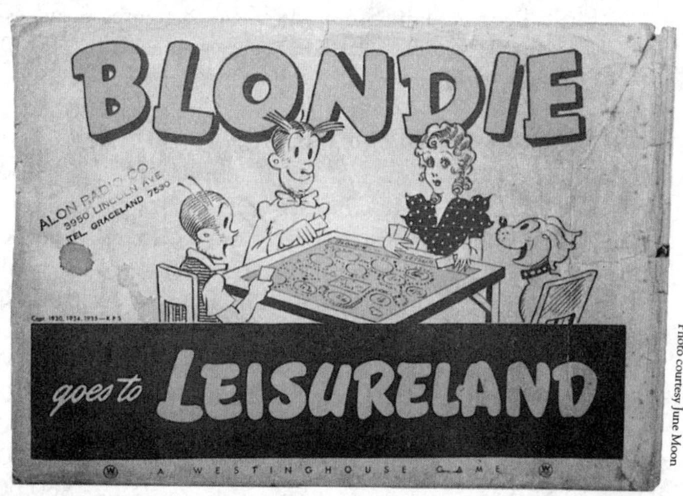

Blondie Goes to Leisureland, Westinghouse premium, 1930s, NM (worn envelope), $45.00.

Bob Cousy Basketball, National Games Inc, 1960s, EX (EX box), J5 ....$95.00
Bonanza, Parker Bros, 1964, EX (EX box) $40.00
Booby-Trap, Parker Bros, 1965, VG (VG box) $20.00
Bop the Beetle, Ideal, 1962, MIB $45.00
Bozo the Clown, card game, Ed-U, 1972, EX (EX box), F8 ..$15.00
Bozo the Clown Circus, Transogram, 1969, NM (EX box), F8 ....$30.00
Break the Bank, Betty-B, 1955, few coins missing, EX (EX box), P3 ....$50.00
Broadside, Milton Bradley, 1962, NM (NM box), P3 ....$40.00
Buccaneers, Transogram, 1957, NM (EX box), F8 ....$60.00
Buffalo Bill Jr, Built-Rite, 1956, NMIB $65.00
Bug-A-Boo, Whitman, 1968, EX (EX box), F8 ....$25.00
Bugaloos, Milton Bradley, 1971, VG (VG box), S16 ....$20.00
Burke's Law, Transogram, 1963, incomplete, VG (VG box), H4 ....$25.00
Bust-Em Target Game, Marx, 1930, NM (EX box), A...$125.00
Buster Brown & Tige, target game, Bliss, early 1900s, VG, A...$575.00
Buster Brown at the Circus, card game, EX (EX box), A..$225.00
Buster Brown Hurdle Race, J Ottmann, EX (VG box), A .$450.00
Busy Bee, card game, Ed-U, 1958, NM (EX box), P3 ....$10.00
Buttons 'N Bows, Transogram, 1960, EX (EX box), J5 .....$85.00
Calling All Cars, Parker Bros, 1938, EX (EX box), from $40 to..$50.00
Camp Granada, Milton Bradley, 1965, MIB $45.00
Candid Camera, Lowell, 1963, EX (EX box), F8 ....$65.00
Candyland, Milton Bradley, 1949, 1st edition, VG (VG box), S16 ....$40.00
Cannonball Run, Cadaco, 1981, EX (EX box), F3 ....$20.00
Captain Caveman, Milton Bradley, 1980, EX (EX box), F3 .$10.00
Captain Gallant of the Foreign Legion, Transogram, 1955, NM (EX box), F8 ....$50.00
Careers, Parker Bros, 1955, EX (VG+ box), T2 ....$25.00
Cargoes, S&C, 1934, 1st version, NM (EX box) $75.00
Carol Burnett, card game, Milton Bradley, NM (NM box) ..$25.00
Casper the Ghost, card game, 1950s-60s, NM (NM box), P3....$15.00
Casper's Picture Lotto, Built-Rite, 1960s, missing few cards, NM (EX box), F8 ....$25.00
Cattlemen, Selchow & Righter, 1977, missing few minor pcs, VG (VG box), S16 ....$35.00
Charlie Brown Plays Baseball, card game, US Games, MIB, H11 ....$20.00
Charlie Brown's All-Star Game, Parker Bros, 1968, VG (VG box), S16 ....$50.00
Charlie's Angels, Milton Bradley, 1977, NM (EX box), F8..$25.00
Chester Gump, Milton Bradley, 1930s, scarce, NM (EX box), A $225.00
Children's Hour, Parker Bros, 1961, EX (EX box), F8......$25.00
Ching Gong, Chinese checkers, Samuel Gabriel, 1937, VG (VG box) $35.00
Chipmunks, card game, Ed-U, 1963, NM (NM box), P3 .$15.00
CHiPs, Milton Bradley, 1977, VG (VG box), S16 ....$30.00
Chitty-Chitty Bang-Bang, Milton Bradley, 1968, NM (EX box), F8 ....$50.00
Chopper Strike, Milton Bradley, 1975, VG (VG box) $38.00
Chuggedy Chug, Milton Bradley, 1955, VG (VG box) $75.00
Chutes & Ladders, Milton Bradley, 1956, VG (VG box), S16 ....$20.00
Chutes Away!, Gabriel, 1978, EX (EX box), M17 ....$65.00
Circus Boy Adventure, 1956, VG (VG box), R2 ....$85.00
Civil War Game, Parker Bros, 1961, M (EX box) $50.00
Classic Major League Baseball, Game Time Ltd, 1987, missing few cards, EX (EX box), S16 ....$55.00
Clean Sweep, Schaper, 1967, EX (EX box), F8 ....$50.00
Clock-A-Word, Topper, 1966, NM (EX box), F8 ....$25.00
Close Encounters of the Third Kind, Parker Bros, 1978, EX (EX box), F8 ....$20.00
Clue, Parker Bros, 1949, orig issue, VG (VG box) $50.00
Clue, Parker Bros, 1963, EX (EX box), T2 ....$25.00
Colorful Game from the Pages of Winnie the Pooh, Parker Bros, 1959, missing few pcs, EX (EX box), J5 ....$65.00
Columbo, Milton Bradley, 1973, EX (EX box), F3 ....$20.00
Combat, Ideal, 1963, NM (EX box) $65.00
Comic Card Game, Milton Bradley, 1972, NM (EX box), F8...$30.00
Comic Conversation, card game, Parker Bros, complete, NMIB, F5 ....$45.00
Concentration, Milton Bradley, 1959, 1st edition, VG (VG box), S16 ....$40.00
Conflict, Parker Bros, 1940, EX (EX box) $150.00
Confucius Say, card game, Milton Bradley, 1937, EX (EX box), S16 ....$45.00
Consetta & Her Wheel of Fate, Selchow & Righter, 1946, NMIB, F8 ....$75.00
Countdown, ES Lowe, 1967, VG (VG box), S16 ....$50.00
Countdown Space Game, Transogram, 1959, rare, VG (VG box) $35.00
Cover 'Em Up, Parker Bros, 1891, VG (VG box), S16 ..$200.00
Cowboys & Indians, card game, Ed-U, 1949, NM (EX box), P3 ....$15.00

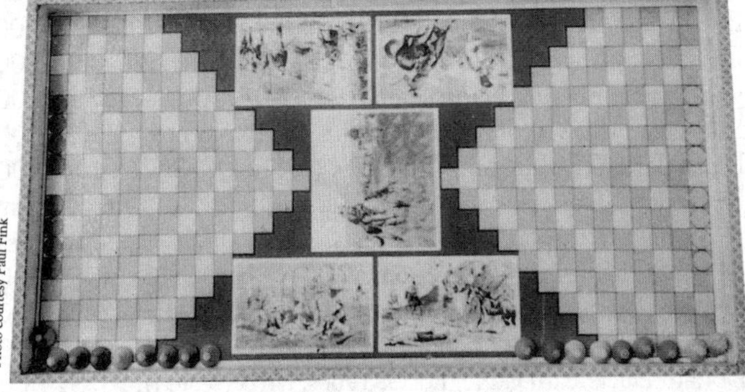

Cowboy Game, Chaffee and Selchow, 1898, EX (EX box), F3, $400.00.

Crazy Clock, Ideal, 1964, NM (EX box), F8 ....$75.00
Crazy Eights, card game, Whitman, 1951, NM (NM box), P3 ....$10.00
Creature Castle, Whitman, 1975, EX (EX box), J2 ....$35.00
Creature Features, Athol Research, 1975, VG (VG box), S16 ....$135.00
Crow Hunt, Parker Bros, 1930, VG (VG box), S16 ....$65.00
Curious George, Parker Bros, 1977, VG (G box), F8 ....$15.00
Cut-Up Shopping Spree, Milton Bradley, 1969, NMIB, F8..$65.00
Daniel Boone, card game, Ed-U, 1965, NM (NM box), P3 ..$15.00
Daniel Boone Wilderness Trail, card game, Transogram, 1960s, EX (VG box), J5 ....$25.00
Dark Shadows Mystery Maze, Whitman, 1968, NM (EX box), F8 ....$50.00
Dark Tower, Milton Bradley, 1981, NM (EX box), F8.....$50.00
Darkie Ten Pins, Milton Bradley, prewar, missing balls & 3 pins, EX (EX box) $175.00
Davy Crockett Adventures, Gabriel, 1955, NM (EX box), A ..$95.00

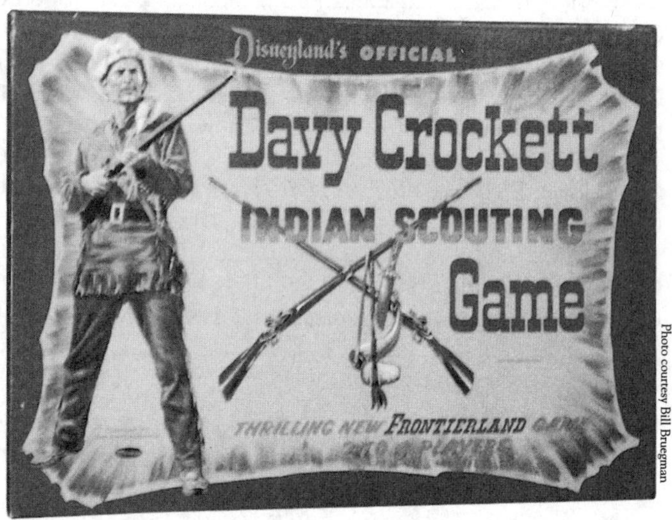

Photo courtesy Bill Bruegman

Davy Crockett Indian Scouting Game, Whitman, NMIB, T2, from $65.00 to $85.00.

Davy Crockett Rescue Race, Gabriel, EX (EX box), T2, from $55 to $75.00
Deputy, Milton Bradley, 1960, NM (NM box), F8...........$90.00
Detectives, Transogram, 1961, NM (EX box), F8.............$55.00
Dice Ball, Milton Bradley, 1934, VG (VG box), S16.......$65.00
Dick Tracy - A Sunday Funnies Game, Ideal, 1972, NMIB ...$35.00
Dick Tracy Master Detective, 1961, EX (EX box), J2 ......$50.00
Dino the Dinosaur, Transogram, 1961, MIB, F3.............$100.00
Disney World, Milton Bradley, 1970s, EX (worn box), J5 ..$25.00
Disneyland, Transogram, 1950s, EX (EX box), F8/J2 ....$50.00
Disneyland Express, card games, Russel, 1950s, set of 6 different games in display box, M, A....................$75.00
Dogfight, Milton Bradley, 1963, VG (VG box), S16........$50.00
Dolly & Daniel Whale, Milton Bradley, 1963, NMIB, J2..$50.00
Don't Spill the Beans, Schaper, 1967, MIB (sealed), I2 ...$25.00
Donald Duck, card game, Ed-U, 1960s, MIB (sealed), F8..$15.00
Dondi Potato Race, Hasbro, 1960, EX (EX box), T2........$50.00
Dondi Prairie Race, Hasbro, 1960, NM (EX box).............$50.00

Photo courtesy Larry Doucet

Dick Tracy Target, Marx, 1930s, 17" dia, EX (EX box), $385.00.

Down You Go, Selchow & Righter, 1954, VG (VG box), F3 ...$20.00
Dragnet, Transogram, 1955, NM (EX box), F8................$50.00
Dream House, Milton Bradley, 1968, rare, EX (EX box)..$60.00
Drew Pearson's Predict-A-Word, Dee-Jay, 1949, VG (VG box) $30.00
Dukes of Hazzard, Ideal, 1981, VG (VG box), S16..........$20.00
Dunce, Schaper, 1955, EX (EX box), T2 ....$30.00
Dungeons & Dragons, Mattel, 1980, NMIB, F8 ....$45.00
Dynomutt, Milton Bradley, 1977, few pcs missing, VG (VG box), F3 ....$20.00
Easy Money, Milton Bradley, 1936, EX (EX box), F3/S16.$30.00
Easy 3's, card game, Ed-U, 1959, NM (NM box), P3........$15.00
Eddie Cantor's Game of Tell It to the Judge, Parker Bros, 1930s, EX (EX box), F8....................$70.00
Electra Woman, Ideal, 1977, EX (EX box), F3 ....$25.00
Electric Bunny Run, Prentice, 1951, EX (VG box), T2 ...$30.00
Electric Whiz Raceway, Electric Game Co, 1950s, missing few pcs, EX (G box), S16 ....$50.00
Ellsworth Elephant, Selchow & Righter, 1960, rare, M (NM box), T2 ....$300.00
Emmett Kelly's Circus, All-Fair, 1950s, NM (VG box)....$75.00
Enter the Dangerous World of James Bond 007, Milton Bradley, 1965, NMIB, F8 ....$55.00
Escape from Colditz, Parker Bros/British, 1960s, VG (VG box)....................$135.00
Everest, J&L Randall, 1961, few pcs missing, VG (VG box), S19 ....$50.00
Fall Guy, Milton Bradley, 1982, EX (EX box), S16 ....$20.00
Family Feud, Milton Bradley, 1984, 7th edition, VG (VG box), F3 ....$10.00
Fibber McGee & the Wistful Vista Mystery, Milton Bradley, 1940, EX (EX box), F8....................$30.00
Finance & Fortune, Parker Bros, 1936, NM (EX box)......$45.00
Fish Pond, Milton Bradley, 1920, EX (EX box) $125.00
Flag, card game, McLoughlin Bros, 1887, VG (VG box), S16 ....$60.00
Flagship Aircraft, Milton Bradley, NM (EX box), A $85.00
Flintstones, card game, Ed-U, 1961, EX (EX box), P3......$10.00

Flintstones, Milton Bradley, 1971, NM (EX box), F8.......**$30.00**
Flip a Basket, Hasbro, 1969, EX (EX box), F8..................**$35.00**
Flip-a-Lid, Hassenfeld Bros, 1950s, VG (VG box), S16 ...**$40.00**
Flipper Flips, Mattel, 1965, EX (EX box), F8....................**$55.00**
Flying Nun, Milton Bradley, 1968, EX (EX box), S16......**$65.00**
Flying the Bean, Parker Bros, 1941, NM (NM box), F3.**$145.00**
Foot Ball Staar, France, tin soccer field w/compo figures & balls, lever action, EX (VG box), A................................**$150.00**
Forest Friends, Milton Bradley, 1956, VG (VG box) **$20.00**

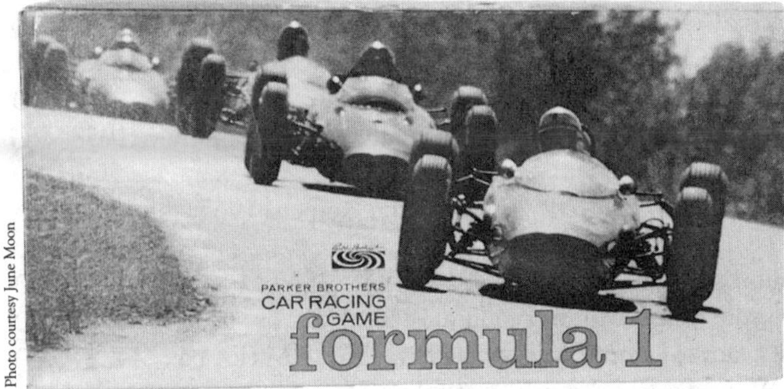

Photo courtesy June Moon

Formula-1 Car Racing Game, Parker Bros, 1963, NMIB, $65.00.

Fortress America, Milton Bradley, 1986, EX (G- box), S16...**$30.00**
Foto-Electric Football, Cadaco, 1965, VG (VG box), P3.**$25.00**
Frantic Frogs, Milton Bradley, 1965, NMIB, F8...............**$75.00**
Frontierland, Parker Bros, 1955, NM (EX box), F8 ....**$55.00**
Frosty the Snowman, Parker Bros, 1979, VG (VG box), S16...**$25.00**
Fu Manchu's Hidden Hoard, 1967, EX (EX box), S16 .....**$65.00**
Funky Phantom, Milton Bradley, 1971, EX (EX box), F3...**$20.00**
G-Men Clue Games, Whitman, EX (EX box), A............**$85.00**
Game of Authors, card game, Parker Bros, 1897, VG (VG box), S16 ....**$40.00**

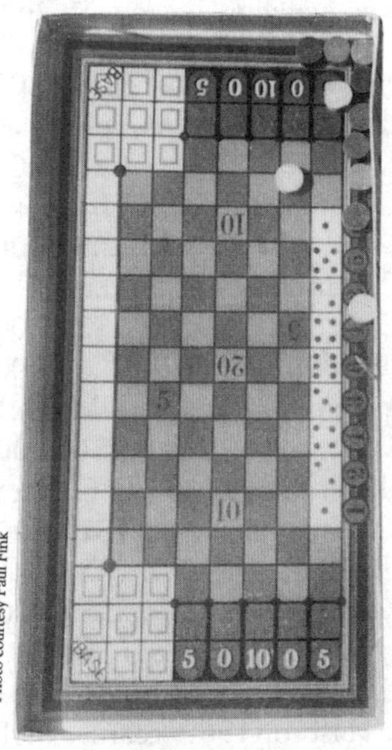
Photo courtesy Paul Fink

Game of Bagatelle, McLoughlin Bros, 1890s, VG (VG box), F3, $400.00.

Game of Bible Rhymes, card game, Goodenough & Woglom, VG (VG box), S16 ....**$40.00**
Game of Captain Kangaroo, Milton Bradley, 1956, EX (EX box), F8 ....**$50.00**
Game of Charlie Brown & His Pals, 1959, EX (EX box), V1 ....**$55.00**
Game of Diamonds & Hearts, McLoughlin Bros, 1886, EX (EX box), V1 ....**$175.00**
Game of Doctor Quack, card game, Russell, 1922, VG (VG box), S16..**$60.00**
Game of Dr Busby, Milton Bradley, VG (VG box), H7 ...**$35.00**
Game of Ferdinand the Bull in the Arena, marble game, WDE, 1938, few marbles missing, VG (VG box), A **$200.00**
Game of General Hospital, Cardinal Industries, 1982, VG (VG box), S16..**$50.00**
Game of Hide & Seek, McLoughlin Bros, 1895, EX (EX box), A **$2,200.00**
Game of Jack & the Beanstalk, McLoughlin Bros, 1898, VG (G box), A..**$865.00**
Game of Louisa, McLoughlin, 1888, EXIB, F3 ....**$625.00**
Game of Merry Christmas, JH Singer, EX (G box), A ...**$925.00**
Game of Moon Tag, Parker Bros, 1957, rare, VG (VG box), S16..**$95.00**
Game of Nations, card game, McLoughlin Bros, 1898, VG (VG box), S16..**$80.00**
Game of Politics, Parker Bros, 1952, VG (VG box), S16.**$40.00**
Game of Poor Jenny, All-Fair, 1927, EX (EX box), F3...**$125.00**
Game of Puss in the Corner, Samuel Gabriel & Sons, 1940s, EX (EX box), S16 ....**$75.00**
Game of Robbing the Miller, McLoughlin Bros, 1888, missing few pcs, VG (VG box), A **$375.00**
Game of the States, Milton Bradley, 1940, 2nd edition, VG (VG box) **$35.00**
Game of the States & Cities, card game, Parker Bros, 1947, VG (VG box), S16 ....**$35.00**

Photo courtesy Paul Fink

Game of the Visit of Santa Claus, McLoughlin Bros 1890s, VG (VG box), $1,600.00.

Game of Tortoise & the Hare, Russell Mfg, 1922, VG (VG box), S16 ....$120.00
Game of War at Sea, McLoughlin Bros, 1898, EX (EX box), A $2,100.00
Game of Winnie Winkle, Milton Bradley, VG (VG box)..$125.00
Game of Yertle by Dr Seuss, Revell, 1960, EX (EX box), M17 .$200.00
Game of Zulu, McLoughlin Bros, EXIB, F3 ....$1,100.00
Garrison's Gorillas, Ideal, 1967, NM (EX box), F8 ....$135.00
Get Smart Skittle Pool, Aurora, 1972, NM (EX box), C1.$55.00
GI Joe Marine Paratroop, Hasbro, 1965, NMIB, F8 ....$75.00
GI Joe Navy Frogman, Hasbro, 1965, NMIB, F8 ....$75.00
Gidget, Standard Toykraft, 1960s, EX (EX box w/Sally Fields), J5 ....$65.00
Gidget Fortune Telling Game, Milton Bradley, 1965, NMIB, F8 ....$50.00
Go to the Head of the Class, Milton Bradley, 1955, 8th edition, NM (EX box), F8 ....$20.00
Godfather, Family Games Inc, 1971, VG (VG box), S16..$30.00
Going to the Fire, Milton Bradley, 1920s, VG (VG box), F5 ....$195.00
Gold Fever, Idea Makers Inc, 1975, VG (VG box), S16 ..$50.00
Goldfinger, Milton Bradley, 1966, NMIB, F8 ....$65.00
Gomer Pyle, Transogram, 1966, NM (VG box), F8 ....$35.00
Good Ol' Charlie Brown, Milton Bradley, 1971, NM (NM box), F8 ....$55.00
Grande Auto Race, Atkins & Co, 1920s, incomplete, rare, VG (VG box), S16 ....$80.00
Gray Ghost, Transogram, 1958, few pcs missing, VG (VG box), S16 ....$75.00
Great American Game of Baseball, Hustler Toys, 1923, litho tin, NM $400.00
Great Grape Ape, Milton Bradley, 1975, EX (VG box), J5 ..$15.00
Great Stampede West, Delight, 1981, incomplete, VG (VG box), S16 ....$45.00
Green Ghost, Transogram, 1965, NMIB, F8....................$90.00
Groucho's You Bet Your Life, Lowell, 1955, EX (EX box), F8 ....$95.00
Guess What?, card game, Arrco Playing Card Co, 1961, M (EX box), T2 ....$10.00
Gypsy Fortune Telling Game, Milton Bradley, 1920, EXIB, F3 ....$150.00
Hair Bear Bunch, Milton Bradley, 1971, NM (EX box), F8..$25.00
Happy Hooligan, target game, Milton Bradley, 1925, EX (VG box), A $300.00
Hardy Boys Mystery Game: Secret of Thunder Mountain, Parker Bros, 1978, few cards missing, VG (VG box) $40.00
Hardy Boys Treasure Game, Parker Bros, 1957, NMIB, F8..$95.00
Hashimoto-San the Japanese House Mouse, Transogram, 1963, EX (EX box), F8 ....$55.00
Hearts, card game, Whitman, 1951, NM (EX box), P3 ....$10.00
Hi-Ho!, Cherry-O, Whitman, 1960, incomplete, VG (VG box), S16 ....$35.00
Hickety-Pickety, Parker Bros, 1924, incomplete, VG (VG box), S16 ....$50.00
Hippety-Hop, Corey Games, 1940, VG (VG box), S16...$65.00
Hit the Beach, Milton Bradley, 1965, VG (lg box version), S16 ....$60.00
Hoko, Spears, 1920s, EX (EX box), F3 ....$95.00
Hokum, card game, Parker Bros, 1927, VG (VG box), S16..$45.00
Hop Off, Parker Bros, 1920, EX (EX box), F3 ....$350.00
Hopalong Cassidy Lasso, Transogram, 1950s, few pcs missing, EX (EX box), A $125.00
Hopalong Cassidy Shooting Gallery, Automatic Toy, 1950, VG (VG box), A $265.00
Hoppity Hooper, Milton Bradley, 1964, EX (EX box), T2 .$45.00
Horse Racing, Milton Bradley, 1953, VG (VG box) $45.00
House Party, Whitman, 1968, EX (EX box), F3 ....$15.00
How Silas Popped the Question, Parker Bros, 1915, VG (VG box), S16 ....$40.00
Howdy Doody, card game, Russell, 1950s, EX (EX box), J5 ..$45.00
Huckleberry Hound, card game, Ed-U, 1961, EX (EX box), P3 ....$15.00
Huckleberry Hound Western Game, Milton Bradley, 1958, VG (G box), T2 ....$25.00
Hulla Baloo, Electric Teen Game, Remco, 1965, rare, NM (EX box), F8 ....$150.00
Hunt for Red October, TSR, 1988, VG (VG box), S16...$20.00
Hurdle Races, Milton Bradley, 1920s, VG (VG box), F3 ..$175.00
I Dream of Jeannie, Milton Bradley, 1965, NM (EX box), F8 .$70.00
I Want To Bite Your Finger - The Dracula Game, Hasbro, 1981, rare, EX (EX box) $60.00
I've Got a Secret, Lowell, 1956, NM (EX box), F8...........$50.00
Ice Hockey, Gotham, 1950, EX (EX box), A.................$125.00
India, Milton Bradley, 1910, VG (VG box), P3 ....$40.00
Indiana Jones & the Temple of Doom, LJN, 1984, EX (EX box), S16 ....$40.00
Intercollegiate Football, Hustler Toy, tin & wood, instructions lithoed on back, 3x9x14", VG, A $150.00
International Game of Spy, All-Fair, 1943, few pcs missing, NM (EX box), F8 ....$70.00
Ipcress File, Milton Bradley, 1966, EX (EX box), F3 ....$25.00
It's a Small World, Parker Bros, 1967, EX (EX box), J2 ...$55.00
It's About Time, Ideal, 1966, EX (EX box), S16 ....$200.00
Jack & the Beanstalk Adventure, Transogram, 1957, G (G box), S16 ....$25.00
Jackpot, Milton Bradley, 1974, VG (G box), F3...............$10.00
Jackson 5ive, Shindana, 1972, rare, NM (NM box), F8 ...$90.00
James Bond Secret Agent 007, Milton Bradley, 1964, rpl pawns, NM (EX box), F8 ....$35.00
James Bond 007 Assault, Victory Games, 1961, EX (EX box), S16 ....$65.00
Japanese Games of Mon, Blind Pilgrim & Cash, McLoughlin Bros, 1890, complete, EXIB, F5 ....$275.00
Jeanne Dixon's Game of Destiny, 1969, MIB (sealed), J2 .$40.00
Jetsons Fun Pad Game, Milton Bradley, 1963, NM (NM box), F8 ....$145.00
Jolly Darkie Target, McLoughlin Bros, prewar, VG (VG box), F3 ....$725.00
Jonny Quest, card game, Milton Bradley, 1964, EX (EX box), F8 ....$70.00
Jungle Book Solitaire, Ed-U, 1966, NM (EX box), F8......$45.00
Junior Auto Race, All-Fair, 1920s, EX (EX box) $175.00
Justice League of America/Flash, Hasbro, 1967, scarce, MIB (sealed), A $350.00
Justice League of America/Wonder Woman, Hasbro, 1967, scarce, NM (NM box), A $575.00

Ka-Bala, Transogram, 1967, NM (EX box), F8................$95.00
King Kong, Ideal, 1976, VG (VG box), S16....................$40.00
Knight Rider, Parker Bros, 1983, NM (EX box), F8.........$20.00
Kojak, Milton Bradley, 1975, VG (VG box), S16............$25.00
Krull, Parker Bros, 1983, EX (EX box), S16......................$20.00
L'Astro Guerre Des Galactica/Battlestar Galactica, Parker Bros/Canadian, 1978, EX (EX box), S16..................$45.00
Land of the Giants, Ideal, 1968, NM (NM box), F8......$250.00
Last Straw, Schaper, 1966, NMIB, F8..............................$25.00
Li'l Abner, Parker Bros, 1969, NM (EX box), F8.............$50.00
Lie Detector, Mattel, 1960, EX (EX box), F8...................$35.00
Lieutenant Combat Town, Transogram, 1963, EX (EX box), F8..$75.00
Little Beaver's 3 Game Set for Boys & Girls, Built-Rite, 1956, MIB, A...$100.00
Little Cowboy, Parker Bros, late 1800s, EX (EX box), F3..$475.00
Little Orphan Annie, Milton Bradley, 1927, scarce, EX (VG box), T2...$265.00
Little Shoppers, Parker Bros, 1915, 2 pcs missing, EX (EX box), F3...$250.00
Lolli Plop Skill Game, Milton Bradley, 1962, NM (EX box), F8..$20.00
Lone Ranger, Parker Bros, 1938, VG (VG box), S16.......$95.00
Lone Ranger Horseshoe Set, Gardner Games, 1950s, EX (EX box), J5...$100.00

Photo courtesy Dunbar Gallery

Lone Ranger Target, Marx, 1938, NM (VG box), from $275.00 to $375.00.

Long Bomb Football, Mattel, 1982, MIB, M17................$50.00
Long Shot Horse Race, Parker Bros, 1962, NM (EX box), F8..$40.00
Looney Tunes, Milton Bradley, 1968, VG (VG box), T2..$30.00
Lost Gold, Parker Bros, 1975, NM (EX box), F8.............$20.00
Lost in Space, Milton Bradley, 1965, EX (EX box), F8....$95.00
Love Boat, Ungame, 1980, VG (VG box), S16..............$20.00

Lucky Stars, Ideal, 1960s, EX (EX box), J2......................$25.00
Lucy Show, Transogram, 1962, MIB, F3.........................$300.00
Lucy's Tea Party, Milton Bradley, 1971, VG (VG box), F3..$25.00
Ludwig Von Drake Presents Walt Disney's Wonderful World of Color, Parker Bros, 1962, NM (VG box), F8............$35.00

Ludwig Von Drake Tiddly Winks, Whitman, EX (EX box), $35.00.

Mad Magazine, Parker Bros, 1979, VG (G box), S16.......$20.00
Mad's Spy Vs Spy, Milton Bradley, 1986, NM (EX box), F8..$30.00
Magilla Gorilla, Ideal, 1964, NMIB, F8........................$150.00
Magnetic Fish Pond, Parker Bros, 1930, EXIB, F3............$75.00
Mail Express, Milton Bradley, 1920, EX (EX box), F3...$325.00
Make-A-Million, card game, Parker Bros, 1945, VG (VG box), S16..$30.00

Photo courtesy John and Sheri Pavone

Man From UNCLE Card Game, Milton Bradley, NMIB, $25.00; 12 O'Clock High Card Game, Milton Bradley, NMIB, $45.00.

Man From UNCLE, Ideal, 1965, NM (EX box), F8.........$45.00
Mandrake the Magician, Transogram, 1966, EX (EX box), F8..$50.00
Mansion of Happiness, Henry P Ives, 1864, EXIB, F5....$250.00
Marathon, Sports Games, 1978, VG (VG box), S16........$20.00
Margie, Milton Bradley, 1961, VG (VG box), S16..........$25.00

Marvel Super Heroes Spin-A-Race, Laramie, 1978, EX, M17 ....$25.00
Mary Hartman, Mary Hartman, Reiss, 1977, NM (EX box), F8 ....$40.00
McHale's Navy, Transogram, 1962, few pcs missing, EX (EX box), F8/J5 ....$30.00
McMurtle Turtle, Cadaco, 1965, EX (EX box), F8 ....$30.00
Melvin the Moon Man, Remco, 1959, NM (EX box), F8 .$90.00
Men in Space, Milton Bradley, 1960, VG (VG box), S16.$95.00
Merv Griffin's Word for Word, Mattel, 1963, NM (NM box), F8 ....$35.00
Miami Vice, Pepper Lane, 1984, EX (EX box), S16 ....$25.00
Mickey Mouse, card game, Ed-U, 1960s, MIB (sealed), F8.$15.00
Mickey Mouse Ball Trap, France, 1930s, EX, A $335.00
Mickey Mouse Kiddy Keno, Jaymar, 1950s-60s, NM (EX box), F8 ....$15.00
Mickey Mouse Scatter Ball, Marks Bros, 1935, NM (EX box), A $350.00
Mickey Mouse Soldier Set, bowling game, Marks Bros, 1930s, rare, M (NM box), M8 ....$725.00
Mickey Mouse Target, Marks Bros, 1930s, EX, J2 ....$125.00
Mickey Mouse Tiddly Winks, Chad Valley, rare, EX (EX box), M8 ....$375.00
Midget Auto Race, Lowe, 1941, NM (EX box) $50.00
Mighty Comics Super Heroes, Transogram, 1966, EX (EX box), F8 ....$75.00
Mighty Mouse Playhouse Rescue, Harett Gilman, 1956, VG (VG box), S16 ....$90.00
Milton the Monster, Milton Bradley, 1966, NMIB, J2 .....$35.00
Miss America Pageant, Parker Bros, 1974, few cards missing, EX (EX box), F8 ....$15.00
Mixies, card game, Ed-U, 1956, NM (NM box), P3 ....$10.00
Monopoly Deluxe, Parker Bros, 1964, EX (EX box) $65.00
Monster Squad, Milton Bradley, 1977, VG (VG box), S16.$75.00
Moon Mullins Automobile Race, Milton Bradley, 1930s, EX (EX box) $175.00
Mork & Mindy, card game, 1979, VG (VG box), S16 .....$35.00
Mosquito, Milton Bradley, 1966, NMIB, F8 ....$40.00

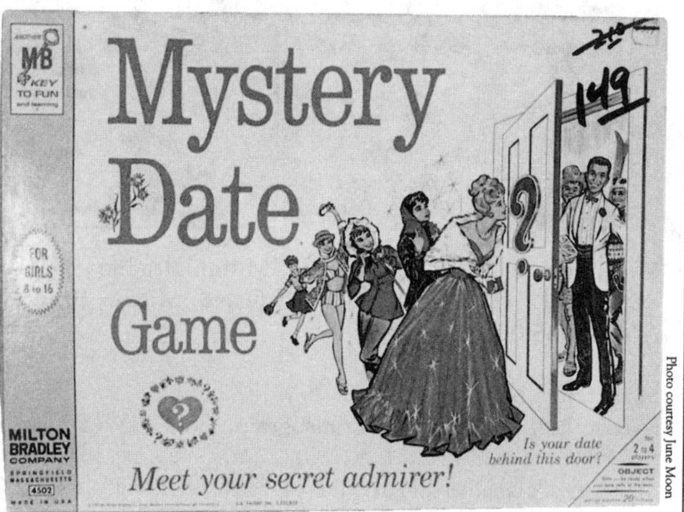

Mystery Date, Milton Bradley, 1965, EX (EX box), $125.00.

Mostly Ghostly, Cadaco, 1975, EX (EX box), P3 ....$20.00
Movie Millions, Transogram, 1938, incomplete, VG (VG box), S16 ....$125.00
Moving Picture, Milton Bradley, 1930s, EX (EX box), F3 .$145.00
Mr Magoo Visits the Zoo, Lowe, 1961, VG (VG box), T2 ..$60.00
Mr Ree, Selchow & Righter, 1946, VG (VG box), S16...$35.00
Murder She Wrote, Warren, 1985, EX (EX box), S16 .....$35.00
My Favorite Martian, Transogram, 1963, VG (VG box), S16...$65.00
Mystic Skull Game of Voodoo, Ideal, 1954, EX (EX box), J2...$65.00
National Derby Pari-Mutuel, Herbert Specialty Co, 1925, NMIB, A $350.00
NBC-TV News Game, Dadan, 1962, NM (EX box), F8 ..$75.00
Nellie Bly, McLoughlin Bros, early 1900s, EX (EX box), F3...$325.00
New Adventures of Gilligan, Milton Bradley, 1974, NMIB, F8 ....$50.00
New Kids on the Block, Milton Bradley, 1990, VG (VG box), S16 ....$20.00
New Price Is Right, Milton Bradley, 1973, missing platform, VG (VG box), F3 ....$20.00
Newlywed Game, Hasbro, 1969, NMIB, T2 ....$20.00
Night Before Christmas, Parker Bros, 1896, EXIB, F3....$850.00
No Time for Sergeants, Ideal, 1964, NM (EX box), F8 ....$80.00
Nodding Nancy, Parker Bros, 1920s, EX (EX box), F3...$275.00
Oh Magoo You've Done It Again, Warren, 1978, NM (EX box), F8 ....$20.00
Old Maid, Milton Bradley, 1900s, EX (EX box), F3 ....$45.00
Old Maid Board Game, Milton Bradley, 1900 (20th century edition), EXIB, F3 ....$275.00
Olive Oyl I'll Catch My Popeye, Hasbro, 1965, NM (NM box), T2 ....$60.00
Our Gang Tipple-Topple, All-Fair, VG (worn box), A .$175.00
Outer Limits, Milton Bradley, 1964, EX (EX box), F3 ...$275.00

Peter Pan Tiddledy Winks, Whitman, NMIB, $25.00.

Ozark Ike's 3 Game Set For Boys & Girls, Built-Rite, 1956, EX (EX box), F8 ....$80.00
Parcheesi, Selchow & Righter, 1938, VG (VG box) $25.00
Park & Shop, Parker Bros, 1960, EX (EX box), S16 ....$60.00
Pathfinder, Milton Bradley, 1977, EX (EX box), S16 ....$50.00
Patty Duke, Milton Bradley, 1964, EX (EX box), S16 ....$45.00
PDQ TV Game of Secret Letters, Milton Bradley, 1965, EX (EX box), F8 ....$20.00
Peg Baseball, Parker Bros, 1930s, EX (EX box), F3, from $65 to $85.00
Perils of Pauline, Marx, 1964, NM (EX box), F8 ....$115.00
Perry Mason Case of the Missing Suspect, Transogram, 1959, EX (EX box), F8/S16, from $50 to $60.00
Peter Coddle & His Trip to New York, Parker Bros, 1888, EX (EX box), P3 ....$60.00
Peter Pan, Parker Bros, 1969, EX (EX box), F8 ....$45.00
Petticoat Junction, Standard Toycraft, 1965, NMIB, F8 ....$165.00
Philip Marlow, Transogram, 1960, NM (EX box), F8 ....$70.00
Pink Panther, Cadaco, 1981, EX (G box), F3 ....$20.00
Pinocchio, card game, Ed-U, 1960s, MIB (sealed), F8 ....$15.00
Pinocchio, Parker Bros, 1971, EX (EX box), F8 ....$25.00
Pinocchio Merry Puppet Game, Milton Bradley, 1939, EX (EX box), A $100.00
Pinocchio Target, American Toy Works, 1940, rpl dart gun, NM (EX box), A $350.00
Pirate & Traveler, Milton Bradley, 1954, EX (EX box), F8 ....$35.00
Pirate Plunder, All-Fair, 1950s, VG (VG box), S16 ....$50.00
Pirates of the Caribbean, Parker Bros, 1965, NM (EX box), F8 ....$50.00
Pit, card game, Parker Bros, 1919, VG (VG box), S16 ....$20.00
Planet of the Apes, Milton Bradley, 1974, VG (VG box), S16 ....$40.00
Planet Patrol, Milton Bradley, 1950s, EX (EX box), M17 ....$75.00
Play Quiz, Trojan Games, 1940s, NM (EX box), T2 ....$30.00
Poison Ivy, Ideal, 1969, VG (VG box), S16 ....$40.00
Pollyanna: The Old Game, Parker Bros, 1916, 2nd edition, VG (VG box) $60.00
Poosh-M-Up Skor-It, marble game, 1940s, EX $75.00
Pop Yer Top!, Milton Bradley, 1968, EX (EX box), F8 ....$30.00
Popeye, card game, 1950s-60s, NM (NM box), P3 ....$15.00
Popeye Bubble Target, Durable Toy & Novelty, 1935, EX, A $385.00
Popeye Electric Target, Schneider, 1930, scarce, missing gun, VG (worn box), A $325.00
Popeye Menu Bagatelle, Durable Toy & Novelty, 1935, EX (G box) $500.00
Popeye Ring Toss, Rosebud, NM (NM box) $125.00
Popeye the Sailor Shipwreck, Funland, EX (EX box), A $200.00
Popeye's Game, Parker Bros, VG (G box), A $185.00
Popeye's Spinach Hunt, Whitman, 1976, NM (EX box), F8 ....$20.00
Poppin' Popeye Target, EX (EX box), A $200.00
Pot O' Gold, All-Fair, 1950s, VG (VG box), S16 ....$50.00
Prediction Rod, Parker Bros, 1970, NM (EX box), F8 ....$40.00
Price Is Right, Lowell, 1958, few pcs missing, EX (EX box), F8 ....$40.00
Prince Valiant Game of Valor, Transogram, 1955, EX (EX box), F8 ....$80.00
Pro-Football, Milton Bradley, 1964, VG (VG box), S16 ....$45.00
Professor Ludwig Von Drake Presents Walt Disney's Wonderful World of Color, Parker Bros, 1962, NM (EX box), F8 ....$40.00
Prospecting, Selchow & Righter, 1953, EX (EX box), F3 ....$55.00
Puff Ball, Spears, 1960s, NMIB, F8 ....$25.00
Punch & Judy Skittles Game, McLoughlin Bros, 1800s, EXIB $100.00
Pursuit, Game Makers Inc, 1940s, EX, S16 ....$75.00
Quick Draw McGraw, card game, Ed-U, 1961, NM (NM box), P3 ....$15.00
Quick Draw McGraw Private Eye, Milton Bradley, 1960, EX (VG box), F8 ....$40.00
Quiz Kids Radio Question Bee, card game, Whitman, 1941, VG (VG box), S16 ....$20.00
Ra-Seba the Egyptian Fortune-Telling Game, Pilgrim Prod, 1950s, NM (EX box), T2 ....$30.00
Rack-O, card game, Milton Bradley, 1966, missing 2 cards, VG (VG box), S16 ....$30.00
Radio Amateur Hour, Milton Bradley, 1930s, VG (VG box), S16 ....$75.00
Raggedy Ann's Magic Pebble, Milton Bradley, 1940, NM (EX box), F8 ....$90.00
Ranger Commandos, Parker Bros, 1944, VG (VG box), S16 ....$50.00
Ranger Rick & the Great Forest Fire, National Wildlife Federation, 1960, rare, NMIB, T2 ....$180.00
Rapid Fire Cannon, target game, Milton Bradley, 1920, tin & wood cannon w/cb figures, EX (EX box), A $135.00
Rat Patrol Desert Combat, Transogram, 1966, NM (EX box), F8 ....$125.00
Rat Patrol Spin-To-Win, Pressman, 1967, NM (EX box), F8 ....$90.00
Red Ryder Whirli-Crow Target, Daisy, few pcs missing, NM (EX box), A $200.00
Red Ryder's 3 Game Set for Boys & Girls, Built-Rite, 1956, MIB, A $125.00
Rex Morgan MD, Ideal, 1972, NM (EX box), F8 ....$35.00
Rifleman, Milton Bradley, 1959, NMIB, P4 ....$75.00
Ring Bonzo, Spear's Comic Quoits, EX (EX box), A $150.00
Ring-A-Rocket Ring Toss, Cragstan, 1970, EX (EX box), V1 ....$165.00
Road Runner, Milton Bradley, 1968, EX (EX box), S16 ....$35.00
Robbing the Miller, McLoughlin Bros, 1888, EXIB, F3 ....$225.00
Robin Hood, Parker Bros, 1973, VG (VG box), S16 ....$30.00
Rocket Patrol Magnetic Target, Am Toy Products, litho tin, 15x14", MIB, P4 ....$95.00
Roly Poly Popeye Target, Knickerbocker, 1958, NM (NM box), A $275.00
Rootie Kazootie, card game, Ed-U, 1953, EX (EX box), F8 ....$25.00
Ropes & Ladders, Parker Bros, 1954, few pcs missing, VG (VG box), S16 ....$30.00
Rose-Petal Place, Parker Bros, 1984, NM (EX box), F8 ....$25.00
Ruff & Reddy Spills & Thrills Circus, Transogram, 1962, EX (EX box), T2 ....$60.00
Sandlot Slugger, Milton Bradley, 1968, VG (VG box), S16 ....$40.00
Scooby-Doo & Scrappy-Doo, Milton Bradley, 1983, EX (EX box), S16 ....$20.00
Sea Raiders, Parker Bros, 1945, EX (EX box), F3 ....$45.00

Photo courtesy June Moon

Scottie, Pilot Plastics, 1950s, NMIB, J6, $25.00.

Sergeant Preston, Milton Bradley, 1956, Canadian version, EX (EX box) $65.00
Shariland, Transogram, 1959, VG (VG box) $45.00
Sharpshooter, Cadaco, 1965, EX (EX box), M17 ....$65.00
Sherlock Holmes, Cadaco, 1974, NMIB, F8 ....$30.00
Shindig, Remco, 1965, EX (EX box), S16....$65.00
Shoot 'Em Down Soldier Set, HG Toys, 1950s-60s, NMIB, F8 ....$70.00
Shotgun Slade, Milton Bradley, 1960, NM (EX box), F8.$70.00
Silly Safari, Topper, 1966, NM (EX box), F8 ....$165.00
Skeezyx, Milton Bradley, 1930, EX (EX box), F3 ....$275.00
Skipper, Mattel, 1964, NMIB, F8....$70.00
Skirmish, Milton Bradley, 1975, American Heritage Series, G (G box), S16....$35.00
Skittle Score Ball, Aurora, 1971, EX (EX box pictures Don Adams from Get Smart), P3....$40.00
Skunk, Schader, 1950s, NMIB, T2....$20.00
Smack-A-Roo, Mattel, 1964, EX (EX box), F8....$40.00
Smurf Game, Milton Bradley, 1981, VG (VG box), S16 .$30.00
Snagglepuss, Transogram, 1961, VG (VG box)....$50.00
Snoop, card game, Ideal, 1965, NM (EX box), F8 ....$25.00
Snoopy, card game, Milton Bradley, 1974, MIB, H11 ....$15.00
Snoopy & the Red Baron, Milton Bradley, 1970, VG (VG box), H11 ....$25.00
Snoopy Come Home, Milton Bradley, VG (VG box), H11 .$15.00
Snow White & the Seven Dwarfs, Cadaco, 1977, EX (EX box), S16 ....$20.00
Snow White & the Seven Dwarfs, Milton Bradley, 1937, rare, NMIB, F8....$300.00
Solarquest, Western Publishing, 1986, EX (EX box), S16 ..$30.00

Photo courtesy Martin and Carolyn Berens

Slap Stick, Milton Bradley, 1967, MIB, B5, $40.00.

Soldiers, target game, J Pressman, EX (EX box) $100.00
Soldiers of Fortune, Marx, VG (worn box), A....$165.00
Soupy Sales Sez Go-Go-Go, Milton Bradley, 1960s, incomplete, VG (VG box), H4 ....$30.00
Space Race, Beswick/England, EX (EX box), A $100.00
Space Shuttle 101, Media/Ungame, 1978, VG (VG box), S16 ....$20.00
Space: 1999, Milton Bradley, 1976, VG (VG box), S16 ..$30.00
Speedway Auto Race, Parker Bros, 1920, EX (EX box), F3 .$250.00
Spin the Spin-nik, Fun Craft, 1960s, NM (EX box), F8...$75.00
Spot-A-Plane, Toy Creations, 1942, 2nd series, incomplete, VG (VG box) $100.00
Sprint, Holland Crafts, 1930s, EX (EX box), F3 ....$75.00
Spudsie Hot Potato, Ohio Art, NMIB, J2 ....$30.00
Square Mile, Milton Bradley, 1962, VG (VG box) $35.00
Stampede!, Cadaco, 1945, VG (VG box), F8....$35.00
Star Trek, Milton Bradley, 1979, VG (VG box), S16 ....$75.00
Steve Canyon, Lowell, 1959, EX (EX box), S16....$75.00
Stratego, Milton Bradley, 1962, VG (VG box), S16 ....$45.00
Strike It Rich, Lowell, 1956, EX (EX box)....$45.00
Stump the Stars, Ideal, 1962, VG (VG box), F3....$20.00
Super Spy, Milton Bradley, 1971, NM (EX box), F8 ....$30.00
Superboy, Hasbro, 1965, rare, few pcs missing, VG (VG box), A $125.00
Supercar Target Game, Magic Wand, 1962, rare, NMIB, F8...$240.00
Supercar to the Rescue, Milton Bradley, 1962, NMIB, F8..$135.00
Superfriends Magnetic Parcheesi Game, Nasta, 1980, MOC, C1 ....$25.00
Superman, card game, Whitman, 1966, NM (EX box), P4..$50.00
Superman, Hasbro, 1965, rare, EX (EX box), A $125.00
Superman, Merry Mfg, 1964, rare, EX (EX box), A....$250.00
Superman Calling, Transogram, 1954, EX (EX box), J2...$200.00
Superman Electronic Question & Answer Quiz Machine, scarce, NM (NM box), A....$150.00
Superman Flying Bingo, Whitman, 1966, MIB....$50.00
Superman II, Milton Bradley, 1981, VG (VG box), S16..$20.00
Superman III, Parker Bros, 1982, EX (EX box), S16....$20.00
Superstition, Milton Bradley, 1977, NM (NM box), F8...$30.00
Surf Side 6, Lowell, 1960, NM (VG box), F8 ....$50.00
Swamp Fox, Parker Bros, 1960, NM (EX box), F8....$95.00
Swayze, Milton Bradley, 1955, VG (worn box), S16 ....$35.00

Swoop, Whitman, 1969, NM (NM box), F8 ....$30.00
Talk to Cecil, Mattel, MIB (sealed), J2 ....$160.00
Talking Football, Mattel, 1971, EX (EX box), M17 ....$100.00

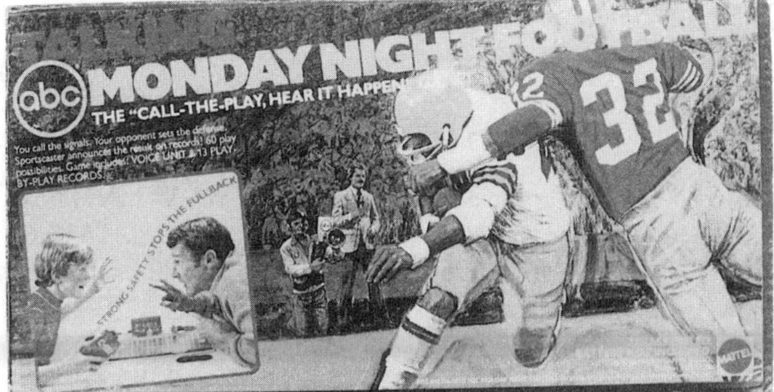

Photo courtesy Martin and Carolyn Berens

Talking Monday Night Football, Mattel, 1977, MIB, B5, $75.00.

Tammy, Ideal, 1965, 2nd issue, NM (NM box) $50.00
Tantalizer, Northern Signal, 1965, VG (VG box) $40.00
Targets in Space, Spear/England, EX (EX box), A $400.00
Tarzan to the Rescue, Milton Bradley, 1977, NM (EX box), F8/S16 ....$20.00
Ten-To-Tal, Selchow & Righter, EX (EX box), P3..........$45.00
Terminator 2 - Judgement Day, Milton Bradley, 1991, VG (VG box), S16...$25.00
Thing Ding Robot, Schaper, EX (EX box), J2 ....$225.00
Three Chipmunks Cross Country, Hassenfeld Bros, 1960, VG (VG box) $35.00

Photo courtesy Martin and Carolyn Berens

Tip-It, Ideal, 1965, MIB, B5, $35.00.

Three Musketeers, Milton Bradley, 1950, NMIB, F3........$60.00
Thunderball, Milton Bradley, 1965, VG (VG box), S16..$55.00
Thunderbirds, Parker Bros, 1967, NM (EX box), F8 ....$95.00
Tic Tac Dough, Transogram, 1957, VG (VG box), F3.....$15.00
Tiddle Tennis, Schonlat, 1930s, EX (EX box), F3 ....$45.00
Tiddly Winks, Whitman, 1958, NM (EX box), P3...........$20.00
Tiltin' Milton, Ideal, 1968, EX (EX box), F8 ....$25.00
Tim Holt 2 Dart Games in 1, American Toys, 1950s, EX (EX box), A...$165.00
Tom & Jerry, Milton Bradley, 1977, VG (VG box), S16 .$20.00
Tom & Jerry, Transogram, 1965, NMIB, F3 ....$100.00
Tomorrowland Rocket to the Moon, Parker Bros, 1956, EX (EX box), F8 ....$65.00
Toonerville Trolley Game, Milton Bradley, 1927, EX (VG box) $150.00
Toppling Tower, Ideal, 1967, EX (EX box), J2 ....$35.00
Touring, Parker Bros, 1926, EX (VG box), P3.................$40.00
Tradewinds, Parker Bros, 1960, VG (VG box), S16.........$60.00
Trap the Rat, Hasbro/Hassenfeld, 1950s, NM (EX box), P3 ..$10.00
Travel w/Woody Woodpecker, Cadaco, 1956, VG (VG box), T2 ....$70.00
Trump, Milton Bradley, 1989, EX (EX box), F3 ....$15.00
Tug of War, Chafee/Selchow, 1898, VG+ (VG+ box), F3 .$425.00
TV Batman, Koideshinkosha/Japan, 1960s, EX (EX box), M17 ....$225.00
Twenty-One TV Quiz, Lowell, 1958, NM (EX box), F8 ..$50.00
Twiggy, Milton Bradley, 1960s, NM (NM box), A $85.00

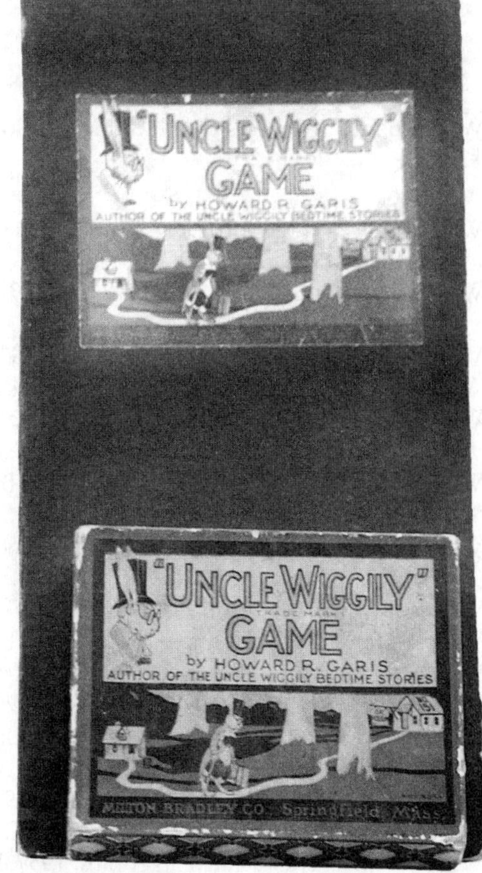

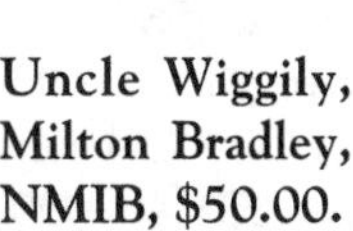

Uncle Wiggily, Milton Bradley, NMIB, $50.00.

Twilight Zone, Ideal, 1964, VG (VG box), S16 ....$65.00
Twin Target, Milton Bradley, 1920s, VG (VG box), F3 ..$225.00
Two for the Money, Hasbro, 1955, VG (worn box), F3 ...$25.00
Two in One Outer Space Rocket Target, Marx, 1950s, NMIB, F8 ....$45.00
Uncle Jim's Question Bee, Toy Creations, 1940s, VG (VG box) $30.00
Underdog to the Rescue, Whitman, 1970s, EX (EX box), J2 ....$40.00
Universe Game, Parker Bros, 1967, NM (EX box), F8 .....$60.00
Vest Pocket Checkers, Embossing Co, 1929, VG (VG box), P3 ....$25.00
Video Village, Milton Bradley, 1960, VG (VG box), F3..$20.00
Vox Pop, Milton Bradley, 1938, VG (VG box), S16........$30.00
Voyage to the Bottom of the Sea, card game, Milton Bradley, 1964, rare, NMIB, F8 ....$65.00
Wacky Races, Milton Bradley, 1969, EX (EX box), F8/S16..$40.00
Wagon Train, Milton Bradley, 1960, EX (EX box), F8, from $35 to $50.00
Wally Gator Game, Transogram, EX (EX box), T2, from $50 to $65.00

Photo courtesy Cindy Sabulis

Walt Disney's Fantasyland Game, Parker Bros, NMIB, $25.00.

Walt Disney's Three Little Pigs, Einson-Freeman, 1933, scarce, NM (EX box)..$200.00
Walt Disney's Uncle Remus, Parker Bros, 1950, NM (EX box), A $125.00
Walt Disney's Zorro, Whitman, 1958, VG (G box) $75.00
Waltons, Milton Bradley, 1974, VG (VG box), S16........$20.00
Watermelon Patch, McLoughlin Bros, 1903, VG (VG box), F3...$1,400.00
Welcome Back Kotter, card game, Milton Bradley, 1976, VG (VG box), S16 ....$35.00
What Shall I Be?, Selchow & Righter, 1968, VG (VG box), S16...$25.00
What's My Line?, Lowell, 1955, NM (EX box), F8...........$70.00
Where's Mrs Beasley, Whitman, 1971, EX (EX box), M17 ..$35.00
Which Witch, Milton Bradley, 1970, EX (EX box) $75.00
White Shadow, Cadaco, 1970s, rare, VG (VG box), from $75 to...$100.00
Who Did It?, Gardiner Games, 1950s, VG (VG box), S16 .$40.00
Who Is the Thief?, card game, Whitman, 1966, EX (EX box), F8 ....$12.00
Wide World Travel Game, Parker Bros, 1957, NMIB......$35.00
Wild Bill Hickok's Cavalry & Indians Game, Built-Rite, 1956, NM (EX box), F8 ....$50.00
Wild West Spin Dart Game, Mettoy, NM (VG box), A.$250.00
Wildlife, ES Lowe, 1971, VG (VG box), S16..................$40.00
Willow, Parker Bros, 1988, MIB, F1................................$20.00
Wimpy Where Are My Hamburgers?, Hasbro, 1965, NM (VG box), T2 ....$60.00
Wizard of Oz, Cadaco, 1974, VG (VG box), S16............$40.00
Woody Woodpecker, Milton Bradley, 1959, NM (EX box), F8 ....$70.00
Woody Woodpecker Up a Tree, Whitman, 1969, VG (VG box), T2...$35.00
Word for Word, Mattel, 1963, VG (VG box), F3............$20.00
Wow Pillow Fight Game for Girls, Milton Bradley, 1964, EX (EX box), F8 ....$45.00
Yacht Race, McLoughlin Bros, 1900s, EX (EX box), F3.$175.00
Yacht Race, Parker Bros, 1961, VG (VG box), S16 ....$85.00
Yoda the Jedi Master, Kenner, 1981, EX (EX box), S16...$50.00
Yogi Bear, card game, Ed-U, 1961, NM (NM box), P3 ....$15.00
Yogi Bear Animal Rummy, Hoyle, 1979, NM (EX box), F8 ..$12.00
Yogi Bear Go Fly a Kite, Transogram, 1961, VG (VG box), T2 ....$50.00
Yogi Bear Score-O-Matic, 1960, EX (EX box).................$75.00
You Don't Say, Milton Bradley, 1963, EXIB, S16............$20.00
Zippy Zepps Air Game, All Fair, NM (EX box), A $600.00
Zoo Game, Milton Bradley, 1920s, EX (worn box), F3.....$55.00
Zoo-M-Roo Space Game, plastic pinball machine, Northwestern Productions, 1950s, NM, P4.....................................$40.00
77 Sunset Strip, Lowell, 1960, NM (EX box), F8 ....$70.00

Gasoline-Powered Toys

Two of the largest companies to manufacture gas-powered models are Cox and Wen-Mac. Since the late '50s they have been making faithfully detailed models of airplanes as well as some automobiles and boats. Condition of used models will vary greatly because of the nature of the miniature gas engine and damage resulting from the fuel that has been used. Because of this, 'new in box' gas toys command a premium.

Advisor: Richard Trautwein (T3).

Baby 2 Quick Racing Boat #18, bl-pnt & mahogany finish, stepped hull design, Super Cyclone engine, 25", EX, A...$2,100.00
Bremer Whirlwind #2, gr & wht, 1939, 18", NM, A...$3,600.00
Bremer Whirlwind #300, red, Brown Jr engine, 1939, VG, A..$1,250.00
Cox, AA Fuel Dragster, bl & red, 1968-70, M $125.00
Cox, Acro-Cub, 1960s, MIB (sealed), J2 ....$85.00
Cox, Chopper, MIB..$100.00
Cox, Commanche, E-Z Flyer series, 1993-95, NMIB........$35.00
Cox, Golden Bee, .49 engine, M $30.00
Cox, Kitty Hawk Spitfire, gr w/yel detail, EX, from $60 to .$80.00
Cox, Navy Helldiver, 2-tone bl, 1963-66, EX, from $65 to .$80.00
Cox, P-40 Kitty Hawk, gr w/yel detail, 1964-65, EX, from $65 to...$80.00

Cox, P-51 Bendix Racer, red & yel, molded landing gear, 1963-64, EX, from $65 to..$80.00
Cox, P-51D Mustang, olive, bubble canopy & bolt-on landing gear, M, from $50 to $70.00
Cox, Pitts Special Biplane, wht, .20 engine, 1968, EX $50.00
Cox, PT-19 Flight Trainer, yel & bl, EX...........................$45.00
Cox, QZ PT-19, Quiet Zone Muffler, red & wht, 1966-69, EX....$50.00
Cox, RAF Spitfire, dk gr w/camoflauge, 1966-69, EX, from $40 to $50.00
Cox, Rivets Racer, w/pilot, red & yel, 1973-73, NM........$50.00
Cox, Ryan ST-3, w/pilot & co-pilot, wht & bl, .20 ignition power, M $65.00
Cox, Shrike, yel, 1968, M..$65.00
Cox, Sky Raider, gray, EX (EX box) $85.00
Cox, Sky-Jumper, helicopter w/pilot & parachute, olive, 1989-95, M...$40.00
Cox, Skymaster, Sure Flyer series, orange w/blk stickers, twin tail, 1976-79, EX..$50.00
Cox, Snowmobile, silver, 1968, M $100.00
Cox, Stealth Bomber, blk, 1987-89, EX............................$30.00
Cox, Super Cub 150, red & cream, upright engine, 1961-62, EX, from $45 to $70.00
Cox, Super Sabre F-100, wht or gray, .20 engine, 1958-63, EX, ea, $60 to $80.00
Cox, Super Stunter, 1974-79, EX......................................$30.00
Cox, Thimble Drome Prop Rod, yel plastic body w/metal chassis, EX, from $85 to...$130.00

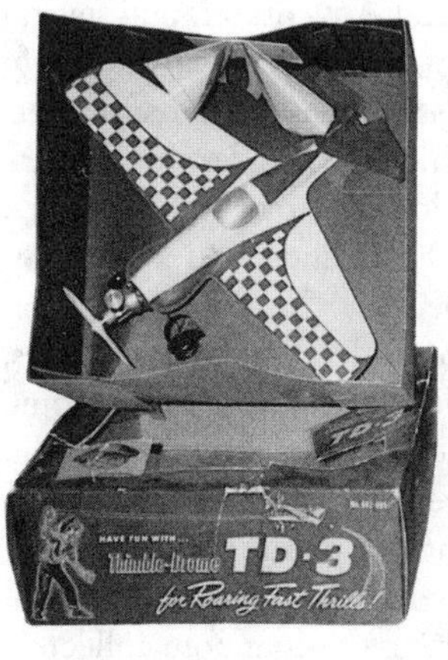

Cox, Thimble-Drome TD-3 Airplane, 1950s, plastic with aluminum wings, MIB, $60.00; Cox, Thimble-Drome TD-1 Airplane, 1950s, all aluminum, MIB, $80.00.

Cox, Thunderbolt, E-Z Flyer series, blk, w/muffler, 1993-95, M...$30.00
Custom Rail Car #2, red-pnt wood body, Hassad engine, 16", EX, A...$2,500.00
Dooling Bros F Racer, bl cast magnesium body w/orig upper & lower hammertone finish, .61 engine, 1948, 16", EX, A........$1,100.00
Dooling Bros F Series Racer #3, red, no engine, 1948, 16", EX, A $1,000.00
Dooling Bros F Series Rail Racer #25, gr & yel, McCoy .60 bl-head engine, 16", VG, A.......................................$1,700.00

Photo courtesy Dunbar Gallery

Dooling Bros. F Series Racer #54, marked Sostilo Offy, black with red and gold detail, M, D10, $2,100.00.

Dooling Bros Frog Cabin Streamliner, cast aluminum, Super Cyclone engine, 1939, 16", EX, A $3,200.00
Dooling Bros Mercury #9, red- & blk-pnt cast aluminum & fiber glass, 1939 repro, 19", EX, A $775.00
Dooling Bros Racer #1, red flat-tail model w/Knoxville Champ logo, 19", EX, A $850.00
Dooling Bros Racer #13, series II, maroon & yel, Super Cyclone engine, 1940, EX, A $2,600.00
Dooling Bros Racer #4, orange, articulated front end, McCoy engine, rstr, EX..$1,500.00
Dooling Bros Racer #6, bl, Super Cyclone engine, rear drive w/front drive conversion, 1939, 18", EX, A..........$2,300.00
Dooling Bros Racer #8, bl, Atwood .60 Champion engine, 1939, 19", EX, A $1,800.00

Dooling Bros. Tether Racing Boat, red with stepped hull design, .61 engine, 1955, 35", EX, A, $500.00.

Photo courtesy Dunbar Gallery

Dreyer Special Racer #2, silver with red seat, 18", NM, D10, $2,600.00.

Giovenale So-Cal Racer #30, wht & red, Hornet .60 engine, 16", EX, A $2,600.00

Photo courtesy Dunbar Gallery

Hiller-Comet #5, red, 1942, 19", EX, D10, $1,800.00.

Hot Rod Roadster, red, Hornet .60 engine, 15", EX, A..**$1,450.00**
McCoy Invader, red, Dooling .61 engine, 1958, 17", EX, A..**$800.00**
McCoy Invader #41, red w/Ed Dowd's racing #300C, White Case .60 engine w/magneto, 1949, 18", EX, A.....**$1,000.00**
McCoy Invader Pan #3, bl-pnt wood w/Goldie's graphics, Hornet .60 engine, 1954, 17", VG, A **$775.00**
Miracle Power Special Racer #1, yel & blk w/red detail, Dooling engine, 17", EX, A....................**$1,800.00**
Reuhl Racer #39, Bakelite body, grille & seat, McCoy .49 engine, 1940, 17", EX, A....................**$2,200.00**
Reuhl Racer #9, blk, McCoy White Case .60 engine, 1940, 17", EX, A....................**$2,000.00**
Rexner Racer #15, maroon w/Rose Tire Co graphics, Super Cyclone engine, 1940, 18", rare, EX, A....................**$4,600.00**
Speed Demon #18, yel-pnt wood, Bunch .60 engine, 1937-38, 20", EX (EX box), A **$5,700.00**
Sprint Car #2, pnt wood w/Marv's Garage graphics, Super Cyclone .60 engine, 19", NM, A **$3,200.00**
Testors, Cosmic Wind, orange, MIB **$50.00**
Testors, OD P-51 Mustang, VG **$30.00**
Testors, Red Albatross, Fly 'Em series, NM....................**$35.00**
Testors, Sopwith Camel, Fly 'Em series, NM **$35.00**
Testors, Sprite Indy Car, wht, 1966-68, M....................**$75.00**
Trackmaster Tether Racer #9, hand-hammered aluminum w/California Racing Assoc graphics, Brown Jr engine, 19", EX, A....................**$2,200.00**
Wen-Mac, Aeromite, blk, Baby Spitfire engine, EX.........**$60.00**
Wen-Mac, Albatross, Flying Wings series, red, wht & bl, EX...**$40.00**
Wen-Mac, Basic Trainer, red, bl, yel & blk w/chrome detail, 1962-64, EX **$50.00**
Wen-Mac, Beechcraft M-35, bl, gr, yel & wht, 1958-64, EX ..**$45.00**
Wen-Mac, Cutlass, bl, blk & yel, 1958-60, EX **$50.00**
Wen-Mac, Eagle, Flying Wings series, red, wht & bl, 1963-64, EX....................**$40.00**
Wen-Mac, Falcon, red, wht & bl, 1963-64, EX **$45.00**
Wen-Mac, Giant P-40 Flying Tiger, wht, 1959-60, EX....**$45.00**
Wen-Mac, Marine Corsair, red, 1968-64, EX **$40.00**
Wen-Mac, Mustang Fast-Back, bl, 1968, EX **$125.00**
Wen-Mac, Navy SNJ-3, lt bl, 1963-64, EX....................**$50.00**
Wen-Mac, RAF Day Fighter, wht, 1963-64, EX....................**$50.00**
Wen-Mac, SBD-5 Navy Dive Bomber, 1962-64, EX........**$50.00**
Wen-Mac, Turbojet, red & cream w/chrome detail, 1958-64, EX....................**$45.00**
Wen-Mac, Yellow Jacket Corsair, yel, 1959-64, EX **$40.00**
Wing Ding Tether Boat #14, mahogany finish w/gold lettering, stepped hull design, Hornet .60 engine, 28", EX, A .**$2,400.00**

GI Joe

GI Joe, the most famous action figure of them all, has been made in hundreds of variations since Hasbro introduced him in 1964. The first of these jointed figures was 12" tall; they can be identified today by the mark each carried on his back: GI Joe T.M. (trademark), Copyright 1964. They came with four different hair colors: blond, auburn, black, and brown, each with a scar on his right cheek. They were sold in four basic packages: Action Soldier, Action Sailor, Action Marine, and Action Pilot. A Black figure was also included in the line, and there were representatives of many nations as well — France, Germany, Japan, Russia, etc. These figures did not have scars and are more valuable. Talking GI Joes were issued in 1967 when the only female (the nurse) was introduced. Besides the figures, uniforms, vehicles, guns, and accessories of many varieties were produced. The Adventure Team series, made from 1970 to 1976, included Black Adventurer, Air Adventurer, Talking Astronaut, Sea Adventurer, Talking Team Commander, Land Adventurer, and several variations. Joe's hard plastic hands were replaced with kung fu grips, so that he could better grasp his weapons. Assorted playsets allowed young imaginations to run wild, and besides the doll-size items, there were wristwatches, foot lockers, toys, walkie-talkies, etc., made for the kids themselves. Due to increased production costs, the large GI Joe was discontinued in 1976.

In 1982, Hasbro brought out the 'little' 3¾" GI Joe figures, each with its own descriptive name. Of the first series, some characters were produced with either a swivel or straight arm. Vehicles, weapons, and playsets were available, and some characters could only be had by redeeming flag points from the backs of packages. This small version proved to be the most successful action figure line ever made. Loose items are common; collectors value those still mint in the original packages at two to four times higher.

In 1993 Hasbro reintroduced the 12" line while retaining the 3¾" size. The highlights of the comeback are the 30th anniversary collection of six figures which are already selling in the collector's market at well above retail ($29.00): Soldier, $100.00; Sailor, $140.00; Marine, $90.00; Pilot, $140.00; Black Soldier, $250.00; and Green Beret, $285.00.

Production of the 3¾" figures came to an end in December 1994. For more information we recommend *Collectible Male Action Figures* by Paris and Susan Manos (Collector Books); *Encyclopedia to GI Joe* and *The 30th Anniversary Salute to GI Joe* both by Vincent Santelmo; *Official Collector's Guide to Collecting and Completing, Official Guide to Completing 3¾" Series and Hall of Fame: Vol II*, and *Official Guide to GI Joe: '64 – '78*, all by James DeSimone. There is also a section on GI Joe in *Dolls in*

Uniform, a publication by Joseph Bourgeois (Collector Books). Note: all items are American issue unless indicated otherwise. (Action Man was made in England by Hasbro circa 1960 into the 1970s.)

Advisor: Cotswold Collectibles (C6).

Other Sources: D4, D8, M15, O1, P3, S17, T1, T2

See also Games; Lunch Boxes; Windups, Friction, and Other Mechanicals.

Key: A/M — Action Man

12" GI Joe Figures and Figure Sets

Photo courtesy Cindy Sabulis

Action Marine, complete, MIB, $325.00.

Action Marine, orig outfit, hat & boots, EX....................$130.00
Action Marine, 30th Anniversary, 1994, NRFB $90.00

Action Pilot, complete, MIB, H4....................................$450.00
Action Pilot, New York Convention, 1994, only 350 made, MIB..$500.00
Action Pilot, 30th Anniversary, 1994, NRFB, H4 ....$140.00
Action Sailor, complete, EX (VG box) $325.00
Action Sailor, orig outfit, boots & hat, EX.....................$125.00
Action Sailor, 30th Anniversary, 1994, NRFB, H4 ....$140.00
Action Soldier, complete, NMIB...................................$300.00
Action Soldier, orig outfit, boots & hat, EX, H4............$100.00
Action Soldier, 30th Anniversary, 1994, NRFB, H4 .....$100.00
Action Soldier (Black), 30th Anniversary, 1994, NRFB, H4 ....$250.00
Adventure Team Adventurer, w/Kung Fu grip, complete, EX (EX box), H4 ....$150.00
Adventure Team Adventurer (Black), complete, NM (VG box)...$325.00
Adventure Team Adventurer (Black), nude, EX..............$90.00
Adventure Team Intruder Soldier, nude, VG, H4............$30.00
Adventure Team Land Adventurer, orig outfit, EX $130.00
Adventure Team Man of Action, orig outfit, no beard, EX .$140.00
Adventure Team Sea Adventurer, orig outfit, EX..........$155.00
Adventure Team Talking Astronaut, complete, EX, H4..$200.00
Adventure Team Talking Commander, orig outfit, EX..$185.00
Air Security, complete, rare, NM, H4 ....$1,000.00
Australian Jungle Fighter, #8205, complete, M (VG box)...$800.00
Battle of the Bulge, Toys-R-Us, NRFB, H4 ....$60.00
British Commando, #8204, complete, M (EX box).....$1,100.00
British Commando w/Chevrons, complete, VG $300.00
Combat Soldier, A/M, complete, M (VG box) $100.00
Crash Crew, complete, EX $180.00

Photo courtesy Joseph Bourgeois

Man of Action, Kung Fu hands, complete, MIB, $325.00.

Deep Freeze, complete, NM, H4 ....$225.00
Deep Sea Diver, complete, G, H4 ....$150.00
Deep Sea Diver, complete, MIB $885.00
Duke, Target limited edition, 1991, 12", NRFB, H4 ....$60.00
Fight for Survival, 1969, complete, EX (EX box), H4 ....$275.00
Fighter Pilot, complete, NM...$550.00
French Resistance Fighter, #8103, complete, M (M repro box) $450.00
French Resistance Fighter, complete, NM $325.00
German Soldier, #8100, complete, MIB $1,750.00
German Stormtrooper, complete, VG $350.00
Green Beret, complete, EX, H4......................................$250.00
Heavy Weapons Deluxe Soldier, missing few pcs, EX, H4..$350.00
Home for the Holiday (African American), Wal-Mart, NRFB, H4 ....$70.00
Home for the Holiday (Caucasian), Wal-Mart, NRFB, H4 ..$50.00
Japanese Imperial Soldier, complete, M $625.00
Joseph Colton Artic Explorer, 30th Anniversary, mail-in, complete w/stand, MIP, H4...$130.00
LSO, complete, EX, H4 ....$250.00
Man of Action (Kung Fu), complete, NM (VG box).....$280.00
Marine, Toys-R-Us, NRFB, H4 ....$60.00
Marine Demolition, complete, NM, H4 ....$200.00
Marine Jungle Fighter, complete, NM, H4 ....$850.00
Military Policeman, complete, EX, H4 ....$200.00
Mountain Troops, complete, VG, H4............................$165.00
Navy Seal, FAO Schwartz, 12", rare, NRFB, H4............$150.00
Nurse, MIB (sealed), H4 ....$5,000.00
Russian Infantryman, #8102, complete, M (EX box) ..$2,700.00
Sabotage Set w/Action Marine, complete, EX, H4 ....$250.00
Scramble Pilot, complete, EX, H4.................................$300.00

Sea Adventurer, hard hands, complete, EX (EX box), $265.00.

Sea Sled & Frogman, complete, MIB, H4.......................$350.00
Shore Patrol, complete, VG $265.00
Ski Patrol, complete, EX, H4 ....$250.00
Space Ranger Captain, A/M, complete, MIB $100.00
Space Ranger Patroller, A/M, complete, MIB..................$90.00
Special Forces, #7532, complete, M (NM box) $975.00
Special Talking GI Joe Adventure Pack, French Resistance Fighter outfit, MIB $1,350.00
Storm Shadow, Hall of Fame, NRFB, H4..........................$50.00
Talking Action Soldier, #7590, complete, NM (VG box)..$400.00
Talking Astronaut, complete, EX, H4 ....$325.00
Tank Commander, complete, EX, H4............................$450.00
West Point Cadet, complete, EX, H4 ....$285.00

Accessories for 12" GI Joe

.30 Caliber Machine Gun & Tripod, w/ammo box, EX, H4 ..$30.00
.45 Pistol, blk revolver-type, EX, H4 ....$6.00
Action Flame Thrower, A/M, gr, w/helmet sticker, M (EX card) $60.00
Action Marine Shirt & Pants, camouflage, VG, H4...........$8.00
Action Soldier Camouflage Netting, MOC, H4..............$45.00
Adventure Team Danger of the Depths, complete, MIB, H4 ...$300.00
Adventure Team Dangerous Removal, 1973, complete, MIB ..$125.00
Adventure Team Fire Suit, silver, EX, H4 ....$25.00

Adventure Team Flying Rescue Action Pack, MIB, $65.00.

Adventure Team Headquarters Radio, EX, H4................$10.00
Adventure Team Infiltration Equipment, complete, NMIB .$300.00
Adventure Team Jungle Survival, complete, MIB, H4.....$95.00
Adventure Team Pants, blk, gr or tan, EX $9.00
Adventure Team Raft, yel, EX $12.00
Adventure Team Seismograph, #7319-6, unused, NMOC, J2...$75.00
Adventure Team Training Center, missing few pcs, VG, H4 .$70.00
Adventure Team Volcano Jumpsuit, EX, J2.....................$20.00
Adventure Team Weight Belt, EX $15.00
Adventures of 1969, red parka & gold pants, EX, H4.......$40.00
Adventures of 1969 Fight For Survival backpack, bl, EX, H4..$30.00

Air Cadet, #7822, complete, MIB...$1,450.00
Air Cadet Hat, EX, H4...$25.00
Air Force Airvest, #7809, MOC (sealed), J2...$125.00
Air Force Cadet Jacket, w/bar & wings, VG+, H4...$50.00
Air Force Dress Jacket, MOC...$200.00
Air Force Dress Uniform, #7803, complete, M (EX box)...$1,450.00
Airborne Military Police Pants, tan, EX, H4...$25.00
Annapolis Cadet Belt, EX, H4...$40.00
Annapolis Cadet Hat, EX, H4...$25.00
Annapolis Cadet Jacket, G, H4...$25.00
Army Communications Radio, gr, EX, H4...$15.00
Army Field Jacket, gr, EX, H4...$20.00
Army Poncho, gr, EX...$20.00
Astro Locker, EX, H4...$200.00
Australian Hat, EX, H4...$30.00
Australian Jacket, EX, H4...$35.00
Australian Medal, w/sticker, EX...$22.00
Australian Shorts, EX, H4...$30.00
Bayonet, NM, H4...$30.00
Bivouac Machine Gun Set, #7514, MOC...$60.00
Bivouac Sleeping Bag, #7515, MOC...$55.00
British Commando Equipment, #8304, MOC...$250.00
British Gas Mask Case, EX, H4...$18.00
British Greatcoat, A/M, MOC...$30.00
British Helmet, EX, H4...$40.00
Cadet Pants, wht, EX, H4...$70.00
Capture of the Pygmy Gorilla Set, complete, EX...$100.00
Carbine, A/M, MIP...$15.00
Combat Camouflage Netting Set, #7511, MOC...$25.00
Combat Mess Kit, #7509, complete, MOC...$70.00
Combat Set, #7502, complete, MOC...$150.00
Command Post Poncho, #7519, MOC...$55.00

Photo courtesy Paris and Susan Manos

Danger of the Depths Sea Adventurer Equipment, complete, NMIB, $100.00.

Communications Field Set, #7703, MOC...$85.00
Convention Outfit, 1990, complete, M, rare, H4...$200.00
Crash Crew Extension Ladder Holder, EX, H4...$40.00
Crash Crew Jacket & Pants, EX, H4...$30.00
Crash Crew Set, #7820, M (VG box)...$260.00
Crash Crew Set, #7820, missing few pcs, EX, H4...$70.00
Deep Sea Diver, complete, EX...$150.00
Deep Sea Diver Helmet, EX...$25.00
Deep Sea Diver Weight Belt, EX...$25.00
Demolition Set, complete, M (EX box)...$250.00
Detonator from Sabotage Set, brn strap hdl, EX, H4...$30.00
Dog Tag, VG...$25.00
El Alamein Weapons Arsenal, Lewis machine gun, Sten sub machine gun, Mausser, Ger & Brit grenades, M (VG box)...$70.00
Fantastic Freefall Helmet, gold, complete, EX, H4...$45.00
Field Phone, brn vinyl, lid seam split o/w EX, H4...$5.00
Fighter Pilot Helmet, EX, H4...$80.00
French Greatcoat, French Foreign Legion, A/M, MOC...$30.00
French 7.65 Lt Machine Gun, A/M, MIP...$15.00
Gas Mask from Sabotage Set, EX, H4...$40.00
German Field Pack, EX, H4...$25.00
German Lugar Pistol, EX, H4...$20.00
German Stormtrooper Equipment, #8300, complete, MOC...$265.00
Green Beret Bazooka, EX, H4...$30.00
Green Beret Hat, EX, H4...$45.00
Green Beret Hat, no emblem, EX, H4...$35.00
Green Beret M-16 Rifle, w/strap, EX, H4...$40.00
Grenade Launcher, w/lugar, silencer & removable stock, A/M, MOC...$30.00
Grenade Launcher Rifle, w/strap, EX...$35.00
Heavy Weapons Vest, EX, H4...$90.00
Highway Hazard Accessories, A/M, complete, M (VG card)...$20.00
Highway Hazard Uniform, A/M, MOC...$20.00
Indian Brave, A/M, complete, M (EX box)...$60.00
Indian Chief, A/M, complete, M (VG box)...$60.00
Japanese Backyard Patrol Uniform, complete, MIP, H4...$50.00
Japanese Jacket, EX, H4...$24.00
Jeep Searchlight, EX, H4...$15.00
Jettison to Safety, Canadian, complete, M (VG box)...$110.00
Life Ring, MOC...$45.00
LSO Coveralls, VG...$40.00
LSO Head Piece w/Earphones, cloth, EX, H4...$40.00
M-1 Rifle, wht, w/strap, EX...$24.00
M-60 Machine Gun, no bipod, EX, H4...$30.00
Mae West Life Vest, yel cloth, EX...$100.00
Marine Flame Thrower, gr, EX, H4...$25.00
Marine Flame Thrower, MOC...$100.00
Marine Parachute Set, #7705, complete, M (NM box)...$225.00
Marine Paratroopers Small Arms Set, #7706, complete, EX, J2...$100.00
Marine Pup Tent, EX, J2...$35.00
Medic Flag, EX...$32.00
Medic Helmet, w/strap, VG+...$40.00
Medic Shoulder Bag, EX...$30.00
Military Police, #7521, complete, M (NM box)...$1,000.00
Military Police Arm Band, EX, H4...$25.00
Military Police Duffle Bag, #7523, MOC...$60.00

Military Police Helmet, w/strap, VG+, H4 .... $20.00
Military Police Jacket, brn, EX, H4 .... $22.00
Military Police Scarf, red, EX, H4 .... $25.00
Military Police Trousers, brn, MOC $70.00
Mine Detection Set, A/M, complete, MIB $150.00
Mortar, A/M, complete, MOC $65.00
Mortar Launcher, no shells, EX, H4 .... $50.00
Mountain & Artic Set, A/M, complete, MIB $55.00
Mountain Troops, #7530, complete, M (EX box) $175.00
NATO Night Maneuvers Arsenal, A/M, complete, MOC..$70.00
Navy Attack Life Jacket, #7611, EX, J2 .... $30.00
Navy Basics, #7628, MOC $100.00
Navy Frogman Set, #7602, complete, MIB (sealed) $765.00
Navy Semaphore Flag, EX, H4 .... $50.00
Panzer Caption Outfit, A/M, MIP $125.00
Parachute, wht cloth w/strings, EX, H4 .... $25.00
Parachute Pack, bl pack w/red & wht parachute, EX, H4.$50.00
Parachute Regiments, A/M, complete, MIP $75.00
Paratrooper Accessory Set, MIP $275.00
Pilot Survival Set, #7801, complete, MIB $950.00
Polar Explorer, A/M, complete, MIB $55.00
Pursuit Craft Pilot, A/M, complete, M (VG pkg) $100.00
Radar Unit, yel, EX, H4 .... $8.00
Rescue Raft Backpack, complete, G (VG box), H4 .... $25.00
Rifle, blk, w/scope, EX $15.00
Royal Air Force, A/M, complete, M (EX box) $70.00
Russian Ammo Disk, EX, H4 .... $20.00
Russian Belt, EX, H4 .... $30.00
Russian Binoculars & Case, w/strap, EX, H4 .... $35.00
Russian Infantryman Equipment, #8302, MOC $300.00
Russian Soldier Equipment, #8302B, MIP $250.00
Sabotage Set, #7516, complete, EX (VG photo box) $725.00
Sabotage Set, A/M, complete, M (VG pkg) $70.00
Sailor Cap, EX, J2 .... $15.00
SAS Secret Mission, A/M, complete, M (EX box) $85.00
Scramble Pilot Air Vest & Accessories, MOC $100.00
Scramble Pilot Clipboard, w/paper, EX, H4 .... $30.00
Scramble Pilot Coveralls, gray, VG $35.00
Scramble Pilot Life Vest, orange vinyl, EX $16.00
Scramble Pilot Parachute Pack, MOC $90.00
Scramble Pilot Set, #7807, complete, M (NM box) $650.00
Scuba Bottom, #7604, MOC $125.00
Scuba Tank, NM, J2 .... $25.00
Sea Rescue Set, #7601, complete, MIB $650.00
Search for the Adominable Snowman, complete, MIB (sealed) $400.00
Secret Mountain Outpost, complete, MIB $200.00
Secret of Mummy's Tomb Set, complete, EX (EX box) .$225.00
Shark, EX $10.00
Shore Patrol Dress Pants, #7641, MOC $65.00
Shore Patrol Jumper, VG $25.00
Shore Patrol Sea Bag, #7615, MOC $40.00
Shore Patrol Set, #7612, M (EX box) $1,000.00
Ski Patrol Bear Helmet, w/strap, EX, H4 .... $30.00
Ski Patrol Boots, EX, H4 .... $15.00
Ski Patrol Ice Pick, w/rope, EX, H4 .... $16.00
Ski Patrol Jacket & Pants, wht, EX, H4 .... $40.00
Ski Patrol Skis & Pole, EX, H4 .... $60.00

Shark's Surprise with Sea Adventurer, MIB, $275.00.

Sleeping Bag, EX $20.00
Space Coveralls, wht, EX, H4 .... $30.00
Space Rifle, A/M, MIP $10.00
Special Operations Kit, A/M, complete, M (VG card) $40.00
Stretcher, wht, VG, H4 .... $35.00
Super Joe Helipak, 1977, MIB, J2 .... $60.00
Super Joe Magna Tools, #7538, complete, NMIB, J2 .... $50.00
Super Joe Sonic Scanner, #7538, complete, NMIB, J2 ..... $50.00
Treasure Chest, gold, EX, H4 .... $8.00
US Air Force Dress Uniform, #7803, complete, M (EX box)..$1,450.00
US Navy Flag & Pole, NM $30.00
USN Life Ring, wht plastic, EX, H4 .... $25.00
Weapons Rack, no weapons, EX $22.00
West Point Cadet Hat, no plume, EX, H4 .... $12.00
West Point Cadet Jacket, EX, H4 .... $30.00
White Tiger Set, complete, EX $90.00
Workshop Accessories, A/M, M (VG card) $20.00
Wrist Camera, EX, H4 .... $10.00
2.30 Caliber Machine Gun & Tripod, w/ammo, EX, H4..$30.00

1964 – 1969 Paperwork

Adventure Team Club Certificate, VG, H4 .... $20.00
Adventure Team Club Magazine, G $20.00
Air Force Manual, lg, EX, H4 .... $6.00
Air Force Manual, sm, EX, H4 .... $6.00
Air Manual for Action Pilot, narrow, EX $18.00
Air Manual for Action Pilot, wide, EX $10.00
Army Manual, lg, EX, H4 .... $3.00
Army Manual, sm, EX, H4 .... $4.00
Army Manual for Action Soldier, narrow, VG $12.00
Comic Book from Talking Dolls, EX, H4 .... $30.00
Counter Intelligence Manual, EX $25.00
Equipment List for Army, Marine, Pilot or Sailor, fold-out, EX, H4, ea $3.00
Instructions, Danger of the Depths $10.00
Instructions, Drag Bike, EX $9.00
Instructions, Fate of the Trouble Shooter, EX $14.00
Instructions, Sea Wolf Sub, EX, H4 .... $10.00
Instructions, Signal Flasher, in color $9.00

Instructions, Sky Dive to Danger, EX....$10.00
Instructions, Yel Helicopter, EX....$12.00
Marine Manual, narrow, VG....$14.00
Marine Manual, wide, EX....$8.00
Navy Manual for Action Sailor, narrow, EX....$14.00
Navy Manual for Action Sailor, wide, EX....$8.00
Official Gear & Equipment Manual, EX, H4....$15.00
Pamphlet, Join the GI Joe Club....$5.00

Vehicles for 12" GI Joe

Action Pack Turbo Copter, MIB (sealed), H4....$50.00
Action Pilot Space Capsule, complete, M (EX box)....$250.00
Adventure Team Avenger Pursuit Craft, complete, MIB, H4....$175.00
Adventure Team Helicopter, yel, VG....$70.00
Adventure Team Sandstorm Jeep, gr, EX (EX box)....$275.00
Adventure Team Skyhawk, MIB (sealed)....$150.00
Adventure Team Underwater Explorer, EX, J2....$35.00
Amphibious Duck, complete, EX (EX box), H4....$750.00
Big Trapper, VG, H4....$75.00
British Armored Car, Irwin, EX, H4....$275.00
Crash Crew Truck, VG (G box), H4....$1,300.00
Fire Engine, A/M, MIP....$75.00
German Staff Car, #5652, blk plastic, no spare tire, EX (worn illus box)....$700.00
Iron Knight Tank, #9031, EX (EX box)....$250.00
Iron Knight Tank, A/M, M (NM box)....$175.00
Jeep Trailer, A/M, missing canopy o/w MIB....$100.00
Jet Helicopter, complete, EX (EX box), H4....$400.00
Mine Sweeper, missing few pcs, EX (EX box), H4....$350.00
Motorcycle & Sidecar, complete, MIB, H4....$425.00
Official Jeep Combat Set, complete, EX (EX box)....$350.00
Sea Wolf Submarine, EX (VG box)....$265.00
Skyhawk, EX (EX box)....$110.00
Space Capsule, Sears Exclusive, complete, MIB, H4....$400.00
Space Speeder, A/M, converts to 4 vehicles, M (EX box)..$65.00
Survival Raft, A/M, complete, MIB....$45.00
Team Vehicle, yel ATV, VG (G box)....$85.00
Windboat, Canadian issue, bl w/yel mast & sail, M (NM box)....$60.00

3¾" GI Joe Figures

Ace, 1983, complete, EX, H4....$10.00
Ace, 1983, MIP....$25.00
Airborne, 1983, complete, EX, H4....$16.00
Airborne, 1983, MIP....$50.00
Annihilator, 1989, MOC, H4....$15.00
Annihilator, 1989, w/accessories, EX....$10.00
Astro Viper, 1988, MIP....$12.00
Astro Viper, 1988, w/accessories & ID card, EX, H4....$6.00
Barbecue, 1983-85, complete, EX....$13.00
Barbecue, 1983-85, MOC....$35.00
Barbecue Eco Warrior, 1991, MOC, H4....$15.00
Baroness, 1984, w/accessories, EX, H4....$30.00
Bazooka, 1983-85, complete, EX, H4....$12.00
Bazooka, 1983-85, MOC, H4....$35.00
Beachhead, 1983-85, MIP, H4....$30.00
Big Boa, 1986, complete, EX, H4....$8.00
Big Boa, 1987, MIP....$25.00
Blizzard, 1988, w/accessories, EX....$8.00
Budo, 1988, w/accessories & ID card....$10.00
Buzzer, 1985, MIP....$35.00
Captain Grid Iron, 1990, MIP....$12.00
Charbroil, 1988, red eyes, MOC....$15.00
Chuckles, 1986, w/accessories, EX....$8.00
Chuckles, 1987, MOC....$26.00
Clutch, 1988, MOC....$18.00
Cobra Commander, 1983, MIP....$125.00
Cobra Commander, 1983, w/accessories & ID card, EX...$28.00
Cobra HISS Driver, 1982, MIP (factory bag), H4....$15.00
Cobra HISS Driver, 1983, w/accessories & ID card, EX, H4....$12.00
Cobra Soldier, 1983, MIP....$62.00
Cobra Stinger Driver, 1982, MIP (factory bag), H4....$15.00
Countdown, 1989, MOC....$18.00
Cover Girl, 1983, MIP....$45.00
Crankcase, 1985, w/accessories, EX, H4....$8.00
Crazylegs, 1986, MOC, H4....$15.00
Crimson Guard, 1984, w/accessories, EX....$14.00
Croc Master, 1987, MOC....$22.00

Cross Country, 1986, EX, $8.00.

Crystal Ball, 1986, MOC, H4....$15.00
Crystal Ball, 1986, w/accessories & ID card, EX, H4....$8.00

Cutter, 1984, MOC $15.00
D-Day, 1995, MOC $7.00
Darklon, 1989, w/accessories & ID card, EX, H4 .... $10.00
Dee-Jay, 1988, w/accessories, EX, H4 .... $6.00
Dee-Jay, 1989, MOC $14.00
Deep Six, 1989, MOC $14.00
Deep Six w/Finback, 1992, MOC $15.00
Dial Tone, 1986, w/accessories, EX $9.00
Doc, 1983, w/accessories, EX $16.00
Dodger, 1987, w/accessories, EX $8.00
Dojo, 1992, MOC $10.00

Dreadnok, 1985, MOC, $35.00.

Dr Mindbender, 1983-85, MOC, H4 .... $25.00
Dr Mindbender, 1986, w/accessories, EX $10.00
Duke, 1985, MOC $100.00
Dynomite, 1995, MOC $7.00
Eels, 1985, MOC $52.00
Eels, 1992, MOC $10.00
Fast Draw, 1987, w/accessories, EX $11.00
Firefly, 1984, w/accessories, EX $25.00
Flash, 1982, w/accessories, EX, H4 .... $20.00
Flint, 1985, MOC $55.00
Footloose, 1985, MOC $30.00
Frag Viper, 1989, MOC $15.00
Fridge, 1986, MIP (factory bag) $30.00
Fridge, 1987, no accessories, EX, H4 .... $20.00
Fridge, 1987, w/accessories & ID card, EX, H4 .... $25.00
Frostbite, 1985, w/accessories, EX, H4 .... $10.00
Gnawgahyde, 1989, MOC $20.00

Green Beret, limited edition made for NY Convention, 1 of 5,000, MIB, H4 .... $50.00
Grunt, 1982-83, w/accessories, EX, H4 .... $20.00
Gyro Viper, 1987, w/accessories, EX, H4 .... $10.00
Hardball, 1988, MOC $18.00
Hardtop, 1987, w/accessories, EX $32.00
Hawk, 1987, w/accessories, EX $14.00
Heavy Duty, 1991, MOC $8.00
Iceberg, 1983-85, MOC $32.00
Iceberg, 1986, MOC $32.00
Iceberg, 1986, w/accessories & ID card, EX, H4 .... $10.00
Interrogator, 1991, w/accessories, EX $6.00
Iron Grenadiers, 1988, MOC $18.00
Jinx, 1987, MIP (factory bag) $12.00
Jinx, 1987, w/accessories, EX $9.00
Keel Haul, 1989 mail-in, MOC $10.00
Lady Jaye, 1985, MOC $75.00
Lamphrey, 1985, w/accessories, EX $10.00
Leatherneck, 1983-85, MOC, H4 .... $25.00

Leatherneck, 1986, EX, $8.00.

Lifeline, 1985, w/accessories, EX, H4 .... $10.00
Lifeline, 1986, MOC (Chinese) $18.00
Low-Light, 1983-85, MOC, H4 .... $25.00
Low-Light, 1986, w/accessories, EX, H4 .... $10.00
Mainframe, 1986, MOC $32.00
Mainframe, 1986, w/accessories, EX, H4 .... $10.00
Major Bludd, 1983, w/accessories & ID card, EX $15.00

Maverick, 1988, MOC $27.00
Mega Marine Blast-Off, 1993, MOC $12.00
Mega Marine Cyber-Viper, 1993, MOC $12.00
Mega Marine Mega-Viper, 1993, MOC $12.00
Mega Marine Mirage, 1993, MOC $12.00
Mega Monster Bio-Viper, 1993, MOC $15.00
Mega Monster Monstro-Viper, 1993, MOC $15.00
Mercer, 1987, w/accessories, EX $8.00

Mercer, 1987, MOC, $35.00.

Metal-Head, 1990, MOC $15.00
Monkey Wrench, 1983-85, MOC, H4 .... $20.00
Motor Viper, 1986, MOC $22.00
Motor Viper, 1986, w/accessories, EX, H4 .... $8.00
Mutt & Junkyard, 1984, MOC $50.00
Night Creeper, 1990, w/accessories, EX $6.00
Night Force Lt Falcon, 1988, w/accessories, EX $15.00
Night Force Outback, 1988, w/accessories, EX $15.00
Night Viper, 1986, w/accessories, EX $8.00
Ninja Force Bushido, 1993, MOC $8.00
Ninja Force Night Creeper, 1993, MOC $8.00
Ninja Force Snake Eyes, 1993, MOC $12.00
Ninja Force Zartan, 1993, MOC $12.00
Outback, 1987, MOC $18.00
Outback, 1987, w/accessories, EX, H4 .... $8.00
Ozone, 1993, MOC $5.00
Payload, 1987, w/accessories, EX $32.00
Psyche-Out, 1987, MOC $22.00
Python Tele Vipers, 1988, MOC, H4 .... $12.00
Quick Kick, 1985, MOC $35.00
Range-Viper, 1990, MOC $12.00
Raptor, 1987, MOC $20.00
Raptor, 1987, w/accessories & ID card, EX, H4 .... $8.00
Recoil, 1989, MOC $15.00
Recondo, 1984, w/accessories & ID card, EX, H4 .... $12.00
Recondo, 1989, MOC $40.00
Red Star Oktober Guard, MOC $15.00
Repeater, 1988, w/accessories, EX $10.00
Rip Cord, 1984, MOC $45.00
Ripper, 1985, MOC $36.00
Ripper, 1985, w/accessories, EX, H4 .... $10.00
Road Pig, 1988, MOC $20.00
Road Pig, 1988, w/accessories & ID card, EX, H4 .... $10.00
Roadblock, 1986, MOC $36.00
Rock 'N Roll, 1983, w/accessories, EX $18.00
Salvo, 1990, w/accessories, EX $8.00
Scarlett, 1982, w/accessories, EX $32.00
Sci-Fi, 1986, w/accessories, EX $9.00
Sci-Fi, 1991, MOC $15.00
Scoop, 1989, MOC $15.00
Scrap Iron, 1984, w/accessories, EX $14.00
Sergeant Savage, 1995, MOC $6.00
Sergeant Slaughter, 1985 mail-in, w/accessories & ID card, EX $26.00
Shipwreck w/Parrot, 1985, MOC $70.00
Shockwave, 1988, MOC $22.00
Short Fuse, 1982, w/accessories, EX, H4 .... $20.00
Skidmark, 1988, w/accessories & ID card $8.00
Sky Patrol Drop Zone w/Parachute Pack, 1990, MOC $18.00
Slaughter's Marauders Footloose, MOC $18.00
Slaughter's Renegades Mercer/Taurus/Red Dog, 1987, MOC $30.00
Slip Stream, 1986, w/accessories, EX $10.00
Slip Stream, 1987, w/accessories & ID card, EX $10.00
Snow Job, 1984, w/accessories, EX $15.00
Snow Serpent, 1985, MOC $50.00
Sonic Fighter Dial-Tone, 1990, MOC $18.00
Stalker, 1983, MOC $65.00
Stalker, 1983, MOC (Japanese) $20.00
Stalker, 1989, w/accessories & ID card, EX, H4 .... $8.00
Steeler, 1983, MOC $35.00
Strato Viper, 1982, MOC, H4 .... $10.00
Strato Viper, 1986, MIP (factory bag), H4 .... $10.00
Strato Viper, 1986, w/accessories, EX, H4 .... $8.00
Street Fighter Blanka, 1993, MOC $10.00
Street Fighter Guile, 1993, MOC $10.00
Street Fighter Ryu, 1993, MOC $10.00
Stretcher, 1990, MOC $15.00
Sub-Zero, 1990, MOC $15.00
Super Trooper, 1988 mail-in, w/accessories, EX $22.00
T'Jbang, 1992, MOC $10.00
Talking Battle Cobra Commander, 1991, MOC $12.00
TARGAT, 1989, MOC $18.00
Taurus, 1987, w/accessories, EX, H4 .... $5.00
Techno-Viper, 1987, w/accessories, EX $13.00
Tele-Viper, 1985, MOC $42.00

Tele-Viper, 1989, MOC $15.00
Thrasher, 1986, w/accessories, EX $8.00
Tiger Force Duke, 1988, w/accessories, EX $12.00
Tiger Force Roadblock, 1988, w/accessories, EX....................$10.00
Tiger Force Tiger Shark, 1988, MIB....................$18.00
Tiger Force Tripwire, 1988, w/accessories, EX $10.00
Topside, 1990, MOC, H4 ....$15.00
Torch, 1985, MOC....................$35.00
Torpedo, 1983, MOC $60.00
Toxo Viper, 1988, MOC $15.00
Toxo-Zombie Eco Warrior, 1991, MOC, H4....................$15.00
Tripwire, 1983, w/accessories, EX....................$16.00
Tunnel Rat, 1987, MOC $25.00
Vapor, 1990, MOC....................$15.00
Viper, 1985, w/accessories, EX $10.00
Wet Suit, 1986, MOC $45.00
Wild Bill, 1983, w/accessories & ID card, EX, H4 ....$12.00
Wild Bill, 1992, MOC....................$10.00
Wild Weasel, 1984, w/accessories, EX....................$15.00
Windmill, 1988, w/accessories, EX, H4 ....$8.00
Zandar, 1983-85, MOC, H4 ....$24.00
Zandar, 1986, w/accessories, EX $8.00
Zarana, 1985, w/accessories, EX, H4 ....$10.00
Zartan, 1984, w/accessories, EX, H4....................$35.00
Zartan w/Swamp Skier, 1984, MIB $100.00

Accessories for 3¾" GI Joe

Air Defense Battle Station, 1985, EX (EX pkg)....................$20.00
Ammo Dump Unit, 1985, EX (EX pkg) $20.00
Armadillo Mini Tank, 1984, EX....................$8.00

Photo courtesy Martin and Carolyn Berens

Armored Missile Vehicle Wolverine with Covergirl, 1983, MIB, B5, $130.00.

Artic Blast, 1988, w/instructions, EX, H4 ....$12.00
Attack Vehicle Vamp w/Clutch, 1982, EX, H4....................$40.00
Battle Gear Accessory Pack #1, 1983, MIP $16.00
Battlefield Robot Devastator, 1988, NRFB, H4....................$30.00
Battlefield Robot Radar Rat, 1988, NRFB, H4 ....$30.00
Battlefield Robot Tri-Blaster, 1988, NRFB, H4....................$30.00
Bomb Disposal Unit, 1985, MIP....................$20.00
Cobra Claw, 1984, EX $20.00
Cobra Condor Z25 Plane, 1988, MIB, H4 ....$80.00

Photo courtesy Martin and Carolyn Berens

Cobra Emperor with Air Chariot, 1986, NRFB, B5, $60.00.

Cobra HISS, 1983, w/driver & ID card, EX, H4 ....$35.00
Cobra Pom Pom Gun, 1983, EX, H4....................$15.00
Cobra Rifle Range Set, complete, EX, H4....................$6.00
Cobra Wolf w/Ice Viper, 1985, EX, H4....................$18.00
Condor, Z25, 1989, w/instructions, EX, H4 ....$25.00
Crusader Space Shuttle, 1988, NRFB, H4 ....$175.00
Desert Fox w/Skidmark, 1988, complete, EX, H4 ....$15.00
Dictator, 1989, w/instructions, EX, H4 ....$10.00
Dragonfly Helicopter w/Wild Bill, 1983, complete, EX, H4 .$40.00
Earth Borer Cobra Action Pack, 1987, MOC, H4....................$15.00
Evader, 1989, complete, EX....................$15.00
Falcon Glider w/Grunt, complete, EX....................$100.00
Fang II, 1989, complete, EX, H4 ....$10.00
Flame Thrower, 1983, EX, H4 ....$5.00
Forward Observer Unit, 1985, w/accessories, EX $8.00
Heavy Artillery Laser w/Grand Slam, 1982, NRFB....................$110.00
Hovercraft, 1984 mail-in, MIP $40.00
Jet Pack JUMP & Platform, 1982, MIP (Canadian)....................$50.00
LCV Recon Sled, 1983, EX, H4 ....$5.00
Machine Gun, 1983, EX, H4 ....$5.00
Mauler MBT Tank, 1985, NRFB, H4 ....$80.00
Missile Defense Unit, 1984, MIP....................$20.00
Missile Launcher, 1983, EX, H4 ....$5.00
Mobile Missile System, complete, EX $45.00
Mobile Support Vehicle, no accessories, VG $50.00
Motorized Battle Wagon, 1991, MIP....................$35.00
Mountain Climber Motorized Action Pack, 1986, EX, H4.$6.00
Mountain Howitzer, 1984, w/accessories, EX $8.00
P-40 Warhawk w/Pilot Savage, 1995, MIP $35.00
Parasite, 1991, Cobra personnel carrier, EX, H4 ....$8.00
Persuader w/Backstop, 1987, EX, H4....................$18.00
Phantom X-19 Stealth Fighter, 1988, MIB, H4 ....$70.00
Pogo, 1987, complete, EX, H4 ....$8.00

Polar Battle Bear, 1983 mail-in, MIP $10.00
Python Conquest, 1988, complete, EX, H4 ....$15.00
Python Stun, 1988, complete, EX, H4 ....$10.00
Q Force Battle Gear, Action Force, MIP..............................$5.00
Rope Crosser Action Pack, 1987, MOC..............................$5.00
SAS Parachutist Attack, Action Force, MIP $35.00
Sea Ray w/Sea Slug, complete, EX, H4 ....$15.00
Shark w/Deep Six, complete, EX, H4..............................$25.00
Sky Patrol Airwave, 1990, MIP $18.00
Skyhawk, complete, EX (G box) $18.00
Snow Cat w/Frostbite, 1984, EX, H4..............................$25.00
Space Force Battle Gear, Action Force, MIP $3.00
Swamp Skier w/Zartan, 1983, complete, EX $55.00
Tiger Cat w/Frostbite, 1988, complete, EX, H4 ....$20.00
Tiger Fish, 1988, complete, EX, H4 ....$10.00
Tiger Shark, 1988, complete, EX, H4..............................$12.00
Transportable Tactical Battle Platform, 1985, complete, EX....$28.00
Weapons Transport, 1984, EX, H4......................................$12.00
Whirlwind Twin Battle Gun, 1983, EX, H4 ....$20.00

Miscellaneous

Activity Box, Whitman, 1965, complete, MIB $125.00
Box, Talking Action Sailor, no insert, VG......................$150.00
Combat Man Equipment Case, EX, J2 ....$45.00
Combat Watch, Gilbert, 1964, shows standard & military time, w/compass & sighting lens, MIB $265.00
Electric Drawing Set, 1965, complete, MIB......................$80.00
Footlocker, 1964, gr wood carrying case w/plastic compartment, complete w/layout guide & display wrapper, 13" L, NM $240.00
Mobile Field Walkie-Talkie Set, MIB, B5 ....$50.00
Official Commando Medal & Bar Pin, KMT Inc, 1982, rare, MOC, F1 ....$10.00
Official Fan Club Kit, 1964, complete, NMIP, H4.........$125.00
Official Field Belt Playset, Nasta, 1982, NRFB, H4..........$30.00
Official ID Bracelet, KMT Inc, 1982, rare, MOC, F1 ....$10.00

Photo courtesy Paris and Susan Manos

Poncho and Hood, MIB, minimum value, $30.00; Bop Bag, MIB, minimum value, $60.00.

Official Inter-Com Telephone Set, Hasbro, 1982, NRFB, H4...$30.00
Official Space Capsule & Astronaut Set, made for 1995 convention, complete w/figure, CD & raft, MIB, H4.........$175.00
Official Space Capsule & Authentic Space Suit, 1966, missing record o/w complete & NM (NM box)...................$200.00
Pamphlet, How To Build Your GI Joe Battle Scenes, Hassenfeld Bros, 1964, EX, M17 ....$16.00
Pencil & Paint Set, 1960s, MIB (sealed), J2 ....$150.00
Pocket Patrol Pack, Hasbro, 1983, holds 3 figures in belt, MOC, F1 ....$20.00
Punch-Out Booklet, GI Joe Action Soldier, Whitman, 1965, unpunched, NM, M17 ....$95.00
Radio Command Unit, NM, J6 ....$100.00
Rings, Artic Force, Shuttle Crew, Artillery or Tank Corps, EX, H4, ea $2.00

Guns

Until WWI, most cap guns were made of cast iron. Some from the 1930s were nickel plated, had fancy plastic grips, and were designed with realistic details like revolving cylinders. After the war, a trend developed toward using cast metal, a less expensive material. These diecast guns were made for two decades, during which time the TV western was born. Kids were offered a dazzling array of weapons, endorsed by stars like the Lone Ranger, Gene, Roy, and Hoppy. Sales of space guns, made popular by Flash Gordon and Tom Corbett, kept pace with the robots coming in from Japan. Some of these early tin lithographed guns were fantastic futuristic styles that spat out rays of sparks when you pulled the trigger. But gradually the space race lost its fervor, westerns were phased out, and guns began to be looked upon with disfavor by the public in general and parents in particular. Since guns were meant to see a lot of action, most will show wear. Learn to be realistic when you assess condition; it's critical when evaluating the value of a gun.

Advisor: Bill Hamburg (H1).

Other Sources: C10, I2, H7, K4, M16

Actoy Restless Gun Cap Pistol, 1959, diecast w/NP finish, olive-gold swirl grips, 9", VG, P4....................................$135.00
Arliss X-100 Mystery Dart Gun, 1950, plastic, complete, 4", MOC..$175.00
Aurora Super Rocket Gun, 1950s, steel, fires wooden bullets w/pull-back mechanism, 8", M (NM box), P4 ....$60.00
AVC Triple Colt Zumbador Cap Pistol, 1970, diecast w/blk-pnt finish, wht plastic grips, 9", M (NM box), P4 ....$75.00
BCM Space Outlaw Cap Firing Ray Gun, 1960, diecast w/silver finish, red plastic windows, 10", EX $225.00
Buddy L M-99 Cracker Rifle, 1947-49, plastic & aluminum w/logo on purple swirl stock, 26", EX $75.00
Cossman Spud Gun, 1960, diecast w/silver finish, fires potato plugs, 6", EX, P4..$35.00
Crescent Lugar Cap Pistol, 1960s, diecast w/gray finish, brn plastic grips, 6½", EX, P4 ....$35.00
Crescent Super Cowboy Cap Pistol, 1969, diecast w/silver finish, brn plastic grips, 9", M (M box) $60.00

Daisy Zooka Pop Pistol, 1950, red, yel & bl pressed steel, 7½", VG $135.00
Futuristic Products Strato Gun, 1950s, diecast w/chrome finish & red detail, 9", EX $250.00
Haji Space Gun, 1960s, litho tin, 5", G, P4 ....$25.00
Hamilton Westerner Cap Pistol, 1950s, diecast w/blk plastic grips, 9½", VG, P4 ....$50.00
Hiller Atom Ray Gun Water Pistol, 1948, diecast w/silver finish, brass nozzle & end cap, 6", rare, VG $75.00
Hubley Army .45 Cap Pistol, 1960, diecast w/NP finish, wht plastic grips, automatic style, 6½", VG, P4 ....$60.00
Hubley Atomic Disintegrator Cap Pistol, 1954, diecast w/zinc finish, red plastic grips, 8", EX $350.00
Hubley Buffalo Rifle, 1954, diecast w/steel barrel & brn plastic stock, flintlock style, 25", VG $75.00
Hubley Champ Automatic Cap Pistol, 1940, NP CI w/brn plastic grips, automatic style w/pop-up cap magazine, 5", VG $45.00
Hubley Colt .45 Cap Pistol, 1958, diecast w/NP finish, wht plastic grips, 13", NM $200.00
Hubley Colt .45 Cap Pistol, 1958, diecast w/NP finish, wht plastic grips, complete w/8 bullets, 13", NM (NM box) $325.00
Hubley Cowboy Cap Pistol, 1940, NP CI, wht checked plastic grips w/star logo, friction break, 8", EX $150.00
Hubley Cowboy Dummy Cap Pistol, 1940, NP CI, brn plastic colt grips, friction break, 8", VG $165.00
Hubley Cowboy Pistol, 1950s, diecast w/NP finish, wht plastic grips w/blk steer, revolving cylinder, 12", VG, P4 ...$135.00
Hubley Dandy Police .38 Cap Pistol, 1937, NP CI, swing-out revolving cylinder, 5¾", EX $135.00
Hubley Deputy Cap Pistol, 1957, metal w/silver finish, 11", VG, P4 ....$95.00
Hubley Dick Cap Pistol, 1930, NP CI, automatic style w/side loading, 4", EX, P4 ....$75.00

Hubley Texan Jr. Cap Pistol, gold-plated metal with red star on black plastic grips, 9", MIB, $175.00.

Hubley Electra-Matic .50 Pistol, 1960, bl plastic w/brn plastic grips, battery-op, 7", NM (EX box), P4 ....$165.00
Hubley Flintlock Jr Cap Pistol, 1955, diecast w/NP finish, brn plastic swirl grips, 7½", M (NM box), P4 ....$45.00
Hubley Model 1860 .44 Cap Pistol, 1959, diecast w/wht plastic grips, 13", EX, P4 ....$225.00
Hubley Panther Pistol, diecast w/plastic grip, complete w/arm band, NM (NM box) $125.00
Hubley Remington .36 Cap Pistol, 1959, diecast w/NP finish, repro blk grips, 10", EX $100.00
Hubley Rodeo Cap Pistol, 1950s, diecast w/NP finish, wht plastic stag grips, 8", NM, P4 ....$45.00
Hubley Sniper Cap Pistol, 1965, blk plastic w/diecast works, 22", EX $65.00
Hubley Texan Cap Pistol, 1940, NP CI w/rearing horse logo, wht plastic steer grips, lever release, 9", VG, P4 ......$225.00
Hubley Texan Cap Pistol, 1950s, diecast w/gold finish, repro wht plastic steer grips, revolving cylinder, 9", VG, P4....$125.00
Hubley Tiny Tommy Machine Gun, plastic, 10", NM (NM box) $75.00
Ideal Clipfire .223 Cap Pistol, 1966, plastic w/metal works, 13", VG $25.00
Ideal Pirate Pistol, 1950s, bl & red plastic, flywheel friction, 9", EX $45.00
Irwin Flashing Rocket Ship Space Pistol, 1950s, bl plastic, flashes & clicks signals, 7", NM (NM box) $200.00

Photo courtesy John Turney

Irwin 6-Shooter Cowboy Water Pistol, plastic, MIB, $65.00.

Ives Butting Match, CI, 1885, 5", EX $475.00
Ives Chinese Must Go, CI, 1880, 4¾", G- $375.00
Ives Clown on Powder Keg, CI, 1890s, 3¾", VG $400.00
Ives Devil's Head Bomb, CI, 1880, 2⅛", EX $275.00
Ives Dog Head Bomb, CI, 1880, 2⅛", EX $250.00
Ives Double-Face Man, CI, 1890, 1⅝", VG $145.00
Ives Hobo Bomb, CI, 1890s, 2", G- $125.00
Japan Baby Space Gun, friction, litho tin, fires w/siren sound, 6", NM (NM box) $75.00
Kenton Cannon, CI, 1900 4⅞", VG $450.00

Kenton Lawmaker Cap Pistol, 1941, CI w/silver-pnt finish, wht plastic grips, friction break, rare, EX, P4 ....$165.00
Kenton Lightning Express, CI, 1800, 5", EX..................$650.00
Kilgore Big Horn Cap Pistol, 1950s, diecast w/silver finish, revolving cylinder, 7", M (NM box), P4.................$100.00
Kilgore Buck Cap Pistol, 1955, diecast w/silver finish, blk plastic deer grips, 7", M (M box), P4 ....$65.00
Kilgore Deputy Cap Pistol, 1950s, diecast w/silver finish, revolving cylinder, 6", NM, P4 ....$75.00
Kilgore Mountie Cap Pistol, 1950, diecast w/blk fr & silver highlights, wht plastic grips, 6", MIB, P4 ....$50.00
Kilgore Mustang Tophand Twins, 1960, diecast w/gold finish, wht & brn cameo grips, friction break, 9", MIB $250.00
Kilgore Police Chief Cap Pistol, 1938, NP CI, automatic style, 5", EX, P4..$85.00
Kilgore Private Eye Cap Pistol, 1950s, diecast w/silver finish, lift-up cap door, 6½", NM (VG box), P4........................$45.00
Kuzan's Astro Zapper Space Gun, plastic, complete, 11", NM (EX box), A $85.00
Langston Super Nu-Matic Jr, 1950, diecast w/red-pnt finish, shoots rolls of paper, EX, P4 ....$55.00
Larami Control Group 95E International Secret Spy Dart Gun, 1960s, wht plastic w/blk trim, complete, 10", MOC, P4..$35.00
Leslie-Henry Marshal Cap Pistol, 1950s, diecast w/NP finish, wht plastic grips w/blk shamrock, 10", EX, P4.........$125.00
Leslie-Henry Texas Cap Pistol, 1950s, diecast w/NP finish, wht plastic horse head grips, lever release, 9", M, P4........$90.00
Lone Star Derringer Dueling Set, diecast w/blk-pnt finish, red plastic grips, 3¼", M (EX box), P4............................$65.00
M&L Space Rocket Gun, 1950s, gray plastic w/space design on grips, fires missiles, 9", MIB, P4................................$135.00
Marksman (Morton Harris) 20 Shot Repeater Air Pistol, 1935, metal w/blk-pnt finish, automatic style, 9", NMIB, P4 .$50.00
Marx Airborne Commando Burp Gun, plastic, crank action, 14", NMIB, A $50.00
Marx Blue & Gray Shell Shooting Civil War Cavalry Pistol, 1960-61, bl plastic w/brn grips, 10", VG, P4.............$50.00

Marx Sharps Cavalry Carbine, 1960, brn & blk plastic w/diecast works, 27", VG..$75.00
Marx Siren Signal Pistol, 1950, yel plastic pistol w/siren sound & built-in whistle, 7", NM (EX box) $75.00
Marx Thundergun Cap Pistol, 1958, diecast w/blk finish, wht plastic grips w/horse & steer head, 12", EX.............$165.00
Marx Tommy Gun, 1950s, diecast w/gray finish, brn plastic stock, 6", MOC, P4...$30.00
Marx Western Saddle Rifle, 1950s, diecast w/dk gray finish, brn plastic stock, 7½", MOC, P4 ....$25.00
Mattel Burp Gun, 1955, plastic & stamped metal, w/up, fires perforated roll caps, 13", EX, P4 ....$75.00
Mattel Colt Six-Shooter Shootin' Shell Rifle, 1960, brn & blk plastic w/bl metal barrel, diecast works, 31", MIB ...$325.00
Mattel Fanner 50 Cap Pistol, 1958, 2nd version, diecast w/silver finish, complete w/bullets, NM (NM box) $225.00
Mattel Fanner 50 Swivelshot Trick Holster Set, 1958, diecast w/plastic stag grips, brn leather holster, MIB...........$250.00
Mattel Firebolt Two-Way Gun, 1959, blk plastic fr w/brn stock, 27", EX (NM box) $125.00
Mattel Official Winchester Crackfire Rifle, 1965, brn & blk plastic w/diecast works, brass-colored lever, 32", MIB, P4 ....$225.00
Mattel Official Winchester Saddle Gun, 1960, plastic & metal w/brn plastic stock, 33", EX (EX box).....................$275.00

Mattel Shootin' Shell Buckle Gun, 1959, MIB, $125.00.

Mattel Shootin' Shell Fanner Cap Pistol, 1959, diecast w/chrome finish, plastic stag grips, 9", EX, P4...........$85.00

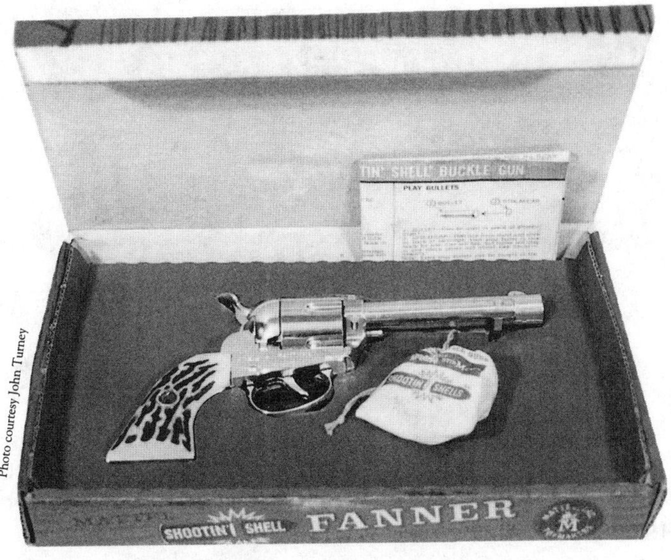

Mattel Shootin' Shell Fanner Cap Pistol, 1959, diecast with chrome finish, plastic grips, 9", MIB, $200.00.

Mattel Shootin' Shell Frontier Double Holster Set, 1958, diecast w/chrome finish, brn leather holster, complete, EX...$285.00
Mattel Shootin' Shell Snub-Nose .38 Cap Pistol, 1959, diecast w/chrome finish, brn plastic grips, 7", EX $50.00
Mattel Shootin' Shell Winchester Rifle, 1965-67, plastic w/diecast works, 26", VG..$50.00
Mattel-O-Matic Air Cooled Machine Gun, 1957, plastic w/diecast works, mounted on tripod, 16", M..............$75.00
Newell Atomic 5 Space Pistol, 1950s, red plastic, shoots table tennis balls, 9", NM (EX box) $75.00
Nichols Cowhand Cap Pistol, 1961, diecast w/NP finish, brn plastic grips, 9", G, P4..$25.00
Nichols Dyna-Mite Derringer, 1950s, diecast w/NP finish, wht plastic grips, 3¼", MIB, P4 ....$55.00

Photo courtesy John Turney

Nichols Hide-A-Mite Derringer, MOC, $65.00.

Nichols Model 61 Shooting Bullet Cap Pistol, 1960, diecast w/chrome finish, 10½", rare, NM $325.00
Nichols Pasadena Stallion .38 Cap Pistol, 1951, diecast w/NP finish, blk plastic grips, 9½", EX, P4 ....$95.00
Nichols Spitfire Saddle Rifle, 1950s, diecast w/brn plastic stock, tan holster, 9", M (NM box) $50.00
Nichols Stallion .22 Cap Pistol, 1950s, diecast w/blk plastic grips, 7", M...$65.00
Nichols Stallion .32 Six Shooter Cap Pistol, 1950s, diecast w/NP finish, blk plastic stag grips, 8", M (NM box) $125.00

Photo courtesy John Turney

Nichols Stallion .38 Six-Shooter Cap Pistol, 1955, diecast with nickel-plated finish, white plastic grips, 9½", MIB, $150.00.

Nichols Stallion .38 Six Shooter Cap Pistol, 1955, diecast w/NP finish, wht plastic grips, 9½", VG...........................$100.00

Nichols Stallion .45 MK II Cap Pistol, 1955, diecast w/NP finish, wht plastic grips w/extra set of blk, 12", MIB....$325.00
Nichols Stallion 300 Saddle Rifle, 1958, diecast w/chrome finish, blk plastic stock, deer & cowboy on fr, 27", MIB........$350.00
Nichols Top Hand 250 Gun & Holster, 1955, diecast w/NP finish, wht plastic stag grips, brn leather holster, 9", MOC ...$175.00
Ohio Art Astro Ray Flashlight Target Gun, 1955, red & wht plastic, 10", missing 1 dart, NM (G box) $75.00
Park Plastics Sky Lab Manned Space Craft w/Launcher, 1970s, bl plastic gun fires 3" saucers, 5½", M (NM box), P4 ..$45.00
Park Plastics Squirt Ray Automatic Repeater, 1950s-60s, translucent yel w/brass nozzle, 5½", M, P4................$25.00

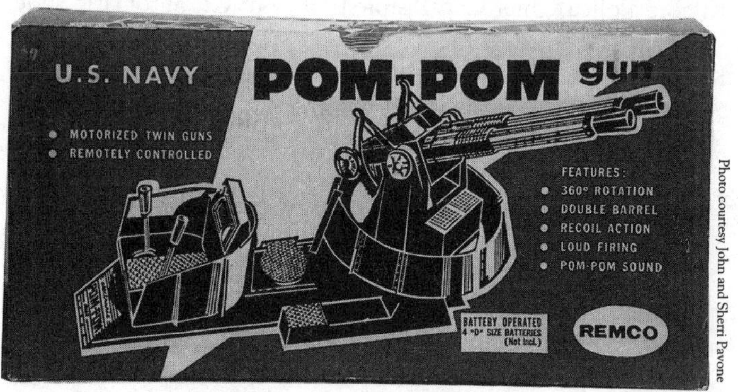

Photo courtesy John and Sherri Pavone

Remco Pom-Pom Gun, battery operated, EX (EX box), $125.00.

Remco Signal Ray Gun, 1955, yel & bl plastic, complete w/color disk & compass, 9", NM (EX box) $75.00
Renwal Stratoblaster, blk plastic w/missiles & rockets emb on grips, 27", NM (VG box) $175.00
Royal Plastics Ltd Space Flashlight Clicker Gun, 1950s, gr w/yel trigger & hammer, battery-op, 7", VG $35.00
Schmidt Buck 'N Bronc Marshal Cap Pistol, 1950, diecast w/NP finish, copper stag grips, 10", EX $135.00
SH New Flash Gun, fires w/lights & sound, litho tin, battery-op, 9", NM (NM box pictures Robby the Robot)..........$175.00

Photo courtesy June Moon

Stevens No. 25-50 Shot Pistol, 1930s, cast iron, EX, J6, $75.00.

Stevens Sea Serpent, CI, 1890, 3½", EX $950.00
Stevens 49-ER, gold-plated metal w/ornate design, wht plastic grips w/emb conestoga & cowboy, 9", M (EX box) .$425.00
Superior/T Cohn Western Cap Shooting Rifle, 1950s, brn swirl plastic w/diecast receiver & works, NM, P4..............$60.00
Tim-Me Laser Ray Gun, plastic, 10", MIB........................$45.00
TN X-Ray Gun, litho tin, fires w/pom-pom barrel action & flashing light, battery-op, 16", NM (EX box) $200.00
Topper Sixfinger, 1965, plastic finger shape, fires missiles, complete, 3½", MOC $45.00
TS Rocketship Water Gun, 1960s, bl plastic w/translucent gold trim, 9", M $50.00
Unknown Maker, Astro Ray Gun, 1960s, red or bl plastic w/visible gears, 9", MIP, P4, ea $35.00
Unknown Maker, Atomic Gun, 1960, litho tin, 5", EX, P4 .$40.00
Unknown Maker, Atomic Water Pistol, plastic w/rubber squeeze bottom, 3½", NMOC, A...$65.00
Unknown Maker, Coin Shooter, 1950, cast aluminum pistol shoots pennies or dimes, 8", EX, P4 ....$50.00
Unknown Maker, Electro Flashlight Signal Gun, 1950s, plastic, battery-op, 6", NM (EX card)...................................$75.00
Unknown Maker, Space Outlaw Water Pistol, 1970, plastic, MIP, P4...$45.00
Wham-O Air Blaster, 1960s, bl & wht plastic, 11", EX....$45.00
Wyandotte Repeating Cap Pistol, 1935, pressed steel w/red-pnt finish, 8½", VG, P4 ....$50.00

Character

Agent Zero-M Movie-Shot Cap Gun, Mattel, 1965, plastic w/diecast works, movie camera converts into gun, NM ..$60.00
Agent Zero-M Night Fighter Tommy Burst Machine Gun, 1964, 27", EX $85.00
Agent Zero-W Fanner 50 Holster & Pistol Set, Mattel, 1967, diecast w/plastic wood-grain grips, brn vinyl holster, EX............$100.00

Al Capone Gun Set, Spain, NMOC, $45.00.

Bat Masterson Holster Set w/Cane & Vest, Carnell, 1958, diecast w/NP finish, blk leather holster, complete, MIB $450.00
Batman Escape Gun, New Zealand, 1966, plastic, launches spinners & shoots darts, 5", NM $75.00
Batman Rocket Gun, Baravelli/Italian, 1960s, hard red plastic w/gold & silver highlights, 24", NMIB $350.00

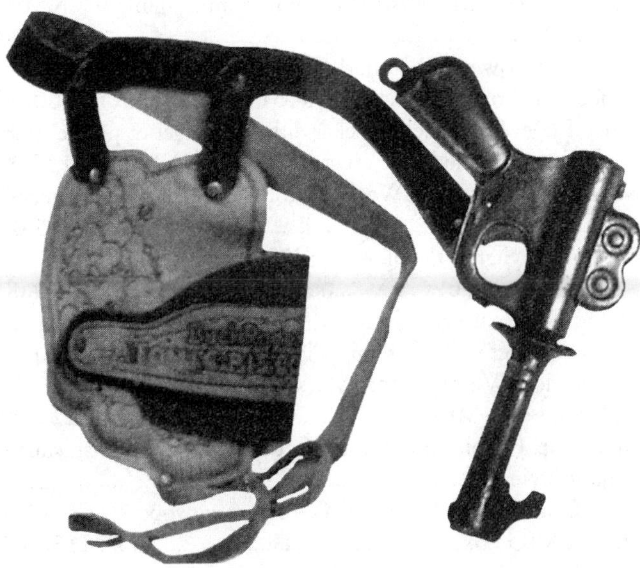

Buck Rogers Atomic Pistol and Holster, Daisy, NM, $425.00.

Buck Rogers Liquid Helium Water Pistol, Daisy, red-& yel-litho metal, 7", EX..$350.00
Buck Rogers Sonic Ray Flashlight Ray Gun, Norton-Honer, 1952, blk plastic w/red & gr trim, battery-op, 7", EX, P4..$85.00
Buck Rogers U-235 Atomic Pistol, Daisy, 1948, pressed steel w/gold-pnt finish, red spark windows, 10", VG........$225.00
Buck Rogers U-238 Atomic Pistol Holster Set, Daisy, 1948, pressed steel w/gold finish, leather holster, 10", MIB.$750.00
Buck Rogers XZ-31 Rocket Pistol Pop Gun, Daisy, 1934, pressed steel w/bl finish, chrome trim, 9½", EX $300.00
Buck Rogers XZ-35 Pop Pistol (Wilma gun), Daisy, 1935, pressed steel w/bl finish, 8", G................................$175.00
Canyon Ranger Holster Set, 2 Texan Jr cap guns in simulated cowhide holsters, EX (EX box), A $100.00
Captain America Clicker Gun, Larami, 1974, bl plastic, MIP, F8 ....$15.00
Captain Space Solar Scout Atomic Ray Gun, Marx, 1950, red plastic, battery-op, 26", not working o/w NM (G box) $175.00
Cheyenne Cap Pistol, Kilgore, 1950s, diecast w/silver finish, plastic stag grips, friction break, 9", G, P4.................$45.00
Dan Dare Planet Gun, Merit, 1969, plastic, MIB $140.00
Dan Dare Space Gun, Lone Star, red-pnt metal, 7½", VG ...$100.00
Davy Crockett Gun & Holster, France, red plastic & metal dart gun w/fancy scroll design, litho cb holster, 12", NM .$200.00
Davy Crockett Pistol & Knife, Multiple, plastic, NM (NM card), A $75.00
Davy Crockett Water Gun, unknown maker, 1950s, blk plastic flintlock-style w/metal nozzle, NM, P4 ....$50.00
Dick Tracy Automatic Repeater Water Gun, Larami, 1971, red tommy-gun shape, NMIP, D11 ....$40.00

Dick Tracy Bullet Gun, Ja-Ru, NMOC, D11....................$25.00
Dick Tracy Crimestopper Machine Gun, Larami, 1973, plastic, 14", NMIP, D11...$40.00
Dick Tracy Jr Click Gun, Marx, 1935, blk-pnt tin w/decal, 4", NM (EX box)...$125.00
Dick Tracy Machine Pistol, Larami, tommy-gun, 9", NMIP, D11..$40.00
Dick Tracy Power-Jet Squad Gun, Mattel, 1962, plastic & diecast w/brn stock, pump style, 31", M (NM box).$200.00
Dragnet Target Set, Knickerbocker, litho tin target & plastic snubnose pistol w/gold badge on grips, complete, NM........$125.00
Flash Gordon Ray Gun Water Pistol, Nasta, 1975, plastic, 9", MOC, J5...$45.00
Flash Gordon Signal Pistol, Marx, 1953, pressed steel w/lt bl finish & red trim, 6½", EX..$350.00
Flash Gordon Space Set, Ja-Ru, 1981, complete w/4½" wht plastic gun, laser radio & Flight Plan book, MOC, P4.....$30.00
Flash Gordon Water Pistol, Marx, yel plastic w/emb handle, 7½", unused, MIB...$225.00
G-Man Cap Pistol, Kilgore, 1935, diecast w/NP finish, automatic style, EX..$125.00
G-Man Gun, Marx, 1930, red & blk tin w/wood stock, w/up, 24", EX (G box)..$150.00
G-Man Siren Alarm Pistol, Marx, 1936, bl-pnt pressed steel w/G-Man decal, 8½", scarce, NM (EX box)...........$225.00
G-Men Gun, Japan, 1950s, litho tin rifle w/cb strap, w/up, 16", NM (NM box)..$100.00
Gene Autry Cap Pistol, Kenton, 1940, CI w/wht plastic simulated pearl grips, 6½", VG, P4................................$135.00
Gene Autry Flying A Ranch Holster Set, Leslie-Henry, 1950s, 9" NP gun w/wht plastic horse grips, complete, MIB.....$900.00
Gene Autry Pistol, Leslie-Henry, diecast w/silver finish, wht plastic grips w/scroll design, fires smoke, 8", NMIB.$250.00
Gene Autry Repeating Cap Pistol, Kenton, CI w/simulated pearl grips, 6½", EX (G box)..$300.00
Gene Autry Repeating Cap Pistol, Kenton, NP CI w/red plastic grips, unused, 6½", MIB...$350.00
Green Avenger Squirt Gun, Barton, 1960s-70s, shaped like brass knuckles w/plunger in palm, NMIP, F8.....................$25.00
Gunsmoke Cap Pistol, Leslie-Henry, 1950s, diecast w/NP finish, brn plastic horse head grips, lever release, 9", NM..$150.00
Hawaii Five-O Dart Gun Set, Laramie, 1973, complete, MOC, M17...$30.00
High Chapparral, Redondo, 1960s, diecast w/silver finish, brn eagle grips, 8½", NM...$50.00
Hopalong Cassidy Cap Pistol, Schmidt, 1950, diecast w/gold finish, bust of Hoppy on blk grips, 9", VG...................$300.00
Hopalong Cassidy Gold Cap Pistol, Wyandotte, 1950s, diecast w/gold finish, plastic grips w/signature, 7½", rare, VG..$375.00
Hopalong Cassidy Gun & Holster, Wyandotte, blk leather holster w/studs, complete w/2 8½" cap guns, NMIB..$1,200.00
I Spy Rapid-Fire Pellet Gun, 1966, complete w/holster, MOC..$65.00
James Bond 007 Pistol, unknown maker, 1969, plastic w/metal works, 12½", EX..$60.00
James Bond 007 Sharpshooter Set, Multiple/Glidrose, 1966, w/plastic pistol, ammo & villain targets, EX (EX card)..........$225.00
Johnny Eagle Lieutenant Automatic, Topper/Deluxe Reading, 1965, bl plastic w/brn grips, 8½", NM, P4.................$60.00
Johnny Eagle Magumba Pistol, Topper, complete, EX, J2..$100.00
Johnny Seven OMA Gun, Topper/Deluxe Reading, 1964, plastic w/diecast works, complete, 36", EX (VG box)...$150.00
Juguetes Bernabeu Colt Cap Pistol, 1960s, plastic w/silver-pnt finish, wht grips w/cowboy & Indian, 11½", MIB, P4......$65.00

Kit Carson Cap Gun and Holster, unmarked, 9", EX, $150.00; Wild Bill Hickok and Jingles Cap Guns and Holster, Hubley, EX, $275.00.

Kit Carson Cap Pistol, Kilgore, 1950s, diecast w/silver finish, wht & tan plastic grips w/cowboy, 8", EX..................$75.00
Lone Ranger Click Pistol, Marx, 1938, steel w/Lone Ranger decal, 8", EX (EX box)..$175.00
Lone Ranger Gun & Holster Set, Esquire, metal cap gun w/heavy cb holster & belt, unused, M (EX box), A................$275.00
Lone Rider Cap Pistol, Buzz-Henry, 1950, diecast w/NP finish, inset wht plastic horse grips, 8", EX........................$100.00
Lost in Space Roto-Jet Gun, 1960s, silver plastic w/red & blk highlights, 3", EX, F8..$95.00

Photo courtesy Bill Bruegman

Man From UNCLE Picture Projector Gun, prototype, Marx, MIB, $750.00.

Marshal of the West Gun Set, Daisy, complete w/2 8" diecast pistols & dbl holster, NM (NM box).......................$100.00
Outlaw Kid Presentation Set, BCM, 2 7" diecast pistols in red velvet-lined box, missing brush & caps, NM (EX box)....$100.00
Pecos Kid Cap Pistol, Lone Star, 1960s, diecast w/red-brn plastic grips, lever release, 8½", M (EX box), P4.................$50.00
Planet of the Apes Rapid Fire Rifle, Mattel, 1965-67, plastic w/brn wood-grain finish, Ape logo on decal, 26", NM, P4......$65.00

Planet of the Apes Tommy-Burst Machine Gun, Mattel, 1967-70, plastic w/wood-grain finish, 25", VG, P4 ....$65.00
Popeye Gun & Holster Set, Halco, 1961, w/2 5" diecast pistols & dbl holster, unused, NM (NM diecut cb card), A ...$150.00
Popeye Pirate Pistol, Marx, 1935, litho tin click gun, 10", NM (EX box) $400.00
Punch & Judy Cap Gun, Ives, 1882, CI w/Punch & Judy figures mounted on top, 4", EX, A $1,000.00
Rambo First Blood Part II 45'er Gun Set, LarGo, 1985, 7", MOC, M17 ....$35.00
Rangeland Western Holster Set, C Ray Lawyer, 1950s, Hubley Texan Jr cap gun & wht holster w/studs & jewels, MIB............$325.00
Red Ranger Dummy Cap Pistol, Wyandotte, 1950s, diecast w/NP finish, wht horse head & horseshoe grips, 9", M........$125.00
Red Ranger Jr Dummy Cap Pistol, Wyandotte, 1955, diecast w/NP finish, wht horse head grips, 8", M (EX box).$100.00
Red Ranger Repeating Cap Pistol, Wyandotte, gold-plated metal w/emb image, 8½", NM (EX box)............$225.00

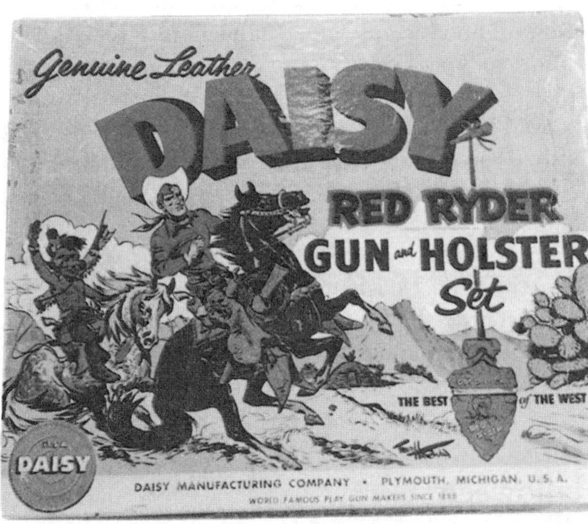

Red Ryder Gun and Holster Set, Daisy, MIB, $250.00.

Roy Rogers Forty Niner Pistol and Spurs, Leslie-Henry, complete, rare, NMIB, $850.00.

Roy Rogers Cap Shooting Carbine Rifle, Marx, plastic w/emb facsimile signature, 25", EX (EX box) $275.00
Roy Rogers Cowpoke Pistols & Holster, complete w/2 pistols & leather holster, EX $225.00
Sgt Eddy FBI Jr Holster Set, Hubley, 1955, diecast w/NP finish, blk leather holster, EX $50.00
Space Pilot Super-Sonic Gun, Merit, 1953, plastic w/color disks in barrel, battery-op, 9", NM (NM box) $175.00
Space Ranger Pistol, Lone Star, red-& bl-pnt diecast, telescopic sight, 7", EX $125.00
Space-Outlaw Atomic Pistol, England, chrome-type finish w/emb rockets & stars, red bubble above grip, 10", NMIB $250.00
Space: 1999 Water Gun, 1976, red, wht & bl plastic w/removable tanks, 9", NM, P4............$55.00
Tom Corbett Space Pistol, Marx, litho tin, 10", NM (EX box)............$325.00

Tom Mix Cap Gun and Holster with Sells Floto Circus Pin-Back Button, cast-iron gun marked made in USA, EX, J6, $85.00.

Tonto Indian Outfit, Esquire, 1950s, complete w/8" Hubley pistol, headdress, knife, sheath & belt, MIB............$350.00
Untouchables Machine Gun, Spanish issue, 22", EX (EX box)............$75.00
Wanted Dead or Alive Mares Laig Cap Pistol, Marx, 1959, blk plastic w/brn stock, diecast works, 19", EX $150.00
Zorro Pistol, Marx, 1950s, plastic, 10½", NMOC............$75.00

BB Guns

Values are suggested for BB guns that are in excellent condition.
Advisor: Jim Buskirk.

Daisy (Early), break action, wire stock, B6 ....$450.00
Daisy (Early), top lever, wire stock, B6 ....$600.00
Daisy '1000' Shot, lever action, wood stock, B6 ....$250.00
Daisy '500 Shot,' lever action, wood stock, B6 ....$250.00
Daisy Model A, break action, wood stock, B6 ....$200.00
Daisy Model B, lever action, wood stock, B6 ....$80.00
Daisy Model C, break action, wood stock, B6............$200.00
Daisy Model H, lever action, wood stock, B6 ....$80.00
Daisy Model 1938B, Christmas Story/Red Ryder, B6 ....$65.00
Daisy Model 21, 1968, dbl barrel, plastic stock, B6 ....$350.00

Daisy No 11, lever action, wood stock, B6 ....$65.00
Daisy No 12, break action, wood stock, B6 ....$50.00
Daisy No 25, pump action, pistol-grip, wood stock, B6 ....$45.00
Daisy No 25, pump action, pistol-grip wood stock, B6 .....$45.00
Daisy No 25, pump action, straight wood stock, B6..........$50.00
Daisy No 30, lever action, wood stock, B6 ....$80.00
Daisy No 40, 'Military,' lever action, wood stock, B6.....$175.00
Daisy No 40, 'Military,' w/bayonet, lever action, wood stock, B6 ....$400.00
Daisy No 50, copper-plated, lever action, blk wood stock, B6...$80.00
Daisy No 100, Model 38, break action, wood stock, B6....$25.00
Daisy No 101, Model 33, lever action, wood stock, B6 ....$40.00
Daisy No 101, Model 36, lever action, wood stock, B6 ....$35.00
Daisy No 103, Model 33, Buzz Barton, B6 ....$200.00
Daisy No 103, Model 33, lever action, wood stock, B6 ..$150.00
Daisy No 104, dbl barrel, wood stock, B6 ....$550.00
Daisy No 105, 'Junior Pump Gun,' wood stock, B6 ....$150.00
Daisy No 106, break action, wood stock, B6 ....$25.00
Daisy No 107, 'Buck Jones Special,' pump action, wood stock, B6..$100.00
Daisy No 107, pump action, plastic stock, B6 ....$20.00
Daisy No 108, Model 39, 'Carbine,' lever action, wood stock, B6 ....$65.00
Daisy No 111, Model 40, Red Ryder, aluminum lever, B6 ....$50.00
Daisy No 111, Model 40, Red Ryder, iron lever, B6 ....$80.00
Daisy No 111, Model 40, Red Ryder, plastic stock, B6.....$30.00

Photo courtesy Jim Buskirk

Daisy No 140, 'Defender,' lever action, wood stock, B6, $200.00.

Daisy No 195, Buzz Barton, lever action, wood stock, B6.$65.00
Daisy No 195, Model 36, Buzz Barton, lever action, wood stock, B6..$70.00
King Model 5533, lever action, wood stock, B6...............$35.00
King No 1, break action, wood stock, B6 ....$50.00
King No 2, break action, wood stock, B6 ....$45.00
King No 4, lever action, wood stock, B6........................$150.00
King No 5, 'Pump Gun,' wood stock, B6........................$125.00
King No 5, lever action, wood stock, B6........................$150.00
King No 10, break action, wood stock, B6 ....$30.00
King No 17, break action, wood stock, B6 ....$125.00
King No 21, lever action, wood stock, B6 ....$55.00
King No 22, lever action, wood stock, B6 ....$55.00
King No 24, break action, wood stock, B6 ....$175.00
King No 24, lever action, wood stock, B6 ....$65.00
King No 55, lever action, wood stock, B6 ....$70.00
King No 2136, lever action, wood stock, B6 ....$20.00
King No 2236, lever action, wood stock, B6 ....$20.00
Markham/King 'Chicago,' break action, all wood, B6 ....$200.00
New King, repeater, break action, wood stock, B6 ....$125.00
New King, single shot, break action, wood stock, B6 .....$100.00

Related Items and Accessories

Box, Roy Rogers Forty Niner Pistol, Leslie-Henry, EX...$250.00
Bullets, Hubley Texan .38, 1957, 6 brass-colored bullets in wht plastic belt, NM, P4 ....$20.00
Bullets, Nichols Six Stallion .38 Cartridges, 6 2-part bullets w/brass casing in clear plastic box, M, P4..................$20.00
Bullets, Nichols Stallion, 1950s, 6 2-part bullets w/brass casing on wht plastic strip, M, P4.......................................$20.00
Bullets, Topper/Deluxe Reading Johnny Eagle Pistol Cartridges, 1965, set of 12, MOC $65.00
Caps, Hubley Texan .38 Six Shooters, 100 per box, M, P4 .$5.00
Caps, Kilgore Bang Caps No 2502, 10 rolls per box, M, P4 .$5.00
Caps, Kilgore Disk Caps, 20 rolls per box, M $5.00
Caps, Kilgore Perforated Roll Caps No 150, 5 rolls per box, M $5.00
Caps, Kilgore Roll Caps No 514, punch-out sheet of 104, M, P4...$5.00
Caps, Kilgore Stick-On Round Caps No 533, 3 rolls per box, M $5.00
Caps, Marx Thundercaps-Supersound Perforated Roll Caps, 1950s, 5 rolls per box, M, P4..$5.00
Caps, Mattel Greenie Stick-M-Caps, 1958, 8 sheets of 60 per box, M, P4...$10.00
Caps, Nichols Fury 500 Shot Roll Caps, 1 roll per box, M, P4....$5.00
Caps, Nichols Stallion Round Caps, 1950s, 100 rolls per box, M, P4 ....$5.00
Caps, Nichols Tophand 250 Shot, 1 roll per box, M, P4 ....$5.00
Caps, Superb Brand Doughboy Big 72 Mammoth Caps, 1930s-40s, sheet of 72, M, P4 ....$5.00
Caps, Universal Playthings Skippy Round Caps, 1950s, 100 per box, M, P4..$5.00

Halloween

Halloween is a uniquely American holiday melded from the traditions of superstitions brought to the new world from Germany and Scotland. St. Matrimony was reportedly the patron saint of this holiday, as it was at this time of the year when the harvest was safely in that betrothals and weddings took place. Most activity for the holiday focused on getting young eligible people married. Trick or treat was a way of getting rid of bothersome younger siblings. Robert Burns, the poet of Scotland was a major influence on the folklore of the holiday. In this country today, Halloween is a holiday with little or no association with earlier religious rites of any group. It's an evening of fun, frolic, and fantasy filled with lots of sugar and calories!

Advisor: Pamela E. Apkarian-Russell, The Halloween Queen (H9).

See also Halloween Costumes; Candy Containers (for glass examples).

Balancing Toy, pumpkin man, celluloid, EX, H9 ....$200.00
Balancing Toy, witch, wood, EX, H9 ....$25.00
Book, Anna Witch, by Madeleine Edmondson, 1982, 1st edition, hardcover, 88 pgs, orig dust jacket, EX $40.00

Book, Best Witches, by Robert Heitmann, 1960, 30 pgs, EX, A...$40.00

Book, Dennison's Bogie Book, 1924, EX, $95.00.

Book, Georgie's Halloween, by Robert Bright, 1958, 30 pgs, EX...$25.00
Book, Hallowe'en Tales, by Ethel Owen, 1928, 127 pgs, orig dust jacket, EX...$65.00
Book, Old Witch Rescues Halloween, by Wendy & Harry Devlin, 1972, 30 pgs, NM...$20.00
Book, Pleasant Fieldmouse's Halloween Party, by Jan Wahl, 1974, 32 pgs, NM...$20.00
Book, Witch Family, by Eleanor Estes, 1960, 186 pgs, orig dust jacket, NM...$30.00
Candy Box, witch atop rectangular box, compo, German, 1920s, 2¼", EX, A...$400.00
Candy Container, champagne bucket w/jack-o'-lantern face, cb, German, 3¼", EX...$600.00
Candy Container, devil head, compo, German, 1910, 6", rare, M...$2,000.00
Candy Container, jack-o'-lantern man riding squash, compo, mk Germany, 4x4", EX, A...$200.00
Candy Container, jack-o'-lantern sailor on lemon, compo, German, 1930, 3", NM...$400.00
Candy Container, jack-o'-lantern soldier on pear, compo, German, 1920, 3", NM...$400.00
Candy Container, jack-o'-lantern soldier on pickle, compo, German, 1920, 3", NM...$400.00
Candy Container, winking jack-o'-lantern, compo, mk Germany, 4", rare, EX...$300.00
Candy Container, witch head w/cat body, compo, German, 1920, 5½", EX...$500.00
Candy Container, witch on broom, compo, German, 1930s, 10", EX...$400.00
Candy Holder, cat pulling pumpkin coach, cb, double-sided, EX, H9...$45.00
Crepe Paper Roll, owl motif, Dennison's, 1920, 7½-ft L, NMIP...$50.00
Crepe Paper Roll, skeleton pattern, Dennison's, 1920s, 7½-ft L, NMIP...$50.00
Crepe Paper Roll, witches in pumpkin patch, Dennison's, 1920s, 10-ft L, NMIP...$50.00
Crepe Paper Roll, witches making potions above girls w/mirrors, Dennison's, 1920s, 10-ft L, NMIP...$50.00
Diecut, blk cat, Beistle, 1930s, 10x23", NM (shrink-wrapped)...$20.00
Diecut, blk cat, German, 1920s, 6x5¼", NM, A...$60.00
Diecut, devil, German, 1920, 5½x2½", NM, A...$100.00
Diecut, devil w/wings, German, 1920s, 15x21", rare, EX...$100.00
Diecut, ghost, Dennison's, 1920s, 20", EX...$100.00
Diecut, jack-o'-lantern, Beistle, 1930s, 9", EX...$60.00
Diecut, jack-o'-lantern man w/cat at his feet, Beistle, 1920s, 16", EX...$50.00
Diecut, skeleton, Beistle, 1930s, 9½", EX, A...$110.00
Diecut, witch face, German, 1920s, 13", NM, A...$100.00
Diecut, witch on broom, German, 1920s, 8", NM...$85.00
Diecut, witch on jack-o'-lantern, mechanical, 9", EX, A...$100.00
Diecut Set, clown, boy, girl w/cat & witch (missing cat & owl), German, 15", EX (VG box)...$300.00
Display, Spook Pops, E Rosen, cb, push haunted house back & forth & ghosts appear, 8x7", EX, A...$195.00
Fan, blk cat, double-sided, German, 1920s, 13", EX...$100.00
Fan, witch, double-sided, German, 1920s, 13", EX, A...$95.00

Figure, jack-o'-lantern drummer, German, crank-operated, EX, $1,800.00.

Figure, donkey w/jack-o'-lantern in his mouth, hard plastic, EX, H9 ....$95.00
Figure, owl, pulp, American, 1940s, 6½", NM $150.00
Figure, scarecrow, celluloid, EX, H9 ....$95.00
Figure, witch, compo w/spring arms, German, 1920s, 7", NM, A $600.00
Figure, witch on base, compo, West Germany, EX, H9..$100.00
Figure, witch on rocketship, hard plastic, EX, H9 ....$100.00
Figure, witch pulling cart w/ghost, celluloid, EX, H9 .....$250.00
Figure, witch w/lg hat, pulp, 1950s, EX $160.00
Game, Jack-o'-Lantern Fortune, Beistle, 1920s, EX....$40.00
Game, Pick a Pumpkin, 1916, matted & framed, 12" dia, EX $400.00
Game, Witch-EE, Selchow & Righter, 1920s, EX (EX box), A $275.00
Game, Zingo Halloween Fortune & Stunt Game, Beistle, 1935, NM $45.00
Horn, blk cat face, German, 1920s, 9", EX, A $225.00

Photo courtesy Pamela Apkarian-Russell

Horn, cardboard, 1921, EX, $20.00.

Horn, cats & witches, tin, short, EX, H9 ....$15.00
Jack-o'-Lantern, cb & crepe paper, smiling face surrounded by creatures, Beistle, 1920s, 12", EX $100.00
Jack-o'-Lantern, cb w/papier-mache wash, smiling face, gr & red, orig insert, German, 1920s, 5½", NM, A....$550.00
Jack-o'-Lantern, cb w/tissue insert, smiling face, double-sided, American, 1940s, 13", EX, A $150.00
Jack-o'-Lantern, compo, jack-o'-lantern head in tree, orig insert, German, 6", EX $1,000.00

Jack-o'-Lantern, papier-mache, skull head, German, 1920s, rare, EX, A $750.00

Photo courtesy Dunbar Gallery

Jack-O'-Lantern, plastic, battery operated, 1950s, 6", NMIB, D10, $75.00.

Jack-o'-Lantern, pulp, pumpkin man w/eyelashes, mk DRGM-German, 1920s, 6½", NM, A $325.00
Jack-o'-Lantern, pulp, smiling face, orig insert, American, 1940s, 7", NM $150.00
Jack-o'-Lantern, pulp, smiling face w/pug nose, orig insert, American, 5", NM $200.00

Photo courtesy Dunbar Gallery

Lantern, American, 1940s – 50s, 8", NM, D10, $375.00.

Lantern, blk cat, full body, German, 1920s, 6¼", NM ...$400.00

Lantern, Chinaman, compo, orig inserts, German, 1910, 4", rare, EX, A $650.00
Lantern, witch, papier-mache, German, 1920s, 18", rare, EX, A $900.00
Light Set, celluloid & plastic w/jack-o'-lanterns on 1 side & witches on the other, Noma, 1930s, VG (VG box), A $135.00
Magazine, Dennison's Party Magazine, Oct/Nov, 1928, NM .. $110.00
Noisemaker, bell shaped w/different images, tin, American, 7", EX $60.00
Noisemaker, bell-shaped w/images of witch, blk cat & owl around clocks, tin w/wood hdl, 1930s, 4½" dia, EX ... $65.00
Noisemaker, blk cat face, tin, EX, H9 .... $15.00
Noisemaker, frying pan shape w/blk cat face, tin, sm, EX, H9 .... $15.00
Noisemaker, pumpkin head, pressed cb w/wood hdl, Germany, 1930, 6", NM $150.00
Noisemaker, ratchet-type w/witch, jack-o'-lantern & owl on moon, tin, EX, H9 .... $12.00
Parade Stick, cat face, pulp, American, 1940s, 21", EX, A . $375.00
Party Outfit, w/place cards, lampshades, cards for games, etc, Beistle, 1920, missing few pcs, EXIB, A $145.00
Pin, hand-painted, movable arms & legs, German, 1¾", EX, A $165.00
Ratchet, witch figure, wood, German, 1930s, 11x6", EX, A ... $190.00
Squeaker, jack-o'-lantern veggie man, double-sided, German, 1930s, 6", nonworking o/w EX $150.00
Squeaker, witch, double-sided, German, 5", nonworking o/w EX $150.00

Photo courtesy Pamela E. Apkarian-Russell

Table Decoration, crepe paper, 4", EX, $40.00.

Tambourine, image of blk cats on wall, tin, Chein, 1920s, 7" dia, EX $100.00
Tambourine, image of children in pumpkin patch, tin, Chein, 1920s, 7" dia, EX $100.00
Tambourine, image of jack-o'-lantern, tin, 1940, 6" dia, EX $100.00
Tambourine, image of laughing devil's face, tin, EX, H9 .. $95.00
Tambourine, image of 2 blk cats & jack-o'-lantern, tin, EX, H9 .... $95.00

Photo courtesy Pamela E. Apkarian-Russell

Tambourines, tin, EX, $50.00 each.

Halloween Costumes

During the '50s and '60s Ben Cooper and Collegeville made Halloween costumes representing the popular TV and movie characters of the day. If you can find one in excellent to mint condition and still in its original box, some of the better ones can go for over $100.00. MAD's Alfred E. Neuman (Collegeville, 1959 – 60) usually carries an asking price of $150.00 to $175.00, and The Green Hornet (Ben Cooper, 1966), $200.00. Earlier handmade costumes are especially valuable if they are 'Dennison-Made.'

Advisor: Pamela E. Apkarian-Russell, The Halloween Queen (H9).

Addams Family (Morticia), Ben Cooper, 1962, MIB $100.00
Alf, Collegeville, MIB, H9 .... $20.00
Alfred E Neuman, Ben Cooper, 1960s, mask only, M $50.00
Alien, mask only, latex, EX, F1 .... $90.00
Andromeda Lady Space Fighter, complete, EX (EX box). $35.00
Aquaman, Ben Cooper, 1967, complete, NM (EX box), J5 .... $125.00
Archie, Ben Cooper, 1969, complete, NMIB, F8 .... $55.00
Barbie, Ben Cooper, MIB, H9 .... $50.00
Barbie Super Star Bride, Collegeville, 1975, MIP, D2 ...... $85.00
Bart Simpson, Ben Cooper/Canada, 1989, MIB, K1 .... $10.00
Batfink, Collegeville, 1965, 1-pc fabric suit, MIP (sealed), T2 .... $60.00
Batgirl, Ben Cooper, 1973, complete, EX (EX box) $85.00
Batman, Ben Cooper, 1969, complete, NMIB, T2 .... $95.00

Batman, Ben Cooper, 1973, M (worn box), $35.00.

Battlestar Galactica (Cylon), Collegeville, 1978, complete, EX (VG box), F8 ....$25.00
Beanie & Cecil (Beanie), Ben Cooper, complete, EX (G box) $100.00
Big Bird, Ben Cooper, MIB, H9 ....$20.00
Birdman, Ben Cooper, 1967, complete, EX (EX box) $40.00
Blue Meanie (Beatles Yellow Submarine), Collegeville, NMIB $75.00
Bozo the Clown, Ben Cooper, 1966, complete, EX (EX box), F8 ....$35.00
Bret Maverick, Collegeville, 1959, MIB $65.00
California Raisin, Collegeville, 1988, MIB, W6 ....$15.00
Captain America, Ben Cooper, 1967, rare, MIB, A $100.00
Casper the Ghost, Ben Cooper, 1961, complete, NMIB, T2 ....$30.00
Catanooga Cats, Ben Cooper, 1969, complete, EX (EX box), F8 ....$65.00
Chuck Norris, Ben Cooper, 1985, MIB, M17 ....$20.00
Cowboy in Africa, 1967, complete, EX, F8 ....$40.00
Cryptkeeper, Ace Novelty, 1994, mask only, latex, EX $45.00
Daisy Mae, 1950s, outfit only, EX, J5 ....$15.00
Daniel Boone, Ben Cooper, complete, EX $65.00
Daredevil, Ben Cooper, 1966, rare, MIB $85.00
Dick Dastardly, Ben Cooper, 1969, MIB $45.00
Donald Duck, Collegeville, complete, NMIB $40.00
Dr Doom, Ben Cooper, 1967, scarce, MIB, A $125.00
Dracula, 1960s, complete, NM, F8 ....$50.00
Droopy, Halco, 1950s, complete, rare, EX (EX box) $85.00
Farrah Fawcett, Collegeville, 1977, complete, EX (EX box) $40.00
Father Murphy, 1981, complete, NMIB $35.00
Frankenstein, Ben Cooper, 1960s, complete, NM (EX box) $60.00
Fred Flintstone, Ben Cooper, 1960s, mask only, VG, J5 ....$15.00
Freddy Krueger, Don Post, 1986, mask only, latex, EX, F1 ....$40.00
Funky Phantom, Ben Cooper, 1971, complete, EX (EX box) $50.00
Garrison's Gorillas, Ben Cooper, 1967, scarce, MIP, T2 ....$35.00
Glow Worm, Ben Cooper, 1984, MIB, H9 ....$20.00
Godzilla, Ben Cooper, 1978, complete, EX $85.00
Grandpa Munster, mask, Illusive Concepts, latex, EX, F1 ....$35.00
Great Grape Ape, Ben Cooper, 1975, complete, NMIB, F8 ....$65.00
Green Hornet & Kato, mask set, MOC, T2 ....$300.00
Green Lantern, Ben Cooper, 1967, complete, EX (EX box) $50.00
Gumby, Collegeville, EX (G box) $50.00
Herman & Katnip (Herman), Collegeville, 1960s, complete, VG (VG box), F8 ....$30.00
Howdy Doody, Ben Cooper, 1976, complete, EX (VG box) $50.00
I Dream of Jeannie, Ben Cooper, 1973, complete, NMIB, M17 ....$125.00
Iron Man, Ben Cooper, 1966, complete, M $60.00
Isis, Ben Cooper, 1976, complete, NMIB, F8 ....$30.00
Jane Jetson, Ben Cooper, 1960s, complete, EX (VG box) $50.00
Jed Clampett, 1963, complete, NM, F8 ....$50.00
Jolly Green Giant, Halco, 1950s-60s, complete, EX (EX box), F8 ....$50.00
King Kong, Ben Cooper, 1976, MIB, H4 ....$80.00
KISS (Gene Simmons), Collegeville, 1978, MIB $100.00
Kung Fu, Ben Cooper, 1970s, complete, EX (VG box), J5 ....$25.00
Lily Munster, Ben Cooper, 1966, complete, unused, NM (EX box) $100.00
Little Mermaid, MIP $25.00
Little Orphan Annie, 1930s, mk Leapin' Lizards!, complete w/bag & party favors, EX (EX box) $175.00
Man From UNCLE, Halco, complete, EX (EX box) $75.00
Mandrake the Magician, Collegeville, 1950s, complete, EX (EX box), F8 ....$70.00
Maverick, 1959, complete, EX, F8 ....$50.00
Max Headroom, 1986, mask only, M $20.00
Mr Fantastic, Ben Cooper, 1967, complete, EX (EX box) $50.00
Muhammad Ali, Collegeville, 1977, complete, NM (EX box) $125.00
Mummy, Bland Charnas, 1979, complete, EX (EX box) $35.00
Oscar the Grouch, Ben Cooper, MIB $30.00
Pink Panther, Ben Cooper, 1964, complete, NMIB $50.00
Predator, mask, latex, rare, EX, F1 ....$100.00
Raggedy Ann, Ben Cooper, TV-Comic series, 1973, MIB $40.00
Rocketeer, Ben Cooper, MIB $95.00
Shazam, Ben Cooper, 1967, complete, EX (EX box), F8 ....$35.00
Space Ghost, Ben Cooper, 1966, MIB, from $40 to $50.00

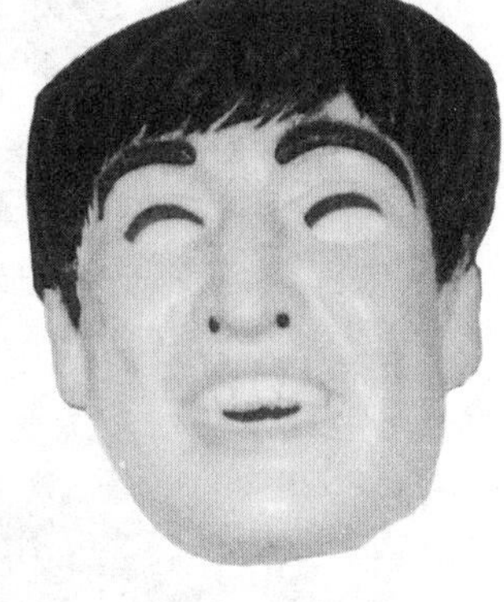

Three Stooges, mask, NMIP, $100.00; Beatles, mask, flocked hair, EX, $100.00.

Spider-Man, Ben Cooper, 1972, complete, EX (EX box), T2 .....**$50.00**
Spider-Woman, Ben Cooper, 1970s, complete, scarce, NM (NM box)..........**$100.00**
Spock, Ben Cooper, 1970s, complete, EX (EX box).......**$100.00**
Tarzan, Ben Cooper, 1975, complete, M (VG box)..........**$95.00**
Teenage Mutant Ninja Turtles, Premo & Remco Toys/China, mask only, EX **$5.00**
Tin Man, Ben Cooper, 1967, complete, EX (EX box), A ..**$125.00**
Tonto, Halco, 1950s, complete, VG (VG box), F8 ....**$30.00**
Top Cat, Ben Cooper, 1965, complete, NMIB, F8 ....**$75.00**
Underdog, Ben Cooper, 1969, MIB..........**$50.00**
Universal Monsters Mutant, Collegeville, rare, MIB, P12 ..**$145.00**
Winky Dink, Halco, 1950s, complete, rare, NM, F8 ....**$95.00**
Wonder Woman, Ben Cooper, 1976, complete, EX (EX box), from $50 to..........**$65.00**
Woody Woodpecker, Collegeville, 1950s, complete, EX (EX box)..........**$50.00**
Zorro, Ben Cooper, 1955, complete, NM (EX box), A.....**$75.00**
20,000 Leagues Under the Sea (Captain Nemo), Ben Cooper, 1950s, complete, EX (EX box), F8 ....**$65.00**

Hartland Plastics, Inc.

Originally known as the Electro Forming Co., Hartland Plastics Ind. was founded in 1941 by Ed and Iola Walters. They first produced heels for military shoes, birdhouses, and ornamental wall decor. It wasn't until the late 1940s that Hartland produced their first horse and rider. Figures were hand painted with an eye for detail. The Western and Historic Horsemen, Miniature Western Series, Authentic Scale Model Horses, Famous Gunfighter Series, and the Hartland Sports Series of Famous Baseball Stars were a symbol of the fine workmanship of the '40s, '50s, and '60s. The plastic used was a virgin acetate. Paint was formulated by Bee Chemical Co., Chicago, Illinois, and Wolverine Finishes Corp., Grand Rapids, Michigan. Hartland figures are best known for their uncanny resemblance to the TV Western stars who portrayed characters like the Lone Ranger, Matt Dillon, and Roy Rogers. For more information we recommend *Hartland Horses and Riders* by Gail Fitch. See Also Clubs, Newsletters, and Other Publications.

Advisor: Judy and Kerry Irvin (K5).

Alkine Ike, NM, K5..........**$150.00**
Annie Oakley, NM, K5..........**$275.00**
Bill Longley, NM, K5..........**$600.00**
Brave Eagle, NM, K5..........**$200.00**
Brave Eagle, NMIB, K5..........**$300.00**
Bret Maverick, miniature series, NM, K5..........**$75.00**
Bret Maverick, NMIB, K5..........**$750.00**
Bret Maverick, w/coffeedunn horse, NM, K5..........**$650.00**
Bret Maverick, w/gray horse, rare, NM, K5..........**$700.00**
Buffalo Bill, NM, K5..........**$300.00**
Bullet, NM, K5..........**$45.00**
Bullet, w/tag, NM, K5..........**$75.00**
Cactus Pete, NM, K5..........**$150.00**
Champ Cowgirl, NM, K5..........**$150.00**
Cheyenne, miniature series, NM, K5..........**$75.00**
Cheyenne, w/tag, NM, K5..........**$190.00**
Chief Thunderbird, rare shield, NM, K5..........**$150.00**
Cochise, NM, K5..........**$150.00**
Commanche Kid, NM, K5..........**$150.00**
Dale Evans, gr, NM, K5..........**$125.00**
Dale Evans, purple, NM, K5..........**$300.00**
Dale Evans, rare bl version, NM, K5..........**$400.00**
Davy Crockett, NM, K5..........**$550.00**
General Custer, NMIB, K5..........**$200.00**
General Custer, repro flag, NM, K5..........**$150.00**
General George Washington, NMIB, K5..........**$175.00**
General Robert E Lee, NMIB, K5..........**$175.00**
Gil Favor, prancing, NM, K5..........**$80.00**
Gil Favor, semi-rearing, NM, K5..........**$600.00**
Hoby Gillman, NM, K5..........**$225.00**
Jim Bowie, w/tag, NM, K5..........**$250.00**
Jim Hardy, NMIB, K5..........**$275.00**
Jockey, NM, K5..........**$150.00**
Jockey, repro crop, NM, K5..........**$100.00**
Josh Randle, NM, K5..........**$650.00**
Lone Ranger, champ, blk breast collar, NM, K5..........**$125.00**
Lone Ranger, miniature series, NM, K5..........**$75.00**
Lone Ranger, NM, K5..........**$150.00**
Lone Ranger, rearing, NMIB, K5..........**$300.00**
Matt Dillon, w/tag, NMIB, K5..........**$275.00**
Paladin, NMIB, K5..........**$350.00**
Rebel, miniature series, repro hat, NM, K5..........**$100.00**

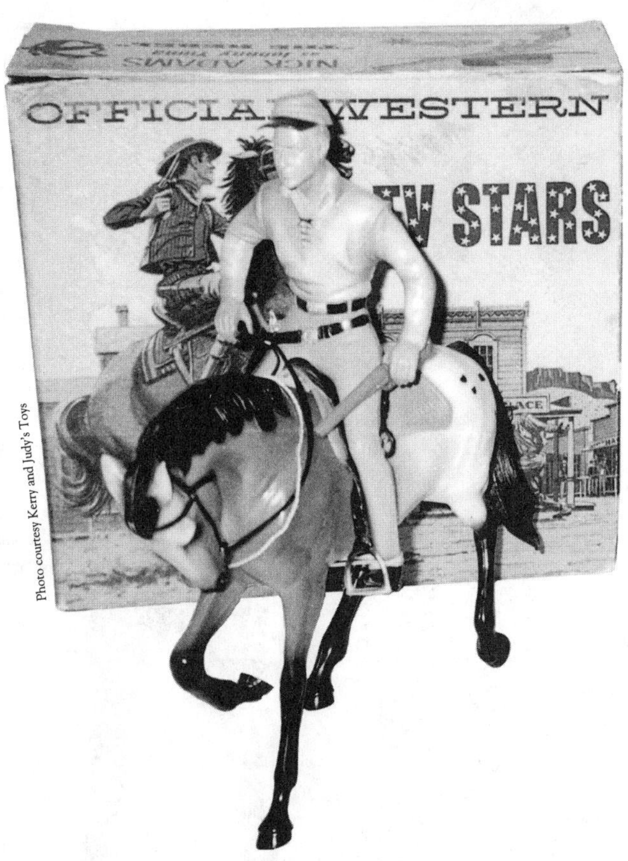

Photo courtesy Kerry and Judy's Toys

Rebel, NMIB, K5, $1,200.00.

Rifleman, miniature series, repro rifle, EX, K5 ....$75.00
Rifleman, NMIB $350.00
Ronald MacKenzie, NM, K5 ....$1,200.00
Roy Rogers, semi-rearing, NMIB, K5 ....$350.00
Roy Rogers, walking, NMIB, K5 ....$250.00
Seth Adams, NM, K5 ....$275.00
Sgt Lance O'Rourke, NMIB, K5 ....$250.00
Sgt Preston, repro flag, NM, K5 ....$750.00
Tom Jeffords, NM, K5 ....$175.00
Tonto, miniature series, NM, K5.......................................$75.00
Tonto, NM, K5 ....$150.00
Tonto, rare semi-rearing, NM, K5...................................$650.00
Warpaint Thunderbird, w/shield, NMIB, K5..................$350.00
Wyatt Eart, w/tag, NMIB, K5...$275.00

STANDING GUNFIGHTERS

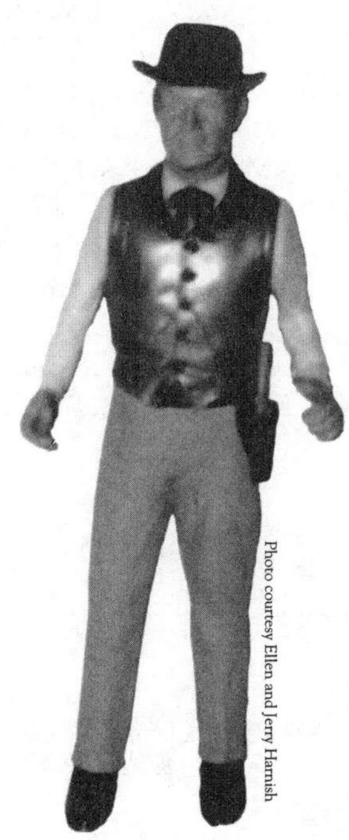

Bat Masterson, NMIB (not shown), K5, $500.00.

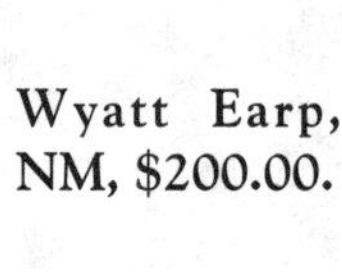

Wyatt Earp, NM, $200.00.

Bret Maverick, NM, K5 ....$150.00
Chris Colt, NM, K5 ....$150.00
Clay Holister, NM, K5 ....$225.00
Dan Troop, NM, K5 ....$400.00
Jim Hardy, NM, K5...$150.00
Johnny McKay, NM, K5...$800.00
Paladin, NM, K5...$400.00
Vint Bonner, w/tag, NMIB, K5 ....$650.00

Horses

Horse riding being the order of the day, many children of the 19th century had their own horses to ride indoors; some were wooden while others were stuffed, and many had glass eyes and real horsehair tails. There were several ways to construct these horses so as to achieve a galloping action. The most common types had rocker bases or were mounted with a spring on each leg.

Platform Horse, cvd wood, blk w/red saddle & yel blanket, red platform w/CI spoke wheels, 30", EX, A...............$1,000.00

Platform Horse, Germany, straw-filled burlap with glass eyes, four-wheeled wooden base, 23x22", EX, A, $475.00

Platform Horse, stuffed brn burlap w/hair mane & tail, glass eyes, wooden platform w/CI wheels, 25", EX....................$525.00
Rocking Horse, Hi-Prancer hobby horse, early 1950s, wht w/blk detail, red saddle, wooden stand, VG, from $150 to $200.00
Rocking Horse, hide-covered w/leather saddle & tack, glass eyes, red-pnt base, 34", EX, A $550.00

Rocking Horse, hide-covered w/red upholstered inset seat, hair mane & tail, 34", runners incomplete o/w VG, A...**$175.00**

Rocking Horse, New England, 1800s, pnt wood, dapple gray w/red saddle, heart-shaped supports, 51", EX, A ..**$1,200.00**

Rocking Horse, pnt pine w/hair mane & tail, leatherette saddle on cloth blanket w/gold fringe, red-pnt platform, 36", EX **$1,000.00**

Hot Wheels

When they were introduced in 1968, Hot Wheels were an instant success. Sure, their racy style and flashy custom paint jobs were instant attention-getters, but what the kids loved most was the fact that they were fast! The fastest on the market! It's estimated that more than two billion Hot Wheels have been sold to date — every model with a little variation, keeping up with new trends in the big car industry. The line has included futuristic vehicles, muscle cars, trucks, hot rods, racers, and some military vehicles. Lots of these can still be found for very little, but if you want to buy the older models (collectors call them 'Red Lines' because of their red sidewall tires), it's going to cost you a little more, though many can still be found for under $25.00. By 1971, earlier on some models, black-wall tires had become the standard.

A line of cars with Goodyear tires called Real Riders were made from 1983 until about 1987. (In 1983 the tires had gray hubs with white lettering; in 1984 the hubs were white.) California Customs were made in 1989 and 1990. These had the Real Rider tires, but they were not lettered 'Goodyear' (and some had different wheels entirely).

Chopcycles are similar to Sizzlers in that they have rechargable batteries. The first series was issued in 1973 in these models: Mighty Zork, Blown Torch, Speed Steed, and Bruiser Cruiser. Generally speaking, these are valued at $35.00 (loose) to $75.00 (MIB). A second series issued in 1974 was made up of Ghost Rider, Rage Coach, Riptide, Sourkraut, and Triking Viking. This series is considerably harder to find and much more expensive today; expect to pay as much as $250.00 to $350.00 for a mint-in-box example.

Though recent re-releases have dampened the collector market somewhat, cars mint and in the original packages are holding their values and are still moving well. Near mint examples (no package) are worth about 50% to 60% less than those mint and still in their original package, excellent condition about 65% to 75% less.

Advisor: Steve Stephenson.

'31 Classic Woody, red line tires, metallic bl w/cream interior, textured blk roof, 1969, M...............**$25.00**

'31 Doozie, blk walls, red w/red-brn interior/fenders, 1983, MIP **$8.00**

'32 Ford Delivery, blk walls, yel w/orange/red/magenta tampo, 1989, M...............**$8.00**

'34 3-Window Coupe, blk walls, chrome, turq fenders/interior, #1 Speed Gleamer tampo, 1995, MIP...............**$5.00**

'35 Classic Caddy, blk walls, tan w/brn interior, 1982, M...**$6.00**

'36 Classic Coupe, red line tires, metallic pk w/blk interior, blk roof, rare color, 1969, NM...............**$100.00**

'37 Bugatti, blk walls, blk w/red side tampo only, 1981, M.**$3.00**

'40s Woodie, blk walls, orange w/tan interior, wood-grain panels, 1981, M...............**$10.00**

'56 Hi-Tail Hauler, blk walls, lt bl w/yel interior, yel/bl flame tampo on hood, 1979, M **$8.00**

'57 Classic T-Bird, red line tires, metallic olive, med interior, 1969, NM...............**$40.00**

'57 T-Bird, blk walls, red w/blk interior, yel/magenta T-Bird tampo, 1985, M (EX+ card) **$10.00**

'80s Corvette, blk walls, blk, red/pk tampo, gray bag, 1987, MIP...............**$8.00**

'80s Firebird, blk walls, dk red, yel tampo, 1983, MIP.......**$10.00**

A-OK, blk walls, dk metallic red, dk maroon fenders/interior, rare gray hubs w/Goodyear tires, MIP **$500.00**

Alive '55, red line tires, lt bl, dk interior, 1973, NM......**$150.00**

Ambulance, red line tires, metallic aqua, cream interior, 1970, NM...............**$40.00**

American Hauler, red line tires, dk bl, 1976, VG+ **$5.00**

American Tipper, red line tires, red, 1976, NM...............**$20.00**

American Victory, blk walls, lt bl w/dk bl tampo, 1983, MIP **$30.00**

American Victory, red line tires, lt bl, red/wht #9 tampo, 1975, M (NM Flying Colors card)...............**$75.00**

AMX/2, red line tires, metallic magenta w/blk interior, 1971, EX+ **$10.00**

Assault Crawler, blk walls, olive, camouflage tampo, 1987, MIP **$8.00**

Auburn 852, blk walls, red w/brn fenders/interior, 1979, MIP **$10.00**

Backwoods Bomb, red line tires, lt bl, clear bl windshield, complete, 1975, M (NM Flying Colors card)...............**$85.00**

Baja Breaker, blk walls, gray w/blk interior, red/bl/yel tampo, 1978, EX+ **$3.00**

Beach Bomb, red line tires, metallic red w/lt gray interior, orig boards, scarce color, 1969, NM **$75.00**

Beach Patrol, blk walls, California Custom, fluorescent gr w/red interior, magenta/wht/pk tampo, 1990, M **$10.00**

Beatnik Bandit, red line tires, metallic purple, 1968, NM ..**$20.00**

Brabham Repco F1, red line tires, metallic red w/rare cream interior, missing decals, 1969, NM **$35.00**

Photo courtesy June Moon

Bugeye, red line tires, metallic green, 1971, EX, $35.00.

Breakaway Bucket, red line tires, dk bl w/blk interior, orange/yel tampo, 1974, M (NM Flying Colors card) $145.00
Bronco Four-Wheeler, blk walls, bl w/Rose & Buick racing logo, 1991, MIP..................$8.00
Bugeye, red line tires, metallic red w/blk interior, 1971, EX...$28.00
Buzz Off, blk walls, gold chrome, Gold One tampo, 1977, NM..$10.00
Buzz Off, red line tires, dk bl w/yel pinstripe, metal base, 1974, M (NM Flying Colors card) $110.00
Bye-Focal, red line tires, metallic lt gr, med interior, complete, scarce, 1971, M..............$100.00
Cadillac Seville, blk walls, metal-flake gold, 1983, M $4.00
Camaro Z-28, blk walls, red, bl/blk/yel tampo, 1986, MIP..$4.00
Carabo, red line tires, lt gr w/blk interior, orange/bl tampo, 1974, M (EX Flying Colors card) $80.00
Cement Mixer, red line tires, metallic orange w/blk interior, orange bed/barrel, orig stickers, scarce color, 1970, NM.............$25.00
Chapparal 2G, red line tires, metallic magenta w/blk interior, orig wing, no decals, 1969, NM..............$15.00
Chevy Citation, blk walls, wht w/blk interior, lt red tampo, 1985, MIP (French)..............$20.00
Chevy Monza, red line tires, Super Chrome, yel/blk tampo, M (NM card)..............$40.00
Chevy Monza 2+2, blk walls, orange, blk tampo, 1983, scarce MIP (French)..............$75.00
Chief's Special, red line tires, red w/blk interior, 1975, M (NM Flying Colors card) $75.00
Classic Cord, red line tires, metallic lt gr w/blk interior, 1971, NM..............$150.00
Classic Nomad, blk walls, metallic dk aqua w/cream interior, MIP..............$8.00

Photo courtesy June Moon

Classic Nomad, red line tires, metallic green, 1970, NM, $55.00.

Classic Nomad, red line tires, metallic purple w/cream interior, #9 flower decals, 1970, NM..............$45.00
Corvette Split Window, blk walls, lt bl, yel/lt brn/magenta tampo, 1993, MIP..............$15.00
Corvette Stingray, blk walls, metallic dk red w/tan interior, yel/wht/lt bl tampo, no ZR1, 1989, MIP..............$5.00
Corvette Stingray, blk walls, yel, dk bl/orange/magenta tampo, 1988, MIP..............$5.00
Custom AMX, red line tires, metallic pk w/cream interior, 1969, VG+ $20.00
Custom Baracuda, red line tires, metallic dk aqua, dk interior, 1968, EX+ $30.00
Custom Camaro, red line tires, metallic red, dk interior, 1968, NM..............$60.00
Custom Continental MK III, metallic yel w/cream interior, 1969, EX+ $25.00
Custom Corvette, red line tires, metallic lt bl, med interior, 1968, NM..............$50.00
Custom Cougar, red line tires, metallic gold, med interior, blk roof, 1968, NM $50.00
Custom Dodge Charger, red line tires, metallic purple w/cream interior, 1969, EX+ $40.00
Custom Eldorado, red line tires, metallic olive w/cream interior, blk roof, 1968, NM $40.00
Custom Firebird, red line tires, metallic purple, med interior, 1968, M..............$55.00
Custom Fleetside, red line tires, metallic purple w/blk interior, 1968, M (NM card)..............$180.00
Custom Mustang, blk walls, metallic brn, 1993, MIP $9.00
Custom Mustang, red line tires, metallic red w/red interior, rare open scoops, slight toning, 1968, EX $175.00
Custom Police Cruiser, red line tires, blk & wht w/cream interior, 1969, M $40.00
Custom T-Bird, red line tires, metallic brn, blk roof, 1968, M (NM card)..............$180.00
Custom VW, red line tires, metallic magenta w/cream interior, 1968, NM..............$35.00
Delivery Truck, blk walls, wht, Air France, 1990, MIP $8.00
Deora, red line tires, metallic aqua, lt interior, 1968, MIP $100.00
Double Vision, red line tires, lemon yel w/cream interior, 1973, NM..............$80.00
Dream Van XGW, blk walls, olive, blk/wht Fortune tampo, MIP..............$10.00
Dump Truck, red line tires, metallic yel w/blk interior, brn bed, yel dump, 1970, NM..............$30.00
Dune Daddy, red line tires, lt gr w/blk interior, flower tampo, M (NM Flying Colors card) $90.00
El Ray Special, red line tires, rare dk bl, yel/orange #1 tampo, 1974, M (NM Flying Colors card) $850.00
Emergency Squad, blk walls, red w/blk interior, yel/wht tampo, 1977, MIP $10.00
Emergency Squad, red line tires, red, gray windshield, 1976, M (NM Flying Colors card) $40.00
Emergency Squad, red line tires, red, gray windshield, 1976, M (NM Flying Colors card) $50.00
Ferrari 312P, red line tires, red w/blk interior, bl/wht tampo, metal base, 1974, M (EX+ Flying Colors card)........$100.00
Fiat Ritmo, blk walls, dk aqua, wht/yel Walt Disney tampo, MIP..............$15.00
Fire Chief Cruiser, red line tires, metallic red w/cream interior, 1970, EX+ $12.00
Fire Eater, blk walls, yel, yel/blk tampo, 1982, M...............$2.00
Fire Engine, red line tires, metallic red w/blk interior, complete, 1970, NM..............$24.00
Firebird Funny Car, blk walls, yel, orange/blk/bl tampo, 1989, MIP..............$5.00
Ford Aerostar, blk walls, wht, Quantas, 1991, MIP............$8.00

Ford J-Car, red line tires, metallic purple w/blk interior, orig stickers, 1968, NM **$15.00**

Formula 5000, red line tires, wht, bl/red #76 tampo, 1976, M (NM Flying Colors card) **$35.00**

Front Runnin' Fairmont, blk walls, red, yel/wht/blk #27 tampo, 1982, MIP **$18.00**

Fuel Tanker, red line tires, wht, med interior, complete, 1971, EX+ **$35.00**

GMC Motor Home, blk walls, olive, wht/blk Greentown/map tampo, MIP **$15.00**

Grass Hopper, red line tires, lt gr w/blk interior, orange/bl tampo, exposed engine, 1974, M (NM Flying Colors card) **$80.00**

Greased Gremlin, blk walls, red, bl/yel/wht #5 tampo, 1979, M **$12.00**

Gremlin Grinder, red line tires, gr, orange/yel/blk tampo, 1975, M (EX+ Flying Colors card) **$80.00**

Gulch Stepper, blk walls, yel w/tan roof, orange/red/purple tampo, 8-spoke construction tires, 1985, MIP.............**$9.50**

Gun Slinger, red line tires, olive, gun clip, 1976, M (NM Flying Colors card) **$50.00**

Hairy Hauler, red line tires, metallic lt gr w/cream interior, EX wheels, 1971, NM **$20.00**

Hare Splitter, blk walls, red w/blk hood, blk/wht stripes, Hot Wheel logo tampo, MIP **$15.00**

Heavy Chevy, red line tires, chrome, Club Car, complete, added decal, 1970, NM **$50.00**

Hi-Way Robber, red line tires, lt gr w/blk interior, 1973, EX....**$70.00**

Hot Bird, blk walls, bl w/yel bird on hood, orange/yel tampo, scarce color, 1980, VG **$22.00**

Hot Heap, red line tires, metallic dk red, med interior, dk red, 1968, NM...**$35.00**

Ice T, red line tires, dk bl w/blk interior, complete, 1973, EX+ **$80.00**

Incredible Hulk, blk walls, yel, gr/blk/wht tampo, 2 rear windows, 1979, NM...**$12.00**

Indy Eagle, red line tires, metallic red w/rare cream interior, missing decals, 1969, NM **$50.00**

Inside Story, blk walls, gray, red/yel/bl tampo, 1979, M......**$6.00**

Jack Rabbit Special, red line tires, wht w/blk interior, 1970, NM **$22.00**

Jaguar XJS, blk walls, gray, no tampo, 1983, MIP **$25.00**

Jeep Scrambler, blk walls, yel, blk/red tampo, MIP...........**$10.00**

Photo courtesy June Moon

Jet Threat, red line tires, metallic yellow, 1971, NM, $55.00.

Jet Threat II, red line tires, plum, yel tampo, 1976, M (NM Flying Colors card) **$60.00**

Khaki Kooler, blk walls, olive, metal base, 1977, M (NM Flying Colors card) **$60.00**

Khaki Kooler, red line tires, wht Army tampo, 1976, M ..**$40.00**

King Kuda, red line tires, chrome, med interior, 1970, EX+...**$25.00**

Lamborghini Countach, blk walls, wht, red/bl/yel tampo, hood tampo, 1988, MIP **$9.00**

Land Lord, blk walls, orange, orange/red/blk tampo, 1982, MIP..**$5.00**

Letter Getter, blk walls, wht, plastic base, 1979, NM **$5.00**

Light My Fire, red line tires, metallic red, med interior, orig stickers, added decals, 1970, EX **$24.00**

Lotus Turbine, red line tires, metallic aqua w/blk interior, orig decals, 1969, M **$20.00**

Photo courtesy June Moon

Mantis, red line tires, metallic green, 1970, NM, $35.00.

Maserati Mistral, red line tires, metallic red w/cream interior, 1969, NM..**$75.00**

Mazda MX5, blk walls, red, no tampo, 1991, MIP (International card) **$4.00**

McLaren M6A, red line tires, orange w/blk interior, rare color, no stickers, 1969, NM...**$22.00**

Mercedes C-111, red line tires, metallic magenta, med interior, 1972, M...**$130.00**

Mercedes C-111, red line tires, red w/cream interior, 1973, EX+...**$250.00**

Mercedes SL, blk walls, chrome, 1991, MIP (International card) **$8.00**

Mercedes 280 SL, red line tires, red w/dk gray interior, 1973, EX..**$65.00**

Mercedes 540 K, blk walls, red w/blk interior, 1982, MIP ..**$5.00**

Mirada Stocker, blk walls, red w/tan interior, blk/yel/wht #10 tampo, 1981, NM **$8.00**

Mod Quad, red line tires, metallic yel w/blk interior, 1970, M **$30.00**

Mongoose, blk walls, metallic bl, 1993, MIP.....................**$10.00**

Mongoose, red line tires, red w/blk interior, 1970, NM....**$35.00**

Mongoose II, red line tires, metallic bl, 1971, NM **$70.00**

Mongoose Rear Engine Dragster, red line tires, bl, clear front wheels, 1972, M (NM card) **$450.00**

Monte Carlo Stocker, blk walls, yel, bl/red/wht #38 tampo, 1977, NM...**$16.00**

Photo courtesy June Moon

Mongoose, red line tires, metallic blue with Tom McEwen decal, 1973, EX, $55.00.

Monte Carlo Stocker, red line tires, yel w/blk interior, red/wht/bl #38 tampo, 1975, M (NM Flying Colors card)..........$100.00
Motocross I, red line tires, red, yel/blk tampo, 1975, NM..$100.00
Moving Van, red line tires, metallic gr, blk interior, gray trailer, complete, 1970, EX+..........$25.00
Mustang Boss Hoss, red line tires, metallic purple w/cream interior, 1971, NM..........$125.00
Mutt Mobile, red line tires, metallic gold, 1971, EX..........$35.00
Neet Streeter, blk walls, lt bl w/blk interior, red/wht/bl tampo, 1977, M..........$16.00
Neet Streeter, red line tires, lt bl, red/wht/bl tampo, 1976, NM..........$27.00

Photo courtesy June Moon

Nissan 300ZX with Ultra Gold, 1992, NM, $25.00.

Nitty Gritty Kitty, red line tires, metallic red, med interior, orig stickers, 1970, VG+..........$20.00
Noodlehead, red line tires, metallic dk magenta w/cream interior, 1971, EX+..........$65.00
Odd Job, red line tires, lt bl w/blk interior, complete, 1973, NM..........$150.00
Odd Rod, blk walls, red, no tampo, M (EX+ card)..........$15.00
Olds 442, red line tires, metallic magenta w/cream interior, orig wing, 1971, NM..........$280.00
Oscar Meyer Wienermoble, blk walls, red w/yel base, 1993, MIP..........$3.00
Oshkosh Snowplow, blk walls, orange, orig plastic cab, orig construction tires, 1991, M..........$2.00

P-911, blk walls, wht, red/blk/aqua #6 tampo, 1980, NM...$5.00

Photo courtesy June Moon

Paddy Wagon, red line tires, blue, 1970, NM, $25.00.

Paramedic, blk walls, yel, metal base, red/wht tampo, 1977, M..........$20.00
Paramedic, red line tires, wht, red/yel tampo, bl windshield, 1975, M (NM Flying Colors card)..........$60.00
Peeping Bomb, red line tires, metallic yel w/blk interior, 1970, NM..........$10.00
Peugeot 205 Rallye, blk walls, wht, #2 tampo, 1989, M (NM International card)..........$10.00
Peugeot 405, blk walls, blk, no tampo, 1991, M (NM International card)..........$3.00
Phantomachine, blk walls, chrome, red/bl/orange tampo, 1987, M (NM International card)..........$8.00
Pit Crew Car, red line tires, wht w/cream interior, complete, 1971, EX+..........$45.00
Pontiac J-2000, blk walls, yel, red/orange/blk tampo, 1983, M (EX+ International card)..........$8.00
Porsche 917, blk walls, orange, yel/purple/red tampo, 1977, NM..........$8.00
Porsche 917, red line tires, metallic pk w/dk interior, missing decals, 1970, M..........$100.00
Porsche 930, blk walls, red, wht/blk/yel tampo, 1991, M....$3.00
Power Pad, red line tires, metallic magenta w/blk interior, NM..........$40.00
Pro Circuit #01, blk walls, wht, gray Pro Circuit Indy wheels, 1993, NM..........$10.00
Prowler, red line tires, Super Chrome w/blk interior, orange/yel Devil tampo, 1976, NM+..........$25.00
Purple Passion, blk walls, purple, 2-tone gr tampo, 1978, NM..........$10.00
Race Bait 308, blk walls, red, blk/yel/wht tampo, 1978, NM+..........$3.00
Racer Rig, red line tires, metallic red w/blk interior, 1971, EX..........$40.00
Range Rover, blk walls, wht, Getty promo, 1991, MIP.......$3.00
Red Baron, blk walls, red, 1977, NM..........$5.00
Red Baron, red line tires, red w/blk interior, 1974, NM ...$15.00
Renault 5 Turbo, blk walls, bl, yel/orange/wht tampo, 1991, MIP (International card)..........$4.00

Road Torch, blk walls, red, blk/wht/yel #8 tampo, 1987, M (NM International card)....................$7.00
Rock Buster, blk walls, Super Chrome, 1977, NM............$22.00
Rock Buster, red line tires, yel, red/wht/bl #10 tampo, 1976, NM....................$30.00
Rocket Bye Baby, red line tires, metallic aqua w/gray interior, dull chrome, 1971, EX+....................$25.00
Royal Flash, blk walls, wht, red/bl tampo, 1979, NM+ $4.00
S'Cool Bus, blk walls, yel, Vintage, 1993, M (NM+ card)..$10.00
Sand Crab, red line tires, metallic yel w/blk interior, 1970, NM....................$12.00
Sand Drifter, red line tires, yel w/blk interior, orange/magenta flame tampo, 1975, M (NM Flying Colors card) $100.00
Science Friction, blk walls, wht, blk/yel/red Space Cop tampo, 1978, NM....................$3.00
Seasider, red line tires, metallic yel w/blk interior, orig orange over wht boat, 1970, NM $45.00
Second Wind, blk walls, bl, blk eagle tampo, MIP $12.00
Sheriff Patrol, blk walls, blk w/tan interior, yel/bl/wht #59 tampo, 1990, MIP $5.00
Short Order, red line tires, metallic dk aqua w/blk interior, 1971, NM....................$60.00
Show Hoss II, blk walls, yel, dk red/wht/blk tampo, 1977, NM $30.00
Side Kick, red line tires, metallic yel, blk rear louvers, 1972, NM $60.00
Silhouette, red line tires, metallic magenta w/cream interior, 1968, NM....................$30.00
Sky Show Fleetside, red line tires, gold w/blk interior, orig ramp/decals/rubber band/yel airplane, complete, 1970, NM+....................$360.00
Snake, blk walls, metallic emerald gr, Vintage, 1993, MIP.$12.00
Snake, red line tires, yel w/blk interior, complete, 1970, NM...$60.00
Snake II, red line tires, wht, complete, 1971, NM $40.00
Snake Rail Dragster, red line tires, wht, complete, blk front wheels, 1971, EX+ $45.00
Special Delivery, red line tires, metallic bl w/wht interior, 1971, NM....................$34.00
Speed Seeker, blk walls, wht, red/gr/blk snake tampo, Ultra Hot Wheels, 1987, M (NM International card)..................$6.00
Spider-Man, blk walls, blk, 1979, M....................$15.00
Spoiler Sport, blk walls, gr, blk/yel/dk red tampo, 1980, MIP..$8.00
Staff Car, red line tires, olive w/blk interior, wht tampo, rare, 1976, EX $250.00
Steam Roller, red line tires, wht, red/bl tampo, 3 stars, 1974, M (NM Flying Colors card) $75.00
Street Eater, red line tires, yel, red/orange flame tampo, 1975, M (NM Flying Colors card) $250.00
Street Snorter, red line tires, fluorescent pk w/blk interior, 1973, VG+....................$50.00
Strip Teaser, red line tires, metallic aqua, 1971, EX $15.00
Super Van, red line tires, plum, scarce yel/orange/bl motorcycle tampo, 1975, NM $110.00
Sweet 16, red line tires, dk bl w/blk interior, 1973, EX+ .$115.00
Swingin' Wing, red line tires, metallic lt gr w/wht interior, 1970, NM....................$25.00
T-4-2, red line tires, metallic gr, med interior, orig top, 1971, M $50.00

Super Van, black walls, black with flame tampo, 1975, EX, $15.00.

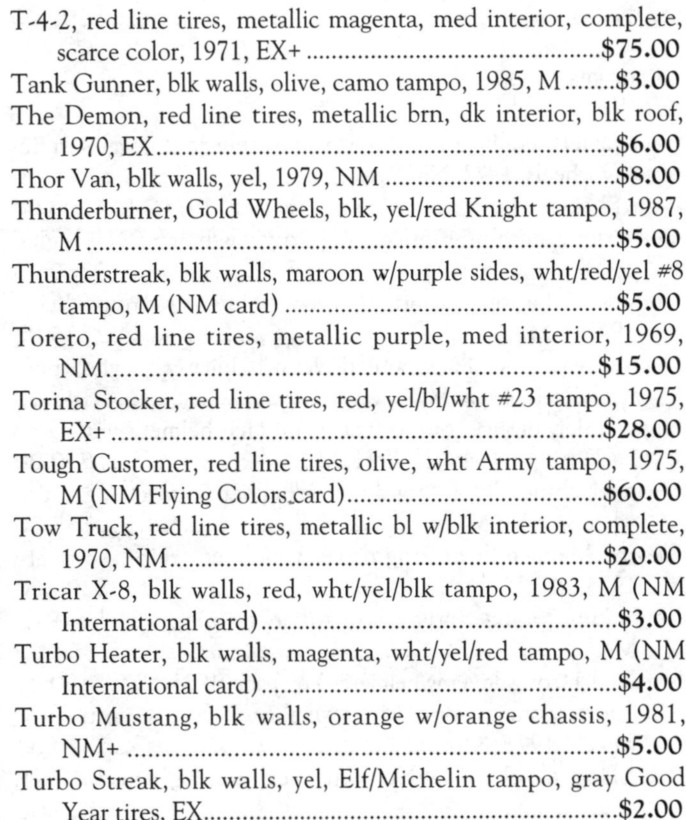

T-4-2, red line tires, metallic magenta, med interior, complete, scarce color, 1971, EX+ $75.00
Tank Gunner, blk walls, olive, camo tampo, 1985, M $3.00
The Demon, red line tires, metallic brn, dk interior, blk roof, 1970, EX....................$6.00
Thor Van, blk walls, yel, 1979, NM $8.00
Thunderburner, Gold Wheels, blk, yel/red Knight tampo, 1987, M $5.00
Thunderstreak, blk walls, maroon w/purple sides, wht/red/yel #8 tampo, M (NM card) $5.00
Torero, red line tires, metallic purple, med interior, 1969, NM....................$15.00
Torina Stocker, red line tires, red, yel/bl/wht #23 tampo, 1975, EX+....................$28.00
Tough Customer, red line tires, olive, wht Army tampo, 1975, M (NM Flying Colors card)....................$60.00
Tow Truck, red line tires, metallic bl w/blk interior, complete, 1970, NM....................$20.00
Tricar X-8, blk walls, red, wht/yel/blk tampo, 1983, M (NM International card)....................$3.00
Turbo Heater, blk walls, magenta, wht/yel/red tampo, M (NM International card)....................$4.00
Turbo Mustang, blk walls, orange w/orange chassis, 1981, NM+ $5.00
Turbo Streak, blk walls, yel, Elf/Michelin tampo, gray Good Year tires, EX....................$2.00

Twin Mill, red line tires, metallic blue, 1969, EX, $35.00.

Turbofire, red line tires, metallic aqua w/cream interior, 1969, EX+ $6.00
Twin Mill II, blk walls, Super Chrome, 1977, NM+.........$20.00
Twin Mill II, red line tires, orange, red/wht/bl tampo, 1976, NM+ $15.00
Upfront 924, blk walls, wht w/blk interior, red/blk tampo, MIP (French) $12.00
Vette Van, blk walls, blk, yel/red/wht tampo, 1980, M $10.00
Warpath, red line tires, wht, red/bl tampo, metal base, M (NM Flying Colors card) $130.00
Waste Wagon, red line tires, metallic magenta, dk interior, 1971, EX+ $50.00
What 4, red line tires, metallic gr w/lt gray interior, 1971, NM $40.00
Whip Creamer, blk walls, metallic red, Vintage, 1993, MIP..$3.00
Wind Splitter, blk walls, metallic gr, yel/blk tampo, 1984, M (NM International card) $5.00
Winnipeg, red line tires, yel, orange/bl tampo, 1974, M (NM Flying Colors card) $200.00

Rumblers

Bold Eagle, metallic gr, lime gr driver w/helmet & goggles, training wheels, 1972, NM $70.00
Bone Shaker, wht, w/driver, training wheels, 1973, M...$200.00
Centurion, metallic orange, orig driver w/helmet & goggles, 1973, M $200.00
Choppin' Chariot, yel, orig driver w/helmet, training wheels, 1972, NM $35.00
Devil's Deuce, metallic gr, orig driver w/helmet & goggles, training wheels, 1972, M $40.00
High Tailer, orange, orig driver w/full-face helmet, wht #5 on back, training wheels, 1971, M $30.00
Mean Machine, dk bl, orig driver w/helmet & goggles, training wheels, 1971, M $35.00
Preying Menace, lt gr, orig driver w/helmet, training wheels, 1973, M $200.00
Revolution, orange, orig driver w/hat, training wheels, 1972, M $50.00
Rip Cord, bl, orig driver w/helmet, #5 on back, 1973, NM ..$150.00
Rip Snorter, orange, orig driver w/helmet & boots, no training wheels, 1971, NM $20.00
Road Hog, dk bl, orig driver w/helmet, training wheels, 1971, M $25.00
Roamin' Candle, orange-brn, orig driver w/full-face helmet, #5 on back, training wheels, M $50.00
Torque Chop, orange, orig driver w/helmet & goggles, no training wheels, 1971, NM $25.00
3 Squealer, orange w/blk tank, orig driver w/helmet & goggles, training wheels, M $40.00

Sizzlers

Angeleno M70, chrome, prof rstr, 1970, NM $15.00
Anteater, metallic red, orange-red, NMIB $35.00
Backfire, metallic rose, 1971, EX $18.00
Camaro Trans-Am, metallic orange, orig stickers, NMIB...$60.00
Cuda Trans-Am, metallic orange, MIB $90.00
Cuda Trans-Am, metallic orange, 1971, EX+ $35.00
Dark Shadow, yel, orig headlight bulb, scarce, 1976, NM ..$50.00
Double Boiler, metallic yel, scarce, 1972, NM $40.00
Firebird Trans-Am, metallic lt gr, orig wing/stickers, 1970, NM $45.00
Ford Mark V, metallic bl, orig stickers, 1970, EX (EX box) ..$30.00
Hot Head, metallic lt gr, 1970, NM $45.00
Hot Wings, metallic olive, 1971, EX+ $30.00
Indy Eagle, metallic bl, EX $15.00

Miscellaneous

Big Belt & Matchmaker, M (EX box) $30.00
Chopcycles, Blown Torch, brn, M (EX+ card) $75.00
Chopcycles, Mighty Zork, metallic gr, M (NM card) $75.00
Chopcycles, Speed Steed, metallic gr, M (NM card)........$75.00
Club & Membership Certificate & Wallet Card, unused, NM $20.00
Collector's Case, blk, 24-car, 1970, EX $12.00
Collector's Case, blk, 48-car, 1970, EX+ $25.00
Collector's Case, Flying Colors, bl & wht, 24-car, EX......$20.00
Collector's Case, pop-up, orange, 12-car, 1968, EX..........$20.00
Collector's Case, yel, adjustable, 12-car, 1969, EX+.........$25.00
Collector's Case, yel, adjustable, 48-car, 1969, EX $40.00
Gran Toro, Chaparral 2G, wht, complete, 1970, M.......$100.00
Gran Toro, Ferrari Can-Am, metallic red or gray, complete, 1970, NM, ea $90.00
Gran Toro, Ford Mark V, metallic bl, 1970, NM $90.00
Gran Toro, Lamborghini Mura P400, metallic gr, 1970, NM...$90.00
Gran Toro, T'rantula, metallic gr, complete, 1970, M ...$225.00
HELP Machines Set, blk walls, unlisted version, #9031, MIB $60.00
Hi-Rakers 3-pack, '40s Woodie, Turbo Mustang, Stutz Blackhawk, scarce, M (NM card) $125.00
Hot Birds, Cloud Hopper, Maching Bird, Ski Gull or Star Grazer, M (EX card), ea $65.00
Live Wire, metallic yel, 1971, EX+ $15.00
March F-1, metallic gr, orig wing, partial orig stickers, 1971, EX+ $15.00
Micro Park 'N Plates, Firebird, metal-flake red, yel license plate, M (EX+ card) $6.00
Micro Park 'N Plates, IROC-Z, bl, M (EX+ card) $6.00
Mongoose & Snake Drag Race Set, reissue, 1994, M (NM sealed box) $40.00
Moon Ghost, wht, scarce, 1976, EX $45.00
Mustang Boss 302, metallic gold, orig wing/stickers, 1970, NM $40.00
Patch, iron-on, HW logo, 1969, NM $10.00
Place Mat, vinyl, colorful images, set of 4, B5 ....$15.00
Revvers Buzzin' Bomb, bl, missing slicks, EX $12.00
Revvers Haulin' Horses, dk bl, EX+ $18.00
Revvers Stingin' Thing, lt bl, EX $12.00
Sideburn, metallic dk bl, 1971, NMIB $22.00
Speedometer, 1970, EX $8.00
Spoil Sport, metallic lt bl, 1971, NMIB $35.00
Straight Scoop, metallic red, 1971, NM+ $22.00
Stunt Action Set, w/Gorgeous & Custom Camaro, no collector's car, 1969, NM (EX box) $180.00

Housewares

Back in the dark ages before women's lib and career-minded mothers, little girls emulated mommy's lifestyle, not realizing that by the time they grew up, total evolution would have taken place before their very eyes. They'd sew and bake, sweep, do laundry, and iron (gasp!), and imagine what fun it would be when *they* were big like mommy. Those little gadgets they played with are precious collectibles today, and any child-size houseware item is treasured, especially those from the '40s and '50s. If you're interested in learning about toy sewing machines, we recommend *Toy and Miniature Sewing Machines*, *Book I* and *II* by Glenda Thomas (Collector Books).

Advisor: Lorraine Punchard (P13) author of *Playtime Kitchen Items and Table Accessories*.

Cleaning and Laundry

Automatic Dishwasher, Marx, MIB **$150.00**
Clothes Presser, 1930s, yel & gr tin w/wooden roller, w/up & electric, EX **$85.00**
Iron, Wolverine, 1950s, electric, MIB, H12 .... **$35.00**
Ironing Board, Sunnie Miss, Ohio Art, 1960s, tin, 20", VG, N2 .... **$20.00**
Ironing Set, Wolverine, 1940s, complete, MIB, H12 .... **$35.00**
Laundry Set, Sunny Suzy, 6-pc, EX **$100.00**
Laundry Set, w/table, wringer & washtub, Kate Greenaway figures stenciled on table, 1910-20, EX, G16 .... **$100.00**
Laundry Set, wood, table mk Peerless, w/2 washtubs, clothes wringer, washboard & clothespins, 15½" table, G **$750.00**
Sad Iron, Dolly Dover, EX **$50.00**

Washing Machine, Pretty Maid, Marx, EX, $150.00.

Sweeper, Little Queen, Bissell, tin w/wood hdl, functional, 25½", EX **$50.00**
Washboard, tin & wood, EX, H12 .... **$20.00**
Washing Machine, Maytag, gray-pnt CI w/aluminum interior tub & mixer, 7", EX, A **$500.00**
Washing Machine, Wolverine, glass & tin, 10", EX **$65.00**

Cooking

Bake-a-Cake Set, Wolverine, MIB **$265.00**
Baking Set, Mother's Little Helper, early, complete w/rolling pin, egg beater, bowls, cutters & baking sheets, MIB, H12 .... **$150.00**
Betty's Pastry Set, Transogram, 1940, complete, EX (EX box) **$50.00**
Canister Set, metal, Coffee, Tea, Sugar, Flour, Cake & Bread in script, 6-pc, EX **$140.00**
Coffee Grinder, metal & wood, sm **$55.00**
Cooking Set, Mirro, 1940s, 16-pc, complete, MIB, H12 .... **$150.00**
Little Mother's Kitchen, Cragstan, 1950s, tin, complete, EX (EX box), A **$235.00**
Mixer, Sunbeam, w/2 bowls, EX **$225.00**
Potato Masher, Steffen, wire w/bl & wht hdls, EX **$15.00**
Refrigerator, Wolverine, litho tin, 15", VG, from $15 to **$20.00**
Rolling Pin, wood w/bl & wht wood hdls, EX **$15.00**
Stove, Baby, name emb on oven door, EX **$350.00**

Stove, Dolly's Favorite, Favorite Stove and Range Co., cast iron with nickel-plated door, heavily scrolled and embossed, 14x18½", VG, A, $400.00.

Stove, Eagle, sm, EX **$185.00**
Stove, Eclipse, EX **$185.00**
Stove, Grand Jewel, plated CI w/utensils & top covers, allover ornate emb design, 4-footed w/side grates, 18", G **$150.00**
Stove, Hoosier, 15x15", VG **$75.00**
Stove, Kenton Eagle, CI, heavily scrolled, 4-ft, 11½x10", G, A **$125.00**

Stove, Kenton Royal, CI & steel, 4 burners, working grates, ornate front, 10", rpt, no stovepipe, G $50.00
Stove, Lionel, porcelain & CI, cream & gr, 4-legged, cream & gr, 32x26", EX, A..$550.00
Stove, Little Fanny, EX $300.00
Stove, Little Willie, EX $85.00

Stove, Qualified Range Co., aluminum and tin with latch front door and temperature dial, 21½x13", EX, A, $775.00.

Stove, Rival, 12" L, no shelves, EX....................................$900.00
Stove, Susie Homemaker, VG+ $65.00
Teakettle, porcelain, rnd w/flat bottom, S-shaped spout, bail hdl, EX $175.00
Toaster, metal, 2-slice w/curved top, electric, EX.............$40.00
Waffle Iron, Little Deb, suction-cup plug, 6" dia, VG $65.00
Waffle Iron, pnt & plated CI w/wooden hdls, 7¾", EX, from $100 to...$125.00

Waffle Iron, Stover Junior, cast iron with wooden handles, EX, $175.00.

Nursery

Photo courtesy David Longest

Carriage, lithographed tin, NM, $600.00 (Felix doll not included).

Carriage, wicker, horizontal upholstered seat w/delicate scrolled & beaded sides, 4 spoked wheels, turned hdl, 35", G $180.00
Carriage, wicker, Kelly Bros, w/parasol & side compartments, metal spoke wheels, upholstered interior, rstr, EX...$700.00
Carriage, wicker, ornate spirals, footrest moves w/back to sit up or lie down, parasol, metal wheels, 36", EX $1,100.00
Carriage, wood, gold-pnt w/red leather upholstered seat, blk collapsible top, wooden spoke wheels, 25", orig pnt, A $415.00
Carriage, wood, Joel Ellis type, blk w/folding leather hood, 2 wooden spoke wheels, 22" w/38" front hdl, orig pnt, EX $325.00
Carriage, wood, railed sides, collapsible fringed top, wooden spoke wheels, 22", orig orange pnt, A $275.00
Carriage, wood, shaped sides, red w/blk & bl stencil, pnt wood canopy, 4 lg wheels, 27", EX...................................$400.00
Cradle, wrought iron, France, blk scroll work w/wht lace covering & head drape, 27x19", EX...............................$225.00
Grooming Set, 1920s-30s, hand-pnt celluloid brush, comb & rattle w/bl ribbon flowers, M (M floral box), H12...$125.00
Stroller, litho tin w/image of puppies & ducks, 1940-50, 6½", NM, G16 ....$110.00
Swing, 1920s-30s, metal, bl & cream, 10x6", EX $50.00

Sewing

Sewing Basket, sq wicker basket w/lid on 4 tall legs, w/bottom shelf, 17x9", EX, A $55.00
Sewing Cabinet, Martha Washington, ca 1930, dk wood w/3 drawers, 2 flip-top side compartments, 18", EX $250.00

Sewing Kit, lid illus w/Victorian girls & Christmas pram, w/mirror, needles, thread, thimble & button, MIB, H12..$135.00

Sewing Machine, Casige #2125, Germany, 1960s, gr, wht eagle logo, EX, from $50 to....$85.00

Sewing Machine, Casige #4 Juvenile, Germany, early 1900s, EX, from $125 to....$150.00

Sewing Machine, Crystal, Cragstan, manual or battery-op, foot pedal, tension regulator, EX, from $25 to....$45.00

Sewing Machine, Crystal/Baby, Japan, various colors, EX, from $75 to....$100.00

Sewing Machine, Decker, Saarbruken Germany, cast aluminum, leopard-type print footed base, 1950s, EX, from $150 to....$175.00

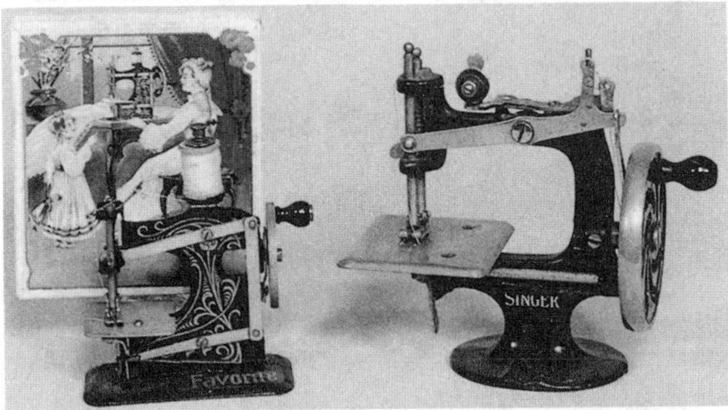

Sewing Machines, Favorite, Germany, black painted tin with gold highlights, nickel-plated fabric plate and crank, 5½", NMIB, A, $275.00; Singer, black painted cast iron with nickel-plated fabric plate and crank, 6½", NM, A, $135.00.

Sewing Machine, Jet Sew-O-Matic, Straco/West Germany, metal, manual, wht on red base, EX, from $45 to....$65.00

Sewing Machine, Junior Miss, Artcraft, 1940s, maroon enamel finish, mounted on wooden base, EX, from $75 to..$100.00

Sewing Machine, Little Betty, Straco/England, metal, manual, EX, from $65 to....$85.00

Sewing Machine, Little Lady, 1950s, various colors, EX, from $75 to....$100.00

Sewing Machine, Muller Lori, W Berlin, Germany, metal, manual, various colors & decals, EX, from $100 to....$125.00

Sewing Machine, Muller Regina, Germany, metal, manual, storage compartment in base, various colors, EX, from $120 to....$140.00

Sewing Machine, Sew E-Z, FW Muller, Germany/US Zone, post-WWII, metal w/wooden base, EX, from $50 to....$65.00

Sewing Machine, Sew Mistress, Japan, battery-op, various colors, EX, from $45 to....$65.00

Sewing Machine, Singer Chainstitch #CO43-EO76, 1980s, plastic, manual or battery-op, EX, from $20 to....$35.00

Sewing Machine, Vulcan Countess, England, metal, wht on red base, manual, detachable extension table, EX, from $75 to....$95.00

Sewing Machine, Vulcan Senior, England, metal, manual, w/detachable extension table, EX, from $85 to....$100.00

Table Service

Castor Set, 4 glass condiment bottles w/stoppers in metal stand, rare sz, 2½", VG, A....$75.00

Decanter Set, brass, 6 goblets, decanter w/lid, fruit bowl, bucket & serving tray, MIB, H12....$40.00

Dinner Set, Ridgways, Maiden Hair Fern lettered on banner, wht w/brn ferns, 27 pcs, VG, A....$45.00

Lemonade Set, Mirro, 1930s, 6 glasses w/pitcher, hammered tray, 6 spoons & straws, MIB, H12....$125.00

Platter, Blue Willow, oval, 6", H12....$45.00

Tea Set, Allerton's England, pk flowers w/mauve designs & gr leaves, mauve lustre trim, 12 pcs, VG....$175.00

Tea Set, Blue Willow, service for 6, MIB, H12....$275.00

Tea Set, early 1900s, gold leaves on wht porcelain w/jet blk hdls, service for 6, MIB, H12....$325.00

Tea Set, German, cranberry w/hand-pnt flowers, gold trim, 12 pcs, M, H12....$75.00

Tea Set, Ideal, 1950s, tin & plastic, service for 4, rare, MIB, H12....$165.00

Photo courtesy John Turney

Tea Set, Little American Maid, Akro Agate, MIB, $350.00.

Tea Set, Little Miss Homemaker, Plastic Art, 15 pcs, MIB..$35.00

Tea Set, Morimura Bros, 1917, Moss Rose pattern w/blk, gr & gold trim, service for 6, MIB, H12....$225.00

Tea Set, Noritake, hand-pnt yel & blk Art Deco design w/gold trim, service for 4, MIB, from $350 to....$450.00

Tea Set, Staffordshire, red sponged design, teapot, cream & sugar, 6 cups, plates & saucers & waste bowl, EX....$575.00

Tea Set, 1880s, persimmon & coral flowers w/gold trim, service for 6, MIB, H12 ....$425.00
Tea Set, 1930s, autumn flowers on lt gr, service for 5, MIB, H12..$165.00
Teapot, Blue Willow, 3", H12 ....$50.00

Miscellaneous

Adding Machine, Wolverine, ca 1937-38, MIB $95.00
Cruet Set, late 1800s, Victorian style w/pewter holder & filigree top, orig glass bottles, 6½", M, G16........................$275.00
Dresser Set, water pitcher & bowl, soap dish, lotion, powder & pin containers, china w/brn & purple flowers, EX...$250.00
Kitchen Scale, mk Germany, early 1900s, litho tin, 3½", G16..$125.00
Lawn Mower, Arcade, push-type w/wooden hdl, CI cutter, 22", VG $55.00
My Merry Shoe Shining Set, Merry Mfg, dated 1953, MIB ..$35.00
Spinning Wheel, early, oak, fully functional, 28", EX....$255.00
Telephone, Speed Phone, red metal w/bell, NM $65.00
Tool Set, Ideal, 1960s, metal, 5-pc, MIB, H12.................$15.00
Typewriter, Smith Corona, 1950s, MIB, H12 ....$40.00
Wall Clock, Gilbert, ca 1870, octagonal, rosewood veneer, paper label on back, 6½" dia, EX $125.00

Jack-in-the Boxes

Very early jack-in-the-box toys were often made of papier-mache and cloth, fragile material to withstand the everyday wear and tear to which they were subjected, so these vintage German examples are scarce today and very expensive. But even those from the '50s and '60s are collectible, especially when they represent well-known TV or storybook characters. Examples with lithographed space themes are popular as well.

See also Character, TV, and Movie Collectibles; Disney.

Boy, ca 1910, wood box w/image of children & St Bernard, compo figure w/cloth clothes, 8", EX, A $325.00
Jester, Lorraine Novelty Mfg, plays 'Pop Goes the Weasel,' litho metal w/cloth figure, NM $35.00
Jesters, 2 hand-pnt papier-mache figures w/fabric hats & fur-lined clothing, paper litho on wood box, 6", G, A ..$700.00
Jolly Jack, litho metal w/cloth clothes on figure, EX (EX box) $65.00
Man in Gray Top Hat, German, paper-covered wood box, papier-mache figure w/gray hair, no squeaker, 4½" sq, EX $375.00
Man in Red Top Hat, German, paper-covered wood box, papier-mache figure w/gray hair, w/squeaker, 5" sq, EX $450.00
Poodle Wearing Glasses, German, paper label on wood box, papier-mache figure w/wht fur trim, w/squeaker, 4" sq, EX...$300.00
Santa Claus, ca 1910, Santa in cloth suit & fur beard in chimney box, 9½", EX..$350.00
Talking Clown, Mattel, 1971, says several phrases, eyes move, NM $40.00

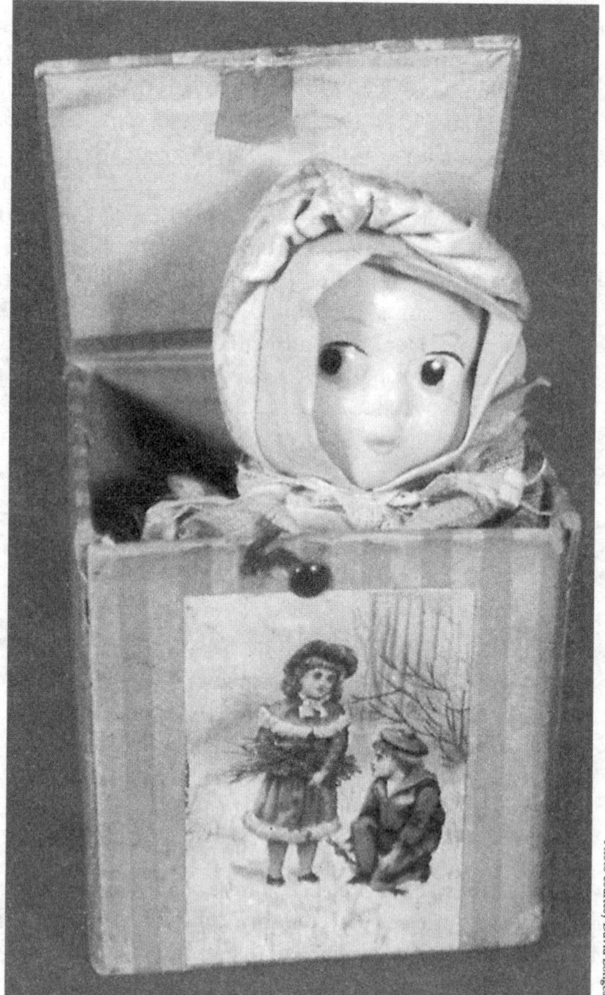

Photo courtesy David Longest

Girl, composition figure with cloth clothes, paper-covered wooden box, EX, $300.00.

Keystone

Though this Massachusetts company produced a variety of toys during their years of operation (ca 1920 – late '50s), their pressed-steel vehicles are the most collectible, and that's what we've listed here. As a rule they were very large, with some of the riders being 30" in length.

Aerial Ladder Truck, 12", G, A.....................................$550.00
Aerial Ladder Truck #1, w/up, spring-loaded ladder, 18", VG, A $200.00
Aerial Ladder Truck #2, w/climbing fireman figure, 16", VG, A $200.00
Aerial Ladder Truck #79, crank-op siren w/battery-op headlights & searchlight, 30", VG...$600.00
Airmail Single-Engine Plane #NX-265, 23", VG, A $550.00
Ambulance, 1929, khaki w/canvas sides & curtains, 28", rstr, A..$695.00
American Railway Express Truck, blk w/red chassis, aluminum hubs, red grip hdl, side compartment opens, 26", EX, A $1,155.00

Bluebird Racer, w/up, 19", rpt, G, A $400.00
Cargo Truck, open cab, tall canvas cover over bed, 26½", VG....................$150.00
Chemical Pump Engine, red, open cab, hand-op siren, 28", G, A $1,600.00
Circus Truck, w/animals in 3 removable cages, 26½", G, A....................$2,750.00
Coast-to-Coast Bus #84, 32", G, A $1,400.00
Dugan Bros Bakery Truck, rider, doorless cab, enclosed bed w/rear doors, 26", VG, A....................$3,300.00
Dump Truck, #38, 1927, blk w/red chassis & wheels, 26½", G, A $350.00
Dump Truck, blk w/red chassis & hubs, doorless cab, lever controls, 26", VG, A....................$660.00
Dump Truck, 1938, gr cab w/red dump, 25", G, A $300.00
Fire Department Combination Truck #49, w/2 ladders & bell, T-type steering wheel & seat, 28", G, A....................$325.00
Fire Truck, 1930s, red w/NP grille & bell, battery-op headlights, orig hose, 30", G+, A....................$750.00
Greyhound Bus, bl w/blk rubber tires, destination plate mk Limited & front plate mk 228, w/up, 17", scarce, VG, A....................$650.00
Inter-City Bus, bl w/red wheels, 24", G, A....................$200.00
Koaster Truck #55, blk open cab w/red flatbed used for riding, blk rubber tires w/red hubs, 26", VG, A....................$635.00
Locomotive #1400, rider, 1941, red & blk, VG $250.00
Packard Flatbed Truck, w/wench, 26", rstr, A $500.00
Police Patrol Truck, 28", EX, A $1,400.00

Railroad Wrecking Car #6600, 20", EX, D10, $475.00.

Railroad Engine, rider, red & blk, EX, A $275.00
Railroad Wrecking Car #6000, 1929, 20¾", G, A....................$200.00
Steam Roller #60, blk w/red corrugated roof & trim, brass bell, simulated spoke wheels, 19½", EX, A....................$660.00
Steam Shovel, rider, red & blk w/metal wheels, 21", G....................$250.00
Tank Department Truck, 24", rstr, A....................$800.00
US Army Truck, open cab w/canvas cover, 26", G $575.00
US Mail Truck #45, 1926, blk & khaki w/red wheels, 26", G, A....................$865.00
Water Tower Truck, ca 1928, red w/blk rubber tires & red hubs, 33", EX....................$2,000.00
Wrecker, 27", rstr, A....................$700.00

Lehmann

Lehmann toys were made in Germany as early as 1881. Early on they were sometimes animated by means of an inertia-generated flywheel; later, clockwork mechanisms were used. Some of their best-known turn-of-the-century toys were actually very racist and unflattering to certain ethnic groups. But the wonderful antics they perform and the imagination that went into their conception have made them and all the other Lehmann toys favorites with collectors today. Though the company faltered with the onset of WWI, they were quick to recover and during the war years produced some of their best toys, several of which were copied by their competitors. Business declined after WWI. Lehmann died in 1934, but the company continued for awhile under the direction of Lehmann's partner and cousin, Johannes Richter.

Advisor: Scott Smiles (S10).

AHA Delivery Van, 8", NMIB $1,000.00
Ajax Acrobat, litho tin figure w/cloth costume, 9½", EX ..$1,600.00
Alabama Coon Jigger, 1910, Black man dances on stage, litho tin, rare version w/checked pants, NM, A $950.00
ALSO Automobile, 1910, yel & red open auto w/driver, 4", NM, A $600.00

AM POL, lithographed tin, 5¾", NM, A, $1,700.00; New Century Cycle, lithographed tin, 5", EX, A, $650.00.

Autin Delivery Cart, 1914-35, Am boy & pedal car, 4", VG $425.00
Autobus, red & wht dbl-decker bus w/driver, litho tin, 7", G, A....................$1,200.00
Autohutte (Two Car), Sedal EPL #760 & the Gallop parked in wht garage w/red roof, 6", MIB $2,300.00
Baker & Chimney Sweep, 1900-35, baker on front of 3-wheeled car w/chimney sweep on back, 5½", EX $4,500.00
Balky Mule, 1910, clown bounces as cart advances w/crazy action, litho tin, 8", EX $500.00
Berolina Convertible, w/driver, litho tin, 7", NM.......$2,800.00

Buster Brown, seated in open auto, litho & pnt tin, 4", EX $1,800.00
Cat & Mouse, blk & wht cat chases mouse, tin, NM..$1,400.00
Climbing Miller, 1915, climbs pole & blades spin, tin, 17", EX (G box), A..$250.00
Crawling Beetle, Pat 1895, 4½", EX (EX box) $375.00

Dancing Sailor, lithographed tin with cloth clothes, cap reads SMS Bradenburg, 7", MIB, $1,200.00.

Echo Motorcycle w/Driver, litho & hand-pnt tin, 8¾", EX, A..$1,800.00
EHE & Co Vehicle, open bed truck w/driver, advances in circular motion, 7", NM, A...$800.00
EPL-1 Dirigible, litho tin w/celluloid props, 2 observation decks, 7½", EX (worn box), A $500.00
EPL-11 Zeppelin, litho tin w/celluloid props, 9½", EX, A..$1,100.00
Express Porter, 1910, porter pulls trunk on 2-wheeled cart, 6", EX, A $700.00
Galop Racer #1, w/driver, yel w/bl stripe, 5½", NM $550.00
Gnome Series Shell Truck, red & yel, NM....................$350.00
Going to the Fair, man pushing lady in promenade chair, pnt & litho tin, 5", NM $5,000.00
Gustav the Miller, pull string & figure climbs pole to mill, litho tin, 18", EX $250.00
Halloh Rider on Cycle, flywheel mechanism, 8", EX..$2,100.00
Kadi, 2 Chinese men carrying tea chest, litho tin, 7", EX....$1,250.00
Lehmann Family (Walking Down Broadway), couple w/dog on leash, litho tin, 6½", EX.......................................$5,700.00
Lila Hansom Cab, w/driver, 2 lady passengers & dog, pnt & litho tin, 5½", EX...$2,000.00
Lo & Li, seated clown plays accordion for jigger on platform, scarce, EX $6,000.00

Heavy Swell, lithographed tin with cloth clothes, 8¾", M, $2,000.00.

Magic Ball Dancer, ballerina w/arms extended on gyroscope stabilizer, pnt & litho tin, 6", EX $3,300.00
Mikado Family, man pulling female passenger in rickshaw, hand-pnt & litho tin, 7", NMIB...................................$4,400.00
Miss Blondin, lady tightrope walker, litho tin, 10½", NMIB...$6,200.00
NA-OB, donkey cart w/driver, litho tin, 6½", EX..........$450.00
Naughty Boy, 1903, wht & bl auto w/driver & boy facing each other at center wheel, 5", NMIB $2,000.00
New Century Cycle, man holding umbrella over driver of 3-wheeled vehicle, 5", NMIB.................................$1,500.00
OHO, 1903, open auto w/driver, litho tin, 3¾", G $350.00
Paak-Paak Quack Quack Duck Cart, mother duck pulling 3 ducklings in 2-wheeled cart, 7", VG, A $500.00
Paak-Paak Quack-Quack Duck Cart, Pat 1903, mamma duck pulling 3 ducklings in 2 wheeled cart, litho tin, 8", EX (G box)...$650.00
Paddy the Pig, man on pig, litho tin, 5", NMIB $3,200.00
Performing Sea Lion, litho tin, 8", EX, A $155.00
Primus Roller Skater, boy on skates, litho tin, 8½", rare, NM $7,500.00
Rad Cycle, uniformed driver on 3-wheeled vehicle, litho & hand-pnt tin, EX, A $650.00
Sailor, 1903, advances & rocks back & forth or turn him upside-down & he bounces on his hat, 8", NM..................$750.00
Shenandoah Dirigible, litho tin w/celluloid props, 7", VG, A...$650.00
Skirolf, man in gray brimless hat & bl suit on skis, pnt & litho tin, 7", EX..$3,300.00
Snik-Snak, man walking 2 dogs, litho tin, 8", EX $7,500.00
Swing Doll, china doll in cloth dress seated in tin swing, 7", EX $2,300.00

Tap-Tap Man w/Wheelbarrow, advances forward, litho & pnt tin, 6½", VG, A..$300.00
Terra Towing Co Vehicle, mk EPL-720, EX..................$900.00
Titiania Sedan, driver in red & bl auto w/electric headlights, litho tin, 10", VG...$2,500.00
Tom the Climbing Monkey, 1903, plain vest, hand-pnt face, 7½", MIB...$300.00
Tom the Climbing Monkey, 1903, polka-dot vest, litho face, 7½", M..$200.00
Toy Balloon Luna, hot-air balloon w/rider holding flag in gondola, litho tin, 5", NMIB......................................$7,000.00

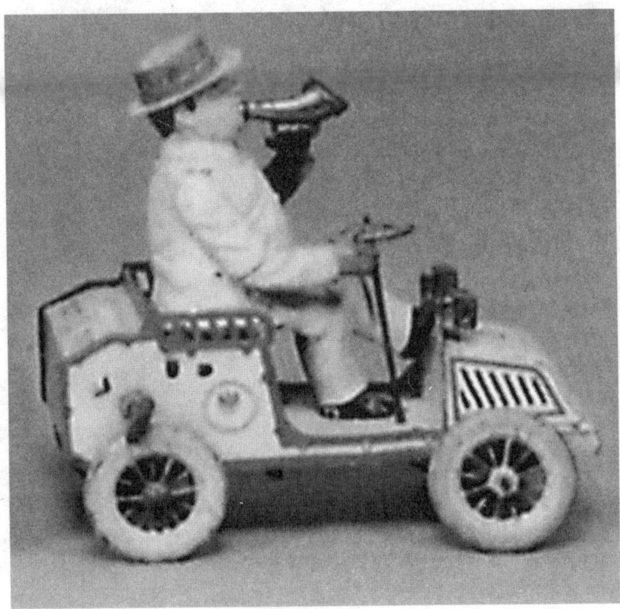

Tut-Tut, lithographed and painted tin, 6½", VG, A, $900.00.

Tut-Tut, driver in open auto, litho & pnt tin, 6½", NMIB....$1,800.00
Velleda Touring Car, driver in orange open touring car w/folding seats, litho tin, 10", EX $4,300.00
Wild West Bucking Bronco, litho tin, 7", NMIB........$1,600.00
Zebra Cart, advances as cowboy bounces up & down in seat, 7½", MIB...$350.00
Zig-Zag, 2 men in rocking car w/lg wheels, litho & pnt tin, 4", VG, A..$1,100.00
Zulu Ostrich Mail, driver on ostrich-driven cart, litho tin, 7", G, A $500.00

Lunch Boxes

When the lunch box craze began in the mid-1980s, it was only the metal boxes that so quickly soared to sometimes astronomical prices. But today, even the plastic and vinyl ones are collectible. Though most lunch box dealers agree that with few exceptions, prices have become much more reasonable than they were at first, they're still holding their own and values seem to be stabilizing. So pick a genre and have fun. There are literally hundreds to choose from, and just as is true in other areas of character-related collectibles, the more desirable lunch boxes are those with easily recognized, well-known subjects — western heroes, TV, Disney and other cartoon characters, and famous entertainers. Thermoses are collectible as well. In our listings, values are just for the box unless a thermos is mentioned in the description. If you'd like to learn more about them, we recommend *A Pictorial Price Guide to Metal Lunch Boxes and Thermoses* and a companion book *A Pictorial Price Guide to Vinyl and Plastic Lunch Boxes* by Larry Aikins. For more pricing information, Philip R. Norman (Norman's Olde Store) has prepared a listing of hundreds of boxes, thermoses, and their variations. He is listed in the Categories of Special Interest under Lunch Boxes.

Advisor: Terri Ivers (I2).

Other Sources: C1, C10, G7, J6, J7, M15, T1, T2

Metal

Action Jackson, 1973, w/thermos, NM, N2....................$200.00
Adam 12, 1972, VG, I2 ....$45.00
Addams Family, 1974, w/thermos, EX, I2 ....$100.00
America on Parade, 1976, w/thermos, EX, N2..................$60.00
Animal Friends, 1978, yel or blk letters, M, N2, ea $90.00
Annie Oakley, 1955, w/thermos, EX, N2........................$300.00
Apple's Way, 1975, w/thermos, M, N2 ....$150.00
Astronaut Space Dome, 1960, w/thermos, EX................$175.00
Atom Ant, 1966, G, I2 ....$60.00
Atom Ant, 1966, w/thermos, EX, from $175 to.............$200.00
Back in 1976, 1975, w/thermos, EX, N2 ....$60.00
Basketweave, 1968, M, N2 ....$100.00
Batman & Robin, 1966, G, I2 ....$95.00
Batman & Robin, 1966, w/thermos, M, N2....................$600.00
Battle Kit, 1965, w/thermos, EX, N2 ....$95.00
Battle of the Planets, 1979, w/thermos, M, N2 ....$175.00
Battlestar Galactica, 1978, w/thermos, EX, I2, from $45 to ..$55.00
Beatles, 1965, bl, VG, I2 ....$380.00
Bedknobs & Broomsticks, 1972, VG, I2 ....$30.00
Bedknobs & Broomsticks, 1972, w/thermos, EX, N2........$65.00
Bee Gees, 1978, EX, I2 ....$40.00

Beverly Hillbillies, 1963, with thermos, M, $500.00.

Bionic Woman, 1978, EX, I2 .... $85.00
Black Hole, 1979, EX, I2 .... $70.00
Bobby Sherman, 1972, w/thermos, EX, I2 .... $80.00
Bonanza, 1963, gr rim, EX, I2 .... $140.00

Photo courtesy June Moon

Bonanza, 1965, brown rim, VG, $65.00.

Boston Bruins, 1973, w/thermos, EX, N2 .... $600.00
Brady Bunch, 1970, VG, I2 .... $200.00
Brady Bunch, 1970, w/thermos, M, N2 .... $700.00
Buck Rogers in the 25th Century, 1979, w/thermos, EX, I2 .... $45.00
Bugaloos, 1971, EX, I2 .... $100.00
Bullwinkle & Rocky, 1962, w/thermos, EX, N2 .... $600.00
Cable Car, 1962, dome top, w/thermos, EX, N2 .... $275.00
Captain Astro, 1966, EX, N2 .... $300.00
Care Bears, 1983, bl rim, w/thermos, G, I2 .... $20.00
Care Bears, 1983, bl rim, w/thermos, M, N2 .... $40.00
Cartoon Zoo, 1962, G, I2 .... $80.00
Casey Jones, 1960, dome top, w/thermos, VG, I2 .... $455.00

Photo courtesy Larry Doucet

Dick Tracy, 1967, with thermos, M, $375.00.

Chan Clan, 1973, w/thermos, EX, I2 .... $100.00
Charlie's Angels, 1978, w/thermos, M, N2 .... $175.00
Chitty-Chitty Bang-Bang, 1968, w/thermos, EX, N2 .... $85.00
Color Me Happy, 1984, EX, N2 .... $150.00
Corsage, 1963, peach rim, w/thermos, M, N2 .... $100.00
Curiosity Shop, 1972, w/thermos, EX, N2 .... $75.00
Daniel Boone, 1965, w/thermos, M, N2 .... $300.00
Dark Crystal, 1982, w/thermos, M, I2 .... $50.00
Davy Crockett at the Alamo, 1955, M, N2 .... $1,000.00

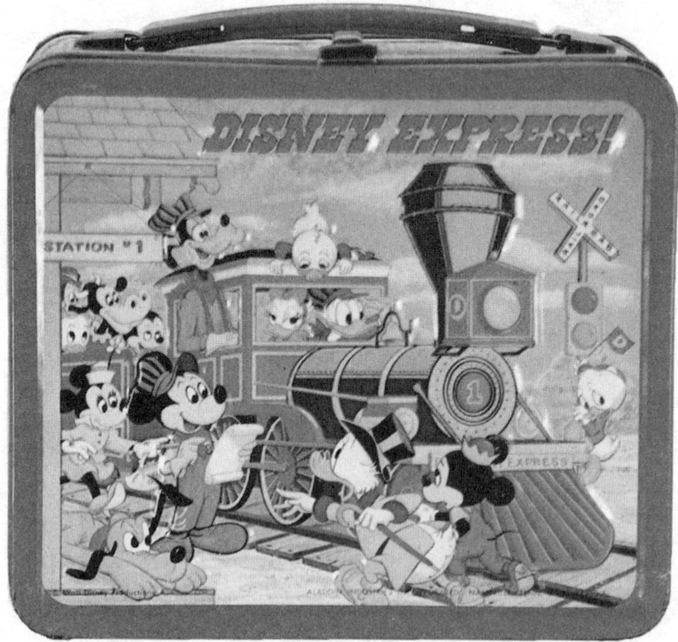

Disney Express, 1979, VG, $22.00.

Disney Express, 1979, w/thermos, M, N2 .... $75.00
Disney Firefighters, 1969, dome top, w/thermos, EX, N2 .... $150.00
Disneyland Castle, 1957, w/thermos, M, N2 .... $500.00
Doctor Dolittle, 1967, w/thermos, EX, N2 .... $100.00
Dr Seuss, 1970, w/thermos, M, N2 .... $300.00
Dragon's Lair, 1983, VG, I2 .... $25.00
Dudley Do-Right, 1962, w/thermos, EX, N2 .... $575.00
Dukes of Hazzard, 1980, w/thermos, M, N2 .... $50.00
Dynomutt, 1976, EX, I2 .... $45.00
Emergency, 1977, dome top, w/thermos, EX, N2 .... $150.00
ET, 1982, w/thermos, EX, N2 .... $20.00
Exciting World of Metrics, 1976, w/thermos, M, N2 .... $100.00
Fall Guy, 1981, w/thermos, EX, I2 .... $35.00
Family Affair, 1969, w/thermos, EX, I2 .... $135.00
Fireball XL-5, 1964, w/thermos, NM $200.00
Flag-O-Rama, 1954, EX, N2 .... $400.00
Flintstones, 1964, w/thermos, M, N2 .... $400.00
Flintstones, 1971, w/thermos, M, N2 .... $225.00
Flintstones & Dino, 1962, orange, VG, I2 .... $140.00
Flipper, 1967, w/thermos, EX, N2 .... $200.00
Fox & the Hound, 1982, w/thermos, EX, N2 .... $25.00
Fraggle Rock, 1984, EX, I2 .... $25.00
Funtastic World of Hanna Barbera, 1977, w/thermos, EX, N2 .... $75.00

Flying Nun, 1968, EX, $125.00.

Gene Autry, 1954, w/thermos, EX, N2 ....$400.00
Ghostland, 1977, EX, N2 ....$65.00
GI Joe, 1967, w/thermos, M, N2 ....$350.00
Globetrotters, 1959, dome top, w/thermos, M, N2 ....$500.00
Gomer Pyle, 1966, VG, I2 ....$155.00
Gomer Pyle, 1966, w/thermos, NM, N2 ....$250.00
Gremlins, 1984, VG+, I2 ....$16.00
Gremlins, 1984, w/thermos, EX, N2 ....$20.00
Gunsmoke, 1959, VG, I2 ....$150.00
Gunsmoke, 1962, w/thermos, EX, N2 ....$250.00
Hansel & Gretel, 1982, EX, N2 ....$85.00

Hogan's Heroes, 1966, dome top, EX, $300.00.

Happy Days, 1976, VG, I2 ....$30.00
Heathcliff, 1982, w/thermos, EX, N2 ....$20.00
Hee-Haw, 1970, w/thermos, M, N2 ....$150.00
Hong Kong Phooey, 1975, w/thermos, EX, N2 ....$75.00
Hopalong Cassidy, 1954, w/thermos, EX, N2, from $300 to ...$325.00
Hot Wheels, 1965, w/thermos, VG, I2 ....$95.00
Howdy Doody, 1954, EX, N2 ....$400.00
Huckleberry Hound & Quick Draw McGraw, 1961, VG, I2 ...$70.00
Incredible Hulk, 1978, EX, I2 ....$30.00
Indiana Jones & the Temple of Doom, 1984, w/thermos, VG, I2 ....$30.00
Jack & Jill, 1982, EX, N2 ....$400.00
Julia, 1969, w/thermos, EX, N2 ....$100.00
Jungle Book, 1966, w/thermos, M, N2 ....$200.00
Junior Miss, 1963, floral, w/thermos, M, N2 ....$400.00
Junior Miss, 1966, yel, w/thermos, M, N2 ....$125.00
King Kong, 1977, w/thermos, EX, N2 ....$60.00
Knight Rider, 1981, w/thermos, M, N2 ....$85.00
Korg 70,000 BC, 1975, G, I2 ....$40.00
Land of the Giants, 1968, w/thermos, M, N2 ....$300.00
Land of the Lost, 1975, w/thermos, M, N2 ....$250.00
Land of the Lost, 1975, w/thermos, VG, I2 ....$100.00
Lawman, 1961, w/thermos, M, N2 ....$300.00
Little House on the Prairie, 1978, EX, I2, from $45 to $55.00
Little Red Riding Hood, 1982, EX, N2 ....$100.00
Lone Ranger, 1954, EX, N2 ....$400.00
Ludwig Von Drake, 1962, w/thermos, EX, N2 ....$200.00
Luggage Plaid, 1955, EX, N2 ....$65.00
Luggage Tweed, 1957, bl, EX, N2 ....$75.00
MacPherson Plaid, 1964, w/thermos, M, N2 ....$50.00
Magic of Lassie, 1978, w/thermos, EX, I2 ....$85.00
Man From Uncle, 1966, w/thermos, EX, N2 ....$150.00
Marvel Super Heroes, 1976, EX, I2 ....$45.00
Mickey Mouse Club, 1976, yel rim, w/thermos, M, N2 ..$200.00
Mickey Mouse Club, 1977, red rim, w/thermos, M, N2 ..$100.00
Miss America, 1972, w/thermos, EX, N2 ....$75.00
Mod Tulips, 1962, dome top, M, N2 ....$600.00
Mork & Mindy, 1979, VG, I2 ....$35.00
Mr Merlin, 1981, w/thermos, VG, I2 ....$30.00
Munsters, 1965, G, I2 ....$75.00
Munsters, 1965, w/thermos, NM, N2 ....$250.00
Muppet Movie, 1979, w/thermos, EX, N2 ....$35.00
National Airlines, 1968, M, N2 ....$200.00
NFL, 1977, w/thermos, EX, N2 ....$25.00
Osmonds, 1973, w/thermos, EX, N2 ....$75.00
Our Friends, 1982, w/thermos, EX, N2 ....$700.00
Pebbles & Bamm-Bamm, 1971, EX, I2 ....$80.00
Pebbles & Bamm-Bamm, 1971, w/thermos, EX, N2 ....$90.00
Pete's Dragon, 1978, EX, I2 ....$45.00
Pete's Dragon, 1978, w/thermos, EX, N2 ....$50.00
Pets & Pals, 1962, w/thermos, EX, N2 ....$25.00
Pink Panther & Sons, 1984, w/thermos, VG, I2 ....$35.00
Pinocchio, 1971, VG, I2 ....$60.00
Planet of the Apes, 1974, w/thermos, EX, N2 ....$95.00
Police Patrol, 1973, w/thermos, M, N2 ....$250.00
Popeye, 1964, EX $100.00
Popeye, 1980, w/thermos, VG, I2 ....$40.00
Popples, 1986, w/thermos, VG, I2 ....$20.00

Porky's Lunch Wagon, 1959, dome top, EX, I2 ....$400.00
Raggedy Ann & Andy, 1973, VG, I2 ....$35.00
Raggedy Ann & Andy, 1973, w/thermos, NM, N2 ....$60.00
Rat Patrol, 1967, EX, I2 ....$145.00
Rat Patrol, 1967, w/thermos, M, N2 ....$300.00
Rescuers Down Under, 1977, VG, I2 ....$35.00
Return of the Jedi, 1983, w/thermos, NM $125.00
Rifleman, 1961, w/thermos, EX, N2 ....$400.00
Ronald McDonald Sheriff of Cactus Canyon, 1982, VG, I2 ...$25.00
School Days, 1984, features Mickey & Donald, w/thermos, EX, N2 ....$300.00
Scooby Doo, 1973, yel rim, w/thermos, M, N2 ....$175.00
Secret Wars, 1984, VG, I2 ....$40.00
Sesame Street, 1980, yel or gr rim, w/thermos, M, N2, ea ..$50.00
Six Million Dollar Man, 1978, w/thermos, EX, I2 ....$95.00
Skateboarder, 1977, w/thermos, EX, I2 ....$55.00
Sleeping Beauty, Canadian, 1960, EX, N2 ....$700.00
Smurfs, 1983, w/thermos, EX, N2 ....$150.00
Snoopy's Doghouse, 1968, dome top, w/thermos, M, N2 .$150.00
Snow White & the Seven Dwarfs, 1975, VG, I2 ....$45.00
Snow White & the Seven Dwarfs, 1975, w/thermos, EX, N2...$75.00
Space Shuttle Orbiter Enterprise, 1977, w/thermos, EX, N2 ....$75.00

Space: 1999, 1975, no thermos, EX, $35.00.

Space: 1999, 1975, w/thermos, VG, I2 ....$45.00
Sport Goofy, 1983, VG, I2 ....$20.00
Sport Goofy, 1984, w/thermos, M, N2 ....$90.00
Sport Skwirts, 1982, EX, I2 ....$40.00
Sports Afield, 1957, EX+, from $200 to..............$225.00
Star Wars, 1978, w/thermos, EX, N2..............$65.00
Street Hawk, 1985, w/thermos, EX, N2 ....$175.00
Super Powers, 1984, w/thermos, VG, I2..............$50.00
Supercar, 1962, w/thermos, VG, I2 ....$335.00
Superfriends, 1976, w/thermos, EX, N2 ....$50.00
Superman, 1967, VG, I2..............$130.00
Tapestry, 1963, EX, N2..............$70.00
Tarzan, 1966, w/thermos, EX, N2 ....$125.00
Three Little Pigs, 1982, EX, N2, from $80 to..............$95.00
Thundercats, 1985, VG, I2 ....$20.00
Thundercats, 1985, w/thermos, NM, N2..............$50.00
Track King, 1975, w/thermos, EX, N2 ....$300.00
Traveler, 1964, brn rim, EX, N2..............$60.00
Treasure Chest, 1961, dome top, w/thermos, EX, N2.....$375.00
Underdog, 1974, w/thermos, EX, N2 ....$1,000.00
Universal Movie Monsters, 1979, w/thermos, EX, N2 ...$100.00
US Mail, 1969, w/thermos, EX, N2 ....$60.00
Voyage to the Bottom of the Sea, 1967, w/thermos, EX, N2..$275.00
Wagon Train, 1964, w/thermos, M, N2 ....$500.00

Photo courtesy Kenn Norris

Walt Disney School Bus, 1960s, dome top, EX, $50.00.

Waltons, 1973, w/thermos, EX, N2 ....$90.00
Welcome Back Kotter, 1977, w/thermos, VG, I2 ....$60.00
Wild Frontier, 1977, EX, N2 ....$60.00

Photo courtesy June Moon

Wild Wild West, 1969, with thermos, EX, $200.00.

Winnie the Pooh, 1976, w/thermos, EX, N2 ....$200.00

Photo courtesy June Moon

Yellow Submarine, 1968, EX, $275.00.

Yogi Bear & His Friends, 1963, w/thermos, EX, N2 ....$150.00
Zorro, 1958, VG, I2 ....$145.00
Zorro, 1966, red rim, w/thermos, EX, N2 ....$250.00

Plastic

A-Team, 1985, red, w/thermos, EX, I2.............................$25.00
Alf, 1987, red, w/thermos, NM, I2 ....$18.00
American Gladiators, 1992, red, EX, I2 ....$15.00
Barbie, Thermos, 1990, purple, w/thermos, EX, I2.............$6.00
Batman, 1982, bl, VG, I2..$5.00
Batman Returns, 1992, blk, w/thermos, EX, I2 ....$16.00
Benji, 1974, bl, VG, I2, from $5 to.....................................$8.00
Cabbage Patch Kids, 1983, yel, w/thermos, EX, I2 ....$10.00
Cabbage Patch Kids, 1990, pk, w/thermos, VG, I2...........$12.00
California Raisins, Thermos, 1987, yel, w/thermos, EX, W6..$10.00
Chip 'n Dale Rescue Rangers, lt bl, NM, I2 ....$10.00
Chipmunks, 1984, yel, w/thermos, EX, I2 ....$5.00
Dick Tracy, 1990, red, w/thermos, EX, I2 ....$5.00
Flintstones Movie, 1994, rock shape, w/thermos, NM, I2 .$15.00
Garfield, 1978, yel, EX, I2...$8.00
Ghostbusters, 1986, purple, EX, I2 ....$20.00
Hobnobbins, 1989, pk, w/thermos, G, I2 ....$10.00
Hot Wheels, 1984, red, EX, I2..$30.00
Jem, 1986, purple, w/thermos, EX, I2, from $10 to $14.00
Looney Tunes, 1988, purple, w/thermos, VG, I2 ....$10.00
Masters of the Universe, 1983, bl, VG, I2.........................$10.00
Miss Piggy, 1980, yel, EX, I2..$15.00
Mr T, 1984, orange, w/thermos, EX, I2 ....$30.00
My Little Pony, 1989, bl, w/thermos, EX, I2.....................$12.00
New Kids on the Block, 1990, orange, w/thermos, EX, I2 .$15.00
Nosy Bears, 1988, bl, VG, I2...$3.00
Popeye & Son, 1987, yel, 3-D, M, I2..................................$55.00
Pound Puppies, 1986, red, VG, I2 ....$10.00
Rainbow Brite, 1983, yel, w/thermos, VG, I2 ....$10.00
Return of the Jedi, 1983, red, VG, I2 ....$15.00
Scooby Doo, 1984, bl, w/thermos, EX $50.00
Simpsons, 1990, red, w/thermos, M, I2 ....$15.00
Smurfette, 1984, pk, EX, I2..$8.00
Superman, 1980, dome top, w/thermos, EX, I2 ....$40.00
Talespin, 1986, bl, w/thermos, EX.....................................$25.00
Teenage Mutant Ninja Turtles, 1990, purple, w/thermos, M, I2 ....$15.00
Tiny Dinos, 1987, pk, w/thermos, M, I2............................$14.00
Tiny Toon Adventures, 1990, purple, w/thermos, EX, I2 .$10.00
Transformers, 1984, red, w/thermos, EX, I2 ....$10.00
Treasure Trolls, 1992, purple, w/thermos, NM, I2 ....$6.00
Voltron, 1984, bl, w/thermos, NM, I2 ....$15.00
Who Framed Roger Rabbit?, 1987, red or yel, VG, I2, ea ...$5.00
World of Teddy Ruxpin, yel, w/thermos, EX, I2 ....$13.00
101 Dalmatians, Aladdin, 1990, w/thermos, EX, I2.........$10.00

Vinyl

Adopt a Norfin Troll, 1992, shows baseball player & gymnast, purple softie w/zipper closure, w/thermos, NM, I2 .....$15.00
Animaniacs, hot pk, EX, I2 ....$20.00
Annie, 1981, w/thermos, VG, I2 ....$45.00
Barney & Baby Bop, 1992, softie w/shoulder & hand straps, zipper closure, EX, I2 ....$8.00
Batman the Dark Knight, 1991, softie, w/thermos, NM, I2 .$15.00
Beauty & the Beast, pk & purple softee, w/thermos, VG, I2 ..$8.00
Betsy Clark, w/thermos, M, I2 ....$90.00
Dawn, 1970, w/thermos, EX, I2.......................................$175.00
Peanuts, 1969, red, w/thermos, M, I2 ....$130.00

Pebbles and Bamm-Bamm, 1971, EX, $125.00.

Princess, 1963, yel, w/thermos, EX, I2............................$140.00
Strawberry Shortcake, 1980, checked design, VG, I2.......$35.00
Tammy, Aladdin, 1962, w/thermos, EX...........................$125.00
Tammy & Pepper, Aladdin, 1964, w/thermos, EX $125.00
Teenage Mutant Ninja Turtles, 1988, bl softee, EX, I2 ......$8.00

Roy Rogers Saddlebag, 1960, EX, $225.00.

THERMOSES

A-Team, 1983, plastic, M, N2 ....$20.00
Adam 12, 1972, plastic, EX, I2 ....$25.00
America on Parade, 1976, plastic, M....$25.00
Annie, 1982, plastic, M, N2 ....$12.00
Annie Oakley, 1955, metal, cork stopper, EX, I2 ....$65.00
Apple's Way, 1975, plastic, EX, N2 ....$15.00
Archies, 1969, plastic, M $50.00
Archies, 1969, plastic, NM, I2....$40.00
Atom Ant, 1966, metal, EX $50.00
Babar, 1988, plastic, M, I2 ....$3.00

Barbie, 1961, EX, $35.00.

Barbie, Midge & Skipper, 1965, metal, EX, I2 ....$50.00
Barbie & the Rockers, 1987, plastic, EX, I2 ....$3.00
Barbie Campus Queen, 1967, metal, EX, I2 ....$22.00
Batman & Robin, 1966, metal, M $75.00
Battle of the Planets, 1979, plastic, M, N2....$18.00
Beatles, 1965, metal, M $225.00
Bee Gees, 1978, plastic, EX, N2 ....$15.00
Beverly Hillbillies, 1963, metal, EX, I2 ....$60.00
Bionic Woman, 1977, plastic, M....$18.00
Bonanza, 1968, metal, EX....$50.00
Boston Bruins, 1973, metal, EX....$120.00
Brady Bunch, 1970, metal, M....$75.00
Buck Rogers in the 25th Century, 1979, plastic, M....$16.00
Cabbage Patch Kids, 1984, plastic, M $8.00
Care Bear Cousins, 1984, plastic, M....$9.00
Carousel, 1965, metal, no liner, G, I2 ....$35.00
Cartoon Zoo, 1962, metal, EX, N2....$150.00
Cartoon Zoo (Touche Turtle, Lippy Lion & Wally Gator), Universal, 1950s, metal lunch chest, missing glass liner o/w EX $75.00
Charlie's Angels, 1978, plastic, M....$18.00
Close Encounters of the Third Kind, 1977, plastic, M....$20.00
Corsage, 1964, metal, M $25.00
Cowboy in Africa, 1968, metal, EX, I2 ....$75.00
Cracker Jack, 1979, plastic, EX....$15.00
Crash Dummies, 1992, plastic, EX, I2 ....$8.00
Davy Crockett & Kit Carson, 1955, metal, EX....$85.00
Dawn, 1970, plastic, EX, I2 ....$30.00
Dick Tracy, 1967, metal, M....$65.00
Dino Riders, 1988, plastic, EX, I2....$4.00
Disney Express, 1979, plastic, M....$8.00
Disneyland Castle, 1957, metal, M....$60.00
Drag Strip, 1975, plastic, EX, I2 ....$24.00
Dudley Do-Right, 1962, metal, EX, N2 ....$150.00
Dukes of Hazzard, 1980, plastic, M....$12.00
Emergency, 1973, plastic, M....$20.00
Empire Strikes Back, 1981, plastic, VG, I2 ....$10.00
ET, 1982, plastic, EX....$8.00
Evel Knievel, 1974, plastic, EX, I2 ....$30.00
Exciting World of Metrics, 1976, plastic, M $15.00
Fall Guy, 1981, plastic, EX, N2 ....$10.00
Fat Albert, 1973, plastic, M, N2....$30.00
Fess Parker as Daniel Boone, 1965, metal, EX, I2 ....$75.00
Firehouse, 1959, metal, EX, I2....$110.00
Flintstones, 1964, metal, EX....$45.00
Flipper, 1967, metal, M....$75.00
Fox & the Hound, 1982, plastic, M, N2....$10.00
Funtastic World of Hanna Barbera, plastic, 1977, M....$18.00
Get Smart, 1966, metal, EX, N2....$75.00
GI Joe, 1967, metal, M $80.00
GI Joe, 1982, plastic, M $8.00
Go Bots, 1984, plastic, M, I2 ....$10.00
Goober & the Ghost Chasers, 1974, plastic, M $25.00
Green Hornet, 1967, metal, EX, I2 ....$150.00
Guns of Will Sonnett, 1968, metal, EX, N2 ....$75.00
Gunsmoke, 1962, metal, M $90.00
Happy Days, 1977, plastic, EX, N2....$15.00
Harlem Globetrotters, 1971, metal, M, N2....$70.00

Heathcliff, 1982, plastic, EX, I2 .... $10.00
Hogan's Heroes, 1966, metal, EX $90.00
Hong Kong Phooey, 1975, plastic, EX, I2 .... $15.00
Hopalong Cassidy, 1954, metal, M $125.00
Howdy Doody, 1977, plastic, EX, I2 .... $25.00
Incredible Hulk, 1978, plastic, EX, N2 .... $12.00
Indiana Jones & the Temple of Doom, 1984, plastic, VG, I2 .... $10.00
It's a Small World, metal, EX, I2 .... $90.00
Jet Patrol, 1957, metal, EX, N2 .... $100.00
Johnny Lightning, 1970, plastic, EX, N2 .... $30.00
Junior Miss, 1966, metal, EX, N2 .... $35.00
Junior Nurse, 1963, metal, EX, I2 .... $75.00
King Kong, 1977, plastic, NM, I2 .... $25.00
KISS, 1977, plastic, EX, N2 .... $50.00
Kung Fu, 1974, plastic, M $18.00
Lawman, 1961, metal, M, N2 .... $75.00
Legend of the Lone Ranger, 1980, plastic, M $20.00
Life & Times of Grizzly Adams, 1977, plastic, EX, I2 .... $28.00
Little House on the Prairie, 1978, plastic, M $20.00
Magic Kingdom, 1980, plastic, EX $7.00
Magic of Lassie, 1978, plastic, EX, N2 .... $20.00
Man From UNCLE, 1966, metal, M $70.00
Mary Poppins, 1964, metal, EX, I2 .... $45.00
Mickey Mouse Club, 1976, plastic, EX, I2 .... $10.00
Mighty Mouse, 1979, plastic, EX, I2 .... $25.00
Miss America, 1972, plastic, M $30.00
Monroes, 1967, metal, EX $60.00
Mork & Mindy, 1978, plastic, EX, I2 .... $15.00
Munsters, 1965, metal, M $130.00
NFL Quarterback, 1964, metal, EX, N2 .... $65.00
Osmonds, 1973, plastic, EX, N2 .... $20.00
Partridge Family, 1971, metal, M $45.00
Pets & Pals, 1962, metal, EX, N2 .... $25.00
Pinocchio, 1971, plastic, EX, I2 .... $30.00
Police Patrol, 1973, plastic, M $35.00
Popeye, 1964, metal, M $50.00
Raggedy Ann & Andy, 1973, plastic, M, N2 .... $18.00
Rambo, 1985, plastic, M $10.00
Road Runner, 1970, metal, M, N2 .... $50.00
Robot Man & Friends, 1984, plastic, EX, I2 .... $12.00
Ronald McDonald, 1982, plastic, M $12.00
Scotch Plaid, 1959, metal, EX, N2 .... $20.00
Sesame Street, 1985, plastic, EX, I2 .... $3.00
Sigmund & the Sea Monsters, 1974, plastic, EX, I2 .... $40.00
Smokey Bear, 1975, metal, M $90.00
Sport Goofy, 1984, plastic, EX, N2 .... $15.00
Star Trek, 1979, plastic, M $18.00
Strawberry Shortcake, 1985, plastic, M $8.00
Superman, 1967, metal, EX, I2, from $60 to $70.00
Superman, 1978, plastic, M $15.00
Tarzan, 1966, metal, EX $50.00
Teenage Mutant Ninja Turtles, 1990, plastic, NM, I2 .... $4.00
Thundercats, 1985, plastic, M $14.00
Tom Corbett Space Cadet, 1952, metal, EX, N2, from $75 to $85.00
Underdog, 1974, metal, EX, N2 .... $300.00
US Mail, 1969, plastic, M $22.00
Voyage to the Bottom of the Sea, 1967, metal, EX $70.00
Waltons, 1973, plastic, EX, I2 .... $16.00
Washington Redskins, 1970, metal, 1970, M $150.00
Welcome Back Kotter, 1976, plastic, M $20.00
Winnie the Pooh, 1976, plastic, M $70.00
Woody Woodpecker, 1972, plastic, G, I2 .... $30.00
Yogi Bear & His Friends, 1963, metal, M, N2 .... $50.00

Marbles

Antique marbles are divided into several classifications: 1) transparent swirl (solid core, latticinio core, divided core, ribbon core, lobed core, and coreless); 2) Lutz or Lutz-type (with bands having copper flecks which alternate with colored or clear bands; 3) peppermint swirl (made of red, white, and blue opaque glass); 4) Indian swirl (black with multicolored surface swirls); 5) banded swirl (wide swirling bands on opaque or transparent glass); 6) onionskin (having an overall mottled appearance due to its spotted, swirling lines or lobes: 7) end-of-day (single pontil, allover spots, either two-colored or multicolored); 8) clambroth (evenly spaced, swirled lines on opaque glass); 9) mica (transparent color with mica flakes added); 10) sulfide (nearly always clear, colored examples are rare, containing figures). Besides glass marbles, some were made of clay, pottery, china, steel, and even semiprecious stones.

Most machine-made marbles are still very reasonable, but some of the better examples may sell for $50.00 and up, depending on the colors that were used and how they are defined. Guineas (Christensen agates with small multicolored specks instead of swirls) sometimes go for as much as $200.00. Mt. Peltier comic character marbles often bring prices of $100.00 and more with Betty Boop, Moon Mullins, and Kayo being the rarest and most valuable.

From the nature of their use, mint-condition marbles are extremely rare and may be worth as much as three to five times more than one that is near-mint, while chipped and cracked marbles may be worth half or less. The same is true of one that has been polished, regardless of how successful the polishing was. If you'd like to learn more, Everett Grist has written three books on the subject that you will find helpful: *Antique and Collectible Marbles*, *Machine Made and Contemporary Marbles*, and *Everett Grist's Big Book of Marbles*. Also refer to MCSA's *Marble Identification and Price Guide*, recently re-written by Robert Block (Schiffer Publishing). See Clubs, Newsletters, and Other Publications for club information.

Artist-made, angelfish or sea horse, David Salazar, 1⅜", M, B8, ea $100.00
Artist-made, end-of-day or swirl, Jody Fine, 1½", M, B8, ea ... $50.00
Artist-made, end-of-day or swirl, Mark Matthews, 1½", M, B8, ea $75.00
Artist-made, end-of-day w/Lutz, aventurine or mica, Rolf & Genie Wald, 1½", M, B8, ea $50.00
Artist-made, end-of-day w/Lutz or mica, Bill Burchfield, 1½", M, B8, ea $75.00
Artist-made, peppermint w/mica, Mark Matthews, ⅝" to ¾", M, B8 .... $50.00

Akro Agates, MIB, $250.00.

Artist-made, single flower or 3 flowers, Harry Boyer, 1½", M, B8, ea $50.00
Artist-made, swirl w/Lutz, aventurine or mica, Rolf & Genie Wald, 1⅛", M, B8, ea $25.00
Artist-made, swirl w/Lutz or mica, Bill Burchfield, 1½", M, B8, ea $75.00
Artist-made, swirls & ribbons, Harry Boyer, 1⅝", M, B8 .$50.00
Clambroth swirl, any color variation, ½" to ⅞", M, B8, ea ...$250.00
Comic, Andy Gump, Peltier Glass, M, B8....$125.00
Comic, Annie, Peltier Glass, M, B8....$150.00
Comic, Betty Boop, Peltier Glass, M, B8....$200.00
Comic, Emma, Peltier Glass, M, B8....$75.00

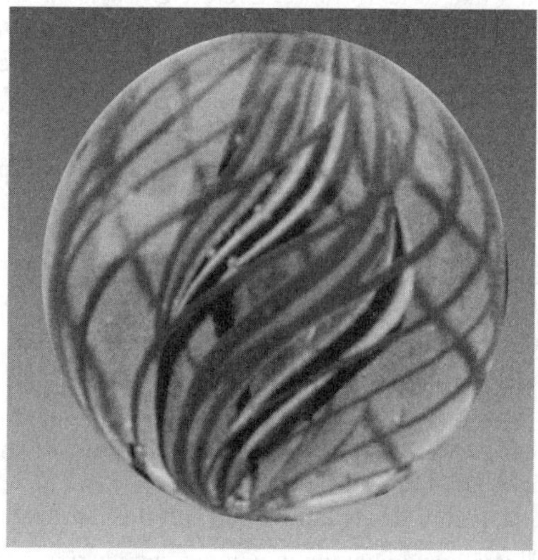

Divided core swirl, red cage-type outer bands with multicolored inner bands, 1⅜", rare, NM, A, $250.00.

Comic, Herbie, Peltier Glass, M, B8....$150.00
Comic, Kayo, Peltier Glass, M, B8....$450.00
Comic, Koko, Peltier Glass, M, B8....$125.00
Comic, Moon Mullins, Peltier Glass, M, B8....$300.00
Comic, Skeezix, Peltier Glass, M, B8....$150.00
Comic, Smitty, Peltier Glass, M, B8....$125.00
Divided core swirl, peewee, any color variation, ⅜" to ½", M, B8, ea....$25.00
Divided core swirl, 4 yel outer bands w/3 mc inner bands, 1 1/16", NM, A....$100.00
End-of-day, cloud-type w/mica, wht w/red & bl blend, 1⅝", NM, B8....$300.00
End-of-day, onionskin, wht base w/2 transparent pk, 1 bl & 1 gr panel, 1⅝", NM, A....$350.00

End-of-day, onionskin, two transparent pink and two blue panels, opaque white core, 1¾", NM, A, $175.00.

End-of-day, peewee, any color variation, ⅜" to ½", M, B8, ea....$50.00
End-of-day, red & wht, 1½", NM, B8....$225.00
End-of-day, single pontil cloud w/mica, mc, 1⅝", NM, B8....$550.00
End-of-day, wht w/2 bl & 2 red panels, 1⅞", NM, B8....$250.00
Game Marbles, Vitro Agate, set of 60 in various colors, MIB, A....$100.00
Indian swirl, any color variation, ½" to ⅞", M, B8, ea...$125.00
Joseph's coat, transparent bl base w/mc swirl, 15/16", VG, A....$65.00
Joseph's coat, transparent clear base w/mc swirl, shrunken core w/aventurine, 19/32", M, A....$165.00
Latticinio core, lt bl transparent base w/4 mc outer bands, gr core, 1 9/16", rare, EX, A....$125.00
Latticinio core, 2 gr on wht & 2 red on wht outer bands, wht core w/2 yel & 1 red band, 1¼", rare, M, A....$185.00
Latticinio swirl, peewee, any color variation, ⅜" to ½", M, B8, ea....$25.00
Latticinio swirl, 3 translucent turq & 3 red & wht outer bands, wht core, 1⅞", NM, B8....$150.00
Latticinio swirl, 6 red & wht outer bands, yel core, 1⅝", NM, B8....$150.00

Lucky Boy Marble Set, set of 28 tiger eye marbles, MIB, A ...$300.00

Lutz, banded colored glass, any color, ½" to ⅞", M, B8, $200.00.

Lutz, banded opaque, any color, ½" to ⅞", M, B8 ....$400.00
Machine-made, aqua or clear slag, Akro Agate, 9⁄16" to 11⁄16", M, B8, ea $8.00
Machine-made, aventurine, Akro Agate, 9⁄16" to 11⁄16", M, B8.$25.00
Machine-made, bl oxblood, Akro Agate, 9⁄16" to 11⁄16", M, B8 .$65.00
Machine-made, brn slag, MF Christensen, 1 3⁄16", NM, B8..$75.00
Machine-made, carnelian oxblood, Akro Agate, 9⁄16" to 11⁄16", M, B8 ....$80.00
Machine-made, corkscrew, Akro Agate, 4-color, 9⁄16" to 11⁄16", M, B8 ....$30.00
Machine-made, corkscrew, Akro Agate, 5-color, 9⁄16" to 11⁄16", M, B8 ....$60.00
Machine-made, guinea, Christensen Agate, transparent base w/melted flecks of color, 11⁄16", M, B8 ....$475.00
Machine-made, lemonade corkscrew or swirl, Akro Agate, 9⁄16" to 11⁄16", M, B8, ea $12.50
Machine-made, limeade corkscrew or swirl, Akro Agate, 9⁄16" to 11⁄16", M, B8, ea $20.00
Machine-made, limeade oxblood, Akro Agate, 9⁄16" to 11⁄16", M, B8 ....$100.00
Machine-made, National Line Rainbo, bumblebee, Peltier Glass, 9⁄16" to 11⁄16", M, B8 ....$12.50
Machine-made, National Line Rainbo, Liberty, Peltier Glass, 9⁄16" to 11⁄16", M, B8 ....$75.00
Machine-made, National Line Rainbo, Superman, Peltier Glass, 9⁄16" to 11⁄16", M, B8 ....$125.00
Machine-made, National Line Rainbo, tiger, Peltier Glass, 9⁄16" to 11⁄16", M, B8 ....$20.00
Machine-made, National Line Rainbo, zebra, Peltier Glass, 9⁄16" to 11⁄16", M, B8 ....$10.00
Machine-made, opaque swirl, Christensen Agate, 2-color, 9⁄16" to 11⁄16", M, B8 ....$15.00
Machine-made, opaque swirl, Christensen Agate, 3-color, 9⁄16" to 11⁄16", M, B8 ....$35.00
Machine-made, orangeade corkscrew or swirl, Akro Agate, 9⁄16" to 11⁄16", M, B8, ea $30.00
Machine-made, oxblood slag, MF Christensen, 9⁄16" to 11⁄16", M, B8 ....$110.00
Machine-made, Popeye corkscrew, Akro Agate, purple & yel or red & bl, 9⁄16" to 11⁄16", M, B8, ea $65.00
Machine-made, Popeye corkscrew, Akro Agate, red & yel or gr & yel, 9⁄16" to 11⁄16", M, B8, ea $12.00
Machine-made, Popeye patch, Akro Agate, red, gr, wht & clear, ¾", rare, NM, B8 ....$150.00
Machine-made, pumpkin oxblood, Akro Agate, ⅝", rare, M, A $155.00
Machine-made, silver oxblood, Akro Agate, 9⁄16" to 11⁄16", M, B8 ....$40.00
Machine-made, sunburst, Master Marble, clear, 9⁄16" to 11⁄16", M, B8 ....$10.00
Machine-made, swirl, MF Christensen, any color variation, 9⁄16" to 11⁄16", M, ea, from $40 to $50.00
Machine-made, swirl, Ravenswood Novelty Works, mc, 9⁄16" to 11⁄16", M, B8 ....$10.00
Machine-made, tiger eye, Master Marble, 9⁄16" to 11⁄16", M, B8 ....$20.00
Machine-made, yel slag, Akro Agate, 9⁄16" to 11⁄16", M, B8..$12.00
Machine-made, yel swirl, lt bl base, MF Christensen, 19/32", NM, A $25.00
Master Made Marble Set, 1940s, complete w/100 wht, bl & gr solid core marbles, ⅝", EX (EX box), A..........$150.00
Peppermint swirl, any color variation, ½" to ⅞", M, B8, ea ..$125.00
Ribbon core swirl, any color variation, ½" to ⅞", M, B8, ea $150.00
Solid core swirl, peewee, any color variation, ⅜" to ½", M, B8, ea $40.00
Solid core swirl, transparent aqua base w/3 sets of opaque wht outer bands, opaque wht core, 9⁄16", NM, A $65.00
Solid core swirl, 12 yel outer bands w/red, gr & bl middle bands, wht 3-layer solid core, 1¼", NM, B8 ....$75.00

Sulfide, duck seated on mound of grass, 1¼", NM, $50.00.

Solid core swirl, 2 red on wht & 2 gr on wht outer bands, translucent yel core, 1$\frac{3}{16}$", rare, M, A $165.00
Solid core swirl, 4 sets of orange outer bands w/pk, gr & bl bands on opaque core, 1⅝", NM, A $125.00
Solid core swirl, 8 yel outer bands, red, gr & bl bands on wht core, 1½", NM, B8 ....$125.00
Sulfide, alligator, 1¾", M $160.00
Sulfide, angel face w/wings, 1¾", M $1,000.00
Sulfide, camel (1 hump), standing on mound of grass, 1½", NM, B8...$200.00
Sulfide, child sitting, 1¾", M $600.00
Sulfide, child w/sailboat, 1¾", M $650.00
Sulfide, cow, 1⅞", NM $200.00
Sulfide, crucifix, 1¾", M..$600.00
Sulfide, dog w/bird in mouth, 1¾", M............................$900.00
Sulfide, dove, 1⅝", M $165.00
Sulfide, elephant, standing, sea gr glass, 1¾", NM $400.00
Sulfide, fish, 1½", M $175.00
Sulfide, George Washington, bust, 2⅜", NM $650.00
Sulfide, Jenny Lind, 1½", NM...$750.00
Sulfide, lamb, 1¾", NM..$125.00
Sulfide, lion, standing on mound of grass, 2", NM, B8 ...$125.00
Sulfide, Little Boy Blue, 1¾", M $700.00
Sulfide, Nipper dog, 1¾", EX $350.00
Sulfide, papoose, 1¾", M..$700.00
Sulfide, parrot, 1½", EX, A...$100.00
Sulfide, peasant boy, on stump w/legs crossed, 1½", NM, B8 ....$400.00
Sulfide, rabbit, sprinting over grass, 1⅞", NM $150.00

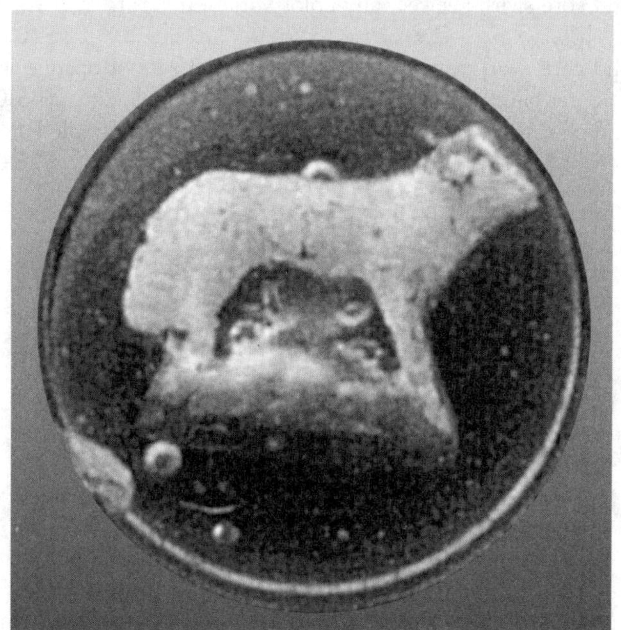

Sulfide, ram, 2", very rare, NM, A, $2,200.00.

Sulfide, Santa Claus, 1¾", M $1,200.00
Sulfide, sheep, standing on mound of grass, 1¼", NM, B8 ...$150.00
Sulfide, squirrel w/nut, 2", EX $200.00
Sulfide, standing on mound of grass, 1⅞", NM, B8 ....$150.00
Sulfide, woman (Kate Greenaway), 1½", NM, B8 ....$450.00
Sulfide, #3, 1$\frac{11}{16}$", rare, NM, A......................................$250.00

Marx

Louis Marx founded his company in New York in the 1920s. He was a genius not only at designing toys but also marketing them. His business grew until it became one of the largest toy companies ever to exist, eventually expanding to include several factories in the United States as well as other countries. Marx sold his company in the early 1970s; he died in 1982. Though toys of every description were produced, collectors today admire his mechanical toys above all others.

Advisor: Scott Smiles (S10), windups; Tom Lastrapes (L4), battery-ops.

See also Advertising; Banks; Character, TV, and Movie Collectibles; Dollhouse Furniture; Games; Guns; Plastic Figures; Playsets; and other categories. For toys made by Linemar (Marx's subsidiary in Japan), see Battery-Operated Toys; Windups, Friction, and Other Mechanicals.

Battery-Operated

Aircraft Carrier, 20", EX (EX box), L4 ....$450.00
Alley the Roaring Stalking Alligator, MIB, L4...............$475.00
Barnyard Rooster, 1950s, several actions, 10", EX..........$200.00
Batcraft, 1966, helicopter w/Batman at controls, advances w/lights & sound, plastic, 6", NM (NM box), A $250.00
Bengali the Exciting New Growling Prowling Tiger, 1961, 3 actions, plush over tin, 18½", EX.............................$200.00
Big Bruiser Super Highway Service Truck, 1960s, several actions, 23", EX $300.00
Big Parade, soldiers march together w/drummer in center, plastic, 15" L, VG (worn box), A $150.00

Buttons the Puppy with a Brain, 1960s, several actions, tin and plush, 12", EX, $400.00.

Bixby & the Bunny, 1950s, several actions, rare, EX......**$400.00**
Brewster the Rooster, 1950s, several actions, 9½", EX...**$225.00**
Clang-Clang Locomotive, 1950s, 3 actions, 10½", EX.....**$65.00**
Colonel Hap Hazard, 1968, several actions, 11", EX......**$700.00**
Crazy Express, 1960s, 17", EX...**$100.00**
Fred Flintstone on Dino, bump-&-go action, 19", NM (EX box), A..**$800.00**
Futuristic Airport, plane circles airport, remote control, 16x16" base, EX (EX box) **$400.00**
Great Garloo, MIB, L4 ....**$750.00**
Hootin' Hollerin' Haunted House, several actions, litho tin, 11", EX, A...**$1,000.00**
Jetspeed Racer #7, advances w/lighted engine & sound, tin w/plastic driver, 17", EX (VG box), A.....................**$850.00**
Marx-A-Serve Table Tennis, rare, MIB, L4 ....**$200.00**
Mickey Mouse Krazy Kar, Mickey in high-wheel cart advances w/bump-&-go action, plastic, EX (EX box) **$75.00**
Mickey the Musician, 1950s, plays xylophone on sq base, plastic & tin, 12", EX...**$275.00**
Mighty Kong, 1950s, several actions, plush over tin, remote control, 11", EX **$500.00**

Mighty Kong, 1950s, several actions, tin and plush, remote control, 11", MIB, $600.00.

Yeti the Abominable Snowman, advances with several actions and grunts, tin, plush, and vinyl, 11", NMIB, A, $735.00.

Motorcycle Delivery, 1929, w/driver, litho tin, rare, EX (EX box)..**$925.00**
Nutty Mad Car, advances on rear wheels, stops & shakes w/monster sound, litho tin, 9", EX, A......................**$200.00**
Nutty Mad Indian, 1960s, rocks while beating drum, tongue moves & makes war hoop sounds, tin & vinyl, 12", MIB.........**$175.00**
Roadster, red & yel litho tin, 15", EX, A....................**$1,375.00**
Teddy Bear Swing, TN, 1950s, 3 actions, NMIB, L4......**$425.00**
Whistling Spooky Kooky Tree, 1960s, bump-&-go w/several other actions, litho tin, 14", NM (NM box) **$2,000.00**

Pressed Steel

Contractor's Dump Truck, red & bl w/yel dump gate, litho tin wheels, 17", M, A **$250.00**
Deluxe Delivery Truck, red & yel w/blk-pnt tires, complete w/cb advertising boxes in back, 11", NM (NM box), A ..**$350.00**
Dump Truck, bl & orange w/high side extensions, MIB.**$300.00**
Easter Truck, 1930s, turq, pk & yel w/chick & rabbit stamped on stake sides, 10", rare, NM, A **$950.00**
Hauler & Stake Truck, bl cab, MIB **$400.00**
Hi Way Express Truck, red & yel, mk New York...Chicago...San Francisco, 16", NM, A...**$350.00**

Hi-Lift Loader, bright yellow with blue plastic tires, MIB, $200.00.

Lazy Day Farms Truck, yel & red w/blk Lumar tires, complete w/2 plastic steers, 18", NM, A................................**$165.00**
Load & Dump Truck, yel, red & wht, 17", MIB, A **$300.00**
Lumar Contractor's Dump Truck, red & bl w/yel lettering on doors, M **$300.00**
Marine Corps Truck, canvas top, complete w/2 plastic soldiers, 13", NM (NM box), A **$250.00**
Railway Express Truck, features hi-lift tailgate, complete w/advertising boxes & wooden crates, 20", NM (EX box), A **$700.00**
Rapid Express Wagon, 1930s, yel w/Rapid Express decals, 8", scarce, NM, A...**$200.00**

Photo courtesy John Turney

Powerhouse Dump Truck, green and tan with black tires, MIB, $300.00.

US Mail Truck, red, wht & bl w/blk Lumar tires, dbl opening rear doors, 26", EX, A $300.00
US Mail Truck, red, wht & bl w/blk-pnt tires, 12", EX, A..$160.00
USA Army Truck, 1920s, WWI Mack-type, canvas top, 10½", NM (G box), A $1,300.00
Willy's Jeep & Trailer, bl & red w/tin balloon tires, battery-op headlights, 21", NM (NM box), A..........................$350.00

Windups, Frictions, and Other Mechanicals

Aero Oil Co Truck, litho tin w/C-style cab, friction, 5¼", NM, A $600.00
Amos 'N Andy, 1930, non-moving eye version, advances & moves side to side, litho tin, 11", NM (EX boxes), from $1,200 to...$1,300.00
Amos 'N Andy Fresh Air Taxi, 1930, litho tin, 8½", M (EX box), from $1,300 to $1,400.00
Andrew Brown, 1930, waddling motion, non-moving eye version, litho tin, 12", EX, A..$725.00
Animal Express, 1930s, 3 litho tin cars mk Bunny Express, complete w/track, scarce, NM (NM box), A...............$1,000.00
Archie Jalopy, Mexico, litho tin w/comical sayings in Spanish, 7", EX...$300.00
Army Dive Bomber #482, 1930s, advances & flips over, litho tin, 7½" wingspan, scarce, NM (G box), A.............$400.00
Army Tank Corps No 12, 1920s, advances w/sparks, litho tin, 10", NM, A $400.00
Army Tractor w/Cannon, 1927, litho tin w/rubber treads, 13", rare, EX (G box), A...$875.00
Astro (Jetsons), 1960s, advances on wheels, plastic, friction, 4", rare, EX, A $375.00
Barney Rubble's Wreck, 1962, litho tin w/vinyl-headed figure, friction, 7", NM $450.00
Beat It! the Komical Kop, 1930s, litho tin, 8", NMIB....$900.00
Bedrock Express Train, 1962, litho tin, 12", EX $250.00
Big Barn Tractor Set, litho tin, complete, EX (EX box), A...$300.00

Photo courtesy Scott Smiles

Beat It Komical Kop, 1930s, travels with crazy action as cop's head spins, lithographed tin, 8", EX, $700.00.

Big Parade, 1930s, soldiers, marching band & ambulance circle track as plane flies above, tin, 24", NM (worn box) .$950.00
Blondie's Jalopy, 1935, bump-&-go action, litho tin, 16½", scarce, NM, A $2,600.00

Photo courtesy Scott Smiles

Butter and Egg Man, 1930s, lithographed tin, EX, from $800.00 to $900.00.

Bluto Horse Cart, 1930s, tin w/celluloid figure, 7", NM (EX box), A...$700.00

BO Plenty, advances while holding Baby Sparkles, tips hat, litho tin, 9", MIB, A...$475.00

Buck Rogers Rocket Police Patrol, 1934, advances w/sparks & sound, litho tin, 11½", NM, A...$1,500.00

Buck Rogers 25th Century Rocket Ship, litho tin, 12", NM (VG box)...$2,000.00

Bunny Express, 1935, litho tin, complete w/tracks, 16", NM (NM box mk Animal Express), A...$1,000.00

Busy Delivery (known as Black Pinocchio Busy Delivery), 1939, peddles cart in all directions, litho tin, scarce, VG .$500.00

Busy Miners, 1930s, coal car w/2 miners travel track to engine house & mine, litho tin, 16½", NM (G box)...$350.00

Busy Parking Station, 1930, car travels track in & out of garage, litho tin, 15", NM (G box)...$250.00

Cannonball Keller Mechanical Roadster w/Trailer, red litho tin w/bl plastic trailer, NM (EX box), from $325 to ...$350.00

Careful Johnnie, 1950s, plastic & tin, 6½", EX...$150.00

Charleston Trio, 1921, jigger dances, boy plays violin & dog w/cane jumps atop cabin, litho tin, 10", EX...$750.00

Charlie McCarthy, 1930s, sways back & forth as mouth opens & closes, litho tin, 8½", NM (G box)...$450.00

Charlie McCarthy in His Benzine Buggy, 1938, Charlie's head spins as car advances, litho tin, 7", EX...$650.00

Chompy the Beetle, advances as mouth opens & eyes roll, litho tin, 6", NM, A...$100.00

Climbing Fireman, plastic & tin version, fireman climbs ladder, EX (EX box)...$250.00

Climbing Fireman, tin version, fireman climbs up ladder, 9", MIB...$300.00

Coast Defense, 1924, plane circles above base w/several actions, litho tin, 9" dia base, NM (G box)...$1,000.00

Cocker Spaniel, advances w/wagging tail, litho tin, friction, 12", scarce, NM, A...$175.00

College Jalopy, advances w/crazy action, litho tin, 6", EX, A...$250.00

Comet Racer #5, Bluestreak Racer #3, and Racer #4, 1930s, lithographed tin, 3½", EX, from $75.00 to $100.00 each.

Coo-Coo Car, 1920s, advances in circular motion as full-figure driver bounces up & down, 7½", EX...$400.00

Cowboy Rider, 1941, rearing horse vibrates as cowboy spins lariat overhead & aims gun, NM (EX box)...$350.00

Cowboy Rider, 1941, rearing horse vibrates as cowboy spins lariat overhead & aims gun, litho tin, 8", EX+...$250.00

Dagwood Solo Flight Aeroplane, 1935, forward & reverse action, litho tin, 9", NM (G box)...$1,200.00

Dagwood the Driver, advances w/crazy action as Dagwood's head spins, litho tin, 8", NMIB, from $1,500 to...$2,000.00

Dapper Dan Coon Jigger, 1910, non-bank version, dances on stage, litho tin, 10", NM (EX box)...$1,200.00

Dick Tracy Police Station, box only, 1950s, G, A...$250.00

Dick Tracy Police Station, 1950s, litho tin, complete w/car, NM, A...$450.00

Dick Tracy Police Station with Car, 1950s, NMIB, $500.00.

Dick Tracy Siren Squad Car, metallic gr w/various characters lithoed in windows, battery-op light, 11", scarce, NMIB, A...$500.00

Dippy Dumper, 1930s, travels in circle as driver gets thrown out & dumpster lifts, tin & celluloid, 9", VG, A...$500.00

Disney Parade Roadster, litho tin w/plastic Mickey, Donald, Goofy & Huey seated in car, 11½", EX (G box)...$450.00

Disney Turnover Tank, WDP/Mexico, 1950s, Goofy forces tank to turn over, litho tin, 4", rare, EX...$750.00

Disneyland Jeep, litho tin, friction, 10", EX, A...$200.00

Disneyland Jeep, litho tin, friction, 10", EX (G box)...$300.00

Donald Duck & His Nephews, Donald pulls nephews attached by rod, plastic w/hand-pnt details, 11", NM (EX box), A...$575.00

Donald Duck Dipsy Car, litho tin w/plastic figure, EX (EX box)...$500.00

Donald Duck Drummer, rocks back & forth while playing drum, litho tin, NM (EX box), A...$800.00

Donald Duck Duet, 1946, Goofy dances on platform as Donald plays drum, litho tin, 10½", NM (EX box)...$950.00

Donald Duck Duet, 1946, Goofy dances on platform as Donald plays drum, litho tin, 10½", VG...$500.00

Donald Duck Twirly Tail, 1950s, vibrates around w/spinning tail, plastic, 6", NMIB...$600.00

Donald the Skier, 1948, advances on snow skis w/arm movement, plastic w/tin skis, 10½", NM (EX box), A...$650.00

Donkey Cart, farmer drives donkey-drawn cart, litho tin, 10", NM (EX box), A...$275.00

Dopey Walker, 1938, advances & vibrates as eyes move up & down, litho tin, 8", EX...$350.00

Doughboy Tank, 1930s, advances as soldier pops up from hat & fires gun, litho tin, 9½", VG (worn box)...$300.00

Drummer Boy, advances & plays bass drum, litho tin, 8½", EX...$350.00

Dum Dum & Touche Turtle, 1963, Dum Dum rides Touche Turtle cart, plastic, friction, 4", rare, NMIB............$300.00
Dumbo, WDP, 1941, performs somersaults, litho tin, 4", EX (EX box)..$750.00
Ferdinand & Matador, WDE, 1939, advances as bull attacks matador's cape, litho tin, 7", EX (EX box)..............$875.00
Ferdinand the Bull, 1938, vibrates around w/spinning tail, litho tin, complete w/cloth flower & bee, 6", MIB...........$475.00
Figaro, see Rollover Figaro
Fire Chief Car, litho tin, battery-op roof light, 11", NM .$175.00
Flash Gordon Rocket Fighter, 1939, litho tin, 12", VG .$450.00
Flintstone Flivver, 1962, Fred driving, litho tin w/vinyl figure, 4", EX...$200.00
Flintstone Log Car, 1977, Fred driving, plastic, friction, 5", MIB $175.00
Flintstone Pals, Barney on Dino, litho tin & vinyl, 8½", MIB $500.00
Flintstone Pals, Fred on Dino, litho tin & vinyl, 8½", MIB ..$500.00
Flintstone Tricycle, Dino peddles trike w/bell sound, litho tin w/celluloid figure, 4½", MIB $800.00
Flipo the Dog, 1940, jumps & does flips in the air, litho tin, 4", NM (EX box)..$250.00
Funny Face Walker, 1928, advances w/animated face change, litho tin, 10½", VG $600.00
Funny Flivver Car, 1925, eccentric car w/comical driver advances in erratic motion, litho tin, 7", EX (worn box) $550.00
Funny Tiger, advances & plays drum, litho tin, 7", VG (VG box)...$200.00
G-Man Pursuit Car, advances w/sound, litho tin w/gun protruding through windshield, 14", EX, A $700.00
Gang Busters Police Car, 1936, advances w/sound, litho tin, 14½", rare, EX, A $1,000.00

George the Drummer Boy, 1930s, with moving eyes, lithographed tin, 9", NM, $300.00.

Photo courtesy Scott Smiles

George the Drummer Boy, 1930s, stationary eyes, litho tin, 9½", NM (EX box)...$300.00
GI Joe & His Jouncing Jeep, litho tin, EX (G box), H7 .$425.00
Giant Reversing Tractor Truck, 1950s, litho tin w/rubber treads, lever action, 14", NM (G box), A...........................$275.00
Goofy the Walking Gardener, Goofy pushes cart, litho tin, 9x8", EX $450.00
Goofy's Stock Car, litho tin w/image of Donald, Daisy, Pluto & Minnie, friction, 6", NM, A $250.00
Great Son of Garloo, advances w/arm & leg movement, plastic, 6", NM (NM box), A $850.00
Guided Missile Truck, litho tin, friction, complete w/14" missile, NM, A $150.00
Harold Lloyd Funny Face Walker, 1929, sways as facial expressions change, litho tin, 10½", EX, A $1,000.00
Hee-Haw Balky Mule, 1929s, advances w/crazy action, litho tin, 10½", VG (G box), A $300.00
Hey Hey Chicken Snatcher, 1927, Black man carries chicken as dog bites his pants, litho tin, 8½", EX, from $1,100 to........$1,250.00
Hi-Yo Silver the Lone Ranger, litho tin, MIB $450.00
Highboy Climbing Tractor, 1950s, plastic blade version, w/driver, 8", EX (G box), A $125.00
Honeymoon Express, 1927, litho tin, 9½" dia base, EX (EX box), from $200 to..$225.00
Honeymoon Express, 1937, litho tin, EX (EX box), from $150 to...$175.00
Honeymoon Express, 1940, litho tin, EX (EX box), from $175 to...$200.00

Photo courtesy June Moon

Honeymoon Express, 1947, lithographed tin, EX, from $100.00 to $125.00.

Hop-A-Long Cassidy, rider w/lariat on rocking base, 10", VG $400.00
Hopping Astro, litho tin, 4", NM, A $250.00
Hopping Elroy, 1963, litho tin, 4", MIB $1,000.00
Hopping George Jetson, litho tin, 4", NM, A.................$275.00
Hoppo the Waltzing Monkey, 1930, monkey in circus tuxedo plays cymbals, litho tin, EX $225.00
Hy & Lo Karnival Kar, 2-tiered base w/swinging rods that catch & raise car, metal, 7", VG (VG box), A.................$400.00

Huckleberry Hound Car, 1962, lithographed tin with vinyl figure, friction, 4", NM (EX box), A, $300.00.

International Agent Car, litho tin w/vinyl-headed figure, friction, 4", EX (EX box), A **$100.00**

Jetson Express, George & family in windows, litho tin, 13", EX.. **$375.00**

Joe Penner & His Duck Goo Goo, 1934, advances w/shuffling feet & tips hat, litho tin, 8½", NM.......................... **$475.00**

Joy Rider, 1929, advances in erratic motion as driver's head spins, litho tin, 7½", VG **$375.00**

Jumpin' Jeep, Army jeep w/soldiers travels w/crazy action, litho tin, 6", EX **$200.00**

Kitty Kat, 1930, push down on tail for action, litho tin, 8", scarce, NM (EX box), A.. **$275.00**

Photo courtesy June Moon

Knockout Champs, boxers on revolving disk in boxing ring, lithographed tin with celluloid figures, 7x7", NMIB, $700.00.

Limping Lizzie Auto, advances in swaying motion w/rattling sound, blk w/wht lettering, 7", EXIB........................ **$325.00**

Little Orphan Annie Skipping Rope, 1930s, litho tin, 6", EX, from $500 to **$600.00**

Little Orphan Annie's Dog Sandy, dog w/book bag in mouth, litho tin, 5½", VG, A **$250.00**

Lizzie of the Valley Jalopy, blk litho tin w/allover lettering, 7", EX **$300.00**

Looping Plane, 1930, advances & flips over, litho tin, 7½" wingspan, EX (EX box) **$300.00**

Looping Plane, 1930s, advances & flips over, litho tin, 7½" wingspan, EX, A **$150.00**

Lucky Stunt Flyer, 1930, plane circles above base & performs flips, litho tin, 6½" base, EX, A **$500.00**

Mammy's Boy, ca 1925, Black man w/cane sways as eyes shift, litho tin, 11", EX **$700.00**

Mary Poppins, 1964, whirls around, plastic, 8", NMIB...**$225.00**

Mechanical Roadster, 1950s, tin convertible w/plastic windshield, 6½", NM (EX box), A **$300.00**

Merry Makers, 1930, 3 mice band members w/band leader atop piano, w/marquee, 9½", EX (VG box), A **$1,300.00**

Mickey Mouse, see also Whirling Tail Mickey Mouse

Mickey Mouse Dipsy Car, 1949, advances w/crazy action as Mickey's head bobs, litho tin & plastic, 6", NM (EX box), A **$750.00**

Mickey Mouse Express, 1950s, Mickey flies above track w/Disneyville station in center, tin, 9" dia, NMIB, from $900 to **$1,000.00**

Mickey Mouse Scooter, 1959, plastic, friction, 4", NM (NM box), A.. **$250.00**

Mickey the Driver, advances to end of table & turns around, litho tin w/plastic figure, 6½", NM (EX box), A.....**$750.00**

Mickey the Musician, Mickey plays xylophone while rocking back & forth, tin & plastic, 12", NM (EX box), A..**$850.00**

Midget Climbing Fighting Tank, 1950s, litho tin, 5", NM (G box).. **$175.00**

Midget Racer #5, 1930s, litho tin, w/driver, 5", EX, A...**$200.00**

Midget Racer #7, 1930s, litho tin, w/driver, 5", EX, A...**$200.00**

Midget Special #2, 1930s, litho tin, 5", rare, NM...........**$200.00**

Midget Special #7, 1930s, litho tin, 5", EX....................**$150.00**

Mighty Thor Scooter, 1967, plastic, friction, 4", scarce, EX (EX box), A **$1,150.00**

Military Aeroplane, 1950s, mk US Army, litho tin, 18" W, NM (EX box), A **$250.00**

Milton Berle Car, tractor-type vehicle w/figure advances in erratic motion, litho tin & plastic, 6", NMIB, from $425 to.. **$525.00**

Monkey Tricycle, 1930s, lever action, litho tin, 6", EX, A...**$200.00**

Moon Mullins & Kayo Handcar, 1930s, flat litho tin figures work handlebars, 6", no track, NM **$575.00**

Mortimer Snerd, 1939, sways as hat bounces up & down, litho tin, 8½", VG, A.. **$300.00**

Mortimer Snerd Tricky Auto, 1939, advances w/erratic motion, head swivels in complete circle, 7", EX.................. **$500.00**

Mortimer Snerd's Hometown Band, 1930, Mortimer w/lg bass drum, red, wht & bl litho tin, 8½", EX, A.............. **$975.00**

Motorcycle Cop & Car Speedway, 1930s, police cycle chases car around track, litho tin, rare, NM (EX box), A.....**$1,100.00**

Mortimer Snerd, 1939, sways as hat bounces up and down, lithographed tin, 8½", M, $300.00.

Photo courtesy Dunbar Gallery

Mysterious Pluto, 1939, press tail for action, litho tin, 9", NMIB..$650.00

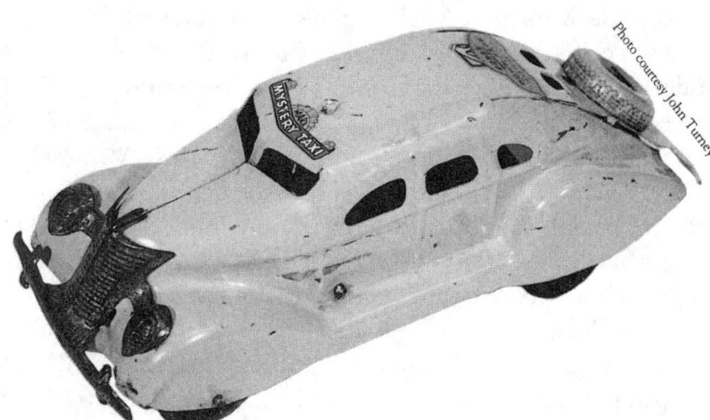

Photo courtesy John Turney

Mystery Taxi, bump-and-go action, VG, $250.00.

Mystic Motorcycle, 1930s, w/driver, non-fall action, litho tin, 4", NM (EX box)..$300.00

New York Honeymoon Express, 1928, train travels track as plane flies above base w/skyscrapers, tin, 9" dia base, NMIB..$1,000.00

Old Jalopy, advances w/undulating motion, litho tin, 7", EX, A...$200.00

Old Mother Goose, 1930, litho tin, 9", NM (VG rare box).$1,925.00

Packard Fire Chief Car, red & cream molded plastic, friction, 10", EX...$75.00

Parade Drummer, advances & plays drum, litho tin, 9", NM, A..$200.00

Pebbles on Dino, advances as Pebbles bounces up & down, plastic, friction, 4", rare, EX......................................$1,800.00

Pecos Bill Ridin' Widowmaker, WDP, 1950s, vibrates as cowboy spins lasso, plastic, 10", NMIB................................$300.00

Peter Rabbit Eccentric Car, lithographed tin and plastic, 5x8", NMIB, $450.00.

Pikes Peak Mountain Climber, 1930s, litho tin, 31" track, EX (worn box)...$550.00

Pinched! 1927, truck goes in circle under 2 bridges, tunnel & station, w/cops & restaurant, tin, 10" sq base, NM..$850.00

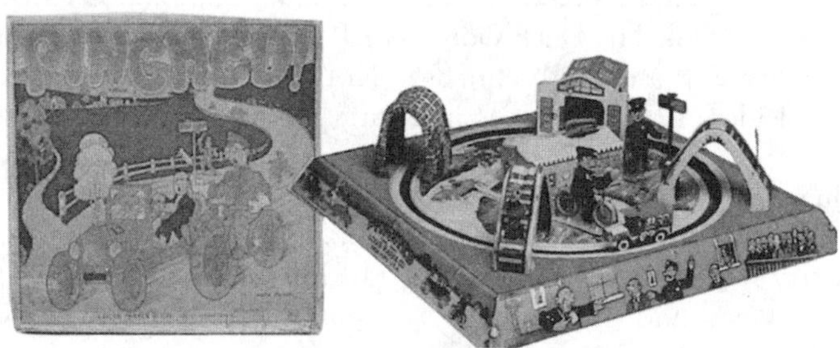

Pinched! 1927, lithographed tin, 10" square base, NMIB, from $1,000.00 to $1,100.00.

Pinnochio, see also Walking Pinnochio

Pinocchio the Acrobat, 1939, performs on spring rod attached to rocking base, litho tin, 11", VG, A..........................$350.00

Pluto, see also Roll-Over Pluto and Wise Pluto

Pluto the Drum Major, 1940s, rocks & shakes bell, litho tin w/rubber ears & tail, 6½", VG, A...........................$275.00

Pluto Twirling Tail, 1950s, vibrates around w/spinning tail, plastic, 6", M..$150.00

Police Motorcycle, 1936, advances w/sound, litho tin, 8½", EX (G box), A..$600.00

Police Motorcycle w/Sidecar, 1930s, litho tin w/full-figure driver, 3", EX...$225.00

Police Patrol Car, gr w/siren & lettering on sides & hood, clockwork mechanism w/battery-op headlights, 14", NM, A............$800.00

Police Squad Motorcycle, advances w/sound & sparks, litho tin, 8¼", NM (G box)....................$550.00
Poor Fish, 1925, advances on wheels & wiggles, litho tin, 8", rare, NM (G- box), A....................$400.00
Popeye & Olive Oyl Jiggers, 1934, Olive Oyl plays accordion & sways while Popeye dances on roof, tin, 10", EX, A..$1,000.00
Popeye & Olive Oyl Jiggers, 1934, Olive Oyl plays accordion & sways while Popeye dances on roof, tin, 10", NMIB..$1,700.00
Popeye Express, 1935, train travels under bridges as Popeye circles in plane overhead, litho tin, EX (EX box) $1,500.00
Popeye Express w/Parrot, parrot pops out of crate in wheelbarrow pushed by Popeye, litho tin, 8½", EX, from $650 to.$750.00
Popeye Handcar, 1925, Popeye & Olive Oyl work handlebar, tin w/rubber figures, 6", NM (EX box), A $850.00
Popeye Jigger, Popeye dances atop roof, litho tin, 9", NMIB, A....................$2,800.00
Popeye the Champ, Popeye & Bluto in boxing ring, litho tin w/celluloid figures, 7x7" ring, EX, from $1,400 to ..$1,500.00
Popeye the Pilot (Popeye Eccentric Airplane), 1930s, litho tin, 8", NMIB, A....................$2,400.00
Popeye the Pilot (Popeye Eccentric Airplane), 1930s, litho tin, 8", EX, from $800 to....................$900.00
Popeye, see also Walking Popeye
Porky Pig, 1939, Porky dressed as cowboy twirls lasso & vibrates around, litho tin, 8½", NMIB, from $700 to $900.00
Porky Pig, 1939, Porky w/umbrella & hat, litho tin, 8½", NM....................$400.00
Power Snap Caterpillar Tractor, 1950s, litho tin, 10", NM (worn box)....................$250.00
Racer #12, 1942, boat-tail style w/driver, litho tin, 16", VG, A $200.00
Racer #3, w/driver, litho tin w/balloon tires, 13", NM (EX box)....................$350.00
Racer #8, w/driver, litho tin w/balloon tires, 13", NM (EX box), A....................$750.00
Red Cap Porter, 1930, Black man w/toothy grin carrying 2 bags, litho tin, 8", EX $650.00
Ride'-Em Cowboy, 1930, horse bucks as cowboy spins lasso, litho tin & celluloid, 7", EX (EX box)....................$300.00
Ring-A-Ling Circus, 1925, ringmaster w/elephant, lion & monkey on pk base, several actions, litho tin, 7" dia, EX, A....................$1,500.00
Ring-A-Ling Circus, 1925, ringmaster w/elephant, lion & monkey on gr base, several actions, litho tin, 7" dia, EX......$1,250.00
Roll-Over Figaro, 1939, advances & rolls over, litho tin, 9", EX, A $250.00
Roll-Over Pluto, 1939, advances & rolls over, litho tin, 9", MIB, A $450.00
Rookie Cop, 1932, travels in circle, falls over & rights itself, litho tin, 8½", EX (EX box) $450.00
Rookie Pilot, 1940, advances in erratic motion, litho tin, 7", EX+, from $475 to $525.00
Sam the Gardener, figure pushes cart, plastic & tin, 8", no tools o/w NMIB....................$250.00
Scottie the Guid-A-Dog, 1930, litho tin, 12½", M (EX box), A....................$750.00
Sheriff Sam Whoopee Car, 1960s, litho tin & plastic, 5½", EX $250.00

Royal Coupe, 1920s, lithographed tin, 9", EX (EX box), $600.00.

Skybird Flyer, 1930s, 2 planes circle tower, litho tin, 8", NM....................$425.00

Skybird Flyer, 1930s, planes circle tower, lithographed tin, 8", NMIB, $500.00.

Skyview Yellow Cab, litho tin, 6½", EX....................$150.00
Smitty Scooter, boy advances on scooter w/realistic action, litho tin, 8", rare, EX, A....................$1,450.00
Smokey Joe the Climbing Fireman, 1930s, fireman climbs ladder attached to base, 11½", EX (EX box), from $350 to.$425.00
Snappy the Miracle Dog, EX, L4....................$175.00
Snoopy Gus Wild Fireman, 1927, travels in erratic pattern as fireman spins on ladder, tin, 8", rare, EX (worn box) ..$1,500.00
Somstepa, 1926, Black man performs jig on stage, litho tin, 8", EX $650.00
Sparkling Climbing Tractor, advances w/sparks, litho tin w/plastic figure, 8½", EX (EX box) $150.00
Sparkling Hot Rod Racer, w/driver, plastic, friction, 7", NM (VG box), A $200.00
Sparkling Luxury Liner, 1949, litho tin & plastic, friction, 15", NM (NM box)....................$200.00
Sparkling Soldier Motorcycle, 1936, advances w/sparking machine gun, litho tin, 8", NM (EX box), A...........$600.00
Speed Boy Delivery (Delivery Motorcycle), 1930s, litho tin, 10", NM (worn box) $650.00
Speedway Coupe, red w/brn top & blk running boards, battery-op headlights, 8", MIB....................$700.00

Spic & Span, 1925, 2 Black minstrels on stage mk The Hams What Am, litho tin, 10½", EX $1,650.00
Steam Roller, red & blk litho tin w/flat figure, 8½", EX..$250.00
Super Hot Rod 777, advances w/flashing motor block, litho tin w/plastic driver, friction, 11", NM (EX box), A $325.00

Photo courtesy June Moon

Super Hot Rod 777, advances with flashing motor block, lithographed tin with plastic driver, friction, 11", M (NM box), $400.00.

Super Sonic Jet, 1960s, plastic, friction, 5", EX, J2 ....$50.00
Super Streamline Racer #12, 1950s, litho tin w/plastic driver, 16", NM (G box) $275.00
Superman Rollover Plane, 1940, advances as Superman causes plane to roll over, litho tin, 6", NM, A $1,700.00
Taxi Cab, mk Yellow Cab Co on door, litho tin, 11", NM (EX box), A $300.00
Tidy Tim the Clean Up Man, mk Keep Your City Spick & Span, litho tin, 8½", EX+ $500.00
Tom & Jerry Scooter, 1972, Tom driving w/Jerry in sidecar, plastic, friction, 4½", MIB, A....$100.00
Tom Corbett Sparkling Spaceship, advances w/sparks, litho tin, 12", NM (NM box), A....$1,500.00
Tower Aeroplane, 1935, 2 planes circle tower, litho tin w/celluloid props, 9", NM (worn box) $400.00
Toyland Milk Wagon, 1929, litho tin w/balloon tires, 10", MIB, A....$1,500.00
Tractor & Trailer, 1930s, aluminum, w/driver, 16", NM (G box) $275.00
Trans-Atlantic Zeppelin, 1930s, litho tin, 10", VG........$250.00
Tricky Motorcycle, 1930s, mystery action, litho tin, 4", MIB $300.00
Tricky Taxi, advances w/non-fall action, tin, gr version, 4½", NM (G box) $200.00
Tumbling Monkey & Trapeze, 1920s, performs on trapeze rings or side bars, 6", NM (EX box) $300.00
Turn-Over Tank, 1925, WWII version, flips over, tin, 9½", scarce, NM (G box)....$375.00
Uncle Wiggily Car, 1935, advances as figure's head turns, litho tin w/Easter motif, 8", EX....$1,000.00
US Army Command Car, litho tin, friction w/battery-op lights & siren, 19", EX (VG box)....$350.00
US Army Turnover Tank No 3, advances & flips over, litho tin, 8", NM, A....$250.00
Wacky Taxi #77, litho tin w/driver & passengers in windows, friction, 7", NM $175.00
Walking Pinocchio, 1939, advances in waddling motion as eyes move, litho tin, 9", NM (G box), A $600.00
Walking Popeye, King Features, 1935, carries 2 cages w/lithoed parrots, 8½", NMIB, A $1,100.00
Walking Tiger, advances w/several actions & roars, plush & celluloid, 8", MIB $125.00
Walt Disney's Television Car, litho tin, friction, 7½", NM (EX box)....$550.00
Wee Scottie, 1930s, litho tin, 5", EX (EX box) $250.00
Whirling Tail Mickey Mouse, tail spins when activated, plastic, 7", NMIB $300.00

Photo courtesy Scott Smiles

Whoopee Cowboy, 1932, advances with crazy action, lithographed tin, 8", EX, $350.00.

Wise Pluto, 1939, advances w/non-fall action & simulates sniffing, litho tin w/rubber ears & tail, 8", EX (EX box) .$375.00
Yogi Bear Car, litho tin w/vinyl-headed figure, friction, 4", NM (EX box mk Huckleberry Hound), A....$275.00

Miscellaneous

Army Base, camouflaged airplane hangar w/central headquarters, litho tin, 11x17", EX, A $400.00
Brightlite Filling Station, 1930, tin, complete, 9½" L, NM (EX box), A $2,200.00
Dairy Delivery Truck, bright litho tin w/Marx milk bottle in back, 10", NM (EX box), A $300.00
Farm Machinery Set, 1948, complete w/tractor & driver, rake w/driver, trailer, hayer & soil loosener, tin, NMIB, A $450.00
Fire House, mk General Alarm Fire House, 1930s, litho tin, complete w/car, NMIB $550.00

Photo courtesy Phil Helley

Circus Truck and Animals, plastic, MIB, $325.00.

Fix-All Convertible, Pontiac, plastic, complete, 9", NM (NM box), A $200.00
Fix-All Station Wagon, 1953 Mercury, plastic, complete, 13", scarce, NM (EX box), A $185.00
Fix-All Tractor, complete w/tools & accessories, NM (NM box), A $100.00

Photo courtesy John Turney

Freight Depot, complete with plastic accessories, MIB, $300.00.

Gas Pump, litho tin, w/air pump, oil stand & signs, EX, H7 .... $385.00
Hangar & Plane, litho tin, hangar: 3x7", plane: 5" L, NM, A $200.00
Hen House, litho tin, w/plastic farm animals, 7", NM, A $55.00
Hi-Lift Tractor, litho tin & pressed steel w/plastic figure, MIB $300.00
Marine Corps Truck, gr litho tin, complete w/plastic figures, MIB $300.00
Municipal Airport Service Station, 1930, litho tin, complete w/Liberty Bus Co bus, 6x5", EX, A $600.00
Pathe Movie Camera, 1930, tin camera on tripod w/crank hdl, 6¼", scarce, NM, A $350.00
Radio Airport, 1930s, litho tin, 17x11" base, EX (EX box), A $355.00
Sunny Side Service Station, litho tin, complete w/car, NM $700.00
Super Circus, complete w/litho tin tent & accessories, EX (EX box) $275.00
Toy Town Express Van Lines Truck, mk Dodge above front grille, litho tin, 11", NM (worn box), A $375.00
Travel Bureau Station, litho tin, 17x11", VG, A $85.00
Tri-City Express Service Truck, litho tin, w/cb advertising boxes in back, 14", NM, A $285.00
Twin Pom-Pom Anti-Aircraft Cannon, metal & plastic, complete, 21", EX (EX box), A $125.00
Universal Airport, 1930s, tin station mk Weather Bureau-Ticket Office..., complete w/3 diecast airplanes, EX (G box), A $350.00
US Army Truck, tin w/canvas cover, mk US Army 5th Div on door, complete w/5 plastic soldiers, 16", NM (EX box), A $285.00
US Mail Tractor Trailer, litho tin w/blk tires, MIB $350.00

Photo courtesy John Turney

USMC Amphibious Marine Truck, lithographed tin with canvas cover, MIB, $400.00.

Matchbox

The Matchbox series of English and American-made autos, trucks, taxis, Pepsi-Cola trucks, steamrollers, Greyhound buses, etc., was very extensive. By the late 1970s, the company was cranking out more than five million cars every week, and while those days may be over, Matchbox still produces about seventy-five million vehicles on a yearly basis.

Introduced in 1953, the Matchbox Miniatures series has always been the mainstay of the company. There were seventy-five models in all but with enough variations to make collecting them a real challenge. Larger, more detailed models were introduced in 1957; this series, called Major Pack, was replaced a few years later by a similar line called King Size. To compete with Hot Wheels, Matchbox converted most models over to a line called SuperFast that sported thinner, low-friction axles and wheels. (These are much more readily available than the original 'regular wheels,' the last of which were made in 1969.) At about the same time, the King Size series became known as Speed Kings; in 1977 the line was reintroduced under the name Super Kings.

In the early '70s, Lesney started to put dates on the baseplates of their toy cars. The name 'Lesney' was coined from the first names of the company's founders. The last Matchboxes that carried the Lesney mark were made in 1982. Today many models can be bought for less than $10.00, though a few are priced much higher.

In 1988, to celebrate the company's 40th anniversary, Matchbox issued a limited set of five models that except for minor variations were exact replicas of the originals. These five were repackaged in 1991 and sold under the name Matchbox Originals. In 1993 a second series expanded the line of reproductions.

Another line that's become very popular is their Models of Yesteryear. These are slightly larger replicas of antique and vintage vehicles. Values of $20.00 to $60.00 for mint-in-box examples are average, though a few sell for even more.

Sky Busters are small-scale aircraft measuring an average of 3½" in length. They were introduced in 1973. Models currently being produced sell for about $4.00 each.

To learn more, we recommend *Matchbox Toys, 1947 – 1996* by Dana Johnson; and a series of books by Charlie Mack: *Lesney's Matchbox Toys* (there are two: *Regular Wheel Years* and *Super Fast Years)* and *Universal Years.*

To determine values of examples in conditions other than given in our listings, based on MIB or MOC prices, deduct a minimum of 10% if the original container is missing, 30% if the condition is excellent, and as much as 70% for a toy graded only very good. In the following listings, we have added zeroes ahead of the numbers to avoid the idiosyncrasies of computer sorting.

Advisors: Mark Giles (G2) 1-75 Series; Dan Wells (W1) King Size, Speed Kings, and Super Kings; Matchbox Originals; Models of Yesteryear; Skybusters.

Other Sources: C18, N3

Key:
LW — Laser Wheels (introduced in 1987)
reg — regular wheels (Matchbox Miniatures)
SF — SuperFast

1-75 Series

II, Sleet-N-Snow, SF, bl, wht base/top, silver hubs, 'US Mail' tampo, M (NM card) $12.00
IX, Flamin' Manta, SF, yel, MOC $11.00
Jaguar 3.4 Litre Saloon, reg, gold wheels, red, 1962, M (NM box) $40.00
Mercedes 300SE, SF, gold, unpnt base, cast doors, open trunk, no labels, 5-spoke wheels, 1970, M $19.00
01-C, Road Roller, reg, lt gr, 1958, M (EX box) $50.00
01-D, Aveling Barford Road Roller, reg, 1962, NM $22.00
01-E, Mercedes Truck, reg, blk wheel, orange canopy, 1968, M (NM box) $15.00
01-G, Mod Rod, yel w/orange interior, blk wheels, spotted cat label, 1971, M (EX+ box) $15.00
02-A, Dumper, reg, scarce gr metal wheels, missing driver, 1953, EX+ $60.00
02-B, Dumper, reg, metal wheels, #2 cast, orig driver, 1957, NM+ $44.00
02-C, Muir Hill Dumper, reg, blk wheels, Laing decals, 1961, NM $23.00
02-D, Mercedes Trailer, reg, blk wheels, orange canopy, 1968 M (NM box) $13.00
02-F, Jeep Hot Rod, SF, pk w/cream interior, lt gr base, 4-spoke wheels, 1971, M (EX+ box) $14.50
02-G, Hovercraft, SF, gr w/tan hull, silver scoop, amber windshield, Rescue label, M (EX+ box) $11.00
03-A, Cement Mixer, reg, orig metal wheels, 1953, EX+ .$42.00
03-C, Mercedes Ambulance, red, blk wheels, orig patient, 1968, M $16.00
03-D, Mercedes Benz Ambulance, cream, dk bl windshield, open rear doors, 5-spoke wheels, orig patient, 1970, M $17.00
03-E, Monteverdi Hai, SF, orange w/ivory interior, blk base, bl windshield, #3 label, M (NM box) $10.00
03-F, Porsche Turbo, metallic brn w/cream interior, blk base, 1978, M (NM box) $12.00
04-B, Massey Harris Tractor, reg, metal wheels, no fender version, orig driver, 1957, NM+ $54.00
04-D, Dodge Stake Truck, reg, blk wheels, gr stakes, 1967, M (NM box) $19.00

Photo courtesy Dana Johnson

04-D, Dodge Stake Truck, regular wheels, scarce blue stakes, 1967, M, $60.00.

04-G, Pontiac Firebird, SF, metallic lt bl, unpnt base, amber windshield, dot-dash wheels, 1975, M (EX+ card) $9.00
05-A, London Bus, reg, metal wheels, 1954, EX+ $43.00
05-B, London Bus, reg, metal wheels, 'Buy Matchbox Series' decal, 1957, NM $49.00
05-D, London Bus, reg, blk wheels, 'Longlife' decals, 1965, M $21.00
05-F, Seafire, SF, wht w/bl hull, red exhaust, bl driver, no trailer, Seafire label, 1975, M (NM card) $8.00
06-A, Quarry Truck, reg, metal wheels, 1954, NM+ $50.00
06-C, Euclid Quarry Truck, reg, blk wheels, solid tires, 1964, M $35.00
06-D, Ford Pickup Truck, reg, blk wheels, wht grille, orig top, 1968, M (VG+ box) $25.00
06-E, Ford Pickup, red w/wht top, blk base, silver grille, 1970, EX $16.00
06-F, Mercedes 350SL, SF, orange w/lt yel interior, blk roof, amber windshield, 5-spoke wheels, 1976, M (EX+ box) $11.00
07-A, Milk Float, reg, metal wheels, wht letters/driver/bottles, 1954, EX+ $88.00

07-C, Ford Refuse Truck, reg, blk wheels, scalloped side plates, 1966, M (NM+ box) **$14.00**

07-D, Ford Refuse Truck, SF, orange, blk axle covers, 1970, M (NM box) **$18.00**

07-E, Hairy Hustler, SF, wht, blk base, amber windshield, checks & stripes, 1971, M (VG+ card) **$12.50**

08-F, Ford Mustang, reddish orange w/ivory interior, 1970, NM+ **$30.00**

08-G, Wildcat Dragster, pk, blk base, blk/orange Wildcat labels, 1971, NM+ **$15.00**

08-H, DeTomaso Pantera, SF, wht w/lt orange interior, bl base, #8 hood tampo, side labels, 1975, M (EX+ box) **$4.00**

09-B, Dennis Fire Escape, reg, metal wheels, #9 cast, 1957, NM+ **$60.00**

09-C, Merryweather Marquis Fire Engine, reg, blk wheels, gold ladder, 1959, M (EX+ box) **$25.00**

09-D, Boat & Trailer, reg, blk wheels, 1966, NM **$17.00**

09-E, AMX Javelin, SF, metallic lime w/orange interior, unpnt base, doors open, 5-spoke wheels, M (NM card) **$9.00**

09-F, Ford Escort RS 2000, SF, wht w/tan interior, blk base, clear windshield, Dunlop labels, 1978, MOC **$9.00**

10-B, Mechanical Horse & Trailer, reg, gold wheels, dk tan driver, 1958, NM+ **$60.00**

10-B, Mechanical Horse & Trailer, reg, metal wheels, lt tan driver, 1958, NM **$40.00**

10-D, Pipe Truck, reg, blk wheels, silver grille, 6 orig pipes on tree, 1966, M (NM box) **$18.00**

10-E, Pipe Truck, SF, orange, silver base, gray pipes, 1970, M (EX+ G box) **$18.00**

10-F, Mustang Piston Popper, SF, bl, unpnt base, no tampo, Rolamatics on base, 1973, M (EX card) **$13.00**

11-A, Road Tanker, reg, metal wheels, yel, 1955, NM+ **$60.00**

11-B, Road Tanker, reg, gold wheels, 1958, VG **$20.00**

11-C, Jumbo Crane, reg, blk wheels, red weight box, 1965, M (NM+ box) **$25.00**

11-D, Scaffolding Truck, reg, blk wheel, complete, 1969, M (NM box) **$18.00**

11-E, Scaffolding Truck, SF, silver, complete, 1970, NM+ **$19.00**

11-G, Car Transporter, SF, orange, beige carrier, blk base, red/yel/bl cars, bl windshield, 1976, M (NM box) **$11.00**

12-A, Land Rover, reg, metal wheels, orig driver, 1955, NM+ **$50.00**

12-C, Safari Land Rover, reg, blk wheels, gr w/brn luggage, 1965, M (NM box) **$24.00**

12-D, Land Rover Safari, SF, gold, tan luggage, 1970, M (NM+ box) **$26.00**

12-E, Setra Coach, SF, gold, wht roof, clear windshield, 1970, M (VG+ box) **$13.50**

13-C, Thames Wreck Truck, reg, blk wheels, gray plastic hook, 1961, EX+ **$25.00**

13-D, Dodge Wreck Truck, reg, blk wheels, yel cab w/gr bed, labels, 1965, M (NM+ box) **$25.00**

13-G, Snorkel Fire Engine, SF, red, unpnt base, bl windshield, yel boom/bucket, 1977, M (VG+ card) **$6.00**

14-A, Daimler Ambulance, reg, metal wheels, w/red cross, 1956, EX+ **$36.00**

14-C, Bedford Ambulance, reg, blk wheels, 1962, M **$41.00**

14-D, Iso Grifo, reg, blk wheels, 1968, NM+ **$14.00**

14-E, Iso Grifo, SF, metallic bl w/lt bl interior, unpnt base, 5-spoke wheels, 1969, M (NM box) **$18.00**

14-F, Mini Ha Ha, SF, red, flesh driver, brn helmet, 4 color labels, maltese cross front wheels, 1975, M (NM card) **$13.00**

15-A, Primo Mover, reg, metal wheels, orange, M (VG box) . **$50.00**

15-C, Tippax Refuse Truck, reg, blk wheels, peep hole, slanted edge decal, 1963, EX+ **$19.00**

Photo courtesy Dana Johnson

15-E, Volkswagen 1500 Saloon, SuperFast wheels, red, 1970, M, $25.00.

15-F, Fork Lift Truck, SF, red, blk steering wheel/base, yel hoist, gray forks, Lansing labels, dot-dash wheels, 1972, M ... **$5.00**

16-A, Atlantic Trailer, reg, metal wheels, 1956, NM+ **$42.00**

16-B, Atlantic Trailer, reg, blk wheels, orange, orig towbar, 1957, EX+ **$26.00**

16-C, Scammell Mountineer Snow Plow, reg, blk wheels, orange w/wht decal, 1964, M (VG+ box) **$30.00**

16-D, Case Bulldozer, reg, complete, 1969, M (NM box) ... **$18.00**

17-A, Bedford Removals Van, reg, metal wheels, gr, solid letters, 1956, NM **$44.00**

17-B, Bedford Removals Van, reg, metal wheels, outlined letters, missing tailgate, 1958, VG **$22.00**

17-D, Hoveringham Tipper, reg, blk wheels, blk base, 1963, M **$20.00**

17-E, Horse Box, reg, blk wheels, complete, 1969, EX+ ... **$12.00**

17-E, Horse Box, SF, orig horse, gr box, gray doors, 1970, M NM (G box) **$14.00**

17-F, Londoner Bus, SF, silver, charcoal base, dot-dash wheels, Silver Jubilee labels, 1972, M (VG+ card) **$12.00**

18-A, Caterpillar Bulldozer, reg, orig treads, 1956, NM ... **$55.00**

18-D, Cat D8 Bulldozer, reg, blk plastic rollers, 1964, NM .. **$27.00**

18-E, Field Car, reg, blk wheels, scarce blk base, red hubs, orig top, 1969, M (NM box) **$14.00**

18-F, Field Car, SF, yel w/wht interior, red-brn top, unpnt base, no labels, 5-spoke wheels, 1970, M (EX+ card) **$18.00**

18-G, Hondarora Motorcycle, SF, orange, blk handlebars/seat, silver engine, w/label, wire wheels, 1975, M (VG+ card) **$12.00**

19-D, Lotus Racing Car, reg, blk wheels, gr, labels, 1966, M (NM+ box) **$25.00**

19-E, Lotus Racer, SF, metallic purple, 1970, M (EX+ G box) **$26.00**

19-F, Road Dragster, SF, red w/ivory interior, unpnt base, #8 labels, 1970, NM **$12.00**

20-A, Stake Truck, reg, metal wheels, silver grille, 1956, M .. **$55.00**

20-B, Erf 686 Truck, reg, blk wheels, 1959, EX+ $30.00
20-C, Chevrolet Impala Taxi, reg, blk wheels, orange, ivory decals, unpnt base, 1965, M (NM box)......................$19.00
20-E, Police Patrol, SF, wht, unpnt base, frosted windshield, police labels, maltese cross wheels, 1975, M $10.00
21-C, Commer Milk Truck, reg, blk wheels, gr windows, cow decals, 1961, M (NM+ box) $37.00
21-D, Foden Concrete Truck, reg, blk wheels, 1968, EX+..$18.50
21-E, Foden Cement Truck, SF, yel, gr base, skinny tires, 1970, M (EX+ box) $21.00
21-F, Rod Roller, SF, yel, gr base, w/labels, red rear wheels, 1973, M..$11.00
22-A, Vauxhall Cresta, reg, metal wheels, cream roof, 1956, NM+ $48.00
22-D, Pontiac Grand Prix, SF, metallic purple, 1970, M (NM box)...$26.00
22-E, Freeman Intercity Commuter, metallic magenta w/ivory interior, unpnt base, w/labels, 1970, M $14.00
22-F, Blaze Buster, SF, red w/silver interior, yel ladder, gray base, 5-spoke wheels, Fire labels, scarce, M (EX card)........$18.00
23-A, Berkeley Cavilier Trailer, reg, metal wheels, no number cast, 1956, EX+ $30.00
23-D, House Trailer Caravan, reg, blk wheels, yel, 1965, M (NM box)..$20.00
23-D, VW Camper, SF, bl w/orange interior, unpnt base, clear windshield, no labels, 5-spoke wheels, 1970, NM+ ...$16.00
23-E, Atlas Truck, SF, bl, silver interior, orange dump, unpnt base, amber windshield, dot-dash wheels, 1975, MOC...........$12.00
24-B, Weatherhill Hydraulic Excavator, reg, blk wheels, w/decals, 1959, NM $33.00
24-C, Rolls Royce Silver Shadow, reg, blk wheels, 1967, NM+..$15.00
24-F, Shunter, SF, metallic gr, red metal undercarriage/base, tan panel, Rail Freight labels, 1979, M (EX+ card)............$7.00
25-A, Dunlop Van, reg, metal wheel, w/decals, M $19.56
25-B, VW 1200 Sedan, reg, gold wheels, gr windshield, 1960, VG+ $20.00
25-D, Ford Cortina, reg, blk wheels, no roof rack version, 1968, M (NM+ box)...$12.00
25-G, Flat Car & Container, SF, tan, blk flatbed, doors open, NYK labels, 1979, M (NM card) $7.00
26-A, Concrete Truck, reg, metal wheels, silver grille, 1956, NM...$49.00
26-C, GMC Truck, reg, blk wheels, 1968, M (NM box)..$16.00
26-D, GMC Tipper Truck, SF, red, 4-spoke wheels, 1970, M (NM G box)...$20.00
27-D, Mercedes 230SL, reg, blk wheels, 1966, M (EX+ box) $19.00
27-E, Mercedes 230SL, SF, cream w/red interior, unpnt base, 1970, NM...$18.00
27-F, Lamborghini Countach, SF, red w/silver interior, blk base, amber windshield, #8 lime/blk tampo, 1973, M (EX card) $10.00
28-A, Bedford Compressor Truck, reg, metal wheels, yel, 1956, EX...$35.00
28-C, Jaguar MK 10, reg, blk wheels, unpnt motor, 1964, M (NM+ box) $24.00
28-D, Mack Dump Truck, reg, blk wheels, red hubs, 1968, M (EX+ box) $15.00
28-F, Stout, SF, gold, blk base, silver hubs, 1974, M (EX+ box) $13.00

Photo courtesy Dana Johnson

28-G, Lincoln Continental Mark V, SuperFast wheels, red with white roof, 1979, NM, $6.00.

28-G, Lincoln Continental, SF, red w/tan interior, unpnt base, wht roof, 1979, M (EX+ box)...................................$10.00
29-C, Fire Pumper, reg, blk wheels, plain sides, 1966, M (NM box)...$17.00
29-D, Fire Pumper, SF, red, P1 tampo, w/water gun, 1970, M (EX card)...$12.00
29-E, Racing Mini, SF, bronze w/ivory interior, unpnt base, #29 orange outline label, 5-spoke wheels, 1970, M (NM box)..$14.00
30-A, Ford Prefect, reg, metal wheels, lt olive, minor roof rub, 1956, M (NM box) $56.00
30-E, Beach Buggy, SF, metallic pk w/yel splatter/interior, unpnt base, 1970, M (EX+ box)...$14.00
31-A, Ford Station Wagon, reg, metal wheels, yel, no-window version, 1957, M $52.00
31-C, Lincoln Continental, reg, blk wheels, metallic bl, 1964, M (NM+ box) $17.00
31-D, Lincoln Continental, SF, gr-gold, 1970, EX+.........$23.00
32-B, E-Type Jaguar, reg, blk wheels, clear windows, wire wheels, 1962, NM...$33.00
32-C, Leyland Petrol Tanker, reg, blk wheels, gr w/silver grille, labels, 1968, M...$21.00
32-E, Maserati Bora, SF, burgandy, dk gr base, #8 label, no tow hook, 1972, M (NM card) $10.00
33-A, Ford Zodiac MK II Sedan, reg, gold wheels, dk aqua, no windows version, 1957, NM $49.00
33-D, Lamborghini Miura, SF, gold w/ivory interior, red base, 1969, EX+ $14.00
33-E, Datsun 126X, SF, yel, orange base, blk/red flame tampo, 1973, M (EX card) $10.00
33-F, Police Motorcycle, SF, blk, LAPD label, wht seat, gray driver, silver engine, 1977, M (EX+ card)...................$8.00
34-A, VW Microvan, reg, metal wheels, w/decals, 1957, NM+ $51.00
34-B, VW Camper, reg, blk wheels, lt gr, 1962, EX+ $43.00
34-C, VW Camper, reg, blk wheels, silver, raised roof, 1967, NM+ $24.00
34-E, Formula 1, SF, yel, #16 bl labels, maltese cross wheels, 5-spoke rear wheels, 1971, NM.....................................$13.00
34-F, Vantastic, SF, orange, wht base, bl-gr windshield, fish label, 1975, M (EX+ card) $8.00

35-A, Marshall Horse Box, reg, metal wheels, 1957, NM+..$41.00
35-B, Snowtrac Tractor, reg, plain sides, orig treads, 1964, M (NM box)....$26.00
35-D, Fandango, SF, wht w/red interior, red base, clear windshield, silver prop, #35 label, 1975, M (EX card).......$12.00
36-A, Austin A50, reg, metal wheels, 1957, NM $40.00
36-E, Hot Rod Draguar, SF, metallic red w/lt yel interior, unpnt base, clear windshield, no trunk label, 1970, EX+ $13.00
37-A, Coca-Cola Lorry, reg, metal wheels, no base, lg letters, scarce uneven load, 1957, NM+....$120.00
37-C, Dodge Cattle Truck, reg, blk wheels, metal base, orig cattle still on tree, 1966, M (NM+ box) $14.00
37-E, Cattle Truck, SF, yel, gray box, orig cattle on tree, 1970, M (NM+ box)....$19.00
37-F, Soopa Coopa, SF, metallic bl, unpnt base, maltese cross wheels, 1972, M $12.00
38-A, Karrier Refuse Collector, reg, gold wheels, gray, 1957, M $44.00
38-B, Vauxhall Victor Estate Car, reg, blk wheels, gr interior, 1963, NM+ $27.00
38-C, Honda Motorcycle & Trailer, reg, blk wheels, scarce orange trailer, no decal version, 1967, NM...............$20.00
38-D, Honda Motorcycle & Trailer, SF, pk bike, yel trailer, label, 5-spoke wheels, 1970, NM+ $20.00
38-E, Stingaroo Motorcycle, SF, metallic purple, purple handlebars, 1972, M $13.00
38-G, Ford Camper, SF, orange-red, gr windshield, beige camper (no windshield), 1980, M (NM card)....$6.00
38-H, Model A Ford Van, SF, dk bl w/red roof, blk base, Matchbox-This Van Delivers! tampo, scarce, MIB.............$62.00
39-A, Ford Zodiac Convertible, reg, metal wheels, turq interior, orig driver, 1967, NM $60.00
39-C, Ford Tractor, reg, blk wheels, bl & yel, 1967, EX+.$15.00
39-D, Clipper, SF, metallic magenta w/yel interior, gr base, amber windshield, silver pipes, 1973, M....$9.00
40-A, Bedford Tipper Truck, reg, metal wheels, 1957, NM+ ..$39.00
40-C, Hay Trailer, reg, blk wheels, orig rails, 1967, M (NM+ box) $11.50

Photo courtesy Dana Johnson

40-D, Vauxhall Guildsman, SuperFast wheels, red, 1971, NM, $15.00.

40-E, Horse Box, SF, orange, beige box, dk brn door, blk base, gr windshield, 1977, M (EX+ card) $7.00
41-C, Ford GT Race Car, reg, blk wheels, wht w/yel hubs, #6 decal, 1965, M (NM+ box) $19.00
41-D, Ford GT, SF, wht, blk base, #6 label, 5-spoke wheels, 1970, M (NM+ box)....$19.00
41-E, Siva Spyder, SF, dk bl w/cream interior, striped tampo, blk body strap, 5-spoke wheels, 1972, M (NM box) $16.00
41-F, Chevrolet Ambulance, SF, wht w/gray interior, unpnt base, Pacific Ambulance label, 1978, M (EX+ card) ...$9.00
42-A, Bedford Evening News, reg, blk wheels, 1957, scarce, EX+ $51.00
42-B, Studebaker Lark Wagonaire, reg, blk wheels, lt bl roof, complete, 1965, EX+ $19.00
42-D, Iron Fairy Crane, orange, metallic lime boom, 1970, NM+....$40.00
42-E, Tyre Fryer, SF, metallic bl w/yel interior, blk base, no label, 5-spoke wheels, 1972, NM+ $11.00
42-F, Container Truck, SF, red top/doors, beige container, unpnt base, bl windshield, Sealand labels, 1977, M (EX card) $9.50
43-C, Pony Trailer, reg, blk wheels, gr base, orig horses, 1968, M (NM box)....$15.00
43-D, Pony Trailer, SF, yel, dk gr base, orig horses, 1970, M..$15.00
43-E, Dragon Wheels, SF, gr, blk base, 5-spoke front wheels, 1972, NM....$16.00
44-A, Rolls Royce Silver Cloud, reg, metal wheels, 1958, NM....$41.00
44-B, Roll Royce Phantom V, reg, blk wheels, tan, 1964, EX+ $24.00
44-D, GMC Refrigerator Truck, SF, yel, red container/axle covers, 1970, M (EX+ box)....$21.00
44-F, Passenger Coach, SF, red, beige top, gr windshield, train wheels, red 431/232 labels, 1978, M (EX card) $9.00
45-A, Vauxhall Victor, reg, gold wheels, yel, no window version, 1958, NM....$35.00
45-B, Ford Corsair, reg, blk wheels, unpnt base, complete, 1965, M (EX+ box) $19.00
45-C, Ford Group 6, SF, metallic purple, gr base, amber windshield, silver motor, #45 label, 1970, M $14.00
46-A, Morris Minor, reg, gold wheels, scarce dk bl, 1958, EX....$90.00
46-B, Pickford's Removal Van, reg, blk wheels, gr, 3-line decal, 1960, M....$35.00
46-C, Mercedes 300SE, reg, blk wheels, metallic bl, 1968, M (NM+ box) $16.00
46-E, Stretcha Fetcha, SF, wht w/yel interior, red base, bl windshield, Ambulance labels, red cross, 1972, M (EX+ card)....$12.00
47-A, 1-Ton Trojan Van, reg, gold wheels, 1958, M........$52.00
47-B, Commer Ice Cream Canteen, reg, blk wheels, bl, striped decals, 1963, M (NM box) $52.00
47-C, DAF Tipper Truck, reg, blk wheels, silvery-yel, lt gray top, 1968, M (NM+ box)....$16.00
47-D, DAF Tipper Truck, SF, silver/yel, 1970, M.............$22.00
47-F, Pannier Loco, SF, dk gr, blk frame/base, 1979, M (VG+ card) $7.00
47-G, Jaguar SS, red, blk base, red hood, Macau, 1982, M (EX+ card) $5.00
48-B, Sport Boat & Trailer, reg, blk wheels, wht deck, red hull, dk bl trailer, gold motor, 1961, M $44.00
48-E, Pi-Eyed Piper, SF, bl, bl windshield, 8 stacks engine, #8 label, 1972, M (EX card) $13.00
49-A, M3 Personnel Carrier, reg, metal rollers, new treads, 1958, NM....$36.00

49-B, Unimog, reg, blk wheels, tan/aqua, 1967, M (EX box) $18.00
49-C, Unimog, SF, metallic bl-gr, red base, MIB....$16.00
50-B, John Deere Tractor, reg, blk wheels, 1964, M (NM box) $27.00
50-C, Kennel Truck, reg, blk wheels, wht grille, complete, 1969, M (NM box) $17.00
51-A, Albion Chieftain, reg, gold wheels, Blue Circle Portland Cement decals, 1958, NM+....$48.00
51-B, John Deere Trailer, reg, gold wheels, complete, 1964, M (NM+ box) $26.00
51-C, 8-Wheel Tipper Trailer, reg, blk wheels, orange/silver, Douglas, 1969, M (NM box) $19.00
51-E, Citroen SM, SF, metallic bl w/cream interior, unpnt base, #8 tampo, 5-spoke wheels, 1972, M (EX+ card) $8.00
52-A, Maserati 4CLT Racer, reg, blk wheels, yel, complete, scarce #5 decal, wire wheels, 1958, VG+ $52.00
52-B, BRM Racing Car, reg, blk wheels, red, w/labels, 1965, EX+ $23.00
52-C, Dodge Charger, SF, metallic gr, no labels, 1970, M..$9.00
52-D, Police Launch, SF, wht w/red hull, orange-yel figures, bl windshield, LA Fire labels, 1976, M (EX+ card)....$7.00
53-A, Aston Martin, reg, metallic lt gr, 1958, NM+ $50.00
53-C, Ford Zodiac MKIV, reg, blk wheels, silver bl, 1968, M....$14.00
53-D, Ford Zodiac, SF, metallic emerald gr, unpnt base, 1970, M (NM box)....$20.00
53-E, Tanzara, SF, wht w/silver interior, unpnt base, amber windshield, red striped tampo, 1972, M (NM box) ...$11.50
53-F, Jeep CJ6, SF, red w/orange-yel interior, tan top, unpnt base, no tampo, 1977, M (EX+ card)....$7.00
54-A, Saracen Personnel Carrier, reg, blk wheels, 1958, M (VG+ box)....$33.00
54-B, S&S Cadillac Ambulance, reg, blk wheels, 1965, NM+ $20.00
54-C, Cadillac Ambulance, SF, wht, blk base, silver grille, 1970, NM+ $20.00
54-D, Ford Capri, SF, metallic purple w/ivory interior, purple hood, unpnt base, 5-spoke wheels, 1971, M (EX+ box)....$14.00
54-E, Personnel Carrier, SF, olive, gr windshield, tan seats, dot-dash silver wheels, 1976, M (EX+ card) $6.00
54-G, NASA Tracking Vehicle, SF, wht, blk base, red door, w/tampo, 1982, M (NM card) $6.00
55-B, Ford Fairlane Police Car, reg, blk wheels, metallic bl, 1963, EX....$35.00
55-C, Ford Galaxie Police Car, reg, blk wheels, decals, red dome, 1966, EX....$14.00
55-E, Mercury Police Car, SF, wht, red dome light, 1970, M (NM box)....$19.00
55-F, Mercury Police Station Wagon, SF, wht, unpnt base, red/yel Police hood labels, red lights, 1971, EX+ $11.00
55-G, Hellraiser, SF, wht w/red interior, unpnt base, clear windshield, stars/stripes label, 1975, NM $11.00
56-A, London Trolley Bus, reg, blk wheels, red poles, 1958, NM $60.00
56-B, Fiat 1500 Sedan, reg, blk wheels, aqua, brn luggage, 1965, M (NM+ box)....$16.00
56-B, Fiat 1500 Sedan, reg, blk wheels, red, 1965, rare, NM+..$90.00
56-C, BMC 1800 Pininfarina, SF, gold, unpnt base, no labels, 1969, M (NM+ box)....$15.50
57-A, Wolseley 1500, reg, gold wheels, pale gr, silver grille, 1958, NM....$43.00
57-C, Land Rover Fire Truck, reg, blk wheels, orig ladder, 1966, NM+ $18.00
57-F, Wildlife Truck, SF, yel, unpnt base, red windshield, lt bl top, orig lion, w/label, 1973, M (NM box)....$10.00
58-A, BEA Coach, reg, gold wheels, British European Airways decals, 1958, EX+ $36.00
58-B, Drott Excavator, reg, all orig, blk plastic tires, 1962, M....$48.00
58-C, DAF Girder Truck, reg, blk wheels, complete, girders still on tree, 1968, M (NM box)....$17.00
58-E, Woosh-N-Push, SF, yel w/red interior, 2 label, maltese cross front wheels, 1972, M $12.00
59-A, Ford Thames Singer Van, reg, gold wheels, lt gr, 1958, EX+ $62.00
59-B, Ford Fairlane Fire Chief Car, reg, blk wheels, 1963, EX $28.00
59-C, Ford Galaxie Fire Chief Car, reg, blk wheels, 1966, NM....$19.00
59-D, Ford Galaxie Fire Chief Car, SF, red, bl light, hood/side labels, 1970, M (EX+ box) $24.00
59-E, Mercury Fire Chief Car, SF, red w/ivory interior, unpnt base, 5-spoke wheels, 1971, M (NM+ box)....$16.00
59-F, Planet Scout, SF, metallic gr, lime base, amber windshield, 1975, M (EX+ box) $10.00
60-A, Morris J-2 Pickup, reg, blk wheels, red/wht decal, no window version, 1958, M (NM+ box) $50.00
60-B, Site Hut Truck, reg, blk wheels, 1966, M (NM box)..$15.00
60-C, Site Hut Truck, SF, bl, 1970, M (EX box)....$22.00
60-D, Lotus Super Seven, SF, orange, flame label, 1971, M (EX+ box)....$16.00
60-E, Holden Pickup, SF, red w/yel-orange interior, amber windshield, 500 label, 1977, NM+ $8.00
61-A, Ferret Scout Car, reg, blk wheels, 1959, M (NM box) ..$34.00
61-B, Alvis Stalwart, reg, blk wheels, gr hubs, 1966, NM...$23.00
61-C, Blue Shark, SF, dk bl, clear windshield, unpnt base, 1971, NM+ $11.00
62-D, Mercury Cougar, SF, metallic gr w/red interior, unpnt base, 1970, M (NM box) $16.00
62-F, Renault 17TL, SF, red, #9 hood label, 5-spoke wheels, 1974, M....$11.00

Photo courtesy Dana Johnson

62-I, Rolls Royce Silver Cloud, SuperFast wheels, white, 1985, NM, $4.00.

63-B, Foamite Airport Crash Render, reg, blk wheels, gold nozzle, complete, 1964, M (NM box) **$34.00**

63-C, Dodge Crane Truck, reg, blk wheels, red hook, 1968, NM+ **$14.00**

63-D, Dodge Crane Truck, SF, yel, blk axle covers, 1970, M (NM box) **$20.00**

63-E, Freeway Gas Tanker, SF, red, blk base, red trailer base, purple windshield, no hook, Chevron, 1973, M (EX+ card) **$11.00**

63-H, Snorkel, SF, red, gray base, unpnt insert, LA City Fire Dept tampo, 1982, M (EX card) **$9.00**

64-A, Scammell Breakdown Truck, reg, blk wheels, metal hook, 1959, NM **$34.00**

64-B, MG 1100 Sedan, reg, blk wheels, 1966, NM **$15.00**

64-C, MG 1100, SF, gr, 1970, rare, M (NM box) **$190.00**

64-D, Slingshot Dragster, SF, pk, blk base/pipes, #9/flame tampo, 1971, M **$16.00**

65-A, Jaguar 3.4 Litre Saloon, reg, gold wheels, 1959, NM . **$42.50**

65-C, Class Combine Harvester, reg, blk wheels, 1967, M (EX+ box) **$14.00**

65-D, Saab Sonnet, SF, metallic bl w/yel interior, unpnt base, 1973, NM **$11.00**

65-E, Airport Coach, SF, bl w/lt yel interior, American Airlines, amber windshield, unpnt base, 1977, M (EX+ card) . **$11.00**

66-A, Citroen DS19, reg, gold wheels, 1959, NM **$56.00**

66-C, Greyhound Bus, reg, blk wheels, amber windshield, 1967, M (NM box) **$22.00**

66-E, Mazda RX500, SF, red w/silver interior, wht base, amber windshield, 5-spoke wheels, #77 tampo, 1971, M (EX card) **$11.00**

67-A, Saladin Armoured Car, reg, blk wheels, 1959, EX+ . **$25.00**

67-D, Hot Rocker, SF, metallic lime, unpnt base, 5-spoke wheels, 1973, M (VG+ card) **$12.00**

68-A, Austin MKII Radio Truck, reg, blk wheels, 1959, NM **$41.00**

68-B, Mercedes Coach, reg, blk wheels, orange, 1965, M (NM+ box) **$20.00**

68-C, Porsche 910, SF, metallic red, amber windshield, #68 hood label only, 1970, NM+ **$12.00**

68-D, Cosmobile, SF, metallic bl w/silver interior, yel base, amber windshield, 1975, M (NM+ box) **$15.00**

69-A, Commer 30 CWT Nestle's Van, reg, gold wheels, 1959, VG+ **$36.00**

69-B, Hatra Tractor Shovel, reg, blk wheels, yel, 1965, NM .. **$21.00**

69-C, Rolls Royce Silver Shadow, SF, metallic bl, orange-brn interior, tan tonneau, 1969, MOC **$16.00**

69-D, Turbo Fury, SF, metallic red, blk base, clear windshield, #69 label, 5-spoke wheels, 1973, M (EX+ box) **$14.00**

70-A, Ford Thames Estate Car, reg, blk wheels, gr windshield, 1959, NM **$35.00**

70-B, Ford Grit Spreader, reg, blk wheels, blk pull, 1966, M (NM+ box) **$16.00**

70-C, Ford Grit Spreader, SF, red/yel, 5-spoke wheels, 1970, NM+ **$18.00**

70-E, Self-Propelled Gun, SF, olive, tan treads, 1976, M (EX+ card) **$7.00**

71-B, Jeep Gladiator Pickup, reg, blk wheels, wht interior, 1964, NM+ **$30.00**

71-C, Ford Heavy Wrecker, reg, blk wheels, red cab, wht bed, gr windshield, red hook, 1968, EX+ **$21.00**

71-F, Cattle Truck, SF, bronze, orange-yel stakes, gr windshield, unpnt base, blk cattle, 1976, M (EX card) **$8.00**

72-A, Fordson Tractor, reg, gold wheels, orange rear hubs, gray plastic wheels in front, 1959, EX+ **$37.00**

72-B, Standard Jeep, reg, blk wheels, 1966, NM+ **$13.00**

72-D, Hovercraft, SF, wht, blk base, bl windshield, w/labels, 1972, NM **$7.00**

73-A, 10-Ton Pressure Refueller, reg, gold wheels, 1959, EX+ **$40.00**

73-B, Ferrari F1 Racer, reg, blk wheels, 1962, missing driver o/w NM **$19.00**

73-C, Mercury Station Wagon, reg, blk wheels, 1968, NM+ **$14.00**

73-D, Mercury Commuter, SF, red, cow label, 1970, M ... **$14.00**

73-E, Weasel, SF, metallic gr, gr insert, silver hubs, 1974, M (EX+ box) **$7.00**

73-F, Model A Ford, cream w/dk gr fenders, gr windshield, spare, 1979, M (VG+ card) **$7.00**

74-A, Mobile Refreshment Canteen, reg, gold wheels, silver, lt bl base/interior, 1959, EX+ **$48.00**

74-B, Daimler Bus, reg, blk wheels, gr, labels, 1966, NM+ **$17.00**

74-D, Toe Joe, SF, metallic lime, unpnt base, gr booms, red hooks, 1972, M (EX+ card) **$8.00**

75-B, Ferrari Berlinetta, reg, blk wire wheels, gr, unpnt base, 1965, M (NM box) **$16.00**

75-D, Alfa Carabo, SF, pk, yel base, w/tampo, 5-spoke wheels, 1971, NM+ **$11.50**

King Size, Speed Kings, and Super Kings

K-01B, Hoverington Tipper Truck, 1964, M (VG+ box). **$44.00**

K-01C, O&K Excavator, red, silver arms/shovel, amber windshield, red hubs, red/wht label, 1970, NM+ **$15.00**

K-02, Esso Scammell Heavy Wrecker, MIB **$54.00**

K-02A, Muir Hill Dumper, 1960, M (NM box) **$55.00**

K-02B, KW Dump Truck, 1964, M (NM box) **$50.00**

K-02C, Scammell Heavy Wreck Truck, wht, gr windshield, 1969, M (NM box) **$56.00**

K-02D, Car Recovery Vehicle, metallic bl, '24 Hour' labels, red ramps, wht interior, w/beige K59 Capri, 1977, M (NM box) **$26.00**

K-03A, Caterpillar Bulldozer, red plastic rollers, orig gr treads, 1960, NM+ **$69.00**

K-03B, Hatra Tractor Shovel, 1965, M **$50.00**

K-03C, Massey Ferguson Tractor & Trailer, red, yel trailer base & wheels, 1970, M **$22.00**

K-03D, Mod Tractor & Trailer, metallic bl, yel seat/grille, stars/stripes labels, 1974, M (NM box) **$14.00**

K-04A, International Tractor, red plastic hubs, 1960, M, VG+ box) **$59.00**

K-04B, GMC Tractor & Freuhof Hopper Train, 1967, M . **$69.00**

K-04C, Leyland Tipper, dk red, silver dump, LE labels, 1969, M **$29.00**

K-04D, Big Tipper, metallic red body, yel dump, striped labels, 1974, M (EX+ box) **$10.00**

K-05, BP Racing Transporter, MIB **$44.00**

K-05A, Foden Tipper Truck, red hubs, 1961, M...............$49.00
K-05B, Racing Car Transporter, 1967, M $26.00
K-05C, Muir Hill Tractor & Trailer, yel, red base, bl driver, clear windshield, labels, 1972, M (EX+ box) $22.00
K-06D, Motorcycle Transporter, metallic dk bl, Team Honda labels, 1 orange 18G Hondarora, 1976, M (NM box).$22.00
K-07A, Curtis Wright Rear Dumper, 1961, M (EX box)..$63.00
K-07B, Refuse Truck, 1967, NM+ (NM box) $34.00
K-07C, Racing Car Transporter, yel, red tailgate, blk interior, Team Matchbox label, w/pk 34E, 1973, M (NM box) $21.00
K-08B, Guy Warrior Car Transporter, yel cab/trailer, red hubs, 1967, M (EX box) $39.00
K-08C, Caterpillar Traxcavator, yel body/rollers, orange bucket & treads, orig driver, 1970, NM+..............................$13.00
K-09A, Diesel Road Roller, orig red driver, 1962, M (NM box) $54.00
K-09B, Class Combine Harvester, gr, red blade, gr/wht labels, no driver version, 1967, M...$35.00
K-09C, Fire Tender, red, amber windshield, gray ladder, 1973, M (EX+ box) $14.00
K-10A, Aveling Barford Tractor Shovel, bl-gr, silver metal hubs, 1963, M $54.00
K-10B, Pipe Truck, 6 orig pipes, 1967, M (EX+ box).......$59.00
K-10C, Car Transporter, red, clear windshield, Auto Transport labels, 1976, M (NM box) $17.00
K-11A, Fordson Tractor & Farm Trailer, bl steering wheel, orange hubs, 1963, M (NM box)...............................$59.00
K-11B, DAF Car Transporter, metallic bl/gold, blk wheel blocks, 1969, M (EX+ box) $89.00
K-11C, Breakdown Truck, scarce red, blk base, wht booms, red hooks, Falck Zonen labels, M (EX+ box)..................$89.00
K-12, Laing Scammell Mobile Crane, MIB.......................$59.00
K-12A, Heavy Breakdown Truck, red hubs, no roof lights, 1963, M (NM box) $59.00
K-12B, Scammell Crane Truck, orange, silver-gray base, 1969, NM+ $29.00
K-12C, Hercules Mobile Crane, yel, yel hook, Laing decals, 1975, M (EX+ box) $26.00
K-13A, Readymix Concrete Truck, red hubs, Readymix decals, 1964, NM+ $23.00
K-13B, Building Transporter, metallic lime, red base, clear windshield, 1971, M (VG+ box)......................................$18.00
K-13C, Aircraft Transporter, red, yel base, amber windshield, wht interior, X4 labels, 1976, M (NM box)..............$21.00
K-14A, Taylor Jumbo Crane, scarce yel weight box, 1964, M (EX box) $35.00
K-14C, Heavy Breakdown Truck, wht, red rear, amber windshield, Shell labels, 1977, M (NM box) $10.00
K-15A, Merryweather Fire Engine, 1964, M....................$39.00
K-15B, The Londoner, red w/yel interior, Swinging London label, w/bell, 1973, M (NM box)...............................$17.00
K-15C, The Londoner, beige, blk interior, Berlin label, 1973, M (VG+ box) $9.00
K-16A, Dodge Tractor w/Twin Tippers, 1966, M (EX box)...$119.00
K-20, Tractor Transport, MIB...$149.00
K-31B, Peterbuilt Refrigerator Truck, Burger King decals, M (NM box)...$50.00
K-34A, Thunderclap, yel background, #34 labels, NM (NM box) $8.00
K-40A, Blaze Trailer, red body, yel base/interior, amber windows, bl lights, EX..$8.00
K-41A, Fuzz Buggy, wht body, blk base, clear windows, yel interior, amber lights, EX $8.00
K-48A, Mercedes 350 SLC, bronze, silver-gray base, yel interior, amber windows, M (EX box) $10.00
K-49A, Ambulance, wht body, red roof/interior, blk base, clear windows, bl lights, orig stretcher/blanket, NM, W1 ..$10.00
K-51A, Barracuda, bl body, yel interior/spoiler, clear windshield, #5 labels, NM $6.00
K-62A, Doctor's Emergency Car, silver-gray base, NM $9.00
K-66A, Jaguar XJ12 Police Patrol, brn interior, bl lights, Maltese cross wheels, bl & orange stripe tampo, NM $9.00
K-78A, Grand Fury Police Car, bl & wht, bl interior, red lights, Polizei decals, orig key, M (NM box) $12.00

K-78B, Gran Fury Fire Chief Car, red, 1990, EX, $8.00.

K-95A, Audi Quattro, metallic bl, blk wheels, 1982, MIB .$6.00

Models of Yesteryear Matchbox

Y-01A, 1925 Allchin Traction Engine, unpnt treads, copper boiler door, 1956, M $59.00
Y-01B, 1911 Ford Model T, red w/blk roof, plastic steering wheel, single brake lever, 1964, NM+..........................$9.00
Y-01C, 1936 Jaguar, silver-bl body/base, blk seats, 1977, M (NM box)..$19.00
Y-02A, 1911 B-Type London Bus, red, unpnt wheels, rare 4-over-4 windows, 1956, EX.......................................$100.00
Y-02B, 1911 Renault, gr, brass dash/wheels, 3-prone spare, 1963, NM...$10.00
Y-02C, 1914 Prince Henry Vauxhall, bl, silver hood, blk grille, 24-spoke wheels, 1970, NM $10.00
Y-03A, London E Class Tramcar, wht roof, News decals, 1957, M...$62.00
Y-03B, 1910 Mercedes Benz Limousine, metallic gr, blk roof, red seats/grille, 1966, M $19.00
Y-04A, 1928 Sentinel Steam Wagon, 1956, NM+ $59.00
Y-04C, 1909 Opel Coupe, wht, tan roof, red seats, 1967, M $12.00
Y-05A, 1929 LeMans Bentley, gold radiator, gr grille/tonneau, 1958, M...$54.00
Y-05B, 1929 4½ Litre Bentley, gr, #5 decal, 1962, M.......$16.00

Photo courtesy Dana Johnson

Y-4D, 1930 Deusenberg Town Car, red with black top, 1976, NM, $40.00.

Y-05D, 1927 Talbot Van, gr, blk base/roof, 12-spoke wheels, Lipton's City Road, 1978, M (NM box) **$15.00**
Y-06A, 1916 AEC-Type Lorry, dk gray, 1957, NM..........**$80.00**
Y-06B, 1926 Type 35 Bugatti, bl, red dash, #6 decal, 1961, NM **$36.00**
Y-07A, 1918 4-ton Leyland Van, red-brn, cream roof, 1957, M **$95.00**
Y-07B, 1913 Mercer Runabout, lilac, 1961, NM+............**$29.00**
Y-07C, 1912 Rolls Royce, silver, red base & seats, 1968, NM+ .**$10.00**
Y-08A, 1926 Morris Cowley Bullnose, tan, brn base, 1958, M.**$82.00**
Y-08B, 1914 Sunbeam Motorcycle w/Sidecar, dk gr seat, 1962, EX...**$14.00**
Y-08C, 1914 Stutz Roadster, metallic bl, 12-spoke silver wheels, 1969, M...**$10.00**
Y-08D, 1945 MG TD, bl w/tan roof, blk interior, 24-spoke chrome wheels, 1978, M (NM box) **$10.00**
Y-09A, 1924, Fowler Big Lion Showman Engine, lt maroon, wht roof, gold spoiler, 1958, NM.....................................**$49.00**
Y-09B, 1912 Simplex, lt gr, tan roof, red seats, 1968, M...**$24.00**
Y-10A, 1908 GP Mercedes, cream, lt gr seats, gold trim, 1958, NM...**$25.00**
Y-10B, 1928 Mercedes Benz 36/220, wht, single spare, 1963, M **$18.00**
Y-10C, 1906 Rolls Royce Silver Ghost, wht, purple-red base, blk seats/grille, silver hubs, 1969, M................................**$12.00**
Y-11A, 1920 Aveling Porter Steam Roller, gr body, blk supports/flywheel, 1958, M **$79.00**
Y-11B, 1912 Packard Landaulet, red, metal steering wheel, brass grille/wheels, 1964, NM+ **$20.00**
Y-11C, 1938 Lagonda Drophead Coupe, copper, gold base, blk interior/grille, silver 24-spoke wheels, 1972, MIB......**$19.00**
Y-12A, 1899 London Horse-Drawn Bus, beige driver/seats, brn horses, 1959, NM+ **$65.00**
Y-12C, 1912 Ford Model T Van, cream, blk base/roof/seat, red wheels, Coco-Cola logo, 1978, M (NM box).............**$32.00**
Y-13A, 1868 Sante Fe Locomotive, gr, 1959, M...............**$73.00**
Y-13B, 1911 Daimler, yel & blk, maroon seats, 1966, M....**$8.00**
Y-14B, 1914 Maxwell Roadster, turq, blk roof/grille, maroon seats, copper gas tank, 1965, M **$15.00**
Y-14C, 1931 Stutz Bearcat, metallic gr, red seats, 24-spoke wheels, 1974, M (NM box) **$15.00**
Y-15B, 1930 Packard Victoria, blk & red, maroon seats, silver disk wheels, M (NM box)...**$12.00**
Y-16A, 1904 Spyder, dk yel, 1961, M **$18.00**

Photo courtesy Dana Johnson

Y-19A, 1933 Auburn 851 Speedster, tan with red interior, 1980, EX, $20.00.

Y-20A, 1937 Mercedes-Benz 540K, wht body/base, red seats, 24-spoke wheels, 1981, M (NM box) **$10.00**
Y-27A, 1922 Foden Steam Wagon, bl, red base, gray roof/top, red wheels, no hook, Pickford's, 1985, NM+ **$8.00**
Y-29A, Walker Electric Van, olive, beige top, olive wheels, tan interior, Harrod's, 1985, M (NM box) **$14.00**
Y-39A, 1820 Passenger Coach & Horses, limited edition, 1990, M (NM box) **$40.00**
Y-66A, Her Majesty's Gold State Coach, limited edition, 1992, M (NM+ box)...**$40.00**

Skybusters

SB-01, Learjet, US Air Force, MIP.....................................**$4.00**
SB-02A, Corsair A7D, metallic gr, wht base, clear windshield, thick axle, 1973, M (NM card) **$10.00**
SB-03A, A300 Airbus, wht, silver base, Air France & #5 label, thick axle, 1973, NM **$5.00**
SB-04A, Mirage F1, metallic red, red base, clear windshield, thin axle, bullseye labels, 1973, NM+ **$4.00**
SB-07A, Junkers 87B, blk, silver base, thin axle, swastika labels, 1973, rare, NM **$100.00**
SB-09A, Cessna 402, metallic gr, wht base/wings, thin axles, clear windshield, 1973, M..**$6.00**
SB-10, Boeing 747, wht & gray, Lufthansa, VG **$3.00**
SB-10A, Boeing 747, wht, dk bl base, thin axle, British Airways logo, 1973, NM+...**$5.00**
SB-13A, DC-10, wht, red base, thin axle, Swissair labels, 1973, NM **$4.00**
SB-15, Boeing 747, bl & wht, MIB..**$5.00**
SB-18A, Wild Wind, lime, wht base, Wild Wind & #7 labels, 1976, M (EX+ card)..**$10.00**
SB-28, Airbus A300, Lufthansa, NM **$5.00**
SB-36, F-117 Stealth Fighter, blk, MIP **$4.00**
SB-38, BAE 146, wht, MIB...**$5.00**

Model Kits

While values for military kits seem to have leveled off and others may have actually gone down, this is certainly not the case with the Aurora monster and character kits which are continuing to increase in value.

Though model kits were popular with kids of the '50s who enjoyed the challenge of assembling a classic car or two or a Musketeer figure now and then, when the monster series hit in the early 1960s, sales shot through the ceiling. Made popular by all the monster movies of that decade, ghouls like Vampirella, Frankenstein, and the Wolfman were eagerly built up by kids everywhere. They could (if their parents didn't object too strongly) even construct an actual working guillotine. Aurora had other successful series of figure kits, too, based on characters from comic strips and TV shows as well as a line of sports stars.

But the vast majority of model kits were vehicles. They varied in complexity, some requiring much more dexterity on the part of the model builder than others, and they came in several scales, from 1/8 (which might be as large as 20" to 24") down to 1/43 (generally about 3" to 4"), but the most popular scale was 1/25 (usually between 6" to 8"). Some of the largest producers of vehicle kits were AMT, MPC, and IMC. Though production obviously waned during the late 1970s and early '80s, with the intensity of today's collector market, companies like Ertl (who now is producing 1/25 scale vehicles using some of the old AMT dies) are proving that model kits still sell very well.

As a rule of thumb, assembled kits (built-ups) are priced at about 25% to 50% of the price range for a boxed kit, but this is not always true on the higher-priced kits. One mint in the box with the factory seal intact will often sell for up to 15% more than if the seal were broken, though depending on the kit, a sealed perfect box may add as much $100.00. Condition of the box is crucial. For more information, we recommend *Aurora History and Price Guide* by Bill Bruegman; *Collectible Figure Kits of the '50s, '60s & '70s*, by Gordy Dutt, and *Classic Plastic Model Kits* by Rick Polizzi (Collector Books).

Advisors: Mike and Kurt Fredericks (F4); John and Sheri Pavone (P3).

Other Sources: B10, J2, J7, T1, P4

See also Plasticville.

Academy, ZZ Gundum, Desert-Zaku Mobile Suit #31, 1974, 1/144MIB, G5 .... **$14.00**
Ace, Tales From the Crypt, Cryptkeeper #55300, 5", MIB, G5 .... **$4.00**
Adams, Hawk Missile Battery #154, 1958, 1/40, MIB, G5 . **$70.00**
Addar, Jaws, Diorama (diver being attacked) #231, 1975, MIB (sealed), G5 .... **$50.00**
Addar, Planet of the Apes, Caesar #106, 1974, 1/11, MIB, G5 . **$90.00**
Addar, Planet of the Apes, Cornelius #101, 1973, 1/11, MIB (sealed), G5 .... **$90.00**
Addar, Planet of the Apes, Dr Zaius #102, 1973, 1/11, MIB (sealed), G5 .... **$60.00**
Addar, Planet of the Apes, Dr Zira #105, 1974, 1/11, MIB (sealed), G5 .... **$80.00**
Addar, Planet of the Apes, Gen Ursus #103, 1974, 1/11, MIB (sealed), G5 .... **$60.00**
Addar, Super Scenes, Jaws, 1975, NM (VG+ box), D9.... **$30.00**
Addar, Super Scenes, Spirit in a Bottle, NM (EX box), D9.. **$43.00**
AEF, Aliens, Bishop #AC-3,1980s, 1/35, MIB, G5 .... **$35.00**
AEF, Aliens, Burke #AC-4, 1980s, 1/35, MIB, G5 .... **$24.00**

Photo courtesy June Moon

Addar, Super Scenes, Planet of the Apes Jail Wagon, MIB, $65.00.

AEF, Aliens, Ferro #AM-11, 1980s, 1/35, MIB, G5 .... **$26.00**
AEF, Aliens, Frost #AM-3, 1980s, 1/35, MIB, G5 .... **$26.00**
AEF, Aliens, Sgt Apone #AM-5, 1980s, 1/35, MIB, G5 .. **$26.00**
AEF, Aliens, Spunkmeyer #AM-12, 1/35, MIB, G5 .... **$24.00**
AEF, Aliens, Warrior Alien #AX-3 (kneeling), 1980s, 1/35, MIB, G5 .... **$40.00**
Airfix, Ankylosaurus #3802, 1981, MIB, G5 .... **$30.00**
Airfix, Apollo Saturn V #9170, 1/44, MIB (sealed), G5 .. **$30.00**
Airfix, Bristol Bloodhound #2309, 1992, 1/76, MIB, G5.. **$11.00**
Airfix, Charles I #2511, 1979, 1/12, MIB, G5 .... **$24.00**
Airfix, Coldstream Guardsman #205, 1960s, 1/12, MIB, G5 .... **$10.00**
Airfix, Corythosaurus #3804, 1970, MIB (sealed), G5 ..... **$30.00**
Airfix, Datsun 280-ZX Champion,1980, M (EX+ sealed box), A **$33.00**
Airfix, James Bond 007 (You Only Live Twice), Little Nellie Autigyro #4401, 1996, 1/24, MIB, G5 .... **$25.00**
Airfix, Lunar Module #3013, 1991, 1/72, MIB (sealed), G5 .. **$10.00**
Airfix, Lunar Module #393, 1975, 1/72, MIB, G5 .... **$11.00**
Airfix, Mounted Bengal Lancer #7501, 1991, 1/12, MIB (sealed), G5 .... **$40.00**
Airfix, Sam-2 Missile, #3303, 1973, orig issue, 1/76, MIB, G5 .... **$40.00**
Airfix, Saturn 1B #6172, 1991, 1/144, MIB (sealed), G5... **$100.00**
Airfix, Skeleton #301, 1970, 1/6, MIB, G5 .... **$20.00**
Airfix, Skeleton #3541, 1979, 1/6, MIB, G5 .... **$14.00**
Airfix, Space: 1999, Hawk Spaceship #5173, 1977, 1/72, MIB, G5 .... **$100.00**
Airfix, Wildlife Series, Robins #4830, 1979, 1/1, MIB (sealed), G5 .... **$30.00**
Airfix, Yeoman of the Guard #2507, 1978, 1/12, MIB (sealed), G5 .... **$24.00**
Alabe, Neanderthal Man #2963, 1976, 1/8, MIB, G5 ...... **$40.00**
Alabe, Stegosaurus #2962, 1976, 1/38, MIB, G5 .... **$40.00**
Alternative Images, Dracula Prince of Darkness, 1992, NM (plain wht box), A **$145.00**
Amai, Captain Scarlet, Patrol Car #1204, 1982, MIB, G5.... **$20.00**
AMT, BJ & the Bear, KW Aerodyne & Trailer #7705, 1980, 1/32, MIB (Sealed), G5 .... **$35.00**
AMT, BJ & the Bear, KW Aerodyne Cabover #5025, 1980, 1/32, MIB, G5 .... **$30.00**

AMT, Farrah's Foxy Vette #3101, 1970s, 1/25, MIB (sealed), G5...$35.00

AMT, Flintstones, Family Sedan #496, 1974, 6", MIB, G5....$90.00

AMT, Get Smart Sunbeam Car #925, 1967, 1/25, MIB, G5 .$90.00

AMT, Hang-Outs, Baseball #615, 1970s, MIB (sealed), G5...$25.00

AMT, Hang-Outs, Cliff Hanger #610, 1970s, MIB, G5 ...$30.00

AMT, Interplanetary UFO #960, 1970s, 1/635, MIB (sealed), G5...$130.00

AMT, Klingon Cruiser #952, 1970s, 1/600, MIB (sealed), G5...$30.00

AMT, Laurel & Hardy, '25 T Touring Car #462, 1976, 1/25, MIB (sealed), G5 ....$55.00

AMT, Laurel & Hardy, '27 Touring Car #461, 1976, 1/25, MIB (sealed), G5 ....$55.00

AMT, Man From UNCLE, Car #912, 1967, 1/25, MIB, G5.....$220.00

AMT, Man in Space Set #953, 1969, 1/200, MIB, G5...$230.00

AMT, Movin' On, Kenworth Truck Tractor #560, 1970s, 1/25, MIB, G5...$40.00

AMT, My Mother the Car #904, 1965, 1/25, MIB, G5....$40.00

AMT, Star Trek, Exploration #958, 1974, orig issue, MIB, G5...$100.00

AMT, Star Trek, Galileo 7 #959, 1974, 1/48, orig issue, MIB (sealed), G5 ....$55.00

AMT, Star Trek, K-7 Space Station #955, 1976, 1/7600, MIB (sealed), G5 ....$90.00

AMT, Star Trek, Klingon Battle Cruiser #952, 1968, 1/600, MIB (Sealed), G5 ....$190.00

AMT, Star Trek, Space Ship Set #953, 1976, 1/2200, MIB (sealed), G5 ....$30.00

AMT, Star Trek, Spock #956, 1973, NM (EX larger box), A...$125.00

AMT, Star Trek, USS Enterprise #921, 1967, orig issue, 1/635, MIB (sealed), G5 ....$190.00

AMT, Star Trek, USS Enterprise #921, 1967, orig issue, 1/635, partially assembled, G5 ....$70.00

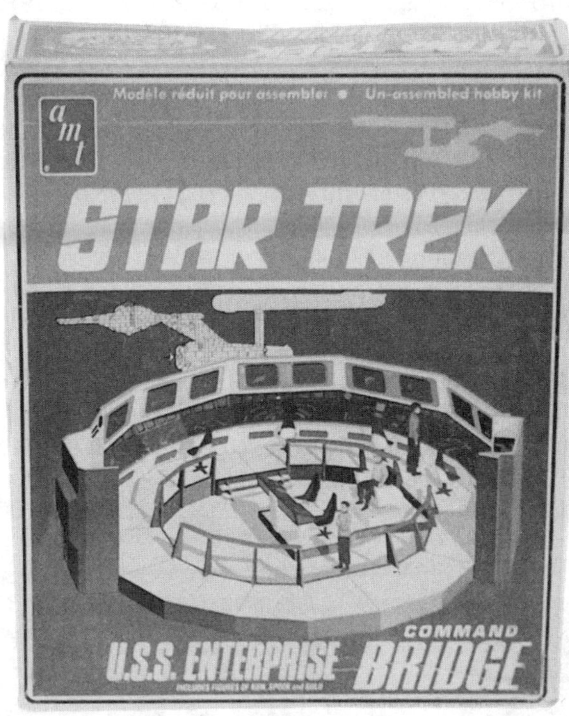

AMT, Star Trek, U.S.S. Enterprise Command Bridge #950, 1975, MIB, $40.00.

AMT, Star Trek: The Motion Picture, Klingon Cruiser, M (EX+ sealed box), D9 ....$35.00

AMT, Star Trek: The Motion Picture, USS Enterprise #970, 1979, 1/535, MIB, G5...$70.00

AMT, Star Trek: The Motion Picture, Vulcan Shuttle #972, 1979, 1/220, MIB (sealed), G5 ....$70.00

AMT, Vegas, '57 Thunderbird #3105, 1979, 1/25, MIB, G5..$25.00

AMT, Wackie Woodie Krazy Kar, 1960s, M (VG sealed box), A...$85.00

AMT/Ertl, A-Team Van #6616, 1983, 1/25, G5 ....$30.00

AMT/Ertl, Airwolf Helicopter, 1984, M (EX sealed box), D9 ....$23.00

AMT/Ertl, Back to the Future, Delorian #6122, 1991, 1/24, MIB (sealed), G5 ....$35.00

AMT/Ertl, Batman (movie), Batmobile #6877, 1989, 1/25, MIB (sealed), G5 ....$14.00

AMT/Ertl, Batman (movie), Batmobile #6972, 1990, motorized, MIB (sealed), G5 ....$20.00

AMT/Ertl, Batman (movie), Batmobile Cacoon #6772, 1989, 1/25, MIB, G5...$16.00

AMT/Ertl, Batman (movie), Batwing #6970, 1990, 1/25, MIB (sealed), G5 ....$30.00

AMT/Ertl, Batman (movie), Joker Goon Car #6826, 1989, 1/25, MIB (sealed), G5 ....$16.00

AMT/Ertl, Batman Returns, Batmissile #6614, 1992, 1/25, MIB (sealed), G5 ....$14.00
AMT/Ertl, Batman Returns, Batskiboat #6615, 1992, 1/25, MIB (sealed), G5 ....$9.00
AMT/Ertl, Bigfoot Monster Truck #6791, 1984, 1/25, partially assembled, G5 ....$6.00
AMT/Ertl, Creepy 'T' Car-Glows #8581 (skull), 1996, 1/25, MIB, G5 ....$10.00
AMT/Ertl, Dick Tracy (movie), Coupe #6107, 1990, 1/25, MIB, G5 ....$10.00
AMT/Ertl, Dodge Viper GTS Coupe #8055, 1994, 1/25, MIB, G5 ....$6.00
AMT/Ertl, Dodge Viper RT/10 #6808, 1992, 1/25, MIB, G5 .$6.00
AMT/Ertl, Ghostbusters II, ECTO 1 #6017, 1989, 1/25, MIB (sealed), G5 ....$24.00
AMT/Ertl, Gigantics, Colossal Mantis #8389, 1996, 1/96, MIB (sealed), G5 ....$14.00
AMT/Ertl, Gigantics #8391, 1996, 1/96, MIB (sealed), G5..$14.00
AMT/Ertl, Knight Rider 2000, KITT 4000 #8084, 1991, 1/25, MIB (sealed), G5 ....$16.00
AMT/Ertl, Luke Skywalker #8783, 1995, MIB (sealed), G5 ..$24.00
AMT/Ertl, Monkees, Monkeemobile #6058, 1990, 1/24, G5.$85.00
AMT/Ertl, Munsters, Koach & Dragula Cars #8059, 1991, 1/25, MIB, G5 ....$100.00

AMT/Ertl, Peterbilt 359, MIB, $35.00.

AMT/Ertl, Rescue 911, Police Car #6417, 1993, 1/25, MIB (sealed), G5 ....$14.00
AMT/Ertl, Rescue 911, Rescue Ambulance #6416, 1993, 1/25, MIB (sealed), G5 ....$14.00
AMT/Ertl, Rescue 911, Rescue Helicopter #6400, 1993, 1/48, MIB (sealed), G5 ....$16.00
AMT/Ertl, Riptide, 1960 Corvette #6621, 1984, 1/25, MIB (sealed), G5 ....$24.00
AMT/Ertl, Robocop 2, Robo 1 Police Car #6059, 1990, 1/25, M (VG+ box), D9 ....$23.00
AMT/Ertl, Star Trek (TV), Galileo II Shuttlecraft #6006, 1991, 1/48, MIB, G5 ....$9.00
AMT/Ertl, Star Trek (TV), Kirk #8773, 1994, 12", MIB (sealed), G5 ....$24.00
AMT/Ertl, Star Trek (TV), McCoy #8774, 1994, 12", MIB (sealed), G5 ....$24.00
AMT/Ertl, Star Trek (TV), Scotty #8777, 1994, 12", MIB (sealed), G5 ....$24.00
AMT/Ertl, Star Trek (TV), USS Enterprise #6676, 1983, 1/635, MIB (sealed), G5 ....$19.00
AMT/Ertl, Star Trek (TV), USS Enterprise Bridge #6007, 1991, 1/32, MIB, G5 ....$14.00
AMT/Ertl, Star Trek III: The Search for Spock, USS Enterprise #6693, 1984, 1/535, MIB, G5 ....$34.00
AMT/Ertl, Star Trek IV: The Voyage Home, USS Enterprise #6693, 1986, 1/535, MIB, G5 ....$34.00
AMT/Ertl, Star Trek V: The Final Frontier, Enterprise/Shuttlecraft #6876, 1989, 1/535, MIB, G5 ....$24.00
AMT/Ertl, Star Trek VI: Undiscovered Country, Enterprise/Shuttlecraft #8617, 1991, 1/535, MIB (sealed), G5 ....$24.00
AMT/Ertl, Star Trek VI: Undiscovered Country, Klingon Cruiser #8229, 1991, 1/600, MIB, G5 ....$9.00
AMT/Ertl, Star Trek: Deep Space Nine, Defiant #8255, 1996, 15½", MIB, G5 ....$19.00
AMT/Ertl, Star Trek: Generations, Klingon Bird of Prey #8230, 1995, 1/650, MIB, G5 ....$24.00
AMT/Ertl, Star Trek: Generations, USS Enterprise #8793, 1995, 1/1400, MIB, G5 ....$19.00
AMT/Ertl, Star Trek: The Motion Picture, Klingon Cruiser #6682, 1984, 1/600, MIB (sealed), G5 ....$16.00
AMT/Ertl, Star Trek: The Motion Picture, Vulcan Shuttle #6679, 1984, 1/220, MIB (sealed), G5 ....$70.00
AMT/Ertl, Star Trek: The Next Generation, Ferengi/Klingon/Romulan #6858, 1989, MIB (sealed), G5 ....$19.00
AMT/Ertl, Star Trek: The Next Generation, Klingon Battle Cruiser #6812, 1991, 1/1400, MIB (sealed), G5 ....$14.00
AMT/Ertl, Star Trek: The Next Generation, USS Enterprise #6619, 1988, 1/1400, MIB (sealed), G5 ....$19.00
AMT/Ertl, Star Wars, Battle of Hoth #8743, 1995, 1/75, MIB, G5 ....$14.00
AMT/Ertl, Star Wars, Cut-away Millenium Falcon #8789, 1996, 1/72, MIB (sealed), G5 ....$26.00
AMT/Ertl, Star Wars, Han Solo #8785, 1995, MIB (sealed), G5 ....$29.00
AMT/Ertl, Star Wars, TIE Fighter Flight Display #8275, 1996, 1/48, MIB, G5 ....$19.00
AMT/Ertl, Thunderbolt 1 Monster Truck #6609, 1/25, G5..$10.00
AMT/Ertl, Viper, Dodge Stealth R/T Turbo #8313, 1994, 1/25, MIB (sealed), G5 ....$24.00
AMT/Ertl, Viper, Viper RT/10 #8311, 1994, 1/25, MIB (sealed), G5 ....$16.00
Anubis, Jonny Quest, Turu the Terrible #9205, 1992, 8½", MIB, G5 ....$60.00
Anubis, Star Trek (TV), Tholian Patrol Ship #9103, 1991, 7½", MIB, G5 ....$40.00
Anubis, Star Trek: The Next Generation #9204, Borg Ship, 1992, 5¼", MIB, G5 ....$70.00
Anubus, Jonny Quest, Robot Spy #9206, 1992, 5½", MIB, G5 ....$60.00
Aoshima, Back to the Future, Delorian #1500, 1989, 1/24, MIB, G5 ....$40.00

Aoshima, Back to the Future II, Delorian #1000, 1989, 1/32, MIB, G5 ....$50.00
Aoshima, Batman (movie), Batmobile #618075, 1989, 1/32, MIB, G5 ....$40.00
Aoshima, Japanese History (Samurai), Warriors in diorama poses, several different, 1980s, 1/35, MIB, G5, ea....$10.00
Apex, Russian Carrier Rocket Sputnik, 1993, 1/44, MIB, G5 ....$24.00
Apex, Russian Carrier Rocket Vostak, 1990s, 1/144, MIB, G5 ....$19.00
Arii, Macross, Fighter VF-1A #325, 1/100, MIB, G5 ....$10.00
Arii, Macross, Quiltra-Queleual Ship #332, 1/2000, MIB, G5 ....$29.00
Arii, Macross, Regult Tactical Scout Type #327, 1/100, MIB, G5 ....$24.00
Arii, Macross, SDF-1 Cruiser Fortress #308, 1/8000, MIB, G5 ....$19.00
Arii, Macross, Valkyrie VF-1D #324, 1/100, MIB, G5 ....$16.00
Arii, Macross, Valkyrie VF-1J #318, 1/100, MIB, G5 ....$16.00
Arii, Macross, Valkyrie VF-1S #319, 1/100, MIB, G5 ....$14.00
Arii, Orguss Flier #503, 1/48, MIB, G5 ....$14.00
Arii, Orguss Tank #504, 1/48, MIB, G5 ....$14.00
Arii, Regult Missile Carrier #328, 1/100, MIB, G5 ....$24.00
Arii, Southern Cross, ATAC-Andrzei Slawsky #603, 1/12, MIB, G5 ....$24.00
Arii, Southern Cross, ATAC-Bowie Emerson #604, 1/12, MIB, G5 ....$24.00
Arii, Southern Cross, ATAC-Charles DeEtouard #602, 1/12, MIB, G5 ....$14.00
Arii, Southern Cross, GMP-Lana Isavia #601, 1/12, MIB, G5 ....$24.00
Arii, Southern Cross, NAD-Jun Yamashita #605, 1/12, MIB, G5 ....$24.00
Atlantic, Goldrake-Toei Animation, Actarus Figure Set #GK1, 1978, MIB, G5 ....$14.00
Atlantic, Goldrake-Toei Animation, Goldrake #GK3, 1978, MIB, G5 ....$16.00
Atlantic, Goldrake-Toei Animation, Golgoth-Robot of Vega #GK4, 1978, MIB, G5 ....$14.00
Atlantic, Goldrake-Toei Animation, Vega Figure Set #GK2, 1978, MIB, G5 ....$14.00
Atlantic, Mao/Chinese Revolution #10010, 1975, 1/75, MIB, G5 ....$19.00
Aurora, Addams Family House #805, minor assembly, G5 ..$270.00
Aurora, Adventure Series, Spartacus #405 1964, 1/8, MIB, G5 ....$270.00
Aurora, Alfred E Neuman #802, 1965, 1/12, partially pnt, G5 ....$220.00
Aurora, American Astronaut, 1967, MIB (sealed), T2 ..$130.00
Aurora, Aston Martin Spy Car #585, 1/25, partially assembled, G5 ....$100.00
Aurora, Astronaut #409, 1967, 1/12, MIB (dk logo), G5 .$90.00
Aurora, Astronaut #409, 1967, 1/12, MIB (yel logo), G5 ....$100.00
Aurora, Batmobile #486, 1966, 1/32, MIB, G5....$500.00
Aurora, Batmobile #486, 1966, 1/32, partially assembled (Model Club box), G5....$230.00
Aurora, Black Falcon Pirate Ship #210, 1/100, MIB, G5 .$50.00
Aurora, Bloodthirsty Pirates, Blackbeard #463, 1965, 1/8, MIB, G5 ....$350.00
Aurora, Bloodthirsty Pirates, Captain Kidd #464, 1965, 1/8, MIB, G5 ....$80.00
Aurora, Bride of Frankenstein #482, 1964, assembled, D9 ....$130.00
Aurora, Captain Action #480, 1966, 1/12, assembled, G5 .$100.00
Aurora, Captain Action #480, 1966, 1/12, MIB, G5....$290.00
Aurora, Captain America #476, 1966, orig issue, 1/12, MIB, G5 ....$400.00
Aurora, Captain America #476, 1966, orig issue, 1/12, partially assembled, G5 ....$260.00
Aurora, Castle Creatures, Vampire #452, 1965, partially assembled, G5 ....$220.00
Aurora, Comic Scenes, Batman #187, 1974, 1/8, MIB (sealed), G5 ....$90.00
Aurora, Comic Scenes, Batman #187, 1974, 1/8, NM (EX box), A $60.00
Aurora, Comic Scenes, Captain America #192, 1974, 1/12, MIB (sealed), G5 ....$160.00
Aurora, Comic Scenes, Incredible Hulk #184, 1974, 1/12, MIB, G5 ....$90.00
Aurora, Comic Scenes, Lone Ranger #188, 1974, M (VG+ sealed box), A $40.00
Aurora, Comic Scenes, Robin Teen Wonder #193, 1974, 1/8, MIB, G5 ....$125.00
Aurora, Comic Scenes, Spider-Man, 1974, assembled, D9 ..$45.00
Aurora, Comic Scenes, Superboy #186, 1974, 1/18, MIB, G5 ....$100.00
Aurora, Comic Scenes, Superman #185, 1974, 1/18, MIB, G5 ....$90.00
Aurora, Comic Scenes, Tarzan #181, 1974, 1/11, MIB (sealed), G5 ....$70.00
Aurora, Comic Scenes, Tonto #183, 1974, 1/12, M (EX+ sealed box), A $40.00
Aurora, Creature From the Black Lagoon #426, 1963, assembled, D9....$65.00
Aurora, Creature From the Black Lagoon #483, 1969, orig issue, 1/8, partially assembled, G5 ....$190.00
Aurora, Customizing Monster Kit, #2 Mad Dog/Vulture/Etc #464, 1963, 1/8, MIB, G5....$290.00
Aurora, Deals' Wheels, Baron & His (5-Winged) Funfdecker Fokker, 1971, NM (EX box), A $100.00
Aurora, Dick Tracy #818, 1968, box only, Canadian issue, EX, D9....$25.00
Aurora, Dick Tracy #818, 1968, 1/16, partially assembled, G5 ....$180.00
Aurora, Dr Jekyll & Mr Hyde #460, 1964, orig issue, 1/8, partially assembled, G5....$250.00
Aurora, Dr Jekyll as Mr Hyde #482, 1969, orig issue, 1/8, assembled, G5 ....$80.00
Aurora, Dr Jekyll as Mr Hyde #482, 1972, 1/8, MIB (sealed), G5....$210.00
Aurora, Dracula #454, 1972, 1/8, MIB (sealed), G5....$200.00
Aurora, Famous Fighters, Confederate Raider #402, 1958, 1/8, M (G- box), G5 ....$410.00
Aurora, Famous Fighters, Gladiator w/Trident #H406, 1958, 1/8, MIB, G5 ....$200.00

Aurora, Famous Fighters, Roman Gladiator, MIB, $200.00.

Photo courtesy June Moon

Aurora, Famous Fighters, Mace TM Guided Missile #130, 1958, 1/48, MIB, G5 .... $190.00

Aurora, Famous Fighters, Nike Hercules Missile #379, 1958, 1/48, MIB, G5 .... $300.00

Aurora, Frankenstein #423-98, reissue, NMIB, $125.00.

Photo courtesy June Moon

Aurora, Famous Fighters, Three Musketeers (Porthos) #KH9, 1958, 1/8, MIB, G5 .... **$180.00**

Aurora, Famous Fighters, Three Musketeers (Aramis) #KH10, 1958, 1/8, MIB, G5 .... **$180.00**

Aurora, Famous Fighters, US Air Force Pilot #H409, 1958, 1/12, MIB, G5 .... **$290.00**

Aurora, Famous Fighters, Viking #K6, 1958, 1/8, MIB, G5 . **$340.00**

Aurora, Forgotten Prisoner, 1966, incomplete, D9 .... **$35.00**

Aurora, Forgotten Prisoner #453, 1972, 1/8, MIB (sealed), G5 .... **$210.00**

Aurora, Frankenstein, 1961, glow-in-the-dark, assembled, D9 .... **$25.00**

Aurora, Frankenstein #423, 1961, orig issue, 1/8, MIB, G5 .... **$400.00**

Aurora, Frankenstein #449 (no blk rope knot), 1972, 1/8, MIB, G5 .... **$120.00**

Aurora, Frightening Lightning, Frankenstein #XFL449, 1969, 1/8, MIB, G5 .... **$400.00**

Aurora, Frightening Lightning, Phantom of the Opera #FL 451, 1969, 1/8, MIB, G5 .... **$400.00**

Aurora, Gladiator #406, 1964, 1/8, MIB, G5 .... **$155.00**

Aurora, Godzilla #466, 1972, 1/600, MIB, G5 .... **$105.00**

Aurora, Godzilla #469, 1964, orig issue, 1/600, assembled, G5 .... **$110.00**

Aurora, Gold Knight of Nice #475, 1965, 1/8, MIB, G5 .. **$340.00**

Aurora, Great American Presidents, George Washington #852, 1965, 1/12, MIB, G5 .... **$140.00**

Aurora, Great American Presidents, John F Kennedy #851, 1965, 1/12, MIB, G5 .... **$200.00**

Aurora, Guys and Gals, Scotch Lad #419, 1957, MIB, $70.00.

Photo courtesy June Moon

Aurora, Great Moments in Sports, Dempsey vs Firpo #861, 1965, 1/18, MIB (sealed), G5 .... $110.00
Aurora, Great Moments in Sports, Jerry West #865, 1965, 1/8, MIB, G5 .... $210.00
Aurora, Green Beret #413, 1966, 1/8, assembled, G5 .... $60.00
Aurora, Guillotine #800, 1964, orig issue, 1/15, MIB, G5 .... $650.00
Aurora, Guillotine #800, 1965, 1/15, assembled, G5 .... $130.00
Aurora, Guys & Gals, Chinese Mandarin #415, 1957, 1/8, MIB, G5 .... $70.00
Aurora, Guys & Gals, Indian Chief #417, 1957, 1/8, MIB, G5 .... $150.00
Aurora, Hercules & the Lion, 1965, M (EX+ box), A ... $300.00
Aurora, Hunchback of Notre Dame #460, 1964, orig issue, 1/8, partially assembled, G5 .... $160.00
Aurora, Hunchback of Notre Dame #481, 1972, 1/8, MIB, G5 .... $150.00
Aurora, Incredible Hulk #421, 1966, 1/12, partially assembled, G5 .... $210.00
Aurora, Invaders, Flying Saucer #256, 1975, 1/72, MIB (sealed), G5 .... $120.00
Aurora, Invaders, UFO #813, 1968, orig issue, 1/72, MIB, G5 .... $210.00
Aurora, King Kong, 1972, glow-in-the-dark, assembled & pnt, EX, H4 .... $80.00
Aurora, King Kong #465, 1969, orig issue, 1/25, MIB, G5 .. $320.00
Aurora, King Kong #465, 1972, 1/25, MIB, G5 .... $270.00
Aurora, King Kong #468, 1964, orig issue, 1/25, partially assembled, G5 .... $280.00

Aurora, Lost in Space, MIB, T2, from $1,500.00 to $2,000.00.

Aurora, Knights in Shining Armor, Sir Percival #884, 1973, 1/8, MIB, G5 .... $60.00
Aurora, Land of the Giants, Diorama w/crew & snake #816, 1968, 1/48, MIB, G5 .... $530.00
Aurora, Land of the Giants, Snake Scene, 1968, rare, NM (EX box), P3 .... $425.00
Aurora, Land of the Giants, Spindrift 'Rocket Transport,' 1975, 2nd issue, NM (VG+ box), A $300.00
Aurora, Lone Ranger #808, 1967, 1/12, MIB, G5 .... $250.00
Aurora, Lost in Space, Diorama #MA 420, 1966, 1/32, MIB, G5 .... $540.00
Aurora, Lost in Space, Robot #418, 1968, partially assembled, M (VG+ repro box), G5 .... $200.00
Aurora, Man From UNCLE, Illya Kurakin #M412, 1966, 1/12, MIB, G5 .... $190.00
Aurora, Man From UNCLE, Napoleon Solo #M411, 1966, 1/12, MIB, G5 .... $310.00
Aurora, Man From UNCLE, Napoleon Solo #411, 1966, 1/12, NM (VG+ box), A $250.00
Aurora, Monster Scenes, Dr Deadly #631, 1971, 1/13, assembled, G5 .... $80.00
Aurora, Monster Scenes, Frankenstein #633, 1971, 1/13, assembled, G5 .... $100.00
Aurora, Monster Scenes, Pendulum #63, 1971, 1/13, MIB, G5 .... $140.00
Aurora, Monsters of the Movies, Dracula #656, 1975, 1/12, MIB, G5 .... $230.00
Aurora, Monsters of the Movies, Rodan #657, 1975, MIB, G5 .... $450.00

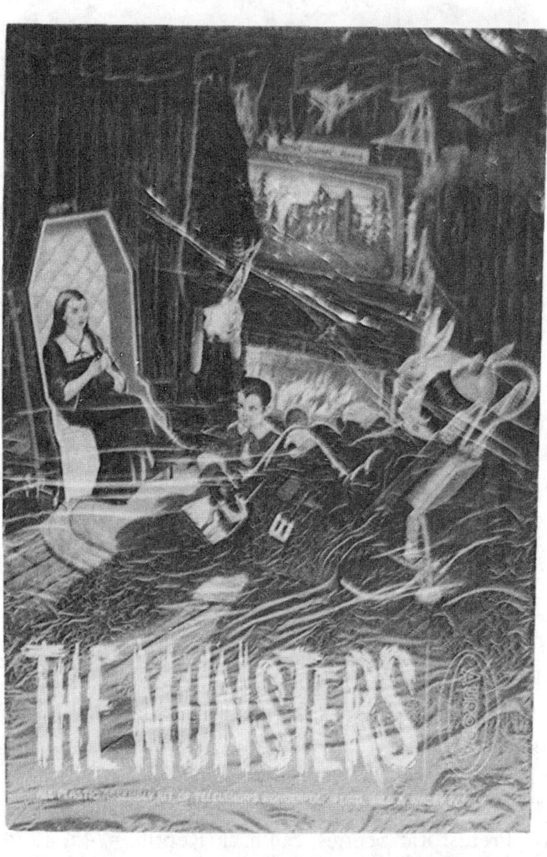

Aurora, Munsters #804, 1964, MIB, $1,250.00.

Aurora, Mummy, 1974, Canadian issue, glow-in-the-dark, NRFB, H4 ....$90.00
Aurora, Mummy #427, 1963, orig issue, 1/8, MIB, G5 ...$220.00
Aurora, Old Ironsides, 1965, M (NM sealed box), A $25.00
Aurora, Phantom of the Opera, Mummy #452, 1972, 1/8, MIB (sealed), G5 ....$70.00
Aurora, Phantom of the Opera #428, orig issue, MIB (foreign box), G5....$120.00
Aurora, Phantom of the Opera #451, 1969, orig issue, 1/8, partially assembled, G5....$140.00
Aurora, Prehistoric Scenes, Allosaurus #736, 1971, orig issue, MIB, G5....$140.00
Aurora, Prehistoric Scenes, Cave #732, 1971, orig issue, 1/12, MIB, G5 ....$90.00
Aurora, Prehistoric Scenes, Cave Bear #738, 1972, 1/13, MIB, G5 ....$90.00
Aurora, Prehistoric Scenes, Cro-Magnon Man #730, 1971, orig issue, 1/12, MIB, G5 ....$90.00

Aurora, Prehistoric Scenes, Cro-Magnon Woman, 1971, original issue, MIB, $100.00.

Aurora, Prehistoric Scenes, Flying Reptile #734, 1971, 1/13, MIB, G5....$60.00
Aurora, Prehistoric Scenes, Neanderthol Man #729, 1971, orig issue, 1/12, MIB (sealed), G5 ....$80.00
Aurora, Prehistoric Scenes, Sabertooth Tiger #733, 1972, 1/13, MIB, G5....$120.00
Aurora, Prehistoric Scenes, Sailback Reptile #745, 1974, 1/13, MIB (sealed), G5....$150.00
Aurora, Prehistoric Scenes, Spiked Dinosaur #742, 1972, 1/13, MIB, G5 ....$80.00
Aurora, Prehistoric Scenes, Tar Pit #735, 1971, orig issue, 1/13, MIB (sealed), G5 ....$190.00
Aurora, Prehistoric Scenes, Three-Horned Dinosaur #741, 1972, 1/13, MIB, G5 ....$90.00
Aurora, Prehistoric Scenes, Wooly Mammoth #743, 1972, 1/13, MIB, G5 ....$180.00
Aurora, Rat Patrol, Battle Diorama #340, 1967, MIB, G5..$120.00
Aurora, Robin the Boy Wonder #488, 1966, box only, EX, D9 ....$32.00
Aurora, Robin the Boy Wonder #488, 1966, 1/18, M (NM sealed box), A $100.00
Aurora, Salem Witch, 1965, assembled, incomplete, D9 .$50.00
Aurora, Spider-Man #182, 1974, 1/11, MIB (sealed), G5..$160.00
Aurora, Spider-Man #477, 1966, orig issue, 1/12, assembled, G5 ....$80.00
Aurora, Superboy #478, 1974, M (VG sealed box), A $65.00
Aurora, Superman, 1963, box only, EX+, D9 ....$65.00
Aurora, Superman, 1964, assembled, D9....$35.00
Aurora, Tarzan #820, 1967, orig issue, 1/11, MIB, G5 ...$190.00
Aurora, Tonto #809, 1967, orig issue, 1/12, MIB, G5 ....$220.00
Aurora, USB Sealab III #721, 1969, 1/93, MIB, G5.......$300.00
Aurora, Viking Ship #320, 1962, 1/80, MIB, G5 ....$60.00
Aurora, Voyage to the Bottom of the Sea, Seaview #707, 1966, M (NM box), P3....$325.00
Aurora, Voyage to the Bottom of the Sea, Flying Sub #817, 1968, 1/60, assembled, G5 ....$60.00
Aurora, Wacky Back Wacker #807, 1965, partially assembled, G5 ....$200.00
Aurora, White-Tail Deer #403, 1962, 1/8, orig issue, MIB, G5....$75.00
Aurora, Whoozis (Denty) #203, 1966, MIB, G5....$90.00
Aurora, Whoozis (Snuffy) #206, 1966, assembled, G5 .....$40.00
Aurora, Whoozis (Suzie) #201, 1966, MIB, G5 ....$60.00
Aurora, Willie Mays, 1965, NMIB, T2 ....$230.00
Aurora, Witch #470, 1972, 1/12, MIB (sealed), G5 ....$250.00
Aurora, Wolfman, 1974, Canadian issue, glow-in-the-dark, NRFB, H4....$100.00
Aurora, Wolfman #450, 1969, orig issue, 1/8, MIB, G5 .$135.00
Aurora, Wolfman #450, 1972, 1/8, MIB, G5 ....$120.00
Aurora, Wolfman's Wagon #458, 1964, partially assembled, missing pcs, no box, G5 ....$290.00
Aurora, X-15 Rocket-Powered Plane #120, 1962, 1/48, MIB (sealed), G5 ....$150.00
Aurora, Zorro #801 (Disney), 1965, 1/12, MIB, G5 ....$400.00
Aurora, 2001: A Space Odyssey, Pan Am Space Clipper #148, 1968, orig issue, 1/144, MIB, G5 ....$220.00
Aurora, 2001: A Space Odyssey, Space Shuttle Orion #252, 1975, 1/144, MIB (sealed), G5 ....$170.00
Bachmann, Animals of the World, Cow & Calf #7201, 1959, MIB, G5 ....$60.00
Bachmann, Animals of the World, Lion #7101, 1959, 1/12, MIB, G5 ....$50.00
Bachmann, Birds of the World, Barn Swallow #9009, 1959, 1/1, MIB, G5 ....$20.00
Bachmann, Birds of the World, Blue Bird, 1960s, M (EX sealed box), A....$35.00

Bachmann, Birds of the World, Hooded Warbler #19013, 1990, 1/1, MIB, G5 .... $20.00
Bachmann, Birds of the World, Painted Bunting #19012, 1990, 1/1, MIB, G5 .... $12.00
Bachmann, Birds of the World, Parakeet #8701, 1970s, 1/1, MIB (sealed), G5 .... $25.00
Bachmann, Birds of the World, Scarlet Tanager #19003, 1990, 1/1, MIB, G5 .... $20.00
Bachmann, Dogs of the World, Cocker Spaniel #8003, 1959, 1/6, MIB, G5 .... $15.00
Bachmann, Dogs of the World, German Shepard, 1960s, M (EX sealed box), D9 .... $35.00
Bachmann, Dogs of the World, Pointer #8006, 1959, 1/5, MIB $40.00
Bachmann, Dogs of the World, Standard Poodle #8007, 1959, 1/6, MIB, G5 .... $40.00
Bachmann, Fisher Boy #6000, 1962, 1/12, MIB, G5 .... $80.00
Bandai, Baltanseizid figure, 1/350, NM (VG+ box), D9 ... $23.00
Bandai, Captain Harlock, Queen Emerelda's Ship #36343, 1980s, 1/1600, MIB, G5 .... $30.00
Bandai, Galaman figure, 1/350, NM (VG+ box), D9 .... $20.00
Bandai, Godzilla #502526, 1984, 1/350, MIB, G5 .... $50.00
Bandai, Gomola figure, 1/350, NM (VG+ box), D9 .... $23.00
Bandai, Gundam, Amuro Ray #36223, 1980, 1/20, MIB, G5 ... $11.00
Bandai, Gundam, Mobile Suit #11 #36199, 1980, 1/44, gr, MIB, G5 .... $20.00
Bandai, Gundam, Mobile Suit Tallgeese #47686, 1995, 1/44, MIB, G5 .... $30.00
Bandai, Kinggidrah #3533, 1990, 1/350, MIB, G5 .... $40.00
Bandai, Kinggidrah #503533, 1984, 1/350, MIB, G5 .... $50.00
Bandai, Pegila #3528, 1990, 1/350, MIB, G5 .... $14.00
Bandai, Prehistoric Animal Series, Stegosaurus #8332, 1973, 1/35, MIB, G5 .... $65.00
Bandai, Silly Dracula #503867, 1985, MIB, G5 .... $20.00
Bandai, Star-Blazers, Desslock's Command Cruiser (#5) #536045, 1980s, MIB, G5 .... $10.00
Bandai, Star-Blazers, Desslock's Command Cruiser #11577, 1989, MIB, G5 .... $25.00
Bandai, Star-Blazers, Space Cruiser Yamato 2520 #46928, 1995, 1/1500, MIB, G5 .... $20.00
Bandai, Thunderbird #536188, 1984, MIB, G5 .... $40.00
Bandai, Thunderbird 2 #536186, 1984, MIB, G5 .... $30.00
Bandai, UFO, SHADO Interceptor #36120, MIB, G5 ..... $80.00
Bandai, Z-Ton figure #503564, 1984, 1/350, NM (VG+ box), D9 .... $19.00
Best Plastics, Winchester 94, 1950s, 1/3, MIB, P4 .... $60.00
Billiken, Batman (Type A or Type B), vinyl, MIB, G5, ea. $200.00
Billiken, Dracula, 1989, vinyl, MIB, G5 .... $280.00
Billiken, Frankenstein, 1988, vinyl, MIB, G5 .... $180.00
Billiken, Gorilla II (King Kong vs Godzilla), 1987, vinyl, NM (EX+ box), A $90.00
Billiken, Invasion of the Saucermen, Saucerman, vinyl, MIB, G5 .... $70.00
Billiken, It Conquered the World, It Alien, 1985, vinyl, MIB, G5 .... $90.00
Billiken, King Kong vs Godzilla, Godzilla, 1986, vinyl, MIB, G5 .... $110.00
Billiken, Laser Blast Alien, 1988, vinyl, MIB, G5 .... $100.00
Billiken, Mole People, 1984, vinyl, NM (EX+ box), A $65.00
Billiken, Mummy, vinyl, MIB, G5 .... $220.00
Billiken, Phantom of the Opera, 1982, vinyl, 1/8, NMIB, A ... $175.00
Billiken, Preditor, 1991, vinyl, MIB, G5 .... $110.00
Billiken, Red King, 1988, vinyl, MIB, G5 .... $80.00
Billiken, She-Creature, 1989, vinyl, NM (EX+ box), A.. $220.00
Billiken, Thing from Another World, Thing, 1984, vinyl, MIB, G5 .... $160.00
Billiken, Ultra Zone, Peguila, 1989, vinyl, MIB, G5 .... $90.00
Billiken, War of Colossal Beats, 1986, vinyl, MIB, G5..... $50.00
Bryan, Silence of the Lambs, Buffalo Bill, resin, MIB, G5 . $50.00
Bryan, The Omen, Damien, 1992, 1/6, resin, MIB, G5 .... $70.00
Dark Horse, Concrete (from comic book) #891-01, 1991, 1/18, MIB, G5 .... $170.00
Dark Horse, Frankenstein #22, 1991, 1/8, MIB, G5 .... $130.00
Dark Horse, King Kong #K1092, 1992, vinyl, MIB, G5 ... $60.00
Dark Horse, King Kong #K22, 1/48, MIB, G5 .... $90.00
Dark Horse, Mummy #220391, 1995, 1/8, MIB, G5 .... $150.00
Dark Horse, Predator II, Predator #240131, 1994, 1/8, MIB, G5 .... $175.00
Dimensional Designs, IT the Terror from Space, 1991, NM (plain wht box), A $125.00
Dimensional Designs, Mad Doctor, 1992, NM (VG+ plain wht box), A $75.00
Dimensional Designs, Outer Limits, Architects of Fear-Thetan, resin, assembled, G5 .... $35.00
Dimensional Designs, Outer Limits, Bellaro Shield-Bifrost, resin, MIB, G5 .... $60.00
Dimensional Designs, Outer Limits, Man Never Born (Andro), resin, MIB, G5 .... $100.00
Dimensional Designs, Outer Limits, Nightmare (Ebonite Guard), resin, MIB, G5 .... $70.00
Dimensional Designs, Outer Limits, Obit-Obit Monster, resin, assembled, MIB, G5 .... $20.00
Dimensional Designs, Outer Limits, Purple Twilight (IKAR), resin, MIB, G5 .... $60.00
Dimensional Designs, Outer Limits, The Mice (Chromite), MIB, G5 .... $100.00
Educational Products, Beating Heart #4000, 1961, 2/1, MIB, G5 .... $10.00
Educational Products, Modern Man Skeleton #5400, 1966, 1/6, MIB, G5 .... $30.00
Eldon, Matador Missile & Launcher, 1960, MIB, P4 .... $75.00
Elfin, Chub Li-Street Fighter #5500, vinyl, 1/8, MIB, G5 .. $60.00
Entex, Battle of the Planets, G-1 Spaceship #8403, 1978, MIB (sealed), G5 .... $40.00
Entex, Battle of the Planets, G-1SP Spaceship #8402, 1978, MIB (sealed), G5 .... $30.00
Entex, Battle of the Planets, Phoenix #8401, 1978, MIB (sealed), G5 .... $110.00
Entex, Message from Space, Comet Fire #8428, 1978, MIB, G5 .... $20.00
Entex, Space Shuttle #8529, 1981, 1/144, MIB (sealed), G5 .. $40.00
Entex, 1st Dune Buggy, 1/20, M (EX box), D9 .... $35.00
Federation Models, Star Trek: The Next Generation, Cardassian Scout Ship #4, 8", MIB, G5 .... $30.00
Fujimi Mokei, Mad Police, Destroyer Car #1, 1980s, 1/30, MIB, G5 .... $50.00

Fujimi Mokei, Mad Police, Farcon Car #4, 1980s, 1/30, MIB, G5 .....$50.00

Fujimi Mokei, Mad Police, Interceptor Car #2, 1980s, 1/30, MIB, G5 .....$50.00

Fujimi Mokei, Mad Police, Venus Car #3, 1980s, 1/30, MIB, G5 .....$50.00

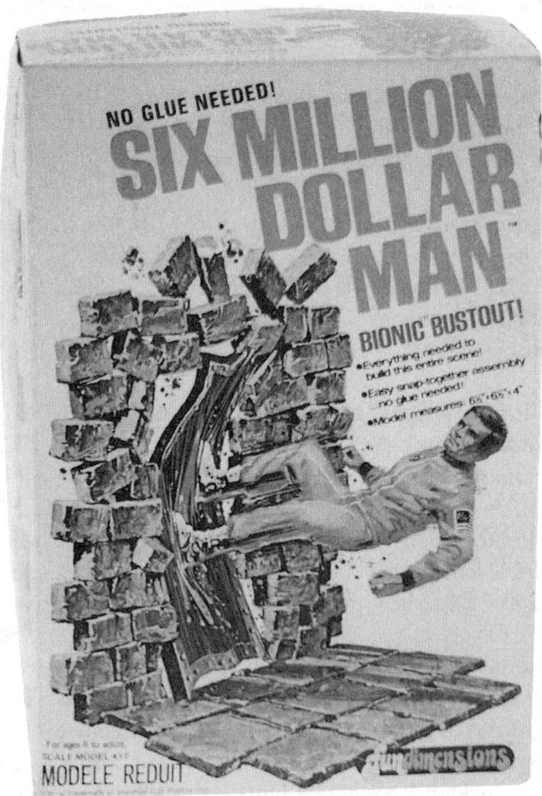

Fundimensions, Six Million Dollar Man, MIB, $40.00.

Fundimensions/MPC, Haunted Glo-Head, Ape Man, 1975, M (G box), D9 .....$35.00

FX, Tales from the Darkside, Gargoyle, resin, 17", MIB, G5 .....$120.00

FX, Tom Tyler as Kharis the Mummy, resin, 12", MIB, G5 .....$70.00

Garage Resin Kit, Star Trek: The Next Generation, Duralyne Hypo Spray, 1/1, MIB, G5 .....$25.00

Garage Resin Kit, Star Trek: The Next Generation, Phaser II, 1/1, MIB, G5 .....$35.00

Geometric Designs, Alien, Alien Warrior #7, 1996, resin, 1/8, MIB, G5 .....$80.00

Geometric Designs, Clash of the Titans, Medusa, vinyl or resin, 1994, 1/6, MIB, G5 .....$60.00

Geometric Designs, I Was a Teenage Werewolf, 1985, NM (EX+ box), A $300.00

Geometric Designs, I Was a Teenage Werewolf, Werewolf, 1990, vinyl or resin, MIB, G5 .....$150.00

Geometric Designs, Star Trek: The Next Generation, Captain Jean Luc Picard, 1992, vinyl or resin, 1/6, MIB, G5 ..$35.00

Geometric Designs, Star Trek: The Next Generation, Lieutenant Worf, 1992, vinyl or resin, 1/6, MIB, G5 ....$35.00

Gerbra, US Navy Vanguard Missile $401, 1950s, 1/48, MIB, G5 .....$200.00

Hasegawa, Boeing F4B-4 Biplane, 1970s, 1/32, MIB (sealed), P3 .....$30.00

Hasegawa, Curtis Soc-3 Seagull Biplane, 1970s, 1/72, MIB (sealed), P3 .....$20.00

Hawk, Explorer 18 Satellite #553, 1968, 1/20, MIB, G5 ..$70.00

Hawk, Gloster FAW 1 Javelin #564, 1967, 1/72, MIB, G5..$20.00

Hawk, Indian Totem Poles, Grave of Ske-Dans Totem #556, 1966, MIB, G5 .....$45.00

Hawk, Indian Totem Poles, Thunderbird #555, 1966, MIB, G5 .....$45.00

Hawk, Jupitor C/Explorer #552, 1966, 1/48, MIB, G5......$50.00

Hawk, Project Vanguard Satellite #515, 1958, 1/5, MIB, G5 ..$100.00

Hawk, Silly Surfers, Hodad Makin' the Scene #543, 1964, assembled, G5 .....$15.00

Hawk, Silly Surfers, Hot Dogger Hangin' Ten #541, 1964, M (G- box), G5 .....$40.00

Hawk, Weird-Ohs, Digger Way-Out Dragster #530, 1963, MIB, G5 .....$40.00

Hawk, Weird-Ohs, Francis the Foul, 1963, incomplete (VG+ box), D9 .....$35.00

Photo courtesy June Moon

Hawk, Weird-Ohs, Francis the Foul #535, 1963, MIB, $50.00.

Hawk, Weird-Ohs, Freddy Flameout #533, 1963, MIB, G5 ..$60.00

Hawk, Weird-Ohs, Sling Rave Curvette #637, MIB, G5 .$40.00

Hawk, Wild Woodie (Surfer Car) #545, 1965, 1/25, MIB, G5 ....$30.00
Horizon, Batman #12, 1989, 1/6, MIB, G5 ....$80.00
Horizon, Bram Stoker's Dracula, Dracula (Bat-Type) #42, 1992, 1/6, MIB, G5 ....$50.00
Horizon, Bram Stoker's Dracula, Dracula (Wolf-Type) #41, 1992, 1/6, MIB, G5 ....$30.00
Horizon, Bride of Frankenstein #3, 1988, assembled, G5 .$25.00
Horizon, DC Comics, Joker #56, 1993, 1/6, partially assembled, G5 ....$30.00
Horizon, Dinosaur Series, Apatosaurus #60, 1993, 1/30, MIB, G5 ....$25.00
Horizon, Dinosaur Series, Stegosaurus #28, 1992, 1/30, MIB, G5 ....$16.00
Horizon, Dracula #4, 1988, MIB, G5 ....$50.00
Horizon, Indiana Jones, Dr Jones #35, 1993, 1/6, MIB, G5..$20.00
Horizon, Indiana Jones, Indiana #34, 1993, 1/6, MIB, G5..$60.00
Horizon, Jurassic Park, Spitter Dilophosaur #62, 1993, 1/4, MIB, G5 ....$90.00
Horizon, Marvel Universe, Cable #52, 1994, 1/6, MIB, G5 ....$40.00
Horizon, Marvel Universe, Cyclops #26, 1993, 1/6, MIB, G5 .$45.00
Horizon, Marvel Universe, Dark Phoenix #16, 1991, 1/6, MIB, G5 ....$40.00
Horizon, Marvel Universe, Dr Doom #17, 1991, MIB, G5 .$40.00
Horizon, Marvel Universe, Green Goblin #55, 1994, 1/6, MIB, G5 ....$40.00
Horizon, Marvel Universe, Incredible Hulk #13, 1990, 1/6, MIB, G5 ....$40.00
Horizon, Marvel Universe, Iron Man #9, 1990, 1/6, assembled, G5 ....$30.00
Horizon, Marvel Universe, Punisher #7, 1988, MIB, G5..$45.00
Horizon, Marvel Universe, Silver Surfer #8, 1989, MIB, G5 ....$30.00
Horizon, Marvel Universe, Spider-Man (2099) #55, 1994, 1/6, MIB, G5 ....$40.00
Horizon, Marvel Universe, Spider-Man #49 (new pose), 1994, 1/6, MIB, G5 ....$30.00
Horizon, Marvel Universe, Spider-Man #6, 1988, MIB, G5 ..$40.00
Horizon, Marvel Universe, Thing #18, 1991, MIB, G5....$50.00
Horizon, Marvel Universe, Thor #25, 1993, 1/6, MIB, G5 ...$50.00
Horizon, Marvel Universe, Wolverine #15, 1990, 1/6, MIB, G5 ....$40.00
Horizon, Marvel Universe, Wolverine #50 (new pose), 1993, 1/6, MIB, G5 ....$15.00
Horizon, Mole People, Mole Man #2, 1988, MIB, G5......$70.00
Horizon, Mummy #39, 1993, MIB, G5....................$60.00
Horizon, Phantom of the Opera #1, 1988, MIB, G5.........$45.00
Horizon, Robocop, ED-209 #11, 1989, 1/9, MIB, G5 ....$70.00
Horizon, Robocop, Robocop #10, 1989, 1/6, MIB, G5 .....$60.00
Horizon, Robocop 3, Robocop #30, 1992, 1/6, MIB, G5 ..$70.00
Horizon, Terminator 2, T-1000 Terminator #22, 1991, 1/5, MIB, G5 ....$20.00
Horizon, Terminator 2 Judgement Day, 1991, M (EX+ box), D9 ....$33.00
Ideal, Jaguar XK-120 Fix-It Car, complete, NM (NM box), A $115.00
Ideal, XP-600 Fix It Car of Tomorrow, 1953-55, partially assembled, M (NM box), P4 ....$285.00

Hubley, Model A Roadster, metal, MIB, $55.00.

Imai, Armored Knights, Archduke II #1394, 1984, orig issue, 1/12, MIB, G5 ....$10.00
Imai, Armored Knights, Pfalzgraf Otto Heinrich #1518, 1/12, MIB, G5 ....$10.00
Imai, Armored Knights, Philipp Graf Von Hessen #1517, 1984, orig issue, 1/12, MIB, G5 ....$13.00
Imai, Captain Blue #1209, 1982, 1/24, MIB, G5 ....$10.00
Imai, Captain Scarlet, Captain Magenta #1210, 1982, 1/24, MIB, G5 ....$10.00
Imai, Captain Scarlet, Captain Ocher #1211, 1982, 1/24, MIB, G5 ....$10.00
Imai, Captain Scarlet, Concerto Angel #1212, 1982, 1/24, MIB, G5 ....$15.00
Imai, Captain Scarlet, Spectrum Helicopter #2015, 1992, MIB, G5 ....$80.00
Imai, Captain Scarlet, Spectrum Pursuit Vehicle #1713, 1988, MIB, G5 ....$40.00
Imai, Joe 90, Mac's Car #1399, 1984, MIB, G5 ....$35.00
Imai, Kaiser Maximillian II #1395, 1984, orig issue, 1/12, MIB, G5 ....$13.00
Imai, Orguss, Cable #52, 1994, 1/6, MIB, G5 ....$40.00
Imai, Orguss, Cyclops #26, 1993, 1/6, MIB, G5 ....$45.00
Imai, Orguss, Dark Phoenix #16, 1991, 1/6, MIB, G5 ......$40.00
Imai, Orguss, Dr Doom #17, 1991, MIB, G5....................$40.00
Imai, Orguss, Incredible Hulk #13, 1990, 1/6, MIB, G5 ...$40.00
Imai, Orguss, Spider-Man #49 (new pose), 1994, 1/6, MIB, G5 ....$30.00
Imai, Orguss, Thing #18, 1991, MIB, G5 ....$50.00
Imai, Orguss, Thor #25, 1993, 1/6, MIB, G5....................$50.00
Imai, Orguss, Wolverine #15, 1990, 1/6, MIB, G5...........$40.00
Imai, Orguss, Wolverine #50 (new pose), 1993, 1/6, assembled, G5 ....$15.00
ITC, Cocker Spaniel #3824, 1959, MIB, G5 ....$30.00
ITC, Collie #3815, 1959, MIB, G5 ....$35.00
ITC, Launcher w/Soviet BB-1 Missile #3812, 1960, 1/32, MIB, G5 ....$140.00
ITC, Marvel Metal Series, Rhinoceros #3853, 1960, MIB, G5 ....$35.00
ITC, Midget Models, Covered Wagon & Stagecoach #3749, 1962, 3½", MIB, G5 ....$30.00

ITC, Neanderthal Man #3808, 1959, 1/8, MIB, G5 ....**$50.00**
ITC, Precious Miniatures, Hansom Cab & Coronation Coach #3772, 1960, 3½", MIB, G5 ....**$30.00**
ITC, Scotch Terrier #3825, 1960, MIB, G5......................**$30.00**
ITC, US Navy Blimp #3723, 1958, 1/336, MIB, G5 ....**$36.00**
ITC, Wire Haired Terrier #3823, 1959, MIB, G5.............**$30.00**
Janus, Tower of London, Boris Karloff, 1991, NM (EX box), A **$120.00**
Kaiyodo, Angurus, 1/250, NM (EX+ box), A **$50.00**
Kaiyodo, Godzilla, 1954, 1/250, soft vinyl, EX (EX box), A .**$60.00**
Kaiyodo, Godzilla, 1991, 1/400, soft vinyl, NM (VG+ box), A **$45.00**
Kaiyodo, Nelonga, 1990s, M (EX box), A........................**$50.00**
KGB, Batman (1960s TV), Batboat (Aurora recast), 1/32, MIB, G5 ....**$50.00**
KGB, Batman (1960s TV), Batcopter, 1/35, MIB, G5 .....**$50.00**
KGB, Batman (1960s TV), Batcycle (Aurora recast), 1/19, MIB, G5 ....**$50.00**
KGB, Batman (1960s TV), Batgirl on Cycle, 1/19, MIB, G5 ...**$50.00**
KGB, Batman (1960s TV), Batplane (Aurora recast), 1/60, MIB, G5 ....**$50.00**
KGB, Fireball XL-5 (TV), 12", MIB, G5 ....**$70.00**
KGB, Space Ghost (TV), 1/12, MIB, G5..........................**$30.00**
Lifelike, Aerial Missiles on Helicopter #9654, 1970s, 1/40, MIB, G5 ....**$50.00**
Lifelike, American Wildlife, Bald Eagle #9350, 1974, MIB, G5...**$14.00**
Lifelike, American Wildlife, Mallard Duck #352, 1970s, M (EX sealed box), A **$13.00**
Lifelike, American Wildlife, Ring Neck Pheasant, 1970s, M (EX sealed box), A **$15.00**
Lifelike, Animals of the World, Shoveler Duck, 1960s, NM (VG+ box), D9 ....**$15.00**
Lifelike, Corythosaurus #9280, 1970s, 1/37, MIB (sealed), G5 ....**$20.00**
Lifelike, Cro-Magnon Man #383, 1973, 1/8, M (VG+ sealed box), D9 ....**$28.00**
Lifelike, Neanderthal Man #382, 1973, 1/8, MIB, G5......**$30.00**
Lifelike, Roman Chariot #9673, 1970s, 1/48, M (G- box), G5...**$20.00**
Lifelike, World of Stegosaurus #9283, 1970s, 1/32, MIB, G5...**$30.00**
Lindberg, American Bald Eagle #315, 1988, 13", MIB, G5 .**$15.00**
Lindberg, Bad Wheels (Lindy Loonies), Bert's Bucket (Scuttle Bucket) #6422, 1971, MIB, G5..............................**$150.00**
Lindberg, Bad Wheels (Lindy Loonies), Fat Max (Road Hog) #6420, 1971, MIB, G5..**$170.00**
Lindberg, Bad Wheels (Lindy Loonies), Sick Cycle (Big Wheeler) #6421, 1971, MIB, G5 ....**$160.00**
Lindberg, Baywatch, Beach Patrol Pickup #72588, 1995, 1/20, MIB (sealed), G5 ....**$20.00**
Lindberg, Brontosaurus #262, 1979, 1/72, MIB (sealed), G5 ....**$15.00**
Lindberg, Lighthouse #331, 1969, w/light, 10", MIB, G5.**$30.00**
Lindberg, Lindy Loonies, Scuttle Bucket #278, 1964, MIB, G5...**$200.00**
Lindberg, Monsters, Krimson Terror #272, 1965, 5", MIB, G5...**$130.00**
Lindberg, Northrop Snark Missile #687, 1988, 1/49, MIB (sealed), G5 ....**$40.00**
Lindberg, Old World Calendar #322, 1973, 12", MIB (sealed), G5 ....**$30.00**
Lindberg, Star Probe, Space Base #1148, 1976, 1/350, MIB, G5 ....**$50.00**
Lindberg, Star Probe, USS Explorer #1149, 1976, 1/200, MIB (sealed), G5 ....**$25.00**
Lindburg, Tyrannosaurus #261, 1987, 1/48, MIB, G5.......**$10.00**
Lunar Models, Angry Red Planet, Giant Amoeba #FG33, 9", MIB, G5...**$100.00**
Lunar Models, Giant Behemoth #FG39, 9", MIB, G5....**$160.00**
Lunar Models, Lost in Space, Chariot #SF009, 1/35, MIB, G5 ....**$120.00**
Lunar Models, Lost in Space, Cyclops/Cave Diorama #FG20, MIB, G5...**$120.00**
Lunar Models, Lost in Space, Space Pod #SF016, 1/35, MIB, G5...**$110.00**
Lunar Models, Penny Robinson & Monster #FG47, 1/8, MIB, G5 ....**$130.00**
Lunar Models, Pumpkinhead (movie), 1989, MIB, G5 ..**$145.00**
Lunar Models, Voyage to the Bottom of the Sea, Seaview (Aurora recast), 1990, 1/300, MIB, G5 ....**$80.00**
Lunar Models, War of the Worlds, Martian War Machine #SF 018, MIB, G5 ....**$60.00**
Magnum PI, Island Hoppers Vanagon #7328, 1982, MIB (sealed), G5 ....**$60.00**
Max Factory, Guyver Bio Fighter Collection, Gastar, 1990s, M (VG+ box), D9 ....**$23.00**
Max Factory, Guyver Bio Fighter Collection, Ramoth, 1990s, M (EX+ box), D9 ....**$28.00**
Max Factory, Nagira Ultra Q the Movie, NM (EX+ box), A **$65.00**
Monogram, Airacobra P-39, 1973, 1/48 scale, MIB (sealed), P3...**$25.00**
Monogram, Backdraft (movie), Fire Chief Car #6250, 1991, 1/32, MIB, G5 ....**$20.00**
Monogram, Backdraft (movie), Fire Engine #6240, 1991, 1/32, G5 ....**$40.00**
Monogram, Battle Star Galactica, Space Fighter Raider #6026, 1978, orig issue, 1/48, MIB (sealed), G5 ....**$100.00**
Monogram, Battlestar Galactica, Cylon Raider #6026, 1979, 1/48, MIB (sealed), G5 ....**$90.00**
Monogram, Battlestar Galactica #6027, 1978, 1/24, MIB, G5...**$100.00**
Monogram, Battlestar Galactica #6028, 1979, MIB, G5 .**$200.00**
Monogram, Blue Thunder, Helicopter #6036, 1984, 1/32, MIB, G5 ....**$30.00**
Monogram, Buck Rogers, Marauder #6031, 1979, M (EX+ sealed box), D9 ....**$33.00**
Monogram, Buck Rogers (TV), Starfighter #6030, 1979, 1/48, MIB, G5 ....**$70.00**
Monogram, Dracula #6008, 1983, 1/8, MIB, G5..............**$45.00**
Monogram, Frankenstein #6007, 1983, 1/8, MIB, G5 ......**$70.00**
Monogram, Go Bots, Buggyman #6067, 1984, MIB (sealed), G5...**$12.00**
Monogram, Go Bots, Cy-Kill #6202, 1984, 1/12, MIB, G5 ....**$40.00**

Monogram, Godzilla, 1978, glow-in-the-dark, NM (EX box), A $85.00
Monogram, Heritage Edition, Apollo Spacecraft #6061, 1984, 1/32, MIB, G5 ....$30.00
Monogram, Heritage Edition, Apollo-Saturn V Rocket #6051, 1983, 1/144, MIB, G5 ....$25.00
Monogram, Kingfisher Navy Catapult Plane, 1966, MIB, P3 ....$20.00
Monogram, Mack Bulldog Stake Truck, 1973, NM (EX box), D9 ....$43.00
Monogram, Miami Vice, Daytona Spyder #2737, 1986, 1/24, MIB (sealed), G5 ....$18.00
Monogram, Miami Vice, Ferrari Testarossa #2756, 1987, 1/24, MIB (sealed), G5 ....$20.00
Monogram, Mummy #6010, 1983, 1/8, MIB (sealed), G5 ..$25.00
Monogram, NASA Space Shuttle #5904, 1986, 1/72, MIB, G5 ....$25.00
Monogram, Paddy Wagon Show Car, 1991, reissue, 1/24, MIB, P3 ....$15.00
Monogram, Rambo, Chopper & Riverboat #6039, 1985, 1/48, MIB (sealed), G5 ....$30.00
Monogram, Rambo, Combat Chopper #6038, 1985, 1/24, MIB (sealed), G5 ....$40.00
Monogram, Rascal Missile #42, 1958, 1/48, MIB, G5 ....$400.00
Monogram, Simon & Simon, Z-28 Camero #1407, 1981, 1/24, MIB (sealed), G5 ....$30.00
Monogram, Space Buggy #194, 1969, 1/48, MIB, G5 .....$100.00
Monogram, Spiked Dinosaur #6042, 1979, 1/13, MIB (sealed), G5 ....$16.00
Monogram, Tyrannosaurus Rex #6077, 1987, 1/13, MIB, G5 ..$25.00
Monogram, US Missile Arsenal #40, 1958, 1/128, MIB, G5 .$210.00
Monogram, Wolfman #6009, 1983, 1/8, MIB (sealed), G5 .....$60.00
Monogram, Wooly Mammoth #6041, 1979, 1/13, MIB, G5 ...$30.00
Monogram, Wooly Mammoth #6075, 1987, 1/13, MIB (sealed), G5 ....$30.00
Monogram, Young Astronauts, Apollo Command Module #5902, 1986, 1/32, MIB, G5 ....$30.00
Monogram, Young Astronauts, Apollo Saturn V Rocket #5903, 1986, 1/144, MIB (sealed), G5 ....$30.00
Monogram, Young Astronauts, First Lunar Landing #5901, 1986, 1/48, MIB (sealed), G5 ....$15.00
Monogram, Young Astronauts, Mercury & Atlas Booster #5910, 1987, 1/110, MIB (sealed), G5 ....$50.00
Monogram, Young Astronauts, Mercury/Gemini Capsules #5909, 1987, 1/48, MIB (sealed), G5 ....$50.00
Monogram, Young Astronauts, Space Shuttle w/Booster #5900, 1988, 1/72, MIB (sealed), G5 ....$110.00
Monogram, Young Astronauts, X-15 Experimental Aircraft #5908, 1987, 1/72, MIB (sealed), G5 ....$20.00
Monstrology Models, Mad Monster, 1992, NMIB, A $75.00
MPC, Advanced Dungeons & Dragons, Dungeon Invaders #2102, 1982, MIB, G5 ....$28.00
MPC, Advanced Dungeons & Dragons, Orc War #2101, 1982, MIB (sealed), G5 ....$30.00
MPC, Alien (movie) #1961, 1979, orig issue, 1/10, MIB, G5 ....$70.00
MPC, Batman #1702, 1984, 1/8, MIB (sealed), G5 ....$50.00
MPC, Beatles Yellow Submarine, 1968, MIB (sealed), P3 ..$300.00
MPC, Black Hole, Cygnus Spaceship #1983, 1979, 1/4255, MIB (sealed), G5 ....$130.00
MPC, Black Hole, Maximillian Robot #1982, 1979, 1/12, MIB (sealed), G5 ....$45.00
MPC, Black Hole, V.I.N.Cent Robot #1981, 1979, M (EX sealed box), D9 ....$28.00
MPC, Cannonball Run, Emergency Van #447, 1981, 1/25, MIB (sealed), G5 ....$35.00
MPC, Cannonball Run, Lamborghini Countach #682, 1981, 1/25, MIB (sealed), G5 ....$35.00
MPC, CB Freak #778, 1975, MIB, G5 ....$50.00
MPC, Disney's Haunted Mansion, Escape From the Crypt #5053, 1974, 1/12, MIB, G5 ....$180.00
MPC, Disney's Haunted Mansion, Grave Robber's Reward #5050, 1974, 1/12, MIB, G5 ....$190.00
MPC, Disney's Haunted Mansion, Vampires Midnight Madness #5051, 1974, 1/12, MIB, G5 ....$110.00
MPC, Disney's Pirates of the Caribbean, Dead Man's Raft #5005, 1972, 1/12, MIB, G5 ....$210.00
MPC, Disney's Pirates of the Caribbean, Fate of the Mutineers #5004, 1972, 1/12, MIB, G5 ....$120.00
MPC, Disney's Pirates of the Caribbean, Ghost of Treasure Guard #5006, 1972, 1/12, MIB, G5 ....$150.00
MPC, Dukes of Hazzard, Daisy's Jeep CJ #662, 1980, 1/25, MIB, G5 ....$50.00
MPC, Dukes of Hazzard, General Lee #3058, 1981, 1/16, MIB (sealed), G5 ....$120.00

Photo courtesy June Moon

MPC, Hot Curl the Surfer's Idol, 1960s, MIB, J6, $95.00.

MPC, Dukes of Hazzard, Rosco's Police Car #663, 1982, 1/25, MIB (sealed), G5 ....$55.00
MPC, Ed Roth's Mail Box Chopper #2400, 1/25, MIB, G5 ..$40.00
MPC, Glo Heads, Ape Man #303, 1975, 1/3, MIB, G5....$60.00
MPC, Happy Days, Fonz Dream Rod #635, 1976, 1/24, MIB (sealed), G5 ....$75.00
MPC, Hardcastle & McCormick, Coyote Super Sportcar #684, 1983, 1/25, MIB (sealed), G5 ....$35.00
MPC, Hardcastle & McCormick, Hardcastle's GMC Truck #450, 1984, 1/25, MIB (sealed), G5 ....$50.00
MPC, Hogan's Heroes, Jeep #402, 1968, 1/25, MIB, G5 ..$80.00
MPC, Hot Rodder Magazine's Tall T w/Stroker McGurk #102, 1964, MIB, G5 ....$130.00
MPC, Incredible Hulk #1932, 1979, 1/9, MIB (sealed), G5..$55.00
MPC, Incredible Hulk Van #3206, 1977, 1/32, MIB (sealed), G5..$16.00
MPC, Ironside's Van #3012, 1970, 1/20, MIB, G5 ....$80.00
MPC, Knight Rider, KITT #675, 1983, 1/25, MIB, G5....$50.00
MPC, Magic Bubble Radar Mast Patrol Boat, 1950s, M (worn box), P4..$55.00

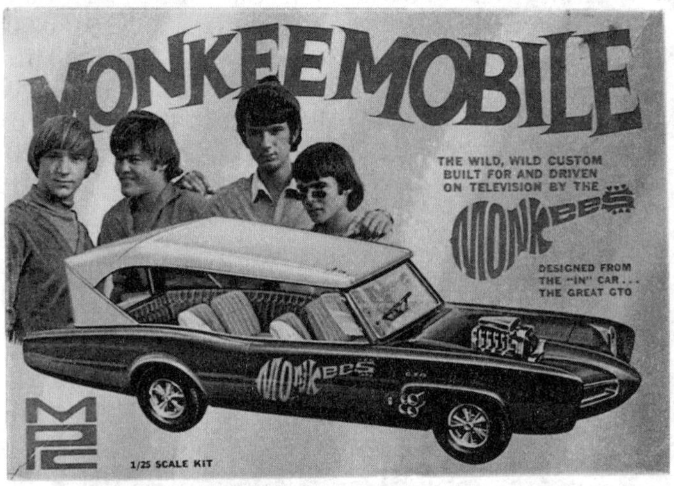

Photo courtesy Bob Gottuso

MPC, Monkeemobile, MIB, B3, $125.00.

MPC, Pilgrim Space Station #9001, 1970, 1/100, MIB, G5..$50.00
MPC, Russian Vostok RD-107 #9000, 1975, 1/100, MIB, G5..$90.00
MPC, Six Million Dollar Man, Bionic Bustout #601, 1975, 1/12, MIB, G5..$45.00
MPC, Six Million Dollar Man, Evil Rider #604, 1975, 1/12, MIB, G5..$55.00
MPC, Six Million Dollar Man #602, 1975, 1/12, MIB, G5..$50.00
MPC, Space: 1999, Alien Creature & Vehicle #1902, 1976, 1/25, MIB, G5..$50.00
MPC, Space: 1999, Eagle I Transporter #1901, 1975, 1/72, MIB, G5..$170.00
MPC, Space: 1999, Hawk Spaceship #1904, 1977, 1/72, MIB (sealed), G5..$160.00
MPC, Spider-Man #1931, 1978, 1/8, MIB (sealed), G5 ...$60.00
MPC, Star Wars, A-Wing Fighter #1973, 1983, 1/48, MIB (sealed), G5..$70.00
MPC, Star Wars, AT-AT #1918, 1981, 1/75, MIB (sealed), G5..$35.00
MPC, Star Wars, Boba Fett's Slave I #1919, 1982, 1/72, MIB (sealed), G5..$25.00
MPC, Star Wars, C-3PO #1913, 1977, orig issue, 1/8, MIB (sealed), G5..$35.00
MPC, Star Wars, C-3PO #1935, 1983, 1/8, MIB (sealed), G5..$30.00
MPC, Star Wars, Luke Skywalker Van, 1977, glow-in-the-dark decal sheet, partially assembled, VG+ box, A............$10.00
MPC, Star Wars, R2-D2 #1912, 1978, 1/8, MIB, G5 ....$50.00
MPC, Star Wars, R2-D2 #1934, 1983, 1/8, MIB (sealed), G5..$40.00
MPC, Star Wars, Shuttle Tydirium #1920, 1983, 1/100, MIB (sealed), G5..$25.00
MPC, Star Wars, Snowspeeder #1917, 1980, orig issue, 1/35, MIB, G5..$40.00
MPC, Star Wars, Y-Wing Fighter #1975, 1984, 1/72, MIB, G5..$60.00
MPC, Strange Changing, Mummy #902, 1974, 1/12, MIB (sealed), G5..$100.00
MPC, Strange Changing, Vampire #901, 1974, 1/12, MIB, G5..$120.00
MPC, Superman #1701, 1984, 1/8, MIB (sealed), G5 ......$60.00
MPC, Titan IIIC #1902, 1970, 1/100, MIB, G5 ....$130.00
MPC, TJ Hooker, Police Car #676, 1982, 1/25, MIB, G5 .$30.00
MPC, Welcome Back Kotter, Sweat Hogs Dream Machine, 1976, 1/25, M (NM sealed box), A $25.00
Nitto, Crusher Joe, Benz 600 SAE Air Car #23015, 1/60, MIB, G5..$15.00
Nitto, Crusher Joe, BMW-A795 Air Car #23016, 1/60, MIB, G5..$15.00
Nitto, Crusher Joe, Dongo Mabot #23001, 1/16, MIB, G5..$10.00
Nitto, Crusher Joe, Fighter 2 #23006, 1/144, MIB, G5.....$15.00
Nitto, Crusher Joe, Powered Suit #23004, 1/35, MIB, G5..$15.00
Nitto, Jerry Heavy Armored Fighting Suit #24110, 1980s, 1/20, MIB, G5..$60.00
Nitto, SF3D, Armored Fighting Suit (#1) #24097, 1980s, 1/20, MIB, G5..$50.00
Palmer, African Tribal Mask #711A, 1950s, MIB, G5 .....$70.00
Palmer, Animals of the World, African Lion #21, 1950s, MIB, G5..$40.00
Palmer, Animals of the World, Kodiak Bear #22, 1950s, MIB, G5..$30.00
Palmer, Animals of the World, White Tail Deer #25, 1950s, MIB, G5..$30.00
Palmer, Revolutionary War Cannon #34, 1950s, 1/24, MIB, G5..$20.00
Palmer, Spirit of '76 Diorama #76, 1950s, 1/24, MIB, G5..$95.00
Palmer, US Navy Vanguard Missile #106, 1958, 1/48, MIB, G5..$230.00
Paramount, Her Majesty's State Coach #1, 1960s, 1/30, MIB, G5..$25.00
Paramount, Lord Mayor of London's Coach #2, 1960s, 1/30, MIB, G5..$25.00
Paramount, Royal Barouche w/Coachmen #V2, 1960s, 1/30, MIB, G5..$30.00

Photo courtesy John and Sherri Pavone

Parks, Born Losers, Hitler, MIB, $50.00.

Plastic Age Concepts, Chiller Hand, 6", MIB, G5 ....**$35.00**
Plastic Age Concepts, The Incredible Mr Limpet (movie), Fish 'n Crab Diorama, MIB, G5 ....**$50.00**
Precision, Trophy Kit, Royal Bengal Tiger, 1958, M (EX+ box), D9 ....**$85.00**
Pyro, Burmese Paddy Boat #318, 1960s, 1/45, MIB, G5 ...**$20.00**
Pyro, Curler Surfcycle w/Figure #177, 1970, 1/8, MIB (sealed), G5 ....**$80.00**

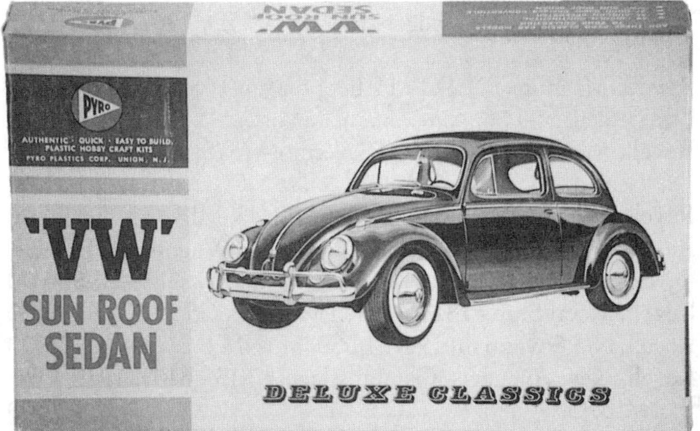

Pyro, Deluxe Classics, VW Sun Roof Sedan, MIB, $60.00.

Pyro, Gladiator 3-Wheel Sho-Cycle #175, 1970, 1/16, MIB (sealed), G5 ....**$55.00**
Pyro, Indian Chief #281, 1960s, 1/8, MIB, G5.................**$60.00**
Pyro, Indian Medicine Man #272, 1950s, 1/8, MIB, G5...**$70.00**
Pyro, Indian Medicine Man #282, 1960s, 1/8, MIB, G5...**$70.00**
Pyro, Indian Warrior #283, 1960s, 1/8, MIB, G5 ....**$50.00**
Pyro, Mark Trail's Nature Series, Mallard Duck #282, 1958, 10", MIB, G5 ....**$40.00**
Pyro, Peacemaker 45, 1960, 1/1, MIB (sealed), P4 ....**$100.00**
Pyro, Rawhide, Cowpuncher Gil Favor #276, 1958, 1/8, MIB, G5 ....**$80.00**
Pyro, Texas Cowboy #284, 1960s, 1/8, MIB, G5...............**$60.00**
Pyro, Wyatt Earp (TV), US Marshall Wyatt Earp #278, 1958, 1/8, MIB, G5...**$120.00**
Remco, Flintstones Paddy Wagon, 1961, plastic, battery-op, complete, EX (EX box), A **$185.00**
Renwal, Senses (The), 1960s, M (EX+ sealed box), D9...**$45.00**
Resin From the Grave, Plan 9 From Outer Space, Inspector Clay, 1990, M (EX box), A **$110.00**
Revell, Aerobee Hi Research Rocket #1814, 1958, 1/40, MIB, G5 ....**$90.00**
Revell, Alien Invader #8001, 1979, w/lights, 1/144, MIB (sealed), G5 ....**$45.00**
Revell, Apollo Astronaut on Moon #1860, 1970, 1/10, MIB, G5 ....**$100.00**
Revell, Apollo Columbia/Eagle #1862, 1969, MIB (sealed), G5 ....**$45.00**
Revell, Apollo Lunar Spacecraft #1838, 1969, MIB (sealed), G5 ....**$175.00**
Revell, Apollo-Soyuz Link-up #1800, 1975, 1/96, MIB (sealed), G5 ....**$80.00**
Revell, Apollo-Soyuz-Club Box #1800, 1975, 1/96, partially assembled, G5 ....**$30.00**
Revell, Ariane 4 Rocket #4762, 1985, 1/144, MIB, G5....**$35.00**
Revell, Astronaut in Space #1841, 1968, 1/12, MIB, G5 .**$25.00**
Revell, Bomarc Missile #1806, 1957, 1/47, MIB, G5........**$80.00**
Revell, Bonanza, Ben, Hoss & Little Joe #1931, 1966, 1/7, MIB, G5 ....**$160.00**
Revell, CHiPs, Helicopter #6102, 1980, M (NM sealed box), A...**$23.00**
Revell, CHiPs, Kawasaki #7800, 1980, 1/12, MIB (sealed), G5..**$30.00**
Revell, CHiPs, Ponch's Firebird #6226, 1981, 1/25, MIB (sealed), G5 ....**$30.00**
Revell, Code Red, Emergency Van #6029, 1981, 1/32, MIB (sealed), G5 ....**$20.00**
Revell, Code Red, Fire Chief's Car #6030, 1981, 1/32, MIB, G5 ....**$20.00**
Revell, Corporal Missile #1820, 1958, 1/40, MIB, G5....**$100.00**
Revell, Disney's Robin Hood Set (#1) #945, 1974, MIB (sealed), G5 ....**$70.00**
Revell, Disney's The Love Bug Rides Again #1326, 1974, 1/25, MIB, G5...**$100.00**
Revell, Douglas DC-7 United, 1974, MIB (sealed), P3 .....**$25.00**
Revell, Dune, Ornithopter #1775, 1985, MIB (sealed), G5 ....**$60.00**
Revell, Dune, Sand Worm #1778, 1985, 1/300, MIB, G5 ..**$70.00**
Revell, Ed 'Big Daddy' Roth, Brother Ratfink on a Bike #1304, 1964, MIB, G5...**$100.00**
Revell, Ed 'Big Daddy' Roth, Dragnut #1303, 1963, MIB, G5 ....**$80.00**

Revell, Ed 'Big Daddy' Roth, Fink Eliminator #6196, 1990, MIB (sealed), G5 ....$60.00
Revell, Ed 'Big Daddy' Roth, Mr Gasser #6197, 1990, MIB (sealed), G5 ....$55.00
Revell, Ed 'Big Daddy' Roth, Rat Fink #1305, 1963, assembled, MIB, G5 ....$40.00
Revell, Ed 'Big Daddy' Roth, Rat Fink #6199, 1990, MIB (sealed), G5 ....$55.00

Photo courtesy Martin and Carolyn Berens

Revell, Ed 'Big Daddy' Roth, Road Agent, MIB, $55.00.

Revell, Ed 'Big Daddy' Roth, Surf Fink #6198, 1990, MIB (sealed), G5 ....$70.00
Revell, Endangered Animals, California Condor #6462, 1991, 15", MIB (sealed), G5....................$25.00
Revell, Endangered Animals, Gorilla #6463, 1991, 7", MIB (sealed), G5 ....$30.00
Revell, Endangered Animals, Komodo Dragon #6461, 1991, 10", MIB (sealed), G5 ....$30.00
Revell, Endangered Animals, Northern White Rhino #6460, 1991, 10", MIB (sealed), G5....................$25.00
Revell, Endangered Animals, Polar Bear #6464, 1991, 9", MIB, G5 ....$45.00
Revell, Evil Eye, 1980, glow-in-the-dark, M (VG sealed box), A....................$35.00
Revell, Flash Gordon & the Martian #1450, 1965, 1/8, MIB, G5....................$170.00

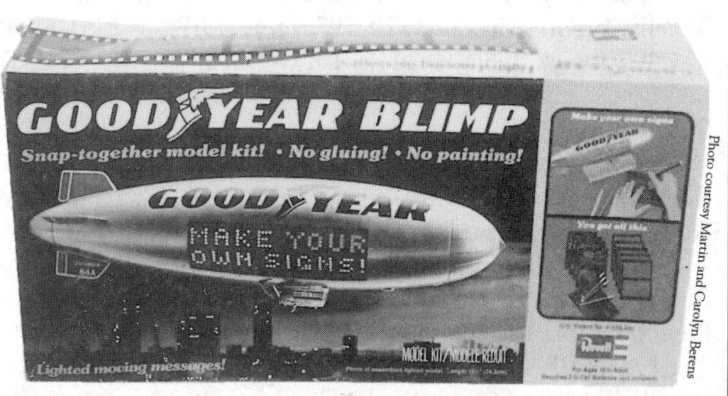

Photo courtesy Martin and Carolyn Berens

Revell, Goodyear Blimp #99000, 1975, MIB, $35.00.

Revell, Friskie the Beagle Puppy #1902, 1958, 1/1, M (G- box), G5 ....$55.00
Revell, Happy Days, '29 Model A Pickup #7374, 1982, 1/25, MIB, G5 ....$30.00
Revell, Hardy Boys Van #1398, 1977, 1/25, MIB (sealed), G5....................$40.00
Revell, Historic PT-109, 1963, 1/72, EX (EX box), A......$30.00
Revell, History Makers, Apollo Saturn-5 Rocket #8605, 1982, 1/96, MIB, G5....................$150.00
Revell, History Makers, Bomarc 1M-99 #8602, 1982, 1/47, MIB, G5 ....$30.00
Revell, History Makers, German V-2 Missile #8601, 1982, 1/54, MIB (sealed), G5 ....$16.00
Revell, History Makers, Jupiter C #8646, 1983, 1/110, MIB (sealed), G5 ....$60.00
Revell, History Makers, Nike Hercules #8613, 1982, 1/40, MIB (sealed), G5 ....$35.00
Revell, History Makers, North American X-15 NASA #8610, 1982, 1/64, MIB, G5 ....$25.00
Revell, History Makers, Terracruzer & Mace Missile #8628, 1982, 1/32, MIB, G5 ....$60.00
Revell, Hunt for the Red October, F/A-18 Hornet #4704, 1990, 1/48, MIB (sealed), G5 ....$15.00
Revell, Incredible Flying Machine, 1980, M (EX sealed box), D9....................$35.00
Revell, Jacques Cousteau, PBY Flying Boat #576, 1976, 1/72, MIB, G5....................$30.00
Revell, James Bond 007, Moonraker Space Shuttle #4306, 1979, M (VG+ sealed box), D9....................$23.00
Revell, John Travolta's 1979 Pontiac Firebird #1387, 1979, 1/25, MIB, G5 ....$35.00
Revell, Jupiter C, History Makers Series II, 1983 reissue, 1/110, MIB (sealed), P4....................$50.00
Revell, Jupiter Missile w/Truck & Trailer, 1958, 1/110, MIB, P4 ....$185.00
Revell, Lacross Missile #1816, 1958, 1/40, MIB, G5 ......$200.00
Revell, Laser Battle Stations #4534, 1984, 1/144, MIB, G5 ....$30.00
Revell, Los Angeles Dodgers Electra #255D, 1962, 1/15, MIB, G5 ....$240.00
Revell, Magnum PI, TC's Helicopter #4416, 1981, 1/32, MIB (sealed), G5 ....$26.00
Revell, Magnum PI, 308 GTS Ferrari #7378, 1982, 1/24, MIB (sealed), G5 ....$20.00
Revell, Mercury/Gemini #1834, 1964, 1/48, MIB, G5......$70.00
Revell, Miniature Masterpieces, Chuck Wagon #507, 1954, 1/48, MIB, G5....................$26.00
Revell, Moon Ship #1825, 1957, 1/96, MIB, G5 ....$140.00
Revell, N/S Savannah, 1960, 1/380, M (NM box), P4.....$75.00
Revell, New Avengers, Gambit's Jaguar XJS #6403, 1979, 1/25, MIB, G5 ....$35.00
Revell, Northrop Snark Missile #1801, 1957, 1/96, MIB, G5 ....$50.00
Revell, Penny Pincher VW Bug, 1980, M (NM sealed box), D9....................$35.00
Revell, Phantom w/Witch Doctor #1451, 1965, 1/8, MIB, G5 ....$110.00
Revell, Robocop, Axoid #1403, 1984, 1/72, MIB, G5......$50.00

Revell, Robotech, Commando #1199 (lg), 1984, 1/48, MIB (sealed), G5 ....$50.00
Revell, Robotech, Nebo #1400, 1984, 1/72, MIB, G5 ......$20.00
Revell, Robotech, Orbot #1401, 1984, 1/72, MIB (sealed), G5 ....$25.00
Revell, Robotech, Sniper Squad 2-in-1 Kit #1139, 1/170, MIB, G5 ....$25.00
Revell, Robotech, Space Fortress SDF1 #1144, 1985, 1/5000, MIB, G5 ....$60.00
Revell, Robotech, Trigon #1405, 1985, 1/48, MIB, G5....$30.00
Revell, Robotech, Vexar #1402, 1984, 1/72, MIB (sealed), G5 ....$30.00
Revell, Robotech, VF-1D Guardian #1408, 1985, 1/100, MIB (sealed), G5 ....$35.00
Revell, Robotech, VF-1J Fighter #1406, 1985, 1/100, MIB, G5....................$45.00
Revell, Robotech, VF-1S Battloid #1407, 1985, 1/100, MIB, G5....................$30.00
Revell, Saint's Jaguar XJS #6402, 1979, 1/25, MIB, G5....$25.00
Revell, Sand Crawler #1776, 1985, 1/25, MIB (sealed), G5....................$50.00
Revell, Search Patrol 2-in-1 Kit #1140, 1984, 1/170, MIB, G5 ....$25.00
Revell, Space Explorer Solaris #1851, 1969, 1/160, MIB, G5....................$120.00
Revell, Space Pursuit #1850, 1969, MIB, G5..................$240.00
Revell, Space Shuttle Challenger #C4526, 1982, 1/32, MIB, G5....................$20.00
Revell, Space Transport Sanger #4804, 1991, 1/288, MIB (sealed), G5 ....$35.00
Revell, Stingray (TV), Stingray Corvette Coupe #7377, 1987, 1/25, MIB (sealed), G5 ....$30.00
Revell, Terrier Missile #1813, 1958, 1/40, MIB, G5.......$200.00
Revell, US Army Hawk Missile, 1958, 1/40, MIB, G5...$170.00
Revell, US Army Nike Hercules #1804, 1958, 1/40, MIB, G5 ....$60.00
Revell, USN Bendix Talos Missile #1808, 1957, 1/40, MIB, G5 ....$80.00
Revell, VF-1A Fighter #1409, 1985, 1/100, MIB (sealed), G5 ....$40.00
Revell, X-17 Research Missile #1810, 1957, 1/40, MIB, G5...$65.00
Revell, XSL091 Manned Spaceship #1800, 1957, 1/96, partially assembled, G5 ....$400.00
Revell, 1941 (movie), P-40 Flying Tiger #4506, 1979, 1/32, MIB (sealed), G5 ....$40.00
Screamin', Advanced Dungeons & Dragons, Red Dragon of Krynn #4100, 1992, 1/15, MIB, G5 ....$70.00
Screamin', Air Assault Martian #4030, 1995, 1/8, MIB, G5.$50.00
Screamin', Army of Darkness (movie), Ash #1100, 1993, 1/4, MIB, G5 ....$70.00
Screamin', Bettie Page-Jungle Fever #5300, 1994, 1/6, MIB, G5....................$85.00
Screamin', Contemplating Conquest #4040, 1995, 1/8, M, G5....................$45.00
Screamin', Halloween (movie), Michael Myers #1600, 1996, 1/6, assembled, G5 ....$30.00
Screamin', Hellraiser (movies), Chatter Cenobite #800, 1991, 1/4, MIB, G5 ....$50.00
Screamin', Hellraiser (movies), Mystery Box #9100, 1/1, MIB, G5 ....$40.00
Screamin', Hellraiser (movies), Pinhead Cenbite #500, 1989, 1/4, MIB, G5 ....$80.00
Screamin', Mars Attacks, Attacking Martian, 1995, 1/8, M, G5 ....$40.00
Screamin', Mars Attacks, No Place To Hide, 1/8, assembled, G5....................$50.00
Screamin', Mars Attacks, Target Earth, 1/8, assembled, G5 ....$30.00
Screamin', Mary Shelley's Frankenstein #1400, 1994, 1/4, assembled, G5 ....$30.00
Screamin', Rocketeer #2100, 1991, 1/4, MIB, G5 ....$140.00
Screamin', Slaughter in the Streets, 1/8, assembled, G5...$50.00
Screamin', Star Wars, Boba Fett #3800, 1994, 1/4, MIB, G5 ....$50.00
Screamin', Star Wars, C-3PO #3500, 1993, 1/4, MIB, G5..$45.00
Screamin', Star Wars, Stormtrooper #3600, 1993, 1/4, MIB, G5 ....$45.00
Screamin', Suburban Commando, General Suitor Mutant #3100, 1991, 1/4, MIB, G5 ....$55.00
Strombecker, Disney's Man in Space, RM-1 Rocketship #D34, 1957, 1/72, MIB, G5....................$300.00
Strombecker, Disney's Man in Space, Satellite Launcher #D35, 1957, 1/262, MIB, G5....................$180.00
Strombecker, Disneyland Stagecoach #D28, 1950s, MIB, G5....................$210.00
Strombecker, Lunar Recon Vehicle #D37, 1958, 1/91, MIB, G5....................$180.00
Takara, Crusher Joe, Hunter Diskhound #443006, 1/25, MIB, D5....................$20.00
Takara, Dougram/Sun Fang, Combat Vehicle Set #440024, 1980s, 1/72, MIB, G5....................$10.00
Testors, Ares S4 UFO Revealed #576, 1994, 1/48, MIB (sealed), G5 ....$15.00
Testors, Davey the Cyclist #731, 1993, MIB (sealed), G5..$15.00
Testors, Grey Extraterrestrial #761, 1995, 1/6, MIB (sealed), G5 ....$12.00
Testors, Grodies! (Weird-Ohs), Flameout Freddie #533, 1983, MIB, G5....................$10.00
Testors, Grodies! (Weird-Ohs), Steel Pluckers #547, 1983, MIB, G5 ....$50.00
Testors, Top Gun, A-4 Aggressor #291, 1987, 1/48, MIB, G5....................$10.00
Testors, Weird-Ohs, Beach Bunny Catchin' Rays #751, 1994, MIB (sealed), G5 ....$30.00
Testors, Weird-Ohs, Daddy the Suburbanite #732, 1993, MIB (sealed), G5 ....$20.00
Testors, Weird-Ohs, Digger/Way-Out Dragster #730, 1993, MIB, G5....................$10.00
Testors, Weird-Ohs, Endsville Eddie #737, 1993, MIB (sealed), G5 ....$35.00
Tomy, Lensman, Boskone Fighter Goblin #7204, 1/72, MIB, G5....................$40.00
Tomy, Lensman, Cycroader II Spacecraft #7202, 1984, 1/72, MIB, G5 ....$40.00
Tomy, Lensman, Galactic Fighter Striker I #7201, 1/72, MIB, G5 ....$40.00

Tomy, Lensman, Grappler & Shuttle Truck #7203, 1984, 1/72, MIB, G5 ....$40.00
Toy Biz, Ghost Rider #48660, 1996, MIB, G5 ....$30.00
Toy Biz, Incredible Hulk #48656, 1996, MIB (sealed), G5 ....$25.00
Toy Biz, Silly Surfer #48653, 1996, MIB (sealed), G5 ......$30.00
Toy Biz, Spider-Man-Level One #48651, 1996, MIB (sealed), G5 ....$20.00
Toy Biz, Storm #48659, 1996, MIB (sealed), G5 ....$30.00
Toy Biz, Thing #48652, 1996, MIB (sealed), G5 ....$20.00
Toy Biz, Venom #48654, 1996, MIB (sealed), G5 ....$25.00
Toy Biz, Wolverine #48657, 1996, MIB (sealed), G5 ....$300.00
Tsukuda, Alien, Chest Buster #SVM31, 1995, 1/1, MIB, G5 ....$100.00
Tsukuda, Frankenstein #38, 1985, 1/6, MIB, G4 ....$110.00
Tsukuda, Ghostbusters, Stay Puft Man (sm), 1984, MIB, G5 ....$40.00
Tsukuda, Ghostbusters, Terror Dog #16, 1984, 1/6, MIB, G5 ....$120.00
Union, Shuttle Challenger #16, 1980s, 1/288, MIB (sealed), G5 ....$10.00
Union, Shuttle Columbia #14, 1981, 1/288, MIB (sealed), G5 ....$10.00
UPC, State Coach of England, 1960s, w/8 horses & 6 figures, 1/40, NM (EX box), D9 ....$23.00
Wave, Gargantuas Sandra vs Gaira, NM (EX box), A...$110.00

Movie Posters and Lobby Cards

This field is a natural extension of the interest in character collectibles, and one where there is a great deal of activity. There are tradepapers that deal exclusively with movie memorabilia, and some of the larger auction galleries hold cataloged sales on a regular basis. The hottest genre right now is the monster movies, but westerns and Disney films are close behind.

Advisors: John and Sheri Pavone (P3).

A Man Called Flintstone, 1966, insert, 36x14", rolled, NM, P3 ....$50.00
Addams Family, 1991, 41x27", rolled, NM, P3 ....$12.00
Adventures of Captain Marvel, Chapter 1 — Curse of the Scorpion, lobby card, 1941, 11x14", EX, A $450.00
Alien 3, 1992, 41x27", rolled, NM, P3 ....$15.00
Aristocats, lobby card (Mexican), 1960s, 13x16", EX, A .$25.00
Atom Man Vs Superman Into the Empty Doom, lobby card, 1950s, 11x14", EX, A $150.00
Babes in Toyland, 1961, 41x27", rolled, EX, P3 ....$35.00
Battle for the Planet of the Apes, 1973, 40x30", rolled, EX, P3 ....$50.00
Bedknobs & Broomsticks, 1971, 41x27", NM, P3 ....$30.00
Ben, 1972, 28x22", EX, P3 ....$20.00
Beneath the Planet of the Apes, 1970, 41x27", EX, P3 ....$50.00
Beverly Hillbillies, 1993, 41x27", rolled, NM, P3 ....$10.00
Big Top Pee Wee, 1988, 41x27", rolled, NM, P3 ....$20.00
Billy the Kid Meets Dracula/Jesse James Meets Frankenstein's Daughter, 1965, 41x27", EX, P3 ....$55.00

Photo courtesy John and Sheri Pavone

Beast From Haunted Cave, 1959, lobby card, NM, P3, $15.00.

Captain Marvel — The Guillotine, lobby card, 1941, 11x14", EX, J5 ....$85.00
Captain Midnight — Menacing Fates, lobby card, 1942, 11x14", EX, J5 ....$85.00
Chitty-Chitty Bang-Bang, 1968, 41x27", EX, P3 ....$35.00
Conquest of the Planet of the Apes, 1972, 60x40", rolled, NM, P3 ....$85.00
Count Dracula & His Vampire Bride, 41x27", EX+, P3 ...$40.00
Creature Walks Among Us, lobby card, 1956, 11x14", EX, A $100.00
Curse of the Mummy's Tomb, 1964, 41x27", VG, P3.......$25.00
Dick Tracy Vs Phantom Empire, 1952, 1-sheet, NM, D11 ..$100.00
Dick Tracy's Dilema, lobby card, 1947, 11x14", EX, from $75 to $100.00
Dick Tracy's G-Men, lobby card, 1955, 11x14", M, D11..$40.00
Empire of the Ants, 1977, 41x27", EX, P3 ....$20.00
Escape From the Planet of the Apes, 1971, 41x27", EX, P3 .$55.00
Flipper, 1963, 41x27", EX, P3 ....$30.00
Frankenstein Created Woman/Mummy's Shroud, 1967, 41x27", EX, P3 ....$45.00
Freddy's Dead — The Final Nightmare, 1991, 41x27", rolled, NM, P3 ....$15.00
Godzilla Vs the Smog Monster, 1972, 41x27", EX, P3 .....$60.00
Golden Eye, 41x27", rolled, NM, P3 ....$15.00
Gone With the Wind, 1974 reissue, rolled, 40x30", NM, from $75 to $100.00
Grease, 1978, 41x27", EX, P3 ....$45.00
Green Hornet Strikes Again — Blazing Fury, lobby card, 1940, 11x14", EX, A $80.00
Halloween II, 1981, 41x27", EX, P3 ....$45.00
Hold On, 1966, 41x27", rare, VG+, P3 ....$45.00
It's Alive, 1974, 41x27", EX, P3 ....$20.00
Jewel of the Nile, 1985, 41x27", EX, P3 ....$15.00
King Kong, 1976, 41x27", EX+, P3 ....$40.00
King Kong Escapes, 1968, 41x27", NM, P3 ....$110.00
Last Action Hero, 1993, 41x27", rolled, NM, P3 ....$10.00
Lion King, 41x27", rolled, M, P3 ....$45.00

Lion King Happy Holidays, insert, 22x17", NM, P3 ....$10.00
Love Bug, 1969, 41x27", EX, F8 ....$20.00
McHale's Navy, 1964, 41x27", EX, P3 ....$55.00
McHale's Navy Joins the Air Force, 1965, 41x27", VG+, P3 ...$30.00
Munsters Go Home, lobby card (Mexican), 1960s, 13x16", EX, A $40.00
New Adventures of Batman & Robin — The Wizard Strikes Back!, lobby card, 1949, 11x14", EX, A.........$150.00
Pocahontas, 41x27", NM, P3.........$45.00
Purple Monster Strikes Again — Man in the Meteor, lobby card, 1940s, 11x14", EX, from $75 to.........$100.00
Return From Witch Mountain, 1978, 41x27", EX+, P3 ...$25.00

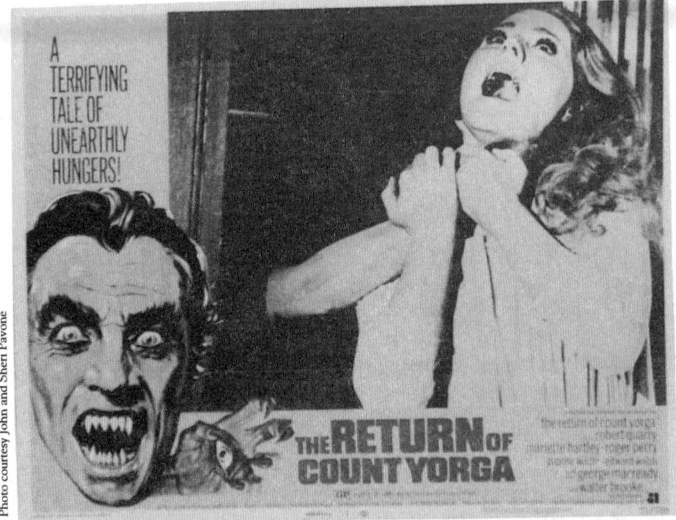

Photo courtesy John and Sheri Pavone

Return of Count Yorga, 1971, lobby card set, NM, $45.00.

Tarzan the Fearless, 1933, linen-backed, 41x27", NM, A, $800.00.

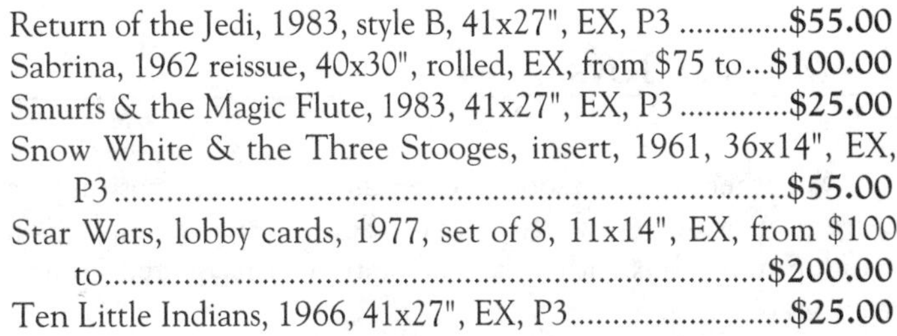
Return of the Jedi, 1983, style B, 41x27", EX, P3 ....$55.00
Sabrina, 1962 reissue, 40x30", rolled, EX, from $75 to...$100.00
Smurfs & the Magic Flute, 1983, 41x27", EX, P3 ....$25.00
Snow White & the Three Stooges, insert, 1961, 36x14", EX, P3 ....$55.00
Star Wars, lobby cards, 1977, set of 8, 11x14", EX, from $100 to.........$200.00
Ten Little Indians, 1966, 41x27", EX, P3.........$25.00

Photo courtesy John and Sheri Pavone

The Beast Must Die, 1974, lobby card set, NM, $40.00.

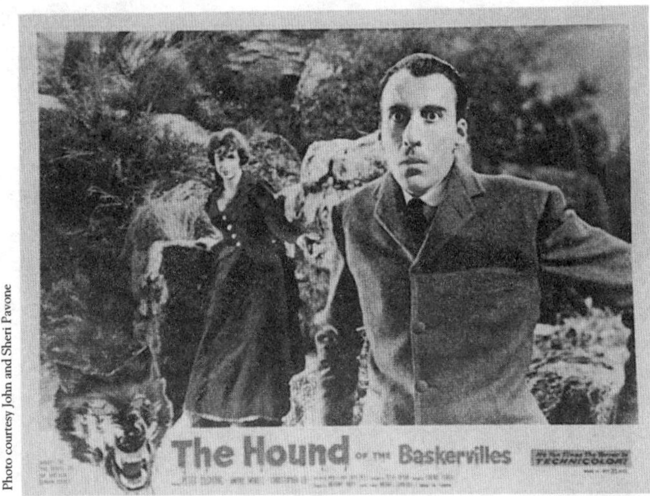

Photo courtesy John and Sheri Pavone

The Hound of the Baskervilles, 1959, lobby card, EX, P3, $20.00.

Time Machine, 1972, reissue, 41x27", EX, P3 ....$30.00
Tom & Jerry Festival of Fun, 1962, 1-sheet, 41x27", EX, J5..$125.00
Total Recall, 1990, 41x27", EX+, P3.........$15.00
Trail of Robin Hood, lobby card (Mexican), 1950s, 12x16", EX, J5 ....$35.00
Who Slew Auntie Roo?, 1971, 41x27", EX, P3.........$30.00
Who's Harry Crumb, 1988, 41x27", NM, P3 ....$10.00
Young Frankenstein, 1974, 41x27", EX, P3.........$55.00
101 Dalmatians, lobby card (Mexican), 1950s, 13x16", EX, A $25.00

Musical Toys

Whether meant to soothe, entertain, or inspire, musical toys were part of our growing-up years. Some were as simple as a windup music box, others as elaborate as a lacquered French baby grand piano.

See also Disney; Character, TV, and Movie Collectibles.

Accordion, Everest, 1940s, 5x6", NMIB $50.00
Accordion, Hohner, 2-octave, leatherette case, 10", EX ..$235.00
Chime, Chein, 1920s-30s, litho tin w/various images of children w/animals, EX $100.00
Drum, Donaldson Bros, c 1894, paper litho image of 6 Brownies in band on wooden drum, 8x10" dia, EX $975.00
Drum, mk Nonpariel, tin, images of Admiral's Flagship & Armored Aeroplane, 5¼" dia, VG $200.00
Drum, tin w/wood rims, Canadian flags w/crest on maple leaf background, metallic, 8" dia, VG $175.00
Drum, tin w/wood rims, children marching in patriotic parade, 8" dia, G $550.00
Drum, tin w/wood rims, litho paper inserts of Washington crossing the Delaware, 13" dia, VG $900.00
Drum, tin w/wood rims, Santa leading an animal orchestra, gold on red, 6" dia, VG $255.00
Drum, tin w/wood rims, Union Soldiers in battle, 13" dia, VG $500.00
Drum, wood veneer shell w/wood rims, images of various battleships, 10" dia, VG $550.00
Drum, wood veneer shell w/wood rims, oval images of cavalry officer, artillery, battleship, etc, 13" dia, EX $575.00

Drum, wood with image of children on parade, 10" dia, EX, A, $575.00.

Farmer in the Dell Music Maker, Mattel, 1950s, litho tin, crank operated, EX, J6 ....$125.00
Futureland Grand Piano #412, Mattel, 1948, red & yel plastic, 12x9", MIB $150.00
Golden Banjo, Emenee, 1960s, NMIB $125.00
Merry Music Box, Mattel, 1953, litho tin, 8x6½", NM $75.00
Musical Church, Reed, piano on 1 side, steeple on the other, 14x12½", VG, A $200.00
Piano, Schoenhut, wood w/image of cherubs & children dancing, 8 keys, EX $200.00
Toyland Band, Ohio Art, 1950s, tin drum set, 8", EX (EX box), A $55.00

Photo courtesy Martin and Carolyn Berens

Victrola, Atlas, with two double-sided picture disks, EX, B5, $125.00.

Whirl-A-Tune, Mattel, 1951, litho tin, MIB $75.00

Nodders

Nodders representing comic characters of the day were made in Germany in the 1930s. These were small doll-like figures approximately 3" to 4" tall, and the popular ones often came in boxed sets. But the lesser-known characters were sold separately, making them rarer and harder to find today. While the more common nodders go for $125.00 and under, The Old Timer, Widow Zander, and Ma and Pa Winkle often bring about $350.00 — Happy Hooligan even more, about $625.00. (We've listed the more valuable ones here; any German bisque nodder not listed is worth $125.00 or under.)

Advisor: Doug Dezso (D6).

See also Character Bobbin' Heads; Sports Collectibles.

Ambrose Potts, NM $350.00
Auntie Blossom, NM $150.00
Auntie Mamie, NM $350.00
Avery, NM $200.00
Bill, NM $200.00

Buttercup, NM, $250.00.

Chubby Chaney, NM $250.00
Corky, NM....$475.00
Dock, NM $200.00
Fanny Nebbs, NM....$250.00
Ferina, NM....$350.00
Grandpa Teen, NM $350.00
Happy Hooligan, NM $625.00
Harold Teen, NM....$150.00
Jeff Regus, med or lg, ea....$250.00
Jeff Regus, sm $175.00
Josie, NM $425.00
Junior Nebbs, NM....$575.00
Lilacs, NM $425.00
Lillums, NM....$150.00
Little Annie Roonie, movable arms, NM $250.00
Little Egypt, NM....$350.00
Lord Plushbottom, NM....$150.00
Ma & Pa Winkle, NM, ea $350.00
Marjorie, NM....$425.00
Mary Ann Jackson, NM $250.00
Max, NM $200.00
Min Gump, NM....$150.00
Mr Bailey, NM....$150.00
Mr Bibb, NM $400.00
Mr Wicker, NM....$250.00
Mushmouth, NM....$350.00
Mutt or Jeff, med or lg, NM, ea $250.00
Mutt or Jeff, sm, NM, ea....$175.00
Nicodemus, NM....$350.00
Old Timer, NM....$350.00
Our Gang, 6-pc set, MIB....$1,200.00
Pat Finnegan, NM $400.00
Pete the Dog, NM....$250.00
Pop Jenks, NM....$200.00

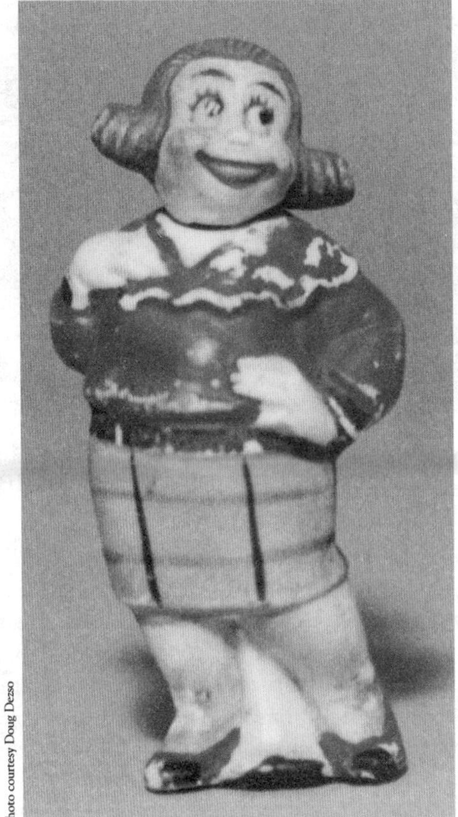

Patsy, NM, $425.00.

Rudy Nebbs, NM $250.00
Scraps, NM $250.00
Uncle Willie, NM....$350.00
Widow Zander, NM....$400.00
Winnie Winkle, NM $150.00

Optical Toys

Compared to the bulky viewers of years ago, contrary to the usual course of advancement, optical toys of more recent years have tended to become more simplified in concept.

See also View-Master and Tru-View.

Automatic Space Viewer, Stephens, 1950s, complete w/picture gun, theater & 7 films, EX....$175.00
Bionic Video Center, Kenner, 1976, shows movie w/hand-crank cassette, MIB, J6 ....$125.00
Charlie Chaplin Ombro-Cinema, France, 1900s, wood fr w/celluloid silhouette inserts, crank action, 12x18", EX, A $550.00
Columbus Lantern, Germany, pnt tin egg-shape w/eagle & lettered decals, kerosene lamp base, 10", EX, A $3,400.00
Easy-Show Movie Projector, Kenner, 1966, features various characters, complete, MIB, A....$150.00
Flashy Flickers Magic Picture Gun, Marx, complete w/projector & 4 films, EX (EX box), M17....$125.00
Flintstones Magic Movies, Embree, 1965, complete, scarce, NMIB....$250.00

Photo courtesy John and Sheri Pavone

Give-A-Show Projector, Kenner, 1969, features several characters, battery operated, complete, NMIB, $65.00.

Give-A-Show Projector Slides, Kenner, 1963, various characters, complete, NMIB, T2..$30.00
Jolly Theatre, 16mm projecter w/built-in screen, features Krazy Kat, Our Gang, Three Stooges, etc, NMIB, A $150.00
Komic Camera, features several comic characters, complete w/viewer & 3 films, EX (EX box), A.......................$140.00
Magic Lantern, Ernst Plank, tin w/CI feet, w/9 glass slides, EX (G wood box), A $135.00
Magic Lantern, Ernst Plank, tin w/CI feet, w/assorted glass slides, EX (G wood box), A...................................$165.00

Magic Lantern, JS, red painted tin with kerosene lamp base, extended lens and round colored glass slide, EX (VG wood box), A, $275.00; Magic Lantern, GVF, wood with tin roof, stack, and lenses, ornate cast iron feet, EX (G wood box), A, $350.00.

Magic Lantern, JS, tin w/CI feet, kerosene lamp w/glass chimney, projector lens & glass slides, 9", EX (G wood box), A $135.00
Magic Mirror, McLoughlin Bros, paper litho image appears on mercury glass tube, EX (EX wood box), A............$1,500.00
Movieland Drive-In Theater, Remco, 1959, complete, EX..$150.00
Movieland Drive-In Theatre, Remco, few pcs missing, EX (EX box)...$200.00
See-A-Show Viewer, Kenner, 1966, features Superman, complete, MIB (sealed), J5 ....$85.00
Three Stooges Jolly Theatre, Excel, 1947, complete, w/projector, film & uncut figures, EX (EX box), A......................$200.00
Top Cat Viewer, Marx, 1962, look through windows of house for colorful action scenes, plastic, EX (EX box), A.......$100.00

Paper Dolls

Turn-of-the-century paper dolls are seldom found today and when they are, they're very expensive. Advertising companies used them to promote their products, and some were printed on the pages of leading ladies' magazines. By the late 1920s most paper dolls were being made in book form — the doll on the cover, the clothes on the inside pages. Because they were so inexpensive, paper dolls survived the Depression and went on to peak in the 1940s. Though the advent of television caused sales to decline, paper doll companies were able to hang on by making paper dolls representing Hollywood celebrities and TV stars. These are some of the most collectible today. Even celebrity dolls from more recent years like the Brady Bunch or the Waltons are popular. Remember, condition is very important; if they've been cut out, even when they're still in fine condition and have all their original accessories, they're worth only about half as much as an uncut book or box set.

For more information, refer to *Price Guide to Lowe and Whitman Paper Dolls* by Mary Young, *Collecting Toys* by Richard O'Brien, and *Toys, Antique and Collectible*, by David Longest.

Advisor: Mary Young (Y2).

Airline Stewardess, Lowe #4913, 1957, uncut, M.............$35.00
Alice Faye, Merill #4800, 1941, uncut, M $300.00
Ann Sheridan, Whitman #986, 1944, uncut, from $150 to....$250.00
Ann Southern, Saalfield #2438, 1943, uncut, M............$150.00
Annie Oakley w/Tagg & Lofty, Whitman #2056, 1955, uncut, M...$70.00
Ava Gardner, Whitman #965, 1949, uncut, M $125.00
Baby Sparkle Plenty, Saalfield #2500, 1948, unpunched, NM, D11...$50.00
Badgett Quadruplets, Saalfield #2348, 1941, uncut, M ..$150.00
Betsy McCall Dress 'n Play, Standard Toycraft #801, uncut, EX, V2...$30.00
Betty Grable, Whitman #962, 1946, M $175.00
Bewitched, Magic Wand, 1965, cut, EX (EX box), F8......$55.00
Blondie, Whitman #2054, 1955, 8 pgs, uncut, M $80.00
Bob Cummings Fashion Models, Lowe #2407, 1957, uncut, M $65.00
Brady Bunch, Whitman #4784, 1972, uncut, boxed set, M .$20.00
Bride Doll, Lowe #1043, 1946, uncut, M $50.00
Campus Queens, Lowe #962, uncut, M...........................$18.00
Career Girls, Lowe #958, 1950, uncut, M $35.00
Carmen Miranda, Whitman #995, 1942, uncut, M........$175.00
Charlie Chaplin & Paulette Goddard, Saalfield #2356, 1941, uncut, M $300.00

Photo courtesy June Moon

Brady Bunch, Whitman #1976, 1973, uncut, M, from $50.00 to $65.00.

Photo courtesy Bill Bruegman

Buffy & Jody, Whitman #4764, 1970, NMIB, from $25.00 to $50.00.

Chatty Baby, Whitman #1872, 1963, partially punched out, EX, F8 ....$20.00

Cinderella, Saalfield #2590, 1950, uncut, M....................$75.00

Claudette Colbert Paper Dolls & Dresses, Saalfield #2503, 1945, uncut, M $150.00

Connie Francis, Whitman #1956, 1963, uncut, M $55.00

Cowboy Cut-Out Book, Lowe #537, 1943, stand-ups, M .$25.00

Cradle Crowd, Whitman #1173, 1948, uncut, M $50.00

Cuddles & Rags, Lowe #1283, 1950, uncut, M $50.00

Davy & Dorothy, Whitman #917, 1933, uncut, M..........$45.00

Deanna Durbin, Merrill #3480, 1940, uncut, M $150.00

Debutantes, Whitman #1013, 1942, uncut, M.................$35.00

Dolls of Many Lands, Whitman #3046, 1931, MIB $85.00

Dolly Jean Her Paper Doll House Furniture & Clothes, Saalfield #877, 1932, uncut, M $140.00

Doris Day Doll, Whitman #1977, 1957, magic stay-on clothes, uncut, M....................$90.00

Dorothy Provine, Whitman #1964, 1962, uncut, M.........$60.00

Down on the Farm, Lowe #1956, 1940s, uncut, M $25.00

Dream Girl, Merrill #3448, 1947, uncut, M......................$75.00

Dude Ranch, Lowe #L126, 1944, uncut, M......................$18.00

Evelyn Rudie, Saalfield #4425, 1958, uncut, NM, from $50 to $60.00

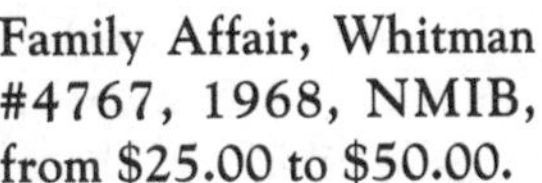
Family Affair, Whitman #4767, 1968, NMIB, from $25.00 to $50.00.

Photo courtesy Bill Bruegman

Fashion Previews, Lowe #1246, 1949, uncut, M $40.00

Faye Emerson, Saalfield #2722, 1952, uncut, NM, J5 ....$85.00

Ferdinand the Bull, Whitman #925, 1938, stand-ups, M, from $75 to $100.00
Flying Nun, Saalfield #5121, 1968, uncut, M $60.00
Gene Autry's Melody Ranch, Whitman #990, 1950, uncut, M $100.00
Gisele MacKenzie, Saalfield #4421, 1957, uncut, M....................$75.00
Green Acres, Whitman #4773, 1968, uncut, NMIB, P3 ..$75.00
Hayride, Lowe #1061, uncut, M $16.00
Hedy Lamarr, Merrill #3482, 1942, uncut, NM, from $150 to....................$200.00
Hee Haw, Saalfield #5139, uncut, M....................$45.00
Here Comes the Bride, Lowe #1053, uncut, M $30.00
Here's Sally/Here's Sunny, Whitman #915, 1939, uncut, M $75.00
Holidays Paper Dolls, Lowe #1326, uncut, M $18.00
Hollywood Personalities, Lowe, #1049, 1941, uncut, M.$300.00
Honeymooners, Lowe #2560, 1956, uncut, M $250.00
It's a Small World, Whitman #1981, 1966, unpunched, EX, F8 ....$20.00
Jane Whithers A-Big-As-Life Doll, Whitman #977, 1936, uncut, M....................$200.00
Janet Leigh, Lowe #2405, 1957, uncut, M....................$75.00
Janet Lennon, Whitman #1964, 1958, uncut, M....................$50.00
Janet Lennon, Whitman #4613, 1962, MIB $50.00
Jeanette MacDonald, Merrill #3460, 1941, uncut, M.....$250.00
Joan Carroll, Saalfield #2426, 1942, uncut, M....................$90.00
Judy Garland, Whitman #980, 1941, uncut, M $200.00
Judy Garland, Whitman #996, 1945, uncut, NM, A $250.00
Julie Andrews, Saalfield #4424, 1958, uncut, M....................$85.00
Kissy Paper Doll, Saalfield #1337, 1963, uncut, M $40.00
Let's Play House w/the Dionne Quints, Merrill #3500 (A,B,C,D, E), 1940, uncut, M, ea $80.00
Life Size Paper Doll, Whitman #958, 1936, uncut, M....$125.00
Little Dressmaker Doll Book (Patty), Lowe #1885, 1966, uncut, M....................$10.00
Little Lulu, Whitman #1971, 1971, uncut, NM, J5 ....$30.00
Little Orphan Annie Cut-Out Doll & Dresses, Gabriel/Harold Lloyd, cut, VG (VG box), A....................$200.00
Little Orphan Annie's Paper Dolls (Junior Commandos), Saalfield #2436, 1943, uncut, M $150.00
Lucille Ball, Desi Arnaz & Little Ricky, Whitman #2116, 1953, cut, complete, EX, F8....................$48.00
Lucille Ball & Desi Arnaz, Whitman #2106, 1953, cut, complete, EX, F8....................$40.00
Lucky Locket Kiddles Magic Paper Dolls, Whitman #4774, cut, MIB $25.00
Major Matt Mason, Whitman #1928, 1969, M....................$25.00
Margaret O'Brien, Whitman #964, 1946, uncut, M $100.00
Mary Martin, Saalfield #2492, 1944, uncut, NM, A.......$225.00
Mary Poppins, Whitman #1982, 1964, unused, NM, F8...$28.00
Mickey Mouse Cut-Out Doll Book, Saalfield #980, 1935-36, uncut, M $400.00
Mod Fashions Featuring Jane Fonda, Saalfield #4469, 1966, uncut, M....................$50.00
Mommy & Me, Saalfield #2424, 1943, uncut, M....................$40.00
Mommy & Me, Whitman #977, 1954, uncut, M....................$30.00
Mopsy & Popsy, Lowe #2713, 1971, uncut, M....................$10.00
Munsters, Whitman #1959, 1966, uncut, EX....................$100.00

Photo courtesy Cindy Sabulis

Magic Mary Ann, Milton Bradley #4010-2, 1950, NMIB, $25.00.

My Book of Paper Dolls, Saalfield #1171, 1920s-30s, red cover, uncut, M....................$75.00
Natalie Wood, Whitman #2086, 1958, uncut, M....................$125.00
National Velvet, Whitman #1948, 1962, uncut, M....................$50.00
New York World's Fair Goodwill Dolls, Whitman #6901, 1939, uncut, M $110.00
Partridge Family, Artcraft #5137, 1971, uncut, M, H4.....$50.00
Patsy Ann & Her Trunk Full of Clothes, Whitman #992, 1939, uncut, M $100.00
Patti Page, Lowe #2406, 1957, uncut, M....................$75.00
Patty Duke, Whitman #1141, 1960, uncut/uncolored, M.$30.00
Patty Duke Fashion Wardrobe, Whitman #4609, 1965, MIB .$50.00
Pebbles & Bamm-Bamm Magic Dolls, Whitman #4796, 1965, cut, NMIB, F8....................$30.00
Pepe & the Senoritas, Saalfield/Artcraft #4408, 1961, uncut, NM, from $50 to....................$60.00
Pepper Around-the-Clock Wardrobe, Whitman #4640, 1965, uncut, M....................$45.00
Peter & Pure, Lowe #528, 1942, uncut, M $12.00
Petunia & Patches, Saalfield #2160, 1937, uncut, M $175.00
Pixie Doll & Pup, Lowe #2764, uncut, M $35.00
Playmates, Lowe #123, uncut, M....................$25.00
Polly Patchwork & Her Friends, Lowe #1024, 1941, uncut, M $50.00
Princess Diana, Whitman #1530, 1985, uncut, M $40.00
Punky Brewster, Whitman #1532, 1986, uncut, M....................$10.00
Rainbow Dolls, Whitman #990, 1934, uncut, M $95.00
Riders of the West, Saalfield #2716, 1950, uncut, M........$35.00
Rita Hayworth (The Loves of Carmen), Saalfield #2712, 1948, uncut, M $125.00
Rita Hayworth Dancing Star, Merrill #3478, 1942, uncut, M....................$300.00
Roy Rogers & Dale Evans, Whitman #1172, 1952, uncut, M....................$100.00

Robin Hood and Maid Marian, Saalfield #2748, 1956, uncut, M, $75.00.

Roy Rogers & Dale Evans, Whitman #2197, 1952, stand-ups, uncut, M....$75.00
School Girl, Saalfield #2400, 1942, uncut, M....$40.00
Sharie Lewis, Saalfield #4447, 1958, uncut, M....$70.00
Sheree North, Saalfield #4420, 1957, uncut, NM....$90.00
Shirley Temple Dolls & Dresses, Saalfield #2112, 1934, uncut, M....$250.00
Shirley Temple In Paper Dolls (The New), Saalfield #2425, 1942, uncut, M....$200.00
Shirley Temple Standing Dolls, Saalfield #1715, 1935, uncut, M....$250.00
Soldiers & Sailors, Lowe #2573, 1943, stand-ups, M....$40.00
Sonja Henie, Merrill #3475, 1939, uncut, M....$275.00
Square Dance, Lowe #968, 1950, uncut, M....$25.00
Sunbonnet Sue, Lowe #521, 1943, uncut, M....$40.00
Sweet-Treat Kiddles, Whitman #1993, uncut, M....$50.00
Tammy & Her Family, Whitman #1997, 1964, uncut, M.$45.00
Tammy & Her Family, Whitman #4733, 1964, uncut, M.$45.00
Teen Shop, Saalfield #2701, 1948, uncut, M....$25.00
That Girl Starring Marlo Thomas, Saalfield #4479, 1967, uncut, M....$60.00
Toni Hair-Do Cut-Out Dolls, Lowe #1284, 1950, uncut, M..$65.00
Turnabout Dolls, Lowe #1025, 1943, uncut, M....$50.00
TV Style Show, Lowe #955, uncut, M....$35.00
Twins Bob & Jean, Lowe #128, 1944, uncut, M....$30.00
Tyrone Power & Linda Darnell, Merrill #3438, 1941, uncut, M....$275.00

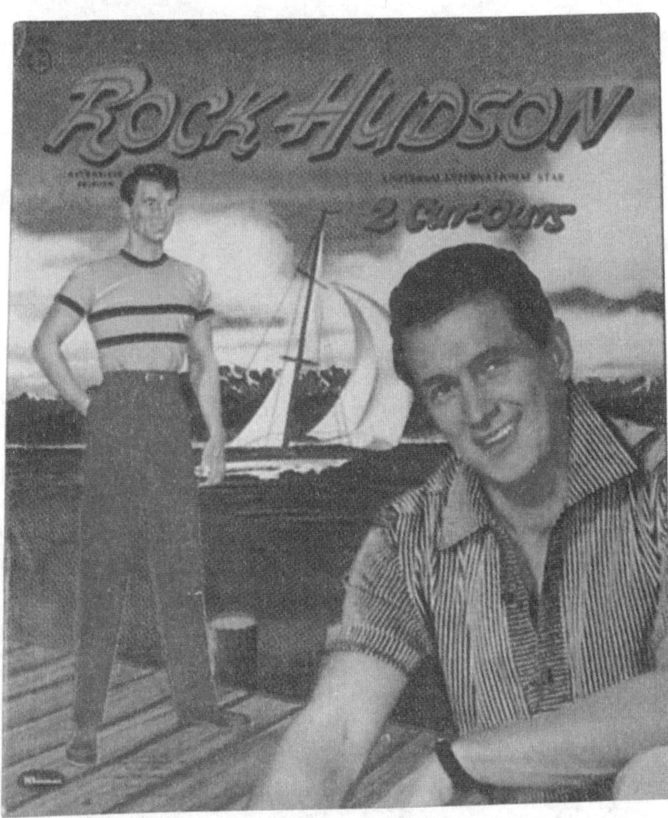

Rock Hudson, Whitman #2087, 1957, complete and uncut, NM, $65.00.

Wedding Party, Saalfield #2721, 1951, uncut, NM, $50.00.

Walt Disney Silly Symphony Cut-Out, Whitman #989, 1933, uncut, M $400.00
Walt Disney's Donald Duck & Clara Cluck, Whitman #969, 1937, uncut, M $450.00
Walt Disney's Sleeping Beauty, Whitman #1981, 1959, uncut, M....................$60.00
Wedding Dolls, Whitman #1953, 1958, uncut, M....................$40.00
Wedding Party, Lowe #1331, uncut, M....................$35.00
Ziegfield Girls, Merrill #3466, 1941, uncut, M $40.00

Paper-Lithographed Toys

Following the development of color lithography, early toy makers soon recognized the possibility of using this technology in their own field. Both here and abroad, by the 1880s toys ranging from soldiers to involved dioramas of entire villages were being produced of wood with colorful and well-detailed paper lithographed surfaces. Some of the best known manufacturers were Crandall, Bliss, Reed, and McLoughlin. This style of toy remained popular until well after the turn of the century.

Advisors: Mark and Lynda Suozzi (S24).

See Also Black Americana; Boats; Circus Toys; Dollhouses; Games; Musical Toys; Pull Toys; Puzzles and Picture Blocks.

Photo courtesy David Longest

Alphabet Blocks, 1890s, wood, VG, $50.00 each.

Baby's Rattle Blocks, Germany, set of 4, 4" sq, NMIB....$300.00
Brownie Blocks, McLoughlin/Palmer Cox, 1891, shows Brownies in various activities, set of 20, 11x13", EX $1,250.00
Clock Blocks, Strauss, 1904, learning clock reverses to months & seasons, 8½" sq, EX (EX cb box) $200.00
Columbus Blocks, McLoughlin, early 1900s, EX (VG box) $800.00
Converse Circus Acrobat Toy, ca 1885, stenciled paper & wood pull toy, 12", EX, S24 ....$825.00
Crandall's District School, ca 1876, pnt wood, 10 articulated students, teacher, desk & books, VG (VG hinged box), S24 ....$1,100.00
Crandall's Great Show, The Acrobats, 1875, complete, EX (EX box), from $1,000 to $1,150.00
Golden Letter Blocks, McLoughlin Bros, 18 blocks w/alphabet & images, 15x8x3", VG (VG wooden box)............$525.00
Little Wonder Trolley, Bliss, images of children at windows, 13", EX $1,250.00

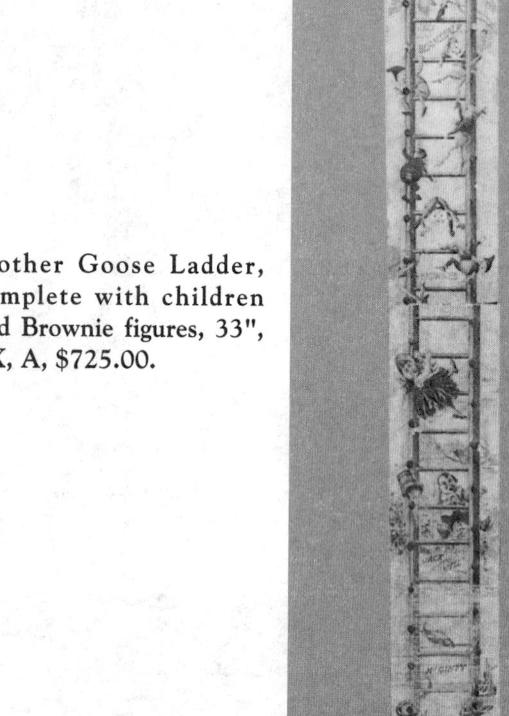

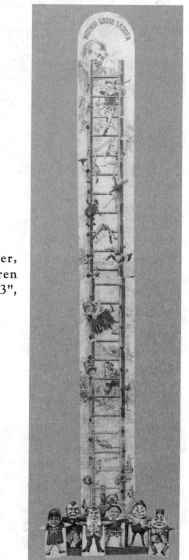

Mother Goose Ladder, complete with children and Brownie figures, 33", EX, A, $725.00.

Nesting Blocks, McLoughlin, ca 1890, alphabet letters w/pictorial nursery rhymes, stacks to 36", EX, S24 ....$1,900.00
Obleisk Alphabet Blocks, Pat 1882, letters over hieroglyphics & various animal scenes, set of 8, VG $1,100.00
Old Guard Soldiers, Ives, w/cannon, EX $1,300.00
Paddle Wheeler, colorful image of passengers waving, mk City of New York on side wheel, 19½", VG, A $225.00
Play & Learn Block Set, McLoughlin, 2-sided, set of 16, 7½" sq, EX (damaged box) $700.00
Pretty Village Boathouse Set, McLoughlin, ca 1898, EX (EX box) $150.00
Pretty Village Church Set, McLoughlin, ca 1898, EX (EX box) $150.00
Pretty Village Colonial Park, McLoughlin Bros, 1897 & 1900, EX (EX box) $275.00
Pretty Village Small Set No 2, McLoughlin Bros, 1890, EX (EX box) $250.00

Punch and Judy Theatre, Forbes, pull knobs on front for pop-up action, EX, A, $875.00.

Read & Learn Block Set, Bliss, 8 cylindrical blocks w/letters & other graphics, 4", G (G box)...............................**$2,400.00**
Train Set, Milton Bradley, 1881, Hercules loco & tender w/City of Springfield coach, complete w/blocks in coach, VG .**$5,700.00**
Train Set (Columbian Expo Chicago Floor Train), Bliss, ca 1885, 'US Grant' engine, tender & passenger coach, 36", EX......**$5,500.00**
Universal Dairy Truck, wood w/paper litho logo, dairy farm scene & driver, 10", NMIB, A **$225.00**

Pedal Cars and Other Wheeled Goods

Just like Daddy, all little boys (and girls as well) are thrilled and happy to drive a brand new shiny car. Today both generations search through flea markets and auto swap meets for cars, boats, fire engines, tractors, and trains that run not on gas but pedal power. Some of the largest manufacturers of wheeled goods were AMF (American Machine and Foundry Company), Murray, and Garton. Values depend to a very large extent on condition, and those that have been restored may sell for upwards of $1,000.00, depending on year and model.

Advisor: Nate Stoller (S7).

Atomic Missile, Murray, 1950s, wht plane-type vehicle w/bl & orange trim, chain drive, 2 levers, 44", rstr...........**$2,500.00**
Austin J40, England, 1950s, lt bl w/NP grille, bumpers & hood ornament, leatherette upholstery, 61", VG, A **$1,600.00**
Bel Air Chevy Convertible, 1955, Official Pace Car/500 Mile Race, red & wht, wht-wall tires, EX, A **$4,500.00**
BMC Special Race Car #8, rubber tires, 41", G, A **$1,250.00**
BMC Station Wagon, Jetliner, 1950s, gr pressed steel, chain drive, hard rubber wheels, silver hubs, 40", rpt, EX+ .**$950.00**
Buick, Murray, 1949, bright bl w/chrome trim, wht-walls w/bl wheels & chrome hubs, 39", rstr **$2,500.00**
Buick Roadster, Am National, 1927, gray-gr w/red trim, rumble seat & opening door, w/picnic jug & basket, 68", rstr.......**$7,500.00**

Bel Air Chevy Convertible, 1955 model, 1930s, red and cream, 38", restored, A, $2,400.00.

Cadillac, Am National, 1920, orig red pnt, hood opens to motor, rear spring suspension, spoke wheels, 48", rare, EX .**$7,500.00**
Car, Gendron, wood & pressed steel, w/fenders & running boards, open seat, scalloped hood w/windshield, 39", G, A..**$2,100.00**
Caterpillar Diesel Tractor, New London Metal Products, 1950s, yel w/blk detail, rubber treads, rstr, S7, from $3,000 to ..**$6,000.00**
Chrysler, Steelcraft, 1941, deep bl w/wht radiator grille & hubs, chrome steering wheel, windshield & trim, S7 ....**$2,500.00**
Chrysler Airflow Fire Engine, modeled after 1936 vehicle, red w/wht detail, 2 wooden ladders, 50", rstr.............**$1,150.00**
Cord Roadster, Gendron, 1931, dk bl w/lt bl & red pinstripe, wht balloon tires w/red spokes, 58", rstr **$4,500.00**
Dodge Roadster, Am National, 1926, tan & blk w/red trim, spoke wheels, red pleated seat, w/horn, 52", rstr ..**$4,500.00**
Earth Mover, Murray, 1961, yel w/blk lettering & detail, Play-load Dump, rstr, S7, from $1,100 to.....................**$1,500.00**
Fire Chief Car, Gendron, orig pnt, decals & bell, 35", EX...**$2,500.00**
Fire Truck, Am National, 1935, red 2-passenger mk AFD, pneumatic spoked tires, w/boots & helmet, hose reel, 70", rstr...**$10,000.00**

Fire truck #B640, Steelcraft, 1941, red with white detail, two wooden ladders, chrome bell, restored, S7, from $1,500.00 to $2,500.00.

Ford, early, pressed steel w/wood seat & grille, maroon w/yel striping, rubber tires w/spokes, 32", VG, A...........**$1,000.00**
Ford, Garton, 1937, gr w/cream detail & interior, rstr, S7, from $1,500 to...**$1,800.00**

Lincoln Zephyr, Garton, ca 1937, cream w/orange trim & red pinstripe, cream wheels w/chrome hubs, 45", rstr.$4,000.00
Little Joe, Steelcraft, 1950s, red & gray pressed steel, metal rods, hard rubber tires, Peugeot crest, 37", rpt, EX $750.00
Locomotive, Pioneer, early, pressed steel & wood w/wire wheels, 54", rare, rpt, VG $950.00
Locomotive, 1930s, blk & red, electric headlight, 26", G..$350.00
Mack Dump Truck, yel open cab w/blk trim, heavily decaled, mk Playboy Trucking Co, 50", rstr, A $2,200.00
Mustang, w/rear wire luggage rack, 40", EX..........$1,750.00
Paige Roadster, Am National, 1925, brn w/orange trim, V-shaped radiator hood, 53", orig condition w/rpt fenders $4,200.00

Photo courtesy Nate Stoller

Racer #8, BMC, 1950s, yellow with white hubs, chrome steering and pipes, Gilmore Speedway Special and logo on sides, restored, S7, $2,500.00.

Red Bird Roadster, Am National, 1924, red w/yel pinstripe & blk trim, tool-box trunk, 50", orig pnt, VG..........$2,700.00
Rickenbacker Fire Chief Car, Am National, 1920s, pressed steel w/wood chassis, red & yel striping, 42", G, A $1,800.00

Roadster, American National, 1920s, gray and black with red striping, rubber tires with hubs, side spare, 70", restored, A, $8,000.00.

Roadster, Steelcraft, 1932, gray w/red fenders, rear spare, 53", rstr..........$3,500.00
Skippy Pontiac, Gendron, ca 1935, orig red pnt w/wht Pontiac logo, red spoke wheels, electric lights, 45", G $3,400.00
Skippy Speedster, Gendron, ca 1935, orig red pnt w/wht trim, red-striped wht wheels, fender lights, squeeze horn, 45" $2,600.00
Sky Kar, Evans, red & wht, VG $525.00
Soap Box Derby Racer, 1934, St Paul Daily News, exterior exhaust pipe, EX..........$350.00
Speed Truck, pnt pressed steel w/dump body, 48", EX ...$450.00

Spirit of America Airplane, Steelcraft, marked NC 66 on tail, orange with black detail, black rubber tires with orange painted wheels, 53", EX, A, $10,000.00.

Spirit of St Louis, Am National, 1932, gray & red w/bl & yel trim, pneumatic tires w/red spokes, 36" wingspan, rstr, A..........$4,500.00
Streamliner, Steelcraft, blk-pnt pressed steel w/chrome-plated detail, tufted red leather upholstery, 49", rstr, A ..$2,500.00
Stutz Roadster, Steelcraft, 1929, lt gr w/red pinstripe & blk trim, cowl lights, spoked wht-walls, 52", rstr $4,000.00
Sunbeam Racer #8, Gendron, ca 1932, red & blk, wht pinstripe, yel wheels, wht balloon tires, side exhaust, 70", rstr.......$3,600.00
T-Bird, Murray, 1960s, dusty rose pressed steel w/steel rods for action, hard rubber wheels & hubs, 32", rpt, NM...$1,600.00
Torpedo Convertible, Murray, 1949, wht w/red interior & hubs, chrome trim w/4 side vents, rstr..........$3,000.00
US Mail Airplane, red sheet metal w/wood seat, blk rubber tires w/red wheels, 39", VG, A..........$400.00
White Trucking Dump Truck, Am National, ca 1935, bl & orange, tires w/silver sidewalls, orange wheels, 54½", rstr $3,200.00

Scooters

Buddy L, blk sturdy platform on 3 wheels, blk & red jtd derrick-type hdl w/wood grip, rubber tires w/red hubs, rstr .$2,300.00
Coaster Craft, orig red pnt w/flared rear fender, red wheels w/yel stripe, rear wheel kickstand, unused, M $200.00
Henley, rectangular platform on base w/4 metal spoked wheels, vertical hdl, 33", G $125.00
Skippy, Gendron, ca 1940, red streamlined style w/wht pinstripe, front & rear fenders, wht tires, 43", rstr $2,750.00

Wagons

Badger Coaster, wood, wood spoke wheels w/steel bands, 42", VG, A $350.00

Birdsell, South Bend Inc, ATC Ferrill & Co, gr-pnt wood w/spoke wheels, mounted bench seat w/backrest, 40", EX, A $2,300.00

Covered Wagon, wood, wrought-iron hoops, canvas cover, wood spokes, w/water barrel & red lantern, 46x48", EX, A .$375.00

Express Wagon, orange-pnt tin w/wood bottom, metal spoked wheels, wood hdl & twisted wire pull rod, 32", VG..$165.00

Georgie, gray-pnt wood w/pnt landscapes on ends, Georgie lettered on sides w/gold trim, wood spoke wheels, 28" bed $650.00

Hercules, 1930s, pnt wood & pressed steel w/removable stake sides, rear dual rubber wheels, 48", EX....................$200.00

Pioneer, red tin w/wood bottom & pull hdl, metal spoked wheels, 25", EX....................$550.00

Sherwood Spring Coasters, pnt wood w/stenciled lettering, sm spoke wheels, spring-loaded, 41", G+, A $400.00

Skippie Deluxe, ca 1935, streamlined w/front headlights & hdl, wht trim, red & wht wheels w/chrome hubs, 40", rstr......$2,500.00

Penny Toys

Penny toys were around as early as the late 1800s and as late as the 1920s. Many were made in Germany, but some were made in France as well. With few exceptions, they ranged in size from 5" on down; some had moving parts, and a few had clockwork mechanisms. Though many were unmarked, you'll sometimes find them signed 'Kellermann,' 'Meier,' 'Fischer,' or 'Distler,' or carrying an embossed company logo such as the 'dog and cart' emblem. They were made of lithographed tin with exquisite detailing — imagine an entire carousel less than 2½" tall. Because of a recent surge in collector interest, many have been crossing the auction block of some of the country's large galleries. Our values are prices realized at several of these auctions.

Advisor: Jane Anderson (A2).

Black Man in Rocking Chair, marked Germany, 2", EX, $325.00.

Airplane, Distler, w/pilot, red & yel w/4 side props, orig pull string, EX, A....................$1,200.00

Airplane Spiral Toy, Einfalt, 2 planes attached to spiral rod, gr & maroon, 6½", EX, A....................$450.00

Armored Tank Car, Distler, WWI version, VG, A........$165.00

Baby Carriage, Fischer, w/baby, yel & blk w/wht spoke wheels, 3", EX, A....................$275.00

Baby Carriage, Meier, w/child holding doll, gr w/red spoke wheels, NM, A....................$700.00

Biplane, Distler, yel & red w/figure seated on wing, EX, A ..$700.00

Biplane Horn, France, blowing makes sound & rotates props, 4", EX, A $225.00

Boy Playing Bugle on Rocking Horse, Meier, EX, A $900.00

Carousel, Distler, complete w/2 zeppelins & 2 hot air balloons, NM, A $385.00

Carousel, Germany, complete w/3 children in swings, 3", EX, A....................$275.00

Chinese Man on Cart w/Parasol, Distler, parasol rotates as 4-wheeled cart is pulled, 2¾", EX, A $475.00

Clown in Barrel, Stock & Co, 2¾", NM, A $900.00

Clowns Playing Ball, Meier, 2 seated clowns playing catch on wht rectangular base, VG, A....................$825.00

Couple in Swing, Meier, couple in double swing on platform, 3¼", EX, A $300.00

Delivery Truck, Fischer, w/driver, panel van w/C-style cab, spoke wheels, EX, A $250.00

Delivery Van, w/driver, red, yel & bl w/spoke wheels, open driver's seat, 3⅝", EX, A $275.00

Dirigible, Distler, mc w/side-mounted props, passenger & pull cord, 3", EX....................$875.00

Donkey Cart, Germany, gray donkey, tan cart w/2 red wheels, 4¾", EX, A $150.00

Donkey on Platform, Germany, gray donkey w/red blanket, 4 disk wheels, 2½", EX, A $250.00

Double-Decker Bus, Distler, w/driver, red & yel w/wht spoke wheels, VG, A $400.00

Double-Decker Bus, Germany, w/driver, red w/gold trim, silver-tone spoke wheels, 4¼", VG, A....................$165.00

Double-Decker Omnibus, Meier, passengers inside & on top, conductor emb of rear platform, 3", EX, A...........$1,000.00

Double-Decker Omnibus, Meier, red w/gold spoke wheels, cut-out passengers on upper level, NM, A $1,500.00

Dray w/Sheep, Meier, w/driver, 3", EX, A......................$400.00

Felix the Cat, Germany, Felix atop gr base, rare, VG, A ..$2,800.00

Ferris Wheel Whistle, Germany, revolves, 4", VG, A....$175.00

Fire Hose Truck, Meier, w/3 firemen, red & gold w/yel back-to-back seats, gray spoke wheels, 3½", VG, A..............$185.00

Fire Pumper Truck, Meier, w/driver, red chassis w/gold-tone nose & vertical tank, silver wheels, 3½", EX, A......$275.00

Gas Station & Car, JDN, yel & red station mk Gas & Oil, gr car, NM, A....................$450.00

Geese Pecking in Shed, Meier, 2 geese protruding from slant-roof shed pecking for food, 2¼", EX, A $200.00

Giraffe on Platform, Meier, spoke wheels, 4", VG, A.....$250.00

Gnome Feeding Parrot on Platform, Meier, gr w/red spoke wheels, EX, A $650.00

Gnome Seated on Egg, Meier, egg lifts up to reveal rabbit, gr rectangular base, EX, A....................$1,650.00

Gnomes, Meier, 2 gnomes cutting wood on beveled base, 4", EX, A $400.00
Gnomes, Meier, 2 gnomes hammering on gr rectangular base, EX, A $275.00
Gnomes, Meier, 2 gnomes sawing on gr rectangular base, EX, A $325.00
Goat on Platform, Meier, wht & blk goat w/red bell collar, silver-tone platform, 3", EX, A $275.00
Gondola w/Rower & Lady Passenger on Platform, bl w/gold spoke wheels, NM, A $2,300.00
Goose on Platform, Germany, realistic colors, gr platform w/red spoke wheels, EX, A $525.00
Grand Hotel Omnibus, Meier, red w/yel highlights, gold spoke wheels, EX, A $385.00
Horse & Jockey on Platform, Germany, disk wheels, 3", EX $200.00
Horse & Jockey on Platform, Germany, spoke wheels, 5", EX $500.00
Horse-Drawn Ambulance, Meier, mc w/red cross emblem on sides, red spoke wheels, driver on 1 of 2 horses, EX, A $200.00
Horse-Drawn Cannon Carrier, Meier, w/driver, gray w/red spoke wheels, 2 horses, EX, A $150.00
Horse-Drawn Carriage, Fischer, w/driver, blk w/gold spoke wheels, single horse, EX, A $125.00
Horse-Drawn Delivery Wagon, Germany, yel w/red spoke wheels, single horse, EX, A $135.00
Horse-Drawn Dray Wagon, Germany, w/driver, yel w/red striping, wht spoke wheels, single horse, VG, A $135.00
Horse-Drawn Fire Patrol Wagon, Meier, gr wagon w/red bench & gold spoke wheels, 5 firemen, 5½", EX, A $575.00
Horse-Drawn Hansom Cab, Meier, gr & blk cab w/gold trim, red spoke wheels, dappled horse, 3¾", EX, A $200.00
Horse-Drawn Landau, Meier, w/driver, gr & yel w/red spoke wheels, single horse, EX, A $175.00
Horse-Drawn Military Cart w/Boat, Meier, spoke wheels, 2 horses w/1 rider, 4¾", EX, A $200.00
Horse-Drawn Oil Tank Wagon, gr tank on bl flatbed w/silver spoke wheels, bench seat, single horse, EX, A $265.00
Horse-Drawn Postal Van, Meier, metallic gold, dappled horse, 5½", EX, A $250.00
Horse-Drawn Postal Van, Meier, yel w/red spoke wheels, rider on 1 of 2 horses, VG, A $300.00
Horses w/Riders, Meier, 3 horses & riders on gr rectangular base, NM, A $1,900.00
Lamb on Platform, Meier, lamb w/red bell collar, red disk wheels, 3", EX, A $375.00
Launch, Germany, wht w/bl trim, #48 on bow, 2 flags at rear, 7½", VG, A $275.00
Launch w/Sailor, Meier, gr boat w/bl house, gold flags & 2 wheels, sailor stands behind compass, 4½", VG, A $1,000.00
Limousine, Distler, bl & wht w/gold trim, luggage rail on roof, spoke wheels, 4¼", EX, A $400.00
Locomotive, Meier, w/cowl & smokestack, 4", EX, A $200.00
Man Feeding Dog, Germany, man feeding dog from basket on red rectangular base, EX, A $635.00
Merry-Go-Round, Meier, complete w/4 horses & riders, EX, A $700.00
Merry-Go-Round, Meier, complete w/6 bicyclists, EX, A ..$1,900.00
Monkey & Chicken on Beveled Platform, Meier, mc figures on cream platform, 4½", VG, A $450.00
Motorcycle, Kellermann, mk CKO, 2¾", NM $1,100.00
Motorcycle w/Sidecar, w/driver & passenger, 4", EX, A ..$1,650.00
Mule & Clown on Platform, Germany, mule rears up to kick clown, 4", EX, A $300.00
Ocean Liner, Meier, red, wht & bl w/2 stacks, flags fore & aft, w/lifeboat graphics, 4¾", EX, A $300.00
Phonograph, Meier, complete w/horn & side lever which activates musical sound, EX, A $150.00
Porter Pushing Trunk on Dolly, Fischer, 3½", EX, A $385.00
Rabbit, Germany, in parade uniform on gr sq base, EX, A..$750.00
Rabbit & Babies on Platform, mother rabbit w/2 babies on her back, spoke wheels, EX, A $1,150.00

Rabbit on Platform, marked Gesch, spoke wheels, 3¼", $300.00.

Racer #11, mk Germany, w/driver, wht, 4", EX, A......$1,750.00
Racer #2, Meier, w/driver, bl, 3", EX, A $2,000.00
Saloon Car, Distler, w/driver & cut-out passengers in windows, bl & yel w/wht spoke wheels, EX, A $200.00
Saloon Car, Fischer, brn w/silver spoke wheels, EX, A...$175.00

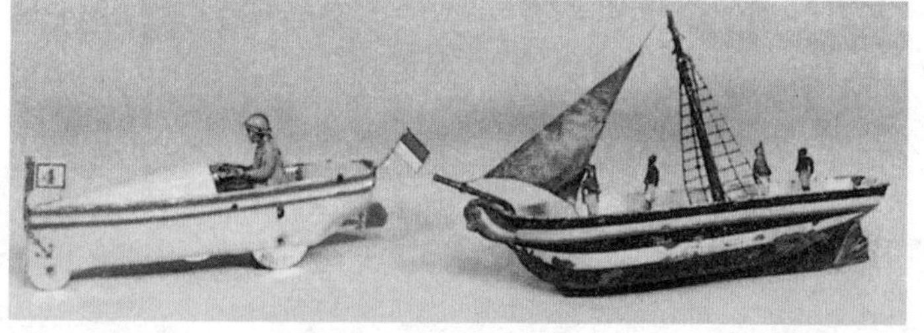

Speedboat, Meier, white with red stripes, EX, A, $925.00; Sailing Vessel, Issmayer, late 1800s, hand painted, VG, A, $400.00.

Saloon Car, Meier, w/driver & cut-out passengers in windows, wht w/gold highlights, gray spoke wheels, EX, A $650.00
Sedan, Germany, bl w/cream roof, disk wheels, EX, A...$150.00
Sewing Machine, Meier, bl w/red hdl, yel table w/gold decorative brace, red treadle, 3¼", EX, A $135.00
Stake Truck, Germany, w/driver, orange w/red & yel trim, spoke wheels, 5¼", VG, A $135.00
Steam Engine, Distler, pnt tin, operating piston & wheel, 4", EX, A $385.00
Sulky, Distler, w/jockey, NM, A $385.00
Swan on Platform, Meier, gold spoke wheels, EX, A......$750.00
Tap Dancer, Distler, man atop gr base, EX, A $285.00
Taxi Cab, Distler, w/driver, wht & gold w/red interior, simulated soft top, spoke wheels, EX, A $500.00
Tiger on Platform, Germany, realistic tiger on platform w/lg gold-tone spoke wheels, 4", EX, A $400.00
Toadstool, Fischer, butterfly atop red toadstool on sq gr base, EX, A $650.00
Touring Car, Germany, w/driver, bl w/red striping, silver spoke wheels, EX, A $125.00
Touring Car, Germany, w/driver, wht w/red & gold highlights, wht spoke wheels, EX, A $350.00
Touring Car, Meier, w/driver & lady passenger, bl & red w/gray spoke wheels, EX, A $800.00
Touring Car, Meier, w/driver & 2 lady passengers, 4", NM, A...$1,100.00
Tractor, Distler, w/driver, 4¼", EX, A $300.00
Train, Hess, locomotive & tender w/3 passenger cars, 9¼", EX, A $275.00
Train Set, GC & Co, locomotive & tender on platform, log car, passenger car & freight car, EX, A $225.00
Watering Can, Meier, images of children at play, spring-loaded lid, 3", VG, A $225.00
Zeppelin, Distler, gr w/red highlights, EX, A $400.00
Zeppelin, Germany, 2 gondolas below w/men at steering wheels, 6", VG, A...$450.00
Zeppelin, mk Gesch, passengers in 2 open gondolas, yel w/4 red props, 4", EX, A $950.00

Pez Dispensers

Pez was originally designed as a breath mint for smokers, but by the '50s kids were the target market, and the candies were packaged in the dispensers that we all know and love today. There are already more than three hundred variations to collect, and more arrive on the supermarket shelves every day. Though early on collectors seemed to prefer the dispensers without feet, that attitude has changed, and now it's the character head they concentrate on. Feet were added in 1987, so if you were to limit yourself to only 'feetless' dispensers, your collection would be far from complete. Some dispensers have variations in color and design that can influence their values. Don't buy any that are damaged, incomplete, or that have been tampered with in any way; those are nearly worthless. For more information refer to A *Pictorial Guide to Plastic Candy Dispensers Featuring Pez* by David Welch and *Collecting Toys #6* by Richard O'Brien. Values are for mint-condition dispensers unless noted otherwise.

Advisor: Richard Belyski (B1).

Other Sources: B10, O1, P10

Angel, no ft..$75.00
Arlene, w/ft, pk, from $1 to $3.00
Baloo, w/ft $25.00
Bambi, no ft..$75.00
Barney Bear, no ft, H4 ....$35.00
Barney Bear, w/ft..$25.00
Baseball Glove, no ft $225.00
Batgirl, no ft, soft head, MIP $185.00
Batman, no ft, H4 ....$15.00
Batman, no ft, w/cape, B1....................................$150.00
Batman, w/ft, bl or blk, ea, from $3 to $5.00
Betsy Ross, no ft...$185.00
Bouncer Beagle, w/ft, B1 ....$6.00
Boy, w/ft, brn hair $3.00
Bozo, no ft, diecut $200.00
Bubble Man, w/ft..$20.00
Bugs Bunny, no ft, H4..$20.00
Bugs Bunny, w/ft, from $1 to...................................$3.00
Bullwinkle, no ft $275.00
Candy Shooter, red & wht, w/candy & gun license, unused....$125.00
Captain America, no ft $85.00
Captain Hook, no ft..$85.00
Casper, no ft..$200.00
Charlie Brown, w/ft, from $1 to $3.00
Charlie Brown, w/ft & tongue $10.00
Chick, w/ft, from $1 to $3.00
Chick in Egg, no ft, H4..$25.00
Chick in Egg, no ft, w/hair $125.00
Chip, w/ft, B1...$100.00
Clown, w/ft, whistle head $10.00
Clown w/Collar, no ft $65.00
Cockatoo, no ft, bl face, red beak $65.00
Cool Cat, w/ft $65.00
Cow (A or B), no ft, bl, ea $65.00
Creature From the Black Lagoon, no ft..................$250.00
Crocodile, no ft $75.00
Daffy Duck, no ft..$15.00
Daffy Duck, w/ft, from $1 to $3.00
Dalmatian Pup, w/ft $50.00
Daniel Boone, no ft $200.00
Dino, w/ft, purple, from $1 to $3.00
Dinosaur, w/ft, 4 different, ea, from $1 to $3.00
Doctor, no ft $275.00
Donald Duck, no ft $15.00
Donald Duck, no ft, diecut $175.00
Donald Duck's Nephew, no ft.................................$30.00
Donald Duck's Nephew, w/ft, gr, bl or red hat, B1, ea $10.00
Donkey, w/ft, whistle head $10.00
Droopy Dog (A), no ft, plastic swivel ears, MIP $25.00
Droopy Dog (B), w/ft, pnt ears, MIP, B1 ....$6.00
Dumbo, w/ft, bl head..$25.00
Eerie Spectres, Zombie, no ft $250.00
Elephant, no ft, orange & bl, flat hat $100.00
Fat-Ears Rabbit, no ft, pk head $20.00

Eerie Spectres, Air Spirit and Diabolic, $250.00 each.

Fat-Ears Rabbit, no ft, yel head.......................................$15.00
Fishman, no ft, gr.......................................$185.00
Foghorn Leghorn, w/ft.......................................$95.00
Football, MIB (sealed), A.......................................$200.00
Fozzie Bear, w/ft, from $1 to.......................................$3.00
Frankenstein, no ft.......................................$300.00
Fred Flintstone, w/ft, B1, from $1 to.......................................$3.00
Frog, w/ft, whistle head, B1.......................................$40.00
Garfield, w/ft, orange w/gr hat, from $1 to.......................................$3.00
Garfield, w/ft, teeth, B1, from $1 to.......................................$3.00
Garfield, w/ft, visor, from $1 to.......................................$3.00
Gargamel, w/ft.......................................$5.00
Girl, w/ft, blond hair, B1.......................................$15.00
Gonzo, w/ft, from $1 to.......................................$3.00
Gorilla, no ft, blk head.......................................$75.00
Green Hornet, 1960s, from $200 to.......................................$250.00
Gyro Gearloose, w/ft, B1.......................................$6.00
Henry Hawk, no ft.......................................$65.00
Hulk, no ft, dk gr.......................................$60.00
Hulk, no ft, lt gr, remake.......................................$3.00
Indian, w/ft, whistle head, B1.......................................$15.00
Indian Brave, no ft, reddish.......................................$175.00
Indian Chief, no ft, yel headdress.......................................$125.00
Indian Maiden, no ft.......................................$150.00
Inspector Clouseau, w/ft.......................................$5.00
Jerry Mouse, w/ft, plastic face, B1.......................................$15.00
Jerry Mouse, w/ft, pnt face.......................................$6.00
Jiminy Cricket, no ft.......................................$275.00
Joker (Batman), no ft, soft head.......................................$200.00
Kermit the Frog, w/ft, red, from $1 to.......................................$3.00
Knight, no ft.......................................$300.00
Koala, w/ft, whistle head.......................................$40.00
Lamb, no ft.......................................$15.00
Lamb, w/ft, from $1 to.......................................$3.00
Lamb, w/ft, whistle head.......................................$20.00
Lazy Garfield, w/ft.......................................$5.00
Li'l Bad Wolf, w/ft.......................................$20.00
Lion w/Crown, no ft.......................................$75.00
Lion's Club Lion, minimum value.......................................$2,000.00
Lucy, w/ft, from $1 to.......................................$3.00
Make-A-Face, works like Mr Potato Head, minimum value.......................................$2,500.00
Mary Poppins, no ft.......................................$1,300.00

Merlin the Mouse, $20.00; Santa (A), $100.00.

Mexican, no ft, B1.......................................$250.00
Mickey Mouse, no ft, removable nose or cast nose, ea, from $10 to.......................................$15.00
Mickey Mouse, w/ft, from $1 to.......................................$3.00
Mimic Monkey (monkey w/ball cap), no ft, several colors, ea.......................................$40.00
Miss Piggy, w/ft, ea, from $1 to.......................................$3.00
Miss Piggy, w/ft, eyelashes.......................................$15.00
Monkey Sailor, no ft, w/wht cap.......................................$50.00
Mowgli, w/ft.......................................$20.00
Mr Ugly, no ft.......................................$45.00
Muscle Mouse (gray Jerry), w/ft, plastic nose.......................................$15.00
Nermal, w/ft, gray.......................................$3.00
Nurse, no ft, brn hair.......................................$175.00
Octopus, no ft, blk.......................................$75.00
Odie, w/ft.......................................$5.00

Olive Oyl, no ft $200.00
Panda, no ft, diecut eyes $30.00
Panda, w/ft, remake, from $1 to $3.00
Panda, w/ft, whistle head $10.00
Papa Smurf, w/ft, red $6.00
Parrot, w/ft, whistle head $10.00
Pebbles Flintstone, w/ft, B1, from $1 to $3.00
Penguin, w/ft, whistle head $10.00
Penguin (Batman), no ft, soft head, NM $175.00
Peter Pez (A), no ft $65.00
Peter Pez (B), w/ft, from $1 to $3.00
Pilgrim, no ft $185.00
Pink Panther, w/ft $5.00
Pinocchio, no ft $150.00
Pirate, no ft $45.00
Pluto, no ft, red $10.00
Pluto, w/ft, from $1 to $3.00
Popeye (B), no ft $115.00
Popeye (C), no ft, w/removable pipe $110.00
Practical Pig (B), no ft $30.00
Psychedelic Eye, no ft $700.00
Psychedelic Flower, no ft $750.00
Psychedelic Hand, remake, blk or pk, MOC, ea $20.00
Pumpkin (A), no ft, from $10 to $15.00
Pumpkin (B), w/ft, from $1 to $3.00
Raven, no ft, yel beak $60.00
Rhino, w/ft, whistle head $10.00

Ringmaster, no ft $300.00
Road Runner, w/ft $15.00
Rooster, w/ft, whistle head, B1 .... $40.00
Rooster, w/ft, wht or yel head, ea $30.00
Rudolph, no ft $75.00
Santa Claus (A), no ft, steel pin $125.00
Santa Claus (B), no ft $125.00
Santa Claus (C), no ft, from $5 to $15.00
Santa Claus (C), w/ft, B1, from $1 to $3.00
Scrooge McDuck (A), no ft $35.00
Scrooge McDuck (B), w/ft, B1 .... $6.00
Sheik, no ft $30.00
Skull (A), no ft, from $5 to $10.00
Skull (B), w/ft, from $1 to $3.00
Smurf, w/ft $5.00
Smurfette, w/ft $5.00
Snoopy, w/ft, from $1 to $3.00
Snow White, no ft $200.00
Snowman (A), no ft $10.00
Snowman (B), w/ft, from $1 to $5.00
Space Trooper Robot, no ft, full body $325.00
Spaceman, no ft $200.00
Speedy Gonzales (A), w/ft $15.00
Speedy Gonzales (B), no ft, from $1 to $3.00
Spider-Man, no ft, from $10 to $15.00
Spider-Man, w/ft, from $1 to $3.00
Spike, w/ft, B1 .... $6.00
Star Wars, Darth Vader, C3PO, Storm Trooper or Chewbacca, B1, ea, from $1 to $3.00
Sylvester (A), w/ft, cream or wht whiskers, B1, ea $5.00

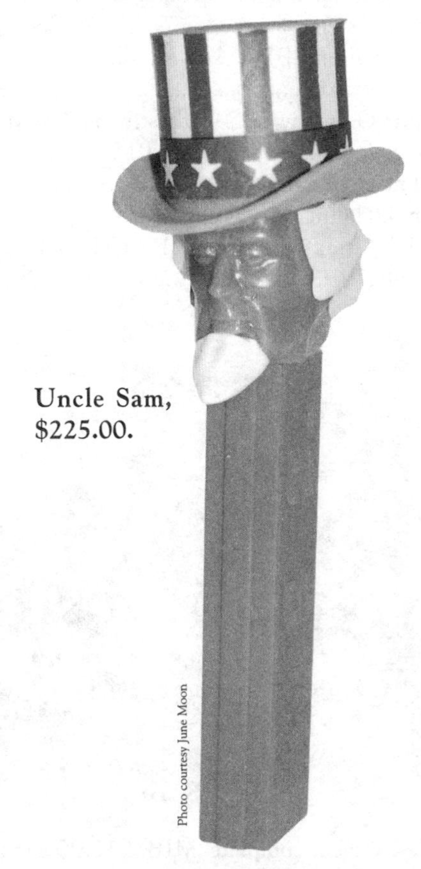

Uncle Sam, $225.00.

Photo courtesy June Moon

Sylvester (B), w/ft, from $1 to $3.00
Teenage Mutant Ninja Turtles, w/ft, 8 variations, ea, from $1 to $3.00
Thor, no ft....................$300.00
Thumper, w/ft, no copyright....................$45.00
Tiger, w/ft, whistle head $10.00
Tinkerbell, no ft....................$250.00
Tom, no ft $35.00
Tom, w/ft, plastic face....................$15.00
Tom, w/ft, pnt face....................$6.00
Truck, many variations, B1, ea, minimum value....................$1.00
Tweety Bird, no ft $10.00
Tweety Bird, w/ft, from $1 to $3.00
Tyke, w/ft, B1 ....$15.00
Valentine Heart, B1, from $1 to $3.00
Whistle, w/ft, from $1 to....................$3.00
Wile E Coyote, w/ft $45.00
Winnie the Pooh, w/ft $75.00
Witch, 3-pc, no ft $10.00
Wolfman, no ft $300.00
Wonder Woman, no ft, soft head....................$185.00
Wonder Woman, w/ft, from $1 to $3.00
Woodstock, w/ft, from $1 to $3.00
Woodstock, w/ft, pk feathers $10.00
Yappy Dog, no ft, orange or gr, ea $65.00
Yosemite Sam, w/ft, from $1 to....................$3.00

MISCELLANEOUS

Bank, truck #1, metal $200.00
Bank, truck #2, metal....................$40.00
Body Parts, fit over stem of dispenser & make it look like a person, many variations, B1, ea $5.00
Bracelet, pk....................$5.00
Clicker, US Zone Germany, 1950, litho tin, 3½", NM..$300.00
Coloring Book, Safety #2, non-English, B1....................$15.00
Power Pez, rnd mechanical dispenser, B1 ....$5.00
Puzzle, Sprinkbok/Hallmark, 500 pcs $15.00
Tin, Pez Specials, stars & lines on checked background, gold colors, 2½x4½", rare, EX $225.00

Puzzles, Ceaco, complete, MIB, $30.00 each.

Watch, pk face w/yel band or yel face w/bl band, ea.........$10.00

Pin-Back Buttons

Pin-back buttons produced up to the early 1920s were made with a celluloid covering. After that time, a large number of buttons were lithographed on tin; these are referred to as tin 'lithos.'

Character and toy-related buttons represent a popular collecting field. There are countless categories to base a collection on. Buttons were given out at stores and theatres, offered as premiums, attached to dolls, or received with a club membership.

In the late '40s and into the '50s, some cereal companies packed one in each box of their product. Quaker Puffed Oats offered a series of movie star pin-backs, but probably the best known are Kellogg's Pep Pins. There were eighty-six in all, so theoretically if you wanted the whole series as Kellogg hoped you would, you'd have to buy at least that many boxes of their cereal. Pep pins came in five sets, the first in 1945, three more in 1946, and the last in 1947. They were printed with full-color lithographs of comic characters licensed by King Features and Famous Artists — Maggie and Jiggs, the Winkles, and Dagwood and Blondie, for instance. Superman, the only D.C. Comics character, was included in each set. Most Pep pins range in value from $10.00 to $15.00 in NM/M condition; any not mentioned in our listings fall into this range. There are exceptions, and we've made sure they're evaluated below.

Nearly all pin-backs are collectible today with these possible exceptions: common buttons picturing flags of various nations, general labor union buttons denoting the payment of dues, and common buttons with clever sayings. Be sure that you buy only buttons with well-centered designs, well-alligned colors, no fading or yellowing, no spots or stains, and no cracks, splits, or dents. In the listings that follow, sizes are approximate.

Advisor: Doug Dezso (D6), Kellogg's Pep Pins only.

Other Sources: C10, D11, S20

See Also Political; Premiums; Sporting Collectibles.

Batfink Is My Heroe, Hal Seiger, 1967, blk & red on wht, 3" dia, EX, A $80.00
Batman, This Is the Year of Batman, red, wht & bl w/image & logo, 1966, 1½", EX, J5....................$40.00
Beatles, blk & wht group photo w/pk rim, 3" dia, VG, R2..$20.00
Beatles, I Like the Beatles & faces, flasher, bl, 2½", EX, B3 ....$25.00
Beatles, I Still Love the Beatles, red, wht & bl, 3½", EX..$25.00
Beauty & the Beast, heart shape, 1991, M8 ....$5.00
Betty Boop, Cabaret Cinema, 1960s, blk on cream, 1½", VG, A....................$65.00
Betty Boop, Max Fleischer's Talkatoons, image of Betty holding parasol,¾", EX $40.00
Bullwinkle, Charge, Bring Back the Bullmoose Party!..., image of Bullwinkle yelling, 2¼", EX, J5 ....$35.00
Chip 'N Dale Rescue Rangers, 1990, 3", M8....................$5.00
Creepy Magazine Fan Club, 1968, monster in center, 2½" dia, EX, M17....................$25.00
Dale Evans, 1950s, blk & wht photo on gr, 1½" dia, EX, A.$40.00

Davy Crockett King of the Wild Frontier, 1950s, blk & wht photo on yel, 1¼" dia, EX, A $65.00

Dick Tracy Detective, 1930s, image of Tracy in profile w/gun, EX, D11 ....$40.00

Famous Monsters Fan Club, 1974, Phantom of the Opera in center, 2½" dia, EX, M17 ....$25.00

Gene Autry, 1950s, photo on bl, purple or red background, 1¼" dia, EX, J5, ea $25.00

Home of Dick Tracy-Woodstock, Illinois, image of Tracy talking on wrist radio, 5¼", M, D11 ....$20.00

Hopalong Cassidy, Best Wishes from Hoppy, gray & blk, 1¾", rare, C10 ....$125.00

Hopalong Cassidy, Daily in the Chicago Tribune, red background, 1¼", NM, $45.00.

Hopalong Cassidy, Savings Rodeo, Bronc Buster or Tenderfoot, 1950s, C10, ea...$45.00

Howdy Doody, 1950s, red, wht & bl image of Howdy Doody's face on wht, 1" dia, EX, A $85.00

I Love Dick Tracy, red heart w/bl letters on wht, NM, D11 .$15.00

John Travolta for President, Midland Records, 1976, image of John wearing Uncle Sam top hat, 1⅜", EX, M17......$20.00

Lion King, 1993, features all characters, 3" dia, NM, M8...$5.00

Little Mermaid, purple lettering, 1980s, 3" dia, NM, M8 ...$5.00

Lone Ranger, Sunday Herald and Examiner, 1930s, EX, J6, $30.00.

Photo courtesy June Moon

Lone Ranger, blk & wht image & lettering on yel background, 1¾", J6 ....$65.00

Lost in Space 30th Anniversary, Dec 2-3, 1995, limited edition, 1½", M, P4...$15.00

Mickey Mouse, Mod Mickey, Beny-Albee, late 1960s, 3½", NM...$20.00

Our Gang, 1930s, bl & wht w/image of Spanky & Our Gang Club, ¾", EX, J5 ....$75.00

Our Gang, 1930s, blk & wht image of Jackie & I Am a Member of Jackie Cooper's Gang, 1¼", M, J5.........................$85.00

Peanuts, Snoopy & Woodstock, Try & Understand Me, image of Snoopy & Woodstock upsidedown, 2", H11 ....$5.00

Peanuts, Snoopy Come Home, 1972, yel, 6", M, H11 ......$15.00

Peanuts, Snoopy Fan Club, bl w/image of Snoopy walking in grass, 2", M, H11 ....$6.00

Peanuts, Snoopy for President, red, wht & bl w/image of Snoopy in top hat, 3", M, H11 ....$15.00

Peanuts, We Love You Charlie Brown, 1¼", M, H11.........$5.00

Peanuts, You're a Good Man Charlie Brown, Charlie Brown on mound, orange background, 1¼", VG, H11 ....$12.00

Pocahontas, I Was There, Wang Center, Boston, 1995, rectangular, NM, M8 ....$8.00

Pocahontas, Sing Along Songs video button, 1995, rectangular, NM, M8 ....$8.00

Red Ryder Pony Contest, 1940s, black on yellow, J6, $25.00.

Photo courtesy June Moon

Rocky Jones, Silvercup Bread premium, 1950s, photo on blue background, $35.00.

Photo courtesy June Moon

Rin-Tin-Tin, Screen Gems, 1956, head shot, NM, P4 .....$20.00
Robin Hood Hustlers Club of America, 1930s, full-color image on cream background,⅞" dia, EX, M17 ....$20.00
Roy Rogers & Trigger, 1950s, blk & wht photo on yel, w/attached red & yel ribbon, 1¾" dia, EX, A $50.00
Simba, I'm Gonna Be King, 1993, 2¼" dia, NM, M8 ....$5.00
Snow White Jingle Club, WDE, 1938, image & lettering on wht, 3" dia, scarce, NM, A $450.00
Superman, image on wht background, Read Superman Comics on back, 1939, NM, A $45.00
Talespin, image of Baloo, 1980s, 3" dia, NM, M8 ....$3.00
Toy Story, Buzz Lightyear, theatre employee button, 3", rare, NM, M8 ....$15.00

Universal Monsters: Wolf Man, Mummy, and Frankenstein, 1960s, three from a set of six, EX, $10.00 each.

Winky Dink, 1950s, yel & pk image on blk, 1" dia, EX, A ..$75.00
Yogi Bear for President, 1964, red, wht & bl, 3", EX $50.00

KELLOGG'S PEP PINS

BO Plenty, NM $30.00
Corky, NM $16.00
Dagwood, NM $30.00
Dick Tracy, NM $30.00
Fat Stuff, NM $15.00
Felix the Cat, NM $85.00
Flash Gordon, NM $30.00
Flat Top, NM $30.00
Goofy, NM $10.00
Gravel Gertie, NM $15.00
Harold Teen, NM $15.00
Inspector, NM $12.50
Jiggs, NM $25.00
Judy, NM $10.00
Kayo, NM $20.00
Little King, NM $15.00
Little Moose, NM $15.00
Maggie, NM $25.00
Mama De Stross, NM $30.00
Mama Katzenjammer, NM $25.00
Mamie, NM $15.00
Moon Mullins, NM $10.00
Olive Oyl, NM $30.00
Orphan Annie, NM $25.00
Pat Patton, NM $10.00
Perry Winkle, NM $15.00
Phantom, NM $80.00
Pop Jenks, NM $15.00
Popeye, NM $30.00
Rip Winkle, NM $20.00
Skeezix, NM $15.00
Superman, NM $42.00
Toots, NM $15.00
Uncle Walt, NM $20.00
Uncle Willie, NM $12.50
Winkles Twins $90.00
Winnie Winkle $15.00

Plastic Figures

Plastic figures were made by many toy companies. They were first boxed with playsets, but in the early '50s, some became available individually. Marx was the first company to offer single figures (at 10¢ each), and even some cereal companies included one in boxes of their product. (Kellogg offered a series of 16 54mm Historic Warriors, and Nabisco had a line of ten dinosaurs in marbleized, primary colors.) Virtually every type of man and beast has been modeled in plastic; today some have become very collectible and expensive. There are lots of factors you'll need to be aware of to be a wise buyer. For instance, Marx made cowboys during the mid-'60s in a flat finish, and these are much harder to find and more valuable than the later figures with a waxy finish. Marvel Super Heroes in the fluorescent hues are worth about half as much as the earlier, light gray issue. Because of limited space, it isn't possible to evaluate more than a representative few of these plastic figures in a general price guide, so if you'd like to learn more about them, we recommend *Geppert's Guide* by Tim Geppert. See the Clubs, Newsletters, and Other Publications section for information on how to order the *Plastic Figure & Playset Collector* magazine.

Advisors: Mike and Kurt Fredericks (F4); Bob Wilson, Phoenix Toy Soldier Co. (P11).

See also Playsets.

ACTION AND ADVENTURE

Photo courtesy June Moon

Archer, Spacemen, 1950s, 4", M, $55.00 each.

Ajax, Spaceman, w/helmet, MIP, P11 ....$9.00
Archer, Space People, complete w/man & 2 women (1 holding a baby), 3" to 4", NMIB, A $150.00
Archer, Spaceman, female w/baby, P11 ....$45.00
Dulcop, Royal Canadian Police, P11 ....$5.00
Dulcop, Sheriff of Nottingham, P11 ....$7.00
Ideal, Pirates, 4-pc set, P11 ....$35.00
Marx, Alien, 35mm, P11 ....$5.00
Marx, Alien, 45mm, crawling, P11 ....$22.00
Marx, Alien, 45mm, P11 ....$7.00
Marx, Arabs, 60mm, crouching, firing or riding, red-brn, P11, ea....................$37.00
Marx, Arabs, 60mm, crouching, firing or riding, silver, P11, ea....................$35.00
Marx, Arabs, 60mm, other, red-brn, P11 ....$32.00
Marx, Arabs, 60mm, other, silver, P11....................$30.00
Marx, Arabs, 60mm, wht, hard plastic, P11 ....$70.00
Marx, Arctic, Eskimo, P11....................$5.00
Marx, Arctic, scientist, P11 ....$6.00
Marx, Arctic, scientist, w/ice ax, P11....................$10.00
Marx, Astronauts, 35mm, 1" ring on head, P11 ....$4.00
Marx, Astronauts, 54mm, Apollo, flag planter, P11 ....$5.00
Marx, Astronauts, 54mm, Apollo, wht or orange, P11, ea..$2.00
Marx, Astronauts, 54mm, in sm Stanford spacesuit, P11..$17.00
Marx, Astronauts, 54mm, Moon Base, silver, P11 ....$5.00
Marx, Astronauts, 54mm, Moon Base, silver, 15-pc set, NM, F5 ....$90.00
Marx, Astronauts, 54mm, Moon Base, silver, 7-pc set, NM, F5 ....$50.00
Marx, Astronuats, 54mm, in lg Republic suit, P11 ....$23.00
Marx, Astronuats, 54mm, seated, orange or red, P11, ea $7.00
Marx, Astronuats, 54mm, tan, P11....................$6.00
Marx, Ben Hur, 54mm, cream, 16-pc set, P11 ....$70.00
Marx, Ben Hur, 54mm, fighting, P11 ....$8.00
Marx, Ben Hur, 54mm, gray, 16-pc set, P11 ....$80.00
Marx, Ben Hur, 54mm, passive, P11....................$5.00
Marx, Ben Hur, 54mm, tan, 16-pc set, P11....................$75.00
Marx, Cape Canaveral Personnel, 54mm, tan, 13-pc set in 7 poses, NM, F5 ....$40.00
Marx, Cape Canaveral Personnel, 54mm, waxy beige, 15-pc set in 10 poses, NM, F5 ....$35.00
Marx, Eskimos, 54mm, paddling, bl, P11 ....$10.00
Marx, Eskimos, 54mm, pulling seal, bl, P11 ....$10.00
Marx, Eskimos, 54mm, pulling seal, gray, separated rope, P11..$10.00
Marx, Eskimos, 54mm, others, bl, P11....................$9.00
Marx, Eskimos, 54mm, others, yel, P11 ....$8.00
Marx, Fox Hunt, 60mm, fox running, P11 ....$9.00
Marx, Fox Hunt, 60mm, horse walking, P11....................$18.00
Marx, Fox Hunt, 60mm, hound running, P11....................$9.00
Marx, Fox Hunt, 60mm, hound sniffing, P11....................$9.00
Marx, Fox Hunt, 60mm, man w/top hat, P11 ....$14.00
Marx, Robin Hood, 54mm, Friar Tuck, cream, P11..........$10.00
Marx, Robin Hood, 54mm, Little John, cream, P11 ....$10.00
Marx, Robin Hood, 54mm, Maid Marian, cream, P11 .....$10.00
Marx, Robin Hood, 54mm, Merry Men, shooter, P11 ....$6.00
Marx, Robin Hood, 54mm, Robin Hood, cream, P11.......$15.00
Marx, Space Cadet, 45mm, P11 ....$3.00
Marx, Space Cadet, 45mm, w/gun, P11 ....$5.00
Marx, Space Patrol, 45mm, driver, P11 ....$12.00
Marx, Space Patrol, 45mm, driver, seated, tan or orange, P11, ea $15.00
Marx, Space Patrol, 45mm, female, tan or orange, P11, ea.$18.00
Marx, Space Patrol, 45mm, gray, P11....................$12.00
Marx, Space Patrol, 45mm, other, P11....................$8.00
Marx, Space Patrol, 45mm, tan or orange, P11, ea $8.00
Marx, Space Patrol, 45mm, w/hoops or pistol, gray, P11 ..$15.00
Marx, Space Patrol, 45mm, w/hoops or pistol, tan or orange, P11, ea $10.00

Photo courtesy June Moon

Marx, Spacemen, silver with clear plastic helmets, J6, $10.00 each.

Marx, Spacemen, 45mm, bl, P11 ....$3.00
Marx, Spacemen, 45mm, metallic bl, P11 ....$5.00
Marx, Spacemen, 45mm, yel, P11 ....$5.00
Marx, Spacemen, 50mm, Rex Mars, yel, 13-pc set, NM, F5..$130.00
Marx, Sports, 54mm, football, 17-pc set....................$50.00

Marx, Sports, baseball player, NM, $3.50.

Marx, Sports, 60mm, bowler, wht, NM, F5 .... $2.50
Marx, Sports, 60mm, boxer, wht, NM, F5 .... $3.50
Marx, Sports, 60mm, diver, P11 .... $8.00
Marx, Sports, 60mm, figure skater, wht, NM, F5 .... $2.50
Marx, Sports, 60mm, golfer, wht, NM, F5 .... $3.50
Marx, Sports, 60mm, hockey player, matt lt bl, NM, F5 .. $12.50
Marx, Sports, 60mm, runner, waxy wht, NM, F5 .... $2.50
Marx, Sports, 60mm, swimmer, matt lt bl, NM, F5 .... $8.50
Marx, Tom Corbett, P11 .... $3.00
Marx, Untouchables, 54mm, P11, ea $15.00
Marx, Vikings, 54mm, flat, gr, P11 .... $4.00
Marx, Vikings, 54mm, semiflat, gr, P11 .... $3.00
Premier, Spaceman, 3", hard plastic, P11 .... $5.00

Animals

Beton, Western, 45mm, horse, soft plastic, P11 .... $3.00
Beton, Western, 54mm, horse, hard plastic, P11 .... $5.00
Beton, Wild Animals, lion, NM, P11 .... $5.00
Marx, Circus Amimals, giraffe, tan, NM, P11 .... $7.00
Marx, Circus Animals, bear, NM, P11 .... $3.00
Marx, Circus Animals, buffalo, NM, P11 .... $7.00
Marx, Circus Animals, camel, NM, P11 .... $7.00
Marx, Circus Animals, dogs, 4 types, NM, P11, ea $2.00
Marx, Circus Animals, elephant w/howdah, NM, P11 ..... $10.00
Marx, Circus Animals, elephants, 2 types, NM, P11, ea $3.00
Marx, Circus Animals, giraffe, baby, NM, P11 .... $3.00
Marx, Circus Animals, giraffe, NM, P11 .... $3.00
Marx, Circus Animals, giraffe, tan, NM, P11 .... $7.00
Marx, Circus Animals, gorilla, NM, P11 .... $3.00
Marx, Circus Animals, horse, NM, P11 .... $3.00
Marx, Circus Animals, leopard, NM, P11 .... $3.00
Marx, Circus Animals, lion, NM, P11 .... $3.00
Marx, Circus Animals, monkey, in hat, NM, P11 .... $2.00
Marx, Circus Animals, monkeys, 6 types, NM, P11, ea $3.00
Marx, Circus Animals, polar bear, baby, NM, P11 .... $3.00
Marx, Circus Animals, polar bear, NM, P11 .... $3.00
Marx, Circus Animals, tiger, cream, NM, P11 .... $7.00
Marx, Circus Animals, tiger, tan, NM, P11 .... $7.00
Marx, Circus Animals, zebra, NM, P11 .... $3.00
Marx, Farm Animals, colt, 2nd issue, NM, P11 .... $2.00
Marx, Farm Animals, cow, 2nd issue, P11 .... $3.00
Marx, Farm Animals, dog, 2nd issue, NM, P11 .... $2.00
Marx, Farm Animals, goat, red-brn, NM, F5 .... $7.50
Marx, Farm Animals, hog, 2nd issue, NM, P11 .... $2.00
Marx, Farm Animals, lamb, 2nd issue, NM, P11 .... $1.00
Marx, Farm Animals, mare & foal, red-brn, NM, F5 .... $16.50
Marx, Farm Animals, pig, red-brn, NM, F5 .... $7.50
Marx, Farm Animals, piglet, 2nd issue, P11 .... $1.00
Marx, Farm Animals, rooster, 2nd issue, P11 .... $2.00
Marx, Farm Animals, sheep, red-brn, NM, F5 .... $7.50
Marx, Farm Animals, various, brn, 14-pc set, NM, F5 ...... $22.00
Marx, Farm Animals, various, red-brn, 8-pc set, NM, F5 . $12.50
Marx, Pet Shop, dogs, 6-pc set, EX $10.00
Marx, Prehistoric, Dinosaurs #PL-0750, lt gr, 6-pc set, NM, F5 .... $25.00
Marx, Prehistoric, Dinosaurs #PL-0755, lt gr, hard plastic, 7-pc set, NM, F5 .... $40.00

Marx, Fun-On-Wheels, with three of eight figures, NMIB, $35.00.

Marx, Prehistoric, Dinosaurs #PL-0755, lt gr, soft plastic, 7-pc set, NM, F5 .... $24.00
Marx, Prehistoric, Dinosaurs #PL-0755, waxy lt gray, 7-pc set, NM, F5 .... $12.50
Marx, Prehistoric, Dinosaurs #PL-0977, lt gr, 4-pc set, NM, F5 .... $16.50
Marx, Prehistoric, Dinosaurs #PL-0977, lt gray, 8-pc set, NM, F5 .... $80.00
Marx, Prehistoric, Dinosaurs; Allosaurus, dk brn, NM, F5 . $8.50
Marx, Prehistoric, Dinosaurs; Allosaurus, gray, 1st issue, M, F5 .... $3.50
Marx, Prehistoric, Dinosaurs; Allosaurus, lt gr, 1st issue, NM, F5 .... $4.50
Marx, Prehistoric, Dinosaurs; Ankylosaurus, dk brn, NM, F5 . $12.50
Marx, Prehistoric, Dinosaurs; Ankylosaurus, 1st issue, lt gr or lt gray, NM, F5, ea $3.50
Marx, Prehistoric, Dinosaurs; Brontosaurus, dk brn, NM, F5 . $18.50
Marx, Prehistoric, Dinosaurs; Cynognathus, lt gr, NM, F5 . $5.50
Marx, Prehistoric, Dinosaurs; Dimetrodon, dk brn, NM, F5 . $10.00
Marx, Prehistoric, Dinosaurs; Dimetrodon, matt lt gr, NM, F5 . $5.50
Marx, Prehistoric, Dinosaurs; Hadrosaurus, dk gray, NM, F5 ..... $3.50
Marx, Prehistoric, Dinosaurs; Hadrosaurus, gray, NM, F5 .. $4.50
Marx, Prehistoric, Dinosaurs; Iguanodon, lt gr, NM, F5 ... $18.50
Marx, Prehistoric, Dinosaurs; Iguanodon, lt gray, NM, F5 .. $12.50
Marx, Prehistoric, Dinosaurs; Kronosaurus, lt gr, NM, F5 ... $12.50
Marx, Prehistoric, Dinosaurs; Kronosaurus, silver, NM, F5 .. $22.00
Marx, Prehistoric, Dinosaurs; Moschops, matt lt gr, NM, F5 .... $15.00
Marx, Prehistoric, Dinosaurs; Parasaurolophus, matt gray, NM, F5 .... $18.50
Marx, Prehistoric, Dinosaurs; Plateosaurus, mint gr, NM, F5 ... $3.50
Marx, Prehistoric, Dinosaurs; Sphenagodon, gray, NM, F5 .. $6.50
Marx, Prehistoric, Dinosaurs; Stegosaurus, lt gray, 1st issue, EX, F5 .... $4.50

Marx, Prehistoric, Dinosaurs; Stegosaurus, matt brn, NM, F5....$10.00
Marx, Prehistoric, Dinosaurs; Struthiomimus, brn, NM, F5.$22.00
Marx, Prehistoric, Dinosaurs; Styracosaurus, lt gr, NM, F5..$10.00
Marx, Prehistoric, Dinosaurs; Trachodon, foot raised, dk brn, NM, F5.......$12.50
Marx, Prehistoric, Dinosaurs; Trachodon, foreleg down, gray, 1st issue, NM, F5 ....$3.50
Marx, Prehistoric, Dinosaurs; Triceratops, brn, 1st issue, NM, F5.......$16.50
Marx, Prehistoric, Dinosaurs; Triceratops, dk gray marble, 1st issue, NM, F5 ....$12.50
Marx, Prehistoric, Dinosaurs; Triceratops, lt gray, NM, F5...$3.50
Marx, Prehistoric, Dinosaurs; Tyrannosaurus Rex, sleek pose, matt dk gray, NM, F5.......$22.00
Marx, Prehistoric, Saber-toothed Tiger; Smilodon, lt gr, NM, F5 ....$16.50
Marx, Prize Livestock, Angus bull, tan, NM, F5 ....$8.50
Marx, Prize Livestock, Clydesdale, male, matt tan, NM, F5..$5.50
Marx, Prize Livestock, Merino ewe, matt tan, NM, F5 ....$6.50
Marx, Prize Livestock, Merino ram, matt cream, NM, F5...$6.50
Marx, Prize Livestock, Polland China sow, matt cream, NM, F5 ....$7.50
Marx, Western, Indian pony running, matt chocolate brn, NM, F5.......$8.50
Marx, Western, Indian pony standing, matt beige, NM, F5..$6.50
Marx, Western, 54mm, pack horse, red-brn, NM, F5 ....$10.00
Marx, Western, 54mm, saddled horse rearing, beige, NM, F5 ....$5.50
Marx, Wild Animals, alligator, red-brn, NM, F5 ....$3.50
Marx, Wild Animals, bear, beige, EX, F5 ....$4.50
Marx, Wild Animals, bear cub w/honey jar, tan, NM, F5...$3.50
Marx, Wild Animals, bobcat, tan or matt cream, NM, F5, ea ..$3.50
Marx, Wild Animals, bobcat stalking rabbit & skunk, red-brn, 3 pcs, NM, F5.......$10.00
Marx, Wild Animals, elephant & Indian, gray, NM, F5 ..$20.00
Marx, Wild Animals, fawn, tan, NM, F5 ....$3.50
Marx, Wild Animals, giraffe, beige, NM, F5.......$14.50
Marx, Wild Animals, grizzly bear, brn, NM, F5 ....$10.00
Marx, Wild Animals, kangaroo, beige, NM, F5 ....$16.50
Marx, Wild Animals, kangaroo, matt gray, NM, F5 ....$8.50
Marx, Wild Animals, lion, brn, NM, F5 ....$14.50
Marx, Wild Animals, ostrich, matt tan, NM, F5.......$6.50
Marx, Wild Animals, seal, brn, NM, F5 ....$7.50
Marx, Wild Animals, tiger, beige, NM, F5.......$16.50
Marx, Wild Animals, tiger, cream, NM, F5 ....$5.50
Timmee, Western, horses #TM238, 5-pc set.......$5.00

Campus Cuties and American Beauties

Marx, American Beauties, ballerina, hula dancer & reclining nude, set of 3, NM $90.00
Marx, Campus Cuties, Dinner for Two, M.......$8.00
Marx, Campus Cuties, Lazy Afternoon, M.......$8.00
Marx, Campus Cuties, Lodge Party, M $8.00
Marx, Campus Cuties, Nighty Night, M $8.00
Marx, Campus Cuties, On the Beach, M $8.00
Marx, Campus Cuties, On the Town, M.......$8.00
Marx, Campus Cuties, Shoppin Alone, M $8.00
Marx, Campus Cuties, Shoppin Anyone, M $8.00
Marx, Campus Cuties, Stormy Weather, M $8.00

Comic, Disney, and Nursery Characters

Marx, Comic Strip, Blondie, 1st issue, pk, NM, F5.......$7.50
Marx, Comic Strip, Blondie; Daisy the Dog, waxy lt bl, NM, F5 ....$30.00
Marx, Disney, 6", Donald Duck, P11.......$7.00
Marx, Disney, 6", Minnie Mouse, NM, F5 ....$10.00
Marx, Disney, 6", Peter Pan, NM, F5 ....$12.50
Marx, Disney, 6", Snow White, cobalt, VG+, F5.......$4.50
Marx, Disney, 60mm, Goofy, pk, NM, F5 ....$12.50
Marx, Disney, 60mm, Huey, Louie or Dewey, beige, NM, F5, ea.......$5.50
Marx, Disney, 60mm, Monty Mouse or Morty Mouse, beige, NM, F5, ea $5.50
Marx, Disney, 7", Zorro, P11 ....$10.00
Marx, Disneykid, Peter Pan; Wendy, 1960s, scarce, EX, M8..$50.00
Marx, Disneykings, Babes in Toyland; Soldiers, 1960s, NMIB, M8, ea $40.00

Photo courtesy Michael Stern

Marx, Disneykins, Bambi, NMIB, $15.00.

Marx, Disneykins, Lady & the Tramp, 2nd series; Boris, 1960s, NM, M8 ....$65.00
Marx, Disneykins, Peter Pan, 1st series; Captain Hook, Peter Pan or Tinkerbell, 1960s, EX, M8, ea $10.00
Marx, Disneykins, Snow White & the Seven Dwarfs, 1st series; any, 1960s, EX, M8, ea $10.00
Marx, Fairytales, 60mm, Goldilocks & the 3 Bears; Baby Bear, bl, P11 ....$4.00
Marx, Fairytales, 60mm, Goldilocks & the 3 Bears; Mama Bear, bl, P11 ....$4.00
Marx, Fairytales, 60mm, Jack & the Beanstalk; Giant, pk, P11 ....$4.00
Marx, Fairytales, 60mm, Jack & the Beanstalk; Jack on the beanstalk, pk, P11 ....$4.00
Marx, Fairytales, 60mm, Simple Simon, bl, NM, F5.......$12.50
Marx, Fun-on-Wheels, Beagle, Cow, French Poodle, Poo Poo the Poodle or Scottie, NM, F5, ea $4.50

Marx, Fun-on-Wheels, 3", Lady & the Tramp; Lady, 1960s, EX, M8 .... $20.00
Marx, Hanna-Barbera, 54mm, Flintstones; Townspeople, P11, ea $3.00
Marx, Hanna-Barbera, 60mm, Flintstones; Barney, cream, EX, F5 .... $3.50
Marx, Hanna-Barbera, 60mm, Flintstones; Dino, lt bl, NM, F5 .... $14.50
Marx, King Features, 60mm, Blondie, Alexander or Daisy the Dog, lt bl, NM, F5, ea $30.00
Marx, King Features, 60mm, Popeye; Olive Oyl, pk, NM, F5 .... $10.00
Marx, King Features, 60mm, Popeye, matt bl, NM, F5 .... $30.00

Photo courtesy Michael Stern

Marx, New Disneykins Play Set, rare, M (worn box), $225.00.

Marx, Nursery Rhymes, 60mm, Humpty Dumpty, matt gr, NM, F5 .... $12.50
Marx, Nursery Rhymes, 60mm, Humpty Dumpty, pk or gr, P11, ea $4.00
Marx, Nursery Rhymes, 60mm, Jack & Jill, pk, EX+, F5, ea $10.00
Marx, Nursery Rhymes, 60mm, Jack Be Nimble, pk, EX+, F5 .... $10.00
Marx, Nursery Rhymes, 60mm, Little Bo Peep, pk, NM, F5 .... $10.00
Marx, Nursery Rhymes, 60mm, Little Bo Peep; sheep, pk, NM, F5 .... $10.00
Marx, Nursery Rhymes, 60mm, Little Boy Blue, pk, EX+, F5 .... $8.50
Marx, Nursery Rhymes, 60mm, Little Miss Muffet, hand-pnt, P11 .... $4.00
Marx, Nursery Rhymes, 60mm, Little Miss Muffet, pk, NM, F5 .... $12.50
Marx, Nursery Rhymes, 60mm, Little Red Riding Hood, pk, NM, F5 .... $10.00
Marx, Nursery Rhymes, 60mm, Mary Had a Little Lamb, gr, P11 .... $4.00
Marx, Nursery Rhymes, 60mm, Mary Had a Little Lamb, pk, NM, F5 .... $10.00
Marx, Nursery Rhymes, 60mm, Old Mother Hubbard, hand-pnt, P11 .... $4.00
Marx, Nursery Rhymes, 60mm, Red Riding Hood; Wolf, pk, EX+, F5 .... $8.50
Marx, Nursery Rhymes, 60mm, Simple Simon; Simon, hand-pnt, P11 .... $4.00
Marx, Nursery Rhymes, 60mm, Simple Simon; Pieman, hand-pnt, P11 .... $4.00
Marx, Nursery Rhymes, 60mm, Three Little Kittens; kitten #1, hand-pnt, P11 .... $4.00
Marx, Nursery Rhymes, 60mm, Three Little Kittens; mother w/mittens, bl, P11 .... $4.00
Marx, TV Tinykins, 35mm, Flintstones; Baby Puss, hand-pnt, NM (EX box), F5 .... $30.00
Marx, TV Tinykins, 35mm, Flintstones; Betty Rubble, hand-pnt, NM, F5 .... $16.50
Marx, TV Tinykins, 35mm, Flintstones; traffic cop, hand-pnt, NM, F5 .... $18.50
Marx, TV Tinykins, 35mm, Flintstones; Wilma, hand-pnt, NM (EX box), F5 .... $30.00
Marx, TV Tinykins, 35mm, Huckleberry Hound; Dixie, hand-pnt, NM (G box), F5 .... $22.00
Marx, TV Tinykins, 35mm, Huckleberry Hound; Huck, hand-pnt, NM, F5 .... $25.00
Marx, TV Tinykins, 35mm, Huckleberry Hound; Mr Jinx, hand-pnt, NM, F5 .... $20.00
Marx, TV Tinykins, 35mm, Quick Draw McGraw; Augie Doggie, hand-pnt, NM, F5 .... $20.00
Marx, TV Tinykins, 35mm, Quick Draw McGraw; Snooper Cat, hand-pnt, NM, F5 .... $16.50
Marx, TV Tinykins, 35mm, Yogi Bear; Boo Boo, hand-pnt, NM, F5 .... $14.50
Marx, TV Tinykins, 35mm, Yogi Bear; Cindy Bear, hand-pnt, NM, F5 .... $14.50
Marx, TV Tinykins, 35mm, Yogi Bear; Ranger Smith, hand-pnt, NM, F5 .... $14.50
Marx, TV Tinykins, 35mm, Yogi Bear, hand-pnt, EX, F5 .... $8.50

Famous People and Civilians

Marx, Airport, 35mm, civilian, P11 .... $1.00
Marx, Airport, 35mm, 23-pc set $25.00
Marx, Airport, 54mm, worker, P11 .... $2.00
Marx, Circus, balloon vendor, P11 .... $10.00
Marx, Civilians & Workmen, 3¼", construction workers, cream, 6-pc set, NM, F5 .... $25.00
Marx, Civilians & Workmen, 35mm, milk delivery man, cream, NM, F5 .... $6.50
Marx, Civilians & Workmen, 45mm, construction workers, cream, 8-pc set, P11 .... $15.00
Marx, Civilians & Workmen, 48mm, construction camp workers, cream, 6-pc set, NM, F5 .... $25.00
Marx, Civilians & Workmen, 54mm, chauffer w/movable arms, cream, NM, F5 .... $2.50
Marx, Civilians & Workmen, 54mm, skyscraper civilians, cream, set of 16, NMIP, F5 .... $130.00
Marx, Family, 60mm, adult, cream, flat, P11 .... $4.00
Marx, Family, 60mm, adult, waxy, P11 .... $3.00
Marx, Family, 60mm, baby, cream, P11 .... $1.00

Marx, Family, 60mm, ball player, P11 ....$4.00
Marx, Family, 60mm, child, seated, P11 ....$1.00
Marx, Family, 60mm, diver, P11 ....$4.00
Marx, Family, 60mm, teenager, P11 ....$3.00
Marx, Farm, 35mm, farm woman w/bucket, cream, NM, F5 ..$4.50
Marx, Farm, 35mm, farmer & wife $4.00
Marx, Farm, 54mm, farmer driving, orange, P11 ....$6.00
Marx, Farm, 54mm, various, matt cream, set of 6, NM, F5 ....$20.00
Marx, Farm, 60mm, farmer milking, P11 ....$2.00
Marx, Farm, 60mm, farmer w/shovel, P11 ....$5.00
Marx, Farm, 60mm, farmer's wife, P11 ....$4.00
Marx, Farm, 60mm, scarecrow, P11 ....$10.00
Marx, Gas Station, 35mm, 6-pc set $5.00
Marx, Gas Station, 60mm, attendant, crouching, P11 ....$2.00
Marx, International VIPs, 60mm, Duke of Edinburgh, wht, sq base, NM, F5 ....$32.00
Marx, International VIPs, 60mm, Prince Charles, wht, sq base, NM, F5 ....$20.00
Marx, International VIPs, 60mm, Princess Anne, wht, sq base, NM, F5 ....$20.00
Marx, International VIPs, 60mm, Princess Margaret, wht, sq base, NM, F5 ....$20.00
Marx, International VIPs, 60mm, Queen Elizabeth II, wht, sq base, NM, F5 ....$30.00
Marx, Railroad, 35mm, workers, 6-pc set $6.00
Marx, Railroad, 45mm, civilian, P11 ....$4.00
Marx, Religious, 60mm, Bartholomew, ivory, NM, F5 ....$12.50
Marx, Religious, 60mm, Cardinal Spellman, ivory, sq base, NM, F5 ....$12.50
Marx, Religious, 60mm, Matthew, ivory, NM, F5 ....$12.50
Marx, Religious, 60mm, Peter, ivory, sq base, NM, F5 ....$12.50
Marx, US Presidents, 60mm, President FD Roosevelt, wht, sq base, NM, F5 ....$20.00
Marx, US Presidents, 60mm, President JF Kennedy, wht, sq base, NM, F5 ....$20.00
Marx, US Presidents, 60mm, President John Adams, wht, NM, F5 ....$4.50
Marx, US Presidents, 60mm, President Nixon, wht, sq base, NM, F5 ....$12.50

Military and Warriors

Airfix, Gurkas, 14-pc set, P11 ....$19.00
Airfix, Modern, British Infantry, 7-pc set, P11 ....$3.00
Airfix, Modern, German Infantry, 7-pc set, P11 ....$3.00
Airfix, Modern, NATO, 7-pc set, P11 ....$3.00
Airfix, Modern, Russian Infantry, 7-pc set, P11 ....$3.00
Airfix, Modern, SAS, 7-pc set, P11 ....$3.00
Airfix, NATO, 7-pc set, P11 ....$3.00
Airfix, Waterloo Highlanders, 29-pc boxed set, P11 ....$25.00
Airfix, WWII, Afrika Korps, khaki, 7-pc set, P11 ....$7.00
Airfix, WWII, Australian Infantry, P11, ea $2.00
Airfix, WWII, British Commando, 7-pc set, P11 ....$5.00
Airfix, WWII, British Infantry, boxed set, complete, P11 ..$50.00
Airfix, WWII, British Infantry, 7-pc set, P11 ....$6.00
Airfix, WWII, British Paratroopers, 14-pc set, P11 ....$14.00
Airfix, WWII, British Paratroopers, 7-pc set, P11 ....$5.00
Airfix, WWII, British Support, complete 68-pc set, P11 ..$48.00
Airfix, WWII, British 8th Army, khaki, 7-pc set, P11 ....$7.00
Airfix, WWII, German Infantry, bl, 8-pc set, P11 ....$7.00
Airfix, WWII, German Infantry, gray, 8-pc set, P11 ....$4.00
Airfix, WWII, German Infantry, 14-pc boxed set, P11 ....$14.00
Airfix, WWII, German Mountain Troops, 22-pc set, P11 .$24.00
Airfix, WWII, German Paratroopers, 14-pc set, P11 ....$10.00
Airfix, WWII, Ghurkas, 14-pc set, P11 ....$19.00
Airfix, WWII, Italian Infantry, 7-pc set, P11 ....$20.00
Airfix, WWII, Japanese, tan, 7-pc set, P11 ....$6.00
Airfix, WWII, Russian Infantry, gray, 7-pc set, P11 ....$6.00
Airfix, WWII, Russian Infantry, orange, 7-pc set, P11 ....$3.00
Airfix, WWII, US Infantry, 7-pc set, P11 ....$5.00
Airfix, WWII, US Paratroopers, gr, 13-pc set, P11 ....$11.00
Atlantic, German AA gun w/3 figures, P11 ....$7.00
Atlantic, Heavy Artillery, w/3 figures, P11 ....$8.00
Atlantic, Heavy Artillery, 2 w/6 figures, MIB, P11 ....$18.00
Atlantic, Sailors, 10-pc boxed set, P11 ....$9.00
Beton, soldier, 45mm, mounted, P11 ....$5.00
Beton, soldier, 60mm, flag bearer, P11 ....$5.00
Beton, soldier, 60mm, hard plastic, P11 ....$4.00
Beton, soldier, 60mm, separate base, P11 ....$5.00
Beton, soldier, 60mm, soft plastic, P11 ....$3.00
Dulcop, Norman Knight, mounted, P11 ....$6.00
Ideal, British Red Coat walking w/slung rifle, 70mm, red, NM, F5 ....$12.50
Ideal, British Red Coat walking w/sword drawn, 70mm, red, NM, F5 ....$12.50
Ideal, Colonial, 70mm, officer w/sword raised, bl, NM, F5 ..$12.50
Ideal, GI, 60mm, hard plastic, P11 ....$5.00
Ideal, GI, 60mm, soft plastic, P11 ....$3.00
Ideal, Knights, 60mm, gold, 12-pc set, P11 ....$75.00
Ideal, Knights, 60mm, silver, 12-pc set, P11 ....$75.00
Marx, Air Force, 45mm, cream, P11 ....$2.00
Marx, American Revolution, 54mm, Redcoat, Heritage Series, officer firing, P11 ....$3.00
Marx, American Revolution, 54mm, Redcoat, officer firing, P11 ....$5.00
Marx, American Revolution, 54mm, Redcoat, other, P11 .$4.00
Marx, American Revolutionary War, 54mm, British Redcoat marching/rifle, red, NM, F5 ....$7.50
Marx, American Revolutionary War, 54mm, soldiers, lt bl, set of 30 in 9 poses, NM, F5 ....$68.00
Marx, American Revolutionary War, 60mm, Paul Revere on horse, wht, NM, F5 ....$48.00
Marx, Cadets, 60mm, no plume, P11 ....$1.00
Marx, Cadets, 60mm, w/plume, P11 ....$5.00
Marx, Civil War, cavalry horses running, blk, 4-pc set, NM, F5 ....$11.50
Marx, Civil War, cavalry horses running, brn, 4-pc set, NM, F5 ....$11.50
Marx, Civil War, 54mm, Centennial, P11 ....$5.00
Marx, Civil War, 54mm, Confederate, flag bearer, Heritage Series, P11 ....$10.00
Marx, Civil War, 54mm, Confederate, flag bearer, P11 ...$25.00
Marx, Civil War, 54mm, Confederate, General Lee, P11...$5.00
Marx, Civil War, 54mm, Confederate, sword overhead or advancing w/bayonet, P11, ea $4.00

Marx, Colonials, 54mm, firing, Heritage Series, P11 ....$3.00
Marx, Colonials, 54mm, firing, P11 ....$5.00
Marx, Colonials, 54mm, firing, yel, P11 ....$10.00
Marx, Colonials, 54mm, flag bearer, Heritage Series, P11 ..$9.00
Marx, Colonials, 54mm, other, Heritage Series, P11 ....$2.00
Marx, Colonials, 60mm, rider, wht, P11 ....$25.00
Marx, Colonials, 60mm, winter dress, dk bl, P11 ....$12.00
Marx, Colonials, 60mm, winter dress, wht, P11 ....$15.00
Marx, Colonials, 60mm, other, dk bl, P11 ....$8.00
Marx, Colonials, 60mm, other, tan, P11 ....$8.00
Marx, Colonials, 60mm, other, wht, P11 ....$10.00
Marx, German, 6", P11 ....$3.00
Marx, Goldmarx Ancient Warriors, 6", Egyptian w/spear & shield, 2nd issue, NM, F5 ....$32.00
Marx, Goldmarx Ancient Warriors, 6", Knight Crusader w/bullet helmet, NM, F5 ....$28.00
Marx, Goldmarx Ancient Warriors, 6", Knight w/axe & shield raised, NM, F5 ....$26.00
Marx, Goldmarx Ancient Warriors, 6", Maximus w/sword raised, NM, F5 ....$25.00
Marx, Goldmarx Ancient Warriors, 6", Roman Soldier w/sword raised, rectangular shield, NM, F5 ....$28.00
Marx, Goldmarx Ancient Warriors, 6", Roman Soldier w/whip & sword, NM, F5 ....$25.00
Marx, Goldmarx Ancient Warriors, 6", Roman Warrior w/sword raised, rectangular shield, NM, F5 ....$28.00
Marx, Goldmarx Ancient Warriors, 6", Roman Warrior w/whip & sword, NM, F5 ....$25.00
Marx, Goldmarx Ancient Warriors, 6", Septimus Pius w/spear, EX, F5 ....$14.50
Marx, Goldmarx Ancient Warriors, 6", Viking Warrior w/mace & shield, NM, F5 ....$25.00
Marx, Japanese, 6", P11 ....$6.00
Marx, Knights, 54mm, any, 2nd series, P11 ....$1.00
Marx, Knights, 54mm, mounted w/flag, gr, 1st series, P11 ..$8.00
Marx, Knights, 54mm, mounted w/flag, silver, 1st series, P11 ....$4.00
Marx, Knights, 54mm, other, bl or gr, 1st series, P11 ....$4.00
Marx, Knights, 60mm, riding, P11 ....$18.00
Marx, Knights, 60mm, w/crossbow, P11 ....$10.00
Marx, Knights, 60mm, w/lance, P11 ....$5.00
Marx, Medieval Knights, 6", knight on guard w/sword & shield, silver, NM, F5 ....$12.50
Marx, Medieval Knights, 6", knight w/battle axe raised overhead, silver, EX, F5 ....$6.50
Marx, Mexican War, 60mm, US soldier aiming rifle, metallic bl, NM, F5 ....$16.50
Marx, Mexican War, 60mm, US soldier marching, metallic bl, NM, F5 ....$10.00
Marx, Mexican War, 60mm, US soldier reading orders, metallic bl, NM, F5 ....$12.50
Marx, Mexican War, 60mm, US soldier w/rifle, metallic bl, NM, F5 ....$12.50
Marx, Warriors of the World, 60mm, Ancient Chinese Warriors; Chang Fei, scarce, NM (NM box), F5, from $35 to $50.00
Marx, Warriors of the World, 60mm, Ancient Chinese Warriors; Chao Yun, scarce, NM (NM box), F5, from $35 to $50.00
Marx, Warriors of the World, 60mm, Ancient Chinese Warriors; Huang Chung, scarce, NM (NM box), F5, from $35 to $50.00
Marx, Warriors of the World, 60mm, Ancient Chinese Warriors; Kuan Yu, scarce, NM (NM box), F5, from $35 to $50.00
Marx, Warriors of the World, 60mm, Ancient Chinese Warriors; Lue Po, scarce, NM (NM box), F5, from $35 to $50.00
Marx, Warriors of the World, 60mm, Ancient Chinese Warriors; Yau Fai, scarce, NM (NM box), F5, from $35 to $50.00
Marx, Warriors of the World, 60mm, Cadets; Roger Case marching w/rifle, NM (EX box), F5 ....$15.00
Marx, Warriors of the World, 60mm, Cadets; Walter Shea, NM (NM box), F5 ....$26.00
Marx, Warriors of the World, 60mm, Civil War; Joe Bates marching w/rifle, NMIB, F5 ....$20.00
Marx, Warriors of the World, 60mm, Indians; Long Bow kneeling w/bow, F5 ....$22.00
Marx, Warriors of the World, 60mm, Indians; Slipping Bird attacking w/tomahawk, NM, F5 ....$12.50
Marx, Warriors of the World, 60mm, Indians; Strong Eagle standing w/bow, NMIB, F5 ....$20.00
Marx, Warriors of the World, 60mm, Mexican Soldiers; Anton Fuentes advancing w/sword, NMIB, F5 ....$35.00
Marx, Warriors of the World, 60mm, Mexican Soldiers; Bernal Veramendi swinging rifle, NM, F5 ....$22.00
Marx, Warriors of the World, 60mm, Pirates; Caesar charging w/knife in teeth, NM (NM box), F5 ....$25.00
Marx, Warriors of the World, 60mm, Pirates; Cripple Jack pegleg w/cutlass & crutch, NM (EX box), F5 ....$22.00
Marx, Warriors of the World, 60mm, Pirates; Steve Bonnet w/pistol, hand on sword, NM (NM box), F5.............$25.00
Marx, Warriors of the World, 60mm, Pirates; Steve Bonnet w/pistol, hand on sword, NM, F5 ....$12.50
Marx, Warriors of the World, 60mm, Pirates; Thomas Veale digging w/shovel, NM (EX box), F5 ....$20.00
Marx, Warriors of the World, 60mm, Revolutionary War; American Minuteman R Jayes, NMIB, F5 ....$20.00
Marx, Warriors of the World, 60mm, Revolutionary War; American drummer John Reeves, NMIB, F5 ....$22.00
Marx, Warriors of the World, 60mm, Revolutionary War; American fife player J Wilson, NMIB, F5 ....$22.00
Marx, Warriors of the World, 60mm, Revolutionary War; American flag bearer Michael Campbell, NM (NM box), F5 ....$30.00
Marx, Warriors of the World, 60mm, Revolutionary War; American officer Richard Travis, NMIB, F5 ....$22.00
Marx, Warriors of the World, 60mm, Revolutionary War; American officer Richard Travis w/sword, NM, F5 ....$16.50
Marx, Warriors of the World, 60mm, Revolutionary War; British soldier Henry Knox at attention, NMIB, F5 ..$32.00
Marx, Warriors of the World, 60mm, Revolutionary War; British soldier Horace Swire kneeling w/rifle, NMIB, F5 ....$36.00
Marx, Warriors of the World, 60mm, Revolutionary War; British soldier Richard Ellis w/rifle at waist, NMIB, F5.............$32.00
Marx, Warriors of the World, 60mm, Revolutionary War; British soldier Edward Sharp standing w/rifle, NMIB, F5 ....$38.00

Marx, Warriors of the World, 60mm, Revolutionary War; British officer James Black, NMIB, F5....................... $36.00
Marx, Warriors of the World, 60mm, Romans; Flavius Stilecho w/banner, NMIB, F5....................... $25.00
Marx, Warriors of the World, 60mm, Romans; Laelius standing at guard w/spear, NMIB, F5....................... $25.00
Marx, Warriors of the World, 60mm, Romans; Marius w/sword & oval shield, NM (VG+ box), F5....................... $15.00
Marx, Warriors of the World, 60mm, Romans; Marius w/sword & shield, NM, F5....................... $12.50
Marx, Warriors of the World, 60mm, Romans; Maximus w/sword raised, NM (EX box), F5....................... $20.00
Marx, Warriors of the World, 60mm, US Combat Soldiers; Harry Byrd prone w/rifle, NM (EX box), F5....................... $20.00
Marx, Warriors of the World, 60mm, US Combat Soldiers; Joe Dixon aiming rifle, NM (EX box), F5....................... $20.00
Marx, Warriors of the World, 60mm, Vikings; Bjorni advancing w/spear raised, NM, F5....................... $12.50
Marx, Warriors of the World, 60mm, Vikings; Eric the Red advancing w/club & shield, NM, F5....................... $14.50
Marx, Warriors of the World, 60mm, Vikings; Gustaf w/spear & shield, NM (EX box), F5....................... $22.00
Marx, Warriors of the World, 60mm, Vikings; Ketil attacking w/axe & shield, NM (VG box), F5....................... $22.00
Marx, Warriors of the World, 60mm, Vikings; Thorfinn attacking w/axe & shield, NM (VG box), F5....................... $20.00
Marx, Warriors of the World, 60mm, WWI, French; A Delcasse running w/rifle, NM (NM box), F5....................... $30.00
Marx, Warriors of the World, 60mm, WWI, French; Christian Gerard throwing grenade, NM (NM box), F5....................... $36.00
Marx, Warriors of the World, 60mm, WWI, French; J Clemenceau swinging rifle, NM (NM box), F5....................... $32.00
Marx, Warriors of the World, 60mm, WWI, French; Leon Pichon marching w/slung rifle, NM, F5....................... $18.50
Marx, Warriors of the World, 60mm, WWI, French; Maurice Valery standing w/rifle, NM (NM box), F5....................... $36.00
Marx, Warriors of the World, 60mm, WWI, French; Theophile Poincare w/pistol, NM (NM box), F5....................... $30.00
Marx, Warriors of the World, 60mm, WWI, German; Anton Dunckern w/sword & pistol, NM (NM box), F5....................... $38.00
Marx, Warriors of the World, 60mm, WWI, German; Friedrich Baden goose-stepping, NM (NM box), F5....................... $38.00
Marx, Warriors of the World, 60mm, WWI, German; Friedrich Baden goose-stepping, NM, F5....................... $22.00
Marx, Warriors of the World, 60mm, WWI, German; Hans Ehlers stabbing w/bayonet, NM (NM box), F5....................... $38.00
Marx, Warriors of the World, 60mm, WWII, German; Albert Galland advancing w/rifle, NM (NM box), F5....................... $32.00
Marx, Warriors of the World, 60mm, WWII, German; Ludwig Spear walking w/rifle, NM (NM box), F5....................... $32.00
Marx, Warriors of the World, 60mm, WWII, German; Martin Ferbach aiming rifle, NM (NM box), F5....................... $32.00
Marx, Warriors of the World, 60mm, WWII, German; Walter Hess throwing grenade, NM, F5....................... $16.50
Marx, WWII, 45mm, Amerians; GI on a stretcher, P11....................... $3.00
Marx, WWII, 45mm, American; GI flag bearer, P11....................... $1.00
Marx, WWII, 45mm, Americans; GI in camp pose, P11....................... $1.00
Marx, WWII, 45mm, Americans; marine flag bearer, P11....................... $10.00
Marx, WWII, 54mm, Americans; paddler, P11....................... $8.00
Marx, WWII, 54mm, Americans; paratrooper, P11....................... $8.00
Marx, WWII, 54mm, Japanese; flag bearer or shooter, dk tan, P11....................... $6.00
Marx, WWII, 54mm, Japanese; flag bearer or shooter, lt tan, P11....................... $4.00
Marx, WWII, 54mm, Japanese; other, dk tan, P11....................... $3.00
Marx, WWII, 54mm, Japanese; other, flesh, P11....................... $2.00
Marx, WWII, 54mm, Japanese; other, lt tan, P11....................... $3.00
Marx, WWII, 6", Americans; marine butting w/bayoneted rifle, gr, NM, F5....................... $5.50
Marx, WWII, 6", Germans; soldier kneeling w/rifle, gray, EX, F5....................... $4.50
Marx, WWII, 6", Germans; soldier running w/ammo belt, brn, EX, F5....................... $5.50
Marx, WWII, 6", Japanese; soldier aiming rifle, caramel, EX, F5....................... $6.50
Marx, WWII, 6", Japanese; soldier running w/bayonet & pistol, caramel, EX, F5....................... $4.50
Marx, WWII, 6", Japanese; soldier throwing grenade, caramel, EX, F5....................... $6.50
Marx, WWII, 6", Russian; aiming rifle, mint gr, NM, F5....................... $12.50
Marx, WWII, 60mm, Americans; combat soldier advancing w/rifle, gr, NM, F5....................... $5.50
Marx, WWII, 60mm, Americans; combat soldier crawling w/rifle, gr, NM, F5....................... $12.50
Marx, WWII, 60mm, Americans; combat soldier marching w/rifle, NM, F5....................... $4.50
Marx, WWII, 60mm, Americans; combat soldier throwing grenade, gr, NM, F5....................... $10.00

Nutty Mads

Marx, All Heart Hogan, pk w/cream swirl, NM, F5....................... $20.00
Marx, Bull Pen Boo Boo, maroon, 1st issue, NM, F5....................... $35.00
Marx, Bull Pen Boo Boo, sand, rare color, NM, F5....................... $28.00
Marx, Chief Lost Teepee, red, EX+, D9....................... $10.00
Marx, Dippy the Deep Diver, lime gr, NM, F5....................... $25.00
Marx, End Zone, pk, NM, F5....................... $25.00
Marx, Lost Teepee, maroon, 1st issue, NM, F5....................... $35.00
Marx, Manny the Reckless Mariner, lime gr, NM, F5....................... $20.00
Marx, Manny the Reckless Mariner, lt gr, 1st issue, NM, F5....................... $35.00
Marx, Rocko the Champ, lime gr, NM, F5....................... $25.00
Marx, Rocko the Champ, pk, EX+, F5....................... $16.50
Marx, Roddy the Hot Rod, chartreuse gr, 1st issue, NM, F5....................... $35.00
Marx, Suburban Sidney, dk gr, 1st issue, NM, F5....................... $32.00
Marx, Suburban Sidney, fluorescent red, NM, F5....................... $22.00
Marx, Waldo the Weight Lifter, pk, NM, F5....................... $25.00

Western and Frontier Heroes

Atlantic, Apache Camp #1206, 18-pc boxed set, P11....................... $20.00
Ausley, Indian, movable arms, P11....................... $20.00
Beton, Cowboy, 45mm, hard plastic, P11....................... $5.00
Beton, Cowboy, 45mm, on horse, hard plastic, P11....................... $9.00
Beton, Cowboy, 45mm, on horse, soft plastic, P11....................... $5.00
Beton, Cowboy, 45mm, soft plastic, P11....................... $2.00
Beton, Indian, 45mm, hard plastic, P11....................... $5.00

Beton, Indian, 45mm, soft plastic, P11 ....$2.00
Beton, Indian, 60mm, on horse, P11 ....$10.00
Beton, Indian, 60mm, P11 ....$3.00
Dulcop, California Mexicans, Mexican, w/separate weapon, P11 ....$4.00
Dulcop, Cowboy, P11 ....$2.00
Dulcop, Pioneer, P11 ....$2.00
Ideal, Cavalry, officer, mounted, P11 ....$8.00
Ideal, Indian, 54mm, mounted, P11 ....$2.00
Marx, Cavalry, 54mm, bugler, lt bl, P11 ....$20.00
Marx, Cavalry, 54mm, bugler, turq, P11 ....$15.00
Marx, Cavalry, 54mm, long coat, lt bl, P11 ....$15.00
Marx, Cavalry, 54mm, long coat, mounted, turq, P11 ....$10.00
Marx, Cavalry, 54mm, long coat & sword, turq, P11 ....$20.00
Marx, Cavalry, 54mm, mounted, shooting, turq, P11 ....$6.00
Marx, Cavalry, 54mm, w/guidon, turq, P11 ....$18.00
Marx, Cavalry, 54mm, w/pistol, turq, P11 ....$15.00
Marx, Cavalry, 60mm, firing, P11 ....$12.00
Marx, Cavalry, 60mm, mounted, P11 ....$18.00
Marx, Cowboy, 3", P11 ....$7.00
Marx, Cowboy, 54mm, gray, P11 ....$3.00
Marx, Cowboy, 54mm, red-brn, P11 ....$4.00
Marx, Cowboy, 54mm, other, P11 ....$2.00
Marx, Cowboy, 60mm, chubby, P11 ....$3.00
Marx, Cowboy, 60mm, Ranch Cowboys, w/horse & steer, 6-pc set $15.00
Marx, Cowboy, 60mm, Rodeo Cowboys, 8-pc set $20.00
Marx, Cowboy, 60mm, specialty, P11 ....$5.00
Marx, Cowboy, 60mm, Town Cowboy #MX244 ....$2.00
Marx, Cowboy, 60mm, Town Cowboys, 10-pc set $25.00
Marx, Cowboy, 60mm, woman, P11 ....$4.00
Marx, Cowboy, 60mm, yel, P1 ....$3.00
Marx, Famous, 35mm, Gunsmoke; Matt Dillon, P11 ....$10.00
Marx, Famous, 45mm, Davy Crockett, no name, P11 ....$5.00
Marx, Famous, 45mm, Davy Crockett, w/name, P11 ....$15.00
Marx, Famous, 54mm, General Custer w/pistol, dk bl, NM, F5 ....$65.00
Marx, Famous, 54mm, Lone Ranger; Lone Ranger & Tonto, 2-pc set $65.00
Marx, Famous, 54mm, Lone Ranger; Lone Ranger on Silver, matt cream, F5 ....$38.00
Marx, Famous, 54mm, Lone Ranger; Tonto w/feather, cream, NM, F5 ....$30.00
Marx, Famous, 54mm, Roy Rogers; Bullet standing, P11 ....$14.00
Marx, Famous, 54mm, Roy Rogers; Dale Evans, P11 ....$10.00
Marx, Famous, 54mm, Roy Rogers; Pat Brady, VG, P11 ....$4.00
Marx, Famous, 54mm, Roy Rogers; Roy, Dale & Bullet, 3-pc set $60.00
Marx, Famous, 54mm, Roy Rogers; Roy mounted, P11 ....$22.00
Marx, Famous, 54mm, Wyatt Earp $35.00
Marx, Famous, 60mm, Lone Ranger; Tonto w/feather, cream, NM, F5 ....$20.00
Marx, Famous, 60mm, Rin-Tin-Tin; Corporal Rusty, bl, EX, F5 ....$20.00
Marx, Famous, 60mm, Rin-Tin-Tin; Corporal Rusty, cream, NM, ...$25.00
Marx, Famous, 60mm, Rin-Tin-Tin; dog, bl, NM, F5 ....$30.00
Marx, Famous, 60mm, Rin-Tin-Tin; dog, wht, NM, F5 ....$35.00
Marx, Famous, 60mm, Rin-Tin-Tin; Lt Rip Masters, cream, NM, F5 ....$38.00
Marx, Famous, 60mm, Roy Rogers; Bullet seated, P11 ....$10.00
Marx, Famous, 60mm, Roy Rogers; Dale Evans, cream, NM, F5 ....$16.00
Marx, Famous, 60mm, Roy Rogers; Pat Brady w/hat in hand, NM, F5 ....$14.50
Marx, Famous, 60mm, Roy Rogers; Roy seated, cream, P11 ....$6.00
Marx, Famous, 60mm, Roy Rogers; Roy seated, waxy, P11 ....$5.00
Marx, Famous, 60mm, Roy Rogers; Roy seated, wht $7.00
Marx, Famous, 60mm, Roy Rogers; Roy w/1 pistol up, P11 ....$10.00
Marx, Indian, 45mm, mounted, shooting, P11 ....$5.00
Marx, Indian, 45mm, scalping, P11 ....$6.00
Marx, Indian, 54mm, sitting w/pipe, yel or red brn, ea $4.00
Marx, Indian, 54mm, 13-pc set w/totem pole, butterscotch, P11 ....$14.00
Marx, Indian, 54mm, 9-pc set w/totem pole (no specialty poses), butterscotch, P11 ....$7.00
Marx, Indian, 54mm, 9-pc set w/totem pole (no specialty poses), caramel, P11 ....$14.00
Marx, Indian, 60mm, camp poses, P11, ea $5.00
Marx, Indian, 60mm, firing, P11 ....$7.00
Marx, Indian, 60mm, mounted, climbing, P11 ....$6.00
Marx, Indian, 60mm, shot, w/club & bow or w/tomahawk & rifle, P11, ea $9.00
Marx, Indian, 60mm, other, P11 ....$3.00
Marx, Pioneer, 54mm, dk sky bl, P11 ....$3.00
Marx, Pioneer, 54mm, firing, flat, gray, P11 ....$8.00
Marx, Pioneer, 54mm, firing, lt bl, P11 ....$4.00
Marx, Pioneer, 54mm, firing, med bl, P11 ....$5.00
Marx, Pioneer, 54mm, firing, metallic bl, P11 ....$8.00
Marx, Pioneer, 54mm, firing, silver, P11 ....$3.00
Marx, Pioneer, 54mm, firing, turq, P11 ....$2.00
Marx, Pioneer, 54mm, Heritage Series, firing, P11 ....$4.00
Marx, Pioneer, 54mm, other, med bl, P11 ....$4.00
Marx, Pioneer, 54mm, other, metallic bl, P11 ....$6.00
Marx, Pioneer, 54mm, other, silver, P11 ....$2.00
Marx, Pioneer, 54mm, other, turq, P11 ....$1.00
Marx, Pioneer, 54mm, tan, ea $4.00
Marx, Pioneer, 54mm, turq, hard plastic, 19-pc set, P11 ....$38.00
Marx, Pioneer, 54mm, 10-pc set, lt bl, P11 ....$31.00
Timmee, Cowboys & Indians, 5-pc set $5.00
Timmee, Pioneers, #TM81-86, 8-pc set $5.00

Plasticville

From the 1940s through the '60s, Bachmann Brothers produced plastic accessories for train layouts such as buildings, fences, trees, and animals. Buildings often included several smaller pieces — for instance, ladders, railings, windsocks, etc. — everything you could ever need to play out just about any scenario. Beware of reissues.

Advisor: Gary Mosholder, Gary's Trains (G1).

#AD-4 Airport Administration Building, wht sides, bl roof, G1 ....$45.00

#AP-1 Airport Hangar, EX (EX box), G1 ....$25.00
#BK-1 Bank, EX (EX box), G1 ....$30.00
#BK-1 Bank, gray sides, gr roof, G1 ....$30.00
#BL-2 Bridge & Pond, EX (EX box), G1 ....$8.00
#BN-1 Barn, red roof, EX (EX box), G1 ....$15.00
#BR-2 Trestle Bridge, G1 ....$18.00
#CC-8 Church, EX (EX box), G1 ....$15.00
#CC-9 Church, EX (EX box), G1 ....$15.00
#DE-7 Diner, EX (EX box), G1 ....$20.00
#DH-2 Hardware/Pharmacy, G1 ....$18.00
#FB-1 Frosty Bar, yel sides, wht roof, G1..........................$15.00
#FB-4 Fire House, EX (EX box), G1 ....$15.00
#FG-12 Picket Fence, EX (EX box), G1 ....$15.00
#GO-2 Gas Station (sm), wht sides, red roof, wht insert, G1.$15.00
#GO-3 Gas Station (lg), w/Plasticville logo & pumps, G1.....$25.00
#HS-6 Hospital, w/furniture, EX (G box), G1 ....$25.00
#LC-2 Log Cabin, EX (G box), G1 ....$22.00
#LH-4 Two-Story Colonial House, wht w/gr roof & trim, EX (G box), G1 ....$20.00
#LM-3 Freight Station Kit, brn platform, EX (G box), G1..$15.00
#MH-2 New England Rancher, wht w/yel trim & brn roof, EX (G box), G1 ....$18.00
#ON-5 Outdoor Necessities, G1 ....$15.00
#PD-3 Police Station, lt gray, EX (EX box), G1 ....$20.00
#PH-1 Town Hall, EX (EX box), G1 ....$35.00
#PO-1 Post Office, gray front & roof, G1..........................$18.00
#RH-1 Ranch House, yel w/wht roof, EX (EX box), G1...$18.00
#SC-4 School, EX (EX box), G1 ....$20.00
#SM-6 Supermarket, sm, EX (EX box), G1 ....$15.00
#SW-2 Switch Tower, brn sides, gray roof, G1 ....$6.00
#WW-3 Wishing Well, brn, G1 ....$3.00
#YW-4 Yard Pump, brn, G1...$3.00
#1090 Telephone Booth, EX, G1 ....$15.00
#1302 Farm Implement Set, yel vehicles w/red trim, G1..$40.00
#1403 Signal Bridge, EX (EX box), G1 ....$10.00
#1405 Street Signs, EX (EX box), G1 ....$15.00
#1406 Playground Equipment, EX (EX box), G1 ....$25.00
#1408 Windmill, lt gray, EX (EX box), G1.......................$40.00
#1502 Cape Cod House, pk, G1 ....$35.00
#1502 Cape Cod House, red & wht, EX (EX box), G1 ....$15.00
#1503 Add-A-Floor, G1 ....$30.00
#1504 Mobile Home, wht sides, turq roof & trim, G1 ......$55.00
#1600 Church, EX (EX box), G1 ....$15.00
#1606 Animals, set of 18, EX (G box), G1 ....$15.00
#1608 School, EX (EX box), G1 ....$20.00
#1615 Water Tank, brn w/gray base, EX (EX box), G1 ....$15.00
#1616 Suburban Station, EX (VG box), G1 ....$12.00
#1617 Farm Buildings & Animals, G1 ....$25.00
#1618 TV Station, EX (EX box), G1 ....$40.00
#1621 Motel, w/flowers, EX (G box), G1..........................$15.00
#1622 Dairy Barn, red & gray, EX (EX box), G1 ....$15.00
#1623 Loading Pen, G1 ....$45.00
#1624 House, under construction, lt gray, G1 ....$45.00
#1626 Corner Store, G1 ....$45.00
#1627 Hobo Shack, EX (EX box), G1 ....$200.00
#1700 Colonial House, EX (EX box), G1 ....$20.00
#1703 Colonial Mansion, wht sides, red roof, G1.............$30.00
#1804 Greenhouse, w/flowers, EX (EX box), G1 ....$75.00
#1805 Covered Bridge, G1 ....$18.00
#1806 Roadside Stand, w/pnt, G1 ....$30.00
#1857 Drug Store, G1 ....$25.00
#1901 Union Station, EX (EX box), G1 ....$25.00
#1904 Cathedral, EX (EX box), G1 ....$30.00
#1906 Factory, tan sides, gray roof, G1.............................$35.00
#1908 Split-Level House, EX (EX box), G1 ....$25.00
#1911 Suburban Station, brn platform, EX (EX box), G1 .$12.00
#1912 New England Ranch, G1 ....$28.00
#1922 Two-Story House, G1 ....$20.00
#1957 Coaling Station, EX (EX box), G1 ....$25.00

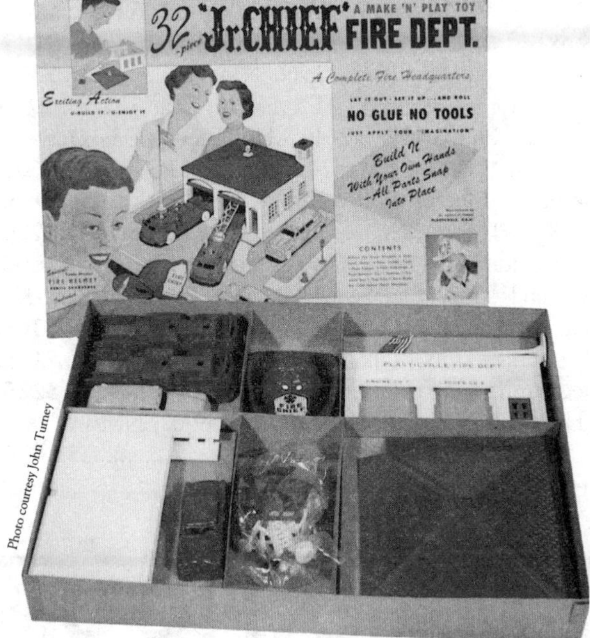

Jr. Chief Fire Dept. complete, MIB, $200.00.

Playsets

Louis Marx is given credit for developing the modern-age playset and during the '50s and '60s produced hundreds of boxed sets, each with the buildings, figures, and accessories that when combined with a child's imagination could bring any scenario alive, from the days of Ben Hur to medieval battles, through the cowboy and Indian era, and on up to Cape Canaveral. Marx's prices were kept low by mass marketing (through retail giants such as Sears and Montgomery Wards) and overseas production. But on today's market, playsets are anything but low priced; some mint-in-box examples sell for upwards of $1,000.00. Just remember that a set that shows wear or has even a few minor pieces missing quickly drops in value. The listings below are complete unless noted otherwise.

Advisors: Bob Wilson, Phoenix Toy Soldier Co. (P11); Mike and Kurt Fredericks (F4).

Adventures of Robin Hood #4722, Marx, 1956, EX (EX box), F5 ....$450.00
Adventures of Robin Hood #4723, Marx, EX (EX box), P11..$450.00
Alamo #3546, Marx, 1960, NM (NM box), F5 ....$900.00
Alaska Playset #3708, Marx, 1959, MIB......................$950.00
American Airlines International Jetport, box only, Marx, Series 1000, EX, P11 ....$35.00
American Patrol Set #6007, Marx/Sears Exclusive, 1964, MIB, F5 ....$1,200.00
Arctic Explorer #3702, Marx, Series 2000, 1958, EX (VG box), F5 ....$750.00
Armored Attack Set, Marx, MIB, A $225.00
Astro Jet Airport, 1961, NMIB $485.00
Bat Masterson Indian Fighter, Multiple, unused, NM (EX box) $185.00
Batman Batcave, Ideal/Sears, 1966, NM, A $300.00
Battle of Navarone, Marx, 1977, EX (EX box), from $100 to ...$125.00
Battle of the Blue & Gray #2646, Marx, EX+ (VG box)..$400.00
Battle of the Blue & Gray #4745, Marx, EX (G box).....$600.00
Battle of the Blue & Gray #4746, Marx, Series 1000, 1958, EX (EX box) $700.00
Battleground #4204, Marx, few pcs missing, EX, P11 ....$90.00
Battleground #4752, Marx, Series 2000, 1958, EX (EX box) $350.00
Battleground #4754, Marx, 1962, NM (NM box), A.....$365.00
Battleground #4756, Marx, few pcs missing, EX, P11.....$125.00
Battleground #4756, Marx, 1967, NM (EX box), F5......$225.00
Ben Hur #4702, Marx, Series 2000, 1959-62, NM (VG+ box), F5 ....$1,000.00
Big Top Circus, Marx, NMIB.......................................$650.00
Bomb-A-Ship, Thomas, EX (EX box), P11 ....$175.00

Photo courtesy Bob Wilson

Boy's Camp, box only, Marx, P11, $100.00.

Boy's Camp #4103, Marx, 1956, EX (G box), F5 ....$700.00
Bradley's Toy Town Post Office, VG (VG box) $100.00
Bridge & Trestle Set, Marx, NMIB, P11 ....$20.00
Buddy L Roundup, unused, NMIB $450.00
Cape Canaveral #2656, Marx, MIB, P11 ....$720.00
Cape Canaveral #4528, Marx, 1959-60, EX (EX box) ...$375.00
Cape Canaveral Missile Set #4526, Marx, MIB, P11 .....$900.00
Cape Canaveral/Project Apollo #4521, Marx, 1961, NM (NM box) $250.00
Captain Gallant of the Foreign Legion #4729, Marx, NM (VG box) $1,200.00
Captain Space Solar Port, box only, Marx, 1954, EX, P11 ..$60.00
Civil War Centennial #5929, Marx/Sears, few pcs missing, VG (G box) $400.00
Construction Camp #4440, Marx, 1954, EX (VG box), F5 ..$285.00

Photo courtesy Bob Wilson

Cowboy and Indian Camp #3849, Marx, EX (EX box), $380.00.

Cowboys & Indians Fort & Campsite Set, Elastolin, NM .$1,265.00
Davy Crockett at the Alamo #3544, Marx, 1955, NM (EX box) $750.00
Davy Crockett Covered Wagon Kit & Armed Escort, Lido, unused, NM (VG box) $200.00
Davy Crockett Western Set, Archer, NM (NM box), A .$150.00
Desert Fox #417MO, Marx, EX (EX box), P11 ....$450.00
Disneyland #4368, Marx, scarce, NM (EX box), A........$750.00
Dow Service Center w/Sky-View Parking, Marx, NM ...$265.00

Elevator Tower Garage, Keystone, w/Renwal cars, EX, A .$300.00
Fighting Knights Carry-All Set #4635, Marx, 1968, MIB..$115.00
Fighting Marine Combat Unit #1172, Marx, NM (NM box), A....................$350.00
Fire Department, Keystone, litho tin w/plastic accessories, NM, A....................$400.00
Flintstones #4672, Marx, 1961, orig issue, EX (EX box), F5.....$350.00
Fort Apache, Marx, miniature, NMIB, A $100.00

Photo courtesy John Turney

Fort Apache, Series 500, MIB, $450.00.

Fort Apache #3632C, box only, EX, P11 ....$50.00
Fort Apache #3647, Series 500, box only, VG, P11 ....$30.00
Fort Apache #3680, Marx, NM (EX box)....................$200.00
Fort Apache #3681, box only, Marx, 1973, EX, P11 ....$20.00
Fort Apache #3681, Marx, 1973, EX (EX box), F5.........$185.00
Fort Apache #3686, Marx/Sears, 1975, EX (EX box), F5 .$150.00
Fort Apache #3698-6063, Marx/Sears Exclusive, Deluxe edition, 335 pcs, M (EX box) $1,200.00
Fort Apache #5962, Happi-Time, 1963, NM (EX Sears-Allstate box)....................$500.00
Fort Apache Carry-All Set #4685, Marx, 1968, NM (NM metal case) $100.00
Fort Boone, MPC, unused, MIB $225.00
Fort Cheyenne, Ideal, opens to playset w/vacuform pcs, EX, P11....................$20.00
Fort Dearborn #3510, Marx, 1952, NM (NM box) $400.00
Fort Dearborn #3514, Marx, EX....................$200.00
Fort Dearborn #3514, Marx, NM (EX box) $325.00
Fort Laramie #4876, Ideal, 1957, VG (VG box).............$500.00
Fort Liberty, Hong Kong, 1970, NMIB, J6....................$85.00
Fort Mohawk #3752, Marx, Series 1000, 1958, NM (NM box), minimum value....................$850.00
Freight Terminal #5420, Marx, MIB, P11....................$700.00
Galaxy Command, Marx, MIB....................$325.00
Gallant Gladiator Warship, Remco, few pcs missing, EX (EX box), P11 ....$235.00
Guid-A Traffic PFPC #32, Marx/Sears, 1952, EX, P11 ..$100.00
Gunsmoke Dodge City #4628, Marx, Series 2000, 1960, rare, MIB....................$2,500.00
Keystone Service Station #143, 1940s, NM (worn box), A ..$385.00
Knights & Castle Miniature Playset, Marx, 1960s, NM (EX box), A....................$100.00
Knights & Vikings Castle #4743, Marx, EX (NM box) .$250.00

Photo courtesy John Turney

International Airport Set, Marx, MIB, $450.00.

Little Red School House #3381, Marx, rare, NMIB $600.00
Marine Beach-Head #4732, Marx, NM (NM box), A ...$250.00
Matchbox Service Station #MG-1, NM (NM box), A $50.00
Medieval Castle #4700, Marx, MIB, P11 ....$850.00
Medieval Castle Fort #4709, Marx, EX (EX box)...........$350.00
Mickey Mouse Old Fashion Pirate Ship, Ideal, missing several figures, EX (EX box) $275.00
Missile Attack Force #4500, MPC, NMIB......................$250.00
Missiles to the Moon, MPC, Deluxe issue, NMIB..........$350.00
Modern Farm, Marx/Sears, EX (EX box) $250.00
Noah's Ark Miniature Play Set, Marx, NM (NM box), A..$125.00
Planet of the Apes #1331, Multiple, NM (NM box), A.$200.00
Prehistoric Playset #3398, Marx, 1971, MIB..................$125.00
Prehistoric Times #3390, box only, Marx, EX, P11 ....$50.00
Prehistoric Times #3390, Marx, NM (NM box).............$200.00
Prince Valiant Castle Fort #4706, Marx, 1954-55, EX (G box), F5 ....$385.00
Project Mercury Cape Canaveral #4524, Marx, NM (EX box), from $250 to $300.00
Radar Rocket Ship #255, Keystone, NM (NM box), A .$185.00
Revell Circus #51, NM (EX box), A..............................$100.00
Revolutionary War #3401, Marx, Series 500, NMIB, P11 .$1,100.00
Rex Mars #7040, Marx, EX (EX box), P11 ....$1,200.00
Rifleman Ranch #3998, Marx, 1961, Series 1000, EX (EX box), F5 ....$750.00
Rin-Tin-Tin #3627, Marx, EX (EX box) $450.00
Rin-Tin-Tin #3658, Marx, EX (VG box) $325.00
Riverside Construction Set #48-23291, Marx/Montgomery Wards, EX (EX box), F5..$300.00
Roadside Steel Service Station #624, T Cohn, NM (NM box), A $300.00
Robin Hood Castle Set #4719, Marx, 1956, MIB...........$450.00
Roy Rogers Fix-It Chuck Wagon & Jeep, Ideal, 1950s, EX (EX box)..$400.00
Roy Rogers Hauler & Van Trailer w/Nellybelle Jeep, Marx, 15" trailer, NM (NM box), A...$900.00
Roy Rogers Rodeo Ranch #3990, box only, Marx, 1950s, VG $95.00
Roy Rogers Rodeo Ranch #3990, Marx, 1950s, NM (EX box), from $200 to $300.00
Roy Rogers Rodeo Ranch #3992, Marx, NMIB.............$275.00
Roy Rogers Western Town #4229, Marx, MIB, P11 ...$1,200.00
Royal Canadian Mounties, Ideal, 1957, few pcs missing, EX (EX box)..$350.00

Sands of Iwo Jima Playset #6062, Sears, 1964, EX (G box)..$985.00
Sears Automotive Center, Marx, battery-op elevator, NM..$450.00
Service Center #3465, Marx, EX (EX box), A $385.00
Service Station, Keystone, litho tin w/plastic accessories, 7x16", scarce, NM, A..$300.00
Service Station #866, Superior, NM (NM box), A $225.00
Sgt Rock Vs the Bad Guys, Remco, 1982, NMIB, J6........$85.00
Silver City Frontier Town #4220, Marx, 1955, M (VG box), F5 ....$500.00
Superior Service Station, T Cohn, NM, A....................$250.00

Superior Space Port, T. Cohn, 1952, MIB, $750.00.

Tom Corbett Space Academy #7010, Marx, EX (EX box) ..$375.00
Tricky Action Construction Set, Marx, MIB, P11 ....$150.00
US Air Force Missile Rocket Command #3007, MPC, NMIB $175.00
US Armed Forces Training Center, Marx, Series 500, MIB (sealed) $450.00
US Army Front Line Command #5033, MPC, NMIB ...$200.00
US Army Training Center #4133, Marx, NM (EX box) ..$155.00

Photo courtesy Bill Bruegman

Voyage to the Bottom of the Sea Seaview Submarine Set, Remco, MIB, from $1,000.00 to $1,500.00.

Wagon Train #4805, Marx/Sears Exclusive, Series 2000, 1960, MIB, minimum value $3,000.00
Walt Disney Alamo #3540, Marx, EX (EX box) $600.00
Westward Ho, Miner Industries, MIB, P11 ....$25.00
Wizard of Oz Munchkinland, Mego, 1976, MIB, J6 ....$450.00
Zorro #3753, Marx, NMIB $1,100.00

Photo courtesy June Moon

World War II Battleground, Marx #4204, 1978, MIB, J6, $125.00.

Political

As far back as the 19th century, children's toys with a political message were on the market. One of the most familiar was the 'Tammany Bank' patented by J. & E. Stevens in 1873. The message was obvious — a coin placed in the man's hand was deposited in his pocket, representing the kickbacks William Tweed was suspected of pocketing when he was the head of Tammany Hall in New York during the 1860s.

Advisors: Michael and Polly McQuillen (M11).

Agnew, Spiro; wristwatch, All American Time Co, caricature face, non-working, M11 ... **$40.00**

Agnew, Spiro; wristwatch, Swiss made, sq face, expandable metal band, non-working, M11 ... **$50.00**

Bush, George; figure for car window, New Waves, bobbing hand under 9" face, NM, M11 ... **$10.00**

Bush, George; monkey toy, plush monkey w/hat, gripping arms, Bush for President '88 on back, 4", NM, M11 ... **$5.00**

Bush, George; squeeze doll, Santa w/Bush's face, rubber, EX, M11 ... **$20.00**

Carter, Jimmy; bank, plastic peanut w/teeth, 12½", EX ... **$15.00**

Carter, Jimmy; peanut ring, C10 ... **$25.00**

Carter, Jimmy; wristwatch, 1977, From Peanuts to President, caricature face, flexible metal band, M11 ... **$35.00**

Cleveland/Harrison, wooden block game, VG, M11 ... **$240.00**

Clinton, Bill; game, Barrel of Clintons, NM, M11 ... **$12.00**

Clinton/Dole, squeeze toy, The Great Debate, candidates pointing into ea other's face, metal, EX, M11 ... **$15.00**

Dukakis, Michael; monkey toy, plush monkey w/hat, gripping arms, Win in '88 on back, 4", NM, M11 ... **$5.00**

Eisenhower, Dwight D; harmonica, red, wht & bl plastic w/I Like Ike on both sides, 6", VG, M11 ... **$25.00**

Eisenhower, Dwight D; nodder, 1950s, pnt compo elephant w/I'm for Ike, 6½", NM, M11 ... **$100.00**

Eisenhower, Dwight D; Presidential Campaign Car, Lionel, 12", EX, M11 ... **$150.00**

Eisenhower, Dwight D; walking elephant, plush, battery-op, EX, M11 ... **$125.00**

Goldwater, Barry; board game, 1964 Presidential Election Game, MOC, M11 ... **$30.00**

Goldwater, Barry; figure, Remco, 1964, NMIB ... **$35.00**

Goldwater, Barry; sunglasses, blk cb, NM, M11 ... **$12.00**

Hoover, Herbert; hat, gr felt, Hoover for President on band, 5", VG, M11 ... **$50.00**

Johnson, Lyndon B; bubble gum cigar, 1964, MIP, M11 ... **$6.00**

Johnson, Lyndon B; figure, Remco, plastic, 5", MIB, M11 .. **$30.00**

Kennedy, Jackie; mask, 1960, thin plastic, EX, M11 ... **$40.00**

Kennedy, John F; balloon, Vote Kennedy, wht on bl, unused, M11 ... **$10.00**

Kennedy, John F; board game, The Kennedys, Mt Rushmore caricatures on box, NM, M11 ... **$55.00**

Kennedy, John F; charm bracelet, 1963, MOC ... **$50.00**

Photo courtesy Martin and Carolyn Berens

Carter, Jimmy; figure, windup walker, plastic, EX, B5, $30.00; Radio, MIB, B5, $55.00.

Photo courtesy Tim Hunter

Kennedys, nodders, $275.00 for the pair.

Kennedy, John F; mask, 1960, thin plastic, EX, M11 ....$40.00
Kennedy, John F; toy boat, Empire, 1960s, soft plastic, 7", EX, M11 ....$75.00
Kennedy, Ted; doll, 1980, cloth caricature, 5½", EX, M11 ....$15.00
Lincoln, Abraham; doll, Effanbee, 1983, 17", MIB, M15 .$70.00
Lindsay, John; comb, bl plastic gun figure w/Aim for Lindsay, NM, M11 ....$20.00
MacArthur, General Douglas; writing pad & candy, EX (EX portrait tin), M11 ....$55.00
McGovern, George; top, plastic, McGovern Is Tops for America, EX $20.00
McKinley/Hobart, top, wood w/photos on paper label, G, M11 ....$175.00
Nixon, Richard; clicker, photo & Click w/Dick, NM, M11 .....$10.00
Nixon, Richard; dart board, Stick Dick, 11½" sq, NM, M11 ....$25.00
Nixon, Richard; doll, Tricky Dick, rubber, 5", NMOC, M11 ...$20.00
Nixon, Richard; hand puppet, 1968, plastic head w/cloth body, NM, M11 ....$35.00
Nixon, Richard; music box, 1972, w/up dancer, plays Ta Ra Ra Boom De Yea, NM, M11 ....$175.00
Reagan, Ronald; voodoo doll, MIP, M11 ....$25.00
Roosevelt, Franklin D; bank, Happy Days, barrel shape, 5", EX, M11 ....$15.00
Roosevelt, Teddy; board game, Rough Riders, Parker Bros, 1900, scarce, EX (VG box), M11 ....$125.00
Roosevelt, Teddy; game, Germany, 1904, drop balls into Teddy's mouth, mirror back w/glass cover, 2¼" dia, VG, M11 ..$850.00
Uncle Sam, mask, Sloan & Woodard, 1904, litho cb, 13", rare, EX $75.00
Washington, George; doll, Effanbee, 1983, 16", MIB, M15 ..$60.00
Wilson, Woodrow; puzzle, diecut profile, w/envelope, VG, M11 ....$70.00

Premiums

Those of us from the pre-boomer era remember waiting in anticipation for our silver bullet ring, secret membership kit, decoder pin, coloring book, or whatever other wonderful item we'd seen advertised in our favorite comic book or heard about on the Tom Mix show. Tom wasn't the only one to have these exciting premiums, though, just about any top character-oriented show from the 1930s through the '40s made similar offers, and even through the '50s some were still being distributed. Often they could be had free for a cereal boxtop or an Ovaltine inner seal, and if any money was involved, it was usually only a dime. Not especially durable and often made in somewhat limited amounts, few have survived to the present. Today some of these are bringing fantastic prices, but the market at present is very volatile.

Condition is very important in assessing value; items in pristine condition bring premium prices.

Advisor: Bill Campbell (C10).

Other Sources: J5

See also Advertising; Cereal Boxes and Premiums; Pinback Buttons.

Buck Jones, ring, 1930s, brass horseshoe design w/image of Buck in center, EX $100.00
Buck Rogers, badge, Chief Explorer, Cream of Wheat, 1935, gold & red, M, A $300.00
Buck Rogers, badge, Solar Scout Membership, inscr To My Solar Scout... on back, no wire hook o/w NM, A $65.00
Buck Rogers, figures, Buck, Wilma & Killer Kane, Coco Malt, 1932, pnt lead, 3", VG, A $650.00
Buck Rogers, manual, Solar Scouts, Cream of Wheat, 1936, 8x5", NM, A $425.00
Buck Rogers, ring, Saturn, 1940s, EX, A $340.00
Buck Rogers, Solar Scouts Manual, Cream of Wheat, 1936, rare, EX, P4 ....$125.00
Buck Rogers, space helmet, 1930s, red rubber, rare, M, A ..$545.00
Captain Action, card game, Kool-Pops mail-in, 1967, EX+ (EX box), A $135.00
Captain Action, flicker rings, 6 different, NM, ea $50.00
Captain Hawks, medal, Flight Captain, 1935, NM, A $60.00
Captain Hawks, medal, Flight Lieutenant, 1935, NM, A .$80.00
Captain Marvel, Magic Flute, Lee-Tex, 1946, MOC $150.00

Captain Marvel, Magic Whistle, 1947, lithographed cardboard, NM, A, $165.00.

Captain Marvel, tie clip, 1946, NMOC, A $100.00
Captain Marvel, toss bag, EX $105.00
Captain Midnight, decoder, SQ Plane, 1955, rare, NM, A ...$280.00
Captain Midnight, Detect-O-Scope (5-Way), 1941, scarce, M (orig mailing tube), A $190.00
Captain Midnight, Key-O-Matic Code-O-Graph, 1949, gold-colored tin & plastic, no key o/w VG, P4 ....$65.00
Captain Midnight, manual, Secret Squadron, 1957, w/whistle, EX (orig envelope), A $145.00
Captain Midnight, manual, 1940, VG+, J5 ....$85.00
Captain Midnight, Mirro-Flash Code-O-Graph, 1945, EX, A $80.00
Captain Midnight, Mirro-Flash Code-O-Graph, 1946, gold-colored tin & plastic, VG, P4 ....$70.00
Captain Midnight, mug, Ovaltine, 1947, plastic, M (orig mailing tube), A $300.00
Captain Midnight, mug, Ovaltine, 1955, red plastic w/decal, MIB, A $200.00

Photo courtesy June Moon

Captain Midnight, mug, Ovaltine, 1955, red plastic with decal, EX, $100.00.

Captain Midnight, patch, Secret Squadron, 1955, cloth, MIP, A....$85.00
Captain Midnight, ring, Marine Corps, 1942, scarce, NM, A...$300.00
Captain Midnight, ring, Mystic Eye, EX....$195.00
Captain Midnight, ring, Seal, NM, C10....$400.00
Captain Midnight, ring, Secret Compartment, NM, C10 .$175.00
Captain Midnight, ring, Whirlwind Whistle, 1941, scarce, VG, A....$275.00
Captain Midnight, Secret Squadron Mystery Dial Code-O-Graph, Ovaltine, 1940, EX, A....$75.00
Captain Midnight, Spy-Scope, 1948, scarce, M (orig mailing tube), A....$255.00
Captain Midnight, Trick & Riddle Book, Skelly, 1939, 2x3", EX, J5....$35.00
Cisco Kid, Humming Lariat, Archway Cookies, 1953, unused, MIP, A....$40.00
Cisco Kid, puzzle, Tip Top Bread, 1950, 8x7", NM (orig mailer), A....$100.00
Davy Crockett, ring, face, 1950s, bronze, NM, A....$40.00
Davy Crockett, ring, rifle, 1950s, bronze, NM, A....$75.00
Dick Steel, badge, News Service Reporter, 1940, NM, A...$50.00
Dick Tracy, badge, Inspector General, 1938, scarce, NM, A..$400.00
Dick Tracy, badge, Secret Service Patrol Captain, Quaker, 1930-39, EX, D11....$200.00
Dick Tracy, badge, Secret Service Patrol Inspector General, Quaker, 1930-39, scarce, EX, D11....$500.00
Dick Tracy, badge, Secret Service Patrol Sargeant, 1938, NM, A....$75.00
Dick Tracy, book, Dick Tracy & the Crook Without a Face, Pan-Am Oil Co, 1938, softcover, rare, EX, D11....$200.00
Dick Tracy, book, Dick Tracy the Detective & Dick Tracy Jr, Perkins, 1933, softcover, rare, NM, D11....$200.00
Dick Tracy, book, Secret Detective Methods & Magic Tricks, Quaker, 64 pgs, NM, D11....$65.00
Dick Tracy, booklet, Dick Tracy's Secret Detective Methods & Magic Tricks, 1939, NM (orig mailer), A....$125.00
Dick Tracy, comic book, Motorola, 1953, M, D11....$20.00
Dick Tracy, Crimestopper Club Kit, 1961, MIB, A....$100.00
Dick Tracy, decoder card, Post, 1950s, NM, D11....$40.00
Dick Tracy, Flagship Plane, Quaker, 1930-39, balsa wood, VG (orig mailing box), D11....$250.00
Dick Tracy, Jr Dick Tracy Crime Detection Folio, 1942, scarce, MIP (unopened), D11....$500.00
Dick Tracy, magnifying glass, EX, J2....$30.00
Dick Tracy, pin-back button, Secret Service Member, Quaker, 1930-39, bl & gold, EX, D11....$30.00
Dick Tracy, ring, monogram, 1930s, rare, VG, A....$700.00
Dick Tracy, Secret Code Book, Secret Service Patrol, Quaker, 1938, G, D11....$15.00
Dick Tracy, watch fob w/belt chain, Jr Detective, 1934, rare, EX, A....$165.00
Doc Savage, lapel stud, Doc Savage Club, 1930s, bronze, ¾", scarce, NM, A....$250.00
Don Winslow, Magic Slate Secret Code Book, 1940, VG, A....$70.00

Photo courtesy June Moon

Dragnet, badge, Sergeant #714, brass, NM, $25.00.

Frank Buck, Adventurers Club Handbook, Pepsodent, 1934, NM (EX mailer), A....$200.00
Frank Buck, Explorer Sun Watch, Wheaties, 1949, MIB, A..$130.00
Frank Buck, Explorer Sun Watch, Wheaties, 1949, NM, A....$55.00
G-Man, see Melvin Pervis
Gene Autry, ring, Flag, NM, C10....$95.00
Green Hornet, flicker rings, 7 different, NM, C10, ea....$35.00
Green Hornet, ring, Seal, General Mills, 1947, EX+, C10 .$950.00
Green Hornet, whistle, Chicken of the Sea, 1966, replica of the Hornet's Sting, plastic, 3", EX, from $500 to....$600.00
Hopalong Cassidy, badge, Post Raisin Bran, 1950, litho tin, NM, A....$100.00
Hopalong Cassidy, badge, Ranch Boss, w/tab, Post Raisin Bran, NM, C10....$35.00
Hopalong Cassidy, ring, face, 1950, M, A....$70.00
Hopalong Cassidy, ring, hat/compass, 1950, M, A....$295.00
Hopalong Cassidy, ring, photo, EX+, C10....$25.00
Howdy Doody, flicker rings, Nabisco Rice Honey's, 1950s, complete set of 8, NM, A....$300.00

Howdy Doody, puppet, Wonder Bread, paper, 11", EX, J2 .$75.00
Jack Armstrong, booklet, Oriental stamp offer, EX, J2 .....$20.00
Jack Armstrong, brooch, gardenia, 1939, plastic, 3", NM, A...$85.00
Jack Armstrong, Explorer Telescope, EX, J2 ....$45.00
Jack Armstrong, game, Adventures w/the Dragon, EX (EX envelope), J2 ....$175.00
Jack Armstrong, map game, Dragon Talisman, 1936, NM, A .$80.00
Jack Armstrong, propeller gun, Gold Medal Foods, metal gun shoots tin propellers, 5½", scarce, EX (EX mailer), A .$100.00
Jack Armstrong, ring, dragon's eye, 1940s, w/instructions, EX, A $450.00
Jack Armstrong, ring, Egyptian whistle, 1940s, NM, A..$150.00
Jack Armstrong, Safety Signal-Light Kit, Wheaties, 1940, complete, NM (G box), A $335.00
Jimmie Allen, mail pouch, Cleo Cola, 1930, cloth pouch w/header card to send for sundial compass watch, rare, EX, A $200.00
Jr G-Man, see Melvin Pervis
Little Orphan Annie, see Radio Orphan Annie
Lone Ranger, badge, Chief Scout, 1935, scarce, EX, A ..$300.00

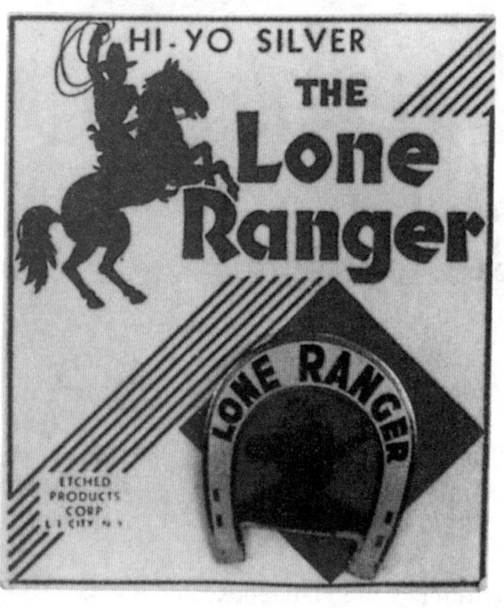

Lone Ranger, badge, horseshoe, 1930s, MOC, A, $350.00.

Lone Ranger, badge, Supplee Club, 1939, G, A $25.00
Lone Ranger, Blackout Kit, Kix Cereal, 1942, rare, NM (orig envelope), A $250.00
Lone Ranger, Club Kit, 1939, NM (orig envelope), A...$340.00
Lone Ranger, Frontier Town, General Mills, 1948, complete w/map, unpunched, NM, A....................$215.00
Lone Ranger, Hunt Map, Silvercup Bread, 1940, rare, NM (EX envelope), A $425.00
Lone Ranger, pedometer, General Mills, 1948, aluminum, M (orig mailer), A....................$75.00
Lone Ranger, ring, atomic bomb, 1945, NM, A $145.00
Lone Ranger, ring, filmstrip saddle, 1950, no film, NM, A .$100.00
Lone Ranger, ring, flashlight, 1947, NM (EX box), A ...$185.00
Lone Ranger, ring, Marine, 1940s, w/secret compartment, no photos, NM, A....................$175.00
Lone Ranger, TV viewer on key chain, Plastic Novelties, 1950, bl, 1½" TV, NM, A $75.00
Mandrake the Magician, pin, Magic Club, Tastee Bread, 1934, metal, 1", EX, A $75.00
Melvin Pervis, badge, G-Man, emb brass shield w/eagle atop, bl enamel trim, 2", NM+, A $45.00
Melvin Pervis, badge, Jr G-Man Corps, enameled shield w/eagle atop, blk & gold lettering, 1½", NM, A....................$65.00
Melvin Pervis, badge, Lieutenant Secret Operator, EX+, J2 .$48.00
Melvin Pervis, ring, Scarab, EX+ $1,100.00
Melvin Pervis, ring, Scarab, G $800.00
Melvin Purvis, manual, Secret Operator, 1936, NM, A ...$65.00
Melvin Purvis, manual, Secret Operator, 1937, EX, J2.....$50.00
Melvin Purvis, ring, Jr G-Man, 1937, NM, A $50.00
Popeye, harmonica, Popsicle, 1929, tin & Bakelite, 4", NM (EX box), A....................$425.00
Radio Orphan Annie, badge, Code Captain, 1939, w/secret compartment, NM, A $80.00
Radio Orphan Annie, belt & buckle, Code Captain, 1940, scarce, NM, A....................$175.00
Radio Orphan Annie, book, Radio Orphan Annie's Secret Society, 1934, EX (orig envelope), A....................$75.00
Radio Orphan Annie, book, Secret Society Signs & Signals, 1935, EX, J2 ....$115.00
Radio Orphan Annie, clicker, Secret Guard Mysto Snapper, Quaker, 1941, litho tin, 2", NM $65.00
Radio Orphan Annie, decoder, Mysto-Magic, 1939, EX, J2 .$50.00
Radio Orphan Annie, decoder, Whirlomatic, 1942, unused, complete w/instructions, EX, A $225.00
Radio Orphan Annie, manual, Secret Guard, Quaker, 1941, NM, A $125.00
Radio Orphan Annie, mug, Ovaltine, 1935, complete w/shake-up pamphlet, MIB, A $220.00
Radio Orphan Annie, pamphlet, Radio Orphan Annie's Secret Society, 1937, NM, A....................$80.00
Radio Orphan Annie, pamphlet, Special Secrets for Silver Star Members, 1937, NM, A....................$85.00
Radio Orphan Annie, ring, March birthstone (aquamarine), mk March-Wisdom on sides, NM, A $250.00
Radio Orphan Annie, ring, Mystic Eye Look-Around, EX, J2 ....$115.00
Radio Orphan Annie, Shado-Ettes, 1938, litho paper, set of 6, complete w/instruction sheet, NM (orig envelope), A.......$155.00
Radio Orphan Annie, Talking Stationery, 1937, complete, scarce, M, A....................$130.00
Radio Orphan Annie, whistle, 1930s, brass slide-type w/Sandy's head at top, 3", EX....................$100.00
Red Ryder, token, 1938, brass w/raised image of Red Ryder & Little Beaver, EX, J5 ....$65.00
Red Ryder, trading cards, Lamont Gloves, 1952, set of 4 on uncut card, rare, VG, A $40.00
Rin-Tin-Tin, compass/mirror, VG, S20 ....$50.00
Rin-Tin-Tin, flag, Fighting Blue Devils, 1950s, bl & yel w/crossed swords & B Company, 8x11", VG, J5 ....$45.00
Roy Rogers, badge, Deputy Sheriff, 1950, w/secret compartment & whistle, NM, A....................$125.00
Roy Rogers, membership card, Riders Club, 1950s, M, A...$40.00
Roy Rogers, punch-out set, Roy Rogers Double R Bar Ranch, Post, 1950s, litho paper, unpunched, NM (orig envelope), A $125.00

Roy Rogers, ring, branding iron, 1950s, NM, from $150 to..**$200.00**
Roy Rogers, ring, microscope, 1950s, NM, A **$125.00**
Sgt Preston, distance finder, Post Cereal, 1955, 5", M (EX mailer), A...**$95.00**
Sgt Preston, Ore Detector, Quaker, red plastic w/decal in center, battery-op, NM (EX box), A.................................**$125.00**
Sgt Preston of the Yukon, Map of the Yukon Territory, 1955, foldout, 9x7", M (EX envelope), A **$75.00**
Shadow, lapel stud, Shadow Club, 1930s, scarce, EX, A ..**$250.00**
Shadow, ring, bl coal, 1941, scarce, NM, A...................**$375.00**
Sky King, decoder, 1950s, Spy-Detecto Writer, silver version w/brass dial, 2", EX, J5 ....**$65.00**
Sky King, ring, Aztec, EX+..**$880.00**
Sky King, ring, Magni-Glo, EX, J2 ....**$100.00**
Sky King, ring, Mystery Picture, NM **$100.00**
Sky King, ring, Navajo Treasure, VG, A.........................**$75.00**
Sky King, ring, Radar, 1940s, NM, A............................**$130.00**
Sky King, ring, TV, 1940s, complete w/4 photos, NM, A..**$175.00**
Sky King, Secret Signalscope, Peter Pan Peanut Butter, 1947, complete, NM (EX box), A....................................**$155.00**
Sky King, Spy Detecto Writer, 1950, metal, gold version, 2½", NM, A **$130.00**
Sky King, Spy Detecto Writer, 1950, metal, silver version, 2½", NM, A **$140.00**
Space Patrol, binoculars, Ralston Purina, plastic rocket-shape mk Space Patrol, 6", NM (NM box), A..................**$150.00**
Space Patrol, Man-From-Mars Totem Head, Wheaties, 1950, litho cb, complete, unassembled, NM (EX envelope), A **$125.00**

Space Patrol, Outer Space Helmet, Ralston, 1950, lithographed cardboard, complete with Mystic-Strato viewer, NM (original envelope), A, $150.00.

Space Patrol, periscope, Ralston, 1950s, cb w/space graphics, 25", NM (orig envelope), J5..................................**$450.00**
Space Patrol, ring, Hydrogen Ray Gun, M.....................**$290.00**
Space Patrol, Space-O-Phones, 1950, bl & yel plastic, M (EX mailer), A **$100.00**
Straight Arrow, Mystic Wrist Kit Bracelet, NM, J2 ....**$160.00**
Straight Arrow, puzzle, National Biscuit Co, 1947, NM (orig envelope), A **$45.00**
Straight Arrow, Tom-Tom War Drum, Nabisco, 1949, MIB, A **$400.00**
Superman, club packet, Supermen of America, Action Comics, 1948, complete, NM (EX envelope), A **$350.00**
Superman, flicker ring, NM, C10..................................**$200.00**
Superman, Krypton Rocket, Kellogg's, 1950, plastic, complete, MIB, A **$285.00**
Superman, ring, F-87 plane, Kellogg's, 1950, EX, A.......**$185.00**
Superman, ring, F-87 plane, Kellogg's, 1950, M (EX box), A **$600.00**
Superman, ring, Pep Airplane, Kellogg's, 1940s, scarce, NM, A **$185.00**
Terry & the Pirates, ring, gold detector, 1940s, NM, A .**$100.00**
Tom Corbett Space Cadet, badge, 1950s, Usalite flashlight, gray & red plastic rocket ship, 2", EX, A **$40.00**
Tom Corbett Space Cadet, coin, gr, EX, J2 ....**$25.00**
Tom Corbett Space Cadet, ring, face, 1952, NM, A **$130.00**
Tom Corbett Space Cadet, ring, rocket, 1950s, w/expansion band, scarce, M, A **$1,000.00**
Tom Mix, badge, Dobie County Sheriff, 1946, w/siren, NM, A...**$75.00**
Tom Mix, badge, Ranch Boss, 1938, M, A **$375.00**
Tom Mix, badge, Straight Shooters, 1937, VG, A **$55.00**
Tom Mix, belt & buckle, Champion, 1936, NM, A.......**$175.00**
Tom Mix, belt & buckle, secret compartment, 1946, NM, A .**$140.00**
Tom Mix, decoder, Six Gun, 1941, EX, from $90 to......**$125.00**
Tom Mix, manual, Life of Tom Mix, 1933, NM, A..........**$65.00**
Tom Mix, parachute plane, Ralston Purina, 1940, balsa, 8½", rare, EX (orig box), A..**$255.00**
Tom Mix, periscope, Ralston Straight Shooters, 1939, cb w/litho tin ends, 9", EX, P4 ....**$40.00**
Tom Mix, RCA TV viewer, 1949, mk Tom Mix Ralston Straight shooters, w/instructions, 1¼", NMIB.........**$225.00**
Tom Mix, ring, sliding whistle, 1940s, NM, A **$75.00**
Tom Mix, ring, Stan Hope Magic Photo, 1930s, NM **$400.00**
Tom Mix, ring, tiger eye, 1950s, NM, A.........................**$200.00**
Tom Mix, Rocket Parachute, 1936, NM (EX box), A ...**$125.00**
Tom Mix, spurs, 1947, glow-in-the-dark, NM (G box), A...**$185.00**
Tom Mix, watch fob, 1940, gold-plated metal w/ore in center, 2", NM, A **$70.00**
Zorro, ring, 1960s, VG **$75.00**
Zorro, Sun Pictures, WDP, 1950s, negatives to develop in the sun, scarce, MIP, A **$35.00**

Pressed Steel

Many companies were involved in the manufacture of pressed steel automotive toys which were often faithfully modeled after actual vehicles in production at the time they were made. Because they were so sturdy, some from as early as the 1920s have survived to the present, and those that are still in good condition are bringing very respectable prices at toy auctions around the country. Some of the better known manufacturers are listed in other sections.

See also Aeronautical; Buddy L; Keystone; Marx; Pedal Cars and Other Wheeled Goods; Structo; Tonka; Wyandotte.

Cars and Busses

Airflow Sedan, Cor-Cor, 1930s, brn 4-door w/blk rubber tires, 16", EX....$1,100.00

American Deluxe Coast to Coast Bus, Dayton, friction, yel & blk, 26", G, A....$850.00

Chrysler Airflow, Cor-Cor, 1937, red w/blk roof, chrome radiator, bumper & lights, 16½", rstr, A....$1,150.00

Desoto, Kingsbury, 1939, orange w/chrome detail, sliding moon roof, wht rubber tires, 14", prof rstr, A....$575.00

Flivver Sedan, Cowdery Works, blk w/red & silver spoke wheels, center door, 11", MIB, A....$600.00

Golden Arrow Racer, Kingsbury, metallic gold with black rubber tires, 21", G, A, $600.00; Campbell's Bluebird Racer, Kingsbury, blue with silver wind reflectors, American flag decal on side, 18", restored, A, $875.00.

Graham Auto, Cor-Cor, 1933, aqua w/blk roof, fenders & running boards, electric headlights, 20", prof rstr, A.$1,375.00

Graham Auto, Cor-Cor, 1933, brn & beige w/blk roof, full running boards, blk rubber tires, 20", rstr, A....$935.00

Greyhound Bus, Kingsbury, bl flat-nose style w/Greyhound logo in wht, wht rubber tires w/chrome hubs, 18", rstr....$250.00

Inter-City Bus, Cor-Cor, gr w/orange disk wheels, bench seats, 23½", EX, A....$1,000.00

Lincoln Sedan, 1928 model, Turner, two-tone green with black roof and sun visor, black rubber tires with green-painted hubs, 26", restored, A, $1,000.00.

Lincoln Zephyr Coupe & Camper Trailer, Kingsbury, 1936, gr, 22½", EX, A....$450.00

Packard Sedan, Turner, red w/brn top & gold striping, 26", EX, A....$2,400.00

Passenger Bus, Kingsbury, clockwork, bl w/orange stripe, wht rubber tires, 16", NM, A....$3,600.00

Pierce Arrow, Girard, orange, gr & beige w/luggage rack, blk rubber tires, electric headlights, 13½", EX, A....$350.00

Roadster, Kingsbury, 1930s, tan & red, wht rubber tires w/gr hubs, 12", EX, D10, from $800 to....$1,200.00

Roadster, Schieble Toys, bl w/wht rubber tires & spare, full running boards, 18", VG, A....$385.00

Sight-Seeing Bus, Cor-Cor, 1929, electric headlights, 24", G, A....$400.00

Firefighting

Aerial Ladder Truck, Kingsbury, clockwork, red w/yel spoke wheels, 2 yel wood ladders, 13", G, A....$325.00

Aerial Ladder Truck, Model Toys, later model, open cab w/aluminum ladder, 34", EX, A....$200.00

Aerial Ladder Truck, Steelcraft, lever action, red w/City Fire Dept decal, 26", EX, A....$1,500.00

Ahrens Fox Fire Engine, Turner, 1920, chartreuse & red w/gold trim, 15", EX....$300.00

American La France Water Tower Truck, Sturditoy, 1920s, 34", EX, A....$1,800.00

Chemical Fire Truck, Sturditoy #7, ca 1929, 27", VG, A....$3,100.00

Fire Chief Car, Kingsbury, 1930s, w/driver, red w/wht rubber tires, 10", EX, D10....$950.00

Ladder Truck, Kingsbury, red and yellow, white rubber tires with red painted hubs, with ladders, hose reel, and two containers, 37", restored, A, $825.00.

Ladder Truck, Schieble, wht w/red ladders & supports, red trim, spoke wheels, 21", VG, A....$300.00

Mack Ladder Truck, Steelcraft, red w/City Fire Dept decal, blk tires w/red hubs, 25", EX....$1,100.00

Pumper Truck, mk Dayton Hillclimber, red w/gold tank, 12", VG....$300.00

Pumper Truck, Schieble, red w/gold-pnt wood boiler, gold spoke wheels & trim, 14", G, A....$400.00

Pumper Truck, Wilkins, w/up, red open truck w/bench seat, silver trim, gold boiler, wht rubber tires, 9½", EX, A..$225.00

Trucks and Vans

Bulldog Mack Dump Truck, Steelcraft, red w/blk chassis, 27", G, A....$900.00

Delivery Truck, Kingsbury, w/up, C-style cab w/canvas sides on open bed, rubber tires, 10", G, A....$450.00

Dredger Truck, Kelmet, red & blk w/open cab, rear boiler under corrugated roof w/wench, spoke wheels, 24", G, A..$775.00

Dump Truck, Girard, 1930s, wht w/blk rubber tires, side dump action, 11", EX....$175.00

Dump Truck, Sturditoy #1, 1929, gr w/blk fenders, red chassis & wheels, 27", G, A....$750.00

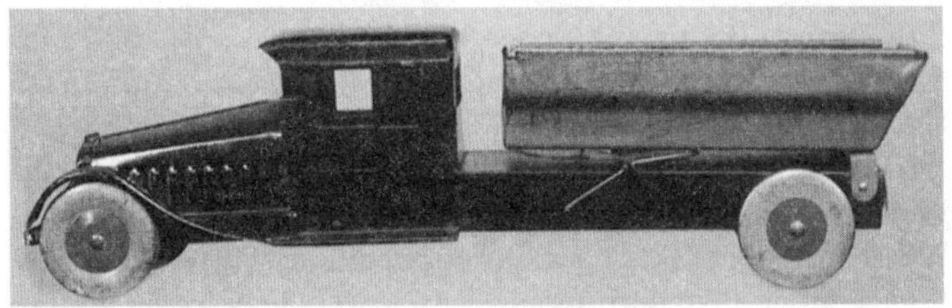

Dump Truck, Cor-Cor, black cab with green dump, painted metal tires, 23", VG, A, $700.00.

Dump Truck, Triang, gr cab & red dump, orig decal, 12", EX (EX box), H7 .... $250.00
Dump Truck, Turner, friction, bl w/blk dump, red top & hubs, 26", EX, A $1,100.00
Dump Truck, 1920s, blk cab & fr w/orange dump, metal wheels w/orange hubs, 23", VG, H7 .... $950.00
Grocery Van, Kingsbury, clockwork, mk Groceries on side, wht rubber tires, VG, A $350.00
Little Jim Tanker Truck, Steelcraft, open cab, 26", rstr, A $475.00
Lumar Van Lines Delivery Truck, 1950s, mk Coast to Coast, red, yel & bl w/blk rubber tires, 19", EX, A $225.00
Mack Dump Truck, Boycraft, red enclosed cab & chassis w/gr dump, blk rubber tires w/gr hubs, 22", EX $600.00
Mack Dump Truck, Steelcraft, C-style cab, red w/blk chassis & fenders, 26", rstr, A $450.00
Mack Dump Truck, Turner, orange cab w/gr bed, blk rubber tires w/orange hubs, 26", NM, D10 .... $850.00
Railway Express Truck, Steelcraft, red cab w/enclosed gr screen body, 24", G, A $600.00
Shell Motor Oil Stake Truck, Metalcraft, red w/yel bed, blk rubber tires w/chrome hubs, 12", VG, D10 .... $650.00
Shell Tanker Truck, Mini-Toys/Canada, yel & red w/decals on sides & back, 28", rare, NM, A $650.00

Stake Truck, Cor-Cor, black and brown, black rubber tires with painted hubs, VG, A, $775.00.

Stake Truck, Kingsbury, w/up, open cab w/bench seat, bl w/wht rubber tires & bl hubs, 9", VG, A $400.00
Stake Truck w/Trailer, Hubley, Mighty Metal series, bl w/blk plastic tires, 20", NM (VG box), A $125.00
Tanker Truck, Sturditoy, doorless cab pulling tank on trailer, red, 33", EX, A $4,700.00
Telephone Service Truck, Lincoln Toys/Canada, gr, 14", VG $225.00
Truck, Cor-Cor, blk w/gr van body & rear platform, pnt metal wheels, 23", VG, A $825.00

Photo courtesy John Turney

U-Haul Truck Set, Ny-Lint, complete, MIB, $450.00.

US Army Truck, Steelcraft, open cab w/canvas-covered bed, 22", G $700.00
US Mail Truck, Sturditoy, blk cab w/red chassis, gr w/screened sides, 26", rstr, A $700.00
Wrecker, Hercules, blk & red w/balloon tires, open bench seat, 19", VG, A $935.00
Wrecker, Schieble, friction, long-nose style w/enclosed cab, 20", G, A $550.00
Wrecker, Sturditoy, red w/Sturditoy Trucking Co decal, blk rubber tires w/red hubs, 30", EX $2,300.00

Miscellaneous

Austin Western Telescoping Crane, Nylint, 1950, red & yel w/blk rubber tires, EX $125.00

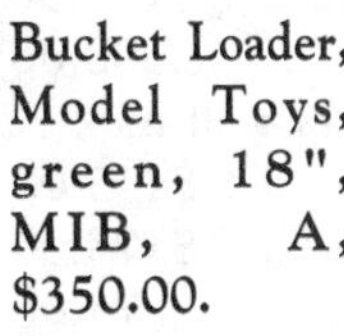

Bucket Loader, Model Toys, green, 18", MIB, A, $350.00.

Caterpillar Tractor, 1920, w/up, CI driver, 8½", VG, A...$350.00
Elgin Street Sweeper, Nylint, NMIB...$250.00
Jaeger Cement Mixer, Doepke, yel w/blk rubber tires, G, A...$100.00
Mobile Home, Nylint, turq, NMIB...$275.00
Road Grader, Nylint, 1950s, red w/blk tires, NM, J6...$100.00
Steam Shovel, Sturditoy, 22", G, A...$200.00
Travel Loader, Nylint, orange, VG...$125.00
Trolley Car, mk Dayton Hillclimber, geared inertia mechanism, 19", VG, A...$165.00
Turbo Roller, Nylint, VG...$75.00

Promotional Vehicles

Miniature Model T Fords were made by Tootsietoy during the 1920s, and though they were not actually licensed by Ford, a few of these were handed out by Ford dealers to promote the new models. In 1932 Tootsietoy was contacted by Graham-Paige to produce a model of their car. These 4" Grahams were sold in boxes as sales promotions by car dealerships, and some were sold through the toy company's catalog. But it wasn't until after WWII that distribution of 1/25 scale promotional models and kits became commonplace. Early models were of cast metal, but during the 1950s, manufacturers turned to plastic. Not only was the material less costly to use, but it could be molded in the color desired, thereby saving the time and expense previously involved in painting the metal. Though the early plastic cars were prone to warp easily when exposed to heat, by the mid-'50s, they had become more durable. Some were friction powered, and others held a battery-operated radio. Advertising extolling some of the model's features was often embossed on the underside. Among the toy manufacturers involved in making promotionals were National Products, Product Miniatures, AMT, MPC, and Jo-Han. Interest in '50s and '60s models is intense, and the muscle cars from the '60s and early '70s are especially collectible. The more popularity the life-size model attained, the more popular the promotional is with collectors.

Check the model for damage, warping, and amateur alterations. The original box can increase the value by as much as 30%. Jo-Han has reissued some of their 1950s and 1960s Mopar and Cadillac models as well as Chrysler's Turbine Car. These are usually priced between $20.00 and $30.00.

1948 Hudson Sedan, gr, 13", VG...$750.00
1953 Buick Roadmaster, AMT, 1/25, EX...$135.00
1953 Chevy Bel Air, bank, brn, plastic, EX+...$90.00
1955 Ford T-Bird Coupe, red, chrome hubs & wht-wall stickers, EX+...$135.00
1956 Cadillac, AMT, 2-tone bl, M...$175.00
1957 T-Bird, red w/blk & white striped seat, EX...$75.00
1958 Chevy Apache Pickup, yel, detailed undercarriage, 1/25, M...$225.00
1958 Chevy Belair, PMC, red, 1/25, EX+...$100.00
1959 Chrysler New Yorker, gr, 1/25, EX+...$60.00
1959 Corvette Convertible, AMT, wht, 1/25, rstr, M19...$425.00
1960 Chevy Nova, lt metallic bl, EX+...$130.00
1961 Ford Hubley Wagon, wht & yel, NM...$65.00
1961 Pontiac Bonneville Coupe, off wht, EX...$200.00
1962 Oldsmobile, MIB...$35.00
1962 Rambler Classic Station Wagon, Johan, NMIB...$75.00
1963 Ford Galaxie Convertible, beige, 8½", EX, A...$50.00
1964 Ford Fairlane, AMT, bl, 8", EX, A...$45.00
1964 Ford T-Bird, AMT, wht, friction, 8½", EX, A...$45.00
1964 Pontiac Plymouth Grand Prix, AMT, gray w/bl top, friction, EX, A...$60.00
1965 Chevy Impala, blue, 8½", EX, A...$65.00
1965 Ford T-Bird, AMT, yel, friction, 8½", EX, A...$70.00
1965 Mercury, AMT, tan, friction, 8¾", EX, A...$45.00
1965 Plymouth Baracuda, AMT, bl, friction, 7¾", EX, A...$60.00
1966 Buick Riveria, tan, 8½", EX, A...$45.00
1966 Ford Galaxie, AMT, lt bl, friction, VG, A...$40.00
1966 Ford Mustang, AMT, brn, 7½", EX, A...$55.00
1966 Ford Mustang, red, 7½", VG, A...$75.00
1966 Plymouth Baracuda, AMT, yel, friction, EX, A...$50.00
1967 Buick Riveria, AMT, bl-gr, friction, 8½", VG, A...$45.00
1968 Olds 442, red w/wht interior, MIB...$115.00

Photo courtesy Dunbar Gallery

1970 Cadillac, yellow, MIB, $125.00.

1970 Ford LDT, dk bl, EX+...$85.00
1971 Chevelle, MPC, red, 2-door, 1/25, MIB, M19...$190.00
1972 Chevy Fleetside Pickup, med bl, MIB...$165.00
1973 Chevy Camaro, Buccaneer Red, MIB...$120.00
1974 Olds Cutlass, Colonial Gr, MIB...$35.00
1975 Ford Mustang, silver, MIB...$35.00
1976 Dodge Dart, Vintage Red, MIB...$50.00
1977 Cadillac Coupe DeVille, metallic gr, M...$20.00
1978 Chevy Monza, dk camel, MIB...$14.00
1984 Chevy Corvette, silver, MIB...$20.00
1989 Buick Reatta, red, 1/24, MIB...$45.00
1989 Chevy Silverado C-1500, Ertl, red, 1/25, MIB, M19...$25.00
1991 Chevy Camaro, blk or teal, MIB, ea...$14.00
1991 Chevy Storm, Ertl, teal, 1/25, MIB...$25.00
1992 Corvette Convertible, Ertl, red, 1/25, MIB...$25.00
1993 Chevy Dually, blk, MIB...$65.00
1994 Dodge Viper Coupe, yel, MIB...$24.00
1995 Ford Explorer, blk, MIB...$24.00
1996 GMC Jimmy, blk, MIB...$24.00

Pull and Push Toys

Pull and push toys from the 1800s often were made of cast iron with bells that were activated as they moved along on wheeled platforms or frames. Hide and cloth animals with glass or shoe-button eyes were also popular, and some were made of wood.

See also specific companies such as Fisher-Price.

Airship Roundabout, stained tin, 3 airships rotate when pulled, 8", VG, A **$1,000.00**

Photo courtesy Dunbar Gallery

Child and Bear, Althof-Bergmann, ca 1874, painted tin, 7", EX, D10, from $1,000.00 to $1,800.00.

Dog on Wheels, German, cloth-covered, glass eyes, 7", EX, A **$200.00**

General Lee Invasion Barge, Cass Toys, litho wood, features moving turret, 12", EX (worn box), A **$100.00**

Goat Bell Toy, Gong Bell, 1890s, goat pulls bell between 2 wheels, EX, D10 .... **$550.00**

Goat Cart, Harris, red w/upholstered seat, yel spoke wheels, w/driver, 9¼", VG, A **$275.00**

Goat on Platform, hide-covered w/felt collar & blanket, gr-pnt wood platform w/CI wheels, 10", EX, A **$1,000.00**

Goat on Platform, 1880s, 5", EX, D10 .... **$450.00**

Grasshopper, Hubley, gr-pnt CI w/articulated legs, complete w/pull string, 9", VG, A **$775.00**

Horse & Jockey on Platform, Althof-Bergmann, pnt tin, 4", EX, D10 .... **$650.00**

Horse & Jockey on Platform, Fallows, 1880, pnt tin, 9½", EX, D10, from $1200 to **$1,800.00**

Horse & Jockey Push Toy, Fallows, 1880s, pnt tin w/wood stick, 18", EX, D10, from $500 to **$1,250.00**

Horse & Jockey w/Pony Platform, Geo Brown, 1870s, pnt tin, EX, D10 .... **$4,500.00**

Horse on Platform, CI horse on wood platform w/4 red spoke wheels, 9", EX, A **$1,500.00**

Horse on Platform, cvd wood w/oilcloth saddle blanket, stenciled platform w/CI wheels, 15", VG, A **$450.00**

Horse-Drawn Carriage, Althof-Bergmann, hand-pnt tin carriage w/4 spoke wheels, 1 horse, 11½", NM, A **$775.00**

Photo courtesy Dunbar Gallery

Horse-Drawn Carriage, Francis, Field and Francis, 1850s, painted tin, large spoke wheels, single horse, 8½", VG, D10, $650.00.

Horse-Drawn Carriage, Merriam, 1860s, bl-pnt tin, 2 brn horses, 14", EX, D10 .... **$3,200.00**

Horse-Drawn Cart, Althof-Bergmann, 1870s, pnt tin, yel cart w/2 spoked wheels, 1 horse, 9", VG, D10, from $200 to **$400.00**

Horse-Drawn Cart, Geo Brown, 1870s, pnt tin, 1 horse, 14", EX, D10, from $200 to **$400.00**

Horse-Drawn City Delivery Wagon, Converse, litho tin, 2 dapple-gray horses, 19", EX, A **$1,200.00**

Photo courtesy Dunbar Gallery

Horse-Drawn Coal Wagon, Hou and Stafford, 1860s, painted tin, with driver and white horse, 14", EX, D10, $5,500.00.

Horse-Drawn Coal Wagon, wood open bed wagon w/bench seat & spoke wheels, blk fabric-covered horse on platform, EX, A **$275.00**

Horse-Drawn Contractor's Dump Wagon, Arcade, 1920s, pnt CI, blk w/yel spoke wheels, 2 wht horses, 14", G, A **$175.00**

Horse-Drawn Contractor's Supply Wagon, wood w/spoke wheels, 2 felt-covered wht horses on separate platforms, 25", EX, A **$525.00**

Horse-Drawn Delivery Wagon, Am, tin w/paper sides showing children at play, spoke wheels, 2 brn horses, 11½", VG, A **$400.00**

Horse-Drawn Dray Wagon, Kenton, CI, gr stake wagon w/driver, red spoke wheels, 1 blk & 1 wht horse, 10", EX, A .**$200.00**

Horse-Drawn Dray Wagon, Pratt & Letchworth, CI open-bed wagon w/wood floor, spoke wheels, w/driver & 1 horse, 10", VG, A **$200.00**

Horse-Drawn Express Wagon, ca 1890, pnt wood, 36", EX, D10, from $2,000 to **$3,000.00**

Horse-Drawn Express Wagon, Geo Brown, 1870s, pnt tin, red & gr w/wht horse, 11", EX, D10, from $1,000 to......**$1,500.00**

Photo courtesy Dunbar Gallery

Horse-Drawn Fire Pumper, Fallows, 1880s, painted tin, with driver and two white horses, 7½", VG, D10, $1,850.00.

Horse-Drawn Fire Pumper, Ives & Blakeslee, 1890, pnt CI w/4 spoked wheels, 1 blk horse & 1 NP, no driver, 20", VG, A **$925.00**

Horse-Drawn Milk Wagon, City Dairy, litho tin & wood, red & blk w/yel trim, blk cloth-covered horse, 20", EX, A ..**$385.00**

Horse-Drawn Milk Wagon, Converse, emb tin w/2 wood dapple-gray horses, 18", EX, A **$500.00**

Horse-Drawn Milk Wagon, Fallows, 1880s, Pure Milk stenciled on red wagon w/driver, brn horse, 13", D10, from $2,000 to **$3,000.00**

Horse-Drawn Milk Wagon, Rich Toys, Borden's, litho tin & wood, orig driver, single horse, 18", EX, A **$355.00**

Horse-Drawn Milk Wagon, Rich Toys, Borden's Farm Products, pnt wood, 9½", EX, A **$200.00**

Horse-Drawn Milk Wagon, Rich Toys, Sealtest Dairy Products, litho tin wagon w/wooden horse, 20", NM, A........**$330.00**

Horse-Drawn Milk Wagon, Rich Toys, 1930, Sheffield Farms Co, pnt wood, articulated horse, 6 bottles/carrier, 20½", VG.......**$635.00**

Horse-Drawn Railroad Omnibus, Merrium, 1870s, pnt tin, w/driver & 2 horses, 12", EX, D10, from $4,500 to .**$6,500.00**

Horse-Drawn Surrey, Pratt & Letchworth, 1900, CI, open carriage w/driver, spoke wheels, 1 horse, 14", VG, A........**$1,000.00**

Horse-Drawn Trolley, Althof-Bergmann, 1870s, pnt tin, red & bl w/2 wht horses, 10", EX, D10 ....**$1,850.00**

Horse-Drawn Wagon, Rich Toys, Rich's Little Milk Man, wht & red w/closed door, 20", NM, A **$330.00**

Horse-Drawn 8th Avenue & Central Park Trolley, Geo Brown, mc tin, 12", D10, from $2,500 to **$3,500.00**

Lamb on Platform, hide-covered w/wooden legs & glass eyes, 2-part tin wheels attached to feet, 10", EX, A **$525.00**

Lamb on Platform, wool-covered figure w/glass eyes, 4-wheeled platform, squeaker mechanism in head, 13", EX, A..**$1,375.00**

Lion Bell Toy, hide-covered w/fur ruff, pnt tin & wire wheels, 10", EX, A........**$165.00**

Photo courtesy Dunbar Gallery

Jockey and Dog on Platform, Fallows, 1880s, painted tin, 9½", EX, D10, $2,450.00.

Mule-Drawn Sulky, J&E Stevens, 1895, CI, Black man moves whip when pulled, rpt cart, EX, A **$450.00**

Old Dutch Girl, Hubley, 1932, CI, Dutch girl in bl & wht dress & wht bonnet on wheeled base, 9", VG, A........**$4,100.00**

Patriotic Boy Bell Ringer, Althof-Bergmann, 1880, hand-pnt tin boy mounted on 2 wheels pulling lg bell, 8½", EX, A........**$4,950.00**

Polar Bear on Platform, mohair-covered w/glass eyes, mica-covered platform w/2-part tin wheels, 11", EX, A ...**$825.00**

Porky & Petunia (Galloping Pals) Bell Toy, Brice No 920, litho paper on wood, EX (worn box), A **$200.00**

Reindeer, hand-pnt tin reindeer attached to 2 gold spoke wheels, plays music when pulled, 9", EX, A........**$550.00**

See-Saw, Gong Bell, CI, Black man & clown mounted on platform w/spoke wheels, 6¼", EX, A **$650.00**

Steam Locomotive, Fallows, 1880s, mk Venus, pnt tin, 6", G, A........**$325.00**

Steer on Platform, cowhide covered, wooden platform, moos when head is turned, 17", VG, A, $775.00; Rooster Pulling Cart, Gibbs, wood with lithographed paper detail, red cart, 16", EX, A, $650.00.

Teddy Bear Bell Toy, Watrous, CI & strap metal, bear on platform w/4 spoke wheels, 6", EX, A **$400.00**

Turtle & Frog, bell toy, CI, 6½", G, A **$300.00**

Puppets

Though many collectible puppets and the smaller scale marionettes were made commercially, others were handmade and are today considered fine examples of folk art which sometimes sell for several hundred dollars. Some of the most collectible today are character-related puppets representing well known television stars.

Advisor: Bill Bruegman (T2), finger puppets, hand puppets, and push-button puppets; Steven Meltzer (M9), marionettes and ventriloquist dolls.

See also Advertising; Black Americana; Political.

Finger Puppets

Adventure Boy, Remco, 1970, complete w/Skymobile, MIB, F8 ....**$65.00**
Crypt Keeper, rubber, set of 3, M, H4 ....**$12.00**
Lamp Chop, 1960, VG, N2 ....**$35.00**
Marvel Super Heroes, w/Captain America, Hulk, Spider-Man & Thor, Imperial Toy, 1978, vinyl, 3", NM, J5 ....**$40.00**
Monkees, Davy & Mickey, Clever Finger Dolls by Remco, MOC (sealed), B3 ....**$95.00**
Monkees, Mickey, MIB (Sears box), B3 ....**$35.00**
Pebbles & Bamm-Bamm, Knickerbocker, 1972, VG, pr **$10.00**
Peter Pan, 1960s, VG, N2 ....**$25.00**
Ricky Jr (Little Ricky from I Love Lucy), Zany Toys, 1952, vinyl w/cloth outfit, fleece blanket, 8", NMIB, from $400 to **$500.00**
Spider-Man, 1970, NM **$12.00**
Thor, Imperial, 1978, vinyl, 3", EX, M17 ....**$20.00**
Yellow Kid, early 1900s, cloth over wood scissor-type mechanism, compo head, 8", rare, VG, A **$500.00**

Hand Puppets

Alf, 1988, w/tag, EX, B10 ....**$15.00**
Alvin (Alvin & the Chipmunks), Knickerbocker, 1963, cloth & vinyl, 12", NM, F8 ....**$50.00**
Archie, 1973, plastic & vinyl, NM, C1 ....**$45.00**
Baby Huey, Gund, 1960, cloth & vinyl, 10", EX **$40.00**
Banana Splits, Bingo, 1968, plastic, EX, J5 ....**$45.00**
Batman, Ideal, 1966, cloth & vinyl, NM, P12 ....**$75.00**
Batman & Robin, Ideal, 1966, cloth & vinyl, 11", rare, EX (in single lg box), from $200 to **$300.00**
Bozo the Clown, Mattel, 1963, talker, EX, J2 ....**$55.00**
Bozo the Clown, Mattel, 1963, talker not working o/w EX, T2 ....**$30.00**
Bugs Bunny, Mattel, 1962, talker, 13", VG, F8 ....**$25.00**
Captain America, Ideal, 1966, plastic & rubber, 11", NM, A **$100.00**
Captain America, Imperial, 1979, cloth & vinyl, MIP **$20.00**
Captain Kangaroo, Rushton, 1960s, cloth & vinyl, EX, D9 ....**$25.00**
Charlie McCarthy, American, cloth & compo, w/monocle, 12", EX, from $50 to **$75.00**
Dean Martin & Jerry Lewis Puppet Show, 1950s, complete, MIB, ...**$350.00**

Captain Hook, Gund, cloth and vinyl, EX, T2, $30.00.

Dennis the Menace, Gund, 1960, cloth & vinyl, 10", EX, T2 ....**$30.00**
Dilly Dally (Howdy Doody), 1950s, cloth & rubber, EX, A **$75.00**
Donald Duck, Gund, 1960s, cloth & vinyl, squeaker, MIP **$25.00**
Dopey (Snow White), Gund, 1960s, cloth & vinyl, VG, P4 ....**$25.00**
Dopey (Snow White), 1930s, compo & cloth, scarce, EX, M8 ....**$125.00**
Dumbo the Elephant, Gund, 1950s, cloth & vinyl, squeaker, EX, C17 ....**$30.00**
Flub-A-Dub (Howdy Doody), 1950s, cloth & rubber, EX, A **$70.00**
Fred Flintstone, Knickerbocker, 1960s, VG, C17 ....**$25.00**
Galafoochie (Rootie Kazootie's dog), 1950s, cloth & vinyl, EX, A **$50.00**
Gomez (Addams Family), Ideal, 1964, cloth & vinyl, EX **$75.00**
Grandpa Munster, Ideal, 1964, cloth & vinyl, EX, H4 ....**$95.00**
Green Hornet, Ideal, 1966, plastic & vinyl, 10", EX **$125.00**
Herman Munster, cloth & vinyl, talker, EX **$75.00**
Hopalong Cassidy, 1950s, cloth & vinyl, scarce, NM, J6 ....**$200.00**
Howdy Doody, 1950s, cloth & vinyl, orig red & yel neckerchief, EX, J5 ....**$45.00**
Huckleberry Hound, Kellogg's premium, 1960s, cloth & plastic, EX, C17 ....**$25.00**
Incredible Hulk, Imperial, 1979, cloth & vinyl, MIP **$20.00**
Jiminy Cricket, Gund, 1960s, cloth & vinyl, MIP **$30.00**
Jiminy Cricket, Knickerbocker/Video Craft Ltd, 1962, cloth & vinyl, EX, J5 ....**$50.00**
Laurel & Hardy, Knickerbocker, 1965, cloth & vinyl, NM, F8, pr **$75.00**
Li'l Abner, Daisy Mae, Mammy & Pappy, Allied Toys, 1950s, cloth & vinyl, 9", M (seperate pkgs), A **$150.00**
Linus the Lion-Hearted, Mattel, 1965, talker, NM, J2 ....**$90.00**

Little Audrey, 1950s, cloth & vinyl, EX..............................$25.00
Lucy (Peanuts), Ideal, M..$45.00
Mean Moe (Inkwell Cartoon Character), Gund, 1962, cloth & vinyl, felt hands, EX, J5 ....$50.00
Mickey & Minnie, 1970s, cloth & soft plastic, VG, M8, pr..$15.00
Mickey Mouse, Gund, 1960s, cloth & vinyl, squeaker, MIP.$65.00
Miss Piggy, Fisher-Price, 1979, EX, B10............................$25.00
Morticia (Addams Family), Ideal, 1964, cloth & vinyl, EX..$75.00
Mr Bluster (Howdy Doody), Zany Toys, cloth & vinyl, 10", EX (EX box), A $150.00

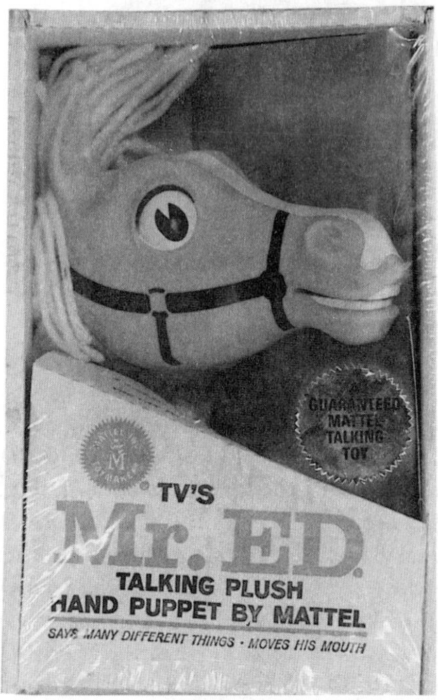

Photo courtesy Bill Bruegman

Mr. Ed, Mattel, 1962, pull-string talker, MIB, T2, $200.00.

Photo courtesy June Moon

Mr. Magoo, 1962, cloth and vinyl, EX, J6, $35.00.

Mr Do Bee & Happy Jack (Romper Room), Hasbro, 1970, cloth & plastic, 11", EX (EX box) $25.00

Myrtle (My Three Sons), Mattel, talker, NM...................$45.00
Olive Oyl, Gund, 1950s, cloth & vinyl, 10", EX, T2........$25.00

Photo courtesy Bill Bruegman

Peter Pan, Gund, cloth and vinyl, EX, T2, $35.00.

Pinocchio, Gund, 1960s, cloth & vinyl, squeaker, MIP ...$50.00
Pinocchio, Knickerbocker, 1962, cloth & vinyl, NM, F8.$35.00
Pokey, Lakeside, 1960s, EX, C17.......................................$45.00
Porky Pig, Mattel, 1964, talker, EX $40.00
Princess Summerfall-Winterspring, Zany Toys, cloth & vinyl, 7", EX (EX box), A $150.00
Raggedy Ann & Andy, Knickerbocker, 1970s, MIP, H12..$15.00
Road Runner & Wile E Coyote, Warner Bros, 1969, vinyl, NM, F8, pr $40.00
Robin, Ideal, 1966, cloth & vinyl, EX, P12/T2, from $185 to...$195.00
Rosie the Robot, Knickerbocker, 1960s, cloth & rubber, NM...$100.00
Sarge (Beetle Bailey), Gund, 1960s, NM, C17 ....$60.00
Sherman (Sesame Street), cloth & vinyl, NM, B10.........$15.00
Spider-Man, Imperial, 1979, cloth & vinyl, MIP..............$20.00
Spike (Tom & Jerry), Multitoy, 1989, MOC, B10............$16.00
Stingray, Lakeside, 1966, cloth & vinyl, Troy Tempest on uniform, NM, F8 ....$65.00
Swee' Pea, Gund, 1950s, cloth & vinyl, NM (EX box) $60.00
Sylvester, 1990, cloth, EX, B10 ....$12.00
Texan Sheriff, Tops in Toys, 1950s, cloth & vinyl, 16", EX, A $65.00
Tinkerbelle, Gund, talker, cloth & vinyl, EX (EX box) ...$75.00
Topo Gigio, American Character, 1960s, 12", NRFB, M15...$125.00
Troll, Gund, cloth & vinyl, EX, C17 ....$45.00
Uncle Fester (Addams Family), Ideal, cloth & vinyl, EX.$75.00
Wendy (Peter Pan), Gund, 1960s, cloth & plastic, squeaker, EX $18.00
Wimpy (Popeye), Presents, cloth & vinyl, MIP................$25.00
Wizard of Oz, Lion, Tin Man, Toto, Wizard or Scarecrow, 1960s-70s, vinyl, NM, F8, ea $20.00

Wonder Woman, Ideal, 1966, cloth & vinyl, 11", MIP, from $200 to $225.00
Yogi Bear, Kellogg's premium, 1960s, cloth & plastic, EX, C17 ....$25.00
Yogi Bear, Mighty Star, plush, NM, C17 ....$20.00

Marionettes

Alice in Wonderland, Peter Puppet/Disney, 1950s, compo head, hands & feet, 14", VG $150.00
Alice in Wonderland (unlicensed), Hazelle's, talker, M, M9....$125.00
Angel, Pelham, MIB, M9 ....$125.00
Astro (Jetsons), Knickerbocker, 1970s, stuffed cloth w/vinyl head, EX, H4..$95.00
Batman, Hazelle's, 1966, cloth & felt costume, 15", EX, A..$400.00
Batman, Madison Ltd, 1976, MIB, H4...........................$125.00
Bengo the Dog, Pelham, MIB, M9 ....$100.00
Bimbo the Clown, Hazelle's, 800 series, EX, M9 ....$95.00
Bimbo the Clown, Pelham, M, M9 ....$135.00
Buckaroo Bill, Hazelle's, talker, EX, M9 ....$175.00
Clippo the Clown, Curtis Craft, MIB, M9......................$100.00
Clippo the Clown, Effanbee, WWII, MIB, M9...............$250.00
Clown, Pelham, talker, MIB, M9 ....$125.00
Cop, Pelham, talker, MIB, M9 ....$125.00
Dagwood, Hazelle's, 1950s, MIB, M9 ....$250.00
Donald Duck, Pelham, wood w/cloth clothes, 10", MIB...$165.00
Emily Ann (Clippo's Girlfriend), Effanbee, M, M9........$160.00
Father, Mother & Son, Effanbee, EX, M9......................$425.00
Flub-A-Dub (Howdy Doody's Pal), Peter Puppet, compo, 12", MIB..$375.00
Freddy MC, Hazelle's, M, M9...$125.00
Gepetto (Pinocchio), Pelham, MIB, M9 ....$160.00
Girl, Pelham, talker, MIB, M9 ....$125.00
Hansel & Gretel, Hazelle's, M, M9, pr..........................$175.00
Hillbilly, Hazelle's, 800 series, M, M9 ....$95.00
Horse, Pelham, EX (EX box), M9 ....$125.00
Howdy Doody, 1950s, compo w/cloth clothes, 16", MIB..$275.00

Huckleberry Hound, Pelham, 1960s, 9", scarce, NM (NM box), A, $450.00.

Jim-Bob & Susy Pigtail, Curtis Craft, 1950, M, M9, pr ..$525.00
Lion Tamer, cvd wood & compo w/cloth clothes, 25", VG, A...$75.00
Little Boy Blue, Hazelle's, 800 series, compo, M, M9 .....$135.00
Mad Hatter (Alice in Wonderland), Peter Puppet, 1950s, compo head & hands w/wooden feet, 14", EX, J5 ....$125.00
Magician, wood & compo w/cloth clothes, papier-mache top hat, 23", EX, A $200.00
Marie Osmond, Madison Ltd, 1978, 8", MIB....................$85.00
Marilyn, Hazelle's, talker, EX, M9.................................$225.00
Mickey Mouse, Pelham, wood, plastic & compo w/cloth clothes, 11", MIB $225.00
Minnie Mouse, Pelham, wood w/cloth clothes, 13", MIB..$225.00
Mr Bluster (Howdy Doody), 1950, compo w/cloth clothes, scarce, EX...$275.00
Nurse, Pelham, M, M9...$95.00
Old Lady, Pelham, MIB, P9...$125.00
Peter Pan, Peter Puppet, 1950s, EX................................$200.00
Pinocchio, Pelham, MIB $135.00
Planet Flyer (Tom Corbett look-alike), Hazelle's, 1950s, NMIB..$200.00
Pluto, WDP, plastic, 8", M, P6 ....$65.00
Pop Singer, Pelham, Hawaiian shirt, M, M9...................$145.00
Pop Singer (3 styles), Pelham, MIB, M9, ea $300.00
Prince Charming, Pelham, MIB, M9 ....$125.00
Princess Summerfall-Winterspring (Howdy Doody), 1950s, compo w/cloth clothes, MIB $195.00
Sailor, Hazelle's, talker, EX, M9.....................................$125.00
Snow White, Peter Puppet, wood w/compo head, cloth clothes, articulated mouth, 15", MIB $245.00
Superman, Madison Ltd, 1976, MIB, H4........................$100.00
Wolf, Pelham, G, M9 ....$250.00
Wombles (Furry Creatures from English TV show), Pelham, MIB, M9, ea $85.00
Wonder Woman, Madison Ltd, 1977, vinyl w/pnt-on top & cloth shorts, 11½", EX...$100.00

Push-Button Puppets

Atom Ant, Kohner, NM, C17..$40.00

Bambi, Kohner, 1960s, NM, T2, $40.00.

Photo courtesy Bill Bruegman

Bamm-Bamm, Kohner, 1960s, EX....................................$25.00
Batman, Kohner, 1960s, NM..$100.00
Bugs Bunny, Kohner, EX, C17..$40.00
Davy Crockett, 1950s, rare, NM...................................$195.00
Dino, Kohner, 1960s, M..$75.00
Disney Pop Pals, Kohner/Hong Kong, Mickey, Donald, Pluto & Goofy, 3", EX...$35.00
Donald Duck Tricky Trapeze, EX, B10...........................$10.00
Felix the Cat, FTCP Inc, wood, EX, B10, from $25 to.....$30.00
Flub-A-Dub, Kohner, 1950s, wood w/felt ears, EX, J5....$175.00
Fred Flintstone, Kohner, 1960s, EX.................................$30.00
Fred Flintstone & Dino, Kohner, 1962, NMIB...............$455.00
Happy the Wonder Dog, Kohner, VG, I2........................$15.00
Hoppy the Hoparoo, Kohner, M......................................$65.00
Howdy Doody, Kohner, 1950s, wood w/plastic head, EX, J5..$150.00
Howdy Doody, Kohner, 1950s, wood w/plastic head, NMIB...$225.00
Huckleberry Hound, EX, B10..$45.00
Lone Ranger on Silver, Kohner, EX...............................$100.00

Lucky the Lion, Gabriel the Giraffe, and Terry the Tiger, Kohner, 1960s, M, J6, $12.00 each.

Magilla Gorilla, Kohner, 1960s, M..................................$65.00
Mickey Mouse, Gabriel, EX, B10....................................$25.00
Olive Oyl, Kohner, NM...$75.00
Pebbles, Kohner, scarce, NMOC, from $35 to.................$45.00
Pluto, Kohner, wood w/plastic base, 5", NM (EX box)...$125.00
Princess Summerfall-Winterspring, Kohner, 1950s, jtd wood, VG, J5..$150.00
Ricochet Rabbit, Kohner, NM, P3...................................$45.00
Robin, Kohner, 1960s, NM...$125.00
Secret Squirrel, Kohner, 1960s, M.................................$75.00
Superman, Kohner, 1960s, NM......................................$100.00
Wilma Flintstone, Kohner, 1960s, NM, J6......................$35.00
Woodsy Owl, Ideal, M...$40.00

Paulette the Poodle, Kohner, 1960s, NM, J6, $12.00; Dancer the Dog, Kohner, 1960s, NM, J6, $10.00; Candy the Cat, Kohner, 1960s, NM, J6, $10.00.

Yogi Bear, Kohner, M...$65.00

Ventriloquist Dolls

Ventriloquist dolls have pull strings from the back of the neck for mouth movement. Dummies have a hollow body, with the head mounted on a pole controlled through an opening in the back of the body. Charlie McCarthy was produced in doll or hand puppet form by Ideal, Juro, and Goldberger (currently). Jerry Mahoney was produced by Juro and later by Paul Winchell's own company. Vinyl-headed ventriloquist dolls are still being produced by Goldberger and include licensed versions of Charlie McCarthy, Mortimer Snerd, Bozo, Emmet Kelly, Laurel and Hardy, Howdy Doody, Danny O'Day, WC Fields, and Groucho.

Jerry Mahoney, head stick dummy, Juro, 32", MIB, $500.00.

Boy, Pelham, M, M9 ....$125.00
Charlie McCarthy, Effanbee, blk tux w/wht vest, shirt & bow tie, blk top hat, pin-back on lapel, w/monocle, 18", EX....$425.00
Charlie McCarthy, Effanbee, tan jacket w/wht shirt & orange print bow tie, wht pants & hat, w/monocle, 15½", M $580.00
Charlie McCarthy, Juro or Goldberger, vinyl head, 30", MIB $85.00
Dopey (Snow White), Ideal, 1938, compo & cloth, 20", EX $800.00
Girl, Pelham, M, M9 ....$125.00
Jerry Mahoney, compo head, 24", NM, D10..................$550.00
Jerry Mahoney, vinyl head (mk Paul Winchell 1966), 22", MIB..$275.00
Knucklehead, 1950s, compo head, 24", MIB, M9...........$950.00
Mickey Mouse, Horsman, 1973, hard plastic head w/soft vinyl hands, blk tux w/red bow tie, 30", EX $175.00
Monk, Pelham, M, M9 ....$225.00
Mortimer Snerd, molded plastic body w/orange hair, blk pants & vest w/wht shirt, red cummerbund, 26", EX..............$65.00
Rover, Pelham, M, M9..$95.00

Puzzles and Picture Blocks

Jigsaw puzzles have been around almost as long as games. The first examples were handcrafted from wood, and they are extremely difficult to find. Most of the early examples featured moral subjects and offered insight into the social atmosphere of their time. By the 1890s jigsaw puzzles had become a major form of home entertainment. Cube puzzles or blocks were often made by the same companies as board games. Early examples display lithography of the finest quality. While all subjects are collectible, some (such as Santa blocks) often command prices higher than games of the same period.

Because TV and personality-related puzzles have become so popular, they're now regarded as a field all their own apart from character collectibles in general, and these are listed here as well, under the subtitle 'Character.'

Advisors: Bob Armstrong (A4); Norm Vigue (V1), character.

See also Advertising.

Photo courtesy Bob Armstrong

Ann Hathaway's Cottage, 1930s, plywood, 566 pieces, MIB, A4, $75.00.

Across the Plough, Atlantic/Kingsbridge, 1950-60, plywood, 150 rnd-knob interlocking pcs, strip-cut, EX (EX box), A4..$15.00
Animal Picture Cubes, McLoughlin Bros, 1897, litho paper on cb, set of 6, VG (VG box), A.................................$135.00
At the End of the Town, J Straus, 1940-50, plywood, 300 rnd-knob strip-cut interlocking pcs, EX (G box), A4.......$25.00
Autumn Leaves Are Falling, G Merrill, 1910-20, plywood, 438 long-rnd push-to-fit pcs, 3 rpl pcs, EX (EX box), A4.$95.00
Autumn Scene, 1930s, cb, 100 long-rnd interlocking pcs, EX (EX box), A4 ....$10.00
Awaiting Spring's Wispful Breezes, B Nowell, 1930s, pressed board, 560 rnd interlocking pcs, color-line cut, NMIB, A4..$90.00
Bearing the Brunt, Schwartz/Special Cut, 1940s, plywood, 750 random interlocking pcs, EX (EX box), A4 ....$120.00
Boughs Are Murmuring in the Breeze, 1930s, plywood, 424 random interlocking pcs, VG (VG box), A4 ....$65.00
Breath of Summer Days, B Nowell, 1930s, pressed board, 412 rnd semi-interlocking pcs, color-line cut, EX (EX box), A4 ....$70.00
Bremgarten on Reuss w/Covered Bridge, C Russell, 1977, plywood, 415 rnd-knob interlocking pcs, color-line cut, NMIB, A4 ....$80.00
Capel Curig, Hayter/Victory Artistic, 1970s, plywood, 500 rnd-knob interlocking pcs, strip-cut, EX (EX box), A4....$65.00
Chatteau, Gimbel Bros, 1930s, plywood, 150 rnd-knob interlocking pcs, strip-cut, EX (EX box), A4.....................$20.00
Child Asleep At Table (Untitled), 1910s, plywood, 203 random semi-interlocking pcs, EX (rpl box), A4 ....$50.00
City of Worchester Picture Puzzle, McLoughlin, 1889, complete, EX (EX box), A..$1,000.00
Colorful Venice, Tuco, 1930s, cb, 350 crooked-line strip pcs, EX (EX box), A4 ....$10.00
Cottage Garden, Macy's, 1930s, plywood, 215 earlet interlocking pcs, color-line cut, 3 rpl pcs, EX (EX box), A4....$50.00
Country Side, 1909, solid wood, 197 push-to-fit pcs, color-line cutting, EX (rpl box), A4 ....$55.00
Cows in Pasture (Untitled), 1909, solid wood, 142 push-to-fit pcs, color-line cutting, EX (orig box), A4.................$35.00
Darkest Hour, 1920s, plywood, 500 random semi-interlocking pcs, EX (rpl box), A4..$110.00
Day in the fields, Madmar/Blue Ribbon, 1930s, 500 long knobby interlocking pcs, EX (EX box), A4 ....$100.00
Declaration of Independence, Parker Bros/Pastime, 1927, plywood, 400 curve-knob semi-interlocking pcs, EX (EX box), A4 ....$120.00
Discussing the News, Ingleside/Scroll Cut, 1909, solid wood, 151 push-to-fit pcs, 1 rpl pc, EX (EX box), A4 ....$35.00
Dissected ABC Puzzle, J Ottoman, 1920, shows Santa coming down chimney & children sleeping, complete, EX (VG box), A..$150.00
Farm Cart w/Horses & Pigs (Untitled), 1930s, 407 semi-interlocking pcs, color-line cutting, 5 rpl pcs, EX (rpl box), A4 ....$80.00
Fate of the Nation, C Dennison, 1909, solid wood, 229 push-to-fit pcs, 1 rpl pc, EX (EX box), A4.............................$55.00
Foreign Maidens, Grunsaco, 1930s, plywood, 331 curve-knob interlocking pcs, semicolor-cutting, EX (EX box), A4..$70.00

Four Seasons-Childhood, HE Hamlen/Little Cut-Up, 1930s, plywood, 151 interlocking pcs, color-line cutting, NMIB, A4..........$30.00

Garden Glories, Tuco, 1940s, cb, 200 crooked-line strip-cut pcs, EX (EX box), A4..........$8.00

General Washington, I Ayer, 1909, solid wood, 50 push-to-fit pcs, color-line cutting, EX (EX box), A4..........$20.00

Girl Capturing Birds w/Hat (untitled), 1910-20, plywood, 362 angular push-to-fit semi-interlocking pcs, EX (rpl box), A4..........$75.00

Photo courtesy Bob Armstrong

Glistening Sheen, HE Hamlen/Little Cut-Up, 1930s, plywood, 204 interlocking pieces, color-line cutting, EX (EX box), A4, $40.00.

Golden Sunset, Leisure Hour, 1909, solid wood, 319 long push-to-fit pcs, color-line cutting, 3 rpl pcs, EX (EX box), A4..........$85.00

Great Fire at Boston, R Chesley, 1972, plywood, 167 rnd-knob interlocking pcs, EX (EX box), A4..........$25.00

Hay Time, Parker Bros/Pastime, 1940-50, plywood, 205 jagged curve-knob interlocking pcs, color-line cut, EX (EX box), A4..........$60.00

Haymaking, Olive Novelty Co, 1920s, plywood, 211 push-to-fit pcs, color-line cutting, EX (EX box), A4..........$55.00

Holland Windmill, 1930s, plywood, 94 1-by-1 long-rnd interlocking pcs, 2 rpl pcs, EX (EX box), A4..........$15.00

Huntsmans Wedding, Hoadley House, 1930s, plywood, 205 1-by-1 curve-knob interlocking pcs, EX (EX box), A4.$40.00

In Blossom Time, Perx Puzzle, 1930s, plywood, 258 rnd-knob interlocking pcs, 2 rpl pcs, EX (EX box), A4..........$40.00

In Full Cry, J Salmon/Academy, 1930s, plywood, 325 rnd-knob interlocking pcs, 1-way strip-cut, EX (EX box), A4..$40.00

Joan of Arc, SN Soule, 1909, solid wood, 135 push-to-fit pcs, color-line cutting, EX (EX box), A4..........$35.00

Lake Louise & Victoria Glazier, R Chesley, 1972-74, plywood, 294 random interlocking pcs, semicolor-line cut, NMIB, A4..........$45.00

Memories Garden, Parker Bros/Pastime, 1920s, plywood, 608 curve-knob semi-interlocking pcs, color-line cut, NMIB, A4..........$200.00

Photo courtesy Bob Armstrong

May Day, early 1900s, solid wood, 564 push-to-fit pieces, 11x8", EX, A4, $85.00.

Minute Man, Parker Bros/Pastime, 1930s, plywood, 201 rnd-knob interlocking pcs, color-line cut, 1 rpl pc, NMIB, A4..........$60.00

Mother's Helper, Book-o'-the Day Libraries, 1930s, plywood, 125 random-knob interlocking pcs, EX (rpl box), A4.$25.00

Mount Vesuvius, Schwartz/Special Cut, 1930s, plywood, 200 random rnd-knob interlocking pcs, EX (EX box), A4..........$30.00

Mounted Parade Band (Untitled), 1930s, plywood, 222 curve-knob interlocking pcs, strip-cut, EX (rpl box), A4....$25.00

Nature's Vivid Trail, L Goff, 1930s, plywood, 325 sq-knob interlocking pcs, semistrip-cut, EX (EX box), A4..........$50.00

Old Ironsides, Glengarry Puzzles, 1930s, plywood, 310 interlocking pcs, semistrip-cut, EX (EX box), A4..........$50.00

Old Silver & Tulips, Madmar/Interlox, 1930s, plywood, 300 long rnd interlocking pcs, EX (EX box), A4..........$55.00

Pals, Cutshalls/Krazy Kut, 1930s, masonite, 231 random semi-interlocking pcs, EX (rpl box), A4..........$35.00

PAR Picture Puzzle, 750 pcs, EXIB, A..........$375.00

Paradise Lake, James Browning, 1950s, plywood, 500 random-knob interlocking pcs, 2 rpl pcs, EX (EX box), A4..$135.00

Quaint Old Holland, Parker Bros/Pastime, 1930s, plywood, 252 curve-knob interlocking pcs, color-line cut, NMIB, A4..........$75.00

Road to the Coast, J Straus, 1930s, plywood, 500 random interlocking pcs, 1 rpl pc, EX (worn box), A4..........$50.00

Saving the Charter, Per-Plex, 1930s, plywood, 155 rnd-knob interlocking pcs, EX (EX box), A4..........$25.00

Ships (Untitled), 1930s, plywood, 247 jagged push-to-fit pcs, color-line cutting, 1 rpl pc, G (G box), A4..........$25.00

Six Way Puzzle Blocks, Germany, 1900, pictures colorful flying machines & zeppelins, 8x11", EX, A..........$275.00

Southern Home, 1930-40, plywood, 272 1-by-1 rnd-knob interlocking pcs, EX (rpl box), A4..........$40.00

Spring, 1910-20, plywood, 231 long-rnd interlocking pcs, semi-color-line cut, 2 rpl pcs, EX (rpl box), A4..........$45.00

Steamboat Natchez, J Straus, 1940s, plywood, 325 sq-knob interlocking pcs, EX (EX box), A4..........$40.00

Sunset Ridge, Milton Bradley/Piedmont, 1930s, 200 interlocking pcs, strip-cut, EX (EX box), A4..........$30.00

Tally-Ho Scroll Puzzle, McLoughlin Bros, image of Father Christmas on stagecoach w/children, 2 rpl pcs, VG (VG box), A......$325.00

The Artist, New Society Scroll Puzzle, plywood, 56 crooked-line pcs, strip-cut, EX (EX box), A4......$16.00

The Chase, Milton Bradley/Piedmont, 1930s, plywood, 200 rnd-knob interlocking pcs, strip-cut, 3 rpl pcs, EX (EX box), A4......$30.00

The Message, Puzzle Library, 1930s, plywood, 412 jagged curve-knob pcs, semicolor-line cut, EX (EX box), A4......$75.00

The Tavern, Northwestern Wood, 1930s, plywood, 300 rnd-knob interlocking pcs, 1-way strip-cut, EX (EX box), A4......$50.00

Tranquility, Perx Puzzle, 1930s, plywood, 142 rnd-knob interlocking pcs, EX (EX box), A4......$25.00

Twilight in Paris, Hayter/Victory Artistic, 1930s, plywood, 600 rnd-knob interlocking pcs, strip-cut, EX (rpl box), A4..$90.00

Photo courtesy Bob Armstrong

Unconquered Places, 1920s, plywood, 324 interlocking pieces, 12x16", VG, A4, $25.00.

Venice, R Purrington, 1930s, plywood, 400 random interlocking pcs, EX (EX box), A4......$80.00

Village on Plain (Untitled), Seaboard, 1950-70, plywood, 200 rnd-knob strip-cut interlocking pcs, EX (EX box), A4......$25.00

War Bonnet Song, Andover Novelty Shop/Nu-F, 1930s, plywood, 570 1-by-1 interlocking pcs, 2 rpl pcs, EX (EX box), A4......$110.00

Water Gates, Haarlem, Parker Bros/Pastime, 1930s, plywood, 576 rnd-knob interlocking pcs, color-line cut, NMIB, A4.$175.00

Welcome Home, J Straus, 1930s, plywood, 300 curve-knob interlocking pcs, EX (EX box), A4......$40.00

When Roses Climb, B Randall, 1931, plywood, 256 random interlocking pcs, semicolor-line cut, EX (EX box), A4......$50.00

Wine Glass Inn, Parker Bros/Golden Eagle, 1930s, plywood, 150 random-knob interlocking pcs, semi-strip cut, NMIB, A4......$30.00

Character

Adventures of Gulliver, fr-tray, Whitman, 1969, complete, 14x11", NM, F8......$35.00

Alien — Nostromo Flight, jigsaw, HG Toys, 1979, complete, EX (VG+ box), D9......$15.00

Andy Panda, fr-tray, Walter Lantz, 1962-63, complete, 11x8", EX, T2......$10.00

Aquaman, jigsaw, Whitman, 1968, 100 pcs, EX (EX box), A.$35.00

Archie — Swinging at the Malt Shop, jigsaw, Jaymar, 1950s, complete, NM (EX box), C1......$35.00

Banana Splits, fr-tray, Whitman, 1969, complete set of 4, EX (EX box), A......$50.00

Barney Google & Snuffy Smith, fr-tray, Jaymar, 1940s-50s, complete, NM, C1......$40.00

Batman, fr-tray, Watkins-Strathmore, 1966, complete, EX, A......$25.00

Batman, jigsaw, APC, 1973, complete, NM (NM canister), from $20 to......$25.00

Batman, jigsaw, Whitman, 1966, missing 2 pcs, EX (EX box), F8......$20.00

Beatles in Pepperland, jigsaw, 100 pcs, MIB (sealed), B3...$200.00

Beatles — Meanies Invade Pepperland, jigsaw, complete, EX (EX box), B3......$150.00

Bee Gees, jigsaw, 1979, MIB, B3......$20.00

Blondie, fr-tray, Built-Rite, 1949, complete, 8x13", EX, M17......$30.00

Bonanza — Expecting Trouble, jigsaw, Milton Bradley, 1964, missing 2 pcs, NM (EX box), F8......$25.00

Broken Arrow, fr-tray, Built-Rite, boxed set of 4, MIB.....$65.00

Broken Arrow, jigsaw, Built-Rite, 1958, complete, NM (EX box), F8......$20.00

Buck Rogers in the 25th Century, jigsaw, Puzzle Craft/John Dille, 1945, complete set of 3, scarce, EX (EX box), A......$300.00

Buffalo Bill Jr, jigsaw, Built-Rite, 1956, 100 pcs, EX (EX box), P4......$25.00

Bugs Bunny, fr-tray, Jaymar, 1940s-50s, image of Bugs eating Elmer's groceries, complete, 10x12", VG, F8......$6.00

Bullwinkle, jigsaw, Whitman, 1960, complete, EX (EX box), F8......$25.00

Captain Kangaroo, jigsaw, Fairchild, 1956, Treasure House scene, 75 pcs, EX (EX box), T2......$15.00

Captain Kool & the Kongs, fr-tray, 1978, M (sealed), J2 .$15.00

Captain Marvel, jigsaw, Fawcett, 1941, complete, EX (EX box), A......$75.00

Chilly Willy, fr-tray, Walter Lantz, 1962-63, complete, 11x8", EX, T2......$10.00

Captain Marvel, jigsaw, L Miller and Son/Fawcett, over 200 pieces, complete, NM (EX box), $125.00.

Chipmunks, fr-tray, Whitman, 1964, complete, EX, J2....$25.00
Cinderella, jigsaw, 1950s, complete, EX (EX canister), N2..$30.00
Circus Boy, fr-tray, 1958, complete, VG, R2 ....$50.00
Close Encounters of the Third Kind, jigsaw, Milton Bradley, 1977, 250 pcs, MIB (sealed), P3 ....$15.00
Combat, jigsaw, Jaymar, 1960s, complete, NMIB, F8.......$20.00
Creature from the Black Lagoon, jigsaw, Golden, 1991, 200 pcs, MIB (sealed), P3 ....$5.00
Davy Crockett Indian Attack, jigsaw, Jaymar, complete, EX (EX box) $35.00
Davy Crockett Seige of the Fort, jigsaw, Jaymar, complete, EX (EX box), J2 ....$35.00
Defenders of the Earth, jigsaw, 1986, complete, EX (EX box), N2 ....$10.00
Dennis the Menace, fr-tray, Whitman, 1960, complete, 11x14", VG+, T2 ....$12.00
Deputy Dawg, jigsaw, Whitman, 1972, 100 pcs, NM (EX box), F8 ....$15.00
Dick Tracy — Manhunt for Mumbles, jigsaw, Jaymar, 1950s-60s, complete, NMIB, C1 ....$65.00
Donald & Mickey on the Moon, fr-tray, Playskool, complete, EX, N2 ....$10.00
Donald Duck in Disneyland, jigsaw, Jaymar, 1950s, 60 pcs, EX (EX box), M17 ....$25.00
Dondi, fr-tray, Jaymar, 1961, complete, 14x11", NM, T2.$15.00
Donny & Marie, fr-tray, Whitman, 1977, complete, NM, C1 ....$20.00
Dr Dolittle, fr-tray, Whitman, 1967, complete, 14x11", NM, F8...$16.00
Dr Kildare, jigsaw, Milton Bradley, 1962, 600 pcs, NMIB, F8.$30.00
Dr Seuss, jigsaw, Random House, 1979, 60 pcs, NMIB, F8......$15.00
Dracula, jigsaw, 1974, complete, EX (EX canister), N2....$20.00
Eddie Cantor, jigsaw, Einson, 1933, complete, NMIB, F8..$30.00
Family Affair, jigsaw, Whitman, 1970, 125 pcs, 20" dia when completed, rare, EX (EX box), M17.......................$100.00
Fantastic Four, fr-tray, Whitman, 1968, 14x11", complete, scarce, NM, A $50.00
Farrah Fawcett, jigsaw, 1977, complete, NM (EX photo box), C1 ....$35.00
Fat Albert, jigsaw, Whitman, 1975, 100 pcs, NM (EX box), F8...$20.00
Featured Funnies, jigsaw, Jaymar, features Popeye, Dick Tracy, Flash Gordon, etc, set of 8, EX (EX box), A...........$375.00
Felix the Cat, fr-tray, Built-Rite, 1949, complete, EX, F8...$35.00
Flintstones, jigsaw, Warren, 1976, set of 4, complete, NM (NM box), F8 ....$25.00
Flipper, jigsaw, Whitman, 1965, complete, NMIB, F8 .....$20.00
Frankenstein, jigsaw, American Publishing, 1974, complete, EX (EX canister), M17 ....$35.00
Frankenstein Jr, jigsaw, Whitman, 1968, 99 pcs, EX (EX box), M17 ....$30.00
Gabby Gator, fr-tray, Walter Lantz, 1962-63, complete, 11x8", EX, T2 ....$10.00
GI Joe, jigsaw, Milton Bradley, 1985, 221 pcs, MIB, F1 ...$15.00
Goofy, fr-tray, Whitman, 1963, complete, 14x11", NM, F8...$20.00
Gulliver's Travels, fr-tray, Saalfield, 1930s, set of 8, complete, EX (EX box), A $100.00
Gunsmoke, jigsaw, Whitman, 1969, 100 pcs, MIB, M15..$35.00
Hardy Boys, jigsaw, 1978, complete, EX (EX box), N2 ....$25.00
Henry, jigsaw, Fairchild, 1973, 100 pcs, NMIB, F8..........$25.00

Hopalong Cassidy, Milton Bradley, boxed set of three, complete, NMIB, $125.00.

Howdy Doody, fr-tray, Whitman, 1953, complete, 15x11", NM, F8 ....$20.00
Howdy Doody ABC Puzzle, jigsaw, Parker Bros, 1950s, 16 giant-sz pcs, VG (VG box), A $130.00
Howdy Doody's One-Man Band, jigsaw, Whitman Jr, 1950s, complete, EX (EX box), P6 ....$50.00
Impossibles, fr-tray, Whitman, 1967, complete, 14x11", EX, F8..$25.00
James Bond 007, Goldfinger, jigsaw, Milton Bradley, 1965, Deluxe edition, complete, NM (EX box), F8............$55.00
Jetsons, fr-tray, Whitman, 1962, complete, EX, J2/M15...$35.00
Johnny Lightning, fr-tray, Whitman, 1970, complete, 14x11", EX, F8...$25.00
Kaptain Kool & the Kongs, fr-tray, 1978, MIP (sealed), J2..$15.00
King Kong, jigsaw, Chad Valley, 200 3-ply wooden interlocking pcs, scarce, NM (EX box), A..................................$600.00
King Leonardo, fr-tray, Jaymar, 1961, complete, 11x13", EX, F8 ....$20.00
King Leonardo, jigsaw, Jaymar, 1962, complete, EX (VG box), F8 ....$20.00
KISS, jigsaw, 1970s, features Paul Stanley, complete, EX (EX box), A $40.00
Krazy Ikes, fr-tray, 1969, complete, 14x11", EX, F8 ....$14.00
Lady & the Tramp — Chicken Capers, jigsaw, Jaymar, 1960s, complete, NM (EX box), F8....................................$16.00
Lariat Sam, jigsaw, Fairchild, 1977, complete, NM (EX box), F8 ....$16.00
Lassie & Timmy, fr-tray, Whitman, complete, EX, J2 ......$25.00
Little King, jigsaw, Jaymar, 1930s, complete, EX (EX box), A...$50.00
Little Lulu, jigsaw, Whitman, 1973, set of 4, MIB, C1 .....$70.00
Lone Ranger Story Puzzle, jigsaw, Parker Bros, 1938, set of 4, EX (EX box), F8 ....$75.00
Ludwig Von Drake, fr-tray, 1960s, set of 4, MIB (sealed), J8.$50.00

Mary Poppins, fr-tray, Jaymar, 1964, complete, NM, F8...**$20.00**
Mary Poppins, jigsaw, Jaymar, 1964, complete, MIB, P6..**$40.00**
Masters of the Universe, fr-tray, Golden, 1984, VG, M15.**$12.00**
Mighty Mouse, jigsaw, Whitman, 1972, 100 pcs, NMIB, F8...**$20.00**
Milton the Monster, jigsaw, Whitman, 1967, NMIB, C1.**$50.00**
Mother Goose Comic Picture Puzzles, fr-tray, Parker Bros, 1950s, set of 4, MIB, J6 ....**$50.00**
Mr I Magination, jigsaw, Jaymar Television Stars series, 1951, 400 pcs, scarce, NMIB, T2 ....**$50.00**
Mr Magoo, fr-tray, Jaymar, 1967, complete, 10x13", EX, F8.**$15.00**
Nancy & Sluggo, jigsaw, Whitman, 1973, complete, NMIB, F8....**$15.00**
New Mickey Mouse Club, fr-tray, Whitman, complete, EX...**$15.00**
Oswald the Rabbit, fr-tray, Walter Lantz, 1962-63, complete, 11x8", EX, T2 ....**$10.00**
Pebbles, fr-tray, Whitman, 1963, complete, 14x11", EX, F8.**$25.00**
Peter Pan, fr-tray, Jaymar, 1950s, complete, EX, M8 ....**$20.00**
Popeye's Comic Picture Puzzle, jigsaw, Parker Bros, set of 4, EX (EX box), A **$100.00**
Prince Valiant, fr-tray, Built-Rite, 1954, complete, 10x12", EX, F8 ....**$15.00**
Princess of Power, fr-tray, 1985, complete, 14x11", EX, N2.**$10.00**
Raggedy Ann & Andy, fr-tray, Milton Bradley, 1955, complete, EX, F8....**$20.00**

Raggedy Ann Picture Puzzles, frame-tray, Milton Bradley, 1944, boxed set of three, complete, 14x11", NMIB, $85.00.

Raggedy Ann Picture Puzzles, fr-tray, Milton Bradley, 1944, set of 3, complete, 14x11", NMIB, J5 ....**$85.00**
Range Rider, fr-tray, Gabriel, 1955, set of 4, 1 missing 2 pcs, EX (VG box), T2....**$30.00**
Road Runner, jigsaw, Whitman, 1980, complete, EX (EX box), J2 ....**$20.00**
Robin Hood, jigsaw, Jaymar, 1973, complete, NMIB, F8.**$15.00**
Robin Hood — Robin's Merry Men, jigsaw, Built-Rite, 1956, complete, NM (EX box), F8....**$20.00**
Roger Ramjet, fr-tray, Whitman, 1966, complete, EX, H4..**$20.00**
Rootie Kazootie, jigsaw, Fairchild, 1950s, set of 3, complete, EX (EX box), F8 ....**$50.00**
Rudolph the Red-Nosed Reindeer, fr-tray, Jaymar, 1950s, complete, 14x11", NM, T2....**$20.00**
Shotgun Slade, jigsaw, Milton Bradley, 1960, 100 pcs, NMIB, F8....**$30.00**
Skyhawks, fr-tray, Whitman, 1970, complete, 14x11", EX, F8....**$18.00**
Sleeping Beauty, fr-tray, Whitman, 1958, various images, complete, 11x14", F8, ea, from $15 to....**$20.00**
Sleeping Beauty, jigsaw, Jaymar, 1960s, complete, NMIB, M8 ....**$20.00**
Smedly, fr-tray, Walter Lantz, 1962-63, complete, 11x8", EX, T2 ....**$10.00**
Snow White & the Seven Dwarfs, jigsaw, Jaymar, 1940s, 300 pcs, NMIB, F8....**$50.00**
Space Kidettes, fr-tray, Whitman, 1967, complete, 14x11", EX, F8 ....**$25.00**
Space Kidettes, jigsaw, Whitman, 1968, complete, VG (VG box), H4....**$20.00**
Steve Canyon in China, jigsaw, Jaymar, 1950s, complete, EX (EX box), I2 ....**$15.00**
Superman, fr-tray, Whitman, 1965, complete, 14x11", EX, A.**$25.00**
Superman, jigsaw, Whitman, 1966, 150 pcs, EX (EX box), F8....**$25.00**
Superman Springs Into Action, jigsaw, Saalfield, 1940, 500 pcs, EX (EX box), from $275 to **$300.00**
Tammy, jigsaw, Whitman, 1964, complete, MIB **$40.00**
Tammy & Pepper, jigsaw, Whitman, 1964, complete, MIB...**$40.00**
Tarzan, jigsaw, Whitman, 1968, complete, EX (EX box), F8.**$20.00**
Three Little Pigs, jigsaw, Parker Bros, 1960s, 140 pcs, MIB (sealed), F8....**$25.00**
Three Stooges — Hold Your Fire, jigsaw, Colorforms, complete, scarce, EX (EX box), A **$475.00**
Tom & Jerry, fr-tray, 1954, complete, EX, J2 ....**$30.00**
Tom & Jerry, jigsaw, Whitman, 1969, complete, NMIB, F8.**$15.00**
Tommy Tortoise & Moe Hare, jigsaw, Built-Rite, 1961, 70 pcs, MIB, T2 ....**$25.00**
Twas the Night Before Christmas, fr-tray, Lowe, 1972, complete, 12x8", M, T2 ....**$6.00**

Uncle Wiggily Picture Puzzles, jigsaw, Milton Bradley, 1900, set of three, complete, NMIB, $200.00.

Twinkles, fr-tray, Whitman, 1962, complete, 14x11", rare, NM, F8 ....$55.00
Underdog, fr-tray, Whitman, 1976, complete, 11x8", EX, F8 ....$15.00
Universal Monsters, fr-tray, Jaymar, 1963, Dracula, Mummy or Frankenstein, complete, NM, H4, ea $150.00
Wacky Races, fr-tray, Whitman, 1969, complete, 14x11", EX, F8 ....$30.00
Willow Ufgood, jigsaw, Random House, 1988, MIB (sealed), D9 ....$5.00
Winnie the Pooh, fr-tray, Whitman, 1979, complete, 14x11", EX, F8 ....$8.00
Woody Woodpecker, fr-tray, Whitman, 1954, complete, VG, M15/T2 ....$25.00
Wyatt Earp, fr-tray, Whitman, 1956, complete, EX, M15 .$25.00
Yogi Bear, jigsaw, Whitman Jr, 1960s, 63 pcs, NMIB, F8 .$25.00

Radios, Novelty

Many novelty radios are made to resemble a commercial product box or can, and with the crossover interest into the advertising field, some of the more collectible, even though of recent vintage, are often seen carrying very respectible price tags. Likenesses of famous personalities such as Elvis or characters like Charlie Tuna house transistors in cases made of plastic that scarcely hint at their actual function. Others represent items ranging from baseball caps to Cadillacs. To learn more about this subject, we recommend *Collector's Guide to Novelty Radios Book I* and *II* by Marty Bunis and Robert F. Breed.

Advisors: Sue and Marty Bunis (B11).

Avon Skin-So-Soft, NMIB, J2 ....$35.00
Big Bird, 2-dimensional figure, NM....................$20.00
Blabber Mouse on Cheese, EX, J2 ....$35.00
Bozo the Clown, plastic, 6", EX, B11 ....$85.00
Bubble Tape, MIB....................$20.00
Bugs Bunny w/Carrot, EX $40.00
Bullwinkle, PAT World Prod, 3-D plastic, 6¼x11⅞" $250.00
Buster the Talking Monkey, Stellar #4221, w/clock, 8x12" $100.00

Cadillac Convertible, 1963 model, AM, MIB, J6, $45.00.

Campbell's Tomato Soup Can, EX, S15....................$35.00

Casper the Ghost, Harvey Cartoons/Sutton, 1972, M, from $50.00 to $75.00.

Champion Spark Plug, MIB $100.00
Charlie McCarthy, Majestic, 1930s, Bakelite w/metal figure of Charlie, 7", EX, A $2,000.00
Chiquita NFL 50th Anniversary, NMIB, J2....................$50.00
Coca-Cola Bottle, EX $35.00
Coca-Cola Can, EX $25.00
Coca-Cola Vending Machine, China, 1989, MIB, J6.......$65.00
Cracker Jack, 2-sided, scarce, NM, P12 ....$125.00
Crayola Rocks, w/headphones, MIB, P12....................$45.00
Delco Battery, MIB $35.00
Double-Cola, can shape, EX, J2....................$35.00
Elvis on Stage, M $75.00
Folgers Coffee Can, plastic, 4", NM, B11....................$75.00

He-Man, Nasta, 1984, 5", M, from $25.00 to $35.00.

Fred Flintstone, Sutton, 1972, molded plastic head figure, NMIB $75.00
Gumby, Lewco, 1970s, NM $150.00
Hamburger, Hong Kong, plastic, EX $65.00
Heinz Ketchup Bottle, NM $50.00
Hershey Syrup Bottle, MIB $75.00
Hopalong Cassidy, Arvin, metal w/diecut plated front featuring Hoppy on Topper w/western designs, 5x8", NM, A .$500.00
Hopalong Cassidy, Arvin, 1950, blk version, 8", EX, A .$500.00
Hot Dog, Hong Kong, plastic, EX $65.00
KISS, M, J6 ....$60.00
Lone Ranger, Airline, 1950, wht plastic w/colorful image of Lone Ranger on Silver, NM, A $1,100.00
Manwich Can, EX $45.00
Michelin Man, Italy, 1960s, rare, NM, P12 ....$400.00
Mickey Mouse, Emerson, 1930s, Syrocco-type material w/emb images of Mickey playing instruments on all sides, 8x8", EX, A $1,800.00
Mickey Mouse, sitting in chair, EX $45.00
Mr Tom Candy Bar, British, M, P12 ....$85.00

Photo courtesy June Moon

Oscar the Grouch, MIB, $45.00.

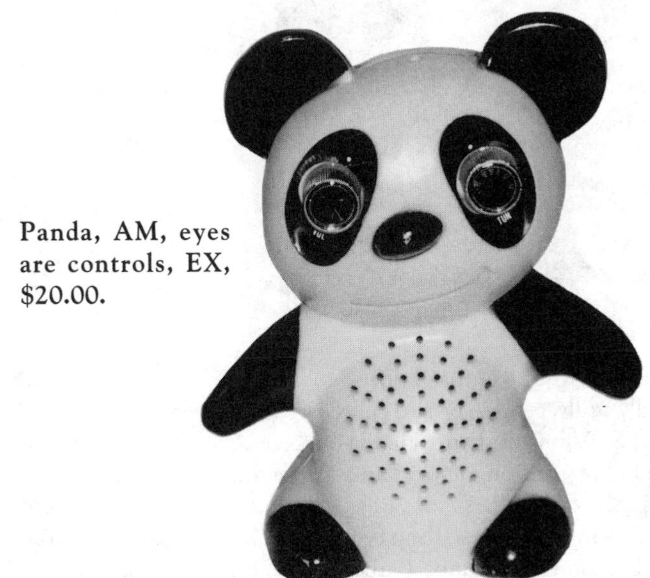

Panda, AM, eyes are controls, EX, $20.00.

Pepsi-Cola Can, EX $25.00
Pepsi-Cola Fountain Despenser, 7", EX $225.00
Planters Cocktail Nuts Can, MIB $55.00
Pound Puppies, 1986, NM, J2 ....$25.00
Raggedy Ann & Andy, Philgee International, 1973, NM .$25.00
Raid Bug, clock radio, M, P12 ....$225.00
RC Cola Can, EX, J6 ....$25.00
Red Goose Shoe, VG $50.00
Six Million Dollar Man Backpack, MIB $25.00
Slot Machine, Stellarsonic, Hong Kong, 4¼x5¼" $75.00
Smurf, NM $10.00
Snoopy, AM, Determined, 1970s, 7", MIB, M17 ....$40.00
Snoopy's Doghouse, Determined, 1975, NM, H11 ....$65.00
Snow White & the Seven Dwarfs, Emerson, Syrocco w/cloth speaker, 7x11", NM, A $3,000.00
Superman in Phone Booth, mk Made in Hong Kong, plastic, 7", NM, B11 ....$175.00

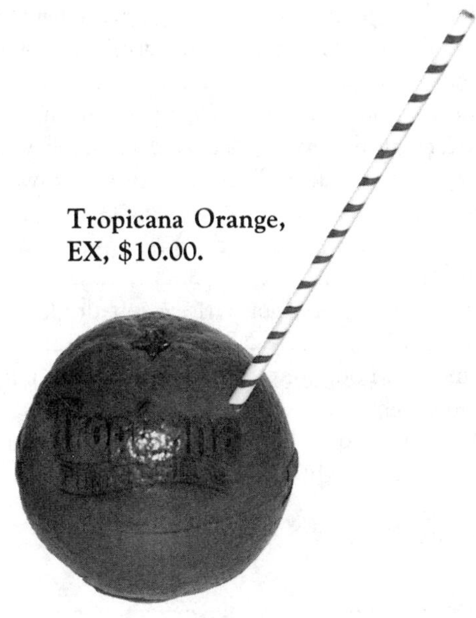

Tropicana Orange, EX, $10.00.

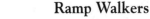

V8 Can, NM, B11 ....$50.00
Welch's Grape Juice Can, M $50.00
Wilson Tennis Balls, can shape $45.00
Yago Sangria, bottle shape, MIB, J2 ....$65.00

Ramp Walkers

Ramp walkers date back to at least 1873 when Ives produced two versions of a cast-iron elephant walker. Wood and composition ramp walkers were made in Czechoslovakia and the U.S.A. from the 1930s through the 1950s. The most common were made by John Wilson of Pennsylvania and were sold worldwide. These became known as 'Wilson Walkies.' Most are two-legged and stand approximately 4½" tall. While some of the Wilson Walkies were made of a composite material with wood legs (for instance, Donald, Wimpy, Popeye, and Olive Oyl), most are made with cardboard thread-cone bodies with wood legs and head. The walkers made in Czechoslovakia are similar but they are generally made of wood.

Plastic ramp walkers were primarily manufactured by the Louis Marx Co. and were made from the early 1950s through the mid-1960s. The majority were produced in Hong Kong, but some were made in the United States and sold under the Marx logo or by the Charmore Co., which was a subsidiary of the Marx Co. Some walkers are still being produced today as fast-food premiums.

The three common sizes are (1) small, about 1½" x 2"; (2) medium, about 2¾" x 3"; and (3) large, about 4" x 5". Most of the small walkers are unpainted while the medium or large sizes were either spray painted or painted by hand. Several of the walking toys were sold with wooden plastic or colorful lithographed tin ramps.

Advisor: Randy Welch (W4).

Advertising

Captain Flint, Long John Silvers, 1989, w/plastic coin weight....$15.00
Choo-Choo Cherry, Funny Face soft drink mix, w/plastic coin weight....$60.00
Flash Turtle, Long John Silvers, 1989, w/plastic coin weight.$15.00
Goofy Grape, Funny Face soft drink mix, w/plastic coin weight .$60.00
Jolly Ollie Orange, Funny Face soft drink mix, w/plastic coin weight $60.00
Quinn Penguin, Long John Silvers, 1989, w/plastic coin weight $15.00
Root'n Toot'n Raspberry, Funny Face soft drink mix, w/plastic coin weight $60.00
Sydney Dinosaur, Long John Silvers, 1989, yel & purple, w/plastic coin weight $15.00
Sylvia Dinosaur, Long John Silvers, 1989, lavender & pk, w/plastic coin weight $15.00

Czechoslovakian

Dog $20.00
Man w/Carved Wood Hat $30.00
Monkey $30.00
Pig $20.00
Policeman....$60.00

Disney Characters by Marx

Big Bad Wolf & Mason Pig....$50.00
Big Bad Wolf & Three Little Pigs $150.00
Donald Duck, pulling nephews in wagon....$35.00
Donald Duck, pushing wheelbarrow, plastic w/metal legs, sm $30.00
Donald Duck & Goofy, riding go-cart....$40.00
Donald's Trio, France, Huey, Louie & Dewey dressed as Indian Chief, cowboy & 1 carrying flowers, NMOC, A $155.00
Fiddler & Fifer Pigs $50.00
Figaro the Cat, w/ball....$30.00
Goofy, riding hippo....$45.00
Jiminy Cricket, w/cello $30.00
Mad Hatter w/March Hare $50.00

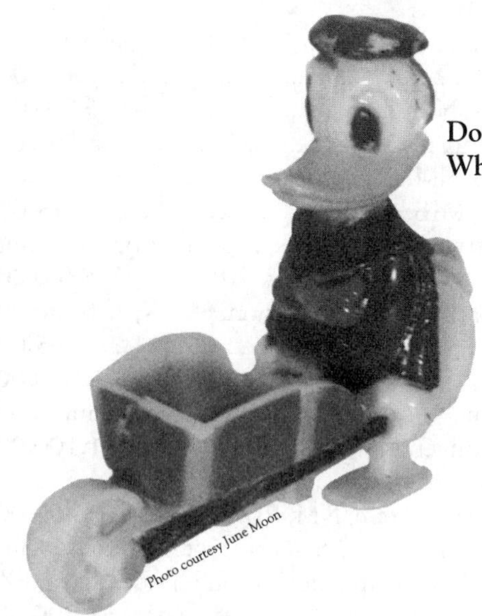

Donald Duck Pushing Wheelbarrow, $25.00.

Mickey & Donald Riding Alligator....$40.00
Mickey Mouse, pushing lawn roller....$35.00
Mickey Mouse & Minnie, plastic w/metal wheels, sm $40.00
Mickey Mouse & Pluto, hunting $40.00
Minnie Mouse, pushing baby stroller $35.00
Pluto, plastic w/metal legs, sm $30.00
Wiggly Walkers, complete set of 4 w/Mickey, Minnie, Pluto & Donald, EX (VG scarce box) $400.00

Hanna-Barbera, King Features & Other Characters by Marx

Astro, Hanna-Barbera $150.00

Astro and George Jetson, $90.00.

Astro & Rosey, Hanna-Barbera....$95.00
Chilly Willy, penguin on sled pulled by parent, Walter Lantz ...$25.00
Fred & Wilma on Dino, Hanna-Barbera....$60.00
Fred Flintstone on Dino, Hanna-Barbera....$70.00
Hap & Hop Soldiers $20.00
Little King & Guards, King Features $70.00
Pebbles on Dino, Hanna-Barbera $70.00

Popeye, Erwin, celluloid, lg $60.00
Popeye Pushing Spinach Can Wheelbarrow $40.00
Santa, w/gold sack $45.00
Santa, w/wht sack $40.00
Santa, w/yel sack $35.00
Santa & Mrs Claus, faces on both sides $50.00
Santa & Snowman, faces on both sides $50.00
Spark Plug $200.00
Top Cat & Benny $65.00
Yogi Bear & Huckleberry Hound, Hanna-Barbera $50.00

Marx Animals With Riders Series

Ankylosaurus w/Clown $40.00
Bison w/Native $40.00
Brontosaurus w/Monkey $40.00
Hippo w/Native $40.00
Lion w/Clown $40.00
Stegosaurus w/Black Caveman $40.00
Triceratops w/Native $40.00
Zebra w/Native $40.00

Plastic

Baby Walk-A-Way, lg $40.00
Baseball Player w/Bat & Ball $40.00
Bear $15.00
Boy & Girl Dancing $60.00
Bull $15.00
Bunnies Carrying Carrot $30.00
Bunny Pushing Cart $60.00
Camel w/2 Humps, head bobs $20.00
Chicks Carrying Easter Egg $30.00
Chinese Men w/Duck in Basket $30.00
Chipmunks Carrying Acorns $30.00
Chipmunks Marching Band w/Drum & Horn $30.00
Cow, w/metal legs, sm $15.00
Cowboy on Horse, w/metal legs, sm $25.00
Dachshund $15.00
Dairy Cow $15.00
Dog, Pluto look-alike w/metal legs, sm $15.00
Double Walking Doll, boy behind girl, lg $60.00

Farmer Pushing Wheelbarrow, $20.00; Pig, $15.00.

Duck $15.00
Dutch Boy & Girl $30.00
Elephant $20.00
Elephant, w/metal legs, sm $20.00
Frontiersman w/Dog $95.00
Goat $20.00
Horse, circus style $15.00
Horse, lg $30.00
Horse, yel w/rubber ears & string tail, lg $30.00
Horse w/English Rider, lg $40.00
Indian Woman Pulling Baby on Travois $95.00
Kangaroo w/Baby in Pouch $30.00
Mama Duck w/3 Ducklings $30.00
Marty's Market Lady Pushing Shopping Cart $60.00
Mexican Cowboy on Horse, w/metal legs, sm $20.00
Milking Cow, lg $40.00
Monkeys Carrying Bananas $60.00
Nursemaid Pushing Baby Stroller $15.00
Pigs, 2 carrying 1 in basket $40.00
Popeye & Wimpy, heads on springs, lg $65.00
Pumpkin Head Man & Woman, faces both sides $75.00
Reindeer $40.00
Sailors SS Shoreleave $20.00
Sheriff Facing Outlaw $65.00
Teeny Toddler, walking baby girl, Dolls Inc, lg $40.00
Tin Man Robot Pushing Cart $125.00
Walking Baby, in Canadian Mountie uniform, lg $50.00
Walking Baby, w/moving eyes & cloth dress, lg $40.00
Wiz Walker Milking Cow, Charmore, lg $40.00

Wilson

Penguin, $25.00; Elephant, $30.00; Pig, $30.00.

Black Mammy $35.00
Donald Duck $175.00
Eskimo $100.00
Indian Chief $45.00
Nurse $30.00
Olive Oyl $175.00
Pinocchio $175.00
Popeye $175.00
Rabbit $60.00
Sailor $30.00
Santa Claus $75.00

Soldier $25.00
Wimpy $175.00

Records

Most of the records listed here are related to TV shows and movies, and all are specifically geared toward children. The more successful the show, the more collectible the record. But condition is critical as well, and unless the record is excellent or better, its value is lowered very dramatically.

33⅓ RPM Records

Amazing Spider-Man Abominable Snowman, Power Records, 1970s, M (M sleeve), from $20 to $25.00
Archies Jingle Jangle, Stereo, 1969, EX (EX sleeve), F8...$15.00
Aristocats, Stereo, 1970, orig soundtrack, complete w/booklet, EX (EX sleeve), F8..$12.00
Around the World With the Chipmunks, Liberty, 1961, VG (VG sleeve), T2...$15.00
Babes in Toyland, 1961, complete w/booklet, NM (EX sleeve), F8 ....$20.00
Big Valley, Paramount, 1966, NM (EX sleeve), F8...........$45.00
Bozo's Christmas Album, 1973, EX (EX sleeve), N2 ....$10.00
Chilling, Thrilling Sounds of the Haunted House, Disneyland, 1964, EX (EX sleeve), F8..$12.00
Chipmunks Sing w/Children, Liberty, 1965, EX (EX sleeve), F8 ....$10.00
Chitty-Chitty Bang-Bang, Stereo, 1968, orig soundtrack, EX (EX sleeve), F8...$12.00
Cinderella, orig soundtrack, #WDL-4007, EX (VG sleeve), P3 ....$8.00
Disneyland & Walt Disney World, Stereo, 1980, M (NM sealed sleeve), F8 ....$18.00

Get Along Gang and the Big Bully, American Greetings #272, 1984, complete with booklet, EX (EX sleeve), from $10.00 to $12.00.

Dr Seuss Presents Bartholomew & the Oobleck, Camden/Stereo, 1960s, EX (EX sleeve), F8 ....$15.00
Dr Seuss Presents Yertle the Turtle, RCA/Stereo, 1960s, EX (EX sleeve), F8 ....$15.00
Dr Seuss' Horton Hatches the Egg, RCA/Stereo, 1960s-70s, NM (NM sleeve), F8..$20.00
Frosty's Winter Wonderland, 1976, soundtrack narrated by Andy Griffith, NM (NM sleeve), F8.........................$20.00
Hefti in Gotham City, RCA, 1966, NM (EX sleeve), F8 .$45.00
Here Come the Hardy Boys, RCA, 1969, NM (NM sleeve), F8...$20.00
House at Pooh Corner, Wonderland, 1960s, stories & songs narrated by Ian Carmichael & Dick Bently, NM (NM sleeve), F8 ....$20.00
Jetsons, Golden, 1960s, features New Songs of the TV Family of the Future, EX (VG sleeve), A $80.00
Li'l Abner, Columbia, 1959, orig soundtrack, NM (EX sleeve), F8/T2, from $10 to...$15.00
Linus the Lionhearted, Premier Albums, 1964, VG (VG sleeve), T2..$30.00
Little Red Riding Hood, 1968, VG (VG sleeve), N2 ....$10.00
Man Called Flintstone, Hanna Barbera, 1966, EX (EX sleeve), F8 ....$35.00
Mandrake the Magician, Garabedian, 1973, EX (EX sleeve), from $15 to..$20.00
Mary Poppins, Buena Vista, 1964, NM (EX sleeve), P3 ...$15.00
Mickey Mouse Christmas Surprises, Mickey Mouse Club, 1950s-60s, EX (EX sleeve), F8 ....$20.00
Monster Mash Sounds of Terror, Pickwick/Stereo, 1974, EX (EX sleeve), F8 ....$15.00
Muppet Movie, 1979, soundtrack from movie, EX (EX sleeve), N2 ....$20.00
Music from Disneyland, Decca, 1950s, NM (EX sleeve), A.$40.00
Peter & the Wolf Narrated by Captain Kangaroo, Everst, 1960, VG (VG sleeve), T2 ....$10.00
Peter Cottontail, 1962, VG (VG sleeve), N2 ....$5.00
Pink Panther, RCA, 1963, orig soundtrack, NM (EX sleeve), T2 ....$8.00
Popeye the Sailor Man, 1960s, VG (VG sleeve), N2 ....$10.00
Roger Ramjet & the American Eagles, RCA, 1966, EX (EX sleeve, from $40 to..$50.00
Six Million Dollar Man, Peter Pan, 1976, EX (EX sleeve), F1 .$10.00
Space: 1999, Power Records, 1975, EX+ (EX+ sleeve), M17...$20.00
Story of Willow, orig soundtrack, complete w/16-pg photo book, EX, F1...$10.00
Superman, Leo the Lion Records, 1966, VG (VG sleeve), from $10 to $20.00
Thor, Golden Records, 1966, EX (EX sleeve), F8.............$24.00
Three Stooges Meet Cinderella, Peter Pan, M (M sealed sleeve), H4 ....$25.00
Three Stooges Songbook, Coral, 1960s, EX (EX sleeve), F8....$40.00
Thunderbirds & Captain Scarlet, Hallmark/Stereo, 1966, rare, NM (NM sleeve), F8 ....$70.00
Winnie the Pooh & the Heffalumps, Disneyland, 1968, complete w/booklet, VG (VG sleeve), F8.........................$12.00
Woody the Woodchuck Christmas Sing Song, 1960s, NM (EX sleeve), F8 ....$12.00

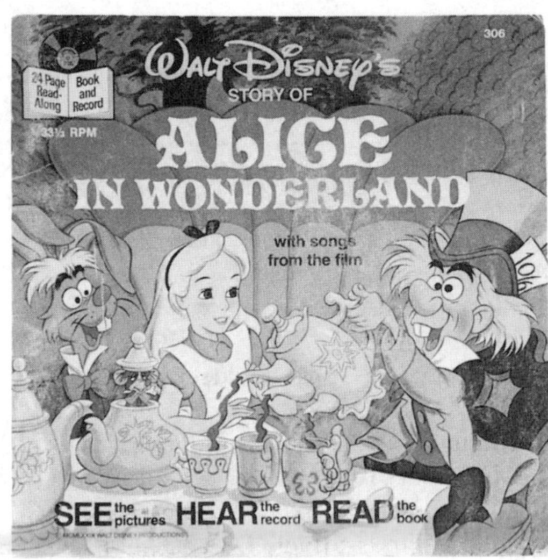

Walt Disney's Story of Alice in Wonderland, Disneyland Records #306, 1979, complete with booklet, EX (EX sleeve), $15.00.

Photo courtesy Peter Muldavin

Jungle Book: Colonel Hathi's March and Trust in Me, Disneyland Records, 1967, $20.00.

Woody Woodpecker, Golden, 1963, EX (NM sleeve), F8 .$30.00

Yogi Bear, Kellogg's premium, 1964, NM (NM mailing sleeve), F8 .$50.00

45 RPM Records

Alice in Wonderland, Golden, 1950s, EX (EX sleeve), J5 .$25.00

Alvin & the Chipmunks, Liberty, 1960s, Chipmunk Song & Almost Good, EX (EX sleeve), F8 .$8.00

Aristocats, 1970, complete w/booklet, EX (EX sleeve), N2 .$10.00

Ballad of Davy Crockett, Golden, 1950s, NM (EX sleeve), F8 .$14.00

Batman, Synthetic Plastics, 1966, EX (EX sleeve w/Batman or Robin), J5, ea .$35.00

Batman & Superman, Wonderland, 1969-71, features theme songs, M (M sleeve), from $40 to .$50.00

Batman Meets Manbat, 1976, complete w/20-pg booklet, EX (EX sleeve), F1 .$10.00

Batman Theme, RCA, 1966, used for jukeboxes, scarce, NM (NM sleeve), A .$375.00

Batman's Pal Robin, 1966, NM (EX figural sleeve), C1 .$30.00

Bozo the Clown, Little Golden, 1960, EX (EX sleeve), T2 .$15.00

Captain Kangaroo's Best Loved Songs, Golden, 1950s, NM (NM sleeve), J5 .$15.00

Davy Crockett Goes to Congress, Columbia, 1950s, NM (EX sleeve), A .$30.00

Ferdinand the Bull, Golden, 1950s, EX (EX sleeve), A .$25.00

Flintstones Lullaby of Pebbles, Golden, 1960s, EX (VG sleeve), F8 .$15.00

Foodini's Trip to the Moon, Caravan, 1949, rare, EX (EX+ sleeve), F8 .$25.00

Frontierland, Golden, 1950s, EX (EX sleeve), J5 .$25.00

Good Night Little Wrangler, Mickey Mouse Club, 1950s, EX (EX sleeve), J5 .$25.00

Heckle & Jeckle, Little Golden, 1958, EX (EX sleeve), T2 .$24.00

Henery Hawk's Chicken Hunt, Capitol, 1960s, EX (EX sleeve), F8 .$12.00

Kukla, Fran & Ollie at the Fair, RCA Camden, 1950s, EX (EX sleeve), J5 .$25.00

Lady & the Tramp, Golden, Siamese Cat Song & Bella Notte, EX (EX sleeve), P3 .$20.00

Little Boy Who Couldn't Find Christmas, Golden, 1950, EX (EX sleeve), A .$55.00

Loopy DeLoop, Golden, 1960, NM (EX sleeve), F8 .$12.00

Mickey Mouse Club, Golden, 1962, Merry Mouseketeers & Talent Round Up, G (EX sleeve), F8 .$3.50

Mighty Mouse, Peter Pan, 1964, story of Mighty Mouse in Toyland, EX (VG sleeve), F8 .$5.00

Peter Pan, Little Nipper/RCA, 1952, 3-record set in spiral-bound story book, EX, J5 .$35.00

Peter Pan, You Can Fly, Golden, 1950s, EX (EX sleeve), J5 .$25.00

Pinocchio, Golden, 1962, story & song from Disney movie, EX (EX sleeve), F8 .$5.00

Popeye, 1964, Skin Diver & Fleas a Crowd, M (EX diecut sleeve), J5 .$15.00

Popeye the Sailor Man, Golden, 1957, VG (VG sleeve), T2 .$12.00

Quick Draw McGraw, Golden, 1960, features That's Quick Draw McGraw!, EX (EX sleeve), F8 .$18.00

Robin Hood, Disneyland, 1973, w/booklet, EX (EX sleeve), F8 .$12.00

Roy Rogers Had a Ranch, Golden, 1950s, EX (EX sleeve), A .$45.00

Space Songs, Peter Pan, 1963, Trip in a Rocket Ship & On the Moon, EX (EX sleeve), F8 .$5.00

Story of Pooh & Tigger, 1968, complete w/booklet, EX (EX sleeve), N2 .$10.00

Tex Ritter Sunday School Songs, Capitol, 1960s, 2 records w/6 songs, EX (EX sleeve), F8 .$12.00

Three Little Kittens, Disneyland, 1962, EX (EX sleeve), F8 .$10.00

Wagon Train, Golden, 1950s, EX (EX sleeve), J5 .$25.00

Winnie the Pooh, Golden, 1960s, features Sing Ho for the Life of a Bear & Cottleston Pie, EX (EX sleeve), F8 .$12.00

Winnie the Pooh & the Heffalumps, 1968, complete w/read-a-long booklet, EX (EX sleeve), F8 .$14.00

Wonder Woman, Shadybrook, 1977, features theme song, M (VG sleeve), A $75.00
Woody Woodpecker & His Talent Show, Capitol, 1949, 2-record set w/booklet, EX (EX sleeve), A $20.00

78 RPM Picture and Non-Picture Records

Alice in Wonderland, Decca, 1944, 3-record set, EX (EX sleeve), F8 ....$55.00
Alice in Wonderland, Golden, 1951, features In a World of My Own, EX (EX sleeve), F8 ....$16.00
Alice in Wonderland, Listen Look Picture Book, 1941, EX (EX sleeve), from $10 to $15.00
Ballad of Davy Crockett, 1950s, M (EX sleeve), P6..........$30.00
Bozo & His Rocket Ship, Capitol, 1947, 2 record set w/storybook, NM (EX cover), P3 ....$25.00
Cheyenne, RCA, 1950s, features Home on the Range & Sons of the Pioneers, scarce, EX (EX sleeve), A..................$100.00
Cinderella, DBR #70, 1950s, NM (EX jacket), A.............$25.00
Cinderella, Listen Look Picture Book, 1941, EX (EX sleeve), from $8 to...$10.00
Corky & the White Shadow, DBR #59, 1950s, M (EX jacket), J5 ....$45.00
Davy Crockett at the Alamo, Columbia, 1950s, 2-record set, NM (EX sleeve), J5 ....$35.00
Donald's Singing Lesson, 1949, EX (EX sleeve), F8 ....$12.00
Fibber McGee & Molly on the Night Before Christmas, Capitol, 1950s, 3-record set, EX (EX sleeve), F8 ....$25.00
Genie the Magic Record, Decca CV 102, 1946, EX (EX sleeve), from $10 to...$15.00
Good Night Little Wrangler, 1950s, NM (EX sleeve), F8 ..$8.00
Great Locomotive Chase, Little Golden, 1950s, EX (VG sleeve), F8..$8.00
Grimm's Fairy Tales Told by Danny Kaye, Golden, 1960s, EX (NM photo sleeve), F8 ....$15.00
Gulliver's Travels, Bluebird, 1939, orig soundtrack, rare, EX (VG sleeve), from $150 to $200.00

Photo courtesy Peter Muldavin

Hopalong Cassidy and the Story of Topper, Capitol CAS-3110, 1952, from $45.00 to $50.00.

Hopalong Cassidy & the Singing Bandit, 1950s, complete w/2 records & photo booklet, NM (VG sleeve), J5 ....$45.00
Howdy Doody & You, RCA, 1950s, 2-record set, NM (NM sleeve), A...$100.00
Howdy Doody's Crystal Ball, RCA, 1950s, 2-record set, NM (EX sleeve), A...$100.00
I Saw Mommy Kissing Santa Claus, Peter Pan, 1965, VG (VG sleeve), P3 ....$10.00
Lady & the Tramp, Little Golden, 1955, features Bella Notte & Siamese Cat Song, EX (EX sleeve), F8 ....$20.00
Little Lulu & Her Magic Tricks, Golden, 1954, EX (EX sleeve), F8 ....$25.00
Little Red Riding Hood, Listen Look Picture Book, 1941, EX (EX sleeve), from $10 to..$15.00
Little Space Girl, Golden, 1959, NM (NM sleeve), T2......$8.00
Lone Ranger: He Finds Silver, Decca K-30, 1951, EX (EX sleeve), from $25 to $35.00
Magic Land of Alla-Kazam, Peter Pan, 1962, NM (EX sleeve), T2..$10.00
Mickey Mouse Newsreel Music, Official Mickey Mouse Club Records, 1950s, unused, NM (EX sleeve), T2............$12.00
Mickey Mouse Picture House Song, Little Golden, 1950s, EX (EX sleeve), F8...$15.00
Mister Ed, Golden, 1960s, features Mr Ed the Talking Horse & Straight from the Horses Mouth, VG (EX sleeve), J5.$65.00
Mousekartoon Time, DBR #68, 1950s, M (EX sleeve), A $50.00
Mr Chip'n Mr Dale & Goofy's Song, Little Golden, 1950s, NM (EX sleeve), F8...$16.00
Myrtle the Turtle, Listen Look Picture Book, 1941, EX (EX sleeve), from $8 to $10.00
Peter Cottontail, Golden, 1950, EX (EX sleeve), T2..........$4.00
Peter Pan Second Star to the Right, Little Golden, 1952, EX (EX sleeve), F8...$15.00
Peter Pan What Made the Red Man Red, Little Golden, 1952, NM (NM sleeve), F8 ....$20.00
Raggedy Ann & Andy, Columbia, 1970s, NM (EX sleeve), J5 ....$25.00
Rin Tin Tin, Little Golden, 1950s, features A Dog's Best Friend & Cold Nose Warm Heart, EX (EX sleeve), F8.........$12.00
Roy Rogers Tells About Pecos Bill, RCA, 1948, 3-record set, M (EX cover), M17 ....$60.00

Photo courtesy Peter Muldavin

Scuffy the Tugboat, Golden, 1948, EX+ (EX+ sleeve), from $8.00 to $12.00.

Sleeping Beauty, Hail to Princess Aurora, Golden, 1959, EX (EX sleeve), F8 ....$8.00
Spanky & the Talking Train, Capitol, 1947, 3-record set w/storybook, NM (EX cover), P3....................$22.00
Superman Song & Tarzan Song, Little Golden, 1950s, NM (EX sleeve), from $40 to $50.00
Three Little Pig, Listen Look Picture Book, 1941, EX (EX sleeve), from $8 to $10.00
Thumbelina, Golden, 1951, VG (VG sleeve), T2 ....$3.00

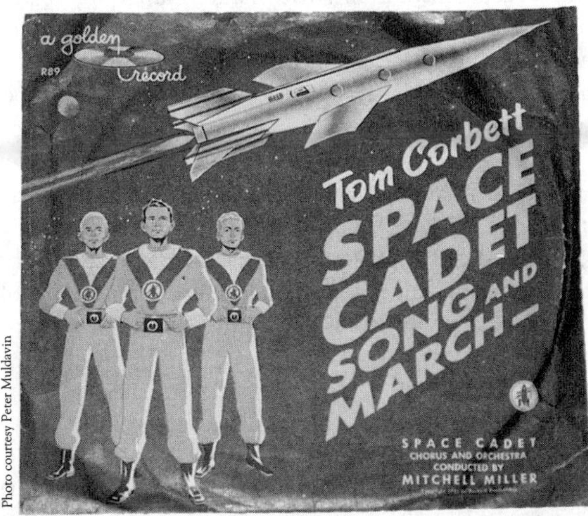

Tom Corbett Space Cadet Song and March, Golden R89, 1951, from $20.00 to $25.00.

Walt Disney's Pinocchio, Victor P18, 1941, from original soundtrack, set of three, rare, from $75.00 to $100.00.

Wagon Train, Golden, 1957, EX (VG sleeve), F8....................$12.00
Walt Disney's Song of Tomorrowland, Golden, 1950s, EX (VG sleeve), F8 ....$14.00
Walt Disney's Story of Robin Hood, Capitol, 1952, complete w/20-pg booklet, EX (EX sleeve), T2 ....$20.00
Westward Ho the Wagons, DBR #67, 1950s, M (NM sleeve), A $50.00
William Tell, Toytime Record & Picture Books, 1941, complete, EX (EX sleeve), from $10 to $12.00

Kiddie Picture Disks

Listed here is a representative sampling of kiddie picture disks that were produced through the 1940s. Most are 6" to 7" in diameter and are made of cardboard with plastic-laminated grooves. They are very colorful and seldom came with original sleeves. Value ranges are for items in very good to near-mint condition. Ultimately, the value of any collectible is what a buyer is willing to pay, and prices tend to fluctuate. Our values are for records only (no sleeves) — note that unlike other records, the value of a picture disk is not diminished if there is no original sleeve.

Advisor: Peter Muldavin (M21).

Alice in Wonderland, Toy Toon Records, 1952, from $10 to....................$15.00
Birthday Song to You, Voco 35215, 1948, 5" sq, from $15 to....................$20.00
Bunny Easter Party, Voco EB ½, 1948, diecut, EX, from $25 to $35.00
Camptown Races: Little Brown Jug, Record Guild of America 2004P, 1949, rare picture sleeve, from $10 to $15.00
Cinderella, Toy Toon Records, 1952, from $10 to $15.00
Goldilocks & the Three Bears, Toy Toon Records, 1952, from $10 to $15.00
I'm Called Little Buttercup, PicturTone, Gilbert & Sullivan series, 1948, from $15 to....................$20.00
Jack & the Bean Stalk, Toy Toon Records, 1952, from $10 to $15.00
Jacob's Dream, Bible Storytime, 1948, from $10 to $15.00
Jesus Loves Me, Bible Storytime, 1948, from $10 to....................$15.00
Laugh Laugh Phonograph, Voco, 1948, rare 6" size, from $20 to....................$25.00
Laugh Laugh Phonograph, Vovo, 1948, 7", from $10 to...$15.00

Little Jack Horner, Pix 104, 1941, 10", from $75.00 to $90.00.

Little White Duck, Red Raven Movie Records, 1956, rare 6" size, from $30 to $40.00

Lord High Executioner, PicturTone, Gilbert & Sullivan series, 1948, from $15 to..$20.00
Old McDonald Had a Farm, Voco, 1948, rare 6" size, from $20...$25.00
Old McDonald Had a Farm, Voco, 1948, 7", from $10 to ..$15.00
Red River Valley, Record Guild of America 2002P, 1949, rare picture sleeve, from $15 to $25.00
Robin Hood, Toy Toon Records, 1952, from $10 to $15.00
Rover the Strong Man, Voco, 1948, diecut, 7", from $25 to $30.00
Shepherd Boy, Bible Storytime, 1948, from $10 to...........$15.00
Singing Mother Goose, Magic Talking Books T-1, 1955, EX (EX cover), from $15 to $20.00
Songs from Mother Goose, Toy Toon Records, 1952, from $10 to $15.00
Superman: The Magic Ring, Musette (Picturetone), 1947, w/book, from $100 to...$120.00

Swing Your Partner, Record Guild of America, Picture-Play Records PR11A, 1948, 10½", from $80.00 to $100.00.

Ten Little Indians, Toy Toon Records, 1952, from $10 to .$15.00
Terry & the Pirates, Record Guild of America F501, 1948, from $35 to $45.00
The Fox, Talking Book Corp, 1919, record mounted on diecut figure, 4", from $80 to..$120.00
The Three Bears w/Uncle Henry, Kidisks KD-77A, 1948, 4", rare, from $15 to $25.00
Tom Cat the Tightrope Walker, Voco, 1948, diecut, from $25 to $30.00
Tom Tom the Piper's Son, Kiddie-Rekord, 1925, rare, from $40 to $50.00
Trial of Bumble, The Bee Part 1, Vogue R745, 1947, 10", from $60 to $75.00
Wandering Minstrel, PicturTone, Gilbert & Sullivan series, 1948, from $15 to..$20.00
When Jesus Was Born, Bible Storytime, 1948, from $10 to $15.00
Winnie-The-Pooh Songs, RCA, 1931-33, very rare, set of 3 w/orig folder, from $300 to $500.00

Reynolds Banks

Reynolds Toys began production in 1964, at first making large copies of early tin toys for window displays, though some were sold to collectors as well. These toys included trains, horse-drawn vehicles, boats, a steam toy, and several sizes of Toonerville trolleys. In the early 1970s, they designed and produced six animated cap guns. Finding the market limited, by 1971 they had switched to a line of banks they call 'New Original Limited Numbered Editions (10 – 50) of Mechanical Penny Banks.' Still banks were added to their line in 1980 and figural bottle openers in 1988. Each bank design is original; no reproductions are produced. Reynolds' banks are in the White House and the Smithsonian as well as many of the country's major private collections. *The Penny Bank Book* by Andy and Susan Moore (Schiffer Publishing, 1984) shows and describes the first twelve still banks Reynolds produced. Values are given for mint-condition banks.

Advisor: Charlie Reynolds (R5).

Mechanical Banks

1M, Train Man Bank, 1971, edition of 30 ....$350.00
2M, Trolley Bank, 1971, edition of 30 ....$450.00
3M, Drive-In, 1971, edition of 10................................$1,000.00
4M, Pirate Bank, 1972, edition of 10 ....$725.00
5M, Blackbeard Bank, 1972, edition of 10......................$650.00
6M, Frog & Fly Bank, 1972, edition of 10 ....$1,200.00
7M, Toy Collector Bank, 1972, unlimited edition $650.00
8M, Balancing Bank, 1972, edition of 10........................$725.00
9M, Save the Girl Bank, 1972, edition of 10..............$2,000.00
10M, Father Christmas Bank, 1972, 1 made ea year at Christmas...$850.00
11M, Gump on a Stump, 1973, edition of 10.............$1,100.00
12M, Trick Bank, 1973, edition of 10.........................$1,000.00
13M, Kid Savings Bank, 1973, edition of 10 ....$1,200.00
14M, Christmas Tree Bank, 1973, edition of 10............$725.00
15M, Foxy Grandpa Bank, 1974, edition of 10..............$975.00
16M, Happy Hooligan Bank, 1974, edition of 10........$1,075.00
17M, Chester's Fishing Bank, 1974, edition of 10 ....$900.00
18M, Gloomy Gus Bank, 1874, edition of 10.............$2,800.00
19M, Kids' Prank Bank, 1974, edition of 10...............$1,100.00
20M, Mary & Her Little Lamb, edition of 20 ....$850.00
21M, Spook Bank, 1974, edition of 10............................$800.00
22M, Decoy Bank, 1974, edition of 10............................$600.00
23M, Decoy Hen Bank, 1974, edition of 10 ....$600.00
24M, Comedy Bank, 1974, edition of 10 ....$975.00
25M, Bozo Bank, 1974, edition of 10 ....$950.00
26M, Reynolds Foundry Bank, 1974, edition of 15 .....$3,400.00
27M, Toonerville Bank, 1974, edition of 10 ....$1,200.00
28M, Bank of Reynolds Toys, 1974, edition of 10..........$425.00
29M, Simple Simon Bank, 1975, edition of 10..............$925.00
30M, Humpty Dumpty Bank, 1975, edition of 20.......$1,250.00
31M, Three Blind Mice, 1975, edition of 15 ....$1,100.00
32M, Clubhouse Bank, 1975, edition of 10 ....$1,100.00
33M, Boat Bank, 1975, edition of 10...........................$1,500.00

34M, St Nicholas Bank, 1975, edition of 50....................$775.00
35M, Forging America, 1976, edition of 13.................$1,200.00
36M, Suitcase Bank, 1979, edition of 22 ....$825.00
37M, North Wind Bank, 1980, edition of 23 ....$1,100.00
39M, Quarter Century bank, 1982, edition of 25........$4,000.00
40M, Columbia Bank, 1984, edition of 25 ....$1,350.00
41M, Whirligig Bank, edition of 30.............................$1,300.00
42M, Miss Liberty, 1986, edition of 36.........................$1,300.00
42M, Miss Liberty on a Pedestal, 1986, edition of 4....$1,600.00
43M, Auto Giant Bank, 1987, edition of 30 ....$2,250.00
45M, Campaign '88 Bank, 1988, edition of 50............$3,000.00
46M, Hollywood, 1989, edition of 35 ....$750.00
47M, Buffalos Revenge, 1990, edition of 35 ....$900.00
48M, Williamsburg Bank, 1991, edition of 35................$725.00

49M, Duel at the Dome, 1992, edition of 50, $1,000.00.

50M, '92 Voting Bank, 1992, edition of 50 ....$3,000.00
51M, Oregon Trail Bank, 1993, edition of 50 ....$800.00

56M, '96 Political Wish Bank, 1996, edition of 50, $900.00.

52M, Norway Bank (Lillehammer), 1994, edition of 50...$825.00
53M, Shoe House Bank, 1994, edition of 50 ....$950.00
54M, J&E Stevens Co, 1995, edition of 50 ....$1,850.00
55M, Hyakutake Bank (The Comet), 1996, edition of 50..$550.00
58M, Uncle Louie, 1997, edition of 50 ....$295.00

59M, Friar's Favorite Bank, 1997, edition of 50, $1,100.00.

Still Banks

1S, Amish Man Bank, 1980, edition of 50......................$135.00
2S, Santa, 1980, edition of 50 ....$80.00
3S, Deco Dog, 1981, edition of 50.....................................$70.00
4S, Jelly Bean King, 1981, edition of 100 ....$250.00
5S, Hag Bank, 1981, edition of 50 ....$160.00
6S, Snowman, 1981, edition of 50 ....$110.00
7S, Mark Twain, 1982, edition of 50 ....$200.00
8S, Santa, 1982, edition of 50 ....$125.00
10S, Redskins Hog Bank, 1983, edition of 50................$125.00
11S, Lock-Up Savings Bank, 1983, edition of 50 ....$45.00
12S, Miniature Bank Building, 1983, edition of 50 ....$195.00
13S, Santa in Chimney, 1983, edition of 50 ....$90.00
14S, Santa w/Tree (bank & doorstop), 1983, edition of 25 .$325.00
15S, Redskins NFC Champs, 1983, edition of 35...........$185.00
16S, Chick Bank, 1984, edition of 50 ....$80.00
17S, Ty-Up Bank, 1984, edition of 35 ....$225.00
18S, Tiniest Elephant Bank, 1984, edition of 50 ....$90.00
19S, Baltimore Town Crier, 1984, edition of 50..............$75.00
20S, Father Christmas Comes to America, July 4th, 1984, edition of 25 ....$325.00
21S, Campaign '84 Bank, edition of 100.........................$250.00
22S, Santa, 1984, edition of 50 ....$100.00
23S, Reagan '85 Bank, 1985, edition of 100 ....$275.00
24S, Columbus Ohio, 1985, edition of 50.........................$60.00
25S, Austrian Santa (bank & doorstop), 1985, edition of 25....$350.00
26S, Halloween Bank, 1985, edition of 50.......................$210.00

27S, 1893 Kriss Kringle Bank (w/tree & candle decorations), 1985, edition of 20 ....$2,400.00
28S, Santa Coming to a Child, 1985, edition of 50........$165.00
29S, Halley's Comet, 1986, edition of 50.......................$190.00
30S, 20th Anniversary Bank, 1986, edition of 86...........$165.00
31S, Father Christmas (bank & doorstop), gr, edition of 25......$280.00
32S, Santa & the Reindeer, 1986, edition of 50.............$160.00
33S, Charlie O'Conner Bank, 1987, edition of 50............$90.00
34S, Chocolate Rabbit Bank, 1987, edition of 50............$95.00
35S, St Louis River Boat, 1987, edition of 60 ....$75.00
36S, German Santa (bank & doorstop), 1987, edition of 25..$275.00
38S, Old Stump Halloween, 1987, edition of 50 ....$85.00
39S, Santa in Race Car, 1987, edition of 100.................$130.00
40S, Technology Education Bank, edition of 88..............$65.00
41S, Super Bowl XXII Redskins, 1988, edition of 50........$90.00
42S, Easter Rabbit Bank, 1988, edition of 50...................$55.00
43S, Florida Souvenir Bank, 1988, edition of 75 ....$90.00
44S, Father Christmas w/Lantern (bank & doorstop), 1988, edition of 35 ....$260.00
45S, Halloween Spook, 1988, edition of 50 ....$70.00
46S, NCRPBC (National Capitol Region Club), 1988, edition of 20 ....$300.00

47S, Santa on Polar Bear, 1988, edition of 75, $110.00.

50S, Pocket Pigs, 1989, edition of 75, $125.00.

48S, Bush-Quayle, 1989, edition of 100..........................$260.00
49S, Shuffle Off to Buffalo, 1989, edition of 75 ....$70.00
51S, Regal Santa (bank & doorstop), 1989, edition of 35 ..$275.00
52S, Tiniest Snowman, 1989, edition of 75 ....$50.00
53S, Santa on Motorcycle, 1989, edition of 75..............$105.00
54S, Rabbit w/Mammy, 1990, edition of 75....................$190.00
55S, Antique Row Sign Post, 1990, edition of 75............$70.00
56S, Duck w/Puppy & Bee Bank, 1990, edition of 75 ....$110.00
57S, 1895 Santa w/Wreath, 1990, edition of 35 ....$250.00
58S, Santa on a Pig, 1990, edition of 75 ....$140.00
59S, St Louis Sally Bank, 1991, edition of 55 ....$65.00
60S, Santa w/Wassail Bowl, 1991, edition of 35............$250.00
61S, Santa Express Bank, 1991, edition of 55................$125.00
62S, Pig on Sled Bank, 1992, edition of 55.......................$85.00
63S, Santa About to Leave, 1992, edition of 25............$290.00
64S, Jack-O'-Lantern, 1992, edition of 60 ....$80.00
65S, Santa in Zeppelin, 1992, edition of 100...................$90.00
66S, Clinton Bank, 1993, edition of 100 ....$300.00
67S, Windy City Bank (Chicago Convention), 1993, edition of 60 ....$85.00
68S, Santa & the Bad Boy (Summer Santa), 1993, edition of 50...$225.00

69S, Arkansas President, 1994, edition of 100, $320.00.

70S, Santa & the Good Kids, 1994, edition of 35 ....$260.00
71S, Penny Santa, 1994, edition of 60 ....$90.00
72S, School Days Bank, 1995, edition of 100 ....$95.00
73S, 1880 Snow Santa, 1995, edition of 50 ....$220.00
74S, Santa on Donkey, 1995, edition of 50 ....$110.00
75S, Clinton/Dole '96 (SBCCA '96), 1996, edition of 100.....$280.00
77S, Foxy Grandpa & Egelhoff Safe, 1997, edition of 60 .$200.00
78S, Halloween Witch Bank, 1997, edition of 50 ....$95.00

Robots and Space Toys

Space is a genre that anyone who grew up in the '60s can relate to, but whether you're from that generation or not, chances are the fantastic robots, space vehicles, and rocket launchers from that era are fascinating to you as well. Some emitted beams of colored light and eerie sounds and suggested technology the secrets of which were still locked away in the future. To a collector, the stranger, the better. Some were made of lithographed tin, but even plastic toys (Atom Robot, for example) are high on the want list of many serious buyers. Condition is extremely important, both in general appearance and internal workings. Mint-in-box examples may be worth twice as much as one mint-no-box, since the package art was often just as awesome as the toy itself.

Because of the high prices these toys now command, many have been reproduced. Beware!

Other Sources: 01

See also Marx; Guns, Miscellaneous.

Acrobat Robot, SH, 1970s, 3 actions, mostly plastic, battery-op, 4½", EX....**$100.00**

Acrobot, Y, robot does acrobatics, plastic, battery-op, EX, L4....**$225.00**

Airport Saucer, MT, saucer circles airport w/flashing control tower, litho tin & plastic, battery-op, 8" dia, NMIB, A....**$235.00**

Animal Satellite MS-7, Japan, litho tin, friction, 5", VG, J2....**$165.00**

Apollo Lunar Module, Japan, litho tin & plastic, battery-op, 9", MIB, L4....**$475.00**

Apollo Space Patrol, battery-op, EX (EX box), L4....**$175.00**

Apollo Super Space Capsule, SH, 1960s, several actions, battery-op, 9", EX....**$200.00**

Apollo-X Moon Challenger, TN, plastic, battery-op, 16", EX....**$185.00**

Apollo-Z Moon Traveler, Alps, 1960s, several actions, battery-op, 9", rare, EX....**$300.00**

Apollo-11 Space Rocket, TN, 1960s, advances w/flashing lights & sound, plastic, battery-op, 14", NMIB, A....**$175.00**

Astro Captain, Daiya, advances w/sound, litho tin, w/up, 7", NM, A....**$350.00**

Astronaut, Rosko, bl version, advances w/lights & sound, litho tin, battery-op, 13", NM (EX box), A....**$1,900.00**

Astronaut w/Walkie-Talkie, TN, 1960s, several actions, litho tin, battery-op, 13", EX....**$1,000.00**

Atlas ICBM Missile Launcher, battery-op, NMIB, L4....**$675.00**

Atom Robot, KO, advances in erratic pattern, litho tin, w/up, 6", NM (NM box), A....**$700.00**

Atom Robot, KO, 1960s, bump-&-go action, litho tin, battery-op, 7", VG, A....**$300.00**

Atom Rocket #7, MT, advances w/lights, sound & rotating antenna, litho tin, battery-op, 9", NM (NM box), A.**$750.00**

Atom-Car, Y, litho tin w/blk rubber tires, friction, 16", rare, NM (EX box), A....**$3,200.00**

Atomic Fighter Robot, SH, 1950s, several actions, battery-op, 11", EX....**$200.00**

Atomic Robot Man, Y, advances as facial expressions change, litho tin & plastic, w/up, 6", EX, A....**$500.00**

Attacking Martian Robot, SH, 1950s, several actions, battery-op, 11½", EX....**$225.00**

Billy Blastoff Space Scout, Eldon, 1968, battery-op, 4½", EX....**$200.00**

Blink-A-Gear Robot, Taiyo, 1960s, 5 actions, 14½", EX (EX box)....**$800.00**

Blue Eagle Space Rocket, battery-op, MIB, L4....**$450.00**

Busy Cart Robot, SH, 1960s, several actions, battery-op, 11", EX....**$500.00**

Chief Robot Man, KO, 1950s, several actions, battery-op, 12", NM....**$900.00**

Cosmo Phone, Italy, yel & red plastic, battery-op, NM (EX box)....**$125.00**

Astronaut, Daiya, advances, stops, and fires machine gun, lithographed tin, battery operated, 14", NM (EX box), A, $1,800.00.

Cragstan Astronaut, Daiya, advances, stops and fires gun, lithographed tin, battery operated, 11", rare, NMIB, A, $3,500.00.

Cragstan Astronaut, red version, litho tin, battery-op, 14",EX (EX box), A $2,200.00
Cragstan Launching Pad w/Rocket & Satellite, battery-op, EX (EX box), L4 .... $375.00
Cragstan Ranger Robot, 1960s, several actions, mostly plastic, battery-op, 10½", rare, NM, minimum value $1,000.00
Cragstan Space Tank, Y, mk Mars Patrol, advances & driver spins in ball in cockpit, litho tin, 6", NM (EX box), A $300.00
Cragstan Space-Mobile, 1960s, several actions, battery-op, 11", EX $500.00
Cragstan Talking Robot, NGS/Japan, 4 phrases, litho tin, friction & battery-op, 11½", NM (NM box), A $1,800.00

Photo courtesy June Moon

Ding-A-Ling Super Return Space Skyway, Topper, 1971, NMIB, J6, $150.00.

Dino Robot, SH, 1960s, several actions, battery-op, 11", rare, NM, minimum value $1,000.00
Docking Rocket, Daiya, 1960s, several actions, battery-op, 16", EX $200.00
Dynamic Fighter Robot, Junior Toy, 1960s, several actions, battery-op, 10", EX $140.00
Earth Man, TN, advances & raises rifle w/flashing lights & sound, remote control, 9", NM $800.00
Earth Satellite, Alps, 1950s, battery-op, 7½", rare, EX... $400.00
Engine Robot, SH, advances w/smoking action & sound, bl plastic w/silver trim, battery-op, 10", EX (EX box), M17 .... $175.00
Esso Energy Rocket, battery-op, MIB, L4 .... $375.00
Fighting Spaceman, SH, 1960s, several actions, battery-op, 12", EX $300.00
Flash Space Patrol Z-206, TPS, 1960s, several actions, battery-op, 8", EX $275.00
Flashy Jim, SNK, 1950s, mk R7 on chest, advances w/light-up eyes, tin, battery-op, 7½", EX (worn box) $1,250.00
Flying Saucer w/Pilot, KO, several actions, litho tin, battery-op, 6" dia, NMIB, H7 .... $500.00
Friendship Rocket #7, battery-op, NMIB, L4 .... $375.00

Giant Robot, SH, advances as lighted gun fires from chest, litho tin, battery-op, 12", NMIB, A $175.00
Golden Gear Robot, SH, 1960s, several actions, battery-op, 9", rare, NM $600.00
Guided Missile Launcher, Irco, 1950s, 3 actions, battery-op, 8", EX $225.00

Hi-Bouncer Moon Scout, Marx, 1968, several actions, battery operated, 11", rare, NMIB, A, $2,200.00.

Hi-Bouncer Moon Scout, Marx, 1968, several actions, remote control, 11", rare, NM $1,000.00
Jumping Robot on Rocket, litho tin, w/up, MIB, L4 .... $575.00
Jupiter Jyro Set, MIB, L4 .... $150.00
Jupiter Robot, Yonezawa, 1950s, several actions, battery-op, 13", rare, NMIB $2,000.00
Jupiter Rocket, Japan, hits object & automatically stands up, litho tin, friction, 9", NM (EX box), A $235.00
King Ding Robot, battery-op, EX, L4 .... $325.00
King Flying Saucer, battery-op, tin, EX (EX box), J2 ..... $150.00
Laughing Clown Robot, battery-op, NM, L4 .... $325.00
Looping Space Tank, Daiya, 1960s, several actions, battery-op, 8", MIB, L4 .... $500.00
Looping Space Tank, Daiya, 1960s, several actions, battery-op, 8", EX $200.00
Luna Hovercraft, TPS, 1960s, 3 actions, litho tin & plastic, remote control, 8", rare, EX $200.00
Lunar Spaceman, Mego, 1960s, several actions, battery-op, 12", EX $200.00
Man in Space, Alps, 1960s, litho tin, battery-op, 7", rare, NM $800.00
Mando Robot, Japan, w/up, EX (EX box), L4 .... $575.00
Marching Drumming Robot (Babes in Toyland look-a-like), battery-op, NM, L4 .... $675.00
Mars Explorer, Japan, litho tin & plastic, battery-op, VG, A $300.00

Mars King, SH, 1960s, several actions, litho tin, battery-op, 9½", rare, NM $800.00
Mars Man Car, TN, litho tin, friction, 5½", EX, A........$400.00
Mars 3 Space Rocket, TN, 1960s, several actions, battery-op, 15", EX..$200.00
Matador Rocket Launcher, K, rocket launches from back of truck, litho tin, friction, EX (VG box), A $235.00
Mercury Explorer w/Magic Color Drome, TPS, 1960s, several actions, litho tin & plastic, battery-op, 8", EX $225.00
Mighty 8 Robot w/Magic Color, MT, 1960s, several actions, battery-op, 12", scarce, NM, minimum value $2,400.00
Missile Robot, SH, 1970s, several actions, battery-op, 9", EX $125.00
Modern Robot, Yoshiya, 1950s, several actions, battery-op, 10½", rare, NM $1,200.00
Mond Roboter, Hong Kong, several actions, battery-op, 12", rare, EX $300.00
Monorail Rocket Ship, Linemar, 1950s, battery-op, 10", EX..$275.00
Monster Robot, SH, 1970s, 3 actions, battery-op, 10", EX $125.00
Moon Astronaut, Daiya, advances w/clicking space gun, litho tin, w/up, 9", VG, A $375.00
Moon City, battery-op, MIB, L4 ....$325.00
Moon Detector, Y, 1960s, advances w/several actions, litho tin, battery-op, 10", rare, NM (NM box), A $1,200.00
Moon Detector, Y, 1960s, advances w/several actions, litho tin, battery-op, 10½", rare, NM......................................$800.00
Moon Explorer, KO, advances w/engine sound & spinning antenna, tin & plastic, crank action, 7", NM (EX box), A $850.00
Moon Explorer Car, Gakken, 1960s, battery-op, 11", MIB, L4 ....$500.00
Moon Explorer M-27, Yonezawa, 1960s, several actions, litho tin, battery-op, 7", rare, NM....................................$700.00
Moon Express, TPS, 1950s, several actions, litho tin, battery-op, 12", EX...$250.00
Moon Grabber, Marx, 1960s, litho tin, battery-op, 8", EX .$85.00
Moon Orbiter, Yonezawa, advances, spins & goes different direction as astronaut flies above, plastic, w/up, 4", NMIB, A..$150.00
Moon Patrol, Gakken, litho tin w/vinyl figure, battery-op, 11½", rare, EX, A $500.00
Moon Patrol 11, Y, 1960s, several actions, tin & plastic, battery-op, 9" dia, EX $200.00
Moon Rocket #3, MT, 1950s, litho tin, friction, 7", NM (EX box), A..$400.00
Moon Rocket XM-12, Y, 1960s, several actions, litho tin, battery-op, 14½", rare, NM $650.00
Moon Traveler Apollo-Z, TN, stop-&-go action w/lights & sound, litho tin, battery-op, MIB $175.00
Mr Atom the Electronic Walking Robot, Advanced Doll & Toy, 1950s, several actions, battery-op, 17", EX......$400.00
Musical Drummer Robot, TN, 1950s, 3 actions, litho tin, battery-op, 8", scarce, NM $8,000.00
Mystery Moon Man, KO, rare variation of Chief Robot Man, bump-&-go w/lights & sound, battery-op, 12", NM (EX box), A $1,550.00
Mystery Space Explorer Tank, AHI, 1950s, several actions, litho tin, battery-op, 8", rare, EX $400.00

Nike Guided Missile Launcher, Thomas Toys, gun fires rocket on swivel base, plastic, spring action, 6", NMIB, A...$85.00
Nike Missile, Daiya, mk Sam-A7 Nike, advances w/sparks, litho tin, friction, 18½", scarce, NM (EX box), A $300.00
Orbit Explorer w/Airborne Satellite, KO, several actions, litho tin & plastic, w/up, 6", VG (G box), A $500.00
Orbit Explorer w/Airborne Satellite, KO, several actions, litho tin & plastic, w/up, 6", NM (NM box), A $775.00
Orbiting Missile, GNK, satellite circles rotating globe on base, litho tin & plastic, w/up, 4", NM (EX box), A $225.00
Pete the Spaceman, Bandai, 1960s, battery-op, 5", EX...$125.00
Pete the Spaceman, Bandai, 1960s, battery-op, 5", MIB, L4...$200.00
Pioneer PX-3 Robot Dog, litho tin, friction, 9", EX $475.00
Piston Action Robot, TN, 1950s, 3 actions, litho tin, remote control, 8", scarce, NMIB $1,800.00
Planet Explorer, battery-op, MIB, L4 ....$475.00
Planet Explorer, MT, 1960s, several actions, litho tin & plastic, battery-op, 9", EX $200.00
Planet Robot, KO, tin, bl w/red hands & feet, battery-op, 9", MIB, A $2,700.00
Planet Special Rocket, Great Britain, 1950s, litho tin, friction, 6", EX (EX box), A..$350.00
QX-2 Walkie Talkies, Remco, 1950s, red & bl plastic, MIB, A $65.00
R-35 Robot, MT, 1950s, several actions, litho tin, battery-op, 7½", NM...$600.00
Rachet Robot, TN, advances w/sparks in chest, litho tin w/coil head, w/up, 8", NM (NM box) $1,100.00
Radar 'N Scope, MT, 1960s, several actions, battery-op, 10", EX $175.00
Radar Rocket Cannon, Remco, battery-op, NMIB, L4 ..$175.00
Radar Scope Space Scout, SH, 1960s, 3 actions, litho tin, battery-op, 9", EX $275.00
Radicon Space Pathfinder, battery-op, MIB, L4..........$1,275.00
Red Rosko Astronaut, TN, advances w/flashing lights in helmet, battery-op, 13", EX..$1,400.00
Robbie the Robot, Japan, tin, rare Army gr color w/red features, w/up, 9", NM, A $925.00
Robot Commando, battery-op, EX (EX box), L4............$500.00

Robert the Robot, Ideal, 1940s – 50s, red and gray plastic, battery-operated, 14", scarce, NMIB, $400.00.

Robot Operated Bulldozer, KO, forward & reverse action, litho tin, battery-op, 7", rare, NM (EX box), A $1,500.00
Robot w/Smoking & Light-Up Lantern, Linemar, rare red & silver version w/eyebrows, remote control, 8", NM (EX box), A $5,800.00
Robotank TR-2, TN, 1950s, several actions, battery-op, 5", EX .$275.00
Robotank-Z, TN, advances w/swinging arms, head turns & lights up, litho tin, battery-op, 10", NM (NM box), A $600.00
Rocket Launching Pad, Y, 1950s, several actions, litho tin, battery-op, 9", rare, EX (G box), A $485.00
Rocket Launching Pad, Y, 1950s, several actions, litho tin, battery-op, 8½", rare, EX $325.00
Rocket Racer #54, Bandai, litho tin Indy-style w/blk rubber tires, friction, 7½", NM (NM box), A $250.00
Rocket XB-115, SH, advances w/lights & sound, litho tin & plastic, friction, 12", MIB, A $175.00
Rotate-O-Matic Super Astronaut, SH, advances w/several actions, lights & sound, litho tin, battery-op, 12", MIB, H12 ....$225.00
Rotator Robot, SH, 1960s, several actions, litho tin, battery-op, 12", EX $250.00
Rudy the Robot, Remco, 1968, several actions, battery-op, 16", EX $225.00
RX-008 Walking Space Robot, Japan, litho tin & plastic, w/up, 7", VG, A $225.00
R1 Robotank, Japan, litho tin & plastic, battery-op, VG, A .$450.00
S-61 Space Explorer, Japan, litho tin, friction, 13", EX, J2 .$65.00
Satellite Launcher Truck, Ideal, 1950s, fires 5" saucers from launcher, red & yel plastic, 16", EX, P4 ....$125.00
Satellite X-107, MT, 1960s, several actions, battery-op, 8", rare, NM $600.00
Saturn V Apollo II Rocket, Hong Kong, plastic & tin, 14", EX (EX box), J2 ....$195.00
Secret Weapon Space Scout Astronaut, SH, 1960s, several actions, litho tin, battery-op, 9", scarce, EX $700.00
Sky Patrol Space Cruiser, TN, 1950s, several actions, litho tin, battery-op, 13", EX $300.00
Sky Robot, SH, 1960s, 3 actions, plastic, battery-op, 9", EX $125.00
Skysweeper Rocket Launcher & Spotlight, Ideal, plastic, EX (EX box), J2 ....$150.00
Smoking Engine Robot, SH, 1970s, advances as pistons in chest move & blow smoke, plastic, battery-op, 10", MIB, A..$300.00
Smoking Engine Robot, SH, 1970s, advances as pistons in chest move & blow smoke, plastic, battery-op, 10", EX....$100.00
Smoking Spaceman, Linemar, 1950s, several actions, litho tin, battery-op, 12", rare, NM $1,800.00
Sonic Ear Space Age Communicator, Ohio Art, 1969, plastic & cb, battery-op, 31", M (NM box), P4 ....$75.00
Sonicon Rocket, MT, 1960s, several actions, litho tin & plastic, battery-op, 13½", EX $400.00
Sounding Robot, SH, advances & makes 3 different sounds, plastic, battery-op, 10", MIB, A $165.00
Space Bus, Bandai, battery-op, NMIB, L4 ....$850.00
Space Capsule #5, MT, 1960s, several actions, litho tin & plastic, battery-op, 10½", EX $300.00
Space Car SX-10, MT, 1960s, several actions, battery-op, 9½", EX $200.00
Space Chariot Vehicle, battery-op, MIB, L4 ....$325.00
Space Conquerer, Daiya, 1960s, several actions, litho tin, battery-op, 14", NM $800.00
Space Dog, Yoshiya, 1950s, silver w/red detail, clockwork mechanism, EX, J6 ....$235.00
Space Explorer, Hong Kong, 1960, advances w/spinning antenna & sound, plastic, friction, 7½", scarce, MIB, A.......$250.00
Space Explorer, SH, silver version, advances & chest opens to reveal Apollo flight, battery-op, 11½", NM (NM box) $350.00
Space Explorer X-7, MT, 1960s, 3 actions, litho tin & plastic, battery-op, 8" dia, EX $175.00
Space Frontier, battery-op, MIB, L4 ....$375.00
Space Launcher w/Atomic Rockets, Marx, NM (NM card), A $125.00
Space Patrol, TPS, bump-&-go action, litho tin, battery-op, 8", NM, A $250.00
Space Patrol R3, w/up, NMIB, L4 ....$675.00
Space Patrol Tank X-11, Yonezawa, 1960s, several actions, battery-op, 8½", EX $350.00
Space Patrol X-16, Amico, 1960s, several actions, battery-op, 8" dia, EX $200.00
Space Patrol XII Tank, battery-op, VG, L4 ....$185.00
Space Patrol 2019, battery-op, MIB, L4 ....$300.00
Space Radar Scout Pioneer, MT, advances as rear screen spins w/siren sound, litho tin & plastic, friction, 6", NMIB, A..............$350.00
Space Ranger Flying Saucer No 3, battery-op, MIB, L4 .$175.00
Space Robot Car, Yonezawa, 1950s, several actions, litho tin, battery-op, 9", scarce, NM $2,000.00
Space Rocket Patrol Car, Courtland, 1950s, advances w/sparks, litho tin, friction, 7", NM (worn box) $175.00
Space Rocket Solar X7, TN, 1960s, battery-op, MIB, L4 ..$200.00
Space Scooter, MT, astronaut on scooter advances w/lights & sound, tin & plastic, battery-op, 8", NM (EX box), A.$200.00
Space Scout S-17, Y, 1960s, several actions, litho tin & plastic, battery-op, 10", rare, EX $500.00
Space Shuttle Challenger, battery-op, MIB, L4 ....$475.00

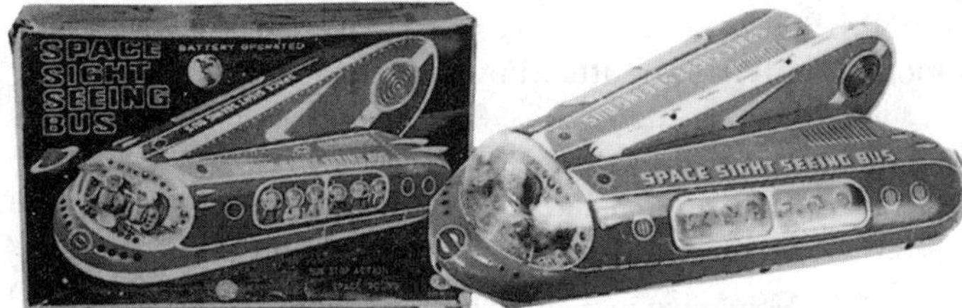

Space Sight Seeing Bus, MT, advances with lights and sound, lithographed tin, battery operated, 13", rare, NM (EX box), A, $925.00.

Space Surveillant X-07, MT, 1960s, several actions, battery-op, 8½", rare, EX $300.00
Space Tank X-4, TN, advances w/sound, litho tin, friction, 7¼", MIB, A $175.00
Space Traveller w/Moving Head, Japan, litho tin w/celluloid figure, friction, 8", NM (EX box), A $300.00
Space Trip, MT, cars navigate track as space station spins, litho tin, battery-op, 19", EX (EX box), A $650.00

Space Trooper, Haji, 1950s, advances w/engine noise, litho tin, w/up, 7", NM (EX box), A....................................$2,200.00
Spacecraft Jupiter, K, advances w/sparks, litho tin w/plastic dome, w/up, 5" dia, NM (EX box), A $155.00
Spaceman, Japan, advances on pk feet, litho tin, w/up, 6", NM (NM box), A $400.00
Spaceman Car, Japan, advances w/sound, litho tin, friction, 6", MIB, A $1,200.00
Spaceship No X-5, MT, 1950s, litho tin, friction, 12", NM (EX box), A $1,000.00
Sparky Robot, KO, 1950s, advances w/sparks & sound, litho tin, 8", NM (EX box), A $585.00
Spitz Junior Planetarium, Harmonic Reed Corp, 1956, plastic globe plugs in & shows stars, planets, etc, EXIB, M17............$150.00
Star Strider Robot, SH, battery-op, MIB, L4..................$225.00
Strange Explorer, DSK, 1960s, battery-op, 7½", MIB, L4 .$300.00
Super Giant Robot, SH, 1960s, several actions, litho tin, battery-op, 15½", EX...$400.00
Super Robot Tank, SH, advances w/dual firing barrels, litho tin, friction, 9", EX, A...$350.00
Super Sonic Space Rocket, KO, 1950s, several actions, litho tin, battery-op, 14", rare, EX..$475.00
Super Space Capsule, SH, advances, stops & door opens to reveal astronaut, tin & plastic, battery-op, 9½", NM, A.....$150.00
Super Space Capsule, SH, 1960s, battery-op, 9½", MIB, L4 .$375.00
Swinging Robot, Yone, swings between girders as mouth opens & closes, litho tin, w/up, 6", MIB, A $400.00
Tobor Robot Mechanico, Argentina, advances in slanting direction w/sparks, litho tin, w/up, 6", NM (EX box), A.$400.00
Twikki Robot (Buck Rogers), plastic, w/up, 7", NM $125.00
Two-Stage Rocket Launcher, Royal Toy, 1950s, soft plastic, complete, MOC, P4...$45.00
Two-Stage Rocket Launching Pad, TN, 1950s, rocket propels after several actions, litho tin, battery-op, 8", EX (EX box) $500.00
UFO X-05, MT, 1970s, battery-op, MIB, L4 ....$175.00
USA-NASA Gemini Space Capsule, MT, 1960s, several actions, battery-op, 9", EX......................................$250.00
Vanguard Satellite Launcher, Remco, 1960s, battery-op, MIB $275.00
Venus Robot, KO, advances w/sound, plastic, remote control, 5¼", M (NM box), A $200.00
Vision Robot, SH, 1960s, several actions, battery-op, 12", EX $300.00
Walking Scaceman, SY, advances w/arms moving in unison, litho tin, w/up, 8", NM (VG box), A.......................$875.00
Walt Disney's Tomorrowland Moon Orbit, Wen-Mac, 1960, battery-op, 20", EX $400.00
Walt Disney's Tomorrowland Rocket Ride, Wen-Mac, 1960, battery-op, 29", rare, EX...$400.00
Wheel-A-Gear Robot, Taiyo, advances w/spinning gears, flashing lights & eyes roll, litho tin, battery-op, 15", NMIB, A $1,300.00
X-001 Space Jet, Bandai, bump-&-go w/flashing lights, sound & smoking engine, litho tin, battery-op, 10", rare, NM, A .$600.00
X-10 Space Vehicle, battery-op, EX, L4 ....$375.00
X-60 Space Rocket on Launching Truck, Rosenthal, 1960, hits object & rocket rises, plastic, friction, 10½", MIB, A.$275.00
Z-101 Flying Saucer, England, 1950s, litho tin, 7" L, scarce, EX, A $250.00
Z-26 Space Patrol, KO, litho tin w/astronaut under clear plastic dome, friction, 6" dia, EX, A $135.00
Zeroid Robot, Ideal, battery-op, scarce, MOC (sealed), A..$465.00
Zintar Robot, Ideal, 1971, advances & performs karate, battery-op, 6", NM (VG box), A...$285.00

MISCELLANEOUS

Bank, Duro, shoots coin from missile to globe, metal, 8" L, NM (NM box mk Strato Bank), A..................................$225.00
Bank, Vacumet Rocketship, 1960s, cast metal w/chrome finish, 13", MIB, P4 ....$165.00
Bubble Bath Set, Space Mates, Watkins, 1960s, EX (EX box), J2 ....$40.00
Cap, Jr Astronaut, 1950s, colorful space scene, NM, J2....$45.00
Chalk, rocket shape, 1950s, NMIB, J2 ....$20.00
Eraser Container, NYG, 1960s, silver plastic rocket w/eraser, 3", M, T2 ....$20.00
Flashlight, gr plastic alien head, NM, J2 ....$30.00
Folder, Mead, colorful space design, NM, J2 ....$20.00
Frisbee, Eureka U1 Flying Saucer, M...............................$55.00
Goggles, Magic Space, 1950s, MOC, J2 ....$50.00
Helmet, Space Patrol, Beemark Plastics, 1950s, complete w/instructions, NMIB, J2...$800.00
Helmet, Zenith Space Commander, 1950s, EX, J2 ....$100.00
Moonmap Puzzle, Rand McNally, 1960s, M (sealed), J2 ..$25.00
Morse Code Set, battery-op, scarce, NMIB....................$125.00
Pencil Case, American Pencil, 1950, cb w/wraparound litho paper outer space scene, 7x10", EX, T2.....................$70.00
Pin, Official Sky Observer Space Satellite, 1950s, 1½" dia, M, P4 ....$5.00
Ring, Jupiter, silver, NM, J2 ....$20.00
Ring, 1960, plastic space gun, gold or wht & bl, M, P4, ea ..$10.00
Rocketship Cap Bombs, Hong Kong, 1960, bl or gr plastic, 5", M, P4, ea $8.00
Space Scientist Drafting Set, 1950s, EX (EX box), J2 ......$80.00
Space Station Rocket Launcher, Amsco, 1950, cb & wood w/rocketship graphics, missing bomb-rockets o/w VG, P4.......$40.00
Spaceship Cap Bombs, Hong Kong, 1960, 2-pc plastic w/metal cap, 5", M, P4...$5.00
Spinner, Space Patrol, M, J2..$25.00
US Space Probe Rocket Bombs, Palmer Plastics, 1960s, soft plastic, complete, MOC, P4...$35.00
Walkie-Talkies, QX-2 Space Model, Remco, 1950s, electromagnetic 2-way phones, MIB...$250.00
Walkie-Talkies, Space Patrol, Randall/England, 1955, plastic, 5", MIB $200.00
Whistle, SS Flying Arrow Spaceship, Hong Kong, plastic, various colors, 4", M, P4, ea...$10.00

Rock 'n Roll

From the '50s on, rock 'n roll music has been an enjoyable part of many of our lives, and the performers themselves have often been venerated as icons. Today some of the all-time great artists such as Elvis, the Beatles, KISS, and the Monkees, for instance, have fans that not only continue to appreciate their music but actively search for the ticket stubs, concert posters, photographs, and autographs of their favorites. More easily found, through, are the items that sold through retail stores at the height of their careers — dolls, games, toys, books, magazines, etc. In recent years, some of the larger auction galleries have sold personal items such as guitars, jewelry, costumes, automobiles, contracts, and other one-of-a-kind items that realized astronomical prices. If you're an Elvis fan, we recommend *Elvis Collectibles* and *Best of Elvis Collectibles* by Rosalind Cranor (Overmountain Press).

Advisors: Bob Gottuso (B3), Beatles, KISS, Monkees; Rosalind Cranor (C15), Elvis.

See also Action Figures; Bubble Bath Containers; Coloring, Activity, and Paint Books; Dolls, Celebrity; Model Kits; Paper Dolls; Pin-Back Buttons; Puppets.

Beatles, Air Bed, UK by Li-Lo, yel w/bl vinyl backing, blk faces & names on pillow, EX, B3 ....**$900.00**

Beatles, ball, blk w/faces & printed signatures on wht oval, The Beatles in red, 9" dia, EX, B3.................................**$850.00**

Beatles, banjo, Mastro, 22", EX (EX box)...................**$2,500.00**

Beatles, bank, Pride Creations, bust figure, 4 different, 8", EX, ea...**$500.00**

Beatles, beach hat, bl & wht or red & wht w/blk faces & signatures, NM, B3, ea...**$125.00**

Beatles, Beatle Twig, Beatle Twig Inc, complete, NM (NM pkg), A **$275.00**

Beatles, Beatlephones, Koss Electronics, EX (EX box)..**$2,000.00**

Beatles, belt buckle, gold-tone metal w/blk & wht photo under plastic, EX, B3/R2..**$40.00**

Beatles, blanket, United Kingdom, Whitney, tan w/red & blk photos under instruments, EX, B3...........................**$250.00**

Beatles, board game, Hullabaloo, 1965, VG (VG box), R2 ..**$75.00**

Beatles, bongos, Mastro, red plastic w/blk & wht group photo, wht top, EX **$2,000.00**

Beatles, book, Apple to the Core, 1972, softcover, NM, F8..**$10.00**

Beatles, book, Beatles Quiz Book, United Kingdom, 1964, softcover, VG, R2..**$10.00**

Beatles, book, Hard Day's Night, 1964, 1st edition, softcover, G, R2..**$10.00**

Beatles, book, Out of the Mouths of Beatles, 1964, softcover, VG, R2...**$15.00**

Beatles, book, The Man Who Gave the Beatles Away, MacMillan, 1975, hardcover, w/dust jacket, NM, F8 ....**$15.00**

Beatles, bracelet, ceramic-type group photo on scalloped brass mounting, Yeh, Yeh, Yeh on back, EX (VG card), B3 .**$100.00**

Beatles, brooch, blk & wht group photo on gold-tone metal, 2" dia, EX, B3 ....**$75.00**

Beatles, brooch, gold-tone banjo w/mop-top figures, movable beaded eyes, pnt hair & strings, EX, B3 ....**$65.00**

Beatles, brooch, United Kingdom, plastic guitar w/blk & wht group photo, 3½", EX, B3..**$75.00**

Beatles, bulletin board, Yellow Submarine, group photo, 17½x23", EX (orig shrink-wrap & sticker), B3 ....**$140.00**

Beatles, Cartoon Kit, Colorforms, 1966, complete, MIB..**$750.00**

Beatles, charms, from gumball machine, blk plastic records w/face on 1 side & label on the other, set of 4, EX....**$25.00**

Beatles, Colouring Set, Kitfix, complete, EX (EX box) ..**$1,500.00**

Beatles, Dimensionals, Yellow Submarine, Craftmaster, makes colorful wall hanging, EX (EX pkg) **$450.00**

Beatles, Disk-Go-Case, record carrier, plastic w/group photo, various colors, rnd, EX, B3 ....**$165.00**

Photo courtesy June Moon

Beatles, dolls, Applause, 1988, in Sgt. Pepper costumes, 22", set of four, complete with stands, M, J6, $385.00.

Beatles, dolls, Beatles Forever by Applause, Raggedy Ann style, set of 4 w/stands & cb stage, 22", M, B3 ....**$450.00**

Beatles, dolls, inflatable cartoon image of ea member, set of 4, EX **$125.00**

Beatles, dolls, Remco, soft bodies, set of 4, NM, B3 ....**$375.00**

Beatles, drum, New Beat, blk outline of Ringo's head, hand & autograph, complete w/stand, 14" dia, EX, B3.........**$675.00**

Beatles, drumstick, 1964, wood, mk 13A Ringo Starr Ludwig USA in bl, EX, B3 ....**$175.00**

Beatles, figures, cartoon series, 1985, HP resin, set of 4, 6", NM, B3..**$150.00**

Beatles, figures, lead, set of 4 in blk leathers w/instruments, litho cb backdrop, NM, B3 ....**$100.00**

Beatles, figures, lead, set of 4 in outdoor snow scene pose from the movie Help!, EX, B3 ....**$95.00**

Beatles, film, Live at Shea Stadium, 8mm, EX, R2 ....**$30.00**

Beatles, flasher rings, set of 4, EX, B3..............................**$60.00**

Beatles, guitar, Big Beat by Selcol, red plastic w/facsimile signatures, 20", VG, A..**$775.00**

Beatles, guitar, Big Six, rare 6-string version, EX (VG box), B3 ....**$765.00**

Beatles, guitar, Four Pop by Mastro, red & pk 4-string w/faces & autographs, complete, 21", EX **$400.00**

Beatles, guitar, Junior, Selcol, red plastic w/name & group image, 14", rare, EX, B3...**$900.00**

Beatles, guitar, New Beat by Selcol, 4-string w/paper group photo & autographs, 32", EX (EX box), B3 ....**$800.00**

Beatles, guitar, New Sound by Selcol, orange & cream 4-string w/blk & red faces & autographs, complete, 23", EX, B3 ....**$455.00**

Beatles, guitar strings, Hofner, NMIP, B3 .... $80.00
Beatles, harmonica, box only, Hohner, EX+, A $140.00
Beatles, headband, Better Wear USA, Love the Beatles, w/photos & autographs, various colors, MIP, B3, from $50 to....... $70.00
Beatles, headband, Dame, 1964, allover head shots & signatures in blk on bl, EX, B3 .... $85.00
Beatles, hummer, cb w/yel plastic tip & mouthpiece, colorful faces & signatures on tube, 11", EX, B3 .... $165.00
Beatles, Kaboodle Kit, yel vinyl w/group photo & signatures, VG, B3 .... $700.00
Beatles, key chain, Yellow Submarine by Pride Creations, plastic, EX, B3 .... $60.00
Beatles, magazine, Beatles at Carnegie Hall, United Kingdom, 1964, VG, R2 .... $40.00
Beatles, mobile, Sunshine Art Studios, cb pop-outs, unused, MIP, B3 .... $140.00
Beatles, necklace, mop-haird figures w/guitars on chain, EX, B3 .... $60.00
Beatles, necklace, silver-colored metal w/blk & wht photo under plastic on oval pendant, EX, B3 .... $100.00
Beatles, nesting dolls, Russian, HP wood, in Sgt Pepper suits, EX $50.00
Beatles, nodders, Carmascots, 1964, compo, signatures on gold bases, set of 4, 8", EX (EX box), B3 .... $850.00
Beatles, nodders, plastic, set of 4, 4", M (sealed on Swingers card), B3 .... $95.00
Beatles, ornaments, hand-blown glass, 4 different, EX, ea... $200.00
Beatles, pencil case, wht vinyl w/head shots & signatures in blk, 4x7", rare, VG, B3 .... $330.00
Beatles, pennant, Canadian, felt, Yeh, Yeh, Yeh, faces inside music notes, red, bl & yel on off-wht, 19½", EX, B3 .... $225.00
Beatles, pennant, felt, I Love the Beatles & hearts in wht on red, 29", VG, B3 .... $125.00
Beatles, photo album, Sgt Pepper's Lonely Hearts Club Band, sm, EX $350.00
Beatles, photo album, Sgt Pepper's Lonely Hearts Club Band, lg, EX $425.00
Beatles, pillow, red guitars & photos on bl, 12x12", rare, EX, B3 .... $250.00
Beatles, Play Ball, Seltaeb, inflatable rubber, 14" dia, NMIP $600.00
Beatles, punch-out portraits, Whitman, 1964, cb, complete, EX, B3 .... $150.00
Beatles, purse, Canadian, 1970s, colorful image of John Lennon on silky material, gold metal clasp, EX, B3 .... $35.00
Beatles, purse, Dame, wht cloth clutch-type w/blk head shots & signatures, leather hdl, orig photo hang tag, EX, B3.. $460.00
Beatles, purse, red vinyl clutch-type w/blk group photo, leather strap, zipper closure, EX, B3 .... $360.00
Beatles, record carrier, Airflite, cb w/paper covering, gr w/wht top & blk hdl, 8½x8½", rare, VG, B3 .... $315.00
Beatles, record carrier, PYX, bl vinyl w/group photo insert, 7x7", NM $200.00
Beatles, scarf, United Kingdom by Blackpool, brn & pk photos & designs on wht, 26x26", rare, NM, B3 .... $225.00
Beatles, scrapbook, Whitman, color photos on front & back, unused, 11x13", EX, B3 .... $75.00
Beatles, spatter toy, Twirl w/the Beatles, NMIP, B3....... $330.00
Beatles, squeeze toy, Yellow Submarine, Spain, 1960s, mk Submarine Amarillo, 2", EX, A $185.00
Beatles, stationery, 1968, Yellow Submarine, 4 sheets (1 w/each member) & matching envelopes, EX, R2 .... $20.00
Beatles, stick-ons, Yellow Submarine, colorful peel-off figures on 9x12" backing, set of 4, MIP (sealed), B3 .... $25.00
Beatles, sticker, from gumball machine, gold & blk w/faces & names, EX, B3 .... $25.00
Beatles, wallet, plastic w/group photo on front, New Jersey tourist map on bk, gold trim, snap-open, NM......... $200.00
Beatles, wig, Lowell, MIP (sealed), B3 .... $125.00
Blondie, International Fan Club Book, 1981, EX, B3....... $10.00
Cheap Trick, bow tie, wht print on blk, EX, B3 .... $30.00
Crosby, Stills & Nash, whistle, ABC Records promotion, Whistling Down the Wire, EX, B3 .... $15.00
Dave Clark Five, dolls, Remco, NMIB, B3 .... $500.00
David Bowie, book, Presenting David Bowie, 1975, paperback, NM, F8 .... $5.00
Dick Clark, iron-on patch, Picture Patch Inc, 1950s, MIP (sealed), P3 .... $20.00
Donny & Marie Osmond, record carrier, Peerless Vidtronic Corp, 1977, yel version, EX, from $20 to $25.00
Elvis, balloon toy, California Toytime, image of Elvis as boxer (Kid Galahad) on red balloon w/cb feet, 4", EX $65.00
Elvis, beach hat, 1956, w/orig photo hang tag, EX, B3 ... $125.00
Elvis, belt, EPE, 1956, vinyl w/full-color image of Elvis w/guitar against record & musical notes, 30", EX $975.00
Elvis, bracelet, Elvis Presley Enterprises, 1977, full-color head shot, EX, B3 .... $15.00

Elvis, cologne and teddy bear, Be My Teddy Bear, marked Elvis Fragrances, Inc., Atlanta, GA (fragrance made in USA, teddy bear made in Hong Kong), plastic tube, 7½", EX, $50.00.

Elvis, guitar, Lapin, 1984, MOC (sealed), B3 .... $75.00
Elvis, guitar, Selcol, 1959, 32", rare, EX, B3 .... $700.00
Elvis, hat, GI Blues, RCA Victor/Paramount, brn paper w/bl & red lettering & photo, EX, B3 .... $100.00
Elvis, key chain, flasher, full figure w/yel background, 2½x2", EX, B3 .... $20.00

Elvis, paint-by-number set, Peerless Playthings, 1956, rare, missing few items, EX (EX box), A....$3,000.00
Elvis, pennant, 1970s, King of Rock'n Roll, The One & Only Elvis, bl & wht on red w/yel stripe, 31", EX....$40.00
Elvis, pennant, 1971, Elvis Summer Festival Sahara..., felt, NM....$75.00
Elvis, ring, 1956, brass w/full-color photo under clear bubble, EX+, A....$200.00

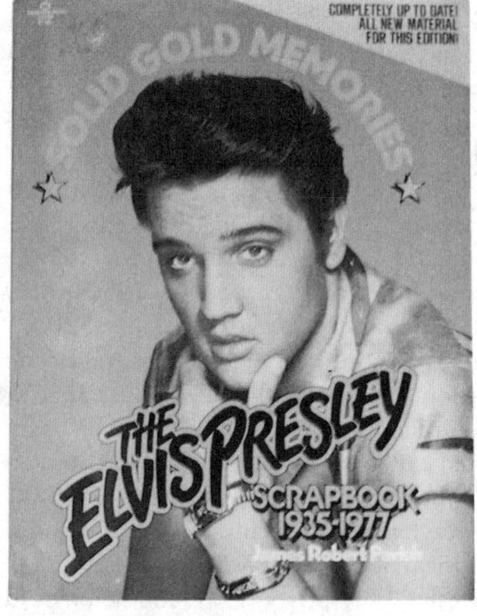

Elvis, scrapbook, Solid Gold Memories, Ballantine Books, 1977, EX, $30.00.

Elvis, sideburns sticker from gumball machine, 1950s, EX..$55.00
Elvis, Ukette, Selcol, early, turn side knob for music, 14", EX (VG rare box), A....$1,200.00
Fleetwood Mac, backstage pass, 1982, EX, B3....$5.00
Grateful Dead, key chain, metal ticket shape, MOC, J8 ..$10.00
Gregg Allman, slingshot, Epic promotion, I'm No Angel, EX, B3....$35.00
Herman's Hermits, doll, Peter Noone, Show Biz Babies, NM....$175.00
Herman's Hermits, sweatshirt, BVD, 1960s, wht w/bl graphics, EX, A....$80.00

KISS, backpack, Thermos, 1979, photo on red canvas, EX, J6, $85.00.

Photo courtesy June Moon

KISS, backstage pass, Return of KISS or Revenge World Tour, laminated, EX, B3, ea....$15.00
KISS, bracelet, gold chain & logo w/red inset, MOC, B3...$35.00
KISS, Colorforms, 1970s, complete, EX (EX box), A.......$65.00
KISS, figures, lead, set of 4 w/instruments & make-up, MIB, B3....$95.00
KISS, guitar pick, wht w/Gene Simmons' autograph & logo in blk, EX, B3....$15.00
KISS, guitar pick, wht w/Paul Stanley's autograph & logo in gold, EX, B3....$15.00
KISS, iron-on transfer, image of the group on stage, unused, NM, H4....$12.00
KISS, jacket, colorful flame design w/photos & logo, child-sz, EX, B3....$95.00
KISS, necklace, 1980, lightning bolt w/silver logo, EX, B3..$25.00
KISS, solo picture disks, 12", EX, B3, ea....$50.00
Marie Osmond, make-up kit, 1976, MOC, V1....$25.00
Monkees, backstage pass, 20th Anniversary Tour, EX, B3 .$8.00
Monkees, beach ball, 1980s, Pool It!, inflatable, EX, R2 ..$25.00
Monkees, book, British Monkee Annual, 1967, hardcover, VG, R2....$40.00
Monkees, book, Circus Boy Annual, 1958, hardcover, VG, R2....$30.00
Monkees, book, Circus Boy Under the Big Top, 1957, hardcover, VG, R2....$18.00
Monkees, book, Love Letters to the Monkees, 1967, paperback, VG, R2....$12.00
Monkees, book, Monkees Go Mod, 1967, paperback, VG, R2....$12.00
Monkees, book, More of the Monkees, 1967, 64 pgs, EX, F8....$35.00
Monkees, bracelet, raised guitar logo on brass disk, MOC, B3....$35.00
Monkees, bracelet, 4 head shots, MOC....$40.00
Monkees, flasher ring, flashes from 2 members to the other 2, VG, B3....$20.00
Monkees, hat, Circus Boy, yel & red plastic w/image of Mickey riding an elephant, VG, R2....$45.00
Monkees, key holder, 1967, color photo & logo, 2½" dia, VG (G card), R2....$45.00
Monkees, oil paint set, Monkee Beat #2001, MIB (sealed), B3....$250.00
Monkees, pennant, Monkees Fan Club, Chicago Chapter 170, 1960s, 10", VG, R2....$30.00
Monkees, Show Biz Babies, set of 4, EX, B3....$400.00
Monkees, sunglasses, w/orig hang tag, EX, B3....$45.00
Monkees, sweatshirt, 1967, pk w/faces, logo & autographs, short sleeves, VG, R2....$75.00
Monkees, tablet, 1967, color photo on cover, 10x8", VG, R2....$25.00
Monkees, tambourine, Chein/Raybert, 1967, litho tin, 9" dia, NM (NM box), A....$255.00
New Kids on the Block, rag dolls, Hasbro, MIB, J8, ea.....$20.00
Rolling Stones, book, Straight Arrow, 1975, softcover, 100 pgs, NM, F8....$15.00
Shaun Cassidy, guitar, MIP....$100.00
Van Halen, binoculars, VH logo, EX, B3....$18.00
Van Halen, scarf, blk, EX, I2....$5.00

Rubber Toys

Toys listed here are made of rubber or a rubber-like vinyl. Some of the largest producers of this type of toy were Auburn Rubber (Indiana), Sun Rubber (Ohio), Rempel (also Ohio), and Seiberling. Because of the very nature of the material, most rubber toys soon cracked, collapsed, or otherwise disintegrated, so they're scarce today.

See also Character, Movie, and TV Collectibles; Soldiers.

Battleship, Auburn, lt gray w/red, bl, & blk trim, 8¼", scarce .$60.00
Building Bricks, Auburn, EX (EX box), J2 .... $50.00
Collie, Auburn, lg, NM+ $15.00
Collie, Auburn, sm, scarce, NM $12.00
Colt, Auburn, brn, EX $8.00
Colt, Auburn, tan, NM $14.00
Farmer, Auburn, M $22.00
Farmer's Wife, M $22.00
Lincoln Convertible, 1946 model, Auburn, red, EX, I2 ...$30.00
Police Set, Auburn, 1950, complete w/2 vehicles, 2 standing policemen & 2 on motorcycles, M (EX box), A......$225.00
Pony Cart w/Pony, Auburn, 5", MIB $65.00
Sedan, 4-door, red w/blk tires, 5", NM $45.00

Telephone Truck, Auburn, turquoise with silver detail, yellow plastic tires, 7", EX, $40.00.

Turkey, Auburn, M $8.00
Western Locomotive, Auburn, 7", VG, I2 .... $15.00

Russian Toys

Many types of collectible toys continue to be made in Russia. Some are typical novelty windups such as walking turtles and pecking birds, but they have also made robots, wooden puzzles, and trains. In addition they've produced cars, trucks, and military vehicles that are exact copies of those once used in Russia and its Republics, formerly known as the Soviet Union. These replicas were made prior to June 1991 and are marked Made in the USSR/CCCP. They're constructed of metal and are very detailed, often with doors, hoods, and trunks that open.

Because of the terrific rate of inflation in Russia, production costs have risen to the point that some of these toys are no longer being made.

Advisors: Natural Way (N1); David Riddle (R6).

Other Sources: O1

Replicas of Civilian Vehicles

Aeroflot (Russian Airline) Service Station Wagon, 1/43 scale, MIB, R6, $18.00.

Belarus Farm Tractor, 1/43 scale, MIB $20.00
Gorbi Limo, 1/43 scale, metal, MIB, R6 .... $25.00
KamA3 Model #5320 Flat Bed Truck, cab tilts forward, 1/43 scale, MIB, R6 .... $35.00
KamA3 Model #53212 Oil Truck, 1/43 scale, MIB, R6....$40.00
KamA3 Model #53213 Airport Fire Truck, 1/43 scale, MIB, R6 .... $40.00
KamA3 Model #5410 Truck Cab, 1/43 scale, MIP, R6 ....$40.00
Lada #212 4x4, trunk, doors & hood open, 1/43 scale, MIB, R6 .... $15.00
Lada #2121 4x4 w/trailer, trunk, doors & hood open, 1/43 scale, MIB, R6 .... $20.00
Lada Auto Service Station Wagon, 1/43 scale, MIB $15.00
Lada Sedan, trunk & hood open, 1/43 scale, MIB, R6......$15.00
Lada Station Wagon, trunk & hood open, 1/43 scale, MIB, R6 .... $15.00
Moskvitch Aeroflat (Soviet Airline) Station Wagon, hood opens, 1/43 scale, MIB, R6 .... $15.00
Moskvitch Auto Service Station Wagon, hood opens, 1/43 scale, R6 .... $15.00
Moskvitch Medical Services Sedan, 1/43 scale, MIB, R6 .$15.00
Moskvitch Panel Station Wagon, hood opens, 1/43 scale, MIB, R6 .... $15.00
Moskvitch Sedan, hood opens, 1/43 scale, MIB, R6 ....$15.00
Moskvitch Slant-Back Sedan, 1/43 scale, MIB, R6 ....$15.00
Moskvitch Soviet Traffic Sedan, hood opens, 1/43 scale, MIB, R6 .... $15.00
Moskvitch Station Wagon, hood opens, 1/43 scale, MIB, R6 .... $15.00
Moskvitch Taxi Sedan, hood opens, 1/43 scale, MIB, R6...$15.00
OMO, 1937 Fire Truck, #1 in series of 6, 1/43 scale, MIB, R6 .... $40.00

OMO, 1937 Fire Truck, #2 in series of 6, 1/43 scale, MIB, R6 .... $40.00
RAF Ambulance Van, back & 3 doors open, 1/43 scale, MIB, R6 .... $20.00
RAF Traffic Police Van, 1/43 scale, MIB, R6 .... $20.00
Volga Ambulance Station Wagon, back & 3 doors open, 1/43 scale, MIB, R6 .... $22.00
Volga Sedan, trunk, hood & doors open, 1/43 scale, MIB, R6 .... $20.00
Volga Taxi Sedan, trunk, hood & doors open, 1/43 scale, MIB, R6 .... $20.00
Volga Taxi Station Wagon, trunk, hood & doors open, 1/43 scale, MIB, R6 .... $20.00
Volga Traffic Police Sedan, 1/43 scale, MIB, R6 .... $22.00

Replicas of Military Vehicles

Armored Car, 1/43 scale, MIB, R6 .... $15.00
Armored Personnel Carrier, 1/43 scale, MIB, R6 .... $15.00
Armored Troop Carrier, 1/86 scale, MIB, R6 .... $15.00
Cannon, 1/86 scale, MIB, R6 .... $15.00
Cannon (100mm), 1/43 scale, MIB, R6 .... $15.00
Cannon (76mm), 1/43 scale, MIB, R6 .... $15.00
Command Car, 1/86 scale, MIB, R6 .... $15.00
N-153 Biplane Fighter, 1/72 scale, MIB, R6 .... $40.00
N-16 Fighter, 1/72 scale, MIB, R6 .... $40.00
Rocket Launcher Armored Truck, 1/86 scale, MIB, R6 ... $15.00
Self-Propelled Cannon, 1/86 scale, MIB, R6 .... $15.00
SU-100 Self-Propelled Cannon, 1/43 scale, MIB, R6 .... $15.00

T-34-85 Tank, metal, rarest of the set of six, MIB, R6, $25.00.

Tank, battery-op, 1/72 scale, MIB, R6 .... $45.00
Tank, 1/86 scale, MIB, R6 .... $12.00
Troop Truck, 1/86 scale, MIB, R6 .... $15.00

Miscellaneous

Bird, metal, w/up, MIB, N1 .... $5.00
Car on Garage Lift, MIB, N1 .... $8.00
Car Set, metal, 6-pc, MIB, N1 .... $12.00
Car Track, metal, w/up, MIB, N1 .... $30.00
Chicken, metal, MIB, N1 .... $5.00
Chicken Inside Egg, w/up, MIB, N1 .... $5.00
Doll, Maytryoshki, metal, w/up, MIB, N1 .... $18.00
Doll Set, Maytryoshki, wood, Lenin, Stalin, Kruschev, Brezhnez & Gorbechev, made in China, MIB, N1 .... $30.00
Hen, metal, w/up, MIB, N1 .... $8.00
Jet Fighter, plastic, bl, MIB, N1 .... $5.00
Monster Beetle, metal, MIB, N1 .... $8.00
Moon Buggy w/2 Cosmonauts, plastic & metal, w/up, MIB, N1 .... $15.00
Parking Garage, metal, MIB, N1 .... $30.00
Rooster, metal, w/up, MIB, N1 .... $8.00
Tank, plastic, MIB, N1 .... $5.00
Train Track, metal, w/up, MIB, N1 .... $30.00
WWII Soldiers w/Rifles, cast metal, set of 10, MIB, N1 ... $25.00

Sand Toys and Pails

In the Victorian era a sand toy was a boxed wooden or cardboard scene with a glass front and a mechanism involving a hopper and/or chute leading to a paddle, then to various rods and levers attached to cardboard or tin figures or animals with loosely jointed limbs at the front of the scene. When the sand was poured, the mechanism was activated, and the figures went through a series of movements. These were imported mostly from Germany with a few coming from France and England.

By 1900, having seen the popularity of the European models, American companies were developing all sorts of sand toys, including free-standing models. The Sand Toy Company of Pittsburgh patented and made 'Sandy Andy' from 1909 onward. The company was later bought by the Wolverine Supply & Manufacturing Co. and continued to produce variations of the toy until the 1970s.

Today if you mention sand toys, people think of pails, spades, sifters, and molds, as the boxed scenes have all but disappeared due to their being quite fragile and not surviving use.

We have a rich heritage of lithographed tin pails with such wonderful manufacturers as J. Chein & Co., T. Cohn Inc., Morton Converse, Kirchoff Patent Co., Marx Toy Co., Ohio Art Co., etc, plus the small jobbing companies who neglected to sign their wares. Sand pails have really come into their own and are now recognized for their beautiful graphics and designs. A new book, *Pails by Comparison, Sand Pails and Other Sand Toys, A Study and Price Guide*, by Carole and Richard Smyth (our advisors for this category) is now available from the authors (S22 in Dealer Codes).

Busy Mike, Chein, ca 1935, boy & girl on seesaw, litho tin, 7", EX $275.00
Capt Sandy Andy Loader, Wolverine, tower w/chute & sand car that goes up & down, 13½", EX (EX box), minimum value $275.00
Dutch Mill, Mac Toys, litho tin, 12", NM, A $250.00
Dutch Mill, Mc Dowell Mfg Co/Pittsburg PA, ca 1927, litho tin, 12", EX, from $225 to $350.00
Pail, litho tin, Donald Duck, mk WDE, EX $450.00

Pail, litho tin, Kewpie Beach, image of Scootles building a sand castle, EX $375.00
Pail, litho tin, Ohio Art, Mickey & Minnie coming into shore on raft, 6", VG, A $295.00
Pail, litho tin, Ohio Art, 1935, mk Atlantic City, image of Mickey & friends in rowboat, w/orig shovel, 6", NM, A $1,000.00

Pail, lithographed tin, Ohio Art, 1936, Mickey Mouse at drink stand, 3", NM, from $225.00 to $350.00.

Pail, litho tin, Ohio Art, 1950s, Little Red Riding Hood, VG, N2 ....$50.00
Pail, litho tin, safari scene w/elephant, zebra & tiger, unsigned, 5¼", EX $100.00
Pail, litho tin, T Cohn, Popeye Under the Sea, 12", EX, A..$1,000.00
Pail, litho tin, T Cohn, Popeye Under the Sea, 9", EX, A ...$385.00
Pail, litho tin, T Cohn, 1933, Popeye the Sailor, 4", EX, A.$200.00
Pail, litho tin, T Cohn, 1933, Popeye's Thimble Theater, 12", VG, A $325.00
Pail, litho tin, 1930s, Popeye at the Beach, shows various characters playing in the sand, 3½", EX+, A $350.00
Pail, plastic, Smurfs, 1981, EX, N2 ....$15.00
Sand Crane, Wolverine, 1916, mc litho, NM....................$375.00
Sand Lift, Ohio Art, M....................$120.00
Sand Mill, Chein, sand causes cups to twirl, 11½", M (EX box) $175.00
Sand Mill, Popeye & Olive Oyl, litho tin, 8", EX, A $385.00
Sand Set, Ohio Art, 1940s-50s, litho tin shovel, sifter & 2 molds, MOC, from $80 to $120.00
Seesaw, Chein, 1925, pour sand in top to activate boy & girl on horses, 11", EX....................$180.00
Shovel, Chein, mc pirates, 14", EX $70.00
Shovel, Ohio Art, 1930s, Mickey & Minnie playing in the sand, litho tin, 8", EX $125.00
Sifter, Ohio Art, 1930s, various Disney characters, 8" dia, EX, A.$285.00
Sifter, Ohio Art #187, litho tin, children playing in sea, artist signed by Elaine Ends Hileman, 7½" dia, EX............$80.00
Sifter, T Cohn, litho tin, Flying Spray, red, wht & bl speedboat shape, window hole in cabin forms hdl, EX.............$185.00
Spade, mk RN Made in USA on hdl, 1920s, 2 girls at beach, 11½", EX....................$150.00
Spade, Ohio Art #184, boy in lg sea waders shows girl his sm fish, wood hdl, 28", EX $125.00
Sunny Andy Merry Miller, Wolverine, elf moves & wheel spins, comes w/can of sand, 12", NM (G-box), from $200 to .$325.00

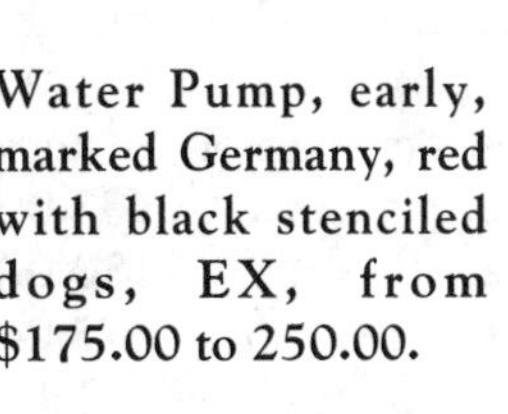
Water Pump, early, marked Germany, red with black stenciled dogs, EX, from $175.00 to 250.00.

Wheelbarrow Loader, Wolverine, 1948, loader travels down ramp & dumps sand into tray, litho tin, MIB $187.00

Santa Claus

Christmas is a magical time for young children; visions of Santa and his sleigh are mirrored in their faces, and their eyes are wide with the wonder of the Santa fantasy. There are many who collect ornaments, bulbs, trees, etc., but the focus of our listings is Santa himself.

Among the more valuable Santas are the German-made papier-mache figures and candy containers, especially the larger examples and those wearing costumes in colors other than the traditional red.

See also Battery Operated; Books; Reynolds Toys; Windups, Friction, and Other Mechanicals; and other specific categories.

Candy Container, 4½", plastic, Sears, 1945, Santa on Skis, NM, from $15 to....................$20.00
Candy Container, 5", wood w/compo face, cloth clothes, Santa sitting on fire wood, Germany, 1920s, NM, A.........$400.00

Candy Container, 6", plastic, Santa in Chimney, 1950s, NM, A..$35.00
Candy Container, 6", plastic, Santa w/horn, 1950s, NM, A....$35.00
Candy Container, 8½", compo & papier-mache, wht fur beard, red felt robe w/wht trim, holding feather tree, EX, A $700.00
Candy Container, 10", compo, gray fur beard, red felt robe w/gray trim, basket on rope belt, holding feather tree, EX, A $1,000.00
Candy Container, 14", compo face, hands & boots, wht fur beard, cloth robe, w/feather tree & pine cone, 1910, NM, A..$600.00
Candy Container, 18", papier-mache, wht fur beard, gray fur hooded robe w/metal buttons, tree in hand, EX, A .$3,850.00
Candy Container, 22", compo & papier-mache, wht fur beard, red cloth robe w/wht trim, basket on belt, w/tree, EX, A $1,375.00
Candy Container, 27", compo & papier-mache, red cloth robe, electrified candles on tree, tin lantern, EX, A......$1,925.00
Clicker, 1930s, litho tin w/image of Santa at base of chimney w/sack of toys, 1¾", EX, A $75.00
Doll, Steiff, 1970s, orig outfit & glasses, brass button & stock tag, 20½", rare, NM, G16..$585.00
Doll, Steiff, 1985-88, all ID, 8", M, G16..$150.00
Doll, 1930s, compo head & hands w/cloth suit, 19", VG, A ..$75.00
Mask, German, papier-mache w/crepe hat & cloth beard, 12x8", NM, A $175.00
Nodder, celluloid, Santa w/lantern, 7", M, A $425.00
Nodder, papier-mache w/sheepskin hair & beard, red fleece coat w/wht fur trim, 25½", EX, A..$1,250.00
Pull Toy, Santa driving truck w/3 trees in back, wood w/compo & cloth Santa, 22", NM, A..$300.00
Pull Toy, Santa on horse-drawn wagon, 2 leather hide-covered horses on wheeled platform, 36", VG, A $935.00
Roly Poly, Irwin, 1930s, celluloid, 3¼", NM, A $65.00

Roly Poly, papier-mache, 4", VG, H7, $250.00.

Photo courtesy Jacquie and Bob Henry

Roly Poly, Viscaloid, 1930s, celluloid, 4", NM, A $65.00
Santa in Basket, celluloid figure in wire mesh basket, 4", EX, A..$100.00
Santa in Truck w/House & Tree in Back, Japan, celluloid, 4", EX, A $75.00
Santa on Sleigh, Japan, celluloid reindeer & sleigh w/cloth Santa, 10", EX, A $100.00
Santa w/Bag of Toys, Japan, 1930s, compo w/cloth clothes, 8", EX, A $75.00
Santa w/Feather Tree, mk Made in Germany, 1920s, compo w/cloth clothes & blk boots, fur beard, 9", EX, A....$425.00
Santa w/Hands in Pockets, pulp, 10", NM, A................$100.00
Santa w/Lantern, Japan, 1930s, celluloid, 5½", VG, A $25.00
Santa w/Toy Bag, pulp, 8½", NM, A $100.00
Santa w/Tree, Japan, 1930s, red felt robe & hat, cloth beard, 4", EX, A $50.00
Santa w/Tree & Basket of Toys, pulp, hand-pnt, 15", EX, A...$325.00

Schoenhut

Albert Schoenhut & Co. was located in Philadelphia, Pennsylvania. From as early as 1872 they produced toys of many types including dolls, pianos and other musical instruments, games, and a good assortment of roly polys (which they called Rolly Dollys). Around the turn of the century, they designed a line they called the Humpty Dumpty Circus. It was made up of circus animals, ringmasters, acrobats, lion tamers, and the like, and the concept proved to be so successful that it continued in production until the company closed in 1935. During the nearly thirty-five years they were made, the figures were continually altered either in size or by construction methods, and these variations can greatly affect their values today. Besides the figures themselves, many accessories were produced to go along with the circus theme — tents, cages, tubs, ladders, and wagons, just to mention a few. Teddy Roosevelt's African hunting adventures inspired the company to design a line that included not only Teddy and the animals he was apt to encounter in Africa but native tribesmen as well. A third line featured comic characters of the day, all with the same type of jointed wood construction, many dressed in cotton and felt clothing. There were several, among them were Felix the Cat, Maggie and Jiggs, Barney Google and Spark Plug, and Happy Hooligan.

Several factors come into play when evaluating Schoenhut figures. Foremost is condition. Since most found on the market today show signs of heavy wear, anything above a very good rating commands a premium price. Missing parts and retouched paint sharply reduce a figure's value, though a well-done restoration is usually acceptable. The earlier examples had glass eyes; by 1920 eyes were painted on. Soon after that, the company began to make their animals in a reduced size. While some of the earlier figures had bisque heads or carved wooden heads, by the '20s, pressed wood heads were the norm. Full-size examples with glass eyes and bisque or carved heads are generally more desirable and more valuable, though rarity must be considered as well.

Value ranges represent items in only fair condition (by the low end) up to those in good to very good condition, i.e., very minor scratches and wear, good original finish, no splits or chips, no excessive paint wear or cracked eyes, and, of course completeness. Animals with painted eyes in fair condition are represented by the low side of the range; use the high side to evaluate glass-eyed animals in very good condition.

During the 1950s, some of the figures and animals were produced by the Delvan Company, who had purchased the manufacturing rights.

Consult the index for Schoenhut toys that may be listed in other categories.

Advisor: Keith and Donna Kaonis (K6).

Humpty Dumpty Circus Animals

Humpty Dumpty Circus animals with glass eyes, ca. 1903 – 1914, are more desirable and can demand much higher prices than the later painted-eye versions. As a general rule, a glass-eye version is 30% to 40% more than a painted-eye version. (There are exceptions.) The following list suggests values for both glass eye and painted eye versions and reflects a low painted eye price to a high glass eye price.

There are other variations and nuances of certain figures: Bulldog — white with black spots or brindle (brown); open-and closed-mouth zebras and giraffes; ball necks and hemispherical necks on some animals such as the pig, leopard, and tiger, to name a few. These points can affect the price and should be judged individually.

Alligator, glass or pnt eyes, $200 to................................**$450.00**
Arabian Camel, 1 hump, glass or pnt eyes, $250 to........**$750.00**
Bactrian Camel, 2 humps, glass or pnt eyes, $200 to...**$1,500.00**

Brown Bear, glass or painted eyes, from $200.00 to $900.00; Kangaroo, glass or painted eyes, from $400.00 to $1,400.00.

Buffalo, carved mane, glass or pnt eyes, $200 to..........**$1,200.00**
Buffalo, cloth mane, glass or pnt eyes, $300 to **$900.00**
Bulldog, glass or pnt eyes, $400 to **$1,600.00**
Burro (made to go w/chariot & clown), glass or pnt eyes, $300 to **$700.00**
Cat, glass or pnt eyes, rare, $600 to.............................**$3,000.00**
Cow, glass or pnt eyes, $250 to **$1,000.00**
Deer, glass or pnt eyes, $300 to **$1,000.00**
Donkey, glass or pnt eyes, $75 to...................................**$200.00**
Donkey, w/blanket, glass or pnt eyes, $90 to..................**$400.00**
Elephant, glass or pnt eyes, $90 to.................................**$300.00**
Elephant, w/blanket, glass or pnt eyes, $200 to..............**$550.00**
Gazelle, glass or pnt eyes, rare, $700 to........................**$3,000.00**
Giraffe, glass or pnt eyes, $200 to...............................**$1,000.00**
Goat, glass or pnt eyes, $150 to **$400.00**
Goose, pnt eyes, $200 to...**$600.00**
Gorilla, pnt eyes, $1,200 to **$3,000.00**
Hippo, glass or pnt eyes, $300 to **$900.00**
Horse, brn, w/saddle & stirrups, glass or pnt eyes, $150 to ..**$400.00**
Horse, wht, platform, glass or pnt eyes, $125 to.............**$400.00**
Hyena, glass or pnt eyes, very rare, $1,000 to **$3,700.00**
Leopard, glass or pnt eyes, $350 to **$800.00**
Lion, carved mane, glass or pnt eyes, $250 to.............**$1,000.00**
Lion, cloth mane, glass eyes, $500 to..........................**$1,200.00**
Monkey, 1-part head, pnt eyes, $250 to **$450.00**
Monkey, 2-part head, wht face, $300 to..........................**$900.00**
Ostrich, glass or pnt eyes, $200 to **$850.00**
Pig, 5 versions, glass or pnt eyes, $200 to **$900.00**
Polar Bear, glass or pnt eyes, $500 to **$1,500.00**
Poodle, cloth mane, glass eyes, $300 to..........................**$500.00**
Poodle, glass or pnt eyes, $125 to **$300.00**
Rabbit, glass or pnt eyes, very rare, $1,000 to.............**$4,000.00**
Rhino, glass or pnt eyes, $250 to.................................**$1,000.00**
Sea Lion, glass or pnt eyes, $400 to.............................**$1,200.00**
Sheep (lamb), w/bell, glass or pnt eyes, $200 to **$750.00**
Tiger, glass or pnt eyes, $250 to.....................................**$900.00**
Wolf, glass or pnt eyes, very rare, $600 to...................**$4,000.00**
Zebra, glass or pnt eyes, $250 to.................................**$1,000.00**
Zebu, glass or pnt eyes, rare, $1,000 to........................**$3,000.00**

Humpty Dumpty Circus Clowns and Other Personnel

Clowns with two-part heads (a cast face applied to a wooden head) were made from 1903 to 1915 and are most desirable — condition is always important. There have been nine distinct styles in fourteen different costumes recorded. Only eight costume styles apply to the two-part headed clowns. The later clowns, ca. 1920, had one-part heads whose features were pressed, and they were no longer tied at the wrists and ankles.

Black Dude, reduced sz, $300 to **$600.00**
Black Dude, 1-part head, purple coat, $250 to...............**$800.00**
Black Dude, 2-part head, blk coat, $400 to....................**$800.00**
Chinese Acrobat, 1-part head, $300 to..........................**$600.00**
Chinese Acrobat, 2-part head, rare, $500 to **$1,000.00**
Clown, early, $150 to **$500.00**
Clown, reduced sz, 1926-35, $75 to...............................**$150.00**
Gent Acrobat, bsk head, rare, $300 to **$750.00**
Gent Acrobat, 1-part head, $500 to...............................**$900.00**
Gent Acrobat, 2-part head, very rare, $800 to **$1,200.00**
Hobo, reduced sz, $300 to...**$600.00**
Hobo, 1-part head, $200 to **$500.00**
Hobo, 2-part head, curved-up toes, $700 to **$1,200.00**
Hobo, 2-part head, facet toe ft, $400 to **$800.00**
Lady Acrobat, bsk head, $300 to...................................**$600.00**
Lady Acrobat, 1-part head, $200 to **$400.00**
Lady Rider, bsk head, $250 to **$500.00**
Lady Rider, 1-part head, $200 to.....................................**$400.00**

Lady Rider, 2-part head, very rare, $700 to **$1,200.00**
Lion Tamer, bsk head, rare, $350 to..............................**$700.00**
Lion Tamer, 1-part head, $250 to **$500.00**
Lion Tamer, 2-part head, early, very rare, $600 to......**$1,500.00**
Ringmaster, bsk, $450 to **$650.00**
Ringmaster, 1-part head, $200 to **$450.00**
Ringmaster, 2-part head, early, very rare, $500 to.......**$1,200.00**

Humpty Dumpty Circus Accessories

There are many accessories: wagons, tents, ladders, chairs, pedestals, tight ropes, weights, and various other items.

Menagerie Tent, ca 1904, $1,800 to **$2,500.00**
Menagerie Tent, 1914-20, $1,200 to **$2,000.00**
Oval Lithographed Tent, 1926, complete, $3,000 to ..**$4,000.00**
Side Show Panels, 1926, pr, $3,000 to........................**$4,000.00**

Schuco

A German company noted for both mechanical toys as well as the teddy bears and stuffed animals we've listed here, Schuco operated from the 1930s well into the '50s. Items were either marked Germany or US Zone, Germany.

Advisor: Candace Gunther, Candelaine (G16).

See also Battery-Operated; Windups, Friction, and Other Mechanicals.

Bear, brn w/cinnamon ears, orig ribbon, 1950, 3½", M, G16..**$200.00**
Bear, brn w/metal eyes, orig paper label, 1950s, 2½", M, G16..**$265.00**
Bear, champagne, 1950s, 2½", NM, G16.......................**$150.00**

Bottle Bear, pink, 3½", NM, $1,000.00.

Bear, cinnamon w/metal eyes, orig ribbon, 1950s, 3½", M, G16..**$225.00**
Bear, in soccer outfit, 1960, 3½", MIB, G16..................**$325.00**
Bear, orange w/metal eyes, shaved muzzle, 1950s, 3½", NM, G16..**$300.00**
Bear, pale gold, orig gr ribbon, 1950, 3½", EX, G16.......**$150.00**
Bear, pale gold w/metal eyes, orig paper label, 1950s, 2½", NM, G16..**$265.00**
Bear, tan w/metal eyes, orig ribbon, 1950s, 3½", NM, G16...**$175.00**
Bear Compact, gold mohair over metal, 1920s, removable head, 3½", G **$650.00**
Berlin Bear, brn, orig banner & crown, 1950s, 2½", NM, G16..**$265.00**
Bigo-Bello Dog, orig clothes, 14", NM, G16..................**$175.00**
Bigo-Bello Tiger, cloth label, 1960s, 9½", EX, G16 ....**$125.00**
Black Scottie, Noah's Ark, 1950, 3", MIB, G16 ....**$225.00**
Blackbird, Noah's Ark, 1950, 3", MIB, G16 ....**$225.00**
Dog Mascott, felt clothes, 1950, 3½", MIB, G16...........**$150.00**
Duck Mascott, bl & wht striped outfit w/red shoes, 1950, 3½", NMIB, G16..**$125.00**
Elephant, Noah's Ark, mohair w/felt ears & blanket, fully jtd, 1950, 2¼", NM, G16..**$150.00**
Fox, Noah's Ark, 1950, 2½", MIB, G16 ....**$285.00**
Janus Bear, 2 faces (googly & bear), cinnamon, 1950s, 3½", M, G16..**$850.00**
Janus Bear, 2 faces (googly & bear), tan, 1950s, 3½", EX, G16..**$700.00**
Ladybug, Noah's Ark, 1950, 3", MIB, G16 ....**$165.00**
Lion, Noah's Ark, 1950, 3½", VG, G16 ....**$125.00**
Monkey, cinnamon w/felt hands & feet, mk Germany, 2½", NM, G16 ....**$200.00**
Monkey, Noah's Ark, 1950, 3½", M, G16......................**$125.00**
Orangutan, Noah's Ark, 1950, 3", very rare, MIB, G16 .**$325.00**
Owl, Noah's Ark, 1950, 3", M, G16...............................**$100.00**
Panda, on all fours, Noah's Ark, 1950, 3", rare, MIB, G16...**$550.00**
Penguin, Noah's Ark, 1950, 3", MIB, G16 ....**$175.00**
Perfume Bear, gold, 1930, 5", M, G16............................**$750.00**
Perfume Monkey, cinnamon w/felt hands & ears, 1930, 5", rpl bottle, EX, G16..**$200.00**
Pig, Noah's Ark, wht w/brn spots, 1950, 1¾", NM, G16..**$200.00**
Raccoon, Noah's Ark, 1950, 3½", M, G16 ....**$200.00**
Siamese Cat, Noah's Ark, orig ribbon, 1950, 3", M, G16..**$300.00**
Squirrel, Noah's Ark, 1950, 2½", M, G16 ....**$175.00**
Tiger, Noah's Ark, 1950, 3", rare, MIB, G16..................**$350.00**
Tumbling Bear, gold, 1950s, 5", NM, G16......................**$850.00**
Turtle, Noah's Ark, 1950, 3", NM, G16 ....**$175.00**
Yes/No Baby Orangutan, 1948, orig FAO Schwarz tag, 8", rare, NMIB, G16..**$700.00**
Yes/No Bear, blk mohair, 1950, 5", NM, G16 ....**$900.00**
Yes/No Bear, caramel w/glass eyes, 1950, 5", NM, G16..**$550.00**
Yes/No Bear, dk brn w/glass eyes, 1950, 5", NM, G16....**$865.00**
Yes/No Bellhop Monkey, 1920s, 13½", NM, G16..........**$950.00**
Yes/No Cat, 5", M, G16..**$650.00**
Yes/No Dog, Pekinese-type, glass eyes, 1930s, 6½", G, G16..**$200.00**
Yes/No Donkey, mohair w/felt ears, orig felt collar & ribbon, 1950, 5", NM, G16..**$485.00**
Yes/No Elephant, mohair w/felt tusks & ears, cloth US Zone tag, 1948, 5", EX, G16..**$400.00**

Yes/No Gnome, w/glasses, mohair & felt w/velvet pants & felt jacket, 1948, 12", EX, G16 ....$800.00
Yes/No Monkey, gray w/orig shirt, jacket & handkerchief, 1920s, 12½", rare, NM, G16 ....$750.00
Yes/No Monkey, limited edition replica of Tricky Monkey, mohair & felt w/glass eyes, 18", M, G16 ....$200.00
Yes/No Panda, orig pk bow, 1950, 5", MIB, G16.........$1,250.00
Yes/No Panda, 1940-50, 8", rare, EX, G16 ....$1,100.00

Yes/No Panda, 1950, original red ribbon, glass eyes, 5", MIB (not shown), $1,250.00.

Yes/No Rabbit, 5", M, G16..$650.00
Yes/No Tricky Bear, tan w/glass eyes, 1948, 8", EX, G16 .$750.00
Yes/No Tricky Elephant, orig ribbon & tag, 1948, 9", EX, G16 ....$475.00
Yes/No Tricky Monkey, orig ribbon, 1948, 10½", EX, G16 ...$295.00
Yes/No Tricky Monkey, orig ribbon & tag, 1948, 14", M, G16 ....$450.00

Slot Cars

Slot cars first became popular in the early 1960s. Electric raceways set up in retail storefront windows were commonplace. Huge commercial tracks with eight and ten lanes were located in hobby store and raceways throughout the United States. Large corporations such as Aurora, Revell, Monogram, and Cox, many of which were already manufacturing toys and hobby items, jumped on the bandwagon to produce slot cars and race sets. By the end of the early 1970s, people were loosing interest in slot racing, and its popularity diminished. Today the same baby boomers that raced slot cars in earlier days are revitalizing the sport. Vintage slot cars are making a comeback as one of the hottest automobile collectibles of the 1990s. Want ads for slot cars appear more and more frequently in newspapers and publications geared toward the collector. As you would expect from their popularity, slot cars were generally well used, so finding vintage cars and race sets in like-new or mint condition is difficult. Slot cars replicating the 'muscle' cars from the '60s and '70s are extremely sought after, and clubs and organizations devoted to these collectibles are becoming more and more commonplace. Large toy companies such as Tomy and Tyco still produce some slots today, but not in the quality, quantity, or variety of years past.

Aurora produced several types of slots: Screachers (5700 and 5800 number series, valued at $5.00 to $20.00); the AC-powered Vibrators (1500 number series, valued at $20.00 to $150.00); DC-powered Thunderjets (1300 and 1400 number series, valued at $20.00 to $150.00); and the last-made AFX SP1000 (1900 number series, valued at $15.00 to $75.00).

Advisor: Gary Pollastro (P5).

Complete Sets

AMT, Cobra Racing Set, NMIB $185.00
Aurora, Home Raceway by Sears #79N9513C, VG, P5 .$225.00
Aurora, Jackie Stewart Oval 8, VG (VG box).................$85.00
Aurora, Stirling Moss 4-Lane Racing Set, EX (EX box), J2....$150.00
Aurora, Stirling Moss, #1313, Table Top Racing Set, 1968, NMIB..$125.00
Aurora AFX, Jackie Stewart Challenger Raceway, NMIB.$75.00
Aurora AFX, Revamatic Slot Car Set, EX (EX box) $75.00
Cox, Ontario 8, #3070, w/Eagle & McLaren, G (orig box), P5 ....$75.00
Eldon, Power 8 Road Racer Show, 1960s, EX (EX box) ...$70.00
Eldon, Raceway Set #24, 1/24th scale, VG, P5..............$175.00
Ideal, Alcan Highway Torture Track, 1968, w/extra car & motor, M (EX box), D9 ....$50.00
Ideal, Dukes of Hazzard Racing Set, complete, MIB $85.00
Ideal, Mini-Motorific Set, #4939-5, EX, P5 ....$85.00
Ideal, Motorific Giant Detroit Race track, w/Corvette, EX+ (EX+ box) $85.00
Marx, Grand Prix Set, G (orig box) $65.00
Motorific, GTO Torture Track, lg, EX (EX box) $100.00
Revell, HiBank Raceway Set, #49-9503, Cougar GTE & Pontiac Firebird, EX (EX box), P5 ....$150.00
Strombecker, European Enduro Home Raceway, 1/32 scale, w/Ferrari P-2, Ford J & 8 ft of track, VG, P5 ....$125.00

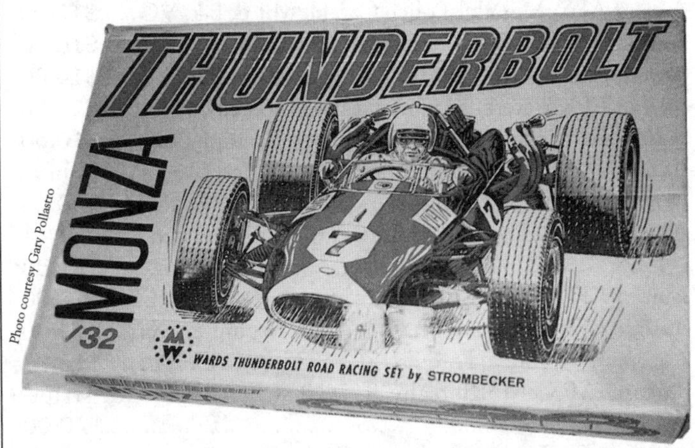

Strombecker, Thunderbolt Monza, Montgomery Ward, VG (VG box), P5, $150.00.

Strombecker, James Bond's 007 Aston Martin, #8630, 1966, NMIB......$225.00
Tyco, International Pro Racing Set, #930086, EX......$125.00
Tyco TCR, Jam Car 500, #6330, 1991, MIB......$60.00

Slot Cars Only

AC Gilbert, Sulky, #1, blk horse, M......$60.00
Aurora, International Semi Tractor, #1580, gray, M......$150.00
Aurora, Javelin, red, wht & bl, NM......$30.00
Aurora, T-Jet Volkswagen, #1404, wht, w/flower, VG......$50.00
Aurora, Thunderbird, Indy Racer, tan, NM......$25.00
Aurora AFX, Autoworld Beamer #5, wht w/bl stripes, NM..$12.00
Aurora AFX, Autoworld McLaren XLR, #1752, orange & gray, EX......$15.00
Aurora AFX, Aztec Dragster, #1963, red, EX......$20.00
Aurora AFX, Camaro Z-28, #1901, red, wht & bl, EX......$15.00
Aurora AFX, Camaro Z-28, lt bl & purple, NMIB......$25.00
Aurora AFX, Capri Trans Am, wht w/bl & lime stripes, EX...$16.00
Aurora AFX, Chevy Nomad, #1760, bl, EX......$20.00
Aurora AFX, Corvette #7, red, wht & bl, EX+......$15.00
Aurora AFX, Datsun Baja Pickup, #211, yel & bl, M......$15.00
Aurora AFX, Dodge Challenger, #1773, lime & bl, NM..$35.00
Aurora AFX, Dodge Charger, bl, NM......$20.00
Aurora AFX, Dodge Charger Daytona, #1900, bl & blk, EX......$25.00
Aurora AFX, Dodge Charger Stock Car, #11, wht w/blk hood, EX......$15.00
Aurora AFX, Dodge Fever Dragster, wht & yel, NM......$20.00
Aurora AFX, Dodge Police Van, wht w/blk stripe, VG......$15.00
Aurora AFX, Dodge Street Van, yel w/orange stripe, EX .$10.00
Aurora AFX, Dragster, red, NM......$25.00
Aurora AFX, Ferrari 512M, #1763, wht & bl, EX......$12.00
Aurora AFX, Ford Baja Bronco, #1909, red, EX......$15.00
Aurora AFX, Ford Escort, #1944, charcoal, bl & red, EX.$14.00
Aurora AFX, Ford Escort, #46, gold & bl w/red stripes, NM..$15.00
Aurora AFX, Grand Am Funny Car, #1702, red, wht & bl, EX......$14.00
Aurora AFX, Javelin AMX, #1906, chrome & red, EX......$40.00
Aurora AFX, Lola T260 Can-Am, NM......$14.00
Aurora AFX, Lotus F1, #1783, blk & gold, EX......$20.00
Aurora AFX, Matador Police Car, bl, wht & blk, VG......$12.00
Aurora AFX, Matador Taxi, wht, EX......$16.00
Aurora AFX, Nissan 300ZX, #33, red wht & bl, NM......$14.00
Aurora AFX, Peterbilt Lighted Rig, #1156, red & yel, EX..$25.00
Aurora AFX, Pinto Funny Car, orange & purple, EX......$10.00
Aurora AFX, Plymouth Roadrunner Stock Car, #1762, bl & wht, EX......$30.00
Aurora AFX, Pontiac Grand Am, #10-191, red, wht & bl, EX......$15.00
Aurora AFX, Porsche Carrera, wht, maroon & blk, EX+ .$12.00
Aurora AFX, Porsche 917, #1757, wht & purple, EX......$14.00
Aurora AFX, Rallye Ford Escort, #1737, gr & bl, EX......$15.00
Aurora AFX, RC Porsche 917-10, wht w/red & bl stripe, NMIB......$20.00
Aurora AFX, Roarin' Rolls, wht & blk, EX......$15.00
Aurora AFX, Shadow Can Am, #1908, MIB......$25.00
Aurora AFX, Speed Beamer #11, red, wht & bl, NM......$15.00
Aurora AFX, Turbo Porsche #3, red, wht & bl, EX......$10.00
Aurora AFX, Turbo Turn On, #1755, orange, yel & purple, EX......$15.00
Aurora AFX, Twi-Night Beamer, wht, red & bl stripes, EX..$10.00
Aurora AFX, Ultra Porsche 917-10 Type A, MIB......$15.00
Aurora AFX, Ultra 5 Shadow, #3007, type A, wht, red, orange & yel, MIB......$25.00
Aurora AFX, Vega Funny Car, NMIB......$25.00
Aurora AFX, Vega Van Gasser, #1754, yel & red, EX......$15.00
Aurora AFX, 1929 Model A Woodie, yel & brn, MIB......$15.00
Aurora AFX, 1957 Chevy Nomad, bl, EX......$22.00
Aurora G-Plus, Camaro (NASCAR), #76, wht, orange & gold, EX......$12.00
Aurora G-Plus, Capri, wht w/gr & bl stripe, EX......$12.00
Aurora G-Plus, Ferrari F1, #1734, red & wht, EX......$25.00
Aurora G-Plus, Indy Special, #1735, blk, red & orange, EX .$18.00
Aurora G-Plus, Lotus F-1, blk & yel, NM......$14.00
Aurora Screacher, Flaming Cuda, wht, red & orange, EX ..$12.00
Aurora Thunderjet, Alfa Romeo Type 33, #1409, yel, EX..$25.00
Aurora Thunderjet, Bushwacker Snowmobile, bl & blk, M..$40.00
Aurora Thunderjet, Camaro, EX......$35.00
Aurora Thunderjet, Chaparral 2F, #1410, lime & bl, EX .$20.00
Aurora Thunderjet, Cheetah, #1403, gr, EX......$35.00
Aurora Thunderjet, Chevy Baja Blazer #4, wht w/bl & red flames, EX......$30.00
Aurora Thunderjet, Cobra GT, #1375, yel w/blk stripe, VG......$35.00
Aurora Thunderjet, Cobra GT Flamethrower, #1495, bl & wht, EX......$25.00
Aurora Thunderjet, Corvette, turq, NM......$45.00
Aurora Thunderjet, Cougar, #1389, wht, NM......$35.00
Aurora Thunderjet, Dino Ferrari, #1381, yel w/red stripe, EX.$30.00
Aurora Thunderjet, Dune Buggy, wht w/red striped roof, EX..$30.00
Aurora Thunderjet, Dune Buggy Roadster, #1398, bl & blk, EX......$32.00
Aurora Thunderjet, Ferrari GTO 250, #1368, red w/wht stripes, EX......$25.00
Aurora Thunderjet, Ford AC Cobra, #3170, wht, red & blk, M......$60.00
Aurora Thunderjet, Ford GT, #1374, bl w/wht stripe, G .$15.00
Aurora Thunderjet, Ford GT, #1374, turq w/blk stripe, EX.$25.00
Aurora Thunderjet, Ford GT Flamethrower, #1494, lt bl, EX......$25.00
Aurora Thunderjet, Ford GT 40, #1374, wht w/blk stripe, EX......$18.00
Aurora Thunderjet, Ford J Car, #1382, bl w/blk stripe, EX..$20.00
Aurora Thunderjet, Ford J Car Flamethrower, wht w/bl stripe, EX......$15.00
Aurora Thunderjet, HO Dune Buggy, wht w/red & wht striped top, EX......$30.00
Aurora Thunderjet, Hot Rod Roadster, tan, NM......$35.00
Aurora Thunderjet, Indianapolis Racer, #1359, red, no chassis, EX......$25.00
Aurora Thunderjet, Jaguar, red, VG......$30.00
Aurora Thunderjet, Lola GT, #1378, blk w/red & wht stripe, EX......$35.00
Aurora Thunderjet, Mack Dump Truck, #1362, yel, cream & gray, NM......$65.00

Aurora Thunderjet, Mako Shark, #1380, turq, EX $24.00
Aurora Thunderjet, Mangusta Mongoose, #1400, gr, EX .$34.00
Aurora Thunderjet, McLaren Elva, #1397, wht, red & blk, EX $24.00
Aurora Thunderjet, McLaren Elva Flamethrower, #1431, blk w/wht stripe, VG..........$20.00
Aurora Thunderjet, Mustang 2+2 Fastback, #1373, yel w/blk & red stripes, EX+ $45.00
Aurora Thunderjet, Pontiac Firebird, #1402, wht, EX $35.00
Aurora Thunderjet, Porsche 904, #1376, turq, VG $18.00
Aurora Thunderjet, Porsche 906GT, red w/wht stripe, VG.$22.00
Aurora Thunderjet, Sand Van Dune Buggy, #1483, pk & wht, EX..........$25.00
Aurora Thunderjet, Snowmobile, #1485-400, M..........$40.00
Aurora Thunderjet, Willie Gasser, #1401, dk gr, VG.......$25.00
Aurora Thunderjet, 1963 Corvette, #1356, red, no rear bumper, VG $25.00
Aurora Thunderjet, 1967 Thunderbird, #1379, EX, from $35 to..........$40.00
Aurora Vibrator, Hot Rod Coupe, #1554, bl, VG $45.00
Aurora Vibrator, Hot Rod Coupe, #1554, yel, VG, P5.....$50.00
Aurora Vibrator, Hot Rod Roadster, #1533, bl, yel or gr, VG, ea $75.00
Aurora Vibrator, International Pickup Truck, #1580, dk gray & blk, EX $150.00
Aurora Vibrator, Mercedes, #1542, yel, EX $50.00
Aurora Vibrator, Mercedes 300SL, #1542, bl, NM..........$75.00
Aurora Vibrator, Mercedes 300SL, #1542, wht, G $60.00
Aurora Vibrator, Van Body Trailer, #1586, dk gray, VG .$15.00
Bachman, James Bond Corvette, silver & bl stripe, VG...$40.00
Bachman, Toyota 2000GT, wht, EX..........$25.00
Classic, Viper, burgandy, EX $80.00
Cox, Ford GT 40, EX..........$75.00
Eldon, Ford Thunderbird, orange, NM..........$35.00
Lionel, Corvette, bl, EX..........$30.00
Monogram, Cooper Ford, #SR3204-598, VG (VG box) ..$60.00
Motorific, Grand Prix, NMIB..........$35.00
Rannalli, Cheetah (Riverside), #6301-1000, VG (w/box), P5 ....$95.00
Revell, Grand Prix Lotus Ford, #R-3152-600, VG (w/box), P5..........$100.00
Strombecker, Cheetah, EX..........$35.00
Strombecker, Jaguar SKE, #9220-595, red, MIB..........$50.00
Strombecker, Pontiac Bonneville, EX..........$40.00
TCR, Blazer, blk & yel w/orange flames, EX..........$15.00
TCR, Jam Car, yel & blk, NM $15.00
TCR, Maintenance Van, wht & red, EX $15.00
TCR, Mercury Stock Car, purple w/chrome, NM..........$18.00
Tyco, A-Team Van, blk w/red stripe, EX..........$38.00
Tyco, Autoworld Carrera, wht w/red, wht & bl stripes, VG .$10.00
Tyco, Bandit Pickup, blk & red, EX..........$12.00
Tyco, Blackbird Firebird, #6914, blk & gold, NM $12.00
Tyco, Blazer, red & blk, VG $10.00
Tyco, Corvette, glow-in-the-dark, any color, EX, ea $10.00
Tyco, Corvette, wht w/red & bl stripes, EX $10.00
Tyco, Corvette Curvehanger, silver chrome w/flames, EX .$15.00
Tyco, Ferrari F-40, #8697, red, VG $12.00
Tyco, Fiero #23, yel, wht & orange stripe, NM..........$12.00
Tyco, Firebird, #6914, cream & red, VG..........$12.00
Tyco, Firebird, blk & gold w/emblem on hood, EX $10.00
Tyco, Firebird Stock Car #35, red & silver lettering, EX..$10.00
Tyco, Firebird Turbo #12, blk & gold, EX..........$10.00
Tyco, Funny Mustang, orange & yel flames, EX $25.00
Tyco, Ghostracer Corvette, blk w/pnt skull, NM $14.00
Tyco, Hardee's Car, orange & bl, EX $14.00
Tyco, Highway Patrol #56, blk & wht, w/sound, NM.......$16.00
Tyco, Indy Diehard, blk & gold, EX..........$12.00
Tyco, Indy Pennzoil, yel, no front spoilers, EX $15.00
Tyco, Javelin, red, wht & bl, EX+ $15.00
Tyco, Jeep CJ7, red & bl, VG..........$12.00
Tyco, Lamborghini, red, VG $12.00
Tyco, Lighted Porsche #2, silver w/red nose, EX..........$20.00
Tyco, Lighted Silverstreak Porsche 908 #3, silver & gray, VG $15.00
Tyco, Lola 260, #8514, red, wht & bl, EX..........$14.00
Tyco, Mack Truck, dk bl & blk, NM $22.00
Tyco, McLaren M8F, #8503, blk & red stripe, EX..........$25.00
Tyco, Mustang #1, orange w/yel flames, EX..........$20.00
Tyco, Porsche Carrera, #8527, yel w/blk hood, VG..........$14.00
Tyco, Porsche 908 #3, gr & silver, EX..........$16.00
Tyco, Rokar 240Z #7, blk, EX $10.00
Tyco, Silverstreak Pickup, silver w/pk & orange stripes, EX..$15.00
Tyco, Silverstreak Porsche 917, lighted, silver w/bl & gr stripes, NM..........$16.00
Tyco, Silverstreak Racing Corvette, #8556, silver w/pk & orange stripe, VG..........$15.00
Tyco, Thunderbird #15, red & yel, VG..........$10.00
Tyco, Turbo Firebird, blk & gold, NM..........$12.00
Tyco, Turbo Hopper #49, blk, VG $10.00
Tyco, Van-Tastic, #8539, bl & wht, VG..........$20.00
Tyco, Z-28 Camaro #7, wht & bl, 5.0 Litre decal, NM $12.00
Tyco, 1940 Ford Coupe, #8534, blk w/flames, NM..........$20.00

Accessories

AMT Service Parts Kit, #2000, VG, P5..........$200.00
AMT Steering-Wheel Controller, #TH-300, 1/24th scale, P5 ....$15.00
Aurora AFX Carrying Case, blk, 2-level, EX $12.00
Aurora AFX Pit Kit, blk, G $15.00
Aurora AFX Speed Steer Breakout Wall, #6056, MIB $20.00
Aurora AFX Speed Steer Intersection Overpass, #6055, 1979, MIB $20.00
Aurora AFX Wall Power Pack, plug or wire style, EX $8.00
Aurora Model Motoring Auto Starter, #1507, 1960, EX (EX box)..........$15.00
Aurora Model Motoring Curved Roadway, #1519, 6 pcs, EX (EX box)..........$15.00
Aurora Model Motoring Guard Rails & Posts, #1532, complete, EX (EX box)..........$10.00
Aurora Model Motoring Loop the Loop Track Set, #1504, EX (EX box) $20.00
Aurora Model Motoring Monza Banked Curve, #1467, EX (EX box)..........$20.00
Aurora Model Motoring Power Pack, 18 or 20 volt, EX, ea.$10.00
Aurora Model Motoring Steering Wheel Controller, EX.$10.00

Aurora Modular Bridge Posts, EX (EX box), J2 ....$15.00
Aurora Terminal Track, 12", EX (EX box), J2..................$15.00
Aurora Thunderjet Bridge Roadway, EX (EX box), J2 .....$10.00
Aurora Thunderjet Carrying Case, butterscotch, VG $15.00
Aurora Thunderjet Country Bridge Roadway, EX (EX box), J2 ....$20.00
Aurora Thunderjet Racing Speed Control, EX (EX box), J2 ....$15.00
Aurora Thunderjet Speed Control Steering Wheel Stile, EX, J2 ....$20.00
Aurora Thunderjet Transformer, VG, J2 ....$20.00
Aurora Vibrator Layout & Service Manual, EX, J2 ....$20.00
Aurora Wide Track Adapter, #1505, O gauge to HO, EX (EX box) $20.00
Eldon Curve Track, MOC (sealed), J2.............................$10.00
Eldon Lane Change, MOC (sealed), J2............................$15.00
Eldon Lap Counter, MOC (sealed), J2............................$10.00
Eldon Power Track, MOC (sealed), J2............................$10.00
Eldon Straight Track, MOC (sealed), J2..........................$10.00
Gilbert, Auto-Rama Speedway (American Flyer) Grandstand Kit, #19349, VG (w/box) $35.00
Gilbert Autorama Automatic Lap Counter, #19339, MIB .$40.00
Gilbert Autorama Fly Over Chicane Kit, #19342, MIB ...$40.00
Monogram Lane Change Track, MIB, J2 ....$20.00
Monogram Tapered Chicane Track, MIB, J2...................$20.00
Revell Curved Track, MIB, J2 ....$15.00
Revell Spin Out Track, MIB, J2 ....$20.00
Revell Straight Track, w/aprons, MIB, J2 ....$15.00
Strombecker Grandstand, #9399, EX..............................$25.00
Strombecker Pagoda Control Tower, #9290, EX $25.00
Strombecker Scale Lap Counter, 1/32nd scale, MIB, P5 ..$25.00
Strombecker Track Customizer, #9150, EX $20.00
Tyco Stick Shift 4-Speed Controller, EX.........................$10.00

Smith-Miller

Smith-Miller (Los Angeles, California) made toy trucks from 1944 until 1955. During that time they used four basic cab designs, and most of their trucks sold for about $15.00 each. Over the past several years, these toys have become very popular, especially the Mack trucks which today sell at premium prices. The company made a few other types of toys as well, such as the train toy box and the 'Long, Long Trailer.'

Advisor: Doug Dezso (D6).

Auto Loader, NMIB, A $400.00
Bekins Vanliner, EX..$1,000.00
Blue Diamond Dump Truck, EX $1,800.00
Camper, 1950s, aluminum w/steel roof, wood interior, 27", VG $225.00
Chevy Milk Truck, EX $300.00
CS Army Overseas Supply Truck, M $700.00
GMC Bekins Truck, VG $400.00
GMC Low Boy Truck, EX $575.00
GMC Machinery Hauler, EX $575.00
GMC Materials Truck, w/4 barrels & 3 timbers, EX $300.00
GMC Mobil Tow Truck, EX $350.00
GMC Rack Truck, EX...$200.00
GMC Searchlight Truck, no lens, VG............................$850.00
GMC Super Cargo Tractor-Trailer, w/10 barrels, NM ...$500.00
GMC Triton Oil Truck, w/3 drums, EX..........................$265.00
Lumber Tandem, complete w/lumber, NMIB, A.........$1,900.00
Mack PIE Truck, EX...$750.00

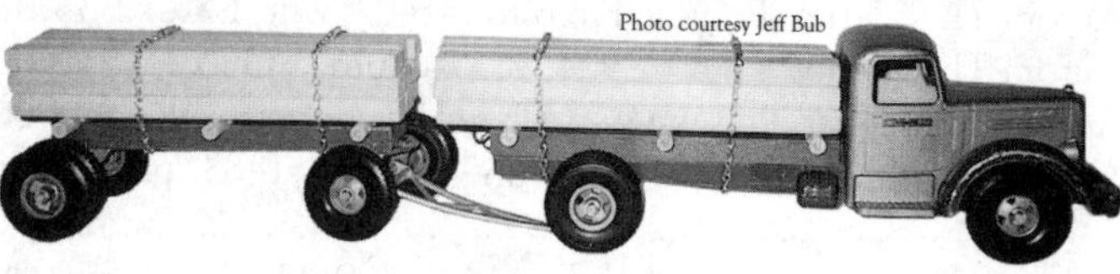
Photo courtesy Jeff Bub

Mack Tandem Timber Truck, green, EX, $850.00.

Pacific Intermountain Express, complete w/aluminum trailer, EX $700.00
SMFD Aerial Ladder Truck, red w/aluminum extension ladders, blk tires, G $500.00
SMFD Mack Aerial Ladder Truck, EX............................$750.00
Smith-Miller Tandem Box Van, NM $1,650.00
Transcontinental Freight Truck, EX $650.00

Snow Domes

Snow domes are water-filled paperweights that come in several different styles. The earliest type was made in two pieces and consisted of a glass globe on a separate base. First made in the middle of the 19th century, they were revived during the '30s and '40s by companies in America, Italy, and Germany. Similar weights are now being imported into the country from the Orient. The most common snow dome on today's market are the plastic half-moon shapes made as souvenirs or Christmas toys, a style that originated in West Germany during the 1950s. Other shapes were made as well, including round and square bottles, short and tall rectangles, cubes, and other simple shapes.

During the 1970s, figural plastic snow domes were especially popular. There are two types — large animate shapes themselves containing the snow scene, or dome shapes that have figures draped over the top. Today's collectors buy them all, old or new. For further information we recommend *Collector's Guide to Snow Domes* by Helene Guarnaccia, published by Collector Books.

Advisor: Nancy McMichael (M18).

Advertising

Air Canada, airplane flying over city in plastic dome, yel ftd base, EX...$60.00
American Express Vacations, Collect a World of Memories, graphic of wht plane in bl sky, wht ftd dome, M........$60.00
Coca-Cola, Santa w/bottle, music box in base, MIB.........$75.00
Days Inn, Catch Some Rays at Days, w/2 Flintstone characters, sm oval plastic dome, M18 ....$10.00
Days Inn, The Whole Family Stays at Days, yel & turq, sm oval plastic dome, M18...$10.00

Michelin Man, Mr Bib in mountians, European issue, MIB..$30.00

Texaco, tanker truck against cityscape in rnd dome, trapezoid base w/dealer advertising, EX $65.00

Character

Betty Boop, seated w/hand up in tall glass dome on rnd blk base, Bully (Germany)/KF Syndicate/Fleischer Studios, 1986, M $18.00

Charlie Chaplin, Enesco, 1989, MIB $25.00

Creature From the Black Lagoon, figural, MIB.................$15.00

Donald Duck, Schmid, 1989, Donald w/single-wheeled riding toy in tall dome atop rnd bl base w/name in wht, M .$10.00

Flintstones, Hanna-Barbera, 1990, Fred, Pebbles, Bamm-Bamm & Dino against bl ground, plastic dome on ftd base, NM $30.00

Garfield, dressed as Uncle Sam, I Want You lettered on base, EX, B5 ....$30.00

Happy Face, Germany, yel w/legs & arms in tall dome w/glitter, rnd blk base, EX...$15.00

Little Mermaid, NM, $20.00.

Photo courtesy Helene Guarnaccia

Lone Ranger Round-Up, Drier, 1940s, lassoing cow in glass dome on rnd base, M $100.00

Mickey Mouse, Bully, 1977, blk & wht striding Mickey in dome, EX $18.00

Mickey Mouse, Monogram Products, in space suit, EX $45.00

Pinocchio, WDP, seated figure w/globe between legs featuring Geppetto's house in snowy landscape, scarce, M.....$100.00

Teenage Mutant Ninja Turtles, dome w/different characters, M, ea $8.00

Yosemite Sam, plays Home on the Range, glass dome on wooden base, MIB $50.00

Figures

#1 Teacher, 'bookworm' atop figural red apple w/heart-shaped window displaying phrase, M....................................$10.00

Cat Playing Drum, drum is water compartment, M18 ......$12.00

Coffeepot, clear plastic w/girl & snowman inside, old, M18...$10.00

Elephant, realistic detail, seated atop dome w/2 elephants inside against gr trees w/dk bl ground, wht oval base, M......$18.00

Monkey, detailed likeness atop dome w/2 monkies on seesaw against gr trees & dk bl ground, wht oval base, M $18.00

Orange w/gr leaves $30.00

Salty Seaman & Captain, standing behind rnd dome w/sailing ship inside, German, M $45.00

Snowman, blk top hat, red ear muffs & lg red smile, carrot nose (broken off), tall, old, M18.......................................$12.00

Holidays and Special Occasions

Birth Announcement, It's a Boy in bl letters floating inside bottle w/bl trim, M $8.00

Birthday, Happy Birthday! lettered on side of bl 3-tiered cake w/red candles, plastic dome, wht rnd ftd base, M.........$8.00

Christmas, figural bear in Santa hat & gr neck ribbon, no plaque, M18 ....$12.00

Christmas, figural boot w/Santa in sled, pine trees & red church inside, old, M18 ....$10.00

Christmas, figural Christmas tree w/lights & balls, old, M18..$15.00

Christmas, figural dog w/gift (water compartment), M18.$12.00

Christmas, figural gift box w/snowman waving inside, lg red bow atop, old, rare, M18 ....$15.00

Christmas, figural Santa climbing out of chimney, plastic, M18...$12.00

Christmas, figural Santa on lamppost, M18 ....$12.00

Christmas, figural Santa w/gift atop lg oval dome, angel & deer inside, old, rare, M18 ....$15.00

Photo courtesy Helene Guarnaccia

Christmas, Santa & snowman on seesaw, NM, from $8.00 to $10.00.

Christmas, Santa on rocket in plastic dome, Marx, 1965, 2x3", M $25.00

Christmas, Santa w/bag of toys in glass dome, mk Made in USA, 7", NM, A $50.00

Christmas, Sat Evening Post, Norman Rockwell Christmas, Dec 4, 1926 on brass plaque on wood base, lg glass dome, M18...$30.00

Christmas, tree in glass dome, mk Made in USA, 4", NM, A .$45.00
Easter, rabbit sitting on fence inside egg-shaped dome atop wooden base, Midwest Imports, 1988, M $8.00
Easter, rabbit w/Easter eggs standing next to pine tree, Austrian glass dome, new, M18 ....$10.00
Graduation, figural graduation cap cocked atop dome w/Congratulations lettered inside, M $8.00
Graduation, Garfield as graduate, Congratulations on base, EX $20.00
Halloween, haunted house in dome atop tall rnd base, Marcel Schurman/San Francisco, M $8.00
Halloween, Trick or Treat!, witch atop haunted house w/skeletons in dome atop mk base, M $10.00
Halloween, 3 ghosts in dome atop cut-out pumpkin, Midwest Imports, M $8.00
New Year, Let's Celebrate, champagne bottle & wht gloves in top hat next to 2 glasses in dome atop rnd base, M $8.00
Wedding, Good Luck on banner around bride & groom cutting wedding cake inside dome atop wht oval ftd base, M .$10.00
Wedding, Weddingland on banner above bride & groom flanked by 2 wedding cakes inside dome, wht oval base, M ...$10.00

Souvenir and Commemoratives

Alaska, polar bear bending over stream, sm oval plastic dome, M18 ....$6.00
Artis Amsterdam, penguins marching in a row, sm oval plastic dome, M18 ....$10.00
Atlanta, blk skyline in front of puffy bl & wht clouds, orange sun & plane, M18 ....$4.00
Bahamas, 500th Anniversary, sailing ship w/1942-1992 on yel banner across sails, lg M18 ....$10.00
Berlin Bleldt Doch Berlin (Berlin Will Always Be Berlin), mc city scene, sm oval plastic dome, M18..........................$8.00
Big Merino Goulburn, NSW, Australia, huge sheep w/national flag at front, sm oval plastic dome, M18 ....$18.00
Blue Ridge Parkway, 2 blk bears on seesaw, gr hills & rainbow at back, sm oval plastic dome, M18 ....$9.00
Buffalo, New York, buffalo before Niagara Falls & rainbow, sm oval plastic dome, M18 ....$8.00
Cancun, Cozumel, Mexico, fish on string in lg plastic dome, M18 ....$8.00
Cancun, Mexico, 2 pk dolphins in lg dome, M18 ....$6.00
Cape Cod, 2 sailboats in sm oval plastic dome, old, M18 ...$7.00
Capri Grotta Azzurra Blue Grotto, lg brilliant bl plastic dome, M18 ....$10.00
Carcassonne, word on plaque, French town w/red roofs, sm oval plastic dome, M18 ....$8.00
Cooper Union (NYC Building), detailed replica, clear all around, broad blk base w/gold decal, rnd, lg, M18.....$18.00
Florida, salt & pepper shakers, 2 different views in pk & bl plastic TVs, M, pr $20.00
Florida, 2 pk flamingos in rnd dome atop pk shell-shaped ashtray, gold trim, M $45.00
Florida Snowman, w/top hat, cane & pipe, plaque on ea side, clear oval plastic dome, orig version, 1980, M18 ....$6.00
Gillette Castle State Park Connecticut, castle inside dome on 3-legged base, old, M18 ....$10.00
Great Smokey Mountains, Bear atop sm dome, old, M18..$12.00
Key West, Florida, gr alligator in clear plastic bottle w/bl top, M...$7.00
Lake George, sailboat on lake scene, lg plastic dome, M18...$6.00

Lake Tahoe, NM, from $8.00 to $10.00.

Louisville Zoo, wht letters on base, bears on Lucite panel, seals at front, turq toaster-shaped dome, M18 ....$5.00
Mayflower II, lg blk letters on plaque, lg sailing ship inside sm oval plastic dome, M18...$12.00
Myrtle Beach, South Carolina, blk letters on band at bottom across sailing scene inside plastic dome, old, M18 ....$8.00
Oberammergau Passion Theatre, Germany, detailed town w/red-domed church inside plastic dome, M18...................$12.00
Paris, Eiffel Tower, Notre Dame & Sacre Coeur at back, glitter, lg plastic dome, M18 ....$7.00
Royal Gorge Colorado, salt & pepper shakers, view of gorge w/pk & bl grounds in popsicle domes, wht rnd bases, M, pr .$30.00
San Gimignano Italy, medieval town w/7 towers & red roofs in lg plastic dome, M18...$10.00
Sears Tower Chicago, lg blk letters in fat bullet-shaped dome, M18 ....$10.00
Six Flags Over Georgia, calendar dome............................$15.00
Space Needle, Seattle Washington, salt & pepper shakers, pk & bl plastic, tall popsicle shape, M18, pr $18.00
St Augustine Florida, fish on string, glitter, low rectangular dome w/blk trim, old, M18 ....$7.00
St Francis Indian Mission, Stone Lake Wisconsin, Mission School building on panel, lg plastic dome, M18 ....$12.00
St Thomas, Virgin Islands, parrot inside sm oval plastic dome, M18 ....$10.00
Sunsphere, Knoxville Tennessee, w/Tower from World's Fair, tall popsicle form, old, rare version, M18..................$13.00
Tarongo Zoo, Australia, tiger atop lg dome w/other tigers inside, M18 ....$10.00
United Nations, UN building inside heart-shaped dome, name lettered on base, M18 ....$10.00
US Constitution, open-work ship inside plastic dome, old, M18 ....$12.00
USS Massachusettes, Fall River MA, lg gray battleship against bl sky panel, w/glitter, 1960s, G-, M18..........................$10.00

Wonderful World of Disney, 1960s, Mickey & Minnie w/castle in background inside plastic dome, EX $50.00

Soldiers

'Dimestore soldiers' were made from the 1920s until sometime in the 1960s. Some of the better known companies who made these small-scale figures and accessories were Barclay, Manoil, and Jones (hollow cast lead); Gray Iron (cast iron); and Auburn (rubber). They're about 3" to 3½" high. They were sold in Woolworth's and Kresge's 5 & 10 Stores (most for just five cents), hence the name 'Dimestore.' Marx made tin soldiers for use in target gun games; these sell for about $8.00. Condition is most important as these soldiers saw lots of action. They're most often found with much of the paint worn off and with some serious 'battle wounds' such as missing arms or legs. Nearly two thousand different figures were made by the major manufacturers, plus a number of others by minor makers such as Tommy Toy and All-Nu. Serious collectors should refer to *Collecting Toys* (1993) or *Toy Soldiers (1992)*, both by Richard O'Brien, Books Americana.

Another very popular line of toy soldiers has been made by Britains of England since 1893. They are smaller and usually more detailed than 'Dimestores,' and variants number in the thousands. O'Brien's book has over two hundred pages devoted to Britains and other foreign makers.

You'll notice that in addition to the soldiers, many of our descriptions and values are for the vehicles, cannons, animals, and cowboys and Indians made and sold by the same manufacturers. Note: Percentages in the description lines refer to the amount of original paint remaining, a most important evaluation factor.

Advisors: Sally and Stan Alekna (A1).

See also Dinky; Plastic Figures.

Auburn Rubber, Charging Soldier, machine gunner, sm, scarce, 99%, A1 ....$49.00
Auburn Rubber, observer w/binoculars, 98%, A1 ....$21.00
Auburn Rubber, searchlight, scarce, 97%, A1 ....$44.00
Auburn Rubber, sound detector, 97%, A1 ....$38.00
Auburn Rubber, tank soldier, running w/ammo box, scarce, 97%, A1 ....$45.00
Auburn Rubber, US Infantry, bugler, 2nd version, 98%, A1 .$22.00
Auburn Rubber, US Infantry, marching, port arms, oval base, early version, scarce, 97%, A1 ....$21.00
Auburn Rubber, US Infantry, officer, 98%, A1 ....$16.00
Auburn Rubber, US Infantry, private, 97%, A1 ....$13.00
Auburn Rubber, US Infantry, private marching, port arms, oval base, early version, 99%, A1 ....$18.00
Auburn Rubber, US Infantry, private marching, port arms, yel w/blk trim, early version, scarce, 98%, A1 ....$25.00
Auburn Rubber, White Guard, officer, wht tunic w/blk pants, M, A1 ....$40.00
Auburn Rubber, White Guard, officer, wht tunic w/red pants, scarce, M, A1 ....$40.00
Auburn Rubber, White Guard, officer, yel w/red trim, 99%, A1 ....$38.00
Auburn Rubber, White Guard, private, wht tunic w/blk pants, scarce, M, A1 ....$40.00
Auburn Rubber, White Guard, private, wht tunic w/red pants, scarce, M, A1 ....$40.00
Barclay, ambulance, bl cross, 98%, A1 ....$41.00
Barclay, armored army car, 98%, A1 ....$25.00
Barclay, aviator, 97%, A1 ....$26.00
Barclay, battleship, #373, scarce, 99%, A1 ....$95.00
Barclay, boy, 98%, A1 ....$15.00
Barclay, bus, red & silver, 1930s, 97%, A1 ....$36.00
Barclay, cadet, 97%, A1 ....$18.00
Barclay, cannon, balloon tires, dk gr, 99%, A1 ....$33.00
Barclay, cannon, balloon tires, khaki, 97%, A1 ....$31.00
Barclay, cannon (field), red spoke wheels, w/closed hatch, sm, 99%, A1 ....$20.00
Barclay, cannon (field), red spoke wheels, 98%, A1 ....$38.00
Barclay, cannon (long range), 98%, A1 ....$41.00
Barclay, cannon (revolving or mortar), khaki, marked Barclay USA under base, very scarce, 99%, A1 ....$98.00
Barclay, cannon car, khaki, wht tires, 97%, A1 ....$22.00
Barclay, cavalryman, gray horse, ca 1930, sm, 95%, A1 ...$31.00
Barclay, convertible w/vacationers, red, wht tires, scarce, 99%, A1 ....$92.00
Barclay, couple in horse-drawn sleigh, 98%, A1 ....$72.00
Barclay, cow grazing, M (in orig tissue & box labeled No 312), A1 ....$29.00
Barclay, cow grazing, M (in orig tissue), A1 ....$17.00
Barclay, cow standing, M (in orig tissue), A1 ....$17.00
Barclay, cowboy firing pistol, orange & bl, 98 %, A1 ....$21.00
Barclay, cowboy firing pistol, orange & gr, 99%, A1 ....$22.00
Barclay, cowboy w/lasso, blk & wht, 99%, A1 ....$24.00
Barclay, cowboy w/lasso (no lasso), 97%, A1 ....$19.00
Barclay, cowboy w/rifle, 96%, A1 ....$18.00
Barclay, cowboy w/rifle, 99%, A1 ....$21.00
Barclay, diver w/axe, repro, solid cast, pnt in correct colors, M, A1 ....$40.00
Barclay, doctor, in wht, flat base, 97%, A1 ....$28.00
Barclay, drum major, short stride, 98%, A1 ....$27.00

Barclay, fireman, worn paint, $20.00.

Barclay, dump truck, red & bl, 1960s, M, A1....................$17.00
Barclay, dump truck (side), orange & gr, 1960s, 97%, A1.$14.00
Barclay, dump truck (side), yel & bl, 1960s, 98%, A1......$15.00
Barclay, Express stake truck, orange, 1930s, 97%, A1 ......$48.00
Barclay, girl in rocker, 98%, A1 ....$19.00
Barclay, girl on sled, 99%, A1 ....$21.00
Barclay, Hertz moving truck, 1960s, 98%, A1 ....$18.00
Barclay, HO scale, boy, 99%, A1 ....$16.00
Barclay, HO scale, brakeman, M, A1 ....$12.00
Barclay, HO scale, dining steward, NM, A1 ....$12.00
Barclay, HO scale, girl, 98%, A1 ....$15.00
Barclay, HO scale, groom, scarce, NM, A1 ....$24.00
Barclay, HO scale, lady w/baby, scarce, NM, A1 ....$18.00
Barclay, HO scale, man, 99%, A1 ....$11.00
Barclay, HO scale, newsboy, M, A1 ....$12.00
Barclay, HO scale, oiler, M, A1 ....$12.00
Barclay, HO scale, porter, 99%, A1 ....$11.00
Barclay, HO Scale, redcap, NM, A1 ....$12.00
Barclay, HO Scale, train conductor, NM, A1 ....$12.00
Barclay, HO scale, train engineer, NM, A1 ....$12.00
Barclay, horse grazing, blk, 98%, A1 ....$15.00
Barclay, Indian brave w/rifle across waist, 96%, A1..........$18.00
Barclay, Indian on horse w/rifle, 98%, A1 ....$33.00
Barclay, Indian w/bow & arrow, 99%, A1 ....$19.00
Barclay, Indian w/bow & arrow kneeling, 99%, A1..........$21.00
Barclay, Indian w/shield & tomahawk, 98%, A1 ....$20.00
Barclay, Japanese garden bridge w/ceramic geisha & 2 ceramic storks on wires, scarce, 98%, A1 ....$42.00
Barclay, Japanese garden house, lg, scarce, 98%, A1 ....$46.00
Barclay, Japanese garden pagoda, scarce, 99%, A1 ....$42.00
Barclay, Japanese garden tori gate, scarce, 98%, A1 ....$42.00
Barclay, knight w/pennant, 99%, A1 ....$24.00
Barclay, knight w/shield, 99%, A1 ....$23.00
Barclay, knight w/sword across waist, NM, A1 ....$35.00
Barclay, knight w/sword over shoulder, NM, A1 ....$35.00
Barclay, knight w/sword overhead, NM, A1 ....$39.00
Barclay, lady, red, NM, A1 ....$12.00
Barclay, lady w/dog, pk, 98%, A1 ....$15.00
Barclay, mailman, 98%, A1 ....$18.00
Barclay, man in overcoat, 99%, A1 ....$15.00
Barclay, man (old) w/cane, NM, A1 ....$19.00
Barclay, man on sled, 98%, A1...$20.00
Barclay, man pulling kids on sled, 98%, A1 ....$59.00
Barclay, man putting skates on girl sitting on bench, very scarce, 99%, A1 ....$165.00
Barclay, man speed skater, M, A1 ....$21.00
Barclay, marine at port of arms, 96%, A1 ....$21.00
Barclay, marine in dress blues, 98%, A1............................$22.00
Barclay, marine officer, bl, scarce, 95%, A1 ....$25.00
Barclay, marine officer, saluting, 90%, A1 ....$18.00
Barclay, minister in hat, walking, very scarce, 94%, A1 ....$71.00
Barclay, minister w/hat in hand, 97%, A1 ....$21.00
Barclay, moving truck, red & silver, no decals, 1960s, 97%, A1..$13.00
Barclay, naval officer in wht, long stride, 97%, A1...........$22.00
Barclay, newsboy, M, A1 ....$20.00
Barclay, officer, gr, 99%, A1 ....$20.00
Barclay, officer, khaki, 99%, A1 ....$17.00
Barclay, officer on horse, in helmet, very scarce, M, A1...$115.00
Barclay, park bench, 99%, A1 ....$15.00
Barclay, policeman, figure-8 base, 99%, A1 ....$24.00
Barclay, policeman, HO scale, NM, A1 ....$12.00
Barclay, Radio Police car, Police stenciled on hood, 1930, 97%, A1 ....$49.00
Barclay, ram, M (in orig tissue), A1 ....$17.00
Barclay, sailor, wht, brn hair, 97%, A1 ....$20.00
Barclay, sailor, wht, red hair, 98%, A1 ....$21.00
Barclay, sailor at attention, M, A1 ....$24.00
Barclay, sailor marching, 95%, A1 ....$19.00
Barclay, Santa on tin skis, 98%, A1 ....$55.00
Barclay, skater, boy, M, A1...$15.00
Barclay, skater, girl, M, A1 ....$21.00
Barclay, ski trooper, brn, scarce, 95%, A1.........................$75.00
Barclay, skier, girl, 98%, A1 ....$25.00
Barclay, skier, man, 98%, A1..$25.00
Barclay, soldier, AA-gunner, khaki, 99%, A1.................$17.00
Barclay, soldier, bomb thrower, khaki, 98%, A1..............$22.00
Barclay, soldier, bugler, khaki, 98%, A1 ....$19.00
Barclay, soldier, bugler, 97%, A1......................................$24.00
Barclay, soldier, charging, khaki, M, A1 ....$18.00
Barclay, soldier, charging, short stride, tin helmet, 97%, A1..$27.00
Barclay, soldier, crawling w/rifle, 94%, A1.......................$25.00
Barclay, soldier, flame thrower, gr, M, A1........................$22.00
Barclay, soldier, flame thrower, red, very scarce, 97%, A1.$128.00
Barclay, soldier, Italian rifleman, 1939, scarce, 97%, A1.$227.00
Barclay, soldier, kneeling, gr, 99%, A1 ....$21.00
Barclay, soldier, leaning over w/phone, scarce, 97%, A1..$72.00
Barclay, soldier, machine gunner charging, cast helmet, 97%, A1 ....$43.00
Barclay, soldier, machine gunner lying flat, cast helmet, 98%, A1 ....$26.00
Barclay, soldier, machine gunner lying flat, tin hat, 95%, A1 ....$24.00
Barclay, soldier, marching, silver pot helmet, 94%, A1 ....$18.00
Barclay, soldier, marching w/pack, cast helmet, scarce, 98%, A1 ....$41.00
Barclay, soldier, marching w/pack, tin helmet, scarce, 97%, A1 ....$33.00
Barclay, soldier, marching w/slung rifle, cast helmet, 93%, A1 ....$33.00
Barclay, soldier, marching w/slung rifle, gr pot helmet, 99%, A1..$22.00
Barclay, soldier, marching w/slung rifle, 99%, A1.............$40.00
Barclay, soldier, marksman, gr, 99%, A1...........................$21.00
Barclay, soldier, parachutist landing, 97%, A1 ....$31.00
Barclay, soldier, raiding in crouch, tin helmet, 99%, A1..$47.00
Barclay, soldier, running looking up, khaki, 99%, A1 ......$17.00
Barclay, soldier, running w/rifle, gr cast helmet, 98%, A1 ..$31.00
Barclay, soldier, sniper kneeling, gr, scarce, 99%, A1 ....$27.00
Barclay, soldier, sniper kneeling, khaki, 97%, A1.............$15.00
Barclay, soldier, sniper kneeling, red, very scarce, 98%, A1....$126.00
Barclay, soldier, tommy gunner charging, red, very scarce, 90-92%, A1 ....$105.00
Barclay, soldier, typist, 98%, A1 ....$34.00
Barclay, soldier, under marching orders, khaki, 99%, A1 .$16.00
Barclay, soldier, w/bazooka, khaki, silver bazooka, 97%, A1 ..$17.00

Barclay, soldier, w/tan bazooka, khaki, 97%, A1 ....**$17.00**
Barclay, soldier, wounded on crutches, 98%, A1 ....**$32.00**
Barclay, soldier, 2 on raft, scarce, 99%, A1 ....**$78.00**
Barclay, soldier, 2-man crew at AA gun, 98%, A1 ....**$39.00**
Barclay, tank, khaki, 98%, A1 ....**$25.00**
Barclay, tank (T41), lg, 98%, A1 ....**$41.00**
Barclay, taxi, die-cast, bl, wht tires, no stencil, NM, A1 ..**$41.00**
Barclay, taxi, die-cast, orange, wht tires, stenciled Taxi, 94%, A1 ....**$35.00**
Barclay, train conductor, 98%, A1 ....**$17.00**
Barclay, train engineer, 99%, A1 ....**$18.00**
Barclay, train porter w/whisk broom, 98%, A1 ....**$25.00**
Barclay, train redcap w/bags, M, A1 ....**$29.00**
Barclay, transport set, 2 cars, 1960s, 93%, A1..................**$60.00**
Barclay, transport set, 2 cars, 1960s, 98%, A1..................**$65.00**
Barclay, US Army plane, w/2 bombs in wire clip, khaki, rare, 99%, A1 ....**$185.00**
Barclay, wedding, bride, sm, 97%, A1 ....**$24.00**
Barclay, wedding groom, 99%, A1 ....**$24.00**
Barclay, West Point cadet, long stride, 98%, A1 ....**$28.00**
Britains, #1 Lifeguards, 5-pc, VG+ (early orig box), A.........**$70.00**
Britains, #2 Royal Horse Guards, 5-pc, EX, A **$150.00**
Britains, #12 Prince Albert's Own 11th Hussars, 5-pc, EX (worn box), A...**$250.00**
Britains, #31 1st Dragoons (The Royals), 5-pc, ca 1930, G (G Wisstock box), A..**$375.00**
Britains, #35 Royal Marines, 16-pc, EX (worn box), A......**$250.00**
Britains, #35 Royal Marines, 8-pc, EX (EX Regiments of All Nations box), A...**$250.00**
Britains, #37 Full Band of Coldstream Guards, 21-pc, VG+ (orig box), A..**$500.00**
Britains, #38 South African Mounted Infantry, 6-pc, VG+, A **$60.00**
Britains, #41 Royal Scot Greys & Grenadier Guards, 14-pc, VG+ (VG box), A...**$70.00**
Britains, #46 Duke of Cambridge's Own 10th Bengal Lancers, 5-pc, ca 1935, G-EX (G Sons of the Empire box), A.....**$350.00**
Britains, #47 Skinners Horses, VG (worn box), A **$110.00**
Britains, #68 2nd Bombay Native Infantry, 10-pc, ca 1900, G (G box), A...**$750.00**
Britains, #75 Scots Guards Marching w/Piper & Officers, 14-pc, VG+ (box top only), A **$110.00**
Britains, #77 Gordon Highlanders w/Pipers, 12-pc, EX (orig box), A...**$170.00**
Britains, #101 Lifeguard Band, 12-pc, EX (worn box), A....**$325.00**
Britains, #109 Dublin Fusliers, 8-pc, ca 1910, G (VG Whisstock box), A...**$600.00**
Britains, #114 The Queen's Own Cameron Highlanders, 8-pc, ca 1940, G-EX (G Whisstock box), A....................**$225.00**
Britains, #121 The Queen's Royal West Surrey Regiment, 10-pc, ca 1925, G-EX (G Whisstock box), A....................**$375.00**
Britains, #127 4th/7th Dragoon Guards, 5-pc, ca 1935, G-EX (VG box), A **$800.00**
Britains, #164 Arabs of the Desert on Horseback, 5-pc, EX (EX Britains Native Warriors box), A..........................**$250.00**
Britains, #164 Bedouin Arabs, 5-pc, VG+ (orig box), A **$160.00**
Britains, #192 French Line Infantry (Active Service), 8-pc, EX (G Whisstock box), A...**$300.00**
Britains, #195 British Infantry at the Trail, 8-pc, EX (EX Regiments of All Nations box), A **$185.00**
Britains, #198 British Army Machine Gun Section, 4-pc, ca 1930, G-EX (G Whisstock box), A **$160.00**
Britains, #206 the Royal Warwickshire Regiment, 8-pc, ca 1930, G-EX (VG Whisstock box), A...............................**$425.00**
Britains, #206 The Royal Warwickshire Regiment, 8-pc, 1935, EX-G, (G Whisstock box), A **$550.00**
Britains, #212 Royal Scots Marching w/Piper, 10-pc, EX+, A **$210.00**
Britains, #225 The Kings African Rifles, 16-pc, EX (orig box), A **$290.00**
Britains, #229 US Cavalry, 10-pc, EX, A.......................**$130.00**
Britains, #313 Royal Artillery Gunners, 8-pc, 1939-41, EX (G Whisstock box), A **$375.00**
Britains, #400 Lifeguards In Winter Cloaks, 14-pc, EX (orig box), A..**$310.00**
Britains, #429 Scots Guards & Lifeguards, winter dress, 6-pc, VG (VG Regiments of All Nations box), A............**$125.00**
Britains, #432 German Infantry, 8-pc, EX, A **$130.00**
Britains, #817 Arabs of the Desert on Foot, 8-pc, EX (EX Britains Native Warriors box), A...........................**$150.00**
Britains, #1257 Yeomen of the Guard (Beefeaters), 9-pc, G-EX (G box), A **$160.00**
Britains, #1283 Grenadier Guards, various positions, 16-pc, EX, A **$90.00**
Britains, #1307 16th Century Knights, 9-pc, VG+, A......**$60.00**
Britains, #1318 British Infantry Machine Gunners, 9-pc, VG (box bottom only), A **$60.00**
Britains, #1327, Grenadier Guards in Action, 6-pc, EX (EX Regiments of All Nations box), A **$100.00**
Britains, #1342 7th Bengal Infantry (3rd Battalion 7th Rajut Regiment), 8-pc, ca 1935, G (Fair box), A.............**$180.00**
Britains, #1343 Royal Horse Guards, winter capes, 5-pc, VG (VG Regiments of All Nations box), A..................**$325.00**
Britains, #1343 Royal Horse Guards The Guards, The Blues, VG+ (worn box), A **$300.00**
Britains, #1349 Royal Mounted Canadian Police, summer dress, 8-pc, EX-NM, A **$160.00**
Britains, #135 Japanese Cavalry, 5-pc, dated 1904, G (VG Whisstock box), A **$1,100.00**
Britains, #1366 French Infantry, active service dress & steel helmets, 1939-41, G (Fair Armies of the World box), A .**$275.00**
Britains, #1395 King's Own Scottish Borders, 8-pc, ca 1935, G-EX (G Armies of the World box), A **$1,000.00**
Britains, #1475 Attendants to the State Coach, 18-pc, M (VG box), A..**$200.00**
Britains, #1512 Army Ambulance, w/driver, stretcher & wounded man, EX, A **$200.00**
Britains, #1517 Scottish Highlanders (Waterloo Period), 8-pc, 1937-41, EX, A...**$500.00**
Britains, #1518 British Line Infantry (Waterloo Period), 9-pc, EX (Fair box), A **$200.00**
Britains, #1554 The Royal Canadian Mounted Police, 8-pc, ca 1940, G-EX, A..**$120.00**
Britains, #1594 Sherwood Foresters (Notinghamshire & Derbyshire Regiments), 8-pc, 1937-1939, G-EX (G+ box), A **$800.00**

Britains, #1603 Republic of Ireland Infantry, 16-pc, EX (VG box), A....$300.00

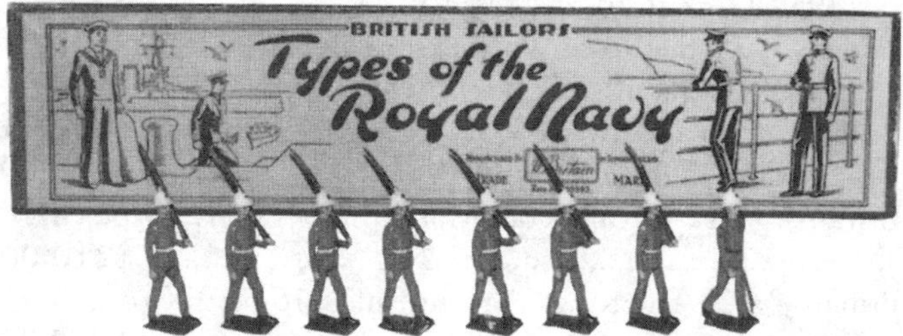

Britains, #1619 British Sailors, 1938 – 41, scarce, EX (EX Types of the Royal Navy box), A, $1,200.00.

Britains, #1633 Princess Patricia's Canadian Light Infantry, Review Order Marching, 8-pc, NM, A....$150.00

Britains, #1637 Canadian Army General's Horse & Foot Guards, 12-pc, VG (VG Regiments of All Nations box), A ..$200.00

Britains, #1663 Mounted Knight of Agincourt w/Lance Rearing, EX (EX box), A....$200.00

Britains, #1730 Gun Detachment, service dress, 8-pc, EX, A ...$170.00

Britains, #1758 Fire Fighters of the Royal Air Forse, 8-pc, 1939-41, EX (G box), A....$850.00

Britains, #1759 Air Raid Precautions Stretcher Party & Gas Detection Service, 9-pc, 1939-41, NM, A....$275.00

Britains, #176 Austrian Dragoons, 5-pc, dated 1902, G (G Types of the Austro-Hungarian Army box), A....$950.00

Britains, #1791 Royal Corps Signal Dispatch Riders, EX (orig box), A....$160.00

Britains, #1791 Royal Signal Corps Dispatch Riders, 4-pc, NM (EX Regiments of All Nations box), A....$220.00

Britains, #1858 British Infantry in Full Battle Dress, 24-pc, NM (separate Regiments of All Nations boxes), A $275.00

Britains, #1892 Indian Army Infantry, 8-pc, 1940-41, G-EX, A.$225.00

Britains, #1893 Indian Army Service Corps, 14-pc, G+ (orig box), A....$250.00

Britains, #1898 British Infantry w/Tommy Guns, 8-pc, EX (EX Regiments of All Nations box), A....$250.00

Britains, #1901 Cape Town Highlanders, 16-pc, VG+, A..$220.00

Britains, #1901 Cape Town Highlanders, 8-pc, EX (EX Regiments of All Nations box), A....$165.00

Britains, #1907 British Army Staff Officers, 5-pc, EX (G Regiments of All Nations box), A....$225.00

Britains, #1907 British Army Staff Officers, 5-pc, VG-NM (orig box), A....$180.00

Britains, #2062 Seaforth Highlanders, 15-pc, VG (repro boxes), A....$225.00

Britains, #2063 Argyle & Sutherland Highlanders, 18-pc, EX (orig box), A....$330.00

Britains, #2071 Royal Marines, 7-pc, NM (EX Regiments of All Nations box), A....$150.00

Britains, #2073 Royal Air Force, 8-pc, NM (EX Regiments of All Nations box), A....$135.00

Britains, #2075 7th Queen's Own Hussars, 5-pc, NM (G Regiments of All Nations box), A....$100.00

Britains, #2077 The King's Troop Royal Horse Artillery w/Walking Team, later version, VG, A....$675.00

Britains, #2087 5th Dragoon Guards, 8-pc, VG (G Regiments of All Nations box), A....$150.00

Britains, #2089 Gloushire Regiment, 8-pc, NM (EX Regiments of All Nations box), A....$100.00

Britains, #2091 Rifle Brigade, 16-pc, EX-NM (orig boxes), A....$250.00

Britains, #2091 Rifle Brigade, 8-pc, EX (EX Regiments of All Nations box), A....$100.00

Britains, #2092 Parachute Regiment, 16-pc, EX (worn box), A....$220.00

Britains, #2092 Parachute Regiment, 8-pc, EX (EX Regiments of All Nations box), A....$150.00

Britains, #2109 Highland Pipe Band of Black Watch, 19-pc, VG+, A....$280.00

Britains, #2111 Black Watch Colour, 6-pc, EX, A $320.00

Britains, #2148 Fort Henry Guards w/Mascot, 14-pc, VG+, A....$120.00

Britains, #2153 Band of the Royal Marines, 12-pc, EX (VG box), A....$350.00

Britains, #2153 Royal Marine Band, 12-pc, VG+ (worn box), A....$290.00

Britains, #2154 British Centurion Tank, gr version, 1956-60, EX (G box), A....$425.00

Britains, #5186 Bahamas Police Band, moders, NMIB, A ..$90.00

Britains, #5290 Royal Scots Dragoon Guards Band, modern, NMIB, A....$110.00

Britains, #5391 US Army Band of Washington, modern, NMIB, A....$80.00

Britains, #5787, Bahamas Police Band, 11-pc, NMIB, A..$125.00

Britains, #8825 Royal Horse Artillery Gun Team, Kings, Troops, 1993 edition, NMIB, A....$130.00

Britains, #9266 French Crusaders Mounted, 4-pc, EX+, A ..$130.00

Britains, #9287 Union Cavalry, 4-pc, VG+, A....$90.00

Britains, #9402 State Open Road Landau, 10-pc, EX-M (VG box), A....$375.00

Britains, #9455 Naval Landing Party, 11-pc, VG-EX, A ..$250.00

Britains, #9497 Medieval Knights in Armour, 6-pc, EX+ (orig box), A....$240.00

Britains, #9497 Tournament Knights Armour, 6-pc, EX-M (EX Historical Series), A....$250.00

Build-A-Cannon Set, Solido #6, NMIB, A $150.00

Courtenay, Sir Walter Thorpe, position 22, EX, A, $375.00; Courtenay, Louis Sieur De Pontchartrain, position 19, EX, A, $375.00; Courtenay, Giles, Lord of Montegu, position 14, EX, A, $400.00; Courtenay, Sir James Douglas, position 6, G, A, $200.00.

Courtenay, Tournament Knight of Sir Nicholas Sarnsfeld KG, mounted, EX, A **$1,600.00**
Courtenay-Greenhill, Bartholomew Lord of Burghershe KG, position Z-11, lunging w/sword, movable visor, M, A.......**$700.00**
Courtenay-Greenhill, Jean Sieur De Aergenton, position Z-14, battle axe raised, helmet on ground, M, A **$350.00**
Courtenay-Greenhill, Sir John Dymock, position, Z-10, sword in right hand, shield in left, movable visor, M, A........**$650.00**
Ducal, #203 Colour Party of the Seaforth Highlanders, 6-pc, EX-M (EX box), A...**$140.00**
Ducal, #210, Band of the Seaforth Highlanders, 12-pc, EX-M (EX box), A **$200.00**
Elastolin, Field Wagon w/2 horses, #0/750/2, VG+, A **$50.00**
Elastolin, German Field Marshall, #650/1, unmk base, EX, A..**$70.00**
Elastolin, German Flag Bearer, #52, type-2 base, EX, A.**$200.00**
Elastolin, German Flag Bearer Mounted, #408/403, yel infantry flag, G+, A..**$160.00**
Elastolin, German Goebels, type-2 base, VG+, A **$150.00**
Elastolin, German Hess in SS Uniform, #30/9, type-1 base, NM, A **$230.00**
Elastolin, German Infantry Flag Bearer, #0/644, type-2 base, VG, A **$40.00**
Elastolin, German Kettle Drummer, #46/32, type-1 base, VG, A **$240.00**
Elastolin, German SA Band Figures, 4-pc, VG+, A **$160.00**
Elastolin, German SA Flag Bearer, #29/49, type-2 base, VG, A...**$90.00**
Elastolin, German SA Flag Bearer, #50/52, tin flag, type-2 base, VG+, A..**$210.00**
Elastolin, German SA Standard Bearer, tin sign, EX, A..**$260.00**
Elastolin, German SA Torch Bearer, #0/40, EX, A **$110.00**
Elastolin, German SS Flag Bearer, #30/52, tin flag, VG, A.**$300.00**
Elastolin, German SS Motorcycle Rider, #29/590, EX, A...**$110.00**
Elastolin, German Standard Marching, #0/485, type-1 base, EX+, A..**$180.00**
Elastolin, Hitler as Messiah, VG, A **$190.00**
Elastolin, Hitler Marching, #30/23, type-3 base, EX+, A..**$200.00**
Elastolin, Mussolini in Stride, #25/21N, VG, A **$120.00**
Elastolin, Mussolini Mounted, #25/406N, type-3 base, EX, A.**$110.00**
Grey Iron, Am Family at Home Series, garage man in gr, postwar, scarce, 99%, A1 ....**$21.00**
Grey Iron, Am Family at Home Series, garage man in wht, scarce, 95%, A1 ....**$18.00**
Grey Iron, Am Family at Home Series, milkman, scarce, 98%, A1 ....**$24.00**
Grey Iron, Am Family at Home Series, old man sitting, M, A1 ....**$15.00**
Grey Iron, Am Family at Home Series, old woman sitting, 98%, A1 ....**$14.00**
Grey Iron, Am Family at Home Series, woman w/basket, 97%, A1 ....**$17.00**
Grey Iron, Am Family on the Farm Series, calf, 99%, A1 ..**$16.00**
Grey Iron, Am Family on the Farm Series, cow, copper & yel, 985, A1 ....**$15.00**
Grey Iron, Am Family on the Farm Series, farmer, 98%, A1...**$17.00**
Grey Iron, Am Family on the Farm Series, farmer's wife, 97%, A1 ....**$16.00**
Grey Iron, Am Family on the Farm Series, gate w/post, scarce, 99% , A1 ....**$29.00**
Grey Iron, Am Family on the Farm Series, goose, 97%, A1..**$14.00**
Grey Iron, Am Family on the Farm Series, hired hand digging, 98%, A1 ....**$22.00**
Grey Iron, Am Family on the Farm Series, horse, blk, 95%, A1 ....**$12.00**
Grey Iron, Am Family on the Farm Series, horse, brn, 98%, A1 ....**$15.00**
Grey Iron, Am Family on the Farm Series, sheep, 99%, A1 .**$16.00**
Grey Iron, Am Family on the Ranch Series, bucking bronco, blk, very scarce, 98%, A1 ....**$58.00**
Grey Iron, Am Family on the Ranch Series, bucking bronco, brn, very scarce, 94%, A1 ....**$53.00**
Grey Iron, Am Family on the Ranch Series, calf, brn, very scarce, 99%, A1 ....**$60.00**
Grey Iron, Am Family on the Ranch Series, colt, blk, very scarce, 98%, A1 ....**$59.00**
Grey Iron, Am Family on the Ranch Series, girl in riding suit, very scarce, 97%, A1 ....**$57.00**
Grey Iron, Am Family Series, bench, M, A1 ....**$14.00**
Grey Iron, Am Family Series, boy in traveling suit, tan, 99%, A1..**$11.00**
Grey Iron, Am Family Series, conductor, 99%, A1 ....**$13.00**
Grey Iron, Am Family Series, engineer, bl, 98%, A1........**$11.00**
Grey Iron, Am Family Series, engineer, gray, aluminum, 99%, A1 ....**$14.00**
Grey Iron, Am Family Series, mailman, 99%, A1 ....**$16.00**
Grey Iron, Am Family Series, man in traveling suit, 99%, A1 ....**$12.00**
Grey Iron, Am Family Series, newsboy, 98%, A1 ....**$14.00**
Grey Iron, Am Family Series, policeman, wht gloves, 98%, A1..**$14.00**
Grey Iron, Am Family Series, porter, scarce, 99%, A1 .....**$19.00**
Grey Iron, Am Family Series, woman in traveling costume, 97%, A1 ....**$12.00**
Grey Iron, aviator, scarce, 92%, A1 ....**$61.00**
Grey Iron, battery & gun limber w/4 horses & several attached soldiers, EX, A1 ....**$21.00**
Grey Iron, Boy Scout, 98%, A1..**$30.00**
Grey Iron, cadet officer, 98%, A1 ....**$35.00**
Grey Iron, cannon, 1st model, spring action, scarce, 98%, A1..**$51.00**
Grey Iron, cannon, 2nd model, nickel barrel, 98%, A1....**$32.00**
Grey Iron, Clever Clown, Sailor Sam, scarce, 90%, A1 ...**$52.00**
Grey Iron, Company C: officer; bugler; drummer; flag bearer; 6 riflemen; EX+, A1 ....**$53.00**
Grey Iron, cowboy, 99%, A1 ....**$26.00**
Grey Iron, cowboy w/lasso, no lasso, scarce, M, A1 ....**$58.00**
Grey Iron, doctor in wht, Red Cross, scarce, 95%, A1 .....**$40.00**
Grey Iron, Ethiopian chief, scarce, 97%, A1....................**$69.00**
Grey Iron, Foreign Legion, bomber, scarce, 94%, A1 ....**$45.00**
Grey Iron, Foreign Legion, machine gunner, scarce, 98%, A1 ....**$49.00**
Grey Iron, holdup man, blk, NM, A1 ....**$30.00**
Grey Iron, Indian chief w/knife, 98%, A1........................**$32.00**
Grey Iron, Indian on horse, early version, scarce, 97%, A1 ..**$52.00**
Grey Iron, Indian w/hatchet, early version, 97%, A1.......**$20.00**

Grey Iron, infantry officer, NM, A1 ....$22.00
Grey Iron, marine, early version, 99%, A1 ....$29.00
Grey Iron, pirate w/sword, gr, 97%, A1 ....$33.00
Grey Iron, Royal Canadian Police w/rifle, early version, 96%, A1 ....$29.00
Grey Iron, sailor, bl, early version, 96%, A1 ....$22.00
Grey Iron, shell stack for artillery, very scarce, EX+, A1 ..$44.00
Grey Iron, ski trooper, scarce, 97%, A1 ....$51.00
Grey Iron, US Cavalry, officer, early version, scarce, 93%, A1 ....$43.00
Grey Iron, US Cavalry, officer, 97%, A1 ....$45.00
Grey Iron, US Doughboy, bomber crawling, postwar, 95%, A1 ....$28.00
Grey Iron, US Doughboy, bomber crawling, 98%, A1 .....$31.00
Grey Iron, US Doughboy, charging, 99%, A1 ....$23.00
Grey Iron, US Doughboy, early version, 98%, A1 ....$22.00
Grey Iron, US Doughboy, officer, 95%, A1 ....$19.00
Grey Iron, US Doughboy, port of arms, brn leggings & rifle, 97%, A1 ....$21.00
Grey Iron, US Doughboy, port of arms, orange leggings w/brn rifle, 95%, A1 ....$19.00
Grey Iron, US Doughboy, shoulder arms, 97%, A1 ....$21.00
Grey Iron, US Infantry, ammo carrier, very scarce, 98%, A1 .$124.00
Grey Iron, US Infantry, shoulder arms, 97%, A1..............$21.00
Grey Iron, US Infantry, signalman w/flags, 97%, A1........$39.00
Grey Iron, US machine gunner, postwar, 97%, A1 ....$19.00
Grey Iron, US machine gunner, 97%, A1.........................$20.00
Grey Iron, US naval officer, bl, postwar, 98%, A1 ....$16.00
Jones, bull, 99%, A1..$6.00
Jones, calf, #236, 93%, A1 ....$10.00
Jones, donkey, #226, 98%, A1 ....$11.00
Jones, farmer, 99%, A1 ....$19.00
Jones, fox, brn, scarce, 98%, A1 ....$23.00
Jones, fox, gray, scarce, 99%, A1 ....$24.00
Jones, fox, reddish brn, scarce, 97%, A1 ....$22.00
Jones, hen, M, A1 ....$13.00
Jones, Hessian on Guard, w/bayonet, 54mm, scarce, 99%, A1 ....$29.00
Jones, horse, '228,' gray, 98%, A1 ....$11.00
Jones, mule, 99%, A1..$12.00
Jones, pig, brn, 99%, A1 ....$12.00
Jones, Scot Highlander (1814), 54mm, scarce, 98%, A1..$28.00
Jones, sheep grazing, 97%, A1 ....$10.00
Jones, soldier, German, kneeling firing long rifle, 99%, A.$195.00
Jones, soldier, kneeling w/AA gun, khaki, scarce, NM, A1 .$115.00
Jones, soldier, prone firing dbl-barrel machine gun, khaki, scarce, 94%, A1 ....$105.00
Jones, soldier, standing firing rifle, khaki, scarce, 97%, A1 ..$120.00
Jones, soldier, wounded, prone, scarce, 98%, A1 ....$145.00
Jones, soldier, 1775, 54mm, port arms, gr & wht, scarce, .$27.00
Jones, soldier, 1775, 54mm, port arms, metallic bl, scarce, 98%, A1 ....$28.00
Jones, US Marine, 18th C, 54mm, very scarce, 99%, A1 .$39.00
Jones, US Marine, 54mm, shoulder arms, scarce, 98%, A1..$21.00
Jones, Waynes Legion Soldier on Guard, no bayonet, 54mm, scarce, 93%, A1 ....$15.00
Jones, Waynes Legion Soldier on Guard w/Bayonet, 54mm, very scarce, M, A1 ....$32.00
Jones, 1775 British Marine, firing musket at angle, 54mm, scarce, 98%, A1 ....$28.00
Jones, 1775 Officer, w/sword at side, scarce, 95%, A1 ......$28.00
Lineol, German Field Hospital w/2-Horse Team, Doctor & Soldier, EX, A $180.00
Lineol, German Infantry Band, 9-pc, VG+, A................$230.00
Lineol, German Officer Goering, SA uniform, VG, A...$390.00
Lineol, German SA Stand Bearer, tin flag, EX, A $240.00
Lineol, German SA Flag bearer, #36/51, tin flag, EX, A .$160.00
Lineol, German SA Trumpeter, tin flag, unmarked base, EX, A $160.00
Lineol, Hindenberg, #5/3, military parade uniform, NM, A..$170.00
Lineol, Mackensen, #5/6, blk beard, VG, A.....................$50.00
Manoil, Airplane, Bonanza B35, very scarce, 97%, A1 ....$75.00
Manoil, Airplane, Ercoupe, very scarce, 98%, A1 ....$77.00
Manoil, Airplane, Navion, very scarce, 98%, A1 ....$77.00
Manoil, calf bawling, 99%, A1 ....$18.00
Manoil, cannon (coastal defense), brace inside to hold halves together, early version, scarce, 98%, A1 ....$33.00
Manoil, cannon (coastal defense), varient breach & sight, late version, 98%, A1 ....$21.00
Manoil, cannon (elevated), red spoke wheels, 97%, A1 ..$21.00
Manoil, cannon loader, 98%, A1 ....$28.00
Manoil, colt, brown, scarce, 96%, A1 ....$26.00
Manoil, Composition, soldier, machine gunner seated, scarce, 94%, A1 ....$52.00
Manoil, Composition, tank, khaki, scarce, 95%, A1 ....$59.00
Manoil, cow grazing, 99 %, A1...$21.00
Manoil, cowgirl, no horse, 98%, A1 ....$29.00
Manoil, diver, #65 on chest, 96%, A1..............................$31.00
Manoil, doctor, wht, gold cross on cap, 98%, A1 ....$31.00
Manoil, doctor, wht, red cross on cap, 95%, A1 ....$28.00
Manoil, ensign, 98%, A1 ....$30.00
Manoil, Happy Farm Series, bench, 97%, A1 ....$14.00
Manoil, Happy Farm Series, Black boy eating watermelon, very scarce, 95%, A1 ....$95.00
Manoil, Happy Farm Series, blacksmith making horseshoes, 97%, A1 ....$25.00
Manoil, Happy Farm Series, blacksmith w/wheel, 99%, A1 ....$29.00
Manoil, Happy Farm Series, brick mason, scarce, 98%, A1 ....$41.00
Manoil, Happy Farm Series, carpenter carrying door, 98%, A1...$67.00
Manoil, Happy Farm Series, carpenter sawing wood, scarce, 96%, A1 ....$25.00
Manoil, Happy Farm Series, couple on park bench, gray, wht,95%, A1 ....$35.00
Manoil, Happy Farm Series, farm woman lifting hen off nest, 96%, A1 ....$23.00
Manoil, Happy Farm Series, farm woman w/butter churn, 97%, A1 ....$24.00
Manoil, Happy Farm Series, farmer at pump, 97%, A1 ....$23.00
Manoil, Happy Farm Series, farmer cutting corn, 97%, A1...$24.00
Manoil, Happy Farm Series, farmer cutting w/scythe, 99%, A1...$29.00
Manoil, Happy Farm Series, farmer sowing grain, 98%, A1 ..$26.00
Manoil, Happy Farm Series, girl, wht dress, 95%, A1 ....$9.00

Manoil, Happy Farm Series, hound dog, 98%, A1 .... $24.00
Manoil, Happy Farm Series, man dumping wheelbarrow, 96%, A1 .... $25.00
Manoil, Happy Farm Series, man juggling barrel, very scarce, 97%, A1 .... $77.00
Manoil, Happy Farm Series, scarecrow, straw hat, 92%, A1 .... $18.00
Manoil, Happy Farm Series, scarecrow, 98%, A1 .... $24.00
Manoil, Happy Farm Series, shoe cobbler, scarce, 94%, A1 .. $29.00
Manoil, hostess, gr, scarce, 98%, A1 .... $72.00
Manoil, marine, 2nd version, 98%, A1 .... $30.00
Manoil, motorcyclist, '52,' 95%, A1 .... $44.00
Manoil, My Ranch Corral Series, cactus, 98%, A1 .... $38.00
Manoil, My Ranch Corral Series, colt, maroon, scarce, 99%, A1 .... $29.00
Manoil, navy gunner, M, A1 .... $42.00
Manoil, nurse, postwar, bl bowl, 94%, A1 .... $21.00
Manoil, officer, 96%, A1 .... $26.00
Manoil, oil tanker, red, scarce, 95%, A1 .... $39.00
Manoil, oil tanker, red & silver, scarce, 98%, A1 .... $43.00
Manoil, parachutist, scarce, 95%, A1 .... $50.00
Manoil, roadster, futuristic, scarce, 95%, A1 .... $68.00
Manoil, roadster, vertical grill, red, scarce, 97%, A1 .... $43.00
Manoil, sailor, 2nd version, 96%, A1 .... $30.00
Manoil, sedan, scarce, 98%, A1 .... $64.00
Manoil, soldier, barbed-wire carrier, 97%, A1 .... $73.00
Manoil, soldier, bomb thrower, 2 grenades in pouch, 98%, A1 .... $33.00
Manoil, soldier, bugler, M, A1 .... $30.00
Manoil, soldier, in gas mask w/flare pistol, scarce, 93%, A1 .. $42.00
Manoil, soldier, in poncho, 97%, A1 .... $47.00
Manoil, soldier, machine gunner, prone, grass on base, 97%, A1 .... $32.00
Manoil, soldier, machine gunner, w/backpack, sm, 95%, A1 . $26.00
Manoil, soldier, mine detector, 98%, A1 .... $39.00
Manoil, soldier, observer, 97%, A1 .... $44.00
Manoil, soldier, parade, 98%, A1 .... $36.00
Manoil, soldier, Postwar, sniper on 1 knee pointing gun up, thin, scarce, 96%, A1 .... $65.00
Manoil, soldier, sharpshooter, prone, camouflaged, 97%, A1 .... $34.00
Manoil, soldier, sitting, 96%, A1 .... $35.00
Manoil, soldier, sniper, camouflaged, pnt flowers, 98%, A1 .. $35.00
Manoil, soldier, sniper kneeling, 97%, A1 .... $28.00
Manoil, soldier, sniper standing, 98%, A1 .... $30.00
Manoil, soldier, stretcher bearer, no medical kit, 98%, A1 . $29.00
Manoil, soldier, w/trench mortar, 97%, A1 .... $28.00
Manoil, soup kitchen, '70,' sm, A1 .... $29.00
Manoil, tractor, loop in front, 97%, A1 .... $28.00
Manoil, tractor, plain front, 97%, A1 .... $24.00
Mignot, American Indians, 7-pc, VG (worn box), A $100.00
Mignot, Ancient Greek Cavalry, 6-pc, M (EX box), A . $300.00
Mignot, Assyrians, #2, 8-pc, VG+ (worn box), A $230.00
Mignot, Austrian Infantry, #43, standing, 12-pc, EX-NM, A $160.00
Mignot, Austrians, #37, VG+ (orig box), A $80.00
Mignot, Austrians, 1914, bl uniforms, 12-pc, EX (EX box), A $170.00
Mignot, Austrians Marching, #37, 12-pc, EX (worn box), A $220.00
Mignot, Bulgares, #51, 12-pc, EX (taped box), A $200.00
Mignot, Chinese Marching, #99, 11-pc, EX (worn box), A .. $210.00
Mignot, Chinois, #242, 12-pc, EX (EX box), A $200.00
Mignot, Egyptian Infantry, VG+ (orig box), A $190.00
Mignot, Egyptians, #1, 12-pc, VG+ (worn box), A $260.00
Mignot, Egyptians, 12-pc, EX (worn box), A $350.00
Mignot, English, #29, firing, 12-pc, EX-NM (orig box), A $170.00
Mignot, English Grenadiers, #210, 12-pc, EX (orig box), A . $200.00
Mignot, English Infantry (1812), #44, NMIB, A $180.00
Mignot, Fourth Swiss Regiment (1812), #41A, EX (orig box), A $170.00
Mignot, Francs Marching, #6, EX (orig box), A $200.00
Mignot, French Guards, #19, VG+ (orig box), A $200.00
Mignot, French 16th Century Marching Infantry, #13, 13-pc, EX (orig box), A $210.00
Mignot, Gardes Francaises Louis XVI, 12-pc, VG (VG box), A $225.00
Mignot, Gauls in Combat, #4, 10-pc, EX (orig box), A . $260.00
Mignot, Grade Fanchise, #17, bl uniform, 12-pc, VG+ (orig box), A $180.00
Mignot, Greek Infantry, 11-pc, VG (VG box), A $250.00
Mignot, Greeks Marching, #3, 12-pc, NMIB, A $260.00
Mignot, Grenadiers de la Garde 1812, 12-pc, NMIB, A ... $150.00
Mignot, Hallebardiers XV Siecle, 12-pc, VG (VG box), A $235.00
Mignot, Henry IV Pikesmen Marching, #14, 12-pc, VG (orig box), A $240.00
Mignot, Highlanders Marching, #76, 12-pc, EX+ (orig box), A $100.00
Mignot, Infantry of the Line, #35, 12-pc, VG (orig box), A $80.00
Mignot, Italian Legere Infantry, #39, EX+ (orig box), A .. $180.00
Mignot, Japanese Infantry, #98, 12-pc, EX+ (orig box), A ... $220.00
Mignot, Lafayette, #439, EX, A $30.00
Mignot, Louis XIV Infantry, #15, bl, VG+ (orig box), A .. $200.00
Mignot, Louis XIV Infantry, #17, 12-pc, VG+, A $200.00
Mignot, Louis XVI Swiss Guards, #21/C, 12-pc, EX+ (orig box), A $170.00

Mignot, Lucotte French Napoleonic Horse-Drawn Gun Team, M (EX box), A, $600.00.

Mignot, Medieval Infantry, 12-pc, NMIB, A $275.00
Mignot, Mousquetaires, 6-pc, EX (EX box), A $325.00
Mignot, Prussian Assault, 12-pc, NMIB, A $300.00
Mignot, Regiment Suisse (1812), 12-pc, NMIB, A $235.00

Mignot, Romans Marching, #5, 12-pc, EX+ (orig box), A...**$260.00**
Mignot, Russian Infantry, 12-pc, EX (EX box), A..........**$300.00**
Mignot, Sakalaves Firing, #245, 14-pc, EX (taped box), A ...**$300.00**
Mignot, Siamese Firing, 12-pc, VG (worn box), A **$350.00**
Mignot, VIII Regiment Bavarois (1812), 12-pc, NMIB, A .**$225.00**
Mignot, West Point Cadets, #500, 24-pc, VG+ (orig box), A **$360.00**
Mignot, West Point Cadets, #501, summer dress, 24-pc, EX, A **$310.00**
Mignot, 13th & 14th Century Archers, 12-pc, EX (worn box), A **$200.00**
Mignot, 210 Grenadiers Anglais, #210, 12-pc, VG (VG box), A...**$150.00**

Sporting Collectibles

Baseball — the great American Pastime — has given us hundreds of real-life sports heroes plus a great amount of collectible memorabilia. Baseball gloves, bats, game-worn uniforms, ephemera of many types, even games and character watches are among the many items being sought out today. And there are fans of basketball, football, and hockey that are just as avid in their collecting.

As you can see, many of our listings describe Kenner's Starting Lineup figures. These small plastic likenesses of famous sports greats were first produced in 1988. New they can be purchased for $5.00 to $8.00 (though some may go a little higher), but they have wonderful potential to appreciate. As the sports' stars fluctuate in popularity, so do their Starting Lineup figures. Some may occasionally sell for several hundred dollars, but on the average most from 1988 run from $25.00 to $50.00. Football and basketball series have been made as well, and in 1993 Kenner added hockey. If you're going to collect them, be critical of the condition of the packaging.

Bobbin' head dolls made of papier-mache were manufactured in Japan during the 1960s until about 1972 and were sold at ball parks, stadiums, and through the mail for about $2.98. They were about 7" high or so, hand painted and then varnished. Some of them represent sports teams and their mascots. Depending on scarcity and condition, they'll run from as low as $35.00 up to $100.00, though there are some that sell for $300.00 or so. A few were modeled in the likeness of a particular sports star; these are rare and when they can be found sell in the $500.00 to $1,000.00 range. Base colors indicate when the doll was made. During 1961 and '62, white bases were used; today these are very scarce. Green bases are from 1962 until '66, and gold bases were used from 1967 until 1972. Mascot-heads are favored by collectors, and football figures are becoming very collectible as well. Our advisor has prepared a *Bobbin' Head Guide,* with a rarity scale and current values. See Dealer Codes for his address.

Advisor: Tim Hunter (H13).

See also Cereal Boxes; Character Clocks and Watches; Games.

Andy Carey, pin-back button, 1950s, photo on gray background, 2" dia, EX, A **$25.00**
Babe Ruth, autographed baseball, Reach, Official American League, NMIB **$1,200.00**

Bill Dickey, windup toy, 1940s, celluloid, NM, J6, $150.00.

Photo courtesy June Moon

Bo Jackson, autographed football, M...............................**$175.00**
Bob Turley, pin-back button, 1950s, photo on gray background, 2" dia, EX, A **$25.00**
Brett Hull, hockey stick, signed, EX...............................**$125.00**
Cleveland Indians, pin-back button, 1950s, Cleveland Indians Am League & baseball design, 1¾" dia, from $25 to.**$45.00**
Dave McNally, record, Theory of Pitching, Sports Stars, 1972, 33 rpm, M (NM jacket), J5.......................................**$25.00**
Hakeem Olajuwon, Houston Rockets jersey, replica, EX .**$175.00**
Hank Aaron, pin-back button, Thanks Milwaukee, 1954-76, full-color image w/blk lettering, 2¼", EX, J5 ....**$15.00**
Harlem Globetrotters, film, Castle Films, 1950s, 8mm, EX (EX box), M17 ....**$25.00**
Harlem Globetrotters, yearbook, 1963, NM, M17............**$25.00**
Jackie Robinson, pin-back button, 1950s, photo on lt bl background, 1¾" dia, EX, A **$60.00**
Joe Dimaggio, baseball shoes, NMIB, D10......................**$400.00**
Joe Dimaggio, pin-back button, 1950s, photo on lt bl background, 1¾" dia, EX, from $50 to..............................**$75.00**
Joe Dimaggio, wallet, 1950s, leather w/cartoon image of Dimaggio & facsimile signature, zipper closure, EX, A **$300.00**
Joe Garagiola, book, Baseball Is a Funny Game, 1960, w/autograph, EX **$25.00**
Joe Namath, doll, Ace Novelty, in San Francisco 49ers uniform, stuffed cloth, 25", EX **$40.00**
Joe Namath, doll, Mego, 1970, 11½", rare, MIB **$325.00**
Los Angeles Dodgers, doll, 1960s, stuffed cloth, 12", VG.**$25.00**
Louisville Slugger, bank, 1970s, red plastic stand holds 10 baseball bats w/Astros, Mets, Reds... logo, EX, A **$35.00**
Michael Jordon, poster, life-size, signed, EX......................**$65.00**
Mickey Mantle, pin-back button, 1950s, photo on lt bl background, 1¾" dia, EX, from $50 to..............................**$75.00**

Mickey Mantle & Roger Maris, poster, 1960s, blk & wht side-by-side photos, 11x17", EX, from $40 to **$60.00**
Muhammad Ali, boxing gloves, When We Were Kings, promotional issue, full-sz, EX **$40.00**
Muhammad Ali & Joe Frazier, film, Joe Frazier Vs Ali, Columbia, 8mm, MIB (sealed), P3 ....**$30.00**
New York Knicks, bear, Good Stuff, 1991, stuffed plush w/uniform & ball, 6", NM **$20.00**
New York Yankees, pin-back button, 1950s, New York Yankees Am League & baseball design, 1¾" dia, from $25 to .**$45.00**
NFL Players, footlocker toy chest, features Dick Butkus, Daryle Lamonica, etc, EX, J2 ....**$100.00**
Nolan Ryan, game, Arcade Strike Zone, electronic baseball w/autograph, EX...**$55.00**
Pee Wee Reese & Jackie Robinson, record, Columbia, 1949, 78 rpm, VG (VG sleeve), A **$50.00**
Phil Rizzuto, pin-back button, 1950s, photo on wht background, 1¾" dia, EX, A...**$40.00**
Roger Maris, pin-back button, 1950s, photo on yel background, 3¼" dia, EX, from $50 to **$75.00**
St Louis Cardinals, doll, 1960s, stuffed cloth w/vinyl head & hands, EX **$65.00**
Ty Cobb, doll, Ideal, 1911, compo head & hands w/stuffed cloth body & limbs, MIB **$400.00**
White Sox, ring, baseball shape, NM, J2..........................**$45.00**
Whitey Ford, pin-back button, 1950s, photo on gray background, w/attached bl & wht ribbon, 2" dia, EX, A...**$40.00**
World Wrestling Federation, belt, aqua w/WWF logo on plastic buckle, EX, F1 ....**$10.00**
World Wrestling Federation, doll, Hulk Hogan, Ace Novelty, 1991, stuffed cloth, 42", EX, F1 ....**$50.00**
World Wrestling Federation, figure, Ultimate Warrior or Big Boss Man, PVC, 3", EX, F1, ea **$5.00**
World Wrestling Federation, kite, Ultimate Warrior, Spectra, 1990, 4½-ft, MIP, F1 ....**$15.00**
World Wrestling Federation, pillow, Hulk Hogan, Big Boss Man or Jake the Snake, Ace Novelty, 1991, 5x5", EX, F1, ea **$5.00**
World Wrestling Federation, Sparkle Art, Hulk Hogan, Colorforms, 1991, MIB, F1 ....**$15.00**
World Wrestling Federation, sticker album w/decoder, Hulk Hogan's Rock 'N Wrestling, Diamond Pub, 1986, 32 pgs, EX, F1...**$20.00**
Yogi Berra, cup, 1960s, wht plastic w/bl image of Yogi on front & Yoo Hoo logo on back, 5", EX, J5 ....**$50.00**

Bobbin' Head Dolls

Atlanta Braves, team mascot, 1967-72, gold base...........**$135.00**
Atlanta Falcons, 1967, rnd gold base **$75.00**
Baltimore Bullets, Little Dribblers.................................**$200.00**
Baltimore Colts, 1966-68, realistic face, rnd gold base ...**$250.00**
Baltimore Orioles, team mascot, 1961-62, wht base, rare, minimum value **$350.00**
Boston Patriots, Type VI, lg shoulder pads, from $300 to **$400.00**
Chicago Bears, Black player, 1965, gold base..................**$350.00**
Chicago Bears, 1967, rnd gold base...............................**$100.00**
Cincinnati Reds, Black Player, 1962-66, gr base **$1,500.00**
Cleveland Indians, team mascot, 1961-62, sq wht base, rare..**$485.00**
Dallas Cowboys, 1965, rnd base **$200.00**
Detroit Tigers, team mascot, 1962-66, gr base, minimum value **$180.00**
Green Bay Packers, 1967, gold base, NM........................**$150.00**
Harlem Globetrotters, 1962 ....**$350.00**
Houston Oilers, 1966-67, rnd gold base **$55.00**
Kansas City Chiefs, 1968, rnd gold base, from $50 to.......**$75.00**
Kansas State Wildcats, rnd gr base **$45.00**
Los Angeles Dodgers, Black player, 1962-66, gr base **$800.00**
Los Angeles Lakers, 1962 ....**$225.00**
Los Angeles Rams, 1966-68, rnd gold base **$75.00**
Mickey Mantle, 1961-62, sq or rnd wht base, ea **$600.00**
Minnesota Vikings, sq gold base, from $100 to..............**$150.00**
New York Mets, 1960-61, sq bl base **$200.00**
New York Yankees, 1961-62, wht base, minimum value ..**$225.00**
Philadelphia Eagles, 1961-62, 1960 Champions emb on gr base, scarce **$135.00**
Roger Maris, 1961-62, sq wht base **$485.00**
Seattle Sonics, 1967, yel uniform **$225.00**
St Louis Cardinals, team mascot, 1961-62, wht base, minimum value..**$400.00**
Washington Redskins, Merger series, rnd gold base **$200.00**
Willie Mays, 1961-62, lt face, rnd wht base **$300.00**

Kenner Starting Lineup Figures

Andre Dawson, 1988, MIP, O1 ....**$15.00**
Babe Ruth & Lou Gehrig, 1989, MIP **$35.00**
Darryl Strawberry, 1988, MIP, O1...................................**$12.00**
Dave Winfield, 1988, MIP, B10 ....**$40.00**
Don Mattingly, 1988, MIP **$30.00**
Gale Sayers, MIP...**$25.00**
Jack Clark, 1988, MIP, B10 ....**$20.00**
Jerome Walton, 1989, w/Rookie of the Year collector card, MIP, H4 ....**$60.00**
Joe Montana, 1990, MIP, H4 ....**$45.00**
John Tyler, 1990, MIP, H4...**$15.00**
Johnny Bench & Pete Rose, 1989, MIP **$45.00**
Johnny Unitas, MIP, B10 ....**$35.00**
Jose Canseco, 1990, MIP, H4 ....**$15.00**
Kevin Mitchell, 1990, MIP, H4...**$15.00**
Larry Bird, 1988, MIP, O1 ....**$110.00**
Magic Johnson, 1988, M, B10 ....**$25.00**
Matt Williams, 1991, w/collector coin, MIP, H4..............**$45.00**
Nolan Ryan, 1988, MIP..**$300.00**
Pete Rose, 1988, M, B10..**$20.00**
Reggie Miller, 1995, MIP, O1...**$35.00**
Rick Reuschel, 1988, MIP, H4 ....**$15.00**
Robby Thompson, 1989, MIP, H4 ....**$10.00**
Steve Sax, 1989, w/Rookie of the Year collector card, MIP, H4 ....**$75.00**
Wade Boggs, 1989, w/Rookie of the Year collector card, MIP, H4 ....**$35.00**
Wally Joyner, 1988, MIP **$15.00**
Will Clark, 1990, MIP, H4 ....**$20.00**
Wilt Chamberlin, MIP, B10 ....**$40.00**

Star Trek

The Star Trek concept was introduced to the public in the mid-1960s via a TV series which continued for many years in syndication. The impact it had on American culture has spaned two generations of loyal fans through its animated TV cartoon series (1977), six major motion pictures, Fox network's 1987 TV show, 'Star Trek, The Next Generation,' and two other television series, 'Deep Space 9' and 'Voyager.' As a result of its success, vast amounts of merchandise (both licensed and unlicensed) has been marketed in a wide variety of items including jewelry, clothing, calendars, collector plates, comics, costumes, games, greeting and gum cards, party goods, magazines, model kits, posters, puzzles, records and tapes, school supplies, and toys. Packaging is very important; an item mint and in its original box is generally worth 75% to 100% more than one rated excellent.

Other Sources: P3

See also Character and Promotional Drinking Glasses; Fast-Food Collectibles; Halloween Costumes; Lunch Boxes; Model Kits.

Figures

Applause, Deep Space 9, Sisko, Odo, Quark or Kira Nerys, 10", MIP, H4, ea....**$10.00**
Applause, Generations, Kirk, Picard, Riker, Data, Worf or Laforge, 10", MIP, H4/F1, ea....**$10.00**
Ertl, Star Trek III, Kirk, 3¾", MOC....**$25.00**
Ertl, Star Trek III, Klingon Leader, 3¾", MOC....**$30.00**
Ertl, Star Trek III, Scotty, 3¾", MOC....**$25.00**
Ertl, Star Trek III, Spock, 3¾", MOC....**$30.00**
Galoob, STNG, Data, 1st series, bl or spotted face, 3¾", MOC....**$125.00**
Galoob, STNG, Data, 2nd series, 3¾", MOC, H4....**$40.00**
Galoob, STNG, Data, 3rd series, 3¾", MOC, H4....**$20.00**
Galoob, STNG, Data, 4th series, 3¾", MOC, H4....**$8.00**
Galoob, STNG, Ferengi, 3¾", MOC, H4....**$12.00**
Galoob, STNG, LaForge, 3¾", MOC, H4....**$12.00**
Galoob, STNG, Picard, 3¾", MOC, H4....**$12.00**
Galoob, STNG, Riker, 3¾", MOC, H4....**$12.00**
Galoob, STNG, Tasha Yar, 3¾", MOC, H4....**$20.00**
Galoob, STNG, Worf, 3¾", MOC, H4....**$12.00**
Mego, 1974-76, Cheron, 2nd series, 8", MOC, from $250 to ..**$300.00**
Mego, 1974-76, Gorn, 2nd series, 8", MOC, from $300 to ..**$350.00**
Mego, 1974-76, Kirk, 1st series, 8", MOC....**$55.00**
Mego, 1974-76, Klingon, 1st series, 8", MOC....**$55.00**
Mego, 1974-76, McCoy, 1st series, 8", MOC, from $150 to....**$175.00**
Mego, 1974-76, Spock, 1st series, 8", MOC....**$55.00**
Mego, 1974-76, The Keeper, 2nd series, 8", MOC, from $250 to....**$300.00**
Mego, 1974-76, Uhura, 1st series, 8", MOC, from $150 to...**$175.00**
Mego, 1979, Motion Picture, Arcturian, 12", MIB, from $100 to....**$125.00**
Mego, 1979, Motion Picture, Decker, 3¾", MOC, from $20 to....**$30.00**

Mego, Cheron, 12", NM, $85.00; Mego, The Keeper, missing footwear, NM, $100.00.

Mego, 1979, Motion Picture, Ilia, 12", MIB, from $75 to ..**$100.00**
Mego, 1979, Motion Picture, Ilia, 3¾", MOC, from $15 to ..**$20.00**
Mego, 1979, Motion Picture, Kirk, 12", MIB, from $100 to....**$125.00**
Mego, 1979, Motion Picture, Kirk, 3¾", MOC, from $40 to....**$50.00**
Mego, 1979, Motion Picture, Klingon, 12", MIB, from $200 to....**$250.00**
Mego, 1979, Motion Picture, McCoy, 3¾", MOC, from $40 to....**$50.00**
Mego, 1979, Motion Picture, Scotty, 3¾", MOC, from $20 to....**$30.00**
Mego, 1979, Motion Picture, Spock, 12", MIB, from $100 to....**$125.00**
Mego, 1979, Motion Picture, Spock, 3¾", MOC, from $40 to....**$50.00**
Playmates, Deep Space 9, O'Brien, Quark, Morn, Gil Dukat or Kira, MOC, F1, ea....**$15.00**
Playmates, Generations, Admiral Kirk, MOC, F1....**$25.00**
Playmates, Generations, Picard, Riker, Worf, Data, Guinan, Bev Crusher, Dr Soran, Troi, LaForge, MOC, F1, ea....**$20.00**
Playmates, STNG, Data, Borg, Troi, LaForge or Picard, 1st series, MOC, F1, ea....**$20.00**

Playsets and Accessories

Command Communications Console, Mego, 1976, MIB..**$150.00**
Communicator Set, Mego, 1974, complete, MIB....**$125.00**
Mission to Gamma VI, Mego, 1975, rare, MIB, from $700 to....**$950.00**
Telescreen Console, Mego, 1975, MIB....**$125.00**
Transporter Room, Mego, 1975, MIB....**$125.00**
USS Enterprise Bridge, Mego, 1975, MIB....**$125.00**

Vehicles

Ferengi Fighter, STNG, Galoob, 1989, NRFB, H4....**$55.00**
Klingon Warship, Dinky, MIB, from $75 to....**$85.00**

Klingon Warship, Star Trek II, Corgi #149, MOC **$25.00**
Shuttlecraft Galileo, STNG, Galoob, 1989, NRFB, H4...**$50.00**
USS Enterprise, Motion Picture, Dinky #803, 1979, 4", MOC **$30.00**
USS Enterprise, Star Trek II, Corgi, 1982, MOC, from $18 to **$25.00**

Miscellaneous

Activity Set, Mix N' Mold casting set, Captain Kirk, Mr Spock or Dr McCoy, MIB, ea **$65.00**
Binoculars, Larami, MOC....................**$80.00**
Book, Mission to Horatius, Whitman, 1968, hardcover, VG, F8 ....**$20.00**
Book, Star Trek Quiz Book, Signet, 1977, softcover, VG, P3 ....**$5.00**
Book, Star Trek 4, Bantam, 1971, softcover, EX, P3...........**$5.00**
Book & Record Set, Passage to Moauv, Peter Pan, 1979, MIP, F1 ....**$10.00**
Bop Bag, Spock, 1975, M....................**$50.00**
Collector Plate, 1st series, Ernst Enterprises, any of crew or crew scene, M, ea **$40.00**
Communicators (Wrist), Motion Picture, 1974, MIB **$100.00**
Doll, Captain Kirk, Knickerbocker, 1979, stuffed cloth w/vinyl head, 12", MIB, H4....................**$50.00**
Doll, Mr Spock, Knickerbocker, 1979, stuffed cloth w/vinyl head, 12", MIB....................**$50.00**
Iron-On Transfers, 4 different, General Mills, 1979, M, ea...**$5.00**
Kite, Star Trek III, M....................**$25.00**
Ornament, Enterprise Ship, Hallmark, 1st series, MIB, H4 .**$350.00**
Patch, Motion Picture, Kirk & Spock, M....................**$35.00**
Playing Cards, Star Trek: The Wrath of Khan, complete, MIB.**$15.00**
Postcard Set, Star Trek: The Motion Picture, 1979, complete, M **$40.00**
Puzzle Cube, STNG, Applause, turn cube to reveal 9 photos, M, F1....................**$5.00**
Rubber Stamp, Motion Picture, M **$8.00**
Sticker Book, Jeopardy at Jutterdon, Whitman, 1979, unused, NM, F8....................**$45.00**
Sticker Book, STNG, Panini, 1992, unused, EX, F1...........**$5.00**
Tablet, 1967, features Captain Kirk w/phaser rifle, unused, NM, T2....................**$20.00**
Wastebasket, Motion Picture, M **$35.00**

Star Wars

The original 'Star Wars' movie was a phenomenal box office hit of the late 1970s, no doubt due to its ever-popular space travel theme and fantastic special effects. A sequel called 'Empire Strikes Back' (1980) and a third hit called 'Return of the Jedi' (1983) did just as well. As a result, an enormous amount of related merchandise was released — most of which was made by the Kenner Company. Palitoy of London supplied England and other overseas countries with Kenner's products and also made some toys that were never distributed in America. Until 1980 the logo of the 20th Century Fox studios (under whom the toys were licensed) appeared on each item; just before the second movie, 'Star Wars' creator, George Lucas, regained control of the merchandise rights, and items inspired by the last two films can be identified by his own Lucasfilm logo. Since 1987 Lucasfilm, Ltd., has operated shops in conjunction with the Star Tours at Disneyland theme parks.

The first action figures to be introduced were Luke Skywalker, Princess Leia, R2-D2, and Chewbacca. Because of delays in production that prevented Kenner from getting them on the market in time for Christmas, the company issued 'early bird' certificates so that they could be ordered by mail when they became available. In all, more than ninety action figures were designed. The last figures to be issued were the 'Power of the Force' series (1985), which though of more recent vintage are steadily climbing in value. A collector coin was included on each 'Power of the Force' card.

Original packaging is very important in assessing a toy's worth. As each movie was released, packaging was updated, making approximate dating relatively simple. A figure on an original 'Star Wars' card is worth more than the same character on an 'Empire Strikes Back' card, etc.; and the same 'Star Wars' figure valued at $50.00 in mint-on-card condition might be worth as little as $5.00 'loose.'

Especially prized are the original 12-back Star Wars cards (meaning twelve figures were shown on the back). Second issue cards showed eight more, and so on. Unpunched cards tend to be valued at about 15% to 20% more than punched cards, and naturally if the proof of purchase has been removed, the value of the card is less. (These could be mailed in to receive newly introduced figures before they appeared on the market.) A figure in a factory (Kenner) bag is valued at $2.00 to $3.00 more than it is worth loose, and an original backing card adds about $1.00 to $2.00. In our listings, you'll find many of these variations noted. These have been included for the information of potential buyers; remember, pricing is not a science — it hinges on many factors. For more information we recommend *Modern Toys, American Toys, 1930 to 1980,* by Linda Baker.

Advisor: George Downes (D8).

Other Sources: B3, B10, D4, D9, J2, J8, O1, P3

See also Character and Promotional Drinking Glasses; Coloring, Activity, and Paint Books; Fast-Food Collectibles; Halloween Costumes; Model Kits; Trading Cards.

Key:
ESB — Empire Strikes Back
POTF — Power of the Force
ROTJ — Return of the Jedi
SW — Star Wars
* — proof of purchase removed

Figures

A-Wing Pilot, POTF, 3¾", MOC (unpunched), H4 .....**$140.00**
Admiral Ackbar, ROTJ, 3¾", MOC, H4....................**$25.00**
Amanaman, POTF, 3¾", MOC, H4....................**$100.00**
Anakin Skywalker, POTF, 3¾", from $30 to....................**$40.00**
Anakin Skywalker, SW, 3¾", w/accessories, NM, H4......**$30.00**
AT-AT Commander, ESB, 3¾", NM (G card), H4.........**$25.00**
AT-AT Commander, ESB, 3¾", w/accessories, NM, H4.**$10.00**

AT-AT Commander, ROTJ, 3¾", MOC* (unpunched), H4 .... $20.00
AT-AT Driver, ESB, 3¾", w/accessories, NM, H4 .... $10.00
AT-AT Driver, ROTJ, 3¾", MOC*, H4 .... $32.00
AT-ST Driver, ROTJ, 3¾", MOC, H4 .... $22.00
AT-ST Driver, ROTJ, 3¾", w/accessories, NM, H4 .... $8.00
B-Wing Pilot, POTF, 3¾", MOC (unpunched), H4 .... $20.00
B-Wing Pilot, ROTJ, 3¾", MOC*, H4 .... $15.00
Barada, POTF, 3¾", complete w/coin, NM, H4 .... $40.00
Barada, POTF, 3¾", MOC, H4 .... $60.00
Ben Obi-Wan Kenobi, POTF, 3¾", MOC (unpunched), H4 .... $130.00
Ben Obi-Wan Kenobi, SW, 3¾", M (NM 20-back card), H4 .... $170.00
Ben Obi-Wan Kenobi, SW, 3¾", no accessories, VG, H4 . $8.00
Ben Obi-Wan Kenobi, SW, 3¾", w/accessories, NM, H4 .. $20.00
Ben Obi-Wan Kenobi, 12", MIB, from $350 to $375.00
Bespin Security Guard, ESB, 3¾", Black or Caucasian, MOC (unpunched), H4 .... $40.00
Bespin Security Guard, ESB, 3¾", Black or Caucasian, w/accessories, NM, H4, ea $8.00
Bib Fortuna, ROTJ, 3¾", MOC, H4 .... $20.00
Bib Fortuna, ROTJ, 3¾", w/accessories, NM, H4 .... $10.00
Biker Scout, ROTJ, 3¾", MOC (unpunched), H4 .... $32.00
Boba Fett, SW, 3¾", MOC (unpunched), H4 .... $165.00
Boba Fett, 12", NM (VG box*), H4 .... $265.00
Bossk, ESB, 3¾", Bounty Hunter outfit, w/accessories, NM, H4. $10.00
Bossk, ESB, 3¾", MOC (unpunched), H4 .... $45.00
C-3PO, SW, 3¾", w/accessories, NM, H4 .... $10.00
C-3P0, 12", EX (VG box*), H4 .... $130.00
Chewbacca, ESB, 3¾", MOC (unpunched), H4 .... $40.00
Chewbacca, POTF, 3¾", MOC, from $125 to $135.00
Chewbacca, SW, 3¾", M (EX 20-back card), H4 .... $100.00
Chief Chirpa, ROTJ, 3¾", MOC (unpunched), H4 .... $30.00
Chief Chirpa, ROTJ, 3¾", MOC*, H4 .... $25.00
Chief Chirpa, ROTJ, 3¾", w/accessories, NM, H4 .... $8.00
Cloud Car Pilot, ESB, 3¾", w/accessories, NM, H4 .... $18.00
Cloud Car Pilot, ROTJ, 3¾", MOC* $35.00
Darth Vader, ROTJ, 3¾", MOC, H4 .... $40.00
Darth Vader, SW, 3¾", w/accessories, NM, H4 .... $15.00
Death Squad Commander, ESB, 3¾", MOC $75.00
Death Squad Commander, SW, 3¾", M (EX 20-back card), H4 .... $90.00
Death Star Droid, ESB, 3¾", MOC $125.00
Death Star Droid, SW, 3¾", w/accessories, NM, H4 .... $15.00
Dengar, ESB, 3¾", NMOC (41-back), H4 .... $55.00
Dengar, ESB, 3¾", w/accessories, NM, H4 .... $8.00
Dengar, ROTJ, 3¾", MOC (unpunched), H4 .... $30.00
Dulok Scout, Ewoks, 3¾", MOC $15.00
Emperor, ROTJ, 3¾", w/accessories, NM, H4 .... $10.00
Emperor, ROTJ, 3¾, MOC $35.00
Emperors Royal Guard, ROTJ, 3¾", w/accessories, NM, H4.. $10.00
FX-7, ESB, 3¾", MOC (unpunched), H4 .... $40.00
FX-7, ESB, 3¾", w/accessories, NM, H4 .... $10.00
Gammorean Guard, ROTJ, 3¾", MOC*, H4 .... $18.00
General Madine, ROTJ, 3¾", MOC, H4 .... $18.00
General Madine, ROTJ, 3¾", w/accessories, NM, H4 .... $8.00
Greedo, ESB, 3¾", MOC, from $85 to $100.00

Greedo, ROTJ, 3¾", MOC, $30.00.

Greedo, SW, 3¾", MOC (21-back), H4 .... $160.00
Greedo, SW, 3¾", w/accessories, NM, H4 .... $10.00
Hammerhead, ESB, 3¾", MOC (unpunched), H4 .... $70.00
Hammerhead, SW, 3¾", w/accessories, NM, H4 .... $10.00
Han Solo, ESB, 3¾", Bespin outfit, w/accessories, NM, H4.. $15.00
Han Solo, ESB, 3¾", Hoth Gear, w/accessories, NM, H4 .. $15.00
Han Solo, POTF, 3¾", Carbonite Chamber outfit, MOC, from $100 to $125.00
Han Solo, ROTJ, 3¾", lg head, MOC*, H4 .... $85.00
Han Solo, ROTJ, 3¾", sm head, Bespin outfit, MOC*, H4.. $50.00
Han Solo, SW, 3¾", MOC (21-back), H4 .... $120.00
Han Solo, 12", NM (VG box*), H4 .... $375.00
IG-88, ESB, 3¾", w/accessories, NM, H4 .... $15.00

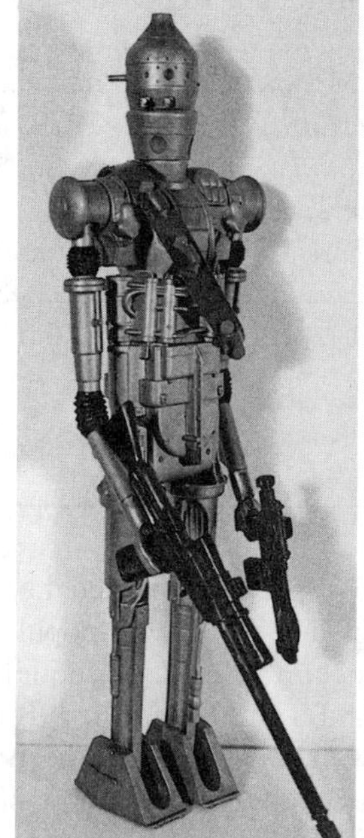

Photo courtesy June Moon

IG-88, 12", complete, M, J6, $285.00.

Imperial Commander, ESB, 3¾", MOC (41-back), H4.... $55.00
Imperial Commander, ESB, 3¾", MOC (47-back), H4.... $30.00

Imperial Commander, ESB, 3¾", w/accessories, NM, H4...$8.00
Imperial Commander, ROTJ, 3¾", MOC, H4...$25.00
Imperial Dignitary, POTF, 3¾", MOC, H4...$80.00
Imperial Gunner, POTF, 3¾", MOC...$100.00
Imperial Stormtrooper, ESB, 3¾", Hoth gear, MOC, MOC (unpunched), H4...$40.00
Imperial Stormtrooper, ESB, 3¾", MOC (41-back), H4...$30.00
Imperial TIE Fighter Pilot, ROTJ, 3¾", MOC (unpunched), H4...$45.00
Imperial TIE Fighter Pilot, ROTJ, 3¾", w/accessories, NM H4...$12.00
Jawa, ESB, 3¾", MOC, from $70 to...$80.00
Jawa, POTF, 3¾", MOC, from $65 to...$75.00
Jawa, ROTJ, 3¾", MOC...$65.00
Jawa, SW, 3¾", MOC (12-back)...$175.00
Jawa, SW, 3¾", w/accessories, NM, H4...$20.00
Jawa, 12", MIB...$225.00
King Gorneesh, Ewoks, 3¾", MOC (unpunched), H4...$22.00
Klaatu, ROTJ, 3¾", MOC* (unpunched), H4...$15.00
Lando Calrissian, ESB, MOC* (31-back), H4...$35.00
Lando Calrissian, ESB, 3¾", w/accessories, NM, H4...$12.00
Lando Calrissian, POTF, 3¾", MOC (unpunched), H4...$95.00
Lando Calrissian, ROTJ, 3¾", MOC (unpunched), H4...$50.00
Lando Calrissian, ROTJ, 3¾", Skiff Guard outfit, MOC (unpunched), H4...$40.00
Lando Calrissian, SW, 3¾", Skiff Guard disguise, no accessories, VG, H4...$5.00
Lobot, ESB, 3¾", MOC (unpunched), H4...$30.00
Lobot, ESB, 3¾", w/accessories, NM, H4...$6.00
Luke Skywalker, ESB, 3¾", Bespin outfit, MOC (unpunched), H4...$90.00
Luke Skywalker, ESB, 3¾", blond hair, MOC (unpunched), H4...$125.00
Luke Skywalker, ESB, 3¾", Hoth gear, w/accessories, NM, H4...$15.00
Luke Skywalker, ESB, 3¾", X-Wing Pilot outfit, M (VG card), H4...$65.00
Luke Skywalker, POTF, 3¾", Battle Poncho, MOC (unpunched), H4...$80.00
Luke Skywalker, POTF, 3¾", Jedi Knight outfit, MOC, from $150 to...$175.00
Luke Skywalker, ROTJ, X-Wing Pilot outfit, MOC...$50.00
Luke Skywalker, ROTJ, 3¾", Hoth gear, MOC (unpunched), H4...$50.00
Luke Skywalker, 12", EX (VG box*), H4...$285.00
Nikto, ROTJ, 3¾", MOC, H4...$20.00
Paploo, POTF, 3¾", MOC...$45.00
Power Droid, ROTJ, 3¾", MOC*, H4...$35.00
Power Droid, SW, 3¾", w/accessories, NM, H4...$8.00
Princess Leia Organa, ESB, 3¾", Bespin outfit, w/accessories, NM, H4...$25.00
Princess Leia Organa, ESB, 3¾", Hoth gear, MOC (unpunched), H4...$50.00
Princess Leia Organa, ESB, 3¾", Hoth Gear, w/accessories, NM, H4...$20.00
Princess Leia Organa, ROTJ, 3¾", Boushh disguise, w/accessories, NM, H4...$18.00
Princess Leia Organa, SW, 3¾", Boushh disguise, w/accessories, NM, H4...$18.00
Princess Leia Organa, SW, 3¾", M (EX 21-back card), H4...$280.00
Princess Leia Organa, 12", NM...$100.00
Prune Face, ROTJ, 3¾", MOC (unpunched), H4...$20.00
Rancor Keeper, ROTJ, 3¾", MOC, H4...$12.00
Rebel Commander, ESB, 3¾", w/accessories, NM, H4...$8.00
Rebel Commando, ESB, 3¾", w/accessories, NM, H4...$8.00
Rebel Commando, ROTJ, 3¾", MOC, H4...$25.00
Rebel Soldier, ESB, 3¾", MOC (unpunched), H4...$40.00
Rebel Soldier, ESB, 3¾", w/accessories, NM, H4...$8.00
Ree-Yees, ROTJ, 3¾", MOC*, H4...$14.00
Ree-Yees, ROTJ, 3¾", w/accessories, NM, H4...$10.00
R2-D2, ESB, 3¾", MOC (unpunched), H4...$45.00
R2-D2, POTF, 3¾", MOC (unpunched), H4...$70.00
R2-D2, ROTJ, 3¾", w/sensorscope, MOC (unpunched), H4...$45.00
R2-D2, 12", remote control, MIB...$125.00
R5-D4, SW, 3¾", M (NM 21-back card), H4...$140.00
R5-D4, SW, 3¾", w/accessories, NM, H4...$8.00
Shaman, Ewoks, 3¾", MOC (unpunched), H4...$22.00
Snaggletooth, ESB, 3¾", MOC (unpunched), H4...$65.00
Snaggletooth, SW, 3¾", M (NM 21-back card), H4...$140.00
Snaggletooth, SW, 3¾", w/accessories, NM, H4...$15.00
Squid Head, ROTJ, 3¾", w/accessories, NM, H4...$8.00
Star Destroyer Commander, ESB, 3¾", MOC (unpunched), H4...$40.00
Star Destroyer Commander, SW, 3¾", w/accessories, NM, H4...$12.00
Stormtrooper, ROTJ, 3¾", MOC, H4...$35.00
Stormtrooper, SW, 3¾", w/accessories, NM, H4...$10.00
Stormtrooper, 12", EX (VG box*), H4...$200.00
Teebo, ROTJ, 3¾", MOC (unpunched), H4...$25.00
Tusken Raider, SW, 3¾", w/accessories, NM, H4...$14.00
Ugnaught, ESB, 3¾", MOC (unpunched), H4...$40.00
Ugnaught, ESB, 3¾", w/accessories, NM, H4...$8.00
Ugnaught, ROTJ, 3¾", MOC*, H4...$30.00
Urgah, Ewoks, 3¾", MOC (unpunched), H4...$22.00
Walrus Man, SW, 3¾", M (EX 21-back card), H4...$150.00
Walrus Man, SW, 3¾", w/accessories, NM, H4...$10.00
Weequay, ROTJ, 3¾", MOC...$18.00
Weequay, ROTJ, 3¾", w/accessories, NM, H4...$8.00
Wicket W Warrick, Ewoks, 3¾", MOC (unpunched), H4...$25.00
Yoda, ESB, 3¾", brn snake, M (VG card), H4...$60.00
Yoda, ESB, 3¾", orange snake, MOC...$50.00
Yoda, ESB, 3¾", orange snake, NM, H4...$20.00
Zuckuss, ESB, 3¾", w/accessories, NM, H4...$8.00
Zuckuss, ROTJ, 3¾", MOC...$45.00
2-1B, ESB, 3¾", w/accessories, NM, H4...$10.00
2-1B, ROTJ, 3¾", MOC...$35.00
4-Lom, ROTJ, 3¾", MOC...$50.00
4-Lom, ROTJ, 3¾", w/accessories, NM, H4...$10.00
8D8, ROTJ, 3¾", MOC, H4...$25.00

Playsets and Accessories

Bespin Control Room, SW, Micro Collection, MIB, H4...$50.00
Bespin Gantry, SW, Micro Collection, EX, H4...$25.00
Cantina Adventure, Sears promo, EX...$200.00
Cloud City, EX (EX box)...$300.00
Darth Vaders Star Destroyer, SW, complete, VG, H4...$60.00

Death Star Compactor, SW, Micro Collection, MIB, $85.00.

TIE Interceptor, ROTJ, MIB, $150.00.

Death Star Space Station, 1977, missing few minor pcs, EX (EX box), F8 ....$50.00
Ewok Village, ROTJ, MIB, H4 ....$100.00
Hoth Generator Attack, SW, Micro Collection, MIB, H4 ..$55.00
Hoth Ion Cannon, SW, Micro Collection, EX, H4 ....$30.00
Hoth Ion Cannon, SW, Micro Collection, MIB, H4 ....$70.00
Hoth Turret Defense, SW, Micro Collection, EX, H4 ....$25.00
Hoth Wampa Cave, Micro Collection, MIB, from $25 to ..$35.00
Imperial Attack Base, EX (EX box), from $55 to $65.00
Jabba the Hut, NRFB (Canadian/French), H4 ....$85.00
Radar Laser Cannon, ROTJ, NMIB, H4 ....$20.00
Sy Snoodles & the Rebo Band, NRFB, H4 ....$100.00
Tripod Laser Cannon, ESB, MIB, H4 ....$20.00

Vehicles

AT-AT, ESB, missing chin guns, VG (VG box), H4 ....$125.00
AT-ST, SW, EX, H4 ....$35.00
Boba Fett's Slave I, ESB, EX (VG box*), H4 ....$130.00
Boba Fett's Slave I, SW, EX, H4 ....$25.00
Darth Vader TIE Fighter, SW, NMIB $75.00
Endor Forest Ranger, NRFB, H4 ....$25.00
Ewok Assault Catapult, NRFB, H4 ....$25.00
Imperial Shuttle ROTJ, NRFB, H4 ....$250.00
Imperial TIE Fighter, SW, Micro Collection, MOC (unpunched), H4 ....$70.00
Imperial Troop Transport, EX (EX box) $65.00
Jawa Sandcrawler, SW, complete, NM, J6, from $300 to ..$350.00
Landspeeder, SW, EX (VG box*), H4 ....$40.00
Millennium Falcon, Micro Collection, Sears Exclusive, MIB $600.00
One-Man Sand Skimmer, POTF, rare, MOC, H4 ....$85.00
Rebel Armored Snow Speeder, ESB, M (EX box) $70.00
Scout Walker, ROTJ, complete, NM (VG box), H4 ....$50.00
Snowspeeder, SW, diecast, VG, H4 ....$25.00
Speeder Bike, ROTJ, NRFB, H4 ....$40.00
Star Destroyer, SW, diecast, VG, H4 ....$30.00
TIE Bomber, diecast, EX, H4 ....$250.00
TIE Fighter, SW, diecast, MOC (unpunched), H4 ....$70.00
Twin-Pod Cloud Car, SW, diecast, EX, H4 ....$25.00
X-Wing Fighter, ROTJ, NMIB, H4 ....$75.00
X-Wing Fighter, SW, Micro Collection, EX, H4 ....$35.00
X-Wing Fighter, SW, Micro Collection, VG (VG box*), H4 ....$70.00
Y-Wing Fighter, ROTJ, MIB, H4 ....$100.00
Y-Wing Fighter, SW, EX, H4 ....$55.00

Miscellaneous

Atari Video Cartridge, ESB, EX, F1 ....$10.00
Atari Video Cartridge, ROTJ Death Star Battle, EX, F1 ..$15.00
Belt, ROTJ, Lee, 1983, EX, D9 ....$8.00
Book, Empire Strikes Back, Ballantine, 1980, softcover, NM, P3 ....$5.00
Book, Empire Strikes Back, Random House, 1985, features Darth Vader on cover, hardcover, EX+, P3 ....$8.00
Book, Return of the Jedi, Ballantine, 1983, 1st edition, softcover, EX+, P3 ....$10.00
Book, Star Wars, Ballantine, 1977, softcover, EX, P3 ....$5.00
Card Game, Return of the Jedi, Parker Bros, 1983, MIB (sealed), P3 ....$10.00
Case, Darth Vader, complete w/header card, NM, H4 ....$35.00
Case, Laser Rifle, NM (EX box) $45.00
Case, SW, vinyl, orig cb insert, EX, H4 ....$16.00
Chewbacca Bandolier Strap, ROTJ, EX (worn box), H4 .$25.00
Comb & Keeper, ROTJ, MOC, B5 ....$18.00
Display, cb backdrop complete w/12 figures & accessories, EX, H4 ....$230.00
Display, Luke Skywalker, cb stand-up, life-size, EX, F1 ....$30.00
Doll, Chewbacca, Kenner, 1977, 21", MIP, J5 ....$125.00
Erasers, ROTJ, Stuart Hall, 1983, set of 3, MOC, D9 ....$5.00
Fun Poncho, Darth Vader or C-3PO, 1977, MIP, C1, ea .$30.00
Game, Escape from Death Star, Kenner, 1977, complete, NM (EX box), F8 ....$25.00
Game, Yoda Jedi Master, 1981, complete, EX (EX box), F8...$25.00
Magnets, ROTJ, set of 4, MOC, B5 ....$25.00
Mask (Don Post), Admiral Ackbar, Wicket W Warrick or C-3P0, hard plastic, EX, F1, ea $50.00
Mask (Don Post), Boba Fett, hard plastic, EX, F1 ....$100.00
Mask (Don Post), Cantina Band Member, hard plastic, EX, F1 ....$60.00
Mask (Don Post), Chewbacca, hard plastic, EX, F1 ....$80.00
Mask (Don Post), Darth Vader, hard plastic, EX, F1 ....$65.00

Mask (Don Post), Emperor's Royal Guard, hard plastic, EX, F1 .$75.00
Mask (Don Post), Klaatu, hard plastic, EX, F1 ....$40.00
Mask (Don Post), Stormtrooper, hard plastic w/smoked eyes, EX, F1 ....$100.00
Mask (Don Post), Tusken Raider, Nein Numb or Gammorean Guard, hard plastic, EX, F1, ea $35.00
Mask (Don Post), Yoda, hard plastic, EX, F1 ....$45.00

Photo courtesy June Moon

Mug, Ben Obi-Wan Kenobi, California Originals, M, J6, $175.00.

Night Light, ROTJ, 6 different, MIP, B5, ea $10.00
Pencil Pouch, ROTJ, Stuart Hall, 1983, vinyl, w/zipper, MIP, D9 ....$12.00
Pin, C-3PO figure, metal, EX, H4 ....$4.00
Pin, Darth Vader figure, metal, EX, H4 ....$4.00
Play-Doh, ESB, complete, MIB, H4 ....$42.00
Presto Magic Transfer Set, ROTJ, NRFB, H4 ....$20.00
Presto Magix Transfer Set, Wicket, set of 120, MIB, B5 ..$28.00
Presto Magix Transfer Set, Wicket, set of 40, MIB, B5 ....$18.00
Record, SW Rebel Mission to Ord Mantel, 1983, 33⅓ rpm, EX, F1 ....$10.00
Record & Book, ROTJ, Buena Vista Records, 1983, 33⅓ rpm, NM (sealed sleeve), D9 ....$10.00
Record Tote, SW, w/6 records, VG, H4 ....$30.00
Speaker Phone, Darth Vader, MIB, P12 ....$145.00
Sticker Album, ROTJ, Topps, 1983, EX, F1 ....$10.00
Sticker Sheet, ROTJ, 1st series, uncut, NM, F1 ....$15.00
Stickpin, R2-D2, 1977, diecast metal figure, NMOC, F8 .$25.00
Transfers, Ewok Village, ROTJ, American Publishing, 1983, MIP (sealed), D9 ....$5.00
3-D Poster Art Set, 1978, complete, M (sealed), F8 ....$25.00

Steam Powered

During the early part of the century until about 1930, though not employed to any great extent, live steam power was used to activate toys such as large boats, novelty toys, and model engines.

See also Boats; Trains.

Accessory, airship roundabout, 3 airships w/gondolas & side-mounted props, litho & pnt tin, 9", EX, A $1,200.00
Accessory, artist, Germany, man w/paint palette on stool at easel, gr base, 4", EX, A $1,000.00
Accessory, blacksmith shop, Germany, hand-pnt tin, 3 men at work inside, 2 roofs w/chimneys, metal base, 9½", VG, A $700.00
Accessory, chimney sweep, Doll, red simulated brick chimney w/figure in blk, 4", VG, A $350.00
Accessory, fan, Ernst Plank, blk table model w/chromed blades, 6", rare, NM, A $275.00
Accessory, house w/horse ride, tin, house w/attached water wheel, emb landscape, sq base, 9" L, G, A $300.00
Accessory, man at printing press, Falk, litho tin figure turns crank on wood & tin press, brn tin base, 5½", VG, A $700.00
Accessory, man pumping tire, Germany, man in goggles & cap pumping tire, yel rectangular base, 5", EX, A $700.00
Accessory, men at work, 2 men sawing plank of wood & 2 men working on wagon wheel w/hammers, 8" & 10", EX, A $350.00
Accessory, mill house, Doll, tin, features man & donkey on revolving platform, water wheel on side, sq base, 8", EX, A .$300.00
Accessory, power station, Doll, tin, figure on revolving base enters & exits through doors, tall chimney, 9", EX, A $335.00
Accessory, power station, Doll, tin, revolving base, 9", EX, A $335.00
Accessory, pulley, Doll, 5 NP wheels on CI stand mounted on base, 15" L, NM, A $250.00
Accessory, shoe shine boy, Germany, Black boy working on shoe in front of simulated brick wall, 4½", G, A $385.00
Accessory, thresher, Bing, yel & red w/gr cranks, 9" L, G-, A $165.00
Accessory, thresher, Marklin, gr & red w/wooden rollers under rear cap, wire mesh bottom, 8" L, EX, A $475.00
Accessory, walking beam pump, Ernst Plank, litho tin, windmill & roof-covered beam pump on rectangular base, 11", NM, A $300.00
Accessory, water fountain, Germany, tin, 4 spigots empty into basin, hand-crank flywheel, sq base, 10½", NM, A .$450.00
Accessory, water wheel, Doll, tin, pulley system activates water wheel & anvils, gr rectangular base, 12", NM, A $750.00
Accessory, wheat sifter, Bing, red w/yel trim, side crank, bl rectangular base, 5½" L, VG, A $700.00
Eureka Steam Engine, Weeden, horizontal w/brass boiler in tin covering w/diecut stars, NP valves & lenses, 14", EX, A...$500.00
Ferris Wheel, Doll, enameled tin, 6 gondolas w/compo figures, 14", EX, A $2,600.00
Ferris Wheel, Falk, red w/gold highlights, 6 double-seat chairs w/figures, 12", rstr, A $500.00
Hot Air Engine, Carette, twin-cylinder vertical engine on maroon-pnt CI base, NP flywheel, 14½", no burner o/w EX, A $935.00
Kaleidoscope, Germany, glass face w/brass frame mounted on wood base, 7½", NM (G box), A $855.00

Locomotive, Weeden, brass boiler w/NP valves & smoke stack, red-pnt spoke wheels & flywheel, 11½", EX, A.......**$475.00**

Organ Grinder, Germany, figure cranks lg wheel, rectangular base, EX, A **$800.00**

Road Roller, Weeden, brass roller on front and cast iron wheels, brass boiler, nickel-plated flywheel, 7" long, EX, A, $850.00.

Sifter, Ernst Plank, pk, yel & gr tin, 2-tier w/4 sifters on each, EP logo on roof marquee, rectangular base, 12", EX, A .**$1,155.00**

Steam Engine, CG&C, horizontal boiler w/CI bracket supporting NP flywheel & levers, CI base, 9", NM, A **$575.00**

Steam Engine, Doll, CI base w/brass boiler, orig burner w/attached plated door, 9", VG, A **$300.00**

Steam Engine, Doll, horizontal, CI base w/brass boiler, orig burner w/attached plated door, 9", VG, A...............**$300.00**

Steam Engine, Doll, horizontal boiler w/dual flywheel, NP detail to levers & rods, CI base, 11½", NM, A..................**$650.00**

Steam Engine, Doll, vertical, CI base w/brass boiler, orig burner, decal on piston, 17", EX, A **$300.00**

Steam Engine, Germany, horizontal, NP twin flywheels & parts, maroon-pnt CI base, 13", EX (EX wood box), A .**$1,155.00**

Steam Engine, Weeden, single cylinder, NP base, 8" L, EX, A **$850.00**

Windmill, Doll, hand-pnt tin, simulated brick base, 19", EX, A **$600.00**

Wishing Well, Fleishmann, crank or steam power, tin, 7", EX (EX box), A **$150.00**

Woman at Trough, Germany, tin, woman & 2 chickens at water trough, 8½", EX, A...**$200.00**

Steiff

Margaret Steiff made the first of her felt toys in 1880, stuffing them with lamb's wool. Later followed toys of velvet, plush, and wool, and in addition to the lamb's wool stuffing, she used felt scraps, excelsior, and kapok as well. In 1897 and '98 her trademark was a paper label printed with an elephant; from 1900 to 1905 her toys carried a circular tag with an elephant logo that was different than the one she had previously used. The most famous 'button in ear' trademark was registered on December 20, 1904. 1904 and '05 saw the use of the button with an elephant (extremely rare) and the blank button (which is also rare). The button with Steiff and the underscored or trailing 'F' was used until 1948, and the raised script button is from the 1950s.

Steiff Teddy bears, perhaps the favorite of collectors everywhere, are characterized by their long thin arms with curved wrists and paws that extend below their hips. Buyer beware: the Steiff company is now making many replicas of their old bears. For more information about Steiff's buttons, chest tags, and stock tags as well as the inspirational life of Margaret Steiff and the fascinating history of Steiff toys, we recommend *Button in Ear Book* and *The Steiff Book of Teddy Bears*, both by Jurgen and Marianne Cieslik; *Teddy Bears and Steiff Animals* 2nd and 3rd series by Margaret Fox Mandel; *4th Teddy Bear and Friends Price Guide* by Linda Mullins; *Collectible German Animals Value Guide* by Dee Hockenberry; and *Steiff Sortiment 1947 – 1995* by Gunther Pefiffer. (This book is in German; however, the reader can discern the size of the item, year of production, and price estimation.) See also Clubs, Newsletters, and Other Publications (for Cynthia's Country Store).

Advisor: Cynthia's Country Store, Cynthia Brintnall (C14); Candelaine (G16).

See also Disney; Santa.

Baby Duck, yel mohair w/brn airbrushed markings, orange felt beak & feet, all ID, 1959-61, 5½", EX, G16............**$195.00**

Bazi Dog, seated, orig collar, all ID, 1950, 7", NM, G16...**$250.00**

Photo courtesy Cynthia Brintnall

Bear, beige mohair, shoe-button eyes, original nose, mouth, and pads, 1903 – 05, 12", minor damage to pads, from $950.00 to $1,450.00.

Bear, gold mohair, FF underscored button, early 1900s, 3½", EX, G16 ....**$750.00**

Bear, gold mohair w/felt pads, glass eyes, all ID, 1950, 6", EX, G16 ....$225.00
Bear, Margaret Strong, cinnamon, all ID, 1982-90, 9", M, G16 ....$125.00
Bear, Margaret Strong, cream, orig button & tag, 1984-86, 9", NM, G16 ....$165.00
Bear, on all fours, caramel mohair w/glass eyes, orig collar, no ID, 4½", EX, G16 ....$100.00
Bear, wht mohair, no ID, 1950, 3½", EX, G16 ....$400.00
Bendy Bear, dk brn, all ID, 1984, 3½", M, G16 ....$45.00
Bendy Bear, reddish brn, bear's head chest tag, 1950s, 3", M, G16 ....$125.00
Bendy Bear, wht, all ID, 1980, 3½", M, G16 ....$45.00
Bendy Bear, wht, no ID, 1960s, 3½", M, G16 ....$60.00
Bendy Panda, incised button & stock tag, 1960s, 3", NM, G16 ....$235.00
Bessy Cow, mohair w/felt horns & udders, glass eyes, orig collar & bell, no ID, 1950s, 9", NM, G16 ....$145.00
Bird, mohair, felt & Dralon w/plastic feet, raised script button, 1950s, 4", EX, G16 ....$145.00
Bison, mohair w/felt horns, all ID, 1950, 8", M, G16 ....$225.00
Boar, blk w/brn face, all ID, 1950s, 11", M, G16 ....$175.00
Boar, velvet, no ID, 1950s, 2¼", EX, G16 ....$85.00
Boxer Dog, brn w/blk face, orig collar, all ID, 1983, 8½", M, G16 ....$100.00
Bully Dog, tan & blk, orig red collar, all ID, 1951-58, 4", EX, G16 ....$125.00
Camel, mohair & felt, all ID, 1950, 5¾", NM, G16 ....$135.00
Cat, blk velvet w/mohair tail, orig ribbon, US Zone tag, 1948, 3", M, G16 ....$200.00
Chick, mohair & felt, no ID, 4½", EX, G16 ....$50.00
Chick, spotted Dralon w/plastic beak & feet, orange felt comb, chest tag, 1969-74, 4¼", M, G16 ....$125.00
Clownie, all ID, 1950-60, 4¾", NM, G16 ....$175.00
Cockie Dog, seated, blk & wht, orig collar, no ID, 4½", EX, G16 ....$85.00
Cocoli Monkey, mohair & felt w/glass eyes, raised script button, 1950s, NM, G16 ....$465.00
Collie, laying down, all ID, 1960, 9", M, G16 ....$225.00
Collie, seated, no ID, 3½", EX, G16 ....$85.00
Cosy Fuzzy Fox, Dralon, all ID, 1968, 8½", NM, G16 ....$50.00
Cosy Kamel, Dralon, all ID, 1968, 10½", M, G16 ....$125.00
Cosy Koala, all ID, 1970, 5", M, G16 ....$65.00
Cosy Trampy, pk Dralon w/airbrushing, orig collar & chest tag, 1982, 8", M, G16 ....$85.00
Country Mouse House w/Mouse, 1967, house: 7x13", mouse: 3", rare, EX, G16 ....$225.00
Crabby Lobster, mohair & felt, all ID, 1950, 6½", NM, G16...$300.00
Dally Dog, tan w/blk spots, orig collar, all ID, 1959-67, 4", EX, G16 ....$145.00
Deer (Buck), beige mohair w/blk glass eyes, FF underscored button, 10", VG, G16 ....$250.00
Deer (Doe), beige mohair w/blk glass eyes, FF underscored button, 9", VG, G16 ....$185.00
Donkey, mohair w/glass eyes, all ID, 1954-58, 5", rare, EX, G16 ....$185.00
Donkey, velvet w/rope tail & leather harness, raised script button & stock tag, 1959-67, 4½", NM, G16 ....$165.00
Dormili Rabbit, tan & wht, all ID, 1986-88, 7", M, G16..$65.00
Dormy Dormouse, mohair & Dralon, all ID, 1968, 7½", M..$95.00
Easter Bunny w/Basket, all ID, 1967, 9", rare, M, G16...$465.00
Elephant, mohair w/felt ears & bib, all ID, 1948, 3½", NM, G16 ....$100.00
Elephant, w/anniversary blanket, all ID, 1959-67, 2½", M, G16 ....$145.00
Fawn, laying down, velvet, FF underscored button, 1930s, 8", EX, G16 ....$335.00
Fawn, velvet, raised script button, stock tag & US Zone tag, 1950, 5", EX, G16 ....$100.00
Floppy Hens, mohair & felt, all ID, 1958, 8" & 7", rare, G16, pr.$300.00
Floppy Kitty, sleeping, tan w/blk stripes, orig ribbon & chest tag, 8", EX, G16 ....$75.00
Floppy Panther, brass button & stock tag, 1972, 17", NM, G16 ....$185.00
Floppy Zotty Bear, sleeping, no ID, 8", NM, G16 ....$65.00

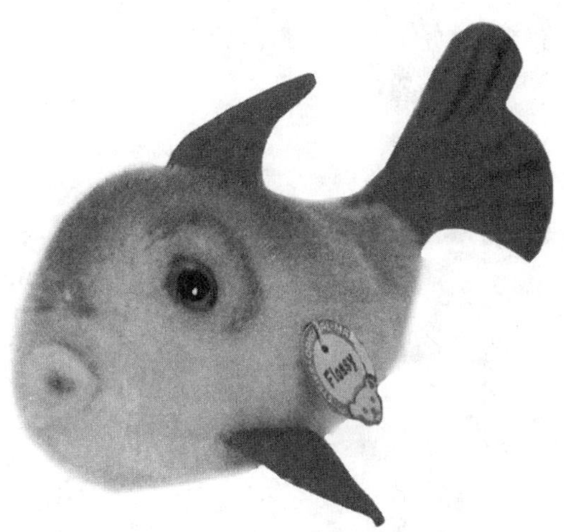

Flossy Fish, 1968, 4", EX, $65.00.

Fox, standing, mohair w/glass eyes, raised script button, 5", EX, G16 ....$80.00
Foxy Dog, no ID, rpl collar, 1950, 7", NM, G16 ....$95.00
Foxy Dog, orig ribbon & chest tag, 1950, 3¼", EX, G16..$85.00
Franzi Parakeet, velvet w/plastic feet, all ID, 1968, 3½", NM, G16 ....$95.00
Froggy Frog, seated, velvet w/glass eyes, all ID, 1968, 3", NM, G16 ....$135.00
Froggy Frog, swimming, mohair, chest tag, 1960s, 10", NM, G16 ....$125.00
Gallo Rooster & Nelly Hen, Dralon, all ID, 1979-81, 6", M, G16, pr $200.00
Giraffe, velvet, all ID, 1959-67, 6", M, G16 ....$145.00
Grissy Donkey, gray & wht Dralon, no ID, 1963-74, 7", EX, G16 ....$40.00
Gussy Cat, blk & wht mohair w/glass eyes, orig ribbon, raised script button, 1950s, 4", NM, G16 ....$165.00
Hansi Parakeet, velvet w/plastic feet, all ID, 1968, 3½", EX, G16 ....$95.00
Hedgehog, incised button & stock tag, 1966-67, 2¼", NM, G16 ....$35.00

Hide-A-Gift Cocker Spaniel, blk & wht, all ID, 1950, 5½", NM, from $175 to $185.00
Hide-A-Gift Rabbit, all ID, 1950, 5½", M, from $175 to ..$185.00
Hucky Raven, metal feet, all ID, 1960-67, 4½", NM, G16 ..$135.00
Hucky Raven, metal feet, raised script button & stock tag, 1960-67, 7½", NM, G16....$225.00
Jackie Bear, all ID, 1986-87, 9", MIB, G16....$165.00
Jackie Bear, raised script button & remnant stock tag, 1950s, 9½", rare, EX, G16....$1,250.00
Jocko Monkey, mohair, raised script button & stock tag, 1950, 3½", NM, G16....$65.00
Jocko Monkey, mohair & felt w/glass eyes, all ID & US Zone tag, 11", M, G16....$225.00
Jolanthe Pig, mohair w/felt ears, incised button, 1960, 5", NM, G16....$125.00
Kangaroo & Joey, mohair w/velvet joey, raised script button, 1950s, 18", EX, G16....$495.00

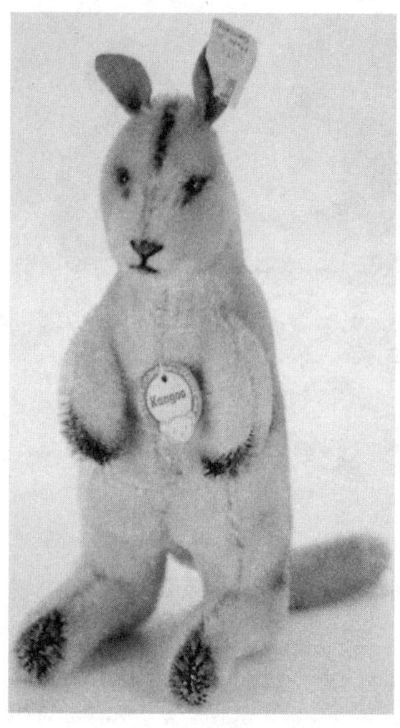

Kangoo Kangaroo, mohair with glass eyes, original tag, and button, 6½", M, $125.00.

Kitty, striped mohair w/velvet muzzle & felt ears, fully jointed, chest tag, 1940s, 4½", NM, G16....$195.00
Koala, tan, chest tag, 1950, 5", NM, G16....$300.00
Lamb (from Mary Had a Little Lamb set), all ID, 1986, 5", M, G16....$75.00
Lamby Lamb, cream wool w/felt ears & glass eyes, orig bl ribbon & bell, all ID, 1953-58, 4", M, G16....$125.00
Leo Lion, puppet, raised script button, 1950, 8", NM, G16.$85.00
Leo Lion, seated, incised button, 1960, 5", NM, G16....$85.00
Leo Lion & Lea Lioness, all ID, 1950, 4", G16, pr....$265.00
Leopard, running, chest tag, 6", M, G16....$150.00
Lion Cub, wool w/glass eyes, raised script button & stock tag, 1950-54, 4", rare, M, G16....$225.00
Lioness, mohair w/glass eyes, fully jtd, raised script button & stock tag, 1951-57, 6", rare, M, G16....$250.00
Lixie Cat, gray w/red & gr cloth outfit, chest tag, 1954, 4¼", EX, G16....$225.00
Lizzy Cat, all ID, 1960, 6½", NM, G16....$135.00
Lizzy Lizard, velvet, no ID, 1950, 8", NM, G16....$250.00
Loopy Fox, puppet, raised script button & stock tag, 1950s, 9", EX, G16....$85.00
Lora Parrot, mohair & felt, incised button & stock tag, 1968, 9", EX, G16....$145.00
Lully Bear, tan mohair w/felt mouth, orig bl ribbon, incised button & stock tag, 1968-77, 11", M, G16....$125.00
Mallard Duck, standing, mc mohair w/orange feet & beak, bl felt tail, raised script button, 1952-57, 4", NM, G16....$125.00
Mama & Baby Bear, limited edition gift set, 1981, mama: 13", baby: 6", MIB, G16....$475.00
Max & Moritz, all ID, 1950s, 3½", rare, MIP, G16....$385.00
Maxi Mole, w/orig shovel, all ID, 1950, 4", M, G16....$85.00
Molly Dog, cream mohair, FF underscored button & stock tag, 1925, 6", NM, G16....$400.00
Moosy Moose, all ID, 1963-64, 4½", rare, M, G16....$425.00
Mucki & Macki Hedgehog, all ID, 10", ea from $145 to .$165.00
Mucki Hedgehog, all ID, 4½", NM, G16....$50.00
Nagy Beaver, stiff mohair, all ID, 1950, 7", M, G16....$140.00
Navy Goat, no ID, 1950s, 5", M, G16....$175.00
Nellie Snail, bl, raised script button & chest tag, 1950s, 6½", NM, G16....$395.00
Ophelia Bear, cream mohair, chest button & stock tag, 1984-89, 17", EX, G16....$175.00
Original Camel, all ID, 1950, 11", NM, G16....$250.00
Original Teddy, blk, all ID, 1985-86, 4", M, G16....$85.00
Original Teddy, caramel, all ID, 1950s, 6", M, G16....$400.00
Original Teddy, caramel, orig ribbon, incised button & stock tag, 1960, 9", M, G16....$100.00
Original Teddy, caramel, raised script button, 1950, 3½", NM, G16....$335.00
Original Teddy, cream, all ID, 1983-88, 13", NM, G16 .$145.00
Original Teddy, dk brn, chest tag, 1950, 6", NM, G16...$600.00
Original Teddy, dk brn, raised script button, 1950s, 3½", NM, G16....$300.00
Original Teddy, gold, chest tag, 1950s, 3½", M, G16....$350.00
Original Teddy, gold, orig red ribbon & stock tag, 6", NM, G16....$400.00
Original Teddy, tan, raised script button & stock tag, sgn Hans Otto Steiff & B Steiff, 1950s, 13", EX, G16....$475.00
Original Teddy, wht, no ID, 1950s, 3½", EX, G16....$285.00
Owl, puppet, mohair & felt, raised script button, 1950, 9", NM, G16....$65.00
Paddy Beaver, all ID, 1985-88, 5", M, G16....$35.00
Paddy Walrus, mohair, chest tag, 1950s, 4½", NM, G16..$100.00
Panda, raised script button, 1950, 8", EX, G16....$750.00
Peggy Penguin, chest tag, 1959, 5", NM, G16....$100.00
Peggy Penguin, raised script button & stock tag, 1959-67, 7½", NM, G16....$150.00
Peky Dog, plush & felt, all ID, 1980-85, 6", M, G16....$55.00
Peky Dog, plush & felt, chest tag, 1950, 3", EX, G16....$75.00
Penguin, mohair w/velvet wings & felt feet, raised script button, 1950s, 4", NM, G16....$145.00
Piccy Pelican, no ID, 1950, 9½", EX, G16....$285.00
Pieps Mouse, wht mohair w/felt ears, paws & tail, red eyes, incised button & stock tag, 1968-78, 3", M, G16....$85.00
Pig, pk velvet, raised script button & stock tag, 1959-67, 4", EX, G16....$85.00

Pip Dog, rattle, velvet w/glass eyes, FF underscored button & stock tag, 3½", NM, G16 ....$750.00
Polar Bear, wht, orig collar & bell, all ID, 1960s, 8", NM, G16....................$275.00
Pony, FAO Schwarz Exclusive, mohair w/felt ears, all ID, 1967-68, 6½", rare, G16....................$350.00
Pony, velvet, chest tag, 1952-57, 4½", NM, G16....................$125.00
Pummy Rabbit, mohair & Dralon, all ID, 1968-76, 6½", M, G16....................$125.00
Rabbit, begging, all ID, 1950, 3¾", VG, G16....................$95.00
Rabbit, mohair & Dralon w/colorful airbrushing, incised button & stock tag, 1960, 5", M, G16....................$85.00
Rabbit, puppet, mohair w/glass eyes, orig ribbon, 1950s, 8", M, G16....................$100.00
Raccy Raccoon, tan & brn mohair, chest tag, 1950, 3½", M, G16....................$125.00
Renny Reindeer, chest tag, 1950s, 4½", M, G16....................$185.00
Richard Steiff, gray, all ID, 1992-95, 12", M (NM box), G16....................$425.00
Robby Seal, all ID, 1950s, 5", M, G16....................$85.00
Rocky Goat, all ID, 1963-67, 5", M, G16....................$175.00
Rooster, puppet, mohair & felt, incised button & stock tag, 1969, 10½", rare, M, G16....................$165.00
Rooster & Hen, egg covers, felt w/shoe-button eyes, 1900s, 6" & 4½", rare, M, G16, pr....................$400.00
Schwarzbar Bear, blk mohair w/felt pads, brass button & cloth stock tag, 1993-95, 6½", M, G16....................$135.00
Scotty Dog, orig collar, raised script button, 1950-57, 4", rare, NM, G16....................$300.00
Shepherd, all ID, 1958, 13", NM, G16....................$285.00
Shepherd, all ID, 1969, 8", NM, G16....................$195.00
Skunk, mohair & velvet w/glass eyes, no ID, 1950, 4", NM, G16....................$150.00
Snobby Poodle, gray, orig collar & chest tag, 1950, 5½", NM, G16....................$125.00
Snobby Poodle, puppet, orig ribbon, all ID, 1955-58, 9", NM, G16....................$100.00
Snucki Goat, all ID, 1978-87, 4", EX, G16....................$95.00
Snucki Ram, tan mohair w/blk face & feet, chest tag, 1950s, 6", NM, G16....................$125.00
Squirrel, mohair w/felt nut, raised script button & stock tag, 1968, 6½", M, G16....................$165.00
Studio Falcon, acrylic & cotton, jtd wings, all ID, 1979, 12", M, G16....................$225.00
Tabby Cat, on wheels, wht w/blk stripes, orig bell, rpl ribbon, US Zone tag, 1948, 8", EX, G16....................$335.00
Teddy Baby, brn, all ID, 1980s, 11½", M, G16....................$225.00
Teddy Baby, tan, all ID, 1985-86, 15", M, G16....................$250.00
Teddy Clown Junior, orig outfit, chest button & stock tag, 1987, 7½", NM, G16....................$200.00
Teddyli Bear, mohair & felt, no ID, 1950, 9", NM, G16..$500.00
Terry Dog, brn & blk, raised script button, 1950s, 8", EX, G16....................$165.00
Terry Terrier, blk & tan mohair, orig red leather collar, all ID, 1948, 9", M, G16....................$325.00
Tiger, running, no ID, 1960s, 11", NM, G16....................$100.00
Tom Cat, blk velvet w/mohair tail, gr glass eyes, orig ribbon, no ID, NM, G16....................$100.00
Tosi Dog, wht mohair w/glass eyes, orig red leather collar, US Zone tag, 1950-53, 6", EX, G16....................$135.00
Treff Dog, tan mohair, jtd head, underscored button & remnant stock tag, 1925, 12½", very worn, G16....................$200.00
Tucky Turkey, all ID, 1952-57, 5", M, G16....................$350.00
Tulla Goose, mohair w/felt beak & feet, bl glass eyes, airbrushed feathers on back, no ID, 1950, 10½", NM, G16......$275.00
Turkey, raised script button, 1950s, 4¼", M, G16....................$285.00
Turtle, footstool, airbrushed mohair, all ID, 1950, 21", NM, G16....................$500.00
Tysus Dinosaur, all ID, 1980s, 7½", MIB, G16....................$125.00
Unicorn, mohair & Dralon, 1983, all ID, 7", NM, G16.$125.00
Waldi Dog, orig collar & chest tag, 1950, 10½", M, G16..$125.00
Weasel, brn & wht Dralon, no ID, 8", tail missing o/w EX, G16..$65.00
Wittie Owl, chest tag, 1950, 4", M, G16....................$110.00
Wolf (from Red Riding Hood set), brass button & stock tag, 1989-91, M, G16....................$75.00
Woolie Bee, red & yel, stock tag, 1975, 1¼", M, G16......$40.00
Woolie Bird, mc w/metal feet, raised script button & stock tag, 1949, 2½", M, G16....................$85.00
Woolie Bird, mc w/plastic feet, no ID, 1960, 1½", M, G16 .$30.00
Woolie Cat, blk & wht, no ID, 1950, 2", EX, G16....................$25.00
Woolie Cat, gray & wht, orig ribbon, raised script button & stock tag, 1970-74, 2½", M, G16....................$85.00
Woolie Chick, plastic feet, incised button & stock tag, 1960s, 2¼", M, G16....................$45.00
Woolie Duck, plastic feet, no ID, 1960s, 1½", M, G16 ....$40.00
Woolie Fish, gr, raised script button & stock tag, 1967, 1½", M, G16....................$40.00
Woolie Fish, red, stock tag, 1968, 1½", M, G16....................$40.00
Woolie Frog, incised button & stock tag, 1960s, 2½", NM, G16....................$35.00
Woolie Guinea Pig, incised button & stock tag, 1960s, 3", M, G16....................$55.00
Woolie Hen, mc w/plastic legs, incised button & stock tag, 1969, 2½", NM, G16....................$55.00
Woolie Ladybug, 1960, 2¼", MIP, G16....................$35.00
Woolie Mouse, gray, raised script button & stock tag, 1950, 1½", M, G16....................$45.00
Woolie Mouse, wht, no ID, 1960, 1½", M, G16....................$35.00
Woolie Owl, brass script button & stock tag, 1971, 3¾", M, G16 .$50.00
Woolie Owl, incised button & stock tag, 1960s, 2½", NM, G16 .$30.00
Woolie Parrot, incised button & stock tag, 1971-75, 2¼", M, G16....................$65.00
Woolie Penguin, no ID, 1950, 2", M, G16....................$65.00
Woolie Raven, mohair w/felt beak & metal legs, raised script button & stock tag, 1949-58, 2", NM, G16....................$55.00
Woolie Skunk, raised script button, 1950s, 1¼", EX, G16...$110.00
Woolie Swan, fluffy version, no ID, 1960s, 2½", EX, G16..$60.00
Wotan Ram, all ID, 1966-67, 4", M, G16....................$275.00
Xorry Fox, raised script button, 1950, 4", VG, G16....................$65.00
Yuku Gazelle, all ID, 1962-63, 7½", rare, NM, G16.......$325.00
Zicky Goat, caramel, orig ribbon & bell, all ID, 1948, 7½", NM, G16....................$285.00
Zotty Bear, frosted mohair w/felt pads & mouth, glass eyes, raised script button, 1950s, 17", rare, NM, G16 ......$600.00
Zotty Bear, tan mohair, orig red ribbon, raised script button & remnant stock tag, 1950, 8", NM....................$300.00

Strauss

Imaginative, high-quality, tin windup toys were made by Ferdinand Strauss (New York, later New Jersey) from the onset of World War I until the 1940s. For about fifteen years prior to his becoming a toymaker, he was a distributor of toys he imported from Germany. Though hard to find in good working order, his toys are highly prized by today's collectors, and when found in even very good to excellent condition, many are in the $500.00 and up range.

Advisor: Scott Smiles (S10).

Aero-Racer, maroon w/beige wings, rubber-band wound propeller & wheels, 9¾", wingspan, EX, A....................$400.00
Air Devil, 1926, w/pilot, 8½", EX, from $500 to............$600.00
Boob McNutt, man in red polka-dot pants & blk jacket, rnd flat hat, 8¾", VG..$500.00
Chek-A-Cab #69, yel & blk w/checked trim, 8½", VG .$650.00
Dandy Jim Clown Dancer, 1921, does the jig & plays cymbals atop circus tent, 10", EX..$600.00
Derrick Truck, w/driver, 8½", EX, A $700.00
Emergency Tow Cab, mk #74 on door, 10", VG, from $250 to...$300.00
Flying Airship, emb aluminum w/brass propellers, 10", EX (VG box), A $900.00
Graf Zeppelin, emb aluminum w/brass propeller, 16", VG (VG box) $1,000.00
Graf Zeppelin Jr #2, emb aluminum w/brass propellers, 10", VG $500.00
Ham & Sam, 1921, Black banjo player standing by piano player, 5½", NM, A $1,200.00

Inter-State Bus, green and yellow, aluminum tires, 11", EX, from $800.00 to $900.00.

Jackie the Hornpipe Dancer, boat advances as sailor dances on deck, 9", EX (EX box) $800.00
Jazzbo Jim, 1920s, figure plays banjo & dances atop cabin roof, 10", VG...$500.00
Jenny the Balky Mule, 1925, advances w/crazy action as farmer bounces in seat, 9½", NM (G box).........................$575.00

Photo courtesy Scott Smiles

Jenny the Balky Mule, 1925, lithographed tin, 9½", EX, $375.00.

Jitney Bus #66, w/driver, gr w/yel lettering & trim, metal tires w/gr hubs, 9¼", EX $650.00
Jolly Pals, 1920, bulldog pulls monkey in cart, 8", EX, A..$475.00
Leaping Lena Car, 1930, w/driver, blk w/wht lettering, 8", G $350.00
Miami Sea Sled, litho tin w/adjustable tiller, 10", EX, from $275 to..$325.00
Parcel Post Special Delivery Truck, orange & red w/blk roof & fenders, 11", NM, A $1,500.00
Play Golf, 1925, 12x7" base, NM (EX box), from $1000 to $1,100.00
Red Flash Racer #31, w/driver, red & yel, 9½", scarce, EX, from $850 to...$900.00
Rollo-Chair, G, from $650 to $750.00
Sail-A-Way Canoe, mk Star SY 1, w/driver, litho tin w/cloth sail & wooden pole, 8", VG....................................$200.00
Santee Claus in Sleigh, 1923, Santa bounces up & down as sleigh advances, 11", EX......................................$1,400.00
Speedboat Ferdinand, w/driver, 10", G, from $200 to $250.00
Tip Top Porter, 1925, Black man pushes 2-wheeled cart, bl & yel, 6½", EX (EX box), A..$300.00
Tip Top Porter, 1925, Black man pushes 2-wheeled cart, bl & yel, 6½", EX (EX box), A.......................................$525.00
Tom Twist the Funny Clown, 8½", EX (EX box), from $1,100 to...$1,200.00
Travelchiks, 4 chicks atop railroad car bend & peck for food, chick passengers, 8", VG (VG box), from $450 to ..$500.00
Wildfire Trotter, driver jumps up & down in seat as donkey cart advances, 8½", EX..$250.00
Yell-O Taxi, w/driver, yel & blk w/disk wheels, 8½", NM, A $900.00

Structo

Pressed steel vehicles were made by Structo (Illinois) as early as 1920. They continued in business well into the 1960s, producing several army toys, trucks of all types, and firefighting and construction equipment.

Army Ambulance, #416, 17", EX...................................$275.00

Cattle Truck, #708, red & wht, MIB $225.00
Cement Mixer, 1950s, 20", EX..$175.00
Delivery Truck, #603, early 1950s, blk & red, Package, Delivery & Service decals on side, 13", EX (EX box), A $200.00
Dump Truck, #141, red & yel w/blk rubber tires, 9", EX (EX box), A..$75.00
End Loader, #340, red w/blk rubber tires, 13", EX, A $100.00
Fire Truck, 1930s-40s, red w/blk rubber tires, 18", EX, D10 .$650.00
Gasoline Truck, #912, 1950s, 13", NM..........................$135.00
Machinery Truck, #607, 1950s, VG...............................$250.00
Overland Freight Trailer, #704, 1950s, EX+ $100.00
Packard Dump Truck, #405, 1930, 18", EX $950.00
Rigger & Hauler, late 1940s, gr w/blk rubber tires, 20", EX, D10, from $200 to $250.00
Stake Truck, 1930s, working headlights, 21", EX $325.00
Tow Truck, #910, red w/decals, complete w/accessories, 11", NM (NM box), A $200.00

Tractor Builder High-Wheel Tractor #11, green with red wheel guards and wheels, 1920, EX, $900.00.

Transport Tractor-Trailer, 1950s, bl cab w/red trailer, blk rubber tires, 21", EX, D10 ....$200.00
US Mail Truck, #428, 17", NM......................................$300.00

Teddy Bears

The history of old teddy bears goes way back to about 1902 – 1903. Today's collectors often find it difficult to determine exactly what company produced many of these early bears, but fortunately for them, there are many excellent books now available that contain a wealth of information on those early makers.

Interest in teddy bears has been increasing at a fast pace, and there are more and more collectors entering the market. This has lead to an escalation in the values of the early bears. Because most teddies were cherished childhood toys and were usually very well loved, many that survive are well worn, so an early bear in mint condition can be very valuable.

We would like to direct your attention to the books on the market that are the most helpful on the detailed history and identification of teddies. *A Collectors History of the Teddy Bear* by Patricia Schoonmaker; *Teddy Bears Past and Present (Volumes I and II)* and *American Teddy Bear Encyclopedia* by Linda Mullins; *Teddy Bears — A Complete Guide to History, Collecting, and Care*, by Sue Pearson and Dottie Ayers; *Teddy Bear Encyclopedia* and *Ultimate Teddy Bear Book* by Pauline Cockrill; and *Big Bear Book* by Dee Hockenberry. The reader can easily see that a wealth of information exists and that it is impossible in a short column such as this to give any kind of a definitive background. If you intend to be a knowledgeable teddy bear collector, it is essential that you spend time in study. Many of these books will be available at your local library or through dealers who specialize in bears.

Advisor: Cynthia's Country Store, Cynthia Brintnall (C14).

See also Schuco; Steiff.

3½", gold mohair, Original Teddy, 1950s, NM $250.00
4½", gold mohair w/lg glass eyes, 1940s, EX.......................$75.00
4¼", tan plush w/glass eyes, orig pk ribbon, East Germany paper label, 1950s, NM, G16...$25.00
5", bright gold mohair w/glass eyes, felt snout & feet, bell on red neck ribbon, 1950s, EX..$75.00
5", wht mohair, plastic brads on outside, EX.....................$75.00
6½", caramel mohair couple w/glass eyes, dressed in peasant-style clothing, fully jtd, German, 1940s, M, G16, pr..........$175.00
6¾", tan mohair w/amber glass eyes, German, 1940-50, VG, G16 ....$150.00

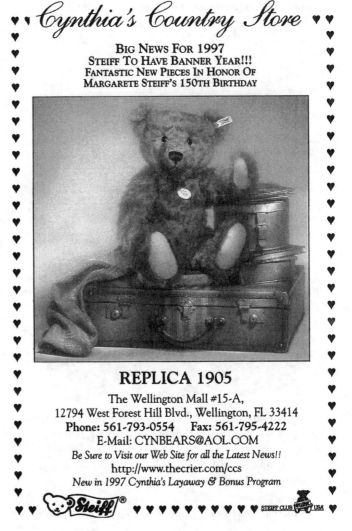

8½", mohair w/shoe-button eyes, excelsior stuffing, jtd at shoulders & hips, long thin arms, Steiff-like, 1905, VG $900.00
10", brn mohair w/glass eyes, orig gold ribbon, East Germany paper label, 1950s, NM, G16 ....$100.00
10", gold short mohair w/long-pile hands & feet, glass eyes, embroidered nose/mouth, straw-stuffed, jtd, post-WWII, EX....$225.00
11", brn mohair w/blk shoe-button eyes, embroidered nose & mouth, felt pads, fully jtd, G, A $125.00
11", dk brn wool plush w/glass eyes, lt tan velvet snout w/metal nose, tan felt pads, straw & cotton mix, jtd, 1940s, EX $100.00
11", Germany, gray & beige plush w/glass eyes, shaved snout, flesh-colored oval pads, straw-stuffed, 1945-52, EX...$250.00
12", blond mohair w/blk shoe-button eyes, embroidered nose & mouth, excelsior stuffing, fully jtd, 1910, G, A........$250.00
12", blond mohair w/glass eyes, embroidered nose, mouth & claws, straw stuffed, fully jtd, 1910, VG $500.00
13", Hermann, lt gold mohair w/glass eyes, swivel head, gold-shaved mohair muzzle, open/closed mouth w/tongue, EX $140.00
14", gold mohair, rexine pads, Chad Valley, M $375.00
15", brn mohair w/glass eyes, pnt details, German, 1927, EX...$350.00
16", pale gold mohair w/glass eyes, silk floss embroidered nose, brn felt pads & feet, jtd, England, 1949, EX $350.00
17", blond mohair w/blk steel eyes, embroidered nose, mouth & claws, felt pads, fully jtd, 1910, VG, A $525.00

17", brown mohair, NM, sold at McMasters 'Playthings Past' catalog auction in 1997 for $7,200.00.

18", blond mohair w/shoe-button eyes, embroidered nose & mouth, excelsior stuffing, fully jtd, Ideal (?), 1910, VG, A $1,000.00
18", brn mohair w/glass eyes, American, 1920s, EX, G16 ..$300.00
20", riding toy, brn mohair w/shoe-button eyes, leather collar mk Teddy B, excelsior stuffing, metal fr, 1920, G, A.....$300.00
21", frosted mohair, open mouth, 1940s, NM $275.00
22", mohair w/glass eyes, excelsior stuffed, swivel head, cloth nose, floss mouth, EX $1,450.00
23", wht shaggy synthetic w/blk & amber eyes glued in 2 layers, sheared plush snout, hands & feet, 1949, EX $75.00
26½", curly yel mohair w/glass eyes, embroidered nose & mouth, excelsior stuffing, fully jtd, 1920, G, A $300.00

Tekno

The Tekno company was formed in Denmark during the late 1920s. The toy vehicles they made were of the highest quality, fully able to compete with the German-made Marklin toys then dominating the market. The earliest Tekno vehicles were made of tinplate, and though some were not marked at all, others were stamped with a number. The factory continued to expand until WWII broke out and restrictions made further building impossible. In 1940 the government prohibited the use of tinplate for toy production, and the company began instead to manufacture diecast vehicles in a smaller (1/43) scale. These were exported worldwide in great volume. Collectors regard them as the finest diecasts ever made. Due to climbing production costs and the resulting increases in retail prices that inevitably hurt their sales, the company closed in 1972. Tekno dies were purchased by Mercury Kirk Joal who used them to produce toys identical to the originals except for the mark.

#356 Porsche, metallic bl w/wht rubber tires, NM....$150.00
#401 Flying Fortress, silver, US, VG $75.00
#408, VW pickup Fire Truck, NMIB $135.00
#409 VW Army Bus, NM (EX box) $125.00
#411 VW Ambulance, MIB $160.00
#415 Ford Tanus, Transit Ambulance, NM (EX box)....$125.00
#423 Ford VB Garbage Truck, red & gr, G $45.00
#426, Volvo FB88 Lumber Semi, MIB $150.00
#428 V8 Wrecking Truck, red & blk, metal tires, rare, G..$175.00
#434 Scania-Vebis Esso Tank Truck, 1965, cream & gray, NM....$50.00
#434 Volvo BP Tanker, wht & gr, M $150.00
#440 Mercury, NMIB $175.00
#443 Vespa Scooter, w/sidecar, M $125.00
#445 Scania Vabis Ladder Truck, red, EX $100.00
#449 Scania Vabis Lumber Truck, MIB $145.00
#452Y Covered Trailer, Tekno Transport, yel w/bl cover, M (G box) $30.00
#459 Falck Zonen Fire Truck, MIB $175.00
#463 Harrow, NM....$15.00
#465 International Harvester Tractor, MIB....$80.00
#481 Ford V8 Wrecker Truck, MIB $190.00
#491 Gyro Coupe, NMIB $90.00
#723 Mercedes-Benz 180, EX (EX box) $110.00
#724 Opel Kadett, EX (G box)....$55.00
#727 Junior Coupe, metallic bl, M $85.00
#731, Buick Ambulance, MIB....$145.00

#734 Chevrolet Truck, EX....$75.00
#739 Dodge Truck, w/topper, yel & red, VG....$125.00
#740 Dodge Milk & Cream Truck, bl & wht, NM....$175.00
#741 Chevrolet Lumber Truck, EX (EX box)....$75.00
#762 Motorcycle, w/sidecar, MIB....$100.00
#775 Small Utility Trailer, MIB....$30.00
#802 Alfa Romeo 2500, NMIB....$175.00
#809 Ford Thunderbird Convertible, MIB....$190.00
#812 Cooper Norton #1, silver, EX....$60.00
#815 Travel Trailer, Sprite, NM....$30.00
#824 MGA Coupe 1600, lt bl, NMIB....$150.00
#827 Saab 96, MIB....$130.00
#833 Ford Mustang, 1967, wht & blk w/Rallye Monte Carlo #169 decals, NM....$65.00
#834K Ford Mustang Kit, 1967, MIB....$30.00
#837 SAAB 99, wht, MIB....$55.00
#838 Volvo 164, EX....$45.00
#851 Scania CR 76 Bus, dk red, MIB....$75.00
#914 Ford D800 Tipping Truck, red side panels, MIB....$45.00
#915 Ford D-Truck, red & silver, MIB....$65.00
#918 Ford Beer Truck D800, NMIB....$50.00
#927 E-Type Jaguar, 1960s, red w/blk top, NMIB....$100.00
#930 Monza GT, silver, MIB....$65.00
#930S, Corvair Monza Coupe, chrome, M....$45.00
#931 Monza Spider, wht, MIB....$65.00
#934TM Toyota 2000 GT, mustard body, MIB....$40.00
#948 Dodge Missile Luancher, M (EX box)....$60.00
#951 Dodge Army Truck, covered, NM (EX box)....$50.00
#956 Dodge Truck w/Searchlight, MIB....$85.00

Three-bay garage with vehicles, 19" long, EX, A, $935.00.

Telephones

Novelty phones representing a well-known advertising or cartoon character are proving to be the focus of a lot of collector activity — the more recognizable the character the better. Telephones modeled after a product container are collectible too, and with the intense interest currently being shown in anything advertising related, competition is sometimes stiff and values are rising.

Advisor: Bill Bruegman (T2).

AC Spark Plug, figural, M....$35.00
Airplane, Northern Telectron, 1970s, NM....$85.00
Alvin, M....$60.00
Batmobile, 1989, blk plastic, 9", NM, M17....$50.00
Bozo the Clown, 1980s, MIB, from $65 to....$75.00
Bugs Bunny, Warner Exclusive, MIB, P12....$100.00
Cabbage Patch Girl, 1980s, EX, from $60 to....$75.00
Charlie Tuna, 1987, MIB, P12, from $50 to....$65.00
Ghostbusters, M, P12....$100.00
Gumball Machine, MIB, P12, from $125 to....$140.00

Keebler Elf, NM, $100.00.

Photo courtesy Martin and Carolyn Berens

Kermit the Frog, candlestick-type, MIB, P12, from $75 to .$85.00
Lazy Pig, MIB, P12....$65.00
Little Green Sprout, EX....$75.00
Mario Brothers, 1980s, MIB....$50.00
Mickey Mouse, Western Electric, 1976, EX....$175.00
Mickey Mouse, 1988, MIB....$50.00
Oscar Mayer Weiner, EX, P12....$65.00
Poppin' Fresh, w/headphones, MIB, P12....$125.00
Sly Dog, 1986, MIB, P12, from $85 to....$110.00
Snoopy & Woodstock, American Telephone Corporation, rotary dial, EX, from $100 to....$125.00
Snoopy & Woodstock, American Telephone Corporation, 1976, touch-tone, EX, H11....$100.00
Snoopy as Joe Cool, 1980s, MIB....$55.00
Spider-Man Climbing Down Chimney, NM, from $165 to ..$200.00
Super Bowl XIX, full-size football, w/handset, NM....$70.00
Superman, rotary dial, early version, M....$500.00
Tang Lips, rnd red base, 9", MIB, from $125 to....$150.00
Winnie the Pooh, sq base, M, from $225 to....$250.00
Ziggy, 1989, MIB....$75.00

Tonka

Since the mid-'40s, the Tonka Company (Minnesota) has produced an extensive variety of high-quality painted metal trucks, heavy equipment, tractors, and vans.

Our values are for items with the original paint. A repainted item is worth much less.

Advisor: Doug Dezso (D6).

Aerial Ladder Truck, 1957, aluminum ladders, 34", M...$300.00
Aerial Sand Loader Set, #992, 1956, complete, EX........$350.00
Air Express, #16, 1959, EX..$225.00
Allied Van Lines Truck, 1956, NM $300.00
Backhoe, #422, 1963, 17", EX......................................$125.00
Big Mike Dual Hydraulic Dump Truck, 1957, 14", EX...$575.00
Boat Transport Semi #41, 1959, 5-pc set, EX $600.00
Camper, #530, 1962, 14", EX $150.00
Car Carrier, #840, 1962, NM $200.00
Car Carrier #40, 1961, w/2 Ford cars & ramp, VG (worn box)..$175.00
Carnation Milk Delivery Van, #750, 1955, EX $475.00
Cement Mixer, #620, 1963, NM.....................................$175.00
COE Allied Van Lines Truck, G $125.00
COE Low Boy & Shovel, M..$300.00
Dump Truck w/Sand Loader, #116, 1961, NM..............$200.00
Farm Set, 1961, NMIB $525.00
Farm Stake Truck, #404, 1962, EX $225.00
Farm Truck w/Horse Trailer, 1959, EX.........................$300.00
Flamer Custom Pickup Truck, 1956, blk, M..................$175.00
Gambles Semi, 1956, EX...$325.00
Gambles Semi, 1958, M $375.00

Gasoline Truck, 1957, red, M, $650.00.

Grain Hauler Semi, #550, 1952, 22", EX $200.00
Hi-Way Dually Pickup Truck, 1959, VG.......................$150.00
Hi-Way Side Dump Truck, 1956, EX.............................$250.00
Jeep Surrey, #350, 1963, M...$100.00
Livestock Truck, 1952, NM $250.00
Low Boy & Shovel, 1955, red & bl, EX $300.00
Lumber Truck, #998, 1956, M.......................................$300.00
Military Tractor, #250, 1964, blk seat, EX+ $100.00
Minute Maid Delivery Truck, 1956, M..........................$550.00
Mobile Dragline, #135, 1961, EX..................................$200.00
Nationwide Moving Van, #39, 1958, EX.......................$275.00
Parcel Delivery Van, 1954, EX......................................$350.00
Pickup Truck, 1955, red, EX...$200.00
Pickup Truck, 1957, bl, EX...$200.00
Power Boom Loader, #115, 1960, EX............................$365.00
Ramp Hoist Truck, 1963, red w/wht trim, EX $450.00
Rescue Van, 1955, NM...$350.00
Sand Loader, 1961, 11½", EX..$50.00
Sportsman Pickup Truck, 1958, G $150.00
Stake Truck, #0860, 1955, EX.......................................$300.00
Standard Oil Tanker Semi, 1961, G $350.00
Star-Kist Van, 1954, 14½", NM....................................$400.00
State Hi-Way Dept Road Grader, 1960, 17", VG............$50.00

State Hi-Way Flatbed Truck with Shovel, M, $450.00.

Steam Shovel, #50, 1947, 21", NM...............................$225.00
Steel Carrier Semi, #145, 1950, 22", EX $265.00
Steel Carrier Truck, 1954, EX.......................................$175.00
Stock Rack Truck w/Animals, 1957, 16", complete, EX...$350.00
Suburban Pumper, #990, 1956, EX...............................$235.00
Terminex Van, 1961, EX...$400.00
Thunderbird Express, #37, 1960, EX............................$350.00
Tonka Toy Transport Van, #140, 1949, EX...................$275.00
Trailer Fleet Set, #675, 1953, w/2 tractors & 5 interchangeable trailers, EX $575.00
Trencher, #534, 1963, 18", EX $85.00
Troop Carrier, #380, 1964, 14", NM.............................$175.00
Winnebego Camper, 1968, VG.....................................$100.00
Wrecker, #2518, 1963, wht w/heavy-duty winch, 12", NM, from $100 to $150.00

Toothbrush Holders

Figural ceramic toothbrush holders have become very popular collectibles, especially those modeled after well-known cartoon characters. Disney's Mickey Mouse, Donald Duck, and the Three Little Pigs are among the most desirable, and some of the harder-to-find examples in mint condition sell for upwards of $200.00. Many were made in Japan before WWII. Because the paint was not fired on, it is often beginning to flake off. Be sure to consider the condition of the paint as well as the bisque when evaluating your holdings. For more information we recommend *Pictorial Guide to Toothbrush Holders* by Marilyn Cooper. Plate numbers in the following listings refer to Marilyn's book.

Advisor Marilyn Cooper (C9).

Andy Gump & Min, Japan, bsk, plate #221, 4" $85.00

Baby Deer, mk Brush Teeth Daily, Japan, plate #12, 4" .**$110.00**
Bear w/Jacket, Japan (Goldcastle), plate #13, 5½" **$95.00**
Betty Boop w/Toothbrush & Cup, KFS, plate #261, 4¾" .**$85.00**
Big Bird, Taiwan (RCC), plate #263, 4½" **$90.00**
Boy Brushing Teeth, Japan, plate #24, 6½" **$100.00**
Candlestick Maker, Japan (Goldcastle), plate #150, 5¼", from $70 to **$80.00**
Cat (Calico), Japan, plate #37, 5½" **$110.00**
Cat on Pedestal, Japan (Diamond T), plate #225, 5⅞" ..**$175.00**

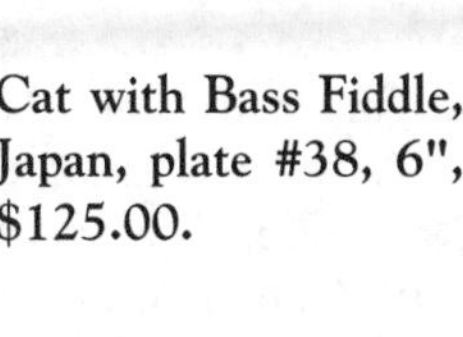
Cat with Bass Fiddle, Japan, plate #38, 6", $125.00.

Photo courtesy Marilyn Cooper

Circus Elephant, Japan, plate #56, 5⅜" **$100.00**
Clown w/Mask, Japan (Goldcastle), plate #62, from $100 to **$135.00**
Cowboy Next to Cactus, Japan, plate #70, 5½" **$95.00**
Dachshund, Japan, plate #71, 5¼" **$80.00**
Dalmatian, Germany, plate #202, 4" **$175.00**
Donald Duck, WDE, bsk, plate #83, 5¼", from $250 to.**$275.00**
Dwarfs in Front of Fence (Sleepy & Dopey), Japan/WD, bsk, 3½" **$1,275.00**
Flapper, plate #230, 4¼" **$130.00**
Girl Powdering Nose, Japan, plate #101, 6¼" **$100.00**
Humpty Dumpty, Pat Pending, bsk, plate #114, 5½" **$175.00**
Lion, Japan, plate #118, 6", from $75 to **$85.00**
Little Red Riding Hood, Germany (DRGM), plate #210, 5½", from $200 to **$225.00**

Mary Poppins, Japan, plate #119, 5¾" **$150.00**
Mickey & Pluto, WDE, plate #122, 4½", from $250 to..**$300.00**
Old King Cole, Japan, plate #125, 5¼", from $85 to......**$100.00**
Old Mother Hubbard, Germany, plate #3, 6¼" **$375.00**
Peter Pumpkin-Eater, Japan, plate #129, 4⅞" **$90.00**
Peter Rabbit, Germany, plate #4, 6¼" **$375.00**
Pinocchio & Figaro, Shafford, plate #242, 5¼" **$475.00**
Popeye, Japan, bsk, plate #244, 5" **$500.00**
Schnauzer, Germany, plate #283, 3⅛" **$115.00**
Siamese Donald Duck, Japan/WD, plate #247, 4¼" **$425.00**
Soldier w/Sash, Japan, plate #149, 6" **$90.00**
Three Bears w/Bowls, Japan (KIM USUI), plate #248, 4" .**$100.00**
Three Little Pigs w/Piano, WD, bsk, plate #250, 5" **$225.00**
Tom, Tom the Piper's Son, Japan, plate #154, 5¾" **$110.00**
Uncle Willie, Japan/FAS, plate #157, 5⅛" **$85.00**

Tootsietoys

The first diecast Tootsietoys were made by the Samuel Dowst Company in 1906 when they reproduced the Model T Ford in miniature. Dowst merged with Cosmo Manufacturing in 1926 to form the Dowst Manufacturing Company and continued to turn out replicas of the full-scale vehicles in actual use at the time. After another merger in 1961, the company became known as the Stombecker Corporation. Over the years, many types of wheels and hubs were utilized, varying in both style and material. The last all-metal car was made in 1969; recent Tootsietoys mix plastic components with the metal and have soft plastic wheels. Early prewar mint-in-box toys are scarce and command high prices on today's market. For more information we recommend *Collector's Guide to Tootsietoys*, Volumes I and II, by our advisor, David E. Richter. The recently released second edition features Tootsietoys from 1910 to 1979 and contains nearly seven hundred color photos.

Advisor: David E. Richter (R1).

Aero-Dawn Plane, #4660, 1934, NM **$70.00**
Ambulance, #0809, Graham Series, wht, NM **$120.00**
Autogyro, #4659, 1934, early wheel type, NM **$135.00**
Battleship, #1034, NM **$30.00**
Bi-Wing Seaplane, #4675, yel, NM **$75.00**
Bleriot Plane, #4482, 1910, NM **$120.00**
Bluebird Racer, #4666, 1932-41, gr, wht rubber wheels or disk wheels, NM, ea **$60.00**
Box Truck, #234, 1940-41 or 1947-48, 3", NM, ea **$25.00**
Buick Estate Wagon, 1948, closed grille, wine & cream, NM .**$70.00**
Buick Roadmaster Sedan, 1949-50 (made in 1949), bl, 6", NM **$55.00**
Buick XP-300, 1953-59 (made in 1951), red, 6", NM **$55.00**
Cadillac (1906), Classic Series, 1960-65, gr & blk, EX **$30.00**
Camper, #2544, 1974-76, gold, NM **$10.00**
Carrier, #1036, NM **$35.00**
Caterpiller Bulldozer w/Blade, #1910, 1956-67, yel w/blk rubber treads, NM **$50.00**
Caterpiller Tractor, #4646, 1931-39, orange w/wht rubber treads, NM **$55.00**

CJ3 Civilian Jeep, 1952-55/1958-61 (made in 1951), orange, 3", NM $30.00
CJ5 Jeep w/Snow Plow, 1961 (made in 1956), bl w/yel plow, rare, 6", NM $50.00
Coast Guard Seaplane, 1950, silver, EX $175.00
Dairy Truck, yel w/wht rubber tires, complete w/3 trailers, 13", VG, A $185.00
DeSoto Airflow, #0118, 1935-39, lt bl, NM $60.00
Dump Truck, #2470, HO Series, 1960s, red cab w/silver bed, NM $35.00
Dune Buggy, 1970-79, M $10.00
Farm Set, #6800, 1958, complete, MIB $475.00
Farm Tractor, #2435, 1974-77, gr, NM $12.00
Farm Tractor, #4654, 1927-32, orange, NM $125.00
Fast Freight Train Set, #186, 1940-41, complete, EX $175.00
Federal Grocery Van, 1924-33, NM $125.00
Federal Milk Van, 1924-33, yel, NM $115.00
Fire Hook & Ladder Truck, #4652, 1927-33, red, bl & metallic gold, NM $110.00
Fire Insurance Patrol Truck, #1042, 1937-41, NM $85.00
Fire Pumper Truck, 1970-79, red & wht, M $8.00
Fire Water Tower Truck, #4653, 1927-33, red, yel & bl, EX .. $110.00
Five-Wheel Roadster, #0511, Graham Series, red & blk, M, from $125 to $150.00
Ford & Trailer, #1043, silver, 1937-41, NM $120.00
Ford Convertible Coupe (1934), orange, EX $95.00
Ford Convertible Sedan (1935), brn, rare, NM $100.00
Ford Econoline Pickup, 1962-69, red, 6", EX $25.00
Ford F6 Oil Truck, 1949, red, 4", NM $25.00
Ford F7000 Stake Truck, 1956, red, 6", NM $45.00

Photo courtesy David E. Richter

Ford Fairlane 500 Convertible, 1957, red, M, $25.00.

Ford LTD, 1970 (made in 1969), bl, 4", NM $30.00
Ford Mainliner Sedan, 1953-54 (made in 1952), red, 3", EX $40.00
Ford Model A (1929), Classic Series, 1960-65, bl, NM $30.00
Ford Model A Sedan, #6665, 1928, gr, NM $65.00
Ford Roadster (1935), #0116, bl, M $70.00
Ford Trimotor Plane, 1932, red, NM $135.00
Ford Wrecker, #0133, 1934, 3", NM $100.00
GMC Scenicruiser, 1955-69, bl & silver, 7", NM $40.00
Greyhound Bus, #1045, 1937-41, bl & silver, w/or w/o tin bottom, NM, ea $85.00
High-Wing Plane, #107, 1932, NM $95.00
Highway Set, #4700, 1949, complete, MIB $450.00
Hudson Pickup Truck, 1947-49, 4", rare, NM $60.00
International K5 Stake Truck, 1947, gr, open sides, 6", NM $45.00
International Parcel Serivce Metro Van, 1959 only, bl, 6", NM $150.00
Jaguar XK 140 Coupe, 1959, bl, 6", NM $40.00
Jumbo Coupe, #1017, 1942-46, red w/wht top, EX $40.00
Jumbo Sedan, #0116, 1942-46, bl w/wht top, NM $50.00
Kaiser Sedan (1947), 1947-49, bl, 6", EX $50.00
Lincoln Capri 2-Door, 1953-58, red w/wht top, 6", NM .. $45.00
Lockheed Constellation, 1951, silver, EX $105.00
Logger w/Cab, 1970-79, red w/silver bed, M $12.00
Mack Anti-Aircraft Gun, #4643, 1931, NM $65.00
Mack Dump Truck (1921), Classic Series, 1960 (?), blk, red & yel, rare, NM $40.00
Mack US Airmail Service Truck (1921), 1931, red & olive w/blk tires, NM, A $85.00
Mercedes 190 SL Coupe, 1959-64 (made in 1956), lt bl, 6", NM $45.00
Mercury Fire Chief Car, 1953-60 (made in 1949), red, 4", EX $45.00
Mercury Sedan, 1953-54 (made in 1952), red, 4", NM $40.00
MG TF Roadster, 1959-67 (made in 1954), bl-gr, 6", EX. $35.00
Miniature Sports Set (1960), #4110, complete, NM (NM box), A $100.00
Offenhauser Racer, 1947-69 (made in 1947), yel, rubber & plastic wheels, NM $30.00
Oldsmobile 88 Convertible, 1950-54 (made in 1949), yel, 4", NM $40.00
Oldsmobile 98 w/Open Fenders, 1955-60 (made in 1955), red w/wht top, 4", NM $40.00

Photo courtesy David E. Richter

Open Touring Car, #232, 1940 – 41, green, NM, $55.00.

Overland Bus, #4680, 1929-33, bl, separate grille, EX $110.00
Packard Sedan, 1956-59 (made in 1956), wht w/bl top, NM $45.00
Packard Sedan w/Tow Hook, 1956-59 (made in 1956), aqua w/wht top, EX $40.00
Playtime Set #5031, 1920s, complete w/11 vehicles, NM (EX box), A $1,400.00
Plymouth 2-Door, 1959-69 (made in 1957), yel, 3", NM . $25.00
Pontiac Sedan, 1950-54 (made in 1950), gray w/red top, 4", NM $45.00
Railway Express Metro Truck, #2465, HO series, 1960s, NM $70.00
RC 180 Machinery Hauler, 1963-66, NM $65.00
RC 180 Transport, 1959-61, tin ramp, single axle trailer $135.00
Sea Champions, 1930s, complete w/battleship, destroyer, aircraft carrier, submarine & cruiser, NMOC, A $100.00
Seaplane, #4660, purple, NM $95.00
Silorsky S-58 Helicopter, 1958-69, red & white, rare, NM ... $100.00

Six-Wheel Convertible Coupe, #0614, Graham Series, maroon w/tan top, M, from $125 to **$150.00**
Sky Fleet Set, 1930s, set of 5 miniature planes, 2¼", EX (EX display card), A **$175.00**
Studebaker Lark Convertible, 1960-64 (made in 1960), lt bl, NM..**$25.00**
Thunderbird Coupe, 1955-67 (made in 1955), wht w/bl top, 4", NM..**$35.00**
Tow Truck, #2485, 1960s, wht w/red trim, NM................**$45.00**
Train Set, #7001 or #193, 1932-37, complete, NM, ea ..**$200.00**
Transport, #1037, EX..**$30.00**
Triumph TR Roadster, 1963-69 (made in 1956), deep aqua, 3", EX..**$20.00**
Twin Coach Bus, 1949-50, yel, 3", EX **$45.00**
Uncle Sam's Soldiers, #1404, 1930, set of 10, NMOC, A...**$450.00**
US Army Armored Car, #4635, 1946-48, camouflage, NM..**$60.00**
US Army CJ3 Jeep, 1947, 4", NM......................................**$35.00**
US Army CJ3 Jeep, 1950, 3", NM......................................**$20.00**
US Army DC-4 Transport, 1941, camouflage, NM........**$175.00**
US Army Plane, #119, 1936, camouflage, NM **$90.00**
US Army Tank (Renault), #4647, 1931-41, camouflage w/wht rubber treads, NM...**$85.00**
US Army Tractor w/Ammo Box, #4654, 1931-32, rare, NM...**$175.00**
USN Los Angeles Dirigible, #1030, 1937, NM **$100.00**
VW Bug, 1960-64 (made in 1960), copper, 3", NM **$20.00**
VW Bug, 1960-64 (made in 1960), copper, 6", NM **$45.00**
Waco Bomber, #718, 1937, red & silver, NM **$145.00**
Wrecker, #0806, Graham Series, wht, NM.....................**$110.00**
Zephyr Railcar, #117, 1935, gr, 4", rare, NM **$125.00**

Tops and Other Spinning Toys

Tops are among the oldest toys in human history. Homer in *The Iliad*, Plato in the *Republic*, and Virgil in *The Aeneid* mention tops. They are found in nearly all cultures, ancient and modern.

There are seven major categories: 1) The twirler — spun by the twisting action of fingers upon the axis. Examples are Teetotums, Dreidels, advertising spinners, and Tippe Tops. 2) The supported top — started with a string while the top is supported upright. These include recuperative, having a string that automatically rewinds (Namurs); separative, with a top that detaches from the launcher; spring launched, which is spun using a wound spring; pump or helix, whereby a twisted rod is pumped to spin the top; and flywheel- or inertia wheel-powered. 3) The peg top — spun by winding a string around the peg of the top which is then thrown. 4) The whip top — which is kept spinning by the use of a whip. 5) The yo-yo or return top. 6) The gyroscope. 7) The Diavuolo or Diabolo.

Advisor: Bruce Middleton (M20).

See also Yo-Yos.

Air Powered, Cracker Jack, Dowsy, Chicago, red, wht & bl, M, M20..**$12.00**
Air Powered, Poll Parrot Shoes, yel, NM, M20 ....**$12.00**
Aladdin Ball & Top, early 1900s, helix rod powered, EX (EX box), M20 ....**$550.00**
Autogyro Horse Race, Britains, lead & wire, flywheel mechanism, w/4 jockeys on horses, 11" L, EX................**$1,000.00**
Circus Horse & Rider, lead w/wire & tin, horse & female rider on rods attached to base, 7", VG+ **$375.00**
Competition Award Patches, top shape, 1st, 2nd & 3rd, M, M20, ea **$50.00**
Dancing Couple, Ives, japanned & polychromed CI figures w/arms entwined, she in lead bell-shaped skirt, 3½", EX **$135.00**
Disk, maroon & red wood flat-top w/natural wood holder, 3½" dia, EX..**$45.00**
Disk, red & natural wood w/gr stripes, w/hdl, 4" dia, EX ..**$75.00**
Game, Big Top, Marx, plastic, battery-op, MIB, M20 ......**$35.00**
Game, Brownie Kic-In, MH Miller, litho tin w/Brownies, top kicks ball into indentations for score, VG (G box), M20 ....**$50.00**
Game, Double Diablos, Parker Bros, 1930s, EX (EX box), M20 ....**$60.00**
Gyro-Cycle Top, British Invention & Manufacture, boy rides circular track, EX (EX box), M20 ....**$600.00**
Hummer, German, litho tin, clown-head knob w/wooden hat, 8", VG..**$580.00**
Hummer, inverted wood beehive-shape w/mc stripes, 2½" dia, VG **$415.00**
Hummer, wht celluloid ball w/mc stripes, tall, hdl, 7", EX..**$415.00**
Namur, wooden ball w/brass string housing, EX, M20......**$20.00**
Peg Top, Duncan Chicago Twister #329, wood, MIP, M20..**$20.00**
Peg Top, Duncan Tournament #349, wood, MIP, M20....**$20.00**
Peg Top, Duncan Twin Spin #310, wood, MIP, M20.......**$20.00**
Peg Top, Duncan Whistler #320, wood, MIP, M20..........**$20.00**
Peg Top, Helix Rod Launcher, advertising Kinney Shoes, VG, M20..**$15.00**
Recuperative, natural wood w/pnt stripes, wood string housing, EX, M20, from $50 to...**$100.00**
Recuperative, wood, 6-sided string housing over ovoid body, G, M20..**$85.00**
Spinner, Alemite Motor Oil, Bakelite, Keep Your Car Humming Like a Top, NM, M20..**$15.00**
Spinner, Brown-Bilt Shoes, Buster Brown, blk & red letters on yel background w/red trim, EX, M20..........................**$45.00**
Spinner, Cracker Jack, M, M20, from $20 to **$75.00**
Spinner, Derby Petroleum Products, M, M20, from $20 to ...**$75.00**
Spinner, man w/mug of beer, Hvem Betaler on hat, litho metal, foreign, spin to see who pays, NM, M20 ....**$85.00**
Spinner, Nolde's American Maid Breads & Cakes, red & wht, NM, M20 ....**$30.00**
Spinner, OTC Trenton Oyster Crackers, bl letters on wht, M, M20..**$50.00**
Spinner, Poll Parrot Shoes, red parrot w/blk shoes on yel background, M, M20..**$30.00**
Spinner, Robin Hood Shoes, M, M20, from $20 to **$75.00**
Spinner, shaped like pointing spaniel, flat, Heads I Win, Tails You Lose, NM, M20 ....**$25.00**
Spinner, Tastykake Cakes & Pies, M, M20, from $20 to..**$75.00**
Spinner, Tip Top Bread, plastic, NM, M20 ....**$10.00**
Supported, pressed board disk w/graphics of boy shooting a toy gun, M **$60.00**
Supported, Rainbow, Seneca, pnt metal 4-tooth disks inside lg disk rotating around shaft, changes color, NM, M20.**$65.00**

Photo courtesy Bruce Middleton

Supported Top, advertises Deininger's Mother's Bread, cast metal, NM, $45.00.

Tip Tray, Canada Dry, red, gr, wht & yel, dimple in center to spin on, G, M20 .... $20.00
Tip Tray, SS Pierce, Wine & Spirit Merchants..., dimple in center to spin on, M, M20 .... $60.00

Trading Cards

Modern collector cards are really just an extension of a hobby that began well before the turn of the century. Advertising cards put out by the food and tobacco companies of that era sometimes featured cute children, their pets, stage stars, battle scenes, presidential candidates, and so forth. Collectors gathered them up and pasted them in scrapbooks.

In the 20th century, candy and bubble gum companies came to the forefront. The cards they issue with their products carry the likenesses of sports figures, fictional heroes, TV and movie stars, Disney characters, Barbie dolls, and country singers!

Distinguishing a collectible trading card from other cards may be a bit confusing. Remember, trading cards are released in only two ways: 1) in a wax or foil pack, generally in multiples of twelve — twenty-four, thirty-six, or forty-eight; or 2) as a premium with another product. The only exceptions to this rule are sets issued as limited editions, with each set individually numbered. Cards issued as factory sets are not trading cards and have no collector value unless they cross over into another collecting area, for example, the Tuff Stuff Norma Jean (Marilyn Monroe) series. In general, from 1980 to the present, wrappers tend to fall into the 50¢ to $2.00 range, though there are some exceptions. For more information we recommend *Collector's Guide to Trading Cards* by Robert Reed.

Advisors: Mark and Val Macaluso (M1).

Other Sources: C1, C10, D11, F1, F8, H4, H11, H12, J6, J7, M8, M17, T2

A-Team, Monty Gum, 1983, set of 100 .... $20.00
Akira, Cornerstone, 1994, set of 100 .... $18.00
Aladdin, Skybox, 1993, set of 90 .... $20.00
Alf, Topps, 1987, 1st series, set of 47 w/22 stickers $12.00
Alf, Topps, 1988, 2nd series, set of 44 w/22 stickers $12.00
Alien Vs Predator, Topps, 1995, set of 72 w/15 stickers $18.00
All My Children, Star Pics, 1991, set of 72 .... $12.00
American Bandstand, Collect-A-Card, 1993, set of 100 .... $15.00
Animaniacs, Topps, 1995, set of 72 w/12 stickers $10.00

Andy Griffith Show, Pacific, 1990, 1st series, set of 110, $25.00.

Archie, Skybox, 1993, set of 120 .... $18.00
Avengers, Cornerstone, 1994, 3rd series, set of 80 .... $18.00
Back to the Future II, Topps, 1989, set of 88 w/11 stickers $12.00
Barbie, Dart/Panini, 1992, set of 196 .... $30.00
Batman (Animated), Topps, 1993, set of 100 .... $30.00
Batman (Movie), Topps, 1989, 2nd series, set of 132 w/22 stickers $15.00
Batman & Robin, Skybox, 1995, set of 90 w/12 stickers $20.00
Batman Returns, Topps, 1992, stadium, set of 100 .... $30.00
Battlestar Galactica, Topps, 1978, set of 132 w/22 stickers $55.00
Beauty & the Beast, Upper Deck, 1993, set of 198 .... $30.00
Beavis & Butthead, Fleer, 1994, set of 150 .... $35.00
Beetlejuice, Dart Flipcard, 1990, set of 100 w/20 stickers $18.00
Berenstain Bears, Kenwis Inc, 1992, set of 72 w/5 stickers $15.00
Betty Boop, Eclipse, 1993, set of 110 .... $25.00
Beverly Hills 90210, Topps, 1991, set of 77 w/11 stickers $18.00
Bill & Ted's Adventure, Pro Set, 1991, set of 140 .... $8.50
Black Hole, Topps, 1979, set of 88 w/22 stickers $15.00
Boris, Comic Images, 1993, 3rd series, set of 90 .... $30.00
Bozo the Clown, Lime Rock, 1994, set of 54 .... $10.00
Buck Rogers, Topps, 1979, set of 88 w/22 stickers $25.00
Cabbage Patch Kids (Astronauts), Coleco, 1989, set of 6 (1 came w/ea doll) $90.00
Campbell's Soup, Collect-a-Card, 1995, set of 72 .... $16.00
Charlie's Angels, Topps, 1977, 2nd series, set of 55 w/11 stickers $35.00
Charlie's Angels, Topps, 1978, 4th series, set of 66 w/11 stickers $30.00
Cinderella, Panini, 1987, set of 225 .... $40.00
Clash of the Titans, Canada, scarce, set of 12 .... $35.00
Close Encounters, Crown, 1978, postcard sz, set of 48 .... $30.00
Coca-Cola (Santa Claus), Collect-a-Card, 1994, set of 100 .... $16.00
Comic Ball Looney Tunes, Upper Deck, 1990, set of 549 .... $20.00
Creature Feature, Topps, 1980, set of 88 w/22 stickers $40.00
Cyndi Lauper, Topps, 1985, set of 33 w/33 stickers $10.00
Dallas, Donruss, 1981, set of 56 .... $12.00

Dallas Cowboy Cheerleaders, Topps, 1981, 5x7", set of 30 ... **$30.00**
Dark Horse, Topps, 1994, set of 100 ... **$20.00**
DC Comics, DC Comics, 1988, scarce, set of 48 ... **$75.00**
DC Legends, Skybox, 1995, set of 150 ... **$55.00**
DC Super Heroes, Taystee, set of 30 ... **$35.00**
Deep Space 9, Skybox, 1994, set of 100 ... **$16.00**
Demolition Man, Skybox, 1991, set of 100 ... **$18.00**
Desert Storm, Pro Set, 1991, set of 260 ... **$20.00**
Desert Storm (Homecoming), Topps, 1991, set of 88 w/11 stickers ... **$10.00**
Dick Tracy, Topps, 1993, set of 88 w/22 stickers ... **$10.00**
Dinamation (Dinosaurs), Star Pics, 1992, set of 80 ... **$16.00**
Dinosaur Attacks, Topps, 1988, set of 55 w/11 stickers ... **$10.00**
Disney Collector Cards, Impel, 1991, set of 210 ... **$30.00**
Donkey Kong, Topps, 1982, set of 16 w/32 stickers ... **$12.50**
Dr Who, Cornerstone, 1995, 2nd series, set of 110 ... **$20.00**
Duran Duran, Topps, 1985, set of 33 w/33 stickers ... **$10.00**
Elvis, River Group, 1992, 1st series, set of 220 ... **$35.00**
Empire Strikes Back, Topps, 1980, 2nd series, set of 132 .. **$38.00**
Empire Strikes Back (Wide Vision), Topps, 1995, set of 144 ... **$40.00**
ET, Topps, 1982, set of 87 w/12 stickers ... **$30.00**
Fievel Goes West, Impel, 1991, set of 150 ... **$15.00**
Flash Gordon, English, set of 180 ... **$45.00**
Flash Gordon, MV Jasinski, 1990, 1st series, limited edition, set of 36 ... **$30.00**
Flintstones, Cardz, 1993, set of 100 ... **$28.00**
Flintstones (Return Of), Cardz, 1994, set of 50 w/10 stickers ... **$15.00**
Fright Flicks, Topps, 1988, set of 90 w/11 stickers ... **$12.50**
Garbage Pail Kids, Topps, 1985, 3rd series, set of 88 stickers ... **$20.00**
Garfield, Skybox, 1992, set of 100 ... **$20.00**
Ghost Rider, Comic Images, 1990, set of 45 ... **$30.00**
Ghostbusters, Panini, 1987, set of 264 ... **$35.00**
GI Joe, Diamond, 1987, set of 225 ... **$20.00**
Gone w/the Wind, Duo Cards, 1996, set of 90 ... **$15.00**
Goonies, Topps, 1986, set of 86 w/22 stickers ... **$15.00**

Grease, Topps, 1978, 2nd series, set of 66 with 11 stickers, from $25.00 to $35.00.

Gremlins, Topps, 1984, set of 82 ... **$15.00**
Growing Pains, Topps, set of 66 w/11 stickers ... **$18.00**
Gunsmoke, Pacific, 1992, set of 110 ... **$15.00**
Happy Days, Topps, 1976, set of 44 w/11 stickers ... **$25.00**
Harley Davidson, Collect-a-Card, 1992, set of 100 ... **$35.00**
Harry & the Hendersons, Topps, 1987, set of 77 w/22 stickers ... **$12.00**
High Chaparral, Monty Gum, 1970, set of 124 ... **$75.00**
Home Alone, Topps, 1992, set of 66 w/11 stickers ... **$12.00**
Home Improvement, Skybox, 1994, set of 80 w/10 stickers ... **$22.00**
Hook, Topps, 1991, set of 99 w/11 stickers ... **$10.00**
Hulk, Comic Images, 1991, set of 90 ... **$25.00**
I Love Lucy, Pacific, 1991, set of 110 ... **$20.00**
In Living Color, Topps, 1992, set of 88 w/11 stickers ... **$15.00**
Indiana Jones & the Temple of Doom, Topps, 1984, set of 88 w/11 stickers ... **$18.00**
James Bond, Eclipse, 1993, 1st series, set of 110 ... **$40.00**
James Bond, Monty Gum, 1987, 2nd series, set of 200 ... **$100.00**
Jaws II, Topps, 1978, set of 59 w/11 stickers ... **$10.00**
Jurassic Park Gold, Topps, 1993, set of 88 w/10 stickers ... **$45.00**
King Kong, Topps, 1976, set of 55 w/11 stickers ... **$35.00**
Knight Rider, Donruss, 1985, set of 66 w/11 puzzle variations ... **$20.00**
Last Action Heroe, Topps, 1993, set of 88 w/11 stickers .. **$20.00**
Legend of Big Foot, Leesley, 1989, set of 100 ... **$12.00**
Lion King, Skybox, 1994, 2nd series, set of 90 ... **$20.00**
Lois & Clark, Skybox, 1995, set of 90 w/6 tattoos ... **$20.00**
Lost in Space, Topps, 1966, set of 55 ... **$550.00**
M*A*S*H, Donruss, 1982, set of 66 ... **$30.00**
Marvel Masterpiece, Skybox, 1993, 1st series, set of 90 ... **$40.00**
Marvel Super Heroes, Topps, 1976, set of 9 w/40 stickers . **$60.00**
Masters of the Universe, Topps, 1984, set of 88 w/22 stickers ... **$22.00**
Maverick, Cardz, 1994, set of 60 ... **$20.00**
Max Headroom, Topps, 1988, scarce, set of 33 w/11 foils ... **$75.00**
Michael Jackson, Topps, 1984, 2nd series, set of 33 ... **$10.00**
Mickey Mouse, Americana, set of 360 ... **$150.00**
Mickey Mouse, Panini, set of 360 ... **$100.00**
Minnie & Me, Impel, 1991, set of 160 ... **$15.00**
Miss USA, Star, 1993, set of 101 ... **$22.00**
Monster Initials, Topps, 1974, set of 132 ... **$400.00**
Mortal Kombat, Topps, 1994, set of 100 ... **$12.00**
Ms Pacman, Fleer, 1981, set of 54 w/28 stickers ... **$50.00**
Muppets, Cardz, 1994, set of 60 ... **$15.00**
New Kids on the Block, Topps, 1990, 1st series, set of 88 w/22 stickers ... **$12.00**
Nightmare on Elm Street, Comic Images, 1988, set of 264 w/album ... **$16.00**
Nintendo, Topps, 1990, set of 53 w/33 stickers ... **$8.00**
Partridge Family, Topps, 1971, bl, set of 55 ... **$95.00**
Partridge Family, Topps, 1971, gr, set of 55 ... **$175.00**
Partridge Family, Topps, 1971, ye,l set of 55 ... **$95.00**
Peanuts (Snoopy for President), Pro Sports, 1992, set of 200 .. **$28.00**
Phantom, Comic Images, 1995, set of 90 ... **$10.00**
Phantom (Movie), Inkworks, 1996, set of 90 ... **$10.00**
Planet of the Apes, Topps, 1975, set of 66 ... **$65.00**
Popeye, Card Creations, 1995, set of 100 ... **$15.00**
Power Rangers, Collect-a-Card, 1994, set of 72 w/12 stickers ... **$20.00**
Power Rangers (Movie), Fleer, 1995, set of 150 ... **$20.00**

Precious Moments, Enesco, 1992, set of 16 (1 given w/ea figurine) $35.00
Raiders of the Lost Ark, Topps, 1981, set of 88 ....$20.00
Rambo, Panini, 1987, set of 240 ....$45.00
Return of Superman, Skybox, 1993, set of 100 ....$24.00
Return of the Jedi, Topps, 1983, 1st series, set of 132 w/66 stickers $25.00
Return of the Jedi (Wide Vision), Topps, 1995, set of 144 ..$40.00
Return to Oz, Topps, 1985, set of 44 stickers $10.00
Robin Hood, Topps, 1991, set of 88 w/9 stickers $12.50
Robocop II, Topps, 1990, set of 88 w/11 stickers $12.50
Rock Stars, Donruss, 1979, set of 66 ....$16.00
Rocketeer, Topps, 1991, set of 99 w/11 stickers $10.00
Rocky II, Topps, 1979, set of 99 w/22 stickers $15.00
Roger Rabbit, Topps, 1988, set of 132 w/22 stickers $20.00
Santa & Snowflakes, TCM, 1995, set of 72 ....$12.00
Saved by the Bell, Pacific, 1992, set of 110 ....$20.00
Seaquest, Skybox, 1994, set of 100 ....$25.00
Sesame Street, Idolmaker, 1992, set of 100 ....$15.00
Shadow Hawk, Comic Images, 1992, set of 90 ....$18.00
Simpsons, Topps, 1990, set of 88 w/22 stickers $22.00
Six Million Dollar Man, Monty Gum, 1975, set of 72 ....$95.00
Sonic Hedgehog, Topps, 1993, set of 33 w/33 stickers $10.00
Space: 1999, Panini, 1976, set of 400 ....$65.00
Spider-Man, Comic Images, 1992, set of 90 ....$20.00
Spider-Man (Team-Up), Comic Images, 1990, set of 45 ..$35.00
Star Trek, Topps, 1976, set of 88 ....$395.00
Star Trek II, Monty Gum, 1983, set of 100 ....$125.00
Star Trek Master Series, Skybox, 1993, set of 90 ....$25.00
Star Trek: The Next Generation, Panini, 1992, set of 240 ..$55.00
Star Wars, OPC, 1978, 1st series, set of 66 ....$100.00
Star Wars, Panini, 1978, set of 256 ....$150.00
Star Wars, Topps, 1977, 2nd series, set of 66 ....$30.00
Star Wars Finest, Topps, 1996, set of 90 ....$35.00
Supergirl, Topps, 1985, set of 44 stickers $6.00
Superman, OPC, 1979, set of 132 ....$35.00
Superman (Movie), Topps, 1979, 2nd series, set of 88 ....$25.00
Superman Doomsday, Skybox, 1994, set of 100 ....$50.00
Superman II, Topps, 1991, set of 88 ....$12.00
Tales from the Crypt, Cardz, 1993, set of 110 ....$30.00
Tarzan, Panini, set of 400 ....$75.00
Teenage Mutant Ninja Turtles, Diamond, 1989, set of 180.$18.00
Terminator 2, Impel, 1991, set of 192 ....$15.00
Three Stooges, FTCC, 1985, set of 60 ....$75.00
Thundercats, Panini, 1980s, set of 264 ....$25.00
Tiny Toons, Topps, 1991, set of 77 w/11 stickers $20.00
Trolls, Topps, 1992, set of 66 w/11 stickers $10.00
Trolls (Norfin), Collect-a-Card, 1992, set of 50 ....$10.00
Twin Peaks, Star Pics, 1992, set of 76 ....$20.00
V, Fleer, 1984, set of 66 ....$25.00
Vampirella, Topps, 1995, set of 90 ....$25.00
Web of Spider-Man, Comic Images, 1991, set of 75 w/album .$85.00
Weird Ohs, Fleer, 1965, set of 66 ....$200.00
Welcome Back Kotter, Topps, 1976, set of 44 ....$25.00
Wizard of Oz, Pacific, 1990, set of 110 ....$20.00
X-Men, Diamond, 1993, set of 150 stickers w/album $18.00
X-Men, Impel, 1992, 1st series, set of 100 ....$25.00
Zero Heroes, Donruss, 1984, set of 66 ....$15.00

Boxes

Addams Family, Topps, 1991 ....$6.00
Aladdin, Panini, 1993 ....$4.00
Andy Griffith, Pacific, 1991, 2nd series $4.00
Animaniacs, Topps, 1995 ....$4.00
Avengers, Cornerstone, 1993 ....$5.00
Back to the Future II, Topps, 1989 ....$6.00
Barbie, Dart Panini, 1991, 1st series $4.00
Batman (Animated), Topps, 1993 ....$5.00
Batman (Movie), Topps, 1989, 1st series $5.00
Beauty & the Beast, Pro Set, 1992 ....$5.00
Betty Boop, Eclipse, 1993 ....$5.00
Beverly Hillbillies, Eclipse, 1993 ....$5.00
Charlie's Angels, Topps, 1977, 3rd series $15.00
CHiPs, Donruss, 1979 ....$8.00
Close Encounters, Topps, 1978 ....$6.00
Coneheads, Topps, 1993 ....$5.00
Dallas, Donruss, 1981 ....$8.00
Deep Space 9, Skybox, 1994 ....$4.00
Desert Storm Victory, Topps, 1991 ....$4.00
Disney, Skybox, 1993, 2nd series $4.00
Dune, Fleer, 1984 ....$5.00
Elvis, River Group, 1992, 1st series $5.00
Empire Strikes Back, Topps, 1980 ....$4.00
Fievel Goes West, Impel, 1991 ....$5.00
Flying Nun, Donruss, 1968, NM $75.00
Garbage Pail Kids, Topps, 1988, 1st series $50.00
Ghostbusters, Topps, 1989 ....$4.00
GI Joe, Diamond, 1987 ....$4.00
Harlem Globetrotters, Comic Images, 1992 ....$4.00
Home Improvement, Skybox, 1994 ....$4.00
Hook, Topps, 1991 ....$8.00
I Love Lucy, Pacific, 1991 ....$6.00
James Bond, Eclipse, 1993, 1st series $5.00
Jurassic Park Gold, Topps, 1993 ....$10.00
Knight Rider, Donruss, 1985 ....$6.00
Leave It to Beaver, Pacific, 1984 ....$10.00
Lois & Clark, Skybox, 1995 ....$4.00
Marvel Super Heroes, FTCC, 1984 ....$6.00
Masters of the Universe, Topps, 1984 ....$6.00
Minnie & Me, Impel, 1991 ....$4.00
Monkees, Cornerstone, 1996 ....$4.00
Muppets, Cardz, 1994 ....$4.00
Nicktoons, Topps, 1993 ....$5.00
Nightmare Before Christmas, Skybox, 1993 ....$5.00
Pagemaster, Skybox, 1994 ....$4.00
Pee Wee's Playhouse, Topps, 1989 ....$10.00
Power Rangers II, Collect-a-Card, 1994 ....$4.00
Ren & Stimpy, Topps, 1994 ....$5.00
Return of Superman, Skybox, 1993 ....$5.00
Robin Hood, Topps, 1991 ....$4.00
Saved by the Bell, Pacific, 1992 ....$4.00
Simpsons, Topps, 1990 ....$5.00
Spider-Man, Comic Images, 1988 ....$15.00
Star Trek, Topps, 1976 ....$50.00
Star Trek III, FTCC, 1984 ....$18.00
Star Trek: Next Generation, Skybox, 1994 ....$5.00

Star Wars, Topps, 1977, 2nd series....$25.00
Superman (Movie), Topps, 1978, 1st series....$10.00
Superman II, Topps, 1991....$6.00
Teenage Mutant Ninja Turtles, Diamond, 1989....$3.00
Terminator 2, Impel, 1991....$4.00
Trolls, Topps, 1992....$4.00
V, Fleer, 1984....$6.00
Wizard of Oz, Pacific, 1990....$5.00
X-Men, Impel, 1992, 1st series....$5.00
Young Indiana Jones Chronicles, Pro Set, 1991....$4.00

Wrappers

Addams Family, Topps, 1991....$1.00
Alien Vs Preditor, Topps, 1995....$1.00
Avengers, Cornerstone, 1994....$1.00
Batman (Animated), Topps, 1993....$1.00
Batman Returns (Stadium), Topps, 1992....$2.00
Bay City Rollers, Topps, 1977....$8.00
Beauty & the Beast, Upper Deck, 1993....$1.00
Beverly Hills 90210, Topps, 1991....$1.00
Bionic Woman, Donruss, 1976....$3.00
Bozo the Clown, Lime Rock, 1994....$1.00
Buck Rogers, Topps, 1979....$2.00
Charlie's Angels, Topps, 1977, 2nd series....$3.00
CHiPs, Donruss, 1979....$1.00
Dark Horse, Topps, 1994....$1.50
Deep Space 9, Skybox, 1994....$1.50
Dinamation, Star Pics, 1992....$1.00
Disney, Skybox, 1993, 2nd series....$1.50
Dukes of Hazzard, Donruss, 1981, 3rd series....$1.50
Elvis, River Group, 1993, 3rd series....$2.00
Empire Strikes Back, Topps, 1980, 3rd series....$1.00
Fern Gully: The Last Rain Forest, Dart Flipcard, 1992....$1.00
Fievel Goes West, Impel, 1991....$1.00
Garbage Pail Kids, Topps, 1985, 1st series....$5.00
Garbage Pail Kids, Topps, 1985, 3rd series....$2.00
Garfield, Skybox, 1992....$1.00
Good Times, Topps, 1975....$3.00
Grease, Topps, 1978....$2.00
Happy Days, OPC, 1976....$2.00
Home Improvement, Skybox, 1994....$1.00
James Bond, Monty Gum, 1987, 2nd series....$2.00
Jurassic Park, Topps, 1993....$1.00
King Kong, Topps, 1976....$2.50
KISS I, Donruss, 1978....$2.00
M*A*S*H, Donruss, 1982....$1.50
Magnum PI, Donruss, 1983....$1.00
Marvel Super Heroes, Topps, 1976....$3.00
Michael Jackson, Topps, 1984, 1st series....$1.00
Mickey Mouse, Panini....$1.00
Minnie & Me, Skybox, 1993, 2nd series....$1.00
Mork & Mindy, OPC, 1978....$1.00
Ms Pacman, Fleer, 1981....$1.50
Muppets, Cardz, 1994....$1.00
Nightmare Before Christmas, Skybox, 1993....$1.00
Pacman, Fleer, 1980....$4.00
Partridge Family, Topps, 1971....$10.00
Popeye, Card Creations, 1995....$1.00
Raiders of the Lost Ark, OPC, 1981....$1.00
Rambo, Panini, 1987....$1.50
Ren & Stimpy, Topps, 1994....$1.00
Return of the Jedi, OPC, 1983....$1.50
Robin Hood, Topps, 1991....$1.00
Rocky II, Topps, 1979....$1.00
Sesame Street, Idolmaker, 1992....$1.00
Six Million Dollar Man, Monty Gum, 1975....$1.50
Snow White & the Seven Dwarfs, Skybox, 1993....$1.00
Space 1999, Panini, 1976....$2.00
Spider-Man, Comic Images, 1992, 2nd series....$1.00
Star Trek, Topps, 1976....$8.00
Star Trek II, Monty Gum, 1983....$3.50
Star Trek IV, FTCC, 1987....$1.50
Star Wars, OPC, 1978, 1st series....$8.00
Star Wars, Topps, 1977, 1st series....$6.00
Star Wars, Topps, 1977, 2nd series....$3.50
Superman (Movie), Topps, 1978, 1st series....$1.50
Superman II, Topps, 1991....$1.00
Tales from the Crypt, Cardz, 1993....$1.00
Three Stooges, FTCC, 1989, 2nd series....$1.00
Tiny Toons, Cardz, 1994....$1.00
Total Recall, Pacific, 1990....$25.00
Trolls Force, Star Pics, 1992....$1.00
Universal Monsters, Topps, 1994....$1.00
Vampirella, Topps, 1995....$1.00
Welcome Back Kotter, Topps, 1976....$1.50
Where's Waldo, Mattel, 1991....$1.00
Wizard of Oz, Pacific, 1990....$1.50
X-Men, Impel, 1992, 1st series....$1.00

Trains

Some of the earliest trains (from ca 1860) were made of tin or cast iron, smaller versions of the full-scale steam-powered trains that transversed America from the east to the west. Most were made to simply be pushed or pulled along, though some had clockwork motors. Electric trains were produced as early as the late 19th century. Three of the largest manufacturers were Lionel, Ives, and American Flyer.

Lionel trains have been made since 1900. Until 1915 they produced only standard gauge models (measuring 2½" between the rails). The smaller O gauge (1¼") they introduced at that time proved to be highly successful, and the company grew until by 1955 it had become the largest producer of toys in the world. Until discontinued in 1940, standard gauge trains were produced on a limited scale, but O and 027 gauge models dominated the market. Production dwindled and nearly stopped in the mid-1960s, but the company was purchased by General Mills in 1969.

The Ives company had been a major producer of toys since 1896. They were the first to initiate manufacture of the O gauge train and at first used only clockwork motors to propel them. Their first electric trains (in both O and #1 gauge) were made in 1910, but because electricity was not yet a common commodity in many areas, clockwork production continued for several years. By 1920, #1 gauge was phased out in favor of standard gauge. The company continued to prosper until the late 1920s when it floundered and was bought jointly by American Flyer and Lionel. American Flyer soon turned their interest over to Lionel, who continued to make Ives trains until 1933.

The American Flyer company had produced trains for several years, but it wasn't until it was bought by AC Gilbert in 1937 that it became successful enough to be considered a competitor of Lionel. They're best noted for their conversion from the standard (wide gauge) 3-rail system to the 2-rail S gauge (7/8") and the high-quality locomotives, passenger and freight cars they produced in the 1950s. Interest in toy trains waned during the space-age decade of the 1960s. As a result, sales declined, and in 1966 the company was purchased by Lionel. Today both American Flyer and Lionel trains are being made from the original dies by Lionel Trains Inc.

For more information we recommend *Collecting Toy Trains, An Identification and Value Guide*, by Richard O'Brien.

Advisors: Bill Mekalian (M4) and Gary Mosholder, Gary's Trains (G1).

See also Buddy L (for that company's Outdoor Railroad); **Paper-Lithographed Toys**.

American Flyer

Accessory, #4B transformer, 100 watts, 1949-56, EX (EX box) .**$35.00**
Accessory, #12B transformer, 250 watts, 1946-52, EX (EX box) **$75.00**
Accessory, #168 hotel, 1953, EX **$200.00**
Accessory, #795 station & terminal, 1954, EX **$450.00**
Car, #779 oil drum loader, 1955-56, NMIB **$150.00**
Car, #981 Central of Georgia boxcar, 1956, EX **$125.00**
Car, #4006 hopper, red, EX (EX box) **$450.00**
Car, #24191 Canadian National reefer, 1958, EX **$250.00**
Car, #24222 Domino Sugar hopper, 1963-64, VG **$450.00**
Car, #24323 Baker's Chocolate tank car, gray ends, 1959-60, NMIB **$350.00**
Car, #24323 Baker's Chocolate tank car, wht ends, 1959-60, rare, MIB **$2,000.00**
Car, #25515 USAF rocket sled, EX **$200.00**
Car, #35515 rocket sled, EX **$150.00**
Loco, #342 DC Switcher, MIB **$575.00**
Loco, #481 Silver Flash, diesel, MIB **$750.00**
Loco, #21551 Northern Pacific A-Unit, NMIB **$375.00**
Loco, #21573 NH EP5, 1958-59, EX (EX box) **$600.00**
Set, #K771 operating stockyard & car, NMIB **$150.00**
Set, #162 Mysto-Magic Factory, 1952, EX **$150.00**
Set, #1218 loco, #1206 boxcars (2), #1205 mail car, VG (G box), from $800 to **$1,200.00**
Set, #23830 Piggyback Unloader & Car, NMIB **$150.00**
Set, Century, #9915 loco w/integral tender, #3178 coaches (2) & #9915 observation car, G **$850.00**
Set, CI loco w/litho tin tender & passenger coach, miniature, M (worn box), A **$2,200.00**
Set, freight; 2-4-2 loco, tender, boxcar, gondola, tank car & flat bed car, 1930-35, VG (VG box) **$700.00**

Set, cast-iron locomotive (black), tin tender (black), railway, and coaches (two red), complete with track, MIB, A, $450.00; Set, cast-iron locomotive (black), tin tender, and passenger coach (red), complete with track, MIB, A, $400.00; Set, cast-iron locomotive and tender (black), #3150, #3151 & #3152 coaches (two orange with brass trim), MIB, A, $475.00.

Set, Minnie Ha Ha, EX **$300.00**
Set, Southern Pacific Alco, MIB, A **$700.00**
Set, tender & 4 passenger cars, red litho tin, EX, A **$275.00**
Set, The Comet, AA loco, 2 coaches & end car, VG **$500.00**
Set, Washington, #21089 loco & tender, #24055 boxcar, #24565 flat car & #24750 coach, EX **$600.00**

Lionel Modern Era 1970 – 96

Accessory, #2163 block target signal, M, G1 .... **$25.00**
Accessory, #2180 road sign, MIB, G1 .... **$5.00**
Accessory, #2312 mechanical semaphore, M, G1 .... **$15.00**
Accessory, #2317 drawbridge, MIB, G1 .... **$125.00**
Accessory, #2320 flag pole, EX, G1 .... **$20.00**
Accessory, #8754 New Haven rectifier, MIB, A **$150.00**
Accessory, #12719 refreshment stand, animated, MIB, G1 .**$60.00**
Accessory, #12865 wisk tractor-trailer, MIB, G1 .... **$18.00**
Accessory, #12891 reefer tractor-trailer, MIB, G1 .... **$18.00**
Car, #5739 B&O tool car, EX, G1 .... **$40.00**
Car, #6100 Ontario Northland hopper, EX, G1 .... **$45.00**
Car, #6138 B&O hopper, EX, G1 .... **$35.00**
Car, #7404 Jersey Central boxcar, M, G1 .... **$50.00**
Car, #7518 Carson City mint car, MIB, G1 .... **$45.00**
Car, #7782 TCA Museum Carlisle Finch, MIB, G1 .... **$30.00**
Car, #782 LRRC 1995 tank car, M, G1 .... **$65.00**
Car, #784 LRRC 1984 covered hopper, MIB, G1 .... **$90.00**
Car, #8690 Lionel Lines trolley car, M, A **$100.00**
Car, #8912 LCAC 1988 Canadian Southern club car, MIB, G1..**$275.00**
Car, #9013 Canadian National hopper, EX, G1 .... **$15.00**
Car, #9054 JC Penney boxcar, EX, G1 .... **$25.00**
Car, #9133 Burlington Northern flat car w/van, MIB, G1 .... **$40.00**
Car, #9160 Illinois Central-N5C caboose, EX, G1 .... **$30.00**
Car, #9162 Pennsylvania Porthole caboose, EX, G1 .... **$35.00**
Car, #9229 Operating Express Mail car, MIB, G1 .... **$40.00**
Car, #9282 Great Northern flat car w/van, MIB, G1 .... **$40.00**
Car, #9301 Operating US Mail car, MIB, G1 .... **$40.00**
Car, #9305 Santa Fe Operating Cowboy car, EX, G1 .... **$25.00**
Car, #9307 Erie Animated Gondola, MIB, G1 .... **$75.00**
Car, #9312 Conrail searchlight car, EX, G1 .... **$25.00**
Car, #9413 Naperville boxcar, MIB, G1 .... **$15.00**
Car, #9415 P&W boxcar, MIB, G1 .... **$20.00**
Car, #9435 LCCA 1981 Central of Georgia club car, MIB, G1..**$40.00**
Car, #9621 NHL Campbell boxcar, MIB, G1 .... **$25.00**

Car, #9726 Erie Lackawanna boxcar, EX, G1 ....$25.00
Car, #9780 Johnny Cash boxcar, MIB, G1 ....$40.00
Car, #9802 Miller High Life reefer, EX, G1 ....$30.00
Car, #16214 Rio Grande auto carrier, MIB, G1 ....$35.00
Car, #16215 Conrail auto carrier, MIB, G1 ....$35.00
Car, #16318 Lionel Lines flat car w/reels, MIB, G1 ....$25.00
Car, #16323 Lionel Lines flat car, MIB, G1 ....$35.00
Car, #16343 Burlington gondola w/coils, MIB, G1 ....$20.00
Car, #16617 Chicago Northwestern boxcar, MIB $40.00
Car, #16623 Katy dbl-door boxcar w/ETD, MIB...............$45.00
Car, #16640 Rutland boxcar, MIB, G1 ....$155.00
Car, #16660 fire car, MIB, G1 ....$35.00
Car, #16801 LRRC 1988 bunk car, MIB, G1 ....$45.00
Car, #16802 LRRC 1989 tool car, MIB, G1 ....$45.00
Car, #16803 LRRC 1990 searchlight car, MIB, G1 ....$65.00
Car, #17605 Reading caboose, M, G1 ....$40.00
Car, #17876 LCCA 1989 CN&L boxcar, MIB, G1..........$60.00
Car, #17881 TTOS 1990 Phelps Dodge club car, MIB, G1 ..$45.00
Car, #17884 TTOS 1990 Columbus-Dayton club car, MIB, G1 ....$50.00
Car, #17900 Santa Fe Unibody tank car, MIB, G1...........$40.00
Car, #19001 Southern Crescent Diner, MIB, G1 ....$100.00
Car, #19203 Detroit-Toledo boxcar, MIB, G1..................$20.00
Car, #19205 Great Northern boxcar, MIB, G1.................$35.00
Car, #19207 CP Rail boxcar, MIB, G1.............................$20.00
Car, #19209 Florida East Coast boxcar, MIB, G1 ....$20.00
Car, #19215 UP dbl-door boxcar, MIB, G1 ....$20.00
Car, #19230 Frisco dbl-door boxcar, MIB, G1 ....$30.00
Car, #19239 Toronto-Hamburg-Buffalo boxcar, MIB, G1..$20.00
Car, #19245 Mickey Mouse boxcar, MIB, G1...................$60.00
Car, #19256 Goofy boxcar, MIB, G1 ....$50.00
Car, #19303 Lionel Lines hopper, MIB, G1.......................$25.00
Car, #19311 Southern Pacific hopper, MIB, G1 ....$25.00
Car, #19408 Frisco gondola w/coils, MIB, G1...................$45.00
Car, #19419 Charlotte mint car, MIB, G1.........................$45.00
Car, #19506 Thomas Newcomber reefer, MIB, G1 ....$20.00
Car, #19508 Leonardo DiVinci reefer, MIB, G1...............$20.00
Car, #19602 Johnson tank car, MIB, G1...........................$45.00
Car, #19656 Milwaukee Road Bunk, MIB, G1 ....$45.00
Car, #19709 Pennsylvania Work caboose, MIB, G1.........$60.00
Car, #19939 Christmas car, 1995, MIB, G1 ....$45.00
Car, #52010 TTOS 1993 Weyerhauser club car, MIB, G1 .$75.00
Car, #52058 Santa Fe, 100 Year Anniversary, MIB..........$60.00
Car, #87004 Southern boxcar, lg gauge, MIB, G1 ....$45.00
Car, #87005 Northern Pacific boxcar, lg gauge, MIB, G1 ..$45.00
Car, #87407 MKT boxcar, lg gauge, MIB, G1 ....$35.00
Car, #87602 Gulf tank car, lg gauge, MIB, G1..................$40.00
Car, #87700 Pennsylvania caboose, lg gauge, MIB, G1 ....$35.00
Loco, #SA1001 QSI Chessie FM diesel engine, MIB, G1 .$200.00
Loco, #8160 Burger King GP20 diesel engine, EX, G1...$125.00
Loco, #8466/67 Amtrak F3 AA diesel engine, MIB, G1 ...$425.00
Loco, #8485 US Marine NW2 diesel engine, EX, G1 ....$125.00
Loco, #8568 Preamble Express F-3 diesel engine, M, A....$75.00
Loco, #8602 Pennsylvania 4-4-2 steam engine, M, G1.....$85.00
Loco, #8610 Wabash 4-6-2 steam engine & tender, MIB, A..$500.00
Loco, #8687 Jersey Central, MIB, A $250.00
Loco, #8702 Southern Cresent steam engine & tender, MIB, A...$375.00
Loco, #8801 Blue Comet engine & tender, MIB, A.......$300.00
Loco, #18011 & #17608 Chessie T1 & caboose, steam, MIB, G1..$900.00
Loco, #18303 Amtrak GG1 diesel engine, MIB, G1 ......$400.00
Loco, #18610 Rock Island 0-4-0 steam engine, MIB, G1 .$150.00
Loco, #33000 GP9 Railscope diesel engine, MIB, G1 ....$225.00
Set, #6-11707 Silver Spike, MIB, A................................$200.00
Set, #6-1387 Milwaukee Special, MIB, A........................$225.00
Set, #6-1463 Coca-Cola Special, MIB, A $250.00
Set, #1260 N&W Continental Limited, MIB, A............$300.00
Set, #1450 SS Rio Grande, MIB, G1 ....$550.00
Set, #1632 Santa Fe Work Train, MIB, G1 ....$375.00
Set, #1652 B&O Freight, MIB, A $150.00
Set, #11704 Southern Freight, MIB (sealed), A $185.00
Set, #11717 CSX freight, MIB, A $200.00
Set, #11758 1989 SSS Desert King, MIB, G1.................$250.00
Set, #11775 Anheuser-Busch, MIB, A............................$300.00
Set, #11809 Trolley, MIB, G1 ....$80.00
Set, #81002 Frontier Freight, lg gauge, MIB, G1 ....$140.00
Set, #81006 Union Pacific Limited, lg gauge, MIB, G1 .$225.00

Lionel Postwar

Accessory, #20 crossing, O gauge, EX, G1...........................$6.00
Accessory, #54 ballast tamper, EX (EX box)...................$200.00
Accessory, #58 rotary snowplow, EX (EX box)...............$575.00
Accessory, #90 control button, EX, G1 ....$5.00
Accessory, #97 coal elevator, NMIB.............................$375.00
Accessory, #110 graduated trestle, EX, G1.......................$15.00
Accessory, #125 whistling station, NMIB......................$150.00
Accessory, #133 lighted station, EX, G1 ....$45.00
Accessory, #147 whistle control, EX, G1 ....$10.00
Accessory, #153 block signal, EX $65.00
Accessory, #164 lumber loader, EX (EX box) $300.00
Accessory, #256 freight station, EX, G1...........................$65.00
Accessory, #260 bumper, red, EX, G1 ....$10.00
Accessory, #264 forklift, operating, EX (EX box)...........$550.00
Accessory, #310 billboard set, EX (EX box), G1..............$25.00
Accessory, #350 engine transfer table, MIB...................$450.00
Accessory, #352 icehouse & car, EX (EX box) $300.00
Accessory, #356 operating baggage station, EX, G1 ....$75.00
Accessory, #364 lumber loader, MIB..............................$300.00
Accessory, #462 derrick platform, NMIB.......................$550.00
Accessory, #464 sawmill, EX, G1 ....$145.00
Accessory, #494 rotating silver beacon, EX, G1 ....$45.00
Accessory, #497 coal station, lt gr roof & base, EX (EX box) $250.00
Accessory, #970 Lionel ticket booth, MIB......................$250.00
Accessory, #1011 transformer, 25 watts, EX, G1 ....$15.00
Accessory, #1033 transformer, 90 watts, w/whistle, EX, G1 .$55.00
Accessory, #1044 transformer, 90 watts, w/whistle, EX (EX box), G1 ....$65.00
Accessory, #1122 automatic 027 switches, EX (EX box), G1 ....$35.00
Accessory, #2001 transformer, 150 watts, w/whistle, EX (EX box), G1...$145.00
Accessory, #3472 milk set, complete, EX, G1...................$55.00
Accessory, #3662 milk set, complete, EX, G1..................$65.00

Accessory, KW transformer, 190 watts, w/whistle, EX (EX box), G1 ....$165.00
Accessory, LW tranformer, 125 watts, w/whistle, EX, G1 .$100.00
Car, #55 Tie Jector, test run, MIB..........$250.00
Car, #60 trolley, blk lettering, MIB, A..........$375.00
Car, #175 rocket launcher, MIB..........$900.00
Car, #3349 turbo flat car, repro missiles, EX, G1 ....$45.00
Car, #3357 hydraulic platform boxcar, EX, G1 ....$75.00
Car, #3360 burro crane, NMIB $600.00
Car, #3361X operating log dump flat car, EX, G1 ....$35.00
Car, #3410 flat car, repro helicopter, EX, G1..........$45.00
Car, #3454 PRR Auto Merchant car, VG..........$75.00
Car, #3494 NYC boxcar, operating, NMIB $200.00
Car, #3519 flat car, repro satellite, EX, G1 ....$55.00
Car, #3535 security car w/rotating searchlight, NMIB, A .$175.00
Car, #3562-50 gondola, yel, EX, G1..........$50.00
Car, #3619 helicopter recon, EX..........$100.00
Car, #455 oil derrick, red top, EX (EX box)..........$325.00
Car, #6014 Frisco boxcar, wht, EX, G1 ....$15.00
Car, #6017 Lionel Lines caboose, EX, G1..........$10.00
Car, #6024 Shredded Wheat boxcar, EX, G1 ....$25.00
Car, #6042 gondola, bl, EX, G1..........$10.00
Car, #6044 Airex boxcar, bl, EX, G1 ....$20.00
Car, #6059 M&StL caboose, red, EX, G1 ....$10.00
Car, #6346 Alcoa quad hopper, EX (EX box)..........$65.00
Car, #6424 flat car, red w/wht autos, EX, G1..........$45.00
Car, #6427 Lionel Lines caboose, EX (EX box), G1..........$35.00
Car, #6457 lighted caboose, EX (EX box), G1..........$30.00
Car, #6462 gondola, blk, EX, G1..........$15.00
Car, #6464-50 M&StL boxcar, EX (EX box), G1..........$60.00
Car, #6464-725 New Haven boxcar, orange, EX, G1 ....$75.00
Car, #6468 automobile car, bl, VG, G1 ....$35.00
Car, #6472 refrigerator car, EX, G1..........$30.00
Car, #6477 bulk car, repro pipes, EX, G1..........$45.00
Car, #6494-150 MoPac boxcar, operating, EX..........$150.00
Car, #6557 smoking caboose, NMIB..........$400.00
Car, #6560 crane car, red, 8 wheels, EX, G1 ....$45.00
Car, #6636 Alaska Railroad hopper car, EX, G1..........$50.00
Car, #6800 flat car w/airplane, test run, NMIB..........$200.00
Car, #6817 flat car w/earth scraper, EX..........$400.00
Car, #6822 searchlight car, gray, EX (EX box), G1 ....$55.00
Loco, #50 gang car, EX $65.00
Loco, #212 USMC, EX..........$125.00
Loco, #218 SF AA, MIB..........$400.00
Loco, #611 Jersey Central NW2, VG..........$165.00
Loco, #613 UP NW2 switcher, EX (worn box) $450.00
Loco, #614 Alaska NW2 switcher, w/dynamic brake unit, EX (EX box) $350.00
Loco, #624 Chesapeake & Ohio, EX (EX box) $350.00
Loco, #1055 Texas Special Alco, EX $40.00
Loco, #2023 Union Pacific Alco, diesel, NMIB $600.00
Loco, #2033 Union Pacific, diesel, NMIB $400.00
Loco, #2245 MKT B-unit, MIB..........$575.00
Loco, #2322 Virginia FM, diesel, EX (EX box)..........$950.00
Loco, #2322 Virginia FM, test run, NMIB..........$700.00
Loco, #2339 Wabash GP7, diesel, MIB $1,000.00
Loco, #2343 Santa Fe B-unit, louver top, MIB..........$700.00
Loco, #2346 B&M GP9, NMIB $575.00
Loco, #2349 Northern Pacific GP-9, diesel, MIB (sealed)...$1,500.00
Loco, #2354 NYC AA unit, EX (EX box) $275.00
Loco, #2356 Southern ABA, NMIB..........$1,200.00
Loco, #2365 C&O GP7, EX (EX box)..........$325.00
Loco, #2367 Wabash F3 AB, EX (EX box)..........$1,200.00
Loco, #2379 Rio Grande F3 AB, EX (EX box) $500.00
Loco, #6220 NW2 switcher, NM $150.00
Loco, #6250 Seaboard NW2 switcher, EX (VG box).....$200.00
Loco & Tender, #665 loco, #736W tender, unrun, NMIB.....$600.00
Loco & Tender, #746 N&W, VG (VG box) $1,300.00
Loco & Tender, #2046, steam, NMIB, A $400.00
Set, #148, #261 loco, #257 tender, #530 conservation car & #529 pullman, MIB, A..........$965.00
Set, #1649 Santa Fe Alco, MIB $1,950.00
Set, #1800 Deluxe General, #1862, #1862T, #1866, #1865 & #1877 flat cars w/horses, NMIB $1,200.00
Set, #2383 Super Chief SF Alco AA, #2562 vista domes (2), #2563 coach & #2561 observation car, NM (NM boxes)...$5,500.00
Set, #11600 Hagerstown, MIB $1,150.00
Set, freight; #2573 Berkshire Freight, NMIB..........$4,200.00

Lionel Prewar

Accessory, #47 crossing gate, EX..........$150.00
Accessory, #61 lamppost, dk gr, EX..........$165.00
Accessory, #66 whistle controller, EX $25.00
Accessory, #76 warning bell shack, VG $175.00
Accessory, #89 flag pole, EX..........$50.00
Accessory, #115 station, late colors, EX..........$400.00
Accessory, #118 tunnel, w/insert, EX..........$100.00
Accessory, #155 freight station, early colors, VG $275.00
Accessory, #155 freight station, late colors, VG $200.00
Accessory, #165 magnetic crane, EX..........$350.00
Accessory, #313 bascule bridge, EX (EX box)..........$750.00
Accessory, #438 switch tower, red & wht, EX, A $300.00
Accessory, #912 Suburban Landscape Villa, EX..........$500.00
Accessory, #914 landscaped park, EX (EX box) $425.00
Accessory, freight station, late colors, VG $200.00
Car, #13 cattle car, EX..........$125.00
Car, #16 ballast dump car, EX $250.00
Car, #17 caboose, EX..........$100.00
Car, #214R refrigerator car, EX $850.00
Car, #32 mail car, EX..........$150.00
Car, #45 tank car, EX $125.00
Car, #98 coal bunker, EX..........$375.00
Car, #112 gondola car, EX..........$100.00
Car, #217 caboose, peacock & red, EX (EX box) $300.00
Car, #218 dump car, EX..........$300.00
Car, #2814R reefer, wht w/bl roof, VG $175.00
Car, #322 observation car, EX..........$200.00
Car, #413 Colorado pullman car, EX..........$2,500.00
Car, #414 Illinois pullman car, EX..........$2,500.00
Car, #442 Tempel Blue Comet observation car, EX..........$900.00
Car, #512 gondola, EX (EX box)..........$150.00
Car, #515 Sunoco tank car, EX (EX box) $200.00
Car, #520 floodlight car, EX..........$225.00
Car, #794 Rail Chief observation car, EX $250.00
Car, #810 crane car, EX (EX box)..........$200.00

Car, #814 boxcar, yel & brn, EX $400.00
Loco, #700E Hudson, EX $4,500.00
Loco & Tender, #001E & #001T, spring latch, EX $425.00
Set, #347, #8 loco, #338 observation car & #337 pullman, olive gr w/maroon trim, MIB, A $1,200.00
Set, #1835 loco (electric), #1835W tender, #310 baggage car, #309 pullman & #312 observation car, EX...........$1,200.00
Set, #1835E loco, #1835W tender, #513 stock car, #511 lumber car & #517 caboose, EX (EX box) $1,200.00
Set, City of Denver, #636W loco, #637 coaches (2) & #638 observation car, EX...$550.00
Set, Flying Yankee, #616 loco, #617 coach & #618 observation car, EX $475.00
Set, Flying Yankee, #616 loco, #617 coaches (2) & #618 observation car, VG (VG box)...$475.00
Set, freight; #225E loco, #2235W tender, #2755 tank car, #2758 boxcar & #2757 caboose, VG $500.00
Set, passenger; #253 loco, #610 pullman & #612 observation car, G $250.00

Miscellaneous

Bing, Budweiser boxcar, litho tin, VG $275.00
Bing, loco & tender, #2663, steam powered, blk w/red striping, NP cylinders, 11½", VG, A....................................$300.00
Bing, loco & tender, steam powered, maroon, 14", VG, A ..$635.00
Bing, set, New York Central, CI engine w/litho tin baggage, passenger & observation car, 31", EX, A $300.00

Photo courtesy Dunbar Gallery

Bing, train and station, 1930s, 18", M, $450.00.

Bowman, loco, #234, steam powered, maroon, 11½", MIB, A...$250.00
Bowman, loco & tender, Great Western, steam powered, 20", VG, A $250.00
Carette, loco & tender, steam powered, gr w/brass boiler, emb coal compartment on tender, 11", VG, A $450.00
Cor Cor, set, engine, tender & pullman, blk & red, VG, A ..$275.00
Dayton, loco & tender, Hillclimber, red w/gold trim, cowl front, 26", EX...$250.00
Dorfan, set, #921, loco & 4 cars, G.............................$1,500.00
Hornby, cars, #6104 Stephenson Rocket coaches (2), MIB .$350.00
Ives, accessory, #322 ringing signal & #331 block signal, gr & cream, EX...$350.00
Ives, baggage car, Limited Vestibule Express, tin, EX $175.00
Ives, boxcar, #64 Canadian Pacific, EX..........................$250.00
Ives, caboose, #67, mk Ives Railway Line, litho tin, gray-pnt tin roof w/red cupola, EX $125.00
Ives, drawing room car, Ives Railway Line Saratoga, gr litho steel w/gray roof, EX $150.00
Ives, freight station, litho block base w/ramp & platform, yel litho body, clerk in window, EX.............................$175.00
Ives, livestock car, mk Ives RR, orange-yel litho tin, gray-pnt roof w/catwalk, EX..$125.00
Ives, loco, #176, CI, clockwork, EX $175.00
Ives, loco & tender, United States, pnt & stenciled tin, bl & red w/gold-tone disk wheels, 13", NM $3,000.00
Ives, loco 0-4-0, CI w/tin wheels, EX $175.00
Ives, parlor car, mk Ives Railway Lines Washington, tin, EX..$350.00
Ives, passenger station, mk Grand Central Station, litho tin w/shingle pattern on roof, CI chimneys, EX $225.00
Ives, reefer car, Refrigerator No 124 Dairy Express Line, litho tin, catwalk on roof, EX..$200.00
Ives, set, blk-pnt CI loco w/red trim pulling 4 litho tin cars, clockwork mechanism, 4½" to 6½", A $550.00
Ives, set, passenger; #3242 loco, #184, #185 & #186 cars, 1925-26, VG $550.00
KTM, loco & tender, 4-8-4 brass loco w/matching 12-wheel tender, M $1,750.00
Marklin, #8189 MiniClub California Zephyr, MIB $550.00
Marklin, loco, #3024, bl w/silver roof, NMIB $300.00
Marklin, loco & tender, #3094, test run, NMIB $150.00
Marklin, set, #3073 loco, #4634, #4654, #4644, #4645, #4631 & #4513, NMIB...$325.00
Marx, loco & tender, #1829 SF, electric, plastic, NM (EX master carton) $150.00
Marx, set, #M10000 loco, coaches (3) & observation car, red & silver, EX...$225.00
Marx, set, #4923, Marline loco, NYC tender, MS Oil tank car, RI gondola, UP stock car & NYC caboose, NMIB (separate)...$150.00

Photo courtesy John Turney

Marx, train set, lithographed tin, MIB, $200.00.

MTH, accessory, #840 powerhouse, NMIB....................$400.00
MTH, car, #219 crane, cream & red, MIB.....................$265.00
MTH, loco, #385, steam, gray w/brass trim, NMIB $475.00
MTH, loco, #392, steam, 2-tone bl, MIB.......................$865.00
MTH, set, pass; Mojave #431, #419, #490 & #418, M ...$575.00
Schoenner, loco, steam powered, blk & gr w/red spoke wheels, NP boiler, 7¾", rpt, A $385.00
Unique, caboose, #105, figures looking out windows, tin, red w/yel lettering, NM...$65.00
Unique, loco & tender, mostly bl tin w/Unique Lines in wht, electric, EX..$75.00
Williams, engine, #960 GE-E 60 Amtrak, M, A $65.00
Williams, loco, #5200 PRR B6SB 0-6-0, steam, MIB.....$375.00

Williams, loco, #6013 Southern PS-4 4-6-2, M..............$475.00
Williams, loco, Camelback 4-6-0, 3-rail, MIB.................$550.00
Williams, loco, Lackawanna Trainmaster, MIB..............$300.00
Williams, loco, Pennsylvania Sharknose Baldwin, NM .$300.00
Williams, loco, Pennsylvania Trainmaster, diesel, gr, MIB....$225.00
Williams, loco, Tuscan SD-45 diesel, MIB.....................$175.00
Williams, loco & tender, PRR E6S 4-4-2, MIB..............$350.00
Williams, locos, Amtrak F-7 A-Units, 1 powered & 1 dummy, MIB..$250.00
Williams, set, NASA Space Shuttle Transporter, MIB..$200.00
Williams, set, passenger; #2519 Southern Pacific Madison loco & 5 cars, MIB..$300.00
Williams, set, passenger; Amtrak Amfleet, MIB.............$225.00
Williams, set, passenger; NY Central baggage car, coaches (2) & observation car, aluminum, MIB.............................$185.00
Williams, set, passenger; Pennsylvania Congressional GGI loco & 5 cars, M (EX separate boxes).............................$650.00
Williams, set, passenger; Pennsylvania Madison, gr, MIB..$265.00

Transformers

Made by the Hasbro Company, Transformers were introduced in the United States in 1984. Originally there were twenty-eight figures — eighteen cars known as Autobots and ten Decepticons, evil robots capable of becoming such things as a jet or a handgun. Eventually the line was expanded to more than two hundred different models. Some were remakes of earlier Japanese robots that had been produced by Takara in the 1970s. (These can be identified through color differences and in the case of the Diaclone series, the absence of the small driver or pilot figures.)

The story of the Transformers and their epic adventures were told through several different comic books and animated series as well as a highly successful movie. Their popularity was reflected internationally and eventually made its way back to Japan. There the American Transformer animated series was translated into Japanese and soon inspired several parallel series of the toys which were again produced by Takara. These new Transformers were sold in the U.S. until the line was discontinued in 1990.

A few years ago, Hasbro announced their plans to reintroduce the line with Transformers: Generation 2. Transformers once again had their own comic book, and the old animated series was brought back in a revamped format. So far, several new Transformers as well as recolored versions of the older ones have been released by Hasbro, and the size of the series continues to grow. Sustained interest in them has spawned a number of fan clubs with chapters worldwide.

Because Transformers came in a number of sizes, you'll find a wide range of pricing. Our values are for Transformers in unopened original boxes. One that has been opened or used is worth much less — about 25% to 75%, depending on whether it has all its parts (weapons, instruction book, tech specks, etc., and what its condition is — whether decals are applied well or if it is worn.

Advisor: David Kolodny-Nagy (K2).

Other Sources: H4, O1, P3

Series 1, 1984

Autobot Car, #TF1023, Sunstreak, yel Countach..........$100.00
Autobot Car, #TF1025, Bluestreak, bl Datsun Z............$300.00
Autobot Car, #TF1025, Bluestreak, silver Datsun..........$100.00
Autobot Car, #TF1027, Jazz, Porsche.............................$100.00
Autobot Car, #TF1029, Ratchet, ambulance....................$80.00
Autobot Car, #TF1031, Trailbreaker, camper................$100.00
Autobot Car, #TF1033, red Countach, MIP..................$100.00
Autobot Car, #TF1035, Hound, jeep............................$100.00
Autobot Car, #TF1037, Mirage, Indy car.......................$100.00
Autobot Car, #TF1039, Prowl, police car......................$100.00
Autobot Car, #TF1041, Wheeljack, Mazzerati...............$100.00
Autobot Car, #TF1055, Camshaft, silver car, mail-in......$40.00
Autobot Car, #TF1057, Downshift, wht car, mail-in, MIP...$40.00
Autobot Car, #TF1059, Overdrive, red car, mail-in.........$40.00
Autobot Car, #TF1061, Powerdasher #1, jet, mail-in.......$20.00
Autobot Car, #TF1063, Powerdasher #2, car, mail-in......$20.00
Autobot Car, #TF1063, Powerdasher #3, drill, mail-in....$40.00
Autobot Commander, #TF1053, Optimus Primus w/Roller, tractor trailer..$170.00
Case, #TF1069, Collector's Case.....................................$15.00
Case, #TF1071, Collector's Case, red 3-D version............$25.00
Cassette, #TF1017, Ravage & Rumble.............................$40.00
Cassette, #TF1019, Frenzy & Lazerbeak...........................$40.00
Decepticon Communicator, #TF1049, Soundwave & Buzzsaw, tape player & gold condor..$80.00
Decepticon Jet, #TF1043, Starscream, gray jet...............$100.00
Decepticon Jet, #TF1045, Thundercracker, bl jet.............$70.00
Decepticon Jet, #TF1047, Skywarp, blk jet......................$70.00
Decepticon Leader, #TF1051, Megatron, Walther P-38....$190.00
Minicar, #TF1000, Bumblejumper (Bumblebee card).......$40.00
Minicar, #TF1000, Bumblejumper (Cliffjumper card).......$40.00
Minicar, #TF1001, Bumblebee, yel VW Bug....................$35.00
Minicar, #TF1003, Bumblebee, red VW Bug....................$25.00
Minicar, #TF1005, Cliffjumper, red race car....................$25.00
Minicar, #TF1007, Cliffjumper, yel race car....................$25.00
Minicar, #TF1009, Huffer, orange semi cab.....................$20.00
Minicar, #TF1011, Windcharger, red Firebird..................$20.00
Minicar, #TF1013, Brawn, gr jeep.....................................$20.00
Minicar, #TF1015, Gears, bl truck....................................$20.00
Watch, #TF1067, Time Warrior, transforming watch w/Autobot insignia, mail-in..$80.00

Series 2, 1985

Autobot Air Guardian, #TF1201, Jetfire, F-14 jet..........$140.00
Autobot Car, #TF1163, Skids, Le Car............................$100.00
Autobot Car, #TF1165, Red Alert, fire chief....................$70.00
Autobot Car, #TF1167, Grapple, crane............................$70.00
Autobot Car, #TF1169, Hoist, tow truck..........................$70.00
Autobot Car, #TF1171, Smokescreen, red, wht & bl Datsun Z..$80.00
Autobot Car, #TF1173, Inferno, fire engine......................$70.00
Autobot Car, #TF1175, Tracks, Corvette..........................$80.00
Autobot Communicator, #TF1199, Blaster, radio/tape player...$50.00
Autobot Scientist, #TF1197, Perceptor, microscope........$50.00

Constructicon, #TF1127, Bonecrusher (1), bulldozer.......$20.00
Constructicon, #TF1129, Scavenger (2), steam shovel $20.00
Constructicon, #TF1131, Scrapper (3), front-end loader .$20.00
Constructicon, #TF1133, Hook (4), crane.......................$20.00
Constructicon, #TF1135, Long Haul (5), dump truck......$20.00
Constructicon, #TF1137, Mixmaster (6), cement mixer..$25.00
Constructicon, #TF1139, Devastator, construction gift set..$200.00
Decepticon Jet, #TF1187, Ramjet.....................................$50.00
Decepticon Jet, #TF1189, Dirge.......................................$50.00
Decepticon Jet, #TF1191, Thrust, maroon jet $30.00
Decepticon Military Operations Commander, #TF1203, Shockwave, lazer gun...$90.00
Deluxe Insecticon, #TF1155, Chop Shop, beetle $90.00
Deluxe Insecticon, #TF1157, Barrage $90.00
Deluxe Insecticon, #TF1159, Benom, bee $90.00
Deluxe Insecticon, #TF1161, Ransack, grasshopper $90.00
Deluxe Vehicle, #TF1193, Whirl, lt bl helicopter............$70.00
Deluxe Vehicle, #TF1195, Roadster, off-road vehicle $60.00
Dinobot, #TF1177, Grimlock, Tyrannosaurus $60.00
Dinobot, #TF1179, Slag, Triceratops $60.00
Dinobot, #TF1181, Sludge, Brontosaurus $40.00
Dinobot, #TF1183, Snarl, Stegosaurus.............................$40.00
Insecticon, #TF1141, Kickback, grasshopper $25.00
Insecticon, #TF1143, Shrapnel, beetle.............................$25.00
Insecticon, #TF1145, Bombshell, boll weevil $25.00
Jumpstarter, #TF1147, Twin Twist, drill tank..................$25.00
Jumpstarter, #TF1149, Topspin, spaceship.......................$25.00
Minicar, #TF1101, Bumblebee, yel VW bug.....................$25.00
Minicar, #TF1102, Bumblebee, yel w/minispy $40.00
Minicar, #TF1103, Bumblebee, red VW bug $20.00
Minicar, #TF1104, Bumblebee, red w/minispy.................$30.00
Minicar, #TF1105, Cliffjumper, red race car....................$20.00
Minicar, #TF1106, Cliffjumper, red w/minispy................$30.00
Minicar, #TF1107, Cliffjumper, yel race car $20.00
Minicar, #TF1108, Cliffjumper, yel w/minispy $30.00
Minicar, #TF1109, Huffer, orange semi cab $20.00
Minicar, #TF1110, Huffer, w/minispy $30.00
Minicar, #TF1111, Windcharger, red Firebird $20.00
Minicar, #TF1112, Windcharger, w/minispy $30.00
Minicar, #TF1113, Brawn, gr jeep, MIP...........................$20.00
Minicar, #TF1115, Gears, bl truck $30.00
Minicar, #TF1116, Gears, w/minispy $30.00
Minicar, #TF1117, Seaspray, hovercraft $20.00
Minicar, #TF1119, Powerglide, plane $15.00
Minicar, #TF1121, Warpath, tank $15.00
Minicar, #TF1123, Beachcomber, dune buggy.................$15.00
Minicar, #TF1125, Cosmos, spaceship $15.00
Motorized Autobot Defense Base, #TF1205, Omega Supreme, rocket launcher base..$140.00
Triple Charger, #TF1151, Blitzwing, tank/plane $60.00
Triple Charger, #TF1153, Astrotrain, shuttle/train..........$60.00
Watch, #TF1207, Autoceptor, Kronoform watch car.......$25.00
Watch, #TF1209, Deceptor, Kronoform, watch jet $25.00
Watch, #TF1211, Listen 'n Fun, w/tape & yel Cliffjumper.$35.00

Series 3, 1986

Aerialbot, #TF1263, Air Raid (1), F-14 jet.......................$20.00
Aerialbot, #TF1265, Skydive (2), F-15 jet........................$20.00
Aerialbot, #TF1267, Fireflight (3), Phantom jet $20.00
Aerialbot, #TF1271, Silverbolt (5), Concorde $50.00

Photo courtesy June Moon

Aerialbot, #TF1273, Superion gift set, $200.00.

Autobot Car, #TF1333, Blurr, futuristic car......................$60.00
Autobot Car, #TF1335, Kup, pickup truck $70.00
Autobot Car, #TF1337, Hot Rod, red race car $200.00
Autobot City Commander, #TF1365, Ultra Magnus, car carrier $70.00
Autobot City Commander, #TF1367, Reflector, Spectro, Viewfinder & Spyglass into camera, mail-in.............$60.00
Autobot City Commander, #TF1369, STARS Control Center, action cb, mail-in...$60.00
Battlecharger, #TF1311, Runamuch, Corvette $15.00
Battlecharger, #TF1313, Runabout, Trans Am................$15.00
Cassette, #TF1315, Ratbat & Frenzy, bat & bl robot........$30.00
Cassette, #TF1317, Rewind & Steeljaw, gold weapons, blk robot & lion...$20.00
Cassette, #TF1318, Rewing & Steeljaw, silver weapons, blk robot & lion $25.00
Cassette, #TF1319, Ramhorn & Eject, gold weapons, rhino & gray robot $25.00
Cassette, #TF1320, Ramhorn & Eject, gold weapons, rhino & gray robot $25.00
Combaticon, #TF1287, Brawl (1), tank $20.00
Combaticon, #TF1289, Swindle (2), jeep $20.00
Combaticon, #TF1293, Vortex (4), helicopter.................$20.00
Combaticon, #TF1295, Onslaught (5), missile transport .$20.00
Combaticon, #TF1297, Bruticus, gift set $300.00
Combaticon, Blast Off (3), shuttle...................................$20.00
Decepticon City Commander, #TF1363, Galvatron, laser cannon...$100.00
Heroes, #TF1131, Rodimus Prime, futuristic RV $60.00
Heroes, #TF1329, Wreck-Car, futuristic motorcycle $80.00
Jet, #TF1353, Scourge, hovercraft....................................$60.00
Jet, #TF1355, Cyclonus Space Jet $60.00
Minicar, #TF1252, Wheelie, futuristic car $20.00

Minicar, #TF1253, Outback, brn jeep $15.00
Minicar, #TF1255, Tailgate, wht Firebird $15.00
Minicar, #TF1257, Hubcap, yel race car $15.00
Minicar, #TF1259, Pipes, bl semi cab $15.00
Minicar, #TF1261, Swerve, red truck $15.00
Motorized Autobot Space Shuttle Robot, #TF1359, Sky Lynz shuttle $90.00
Motorized Decepticon City/Battle Station, #TF1357, Trypticon, dinosaur w/Brunt, robot tank & Full Tilt $130.00
Predacon, #TF1339, Razorclaw (1), lion $60.00
Predacon, #TF1341, Rampage (2), tiger $60.00
Predacon, #TF1343, Divebomb (3), vulture $60.00
Predacon, #TF1345, Tantrum (4), bull $60.00
Predacon, #TF1347, Headstrong (5), rhino $60.00
Predacon, #TF1351, Gnaw, futuristic shark $50.00
Stunticon, #TF1275, Dead End (1), Porsche $15.00
Stunticon, #TF1277, Breakdown (2), Countach $15.00
Stunticon, #TF1279, Wildrider (3), Ferrari $15.00
Stunticon, #TF1281, Drag Strip (4), Indy car $15.00
Stunticon, #TF1283, Motormaster (5), tractor trailer $40.00
Stunticon, #TF1285, Menasor, gift set $300.00
Triple Changer, #TF1321, Springer, armored car/helicopter .$80.00
Triple Changer, #TF1323, Sandstorm, dune buggy/helicopter $60.00
Triple Changer, #TF1325, Broadside, aircraft carrier/plane ...$60.00
Triple Changer, #TF1327, Octane, tanker truck/jumbo jet....$55.00
Triple Charger, #TF1321, Springer, armored car/helicopter ..$90.00

Series 4, 1987

Cassette, #TF1441, Slugfest & Overkill, Stegosaurus & Tyrannosaurus $15.00
Clone, #TF1443, Pounce & Wingspan, puma & eagle.....$40.00
Clone, #TF1445, Fastlane & Cloudraker, dragster & spaceship $40.00
Double Spy, #TF1447, Punch-Counterpunch, Fiero $40.00
Duocon, #TF1437, Battletrap, jeep/helicopter $40.00
Duocon, #TF1439, Flywheels, jet/tank $20.00
Headmaster Autobot, #TF1477, Chromedome w/Stylor, futuristic car $55.00
Headmaster Autobot, #TF1479, Hardhead w/Duros, tank .$40.00
Headmaster Autobot, #TF1481, Highbrow w/Gort, helicopter $40.00
Headmaster Autobot, #TF1483, Brainstorm w/Arcana, jet .$40.00
Headmaster Base, #TF1497, Scorponok w/Lord Zarak & Fasttrack, scorpion, mini-tank $80.00
Headmaster Base, #TF1499, Fortress Maximus w/Cerebros & Spike, Gasket, Grommet, battle station/city $350.00
Headmaster Decepticon, #TF1485, Skullrunner w/Grax, alligator $35.00
Headmaster Decepticon, #TF1487, Mindwipe w/Vorath, bat $35.00
Headmaster Decepticon, #TF1489, Weirdwolf w/Monzo, wolf $35.00
Headmaster Horrocon, #TF1491, Apeface w/Spasma, jet/ape $40.00
Headmaster Horrorcon, #TF1493, Snapdragon w/Krunk, jet/dinosaur $40.00

Monsterbot, #TF1461, Grotusque, tiger $40.00
Monsterbot, #TF1463, Doublecross, 2-headed dragon......$40.00
Monsterbot, #TF1465, Repugnus, insect $40.00
Sixchanger, #TF1495, Sixshot, starfighter jet, winged wolf, lazer pistol, armored carrier, tank $70.00
Targetmaster Autobot, #TF1449, Pointblank w/Peacemaker, race car & gun $30.00
Targetmaster Autobot, #TF1451, Sureshot w/Spoilsport, off-road buggy & gun $30.00
Targetmaster Autobot, #TF1453, Crosshairs w/Pinpointer, truck & gun $30.00
Targetmaster Autobot, #TF1455, Hot Rod & Firebolt, race car & gun $125.00
Targetmaster Autobot, #TF1457, Kup & Recoil, pickup truck & gun $50.00
Targetmaster Autobot, #TF1459, Blurr w/Haywire, futuristic car & gun $60.00
Targetmaster Decepticon, #TF1469, Misfire w/Aimless, spaceship & gun $30.00
Targetmaster Decepticon, #TF1471, Slugslinger w/Caliburst, twin jet & gun $30.00
Targetmaster Decepticon, #TF1475, Scourge w/Fracas, hovercraft & gun $70.00
Technobot, #TF1425, Afterburner (1), motorcycle $15.00
Technobot, #TF1426, Afterburner, w/decoy $20.00
Technobot, #TF1427, Nosecone (2), drill tank $15.00
Technobot, #TF1428, Nosecone, w/decoy $20.00
Technobot, #TF1429, Sate (3), fighter plane $15.00
Technobot, #TF1430, Stafe, w/decoy $20.00
Technobot, #TF1431, Lightspeed (4), race car $15.00
Technobot, #TF1432, Lightspeed, w/decoy $20.00
Technobot, #TF1433, Scattershot (5), spaceship $40.00
Terrocon, #TF1413, Rippersnapper (1), lizard $10.00
Terrocon, #TF1414, Rippersnapper, w/decoy $15.00
Terrocon, #TF1415, Sinnertwin (2), 2-headed dog $10.00
Terrocon, #TF1416, Sinnertwin, w/decoy $15.00
Terrocon, #TF1417, Cutthroat (3), vulture $10.00
Terrocon, #TF1418, Cutthroat, w/decoy $15.00
Terrocon, #TF1419, Blot (4), monster $10.00
Terrocon, #TF1420, Blot, w/decoy $15.00
Terrocon, #TF1421, Hun-grr (5), 2-headed dragon $30.00
Terrocon, #TF1423, Abominus, gift set $70.00
Throttlebot, #TF1401, Goldbug, VW bug $10.00
Throttlebot, #TF1403, Freeway, Corvette $10.00
Throttlebot, #TF1404, Freeway, w/decoy $15.00
Throttlebot, #TF1405, Chase, Ferrari $10.00
Throttlebot, #TF1406, Chase, w/decoy $15.00
Throttlebot, #TF1407, Wideload, dump truck $10.00
Throttlebot, #TF1408, Wideload, w/decoy $15.00
Throttlebot, #TF1409, Rollbar, jeep $10.00
Throttlebot, #TF1410, Rollbar, w/decoy $15.00
Throttlebot, #TF1411, Searchlight, race car $10.00
Throttlebot, #TF1412, Searchlight, w/decoy $15.00

Series 5, 1988

Cassette, #TF1539, Squawkalk & Beastbox, hawk & gorilla .$15.00
Cassette, #TF1541, Grand Slam & Raindance, tank & jet....$15.00

Firecon, #TF1507, Cindersaur, dinosaur $10.00
Firecon, #TF1509, Flamefeather, monster bird $10.00
Firecon, #TF1561, Sparkstalker, monster.....................$10.00
Headmaster Autobot, #TF1555, Hosehead w/Lug, fire engine .$30.00
Headmaster Autobot, #TF1557, Siren w/Quig, fire chief car .$25.00
Headmaster Autobot, #TF1559, Nightbeat w/Muzzle, race car..$25.00
Headmaster Decepticon, #TF1561, Horri-Bull w/Kreb, bull ..$25.00
Headmaster Decepticon, #TF1563, Fangry w/Brisko, winged wolf...$25.00
Headmaster Decepticon, #TF1565, Squeezeplay w/Lokos, crab $25.00
Powermaster Autobot, #TF1567, Getaway w/Rev, MR2 ..$35.00
Powermaster Autobot, #TF1569, Joyride w/Hotwire, off-road buggy $40.00
Powermaster Autobot, #TF2571, Slapdash w/Lube, Indy car ..$40.00
Powermaster Autobot Leader, #TF1617, Optimus Prime w/HiQ, tractor trailer...$90.00
Powermaster Decepticon, #TF1573, Darkwing w/Throttle, dk gray jet...$40.00
Powermaster Decepticon, #TF1575, Dreadwing w/Hi-Test, lt gray jet...$40.00
Powermaster Mercenary, #TF1613, Doubledealer w/Knok (robot) & Skar (bat), missile launcher.....................$80.00
Pretender, #TF1577, Landmine, race car w/shell $60.00
Pretender, #TF1579, Cloudburst, jet w/shell....................$60.00
Pretender, #TF1581, Waverider, submarine w/shell $40.00
Pretender, #TF1583, Skullgrin, tank w/shell....................$40.00
Pretender, #TF1585, Bomb-burst, spaceship w/shell.........$60.00
Pretender, #TF1587, Submarauder, submarine w/shell $40.00
Pretender, #TF1589, Groundbreaker, race car w/shell......$40.00
Pretender, #TF1591, Sky High, jet w/shell $40.00
Pretender, #TF1593, Splashdown, sea skimmer w/shell....$40.00
Pretender, #TF1595, Iguanus, motorcycle w/shell $40.00
Pretender, #TF1599, Finback, sea skimmer w/shell $25.00
Pretender Beast, #TF1601, Chainclaw, bear w/shell.........$30.00
Pretender Beast, #TF1603, Catilla, sabertooth tiger w/shell ...$30.00
Pretender Beast, #TF1605, Carnivac, wolf w/shell $30.00
Pretender Beast, #TF1607, Snarler, boar w/shell $30.00
Pretender Vehicle, #TF1609, Gunrunner, red jet w/vehicle shell $40.00
Pretender Vehicle, #TF1611, Roadgrabber, purple jet w/vehicle shell $40.00
Seacon, #TF1513, Overbit (1), shark.............................$15.00
Seacon, #TF1515, Seawing (2), manta ray $15.00
Seacon, #TF1517, Nautilator (3), lobster $15.00
Seacon, #TF1519, Skalor (4), fish..................................$15.00
Seacon, #TF1521, Tentakil (5), squid.............................$15.00
Seacon, #TF1523, Snaptrap (6), turtle............................$35.00
Seacon, #TF1525, Pirancon, gift set.............................$200.00
Sparkbot, #TF1501, Fizzle, off-road buggy.......................$10.00
Sparkbot, #TF1503, Sizzle, funny car $10.00
Sparkbot, #TF1505, Guzzle, tank $10.00
Targetmaster Autobot, #TF1543, Scoop w/Tracer & Holepunch, front-end loader & 2 guns $25.00
Targetmaster Autobot, #TF1545, Landfill w/Flintlock & Silencer, dump truck & 2 guns.................................$25.00
Targetmaster Autobot, #TF1547, Quickmix w/Boomer & Ricochet, cement mixer & 2 guns $25.00
Targetmaster Decepticon, #TF1549, Quaker w/Tiptop & Heater, tank & 2 guns $20.00
Targetmaster Decepticon, #TF1551, Spinster w/Singe & Hairsplitter, helicopter & 2 guns $20.00
Targetmaster Decepticon, #TF1553, Needlenose w/Sunbeam & Zigzag, jet & 2 guns..$20.00
Tiggerbot, #TF1527, Backstreet, race car $15.00
Tiggerbot, #TF1529, Override, motorcycle.......................$15.00
Triggercon, #TF1533, Ruckus, dune buggy $15.00
Triggercon, #TF1535, Windsweeper, B-1 bomber $15.00
Triggercon, #TF1537, Crankcase, jeep.............................$15.00

Series 6, 1989

Legends, K-Mart Exclusive, #TF1727, Bumblebee, VW bug ...$30.00
Legends, K-Mart Exclusive, #TF1729, Jazz Porsche $40.00
Legends, K-Mart Exclusive, #TF1731, Grimlock, dinosaur..$40.00
Legends, K-Mart Exclusive, #TF1733, Starscream, jet......$45.00
Mega Pretender, #TF1717, Vroom, dragster w/shell $35.00
Mega Pretender, #TF1719, Thunderwing, jet w/shell.......$35.00
Mega Pretender, #TF1721, Crossblades, helicopter w/shell....$25.00
Micromaster Base, #TF1679, Skyhopper & Micromaster, helicopter & F-15..$50.00
Micromaster Base, #TF1681, Groundshaker & Micromaster, self-propelled cannon & stealth fighter.....................$35.00
Micromaster Base, #TF1735, Skystalker, Space Shuttle Base & Micromaster Porsche $55.00
Micromaster Base, #TF1737, Countdown, Rocket Base & Micromaster Lunar Rover..$60.00
Micromaster Patrol, #TF1651, Off-Road Series, 4 different, ea $20.00
Micromaster Patrol, #TF1657, Sports Car Patrol Series, 4 different, ea...$20.00
Micromaster Patrol, #TF1661, Battle Patrol Series, 4 different, ea $20.00
Micromaster Station, #TF1671, Greasepit, pickup w/gas station..$20.00
Micromaster Station, #TF1675, Ironworks, semi w/construction site $20.00
Micromaster Transport, #TF1663, Overload, car carrier ..$15.00
Micromaster Transport, #TF1665, Flattop, aircraft carrier .$15.00
Micromaster Transport, #TF1667, Roughstuff, military transport $15.00
Pretender, #TF1697, Pincher, scorpion w/shell $20.00
Pretender, #TF1699, Longhtooth, hovercraft w/shell.......$20.00
Pretender, #TF1701, Stranglehold, rhino w/shell $20.00
Pretender, #TF1705, Bludgeon, tank w/shell $30.00
Pretender, #TF1707, Doubleheader, twin jet w/shell........$20.00
Pretender Classic, #TF1709, Bumblebee, VW bug w/shell ..$40.00
Pretender Classic, #TF1711, Grimlock, dinosaur w/shell .$40.00
Pretender Classic, #TF1713, Starscream, jet w/shell.........$40.00
Pretender Classic, #TF1715, Jazz, Porsche w/shell $40.00
Pretender Monster, #TF1683, Icepick (1).........................$12.00
Pretender Monster, #TF1687, Wildfly (3), ...$12.00
Pretender Monster, #TF1695, Monstructor, gift set, not produced $1,000.00
Ultra Pretender, #TF1725, Roadblock, tank w/figure & vehicle...$40.00

Ultra Pretender, #TF1727, Skyhammer, race car w/figure & vehicle....$40.00

Series 7, 1990

Action Master, #TF1781, Soundwave: Soundwave (bat), Wingthing....$15.00
Action Master, #TF1785, Grimlock: Grimlock, Anti-Tank Cannon (tank gun)....$15.00
Action Master, #TF1789, Rad: Rad, Lionizer (lion)....$15.00
Action Master, #TF1793, Devastator: Devastor, Scorpulator (scorpion)....$15.00
Action Master, #TF1799, Blaster: Blaster, Flight-Pack (jet pack)....$15.00
Action Master, #TF1805, Shockwave: Shockwave, Fistfight (mini-robot)....$25.00
Action Master, #TF1809, Inferno: Inferno, Hydro-Pack (water laser backpack)....$25.00
Action Master, #TF1817, Prowl: Prowl, Turbo Cycle....$60.00
Action Master, #TF1821, Over-Run: Over-Run, Attack Copter....$40.00
Action Master, #TF1825, Wheeljack: Wheeljack, Turbo Racer.$70.00
Action Master, #TF1829, Gutcruncher: Gutcruncher, Stratotronic Jet....$30.00
Action Master, #TF1833, Optimus Prime: Optimus Prime, Armored Convoy....$80.00
Action Master, #TF1873, Skyfall: Skyfall, Top-Heavy Rhino.$20.00
Micromaster Combiner, #TF1763, Battle Squad: Meltdown, Half-Track, Direct Hit, Power Punch, Fireshot & Vanguish.$15.00
Micromaster Combiner, #TF1767, Metro Squad: Wheel Blaze, Road Burner, Oiler, Slide, Power Run & Strikedown.$15.00
Micromaster Combiner, #TF1771, Tanker Truck: Tanker Truck, Pipeline & Gusher....$15.00
Micromaster Combiner, #TF1775, Missile Launcher: Missile Launcher, Retro & Surge....$15.00
Micromaster Combiner, #TF1777, Anti-Aircraft Base: Anti-Aircraft Base, Blackout & Spaceshot....$15.00
Micromaster Patrol, #TF1751, Race Track Patrol: Barricade, Roller Force, Ground Hog & Motorhead....$10.00
Micromaster Patrol, #TF1755, Air Patrol: Thread Bolt, Eagle Eye, Sky High & Blaze Master....$10.00
Micromaster Patrol, #TF1759, Hot Rod Patrol, Big Daddy, Trip-Up, Greaser & Hubs....$10.00
Micromaster Patrol, #TF1761, Military Patrol: Bombshock, Tracer, Dropshot & Growl....$10.00

Generation 2, Series 1, 1992 – 93

Autobot Car, #TF1863, Jazz, Porsche....$25.00
Autobot Car, #TF1867, Inferno, fire truck....$25.00
Autobot Leader, #TF1879, Optimus Prime w/Roller, tractor trailer w/electronic sound-effect box....$35.00
Autobot Minicar, #TF1881, Bumble, metallic VW bug...$30.00
Autobot Minicar, #TF1883, Hubcap, metallic....$20.00
Autobot Minicar, #TF1887, Seaspray, metallic hovercraft...$15.00
Autobot Obliterator (Europe only), Spark....$45.00
Color Change Transformer, #TF1905, Deluge....$15.00
Color Change Transformer, #TF1911, Gobots....$15.00
Constructicon (orange version), #TF1851, Bonecrusher (1), bulldozer....$7.00
Constructicon (orange version), #TF1855, Scrapper (3), front-end loader....$7.00
Constructicon (orange version), #TF1859, Long Haul (5), dump truck....$7.00
Constructicon (yel version), #TF1851, Bonecrusher (1), bulldozer....$6.00
Constructicon (yel version), #TF1855, Scrapper (3), front-end loader....$6.00
Constructicon (yel version), #TF1859, Long Haul (5), dump truck....$6.00
Decepticon Abliterator (Europe only), Colossus....$45.00
Decepticon Jet, #TF1875, Starscream, gray jet w/electronic light & sound-effect box....$30.00
Decepticon Leader, #TF1913, Megatron, gr tank w/electronic sound-effect treads....$45.00
Dinobot, #TF1869, Grimlock, bl Tyrannosaurus....$25.00
Dinobot, #TF1870, Grimlock, turq Tyrannosaurus....$50.00
Dinobot, #TF1873, Snarl, orig gray Stegosaurus....$30.00
Dinobot, #TF1873, Snarl, red Stegosaurus....$25.00
Small Autobot Car, #TF1899, Skram....$8.00
Small Autobot Car, #TF1903, Turbofire....$8.00
Small Decepticon Jet, #TF1889, Afterburner....$8.00
Small Decepticon Jet, #TF1891, Eagle Eye....$8.00
Small Decepticon Jet, #TF1893, Terradive....$8.00
Small Decepticon Jet, #TF1895, Windrazor....$8.00

Generation 2, Series 2, 1994

Aerialbot, #TF1915, Skydive (1), F-15....$7.00
Aerialbot, #TF1919, Firefight (3), Phantom....$7.00
Aerialbot, #TF1923, Silverbolt (5), Concorde....$18.00
Combaticon, #TF1927, Brawl (1), tank....$7.00
Combaticon, #TF1931, Blast Off (3), shuttle....$7.00
Combaticon, #TF1935, Onslaught (5), missile transport.$18.00
Heroes, #TF1953, Autobat Hero Optimus Prime, M (Japanese box).$35.00
Heroes, #TF1953, Autobot Hero Optimus Prime....$20.00
Heroes, #TF1955, Decepticon Hero Megatron....$20.00
Laser Rod Transformer, #TF1937, Electro....$15.00
Laser Rod Transformer, #TF1937, Electro, M (Japanese box).$20.00
Laser Rod Transformer, #TF1941, Jolt....$15.00
Laser Rod Transformer, #TF1941, Jolt, M (Japanese box)..$20.00
Rotor Force, #TF1945, Leadfoot....$7.00
Rotor Force, #TF1947, Manta Ray....$7.00
Rotor Force, #TF1951, Ransack....$7.00
Stunticon, BotCon '94 Exclusive, #TF1925, Breakdown (2), Countach....$100.00
Watch, #TF1957, Superion....$12.00
Watch, #TF1961, Ultra Magnus....$12.00
Watch, #TF1965, Scorpia....$12.00

Bootleg/Unlicensed Transformers

Action Master Blue Streak w/Action Master Optimus Prime's Vehicle, K2....$30.00
Action Master Jazz, gray & purple or gray & ultramarine bl, K2, ea....$5.00

Action Master Rad, orange & purple, K2 ..... $5.00
Blitzwing, plastic, K2 ..... $6.00
Dai-Atlas (Dai-Atris), same as orig Japanese toy except for recolored stickers, battery-op, K2 ..... $25.00
Dino King, oversized version from Victory series, K2 ..... $25.00
Generation 3 Inferno, plastic, yel arms & legs, K2 ..... $6.00
Gumball Transformer Models, Japanese, set of 4, very rare, MIP, K2 ..... $30.00
G2 Combaticon Blast-Off, giant size, K2 ..... $10.00
Mini Max, sm version of Fortress Maximus, spike forms head, 7", K2 ..... $15.00
Power Master Decepticon Jet, different colors than orig, K2 ... $15.00
Sky Garry, remake of robot from Star Convoy series, no micro-masters or shuttles, K2 ..... $10.00
Star Saber, Brainmaster from Japanese Victory series, no componets to form super robot, K2 ..... $15.00
Superion, lg firearm, gold helmet, 13", K2 ..... $25.00
Transformer Landross, Japanese remake, K2 ..... $15.00

Trolls

The first trolls to come to the United States were modeled after a 1952 design by Marti and Helena Kuuskoski of Tampere, Finland. The first trolls to be mass produced in America were molded from wood carvings made by Thomas Dam of Denmark. As the demand for these trolls increased, several US manufacturers were licensed to produce them. The most noteworthy of these were Uneeda Doll Company's Wishnik line and Inga Scandia House True Trolls. Thomas Dam continued to import his Dam Things line. Today trolls are enjoying a renaissance as baby boomers try to recapture their childhood. As a result, values are rising.

The troll craze from the '60s spawned many items other than just dolls such as wall plaques, salt and pepper shakers, pins, squirt guns, rings, clay trolls, lamps, Halloween costumes, animals, lawn ornaments, coat racks, notebooks, folders, and even a car.

In the '70s, '80s, and '90s, new trolls were produced. While these trolls are collectible to some, the avid troll collector still prefers those produced in the '60s. Remember, trolls must be in mint condition to receive top dollar.

For more information, we recommend *Collector's Guide to Trolls* by Pat Petersen.

Advisor: Roger Inouye (I1).

Astronaut, Dam, 1964, 11", EX, H4 ..... $125.00
Ballerina, Dam, bright red hair, gr eyes, orig outfit, MIP, I1 .. $55.00
Boy & Girl, Sun Rubber, 1964, pnt-on clothes, orange hair, EX, I1, pr, from $125 to $150.00
Boy w/Club, Wishnik, pnt-on clothes, molded club, blk hair, orange eyes, 3", NM, I1 ..... $65.00
Bride & Groom, Uneeda Wishnik, 1970s, 6", VG+, H4, pr . $30.00
Cave Girl, Dam, flannel leopard skin outfit w/matching hair ribbon, wht hair, brn eyes, 3", EX $25.00
Caveman, 'Ughie Ughie,' Scandia House, NM $20.00
Clown, Dam, 1965, pnt-on clothes, yel eyes & red nose, 5½", NM, I1, from $175 to $250.00
Clown Ball Player, Royalty Design, 1968, felt uniform & hat, molded baseball glove, yel hair, blk eyes, 4", EX $15.00
Cook-Nik, Uneeda Wishnik, 1970s, bendable, 5", MOC, H4 ..... $40.00
Cousin Claus, Dam, 1984, orig outfit, wht hair, brn eyes, 10", EX $15.00
Cow, Dam, wht hair, brn eyes, 3½", EX, I1 ..... $45.00
Cowboy, Wishnik, orig outfit & hat, blond hair, amber eyes w/gr pupils, 3½", EX $15.00
Donkey, Dam, wht mane & tail, lg amber eyes, 9", G, I1 . $50.00
Double-Nik Clown, Wishnik, red & wht flannel outfit, red & bl hair, red eyes, EX $60.00
Eskimo, Dam, 1965, red & wht pnt-on clothes, brn hair & eyes, 5½", EX, I1 ..... $75.00
Girl, Dam, in gr felt Liederhosen & yel felt skirt, 9", VG, H4 ..... $60.00
Girl w/Pigtails, unmk, yel felt dress & hat, blond hair, amber eyes, 3", EX $20.00
Good Luck-Nik, Uneeda Wishnik, 1970s, M (orig tube pkg), H4 ..... $30.00
Graduate, Uneeda Wishnik, 1970s, in robe & hat, 6", VG+, H4 ..... $20.00
Grandpa Claus, Dam, 1977, orig outfit, wht hair, brn eyes, 14", EX, from $100 to $125.00
Hula Girl, Dam, redressed, blk hair, brn eyes, 6", EX $20.00
Iggy-Normous, Dam, 1964-65, wht sailor-style suit w/blk tie, blond hair, amber eyes, 12", EX, from $150 to $175.00
Indian Dress, Wishnik, Black w/blk rooted hair, blk eyes, 3½", EX, I1 ..... $75.00
Judge, Uneeda Wishnik, gray hair, orange eyes, 5½", EX, I1 .. $30.00
Leprechaun Man & Woman, Scandia House, 1960s, stuffed bodies, 10", H4, pr $175.00
Miss America, unmk, wht satin & net gown, pearl tiara, wht hair, amber eyes, 3", EX $25.00
Monkey, Dam, wearing sailor suit & hat, brn hair & eyes, extremely rare, I1, from $200 to $300.00
Moonitik, Uneeda Wishnik, mohair body w/rubber feet & shake eyes, 18", extremely rare, I1 ..... $100.00

Norfin Fan Club Troll, Thomas Norfin by Dam, blue and white outfit with gray and red cap, M, $40.00.

Nursenik, Uneeda Wishnik, 1970s, 6", MOC, H4............$50.00
Pick-nik, Uneeda Wishnik, 1970s, bendable, 5", MOC, H4..$40.00
Playboy Bunny, unmk, blk & wht felt ears & outfit, blond hair, clip hands, 3½", EX, I1..$15.00
Poppa-He-Nik, Wishnik, gr felt outfit, gold hair, amber eyes, 5", EX..$25.00
Superman, Uneeda Wishnik, felt costume w/stretch fabric cape, wht hair, amber eyes, 5", EX......................................$75.00
Tailed Troll, Dam, 1965, burlap outfit w/belt & charms, gray hair, brn eyes, M, I1, from $150 to..........................$250.00
Vending Machine Trolls, 1960s, several variations, EX, ea from $5 to..$10.00
Viking, Dam, 1967, wht felt dress w/bl belt, wht hair, brn eyes, 5½", NM, I1, from $150 to......................................$200.00
Werewolf Monster, 1930s, 3", I1 ....$40.00

Miscellaneous

Bank, girl, Dam, 1960s, in gr or yel felt dress, 8", EX, H4, ea..$25.00
Bank, Pirate, Dam, 1960s, hard plastic w/felt clothes, red hair, 8", EX, H4..$30.00
Bank, Santa, Dam, 1960s, hard plastic w/felt clothes, 8", rare, H4 ....$45.00
Bank, Silvestre Bros, 1964, glazed ceramic, 18", M, I1 ...$150.00
Book, It's a Dam, Dam World, 1965, hardcover, 48 pgs, EX, F8...$18.00
Carrying Case, Ideal, w/molded waterfall, M, I1 ....$25.00
Christmas Stocking, Adopt a Norfin Troll, lg vinyl head, M, I2..$25.00
Greeting Card, American Greeting Corp, 1965, w/3" troll tied on card, rare, I1..$100.00
Lamp, Wishnik, complete, 18", rare, I1 ....$250.00
Magnet Toy, Smethport, 1967, colorful illustrations on 10x14" board, no magnet, EX, F8 ....$45.00
Outfit, any style, MIP, I1, ea...$15.00
Paint-By-Number Kit, Russ/Golden, early 1990s, complete, MIB...$10.00
Pencil Topper, astronaut, Scandia House, 1½", MIP, I1 ..$45.00
Playhouse, Wishnik Mini Trolls, Ideal, 1960s, EX, B10 ...$20.00

View-Master and Tru-Vue

View-Master, the invention of William Gruber, was introduced to the public at the 1939 – 1940 New York World's Fair and the Golden Gate Exposition in California. Since then, View-Master reels, packets, and viewers have been produced by five different companies — the original Sawyers Company, G.A.F (1966), View-Master International (1981), Ideal Toys, and Tyco Toys (the present owners). Because none of the non-cartoon single reels and three-reel packets have been made since 1980, these have become collectors' items. Also highly sought after are the three-reel sets featuring popular TV and cartoon characters. The market is divided between those who simply collect View-Master as a field all its own and collectors of character-related memorabilia who will often pay much higher prices for reels about Barbie, Batman, The Addams Family, etc. Our values tend to follow the more conservative approach.

The first single reels were dark blue with a gold sticker and came in attractive gold-colored envelopes. They appeared to have handwritten letters. These were followed by tan reels with a blue circular stamp. Because these were produced for the most part after 1945 and paper supplies were short during WWII, they came in a variety of front and back color combinations, tan with blue, tan with white, and some were marbleized. Since print runs were low during the war, these early singles are much more desirable than the printed white ones that were produced by the millions from 1946 until 1957. Three-reel packets, many containing story books, were introduced in 1955, and single reels were phased out. Nearly all viewers are very common and have little value except for the very early ones, such as the Model A and Model B. Blue and brown versions of the Model B are especially rare. Another desirable viewer, unique in that it is the only focusing model ever made, is the Model D. For more information we recommend *View-Master Single Reels, Volume I,* by Roger Nazeley. Note: though the market was down by a substantial percentage at one point, it appears to have recovered, and prices are now fairly stable.

Advisor: Roger Nazeley (N4).

Other Sources: C1, P3

A-B-C Circus, B-585, 1974, MIP, N4 ....$15.00
Adventures of GI Joe, B-585, MIP (sealed), B10.............$40.00
Adventures of Tarzan, #975, w/book, M, B10.....................$8.00
Alice in Wonderland, B-360, MIP, B10...........................$15.00
Alice in Wonderland, FT-20, MIP, B10 ....$12.00
Apollo Moon Landing, B-633, MIP, B10..........................$15.00
Apple's Way, B-558, MIP (sealed), B10...........................$25.00
Archie, B-574, 1975, MIP, N4 ....$10.00
Aristocats, B-365, 1970, MIP, N4 ....$8.00
Babes in Toyland, B-375, 1961, MIP, N4 ....$35.00
Bad News Bears in Breaking Training, H-77, 1977, MIP, N4.......$20.00
Bambi, B-400, MIP (sealed), B10 ....$20.00
Batman, B-492, 1966, MIP (sealed), B10..........................$40.00
Bedknobs & Broomsticks, B-366, 1971, MIP, N4............$20.00
Beep, Beep, The Road Runner, B-538, 1967, MIP, N4 ....$15.00
Beverly Hillbillies, B-570, 1963, MIP..............................$45.00
Big Blue Marble, B-587, 1976, MIP, N4 ....$20.00
Birth of Jesus, B-875, MIP, B10 ....$12.00
Bonanza, B-471, 1st issue, 1964, MIP, N4.........................$35.00
Brady Bunch Grand Canyon Adventure, 1971, MIP, C1.$75.00
Brave Eagle, B-446, 1955, MIP, N4.................................$30.00
Buck Rogers, L-15, 1980, MIP, N4..................................$20.00
Buck Rogers in the 25th Century, J-1, 1978, MIP, N4 ....$8.00
Bugs Bunny, B-531, 1959, MIP, N4 ....$15.00
Bugs Bunny, B-549, MIP (sealed), B10 ....$22.00
Captain America, H-43, MIP (sealed), B10......................$30.00
Captain Kangaroo, B-560, 1957, MIP, N4 ....$30.00
Casper's Ghostland, B-545, MIP (sealed), B10 ....$25.00
Casper the Friendly Ghost, B-533, 1961, MIP, N4 ....$8.00
Charlotte's Web, B-321, MIP, B10...................................$15.00
CHiPs, L-14, 1980, MIP, N4 ....$20.00
Christmas Carol, B-830, MIP (sealed), B10......................$22.00
Cinderella, B-313, 1953, MIP, N4....................................$12.00
Close Encounters of the Third Kind, J-47, 1977, MIP, N4.$20.00

Daktari, B-498, MIP (sealed), B10 ....$45.00
Daniel Boone, B-479, 1965, MIP, N4 ....$35.00
Dennis the Menace, B-539, MIP, B10................................$22.00
Dinosaurs (TV show), #4138, 1992, MIP, N4.....................$8.00
Disney World Fantasyland, A-948, MIP (sealed), B10.....$25.00
Disney World Liberty Square, A-950, MIP (sealed), B10.$20.00
Donald Duck, B-525, 1957, MIP, N4 ....$15.00
Dr Shrinker & Wonderbug, H-2, 1977, MIP (sealed) $30.00
Dracula, B-324, 1976, MIP, N4 ....$20.00
Dukes of Hazzard, L-17, 1980, MIP, N4 ....$25.00
Eight Is Enouqh, K-76, 1980, MIP, N4 ....$25.00
Emergency!, B-597, MIP (sealed), B10 ....$25.00
Family Affair, B-571, 1969, MIP, N4 ....$40.00
Fangface, K-66, 1980, MIP, N4 ....$8.00
Fantastic Voyage, B-546, MIP, N4 ....$10.00
Fat Albert & the Cosby Kids, B-544, 1974, MIP, N4 ....$5.00
Flintstones, B-514, 1962, MIP, N4 ....$12.00
Flintstones, Beasts of Bedrock, L-6, 1980, MIP, N4 ....$8.00
Flintstones, Pebbles & Bamm-Bamm, B-520, 1966, MIP, N4.....$15.00
Flipper, B-485, MIP, B10 ....$35.00
Frankenstein, B-323, 1976, MIP, N4................................$20.00
Golden Book Favorites, H-14, MIP (sealed), B10 ....$30.00
Goldilocks & the Three Bears, B-317, MIP (sealed), B10 ..$25.00
Green Hornet, B-488, 1966, MIP, N4................................$75.00
Hair Bear Bunch, B-522, MIP (sealed), B10 ....$25.00
Happy Days, B-586, 1974, MIP, N4 ....$20.00
Hare & the Tortoise, B-309, MIP (sealed), B10 ....$20.00
Hawaii Five-O, B-590, MIP (sealed), B10.........................$30.00
Herbie Rides Again, B-578, MIP, B10 ....$15.00
Horses, H-5, 1977, MIP, N4 ....$25.00
James Bond 007, Live or Let Die, B-393, 1973, MIP, N4 .$30.00
Jetsons, L-27, 1981, MIP, N4..$5.00
Jungle Book, B-363, MIP, B10...$15.00
King Kong, The Greatest Monster of All Time, B-392, 1976, MIP, N4 ....$15.00
Land of the Giants, B-494, 1968, MIP, N4 ....$60.00
Land of the Lost #2, H-1, 1977, MIP, N4 ....$30.00
Lassie & Timmy, B-474, 1959, MIP, B10...........................$20.00
Lassie Rides the Log Flume, B-489, 1968, MIP, B10.........$15.00
Legend of Indiana Jones, 4092, 1989, MIP, N4...................$6.00
Little Drummer Boy, B-871, 1958, MIP, N4 ....$15.00
Little Red Riding Hood/Hansel & Gretel, B-301, 1950, MIP, N4 ....$10.00
Love Bug, B-501, 1968, MIP (sealed), B10 ....$25.00
Mary Poppins, B-376, 1964, MIP, N4 ....$15.00
Mickey Mouse, B-528, 1958, MIP, N4 ....$8.00
Mister Magoo, H-56, 1977, MIP, N4 ....$10.00
Monkees, B-493, 1967, MIP, N4 ....$30.00
Mork & Mindy, K-67, 1979, MIP, N4.................................$20.00
Mr Spock's Time Trek, B-555, 1974, MIP, N4 ....$25.00
Nanny & the Professor, 1970, MIP $45.00
Night Before Christmas, B-382, MIP, B10.........................$15.00
Partridge Family, B-569, 1971, MIP, N4 ....$35.00
Peanuts, B-536, MIP (sealed), B10 ....$15.00
Pee Wee's Playhouse, #4074, 1988, MIP, N4.....................$10.00
Pink Panther, J-12, 1978, MIP, B10 ....$15.00
Planet of the Apes, B-507, 1967, MIP, N4.........................$30.00
Pluto, B-529, MIP, N4 ....$10.00
Popeye, B-516, 1962, MIP, N4 ....$10.00
Project Apollo, B-658, MIP, B10 ....$25.00
Ren & Stimpy Show, #1084, 1993, MIP, N4 ....$5.00
Rescuers, H-26, MIP, N4 ....$15.00
Robinson Crusoe, B-438, 1958, MIP, N4...........................$20.00
Rookies, BB-452, MIP (sealed), B10 ....$30.00
Run Joe Run, B-594, 1974, MIP, N4 ....$20.00
Search (TV show), B-591, 1973, MIP, N4..........................$30.00
Shaggy DA, B-368, 1976, MIP, N4 ....$20.00
Six Million Dollar Man, AVB-559, MIP, N4 ....$20.00
Sleeping Beauty, Walt Disney, B-308, 1959, MIP, N4 .....$15.00
Snow White & The Seven Dwarfs, B-300, 1946, MIP, N4...$15.00
Space: 1999, BB-451, MIP, B10 ....$30.00
Star Trek: The Motion Picture; K-57, MIP, B10 ....$25.00
Superman Meets Computer Crook, B-584, MIP (sealed), B10..$30.00
Time Tunnel, B-491, 1966, MIP, N4 ....$50.00
Voltron, Defender of the Universe, 1055, 1984, MIP, N4..$5.00
Who Framed Roger Rabbit, K-37, 1979, MIP, N4...........$35.00
Winnie the Pooh & the Honey Tree, B-362, MIP, B10...$15.00
Wolfman, J-30, 1978, MIP, N4 ....$16.00
Woody Woodpecker, #1011, MIP, N4 ....$5.00
World of Liddle Kiddles, B-577, 1970, MIP, N4 ....$75.00
X-Men, Captive Hearts, #1085, 1993, MIP, N4 ....$15.00
Zorro, B-469, 1958, MIP, N4..$40.00
20,000 Leagues Under the Sea, B-370, 1954, MIP, N4 ....$20.00

Western

No friend was ever more true, no brother more faithful, no acquaintance more real to us than our favorite cowboys of radio, TV, and the silver screen. They were upright, strictly moral, extrememly polite, and tireless in their pursuit of law and order in the American West. How unfortunate that such role models are practically extinct nowadays.

This is an area of strong collector interest right now, and prices are escalating. For more information and some wonderful pictures, we recommend *Character Toys and Collectibles, First* and *Second Series*, by David Longest and *Guide to Cowboy Character Collectibles* by Ted Hake. New publications include *The Lone Ranger* by Lee Felbinger and *The W.F. Cody Buffalo Bill Collector's Guide* by James W. Wojtowicz. With the exception of Hake's, all are published by Collector Books.

Advisors: Donna and Ron Donnelly (D7).

See also Advertising Signs, Ads, and Displays; Books; Cereal Boxes; Character and Promotional Drinking Glasses; Character Clocks and Watches; Coloring, Activity, and Paint Books; Guns; Lunch Boxes; Premiums; Windups, Friction, and Other Mechanicals; and other specific categories.

Annie Oakley, notebook, 1950s, photo image of Annie holding up guns, 10x8", EX, A...$40.00
Annie Oakley, outfit, Pla-Master, 1950, red blouse & fringed skirt w/silkscreen of Annie on pockets, NMIB $200.00
Bat Masterson, cane, 1958, plastic w/ornate chrome-covered plastic hdl, EX, F8...$25.00

Bat Masterson, holster set w/cane & vest, Carnell, 1958, no gun, NMIB, J2 .... **$225.00**

Bonanza, cup, 1960s, litho tin, features Adam & the Ponderosa, EX, T2 .... **$30.00**

Bonanza, Foto Fantastiks Coloring Set, Eberhard Faber, 1965, complete, M (EX box) **$85.00**

Bonanza, Stardust Touch of Velvet Art, Hasbro, complete, NMIB, J2 .... **$85.00**

Brave Eagle, teepee, Roy Rogers Enterprises, 1950s, yel canvas w/red & gr Indian graphics, EX, A **$100.00**

Cheyenne, cowboy gloves, fringed w/name & image of horse head, unused, M, P6 .... **$40.00**

Cisco Kid, hobbyhorse, vinyl w/wood hdl, VG **$50.00**

Dale Evans, Dress-Up Kit, Colorforms, EX (EX box) **$75.00**

Dale Evans, outfit, Yankeeboy, w/skirt, vest, blouse & holster, EX (EX box), A **$300.00**

Daniel Boone, canoe, Multiple International, 1965, rubber, inflatable, 18", EX, A **$85.00**

Daniel Boone, coonskin cap, Fashion Hat & Cap Co Ltd/Canada, NM, M5 .... **$25.00**

Daniel Boone, Fess Parker Cartoon Kit, Colorforms, 1964, complete, M (EX box) **$85.00**

Davy Crockett, Camera Ensemble, Herbert-George, complete w/camera, flash attachment & bulbs, scarce, NM (EX box), A **$400.00**

Davy Crockett, doll, plastic w/hand-pnt features, cloth clothes, moveable head & arms, 8", NM (NM box), A **$150.00**

Davy Crockett, doll, Reliable/Canada, rubber head & hands w/cloth outfit, coonskin cap, shoes & knife sheath, 10", EX **$175.00**

Davy Crockett, doll outfit, Vogue Dolls Inc, complete, EX (EX box), A **$400.00**

Davy Crockett, figure, France, 1950s, Davy w/rifle across chest, hand-pnt lead, 4", EX, A **$125.00**

Davy Crockett, flashlight, 1950s, litho tin w/red plastic top, 3", NM **$65.00**

Davy Crockett, guitar, Peter Puppet/WDP, fiberboard w/color decal, complete w/pick & songbook, 25", EX (EX box) **$200.00**

Davy Crockett, hat, England/WDP, litho cb, NMIB, A ... **$75.00**

Davy Crockett, hobbyhorse, wood w/heavy bouncing springs, 23x33", EX, A **$175.00**

Davy Crockett, Indian Craft Set, Pressman, complete, NM (NM box) **$125.00**

Davy Crockett, knife & sheath, France, 1950s, NMOC, A .. **$100.00**

Davy Crockett, pistol & knife, Multiple, plastic, NM (NM card), A **$75.00**

Davy Crockett, play horse, Pied Piper, assembles to 46", MIB (sealed), A **$100.00**

Davy Crockett, ring, 1960s, from gumball machine, F1 .... **$15.00**

Davy Crockett, Sipcup, Century Plastics, red w/raised image of Davy w/rifle on cream lid, 3", NM (EX box), A **$125.00**

Davy Crockett, T-shirt, Norwick, 1950s, wht w/red, yel & gr image, EX, J5 .... **$25.00**

Davy Crockett, T-shirt transfer, NM, J2 .... **$15.00**

Davy Crockett, Thunderbird Moccasin Kit, Blaine, 1950s, complete, NM (EX box) **$175.00**

Gabby Hayes, Sheriff's Set, 1950s, unused, NMOC, J2 .... **$80.00**

Gene Autry, outfit, Leslie Henry, 1940s, brn suede vest & chaps, red felt trim, w/images, NM (VG box), J5, from $200 to **$300.00**

Gunsmoke, outfit, Matt Dillon, Kaynee, complete, EX (EX display box for 6 outfits) **$155.00**

Gunsmoke, outfit, Matt Dillon, Seneca, 1958, complete, EX (EX box) **$125.00**

Gunsmoke, pencil case, Hasbro, 1961, bl cb, features Matt Dillon, 4x9", EX, T2 .... **$30.00**

Hopalong Cassidy, bank, 1950s, bronze plastic bust, mk Springfield Institution... on back, 4", EX, A **$65.00**

Hopalong Cassidy, belt, Bill Boyd, 1950, emb leather, NMOC, A **$250.00**

Hopalong Cassidy, bicycle horn, w/handlebar clamp, C10.... **$200.00**

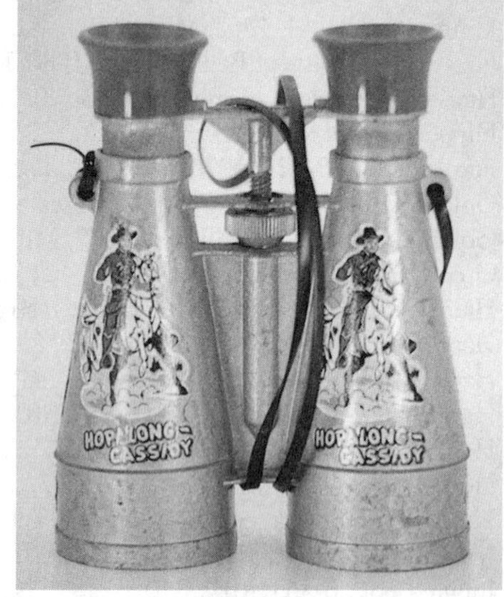

Hopalong Cassidy, binoculars, marked Sports Glass Chicago, metal and plastic with paper decals, EX, $165.00.

Hopalong Cassidy, chaps, 1950s, blk suede w/image of Hoppy, VG, pr **$85.00**

Hopalong Cassidy, Chuck Wagon Set, WS George, 1950, ceramic, complete w/plate, bowl & cup, unused, MIB, A **$600.00**

Hopalong Cassidy, drum, Rubbertone/Wm Boyd, 1950, 2 different images of Hoppy on drum tops, 5" dia, EX **$300.00**

Hopalong Cassidy, figure, chalkware, 14", NM, A **$450.00**

Hopalong Cassidy, figure set, Ideal, 1950, complete w/Hoppy, Topper & accessories, plastic, MIB, A **$250.00**

Hopalong Cassidy, figure set, Timpco/England, lead, set of 4 rare, EX (EX box) **$350.00**

Hopalong Cassidy, film, Danger Trail, Castle Films, 1950s, 16mm, NM, P4 .... **$30.00**

Hopalong Cassidy, iron-on transfer, 1950s, blk steer head w/Deputy below, 2x7", EX, J5 .... **$25.00**

Hopalong Cassidy, jacket & pants, Blue Bell, 1950, denim w/long horn design on pocket, scarce, EX, A **$475.00**

Hopalong Cassidy, mask, Traveler Trading Co, rubber, 8", EX (EX box) **$300.00**

Hopalong Cassidy, Picture Gun & Theater, Stephens, complete w/metal picture gun, theater & 2 slides, NM (EX box) . **$300.00**

Hopalong Cassidy, rocking chair, 1950, chrome w/red vinyl seat, decal of Hoppy & Topper on backrest, NM **$475.00**

Hopalong Cassidy, roller skates, metal w/leather straps, VG . **$250.00**

Hopalong Cassidy, rug & bed cover, 1950, embroidered image of Hoppy & Topper in front of fence, NM, A $225.00
Hopalong Cassidy, spurs, metal w/name screened on leather, EX $225.00
Hopalong Cassidy, sweater, 1951-52, shades of bl w/Hoppy on front & Topper on back, rare, M, T2 ....$250.00
Hopalong Cassidy, tie & handkerchief set, Glick, tie features Hoppy & Topper, unused, NMIB $400.00
Hopalong Cassidy, tie clasp w/initial chain, Anson, 1950, NM (NM box) $250.00
Hopalong Cassidy, tie clip, Anson, 1950, bust image, MIB $250.00
Hopalong Cassidy, vest, 1950s, blk suede w/image of Hoppy, VG...$100.00
Hopalong Cassidy, wallet, 1950, plastic & metal w/image of Hoppy & Topper, VG (VG box), A $250.00
Lone Ranger, bank, 1938, metal book shape w/Lone Ranger on Silver & name emb on leather cover, 3⅜", VG $200.00
Lone Ranger, binoculars, Harrison/TLR, 1949, NM (EX box)..$225.00
Lone Ranger, crayon tin, Milton Bradley, 1950s, mk Lone Ranger Crayons w/image of Lone Ranger & Silver, 6x5", EX, J5 ....$65.00
Lone Ranger, doll, Dollcraft TLR, pnt compo, standing w/guns drawn, wearing chaps & felt mask, 10", NMIB........$800.00
Lone Ranger, flashlight, Usalite/TLR Inc, 1920, litho tin flashlight on orig cb store display, NM $300.00
Lone Ranger, hairbrush & comb set, TLR, 1939, wood brush w/decal of Lone Ranger & Silver, NM (G box), A ..$125.00

Lone Ranger, horseshoe set, Gardner Games, 1950s, rubber w/wooden posts, complete, EX (EX box) $200.00
Lone Ranger, outfit, Esquire, 1950s, complete w/belt, bullet, mask, jail keys & sheriff's badge, MOC, P4 ....$375.00
Lone Ranger, outfit, mk TLR, complete w/hat, mask & bandana, EX $200.00
Lone Ranger, paint box, Milton Bradley, 1938, M $80.00
Lone Ranger, scrapbook, Whitman, 11x17", VG, J2 ....$40.00
Lone Ranger, viewer & film, Acme, 1940, not working, G (worn box), H7...$235.00
Lone Ranger, Water Gun Playset, HG Toys, 1981, MIB, M17 ....$50.00
Maverick, TV Eras-O-Picture Book, Hasbro, 1959, no crayons, NM...$25.00
Range Ryder, outfit, Pla-Master, 1950s, complete, MIB, J6 .$265.00
Red Ryder, Ranch Molding & Coloring Kit, Hobby Craft/Slesinger, 1948, complete, unused, NM (NM box), A $250.00
Rifleman, outfit, Pla-Master, 1959, flannel & corduroy w/felt hat, MIB...$250.00
Rin-Tin-Tin, outfit, Pla-Master, 1955, Corporal Rusty 101st Cavalry, complete, NM (EX box), A $155.00
Roy Rogers, binoculars, w/decal, 5", NM $100.00
Roy Rogers, camera & binoculars, Herbert George, complete w/paperwork & photo, NMIB, A $675.00
Roy Rogers, Cowboy & Indian Kit, Colorforms, complete, NM (VG box) $150.00
Roy Rogers, Fix-It Stagecoach, Ideal, 1955, missing few accessories, NM (NM box), A..$250.00
Roy Rogers, flashlight, Bantam, 1974, red & wht plastic, complete w/Trail Guide pamphlet, 3¼", NM, A............$165.00
Roy Rogers, holster set, Classy, 1955, brn leather w/RR logo in wht, simulated jewel strap, NM (NM box) $1,000.00
Roy Rogers, Horse Trailer & Jeep, Ideal, 1950s, complete, NMIB $365.00
Roy Rogers, horseshoe set, Ohio Art, 1950s, NM $200.00
Roy Rogers, lariat, Lasso, 1950, plastic coated, NMIP, A ..$200.00
Roy Rogers, Modeling Clay Set, Standard Toykraft, complete, NM (NM box), A..$125.00
Roy Rogers, mug, Dayton, 1950, plastic head figure, 4½", NM, A $70.00
Roy Rogers, outfit, cowgirl, Merit Playsuits, 1950s, complete, NMIB...$265.00
Roy Rogers, outfit, Merit Playsuits, 1950s, complete, NMIB...$350.00
Roy Rogers, outfit, Plus Brand, 1950, complete, NM (EX box), A $500.00
Roy Rogers, outfit, Yankeeboy, 1950s, tan pant styled like chaps, vest & folding cloth hat, EX (G box) $275.00
Roy Rogers, paint-by-number set, Avalon, 1950s, unused, EX (EX box) $165.00
Roy Rogers, portable saddle seat, leather seat w/studs & jewels on wooden tripod base, 18x15", EX, A $275.00
Roy Rogers, pull toy, NN Hill, 1955, Roy riding Trigger, wood & tin, 9½", NM (NM box), A..............................$525.00
Roy Rogers, raincoat & hat, yel vinyl w/blk fringe & trim, EX...$350.00
Roy Rogers, Ranch Lantern, Ohio Art, 1950s, battery-op, 12", NMIB...$200.00

Roy Rogers, riding toy, Trigger, Reliable Toy, plush w/plastic face, leather seat, 26" L, EX+, A $375.00

Roy Rogers, sun dial, Thrift Novelty, gold-pnt metal, w/path finder & signal flasher, NMOC, A..........................$350.00

Roy Rogers, tent, Hettrick, 1950s, yel canvas teepee style w/red & brn image of Roy on Trigger, 54", EX.................$250.00

Roy Rogers, Western Telephone, Ideal, 1950s, battery-op, 9", EX $175.00

Roy Rogers, yo-yo, photo image of Roy & Trigger, EX, B5 ..$25.00

Roy Rogers & Dale Evans, Dress-Up Kit, Colorforms, 1950s, complete, EX (EX box) $125.00

Tales of Wells Fargo, coloring set, Transogram, 1959, complete, EX (EX box), J5 ....$65.00

Tonto, outfit, Esquire, 1950s, complete w/headdress, knife & sheath, Hubley pistol & belt, MIB..........................$350.00

Wild Bill Hickok, outfit, Yankeeboy, 1948, complete, MIB..$200.00

Wyatt Earp, guitar, 24", EX, J2.......................................$125.00

Wyatt Earp, paint-by-number set, Life & Legend of Wyatt Earp, Transogram, 1958, unused, MIB $50.00

Zorro, cape, Carnival Creations, NMOC.........................$65.00

Zorro, charm bracelet, gold-color w/blk highlights, complete w/5 charms, NMIB, M8...$65.00

Zorro, cutouts, Aldon, 1950s, 3-D plastic, complete, MIP (sealed), A $100.00

Zorro, flashlight, 1958, blk plastic w/wrist strap, 2" dia, EX, F8 ....$40.00

Zorro, paint-by-number set, Hasbro, MIB (sealed).........$100.00

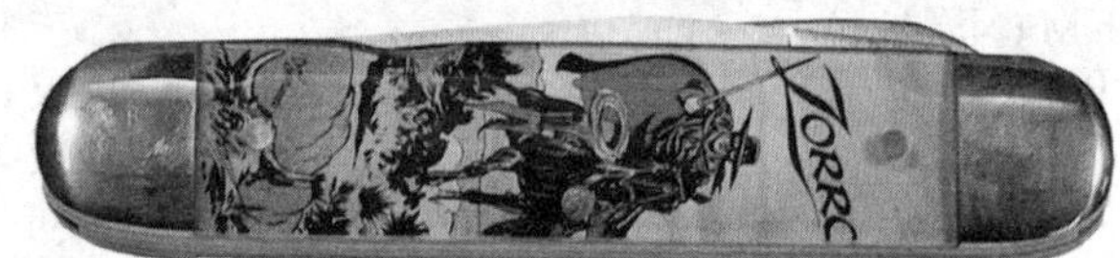

Zorro, pocketknife, Riders of the Silver Screen series, NMIB, $50.00

Windups, Friction, and Other Mechanicals

Windup toys represent a fun and exciting field of collecting — our fascination with them stems from their simplistic but exciting actions and brightly colored lithography, and especially the comic character or personality-related examples are greatly in demand by collectors today. Though most were made through the years of the '30s through the '50s, they carry their own weight against much earlier toys and are considered very worthwhile investments. Various types of mechanisms were used — some are key wound while others depend on lever action to tighten the mainspring and release the action of the toy. Tin and celluloid were used in their production, and although it is sometimes possible to repair a tin windup, experts advise against investing in a celluloid toy whose mechanism is not working, since the material is usually too fragile to withstand the repair.

Many of the boxes that these toys came in are almost as attractive as the toys themselves and can add considerably to their value.

If you especially enjoy windup and friction motorcycle toys, Sally Gibson-Downs and Christine Gentry have written a collectors' guide called *Motorcycle Toys, Antique and Contemporary*, published by Collector Books.

For more information on windups such as identification, value, etc., see Categories of Special Interest under Windups in the back of the book.

Advisors: Richard Trautwein (T3); Scott Smiles (S10).

See also Aeronautical; Automobiles and Other Replica Vehicles; Boats; Chein; Lehmann; Marx; Robots and Space Toys; Strauss.

American

Airport, Wyandotte, planes circle above airport, litho tin w/pressed steel planes, VG, A $175.00

Alpine Express, Ohio Art, 2 buses travel up & down mountains, 33" base, EX (EX box), A.......................................$125.00

Artie the Clown, Unique Art, clown drives comical car w/several actions, litho tin, 9½", EX...............................$450.00

Auto-Lift, Wolverine, lithographed tin, MIB, $325.00.

Auto Speedway, Automatic Toy, cars travel track & stops in garage, litho tin, 17" track, EX (G box), A..............$175.00

Auto Speedway Jr, Automatic Toy, car travels on base & turns around, litho tin, 12" track, NM (G box), A...........$100.00

Baby-Launching Kangaroo, 1950s, mama kangaroo shoots baby out of spring-loaded pouch, plastic, 4½", M, P4 ....$50.00

Billiard Players, Ranger Steel, litho tin, 15", NM (EX box)....$375.00

Blue Bird Racer, Kingsbury, 1930s, pnt pressed steel, w/driver, 18", EX (worn box), A $1,155.00

Bulldozer, Ranger, 1950, w/plow, cart & driver, litho tin, 10", MIB, A $200.00

Capitol Hill Racer, Unique Art, car travels track in & out of station house, litho tin, 17", NM (NM box)................$325.00

Captain Marvel Car, Automatic Toy, 1947, litho tin w/Captain Marvel on sides, 4", EX, A $225.00
Carousel, Converse, horses spin w/music, litho paper on wood w/clockwork mechanism, 28" dia, EX, A.............$3,500.00
Casey the Cop, Unique Art, litho tin, 8½", scarce, EX, A..$550.00
Cats, Ives, 2 cats w/violin & viola, litho paper w/clockwork mechanism, 6", scarce, VG (VG box), A $650.00
Charlie Chaplin, 1925, waddles back & forth w/swinging arms, litho tin, 8½", VG, A $650.00
Chrysler Speedster, Girard, 1925, tin, bl w/yel top, red tires & mounted spare, w/driver, 8½", EX (G- box), A.......$450.00
City of Los Angeles Streamlined Train Set, Nosco, plastic, complete, NM (NM box), A....................$175.00
City Transit Lines Trolley, Conway Skokie, 1950, plastic w/Wrigley's Spearmint Gum ad, friction, 14", rare, NMIB, A $250.00
Cop-Cycle w/Sidecar, Nosco, w/driver & passenger, plastic, friction, 5", NM (VG box), A $500.00
Dancing Cinderella & Prince, Irwin, 1950, plastic, 5½", NM (EX box), A $175.00
Dancing Jigger, wood & compo figure w/cloth clothes dances atop wood base, EX, A $1,000.00
Dandy Andy Rooster, Wolverine, rooster plucks worm from tree trunk as baby chick looks on, wheeled base, tin, 10", NMIB.....$850.00
Do-Do Clown, Do-Do Toy, squeeze bars & clown performs, tin, 8½", EX (EX box), A $150.00
Donald Duck Racer, litho tin w/flat tin figure, wht rubber tires, 4", rare, EX, A....................$650.00
Donald Duck Rail Car, Lionel, 1935, Donald works handlebars as Pluto's head bounces, compo, 10½", NM (EX box) ...$1,900.00
Drum Major, Wolverine, advances & plays drum, litho tin, 14", NM, A $350.00
Easter Bunny Delivery, Wyandotte, bunny on motorcycle w/sidecar, litho tin, 9", EX....................$275.00
Express Bus, Wolverine, 1950s, press down on rear for action, litho tin, 14", NM (EX box), A....................$150.00
Fast Freight Set, Nosco, plastic, complete, NM (NM box), A $150.00
Finnegan, Unique Art, cart advances in erratic motion w/baggage handler on front, litho tin, 13", NM (VG box) $275.00
Fire Ladder Truck, Lindstrom, 1920s, main ladder cranks up, litho tin, VG, H7....................$400.00
Flasho the Mechanical Grinder, Girard, 1925, workman sharpens tool on wheel, litho tin, 4½", EX (worn box), A.......$175.00
Fliver Bug, Buffalo Toy, 1937, travels in figure-8 pattern, red-pnt tin, 6½", NM (EX box) $250.00
Gasoline & Motor Oils Truck, Courtland, 1950s, red, wht & bl, 12½", EX (G box) $225.00
George Washington Bridge, Fritz Bueschell, Greyhound bus crosses bridge, litho tin, 25", NMIB, A................$1,650.00
GI Joe & His K-9 Pups, Unique Art, advances w/puppies in cages, litho tin, 9", VG, A....................$250.00
Golden Racer #1, Kingsbury, 1930s, pnt tin w/blk rubber tires, w/driver, 19", EX, A $1,000.00
Golden Racer #2, Kingsbury, 1930s, pnt tin w/blk rubber tires, w/driver, 19", rpt, VG....................$350.00

Hansom Cab Hillclimber, Dayton Friction Co, tin & wood w/CI spoke wheels, flywheel mechanism, 11", EX, A.......$450.00

Hobo Train, Unique Art, dog tugs on man's pants atop train, litho tin, 8", EX, A $350.00

Photo courtesy Scott Smiles

Home Run King, Selrite, 7", G, $450.00.

Horse Race, Buffalo Toys, 1930, carousel w/horses & Indians, litho tin, lever action, 6½", scarce, NM, A $200.00

Hott & Tott, Unique Art, Black banjo player standing by piano player, litho tin, 8", EX (G box), A $1,400.00

Humphrey Mobile, Wyandotte, 1950, figures pedals trike w/attached shack, litho tin, 9", EX (G box), A $500.00

Jackie Gleason Bus, Wolverine, 1955, litho tin, 13", EX (VG box), A...$975.00

Jazzbo Jim, Unique Art, 1920s, Black man w/checked pants dances on roof of litho tin house, 10", NMIB, A.....$825.00

Jet Roller Coaster, Wolverine, futuristic bus travels up & down ramp, litho tin, 12", NM (EX box) $300.00

Jolly Juggler Clown, Wolverine, 1930s, litho tin, scarce, NM (NM box), A $600.00

Kid Sampson Bell Ringer, B&R, man rings bell on base w/lithoed carnival scenes, tin, 9", EX, A $1,375.00

Kiddy Cyclist, Unique Art, 1930s, boy peddles bike & turns handlebars, litho tin, 9", VG (G box), A $400.00

Koolie Koal Kart, GE Carter, 1920, porter pulls cart, litho tin, 6½", rare, EX (EX box), A $825.00

Limousine, Marklin, 1909, enamelled tin w/cloth upholstered seats, brass side lamps, 2 opening doors, 13", rare, EX, A..$19,000.00

Lincoln Tunnel, Unique Art, cars travel road to tunnel as policeman directs traffic, litho tin, 24", MIB, A......$600.00

Magic Crossroads, Automatic Toy, 2 cars travel track, litho tin, 18" track, EX (G box), A $150.00

Mechanical Super Racing Car, Irwin #105, plastic, yel w/red hood, 12⅛", NMIB, A...$85.00

Merry-Go-Round, Wyandotte, 4 swan boats & airplanes circle base, litho tin, 5½", EX, A $400.00

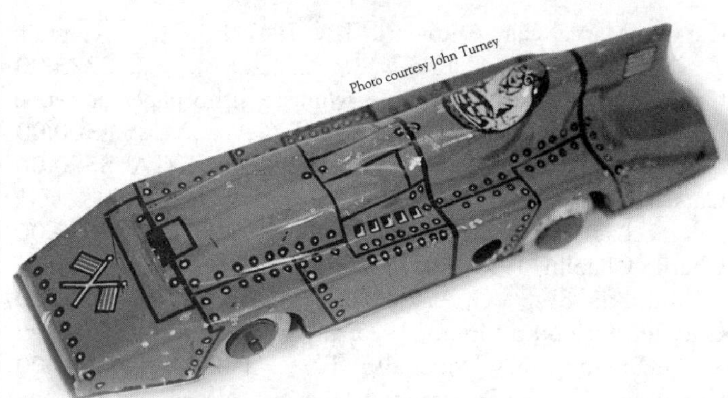

Photo courtesy John Turney

Land Speed Racer, Lindstrom, lithographed tin, NM, $250.00.

Mickey Mouse Hand Car, Lionel, 1930s, Mickey & Minnie work hdl, 8", VG (worn box), A $850.00

Mickey Mouse Racer #5, litho tin w/flat tin figure, wht rubber tires, 4", EX, A..$385.00

Never Stop Seesaw, Gibbs, boy & girl seesaw up & down tower, hand-pnt tin, 14", rare, VG (worn box), A $250.00

Peter Rabbit Chick-Mobile, Lionel, 1930s, Peter Pumps handcar, pnt compo & steel, 10", EX, J5.........................$500.00

Preacher at Pulpit, Ives, Black preacher behind pulpit, wood w/compo figure, 10⅜", EX, A $4,000.00

Pump-Mobile, Nylint, unlicensed Howdy Doody figure driving cart, litho tin, 9", NM (EX box), A $650.00

Racing Car, Irwin, red & yel plastic w/blk tires, 12", NM (NM box), A...$150.00

Rapid Transit Hillclimber, Schiebles, bl-& red-pnt metal w/gray doors, flywheel mechanism, 21", NMIB, A $1,700.00

Red Devil Racer, Budwill, 1950, w/driver, red & yel w/blk balloon tires, tin, NM (EX box), A.............................$350.00

Roaring Roadster, Nosco, w/driver, cream & red plastic w/visible engine, friction, 8", NM (NM box), A $200.00

Santa Car, Lionel, 1935, Santa works handlebars, Mickey Mouse in sack on his back, compo, 11", NM (EX box), A .$3,400.00

See-Saw, Irwin, 2 sm girls on see-saw, plastic, M (NM box), A $100.00

Skeeter Duck, Lindstrom, advances in figure-8 motion & shakes head, litho tin, 9", EX (G box), A............................$75.00

Sky Rangers Tower, Unique Art, airplane & zeppelin circle tower, litho tin, 9", EX, A $800.00

Sparkling Climbing Tractor & Cart, Ranger, 1950, litho tin w/blk rubber treads, 9½", NM (G box)...................$125.00

Sportsman's Convertible, Wyandotte, roof slides up & down, trunk opens, pressed steel, 12", MIB, A $700.00

Streamline Railway, Wolverine, litho tin w/wooden wheels, friction, 17", EX $150.00

Super Motor Bus, Saunders, forward & reverse action w/gyro motor, plastic, 13", NM (EX box), A.......................$150.00

Texas Pete, Seaman, 1950s, cowboy bounces up & down on rocking horse, plastic, 9", NMIB, A $75.00

Toytown Estate Station Wagon, Wyandotte, litho tin w/blk rubber tires, 21", EX, A...$400.00

Transmobile Jr Car Carrier, Wyandotte, red & yel litho tin w/2 plastic cars, 12", NM, A $200.00

Trolley Car Hillclimber, Dayton Friction Co, hand-pnt metal w/diecut figures in windows, 14½", NM, A..........**$1,400.00**

US Army Anti-Tank Car, Courtland, litho tin w/mounted plastic weapon, 7", NM (EX box), A **$100.00**

US Gasoline Co Gas Pump, Hillco Toys, crank pump & gauge moves up, litho tin, 5", EX, H7 ....**$195.00**

US Mail Truck, Kingsbury, red tin w/open driver's seat & enclosed body, spoke wheels, 7", VG, A.................**$875.00**

Waltzing Royal Couple, Irwin, couple glide across floor in realistic motion, plastic, 5", NM (VG box), A **$150.00**

Zilotone, Wolverine, 1930, circus band performer hits keys, plays 6 tunes, tin & steel, 9", NM (EX box), A....**$1,100.00**

ENGLISH

Airplane Carousel, mk Made in England, 2 planes circle tower, litho tin w/pressed steel base, 6", EX.......................**$100.00**

Bandit Chase, police motorcycle chases car & circles it, litho tin cycle & plastic car, NM (EX box), A.......................**$300.00**

Big Dipper Carnival Ride, vehicle navigates track, litho tin, 41" track, EX (EX box), A **$225.00**

Circus Truck, Wells, litho tin w/animals on both sides, 9½", EX, A **$150.00**

Crazy Express Train, litho tin, 11", EX (EX box), A **$100.00**

Drummer on Horseback, figure plays drum as horse advances, litho tin, 5", EX, A **$225.00**

Dump Truck, Wells, dump action, litho tin w/balloon tires, 10", VG, A **$175.00**

Funfair Flyer, car navigates track above carnival base, litho tin, 11", NM, A **$500.00**

Gyro Cycle, Triang, prewar, rider on cycle, litho tin w/compo figure, 8", MIB **$600.00**

Magic Midget MG Racer, Minic-Triang, gr pressed steel w/British flag emblem, litho tin driver, G, A **$1,375.00**

Mickey Mouse Duet, Salco, 1950, Minnie dances atop piano as Mickey plays, VG (VG box) **$500.00**

Mickey Mouse Handcar, Wells, 1935, Mickey & Minnie work handcar, tin & celluloid, 6 sections of track, 13", NMIB, A...**$850.00**

Nautilus Submarine (20,000 Leagues Under the Sea), Sutcliffe, lt gr tin w/gold highlights, 9½", MIB, A..................**$475.00**

Saloon Car, Chad, red w/driver & passengers lithoed in windows, balloon tires, tin, 9", NM (VG box), A **$450.00**

Saloon Car, Minic-Triang, tin, 2-tone, 5", EX (EX box), A...**$275.00**

Sea Wolf Atomic Submarine, Sutcliffe, cast metal, 9", EX (EX box), A...**$135.00**

Taxi Cab, Wells 'O London, maroon & yel, electric headlights & taillights, litho tin, w/driver, 14", VG (partial box), A **$800.00**

Transport Bus, Brimtoy, litho tin dbl-decker w/Brimtoy Trains & Cinderella Sweepers advertising, 8", NM, A.......**$425.00**

FRENCH

Acrobat Cart, rider & horse w/acrobat on 2 wheels, advances w/plink-plunk music, 6", EX, A...............................**$275.00**

Auto Transport, Martin, ca 1920, truck w/driver pulls 2-wheeled wagon, 10½", EX (EX box), A.............................**$1,500.00**

Bear Climbing Pole, Martin, wht bear climbs pole, 14", NMIB, A...**$1,875.00**

Bell Ringer, Martin, jtd flat figure rings bell on post on oblong base, rubber-band drive, pnt tin & lead, 7", VG, A.**$350.00**

Bimbo Clown Car, Joustra, car spins & front end lifts up, litho tin, 4½", NM, A **$175.00**

Black Man Playing Bass Fiddle, standing on trapezoid base, plays plink-plunk music, 9½", EX, A...........................**$1,300.00**

Black Man Pushing Fruit Cart, Martin, mk FM, man leans on flat 4-wheeled cart, litho tin w/cloth clothes, 8", VG, A .**$950.00**

Black Minstrel Seated, figure in top hat shakes bells & plays cymbals w/feet, pnt tin, 7", VG, rpt, A **$700.00**

Boy Pushing Cart, Martin, pushes 2-wheeled cart w/package mk Tres Tres Presse, pnt tin w/cloth clothes, 8", EX, A ..**$1,000.00**

Boy Twirling Balls, no cap, pnt tin, 8½", EX, A............**$550.00**

Boy Twirling Balls, w/cap, pnt tin, 10", EX, A **$900.00**

Champion, Rossignol, Buffalo Bill-type figure shoots rifle at target, lever action, pnt tin, 9", NMIB, A................**$1,900.00**

Chinese Man Pulling Rickshaw, Les Jouets, tin & compo, 6½", NM (G box), A **$225.00**

Chinese Warrior w/Swords, Martin, hat mk FM, figure in bl & blk period costume wields swords, pnt tin & wire, 7", VG...**$1,000.00**

City Bus, JP, gr litho tin w/wht top, destinations listed on sides, 10½", EX, A **$1,100.00**

Clown & Duck Roundego, clown bobs up & down as duck pops in & out of base, pnt tin, 8½", VG, A **$800.00**

Clown Banjo Player, seated on chair w/banjo, plays plink-plunk music, tin, 6", rpt, A **$700.00**

Clown Curtsying, pnt tin w/cloth clothes, 7½", G, A....**$350.00**

Clown Trombonist, straddles drum-like base & plays trombone, plink-plunk music, pnt tin, 8½", VG, A **$1,000.00**

Clown Twirling Parasol, clown rotates as parasol spins on ground, pnt tin, 5½", VG, A.......................................**$500.00**

Clown Twirling Star w/3 Bells, gold star twirls on clown's stomach, pnt tin, 9", VG **$1,100.00**

Clown Twirling Star w/8 Bells, lg lithoed star twirls on clown's stomach, pnt tin, EX, A **$2,000.00**

Clown Viola Player, plays as eyes move, pnt tin w/compo head & cloth outfit, 11", EX, A...................................**$3,800.00**

Clown Violinist, plays plink-plunk music, tin w/bsk head, cloth clothes, 13", VG, A...**$3,400.00**

Clown w/Duck, clown faces quacking duck that flaps wings as they move back & forth, pnt tin, 10", G, A **$550.00**

Clown w/Hoop & Ball, wooden ball spins as hoop rotates & revolves around clown, pnt tin, 5½", G..................**$275.00**

Clowns on Seesaw, legs outstretched on plank attached to drum on base, w/plink-plunk music, pnt tin, 10", G, A.**$1,300.00**

Clowns on 4-Wheeled Platform w/Bells, 2 clowns waving bells while facing each other, pnt tin, 8", VG, A............**$800.00**

Donald Duck (Donald le Canard), Donald as caballero bounces around, plastic, 6½", NM (NM box), A **$300.00**

Dump Truck, Bonnet, open cab w/side dump, disk wheels, w/driver, pnt & emb tin, 8", VG, A **$450.00**

Exposition Universalle, Martin, 1889, man pushes lady w/fan in 3-wheeled chair, inertia wheel, litho tin, 7", EX, A.....**$1,900.00**

Fire Engine, Delahaye, 1900, red-pnt tin w/top-& rear-mounted reels, 2 cloth-dressed compo figures, 15", NMIB, A .**$4,600.00**

Fisherman, Martin, figure sitting atop rock manipulating rod w/fish, pnt tin w/cloth clothes, 7", EX, A............**$1,800.00**

Flying Carpet, couple on carpet fly in circle while suspended on string, pnt tin, 5½", VG, A..................................**$600.00**

Flying Geese, 2 geese fly in circle on string, pnt tin, 8", VG, A...**$300.00**

Girl Skipping Rope, figure attached to rod on base jumps in realistic motion, pnt tin, 6", VG, A.............................**$800.00**

Glaces Extra Ice Cream Truck, compo w/full-figure driver, 4", NM, A..**$125.00**

International Circus Set, clown balances on 2 ladders, litho tin & wood w/cloth clothes, MIB, A..........................**$1,000.00**

Joe Carioca, pnt compo, 8", EX, A...............................**$400.00**

Lady Doing Cake Walk, Martin, moves arms & dances forward, pnt tin, wire & lead w/cloth clothes, 7½", rare, G ..**$1,800.00**

Lady on Roller Skates, figure in long dress & hat moves feet as she advances, pnt tin, 7", VG, A **$850.00**

Lady Pushing Cart (La Petite Marchande), Martin, lady pushes 2-wheeled cart, pnt tin w/cloth clothes, 7", NMIB, A.**$1,100.00**

Lady Pushing Fruit Cart, Creation, pnt compo & tin, 6", NMIB, A...**$350.00**

Lady w/Basket & Umbrella, advances as torso rocks, pnt tin w/cloth skirt, 6½", VG, A.......................................**$400.00**

Lady w/Fan, slowly dances around as torso moves, pnt tin, 7", VG, A..**$850.00**

Lady w/Muff, Martin, slowly advances in rocking motion, tin w/cloth clothes, 8", VG, A..................................**$1,000.00**

Lawyer Behind Desk (L/Eminent Avocat), Martin, cloth-dressed figure addresses court, pnt & litho tin, 9", EX, A.**$2,800.00**

Man Sweeping, Martin, twists & swings broom, pnt tin, wire & lead w/cloth clothes, 7", rare, G, A.........................**$850.00**

Man Swinging Around Pole, clasps legs together as he rotates around pole, pnt tin, 15", VG............................**$1,750.00**

Marble-Drop Toy (Le Treuil), Martin, marbles descend pole causing man to turn crank, pnt tin, 25", VG (VG box), A...**$700.00**

Marechal Ferrand, Martin, 2 men working forge w/anvil, pnt & litho tin, 6½", EX, A..**$2,750.00**

Military Ambulance, litho tin w/Dunlop balloon tires, lift-top roof, 7", EX, A **$175.00**

Monkey w/Music Box, Decamps, hand-pnt papier-mache w/fur-covered body, wood music box, 11", NM, A...........**$350.00**

Mysterious Ball Toy (Boule Mysterier), Ferdinand Martin, 1906, figure inside ball descends down spiral pole, 12", NMIB...**$2,000.00**

Orange Vendor, Martin, lady pushes oranges in 2-wheeled cart, tin w/cloth outfit, 6¾", VG, A...............................**$900.00**

Oriental Soldier, Martin, free-standing figure in gold costume & cap holds weapon, pnt tin, wire & lead, 8", VG, A.**$800.00**

Peacock, walks forward, real peacock feathers over papier-mache, brass feet, 22", EX, A **$450.00**

Pianist, Martin, rocks as hands move over keyboard, plink-plunk music, pnt tin w/cloth clothes, 5", EX, A **$1,100.00**

Pigeon, Bonnet, pnt tin, eccentric wheels, 8", VG, A....**$250.00**

Police Patrol, 1930s, litho tin w/Dunlop balloon tires, lift-top roof, 7", NM, A..**$250.00**

Porter Pushing 2-Wheeled Cart, Martin, porter pushing cart w/lg box, inertia wheel, tin, 5", EX, A **$700.00**

Racer #4, Pinard, red w/blk rubber tires & red spokes, side-mounted exhaust pipe & horn, electric headlamps, 12", VG, A...**$1,650.00**

Rotor Auto, bright yel plastic, friction, 5", EX (G box), A ...**$60.00**

Soldier w/Rifle & Bayonet, Martin, pnt tin, wire & lead w/cloth clothes, 7½", EX, A...**$900.00**

Squirrel in a Cage, Martin, mk FM, squirrel runs in cage attached to housing on flat base, pnt tin, 9", VG, A.............**$400.00**

Torpedo Convertible, JEP, tin roadster w/driver, 10", NMIB, A...**$2,500.00**

Trolley Bus, Joustra, advances w/bell sound, tin w/6 balloon tires, 12", NM (EX box), A **$400.00**

Violin Player (Le Gai Violinist), Martin, man in top hat plays violin, tin w/cloth clothes, EX (EX box), A.........**$1,200.00**

German

A-580 Tank, Arnold, advances w/firing sound, litho tin, 5", EX (G box), A **$175.00**

Aeroplane Ride, US Zone, 3 planes spin around canopy, litho tin w/celluloid props, 8", EX, A...............................**$175.00**

Akustico 2002 Roadster, Schuco, cream w/red interior, 6", EX, A **$175.00**

Bagatelle Player, Gunthermann, pool table w/man at 1 end, numbered pockets at the other, hand-pnt tin, 11", NM, A **$975.00**

Barney Google Riding Spark Plug, Nifty, Barney rocks back & forth as Sparky nods his head, litho tin, 7", EX, A.**$1,400.00**

Black Dancer, lady dances w/hands up, hand-pnt tin, 7", NM, A **$800.00**

Blue Bird Racer, Gunthermann, litho tin, w/driver, 20", scarce, EX, A..**$1,275.00**

Boxers, 2 boxers on gr platform w/red spoke wheels, tin, 7", EX, A **$385.00**

Boy w/Performing Poodle, Gunthermann, boy holds rope as poodle jumps on wheeled platform, hand-pnt tin & lead, 6", VG, A **$850.00**

Bruxelles, GNK, 1958 exposition toy, helicopter circles opposite of cube design, plastic, 6", NM (NM box), A..........**$175.00**

Busy Lizzie, lady advances w/mop, litho tin, 7", EX, A...**$500.00**

Charlie Chaplin, Schuco, dances around w/spinning cane, tin w/cloth clothes, 6", EX (worn box), A **$1,000.00**

Charlie Motorcycle, Schuco, litho tin w/full-figure driver, 5", EX, A **$500.00**

Checker Cab, Bing, orange & blk w/spoke wheels, pick-up flag on side, 6½", EX, A..**$1,250.00**

Circus Elephant, US Zone, balls spiral up column into elephant's basket as parasol spins on trunk, tin, 10", NMIB, A..**$475.00**

Circus Monkey, GNK, monkey w/umbrella advances on drum, litho tin w/paper umbrella, 7½", scarce, NM (EX box), A **$300.00**

Circus Monkey on Tricycle, US Zone, monkey peddles bike & turns handlebars to change direction, litho tin, 4", VG, A..**$150.00**

Civilian Motorcycle, Arnold/US Zone, advances in circular motion w/sparks & sound, litho tin, 8", NM (G box), A **$800.00**

Clown & Child Performing, Gunthermann, clown plays cymbals as child spins on pedestal, hand-pnt tin, 7", G, A...**$500.00**

Clown & Dogs, 2 dogs pull clown on 4-wheeled platform, litho tin, 8", EX, A...**$1,000.00**

Clown Band, US Zone, 1 plays drum & 1 plays cymbals, litho tin, 8½" base, EX, A...**$825.00**

Clown Carousel w/Boats & Whales, Gunthermann, rotates w/plink-plunk music, pnt tin, EX, A...**$9,900.00**

Clown Drummer, boy in clown suit plays bass drum, tin & celluloid w/cloth outfit, 8", NM, A...**$875.00**

Clown Playing Cymbals, seated clown plays cymbals, hand-pnt face, cloth outfit, 6", EX, A...**$1,000.00**

Clown Riding Cart, GK, clown in 3-wheeled cart, litho tin, 5½", EX, A...**$385.00**

Clown w/Billy Goat, clown atop round base tries to train billy goat on wheeled platform, hand-pnt tin, 6½", VG, A...**$1,000.00**

Clowns & Monkey, Gunthermann, 2 clowns swing monkey on bar, litho tin, 8", EX, A...**$1,300.00**

Combinato 4003 Convertible, Schuco, red tin, 7", EX ..**$350.00**

Coupe, Bing, red w/blk running boards & roof, spoke wheels, no driver, 6½", EX, A...**$500.00**

Coupe, Bing, red w/blk running boards & simulated soft top, spoke wheels & mounted spare, female driver, 6", NM, A.**$1,200.00**

Coupe Convertible, Stock, red & beige w/disk wheels & mounted spare, removable top, 8", MIB, A...**$3,000.00**

Cowboy Juggler, Schuco, cowboy juggles 4 attached balls, litho tin w/cloth outfit, 4½", NM, A...**$1,200.00**

Dare Devil Racer, Arnold, car spins in loop, litho tin, 4" car, NM (EX box), A...**$450.00**

Donald Duck Rocket, W Germany, advances as Donald's head moves, tin w/plastic head, 7", scarce, EX (EX box), A...**$1,300.00**

Donald Duck Rocket, W Germany, advances as Donald's head moves, tin w/plastic head, 7", scarce, VG, A...**$400.00**

Examico 4001, US Zone, silver w/red interior, 5½", NMIB...**$225.00**

Express Parcels Truck, Distler, w/driver, gray-& maroon-litho tin w/spoke wheels, EX, A...**$285.00**

Felix the Cat, Gunthermann, pnt tin, 7", EX, A...**$550.00**

Fex 1111, Schuco, bl tin w/blk rubber tires, 2 speeds, 6", NMIB, A...**$400.00**

Fighting Roosters, 1930, roosters travel back & forth on base & peck at each other, litho tin, 10", EX, A...**$500.00**

Fire Chief Car, Hoge, advances w/siren sound, pressed steel, orig decal, 15", VG, A...**$225.00**

Fire House & Ladder Truck, Distler, litho tin, fire house: 11½", truck: 11", EX, A...**$3,200.00**

Fishing Fred, US Zone, man spins on base as fish winds up pole, litho tin, MIB, A...**$450.00**

Ford Model T Doctor's Coupe, Bing, litho tin, w/driver, 6½", NM, A...**$600.00**

Ford Model T Roadster, Bing, 1921, blk w/spoke wheels & mounted spare, w/driver, 6½", EX, A...**$500.00**

Ford Model T Roadster, Bing, 1921 model, blk w/spoke wheels & mounted spare, w/driver, 6½", MIB, A...**$900.00**

Fox Carrying Swan in Cage, Schuco, litho tin w/plush-covered head & cloth clothes, 5", M, A...**$1,100.00**

Friendly Cycle, Technofix, full-figure driver & passenger w/dog between them, litho tin, friction, 8", EX, A...**$300.00**

Gama 520, West Germany, mouse travels around cage & goes through door, tin & plastic, 3" mouse, NM (EX box), A...**$175.00**

Garage & Limousine, Bing, litho tin, garage: 5x7", MIB, A...**$800.00**

Gordon Bennet Coupe, Gunthermann, litho tin open-seater w/driver, spoke wheels, extremely rare, EX, A...**$17,600.00**

Gordon Bennet Coupe, Gunthermann, litho tin w/pnt-tin figures, 6", EX, A...**$6,600.00**

Gordon Bennet Racer #5, Gunthermann, litho tin w/rubber tires, wood & paper bellows, 9", rare, EX, A...**$9,000.00**

Hansom Cab, advances forward, horse pulls cab w/rear mounted driver, 7½", EX, A...**$275.00**

Harold Lloyd Bell Toy, 1930, bell rings & face changes expression, flat tin face, lever action, 6", NM, A...**$400.00**

Hessmobile Racer, Hess, w/driver, litho tin, 8¼", NM, A..**$2,300.00**

Hessmobile Tractor & Log Trailer, Hess, litho tin, complete w/stacked wood, 15½", EX, A...**$275.00**

House Maid, Gunthermann, lady advances w/broom, hand-pnt tin, 7½", NM, A...**$850.00**

Ice Cream Vendor, man pushes ice cream cart w/spoke wheels, litho tin, 6", EX, A...**$600.00**

Jackie Ostrich Cart, Gunda & Kelpert, ostrich pulls boy in 4-wheeled cart, litho tin, 9½", EX, A...**$1,000.00**

Jockey on Horse, rocking motion, hand-pnt tin, 6", EX, A...**$850.00**

Jubilating Singing Bird, GNK, sings w/several other actions, litho tin, 7", NM (EX box), A...**$200.00**

Jumbo the Elephant, US Zone, litho tin, 4", NM (EX box), A...**$500.00**

Lady Chasing Mouse, Gunthermann, lady swats mouse attached to rod w/broom, hand-pnt tin, 7½", EX, A...**$1,100.00**

Lady Gardener, Gunthermann, advances w/rake & watering can, hand-pnt tin, 7", G, A...**$475.00**

Lady w/Umbrella, Gunthermann, Black woman advances w/umbrella & wicker basket, hand-pnt tin, 6", G-, A..**$300.00**

Lighthouse w/Boat, Carette, boat w/driver circles lighthouse, hand-pnt tin, 10" dia, G, A...**$700.00**

Limousine, Bing, 1910, red w/maroon & orange striping, orig driver, tin, 5¼", VG, A...**$700.00**

Limousine, Carette, gr w/red detail, rubber tires w/spokes, orig chauffeur & luggage on top, EX, A...**$2,200.00**

Limousine, Gundka & Kelpert, open front w/enclosed rear, red w/blk roof & yel trim, w/driver, litho tin, 6½", NM, A...**$775.00**

Limousine, Gunthermann, open front w/enclosed rear, gray w/blk roof & running boards, litho tin, w/driver, 12", VG, A...**$2,000.00**

Limousine, Karl Bub, open front w/enclosed rear, maroon w/blk roof & running boards, litho tin, w/driver, 10", NM, A...**$1,000.00**

Maggie & Jiggs, Nifty, 1924, figures travel on platform, litho tin, 7", EX, A...**$1,300.00**

Magic Blossom Top, tulip spins inside dome & opens up to reveal ballerina, tin & plastic, lever action, 10", NMIB, A..**$250.00**

Mammy, Lindstrom, vibrating motion, litho tin, 8", EX, A...**$350.00**

Man in Parachute, Muller & Kadeder, figure sails around bases, pnt & stained tin, 16", VG, A...**$2,500.00**

Mickey Mouse Hurdy-Gurdy, Distler, 1931, Mickey cranks hdl as Minnie dances atop stage on wheels, tin, NM, A .**$10,000.00**

Mickey Mouse Jazz Drummer, 1934, lever action, litho tin, 7", rare, EX, A $2,800.00
Monkey in Race Car, Schuco, tin w/felt shirt & plush hair, 3½", EX, A $800.00
Monkey on Motorcycle, Gama, litho tin w/full-figure driver, 7", VG, A $350.00
Motodrill Clown, Schuco, bl coat version, advances in circular motion, litho tin w/cloth clothes, 5", EX, A $1,400.00
Motodrill Clown, Schuco, gr coat version, advances in circular motion, litho tin w/cloth clothes, 5", NM (NM box), A $2,600.00
Motorcycle, Fischer, litho tin, propels w/chain driver, 7", EX, A $1,750.00

Motorcycle, Technofix, lithographed tin, rare, MIB, $450.00.

Mystery Car & Garage, PN, car enters & exits garage, litho tin, 5" garage, EX (EX box), A $200.00
Oh La La Car, Gescha, advances & driver's head spins, litho tin, 6", NMIB, A $350.00
Open Motor Coach, Bing, 1901, w/driver & 2 passengers, pnt tin w/spoke wheels, 8", EX, A $15,000.00
Open Seat Passenger Car, Hess, w/driver, bl w/gold trim, simulated spoke wheels, 7½", EX, A $1,300.00
Paddy's Pride, pig pulling rider in 2-wheeled cart, litho tin, 8", NM (VG box), A $2,000.00
Performing Bear, Gunthermann, advances forward w/several actions, hand-pnt tin, 6½", NM, A $500.00
Phaeton, Gunthermann, litho tin w/rubber tires & spoke wheels, 4 hand-pnt tin figures, extremely rare, EX $18,000.00
Phaeton, Gunthermann, pnt-& litho-tin, orig driver, spoke wheels, 9", EX, A $4,600.00
Phaeton w/Canopy, Carette, red- & beige-litho tin w/4 figures, rubber tires w/spoke wheels, 8", EX, A $4,400.00
Police Motorcycle & Car, PN, motorcycle circles car, litho tin, MIB, A $525.00
Popeye in Rowboat, Hoge, 1930s, litho tin & pressed steel, complete w/oars, 14", rare, EX $2,500.00
Popeye w/Spinach Can, squats & stands up as he eats his spinach, vinyl w/cloth clothes, 10", NM $175.00
Punch & the Devil, diecut figures clash together on base, litho tin, 7", missing 1 figure o/w VG, A $225.00
Rudy the Ostrich, Nifty, litho tin, 8", G, A $450.00
Schuco Turn Clown, tin w/cloth clothes, several actions, 4½", MIB, A $500.00
Service Station, convertible travels base w/service station & Esso gas pump, litho tin, 6x9" base, NM (VG box). $150.00
Sky Rider, 1950s, 2 planes attached to rod circle above airport hangar, litho tin, 8", NM (EX box), A $150.00
Sparking Racer, Lupor, litho tin w/blk rubber tires, 12", NM (EX box), A $225.00
Speedway Streamlined Racer, Lindstrom, red racer w/wht rubber tires, 6", scarce, EX (worn box), A $375.00
Submarine, Arnold, litho tin, 9", NM (EX box), A $250.00
Sweeping Mammy, Lindstrom, 1935, vibrates around & sweeps, litho tin, 8", NM (EX box), A $450.00
Telesteering Car 3000, Schuco, enameled steel, 4", EX (VG box), A $275.00
Tightrope Clown, clown moves hand-over-hand on rope, compo w/cloth clothes, 8", NM (EX box), A $100.00
Toonerville Trolley, Fontaine Fox, 1922, advances, stops & shakes, litho tin, 6", scarce, EX $850.00
Toonerville Trolley, Fontaine Fox, 1922, advances, stops & shakes, litho tin, 6", scarce, EX (EX box) $1,200.00
Topsy Turvy Tom, Ri N Co, car w/roll bars & clown driver advances & flips over, litho tin, 10", MIB, A $2,800.00
Touring Car, Distler, beige & red w/orange roof, bl spoke wheels, w/driver, litho tin, 7", EX, A $1,100.00
Traffic Man (Flic), Schuco, figure rotates & lifts arm as simulated lights change on base, 5", NM (NM box), A.. $275.00
Train Station, Arnold, locomotive & coach travel track w/station at each end, litho tin, 15", M, A $300.00
Tramway Co Trolley Car, 1920, red w/gray roof & striping, tin, 7", G, A $200.00
Traveling Man, FV, 1950s, man in lg overcoat advances w/suitcase, litho tin, 4½", NM, A $275.00
Trip-Trap, Hans Ebor, mule pulls wagon w/driver, litho tin, 11", EX, A $600.00
Variente Bus & Gas Station, Schuco, tin bus w/plastic & litho tin station, 6" station, VG, A $275.00
Vis-A-Vis, Gunthermann, red open-seater w/driver, tin w/wht rubber tires & blk spokes, 6½", NM, A $3,200.00

Japanese

Abarth 750 Pinin Farina Racer, HTC, litho tin, friction, 10", VG, A $185.00
Airman NR-1800, TN, 1930s, advances w/spinning prop, litho tin, 8" wingspan, EX+, A $325.00
Animal Barber Shop, TPS, cat applies shaving cream & moves razor across rabbit's face, litho tin, 5", NM (NM box), A $475.00
Animal Circus Magic Garage, K, dog enters & exits garage, litho tin, 4x5" garage, EX, A $100.00
Animal Tag, CK, prewar, dog chases cat around kennel, litho tin & celluloid, 7", EX (EX box), A $400.00
Atom Racer #45, Marusan, 1950s, w/driver, litho tin, 8", EX (G box), A $550.00
Auto Cycle, TN, litho tin w/full-figure driver, friction, 5", EX (EX box), A $550.00
Auto Transporter, SSS, complete w/4 cars, litho tin, friction, 12", NM (EX box), A $200.00

Automatic Racing Game, Haji, 3 cars start race from garage, litho tin, plunger action, EX (EX box), A $225.00

Babes in Toyland, Linemar, soldier advances while playing drum, 6", NM (EX box)...$350.00

Babes in Toyland Go-Mobile, Linemar, litho tin w/vinyl-headed figure, friction, 6", MIB $475.00

Baby Tortoise, Occupied Japan, advances in realistic motion, litho tin, 5", NM (EX box)......................................$100.00

Ball Playing Giraffe, TPS, ball bounces from arms to chin, litho tin, 8½", NM (EX box) $325.00

Balloon Santa, Alps, 1950s, lifts balloons & rings bell, 7½", NMIB...$150.00

Batman, 1989, litho tin, NMIB.......................................$100.00

Batman Batmobile, Alps, 1966, litho tin, friction, 8", scarce, EX...$900.00

Batman Batmobile & Batboat w/Trailer, AHI/NPPI, 1974, plastic, friction, EX (EX box) $150.00

Bear Golfer, TPS, bears hits ball across bridge into net, litho tin, 4", NM (EX box) $375.00

Bell Ringing Cat, mk Made in Occupied Japan, litho tin, NM..$300.00

Ben-Hur Trotter, AHI, horse-drawn cart w/gladiator, litho tin, 7", NM (NM box) $300.00

Big Joe Chef, Yone, advances w/chicken on plate, litho tin, 9", NM (NM box)..$150.00

Big League Hockey Player, TPS, 1950s, skates w/realistic movement, litho tin, 6", EX (G box), A..........................$400.00

Bill the Ball Blowing Whale, KO, advances & balances styrofoam ball on top of water spout, litho tin, NM (NM box) $150.00

Bird Cage, prewar, 3 parrots in cage & 1 on top perform several actions, litho tin w/celluloid birds, 10", EX, A $150.00

Black Boy on Tricycle, advances forward & reverse as bell rings, litho tin w/celluloid head, 8½", rare, NM, A $1,400.00

Blacksmith Teddy, TN, sits on base & hammers horseshoe, tin & plush, 6", NM (NM box), A $175.00

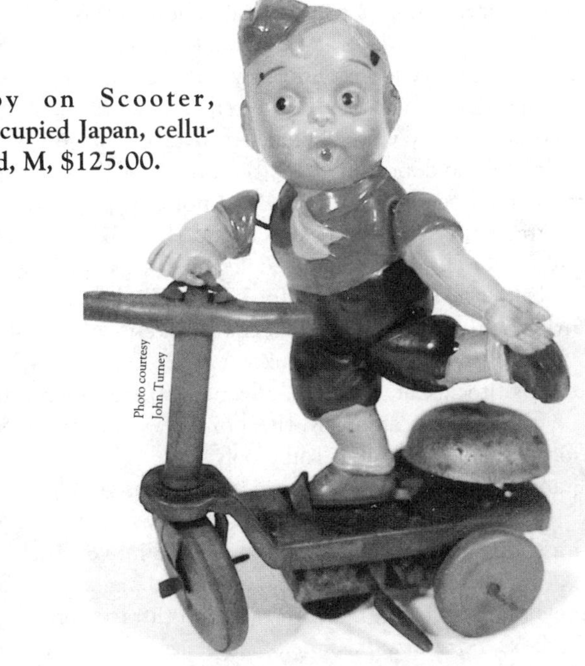

Boy on Scooter, Occupied Japan, celluloid, M, $125.00.

Bobo the Magician (Happy-Go-Lucky Magician), TN, lifts hat & rabbit, chick & egg appear, litho tin, 9", NM (EX box), A $850.00

Boy Feeding Chicken, seated boy feeding chicken on rectangular base, litho tin, 7", NM, A.......................................$500.00

Boy Playing Drum & Bell, prewar, plays drum & bell w/parasol spinning above, tin w/celluloid head, 11", VG, A...$450.00

Bozo the Clown, Alps, plays drum & rocks back & forth, litho tin, 8½", EX (EX box), A..$750.00

Branko Mechanical Acrobat, CK, child performs acrobats on highbar, celluloid & tin, 13", MIB, A.......................$200.00

Bunny Family Parade, mama bunny advances w/3 babies behind her, litho tin, 12", EX (EX box), A..........................$135.00

Cadet, Showa, prewar, advances w/sword, litho tin w/celluloid head, 6½", EX (EX box), A....................................$150.00

Calypso Joe the Drummer, TPS, native beats drum on rocking base, litho tin, 6", scarce, NM (EX box), A.............$375.00

Candy Loving Canine, TPS, dog flips candy in mouth as balls drop into candy box, litho tin, 6", NM (NM box) ..$225.00

Car w/Motorcycle Cop, car advances w/motorcycle attached by rope, litho tin, car: 6", motorcycle: 3", EX (EX box), A..........$225.00

Casper the Ghost, Linemar, litho tin, 4½", scarce, NM.$475.00

Casper the Ghost Tank, Linemar, Casper forces tank to turn over, litho tin, 4", NM (EX box).............................$550.00

Central Railway, ST, 1950s, litho tin, friction, 13", NM (NM box), A...$200.00

Champ on Ice, TPS, 3 bears skate w/realistic leg movement, litho tin, 8", NM (NM box), A $1,100.00

Charlie McCarthy, vibrates around & mouth opens & closes, celluloid, 7", EX, A..$400.00

Circus Bugler, TPS, rare version w/bl pants, sways side to side while playing trumpet, litho tin, 9", MIB $500.00

Circus Car, KO, lithographed tin, MIB, J6, $200.00.

Circus Elephant, pushes ball around w/spinning parasol on his trunk, litho tin, 6", MIB, A $135.00

Circus Jeep, Y, litho tin, friction, 6", EX (VG box)........$200.00

Circus Motorcycle, TT, clown on motorcycle advances & turns automatically, litho tin, 6", NM (EX box), A..........$300.00

Circus Plane, Yone, advances & flips over, clown pilot, litho tin, 3½", MIB $125.00

Circus Trailer, SSS, lion moves in trailer as truck advances, litho tin, friction, 9", NM (NM box), A $200.00
Circus Train, advances as tiger stripes roll inside inserts on side, litho tin, friction, 14", EX (EX box), A $100.00
Climbing Pirate, TPS, pull string for action, litho tin, 5", NM (EX box) $200.00
Climbing Tom-Tom Monkey, MT, native girl shakes back & forth as monkey scoots up & down palm tree, litho tin, 13", EX, A $125.00
Clown in Carriage, CK, prewar, advances & spills forward as clown hangs on, litho tin w/celluloid figure, 5", NMIB, A $125.00
Clown in His Car, Cragstan, car mk Star of the Circus, advances as clown tips hat & waves, litho tin, 6", VG (VG box), A $400.00
Clown on Roller Skates, TPS, skates w/realistic motion, litho tin w/cloth pants, 7", EX (VG box), A $400.00
Clown w/Donkey, clown pulls donkey's tail, pnt celluloid, 7", EX $150.00
Clown w/Monkey Whirligig, prewar, advances in circular pattern w/parasol spinning above, celluloid, 7½", NM, A $250.00
Come Come Santa, Occupied Japan, 2 reindeer pull Santa in sleigh, celluloid w/tin base, 7", EX (EX box), A $550.00
Comical Driver, car advances as monkey driver rocks back & forth, litho tin, friction, 6", EX (EX box), A $200.00
Crawling Baby, prewar, crawls w/realistic action, celluloid, 5", NM $75.00
Crazy Car, CK, prewar, tractor-type vehicle advances as driver's head spins, litho tin w/vinyl-headed figure, 5", VG, A $175.00
Dancing Chef, Occupied Japan, Black chef travels around w/plate of food, celluloid, 5", scarce, MIB, A...........$725.00
Dancing Sam, S&E, stage rotates as figure dances, litho tin, 9", NM (EX box)..................$175.00
Dandy, Mikuni, man tips hat, moves toes & eyes roll, litho tin, 6", EX (G box), A..................$150.00
Daredevil-Acrobat Stunt Motorcycle, Alps, advances & tumbles, litho tin, friction, 5", NM (EX box), A $250.00
Disney Express, Linemar, litho tin, 12", scarce, EX (EX box) $1,200.00
Disney Flivver Car, Linemar, litho tin, rare, NM (EX box) $850.00
Disneyland Happy Birthday Carousel, Ross, litho tin, 9", NM (EX box), A $150.00
Donald Duck, Linemar, vibrates around w/twirling tail, litho tin, 5", NMIB, A $500.00
Donald Duck Climbing Fireman, Linemar, Donald climbs up & down ladder on lithoed base, tin, 5", EX..................$700.00
Donald Duck Delivery Wagon, Linemar, Donald peddles wagon mk Mickey's Delivery, tin & celluloid, 6", VG (worn box), A $500.00
Donald Duck Dipsy Car, Linemar, advances w/crazy action as Donald's head bobs, litho tin, 5½", NM (EX box) ..$800.00
Donald Duck Fire Chief Truck, Linemar, advances in erratic motion, litho tin, 5", NM..................$500.00
Donald Duck Motorcycle, Linemar, advances w/sound, litho tin, friction, 4", NM, A $275.00
Donald Duck Tricycle, advances as bell rings, litho tin w/celluloid figure, 4", MIB $375.00
Donald Duck Whirlygig, prewar, Donald rides on platform as umbrella w/balls spins above, celluloid, 8", NM, A ..$3,600.00
Donald Riding Pluto, mk Made in Japan, Donald riding Pluto on rocking base, celluloid & wood, 7", NM, A..........$3,000.00
Dream Car, Cragstan/Ashitoy, bl-pnt tin w/plastic windshield, friction, 7½", EX (EX box), A $275.00
Dreamland, Kosuge, vehicle navigates track, litho tin, 19" track, EX (VG box), A $275.00
Droopy, MGM, 1960s, vinyl, 4", rare, F8 ....$100.00
Drummer Boy, Nifty, drum major plays drum as head moves side to side, celluloid w/cloth clothes, 12", NM (EX box), A $225.00
Duck Amphibious Taxi, TPS, duck pulls monkey driver & 2 squirrels, litho tin, 6", scarce, NM (VG box), A $975.00
Duck Mailman w/Geese, TPS, advances as geese bob around in boxes, litho tin, 5", scarce, EX..................$250.00
Dump Car w/Track, travels track & loads & unloads contents in bed, litho tin, 28" track, EX (EX box) $150.00
Eagle Racer #57, IY Metal Toys, Indy-type racer mk Speed on wheels, litho tin, w/driver, 11", NM (NM box), A..$950.00
Easter on Parade, MM, rabbit pulls 3 chicks in basket, celluloid w/pressed steel base, 8", NM (NM box), A..............$175.00
Electric Locomotive, TN, mk Union Pacific, advances w/sound, litho tin, friction, 13", NM (EX box), A..................$125.00
Elephant & Clowns, CK, prewar, 1 clown riding on back & 1 on trunk, advances as head sways, celluloid, 7", NMIB, A $550.00
Elephant Circus Car, elephant driver juggles world globe on his nose, litho tin, friction, 7", EX (EX box), A $250.00
Ferdinand the Bull, Linemar, head moves up & down & tail spins, tin w/rubber tail, 5½", scarce, NM (EX box), A..................$900.00
Fire Department Set, SSS, 1957, advances w/siren sound, friction, complete w/5 litho tin vehicles, EX (EX box), A $125.00
Fire Engine, hits object & ladder extends, litho tin, 12", NM (EX box), A $135.00
Fishing Monkey on Whale, TPS, monkey on whale w/fishing rod attached to 2 fish, several actions, litho tin, 9", NMIB, A $375.00
Five Man Smoky Joe, K, fire truck advances w/siren sound, litho tin, friction, 6", NM (NM box), A..................$225.00
Flowers Delivery Car, Bandai, Ford station wagon w/elephant panels on doors, litho tin, friction, 11", EX, A $700.00
Frankonia Race Way Game, MM, 3 horses w/jockeys advance on track, tin & plastic, 10" track, NM (EX box), A $100.00
Gay 90's Cyclist, TPS, man peddles high-wheel bicycle w/ringing bell, litho tin w/cloth outfit, 7", NM (EX box), A $400.00
Girl w/Chickens, TPS, girl feeds chickens w/several actions, litho tin, 5", NM (NM box), A..................$425.00
Goofy's Stock Car, Linemar, advances w/siren sound, litho tin, friction, 6", scarce, NM (EX box), A $850.00
Goofy, see also Whirling Tail Goofy
Grand-Pa's New Car, Yonezawa, advances as grandpa bounces in seat, litho tin, 5", NM (NM box)..................$350.00
Grasshopper, SAN, advances w/realistic movement, litho tin, 7½", NM (EX box), A..................$200.00
Greyhound Escorter, Lowell Toy, litho tin, friction, 6", EX (EX box), A..................$175.00

Groolies Car, Yone, advances as front end jumps up & down, litho tin, 4¾", NM (EX box), A $250.00

Happy Express, MT, prewar, train travels base under 3 bridges, litho tin, 9" dia, EX, A $275.00

Happy Life, Alps, girl in beach chair under umbrella w/duck on sq base, several actions, tin & celluloid, 9", NMIB, A $500.00

Happy the Violinist, TPS, rare version w/bl pants, sways side to side while playing violin, litho tin, 9", MIB, A $475.00

Photo courtesy John Turney

Harley Davidson Auto Cycle, lithographed tin, friction, MIB, $550.00.

Harley-Davidson Motorcycle, TN, litho tin, friction, 9", VG, A $185.00

Hawaiian Dance, CK, prewar, Hawaiian girl performs hula dance, celluloid w/grass skirt, 8", EX (EX box) $175.00

Henry Eating Ice Cream, Linemar, 1950s, vibrates around while eating ice-cream cone, litho tin, 6", scarce, NM, A .$1,000.00

Henry on Elephant, celluloid, 8", VG, A $475.00

Hobby Horse, prewar, advances in circular pattern w/bell noise, litho tin w/celluloid cowboy, 6", EX, A $350.00

Hopping Astro, Linemar, litho tin, 4", rare, NM (EX box), A $3,300.00

Hopping Carry the Crow, Linemar, litho tin, 4", M (EX box), A $150.00

Horse Race, Occupied Japan, boy in clown suit rides horse on base, celluloid & tin, 4", NM (EX box), A $200.00

Hot Rod #3, MT, little boy rides car w/siren sound, litho tin w/rubber-headed figure, friction, 6", EX (EX box), A $100.00

Hot Rod Racer, KO, advances as driver moves back & forth in seat, litho tin, friction, 6", NM (NM box), A....$300.00

Humpty-Dumpty Clown, prewar, clown vibrates around w/umbrella spinning overhead, celluloid, 12", rare, MIB, A....$1,100.00

Hurricane Racer #7, KSG, advances w/sound, tin w/celluloid driver, friction, 5", NM (EX box), A $300.00

Ice Cream Cart, Occupied Japan, man pedals cart, litho tin w/celluloid figure, 3", NM, A $175.00

Ice Cream Vendor, Frankonia, 1950s, boy pedals cart, litho tin w/celluloid figure, 4", MIB, A $200.00

Ice Cream Vendor Truck, KO, 1950s, advances w/bump-&-go action, litho tin, NM (EX box), A....$275.00

Ice Skaters, Occupied Japan, couple skate around, celluloid, 5½", NM, A....$150.00

Indian Chief on Horse, Haji, horse bounces up & down, litho tin, 8", EX, A $250.00

Indianapolis Champion Racer #98, ET, red & wht litho tin w/blk rubber tires, friction, 18", EX, A $2,200.00

Indians in Canoe, advances as 1 figure plays tomtom & 1 oars, litho tin, friction, 9½", VG, A....$175.00

Joe's Kitchen Wagon, H, side panel opens w/bell sound to reveal Joe cooking, litho tin, friction, 9½", EX, A $200.00

Jolly Farmer w/Pig, prewar, farmer pulls pig's tail, tin & celluloid, 7½", MIB, A $250.00

Juggling Clown, TPS, balances ball on rod attached to his nose, litho tin, 7", NM (NM box) $500.00

Jumping Rabbit w/Baby, Mikuni, mama rabbit hops around w/baby on her back, litho tin, 4½", EX (EX box), A....$100.00

Kiddy City Amusement Park, AHI, 3 planes circle tower, litho tin w/celluloid props, 9½" tower, NM (G box), A ..$185.00

King Racer #5, mk 2000 Mile Racer on sides, litho tin w/blk rubber tires, friction, 9", NM (NM box), A $750.00

Ladybug Parade, TPS, litho tin, MIB $150.00

Lester the Jester, Alps, vibrates around & twirls cane, litho tin w/cloth clothes, 9½", EX (G box), A $475.00

Liberty Ferry, travels across river to the Statue of Liberty, litho tin, 26" base, NM (EX box), A $375.00

Livestock Truck, cow nods head as truck advances, litho tin, friction, 8", EX (EX box), A....$200.00

Lone Ranger on Silver (unauthorized), Haji, litho tin, 9", VG, A....$250.00

Lucky Carnival Truck, ATC, advances in circular pattern w/ringing bell on truck bed, litho tin, 6", EX, A....$200.00

Lucky Monkey Playing Billiards, TPS, hits ball w/pool cue, litho tin, 6", NM (EX box), A $350.00

M-105 Maneuvering & Shooting Tank, HTC, advances, shoots darts & changes directions, litho tin, friction, 8", NMIB, A....$100.00

M-12 Tank, litho tin, 7", VG $75.00

Magic Fire Car, MT, advances w/sound & extended bumper, litho tin w/vinyl-headed animal driver, friction, 7", NMIB, A $75.00

Magician Dog Triksie, lifts hat & chick & egg appear, tin & plush w/cloth clothes, 8", EX (EX box), A $475.00

Marching Japanese Soldiers, CK, prewar, 3 compo figures on tin base, 3½", EX (EX box), A....$450.00

MG Sports Car & Track, TPS, litho tin, NM (NM box), A....$200.00

Mickey Mouse Motorcycle, Linemar, advances w/sound, litho tin, friction, 4", NM, A $275.00

Mickey Mouse Whirligig, prewar, advances on wheels as umbrella w/balls spins above, celluloid, 7", NM, A....$1,900.00

Minnie Mouse Knitting, Linemar, Minnie sits in rocking chair & knits, litho tin, 6½", VG, A....$350.00

Minnie Mouse Knitting, Linemar, Minnie sits in rocking chair & knits, litho tin, 6½", MIB, A $1,000.00

Monkey Basketball Player, TPS, flips ball into basket, litho tin, 7½", NM (EX box), A....$475.00

Monkey Golfer, TPS, hits ball across bridge & into net, litho tin, 4½", NM (G box), A....$250.00

 Windups, Friction, and Other Mechanicals/JAPANESE

Motorcycle Auto Race, MS, 5 motorcycles race down track to finish line, litho tin, 15" track, rare, EX, A..............**$650.00**

Mr Dan the Hot Dog Eating Man, TN, 1950s, several actions, litho tin w/red cloth coat & flocked hair, 7", MIB ..**$125.00**

Mr Fox the Magician, Yonezawa, lifts hat to reveal rabbit, litho tin & plush, 10", EX (EX box), A **$500.00**

Old Jalopy, Linemar, advances in erratic motion w/jutting headlights, litho tin, 7", EX (VG box), A **$150.00**

Over the Hill, Alps, race car travels track, litho tin, 14" track, EX (EX box), A **$250.00**

Pango-Pango African Dancer, TPS, vibrates around, litho tin, 6", MIB, A **$300.00**

Pat the Pup, TPS, pat nose & he moves, twirls tail & barks, litho tin, 5", NM (NM box), A...**$135.00**

Peaceful Pigeon, Ichiko, advances w/flapping wings & tail, litho tin, 8", NM (EX box), A **$750.00**

Piggy Cook, Y, shakes salt on eggs & bacon & flips egg, litho tin w/vinyl head, 5½", NM (EX box), A.......................**$200.00**

Pioneer Spirit, Alps, lithographed tin, friction with battery operated lanterns, 11", NM (EX box), A, $150.00.

Planet of the Apes Prison Wagon, AHI, plastic, friction, NM (EX box), A **$100.00**

Playful Pluto & Goofy, Linemar, advance w/spinning tails, litho tin w/rubber tails, EX (EX scarce box), A.............**$1,400.00**

Playland Sky Bus Ride, Yone, 2 buses w/passengers spin around base w/bell sound, tin & plastic, 5½", NM (EX box), A **$125.00**

Pluto Motorcycle, Linemar, advances w/sound, litho tin, friction, 4", NM, A **$250.00**

Police Car, litho tin, friction, 5", NM (NM box) **$75.00**

Popeye, 1929, vibrates around as head & arms move, celluloid, 8½", NM (G box), A **$1,500.00**

Popeye & Brutus, Linemar, Popeye & Brutus box on wheeled platform, litho tin w/celluloid figures, 6", EX, A ..**$1,900.00**

Popeye & Olive Oyl, Linemar, Popeye balances Olive Oyl in chair on his head, litho tin, 9", EX, A **$700.00**

Popeye & Olive Oyl Stretchy Hand Car, Linemar, figures w/spring bodies move up & down, litho tin, 6½", MIB, A **$1,750.00**

Popeye Basketball Player, Linemar, litho tin, 9", EX, A ...**$900.00**

Popeye Roller Skater, Linemar, skates while holding can of spinach, litho tin w/cloth pants, NM (EX box), A..**$2,200.00**

Popeye the Acrobat, Popeye performs on highbar, metal w/celluloid figure, 7", EX, A **$300.00**

Popeye Turnover Tank, Linemar, Popeye forces tank to turn over, litho tin, 4", EX **$350.00**

Porter Doll, MTH, advances w/bobbing head, plastic w/vinyl head, 4", NMIB, A **$300.00**

Professor Von Drake, Linemar, advances w/swinging arms, litho tin, 6", NM (NM box)...**$600.00**

Professor Von Drake Go-Mobile, Linemar, tin w/vinyl-headed figure, friction, 6", MIB, A **$300.00**

Pussy Cat Chasing Butterfly, TPS, blk cat arches back & chases butterfly attached to rod, plush over tin, 5", MIB, A..**$200.00**

Racing Car, OKK, w/driver & passenger, cream-pnt tin w/see-through plastic hood, friction, 10½", NMIB, A **$175.00**

Racing Motorcycle, Stone, motorcycle w/driver circles post w/suction cup bottom, litho tin, 4", NM (EX box), A.........**$250.00**

Racer #5, lithographed tin, friction, M, $300.00.

Reading Santa Claus, Alps, flips pages in book & nods head, tin & vinyl w/cloth clothes, 7", NM (EX box), A.........**$200.00**

Rocking Dog, K, dog in cowboy outfit twirls rope, litho tin, 7", NM (EX box), A **$150.00**

Round Auto Circus Cycle, Ashitoy, 1950s, litho tin w/full-figure clown driver, 4", scarce, NM (NM box), A **$900.00**

Safety First, Alps, Policeman stands on platform & directs traffic w/several actions, tin & celluloid, 12", NMIB, A...**$1,000.00**

Sailor Rowing Boat, KO, rows w/realistic action, litho tin, 7½", EX (EX box), A **$125.00**

Sam the Strolling Skeleton, Mikuni, advances w/swinging arms, litho tin, 5½", MIB, A..**$275.00**

Santa Claus, TN, Santa rings bell & waves Merry Christmas sign, litho tin, 7", NM (EX box), A **$200.00**

Santa Claus, Y, rocks back & forth & lifts lid from box, litho tin w/cloth clothes, vinyl face, 9", NM (EX box), A.....**$300.00**

Santa Claus on Skis, KSK, advances using ski poles, litho tin, 5½", NM (EX box), A....$500.00

Santa Claus on Sled, Occupied Japan, celluloid, 8", EX (EX box)....$175.00

Santa in Chimney, 1950s, spins up & down chimney w/sound, 5", EX, A....$100.00

Santa on Bike, Aoki, advances w/sound, litho tin w/celluloid figure, 4", rare, MIB, A....$100.00

Service Boy, CK, prewar, celluloid, 4", EX (VG box), A..$200.00

Six-Cylinder Piston Action Racing Car, Cragstan/ATC, cream-pnt tin w/see-through plastic hood, friction, 8", NMIB, A....$175.00

Skip Rope Animals, TPS, dog & squirrel turn rope as baby bear jumps, litho tin, 8", NM (EX box)....$250.00

Skippy the Tricky Cyclist, TPS, clown rides unicycle w/realistic action, litho tin w/cloth clothes, 6", EX (EX box), A...$250.00

Smiling Sam the Carnival Man, Alps, lithographed tin with cloth clothes, 9", NM (EX box), A, $375.00.

Soldier w/Gun (Vilco Gun), MT, prewar, vibrates & lifts gun up & down, celluloid, 7", MIB, A....$1,200.00

Speed Fire Engine, litho tin, friction, 6", NM (NM box), A....$175.00

Sports Land Amusement Park Ride, prewar, litho tin, 6½x6½" base, EX, A....$500.00

Stutz Bearcat, advances w/jutting headlamps, litho tin, friction, 6", NM (EX box), A....$450.00

Super Atom Train, Ashitoy, mk Mountain Express, advances w/visible piston action, litho tin, 11", EX (EX box), A....$100.00

Super Cycle, 1950s, litho tin, friction, missing figure, 12", scarce, EX, A....$1,100.00

Super Sonic Race Car No 36, MT, advances w/engine sound, litho tin, friction, 9", NM (NM box), A....$200.00

Superman Turnover Tank, Linemar, Superman forces tank to turn over, litho tin, 4", EX, A....$350.00

Surprise Santa Claus, Y, rocks back & forth & pulls present from bag, litho tin w/cloth clothes, vinyl face, 9", MIB, A .$225.00

Teacup Merry-Go-Round, 3 bears in seats circle on base as umbrella spins above, tin, plastic & plush, 8", NMIB, A....$185.00

Telephone Bear, Alps, bears answers phone & chatters, tin, cloth & plush, 6½", EX (EX box), A....$150.00

Telephone Santa Claus, Alps, Santa answers phone w/3 different sounds, tin w/cloth clothes & vinyl face, 7", MIB, A....$175.00

Tricycle Tot, TPS, girl pushes off right leg to propel tricycle, litho tin w/vinyl head, 5", scarce, M (EX box), A...$175.00

Troy Ruttman Jet Racer, Marusan, w/driver, litho tin, friction, 8", NM (NM box), A....$550.00

Trumpet Player, TN, Black man stands on base & plays trumpet, litho tin w/cloth clothes, 10½", NM (NM box), A.$700.00

Trumpet Player, TN, Black man stands on base & plays trumpet, litho tin w/cloth clothes, 10½", NM, A....$400.00

Twist Dancer, girl dances on stage w/plink-plunk music, litho tin w/cloth clothes, 7", EX (EX box), A....$75.00

Union Pacific Electric Locomotive, TN, advances w/engine & bell sound, litho tin, friction, 13", NM (EX box), A .$150.00

Vacationland Express, Y, train circles carnival as plane flies overhead, litho tin, 5½" sq base, MIB, A....$150.00

Wagon Fantasy Land, TPS, snail pulls monkey driver & 2 squirrels on leaf, litho tin, 12", NM (NM box), A....$400.00

Western Hero, prewar, cowboy on horse w/lasso chases cow in circular motion, celluloid, 7", NM (EX box)....$650.00

Whirling Tail Goofy, Linemar, litho tin w/rubber tail, 5½", NM, A....$400.00

Wilma Flintstone on Tricycle, Linemar, advances w/ringing bell, litho tin w/celluloid figure, 4", NM, A....$350.00

Wimpy, Linemar, hopping action w/nodding head, litho tin, 5", scarce, NM (NM box), A....$8,000.00

X-Mas Car, F, Santa in convertible, litho tin, friction, 5½", NM (EX box), A....$325.00

X-3 Racer, Bandai, w/driver, litho tin w/blk rubber tires, friction, 7", EX (EX box), A....$200.00

Spanish

Autoescuela Donald (Donald Duck), 1965, Donald, Goofy & Nephew travel base in cars, plastic, 18" base, NM (EX box), A....$200.00

Boat w/Revolving Airplanes, Espana, planes fly as boat advances, litho tin, 9", EX, A....$575.00

Bugatti I-907, Paya, 1986, tin, w/driver, 1 of 5000 made, 19", NM, A....$250.00

Disneylandia, Nibo, 1950s, 2 vehicles navigate track, litho tin w/plastic station house in center, 11x18", NMIB, A .$350.00

Donald Duck Walking Car, advances as Donald's head bobs, litho tin w/celluloid figure, 5½", MIB, A....$275.00

Goofy Walking Car, advances as Goofy's head bobs, litho tin w/celluloid figure, 5½", MIB, A....$475.00

Louie Walking Car, advances as Louie's head bobs, litho tin w/celluloid figure, 5½", MIB, A....$250.00

Negro Danzante (rare variation of Pango-Pango African Dancer), litho tin, 6", NM (EX box), A....$275.00

Vaquero Mareado (Spanish version of Rodeo Joe), Rico, crazy action, litho tin, 5", NM (EX box), A....$575.00

Wyandotte

Though the Wyandotte Company (Michigan) produced toys of all types, included here are only the heavy-gauge pressed-steel cars, trucks, and other vehicles they made through the 1930s and '40s.

See also Aeronautical; Boats; Character, TV, and Movie Collectibles; Windups, Friction, and Other Mechanicals.

Ambulance, #340, w/swinging rear door, 11", EX..........**$175.00**
Circus Truck, #503, 11", EX..........**$385.00**
Cord Roadster No 600, 1936, yel w/red top, blk tires w/red wooden hubcaps, 13", EX (G box), A..........**$700.00**
Deluxe Delivery Truck, 1936, 11", EX+..........**$100.00**
Dump Truck, #326, 1931, NM..........**$350.00**
Dump Truck w/Sand Loader, 1941, EX..........**$450.00**
Grader, 1950s, orange w/blk rubber tires, adjustable blade, 19", missing rubber stack o/w EX, P4..........**$135.00**
Hydraulic Dump Truck, rear & side tip, 20", EX+..........**$250.00**
LaSalle Sedan w/Trailer, 1930s, 25½", VG..........**$425.00**
Official AAA Service Car, 1930s, 12", EX..........**$300.00**
Railway Express Truck, 1939, 12", EX..........**$100.00**
Roadster, 1935, red w/wood tires, 6", EX, A..........**$165.00**
School Bus, 1930s, 24", EX+..........**$175.00**
Stake Truck, #325, 1931, 10", EX..........**$200.00**
Toytown Estate Station Wagon, EX..........**$200.00**
Wrecker, 1930s, 10", NM..........**$150.00**

Yo-Yos

Yo-Yos are starting to attract toy collectors, especially those with special features such as Hasbro's 'Glow-Action' and Duncan's 'Whistler.'

Advisor: Lucky Meisenheimer (M3).

Alox Mfg, Flying Disc, wood, 1950s, 2⅛", M, M3..........**$15.00**
Avon, Garfield, plastic, MIP, M20..........**$10.00**
Avon, Teenage Mutant Ninja Turtles, MIP, M20..........**$10.00**
Champion, Style #55, return top, red, VG, M20..........**$12.00**
Cheerio, Beginners 55, wood w/foil sticker, NM..........**$50.00**
Cheerio, Glitter Spin, wood w/foil label & rhinestones, G..........**$100.00**
Cheerio, Official Pro 99, wood w/foil sticker, EX, M3..........**$50.00**
Dell, Big D Sleeper King, plastic, EX..........**$20.00**
Duncan, Beginner, #1044 or #44, wood, MIP, M20, ea..........**$25.00**
Duncan, Beginner, Bosco Bear advertising, sm, G, M20..........**$8.00**
Duncan, Cattle Brand, late 1970s, MOC, M3..........**$12.00**
Duncan, Glow Imperial, orange letters, MIP, M3..........**$18.00**
Duncan, Glow Imperial, red letters, early 1970s, MIP..........**$14.00**
Duncan, Imperial, Kool-Aid premium, MIP..........**$10.00**
Duncan, Lil' Champ, red w/gold raised lettering, 1980s, NM..........**$15.00**
Duncan, Magic Motion, 1975, Hulk, MIP..........**$30.00**
Duncan, O-Boy, wood, 1930s, EX..........**$35.00**
Duncan, Shrieking, Sonic Satellite, #500, MIP, M20..........**$35.00**
Duncan, Super Yo-Yo, tournament, natural wood w/gr stripe, VG, M20..........**$15.00**

Photo courtesy Christopher Cook

Duncan Whistling Yo-Yo, 1930s, lithographed tin, M, $75.00.

Festival, Be a Sport Series, 1970s, MIP, M3..........**$20.00**
Festival, Disney (Goofy), 1970s, MOC, M3..........**$15.00**
Festival, Disney (Mickey, Pluto or Donald), 1970s, MOC, M3, ea..........**$12.00**
Goody, Joy-O-Top, wood w/pnt seal, M..........**$75.00**

Photo courtesy Christopher Cook

Goody Rainbow Filipino Twirler, wood with air-brushed stripe, painted seal, M, $100.00.

Hasbro, Glow Action, 1968, MOC, M3, from $10 to..........**$15.00**
Hi-Ker, flat-top, NM, M3..........**$35.00**
Royal Thunderbird, triangular decal seal, 1960s, NM, M3..........**$70.00**
Spectra Star, Freddy Krueger, 1980s, MOC, M3..........**$7.00**
Spectra Star, Ghostbusters, 1980s, MOC, M3..........**$8.00**
Spectra Star, Pee Wee Herman, 1980s, MOC, M3..........**$9.00**
Spectra Star, Radical Curve Ball #1502, 1988, MIP..........**$6.00**
Whirl King, top standard model, G, M20..........**$10.00**
World's Fair (1939), decal seal, NM, M3..........**$15.00**

Dealer Codes

Most of our description lines contain a letter/number code just before the suggested price. They correspond with the names of the following collectors and dealers who sent us their current selling list to be included in this addition. If you're interested in buying an item in question, don't hesitate to call or write them. We only ask that you consider the differences in time zones, and try to call at a convenient time. If you're corresponding, please send a self-addressed, stamped envelope for their reply. **Because our data was entered several months ago, many of the coded items will have already sold,** but our dealers tell us that they are often able to restock some of the same merchandise over and over. Some said that they had connections with other dealers around the country and might be able to locate a particular toy for you. But please bear in mind that because they may have had to pay more to restock their shelves, they may also have to charge a little more than the price quoted in their original sales list. We must stress that these people are not appraisers, so please do not ask them to price your toys.

If you have lists of toys for sale that you would like for us to use in the next edition, please send them to us at the address as soon as possible. We will process incoming lists as they arrive and because our space is limited, the earlier you send it, the better. Please do not ask us to include you in our Categories of Special Interest unless you contribute useable information. Not only are we limited on available space, it isn't fair to those who do. If you would like to advertise with us but cannot contribute listings, display ads are available (see page 486 for rates). We will hold a previously assigned dealer code over for you who are our contributors/advisors from year to year as long as we know you are interested in keeping it, but if we haven't heard from you by February 1, we will reassign that code to someone else. Because the post office prefers your complete 9-digit zip code, please send us that information for our files.

Direct your correspondence to: **Huxford Enterprises, Inc., 1202 7th St., Covington, IN 47932**

(A1)
Stan and Sally Alekna
732 Aspen Lane
Lebanon, PA 17042
717-228-2361
Fax 717-228-2362

(A2)
Jane Anderson
R.R. 5, Box 5525
Saylorsburg, PA 18353

(A3)
Avalon Comics
Larry Curcio
P.O. Box 821
Medford, MA 02155
617-391-5614

(A4)
Bob Armstrong
15 Monadnock Rd.
Worcester, MA 01609

(A5)
Geneva Addy
P.O. Box 124
Winterset, IA 50273

(A7)
Matt and Lisa Adams
1234 Harbor Cove
Woodstock, GA 30189
770-516-6874

(B1)
Richard Belyski
P.O. Box 124
Sea Cliff, NY 11579
516-676-1183
e-mail: peznews@juno.com

(B2)
Larry Blodget
Box 753
Rancho Mirage, CA 92270

(B3)
Bojo
Bob Gottuso
P.O. Box 1403
Cranberry Twp., PA 16066-0403
Phone or fax 724-776-0621

(B4)
Dick Borgerding, RJB Toys
720 E Main
Flushing, MI 48433
810-659-9859

(B5)
Martin and Carolyn Berens
Collection Connection
P.O. Box 18552
Fairfield, OH 45018
Phone or fax 513-851-9217

(B6)
Jim Buskirk
3009 Oleander Ave.
San Marcos, CA 92069
760-599-1054

(B8)
Stanley A. and Robert S. Block
P.O. Box 51
Trumbull, CT 06611
203-261-3223 or 203-775-0138

(B10)
Tom Bremer
P.O. Box 49
Newark, NY 14513
Phone or fax 315-331-8146

(B11)
Sue and Marty Bunis
RR 1, Box 36
Bradford, NH 03221-9102

(B12)
Bromer Booksellers, Inc.
607 Boylston St.
Boston, MA 02116
617-247-2818 or fax 617-247-2975

(B14)
Scott Bruce
P.O. Box 481
Cambridge, MA 02140
e-mail: scott@flake.com

(C1)
Casey's Collectible Corner
HCR Box 31, Rt. 3
N Blenheim, NY 12131
607-588-6464
e-mail: CASEYSCC@aol.com

(C2)
Mark E. Chase and Michael Kelley
Collector Glass News
P.O. Box 308
Slippery Rock, PA 16057
724-946-2838
Fax 724-946-9012

(C3)
Ken Clee
Box 11412
Philadelphia, PA 19111
215-722-1979

(C4)
Arlan Coffman
1223 Wilshire Blvd., Ste. 275
Santa Monica, CA 90403
310-453-2507

(C6)
Cotswold Collectibles
P.O. Box 716, Dept. SC
Freeland, WA 98249
360-331-5331; fax 360-331-5344
website: http://www.whidbey.net/-cotswold

(C9)
Marilyn Cooper
P.O. Box 55174
Houston, TX 77255
713-465-7773
Author of *The Pictorial Guide to Toothbrush Holders*

(C10)
Bill Campbell
1221 Littlebrook Lane
Birmingham, AL 35235
205-853-822
Fax 405-658-6986

(C11)
Jim Christoffel
409 Maple
Elburn, IL 60119; 630-365-2914
e-mail: jimc@elnet.com

(C12)
Joel J. Cohen
Cohen Books and Collectibles
P.O. Box 810310
Boca Raton, FL 33481
561-487-7888
Fax 561-487-3117
e-mail: cohendisney@prodigy.net

(C13)
Brad Cassity
1350 Stanwix
Toledo, OH 43614
419-389-1100

(C14)
Cynthia's Country Store
The Wellington Mall #15-A
12794 W Forest Hill Blvd.
Wellington, FL 33414
561-793-0554
Fax 561-795-4222 (24 hours)
e-mail: cynbears@aol.com
website:http://www.thecrier.com/ccs

(C15)
Rosalind Cranor
P.O. Box 859
Blacksburg, VA 24063

(C17)
John and Michele Casino
633 Franklin Ave., Suite #169
Nutley, NJ 07110
201-759-2520

(D2)
Marl Davidson (Marl & B)
10301 Braden Run
Bradenton, FL 34202
941-751-6275; fax 941-751-5463
website: http://auntie.com.marl

(D3)
Larry DeAngelo
516 King Arthur Dr.
Virginia Beach, VA 23464
757-424-1691

(D4)
John DeCicco
57 Bay View Dr.
Shrewsbury, MA 01545
508-797-0023

(D6)
Doug Dezso
864 Patterson Ave.
Maywood, NJ 07607
201-488-1311

(D7)
Ron and Donna Donnelly
Saturday Heroes
6302 Championship Dr.
Tuscaloosa, AL 35405

(D8)
George Downes
Box 572
Nutley, NJ 07110
201-935-3388

(D9)
Gordy Dutt
P.O. Box 201
Sharon Center, OH 44274-0201
330-239-1657; fax 330-239-2991

(D10)
Dunbar's Gallery
Leila and Howard Dunbar
76 Haven St.
Milford, MA 01757
508-634-8697
Fax 508-634-8696

(D11)
Larry Doucet
2351 Sultana Dr.
Yorktown Heights, NY 10598
914-245-1320

(D12)
Doris' Dolls & Collectibles
325 E. 10th St.
Mt. Vernon, IN 47620
Phone or fax 812-838-5290

(F1)
Anthony Balasco
P.O. Box 19482
Johnston, RI 02919
401-946-5720; fax 401-942-7980

(F2)
Paul Fideler
20 Shadow Oak Dr., Apt. #18
Sudbury, MA 01776
617-386-0228 (24 hours)

(F3)
Paul Fink's Fun and Games
P.O. Box 488
59 S Kent Rd.
Kent, CT 06757
860-927-4001
website: www.gamesandpuzzles.com

(F4)
Mike and Kurt Fredericks
145 Bayline Cir.
Folsom, CA 95630
916-985-7986

(F5)
Fun House Toy Co.
G.F. Ridenour
P.O. Box 444
Warrendale, PA 15086
724-935-1392 (fax capable)

(F7)
Finisher's Touch Antiques
Steve Fisch, proprietor
10 W Main St.
Wappingers Falls, NY 12590
914-298-8882; fax 914-298-8945

(F8)
52 Girls Collectibles
P.O. Box 36
Morral, OH 43337
614-465-6062

(F9)
Donald Friedman
660 W Grand Ave.
Chicago, IL 60610
708-656-3700 (day) or 312-226-4741 (evening & weekends)
Fax 708-656-6292

(G1)
Gary's Trains
186 Pine Springs Camp Road
Boswell, PA 15531
814-629-9277

(G2)
Mark Giles
510 E Third St.
Ogalala, NE 69153
308-284-4360

(G5)
John F. Green Inc.
1821 W. Jacaranda Pl.
Fullerton, CA 92633-USA
714-526-5467; 800-807-4759

(G6)
Carol Karbowiak Gilbert
2193 14 Mile Rd. 206
Sterling Height, MI 48310

(G7)
PAK-RAT
Andy Galbus
900 8th St. NW
Kasson, MN 55944-1079
507-634-2093
e-mail: lhpakrat@polaristel.net

(G8)
Joan Stryker Grubaugh
2342 Hoaglin Rd.
Van Wert, OH 45891
419-622-4411
Fax 419-622-3026

(G16)
Candelaine (Candace Gunther)
Pasadena, CA 91103-2320
626-796-4568; fax 626-796-7172
e-mail: Candelaine@aol.com.

(H1)
The Hamburgs
Happy Memories Antique Toy Co.
P.O. Box 1305
Woodland Hills, CA 91365
818-346-9884 or 818-346-1269
Fax 818-346-0215

(H3)
George Hardy
1670 Hawkwood Ct.
Charlottesville, VA 22901
804-295-4863
Fax 804-295-4898
Internet: georgeh@comet.net
http://www.comet.net/personal/georgeh/

(H4)
Jerry and Ellen L. Harnish
110 Main St.
Bellville, OH 44813
Phone or fax 419-886-4782 after 7 pm Eastern time

(H6)
Phil Helley
Old Kilbourne Antiques
629 Indiana Ave.
Wisconsin Dells, WI 53965
608-254-8770

(H7)
Jacquie and Bob Henry
Antique Treasures and Toys
Box 17
Walworth, NY 14568
315-597-4719
e-mail: Jhenry5792@aol.com or jacqueline.henry@MCI2000.COM

(H8)
Homestead Collectibles
Art and Judy Turner
R.D. 2, Rte. 150
P.O. Box 173-E
Mill Hall, PA 17751
717-726-3597
Fax 717-726-4488

(H9)
Pamela E. Apkarian-Russell
The Halloween Queen
C.J. Russell & The Halloween Queen Antiques
P.O. Box 499
Winchester, NH 03470
603-239-8875

(H10)
Don Hamm
712 N. Townsend St.
Syracuse, NY 13203
315-478-7035

(H11)
N.F. Huber, the SNO-PEA Trader
Norman Huber, Buyer
931 Emerson St.
Thousand Oaks, CA 91362-2447
805-497-0119
Fax 1-800-SNO-OPY-2

(H12)
Roslyn L. Herman
124-16 84th Rd.
Kew Gardens, NY 11415
718-846-3496 or 718-846-8491

(H13)
Tim Hunter
4301 W. Hidden Valley Dr.
Reno, NV 89502
702-856-4357
Fax 702-856-4354
e-mail: thunter885@aol.com

(I1)
Roger Inouye
765 E Franklin
Pomona, CA 91766

(I2)
Terri Ivers
Terri's Toys and Nostalgia
206 E. Grand
Ponca City, OK 74601
580-762-8697 or 580-762-5174
Fax 580-765-2657
e-mail: toylady@poncacity.net

(I3)
Dan Iannotti
212 W. Hickory Grove Rd.
Bloomfield Hills, MI 48302-1127
248-335-5042

(J1)
Bill Jackameit
972 Kelsey Dr.
Charlottesville, VA 22903
804-923-3398 (Monday – Thursday, 7 pm – 9 pm EST)
e-mail: wj2d@sprintmail.com
website: http://www.freeyellow.com/members/bjdiecast

(J2)
Ed Janey
1756 65th St.
Garrison, IA 52229-9644
319-477-8888

(J3)
Dana Johnson Enterprises
P.O. Box 1824
Bend, OR 97709-1824
503-382-8410

(J5)
Just Kids Nostalgia
310 New York Avenue
Huntington, NY 11743
516-423-8449; fax 516-423-4326

(J6)
June Moon
245 N Northwest Hwy.
Park Ridge, IL 60068
847-825-1411 (24-hr phone)
Fax 847-825-6090
e-mail: junmoonstr@aol.com

(J7)
Jim's TV Collectibles
P.O. Box 4767
San Diego, CA 92164
Phone/fax 619-462-1953

(J8)
Jeff and Bob's Fun Stuff
7324 Reseda Blvd #168
Reseda, CA 91335
818-705-3368

(K1)
K-3 Inc.
Bendees Only; Simpson Mania
2335 NW Thurman
Portland, OR 97210
503-222-2713

(K2)
David Kolodny-Nagy
May through Jan:
3701 Connecticut Ave. NW #500
Washington, DC 20008
202-364-8753

(K3)
Ilene Kayne
1308 S Charles St.
Baltimore, MD 21230
410-685-3923
e-mail: kayne@clark.net

(K4)
Debby and Marty Krim
P.O. Box 2273
W Peabody, MA 01960
508-535-3140; fax 508-535-7522

(K5)
Kerry and Judy's Toys
7370 Eggleston Rd.
Memphis, TN 38125-2112
901-757-1722
Fax 901-757-0126
e-mail: kjtoys@memphisonline.com

(K6)
Keith and Donna Kaonis
60 Cherry Ln.
Huntington, NY 11743
516-261-8337; fax 516-261-8235

(L1)
Jean-Claude H. Lanau
740 Thicket Ln.
Houston, TX 77079
713-497-6034 (after 7:00 pm, CST)

(L2)
John and Eleanor Larsen
523 Third St.
Colusa, CA 95932
916-458-4769 (after 4 pm)

(L4)
Tom Lastrapes
P.O. Box 2444
Pinellas Park, FL 34664
813-545-2586

(L6)
Kathy Lewis
187 N Marcello Ave
Thousand Oaks, CA 91360
805-499-8101
e-mail: chatty@ixnetcom.com

(L7)
Terry and Joyce Losonsky
7506 Summer Leave Ln.
Columbia, MD 21046-2455
301-381-3358

(M1)
Mark and Val Macaluso
3603 Newark Rd.
Marion, NY 14505
315-926-4349; fax 315-926-4853

(M2)
John McKenna
801-803 W Cucharres
Colorado Springs, CO 80905
719-630-8732

(M3)
Lucky Meisenheimer
7300 Sand Lake Commons Blvd.
Orlando, FL 32819
407-354-0478

(M4)
Bill Mekalian
550 E Chesapeake Cir.
Fresno, CA 93720
209-434-3247

(M5)
Mike's General Store
52 St. Annes Rd.
Winnipeg, Manitoba, Canada R2M-2Y3
204-255-3463; fax 204-253-4124

(M7)
Judith A. Mosholder
186 Pine Springs Camp Road
Boswell, PA 15531
814-629-9277

(M8)
The Mouse Man Ink
P.O. Box 3195
Wakefield, MA 01880
781-246-3876; fax 781-245-4511

(M9)
Steven Meltzer
1253 B Third St. Promenade
Santa Monica, CA 90401
310-656-0483

(M10)
Gary Metz
263 Key Lakewood Dr.
Moneta, VA 24121
540-721-2091; fax 504-721-1782

(M11)
Michael and Polly McQuillen
McQuillen's Collectibles
P.O. Box 50022
Indianapolis, IN 46250
317-845-1721

(M13)
Helen L. McCale
Holly Hobbie Collector
1006 Ruby Ave.
Butler, MO 64730-2500

(M14)
Ken Mitchell
710 Conacher Dr.
Willowdale, Ontario
Canada M2M 3N6
416-222-5808 anytime

(M15)
Marcia's Fantasy, Marcia Fanta
R.R.#1, Box 107
Tappen, ND 58487-9635
701-327-4441

(M16)
Gene Mack
408 Yorkshire Blvd.
Syracuse, NY 13219
315-487-9023

(M17)
Mrs. Miller's Memorabilia
70a Greenwich Ave., Box #116
New York, NY 10011
212-614-9774 (leave message)

(M18)
Nancy McMichael
P.O. Box 53262
Washington DC 20009

(M19)
Model Auto
P.O. Box 79253
Houston, TX 77279
Phone or fax 713-468-4461 (phone evenings; fax anytime)

(M20)
Bruce Middleton
5 Lloyd Rd.
Newburgh, NY 12550
914-564-2556

(M21)
Peter Muldavin
173 W 78th St., Apt. 5-F
New York, NY 10024
212-362-9606
website: http://members.aol.com/kiddie78s/

(N1)
Natural Way dba Russian Toy Co.
820 Massachusetts
Lawrence, KS 66044
913-841-0100

(N2)
Norman's Olde & New Store
Philip Norman
126 W Main St.
Washington, NC 27889-4944
919-946-3448

(N3)
Neil's Wheels, Inc.
Box 354
Old Bethpage, NY 11804
516-293-9659; fax 516-420-0483

(N4)
Roger Nazeley
4921 Castor Ave.
Philadelphia, PA 19124
Fax 215-288-8030

(O1)
Olde Tyme Toy Shop
120 S Main St.
Fairmount, IN 46928
317-948-3150; fax 317-948-4257

(P2)
Dawn Parrish
20460 Samual Dr.
Saugus, CA 91350-3812
805-263-TOYS

(P3)
American Pie Collectibles
John and Sheri Pavone
29 Sullivan Rd.
Peru, NY 12972
518-643-0993; toll free 888-458-2200; fax 518-643-8152
e-mail: apc1@worldnet.att.net
website: http://www.serftech. com/apc
Mastercard Visa Discover

(P4)
Plymouth Rock Toy Co.
38 Russell St.
Plymouth, MA 02360
508-746-2842 or 508-830-1880 (noon to 11 PM EDT)
Fax 508-830-0364

(P5)
Gary Pollastro
5047 84th Ave. SE
Mercer, WA 98040
206-232-3199

(P6)
Judy Posner
R.D. 1, Box 273
Effort, PA 18330
717-629-6583
(or winter) P.O. Box 21945C
Englewood, FL 34295
941-497-7149
e-mail: judyandjef@aol.com

(P8)
Diane Patalano
P.O. Box 144
Saddle River, NJ 07458
201-327-2499

(P10)
Bill and Pat Poe
220 Dominica Circle E
Niceville, FL 32578-4068
904-897-4163; fax 904-897-2606
e-mail: mcpoes@aol.com or anem34a@prodigy.com

(P11)
The Phoenix Toy Soldier Co.
Bob Wilson
16405 North 9th Place
Phoenix, AZ 85022
602-863-2891

(P12)
Michael Paquin, That Toy Guy
72 Penn Blvd.
E Lansdowne, PA 19050
610-394-8697 (10 am – 10 pm EST); fax 610-259-8626 (24 hr)

(P13)
Lorraine Punchard
8201 Pleasant Ave. South
Bloomington, MN 55420
612-888-1079

(R1)
David Richter
6817 Sutherland Dr.
Mentor, OH 44060-3917
440-255-6537

(R2)
Rick Rann, Beatlelist
P.O. Box 877
Oak Park, IL 60303
708-442-7907

(R3)
Jim Rash
135 Alder Ave.
Egg Harbor Twp., NJ 08234-9302
609-646-4125 (evenings)

(R4)
Robert Reeves
104 Azalea Dr.
St. Mathews, SC 29135
803-578-5939 (leave message)

(R5)
Reynolds Toys
Charlie Reynolds
2836 Monroe St.
Falls Church, VA 22042
703-533-1322

(R6)
David E. Riddle
P.O. Box 13141
Tallahassee, FL 32308
904-877-7207

(S1)
Sam Samuelian, Jr.
700 Llanfair Rd.
Upper Darby, PA 19082
215-566-7248

(S5)
Son's a Poppin' Ranch
John Rammacher
1610 Park Ave.
Orange City, FL 32763-8869
904-775-2891
website: http://www.bitstorm.net/sap
e-mail: sap@bitstorm.net

(S6)
Bill Stillman
Scarfone & Stillman Vintage Oz
P.O. Box 167
Hummelstown, PA 17036
717-566-5538

(S7)
Nate Stoller
960 Reynolds Ave.
Ripon, CA 95366
209-599-5933
website: http://www.geocities.com/heartland/plains/6385
e-mail: multimotot@aol.com

(S10)
Scott Smiles
848 SE Atlantic Dr.
Lantana, FL 33462-4702
561-582-4947
e-mail: ssmiles664@aol.com

(S12)
Nancy Stewart Books
1188 NW Weybridge Way
Beaverton, OR 97006
503-645-9779

(S14)
Cindy Sabulis
P.O. Box 642
Shelton, CT 06484
203-926-0176
website: http://www.dollsntoys.com
e-mail: toys4two@snet.net

(S16)
Bill Smith
56 Locust St.
Douglas, MA 01516
508-476-2015

(S18)
The Silver Bullet
Terry and Kay Klepey
P.O. Box 553
Forks, WA 98331
360-327-3726

(S19)
Craig and Donna Stifter
P.O. Box 6514
Naperville, IL 60540
630-789-5780

(S20)
Pat and Kris Secor
P.O. Box 158
Clarksville, AR 72830
501-754-5746

(S22)
Carole & Richard Smyth
Carole Smyth Antiques
P.O. Box 2068
Huntington, NY 11743

(S24)
Mark and Lynda Suozzi
P.O. Box 102
Ashfield, MA 01330
Phone or fax 413-628-3241 (9am to 5pm)

(S25)
Steve Stevenson
11117 NE 164th Pl.
Bothell, WA 98011-4003
206-488-2603
Fax 206-488-2841

(T2)
Toy Scouts, Inc.
Bill Bruegman
137 Casterton Ave.
Akron, OH 44303
330-836-0668
Fax 330-869-8668
e-mail: toyscout@akron.infi.net

(T3)
Richard Trautwein
Toys N Such
437 Dawson St.
Sault Ste. Marie, MI 49783
906-635-0356

(T5)
Bob and Marcie Tubbs
6405 Mitchell Hollow Rd.
Charlotte, NC 28277
704-541-5839

(T6)
TV Collector
P.O. Box 1088
Easton, MA 02334
508-238-1179
Fax by pre-set agreement

(V1)
Norm Vigue
62 Bailey St.
Stoughton, MA 02072
781-344-5441

(V2)
Marci Van Ausdall
P.O. Box 946
Quincy, CA 95971
916-283-2770
e-mail: dreams707@aol.com

(W1)
Dan Wells Antique Toys
7008 Main St.
Westport, KY 40077
502-225-9925
Fax 502-225-0019
e-mail: dwatcatDan@aol.com

(W2)
Adrienne Warren
1032 Feather Bed Lane
Edison, NJ 08820

(W4)
Randy Welch
27965 Peach Orchard Rd.
Easton, MD 21601-8203
410-822-5441

(W5)
Linda and Paul Woodward
14 Argo Drive
Sewell, NJ 08080-1908
609-582-1253

(W6)
John D. Weatherhead
5224 S. Guerin Pass
New Berlin, WI 53151
414-425-8810
fax 414-425-7844

(W7)
Larry and Mary White
108 Central St.
Rowley, MA 10969

(Y1)
Henri Yunes
971 Main St., Apt. 2
Hackensack, NJ 07601
201-488-2236

(Y2)
Mary Young
Box 9244
Dayton, OH 45409
937-298-4838

Categories of Special Interest

If you would like to be included in this section, send us a list of your 'for sale' merchandise. These listings are complimentary to those who participate in the preparation of this guide by doing so. Please understand that the people who are listed here want to buy and sell. They are not appraisers. Read the paragraph under the title *Dealer's Codes* for more information. If you have no catalogs or lists but would like to advertise with us, see the display ad rate sheet on page 486.

Action Figures
Also GI Joe, Star Wars and Super Heroes
John DiCicco
57 Bay View Dr.
Shrewsbury, MA 01545
508-797-0023

Captain Action, Star Wars, Secret Wars, and other character-related Western, TV, movie, comic, or paperback tie-ins
George Downes
Box 572
Nutley, NJ 07110
201-935-3388

Figures
Anthony Balasco
P.O. Box 19482
Johnston, RI 02919
401-946-5720
Fax 401-942-7980

GI Joe, Captain Action, and other character-related TV, advertising, Marx, and Mego figures; send $2 for sales catalog
Jerry and Ellen Harnish
110 Main St.
Bellville, OH 44813
Phone or fax 419-886-4782

Advertising
M&M Toppers
Ken Clee
P.O. Box 11412
Philadelphia, PA 19111
215-722-1979

Gary Metz
263 Key Lakewood Dr.
Moneta, VA 24121
540-721-2091
Fax 504-721-1782

Also general line
Mike's General Store
52 St. Annes Rd.
Winnipeg, Manitoba, Canada R2M 2Y3
204-255-3463
Fax 204-253-4124

Advertising figures, novelty radios, Barbies, promotional watches, character toys, and more
Michael Paquin, That Toy Guy
72 Penn Blvd.
E Lansdowne, PA 19050
610-394-8697 (10 am – 10 pm EST) or fax 610-259-8626 (24 hrs)

Coca-Cola and Pepsi-Cola toys
Craig and Donna Stifter
P.O. Box 6514
Naperville, IL 60540
630-789-5780

Automobilia
Especially model kits, promotional model cars, books, and literature
Model Auto
P.O. Box 79253
Houston, TX 77279
Phone or fax 713-468-4461
(phone evenings; fax anytime)

Banks
Ertl; sales lists available
Homestead Collectibles
Art and Judy Turner
R.D. 2, Rte. 150
P.O. Box 173-E
Mill Hall, PA 17751
717-726-3597
Fax 717-726-4488

Modern mechanical banks: Reynolds, John Wright, James Capron, Book of Knowledge, Richards, Wilton; sales lists available
Dan Iannotti
212 W. Hickory Grove Rd.
Bloomfield Hills, MI 48302-1127
248-335-5042

Also children's sadirons, Black Americana dolls and memorabilia
Diane Patalano
Country Girls Appraisal and Liquidation Service
P.O. Box 144
Saddle River, NJ 07458
201-327-2499

Penny banks (limited editions): new, original, mechanical, still, or figural; also bottle openers
Reynolds Toys
Charlie Reynolds
2836 Monroe St.
Falls Church, VA 22042-2007
703-533-1322

Antique tin and iron mechanical penny banks; no reproductions or limited editions; cast-iron architectural bank buildings in Victorian form; buy and sell list available upon request
Mark and Lynda Suozzi
P.O. Box 102
Ashfield, MA 01330
Phone/fax 413-628-3241 (9 am – 5 pm). Mail order and shows only

Barbie and Friends
Wanted: Mackies, holiday, and porcelain as well as vintage Barbies; buying and selling 1959 dolls to present issues
Marl Davidson (Marl & B)
10301 Braden Run
Bradenton, FL 34202
941-751-6275
Fax 941-751-5463
website: http://auntie.com.marl

Especially NRFB dolls 1980 to present, also Barbie Hallmark ornaments
Doris Gerton
Doris' Dolls & Collectibles
325 E 10th St.
Mt. Vernon, IN 47620
Phone or fax 812-835-5290

Battery-Operated
Tom Lastrapes
P.O. Box 2444
Pinellas Park, FL 34664
813-545-2586

Also general line
Mike Roscoe
3351 Lagrange
Toledo, OH 43608
419-244-6935

Boats and Toy Motors
Also Japanese wood toys
Dick Borgerding
RJB Toys
720 E Main St.
Flushing, MI 48433
810-659-9859

Books
Little Golden Books, Wonder Books, many others; 20-page list available
Ilene Kayne
1308 S Charles St.
Baltimore, MD 21230
410-685-3923
e-mail: kayne@clark.net

Specializing in Little Golden Books and look-alikes
Steve Santi
19626 Ricardo Ave.
Hayward, CA 94541
510-481-2586
Author of *Collecting Little Golden Books*, Volumes I and II. Also publishes newsletter, Poky Gazette, primarily for Little Golden Book collectors.

Children's Books
Nancy Stewart Books
1188 NW Weybridge Way
Beaverton, OR 97006
503-645-9779

Breyer
Carol Karbowiak Gilbert
2193 14 Mile Rd. 206
Sterling Height, MI 48310

Bubble Bath Containers
Including foreign issues; also character collectibles, character bobbin' head nodders, and Dr. Dolittle; write for information or send SASE for Bubble Bath Bulletin
Matt and Lisa Adams
1234 Harbor Cove
Woodstock, GA 30189
770-516-6874

Building Blocks and Construction Toys
Arlan Coffman
1223 Wilshire Blvd., Ste. 275
Santa Monica, CA 90403
310-453-2507

Anchor Stone Building Blocks by Richter
George Hardy
1670 Hawkwood Ct.
Charlottesville, VA 22901
804-295-4863
Fax 804-295-4898

California Raisins
Ken Clee
Box 11412
Philadelphia, PA 19111
215-722-1979

California Raisins (PVC); buying collections, old store stock, and closeouts
Larry DeAngelo
516 King Arthur Dr.
Virginia Beach, VA 23464
757-424-1691

John D. Weatherhead
5224 S. Guerin Pass
New Berlin, WI 53151
414-425-8810
Fax 414-425-7844

Candy Containers
Jeff Bradfield
Corner of Rt. 42 and Rt. 257
Dayton, VA 22821
703-879-9961

Also Tonka, Smith-Miller, Shafford black cats, German nodders
Doug Dezso
864 Patterson Ave.
Maywood, NJ 07607
201-488-1311

Cast Iron
Pre-war, large-scale cast-iron toys and early American tinplate toys
John McKenna
801-803 W Cucharres
Colorado Springs, CO 80905
719-630-8732

Victorian bell toys, horse-drawn wagons, fire toys, carriages, penny banks, pull toys, animated coin-operated machines; buy and sell, list available upon request, mail order and shows only
Mark and Lynda Suozzi
P.O. Box 102
Ashfield, MA 01330
Phone/fax 413-628-3241 (9 am – 5 pm)

Cereal Boxes and Premiums
Scott Bruce, Mr. Cereal Box
P.O. Box 481
Cambridge, MA 02140
e-mail: scott@flake.com

Character and Promotional Glasses
Especially fast-foods and sports glasses; publishers of Collector Glass News
Mark Chase and Michael Kelly
P.O. Box 308
Slippery Rock, PA 16057
724-946-2838; fax 724-946-9012

Character Clocks and Watches
Also radio premiums and decoders, P-38 airplane-related items from World War II, Captain Marvel and Hoppy items, Lone Ranger books with jackets, selected old comic books, toys and cap guns; buys and sells Hoppy and Roy items
Bill Campbell
Kirschner Medical Corp.
1221 Littlebrook Ln.
Birmingham, AL 35235
205-853-8227; fax 405-658-6986

Character Collectibles
Dolls, rock 'n roll personalities (especially the Beatles), related character items, and miscellaneous toys
BOJO
Bob Gottuso
P.O. Box 1403
Cranberry Twp., PA 16066
Phone or fax 724-776-0621

Children's plastic character cups by F&F, Deka, etc.; also related advertising and catalogs; SASE required when requesting information
Cheryl and Lee Brown
7377 Badger Ct.
Indianapolis, IN 46260

1940s – 60s character items such as super heroes, TV and cartoon items, games, playsets, lunch boxes, model kits, comic books, and premium rings
Bill Bruegman
Toy Scouts, Inc.
137 Casterton Ave.
Akron, OH 44303
216-836-0668
Fax 216-869-8668
e-mail: toyscout@akron.infi.net

Hanna-Barbera, Warner Bros, Disney, vintage TV and 'toons; also collectible dolls of the '60s and '70s
John and Michele Casino
633 Franklin Ave., Suite #169
Nutley, NJ 07110
201-759-2520

TV, radio, and comic collectibles; sports and non-sports cards; silver and golden age comics
Casey's Collectible Corner
HCR Box 31, Rt. 3
N Blenheim, NY 12131
607-588-6464
e-mail: CASEYSCC@aol.com

Disney, especially books and animation art
Cohen Books and Collectibles
Joel J. Cohen
P.O. Box 810310
Boca Raton, FL 33481
561-487-7888; fax 561-487-3117
e-mail: cohendisney@prodigy.net

Early Disney, Western heroes, premiums and other related collectibles
Ron and Donna Donnelly
Saturday Heroes
6302 Championship Dr.
Tuscaloosa, AL 35405

Dick Tracy collectibles; free appraisals of DT items with SASE and photo or detailed description
Larry Doucet
2351 Sultana Dr.
Yorktown Heights, NY 10598
914-245-1320

Large comprehensive catalog available by subscription ($2 for sample copy, $10 per yr for 4 issues, 1st class); 100% satisfaction guaranteed
52 Girls Collectibles
P.O. Box 36
Morral, OH 43337
614-465-6062

Rocketeer memorabilia
Don Hamm
712 N. Townsend St.
Syracuse, NY 13203
315-478-7035

Snoopy/Peanuts classics, new and old
N.F. Huber, The SNO-PEA Trader
931 Emerson St.
1000 Oaks, CA 91362
805-497-0119; fax 1-800-SNO-OPY-2

Any and all, also Hartland figures
Terri Ivers, Terri's Toys & Nostalgia
206 E. Grand
Ponca City, OK 74601
580-762-8697 or 580-762-5174
Fax 580-765-2657
e-mail: toylady@poncacity.net

Characters from comic strips/comic books, related memorabilia
Jeff and Bob's Fun Stuff
7324 Reseda Blvd #168
Reseda, CA 91335
818-705-3368

TV characters and shows, original network stills from 1955 to 85, soundtrack albums from 1950 to 90
Jim's TV Collectibles
P.O. Box 4767
San Diego, CA 92764
Phone or fax 619-462-1953

Games, models, action figures, dolls, general line; especially Nightmare Before Christmas
June Moon
245 N Northwest Hwy
Park Ridge, IL 60068
847-825-1411 (24-hour phone)
Fax 847-825-6090
Open 2 to 6 PM Tues – Sat
e-mail: junmoonstr@aol.com

TV, Western, Space, Beatles; auction as well as set-price catalogs available
Just Kids Nostalgia
310 New York Ave.
Huntington, NY 11743
516-423-8449
Fax 516-423-4326

Especially bendy figures and the Simpsons
K-3 Inc.
Bendees Only; Simpson Mania
2335 NW Thurman
Portland, OR 97210
503-222-2713

Auction house with consignments welcomed; specializing in western Hartlands, airplanes, boats, cars, trucks, robots, windups, battery-ops, dolls, character items, and playset figures
Kerry and Judy's Toys
7370 Eggleston Rd.
Memphis, TN 31825-2112
901-575-1722

Western stars of radio, movies, and TV
Gene Mack
408 Yorkshire Blvd.
Syracuse, NY 13219
315-487-9023 (anytime)

Disney and other character collectibles
Kathy and Skip Matthews
Second Childhood Antiques & Collectibles
1154 Grand Ave.
Astoria, OR 97103
503-325-6543

Any and all, also gum cards, sports, movie posters, etc.
Mrs. Miller's Memorabilia
70a Greenwich Ave., Box 116
New York, NY 10011
212-614-9774 (leave message)

Especially Disney; send $5 for annual subscription (6 issues) for sale catalogs
The Mouse Man Ink
P.O. Box 3195
Wakefield, MA 01880
781-246-3876; fax 781-245-4511

General line, especially Raggedy Ann, Disneyana, Star Wars, GI Joe
Olde Tyme Toy Shop
Jim May and Debra Coleman
120 S Main St.
Fairmount, IN 46928
317-948-3150
Fax 317-948-4257
Also tin windups, cast iron, old toy stock, cap pistols, and trains

Especially pottery, china, ceramics, salt and pepper shakers, cookie jars, tea sets and children's china; with special interest in Black Americana and Disneyana; illustrated sale lists available
Judy Posner
R.D. #1, Box 273
Effort, PA 18330
717-629-6583
(or winter) P.O. Box 2194 SC
Englewood, FL 34295
941-497-7149
e-mail: judyandjef@aol.com

Buying, selling, and trading original Beatles and Monkees memorabilia
Rick Rann, Beatlelist
P.O. Box 877
Oak Park, IL 60303
708-442-7907

Also battery-ops, character clocks, and novelties
Sam Samuelian, Jr.
700 Llanfair Rd.
Upper Darby, PA 19082
215-566-7248

Lone Ranger collector, buy and sell; publisher of Silver Bullet Newsletter (see Clubs, Newsletters, and Other Publications)
The Silver Bullet
Terry and Kay Klepey
P.O. Box 553
Forks, WA 98331
360-327-3726

Wizard of Oz memorabilia; quarterly mail/phone bid auctions available for $2; always buying Oz
Bill Stillman
Scarfone and Stillman Vintage Oz
P.O. Box 167
Hummelstown, PA 17036
717-566-5538

Especially tinplate toys and cars, battery-op toys, and toy trains
Richard Trautwein
Toys N Such
437 Dawson St.
Sault Ste. Marie, MI 49783
906-635-0356

TV, movie, rock 'n roll, comic character, commercials, radio, theater, etc., memorabilia of all kinds; Send $4 for sale catalog. We are not interested in buying items. All inquiries must include SASE for reply unless ordering catalog.
TV Collector
P.O. Box 1088
Easton, MA 02334
508-238-1179
Fax by pre-set agreement

Games, premiums, cartoon personalities, Dick Tracy, Popeye, Buck Rogers, Flash Gordon, Tarzan, Lone Ranger, and others
Norm Vigue
62 Bailey St.
Stoughton, MA 02072
781-344-5441

Especially Garfield, Smurfs, comic/character collectibles, dolls, monsters, premiums, etc.; lists available
Adrienne Warren
1032 Feather Bed Lane
Edison, NJ 08820
908-381-7083 (EST)

Children's Play Dishes
Author of book
Lorraine Punchard
8201 Pleasant Ave. South
Bloomington, MN 55420
612-888-1079

Chinese Tin Toys
Also buying and selling antiques, old toys and collectibles; custom refinishing and quality repairing
Finisher's Touch Antiques
Steve Fisch, proprietor
10 W Main St.
Wappingers Falls, NY 12590
914-298-8882
Fax 914-298-8945

Comic Books
Also Western pulps, Big Little Books, magazines, Mad and other humor publications; large catalog available
Avalon Comics
Larry Curcio
P.O. Box 821
Medford, MA 02155
617-391-5614

Also Sunday comics, books, pulp magazines, premiums, character collectibles, non-sports cards, and more
Ken Mitchell
710 Conacher Dr.
Wilowdale, Ontario
Canada M2M 3N6
416-222-5808 (anytime)

Cracker Jack
Author of Cracker Jack Toys
Larry and Mary White
108 Central St.
Rowley, MA 10969

Dakins
Jim Rash
135 Alder Ave.
Egg Harbor Twp., NJ 08234-9302

Diecast
Matchbox, extensive lists available
Classic Golf & Collectibles
P.O. Box 8
Lake Havasu City, AZ 86406-0008
520-855-9623

Especially Dinky; also selling inexpensive restorable diecast as well as reproduction parts and decals for many diecast brands
Paul Fideler
20 Shadow Oak Dr., Apt. #18
Sudbury, MA 01776
617-386-0228 (24 hours)
Fax 617-386-0159 (24 hours)

Especially English-made toy vehicles
Mark Giles
510 E Third St.
Ogalala, NE 69153
308-284-4360

Especially Matchbox and other small-scale cars and trucks
Bill Jackameit
200 Victoria Dr.
Bridgewater, VA 22812
804-923-3398 (Monday – Thursday, 7 pm – 9 pm EST)
e-mail: wj2d@sprintmail.com
website: http://www.freeyellow.com/members/bjdiecast

Especially Matchbox, Hot Wheels, Majorette
Dana Johnson Enterprises
P.O. Box 1824
Bend, OR 97709-1824
503-382-8410
Author/publisher of *Matchbox Blue Book, Hot Wheels Blue Book*, and *Collecting Majorette Toys* (prices updated yearly); also *Collector's Guide to Diecast Toys & Scale Models*, 2nd edition, and *Matchbox Toys, 1947 – 1996*, 2nd edition (Collector Books)

Especially Dinky; also obsolete French, German, Italian, and English-made vehicles
Jean-Claude Lanau
740 Thicket Ln.
Houston, TX 77079
713-4971-6034

Matchbox of all types including Dinky, Commando, Convoys, Harley-Davidson, Indy/Formula 1, and Looney Tunes; also Corgi, Hartoy, Hot Wheels, Tomica, and Tyco slot cars
Neil's Wheels, Inc.
Box 354
Old Bethpage, NY 11804
516-293-9659; fax 516-420-0483

Ertl, banks, farm, trucks, and construction
Son's a Poppin' Ranch
John Rammacher
1610 Park Ave.
Orange City, FL 32763-8869
904-775-2891
e-mail: sap@bitstorm.net
website: http://www.bitstorm.net/sap

All types; also action figures such as GI Joe, Johnny West, Matt Mason, and others
Robert Reeves
104 Azalea Dr.
St. Mathews, SC 29135
803-578-5939 (leave message)

Especially Soviet-made toys (marked USSR or CCCP)
David E. Riddle
P.O. Box 13141
Tallahassee, FL 32308
905-877-7207

Hot Wheels
Steve Stevenson
11117 NE 164th Pl.
Bothell, WA 98011-4003
206-488-2603
Fax 206-488-2841

Hot Wheels, Matchbox, and all obsolete toy cars, trucks, and airplanes
Dan Wells Antiques Toys
7008 Main St.
Westport, KY 40077
502-225-9925
Fax 502-225-0019
e-mail: dwatcatDan@aol.com

Dolls
Strawberry Shortcake dolls, accessories, and related items
Geneva Addy
P.O. Box 124
Winterset, IA 50273
515-462-3027

Hard plastic and composition, Ginny and accessories, pincushion dolls, doll dishes; catalogs available
Roslyn L. Herman
124-16 84th Rd.
Kew Gardens, NY 11415
718-846-3496 or 718-846-8491

Chatty Cathy and Mattel
Kathy Lewis
187 N Marcello Ave.
Thousand Oaks, CA 91360
805-499-8101
Author of book: *Chatty Cathy Dolls, An Identification and Value Guide*

Ad dolls, Barbie dolls and other Mattel dolls, premiums, character memorabilia, modern dolls, related items
Marcia Fanta
Marcia's Fantasy
RR 1, Box 107
Tappen, ND 58487-9635
701-327-4441

Gerber Baby dolls; author of book ($44 postpaid)
Joan S. Grubaugh
2342 Hoaglin Rd.
Van Wert, OH 45891
419-622-4411
Fax 419-622-3026

Holly Hobbie dolls and collectibles
Kathe Conley
51 Spencer Rd.
Airville, PA 17302
717-862-3162
Fax per Winchester Group; 410-866-3125

Holly Hobbie dolls and collectibles
Helen L. McCale
1006 Ruby Ave.
Butler, MO 64730-2500

Liddle Kiddles and other small dolls from the late '60s and early '70s
Dawn Parrish
20460 Samual Dr.
Saugus, CA 91350-3812
805-263-TOYS

Dolls from the 1960s – 70s, including Liddle Kiddles, Barbie, Tammy, Tressy, etc.
Cindy Sabulis
P.O. Box 642
Shelton, CT 06484
203-926-0176
website: http://www.dollsntoys.com
e-mail: toys4two@snet.net
Co-author of *The Collector's Guide to Tammy, the Ideal Teen* (Collector Books)

Betsy McCall
Marci Van Ausdall
P.O. Box 946
Quincy, CA 95971
916-283-2770
e-mail: dreams707@aol.com

Celebrity and character dolls
Henri Yunes
971 Main St., Apt. 2
Hackensack, NJ 07601
201-488-2236

Dollhouse Furniture
Renwal, Ideal, Marx, etc.
Judith A. Mosholder
186 Pine Springs Camp Road
Boswell, PA 15531
814-629-9277

Dollhouses
Tin and fiberboard dollhouses and plastic furniture from all eras
Bob and Marcie Tubbs
6405 Mitchell Hollow Rd.
Charlotte, NC 28277
704-541-5839

Elvis Presley Collectibles
Rosalind Cranor
P.O. Box 859
Blacksburg, VA 24063
Author of books: *Elvis Collectibles*, *Best of Elvis Collectibles*

Ertl
Also Tonka, construction and logging toys, pressed steel, diecast toy trucks, Smokey Bear items
Glen Brady
P.O. Box 3933
Central Point, OR 97502
503-772-0350

Fast Food
Early Big Boy, Royal Castle, McDonald's® items
Allan Bradley Music (BMI)
Allan Licht
484 S. Grand
Orange, CA 92866
714-633-2628
Also '50s & '60s toys; Batman; Superman; '60s & '70s cereal boxes

All restaurants
Jim Christoffel
409 Maple
Elburn, IL 60119
630-365-2914
e-mail: jimc@elnet.com

All restaurants and California Raisins
Ken Clee
Box 11412
Philadelphia, PA 19111
215-722-1979

McDonald's® only, especially older or unusual items
John and Eleanor Larsen
523 Third St.
Colusa, CA 95932
916-458-4769

McDonald's®
Terry and Joyce Losonsky
7506 Summer Leave Lane
Columbia, MD 21046-2455
410-381-3358
Authors of *Illustrated Collector's Guide to McDonald's® Happy Meals® Boxes, Premiums, and Promotionals* ($9 plus $2 postage), *McDonald's® Happy Meal® Toys in the USA* and *McDonald's® Happy Meal® Toys Around the World* (both full color, $24.95 each plus $3 postage), and *Illustrated Collector's Guide to McDonald's® McCAPS®* ($4 plus $2 postage)

Source for catalog: McDonald's® Collectibles and Other Fast-Food Toys and Memorabilia
Bill and Pat Poe
220 Dominica Circle E
Niceville, FL 32578-4068
904-897-4163
Fax 904-897-2606
e-mail: mcpoes@aol.com or anem34a@prodigy.com
Send $3.00 for catalogs (2 each year, in January and July); see Clubs, Newsletters, and Other Publications for information on McDonald's® club

Fisher-Price
Brad Cassity
1350 Stanwix
Toledo, OH 43614
419-389-1100

Games
Victorian, cartoon, comic, TV, and nostalgic themes
Paul Fink's Fun & Games
P.O. Box 488
59 S Kent Rd.
Kent, CT 06757
860-927-4001
website: gamesandpuzzles.com

Paul David Morrow
1045 Rolling Point Ct.
Virginia Beach, VA 23456-6371

Circa 1900 to modern
Bill Smith
56 Locust St.
Douglas, MA 01516
508-476-2015

GI Joe
Also diecast and Star Wars
Cotswold Collectibles
P.O. Box 716, Dept. SC
Freeland, WA 98249
360-331-5331
Fax 360-331-5344
website: http://www.whidbey.net/-cotswold

Guns
Pre-WWII American spring-air BB guns, all Red Ryder BB guns, cap guns with emphasis on Western six-shooters; especially wanted are pre-WWII cast iron six-guns
Jim Buskirk
3009 Oleander Ave.
San Marcos, CA 92069
760-599-1054

Parts for 1940 cast-iron and 1950 diecast guns: steer-head grips, 2-pc. silver or silver and brass bullets for Nicholas paint 6-shooter and spitfire rifle
ED Drew
7530 146th Ave. NE
Redmond, WA 98052
206-885-7378

Specializing in cap guns
Happy Memories Antique Toy Co.
The Hamburgs
P.O. Box 1305
Woodland Hills, CA 91365
818-346-9884 or 818-346-1269
Fax 818-346-0215

Also model kits, toy soldiers, and character toys and watches; character watch service available
Plymouth Rock Toy Co.
38 Russell St.
Plymouth, MA 02360
508-746-2842 or 508-830-1880 (noon to 11 pm EDT); fax 508-830-0364

Hartland Plastics, Inc.
Author of book
Gail Fitch
1733 N. Cambridge Ave.
Milwaukee, WI 53202

Specializing in Western Hartlands
Kerry and Judy's Toys
7370 Eggleston Rd.
Memphis, TN 38125-2112
901-757-1722

Halloween Collectibles
Also postcards
Pamela E. Apkarian-Russell
C.J. Russell and The Halloween Queen Antiques
P.O. Box 499
Winchester, NH 03470
603-239-8875

Lunch Boxes
Also Little House on the Prairie items, Star Trek and Star Wars unusual items
PAK-RAT
Andy Galbus
900 8th St. NW
Kasson, MN 55944-1079
507-634-2093
e-mail: lhpakrat@polaristel.net

Norman's Olde and New Store
Philip Norman
126 W Main St.
Washington, NC 27889-4944
919-946-3448

Also characters such as cowboys, TV shows, cartoons, and more
Terri's Toys
Terri Ivers
206 E. Grand
Ponca City, OK 74601
580-762-8697 or 580-762-5174
Fax 580-765-2657
e-mail: toylady@poncacity.net

Marbles
Stanley A. & Robert S. Block
P.O. Box 51
Trumbull, CT 06611
203-261-3223 or 203-926-8448;
Internet: bblock@well.com
World Wide Web: http://pages.prodigy. com/marbles/mcc.html
Prodigy: BWVR62A
Block's Box is the longest continuously running absentee marble auction service in the country; catalogs issued

Marionettes and Puppets
Steven Meltzer
1253 B Third St. Promenade
Santa Monica, CA 90401
310-656-0483

Marx
Figures, playsets, and character toy; send three 32¢ stamps for extensive sales lists
G.F. Ridenour
Fun House Toy Co.
P.O. Box 444
Warrendale, PA 15086
724-935-1392 (fax capable)

Model Kits
Specializing in figures & science fiction
Gordy Dutt
P.O. Box 201
Sharon Center, OH 44274-0201
330-239-1657 or 330-239-2991
Also action figures, monsters (especially Godzilla and Japan automated toys), Star Trek, and non-sports cards

From and of science fiction, TV, movies, figures, space, missiles, comics, etc.
John F. Green Inc.
1821 W. Jacaranda Pl
Fullerton, CA 92633
714-526-5467; 800-807-4759

Character, space, monster, Western, radio and cereal premiums and toys; GI Joe, Captain Action, tin toys and windups
Ed Janey
1756 65th St.
Garrison, IA 52229
319-477-8888

Also plastic toys and radio, movie, or TV tie-ins, movie posters
John and Sheri Pavone
29 Sullivan Rd.
Peru, NY 12972
518-643-0993
Toll-free 888-458-2200
Fax 518-643-8152
e-mail: apc1@worldnet.att.net
Website: http://www.serftech.com/apc
Mastercard Visa Discover

Non-Sport Trading Cards
Mark and Val Macaluso
3603 Newark Rd.
Marion, NY 14505
315-926-4349
Fax 315-926-4853
Send $1 for our 40-page catalog of non-sport cards ca 1970 to date; dealers send large SASE for our 10-page wholesale and closeout list

Paper Dolls
Author of books
Mary Young
Box 9244
Dayton, OH 45409
937-298-4838

Paper Lithographed Toys
Rare 18th-, 19th-, and 20th-century games, paper dolls, books, etc.
Bromer Booksellers, Inc.
607 Boylston St.
Boston, MA 02116
617-247-2818
Fax 617-247-2975

Antique McLoughlin games, Bliss and Reed boats, toy wagons, Ten Pin sets, cube blocks, puzzles, and Victorian doll houses. Buy and sell; lists available upon request. Mail order and shows only
Mark and Linda Suozzi
P.O. Box 102
Ashfield, MA 01330
Phone or fax 413-628-3241 (9am to 5pm)

Pedal Cars
Also specializing in Maytag collectibles
Nate Stoller
960 Reynolds Ave.
Ripon, CA 95366
510-481-2586
website: http://www.geocities.com/heartland/plains/6385
e-mail: multimotot@aol.com

Penny Toys
Jane Anderson
R.R. 5, Box 5525
Saylorsburg, PA 18353

Pez Candy Dispensers
Richard Belyski
P.O. Box 124
Sea Cliff, NY 11579
e-mail: peznews@juno.com

Plastic Figures
Also Dakins, cartoon and advertising figures, and character squeeze toys
Jim Rash
135 Alder Ave.
Egg Harbor Twp., NJ 08234-9302
609-649-4125

Playsets
Also GI Joe, Star Trek, and dinosaurs
Mike and Kurt Fredericks
145 Bayline Circle
Folsom, CA 95630-8077

Political Toys
Michael and Polly McQuillen
McQuillen's Collectibles
P.O. Box 50022
Indianapolis, IN 46250
317-845-1721

Promotional Vehicles
'50s and '60s models (especially Ford); also F&F Post Cereal cars; author of two books on promotional model cars, both available directly from him
Larry Blodget
Box 753
Rancho Mirage, CA 92270
619-862-1979

Puzzles
Wood jigsaw type, from before 1950
Bob Armstrong
15 Monadnock Rd.
Worcester, MA 01609

Specializing in advertising puzzles
Donald Friedman
660 W Grand Ave
Chicago, IL 60610
Day phone: 708-656-3700; evenings and weekends: 312-226-4741; fax 708-656-6292

Radio Premiums
Also Fisher-Price; lists available
Pat and Kris Secor
P.O. Box 158
Clarksville, AR 72830
501-754-5746

Radios
Authors of several books on antique, novelty, and transistor radios
Sue and Marty Bunis
RR 1, Box 36
Bradford, NH 03221-9102

Ramp Walkers
Specializing in walkers, ramp-walking figures, and tin windups
Randy Welch
Raven'tiques
27965 Peach Orchard Rd.
Easton, MD 21601-8203
410-822-5441

Records
78 rpm children's records and picture disks; buys, sells, and trades records as well as makes cassette recordings for a small fee
Peter Muldavin
173 W 78th St., Apt. 5-F
New York, NY 10024
212-362-9606
website: http://members.aol.com/kiddie78s/

Russian and East European Toys
Wooden Matrioskha dolls, toys of tin, plastic, diecast metal; military theme and windups
Natural Way
DBA Russian Toy Co.
820 Massachusetts
Lawrence, KS 66044
913-841-0100

Specializing in Russian toys
David E. Riddle
P.O. Box 13141
Tallahassee, FL 32308
904-877-7207

Sand Toys
Jane Anderson
Rt. 1, Box 1030
Saylorsburg, PA 18353

Carole and Richard Smyth
Carole Smyth Antiques
P.O. Box 2068
Huntington, NY 11743
Authors of book; send $25 plus $3 for postage for a signed copy. New York residents please add 8¼% sales tax.

Schoenhut
Publishers of *Inside Collector* and *Antique Doll World*
Keith and Donna Kaonis
60 Cherry Ln.
Huntington, NY 11743
516-261-8337
Fax 516-261-8235

Slot Cars
Especially HO scale from the 1960s to the present; also vintage diecast
Joe Corea
New Jersey Nostalgia Hobby
401 Park Ave.
Scotch Plains, NJ 07076
908-322-2676
Fax 908-322-4079

Specializing in slots and model racing from the '60s – '70s; especially complete race sets in original boxes
Gary Pollastro
5047 84th Ave. SE
Mercer, WA, 98040
206-232-3199

Snow Domes
Broad assortment from states, cities, tourist attractions, novelties, also glass domes; list available
Nancy McMichael
P.O. Box 53262
Washington DC 20009
Editor of Snow Biz, quarterly newsletter, see Clubs, Newsletters, and Other Publications

Soldiers
Barclay, Manoil, Grey Iron, Jones, dimestore types, and others; also Syrocco figures
Stan and Sally Alekna
732 Aspen Lane
Lebanon, PA 17042
717-228-2361
Fax 717-228-2362

Recasts, conversions, diorama work; price list available
Bryan and Val Davis
3132 E. Prince Rd.
Tucson, AZ 85716
502-323-2598 (9 am – 7 pm, Mountain Standard)

Auburn, Airfix, Atlantic, etc; also Marx plastic figures, playsets, and accessories; lists available with SASE
Phoenix Toy Soldier Co.
Bob Wilson
16405 North 9th Place
Phoenix, AZ 85022
602-863-2891

Sports Bobbin' Head Dolls
Tim Hunter
4301 W. Hidden Valley Dr.
Reno, NV 89502
702-856-4357
Fax 702-856-4354
e-mail: thunter885@aol.com

Star Wars
Also vehicles, model kits, GI Joes, games, ad figures, View-Master, non-sports cards, Star Trek, advertising, antiques, fine art, and much more
June Moon
Jim and Nancy Frugoli
245 N Northwest Hwy
Park Ridge, IL 60068
847-825-1411 (24-hr phone)
Fax 847-825-6090
Open 2 to 6 PM Tues – Sat
e-mail: junmoonstr@aol.com

Steiff
Also Schucos and children's things
Candelaine (Candice Gunther)
Pasadena, CA 91103-2320
626-796-4568; fax 626-796-7172
e-mail: Candelaine@aol.com.

Especially limited editions, '50s and antique. Other teddies and reference books.
Cynthia's Country Store
The Wellington Mall #15-A
12794 W Forest Hill Blvd
Wellington, FL 33414
561-793-0554
Fax 561-795-4222
e-mail: cynbears@aol.com
website: http://www.thecrier.com/ccs

Particularly bears; also Schucos and dolls
Bunny Walker
Box 502
Bucyrus, OH 44820
419-562-8355

Tonka
Also candy containers and German nodders
Doug Dezso
864 Patterson Ave.
Maywood, NJ 07607
201-488-1311

Toothbrush Holders
Also Pez
Marilyn Cooper
P.O. Box 55174
Houston, TX 77255

Tootsietoys
David Richter
6817 Sutherland Dr.
Mentor, OH 44060-3917
Author of *Collector's Guide to Tootsietoys*

Tops and Other Spinning Toys
Yo-yos, advertising spinners, gyroscopes, spinning games, Victorian figural tops; any unique spinning toy; buy, sell, trade
Bruce Middleton
5 Lloyd Rd.
Newburgh, NY 12550
914-564-2556

Trains
Lionel, American Flyer, and Plasticville
Gary's Trains
186 Pine Springs Camp Road
Boswell, PA 15531
814-629-9277

Also Fisher-Price, Tonka toys, and diecast vehicles
Bill Mekalian
550 E Chesapeake Cir.
Fresno, CA 93720
209-434-3247

Buying American Flyer S gauge; toys of all types for sale; satisfaction guaranteed; color photos with SASE; shipping extra; no return calls on sold items; phone until midnight
Linda and Paul Woodward
14 Argo Drive
Sewell, NJ 08080-1908
609-582-1253

Toy mall; general line (toys on 2nd floor)
Bo-Jo's Antique Mall
3400 Summer Avenue
Memphis, TN 38122
901-323-2050

Transformers
Specializing in Transformers, Robotech, Shogun Warriors, Gadaikins, and any other robot; want to buy these MIP — also selling
David Kolodny-Nagy
May through Jan: 3701 Connecticut Ave. NW, Apt #500
Washington, DC 20008
202-364-8753
For copy of *BotCon Transformer Comic Book, Comic Smorgasbord Special*, send $3 + $1.50 for single issues, $2.50 each for 10 or more + $2. Also available: *Transformers: BotCon '94 Ten-Year Retrospective* (130+ pages) at $15 + $2

Trolls
Roger Inouye
765 E. Franklin Ave.
Pomona, CA 91766

View-Master
Also games, slot cars, Pez, lunch boxes, Halloween costumes, dolls, premiums, TV Guides, Mad magazines
Tom Bremer
P.O. Box 49
Newark, NY 14513
Phone or fax 315-331-8146

Roger Nazeley
4921 Castor Ave.
Phil., PA 19124
Fax 215-288-8030

Windups
Also Occupied Japan celluloid toys
Barry Hardin
1834 NW 39th Terrace
Gainesville, FL 32605-3536
352-372-5182

Especially German and Japanese tin toys, Cracker Jack, toothbrush holders, radio premiums, pencil sharpeners and comic strip toys
Phil Helley
Old Kilbourne Antiques
629 Indiana Ave.
Wisconsin Dells, WI 53965
608-254-8770

Also pressed steel toys, battery-ops, candy containers, dolls and children's things, games, soldiers, Noah's ark, space, robots, etc.
Jacquie and Bob Henry
Antique Treasures and Toys
Box 17
Walworth, NY 14568-0017
315-597-4719
e-mail: Jhenry5792@aol.com or jacqueline.henry@MCI2000.COM

Fine character windups; also Black Americana
Stephen Leonard
Box 127
Albertson, LI, NY 11507
516-742-0979

Also friction and battery operated; fast-food toys, displays
Antique Toy Information Service
Send: SASE, good photos (35mm preferred) and $9.95 per toy to:
Scott Smiles
848 SE Atlantic Dr.
Lantana, FL 33462-4702
561-582-4947
e-mail: ssmiles664@aol.com

Yo-Yos
Lucky Meisenheimer
7300 Sand Lake Commons Blvd.
Orlando, FL 32819
407-354-0478

Clubs, Newsletters, and Other Publications

There are hundreds of clubs, newsletters, and magazines available to toy collectors today. Listed here are some devoted to specific areas of interest. You can obtain a copy of many newsletters simply by requesting a sample.

Action Figure News & Toy Review
James Tomlinson, Editor
556 Monroe Turnpike
Monroe, CT 06458
203-452-7286
Fax 203-452-0410

Action Toys Newsletter
P.O. Box 31551
Billings, MT 59107
406-248-4121

The Antique Trader Weekly
Kyle D. Husfloen, Editor
P.O. Box 1050
Dubuque, IA 52004

American Game Collectors Assn.
49 Brooks Ave.
Lewiston, MA 04240

American International Matchbox Collectors & Exchange Club News-Monthly
Dottie Colpitts
532 Chestnut St.
Lynn, MA 01904
617-595-4135

Anchor Block Foundation
908 Plymouth St.
Pelham, NY 10303
914-738-2935

Antique Advertising Association
P.O. Box 1121
Morton Grove, IL 60053
708-446-0904

Antique & Collectors Reproduction News
Mark Cherenka
Circulation Department
P.O. Box 71174
Des Moines, IA 50325; 800-227-5531. Monthly newsletter showing differences between old originals and new reproductions; subscription: $32 per year

Antique Trader Weekly
Kyle D. Husfloen, Editor
P.O. Box 1050
Dubuque, IA 52004
Subscription $32 (52 issues) per year

The Autograph Review (newsletter)
Jeffrey Morey
305 Carlton Rd.
Syracuse, NY 13207
315-474-3516

Autographs & Memorabilia
P.O. Box 224
Coffeyville, KS 67337
316-251-5308
Six issues per year on movie and sports memorabilia

Barbie Bazaar (magazine)
5617 Sixth Ave., Dept NY593
Kenosha, WI 53140
414-658-1004
Fax 414-658-0433
Six issues for $25.95

Barbie Talks Some More!
Jacqueline Horning
7501 School Rd.
Cincinnati, OH 45249

The Baum Bugle
The International Wizard of Oz Club
Fred M. Meyer
220 N 11th St.
Escanaba, MI 49829

Berry-Bits
Strawberry Shortcake Collectors' Club
Peggy Jimenez
1409 72nd St.
N Bergen, NJ 07047

Beyond the Rainbow Collector's Exchange
P.O. Box 31672
St. Louis, MO 63131

Big Little Times
Big Little Book Collectors Club of America
Larry Lowery
P.O. Box 1242
Danville, CA 94526
415-837-2086

Bojo
P.O. Box 1203
Cranberry Township, PA 16033-2203; 412-776-0621 (9 am to 9 pm EST). Issues fixed-price catalog containing Beatles and rock 'n' roll memorabilia

Buckeye Marble Collectors Club
Betty Barnard
472 Meadowbrook Dr.
Newark, Oh 43055
614-366-7002

Bulletin
Doll Collectors of America
14 Chestnut Rd.
Westford, MA 01886
617-692-8392

Canadian Toy Collectors Society
Gary A. Fry
P.O. Box 636
Maple, Ontario, Canada L6A 1S5

Candy Container Collectors of America
P.O. Box 352
Chelmsford, MA 01824-0352
or
Jeff Bradfield
90 Main St.
Dayton, VA 22821

The Candy Gram newsletter
Candy Container Collectors of America
Douglas Dezso
864 Paterson, Ave.
Maywood, NJ 07607
201-845-7707

Captain Action Collectors Club
P.O. Box 2095
Halesite, NY 11743
516-423-1801; Send SASE for newsletter information

Cast Iron Toy Collectors of America
Paul McGinnis
1340 Market St.
Long Beach, CA 90805

Cat Collectors Club
33161 Wendy Dr.
Sterling Heights, MI 48310
Subscription: $18 per year

Cat Talk
Marilyn Dipboye
31311 Blair Dr.
Warren, MI 48092; 810-264-0285

Century Limited
Toy Train Collectors Society
160 Dexter Terrace
Tonawanda, NY 14150
716-694-3771

Coca-Cola Collectors Club International
P.O. Box 49166
Atlanta, GA 30359
Annual dues: $25

Collecting Tips Newsletter
c/o Meredith Williams
P.O. Box 633
Joplin, MO 64802
417-781-3855 or 417-624-2518
Twelve issues per year focusing on fast-food collectibles

Collector Glass News
P.O. Box 308
Slippery Rock, PA 16057
724-946-2838
Fax 724-946-9012
Six issues per year focusing on character glasses, $15 per year

The Cookie Jar Collector's Club News
Louise Messina Daking
595 Cross River Rd.
Katonah, NY 10536
914-232-0383
Fax 914-232-0384

Cookie Jarrin' With Joyce: The Cookie Jar Newsletter
R.R. 2, Box 504
Walterboro, SC 29488

Cynthia's Country Store
Wellington Mall #15A
12794 West Forest Hill Blvd.
West Palm Beach, FL 33414
Fax or phone 407-793-0554
Specializing in Steiff new, discontinued and antique. Publishes quarterly Steiff and bear-related newsletter and limited edition yearly price guide. $15 per year for both. Call or fax for information or if you have any questions. Also specializes in pieces by R. John Wright, other bear manufacturers, toy soldiers and some old toys. Many Steiff color catalogs and books available.

Dark Shadows Collectibles Classified
Sue Ellen Wilson
6173 Iroquois Trail
Mentor, OH 44060
216-946-6348
For collectors of both old and new series

Dionne Quint Collectors Club
(see also *Quint News*)
Jimmy Rodolfos
P.O. Box 2527
Woburn, MA 01888
617-933-2219

Doll Castle News Magazine
P.O. Box 247
Washington, NJ 07882
908-689-7042
Fax 908-689-6320
Subscription: $16.95 per year or $31.95 for 2 years; issued 6 times a year, serves general interests of doll and miniature collectors as well as dollmaking

Doll Investment Newsletter
P.O. Box 1982
Centerville, MA 02632

Doll News
United Federation of Doll Clubs
P.O. Box 14146
Parkville, MO 64152

Dollhouse & Miniature Collectors Quarterly
Sharon Unger, Editor
P.O. Box 16
Bellaire, MI 49615
$20.00 for four issues per year, 45 – 50 pages of information, buy & sell ads, pricing information

Dunbar's Gallery
76 Haven St.
Milford, MA 01757
508-634-8697
Fax 508-634-8698
Specializing in quality advertising, Halloween, toys, coin-operated machines; holding cataloged auctions occasionally, lists available

Ephemera News
The Ephemera Society of America, Inc.
P.O. Box 37
Schoharie, NY 12157
518-295-7978

The Ertl Replica
Ertl Collectors Club
Mike Meyer, Editor
Hwys 136 & 20
Dyersville, IA 52040
319-875-2000

The Fisher-Price Collector's Club
This club issues a quarterly newsletter packed with information and ads for toys. For more information write to:
Fisher-Price Club
c/o Jeanne Kennedy
1442 N. Ogden
Mesa, AZ 85205

FLAKE, The Breakfast Nostalgia Magazine
P.O. Box 481
Cambridge, MA 02140
617-492-5004
Bimonthly illustrated issue devoted to one hot collecting area such as Disney, etc., with letters, discoveries, new releases, and ads; single issue: $4 ($6 foreign); annual: $20 ($28 foreign); free 25-word ad with new subscription

Friends of Hoppy Club and Newsletter
Laura Bates
6310 Friendship Dr.
New Concord, OH 43762-9708
614-826-4850

Game Times
American Game Collectors Assn.
Joe Angiolillo, Pres.
4628 Barlow Dr.
Bartlesville, OK 74006

Garfield Collectors Society Newsletter
c/o David L. Abrams, Editor
744 Foster Ridge Rd.
Germantown, TN 38138-7036
901-753-1026

Gas Toy Collector
P.O. Box 440818
Houston, TX 77244-0818
Membership: $15 per year; sample issue $1.00

Gene Autry Star Telegram
Gene Autry Development Assn.
Chamber of Commerce
P.O. Box 158
Gene Autry, OK 73436

Ginny Doll Club News
Jeanne Niswonger
305 W Beacon Rd.
Lakeland, FL 33803
813-687-8015

Gone With the Wind Collectors Club Newsletter
8105 Woodview Rd.
Ellicot City, MD 21043
301-465-4632

Good Bears of the World
Terri Stong
P.O. Box 13097
Toledo, OH 43613

Grandma's Trunk
P.O. Box 404
Northport, MI 49670
Subscription: $8 per year for 1st class or $5 per year for bulk rate

Headquarters Quarterly, for GI Joe Collectors
Joe Bodnarchuk
62 McKinley Ave.
Kenmore, NY 14217-2414

Hello Again, Old-Time Radio Show Collector
Jay A. Hickerson
P.O. Box 4321
Hamden, CT 06514; 203-248-2887; fax 203-281-1322. Sample copy upon request with SASE

Highballer for Toy Train collectors
c/o Lou Bohn
109 Howedale Dr.
Rochester, NY 14616-1543

Hobby News
J.L.C. Publications
Box 258
Ozone Park, NY 11416

Hopalong Cassidy Fan Club International
Laura Bates
6310 Friendship Dr.
New Concord, OH 43762
614-826-4850; Subscription: $15 (USA) or $20 (Canada and overseas); includes quarterly newsletter and information on annual Cambridge, Ohio, festival

Hopalong Cassidy Newsletter
Hopalong Cassidy Fan Club
P.O. Box 1361
Boyes Hot Springs, CA 95416

Ideal Doll & Toy Collectors Club
P.O. Box 623
Lexington, MA 02173
617-862-2994

International Figure Kit Club
Gordy's
P.O. Box 201
Sharon Center, OH 44274-0201
330-239-1657
Fax 330-239-2991

International Wizard of Oz Club Inc.
P.O. Box 95
Kinderhook, IL 62345

Kit Builders Magazine
Gordy's
P.O. Box 201
Sharon Center, OH 44274-0201
330-239-1657
Fax 330-239-2991

Madame Alexander Fan Club Newsletter
Earl Meisinger
11 S 767 Book Rd.
Naperville, IL 60564

Marble Mania
Marble Collectors Society of America
Stanley Block
P.O. Box 222
Trumbull, CT 06611
203-261-3223

Martha's Kidlit Newsletter
Box 1488A
Ames, IA 50010. A bimonthly publication for children's books collectors. Subscription: $25 per year

Matchbox USA
Charles Mack
62 Saw Mill Rd.
Durham, CT 06422
203-349-1655

McDonald's® Collecting Tips
Meredith Williams
Box 633
Joplin, MO 64802
Send SASE for information

McDonald's® Collector Club
Joyce and Terry Losonsky
7506 Summer Leave Ln.
Columbia, MD 21046-2455; 301-381-3358. Authors of *Illustrated Collector's Guide to McDonald's® Happy Meal® Boxes, Premiums, & Promotions©* ($9 plus $2 postage), and *Illustrated Collector's Guide to McDonald's® McCaps®* ($3 plus $2), both available from the authors.

McDonald's® Collector Club
'Sunshine Chapter'
Bill and Pat Poe, founders
c/o Dominica Circle. E.
Niceville, FL 32578-4068
904-897-4163
Fax 904-897-2606
e-mail: mcpoes@aol.com or anem34a@prodigy.com

McDonald's® Collector Club Newsletter
c/o Tenna Greenberg
5400 Waterbury Rd.
Des Moines, IA 50312
515-279-0741

Model & Toy Collector Magazine
Toy Scouts, Inc.
137 Casterton Ave.
Akron, OH 44303
330-836-0668
Fax 330-869-8668

Modern Doll Club Journal
Jeanne Niswonger
305 W Beacon Rd.
Lakeland, FL 33803

The Mouse Club East
(Disney collectors)
P.O. Box 3195
Wakefield, MA 01880
Family membership: $25 (includes newsletters and 2 shows per year)

The Mouse Club (newsletter)
Kim and Julie McEuen
2056 Cirone Way
San Jose, CA 95124
408-377-2590
Fax 408-379-6903

Movie Advertising Collector (magazine)
George Reed
P.O. Box 28587
Philadelphia, PA 19149

NAOLH Newsletter
National Assn. for Outlaw & Lawman History
Hank Clark
P.O. Box 812
Waterford, CA 95386
209-874-2640

NAPAC Newsletter
National Assn. of Paper and Advertising Collectors
P.O. Box 500
Mt. Joy, PA 17552
717-653-4300

National Fantasy Fan Club
(for Disney collectors)
Dept. AC, Box 19212
Irvine, CA 92713
Membership: $20 per year, includes newsletters, free ads, chapters, conventions, etc.

National Headquarters News
Train Collectors Assn.
300 Paradise Ln.
Strasburg, PA 17579

Novelty Salt and Pepper Club
c/o Irene Thornburg, Membership Coordinator
581 Joy Rd.
Battle Creek, MI 49017
Publishes quarterly newsletter and annual roster. Annual dues: $20 in USA, Canada, and Mexico; $25 for all other countries

Old Toy Soldier
The Journal for Collectors
209 N Lombard Ave.
Oak Park, IL 60302
708-383-6525
Fax 708-383-2182
Subscription: $35 per year for 6 issues (1st class U.S. mail); current sample copy available by sending $3. Written for collectors by collectors, this magazine shares useful information on military and civilian toy figures and the companies that produced them.

On Line With Betsy McCall
Marci Van Ausdall
P.O. Box 946
Quincy, CA 95971
Subscription: $10 per year for 4 issues

Paper Collectors' Marketplace
470 Main St., P.O. Box 128
Scandinavia, WI 54977
715-467-2379
Subscription: $19.95 (12 issues) per year in USA; Canada and Mexico add $15 per year

Paper Doll News
Emma Terry
P.O. Box 807
Vivian, LA 71082

Paper Pile Quarterly
P.O. Box 337
San Anselmo, CA 94979-0337; 415-454-5552. Subscription: $17.00 per year in USA and Canada

The Pencil Collector
American Pencil Collectors Soc.
Robert J. Romey, Pres.
2222 S Millwood
Wichita, KS 67213
316-263-8419

Pepsi-Cola Collectors Club Newsletter
Pepsi-Cola Collectors Club
Bob Stoddard
P.O. Box 1275
Covina, CA 91722
714-593-8750
Membership: $15

Pez Collector's News
Richard and Marianne Belyski, Editors
P.O. Box 124
Sea Cliff, NY 11579
Phone or fax 516-676-1183
e-mail: peznews@juno.com

Piece by Piece
Frances Main, Editor
P.O. Box 12823
Kansas City, KS 66112-9998
For Springbok puzzle collectors; subscription: $8 per year

Plastic Figure & Playset Collector
5894 Lakeview Ct. E
Onalaska, WI 54650

The Pokey Gazette, A Little Golden Book collector newsletter
Steve Santi
19626 Ricardo Ave.
Hayward, CA 94541
510-481-2586

The Prehistoric Times
Mike and Kurt Fredericks
145 Bayline Circle
Folsom, CA 95630
916-985-7986
For collectors of dinosaur toys; six issues (1 yr), $19

The Prize Insider Newsletter, for Cracker Jack collectors
Larry White
108 Central St.
Rowley, MA 01969
978-948-8187

The Puppet Collector's Newsletter
Steven Meltzer
1253 B Third St. Promenade
Santa Monica, CA 90401
310-656-0483

Quint News (see also Dionne Quint Collectors Club)
Dionne Quint Collectors
P.O. Box 2527
Woburn, MA 01888
617-933-2219

Record Collectors Monthly (newspaper)
P.O. Box 75
Mendham, NJ 07945
201-543-9520; fax 201-543-6033

Roy Rogers-Dale Evans Collectors Assn.
Nancy Horsley
P.O. Box 1166
Portsmouth, OH 45662

Schoenhut Collectors Club
For membership information:
Patricia J. Girbach
1003 W Huron St.
Ann Arbor, MI 48103-4217

The Shirley Temple Collectors News
8811 Colonial Rd.
Brooklyn, NY 11209
Dues: $20 per year; checks payable to Rita Dubas

The Silent Film Newsletter
Gene Vazzana
140 7th Ave.
New York, NY 10011
Subscription $18, send $2.50 for sample copy

The Silver Bullet
Terry and Kay Klepey
P.O. Box 553
Forks, WA 98331
360-327-3726
Subscription $15 per year, sample issue $4; back issues available; also licensed mail-order seller of memorabilia and appraiser

Smurf Collectors Club
24ACH, Cabot Rd. W
Massapequa, NY 11758
Membership includes newsletters. LSASE for information.

Snow Biz
c/o Nancy McMichael
P.O. Box 53262
Washington, DC 20009
Quarterly newsletter (subscription $10 per year) and collector's club, annual meeting/swap meet

Steiff Life
Steiff Collectors Club
Beth Savino
c/oz The Toy Store
7856 Hill Ave.
Holland, OH 43528
419-865-3899 or 800-862-8697

The Survivors (Transformers Club)
For membership information:
Send name and address along with SASE or e-mail address to:
Liane Elliot
6202 34th St. NW
Gig Harbor, WA 98335-7205
e-mail: tetra@eskimo.com

The Television History Magazine
William J. Flechner
700 E Macoupin St.
Staunton, IL 62088
618-635-2712

Toy Collector Club of America (for Ertl toys)
P.O. Box 302
Dyersville, IA 52040
800-452-3303

Toy Dish Collectors
Abbie Kelly
P.O. Box 351
Camillus, NY 13031
315-487-7415

Toy Gun Collectors of America Newsletter
Jim Buskirk, Editor and Publisher
3009 Oleander Ave.
San Marcos, CA 92069
760-599-1054
Published quarterly, covers cap guns, spring air BB guns and other toy guns. Dues: $17 per year; SASE for information

Toy Shop
700 E State St.
Iola, WI 54990
715-445-2214
Subscription (3rd class) $23.95 for 26 issues

Toy Trader
100 Bryant St.
Dubuque, Iowa 52003
1-800-364-5593
Subscription in US $24 for 12 issues

Toychest
Antique Toy Collectors of America, Inc.
2 Wall St., 13th Floor
New York, NY 10005
212-238-8803

Toys & Prices (magazine)
700 E State St.
Iola, WI 54990-0001
715-445-2214
Fax 715-445-4087
Subscription: $14.95 per year

The Trick or Treat Trader
CJ Russell and the Halloween Queen Antiques
P.O. Box 499
4 Lawrence St. and Rt. 10
Winchester, NH, 03470
Subscription is $15 a year for 4 issues or $4 for a sample

Trainmaster (newsletter)
P.O. Box 1499
Gainesville, FL 32602
904-377-7439 or 904-373-4908
Fax 904-374-6616

Troll Monthly
5858 Washington St.
Whitman, MA 02382
800-858-7655 or 800-85-Troll

Turtle River Farm Toys
Rt. 1, Box 44
Manvel, ND 58256-9763

The TV Collector
Diane L. Albert
P.O. Box 1088
Easton, MA 02334-1088
508-238-1179
Send $4 for sample copy

View-Master Reel Collector
Roger Nazeley
4921 Castor Ave.
Philadelphia, PA 19124
215-743-8999

Western & Serials Club
Rt. 1, Box 103
Vernon Center, NM 56090
507-549-3677

The Working Class Hero (Beatles newsletter)
3311 Niagara St.
Pittsburgh, PA 15213-4223
Published three times per year; send SASE for information

The Wrapper
Bubble Gum & Candy Wrapper Collectors
P.O. Box 573
St. Charles, IL 60174
630-377-7921

The Yellow Brick Road Fantasy Museum & Gift Shop
Rt. 49 and Yellow Brick Rd.
Chesterton, IN 46304
219-926-7048

Yo-Yo Times
P.O. Box 1519-SCT
Herndon, VA 22070

DON'T MISS YOUR CHANCE TO REACH THOUSANDS OF TOY COLLECTORS

TO RESERVE YOUR AD SPACE FOR THE NEXT EDITION PLEASE CONTACT HUXFORD ENTERPRISES *IMMEDIATELY*

RATES
(Ad Size)

FULL PAGE	**7½" wide x 9¾" tall – $750.00**
HALF PAGE	**7½" wide x 4½" tall – $400.00**
QUARTER PAGE	**3½" wide x 4½" tall – $250.00**
EIGHTH PAGE (or business card)	**3½" wide x 2¼" tall – $150.00**

NOTE: The above rates are for ***camera ready copy only*** *– Add $50.00 if we are to compose your ad. These prices are net – no agency discounts allowed. Payment in full must accompany your ad copy.*

All advertising accepted under the following conditions:

1. *The Publisher will furnish advertising space in sizes and at rates as set forth in this rate sheet upon full payment in advance of its annual advertising deadline as set forth herein.*

2. Submission of Copy. *The publisher shall have the right to omit any advertisement when the space allotted to Advertiser in a particular issue has been filled. In addition, the Publisher reserves the right to limit the amount of space the Advertiser may use in any one edition.*

3. Content and Design. *Publisher reserves the right to censor, reject, alter, or refuse any advertising copy at its sole discretion or disapprove any advertising copy in accordance with any rule the Publisher may now have, or may adopt in the future, concerning the acceptance of advertising matter, but no intentional change in advertising copy will be made without the prior consent of the Advertiser.*

4. Publisher's Liability for Deletions. *Publisher's liability for failure of the Publisher to insert any advertisement in their books shall be limited to a refund of the consideration paid for the insertion of the advertisement or, at Advertiser's option, to such deleted advertisement being inserted in the next edition.*

5. Copyright and Trademark Permission. *Any Advertiser using copyrighted material or trademarks or trade names of others in its advertising copy shall obtain the prior written permission of the owners thereof which must be submitted to the Publisher with the advertising copy. Where this has not been done, advertising will not be accepted.*

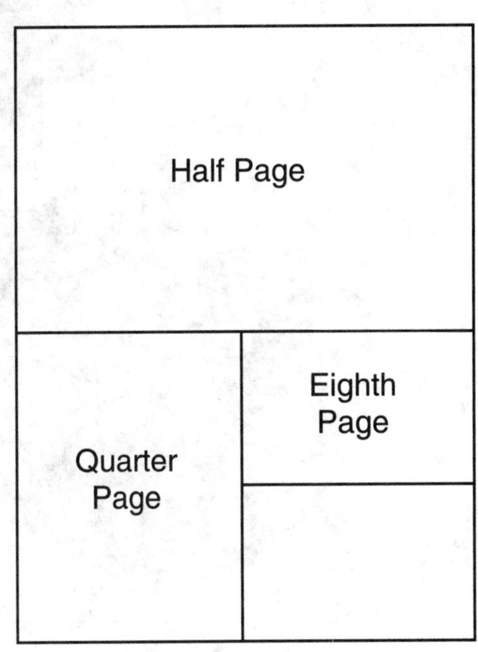

Make checks payable to:

HUXFORD ENTERPRISES
1202 7th St.
Covington, IN 47932

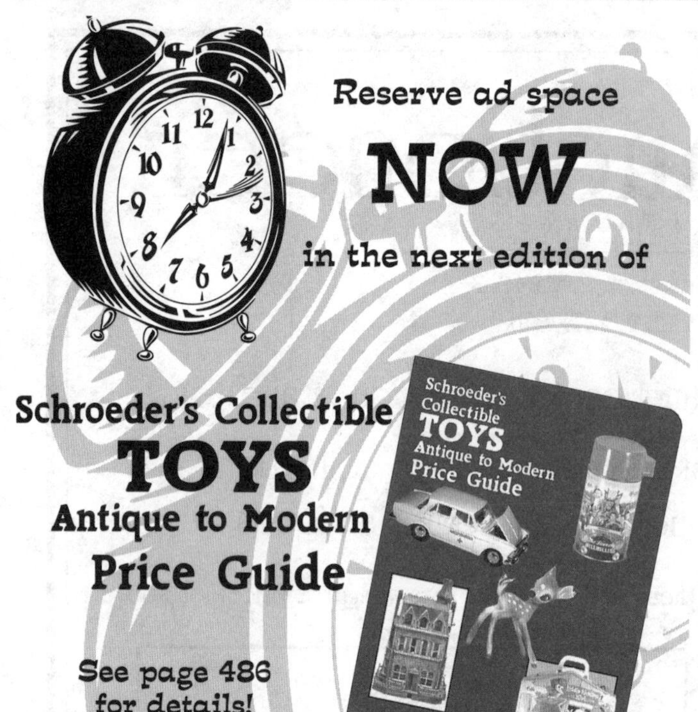

Reserve ad space

NOW

in the next edition of

Schroeder's Collectible
TOYS
Antique to Modern
Price Guide

See page 486 for details!

COLLECTOR BOOKS
A Division of Schroeder Publishing

A Blast from the past... and then some!

AMERICAN PIE COLLECTIBLES

29 Sullivan Road
Peru, New York 12972-4961
(888) 458-2200
(518) 643-0993
Fax(518) 643-8152
apc1@worldnet.att.net
http://www.serftech.com/apc

DUNBAR'S GALLERY
76 HAVEN STREET
MILFORD, MA 01757

508-634-8697 Phone • 508-634-8698 FAX

Sales & Purchases & Auctions By Color Catalog Or At Our Gallery, only 30 minutes from Boston

Toys & Banks, Advertising Signs & Posters, Halloween, Americana

25 Years Experience,
Our Store At Your Door

Call us for information about our items in stock for sale and also upcoming phone/mail auctions.

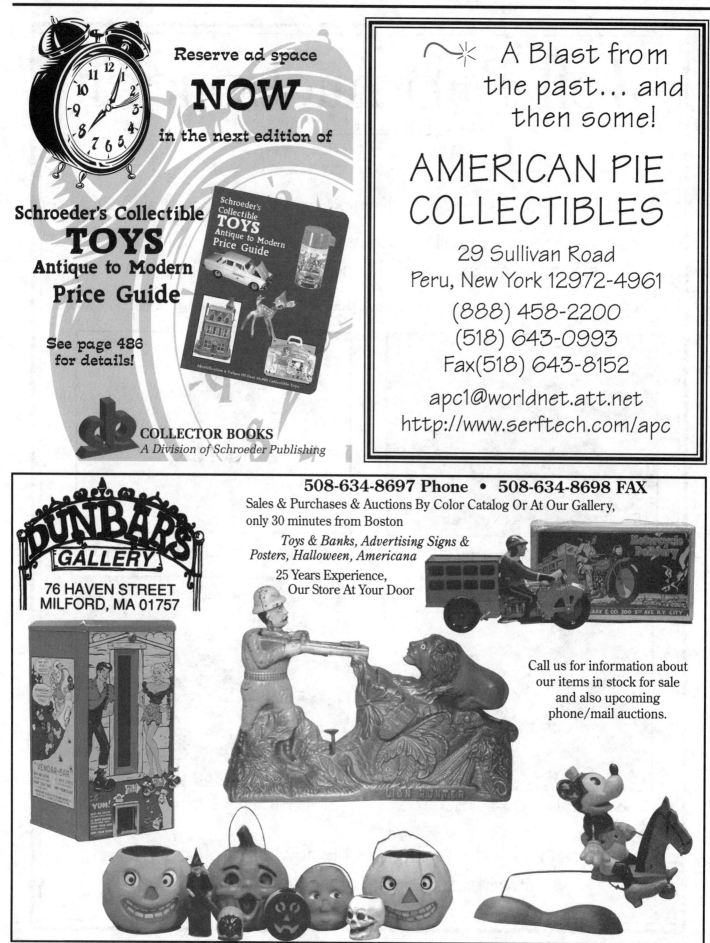

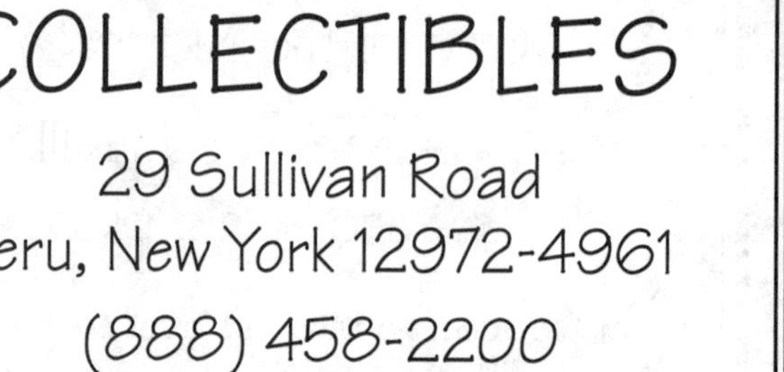

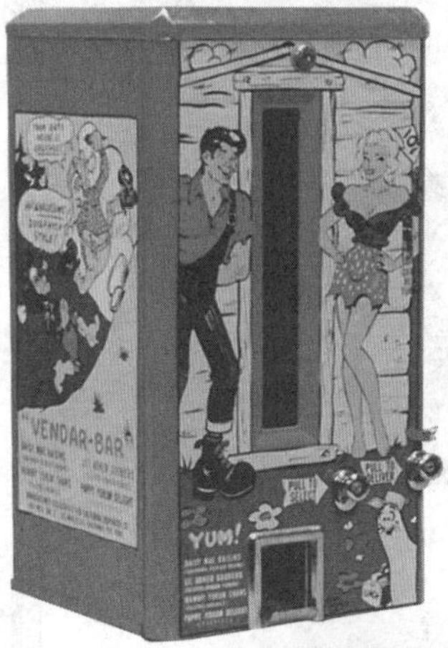

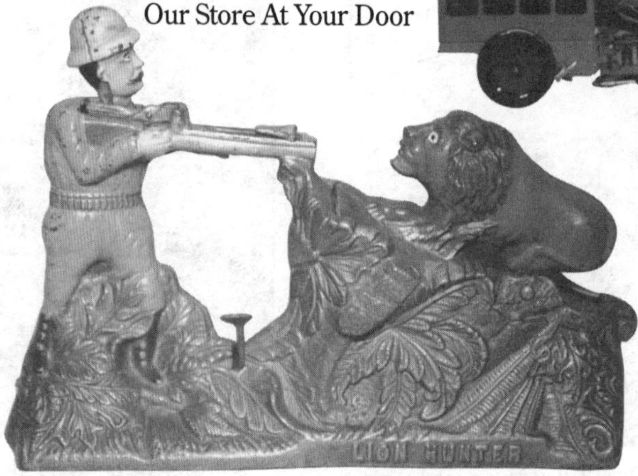

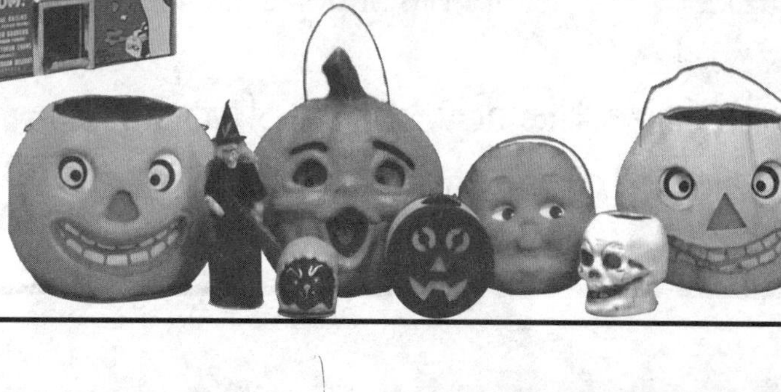

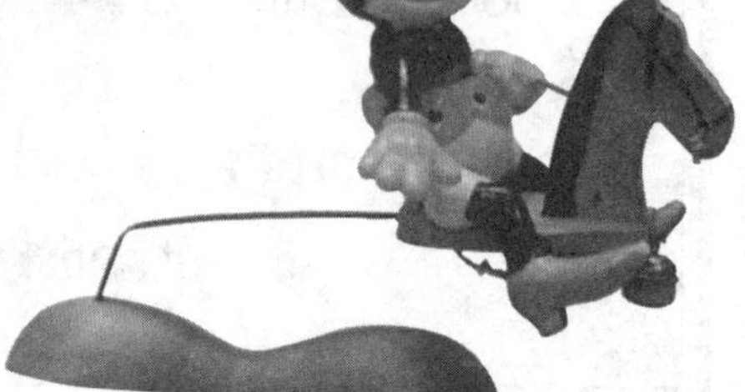

MAIL ORDER CATALOGS

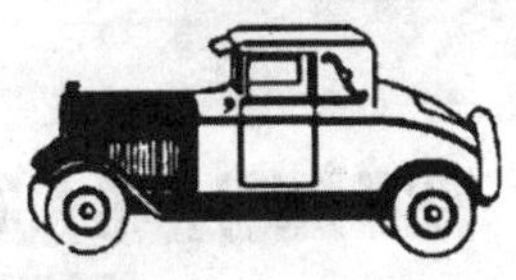

CALLING ALL COLLECTORS!

If you are thinking of either buying or selling, Collection Liquidators Auction Service & Sales is the place for you.

Specialists in Antique Toys, Character Collectibles & Black Americana, we hold three to four Absentee Mail auctions per year, each one offers hundreds of quality collectibles for every level of collector, and unique to the industry, our catalog price is deductible from your successful bid.

We are the only auction house in America which offers, along with a vast assortment of toys & related character collectibles, a large selection of quality Black Americana in each and every sale.

Both buyers and consignors benefit from our personalized approach to providing individualized customer service.

Call or write today and subscribe for our fully illustrated catalogs that size, describe, and condition each and every item (includes prices realized). Send $9.00 ($14 foreign) for a single issue or $24.00($38. foreign) for the next three.

COLLECTION LIQUIDATORS
341 LAFAYETTE STREET SUITE 007
NEW YORK, NY 10012
212-505-2455

By Collectors...For Collectors For Over 30 Years

- * *Board Games*
- * *Tin Toys*
- * *Action Figures*
- * *Scouting*
- * *Coca-Cola*
- * *Disneyana*
- * *Cap Pistols*
- * *Brewery*
- * *Matchbox*
- * *Advertising*
- * *Airlines*
- * *Political*
- * *Harley Davidson*
- * *Zippo Lighters*
- * *Vintage Denim*
- * *Character-Related*
- * *Dinky's*
- * *Straight Razors*

MAIL/PHONE BID AUCTIONS

Nine times each year Manion's *Antiques & Collectables* catalog reaches thousands of customers worldwide!

Call us for Consignment or Subscription information and a *FREE* catalog.

Manion's International Auction House

P.O. Box 12214, Kansas City, Kansas 66112 Tel: (913) 299-6692

E-Mail: **manions@qni.com** Internet: **www.manions.com**

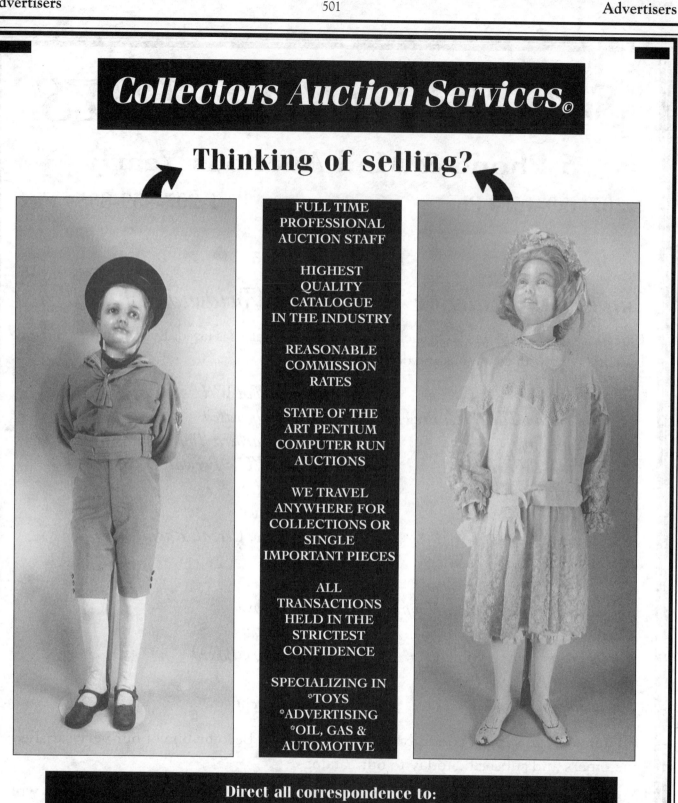

WOW!

There is no better and easier way to get top dollar for your collection or fine quality pieces than by consigning to the *Tiques Telephone Auction.*

Just look at the INCREDIBLE prices we realized in our May 8, 1998 "Toy Town III" Auction.

Elvis Carryall Bag, $1,663.

Beatles "Yellow Submarine" Banks, $4,428.

Bambi Store Display, $2,501.

Beatles "Wing Ding" Sneakers in Box, $3,500.

Mickey Mouse Pocket Watch, $2,070.

1961 Rock 'N Roll Poster, $1,191.

There is no better place to consign than *Tiques Auction.*

- COMPETITIVE RATES.
- FULL COLOR, high quality auction catalogues (acknowledged as the best in the business).
- THE BEST CLIENT LIST of any auctioneer.
- EASIEST BIDDING ACCESS. Clients can bid by phone, fax, mail and LIVE on the INTERNET.
- WEBSITE. Our auctions are always up on our website on The Net.
- NO ONE CAN TOUCH THE PRICES WE GET. That is a fact!
- WE PAY OUR CONSIGNORS RIGHT ON TIME.
- ONE OF THE BEST KNOWN NAMES IN THE BUSINESS. We have been in the collectibles business for over 30 years.

Don't miss the next *Tiques Auction.* Contact us now for all the pertinent info.

Tiques Auction
RR 1 Box 49B, Rte. 34
Old Bridge, NJ 08857
Tel: 732-721-0221
Fax: 732-721-0127

Email: tiquesauc@aol.com
Visit the Tiques Auction at our website: www.tiques.com
Proprietors: Maxine Evans, Stuart Evans & Andrea Evans

Index to Advertisers

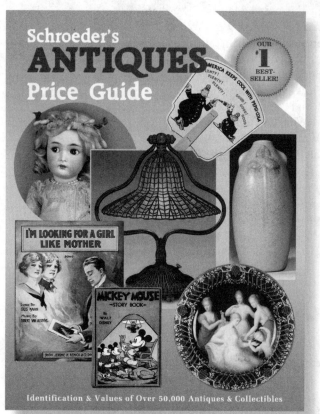